Second Edition

Volume 1

The "Who Is Johnny Dollar?" Matter

A Character Profile and Program Synopsis of
*"America's Fabulous Insurance Investigator,
The Man with the Action-Packed Expense Account"*

"Yours Truly, Johnny Dollar"

by **John C. Abbott**

THE "WHO IS JOHNNY DOLLAR?" MATTER
A CHARACTER PROFILE AND PROGRAM SYNOPSIS OF
*"AMERICA'S FABULOUS INSURANCE INVESTIGATOR,
THE MAN WITH THE ACTION PACKED EXPENSE ACCOUNT"*
"YOURS TRULY, JOHNNY DOLLAR"   VOLUME 1
© 2018 JOHN C. ABBOTT

All rights reserved.

No part of this book may be reproduced in any form or by any means, electronic, mechanical, digital, photocopying or recording, except for the inclusion in a review, without permission in writing from the publisher.

Published in the USA by:

BEARMANOR MEDIA
PO BOX 71426
ALBANY, GA 31708
www.BearManorMedia.com

ISBN: 978 1 62933 324 3 (alk. paper)

BOOK DESIGN AND LAYOUT BY VALERIE THOMPSON.

Table of Contents

V1	I. THE GOLDEN AGE OF RADIO	1
V1	II. WHO IS JOHNNY DOLLAR?	3
V1	BACKGROUND	3
V1	THE DIFFERENT INVESTIGATOR	5
V1	PERSONAL DETAILS	6
V1	OCCUPATIONAL HAZARDS	8
V1	RECREATION AND HOBBIES	9
V1	SOURCES OF INCOME	9
V1	III. THE FINAL CHAPTER MATTER	13
V1	IV. PROGRAM RELATED INFORMATION	23
V1	THE CASES	23
V1	THE ACTORS	24
V1	THE WRITERS AND PRODUCERS	24
V1	RECURRING CHARACTERS	26
V1	V. CASE SYNOPSES	29
V1	CHARLES RUSSELL	31
V1	EDMOND O'BRIEN	89
V1	JOHN LUND	259
V1	BOB BAILEY (5-PART)	435
V2	BOB BAILEY	683
V2	BOB READICK	1043
V2	MANDEL KRAMER	1099
V2	THE AUDITION PROGRAMS	1237
V2	VI. SO, WHO WAS THE BEST JOHNNY DOLLAR?	1251
V2	VII. REPORTS	1253
V2	EXPENSES BY ACTOR	1253
V2	EMPLOYERS AND AGENTS	1254
V2	RECYCLED PROGRAMS	1286
V2	VIII. THE CANONICAL JOHNNY DOLLAR LIST	1295
V2	THE DICK POWELL PROGRAMS	1300
V2	THE CHARLES RUSSELL PROGRAMS	1300
V2	THE EDMOND O'BRIEN PROGRAMS	1301
V2	THE JOHN LUND PROGRAMS	1304
V2	THE GERALD MOHR PROGRAMS	1306
V2	THE BOB BAILEY PROGRAMS	1306
V2	THE BOB READICK PROGRAMS	1318
V2	THE MANDEL KRAMER PROGRAMS	1318
V2	THE UNPRODUCED PROGRAMS	1320
V2	THE MISSING PROGRAMS	1321
V1&2	INDEX	1325

Dedicated to:
All those wonderful actors, actresses, writers, directors, producers, technical staff and sponsors, who made radio a wonderful place for almost 40 years.

Special thanks also go out to Stewart Wright, Dr. Joe Webb, J. David Goldin, and the late Bill Brooks for their support, and encouragement and most of all, for answering my many questions. Thanks guys.

Support for this project was also provided by Jeanette Berard and Klaudia Englund of the Thousand Oaks Library, Anthony L'Abatte at Eastman House, and Janet Lorenz at the National Film Information Service.

I: The Golden Age of Radio

From the day of its invention in the late 1920's, until the early 1960's, radio was a magical place where Americans went to find news, sports, and entertainment. And find them they did. One could find almost any sort of entertainment on the radio. This was the age of quiz shows, talent shows, soap operas, westerns, thrillers, detective shows, dramas, comedies, variety shows, news, gossip and much more. Everyone gathered around the radio duringthe World Series when Red Barber or Vin Scully or Mel Allen would describe every nuance of what was happening on the field. I remember an interview on Ed Walker's *The Big Broadcast* program on WAMU-FM in Washington, where the interviewee noted that in the 1940's and 1950's you could walk down the block and never miss a play when a ball game was on the radio.

Radio presented the presidential campaigns. Radio brought America into President Roosevelt's living room for fireside chats. We heard the blitz of London, the capitulation of the Axis and the demise of the Japanese. Lowell Thomas took us to all sorts of exotic places. Radio took us into committee hearings to hear the Red Scare exposed before our ears. Americans took to radio, and vice versa. Radio was the next big thing in entertainment. Next to talking films, radio was the entertainment for everyone, until the numbing of our senses by television.

Unlike the visual nature of movies and television, radio required three things to be successful:

1. A WELL WRITTEN AND DESCRIPTIVE SCRIPT
2. ACTORS WHO COULD PRESENT THE MATERIAL
3. THE IMAGINATION OF THE LISTENER.

When a writer sat down to create a story, dialog was not enough — you had to describe almost everything. When the character walked across the room, the sound effects men made him walk, but the writer had to tell them how. Every action had a sound, a gun shot, a door opening, a creaking step on the stairs up to the haunted attic. When a girl walked into a room, you knew what she was wearing via the description of the observer in the story. That requirement did not exist for the movies where everything was naked and exposed to the eyes of the viewer.

It was the imagination of the listener that brought many programs to life. When you turned the lights down, and tuned in *Suspense*, or *Inner Sanctum*, it was the mind's eye that provided the illumination of the story. Ask two listeners what Matt Dillon looked like, and you got two distinctly different answers. Ask how big Fibber McGee's closet was and the answer would vary. The listener was totally in control of the visual aspect of a program. If they wanted *The Shadow* to look a certain way — he did. Did Walter Denton, the student nemesis of Miss Brooks on the comedy *Our Miss Brooks* have a dimple on his chin? If you were a young and impressionable teenager who liked dimples — he did. It was your program to color in as you wished.

It is the many-hued nature of radio characters that brought about the contents of this book. We know what Johnny Dollar did — he solved cases for insurance companies. But what was Johnny Dollar the man like?

II: Who Is Johnny Dollar?

In February of 1949, America was introduced to an investigator named Lloyd London. But before the first broadcast was aired, his name was changed to Johnny Dollar. Johnny was not your average run-of-the-mill, hard drinking, hard hitting, one step behind the crook and one step ahead of the local police detective out to track down murderers, gangsters and thugs. Johnny Dollar was different — his beat was freelance insurance investigations. He was hired and paid by insurance companies to look after their financial interests in various matters.

Over the course of the next 12 years, and over 800 broadcasts, Johnny Dollar entertained audiences via the voices of 6 different actors: Charles Russell (1949–1950), Edmond O'Brien (1950–1952), John Lund (1952–1954), Bob Bailey (1955–1960), Bob Readick (1960–1961) and Mandel Kramer (1961–1962). Additionally, two other actors, Dick Powell and Gerald Mohr auditioned for the program.

Many other sources have detailed the actors and writers and directors and producers who created and presented the series. But what do we really know about the character? What was he like? What were his habits, predilections and preferences? After listening audio files or reading scripts for every available case, the following profile of Johnny Dollar emerges.

Background

There is no concise biography of John Dollar, or Johnny Dollar as he preferred to be called. After all, he was a fictitious character. He could be, or would be, whatever the writer chose him to be. With over 30 individual writers or writing partnerships involved in the creation of his adventures, there would be some variability in his past, his likes and dislike and his habits. Only after listening to his adventures the following comes out:

- Early programs in the series tend to indicate that Johnny Dollar started out as an employee of the legendary Pinkerton detective agency.

- In episode 4 of the *The Bennet Matter*, the following information is brought out as Johnny testifies in court that as of 1956, he:
  - Has 10 plus years as a freelance investigator
  - Spent 4 years in the United States Marines
  - Was a New York Police Department Detective Sergeant 2nd Grade.

Adding these factors together and doing a little math:

STORY YEAR	1956
Investigator Experience	-10
US Marines	-4
NYPD Detective experience	-4
High School Graduation Age	-18
YEAR OF BIRTH	1920

- However, in the *The Man Who Waits Matter* aired on 5/22/1960, Johnny mentions that he was just getting started 7 years earlier in 1953.

This would make the Bob Bailey era Johnny Dollar in his middle to late thirties.

In *The Paradise Lost Matter*, and in *The Bad One Matter* Johnny Dollar is asked his age, and the answer is always a mumbled thirty something. Not too old to be found attractive by younger women, not too old to go off romping through the woods and pretty much old enough to be settled in his ways and experienced enough to get the job done. In the series, Bob Bailey was in his early forties, and quite capable of vocally carrying off the part.

Johnny is a very knowledgeable individual, who always seems to have that special bit of knowledge necessary to cinch a case. Some of that knowledge no doubt came from the school of hard knocks. But, in *The Wayward Heiress Matter* Johnny notes that he met Ginnie Van Doren while they were attending college together in the Midwest.

Other than a direct reference to the U.S. Marines in the *Bennet Matter*, a reference of having been a soldier in the CBI (China, Burma, India) Theater of World War II in *The Expiring Nickels and the Egyptian Jackpot* and the Army Air Corps in *The Upjohn Matter*, there is no direct mention about Johnny's specific military experience. However, in three programs, Johnny is at the controls of a small plane with the inference that he might have been an aviator during World War II. In *The Sea Legs Matter*, Johnny tells his cohort Oscar Patrick Vladimir Poscaro, played by Parley Baer, that he has a Pilot's License. In *The Midnite Sun Matter*, Johnny handles the controls of a twin-engine cargo plane, and eventually performs a belly landing after the pilot suffers an attack of appendicitis during a failure of the plane's hydraulic system. In *The Wrong Doctor Matter*, Johnny flies a small plane across the border in pursuit of a drug smuggler. In several cases, Johnny uses SCUBA (Self Contained Underwater Breathing Apparatus) gear, and even an old-fashioned helmeted deep-sea diving suit, indicating some possible military training as a diver.

Johnny does own a personal automobile — a "jalopy" he calls it, that is used on some trips, usually after he buys a tank of gas, on the expense account of course. However, Johnny is more apt to jump into a cab, onto a plane or a train to add items to the expense account. In *The Star of Capetown Matter*, Johnny even rides in a helicopter to get onto an ocean liner while it is in route. The rental of a helicopter also figures into *The Further Buffalo Matter*.

In the beginning of the series, Johnny Dollar was only armed with his wits. As the character, and the nature of the plots developed, Johnny was within close proximity of his gun. It was always on a case with him, either packed in his bags or in a holster. While no specific mention is made, the "typical" detective of the era usually carried his gun in a shoulder holster.

On numerous occasions Johnny makes a reference to his "automatic" of un-noted caliber possibly either a .38 automatic, or a .45 automatic. Other references are made to his .38 revolver, probably a Smith & Wesson .38 caliber Police Special. However, in *The Shy Beneficiary Matter*, he notes that he threw his automatic to the ground. In *The Carboniferous Dolomite Matter*, the local police inspect his .38 automatic and specifically notes that the clip is full, another inference to an automatic. In *The Deadly Swamp Matter*, a reference is made to his "pretty gun" possibly indicating a nickel finish. In *The Can't Be so Matter* the wife of an insurance agent buddy mentions his impressive gun collection, to which her husband is secretly trying to add a single action Army Colt .45 revolver.

In the Bob Bailey and Mandel Kramer programs, Johnny carries a .38 "lemon squeezer". From the 1890's until the 1930's Smith and Wesson manufactured a hammerless .32 and .38 caliber revolver called a "lemon squeezer" because it had a grip safety which required the user to squeeze the grip like a lemon juicer. This type of revolver was reportedly popular with gamblers and detectives because it could be safely fired from inside a coat pocket.

In the post 9/11 era, it is somewhat incongruous to think that Johnny Dollar could jump on an airplane, armed and ready to go.

Johnny was a licensed investigator. He was more than willing to show his ID to the police, sometimes with less-than favorable results. As the red scare developed, Johnny also picked up a secret clearance from the FBI. In *The Top Secret Matter* Johnny lists several other clearances, including several military organizations. Having such clearances allows Johnny to handle much more than the usual insurance cases. He was able to go where the political action was and helped out on a number of cases involving the space race.

THE DIFFERENT INVESTIGATOR

There was more to Johnny Dollar than the theme of the program. Johnny answered to a "higher" power. A Sam Spade or a Richard Diamond was hired, typically by a person, to right some wrong, find a killer or put a crook in jail. All cases were handled with the hope of getting paid. Johnny Dollar however, worked for insurance companies, an industry known for trust and financial propriety.

When Johnny took an assignment, he was not on his own. He was working to protect the interests of the insurance company, and in turn to protect the interests of the policyholder. When a policyholder must be paid, no matter the circumstances, it was Johnny's job to get the facts and make sure the payment was correct. When the circumstances called "foul", Johnny had to look to the interests of the insurance company that was employing him. In several cases, that was a difficult thing to do. In *The Island of Tin-Yutan* Johnny was hired to find a group of missing policyholders in the south Pacific. Once into the investigation, Johnny discovers that the very ones he must protect were the one causing the problems. So, there was the matter of keeping his client's property alive long enough to turn them in to the police.

Like all detectives, Johnny was often working on investigations where the police were or should have been involved. The "typical" radio detective was usually either one step ahead of the police, or the prime suspect of the police. Johnny Dollar was put in the position of working along with the police. For the most part, this was a professional and mutually rewarding experience, as Johnny was able to provide additional footwork to the police, or in some cases go where the police could not go. In a number of cases, Johnny notes that he is able to "cut a deal" with the suspect for the return of jewels or stolen money, something prohibited to the police. In *The Protection Matter* Johnny goes one step further and gets the necessary information by administering a beating to a former gangster.

The relationship with the police was not always cordial. Because of his ability to offer deals and the need to maintain confidentiality, Johnny frequently withheld information from the police. On occasions that put Johnny on a collision path with the police, who were out to solve the crime. Johnny was threatened with arrest and was arrested on several occasions. He was ordered off cases and had his license threatened numerous times as a form of unfair leverage.

Personal Details

As an individual, Johnny Dollar gave no reference to either parents or siblings. In *The Medium, Well Done Matter, Episode 3*, he does state that he does not have a brother, even though he had told a medium that he did. But there were no other familial references in the programs available.

Johnny was a confirmed bachelor but really enjoyed the company of an attractive young lady. There were several women who seemed to play an important or recurring part in Johnny's life:

- Carol Dalhart, daughter of the cantankerous Durango Laramie Dalhart
- Betty Lewis, a business woman bent on trapping Johnny into marriage, which he would have loved to do, except for his job.
- Mary Grace Marshall, a New York fashion designer who only appears once, and is killed after spending a chummy, platonic weekend with Johnny.

Many other relationships were inferred, and many hearts were broken, but Johnny remained a bachelor right to the end. While all of the Johnny Dollars were comfortable around women, Charles Russell played a particularly womanizing character, which by the end of the Edmond O'Brien run had mellowed quite a bit. Maybe he had just grown up by then.

In *The Henry J. Unger Matter* Johnny gave his address as 390 Pearl Street, an apartment in Hartford, Connecticut, the heart of the American insurance industry. There actually is a Pearl Street in Hartford. Today the 390 Pearl Street address is a parking lot. In *The Calgary Matter* his phone number was given out by the operator as Stanley 3469. In the Dick Powell audition program, Johnny says that "he lives in Hartford, Connecticut, or at least that is where he pays rent". The apartment is a walk up and is described as being nicely furnished. As it was described in *The Date with Death Matter* the apartment has a den and a small kitchen with a rear entrance out to the fire escape. It seemed to be your typical professional bachelor apartment.

There is generally no indication of his appearance. We can only assume he is around six feet tall, probably of medium build and very attractive to women. (Was there ever a detective who was repulsive in appearance?) In *Milford Brooks III*, Johnny says that, in case you want to give a Christmas present, he wears a size 42 suit, 15 ½ inch shirt with 33-inch sleeve, and a 7 3/8" hat. No doubt these measurements fit Dick Powell to a "T". In *The Man Who Waits Matter*, Johnny notes that in order to affect a disguise, he had to use dye to darken his light hair, and peroxide to lighten his normally darkly tanned skin. In *The Wayward Truck Matter*, Johnny is told that he fights pretty well for a skinny guy. As with most "men of action" in the 1950's and 60's, Johnny was a cigarette smoker.

Johnny also was one who enjoyed fine dining as many entries in his infamous expense reports were for meals at nice restaurants. At the same time, he was not above grabbing a sandwich on the go or even skipping a meal when the action required otherwise. Johnny was not above finding comfort in a bonded form of nourishment, both in his room at night, or with clients. Both Charles Russell and Edmond O'Brien would, when asked if they were on a case, reply "Yes, a case of Kentucky bonded". The earlier Johnny Dollars tended to be bourbon and cognac drinkers, Bob Bailey and later Johnny's were scotch drinkers. No fizzy, umbrella-topped drinks for these guys.

Johnny Dollar always seemed to be a snappy dresser. While nothing specific was mentioned, he seemed to fit the business suit and hat standard of the day (see above for a wardrobe description). In *The Smoky Sleeper Matter*, Johnny is described as wearing "a blue shirt and a bow tie". In *The Short Term Matter*, Johnny mentions a cashmere sports coat. Even when out fishing, there was no mention of what he was wearing, other than fishing clothes.

On his many adventures, he was always doing things that could only bring joy to the heart (and pocketbook) of the local haberdasher. Things like jumping into the Everglades or the 20-Mile Swamp to protect himself, climbing down into ravines to find a body or wrecked automobile, or traipsing all over town at night, all while dressed in his business attire. A number of expense accounts included replacement clothes.

Johnny Dollar was a departure from the "hard-core" fast-fisted cynical tough-guy detective. He could be tough. In the *The Clinton Matter — Episode 4*, Johnny shows his tough side by demanding that the sheriff of a crooked town resign. In several other cases, he is not afraid to order autopsies be performed, issue court orders or convince someone that his face would look much prettier without Johnny's fist in it.

But at the same time, Johnny could show a tender, even compassionate side. He was not afraid to give someone, especially a pretty girl, a shoulder to cry on. Often Johnny would look the other way when what was right went against what justice called for. In a couple of cases, he even donated his expense account to the local charity or even worked gratis if the case was one where taking his expenses was not the correct thing to do.

Johnny was an admirer of the other sex but remained a confirmed bachelor. The most consistent reason was that it would be unfair to tie someone down to a guy who did not know from day-to-day if he would be home for dinner, or even home. Johnny once told a travel agent that he only bought one-way tickets because sometimes he did not know if he would be coming back. He seemed to have a bit of remorse over his occupation from time to time, but he never strayed from the case or gave up. On at least one occasion, he traveled all over the country to avoid what he thought was going to be a shotgun wedding!

OCCUPATIONAL HAZARDS

There is another aspect to Johnny Dollar that is somewhat troublesome. In every episode, almost without exception (although there were a few) there were two occurrences that could be relied on:

1. SOMEONE WOULD DIE, AND
2. JOHNNY WOULD BE KNOCKED UNCONSCIOUS BY A HIT ON THE HEAD WITH SOMETHING — USUALLY THE BUTT OF A GUN.

It is the second occurrence which must have made Johnny's head look like a phrenologist's nightmare with its numerous bumps, gashes, gullies and chasms inflicted by over 12 year's worth of abuse. One wonders why Johnny did not stammer and lumber around like a punch-drunk fighter.

Another occupational hazard held by all detectives is the risk of being shot and working for insurance companies does not spare Johnny from that danger. Over the course of 12 years, Johnny is shot 13 times. The cases involved are:
- *The Eighty-Five Little Minks*
- *The Lloyd Hammerly Matter*
- *The Baltimore Matter*
- *The San Antonio Matter*
- *The Macormack Matter* — Episode 5
- *The Todd Matter* — Episode 5
- *The Midas Touch Matter* — Episode 5
- *The Denver Disbursal Matter*
- *The Virtuous Mobster Matter*
- *The Perilous Parley Matter*
- *The Informer Matter*
- *The Well of Trouble Matter*
- *The Skimpy Matter*

For the superstitious, bear in mind that there are a number of missing programs that might adjust the above number.

RECREATION AND HOBBIES

For Johnny Dollar, there was only one sport, fishing, either on the job or on vacation. Many of the programs were woven around the Lake Mohave Resort in Arizona, or at Earle Poorman's Sarasota, Florida, beach home. Johnny was willing to wet a line where ever opportunity and a body of water presented itself. Fishing locations included the Gulf of Mexico, the Pacific around southern California, Lake Tahoe, the Esopus River in New York State, and Lake Mohave Resort. Most of the dialog was pretty general, but in the *The Blue Rock Matter* the author of the script, Jack Johnstone goes into a nice bit of detail regarding what type of trout flies to use in the early season. I know the details are correct, as I am more than familiar with the joys and frustrations of being humiliated by a wily trout, while standing in freezing water with a fly rod in my hands! Jack Johnstone was also quite a fisherman, and would often to to the real Lake Mohave, and fish with his real friends Ham Pratt and Buster Favor. Jack even patented a fishing hook called the Sure-Strike hook that was mentioned in several programs.

Johnny also liked beach activities, whether swimming or snorkeling, or discussing a case with a lovely young lady pool-side. In several cases, Johnny seems to be a boxing fan and occasionally goes to the track. In *The Picture Postcard Matter* Johnny takes to a pair of skis. In *The Short Term Matter*, Johnny starts the case by relating the previous weekend's major activity, falling on his back in a chair-lift accident that requires him to wear a steel-ribbed corset, another skiing reference.

SOURCES OF INCOME

The basic premise of the program is the "action packed expense account" created in the process of completing his investigations for his employers. But there is more to be had in examining the details.

The early Johnny Dollars always seemed to be one step ahead of their creditors, although they always seemed to have the cash to jump on an airplane (long before frequent flier miles) or a train (when trains still ran). Johnny even takes a bus on several occasions to get to the scene of the case. Near the end of the Bob Bailey series, Johnny notes the use of his personal American Express credit card. There are also several references to grabbing a hand-full of American Express Travelers Checks on his way to the airport.

The major issue with the expense account, and the underlying theme of the program, tends to be the padding of the expenses for any given case. The term "incidentals" shows up regularly, as do the names of top-grade hotels. There was no *Motel 6* for Johnny Dollar, unless that was the only place available. In *The Parakoff Policy*, Johnny adds $700 to the expense account for a trip to Miami to recover from a cold caught in Ohio. When Dick Powell auditioned for Johnny Dollar, he adds a $318 bracelet for his girlfriend "Butter" to the tab in *Milford Brooks III*.

In retrospect it is interesting to listen to Johnny wrap up a case, having traveled all over the country, with an expense account of less than $200. In a report at the end of the cases, I have recapped the expenses of each of the actors who played Johnny Dollar, and have adjusted them for inflation to 2017 values. The adjusted figures help to see not only the relative cost of the trips but give a perspective on price inflation also. Sometimes there was not even an expense account. On several occasions, Johnny even ended up working gratis for a good cause.

But there is more to the picture. A close listening reveals that in addition to expenses, Johnny's pay was tied to the face value of the policy or the goods stolen. It seems that almost everyone in the world had a huge diamond or emerald necklace in the 1950's, and most of these ended up being stolen. Sometimes, like the Canary Diamonds, they were stolen twice!

It would seem that in cases of fraud or other occurrences that would render a policy null and void, Johnny got a percentage of the face value of the policy. In the case of stolen items, there was a fee based on the insured value of the property recovered. In *The Suntan Oil Matter*, Johnny tells Mrs. Galloway that he gets 10-30% of the value of a piece of stolen jewelry when he recovers it. In some cases, when he was really trying to get out of a case or was just irritated at the agent requesting his time, or Johnny was in need of money, there would be a "fee" or "commission" added to make the case worth his time. In several cases, there was a reward for the arrest of a criminal, which went to Johnny.

Other clients bestowed gifts and rewards on Johnny as well. Alvin Peabody Cartwright was one such client, Durango Laramie Dalhart was another. Both lavished relatively large amounts of cash or expensive gifts on Johnny whom they both counted on, for professional services and as a good friend. In *The Merry Go Round Matter*, Alvin Cartwright gives Johnny a money clip covered with diamonds as a Christmas present.

Another interesting item is the radio broadcasts of his cases. Starting with *The Blooming Blossom Matter*, Mr. Blossom notes that he listens to Johnny's radio programs. In *The Winsome Widow Matter*, the program actually starts with Johnny telling Pat McCracken that he is in Hollywood to meet with Jack Johnstone about the broadcasting of his cases. Johnny even runs into Jack Johnstone's brother Doug in several stories that take place in Corpus Christi, Texas. In a number of later episodes, Johnny is recognized by his voice (which is his undoing in at least one case), and many clients and contacts make reference to hearing the stories on the radio. In *The Big H Matter*, Johnny is even contacted by an elderly radio fan for help. The unmentioned aspect of the Hollywood angle is that Johnny Dollar would likely have been paid for the stories, providing yet another source of income for Johnny.

During the later Bob Bailey series, and especially at the end of the Mandel Kramer episodes, there are blatant plugs for the CBS affiliate located in the city of the investigation. The Bob Bailey, John Lund and Mandel Kramer characters enlist the aid of the local CBS news departments in their investigations. In *The Missing Missile Matter, The Wayward Kilocycles Matter* and *The Vociferous Dolphin Matter* Johnny enlists the aid of CBS sound engineer Bob McKenny to provide technical assistance.

All things considered, in an era when the average household income was less than $6,000, and a $25,000 policy was big stuff, Johnny Dollar tended to live pretty well, but always seemed to act as if the wolf was at the door. Johnny lived in a walkup apartment, and drove a jalopy, and did mention some investments in the stock market. So, one wonders where his money went.

III: The Final Chapter Matter

After the final episode of Yours Truly, Johnny Dollar aired in September 1962, Johnny Dollar disappeared from the airwaves. There was no closure, just the finality of dead air. The abruptness of the end raises an interesting question: what would have happened to Johnny Dollar if Jack Johnstone had been given the opportunity to close out the character gracefully? How would the series have ended, what would have become of the man with the action-packed expense account?

What follows below is my attempt to provide an answer to these questions. There are several typical closure mechanisms available. Johnny could just be killed off or disappear on his last case or he could just get tired and retire. There are many options, but the following scenario, in my mind, outlines the final days of Johnny Dollar.

NOTE: The text below is written with Bob Bailey in mind, so I have tried, probably very poorly, to write as if Bob were reading the text below. Additionally, my mind's ear hears Will Wright as Mr. Farnsworth, and Virginia Gregg as Betty.

THE FINAL CHAPTER MATTER

(Phone rings)

Johnny (yawn) Dollar.

"Mr. Dollar, this is Webster T. Farnsworth and I represent…"

"I'm sorry Mr. Farnsworth, but I am not interested in a new case right now. I have been out of town on a case for five weeks and I'm really tired." I mumbled into the phone.

"Mr. Dollar, I am not calling to hire you for your services. I represent Alvin Peabody Cartwright and"

"Oh, no! What has poor old Alvin gotten himself in to this time?"

"Well Mr. Dollar, I do understand you were previously involved in some insurance matters with Mr. Cartwright. But I am calling on an entirely different matter. I regret to inform you, Mr. Dollar, that Mr. Cartwright has died."

"Died? Alvin? How did it happen? Was foul play involved?"

"No, Mr. Dollar. Alvin's passing was quite natural. He had been ill for some weeks and died peacefully in his sleep four days ago. We have been trying to contact you, but the phone was never answered. Now I understand why. Mr. Dollar, can you come to Los Angeles for the funeral? It is quite important that you do so."

"I'll grab the first flight."

(Theme Music)

Expense Account submitted by special investigator Johnny Dollar to, well this one is really to me. The following is an accounting of expenditures during my involvement in *The Final Chapter Matter*.

"After returning home at 3:00 a.m. from another tiring and very frustrating case, I found a telegram under my apartment door urging me to call a Mr. Farnsworth, an attorney in California. I was not ready for another case, and it was too late to call, so I made a note to return the call in the morning, or rather much later that day after a well-deserved rest. At 10:45 that morning, I received a call from Mr. Webster T. Farnsworth advising me of the passing, four days ago, of my old friend and client Alvin Peabody Cartwright. Poor old Alvin had been in ill health for weeks and had died peacefully in his sleep. I immediately advised Mr. Farnsworth that I would catch the first available flight to Los Angeles to attend the services for my dear old friend. Mr. Farnsworth advised me that I should be prepared to attend the reading of the will the day after the funeral. It was just like Alvin to remember his friends with a last thank you."

"I shaved and showered, packed a fresh suitcase and threw my swimming trunks in for good measure. After a long, cold, and frustrating five-weeks chasing down a gang of insurance scam-artists I needed a rest. So, I planned on spending a week in the sun and surf around San Diego after the funeral."

"EXPENSE ACCOUNT ITEM ONE: cab fare, incidentals and plane fare to Los Angeles: $295.45"

"After wiring Mr. Farnsworth of my travel arrangements, I caught an early evening jet flight to Los Angeles, settled back and napped most of the way. I arrived in Los Angeles at 9:15 p.m. and was unexpectedly met by one of Mr. Farnsworth's associates, who took my bag and informed me that I would be staying at the Cartwright estate. The drive to Alvin's mansion was pleasant and a familiar one, as I had been to the estate several times on business. I was shown to a suite of rooms and informed that there would be a breakfast buffet on the patio for Mr. Cartwright's friends at 9:00 a.m. the next morning. I was still tired, so I went to bed and slept through the night, time change and all."

"At 9:00 a.m., I went downstairs and was met at the bottom of the long winding staircase by George Reed, Alvin's insurance agent and advisor. George was and old friend and we expressed our pleasure to see each other but lamented the circumstances. On the large balcony outside the dining room our mutual friend Pat McCracken, who had acted as the Universal Adjustment Bureau intermediary on several cases involving Alvin, met us for breakfast."

"On the balcony were about a two dozen others, executives of the various companies Alvin had set up over his long and profitable lifetime, his personal staff and old friends. At 10:30 we were all ushered into the Library for a very sedate and short memorial service. Alvin had never wanted a formal funeral, so we were not surprised that there was no coffin in the room. Mr. Farnsworth orchestrated the service at which there were three speakers: his longtime secretary, his legal advisor Mr. Farnsworth, and his friend George Reed. The whole event was over in barely over thirty minutes."

"After the service, I introduced myself to Mr. Farnsworth."

"I am sorry I had to awaken you the other day, Mr. Dollar, but we had been trying to reach you for four days." Farnsworth told me.

"Unfortunately, I was out on a case. In my business I am rarely home. Did you contact my service?" I asked.

"No, we had your home number in Mr. Cartwright's file and there were very explicit instructions to make sure you were called immediately. You must have been a very good friend of Mr. Cartwright's, Mr. Dollar."

"Alvin, er, I mean Mr. Cartwright and I were associated professionally. I handled some insurance related matters for him, and some personal matters as well. He was quite a character."

"Yes. Knowing Mr. Cartwright as I did, I can only imagine what he had you involved in. The poor man was a bit flighty and addled at times, but he had a business mind that was just as sharp in his final weeks as it was forty years ago."

"Flighty is an understatement. Some of his cases made for the funniest of the all the broadcast programs I worked on for Jack Johnstone over at CBS radio."

"Well, I am not much of a radio or television person Mr. Dollar, so I will have to get my staff to find some of the programs to listen to. While I am talking about my staff, I will send a car for you here tomorrow at 9:00 a.m. Mr. Cartwright's Last Will and Testament will be read in my offices at 10:00 a.m. tomorrow, and your presence is most important."

"I had planned to stay until tomorrow afternoon, and then head for the beach in San Diego for a week of vacation."

"Very good. I will see you tomorrow morning, Mr. Dollar."

"During the service, we all had learned that Alvin had wished to be cremated and have his ashes spread at sea. At 1:00 p.m. I joined a small group of chosen friends who were driven to his yacht 'The Alpecar'. We sailed out to the area beyond the Channel Islands and very somberly spread the ashes of Alvin Cartwright over the waters. It was quite fitting that a Sea Otter came up, looked around, winked and then dived down into the waters during the ceremony."

"The rest of the day was spent with George and Pat talking about old times. We managed to find a good restaurant nearby and went out for drinks and dinner."

"EXPENSE ACCOUNT ITEM 2: Dinner for three at the Surfside Restaurant: $57.89. I shocked no one by picking up the check, but Pat wondered aloud how I was going to get Alvin to pay for it."

"At 9:00 a.m. sharp the next morning there was a car and driver to take me to the offices of Mr. Farnsworth in Beverly Hills. In the wood paneled and somber conference room of Farnsworth's office were gathered a variety of people. Some were quite obviously executives of Alvin's various companies, while others looked like they had worked for, or known Alvin personally over the years."

"Most of the bequests were generous amounts given to Alvin's employees, some old friends and his business associates. But it was the last part of the will that left me speechless. Having no immediate family, Alvin had established a foundation to direct the activities of his far-flung financial interests, and he had named me, Special Investigator Johnny Dollar to be Chairman of the Board of the Alvin Peabody Cartwright Foundation. Needless to say, I was flabbergasted. Being an insightful man, Alvin knew that I could not maintain my activities as an investigator and direct a foundation that would oversee almost five hundred million dollars. So, Alvin left me another most unexpected surprise. Alvin provided a $5,000,000 cash bequest to allow me to lessen my schedule and help me make time for my new responsibilities without making for a financial burden! Like I said, I was flabbergasted!"

"After the meeting adjourned I approached Mr. Farnsworth."

"Mr. Farnsworth, are you really sure about this foundation thing? I am not sure that I am the executive type, or at least the type of high power executive you are looking for. I have spent the past twenty years chasing people, being shot at and the hit on the head. I do not want to appear ungrateful or disrespectful, but I think that you and Alvin have made a mistake here."

"No, Mr. Dollar. I believe it is you who are wrong. Let me explain. For the past year, after Mr. Cartwright suspected that he was ill, we looked for someone who could run the foundation in the manner Mr. Cartwright wanted it run. We interviewed over 200 well-qualified executives, and after each meeting, Mr. Cartwright would say that he wished he could find another Johnny Dollar, a man he could trust implicitly. He wanted a man with four qualities. First the man had to be honest above suspicion. Secondly, the man had to be able to stand toe-to-toe with someone, look him in the eye and tell him 'NO!' Thirdly we wanted a man who could wade through the smoke and fluff of a problem and find the facts and act accordingly. Lastly, we wanted a man who would look out for the interests of the foundation and all associated with it. Mr. Cartwright knew you were the man for the job."

"Well, I am flattered, but still I…"

"Mr. Dollar, Johnny. Let me reassure you that you will not flounder alone in this position. You will have the assistance of the finest law firms, accountants and auditors in the country. You will not be alone.

"You may not know this, but Mr. Cartwright followed your cases very closely, to the point of buying a sizeable interest in the Universal Adjustment Bureau. He watched how you dealt both with the small penny-ante policyholders and the industrialists who were out to fleece anyone they could. Mr. Cartwright was positive you were the right man for the job."

"But this is such a change from what I am doing now. I do not even know the others I am supposed to work with, let alone how to evaluate or protect anything. I feel like I have just been launched into space on one of those new guided missiles."

"Johnny, let me tell you a story. I was born on a hardscrabble farm in Alabama. My father never had more than a dollar to his name, but he taught me how to work hard. In high school, I had to literally fight my way on to the basketball team so that I could have a pair of shoes that fit. I worked my way through college and law school. When I got to my first real legal job, I did not think I could pour water from a boot and hit the floor with it. But, a mentor at the firm told me something that got me through. The oldest partner of the firm called me into his office on the first day and told me that the only thing separating me from the other attorneys there was experience. He told me I was just as smart as anyone there, I just did not know the ropes. His advice was to learn how to manage the ropes, and everything else would take care of itself. And it has. Johnny, my advice to you is to learn the ropes and you will excel. There is no magic here. This position is no different than working on one of your investigations. In some ways, it will be the same job you have been doing very well for many years. The only difference is, you get to approve your own expense accounts."

"Well, Mr. Farnsworth if"

"Please, my friends call me Webb, and you are my friend now Johnny."

"Okay, Webb. I guess I need to think like Tarzan and learn the ropes. Thank you very much for your confidence in me. And I promise to take it easy on the expense accounts for once! Did I say that?"

"After completing the necessary paperwork with Mr. Farnsworth, who is now "Webb" and who promised me that I would not be overwhelmed by my new duties, we met with several other members of the foundation, and I was given a very thick binder to read on my vacation."

"Later that day I caught a flight to San Diego for that week at the beach."

"EXPENSE ACCOUNT ITEM TWO, well, with money in my pocket and a new set of responsibilities I think that accounting for my expenses as I have done for so many years is somewhat unnecessary now, as this account is on me."

"I spent a short week at the beach, enjoying the sun, swimming in the pool, snorkeling down near Mexico and doing a little deep-sea fishing. But the binder was always there to lull me to sleep each night. I was tempted to take a quick trip to see my friends Buster and Ham at Lake Mohave Resorts, but I decided to get back to cold, snowy Hartford. After all, I still had not unpacked my bags from my last case."

"EXPENSE ACCOUNT ITEM THREE, well old habits are hard to break."

"I arrived home in Hartford and spent a busy day unpacking, catching up on the mail, paying some bills and making my dry cleaner a happy man with the accumulation of a month's dirty clothes. After a night of strangely fitful sleep, I called my service only to find out that the Universal Adjustment Bureau was looking me."

"I called Pat Fuller at his office and listened to the case, which would have taken me to the jungles of South America once again. I told Pat that, for the first time I would need to think about the case before accepting it."

"I left the offices and walked around snowy Hartford for several hours just thinking. After thinking about the changes in my life over the past week and a long day of contemplation, I went to a public stenographer and had her prepare several letters for the next day."

"On a cold mid-February morning, I made a series of early phone calls, sent some wires and visited a number of my most loyal employers in Hartford to give them an unwanted message, Johnny Dollar has retired. I explained why at each of my stops, and after both congratulations and pleas for my services "for just one more big case" the deed was done. Johnny Dollar, the man with the action-packed expense account was no longer available."

"After the insurance company meetings, I made my way to the office of my dearest and closest gal-friend, Betty Lewis. I surprised the receptionist Lucy by showing up unexpectedly. Lucy told me that Betty was in a meeting that had already gone an hour over the scheduled time, so I decided to sit and wait. After 45 minutes and four magazines, the conference room emptied and Betty finally burst out of the room talking angrily to a younger man about really botching the presentation to a major client."

"What were you thinking? That presentation was nowhere close to the approach you were told to use! And you event spelled the man's name wrong!" the young man is told. Betty was so involved with sending the man off to his office to start trying to fix the damage that she walked right past me, into her office, slamming the door in the process. I looked at a surprised Lucy who then buzzed Betty to tell her that I was here.

"Johnny? Here?" Betty came rushing out, pleasantly surprised to see me yet apologetic about walking past me.

"That's OK, Betty. I sort of sensed you were busy," I told her "but I need your help right now on a major case I am working on."

"Johnny, you know I would do just about anything for you, but today, no, this week has just gone down the drain and I need to recover a botched presentation to keep a major client. It really is important. You understand, don't you?" she said, looking like she was ready to either pull her hair out or cry or both.

"Sure, I understand, but I only need you for an hour, and it has to be today, right now." I told her. "Come on, I'll buy you lunch and you can help me start this project. It will only take a few minutes, and you really could use a break right now. Who knows, you might actually like working on this project."

"Johnny, what is so important that you have to come into my office without an appointment, not that you need one, and take me off on one of your crazy wild-goose-chase insurance investigations? Can't it wait until next week? After all, I have not seen you for, well for months. I really need to salvage this project. I know your job is important to you, but this project is important to me. It is maybe the most important project of my career, and maybe the last one if I cannot salvage it."

"Betty, what I want you to do for me is even more important than your project. It will only take half an hour at most if we skip lunch. Come on, we can start on it now." I told her pulling on her arm.

"Look, Johnny, I can't leave right now. What is so all important that is can't wait for a week?" she told me, starting to get angry.

"Look, all I need you to do is get in a cab with me, run down to City Hall and get a marriage license with me. You will be back in plenty of time to deal with your client. Maybe even with a new perspective on it."

"Johnny, if all you need is someone to sign a paper, I will get Lucy to call our Notary and…what did you say!"

"You heard me, Miss Betty Lewis. Johnny Dollar has retired. I have a new job, and I think that it is about time I stopped stringing you along and settled down. Now are you coming with me?"

Lucy and I picked Betty up and put her on the sofa in her office after she fainted. After recovering for a few minutes, I told Betty of my new job with the foundation and my plans to retire and move to Florida. I told her I wanted to build a little beach house, maybe somewhere close to my friends Earle and Mike Poorman. Then I would spend my days fishing with Earle, tending to my job at the foundation and most importantly of all, trying to be a good husband to Mrs. Betty Dollar. Suddenly the turmoil of the office was forgotten, and after dictating a series of instructions for Lucy, Betty and I ran off to catch a cab for City Hall.

Over the next month I worked on settling my affairs, collecting my outstanding expense account payments, starting the plans for a move to Florida and attending a few board meetings. Betty was even able to rescue her client, at the cost of a brash young up-and-coming account manager who is now probably working on a loading dock somewhere licking his wounds!

On a bright Saturday in April, Miss Betty Lewis became Mrs. Johnny Dollar before an overflow crowd of family, clients and friends. Pat McCracken was my best man and Betty's college roommate was her maid of honor. My old fishing buddies Buster and Ham from Lake Mohave Resort were there. Randy Singer came up from New York and the boys from Virtue, South Carolina were there. That living-doll Carol Dalhart Johnson came, with a note from her Uncle Durango who was ill, her husband William, and a wink-in-her-eye offer to dump William if I would change my mind about marrying Betty. Insurance agents from all over the country were there, some of who owed their jobs to my work. Even my friend Louis De Marsac, "Les Chat Gris" from Paris, France was there, albeit with a gendarme handcuffed to his left wrist, a sly grin on his face and a solemn promise to keep his right hand in his own pockets.

Jack Johnstone and the actors from my CBS Radio program came. Parley Baer and Howard McNear were up to their usual tricks and even put on a little "roast" during the reception. Jack even arranged for the CBS Television staff in New York to come and film the wedding as a present. Some of the footage even made the national evening news with Walter Cronkite that Sunday.

After almost 20 years of investigations for agents and clients all over the country, the gifts from my associates looked like a catalog from a well-heeled department store. At one point, I think I recognized an antique silver tea set on the gift table that had almost gotten me killed. I shot a quick glance to Pat McCracken only to get a quizzical look as Pat went looking for the punch bowl. All in all, a fine day was had by all, even though the party lasted well into the next morning.

The next day Betty and I left for a two-week honeymoon in Bermuda and the Bahamas, where the hotels mysteriously seemed to lose the bills and champagne appeared mysteriously every night. Well rested and happy, Betty and I returned to Hartford to clean out my apartment at 390 Pearl Street. Even after 20 years of odd hours, strange visitors and more than a few late rent payments, the landlady and my old friends in the building were in tears as they watched the moving van being packed.

Unfortunately, another bit of bad news came for us as we were packing up. Carol Dalhart Johnson called to tell me that her uncle, Durango Laramie Dalhart, had died that night. According to his wishes, he was buried quietly with no fanfare on his little farm in Bum Spung, Oklahoma. But there was a letter for me that Durango had written shortly before his death that required my presence.

Betty and I flew to Enid, Oklahoma, and drove to Bum Spung where we met with Carol and William, who is now the attorney for Durango's business interests. We read the letter under a cottonwood tree in the yard of his farm, beside that ramshackle little house he loved so much. In the letter, Durango recalled his life and the adventures he and I had shared together, including the time he chased me across the country as I ran from him, thinking he was after me with a shotgun to make me marry Carol. As a token of thanks for my friendship to both him and to Carol, Durango left me 10,000 shares of Dalhart Industries stock and a position on the board of directors. Once again, my life had taken on a new and unexpected dimension.

So, it is no more "Mr. Special Investigator" for Johnny Dollar. No more long flights, long nights and bullets whizzing past my ears. No more spending hours poring over insurance policies and watching shady characters. My activities have now turned to board meetings and financial dealings.

Betty and I finally were able to get to Sarasota and move into our new house on the beach. Earle and Mike Poorman welcomed us like long-lost children. Our life has settled down to trips for board meetings in Los Angeles and Dallas, regular trips to Lake Mohave Resort, fishing with Earle on the Gulf of Mexico and most of all, enjoying life with a wonderful woman named Betty Dollar. Betty has me eating right, she convinced me to stop smoking and I have almost learned how to beat her at tennis, but I still think she cheats with the scoring.

EXPENSE ACCOUNT TOTAL, well there is no amount of money that can pay for the happiness I now have with Betty. I have lost two wonderful friends, but life has dealt me a new hand, which I, or rather we, are still trying to deal with. I still jump each time the phone rings during the night, but now it is Earle wanting to sneak out early to fish for Tarpon or Snook before it gets too hot. So, as I close out this final matter, I can only say,

Yours Very Truly,
Betty and Johnny Dollar

And this is where the story of Johnny Dollar should have ended. It leaves plenty of opportunity for some enterprising writer to pick up the story and create new life for Johnny Dollar, the man with the action-packed life being lived with one hand in Betty's, and a fishing rod in the other.

IV: Program Related Information

The program stuck to a general premise over the entire run of the series. A client hired Johnny to resolve an insurance matter. Hopefully, Johnny would not spend more than the client was going to save! In the process, a variety of cases, presented by a stellar gathering of voices were presented to the listening audience.

THE CASES

As an independent investigator, Johnny Dollar was free to pick and choose his assignments. Early on, the option tended to be to accept or be poorer than he was. Later in the series, there was reticence over some types of cases, but others — where there was money to be had — were accepted regardless of the circumstances. Most of his cases were for insurance or related financial companies. However, Johnny did work for individuals, as in the case of *Murder Ain't Minor* where King Hart, a gangster hires him. Johnny also worked several cases for himself, as in *The Mickey McQueen Matter* where he looks into the death of his old, personal friend police officer Mickey McQueen.

Over the run of the series, Johnny handled almost every type of insurance matter. Cases included:

- Tracking down missing beneficiaries
- Exposing fraudulent claims
- Investigating applications for large policy amounts
- Finding lost policy holders
- Recovering lost jewels and other property
- Acting a body guard to lovely women — and a few ugly men
- Investigating manufacturing accidents
- Arson, mayhem, murder and the occasional talking dog or singing mouse!

During the mid-late 1950's a number of cases involved espionage by "a certain unfriendly country" (I wonder who that was?). As the space race picked up speed, several cases involved a rocket-fuel or space capsule related theme.

More often than not, murder was involved. Johnny often solved cases that the Police should have. Johnny always seemed to know who to call for information, whether it was to Randy Singer of the NYPD, or some famous scientist or professor who just happened to have a vital piece of information.

The Actors

Reviewing the many other excellent publications that report the broadcast history of Johnny Dollar, there are a number of names that reappear, some in recurring roles. Some of the most noted radio, screen and television actors stepped up to a microphone opposite Johnny Dollar.

Among the many stars were Virginia Gregg, Parley Baer, Howard McNear, Vic Perrin, Harry Bartell, John McIntire, William Conrad, Hy Averback, Sam Edwards, John Dehner, Will Wright, Lou Krugman, Jack Johnstone, William Johnstone, Roy Glenn, Byron Kane, Ed Begley, Jim Nusser, Herb Vigran, and many, many, more — too many to mention. Many of these names represent voices familiar to many. Many made the transition to television. Many were motion picture stalwarts. Some played a recurring role, such as Howard McNear as Alvin Peabody Cartwright and Parley Baer as Jake Kessler and Lawrence Dobkin as Pat McCracken. The interesting thing about radio is that, due to the non-visual presentation, and consummate skill of many of these actors, they could play numerous characters in the same program — each with their own voice and character.

The Writers and Producers

Yours Truly, Johnny Dollar was in a sense brought to life by the writers who penned the stories. The table below lists the writers for the programs that I have detailed in this book. There are others, but I have no information about the writers of the numerous missing programs.

Story Totals by Writer

Writer(s)	Story Count:
Adrian Gendot	1
Allen Botzer	2
Blake Edwards	31
Charles B. Smith	11
David Chandler	1
Don Sanford	3
E. Jack Neuman	25
E. Jack Neuman, Gil Doud	1
E. Jack Neuman, John Michael Hayes	3
Gibson Scott Fox	1
Gil Doud	79
Gil Doud, David Ellis	15
Jack Johnstone	272
Joel Murcot	3
John Dawson (aka E. Jack Neuman)	22
Kathleen Hite	1

Writer(s)	Story Count:
Les Crutchfield	23
Morton Fine, David Friedkin	2
Paul Dudley, Gil Doud	41
Paul Franklin	1
Robert Bainter (Bob Bailey)	1
Robert Ryf	15
Robert Stanley (aka Robert Ryf)	4
Sam Dawson (aka Jack Johnstone)	1
Sidney Marshall	21
Tony Barrett	2

It fell on the producer to coax the characters out of the actors in each program. The table below lists the producers for the programs compiled here:

Producer Show Totals

Producer	Show Total:
Bruno Zirato, Jr.	70
Fred Hendrickson	18
Gordon T. Hughes	17
Jack Johnstone	260
Jaime del Valle	184
Norman Macdonnell	5
Ralph Rose	2
Richard Sanville	8
Anton M. Leader	1
Un-broadcast	1

Based on the above information, if one were to choose a father figure for Johnny, the honor would fall on Jack Johnstone. It was to Jack, who was already a successful writer and producer, that the task fell to revive Johnny Dollar in 1955. Not only did Jack bring in a different format, but he brought in a stellar cadre of radio actors to bring life to the programs.

As more and more writers were lured to the higher salaries paid to television and film writers, eventually Jack undertook both the writing and directing/producing responsibilities for the program. Under Jack's aegis, the program was able to last until September of 1962, when *Yours Truly Johnny Dollar* and *Suspense* ended their runs as the last dramatic programs on radio. Interestingly, Jack wrote the programs for both final broadcasts.

Recurring Characters

Over the run of the series, there were a number of recurring characters, either as contacting agents, clients, or helpers. Some of the more notable are:

Randy Singer, NYPD 18th Precinct: Randy was an old friend who invariably helped Johnny out with information, and an occasional hand out of a deep situation.

Earle Poorman, Sarasota Florida: Earle was a good friend of Johnny, as well as an insurance agent who called him in to resolve difficult cases, and to go fishing in the Gulf of Mexico. Based on conversations with my friend Bill Brooks, who was a friend of Jack Johnstone's, Earle and Mike Poorman were real friends of Jack's.

Ham Pratt & Buster Favor, Lake Mohave Resorts: As the owner and manager of the resort, Ham and Buster were always on hand to provide the necessary local information, and to make sure the boat was ready for fishing after the work was done. Based on conversations with my friend Bill Brooks, who was a friend of Jack Johnstone's, Ham and Buster were friends of Jack Johnstone, and the Lake Mohave Resort actually existed.

Pat McCracken, Universal Adjustment Bureau: The Universal Adjustment Bureau was a fictitious policy claim-clearinghouse. As the manager, Pat was able to provide Johnny both cases and logistical assistance.

Pat Fuller, Universal Adjustment Bureau: Pat Fuller replaces Pat McCracken — who has retired — in *The Bee or Not to Bee Matter.*

Betty Lewis, favorite girlfriend: Betty was a business woman who, while desperately wanting to get Johnny's ankle into a marital bear trap, was smart enough to know that the time was not right. Betty figured in several cases as the "secondary" lead.

Durango Laramie Dalhart, of Bum Spung, Oklahoma: Durango, a retired oil/cattle/real estate millionaire, had the habit of walking around with a small fortune in cash in his pocket — and paying all his bills in cash. On one occasion, he even laundered his money — literally!

Alvin Peabody Cartwright, slightly forgetful eccentric millionaire: This role fit Howard McNear to a "T". Poor Alvin was loaded but so addle brained he would forget whom he was calling in the middle of a phone call. While seemingly gullible, he was no man's fool in the final analysis.

George Reed, Floyds of England: As a representative of the fictitious "Floyds of England (read Lloyds of London) who always had a wacky case to be handled whether it was a singing mouse or a talking dog, Alvin Peabody Cartwright or Durango Dalhart.

Louis De Marsac, "Les Chat Gris" ("The Grey Cat"): This was a French underground character played with a distinct Peter Lorre accent. While the character knew everything that happened in the underground, he quite often cheated himself out of money while dickering over the amount of money he was trying to extort out of Johnny Dollar.

One notable feature of the broadcast series is that on two different occasions during the Bob Bailey episodes (during *The Open Town Matter* and *The Curse of Kamashek Matter*), the star took a few moments to give heartfelt thanks to all of those who had taken the time to write in. Each used the words "You will never know how much your letters meant to us". The announcement also included a promise to answer every letter.

In *The Look Before the Leap Matter* in 1960 during National Brotherhood week, Bob gives a very heartfelt plea for the principles of the event. Bob also gave messages around the Christmas and Thanksgiving holidays as well.

V: Case Synopses

I personally have listened to every available episode of "Yours Truly, Johnny Dollar" I am aware of. My personal collection is over 800 programs. In 2005 I spent a busy week at the Thousand Oaks Library reviewing the scripts in the KNX collection, which added over 75 programs to the book and again in 2017 that added 8 programs — including 6 Bob Readick programs. The information below is a synopsis of the story line for every program I have either listened to or reviewed. I have tried to recap the writer, producer, announcers and music providers when available in the broadcast. I have referenced at least two other external sources where cast and crew information are available there. Unless otherwise noted, all cast and crew information are taken from the actual program or from the script pages for the program.

For this second edition, I have relied on the Old Time Radio Researchers (OTRR) collection of mp3 programs, version 2. This collection includes all the known digital programs and has the most complete versions of the programs.

The format of the synopses is as follows:

SHOW DATE: Date on which the program aired.

SHOW TITLE: The name of the program. Where my name varies from the usual name, it is because I have either corrected spelling or based the name on the title page of the script or uncapitalized articles ("the" instead of "The" "and" instead of "And", etc.)

COMPANY: This is the company or individual who has hired Johnny for the case

AGENT: Where available, the agent of the company

EXPENSE TOTAL: This is the total of expenses for each case.

PRODUCER: This is the producer of the program, where known.

WRITER: This is the writer(s) of the program, where known.

CAST: Where available, the cast members for each program are listed. I have standardized on the actor's names, so there will only be one entry for an actor whether they were announced as "Bill" or as "William".

SYNOPSIS: A rundown of the case — including who done it.

NOTES: Information or facts in the case I find interesting, any AKA's for the story, the announcers and music providers, etc.

The synopses below are divided into seven sections, one section for each of the primary actors, and one for the several audition programs which are available. In each of these programs I have endeavored to spell the names of the directors, writers and actors as accurately as possible. I have relied on the information available from a review of the scripts at the Thousand Oaks Library, J. David Goldin and Terry Salomonson, as well as assorted tools on the Internet, such as the *Internet Movie Database* and the researcher's friend, *Google*.

In the case of characters in the radio programs, I have tried as much as possible to apply a reasonable transliteration to sounds and have relied on the above resources where possible. "Smith and "Jones" are easy, "Ah Mai" and "Arnesson" are a little harder.

Where geographical locations are noted, I have tried to locate them. Native peoples and regions are located and described to the extent possible.

Charles Russell

Charles Russell (1918–1985) was the first regular actor to play the Johnny Dollar character.

The role that Russell played was of a sarcastic, irreverent, droll and somewhat lecherous person. Johnny always got the bad guy, but he always seemed to get the girl as well — sometimes to his undoing and always, it seemed "on" the expense account.

Each of the Russell cases included one alternative title, sometimes two. An additional feature added after the initial programs was an opening comment about the case. An example is the opening of *The Search for Michelle Marsh*: "Sure, they may have plenty of blue blood in Boston, but from what I just saw, they've got plenty of the other kind too."

This Johnny is not so much of a hard-boiled detective. He does his job and yet wonders why. He is not afraid to stick his nose into trouble, but he often wonders why he does it. The first Johnny Dollar has no hesitation to add pleasure and personal items to the expense account, much to the chagrin of his employers.

Charles Russell appeared in 18 movies between 1943 and 1950, and also appeared in several other radio programs, but seems to have ceased acting after 1950. Russell died in January, 1985 in Los Angeles.

The following are the Charles Russell Johnny Dollar cases.

Show: The Parakoff Policy
Show Date: 2/18/1949
Company: East Coast Underwriters
Agent:
Exp. Acct: $1,230.20

Synopsis: Johnny is already in his room when he checks into the Valley Hotel in Benton, Ohio. Johnny asks to leave his card and sees the room number the clerk puts it in and goes to that room. Johnny knocks and announces himself as the bellboy with a special delivery package from Hartford. Inside the room is Eric Barker, the defense attorney for the policyholder Parakoff. Johnny questions Barker and learns that Parakoff killed Harland Wolf, who was the owner of the insurance policy and his business partner. Barker tells Johnny that Mr. Parakoff was caught running away from town with the murder weapon in his possession. Supposedly Parakoff shot Wolf in self-defense after an argument.

Johnny goes to visit Mrs. Marsha Parakoff and is met at the door by a woman with red hair, green eyes, and wearing a negligee. Johnny is invited in and comments on how well she furnishes the living room. Johnny asks her what she knows, but she tells Johnny that the District Attorney had told her to keep quiet. But she willingly tells Johnny all of what is in the newspapers. Her story is that she is the Vice President of the Highland Coal Company. Johnny makes a comment about his anthracite heart feeling very bituminous, but Marsha does not catch the references to coal. She claims she was alone with Wolf talking about the business when her husband came home and shot Wolf with a .38 — hence the case. Marsha asks Johnny to throw some more wood on the fire in the fireplace for her. Johnny goes out to get a damp piece of wood — they burn slower.

Sometime later Johnny calls for a cab and walks down the snow-covered sidewalk where he is stopped and told to get out of town by two police officers. They have the guilty man and do not want any trouble. The men beat Johnny up, but he lifts a wallet from one of them in the confusion. The cabby arrives and takes Johnny to his hotel room where Johnny expenses medicinal supplies (bonded). The next morning Johnny has the contents of the wallet photographed and mails the photos to Hartford. Johnny then meets with the D.A., Edwin Byrum. Johnny tells him what happened to his face and Byrum plays ignorant of any involvement by the local police. Johnny is told that the indictment will be handed down tomorrow.

Johnny phones Barker and arranges to borrow photos of the crime scene. The photos arrive and Johnny examines the pictures, and it turns out that Wolf and Parakoff were standing face-to-face when Parakoff was shot. Bullet placements in Parakoff's body indicate that a left-handed person shot him. Johnny makes an appointment to see Barker at three and goes to look into the owner of the wallet he got the night before.

Johnny goes to the disreputable address of the wallet's owner, Ben Arnold, and finds Arnold's wife there with a black eye. In a small room Johnny finds a police coat with "CPD" on the buttons. Johnny goes to see Barker and tells him about the fake police who beat him up while wearing out-of-town uniforms. Johnny wonders if Marsha set Johnny up.

Johnny figures that if Wolf dies she gets the money from the insurance, being the widow of the beneficiary, and she gets the coal company. Barker admits to Johnny that Marsha and Wolf had been having a romance. Johnny figures that Marsha shot her husband and convinces Wolf to take the blame and claim self-defense. Wolf gets a light sentence, or no sentence and then gets the girl. Johnny notes that the photos indicate a left-handed shooter and Barker tells Johnny that Wolf is left-handed, so he decides to go to see Marsha to see if she is also left-handed.

At the Parakoff house, Johnny builds a fire and asks Marsha to light it, which she does with her right hand. Johnny asks Marsha to call the D.A. and change her story. Johnny tells her that her husband was killed by a left-handed man and that Marsha had killed her husband and phoned Wolf to convince him to take the rap for her.

As Marsha cries Johnny tells her that she changed her story after Wolf was arrested and told the D.A. that Wolf had been after her to leave her husband and threatened to kill him. Marsha begs Johnny to stop and Barker comes into the room and agrees with her.

Barker tells Johnny that he wants the wallet and Johnny tells him of the photos he took, but Barker is not convinced. Johnny tells Barker that he was the one who arranged for the men to beat him up. Johnny notes that Barker is holding the gun in his left hand and accuses him of shooting Parakoff.

Marsha tells Barker to shoot Johnny and rushes for the gun. Johnny throws Marsha into Barker and a fight for the gun begins. Johnny manages to shoot the gun into the ceiling and knocks Barker out.

Johnny has lunch with the D.A. and they agree that the defense was working harder for a conviction that the prosecution and that everyone was guilty: Barker of murder, Marsha of being an accessory before and after the fact, and Wolf for conspiracy to defraud. "Oh, no wonder the nation's jails are getting overcrowded." Johnny notes that he had to take a $700 side trip to Miami Beach to recover from a cold he caught rolling in the snow.

Notes:
- "The next half-hour has its baggage packed to take a trip with America's fabulous freelance Insurance investigator. At insurance investigation he is an expert   At making out his expense account he is an absolute genius."
- Johnny buys two one-way tickets because he is not always sure he will come home.
- $1-dollar tips to taxis and bellman.
- There is 3 inches of snow on the sidewalk, cold weather and Johnny is wearing summer clothes.

- $7.00 of bonded medical supplies is expensed after the beating.
- Johnny notes some skills as a poolroom pickpocket.
- In the final struggle, the .38 murder weapon fires 7 times.
- The mid-program commercial is for the program *Sing It Again*.
- There are several different versions of this program in circulation. One version talks about the special program *Mind in the Shadows*, other previews *Life with Luigi*.
- For many years, the program *Mind in the Shadows* was incorrectly identified as a Johnny Dollar program.
- Mark Warnow provides the music in one of the versions of this program.

Producer: Richard Sanville   Writer: Paul Dudley, Gil Doud
Cast: Unknown

◆ ❖ ◆

Show: **The Slow Boat from China**
Show Date: **2/25/1949**
Company: **Oriental West Cargo Bonding Company**
Agent: **Mr. Fundy**
Exp. Acct: **$1,407.00**

Synopsis: Johnny flies to San Francisco, California in answer to a letter from Oriental Bonding and has lunch on Fisherman's wharf. Johnny cabs to the office of Mr. Fundy, who gives Johnny a ticket to Singapore and tells Johnny that Oriental has insured a cargo of tin, but the ship has been held up for three weeks. The delay was investigated by an expediter who has reported several mechanical failures. Johnny tells Fundy that what he needs is a good plumber.

Johnny is told to look for William Harrison at the Crown Colony Hotel and Harrison will fill in the details. Johnny only has hours to get the boat moving, as more delays will cost them $2,500 per day. Johnny looks forward to a night on the town but is told his plane leaves in two hours.

Johnny reports a loss of $240 from teaching a plane passenger how to play poker on the trip. In Singapore, Johnny gets a room at the Crown Colony Hotel and goes to Harrison's room where the door is open and Johnny finds a calling card from his old friend trouble.

Johnny searches the dresser and the bathroom, where the toothbrush is still wet. In the trashcan Johnny finds a swizzle stick with "The Colliard Tea Bar" stamped on it. Johnny goes to the bar, overlooking the harbor. The bartender gives Johnny bourbon and is told that Harrison has been in every night with the chief engineer of the *Shanghai Wayfarer*, a really nice guy and big tipper. For $20 Johnny gets his name, Frank Moore.

Johnny goes to the docks by rickshaw and tips the driver $1. The gangway-watch stops Johnny with a large knife and tells Johnny that Moore has been stabbed and is in the morgue and that the police are holding a girl.

Johnny visits the British Chief Inspector who has never heard of Harrison. Johnny looks at the body, and comments that Moore had been "sunk with a hole in one". A large stack of crisp $20 bills in the wallet makes Johnny wonder if

Moore was taking money to delay the sailing. A picture, signed by Shandra, the girl who had been released by the police, reminds Johnny that the man who said, "never the twain shall meet" should have met her. Johnny learns that she works in the Wordlow Bar on Malay Street.

Johnny goes to the bar and asks for Shandra and is told that she is not there tonight. Shandra shows up and asks why Johnny is asking for her. She tells Johnny that he either wants secrets or has secrets to sell. Johnny asks if she knows Harrison, but she does not know him and tells Johnny that maybe he was lonely and does not want to be found tonight. She tells Johnny that they should go to her house to have a drink where they do not have to whisper.

At Shandra's house Johnny spots a Louisville Slugger baseball bat on the wall with the words "Remember the US Marines" on it. Johnny and Shandra relax and she wants to know Johnny better, and she does when Johnny stops talking, but Johnny wonders how Shandra knew that Harrison was missing tonight.

Two men with guns break the door open, and Shandra joins them. One man is a bald fat man with three chins, the other a punk with a sneer and arms too long for him. Johnny is tied to a chair and Shandra tells them that Johnny is looking for Harrison and Moore, which is why she called them. The punk tells Johnny that he is using his head better than Harrison did. Johnny is told he can prevent Harrison's death and his if he cooperates. Johnny is offered 750 pounds for the information they want. The man threatens to slit his tongue to make him talk but Johnny replies "Nuts!"

Johnny is beaten and wakes up tied up in the dark where another voice says "hello" and asks who Johnny is. The other man is Harrison, and Johnny tells him that he is trying to find him. Johnny tells him that the men, Roseline and Corgy have offered him 750 pounds for "it", whatever "it" is.

Harrison tells Johnny that "it" is a package that Moore had asked him to drop off with Shandra. She was not there, so he took it to her house where he hid the package in the bottom drawer of a chest. Harrison tells Johnny that Moore had been a good friend, and he wanted to make sure that Shandra got the package rather than those two. Johnny tells him that all three are working together, and Harrison calls himself an idiot. Johnny is sure that Moore was murdered for the package.

The door opens and a voice Johnny recognizes enters the room. Johnny recognizes him as the gangway-watch at the *Shanghai Wayfarer*. The man, named Roark, tells Johnny that he wants the package. Johnny tells him he is only interested in getting the ship underway, and Roark tells him that will happen as soon as he gets the package. Johnny convinces Roark to untie them. Johnny hits him and runs from the room.

Johnny goes to Shandra's house and breaks in. Johnny tells Shandra he knows where the package is, and she tells Johnny that with the package they can be happy for the rest of their life. Johnny goes to the bedroom and takes the package from the chest and opens it to find a stack of money — $500,000 in fresh, green American twenties. Shandra tells Johnny they are counterfeit, made in China. Moore brought them for Roseline to take to the states, but Roseline was delayed, so Moore created the accidents. Moore then decided to keep the money, but Roseline caught up to him and killed him.

A car drives up, so Johnny ties up Shandra and locks her in the closet with a mouth full of money as a gag. Johnny takes the baseball bat and waits by the door. Roseline walks in and is decked with the bat, as is Corgy. Johnny takes their guns when Roark comes in telling Johnny that he will take over. He tosses Johnny his wallet, which contains his US Treasury ID.

Roark tells Johnny that he was too close to the payoff to tell him who he was. The money has been coming through Singapore for months, and Roseline was the ringleader. Johnny asks Roark, since he is with the Treasury, to help him fill out his income tax.

Johnny expenses, among other things, $200 for a new suit and $375 for entertainment while waiting for his plane after the ship sails.

Notes:
- The case title is "The Investigation of Delayed Cargo Aboard the Shanghai Wayfarer".
- This program contains a commercial for *The Jack Benny Program* on Sunday, with Claude Raines.
- The next adventure is *The Star of Hades Diamond* where Johnny will hit the hot spots in Palm Beach and New Orleans. There is no record of a program with this title.
- The Star of Hades was mentioned in *The Diamond Protector Matter*.
- There is a commercial for *Gang Busters* and *Phillip Marlow* at the end of the program.
- Johnny expenses a suit to replace one ruined in the Shanghai River but he was never thrown into the river.
- Mark Warnow provides the music.

Producer:	Richard Sanville	Writer:	Paul Dudley, Gil Doud
Cast:	Unknown		

◆ ❖ ◆

Show: The Robert Perry Case
Show Date: 3/4/1949
Company: American Continental Life Insurance
Agent: Mr. Gordon
Exp. Acct: $1,263.00

Synopsis: Johnny takes a night train to New York and cabs to Mr. Perry's New York City import office at exactly 9:00 a.m. Susan the receptionist buzzes him in and the office explodes. Perry had thought his life was in danger and now he is dead.

Johnny gives the receptionist some water to drink as the occupants of the building stream in. Everyone is told to leave and Johnny explains to Susan that someone hooked up a bomb to the buzzer to kill Perry. Mr. Perry left last night and someone must have come in afterwards and rigged the bomb. Susan tells Johnny that his next appointment was to be with his partner, Van Brooten, who came from Holland to pick up a check dissolving the partnership. Christine the wife, was due later to finalize the upcoming divorce. The fire department arrives and Johnny tells them someone will get burned when the cops arrive. The police arrive and conduct an investigation. At eleven, Van Brooten arrives to pick up the check. Johnny tells Van Brooten that Perry is dead, but Susan is confused. Susan gives Van Brooten the check and he leaves.

Johnny calls American Continental and tells Mr. Gordon what has happened. Johnny is told to stay on the case, and Mr. Gordon asks if the death could have been suicide. Johnny tells Gordon that trying to prove "suicide" to enable the suicide clause would require a "Santa" clause. Johnny will talk to the wife to see if fraud is involved.

Johnny cabs to the apartment of Christine Perry. Christine tells Johnny who he is and why he is there, and Johnny wonders about her motives. She tells Johnny that she knows very little about her husband's friends since she left him. She tells Johnny that she was with a friend, Al Donovan at the Club Caprice. Her husband was there also with Susan. Al Donovan enters the apartment and slugs Johnny after he starts asking questions. Al tells Christine that he was not with her at the club, and that she was supposed to be there with her husband talking about the divorce. Johnny listens from the floor as Christine and Al leave the apartment. This case is becoming interesting.

Johnny follows Al in a cab and after a car ride with Christine, she jumps out and Johnny follows Al to a police precinct. Johnny speaks with the police and they tell Johnny that Al Donovan has made a full confession to bombing the office. Donovan told the police he was in love with Mrs. Perry and planted a bomb in the office. Johnny thinks he is trying to cover up something.

Johnny searches Perry's office and learns that Van Brooten was bald and had been getting toupees from Perry for years. In the files Johnny learns that Al Donovan was Perry's former bodyguard and that he was fired the day before the murder. Mrs. Perry comes in and finds Johnny in the office. She tells Johnny that she wants to talk to someone and thought Johnny might be there. She tells Johnny that Al's confession is bogus. Johnny tells her that Al was Perry's bodyguard until the day before the blast. Christine tells Johnny that she wants to tell the truth and Johnny tells her to call the police. Christine pulls a gun on Johnny and Johnny pulls the phone from the wall as Christine wishes him success in the investigation. After she leaves Johnny discovers that Susan, the receptionist, was a former ordnance technician who wired bomb fuses!

Johnny goes to Susan's apartment and meets her when she comes in. Johnny tells her about Al's confession, but Susan thinks he is covering for Christine. Johnny mentions the Club Caprice and Susan tells him that she was there with Perry. Mrs. Perry was there with a man Susan did not know, but Perry did. Susan tells Johnny that she has worked for Perry for four years. The doorbell rings, Susan answers the door and is shot. Susan is shot once and Johnny can find no one in the hallway. Susan is sure that she will be arrested.

She tells Johnny that the man in the office was a phony and she was shot because she was trying to blackmail him. Susan tells Johnny the man's hotel name and faints.

Johnny goes looking for the phony Van Brooten in the Nelson Hotel. Johnny cannot find any Dutch names so he gets the rooms that the maids have not been able to make up and starts looking. Johnny finds pay dirt in room 427. Johnny gets the man out of the room with a phony fire alarm.

Johnny gets into the room and beats the man, who is named Van Zandt. Van Zandt tells Johnny that the real Van Brooten is drugged in the next room. Van Zandt had known Van Brooten in Amsterdam and knew about the sale of the company. Van Zandt had drugged Perry's cocoa and set up the bomb in the office.

Van Zandt did not know how Susan had known he was a phony. Johnny tells Van Zandt that Perry was sending his partner gray wigs, my red-headed friend! Johnny wires the insurance company that they will have to pay Christine, who was only guilty of trying to stay on the right side of a hot-tempered boyfriend. Christine had lied about the Club Caprice because she had been out with the real Van Brooten who was trying to convince her not to divorce his friend Perry. Johnny expenses a fine of one thousand dollars and no sense for setting off the false alarm.

Notes:
- This program uses a slightly different opening music from previous program.
- This program was done as *Bodyguard to the Late Robert W. Perry* on 3/3/1950.
- There is only one $1 tip.
- The mid-program commercial is about the $60 Million the Red Cross needs.
- The announcer gives a promo for the *Jack Benny Show* with Ronald and Benita Colman next Sunday.
- Mark Warnow provides the music.

Producer: Richard Sanville   Writer: Paul Dudley, Gil Doud
Cast: Unknown

◆ ❖ ◆

Show: Murder is a Merry-Go-Round
Show Date: 3/11/1949
Company: **Nutmeg State Casualty & Bonding Company**
Agent:
Exp. Acct: $692.18

Synopsis: Johnny travels to Talladega, Alabama to investigate a series of accidents at the Funfair and Weatherly Entertainment traveling circus. Johnny cabs to the circus and talks to the employees, but none of the employees is willing to talk about the accidents.

After being slugged, Johnny is awakened by a man who asks him what he is doing there. The man is Shanty Brennan the manager. Over a drink, Johnny tells Brennan that the show is reported to be clean but is plagued by accidents for ten straight nights. The owner, Louisa Pepper, comes in and Johnny feels that she is too friendly. Johnny tells her he is with the insurance company and she wants Johnny to find out who is responsible for the accidents as someone is out to get them, and, the cost of extra protection is costing too much. They know their help and trust them.

Louisa tells Johnny that a former employee, Carter Lacy, is the only one to have a grudge — but he is in jail for attempted murder — or is he? Johnny agrees to find out if Carter is still in jail. Brennan tells Johnny that Carter was jailed for the attempted murder of Myrtle Pepper, Louisa's niece. Johnny finds out that Carter has been paroled and has been following the show for two weeks. Johnny calls the hotels in town and finds one with Carter registered there.

Johnny cabs to the Sunshine Hotel and arranges to meet Carter in a cafe. Carter tells Johnny that he is going to settle some scores. Carter tells Johnny that two of the three key people will be dead soon, and one of the three will help him. Louisa Pepper, Shanty Brennan and Myrtle Pepper the snake charmer, are the targets. Cater tells Johnny that he was an innocent bystander and was hurt, just like the people in the accidents.

Johnny hires a detective to follow Carter and returns to the circus. Johnny looks for Myrtle and tells her he has a message from Carter Lacey. Myrtle lets Johnny in and he tells her about the threat to two of the people at the circus. Myrtle leaves to tell Shanty and Louisa and Johnny finds a black book in her tent. Johnny goes to see Louisa and find Myrtle there. Myrtle has told Shanty, who was going to feed her snakes. All three go to the snake tent and find Shanty Brennan feeding the snakes — literally.

Johnny takes Myrtle and Louisa to their tent and Johnny tries to figure out who is next. Johnny gets Louisa's gun and puts it on the table between Louisa and Myrtle, in case Carter shows up. Johnny gets the car keys so that the car and trailer cannot be moved. Johnny calls the police and a cab.

Johnny cabs to Carter's hotel and finds Carter gone. Johnny picks the lock and finds Myrtle Pepper strangled in Carter Lacey's room. Johnny calls the police and tells them to send in the second team. Johnny finds some old newspaper clippings in the room along with Carter's parole papers.

Johnny leaves and finds Carter in the hallway. Johnny tells Carter that Carter was sent up for grand larceny not attempted murder like Brennan had told Johnny. Johnny tells him about a bankbook he found where $60,000 had been deposited into a bank the same year Carter was sent up for grand larceny. Johnny suspects a double-cross as the money went to a bank account for the Peppers and Brennan.

Johnny goes back to the circus and Louisa lets him into the trailer. Johnny tells her that he had talked to Carter and that Myrtle is dead. Johnny hints that Carter never meant to do anything himself, he would just let others fight among themselves. Johnny tells Louisa that Myrtle was strangled by someone with long fingernails, but Carter bites his nails.

Louisa pulls the gun on Johnny but Carter shows up with a gun. Johnny tells Carter that the state will take care of Louisa, but Carter wants to hear her squeal. Johnny leaves to find a rope when he hears shooting. Johnny starts the car and takes the trailer onto the highway. Johnny is shot at and attracts the police with some reckless driving.

Johnny buys cigars for the local police and pays Carter's hotel bill, as Louisa had shot him.

Notes:
- A word of advice   go to the head of a circus first for information.
- A slow taxi ride gets a nickel tip.
- The mid-way hot dogs are no thoroughbreds.
- There is a commercial about John Lund in *Escape*.
- Expense Account total   only $692.18? "I must be slipping!"
- This program contains a commercial for the *Spike Jones Show*, which has moved to Saturday.
- Mark Warnow provides the music.

Producer:	Richard Sanville	Writer:	Paul Dudley, Gil Doud
Cast:	Unknown		

◆ ❖ ◆

Show: Milford Brooks III
Show Date: 3/25/1949
Company: Honesty Life Insurance Underwriters
Agent: Austin Farnsworth
Exp. Acct: $1,182.23

Synopsis: Johnny cabs to Austin Farnsworth's Hartford, Connecticut office where there is a struggle going on. Johnny slugs the man Farnsworth is fighting with to keep him away from the window so Johnny closes it. Johnny sits on the man's head to keep him from killing Johnny. Johnny is told that the man is Farnsworth's most important client and is insured for two million dollars. The man is Milford Brooks, III and the policy is to allow the heirs to pay the inheritance taxes when he dies. But because of his life style, he has no heirs and no money, so he is trying to get money by killing himself. He came in today and changed the beneficiary and demanded $500,000 in cash. Since there was no loan provision in the policy he told Farnsworth to either get the money or pay off on the policy.

The new beneficiary is a notorious gambler named Harold Hatcher. Farnsworth wants Johnny to protect Brooks. Johnny tells him that since he will have to work twice as hard to keep somebody from killing Brooks, or having him kill himself, he will have to be paid twice as much. Johnny is told to give Brooks something to live for, an interest in life.

Johnny gets an inspiration and pulls out his little black book. Rudi? No, her favorite expression is "Drop dead!" Bernadine? No, she would be the new beneficiary by midnight. Butter! She's the one. Johnny calls Miss Theodora Butts in New York at Hudson 2-4292. Johnny tells Butter he is coming and he asks her to reserve a table for dinner, and that he will be there in a couple hours. Johnny buys a bottle of brandy to keep Brooks quiet on the drive to New York. As they pass the Yale Bowl, Brooks gives a "Boola, Boola" for dear old Eli. Brooks tells Johnny that he loves someone very much and hates someone very much and passes out again.

Johnny muses about the case as he drives the Merit Parkway. He is sure that Brooks owes Hatcher a bundle, so Hatcher must have forced Brooks to make him the new beneficiary. But why the suicide-threat, unless he was trying to get away from Hatcher.

At Butter's apartment Johnny puts Brooks on the couch where he passes out. Over a root beer Johnny tells Butter all about the case. Johnny sees a big boat in the window and wishes he could sail away with Butter — but she tells him it is the 125th street ferry. Johnny tells Butter that he has a Dad's old-fashioned root beer and is ready for one of Mom's new-fashioned kisses. Johnny tells Butter that she is what Brooks is supposed to live for, and she slaps him. Johnny talks his way out of the situation and Butter apologizes. The phone rings, and the call is for Johnny. Farnsworth asks about Brooks and wants to talk to him. Johnny goes to get him, but Brooks has gone out with Butter.

Johnny has lost both Brooks and Butter and so Johnny goes to look for them. Johnny searches the neighborhood and decides to get help from a higher source. Johnny calls Lt. Fisher at Missing Persons. Johnny asks him about Butter and is told to call Dorothy Dix. Johnny asks him about Brooks and is told they think they know where he is — the Hudson River. His coat was found in the 125th street ferry with a pack of matches with the initials "HH".

Johnny goes to the club owned by Hatcher and is met by a blond who asks Johnny who he is looking for. She is Janelle, and she knows Hatcher. Johnny tells him he wants to see Hatcher about a friend — Brooks. She recognizes that Johnny is not a cop or a society friend of Brooks. She tells Johnny where Hatcher's office is and that he won't have any trouble, as Hatcher sent her to check him out — and Johnny is all right. Johnny goes to the office and tells Hatcher who he is and why he is there and about Brook's disappearance.

Johnny asks where Brooks is and Hatcher tells Johnny he was driving around when Brooks disappeared. He tells Johnny that Brooks owes him a couple hundred thousand, so he would not bump off his own assets. Hatcher knows nothing about the insurance policy, but Johnny tells him he will get $2 million if Brooks is found dead. Hatcher tells Johnny that he will never be able to prove anything. The intercom buzzes and Hatcher is told the police are there. The police take Hatcher to headquarters and Johnny goes to talk to Janelle.

Johnny tells her about the conversation and she tells Johnny that she told Hatcher he would get in trouble about the policy. Brooks owes Hatcher money, and there is a note in Hatcher's office that Brooks is supposed to get back when Hatcher is made beneficiary. Johnny is sure that Janelle is trying to sell out Hatcher. They go to the office and Johnny searches the closet until he finds the note in the top desk drawer. Johnny also finds something in his closet that could turn into a bond fire. Johnny tells Janelle he found what he was looking for and leaves.

Johnny gets a cab (dollar tip) and waits until Janelle comes out and gets one also. Johnny follows her to 72nd street where he stops a block behind her and runs to the building, and old garage. Inside Johnny goes upstairs and hears Brooks plotting with Janelle. Johnny rushes in and slugs Brooks and Janelle tells Johnny that he is hers. Johnny tells them that they were silly to plant the matchbook. They should have planted a lighter, as there is one in every suit Hatcher owns and that he never carries matches.

Johnny accuses Brooks of insurance fraud and asks where Butter is. Brooks tells Johnny that he had to take her with him when he left, but he put Butter into a cab to the emergency hospital. Hatcher comes in and tells Johnny that he has had enough fun. He tells Johnny that the police had counted the turnstiles at each end of the ferry, and they matched. So, Brooks was not really missing. He came to the garage because he always knows where Janelle goes. Johnny tells Hatcher that they were trying to frame him and that they made a real mistake by trying the fraud.

Hatcher is ready to shoot Brooks when Johnny tackles him and knocks him out, but not before Brooks is shot. The police arrive and Johnny goes to see Butter in the hospital. She tells him that they had to cut off some of her hair to put on the bandages. Johnny tells her that Brooks is in the same hospital and that he knows a man who has something better than hair. Johnny buys Butter a hat for $640 to cover the bump on her head.

"Expense account total is $1,182.23, which you may say Mr. Farnsworth is a lot of money for one man to spend in a day-and-a-half. But you must bear in mind that the amount at stake was 2 million dollars, and you know the price of steak these days."

Notes:
- This program contains a commercial for the *Jack Benny Program*.
- In the Dick Powell audition, Johnny spent $318 on a bracelet for Butter.
- Music is by Mark Warnow.

Producer:	Richard Sanville	Writer:	Paul Dudley, Gil Doud
Cast:	Unknown		

◆ ❖ ◆

Show: The Stolen Portrait of the Duke of Massen
Show Date: 4/1/1949
Company: Fine Arts Securers
Agent: Frederick Kimble
Exp. Acct: $1,563.40

Synopsis: Johnny flies to London, England to look for a stolen portrait of the Duke of Massen. Johnny loans his coat to a seatmate who is fighting to keep his meal down. The passenger goes to get some water from the stewardess and disappears out the back door of the plane in Johnny's topcoat!

In London, Johnny meets Dexter Morley, who appreciates the fine arts but who does not have the money to buy them or travel to see them. He has set up a program to get the top twelve museums of the world to loan out pictures to him. The Duke's picture was the first one to be shown and was stolen on the first night! Johnny gets the address of the museum and Dexter tells Johnny that he is going to France that day.

Johnny buys a paper to read of his adventures on the front pages. Johnny meets Dexter's assistant, Muriel Harding. Johnny tells her about what happened on the plane and she shows Johnny where the paining was stolen, along with the frame. Muriel has gone over the museum with Scotland Yard and is sure that she can save Johnny a lot of trouble. Muriel provides Johnny with a complete list of all the known art thieves in Europe complete with addresses for the two who are not in prison. Criminology fascinates her.

Johnny cabs to Scotland Yard and meets with Inspector Carrew. Carrew tells Johnny that no one has filed a claim of loss, and they cannot act until someone does. Johnny asks if Muriel is known by Scotland Yard and shows Carrew the list. On his way to the Mount Royal Hotel, Johnny naps and wonders about Muriel and the incident on the plane. At the hotel Johnny is almost run down by a car "Worse than the bloody buzz bombs" replies the doorman. Johnny is sure he has been set up as a pigeon.

After a nap and a shower, Johnny goes to dinner at Ketners. Johnny goes to the flat of the first thief on his list and lets himself in to find a wood burning stove blazing away, the painting of the Duke on a table, and a dead body with its head parted down the middle. Johnny searches for a phone and finds a door that spits bullets at him.

Johnny drops to the floor and hears someone leaving through a window. Johnny goes to see Miss Harding and tells her he has called the police and taken the painting to Scotland Yard. Muriel tells Johnny that the thief probably tried to shoot Johnny, but Johnny is not convinced. Johnny tells her he has a yearning, burning deep inside to break someone's neck. Johnny calls New York collect to report in. While Johnny waits Muriel offers Johnny a drink, but Johnny wants to join her on the couch. Muriel tells Johnny about her days in the Royal Air Force as he kisses her. The phone call comes in and Johnny learns that the frame is also insured for $10,000. Johnny goes back to work after he calms his nerves with Muriel.

Johnny goes back to the flat of the thief and finds a very curious form of ashes — diamonds! Johnny cabs to Morley's office and finds a cabinet shop in the basement — and a gun in Morley's hand. Johnny is sure that Morley was the one who shot at him earlier that day. Johnny tells Morley that he is in charge of a smuggling racket, but Morley only wants the diamonds. Johnny tells him that the diamonds are in a cab with a burnt-out license light, so only Johnny knows which cab it is.

Johnny tells Morley that as each picture is sent to him, the frame would be filled with diamonds and moved around the world. But a burglar interrupted the plan, so now Johnny will get his. When Muriel tries to get in through a window, Johnny slugs Morley with his gun. Muriel tells Johnny that she was only trying to help and had followed him. Johnny shows her the diamonds that are in his pocket.

Johnny flies home to avoid a wedding and buys Muriel a cookbook to divert her interest on criminology. Any expense account errors in Johnny's favor were due to confusion over the exchange rates!

Notes:
- AKA "Who Opened the Season on Canvas Backed Dukes"?
- Johnny notes he pads his expense account to make a living.
- Tip to the cabby, 2 bob (shillings).
- $14 for a bottle of medicinal scotch.
- There is a 5-schilling limit on dinner prices. Johnny's dinner is chicken with creamed, boiled, and roasted brussels sprout!
- Johnny states that "there is a yearning, burning deep inside" to break some one's neck   nice quote of Jerome Kerns.
- There is a small expense item for Bromo Seltzer to fight the brussels sprouts in Gander, Newfoundland.
- This program contains a commercial for Ozzie and Harriet, and a final commercial that Jane Wyman will return to The Family Hour of Stars, *Ozzie and Harriet* return to CBS next Sunday. Add these to the comedy of *Jack Benny, Helen Hayes, Eve Arden, Amos n' Andy, Lum and Abner,* and Sunday makes great news along with *Sam Spade*, and *Life with Luigi*.
- Music is by Mark Warnow.

Producer:	Richard Sanville	Writer:	Paul Dudley, Gil Doud
Cast:	Unknown		

• ❖ •

Show: The Case of the Hundred Thousand Dollar Legs
Show Date: 4/15/1949
Company: Highworthy Insurance Underwriters Association
Agent: Harvey Anthony
Exp. Acct: $948.76

Synopsis: Johnny is paged at the track and expenses the $60 he lost because of a hasty bet. Johnny takes a call from Harvey Anthony, who tells Johnny to fly to Hollywood, California and act as a bodyguard to Marilyn Majors, whose legs are insured for $100,000 for 48 hours as part of a publicity policy. Johnny will be there, if American Airlines co-operates.

Johnny flies to Los Angeles and goes to the penthouse apartment of Marilyn where he finds the door open and the body of Marilyn very dead in a cheesecake position, with a bullet hole where an earring should have been. Johnny calls Anthony to tell him the bad news but it gets worse. Johnny is told that Highworthy also insures her life with double indemnity for death by violence.

While Johnny is on the phone about to call the police, he is told by a young girl (who is wearing a tobacco brown dress so round, so firm, so fully packed) to hang up the phone with a .32 caliber convincer. She tells Johnny that she came there to kill Marilyn but someone beat her to it. The girl takes Johnny to the bedroom and puts him against the wall as she searches for a packet of letters apparently written by her husband who had just committed suicide over them. Johnny gets locked in a closet and uses a nail file and an ink pen to push the carpet down to let air in. Johnny overhears the girl call the police and tell them that the killer is in the closet. Then Johnny hears a man come in, accuse her of blackmailing him and then shoots the girl with 6 shots in the back. He takes the letters and leaves.

Johnny escapes the closet with a hard kick. Johnny looks around the apartment and finds letters from two other men, one named Baron and one named Lawrence, and suspects the "old badger game". The police arrive and naturally blame Johnny for the murders. Johnny shows his ID to the police who call him an insurance dick. Johnny prefers "freelance special insurance investigator — it keeps his rates up. Johnny tells the police what had occurred and why he is there. Johnny's only witness is the dead girl. Johnny tells them about the letters and the man who came in and shot the girl. An officer finds Johnny's nail file, pen and a .32 stuffed in a shoe in the closet. Johnny tries to explain but spends the night in the LA City jail, cell number 36.

Johnny relates how he had envisioned staring at bars on this case, but not jail bars. Police Lt. Roach talks to Johnny and tells him that the evidence points to his innocence. He tells Johnny that the gun in the closet is the one that killed Marilyn. Roach tells Johnny that Marilyn had been playing a high stakes Badger game, and that the fire department should be handling the case. Johnny suggests that there is a third set of letters floating around, as the murderer grabbed the wrong letters. Johnny wants to clear his name and get his job done so he suggests planting a newspaper article stating that the murderer got the wrong letters and that Johnny has them in his hotel room. Roach agrees to publish the story and Johnny asks for fighter cover. Johnny gets out and buys a newspaper with the fake story, his picture and his hotel name in it.

Johnny goes to dinner and returns to his hotel. In his hotel room he finds a woman, Mrs. Alice Lawrence Hill, wearing a negligee. She tells Johnny that her husband is in the lobby and knows that Johnny is in the room. She wants the letters. If she doesn't get them, her husband will shoot Johnny for attacking his wife. Johnny is sure that he will get killed when Hill gets there and tries to talk her out of going further. There is a knock at the door and Mr. Baron comes in with a gun and wants the letters. Baron threatens Johnny and he tells both of them that he does not have the letters. When the phone rings Johnny fakes a conversation with the police to an empty line. Johnny recognizes Baron's voice from the closet and figures Lawrence Hill killed Marilyn.

Johnny mutters dangerous words into the phone to get Baron close enough to bean him with the phone. Johnny kicks the gun under the bed and Johnny beans Baron with a water jar. Johnny pulls Mrs. Hill from under the bed where she is trying to get Baron's gun. Johnny tells Alice that her husband did not see

Johnny come in, because he used the back door. As Johnny gets the gun from under the bed Lawrence Hill comes in. Alice screams at him to shoot, and he shoots Baron. Johnny shoots Hill from under the bed.

After the police finally show up, Johnny yells at Roach for not having protection in the hotel. Johnny tells him who the bodies are and how he shot Hill from under the bed. Roach tells Johnny that no one saw him come in. Johnny tells him that he came in the back door.

Notes:
- Without a script title page to verify the actual title, I am opting to use "Hundred Thousand Dollar" instead of $100,000.
- AKA "Who Put Your Company out on a Limb?"
- Johnny mentions American Airlines.
- He is not carrying his gun in this case.
- This program contains a mid-program commercial for the $50,000 jackpot on the program *Sing It Again*.
- Quote from in jail   "Who ever said stone wall do not a prison make has a better chance of getting out of *Bartlett's Quotations* than I have of getting out of jail."
- Newspaper costs 7 cents.
- The expense account includes $167 for "entertainment" in Hollywood.
- Music is by Mark Warnow.

Producer:	Richard Sanville	Writer:	Paul Dudley, Gil Doud
Cast:	William Conrad, Unknown		

◆ ❖ ◆

Show: The Case of Barton Drake
Show Date: 4/22/1949
Company: American Pioneer Life Insurance
Agent: W.K. Green
Exp. Acct: $1,482.63

Synopsis: After a $100 expense item for being awakened at 9:00 a.m., Johnny goes to "Old Stonewall's" office for his assignment. Johnny is greeted by Chickie, the receptionist, and tries to wrangle a date. Johnny goes in to see "The General", or rather Mr. Green. Green tells Johnny about Barton Drake, who is insured for $30,000 and disappeared almost 7 years ago in 1942 after his car plunged in to a river during an attempt to escape the police. Drake gave his occupation as hardware store manager, but Johnny remembers he was generally acknowledged to be a thief. In one week, Drake will be declared legally dead, and his wife has started proceedings. However, the NYPD Missing Persons Squad saw Barton Drake on the television watching a boxing match!

Johnny drives to Bridgeport to review the files on Drake and then to Drake's home on Long Island, New York where he meets Mrs. Stella Drake — dressed in a negligee and a diamond necklace while eating a genuine English kipper for breakfast at 2:00 p.m. Johnny tells her that she has a good chance of getting her husband back, but Stella is not too happy to hear that her hubby is not dead and works up some appropriate suffering. Johnny is told to leave so that she can think. On the way out, Johnny cuts the phone lines and watches the house.

Johnny follows Stella downtown to a phone booth where (after writing down the number she calls) he listens to her arrange to meet someone at the usual place in twenty minutes. The usual place is the ladies room at Union Station. Mrs. Drake then goes to the Commodore Hotel and gets a room. Johnny gets a room on a different floor and hires the house detective to keep an eye on her.

Johnny buys a portable phonograph and a Frank Sinatra record (65¢). He then calls the number, fakes a radio call-up quiz and arranges to deliver a bunch of goodies to the winner. Johnny plays the Sinatra record "Night and Day", and Mrs. Knott is the winner! When he delivers the prizes, he finds an old lady in a wheelchair. While Johnny is grilling Mrs. Knott about her background, Barton's wife comes in, and Mrs. Knott turns into Barton Drake with a set of brass knuckles.

Johnny wakes up to hear Barton Drake yelling at his wife about trying to collect on the policy. Drake ties Johnny to a chair and drives him to the beach. Johnny is tied up and thrown into a boat and sent to sea. Johnny manages to turn the boat around by using his body as a rudder and ends up on an island. On the island Johnny wakes up to meet Fred Kindly who wants to be paid for the damage to his dock on Slate Island. Fred tells Johnny that for $500 in canned food he will take Johnny to shore. Johnny agrees and signs the contract for food as "Ali Khan".

Johnny gets back to Drake's apartment and finds an empty apartment. Unfortunately, Drake has split with the baggage Johnny bought him. Stella comes in and she tells Johnny that she does not know anything. Johnny tells her that she is guilty of fraud and she tells Johnny that Drake never left New York and had been using the disguise for years. Johnny takes Stella's bag and discovers that she is heading south. Stella tells Johnny that Barton is leaving in an hour and a half on the Orange Blossom Special. Johnny tells Stella that she had been double-crossed — the Orange Blossom Special leaves in 30 minutes.

Johnny makes a quick call to Travelers Aid and tells them to hold his dear old crazy aunt who thinks she is a honey bee, and who is going to throw herself in front of the Orange Blossom Special. Johnny rushes to the station and finds the police and the Travelers Aid folks have Drake surrounded, but they still think that he is just and old lady. Johnny slugs Drake and gets slugged by a policeman.

Johnny goes back to Mr. Green's office and Chickie tells Johnny that "The General" is so happy that Johnny has saved the company $30,000 that he has taken the morning off to celebrate by playing golf. Chickie agrees to help Johnny complete his expense account so that they can go out for the evening. Johnny tells how, after waking up, that the police discovered that Mrs. Knott was Drake when the police took him to the hospital! Drake and his wife were put in jail, as they are guilty of insurance fraud. Mr. Kindly gets $500 of canned food. $500 of canned tomatoes with no labels on the can! Yours — um — Truly, Johnny Dollar.

Notes:
- AKA "How I Played Ducks and Drakes with a Drake Who Ducked."
- $1 tip to the cabby.
- Johnny derisively notes that "Old Stonewall's belt never stopped fighting the battle of the businessman's bulge" and "Those who served can be just as proud as those who fought".
- Appliances Johnny bought were a Sunbeam Mixmaster for $39.50, a Hoover Vacuum for $79.50 and Gladiator suitcases for $89.50.
- Frank Sinatra sings *Night and Day* only long enough to give the title of the song.
- This program contains a mid-program commercial for *Phillip Marlow* (The Cloak of Kamehameha) and *Gang Busters* (The Callous killer).
- There is a public service announcement for the American Cancer Society fund drive.
- Music is by Leith Stevens.

Producer:	Richard Sanville	Writer:	Paul Dudley, Gil Doud
Cast:	Parley Baer, Unknown		

♦ ❖ ♦

Show: **Here Comes the Death of the Party**
Show Date: **7/17/1949**
Company: **Premier Life & Casualty Company**
Agent:
Exp. Acct: **$1,434.67**

Synopsis: "Some people feel that for a quick divorce, bullets are much cheaper than lawyers."

Johnny goes to Reno, Nevada (where the husbands pay off faster than the slot machines) and goes to the Broken Ring Ranch and meets the manager, B. T. Bates, and a young lady named Francine. Johnny is being hired as a "social director" to keep an eye on a guest, Mrs. Nora Craven, who is afraid her husband Arnold wants to kill her. If she dies before the divorce, he gets the $100,000 policy.

While talking to Mr. Bates Johnny hears Nora scream. It seems that a ranch hand, Slim, had given Nora a present, a .38 with a broken barrel and was showing Nora how to use it when it went off. Johnny tries to ride a horse, finds a snake in his room and is wounded at a dance in his role a social director.

Johnny decides on a preemptive strike and takes Nora to town to meet her husband, but he is not there. Johnny goes back to the ranch to find Nora's husband in her room. Johnny is knocked out and wakes up to find Francine in the room — dead. Slim walks in to find Johnny and Francine and tells Johnny that firing the gun for Nora was his idea. Johnny goes to Francine's room to find Nora there. Johnny searches her purse and finds a photostat of a marriage license proving that Francine has been married to Arnold for two years. Arnold arrives and Johnny tells him about his bigamy and killing Francine, who was going to tell Nora. Arnold fires the gun he had given Nora, but the barrel explodes and Arnold is killed.

Notes:
- AKA "The Case of the Poisonous Grapevine".
- Music is by Leith Stevens.
- Story information obtained from the KNX Collection in the Thousand Oaks library.

Producer: Norman Macdonnell **Writer:** Paul Dudley, Gil Doud
Cast: Vivi Janiss, Jack Kruschen, John Dehner, Anne Morrison, Paul Dubov

♦ ❖ ♦

Show: Who Took the Taxis for a Ride?
Show Date: 7/24/1949
Company: Nutmeg State Liability Underwriters
Agent:
Exp. Acct: $1,100.00

Synopsis: "Everybody knows a taxi driver likes being over-tipped, but you can't blame them for not liking being tipped over."

Johnny travels to New York City and then to the Apex Cab Company. Johnny meets with Gordon McKissick who has just had another cab stolen and is rushing to the site. So far 12 cabs have just vanished on the streets of New York. Johnny tells him that he wants facts, but McKissick tells him it might just be competition.

After a cab ride to 13th & East River, Johnny finds cabby George Brandon beaten. All Brandon can tell Johnny is that a small guy who talks funny was involved and then he dies.

Johnny visits the 11 other victims and now has three clues: 1.) A team of a small man and a huge man with a seersucker suit were involved, 2.) Only the uniform hats were stolen, 3.) McKissick is a former bootlegger, bookmaker and an ex-con.

Back at the cab office, Johnny tells McKissick what he has learned, but McKissick is angry at the idea that he was faking the thefts for the insurance. Johnny orders all the cabs off the street until the case is cleared up, or he will have the insurance cancelled. By 5:00 p.m. all the cabs are in, and by 5:30 the place is deserted except for the night watchman.

Marita Guastilla visits at 6:00 looking for a purse lost in a cab. Johnny takes Marita to a local bar to find out what she is really about. She tells Johnny that she only came from Spain two weeks ago and took the cab at ten minutes before four. Johnny suggests that they go and look at the cab registers to see which cab she rode in. But Johnny notes that Sherry is more the drink for

Spanish ladies, but Marita sure can belt down a martini. Johnny is sure that she is in a hurry to get something out of a cab.

Back at the garage, the gate is open and the night watchman is gone. "Bridewell!" moans Marita. Marita runs away and Johnny goes in to find the guard lying on the floor — and a .38 in his ear held by a huge man with a Sidney Greenstreet type voice. He is Mr. Bridewell, and the guard is OK. His partner Victor comes in and is unable to find something in the cabs. Bridewell invites Johnny to go with him to his hotel.

Johnny has made up his mind that there is something hidden in one of the cabs. Johnny goes to Bridewell's hotel where he hears Bridewell's life story and is told that Marita is nothing but a common thief. Victor comes in and is ready to search Johnny for something. Bridewell offer Johnny $7,500, but Johnny replies "Nuts!" Bridewell tells Johnny the story of the "Scarlet Madonna": it is an emerald fashioned in 1256 with an image of the Madonna on one side. It is the Scarlet Madonna because everyone who has owned it has died, including a pirate who had it braided into his beard.

Victor slugs Johnny and searches him. Victor finds Johnny's gun and ID and in the ensuing argument over what to do, Johnny slugs Victor and runs down to the street where he runs into Marita.

In a cab Marita tells Johnny that she owns the Scarlet Madonna and was smuggling the stone into the country. She realized that she was being followed by Victor and Bridewell, so she left the stone in the seat of one of the cabs and is looking for it now. Johnny takes Marita to a small hotel and checks her in. While Marita is taking a bath, Johnny steals her clothes and leaves.

Back at the garage, Johnny finds the night watchman who tells Johnny he had told Bridewell that McKissick had searched the cabs. Johnny goes to the office and discovers McKissick holding the stone and bartering with Victor, who shoots McKissick. Johnny beats Victor and takes the Madonna from McKissick's hand. Bridewell comes in and asks for the Madonna. Bridewell gives Johnny his ID and a letter of authorization. Bridewell turns out to be a British Insurance Investigator "with a fantastic and highly successful career". However, because he looks and sounds like Sidney Greenstreet, people normally assume he is the villain. Bridewell is authorized to recover the stone for the museum from which Marita and Victor had stolen it. Bridewell gives Johnny the address where he had hidden the cabs.

Johnny buys a dressing gown and gives it to Bridewell to give to Marita before he turns her over to the police. Johnny decides to stay in New York to rest up for a while.

Notes:
- AKA "The Disappearance of Twelve Apex Cabs".
- Different opening theme music.
- Music is by Leith Stevens.
- The announcer is Allen Botzer.
- With the "Scarlet Madonna," at stake this sounds just like the *Maltese*

Falcon, with a wonderful imitation of a Sydney Greenstreet like character named Bridewell.
- The drinks with Marita are martinis.
- $1.95 for an evening gown for the naked Marita.
- $6.10 for a bottle of "mouthwash".
- $400 advance for resting on his laurels   or possibly even Bridewell's laurels.
- This program contains a mid-program commercial for the world's greatest scientific enterprise   the armed forces.

Producer:	Norman Macdonnell Writer: Paul Dudley, Gil Doud
Cast:	Herb Butterfield, Jack Kruschen, Paul Dubov, Lillian Buyeff, Lou Krugman, Junius Matthews, Jan Arvan

◆ ❖ ◆

Show:	**How Much Bourbon Can Flow Under the Bridgework?**
Show Date:	7/31/1949
Company:	**National Surety & Life Insurance Company**
Agent:	
Exp. Acct:	$2,063.00

Synopsis: "I had to go all the way to Hawaii to be taught that a pineapple is sometimes just another word for a bomb."

Johnny goes to Honolulu, Hawaii to look into the $100,000 policy on Peter Neeley, who has been drinking because of a half-caste girl named Dai Soon. Johnny goes to a bar and the bartender tells Johnny that Peter has been drinking and that his sister has been trying to break off Peter's relationship with Dai. Johnny goes to Peter's apartment and meets Dai. She tells Johnny about the dock strike that is affecting the Pineapple factory. Peter comes in drunk and gets into a fight with Johnny and loses.

Sylvia Neeley arrives with Mr. Fenger, who manages the Neeley factory. Peter gets angry with Sylvia because Peter wants to change the beneficiary of the policy. Sylvia leaves and Johnny takes Peter to a doctor but is attacked and Peter is kidnapped. Johnny goes back to the apartment to find Dai looking for the insurance policy. Johnny ends up being tied up and given a parting kiss by Dai, who leaves. Later a clerk comes in and unties Johnny and tells Johnny that Dai took a cab. Johnny finds the cab and it takes him to the waterfront where the longshoremen are on strike. Johnny talks his way onto the Island Traveler only to see Dai dive into the water just before the ship explodes "in the biggest explosion since Mona Loa erupted in 1946".

The fire department fights the fire while Johnny feels that Peter was forced to sign the policy because Fenger was losing money at the plant, and that the boat was really shipping munitions rather than fruit. Sylvia and Fenger show up and are anxious about the thought of murder. Johnny gets onto the ship and discovers that the cargo really is fruit. In the process Johnny finds a cat trying to get back into the boat. On a hunch Johnny takes the cat to a local herbalist, Dr. Fu, who confirms Johnny's suspicions about the cat.

Johnny goes to his hotels and is called by Dai, who tells Johnny that she blew up the boat to save Peter, who is OK. Dai tells Johnny that Peter knows that Sylvia and Fenger are smuggling narcotics out in cans of pineapples.

Johnny picks up Peter and they go to Sylvia's and Fenger's apartment, but they are not there. They then go to the plant. Johnny goes in and is shot at by Fenger, who is on top of the pineapple slicer. Johnny works his way up to a control panel, but Fenger has Johnny covered. Johnny throws a pineapple at the control panel, starts the conveyor belt, causing Fenger to be sliced like his pineapples.

Notes:
- AKA "Being the Sabbath, Let's All Go Have a Pineapple Sundae".
- The announcer is Allen Botzer.
- Music is by Leith Stevens.
- Story information obtained from the KNX Collection in the Thousand Oaks Library.

Producer: Norman Macdonnell Writer: Paul Dudley, Gil Doud
Cast: Wilms Herbert, Georgia Ellis, Lawrence Dobkin, Doris Singleton, John Dehner, Don Diamond, Edgar Barrier, Barney Phillips

♦ ❖ ♦

Show: Murder Ain't Minor
Show Date: 8/7/1949
Company: King Hart
Agent:
Exp. Acct: $0.00

Synopsis: "I hope Saint Peter is listening. This report may one day qualify me for that pass through the pearly gates. This case almost rushed me up there."

Johnny comes home late on Saturday night to find a party going on in his apartment — a party of one, King Hart a noted New York gangster. Hart wants Johnny to find a girl named Bonnie Goodwin so that he can change the beneficiary of his $100,000 insurance policy. According to the policy, Bonnie must sign it before the beneficiary can be changed. Johnny wants to turn down the case because he cannot check King's credit, but King has a full wallet. Johnny suggests that King hire Phillip Marlow, Sam Spade or Richard Diamond, who would sing him a song. King is allergic to detectives, so he wants Johnny to find the girl. Johnny is told that Bonnie Goodwin is in Chicago and that Hart had run the accounting department at Leavenworth for five years. Johnny wants the assignment in writing and a $3,000 advance, which Hart agrees to.

With a $3,000 advance in hand, Johnny heads to Chicago, Illinois (traveling first class per Hart's instructions) to look for Bonnie, first checking into the Ambassador Hotel. The first stop is Bonnie's last boarding house, the Muriel Arms. The switchboard operator tells Johnny that Bonnie was last seen around "Emma's Place", a local bar. Johnny goes to Emma's and the bartender, Joe Emma, tells

Johnny to look for Bonnie at the Flagler Apartments. After 18 other stops there is still no sign of Bonnie. (Her heart was no express train because it made a lot of stops") At the last place he checks, Johnny is only a couple of hours behind the last move-out.

As Johnny leaves, a girl carrying a suitcase stops Johnny on the street. She is Janie and claims to be a friend of Bonnie. Johnny notices a tail and they head to a bar in two different cabs. At the bar, Johnny mentions the insurance, at which the girl asks if Hart is dead. When told he is not, she says that Bonnie will never sign away the only thing she has. When Janie leaves, the two goons who followed them enter the bar. Johnny creates a disturbance to stop them and runs out the back door. Janie heads out the back and is killed. The next morning Johnny hears on the hotel room radio that the girl was identified as Bonnie Goodwin, ex-girlfriend of King Hart.

Johnny is upset that he had been looking for Bonnie with Bonnie! King Hart calls Johnny from the airport and tells him that Joe Emma had called him with the news. Johnny tells him to take his case and well...Johnny quits and will report what he knows to the police. Johnny goes to the morgue to find an address in the girl's belongings and learns that her roommate, Janie Page had identified the girl. Johnny goes to see Janie and finds her packing. Janie tells Johnny that Bonnie knew too much about too many people and was afraid. Janie tells Johnny that Hart had wanted to marry Bonnie but she said no. Also, Joe Emma is an enemy of Hart and had split up with Hart over Bonnie.

Johnny works up a plan to expose the killer by planting a false story in the papers about the misidentification of the body. Johnny takes up residence in Janie's apartment, makes some coffee and sandwiches and waits by the phone. The first person to show up is Hart. Hart comes in while Johnny fakes a phone call to the police. Hart tells Johnny that the body in the morgue was not Bonnie's. When Hart gets too close Johnny slugs him with the phone and hides him in the closet.

Johnny is calling the police when Joe Emma and a friend name Angie show up. Joe wants Bonnie, but Johnny tells him she is not there. Joe goes to the closet and Hart jumps from the closet and a fight ensues and Joe and Angie are knocked out. Hart tells Johnny that the body in the morgue is not Bonnie's and wants to know where she is. As the police show up, Johnny agrees to pass a message to Bonnie for him.

Johnny plays cupid and over dinner tells Bonnie how Hart feels about her. Bonnie tells Johnny to tell Hart that she is going back home. Johnny, in an altruistic move gives Bonnie the $3,000 he had gotten from Hart and tells her to get a long way away. Johnny buys a beer for Hart, who is not happy with the results and tells Johnny to forget about the $163.55 in expenses!

Notes:
- AKA "She Was Under Twenty-One, But That Didn't Mean She Was Involved with Nothing but Minor Vices", or "The Case of Bonnie Goodwin".
- The title of this program on the script is *Murder Ain't Minor*.

- References are made to *Sam Spade, Phillip Marlowe* and *Richard Diamond* (who will sing a song for you).
- A reference is made to being taught by an old Pinkerton agent that "being an investigator is like being a mailman with no address on the letter".
- Expenses include $22.50 to replace a radio he turned off with his fist.
- This program contains a mid-program commercial for *Call the Police* and *Sam Spade*.
- Roy Rowan is the announcer.
- Music is by Leith Stevens.

Producer: Gordon T. Hughes Writer: Paul Dudley, Gil Doud
Cast: Paul Dubov, Martha Wentworth, Lou Krugman, Georgia Ellis, Jeanne Bates, Lawrence Dobkin

◆ ❖ ◆

Show: **Death Takes a Working Day**
Show Date: 8/14/1949
Company: **Great Columbian Life Insurance Company**
Agent: **Harry Del Hubbel**
Exp. Acct: **$823.00**

Synopsis: "Take off your lipstick and pucker up sweetheart, here comes the kiss of death."

Johnny drives to the estate of the deceased at Loyal House. The housekeeper, Miss Sarah Trammel meets Johnny and tells him that the widow is out shopping. Miss Trammel has worked for the household for 30 years. "Loyal, er, Mr. Martin was an expert on Victorian furniture" Johnny is told. In answer to the unasked question, yes, Miss Trammel was provided for in the estate. Johnny says he is investigating the murder so the murderer is not paid off. "People waste a lot of murders that way" He tells her.

Police Lt. Markwood is in the library in which only two things were out of place — a suit of armor and a case of shiny new hunting rifles. Lt. Markwood tells Johnny that the body of Mr. Martin was found after dinner and had two bullet holes in it. According to Markwood, there are four suspects, a wife who was too young, the housekeeper who was in love with the deceased, the brother who is broke and brooding and the bodyguard, a detective.

Johnny decides to start with Nick Bulotti, the bodyguard. Johnny meets with him after a horseback ride, and he tells Johnny that he had nothing really to say, but the police told him to stay put.

Marty, the brother was entertaining a bottle of 20-year-old brandy that was much too young for the book he was reading. It seems that the young wife had asked him to come and protect her from her husband. Joy-Anne, the widow comes home and goes swimming in a bikini that would "get her pinched on the Riviera!" Joy-Anne tells Johnny that Marty had introduced her to Loyal. But Loyal gave her everything but love, and when she went looking for it, the housekeeper informed Loyal and he became a madman. The housekeeper was upset with Joy-Anne because she had always assumed that Loyal would marry her. So, Joy-Anne is going to enjoy what little free time she has left.

Johnny goes to check up on the housekeeper who Johnny finds in the library wiping off the desk, in violation of police orders to keep out. She tells Johnny that she always cleaned at that hour of the day, otherwise Loyal would get mad. Markwood comes in and orders Johnny to take her to her room and then come back. On the way, there are 6 shots fired in the library. Johnny goes back to the library and finds an open window and Markwood dead holding a shotgun.

While searching the body, Bulotti comes in. The only clue Johnny can find, which Markwood would have wanted to share, was an entry in his new notebook "Check tattooing diameter. Recheck penetration". Johnny asks Bulotti to keep quiet. He also asks the others who have now gathered to go back to their rooms. Outside Johnny looks for clues and finds a .32 revolver in the grass. The gun has 6 empty chambers and lipstick on the grip. Johnny wonders if it could be a red herring? Sgt. McDougal arrives and Johnny tells him what happened and gives him the gun. The gun is the same caliber which killed Loyal, but why was Markwood holding an unloaded shotgun when he was shot? Johnny gets more puzzling information from McDougal. The autopsy showed two bullet holes, 1 ½ inches apart, which did not penetrate too deeply. Everything pointed to the bullets being fired from 300 yards. The witnesses were split on whether 1 or 2 shots were fired on the night of the killing.

Johnny goes to the ballistics lab and discovers that the ballistics people had found powder burns, called tattooing, on the body indicating a close firing of the weapon. Also, the .32 was the weapon that killed both people. A .32 owned and licensed to Joy-Anne Martin, who looked better in a bathing suit than she will in the electric chair.

Johnny goes to see Joy and gets her out of the shower. When quizzed about the gun owned by her, she says that her gun is in the dresser. When she gets up to get it, the gun is gone. She says it must have been stolen, and there are too many people who would love to frame her. When asked if she remembers anything else, she says that she remembers hearing shots two days before the killing while she was out horseback riding. They came from a walnut grove. Just as Johnny kisses her, the police he had called showed up, and Joy-Anne is taken into custody after she slaps Johnny.

Next morning Johnny goes looking for the walnut grove and pondering why everyone heard one shot, and there were two bullets in the body. In the hollow trunk of a tree Johnny finds a peck of cotton waste with powder burns in it. Johnny is hit on the head and sees Marty running back to the house. Johnny chases Marty back to the house and hears 6 shots. Johnny finds Bulotti standing over Marty. Bulotti says that Marty had drawn on him, so he shot in self-defense. Johnny suggests Bulotti go to police headquarters and register his story.

Johnny calls McDougal and tells him that Marty had just been shot and the killer was on his way to the office. Johnny tells McDougal that Nick and Marty had arranged to fire the .32 into the cotton waste to get the bullets. The bullets were then packed into a shotgun shell and fired at close range by a shotgun.

Johnny tells him that he knew that Bulotti was the accomplice because he had said Marty drew on him, but Marty was unarmed.

Notes:
- AKA "Investigation of the Policyholder Loyal B. Martin".
- AKA "How Not to Take a Vacation in Fairfield County".
- The script title page lists *Death Takes a Working Day* as the show title.
- The announcer is Roy Rowan.
- Music is by Leith Stevens.
- Story information obtained from the KNX Collection in the Thousand Oaks Library.

Producer: Gordon T. Hughes Writer: Paul Dudley, Gil Doud
Cast: Herb Vigran, Lawrence Dobkin, Jack Edwards, Doris Singleton, Lois Corbett, Bill Bouchey

♦ ❖ ♦

Show: **Out of the Fire, Into the Frying Pan**
Show Date: 8/21/1949
Company: **Corinthian Liability & Bonding Company**
Agent:
Exp. Acct: $1,463.00

Synopsis: "Mrs. Perkins won the prize, but I got in the biggest pickle at the county fair."

Johnny is bodyguard to a Grand Blue-Ribbon Champion Spotted Portland China Hog, Rosie Baron of Iowa.

Johnny travels to Carver, Iowa and goes to the county fairgrounds looking for the 980-pound hog he is assigned to protect. Johnny is told that Rosie Baron is known as Rollo around here. As Johnny approaches the swine building, loud noises are heard. As Johnny rushes in, a man rushes out. Once inside, Johnny discovers that a brooch has been stolen from Mrs. Hortense Tiller, whose husband owns Rollo. Johnny is told that someone stole the brooch while Mrs. Tiller was having her photo taken. Sheriff Harry Blewit comes in and accuses Johnny of being in cahoots with the man seen running out because Harry saw something passed between them. Johnny tells the sheriff why he is there (as a piggy-sitter) and suggests to the sheriff to get the pictures developed and look for the thief in the pictures. (Say, that gives me a idea!)

Johnny finds Rollo eating yams and meets Alva Anderson, who raised Rollo the pig. The owner, Worthington Tiller shows up and wants Johnny's picture taken with his wife and the pig. Tiller tells Johnny not to worry about the brooch because it is insured. Tiller also notes that he paid $10,000 for the pig, which is insured for $25,000, and does not want anything to happen to Rollo. When Tiller reminds Johnny of all the publicity he will get, Johnny just hopes his publicity will not be an obituary that reads "Johnny Dollar no longer am, He gave up his life for a great big ham."

To pass the afternoon guarding Rollo, Johnny talks to Alva and vice versa, but the conversation is all about pigs. When Tiller relieves them, they go to dinner, for baked ham, of course. The sheriff finds Johnny and informs him that he had rushed the pictures from the camera to the state capital, and there was a known criminal in it, "Little Rocky" from Arkansas! He has the brooch and is on the loose.

The grand march starts and Johnny goes to watch. As Rollo's truck and trailer pass by, Johnny sees that the driver is Little Rocky from Arkansas. After an unsuccessful attempt to tackle the truck, Little Rocky and Rollo get away.

Johnny is helped up and questions Alva as to where to get rid of a hot pig. Johnny gets the price of pork and is sure that Little Rocky is not interested in selling Rollo. The sheriff finds Johnny and tells him that he saw Johnny's performance and does not believe Johnny was trying hard enough. Johnny asks the sheriff to loan him a car but there is no way, as there is only one county vehicle. On the way to the Ferris wheel to scout out the country (Say, that gives me a idea!) Johnny asks if another pig could smell out the mash in Rollo's feeding trough and lead them to Rollo. — it's possible says the sheriff (Say, that gives me a idea!).

Johnny tricks the sheriff onto the Ferris wheel where Johnny drowns the engine with lemonade and strands Harry at the top. Johnny goes back to the swine building to talk to Tiller. Johnny tells him that the only one who is in trouble now is the insurance company. Tiller does not like it when Johnny accuses Mrs. Tiller of losing the brooch to get the insurance money for it. Tiller tells Johnny that his father had the same thing happen to him. He bought a prize pig at a fancy price and then had it stolen from him. Johnny asks if he should arrest Alva and Tiller tells Johnny that it is up to him.

Johnny searches the fair grounds for Alva. As Johnny goes to the swine building Johnny sees Little Rocky with a bag over his shoulder forcing Alva out the back door. Johnny steals the sheriff's car and follows Rocky to a building outside of town where Rollo and another man are. As Johnny listens at the window, he learns that the man had hidden the brooch in a yam, and the pig must have eaten it. After going through all the yams, they have not found the brooch. The men argue about killing Rollo and Alva is very upset.

Johnny "has a idea", and throws in a yam as a diversion, Johnny rushes in and slugs the thieves and rescues Alva and Rollo. Rollo is delivered to Tiller and is told that the brooch is inside him. Tiller gets Rollo ready for his next appearance — at a slaughterhouse the next day — and Alva is upset at losing Rollo. Johnny and an upset Alva go to dinner, a vegetable dinner. Johnny buys Harry a new badge to appease him. Johnny notes that the sheriff was using a pig to track down Rollo at a distillery on the wrong side of town. Johnny wonders what else you can eat with eggs for breakfast.

Yours — um — Truly, Johnny Dollar.

Notes:
- **AKA "Bodyguard to Grand Blue-Ribbon Champion, Spotted Poland Hog Rosie Baron of Iowa", or "How You Cast My Pearls of Wisdom Before Swine."**

- This program contains a mid-program commercial for *Lux Radio Theater*, *Call the Police* and *Sam Spade*.
- Current pork prices are $23.50 per lb.
- Roy Rowan is the announcer.
- Music is by Leith Stevens.

Producer:	Norman Macdonnell
Writer:	Paul Dudley, Gil Doud
Cast:	Parley Baer, Jack Kruschen, Sammie Hill, John Dehner, Junius Matthews, Anne Morrison, Paul Dubov, Pinto Kolveg (Rollo)

♦ ❖ ♦

Show: **How I Turned a Luxury Liner into a Battleship**
Show Date: 8/28/1949
Company: **Old Caledonia Security Insurance Company**
Agent:
Exp. Acct: $2,747.27

Synopsis: "Well, now I know one quartet that wishes it could sing "My Body Lies Under the Ocean"."

Johnny goes to New York City and buys seasickness pills and passage to Le Havre on the *S.S. Atlanta*. Onboard Johnny has dinner with Roberta Cobb, the owner of a $75,000 diamond bracelet, which she is wearing. While they are talking, Aunt Cobina comes to the table to tell Roberta that her stateroom has been torn apart. Johnny inspects the cabin and calls Murdock, the ship's detective. Once under way, Roberta starts working on the male passengers while Johnny watches the bracelet. Johnny meets one of the passengers, Duke Cornwall, who Johnny is suspicious of because he heard Duke tell a man named Foley that they will have a profitable voyage. Johnny talks to Murdock who is familiar with Cornwall, and Eddie "The Faker" Foley, both of whom are fast operators. Johnny tells Roberta, but she tells Johnny that he is just jealous. Johnny continues to follow Roberta for two more days.

When the boat arrives in Le Havre, Roberta is not wearing the bracelet. Johnny goes to her room and sees the bracelet. Johnny goes in to get it and is knocked unconscious.

Johnny wakes up to Murdock slapping him. Roberta comes in and learns that the bracelet is gone and is angry, especially since Cornwall dumped her. Johnny watches the customs agents search both Cornwall and Foley, but they find nothing. Johnny joins Roberta, Aunt Cobina, Cornwall and Foley on the train to Paris. In Paris Johnny follows Cornwall and Foley through a number of bars until they meet a contact who hands Cornwall a small package containing the bracelet. Johnny follows Cornwall to the Hotel Ritz and up to the second-floor room of Roberta Cobb. Cornwall slaps Roberta and accuses her of passing paste. Johnny tells Roberta that she was flashing the bracelet to set up Cornwall, and that the bracelet was stolen in front of Johnny to collect the insurance. Roberta gives Johnny the fake bracelet. Roberta gets a call from the desk for Johnny. The desk clerk tells Johnny that Aunt Cobina is on her way up. Johnny tells Roberta that "Aunt" Flora Cobina is not her aunt, and that she has a record for selling stolen jewels. Flora comes into the room and Roberta throws a vase at her while Johnny takes the real bracelet from her hair.

Notes:
- The announcer is Roy Rowan.
- Music is by Leith Stevens.
- Johnny notes that he has been a detective for 10 years.
- Story information obtained from the KNX Collection in the Thousand Oaks Library.

Producer:	Norman Macdonnell	Writer:	Paul Dudley, Gil Doud
Cast:	Lynn Allen, Lois Corbett, Lawrence Dobkin, Paul Dubov, John Dehner		

◆ ❖ ◆

Show:	**The Expiring Nickels and the Egyptian Jackpot**
Show Date:	9/4/1949
Company:	**Constant Sun Trading Company**
Agent:	
Exp. Acct:	$5,350.40

Synopsis: "I always say, if you take a trip halfway around the world you gotta expect you'll get your ticket punched."

Johnny travels to French Indochina and then to Calcutta, India (9 dreary hours at 20,000 feet sucking oxygen) to assist an old Army buddy, Chaplain Joe Blessing, who stayed in India to save souls in his church — a recycled Army Quonset hut. Joe tells Johnny that he wants Johnny to save another man's soul. Here in Calcutta, William Briggs has evidence which will free a man condemned to hang the next day in Cairo, Mr. Lionel Brooke-Nickels, who owns the Constant Sun Trading Company. Brooke-Nickels' cousin is Miles Atkinson, a big-wheel in the Egyptian government, who wants the business, and is framing Brooke-Nickels for a murder Miles committed. Johnny is to take Briggs (who is a leper) and the evidence (a loaded and armed Luger) to Cairo via a chartered cargo plane.

On the Horizons Unlimited plane, Joe's assistant Frankie gives Johnny the loaded Luger, which Johnny pockets. Frankie and Johnny compare stories of losing horses during the trip. After a refueling stop in Bombay, they stop in Aden for servicing and pick up a stowaway, Miss Fate Fabian who is quite a dish, as usual. Johnny takes $500 as payment for passage to Cairo, and for her good behavior. Johnny is happy to spend the flight with Fate. An ambulance meets the plane in Cairo, Egypt only it is not an ambulance and both Briggs and Frankie are kidnapped.

After Briggs is taken Johnny attempts to fire at them with the Luger, but Johnny finds that it is missing from his coat. Fate has it in the bathroom, but she does not know how it got there. Johnny takes a wild cab ride into Cairo to find Briggs. Johnny accuses Fate of being involved, but she denies it, even after Johnny tells her all about what is going on.

Johnny goes to the police and meets with the Chief Inspector, who is Miles Atkinson! Miles takes the gun from Johnny and tells Johnny that Frankie has been arrested for killing Briggs. At gunpoint, Miles tells Johnny the entire story of how he killed a man and framed Brooke-Nickels. Fate commends Miles for making a full and voluntary confession and that Miles is going with them. When Miles tries to fire the Luger, but it is empty.

In an attempt to escape, Miles runs for the roof, turning off the lights as he goes. On the roof, Miles tries to hold Fate and Johnny off with a fire hose. Fate opens the hose valve all the way and whips Miles off of the roof and down onto the gallows in the courtyard.

Johnny thanks Fate, who tells Johnny that she had unloaded the gun on the plane. Fate tells Johnny that she is an undercover agent for the Police Inspector General. Johnny and Fate get Brooke-Nickel and Frankie released and Johnny heads back to the airport. Mr. Brooke-Nickel meets with Johnny and agrees to pay all of Johnny's expenses. He also agrees to build a proper church for Joe Blessing. Johnny heads back to Calcutta to say goodbye to Joe and buys a custom blackjack for Fate.

Notes:
- Johnny notes he met Joe Blessing while he was a soldier in the "CBI Theater" which was the "China-Burma-India" Theater.
- Johnny buys a blue-suede blackjack for Fate   how romantic!
- This program contains a mid-program commercial for *"Horace Hite's Youth Opportunity Show".*
- Johnny un-hocks an old Air Medal upon return to Hartford. After all that flying, he needs one.
- Roy Rowan announces that Johnny will take a vacation and will come back on Saturday, October 1. However, there appears to be a program broadcast on Sunday, September 25, 1949.
- Roy Rowan is the announcer.
- Music is by Leith Stevens.

Producer: Gordon T. Hughes   Writer: Paul Dudley, Gil Doud
Cast: Georgia Ellis, Parley Baer, Paul Dubov, Jack Edwards

◆ ❖ ◆

Show: The Search for Michelle Marsh
Show Date: 9/25/1949
Company: Tri-State Life & Casualty Insurance Company
Agent:
Exp. Acct: $786.00

Synopsis: "Sure, they may have plenty of blue blood in Boston, but from what I just saw, they've got plenty of the other kind too."

Johnny goes to Boston, Massachusetts to look for Michelle Marsh, who was reported missing by her sister. Michelle is insured for $25,000. Johnny gets to her last known address just in time to see a man gunned down with carbines by two men in a car. Johnny goes to the victim and the dying man's last words were "Michelle Marsh". Johnny makes a quick visit to her apartment and searches it finding only a book of matches for "Boston's Best Bar by Far, Flannery's Bar".

Back outside, Johnny meets Lt. Bell and gives him a very detailed breakdown of the killers. After all, he is paid to pay attention to details. Johnny learns that the dead man was also a detective with a good business and a bad reputation. Johnny tells Bell about Michelle and why he is looking for her, and what the dead man had told him.

A visit to Michelle's apartment manager, Mrs. Macy, uncovers nothing except that Michelle had irregular hours, and was last seen leaving with a suitcase and a man, supposedly her employer. She only got mail from someone in Chicago.

Johnny questions the neighbors and learns nothing more. Johnny goes to dinner and then to Flannery's Bar and asks for a double rye. Johnny asks for "Blackie" and gives the bartender a description of Michelle's boyfriend. A big guy named Roxy takes Johnny outside and tells him that the description is that of Louie Marine. On the way out of the bar with Roxy, Johnny is met by a hail of carbine fire that is met with submachine gun fire.

Johnny discovers that he had been saved by the police and is probably being used as a pigeon. Johnny goes to his hotel and after reading the afternoon paper he calls Bell and tears him apart for putting Johnny's name, hotel, and why Johnny was in town into the papers. Bell tells Johnny that it must have been a misunderstanding. Bell tells Johnny that the dead detective was named Bernard Knight, and that he was hired by Roxy Morris to find the girl. Johnny is sure that Louie Marine probably killed Knight.

Michelle calls Johnny the next morning. She tells Johnny to stop looking for her. Johnny tells her that she was waiting for Roxy to come from Chicago when Louie showed up. She thinks Johnny is guessing but agrees to meet Johnny at the Gangplank Bar on Chelsea Street near the Navy Yard. Johnny visits a North Boston "Undertaker" and pays for information. Johnny learns that Roxy Morris was suspected of stealing $75,000 in a payroll robbery. Roxy left for Chicago and left the money in Boston.

In the bar Johnny meets Michelle who confirms the story. Michelle adds that Louie Marine had tricked Michelle out of $20,000 by telling her that Roxy had sent him for it. Later Louie told Michelle that he had lied and that he would call the police if she turned him in or told Roxy. Then he made her give him $15,000 more. Now Roxy is back and he wants ALL of the money, which Michelle doesn't have.

Johnny sets up a plan with Michelle and the police: Michelle will arrange to meet Roxy. The undertaker friend will arrange for Louie to meet Roxy. The police will meet all three. The place is the Bunker Hill Monument (Don't fire until you see the red in their eyes) at 3:00 p.m.

Johnny walks up to the observation platform early and finds an unconscious Michelle with a suicide note beside her. Johnny hears a shot and starts down the steps where he meets Roxy and baits him to go up by saying Louie Marine is upstairs. Roxy slugs Johnny and goes back upstairs. Johnny then meets

Louie climbing the stairs, and he escorts Johnny in front of him to the observation deck. Johnny reaches the observation deck to see Roxy leaning over Michelle. Johnny goes up and ends up standing between Louie and Roxy. Suddenly Michelle screams and pulls Johnny's leg out from under him while Roxy and Louie shoot each other.

Johnny carries an unconscious Michelle to the hospital to have the remaining poison pumped from her stomach, apparently, she took too little the first time. Then he goes to Bell to find out why he did not show up until an hour later. The reason: He forgot to set his watch back after the time change to daylight savings time!

Notes:
- AKA "She Came in Like a Lion, But Went Out on The Lam", or "She Should Have Been Banned in Boston."
- The first car was a tan club coupe with Massachusetts tags 3R165.
- The carbines were .30 cal. Army issue.
- Johnny shows up next Saturday night, October 1.
- Music is by Leith Stevens.

Producer: Gordon T. Hughes Writer: Paul Dudley, Gil Doud
Cast: Bill Bouchey, Charles Seel, Dorothy Lovett, Lawrence Dobkin, Myra Marsh, Vic Ryan

♦ ❖ ♦

Show: **The Fishing Boat Affair**
Show Date: 10/1/1949
Company: **Intercontinental Marine Insurance Company**
Agent:
Exp. Acct: $1,264.28

Synopsis: "This you can really call a fish story, and I was the live bait!"

Johnny flies to the Pacific Deep-Sea Canning Company in San Pedro, California where he meets Mr. Walton who wants his $400,000 for the two fishing boats he lost at sea with no survivors and only two bodies. Walton agrees to assist Johnny when insurance fraud is mentioned. Captain George Carpo, Fleet Captain, meets Johnny but he does not know what happened, but he has never lost a boat in five years. Carpo tells Johnny it will be a miracle if he finds the boats.

Johnny goes to the Coast Guard and meets with Lt. SG Myles Endikett. The Coast Guard report says that the bodies show signs of a violent explosion, and that means scuttling to collect the insurance.

Johnny goes to the Cormorant Bar and finds Carpo talking to a woman and then he leaves. Johnny goes in and talks to the girl. Johnny tells her who he is and she tells Johnny he has a tough job. The girl, Anita Vargaves, is willing to talk somewhere else for money, as Carpo lives upstairs. Johnny takes Anita to another bar where Roscoe Walton shows up and is angry because Johnny is with HIS girlfriend. Johnny decides to get lost.

Johnny goes to the local police and asks them to look into dynamite purchases, then goes back to Carpo's place. While walking up the steps he hears 6 shots and runs in to find Carpo shot and barely alive, and Johnny notices that he was beaten. A man walks in and accuses Johnny of killing his friend.

Johnny finds himself with a dead man at his feet, and a gun at this head. Johnny explains what has happened, and the man identifies himself as Cricket, who was there to talk business with Carpo. Johnny tells him who he is and Cricket tells him that he is in the salvage business. Cricket tells Johnny that Carpo's face met with a "Monkey's Fist". Cricket explains the purpose of the knot, and Johnny asks about a woven ship's bumper on the wall. Before the police arrive, they leave and go to Cricket's boat, a surplus Navy PT boat where, over some Tchaikovsky and a drink, Cricket agrees to find the sunken boats for salvage rights and a $5,000 fee, returnable if he is unsuccessful. After agreeing, Johnny goes to Carpo's office where he finds a floor safe with a gold ingot in it. Walton and Anita show up with a gun. Johnny accuses Walton of smuggling Mexican gold, but Walton does not know what he is talking about, so they struggle and Johnny knocks him out with the ingot.

Johnny gets the $5,000, calls the Coast Guard and then heads out to sea with Cricket. After arriving in the San Climente area, they spend an hour searching for the lost boats. The wrecks are located and a diver goes down and confirms that the boats are there.

Johnny has to go down to make it official, so he dons the old-fashioned diving suit, complete with helmet, lead shoes, rubber hoses and a canvas suit, not very zoot!

While on the bottom, Johnny finds the boats and the gold hidden in the ship's bumper. Cricket calls to Johnny over the intercom and tells Johnny he is not going to come up but will suffer an "accident". Johnny tells Cricket that he has found the gold and hidden it, so he has to come up.

Upon arriving at the surface, actually at the end of the hoist, Johnny sees a full-scale battle going on with the Coast Guard. Johnny cuts his suit with a diving knife and he falls on Cricket.

After a cab trip to the police, Cricket tells all: while in Cleveland he had noticed a nationwide series of small gold thefts. He discovered that the gold was being melted into ingots and shipped to the orient. He wanted to intercept the gold and make a tidy profit. It was Carpo who was helping him get the gold and transfer it to the tuna clippers.

Johnny buys chocolates for Anita, who is in jail as an accomplice.

Notes:
- AKA "The Tuna Were Running and So Was Everyone Else", or "I Caught a Fishing Boat but You Should Have Seen the One That Got Away!"
- A "Monkey's Fist" is a type of knot used as a weight at the end of a rope.
- This program contains a commercial for *The Edgar Bergen Program*, which starts on Sunday.

- Cricket is described as a "Thomas Mitchell Type". Mitchell played the forgetful Uncle Billy in "It's a Wonderful Life".
- Wilbur Hatch does the music for this program.
- *The Red Skelton Program* starts tomorrow.
- Paul Masterson is the announcer.

Producer:	Gordon T. Hughes	Writer:	Paul Dudley, Gil Doud
Cast:	Willard Waterman, Lawrence Dobkin, Paul Dubov, Junius Matthews, Edmond MacDonald, Georgia Ellis		

♦ ❖ ♦

Show: The Racehorse Piledriver Matter
Show Date: 10/8/1949
Company: Lloyds Underwriters Association
Agent:
Exp. Acct: $1,449.22

Synopsis: "This is a horse on me. But I did find out that in the race for life and death, the police laboratory is where they make the photo finish."

While buying cigarettes (18 cents) Johnny is approached by Nettie Montana, the short Johnny Longden, a former jockey and small guy. Nettie has an offer for Johnny about a horse and $50,000, but he can't talk in public so they go to Johnny's apartment. In Johnny's apartment Nettie tells Johnny about the racehorse Piledriver. The horse made a lot of money for Nettie, but Piledriver hasn't won since Nettie retired after an accident in Central Park. The current owner has him insured for $50,000 and is going to kill him because he can't win and can't go to stud. Nettie is willing to pay Johnny to save Piledriver. After an OK from the insurance company, Johnny and Nettie head for the Hiawatha Racetrack, outside of Chicago, Illinois.

At the track Nettie warns Johnny to look out for Lilah, as she is dangerous to men like Johnny. Johnny meets Lilah Bushnell, the daughter of the owner, Col. Faraday Bushnell. Johnny tells Lilah that he is interested in buying Piledriver but Lilah assures Johnny that "daddy would nevah sell Pahledrivah as he is one of the family!" Lilah shows the horse to Johnny and he tells her he hopes to make the horse win again. Lilah kisses Johnny just as her boyfriend Leo Corbett shows up and blows up at her. Johnny slugs Leo just as the Colonel shows up. Lilah and Leo leave and the Colonel explains to Johnny that Leo is a fellow horse owner and a very jealous man. Johnny tells the Colonel that he is glad that Leo is not James J. Corbett.

Johnny meets Nettie in a bar and learns that Corbett owns fast horses but is suspected of running his horses slow to build up the odds, and then cashes in by running them fast. Johnny tells Nettie that he offered the Colonel $60,000 for Piledriver pending approval from his private vet from California. Against Johnny's advice, Nettie is going to the stable to personally guard the horse.

Johnny gets a room for $3 and settles in for the night only to be awakened by sirens heading towards the stables. Johnny goes to the barn in the landlady's 1929 Ford and learns that Nettie had gone into the barn. Johnny goes in and finds Piledriver's stall padlocked. Johnny breaks the door and gets the horse out and then finds Nettie in the stall unconscious on the floor. Johnny drags Nettie outside and finds a horseshoe imprint on his very dead head.

Lilah runs up and sees Nettie, and Johnny tells her to get lost. The Colonel runs up and is shocked that Nettie is dead, as he was his best jockey. Johnny accuses the Colonel of trying to kill Piledriver and takes Nettie to the morgue in Chicago.

Later that morning Lilah calls and wants to talk to Johnny. Johnny tells her to pick him up so they can drive to the country. Lilah denies all Johnny's accusations that the Colonel is out to kill Piledriver. She tells Johnny that her father owes Leo $50,000 from betting on Piledriver and Leo has told the Colonel to kill the horse and he has agreed, but Lilah knows he will not. Lilah tells Johnny that she kissed him to prove to Leo that he would not get everything he wants.

Johnny goes to the Chicago police, where Lt. Craig tells Johnny that the autopsy confirmed that Nettie was hit with a new horseshoe, not one on a horse. It also had to have been swung by a person, and not a horse. Johnny calls a meeting at the track offices with the Colonel and Leo. The colonel arrives and is ready to sell Piledriver to Johnny. Leo shows up because Johnny had called him. Johnny tells them that the fire was set and that Nettie's lungs were full of smoke. Johnny wants to test their lungs for residual smoke to see who killed Nettie. The Colonel hesitantly agrees, but Leo bolts out the door. Leo runs out onto the roof with Johnny in hot pursuit. On the grandstand roof, Leo shoots at Johnny, but he is a lousy shot. Leo fights with Johnny and runs again. Leo tries to escape down the downspout, but it collapses and he is killed.

The final expense item is dinner for two with Lilah, $34.80 — only $8 of which was for dinner, the rest was listening to her life story.

Notes:
- AKA "He Would Have Been Off His Feed If I Didn't Know My Oats", or "It's Great to Get a Kick Out of Life as Long As it is Not a Kick in the Head."
- Johnny buys Lucky Strike cigarettes.
- Leo is compared to James J. "Gentleman Jim" Corbett   heavyweight prizefighter.
- This program contains a commercial for the Saturday programs *Phillip Marlow*, *Gang Busters* and *Escape*. There is a singing "CBS" commercial at the end.
- During the proverbial chase scene, there are two races going on   the one on the track "And there they go!" and the one on the roof with both commentaries going on at the same time   very funny!
- Wilbur Hatch provides the music for this program.
- Paul Masterson is the announcer.

Producer: Gordon T. Hughes   Writer: Paul Dudley, Gil Doud
Cast: William Conrad, Doris Singleton, Jerry Hausner, Herb Butterfield, Hal March

Show:	Dr. Otto Schmedlich
Show Date:	10/15/1949
Company:	American Volunteer Liability Insurance Company
Agent:	Homer Shally
Exp. Acct:	$1,211.69

Synopsis: "Well anyway, I learned the answer to the question 'What does a doctor do, when a doctor needs a doctor?'"

Johnny takes a cab to the office of American Volunteer where Homer Shally apologizes for an argument they had about Johnny's $1 tips on his last expense account. The insurance company has issued a malpractice policy on Dr. Otto Schmedlich in Los Angeles (doesn't anything happen in Hartford?). It covers accidental malpractice, but they want to prove criminal malpractice. The company has paid 2 claims to this quack so far and the local authorities are looking into him, but they cannot find anything.

Johnny flies to Los Angeles, California and, after 11 phone calls, goes to Dr. Schmedlich's office where he meets the nurse Doreen, the receptionist, and asks her for a date. Doreen tells Johnny that there is no way she would be caught dead with him. Later that night in a restaurant, Johnny tells Doreen he is an "insurance man" and would like to get a list of the doctor's patients, after all a lot of healthy people go to the doctor and worry about their health. Johnny takes Doreen home and tells the cab to wait. $28 later, Johnny goes to his hotel.

Next morning Johnny gets to the office early to get the list from Doreen. While eyeing the list, surprise, the doctor is also early. After telling the doctor that Johnny is a patient, the doctor gives Johnny an exam for a back problem. The exam the doctor gives includes a hypo of a liquid lullaby. As Johnny goes out, he sees the doctor going through his jacket for the list and his ID.

When Johnny wakes up, he is in a room with padded walls, a bad taste in his mouth and a ringing in his head. Johnny realizes he is in a mental institution and pounds on the door. His nurse, a man named Forgey, tells Johnny that the boss will see him just before supper. The boss is Dr. Doreen Smith.

While he waits, Johnny makes a blackjack out of his shoes and a ripped-up bed sheet. At 4:00, Forgey shows up with Doreen. Johnny slugs Forgey when he comes in and pulls Doreen into the room. Doreen tells Johnny to go back to Hartford. Johnny locks Doreen and Forgey in the cell and takes her keys. Johnny notes that the cell is in an out-of-the-way country house with no other visitors.

Johnny borrows Doreen's car and drives to a gas station. At a phone booth Johnny calls the one name he remembers (A. A. Aaron) and fakes a pharmacy survey, and gets the name of Schmedlich's favorite pharmacy.

Johnny goes to the pharmacy and while talking to the pharmacy manager Mr. Anjoy, Johnny learns that most of Schmedlich's prescriptions are refillable, dangerous, and habit forming. Johnny also memorizes a list of clients from the narcotics book in Anjoy's office.

Johnny finally finds one client at home, Millicent Royal, a blue blood type. She tells Johnny that Dr. Schmedlich is a wonderful doctor. Johnny threatens to tell her father that he thinks she is not being honest and she gets angry. Millicent's estranged husband Bill shows up and Johnny decides to leave.

After a shower, a drink and a thinking session at his hotel room, Johnny wonders why he has not called the police. After four drinks Millicent calls and wants to talk. Johnny tells her to tell him what she wants to say over the phone because, usually when he goes to see someone, they wind up dead. Johnny goes back to Millicent's apartment and, yup, she's dead.

A call to Dr. Schmedlich's phone service tells Johnny that he is going to the office. When Johnny gets there the lights are on and Bill is waiting inside. He tells Johnny that he didn't kill Millicent. He tells Johnny that Dr. Schmedlich had hooked her on narcotics and then blackmailed her to not tell the family. When she called Schmedlich and told him she was going to tell, Schmedlich killed her. Now Bill is going to kill Schmedlich using a hand grenade he had kept from Guadalcanal.

When the Doctor comes in, Bill pulls the pin and throws it at Schmedlich. Johnny kicks Bill, and then kicks the grenade out into the hallway. After the explosion, Bill beats Schmedlich while Johnny watches. Johnny stops Bill with a portable typewriter before he kills Schmedlich. PS, Johnny calls the police.

The final expense items include round-trip air fare to Palm Springs and dinner for three — Johnny, Haig and Haig.

Johnny warns Shally that if he reacts to this expense account like he did to the last one, he will need a doctor.

Notes:
- AKA "An Apple a Day Sent the Doctor Away", or "It Couldn't Have Happened to a Bigger Worm".
- $1 tip to office.
- Shally tells Johnny, "When I want a laugh, I tune in Jack Benny".
- The fee for the office visit to Dr. Schmedlich was $50.
- Russell stammers three, once on "submitted" and once on "identification", once on "word".
- Champagne is described as "rich people's 7-Up".
- This program contains a commercial for *The Edgar Bergen Program*.
- Johnny mentions Haig and Haig scotch at the end.
- Music direction is by Wilbur Hatch.
- The announcer is Paul Masterson.

Producer:	Gordon T. Hughes	Writer:	Paul Dudley, Gil Doud
Cast:	Willard Waterman, Betty Lou Gerson, Lawrence Dobkin, Paul Dubov, Georgia Ellis, Edmond MacDonald		

Show:	**Witness, Witness, Who's Got the Witness**
Show Date:	10/22/1949
Company:	Max Krause Bail Bond & Insurance
Agent:	Max Krause
Exp. Acct:	$500.71

Synopsis: "In this case, most of the principles are out on bail. It put me out on a limb."

Max Krause arrives at Johnny's apartment with a bad cigar and a potential loss of $50,000. Max put up bail for two prosecution witnesses against gangster Leo Porcina, and both have disappeared. Max's insurance contacts recommended Johnny, who has a good reputation, except for padding the expense account, but who doesn't do that, right? Johnny gets a $1,000 advance to find Glenn "Nippy" Cochran and Dan Patterson.

Johnny goes to New York City and heads for the apartment of Nippy's sister, who uses the stage name Mona Doyle. Johnny gets into the building with a delivery boy and goes to Mona's apartment. Johnny tells her why he is there and tells Mona he hires some radio writers to work things out for him. Mona does not know where Nippy is and would not tell Johnny if she did. She tells Johnny that everything she owns has come from Nippy, including being introduced to Leo Porcina. Johnny and Mona have a couple of drinks and then Leo shows up. He offers Johnny the opportunity to work together to find Nippy and Dan, because their disappearance makes him look bad. But Johnny turns him down.

On the way out, Johnny notices the chauffeur of Leo's limo is following him. Johnny takes a cab to Dan Patterson's apartment, but the chauffeur is there when he gets to the apartment. The chauffeur tells Johnny that he is Dan Patterson! Dan suggests they go somewhere to talk and slugs Johnny.

Johnny wakes up with a .45 headache on the floor of the back seat of the limo, with a hose coming in from the exhaust pipe. Johnny is able to plug up the hose with a handkerchief and waits to see what will happen.

Dan stops the limo and takes Johnny out. Johnny slugs him with a rock and takes his gun. When Dan wakes up, he tells Johnny that Leo made him do it, and what Leo says, you do. Johnny gets Dan to tell him that they are in New Jersey. Dan tries to run, and Johnny shoots him and then deposits him with a police doctor.

Johnny goes to New York and calls Mona. She tells Johnny that Nippy has come back and killed Leo. Johnny picks up Mona and goes to Leo's apartment where they find Leo dead, with a knife wound in his chest. Mona tells Johnny that she was in the back room and heard voices. When she came back in, Nippy was standing over Leo.

They go back to Mona's apartment and, after almost being seduced by her charms, and a "Johnny Walker for Johnny Dollar", Johnny wakes up. Johnny wonders why would someone who had turned state's evidence kill someone the state was going to kill? Then he figures it out. Leo was up on tax charges and Mona was holding some of the money for him. If the police found out,

Mona would go to jail, and Nippy provided everything for Mona.

The seduction does not work. "I'm not human, I'm an insurance investigator!" Johnny calls the police and turns Mona in for murder. Johnny plants a phony story in the newspaper outlining how he had used a tape recorder to get the confession. Johnny goes to the hotel, after getting some adhesive tape. In his room, Johnny tapes the phone books to his chest and waits.

Nippy shows up and tells Johnny that Mona's confession is phony. Johnny tells Nippy that a friend killed Leo but that does not fit Nippy. Nippy tries to throw a knife into Johnny's chest, but it bounces off the telephone books. Johnny throws a chair at Nippy and finally knocks him out. Johnny expenses a trip to the doctor to get the adhesive tape removed with alcohol. The expense account also includes $367.25 entertaining Mona for her forgiveness!

Signed: "Yours (clink, clink) ummm Truly, (ahhhhh) Johnny Walker, I mean Dollar!"

Notes:
- AKA "He said 'Give me liberty or give me death", and got both".
- Johnny tells Mona "I have a couple of radio writers work things out for me."
- This program contains a commercial for the program *People's Platform*.
- Several references to Johnny Walker scotch   the best is: "Johnny Walker for Johnny Dollar Johnny on the spot!"
- This story was done as *The Jack Madigan Matter* on 10/21/50 and *The Tom Hickman Matter* on 8/13/52, both with Edmond O'Brien.
- Paul Masterson is the announcer.
- Music direction is by Wilbur Hatch.

Producer:	Gordon T. Hughes Writer:	Paul Dudley, Gil Doud
Cast:	Sidney Miller, James Nusser, Georgia Ellis, Paul Dubov, Ed Max	

♦ ❖ ♦

Show:	**The Little Man Who Wasn't All There**
Show Date:	**10/29/1949**
Company:	**West Coast Underwriters**
Agent:	**Bradford L. Coates**
Exp. Acct:	**$942.08**

Synopsis: "If you're looking for murder, I know a man who can get it for you wholesale."

Johnny receives a postage-due letter assigning him to a case in San Francisco, California. Mr. James Yarbow had a $20,000 policy on his wife, which was cancelled the day before she died due to non-payment of the premium. Yarbow claims to have had a hand in the "accidental" deaths of 12 other West Coast policyholders.

Johnny goes to San Francisco and meets with Mr. Coates. Coates tells Johnny that the 12 deaths in question have totaled $250,000. Mr. Yarbow has had a perfect alibi for each of the 12 deaths. All of the deaths involved an automobile accident, except for one where a pilot died. Johnny asks for a list of policyholders, only to see if it would be easy for Yarbow to get it also. Johnny asks for a $50,000 policy on himself — just in case.

Johnny gets Yarbow's address and the address of the 12 victims, rents a limo with chauffeur and starts interviewing. The "tears were falling like monsoon rains in Burma" at each family, but none of the families knew a man named Yarbow.

Johnny then goes to Yarbow's house and starts watching. When Yarbow leaves his house dressed in a black trench coat and carrying a black satchel, Johnny breaks in through a window and explores the house. Yarbow's house looks like a crime museum, full of guns, books, evidence and Mr. Yarbow!

Yarbow holds Johnny at bay by telling him that the room and the roses in the rug are wired to booby traps. Yarbow tells Johnny that crime is his hobby. He has items from the Black Museum in Scotland and items from all over the country. Yarbow knows who Johnny is and why he is there. Yarbow continues his rant about the unpaid policy on his wife. Yarbow tells Johnny that he gave the money to his wife and she spent it, and he can prove it. When Yarbow lowers his guard to open a drawer, Johnny slugs him while he is standing on a big red rose on the floor. The phone rings and, trying to imitate Yarbow, Johnny answers. On the phone is Martha, calling from the office, who tells Johnny that there has been another accident killing two more policyholders — and Johnny is Yarbow's alibi!

Johnny searches Yarbow for a gun and then looks in the black satchel and finds an old Army tank radio receiver wired to a transmitter in the house, which is what allowed Yarbow to hear Johnny enter the house.

When Yarbow recovers, Johnny tells him that Martha had called, but Yarbow is sure that she told him nothing. Yarbow shows Johnny the insurance policy he was reaching for. Johnny locks Yarbow in the most secure room in the house, the bathroom. Yarbow protests in horror, as he does not want to be locked in the room where his wife died!

Johnny calls the state police and confirms the accident information given him by Martha. Then Johnny calls Coates and arranges to meet him in his office. At the office Johnny and Coates search the personnel files for "Martha" and find three, but only one was in the office that night, Martha Kinsey.

Johnny goes to Martha's apartment and wakes her up and tells her who he is. Martha says nothing other than Yarbow has paid her for information (everyone does it) and Yarbow is smart, he told her so. The only thing Johnny really gets is that Martha is in love with Yarbow.

Johnny then visits the doctor who did the autopsy on Yarbow's wife. She died of a cerebral hemorrhage after falling in the shower. On the way back to Yarbow's, Johnny realizes that 1.) The alibis are too perfect, 2.) Yarbow cared more about the policy money than losing his wife, and 3.) Yarbow is crazy and a murderer! Now Johnny has to get the evidence.

At Yarbow's, Johnny searches the house until he finds the evidence he is looking for, while being careful not to step on the roses on the carpet!

Yarbow is taken from the bathroom and Johnny confronts him the fact that he had nothing to do with the accidents. Martha was the one supplying him with the information Yarbow had used to threaten the insurance company with. Johnny shows Yarbow the evidence of his wife's murder, the one piece of evidence he should not have kept — a piece of pipe with a faucet on it. The pipe he used to murder his wife. Martha comes in and they both attack Johnny. Martha throws an urn and misses, but Yarbow chases the urn as it rolls towards a rose on the rug, which explodes on a booby trap killing Yarbow.

Johnny buys Martha a three-month subscription to *Love Life Magazine* to read in jail. Then there is dinner on fisherman's Wharf diving for pearls in a barrel of blue points at Fisherman's Wharf, diving for Pearl's earring which she lost bending over a barrel trying to see what oysters look like.

Yours, ah Truly, Johnny Dollar.

Notes:
- AKA "The Little Man Who Wasn't All There, or in Most Cases There at All", or "The Unpaid Premium Payoff".
- *The Black Museum* was also the name of a mystery series hosted by Orson Wells.
- This program contains a commercial for *The Groucho Marx Show, Bing Crosby, George Burns* and *Lum and Abner* programs.
- Music direction is by Wilbur Hatch.

Producer:	Gordon T. Hughes	Writer:	Paul Dudley, Gil Doud
Cast:	Jay Novello, Martha Wentworth, Paul Dubov, GeGe Pearson, Lawrence Dobkin		

◆ ❖ ◆

Show: The Island of Tin-Yutan
Show Date: 11/5/1949
Company: Seven Seas Maritime Underwriters Association
Agent: Enos McCartle
Exp. Acct: $3,286.44

Synopsis: "The only reason I took this case on a savage island off the coast of New Guinea is I'd been having a bout with a bottle of "Old Fairy Godmother" and I was hoping to run into a native who would shrink my head!"

Johnny travels to Port Moresby, Papua, New Guinea, buys some new tropical clothes and goes to the offices of Seven Seas where he meets Mr. Narky. Johnny confirms that a group insurance policy was sold to Grand East Development Corporation, who used it to provide $50,000 policies as an inducement to get divers and executives for their pearling fleet. So far, 2 men are dead and 4 are missing. Narky tells Johnny that the police have their own problems, and that the government officials might get to an investigation in three months, so Narky is just waiting for Johnny.

Johnny charters the *Kitty Wake*, captained by Steve Granger for the trip to Tin-Yutan. Granger arranges to leave at 5:00, and Johnny is told to bring a .45!

Once at sea, Johnny starts to enjoy being on the boat. Granger meets Johnny on deck and tells Johnny that there is another unnamed passenger going to Tin-Yutan. On the trip the other passenger stays in his cabin claiming seasickness, but the cabin boy says he eats like a horse.

The next evening the boat arrives at Tin-Yutan. The captain starts the engine and works his way through the reef. Just short of the reef the captain orders an about face. There is a pearling lugger on the beach with a native strangled and hanging from the foremast!

Suddenly the other passenger, Matt Keely shows up on deck with a gun in each hand and orders everyone aft. When Granger orders the crew to abandon ship in Kanaka — the local language, Keely kills them and then orders the boat towards shore. Once on shore, Johnny and Granger are taken to a hut surrounded by 12 dead natives apparently killed by the .30 cal. water-cooled machine gun protruding from the window. In the hut they meet Portez. Johnny tells them that he is there to take care of them and they laugh. Keely offers Granger $500 for his boat which is worth $50,000. Somehow the offer of $500 or death seems fair. They need the boat to get off the island and will be at sea for a couple months. A very ugly, fat woman, Princess Papalya, comes into the room and is brusquely pushed back into the other room by Portez. Granger slugs Keely, then Johnny lunges out for Portez. Granger is shot and then Keely is hit with a chair swung by the Princess! Then the lights go out.

Johnny dreams of being in a hammock, with a pretty girl and a parrot, and wakes up to the first two! (and he remembers his copy of "Tales of the South Pacific" is 17 days overdue from the library). The lovely girl he is with is Ponta, and she tells Johnny that Papalya slugged Johnny and brought him to her village. **Papalya likes Johnny** and saved him for herself! Ponta explains that Keely and Portez were pearl divers who went bad and killed the natives and stole all the pearls. The natives had stopped diving, so Keely kidnapped the princess and held her for ransom until they started diving for pearls again. Johnny learns that the dead natives had tried to save the princess and were killed by Portez and that the Princess is now hiding in the mountains. The ugly part is that now Johnny has to protect Keely and Portez as they are insured by Seven Seas for $50,000 each!

The next morning there is more shooting as the natives try to get at Keely and Portez who Johnny must protect. Johnny wonders why Keely and Portez do not leave, so Ponta gives Johnny a black pearl that Papalya had sent for him. Keely and Portez want it also. But Johnny has a plan. Johnny disguises Ponta to look like the Princess and goes to tell Keely and Portez that he will trade the pearls and the princess if they will leave the next morning.

The next morning Johnny and Ponta leave early to get to the boat but Keely and Portez are there early too. Johnny opts to swim out to the Kitty Wake and waits for daylight. At dawn, Keely sees the natives coming out in his binoculars. So that Keely does not spot the fake princess, Johnny creeps up onto the boat and pushes Keely overboard, and then slugs Portez. When Johnny checks on Keely, the Princess Papalya is beating him with a paddle. She had pulled rank on Ponta because, **"She like Johnny!"**

Keely and Portez are turned over to the police and Johnny recommends that their policies be cancelled. Johnny buys a tattoo for the Princess Papalya. The last expense item — 48 cents for overdue fines at the library. Never did read the book. It would be an utter waste of time for a man who has known Ponta!

Notes:
- AKA "South of the Equator Things Can Get Hot in More Ways Than One!", or "Mother Call My Draft Board, I'm Leaving the Country Again."
- Johnny stutters on the word "sing".
- A pearling lugger is a two-masted ship with a diagonal spar to hold the sail.
- *Tales of the South Pacific* was written by James Michener and A. Grove Day.
- A Kanak is a native Melanesian inhabitant of New Caledonia.
- This program contains a commercial for the CBS programs *Sing It Again, Gene Autry, Vaughn Monroe, Gang Busters, Phillip Marlow, Johnny Dollar* and *Danny Clover the Broadway Cop* the CBS Saturday night lineup.
- Paul Masterson is the announcer.
- Music direction is by Leith Stevens.

Producer: Gordon T. Hughes Writer: Paul Dudley, Gil Doud
Cast: Willard Waterman, Mary Shipp, D. J. Thompson, Tom Holland, Clarke Gordon, Lawrence Dobkin

♦ ❖ ♦

Show: **The Melanie Carter Matter**
Show Date: **11/12/1949**
Company: **Miss Melanie Carter**
Agent:
Exp. Acct: **$0.00**

Synopsis: "The most popular sport on Boston's Charles River is rowing in one-man skulls, or rather it was the most popular sport that is, until they took to beating on one man's skull — MINE!"

Johnny goes to Boston, Massachusetts and meets Melanie Carter, who lives in a chrome and black wheelchair in a flat, right out of the last century. Melanie had gotten a telegram of his assignment, as she has no telephone. Melanie is taken aback when Johnny reminds her of an old flame from her youth. She tells Johnny that she was once happy, but as for today and tomorrow, who knows.

Melanie tells Johnny that many years ago her husband was murdered by his brother, who then died. She not only got all of the insurance, but she also adopted the brother's children and raised them. Now they are destroying her mind by trying to kill her.

Johnny first checks out the financial arrangements for the heirs, and they have a frugal stipend to live on. Johnny then goes to visit the nephew, Chalmers Carter and is met by his wife, Crystal. Johnny is told that her poor hubby is out on business — he is always out on business, but will call before he comes home, but she wants to have fun. Johnny looks like a fun guy in that "nice" suit.

Johnny unfolds a plan: he is a "finder" for a California man who has some oil property to develop, and Johnny is looking for investors with a lot ($120K) of money. Would hubby be interested? Boy would he be interested. "He just needs one big chance!"

Back at his hotel, Johnny finds a note from Chalmers who is at the Bay Shore Trotters Club, watching the horses work out. Johnny gives him the oil spiel, including the 27% tax write-off. When Chalmers says he probably can raise the $120K, "George", a fellow horse watcher reminds Chalmers that he owes George $500,000!

Johnny goes to the niece, Sophia Carter and gives her the spiel. She first must rely on the advice of her business manager but decides she can raise the money.

Johnny goes back to Melanie's flat and finds the door open and Miss Carter standing at the telephone she does not own! She is telling Joe to bring Rocky to her place as she has a job for them. She wants to get rid of someone. Johnny watches the flat from across the street. When Joe and Rocky go in, Johnny follows and listens at the keyhole. Johnny hears "Grandma" tell Joe and Rocky that she has had Dollar followed, and Dollar is trying to get the niece and nephew to kill her. Now she wants Dollar out of the way, and she means "out of the way!" Suddenly Joe sees Johnny's shadow under the door. Joe and Rocky grab Johnny and rough him up before taking him out of the apartment.

Johnny is "taken for a ride" in a cab to Joe's hotel room where the boys tell Johnny that they want a piece of the action. They think that Johnny is hustling the heirs with a phony oil stock scam. They figure that since they are getting money from "Grandma", they want some of Johnny's action too, so Johnny agrees to cut them in. Incidentally they met Grandma when, while breaking and entering, she nailed them with a musket and then hired them for odd jobs. Johnny suggests they go back and watch to see who kills Grandma, so they can work on getting the insurance money.

They all go back to Melanie's flat to find the police there. By claiming he is a *Boston Globe* reporter Johnny finds out that a friend of the Commissioner called for help, and by the time the police got there, the dame was dead. By saying he will get his name in the paper, Johnny gets officer Fred Moser to fake an arrest, which sends Joe and Rocky fleeing. A couple blocks later, Johnny gets a cab to Chalmer's place. He is out on business, but Crystal is alone and wants company! In the middle of an embrace, Chalmers comes in (and he didn't call either!) and threatens to thrash Johnny, so Johnny has to slug him.

Johnny then goes to Sophia's place, breaks in and sees several things, the Charles River he has been crossing all day, an open drawer with the impression of a missing revolver in the dust, and Grandma holding the gun on Johnny. Johnny takes the gun from Grandma after firing 3 shots into the ceiling. In the other hand is a letter she was trying to steal from Sophia's desk. The note is from Melanie's husband to Sophia telling his favorite niece that his wife has finally succeeded in killing him, as she did his brother when he came to his rescue and she ran over him with her carriage. It is not too hard to see that Sophia has been blackmailing Grandma and Sophia was the dead body at the Carter flat, where she had gone to get the $120,000.

Grandma goes to the police on Johnny's arm to give a dignified surrender. Chalmers gets a pipe and slippers to help his home life, Joe and Rocky get a pass on the *River Queen* sightseeing boat and officer Moser gets his name published, on a check for $50. Expense Account total — oh, what's the use, you won't be able to pay it where you are.

Notes:
- AKA "Who'd Like to Rock the Old Doll to Sleep", or "The Un-Nice Niece and the Charming Young Rat Who Put the Few in the Word Nephew".
- Johnny's "nice" suit is New York City $185 right off the rack (that's about $1,900 in 2017 dollars).

Producer:	Gordon T. Hughes	Writer:	Paul Dudley, Gil Doud
Cast:	Lawrence Dobkin, Unknown		

◆ ❖ ◆

Show:	**The Skull Canyon Mine**
Show Date:	**11/26/1949**
Company:	**Old Caledonia Insurance Company**
Agent:	**Oscar Wheaton**
Exp. Acct:	**$947.99**

Synopsis: "I knew when I went to the desert that anyone who plays around with cactus is liable to get stuck. But I didn't remember another way of saying death is going west."

While working on a case at dinner, Johnny is contacted by Oscar Wheaton. Johnny is told that two years ago Old Caledonia had invested in a working gold mine in Twin Buttes, Arizona. Two months ago, profits suddenly dipped by 50%. Johnny is to find out why!

Johnny flies to Twin Buttes and is met by Jackie who drives him in a jeep for 23 miles, over no road, to the mine. Johnny's cover is that he is an efficiency expert hired by the company.

At the mine Johnny meets Nugget the barking dog, and the manager Doyle, who gives him the books to review. Doyle knows of no problems at the mine, but things could be better considering they must cart the ore 8 miles by mule train to the smelter. Then Johnny goes to the mine with Doyle.

On the way in on a burro propelled dynamite cart, Johnny hears drilling. Just before a blast goes off Johnny is told to open his mouth and close his eyes by Doyle, who then instructs the miners to get the ore loaded. Johnny asks to see the rest of the mine, but Doyle tells him that this is the only face being worked.

After a steak dinner (burro steak maybe?) Doyle goes to the mine and Johnny talks to Jackie. She tells Johnny that she is the secretary and bookkeeper. She came out to the mine to marry the former manager, but he disappeared.

Johnny goes to the bunkhouse and meets a muleskinner named Kangaroo, who will be his roommate. Johnny tells him that he plans to go with him the next morning to deliver the gold ore to the smelter. Johnny is starting to suspect that Doyle is working the mine for himself and keeping the profits.

The next morning on the way to the smelter, while Kangaroo is murdering "Mule Train", the mule wagon is buzzed by an airplane at Halfway Rock, and then it is surrounded by horsemen. The pilot lands and introduces himself. He is "El Puerco", the pig, because he is as ugly as one. El Puerco wants the gold, not the unrefined ore in the back, but the $30,000 in pure gold under the wagon seat.

The gold is loaded into the plane. Johnny and Kangaroo are tied to a stake and the mules are tied around them. El Puerco tells them that he will then buzz the mules, and they will kick Johnny and Kangaroo to death. Too bad Kangaroo knows how to calm angry mules, except for the one who kicks Johnny as Kangaroo is warning him to "never trust a mule".

Johnny wakes up to Nugget licking his face, and Jackie tending his head. Jackie's clothes are torn. She tells Johnny that she and Doyle were going to run away, but the plans have changed. Jackie tells Johnny that Kangaroo has taken the mules back to the mine. Jackie also tells Johnny that she suspects that Doyle had killed her intended husband Larry and was milking the mine. She had only acted interested in Doyle to find out more. Now she wants to help Johnny expose Doyle. She knows that there is a refinery in the mine, which is where the pure gold comes from. The charts to the mine are in the safe and she has the combination.

Back at the mine, the Saturday night square dance is in progress. Johnny and Jackie go to the office and find the door of the safe open, along with El Puerco's dead mouth. Johnny goes looking for Kangaroo. A miner tells Johnny that Kangaroo was looking for Doyle, who was in the mine.

At the mine entrance shots are heard and Jackie thinks it was Kangaroo who was shot. Johnny goes in to investigate and finds Doyle dead. He calls for Kangaroo, but another wounded man answers — it is Larry! Johnny gets to him just as he dies. Johnny discovers that Kangaroo was out feeding his mules and was not in the mine.

Johnny figures out that Larry, Doyle and El Puerco were working together and started double-crossing each other.

Final expenses include a cable to Old Caledonia recommending that Jackie be made mine manager, and 32 ounces of snakebite prevention — in case a snake ever bites him.

Expense account total, $947.99. Which is just about as much sense as you can make it without making it a dollar. Yours, (No charge for that double talk) Truly, Johnny Dollar.

Notes:
- AKA "Mr. Bones, Who Was That Lady I Seen You with Last Night?" or "Messing with a Mule Train is One Good Way to Kick Off."
- "Mr. Bones" refers to the old blackface minstrel shows.
- Johnny stammers on "remember" in the introduction.
- Dinner ($12.80) was liver and dumpling soup, veal paprikash, cherry strudel and coffee. The case was an eccentric millionairess who wanted to marry Johnny for his money.
- The song Kangaroo "murdering" refers to *Mule Train* sung by Frankie Laine.
- "Making history at Tanferan" when the horsemen attack refers to the former Tanferan Race track, a Japanese assembly area in WWII.
- The snake bite remedy is an old W. C. Fields routine.
- Paul Masterson is the announcer.
- Music direction is by Leith Stevens.

Producer:	Gordon T. Hughes Writer: Paul Dudley, Gil Doud
Cast:	Doris Singleton, Willard Waterman, Don Diamond, John Dehner, Fred Howard

◆ ❖ ◆

Show:	**Bodyguard to Anne Connelly**
Show Date:	**12/3/1949**
Company:	**Ambassador Life & Casualty Insurance Company**
Agent:	**Franklin Haley**
Exp. Acct:	**$845.30**

Synopsis: "This case looked refreshing at first. It took me to Milwaukee, the brewing capitol of the USA. But it occurred to me later, for a guy who appreciates a good head on a glass of beer, I take lousy care of my own."

Johnny has just started a library "who done it" mystery book "The Playful Siamese" when Franklin Haley calls. Haley thinks crime fiction is trash. "They'll never get a penny of mine (oh yes I will, mutters Johnny!)". It seems that Miss Anne Connelly fell in love with a man named Neal Grafter. On the eve of their wedding, Neal was arrested for grand theft. Neal is being paroled tomorrow. Anne is penniless and has a large policy, therefore Johnny has been assigned to protect her, and leaves on a 6:30 flight to Milwaukee, Wisconsin. Johnny takes the book, with him, but gets little reading time on the flight due to a blown fuse.

He arrives at Anne Connelly's fashionable house and is admitted by Cora the maid. Cora informs Johnny that Miss Connelly "should be home when the joints close. Want a straight slug or a highball?" Cora, it turns out, is Miss Connelly's personal maid and a former specialty dancer. When Johnny tells Cora that he thought Connelly was penniless, which is why Johnny was hired, Cora tells Johnny that Anne needs a bodyguard like she needs a foster mother. She has all sorts of boyfriends, like Ray Merrick with whom she is out with tonight. Cora also tells Johnny that she has never heard of Grafter. When

Johnny comments on her wardrobe, Cora says that she has free use of Connelly's clothes, except for a few upper pieces which are too small.

Johnny waits on the couch and reads his book until Anne and Merrick, who is a lawyer, come home at 2:30 a.m. When challenged about the nice house and the penniless plea, Merrick tells Johnny that they went to the insurance company because they have no idea how long protection would be needed, as there is no telling when Grafter will show up. Ray leaves and tells Johnny to call him if anything comes up.

Everyone goes to bed and Johnny checks the doors, turns out the lights and snuggles up on the couch, like a Fakir, with his book. Later Cora comes out to talk, dressed only in a nightgown. She tells Johnny that Merrick and Connelly were giving him a boatload of untruths. She has personally seen Anne's bankbook, and she can afford J. Edgar Hoover!

While they are talking, a window breaks, there are shots, and Anne screams. While running to her bedroom, Johnny sees an open window and a shadow by the garage. He rushes out to the garage and runs into a huge arm that reaches out and nearly strangles him. It is Neal Grafter.

When Johnny asks Grafter about being in prison, Neal doesn't remember anything about prison. He only remembers a room with bars and screaming people, and doctors. He knows that he didn't kill Anne because she wasn't in her bed. Was she with Johnny! Johnny tries to reason with him, but it only gets his throat grabbed again. Finally, Neal leaves and Johnny goes inside.

Back in the house Johnny pulls the shades and confronts Anne with Neal's talk of doctors and bars, like in a mental hospital. Since it was Cora's bed that was shot at, Johnny realizes that Anne had set Cora up as a pigeon.

Anne admits that Neal was in a mental hospital and had escaped over a month ago. The police had watched for a while but gave up when he didn't show. She had no insurance, so Merrick bought some and called the insurance company to get protection.

The next morning Johnny gets a call from the hospital confirming that Neal was a paranoid schizophrenic, is dangerous, and would try again, probably tonight.

Johnny sets up a lie. Johnny tells Anne and Ray to go out as usual, he and Cora will stay. Johnny hides in the yard by the incinerator as it snows, waiting for Neal. At 4:00 a.m. Johnny sees a shadow by the house. After breaking the window glass, shots are fired into Anne's window. Johnny tackles the shadow at the window and nails his target with a furnace poker. The shadow is Ray Merrick!

Back inside, Johnny calls an ambulance for Anne. Cora is very distraught primarily because Anne still owes her a week's pay. Anne ends up in the hospital with a 50/50 chance and Ray Merrick is in jail for Insurance fraud. Ray was going to kill Anne and blame it on Neal, who was caught that morning and returned to the hospital.

Notes:
- AKA "It May Have Been Love at First Sight, But the Last Sight Was Down the Barrel of a .45 Automatic."
- Johnny is drinking Johnny Walker and soda
- While on the couch Johnny feels like a fakir: A Muslim or Hindu religious mendicant, especially one who performs feats of magic or endurance.
- This program was modified and aired as *The Virginia Beach Matter* on 8/31/1950.
- Bob Stevenson is the announcer
- Music direction is by Leith Stevens

Producer:	Gordon T. Hughes	Writer:	Paul Dudley, Gil Doud
Cast:	Betty Lou Gerson, William Conrad, William Johnstone, Sandra Gould, John Dehner		

◆ ❖ ◆

Show:	**The Circus Animal Show Matter**
Show Date:	**12/10/1949**
Company:	**Britannia Underwriters Association**
Agent:	
Exp. Acct:	**$152.70**

Synopsis: "They say that big game hunting is a sport only for the wealthy. Well, it didn't cost me much, except almost my life."

Johnny travels to Brunswick, Georgia to the animal circus of Maximillian Sandro. Max is working with a singing elephant when Johnny gets there. Sandro tells Johnny that he has just acquired a new black leopard named "Ashanti", which is insured for $20,000. But someone has tried to steal her. Sandro saw the attempt but was not able to trace who did it. Additionally, Tex Randall, who sold Sandro the cat, has upped his price.

When Johnny sees the cat pacing in its cage, "my feet wanted to run but my eyes could not leave the cat". Fortunately, there was a gorgeous set of steel bars in the middle.

Tex shows up. He tells Johnny that he had caught the cat in Togo and was watching it to protect his investment. The price has gone up because the trip was more expensive than first planned. He also had seen the attempted robbery and had received a gaping knife wound for his diligence.

When Tex leaves to go to town, Angela, an "Ava Gardner type woman" shows up. Angela tells Johnny that she is Sandros' daughter, and that she likes cocktails, dining and dancing, which Johnny tells her is on the agenda for later. Angela leaves to get ready for tonight.

While watching the cat pace, Johnny sees a light it the cat's eyes then a knock on his head that does not put him out. He is grabbed from behind in a double hammerlock and pushed towards the cat's cage. Suddenly, cocktail hour is over and the lights are out.

When Johnny wakes up, the cat is gone, and Tex is dead with claw marks across his head. The police are called and while waiting for the police, Johnny searches Sandro's trailer and finds a "friendship tree" made up of Christmas cards, including one from Angela in San Francisco, regretting that she will not be able to be with him this year!

Angela enters the trailer with a well-armed man she calls Ben, who suggests they retire to his hotel room to discuss the location of the cat, and Johnny agrees. At the hotel room, Johnny makes a big mistake — he calls the man "Ben" and is rebuked. Johnny is told that the man's name is Sir Bennett Montford and only his closest friends may call him by the familiar term "Ben". Montford tells Johnny that he is a big game hunter and is well trained in the proper use of a high-powered rifle. He wants to know where the cat is. He gives Johnny a story that the local people in Togo worship the cat, and are offering $100,000 in gold to get the cat back. Montford's assistant Harold is called to help convince Johnny to talk, but Johnny calls Montford's bluff and walks out. Whew!

Back at the circus, Sandro shows up, and tells Johnny that he has been in hiding. He admits to killing Tex, who was trying to kill Johnny, by pushing Tex into the bars of the cage. Johnny suggests going to the cat to lure Montford there ($100,000 of cheese even makes a mouse look dangerous), but Sandro objects until Johnny threatens him with the police.

Johnny and Sandro drive to the barn where the cat is still pacing in its cage. Montford, Angela and Harold show up armed to the teeth. Montford is now prepared to kill the cat to get at a fortune in diamonds hidden in the cage by Tex Randall. Sandro tries to protect his cat by opening the cage to let it escape. As the cat flies across the room, Montford gets a paw full of claws across the face and is killed. Fearing the cat, Angela and Harold disappear. Johnny gives his story to the police who put out an APB for Angela and Harold, Sandro heads to Okefenokee swamp with a group of men to look for the cat.

Johnny has a word of advice for the insurance company: don't insure the men who are looking for the cat! If you want to throw away your money, throw it at me!

Signed "Yours Truly, Johnny ummm 'Frank Buck' Dollar"

Notes:
- **AKA "All they needed was a clown, and then I showed up"**
- **AKA "I Once Thought I'd Run Away with The Circus, This One I Wanted to Run Away From."**
- **Frank Buck was a famous animal hunter and provider for zoos and circuses.**
- **Music is by Leith Stevens.**
- **Bob Stevenson is the announcer.**

Producer:	Ralph Rose	**Writer:**	Paul Dudley, Gil Doud
Cast:	Lynn Allen, Lawrence Dobkin, William Conrad, Parley Baer		

Show:	**Haiti Adventure Matter**
Show Date:	**12/17/1949**
Company:	**American Federated Life Insurance Company**
Agent:	**Harvard Huntington**
Exp. Acct:	**$424.70**

Synopsis: "The encyclopedia says that the island of Haiti can be called San Domingo, Santa Domingo, or Hispaniola. Well after my visit there, I could suggest several more things they can call it, but they probably wouldn't get past the censors."

Johnny is called, just as he is about to go to a show, to the office of Mr. Harvard Huntington. Harvey tells Johnny that Ralph Gordon, the black sheep scion of the Hartford Gordons, is insured for $100,000. The beneficiary is either charity or a wife, if he has one. Ralph is on his boat in Haiti and is dying of a voodoo curse. Ralph's older brother, Thomas who is also in Haiti, reported the information.

Johnny flies to Port-au-Prince, Haiti, buys some tropical clothes, and goes in search of someone to help find Gordon. In a bar, Johnny runs into Cap Regan, American expatriate (courtesy of the Feds), who tells Johnny that Gordon's boat is in the harbor without a crew because they refused to work for a drunken captain. Regan rows Johnny out to Gordon's boat — a filthy yacht — and is met by a woman in a pair of clam diggers and an off-shoulder tee shirt. The woman is Edwina, Ralph's wife. When Johnny explains why he is there and asks to see Ralph, she agrees and takes Johnny below. Johnny only gets as far as the locked cabin door when he is met by abusive shouts and cries for more wine. Edwina explains to Johnny that a woman called Maria LaSalle has put a curse on Ralph after he cursed at her. Edwina gets angry when Johnny suggests she is after the money and the ship's bosun invites Johnny to leave.

Johnny goes to see Thomas Gordon, who agrees that the voodoo curse is trash and requires only a susceptible mind. Thomas tells Johnny that Ralph is only looking for escape through alcohol. "Call on me for anything" and "Let me know what you learn" are the reassuring words of the good doctor as Johnny leaves.

Johnny and Regan go in search of Madam LaSalle and find her hut in a cane field. Madam LaSalle tells Johnny that Gordon will die tonight in the wind and rain, and her magic is the key. When Johnny doubts her magic, she throws something into the fire that causes Johnny to stagger out of the hut gasping for breath and nearly passing out. When he recovers he goes into the hut and finds small pieces of photographic film. So much for magic.

Johnny goes back to the boat in a gathering storm. On the boat, Johnny overhears Edwina talking to someone. Johnny then knocks out the bosun when he comes out on deck. Johnny then accuses Edwina of plotting with Madam LaSalle to kill Ralph, which she denies. She tells Johnny that she is only plotting to divorce Ralph and marry the bosun.

Johnny and Edwina go back to Madam LaSalle and Johnny confronts her with the film scam. When threatened with the police she admits a that a man put her up to the phony curse. She tells Johnny that the man needs the storm so that the portholes on the boat will be closed. Edwina tells Johnny that only the food, which she cooks, and champagne are brought onto the boat. A visit to the local liquor shop confirms that a case of champagne has just been sent to the boat, packed in dry ice. A call to Thomas confirms that dry ice in a closed cabin could asphyxiate a drunken man.

Johnny finds Regan and, for $20, Johnny gets him to row out to the boat in the storm. (It was raining hard enough to require a seeing-eye seal.) When they near the boat, Regan is shot in the leg and Johnny decides to swim for the boat. When Johnny gets to the boat, dear brother Thomas is holding a gun on Johnny! The bosun pushes Thomas off of the boat, and Johnny breaks down the door to Ralph's cabin and carries him up to fresh air.

Thomas goes to jail (he wanted control of the family fortune, not Ralph's insurance). Ralph and Regan go to the hospital.

Notes:
- AKA "The Nights May Be Black Down There, But the Magic Blacker".
- This program was domne as *The Port-au-Prince Matter* on 5/30/1950.
- This program has a commercial for the Orange Bowl teams (Santa Clara and Kentucky) who will be honored on the Vaughn Monroe program to follow.
- Johnny knew that photographic film made of cellulose and nitrate gives off nitric oxide and nitrogen dioxide when burned. Both are worthy of any gas chamber.
- Music by Leith Stevens.

Producer:	Ralph Rose	Writer:	Paul Dudley, Gil Doud
Cast:	Betty Lou Gerson, Daws Butler, Sylvia Syms, Ben Wright, Ken Christy, Howard Culver, Tim Graham		

♦ ❖ ♦

Show: The Department Store Swindle Matter
Show Date: 12/24/1949
Company: Industrial Insurers Incorporated
Agent: Eban Stevens
Exp. Acct: $511.50

Synopsis: "It was the week before Christmas and all through the house, a creature was stirring, and boy what a rat!"

A hand-written message delivered to Johnny's apartment summons him to the office of penny-pinching Mr. Stevens. Evans tells Johnny that the Association of Department Stores of Greater Manhattan has reported a number of robberies. A man impersonating a sales person will take an order for a large item and then disappear. Evan gives Johnny a check for his "usual retainer".

Johnny heads for New York City on the 7:03 "Bankers Special" train where he watches the bankers practice shaking their heads and whispering "no". At the association offices, Judy Whitehall is assigned to help Johnny. Judy tells Johnny that they have a general description of the man and that all the store detectives and sales staffs are watching for him. Just as Johnny is getting his Letter of Identification, Judy and Johnny learn that another store has been hit. They are told that a man was buying a camera when a little girl took his picture. The man then shot a store detective and grabbed the girl and the camera and ran off. The man is still in the store.

Johnny and Judy go to the store and find the manager, Mr. Sandler, going crazy in the camera department. He tells Johnny that the girl was found wrapped in a 9 by 12 oriental carpet ($123.50) but without the camera, which probably was not loaded anyway.

Johnny talks to the little girl, Bobbie, and she is no help as she just cries until Johnny gets her with the old "better-be-nice-to-Santa" trick. Johnny then gets news that the store detective is dead — now it's murder. Johnny goes and tells Santa (5th floor — Dante's Inferno, Jr. Grade) what is going on and then Bobbie and Judy come in. Bobbie tells Santa that all she wants is an air rifle. After telling Santa all about the event, a descriptive drawing of the man is made, including the details of Bobbie's teeth marks in his hand, and it is given to the guards. Johnny has lunch is in the tearoom with Judy. Lunch is the "shoppers special".

After lunch Johnny learns that the store Santa has been found tied up in a closet. It seems that the killer was playing Santa and Bobbie told him all! Then Johnny learns that the Santa costume has been found about the same time as a woman was shot in the junior lingerie department. Sandler tells Johnny that she was lost on the stairs looking for the lady's room, and the man shot her and ran down stairs to sporting goods where he got several guns and ammo. The police arrive, the store is emptied and the police start searching from the roof down. Johnny and Sandler start from the bottom floor. On the first floor Johnny and Sandler are shot at. After getting Sandler to create a diversion, Johnny shoots the display case the man is standing on, but he runs down to the shipping department. Johnny runs after him and, after finding the man and engaging in a fight with a hammer, Johnny nails the man is into a crate and blacks out.

The next morning Johnny wakes up in the hospital with Judy standing beside him. Judy tells Johnny that the man got away, and Johnny gets up and runs to the store. In the shipping department, the manager tells Johnny that the crate Johnny had nailed shut has been shipped out to upstate New York. The funny thing is, the merchandise meant for the box was found on the floor. But the manager tells Johnny that he knows where the box is going. The merchandise was the manager's charitable contribution for the unfortunates who will be spending the holidays away from home...at the state prison in Ossining!

Expenses included $12 dinner for Judy, and $10 for medical supplies for the CBS sound men Bern Surrey and Billy Gould who had to break all the glass during the show. The expense account may be high, but isn't everyone this time of year?

Notes:
- AKA "How I Played Santa Claus and Almost Got Left Holding the Bag", or "Going for A Sleigh Ride Without the Benefit of Snow Can Be Tough Sledding".
- This is the first program to mention a retainer.
- The "shoppers special" is cream cheese, walnuts, watercress and pineapple on whole wheat.
- At the end, the announcer's mike must have been turned off, as he has to start twice.
- Bob Stevenson is the announcer.
- Music by Leith Stevens.

Producer:	Gordon T. Hughes	Writer:	Paul Dudley, Gil Doud
Cast:	Connie Crowder, Georgia Ellis, Jay Novello, Parley Baer, Marlene Ames, Paul Dubov		

◆ ❖ ◆

Show: The Diamond Protector Matter
Show Date: 12/31/1949
Company: American Continental Insurance Company
Agent: Robert Ferry
Exp. Acct: $1,142.89

Synopsis: "This was not only the end of the old year — it was almost the end of mine."

Johnny goes to the office of Robert Ferry who tells Johnny that a rich, old widow has a diamond necklace worth $250,000 that is kept in a bank vault. Robert wants Johnny to take the diamond to her so that she can wear it to a party, after which Johnny will return it to the bank vault. Johnny is not sure until Robert gives him a ticket to Honolulu, Hawaii.

Johnny goes to San Francisco to catch a flight to the islands. Johnny spots a man who looks familiar. The man introduces himself as Wayne Franklin, former thief. Wayne recognized Johnny from a newspaper article that describes how Johnny will be bringing the Star of Hades diamond to Honolulu. Wayne also points out a man who he describes as a detective who is following him.

In Honolulu, Hawaii Johnny goes to the Royal Hawaiian Hotel where Mrs. Bettsworth keeps a beach house. At the beach house Johnny meets Thomasina, Mrs. Bettsworth's niece. She tells Johnny that she was the one who put the article in the paper, and hopes that the diamond will be stolen. If is it, she will get a third of the insurance money, which she will use to help others at Warm Springs Georgia, where she had been a patient. Mrs. Bettsworth arrives with her son Nikki, who is in debt and tries to hit Johnny. Mrs. Bettsworth thinks Johnny's name is funny, so he tells her that he paid two radio writers for the name. Johnny gives her the stone. Johnny tells her about Franklin and how the kids want the money. When she gets uppity, Johnny locks her in her room until the party.

Mrs. Bettsworth is let out for the party, at which Johnny spots Franklin in the orchestra. The lights go out, Mrs. Bettsworth screams and the diamond is gone. The police are called and the guests are searched and released when nothing is found. Johnny suggests to Mrs. Bettsworth that she issue a $10,000 reward for the return of the stone. Suddenly there are shots, and Johnny hurries outside to find that the police have shot Franklin. Franklin tells Johnny that the detective really was his accomplice and dies before telling Johnny where the stone is.

Johnny goes in to talk to Mrs. Bettsworth, who tells Johnny that the diamond is the only important thing. Johnny grabs Thomasina, carries her up the stairs and shows her the diamond in a chandelier. Thomasina gets the diamond and Johnny gives it back to Mrs. Bettsworth. Johnny tells her that when the lights went out, he slid down the banister, grabbed the necklace and hid it in the lights. Johnny tells Mrs. Bettsworth he will take the diamond back, and might tell the police if she does not pay Thomasina the reward, which she gets.

Notes:
- AKA "You Lead a Diamond, Mother, and the Game Will Really Get Started".
- "The Star of Hades Diamond" was mentioned as the next adventure at the end of *The Slow Boat from China*, broadcast on 2/25/1949, however the location of the story has changed from Palm Beach and New Orleans to Honolulu.
- Bob Stevenson is the announcer.
- Music by Leith Stevens.
- Story information obtained from the KNX Collection in the Thousand Oaks Library.

Producer:	Gordon T. Hughes	Writer:	Paul Dudley, Gil Doud
Cast:	Unknown		

◆ ❖ ◆

Show:	**The Firebug Hunter Matter**
Show Date:	1/7/1950
Company:	**Eastern Insurance Company**
Agent:	**Arnold Whelan**
Exp. Acct:	**$410.00**

Synopsis: "I didn't make any New Year's resolutions, but if I had, one of them would have been to take no more arson cases. Ouch! They get hot in more ways than one."

Johnny is in Palm Springs trying to recoup from the New Year when he is called to San Diego, California. Johnny meets with Mr. Sheridan who introduces Johnny to a local investigator named Crowley. Johnny is told that George Duke has policies on five buildings, three of which have burned. Crowley has learned that Duke was convicted of arson in 1941 when he burned a garage.

Johnny goes to the police who suspect Duke and a partner named Menkoff of running a car theft ring, and the burned garage was used to paint and renumber the cars. Johnny then goes to the Ohio Hotel and starts following Duke. On the third night Johnny spots a girl and a drunk go into the hotel. Shortly afterward the girl leaves, and the hotel catches on fire. Johnny calls the fire department and goes to the hotel where he meets Duke coming out. Johnny confronts Duke, who tells Johnny that he was on the fourth floor, and that Johnny can prove nothing.

The fire is out in about forty minutes, and all of the guests but one, Geraldine Marlow, are accounted for. The fire is determined to have started in her room, and a body was found on the stairs. Geraldine arrives and must get into her room to find Carl, who was sick and had passed out. Johnny tells her that Carl started the fire with a cigarette on the bed. The body of Carl is later identified to be a legal Houdini and a gang lord. Crowley calls Johnny and tells him that Carl was poisoned, and Johnny tells him to find out more about Geraldine.

Johnny goes to the hotel and finds Geraldine shot. George Duke is there but claims that someone threw the gun into the room when she was shot. Johnny goes to a local bar to look into Geraldine and Carl. The Bartender tells Johnny that Carl was not with a girl the previous night. Later the body is identified by Carl's fourth wife, Lucille Taylor, based on a watch on the body. Lucille tells Johnny that she last saw Carl at 8:30, and Johnny notes that the fire was at 9:00. Lucille tells Johnny that a girl was to take Carl to meet a man from LA about a payoff, but the man in the room was a stand in, Jules Menkoff, who handled the car ring.

Johnny calls the editors of the newspapers and entertains them while giving them the story that he is investigating the fire and can prove that Carl is still alive. Johnny waits for Jules to appear, but Carl comes to the room. While he is talking to Johnny there is a knock and Jules is there and wants proof that Carl is alive. Carl tells Johnny that he saw Jules start the fire, and Jules calls him a liar and pulls a gun. Both shoot, but Carl shoots Jules.

Johnny apologizes to George Duke, and Carl is held and released when it is learned that he saved Johnny's life.

Notes:
- **AKA "Press Out My Asbestos Dinner Jacket, Mother, I'm Going to Smoke".**
- **Music is by Leith Stevens.**
- **The announcer is Bob Stevenson.**
- **Story information obtained from the KNX Collection in the Thousand Oaks Library.**

Producer:	Gordon T. Hughes	Writer:	Paul Dudley, Gil Doud
Cast:	Fay Baker, Rita Lynn, Herb Butterfield, Willard Waterman, Sidney Miller, Paul Dubov, Edmond MacDonald, Lawrence Dobkin		

Show:	The Missing Chinese Stripper Matter
Show Date:	1/14/1950
Company:	Apex & Great Northern Bonding Company
Agent:	Phineas Perch
Exp. Acct:	$611.44

Synopsis: "This time I went on a personally conducted tour of San Francisco's Chinatown, and Johnny Dollar got a new slant on life."

Johnny goes to San Francisco, California, and meets with Phineas Perch, who has a broken arm. Johnny is told that Wu Sin was given a six-week work permit and Apex has the bond. But Wu Sin has disappeared. Phineas has some information that Wu Sin had been beaten. A girl had called and told Phineas that Wu Sin had called her boss and told him not to look for her.

Johnny goes to the Almond Pit Bar and meets Eddie Foo. Eddie tells Johnny that he was told to hire the girl and was paid to employ her. She was good for business, and he wants her back. Eddie will not tell Johnny who paid him, and is told to come back later. Johnny eats dinner, and in his fortune-cakes is a message that the man Johnny is looking for is a killer named Lo Hoo Pur. Johnny goes to the police and learns that the police have turned the case over to the Feds. Johnny learns that Pur is suspected of arson, but it was not proven. Johnny is told to let it be known that he is looking for Pur, and he will find Johnny.

Johnny goes to a number of bars, and Pur finds him. Johnny asks about the girl and Pur takes Johnny to a back room where he is beaten, pushed into a trashcan, and rolled down a hill.

Johnny wakes up in the hospital where police Lieutenant Fischer tells Johnny that he is being sued. The trashcan he was in hit a 1949 Caddy, and the owner is suing. Johnny is called by Eddie Foo and told that he is in love with Wu Sin, and that she has some problems with immigration. Eddie tells Johnny that she is hiding in Sausalito.

Johnny goes to the address in Sausalito and gets in to talk to Wu Sin. She tells Johnny that she is in trouble but does not know why. Johnny tells her who he is, and that she is being lied to. Wu Sin tells Johnny that a friend will be back at midnight, and Johnny tells her to keep him there.

Johnny goes back to his hotel and find Eddie Foo in his room, dead. Johnny calls Lt. Fischer and leaves a message for him to come to Harbor House Hotel. The lieutenant arrives and Johnny tells him his story. Johnny and Fischer drive to Sausalito armed with a riot gun and tear gas. There is a car in the drive and the lights are on. The police surround the house and are shot at. Johnny gets a gun from Fisher and climbs into an ashcan and rolls into the house. Wu Sin shoots at Johnny but he gets the gun and finds the body of Lo Hoo Pur. Johnny tells her that she finally will be staying in the country.

Wu Sin was brought into the country to work as an entertainer but was taken into Mexico for a form of entertainment not related to this report. Wu Sin killed Lo when he threatened to expose her.

Notes:
- AKA "The Search for the missing Chinese stripper Wu Sin", or "She Didn't Have Much to Hide, So Why Did They Hide Her?" or "This Time I Went on a Personally Conducted Tour of San Francisco and Johnny Dollar Got a New Slant on Life".
- This is the last Charles Russell show.
- The announcer states: "We hope you will be listening at this time next when CBS presents a sparkling new comedy of college life *Young Love*.
- The announcer is Bob Stevenson.
- Music is by Leith Stevens.
- Story information obtained from the KNX Collection in the Thousand Oaks Library.

Producer: Gordon T. Hughes Writer: Paul Dudley, Gil Doud
Cast: David Ellis, Parley Baer, Edmond MacDonald, Vanessa Brown

Edmond O'Brien

Edmond O'Brien (1915–1985) was the second actor to play Johnny Dollar, but his character was a much different person. O'Brien's approach offered a more hard-boiled and cynical persona. Edmond had a much harder voice with a faint New York accent and a clipped manner of speech which added to his persona.

These vocal characteristics portray his voice as that of a hard person. This Johnny Dollar was not one to fool around. There were jokes from this Johnny Dollar, but they were much darker than Charles Russell's quips. In *The Yankee Pride Matter* after Carl Bush tells Johnny that the insurance company is on the short end of the deal, Johnny says he knows all about that, "I bet on Notre Dame last weekend". There was no nonsense allowed from the aggrieved widow or the philandering playboy.

This Johnny Dollar was all business and would not pull either his verbal or physical punches. Not that he was heartless. In *The Virginia Towne Matter*, Johnny totally realized that the girl has been shortchanged and gives her a break in allowing her time to raise the money for the jewelry. At the end of the case, he even donates his expense check to the defense attorney. His cold-blooded nature shows itself in *The Yankee Pride Matter* where Johnny shoots "The Major" to prevent him from leaving the room. In *The Stanley Springs Matter* Johnny shoots Norman Staiger to prevent him from walking out on him. Both instances were against unarmed men and premeditated, yet not fatal. Other Johnny Dollars tended to shoot only after being shot at.

Edmond O'Brien was an accomplished actor who appeared in over 200 films and Television programs and won two Academy Awards. Additionally, O'Brien appeared in over 110 radio programs, including his stint as Johnny Dollar. O'Brien died in 1985.

The following are the Edmond O'Brien Johnny Dollar cases.

◆ ❖ ◆

Show:	**Death Takes a Working Day**
Show Date:	**2/3/1950**
Company:	**Great Columbian Life Insurance Company**
Agent:	
Exp. Acct:	**$823.00**

Synopsis: Johnny drives to the estate of the deceased — a mausoleum like manor — Loyal House.

The housekeeper, Miss Sarah Tompkins meets Johnny and tells him that the widow is out shopping. Miss Tompkins has worked for the household for 30 years. "Loyal, er, Mr. Martin was an expert on Victorian furniture" Johnny is told. In answer to the unasked question, yes, Miss Tompkins was provided for in the estate. Johnny says he is investigating the murder so the murderer is not paid off. "People waste a lot of murders that way" he tells her.

Police Lt. Markwood is in the library in which only two things were out of place — a suit of armor and a case of shiny new hunting rifles. Markwood tells Johnny that the body of Mr. Martin was found after dinner and it had two bullet holes in it. According to Markwood, there are four suspects, a wife who was too young, the housekeeper who was in love with the deceased, the brother is broke and brooding and the body guard, a detective.

Johnny decides to start with Nick Bulotti, the bodyguard. Johnny meets with him after a horseback ride, and he tells Johnny that he had nothing really to say, but the police told him to stay put.

Marty, the brother was entertaining a bottle of 20-year-old brandy that was much too young for the book he was reading. It seems that the young wife had asked him to come and protect her from her husband. Joyanne, the widow comes home and goes swimming in a bikini that would "get her pinched on the Riviera!" Joyanne tells Johnny that Marty had introduced her to Loyal. But Loyal gave her everything but love, and when she went looking for it, the housekeeper informed Loyal and he became a madman. The housekeeper was upset with Joyanne because she had always assumed that Loyal would marry her. So, Joyanne is going to enjoy what little free time she has left.

Johnny goes to check up on the housekeeper, who Johnny finds in the library wiping off the desk in violation of police orders to keep out. She tells Johnny that she always cleans at that hour of the day otherwise Loyal would get mad. Markwood comes in and orders Johnny to take her to her room and then come back. On the way, there are 6 shots fired in the library. Johnny goes back to the library and finds an open window, and Markwood dead holding a shotgun.

While searching the body, Bulotti comes in. The only clue Johnny can find, which Markwood would have wanted to share, was an entry in his new notebook

"Check tattooing diameter. Recheck penetration". Johnny asks Bulotti to keep quiet. He also asks the others who have now gathered to go back to their rooms. Outside Johnny looks for clues and finds a .32 revolver in the grass. The gun has 6 empty chambers and lipstick on the grip. Johnny wonders if it could it be a red herring? Sgt. McDougal arrives and Johnny tells him what happened and gives him the gun. The gun is the same caliber which killed Loyal, but why was Markwood holding an unloaded shotgun when he was shot? Johnny gets more puzzling information from McDougal. The autopsy showed two bullet holes, 1½ inches apart, which did not penetrate too deeply. Everything pointed to the bullets being fired from 300 yards. The witnesses were split on whether 1 or 2 shots were fired on the night of the killing.

Johnny goes to the ballistics lab and discovers that the ballistics people had found powder burns, called tattooing, on the body indicating a close firing of the weapon. Also, the .32 was the weapon that killed both people, a .32 owned and licensed to Joyanne Martin, who looked better in a bathing suit than she will in the electric chair.

Johnny goes to see Joyanne and gets her out of the shower. When quizzed about a gun owned by her, she says that her gun is in the dresser. When she gets up to get it, the gun is gone. She says it must have been stolen, and there are too many people who would love to frame her. When asked if she remembers anything else, she says that she remembers hearing shots two days before the killing, while she was out horseback riding. They came from a walnut grove. Just as Johnny kisses her, the police he had called showed up, and Joyanne is taken into custody after she slaps Johnny.

Next morning Johnny goes looking for the walnut grove and pondering why everyone heard one shot, and there were two bullets in the body. In the hollow trunk of a tree Johnny finds a peck of cotton waste with powder burns in it. Johnny is hit on the head and sees Marty running back to the house. Johnny chases Marty back to the house and hears 6 shots. Johnny finds Bulotti standing over Marty. Bulotti says that Marty had drawn on him, so he shot in self-defense. Johnny suggests Bulotti go to police headquarters and register his story.

Johnny calls McDougal and tells him that Marty had just been shot and the killer was on his way to the office. Johnny tells McDougal that Nick and Marty had arranged to fire the .32 into the cotton waste to get the bullets. The bullets were then packed into a shotgun shell and fired at close range by a shotgun. Johnny tells him that he knew that Bulotti was the accomplice because he had said Marty drew on him, but Marty was unarmed.

Expense account items 2-9 are $624 in entertainment of Joyanne.

Notes:
- AKA "The Loyal B. Martin Matter", or "How to Take a Vacation in Fairfield County".
- O'Brien stammers several times.
- Johnny announces himself to Joy as the Hartford Hawkshaw a reference to a character in the 1863 Tom Taylor play *The Ticket of Leave Man*.

- Cotton waste is the materials left over from the cotton ginning process and used as a rag or absorbent.
- Edmond O'Brien continues the "um" ending for this program.
- Music is by Leith Stevens.

Producer:	Jaime del Valle	Writer: Paul Dudley, Gil Doud
Cast:	Irene Tedrow, Ted de Corsia, John Dehner, Walter Burke, Jeanne Bates, Ed Begley	

♦ ❖ ♦

Show:	The SS Malay Trader
Show Date:	2/10/1950
Company:	Intercontinental Marine Insurance Company
Agent:	
Exp. Acct:	$0.00

Synopsis: Johnny goes to Savannah, Georgia and signs on to the *SS Malay Trader* as a seaman. The ship is a rusty old liberty ship in the process of loading rattan-covered bales.

At the top of the gangplank is an officer cleaning his nails with a knife. He is chief officer Halstaff who assigns Johnny to the 4-8 watch and to his quarters.

In his quarters, Johnny meets Al Roter, a marine investigator for Intercontinental. Al has been onboard since the ship left Singapore. Johnny learns that the company has had some run-ins with customs and bought a lot of crude rubber just before the devaluation of the British pound. Half of it burned with an insurance loss of $100,000. Now the cargo is worth more lost than sold. Al thinks that the ship is heading for Corpus Christi and then to Mexico.

Halstaff calls Johnny and tells him to sign his papers in the shipping office where he meets Amai, (yes, ahhhh me!) a half-caste Malay who is the daughter of the owner. She is also Halstaff's girlfriend and wishes she could go with Johnny to be with her father who is going on the ship. While Johnny is signing his papers, Amai notices that his hands are so nice, and she has seen all kinds.

Johnny takes up his duties and wonders about the interest Amai has in his hands, could they be a tip-off? And why would the owner go on the ship — to smell his rubber burn?

The next day the ship departs and Johnny is sure "the sailor's life is not for me". Later he talks to Al, who feels that something is fishy, but cannot tell what. They go on deck, and while Johnny distracts the lookout, Al goes into the #2 hold. After 10 minutes, Johnny heads back to his cabin and hears a disturbance and running feet. Johnny finds Al Roter dead, with a knife wound in the back of his neck. Johnny goes to the owner and reports a killing and demands the Coast Guard be called. While arguing with the owner, Johnny hears a "man overboard" call. The owner, to find out what is going on, calls Halstaff who tells him that he saw a seasick man leaning over the rail and he fell over when the ship pitched. He is circling the ship now.

Johnny is on his way to radio the Coast Guard when the boilers start exploding. The crew panics, and in the confusion, Johnny gets to inspect the #2 hold area where he finds blood on the cover and a pocketknife, the one Halstaff was using. When he opens the hold, he sees the real reason for the explosions, burning cargo!

At dawn the ship finally sinks and there is no evidence of her presence except the loose hatch covers. Johnny makes his way back to the Malay Traders office in Savannah and sees Amai, who is surprised to see him, as Johnny had been reported missing. Johnny tells her he is missing because he did not report himself in the confusion. Johnny shows her his ID and accuses her of complicity in the destruction of the cargo. She claims total ignorance of a plot. A daughter does not question her father. She cries and Johnny is convinced she is innocent.

Johnny calls a chemist and asks a question about the specific gravity of crude rubber. The chemist says it should float, but Johnny notes that it didn't. Johnny asks Amai about movements from the warehouses, and then tells Amai to tell her father he is in the warehouses and to meet him there.

Johnny goes to the warehouse and finally finds what he is looking for, crates of crude rubber which should have been of the ship, but which will now be sold for a profit after an insurance payoff. Halstaff comes into the warehouse with a gun. Johnny tells him that he has the knife Halstaff used to kill Roter. But Halstaff says that even if he confessed there is no body. "Who says that there is no body?" asks Johnny. When Halstaff tries to search Johnny, a fight ensues and Halstaff ends up in police custody. Johnny had bluffed about the body, but Halstaff sang to the police and the ship owner was innocent of the murder but guilty of insurance fraud.

Expense Account total: because of Al Roter, his friend's death and the ugly taste it left, "this one is on me."

Notes:
- AKA "The Ship with no Port of Call".
- A Liberty Ship was used by the US in WWII to transport goods to the front.
- Rattan: a climbing palm used especially for walking sticks and wickerwork.
- There are a number of ship related terms used in this program: Topping-Lift, a large and strong tackle, employed to suspend or top the outer end of a gaff, or of the boom of a main-sail and fore-sail, such as are used in brigs, sloops, or schooners. A preventer: an additional rope, employed at times to support any other, when the latter suffers an unusual strain, particularly in a strong gale of wind. Definitions from William Falconer's Dictionary of the Marine   the South Seas project.
- Specific gravity: the ratio of the density of a substance to the density of some substance (as pure water) taken as a standard when both densities are obtained by weighing in air.

- Roy Rowan is the announcer.
- Music is by Leith Stevens.

Producer: Jaime del Valle   Writer: Paul Dudley, Gil Doud
Cast: Barton Yarborough, Elliott Reid, Lillian Buyeff, William
               Conrad, Robert Griffin

♦ ❖ ♦

Show: The Gravedigger's Spades
Show Date: 2/17/1950
Company: National Fidelity Life Insurance Company
Agent:
Exp. Acct: $763.90

Synopsis: Johnny is asked to go to North Dakota and notes that he is sent to North Dakota in the winter and Miami in the summer. Johnny is asked to look into two old duffers who are insured for $80,000. They are threatening to kill themselves.

Johnny travels to Highbridge, North Dakota to look into Mr. and Mrs. Trump. They are insured for $80,000 and are going to kill themselves. At the train station, Johnny gets a ride on the local pung to the Trump home, but the driver will only take Johnny to the gate. He is scared and wishes those folks were dead. He has been receiving packages from Africa and India labeled "Dangerous — Do Not Open — DEADLY". He tells Johnny that whatever was in those packages was alive. Johnny says he will call when he is ready to leave but is told there is no phone there.

At the Trump place, Johnny walks up the snow-covered driveway in a fresh set of automobile tracks. A young man greets Johnny and tells him to come in. Johnny is told not to take off his coat, he won't be staying long. The house is hot, humid and filled with orchids. Johnny is told to join the Trumps for coffee. At the dinner table Johnny explains that he has the papers to change the beneficiaries, but asks isn't killing your selves rather drastic?

Mr. Trump explains that noted alienists have found them sound of mind. They have had a happy life and owe the world something. With all the threats of A-bombs and H-bombs and UFOs, which are the prelude to destruction. Mrs. Trump tells Johnny that, after all Mr. Trump knows these things — He READS! They want to leave the world the beginnings of a new humanity. The current beneficiary, their niece Hope is wasteful. The new beneficiary Irwin Harper will use the money to continue their plan. And their plan?

Johnny is taken to the basement to see a maze of lead and concrete bunkers lined with cages of snakes! Johnny is told that when life on earth is erased, the snakes will be released to recreate humanity, just as Masterson said in 1903. Machines will feed the snakes for 100 years if necessary, and Irwin will continue their work with the insurance money. Johnny says that they are entitled to their opinions, but they are still wrong. He will let them sleep on it and let them sign the papers in the morning.

Johnny wants to borrow a car but is told that there is no car here. They have been barred from the property for years, including tonight!

Johnny is shown to his room and spends the night thinking about the situation. Just as he is about to drop off, he hears what he fears. Hisssss. Hisssss. Johnny grabs a shoe and turns on the light, ready to kill the hissing non-venomous radiator. Then Johnny hears a woman scream in the hallway. Johnny slips on his shoes and opens the door to see a girl lying on the floor. He bends over to look and is knocked unconscious.

When Johnny wakes up, the girl is gone and Mr. and Mrs. Trump are telling him he must be careful when he walks in his sleep. They tell Johnny that they saw no woman when they got to Johnny. When Johnny tells them about the tire tracks, they look out the window and see nothing. Johnny tells them that the drifting snow took care of the tire tracks and his footprints, so he must not be there either! The Trumps say it must have been a nightmare. Johnny takes them to his room to sign the papers immediately, but the papers are gone.

The Trumps go back to bed, and Johnny goes to Irwin's room. He tells Johnny that he knows nothing of a girl and heard no scream. Now, Johnny is starting to get mad.

Johnny searches the house looking for Hope. Back in his room, he hears a car trying to start. Johnny jumps from his window into the snow and goes to the car where Hope is trying to get away and they go back inside. Hope is a very attractive girl with an ugly gun she pulls from a shoulder holster. She tells Johnny that she has every right to the money and will do everything to thwart their plans, as the Trumps are fools. She tells Johnny that Irwin will take the money and run, as he already has a ticket to South America. She had gone to him and confronted him with the facts and it was he who slugged her outside of Johnny's room. She tells Johnny that she has thrown the switch to release the snakes, and they are outside freezing right now. Irwin comes into the room with a gun and is ready to kill both of them. Johnny tells Irwin not to move, as a snake has found its way into the house and is coiled up behind him. Irwin accuses him of faking and moves toward Johnny. The snake (yes there was a snake) strikes Irwin. Irwin recognizes it as a bushmaster, the deadliest of their snakes. He manages to shoot the snake, and then kills Hope and dies.

With no snakes and no beneficiaries, the Trumps are left with no purpose. Johnny suggests that Mr. Trump research a machine to fight the UFOs. He calls it the "Flying Cup". Yours uh Truly, Johnny Dollar.

Notes:
- AKA "How the gravedigger's spades came near to being trumps".
- A pung is a low box-like sleigh drawn by a single horse.
- An alienist is the old term for psychiatrists.
- Johnny wants some Old Harper referring to Old Harper bourbon.
- The bushmaster is a deadly South American viper.
- There is a promotion for O'Brien's newest movie, D.O.A.
- This is the first program using the "phone call" opening.

- Roy Rowan is the announcer.
- Music is by Leith Stevens.

Producer: Jaime del Valle Writer: Paul Dudley, Gil Doud
Cast: Peggy Webber, Parley Baer, Hugh Thomas, Dick Ryan, Jess Kirkpatrick, Mary Shipp

❖

Show: The Archeologist
Show Date: 2/24/1950
Company: Great Corinthian Life Insurance Company
Agent:
Exp. Acct: $456.90

Synopsis: Johnny is called and asked why he is not down here, as his train leaves in 45 minutes. Johnny tells the caller he is taking a quick course in ancient history. He wants to be able to speak his language in case he finds him alive.

Johnny travels to the Brighton Arms Hotel in New York City to meet with Marcia Lambert, sister of the missing archeologist Bruce Lambert, who has disappeared after his return from Egypt. Marcia had called the insurance company because she does not want any publicity or police involvement.

Marcia tells Johnny that her brother had been working on a remote dig in Egypt. She had stayed in the village. After telling her that he does not trust her and threatening to walk out, Marcia tells Johnny that they had smuggled some artifacts into the country. The artifacts were an obsidian statue and a scarab, both were possibly very valuable. Her brother is not a strong man as he had been involved in an accident in Egypt and his arm and shoulder are in a cast. She gives Johnny a picture of Bruce for ID purposes.

Johnny goes to check with the crew of their boat, but it has sailed. Johnny checks with customs. They have a record of Lambert coming in with one suitcase and one piece of statuary, no duty paid. Johnny then starts checking with the cabbies and notices a small well-dressed man watching him from behind a newspaper. Cabby #782 remembers seeing Lambert, but he paid him more to keep quiet than Johnny is paying for him to talk. After a $20 bribe, the cabby takes Johnny to a dingy hotel. A bribe to the room clerk gets Johnny a passkey to Lambert's room where he finds the obsidian statue. Johnny wonders why, if this thing is so valuable, does he not care for it better?

His thoughts are interrupted by a small man with a small "lady's gun" who wants to know where Lambert is. The man tells Johnny that Mr. Drummond will pay Johnny $2,000 to find Lambert. The man waves the gun in Johnny's face, and Johnny takes it from him and slugs him for good measure. In the man's jacket Johnny finds an Egyptian passport in the name of Ammon Hixis. Johnny leaves Hixis in the room and leaves a note with the desk clerk telling Lambert not to go into the room, but to call Johnny.

Johnny goes back to Marcia and confronts her with Ammon Hixis' visit. He bawls her out for withholding information and tells her "I just stopped doing things her way." If anyone calls, he will be in his room. In his room, Johnny gets a call from Lambert. Johnny explains who he is and what his sister has told him. Lambert tells Johnny that Marcia is his fiancée, not his sister. Johnny tells him to meet him in Marcia's room.

Johnny gets there first and goes in. Johnny meets Lambert in the corridor to tell him that Marcia is in the bathroom, dead. Johnny takes Lambert up to his room to get his story and to prepare an alibi for the police. Lambert tells Johnny that he had met Marcia in the hospital after his accident, and that she knew about the artifacts. Lambert gives Johnny the scarab to hold on to. He tells Johnny that he does not know Hixis or Drummond. Also, Lambert tells Johnny that his life had been threatened twice on the voyage over.

Johnny and Lambert go back to Marcia's room to meet with the police. In the room the police find a prescription bottle with the name of Dr. Ammon Hixis. Johnny suggests that Lambert be taken to police headquarters. Johnny also suggests that the police doctors x-ray Lambert's casts.

After dinner, Johnny goes to his room and finds Hixis and Drummond there. They weave a tail about the value of the scarab and how it will open up vast new oil fields if they can get it from Lambert. When Johnny tells them that he has it, the story changes. They tell Johnny that they had lied about the gewgaw, they want Lambert. The phone rings and Johnny answers it. The police are calling to tell Johnny that they have x-rayed the cast and found over $300,000 in narcotics in it. They are on their way over. When Johnny tells Drummond that the call was from the police, Drummond tells Johnny how he and Hixis had used Lambert to carry their drugs for them. Marcia was involved also but stupidly fell in love. They decide to wait for Lambert to show. Hixis goes into the bathroom with his gun, and Drummond sits on the bed. There is a knock on the door, and Johnny tells Lambert to come on in, thus tipping the police. The police burst in and Hixis shoots Drummond when he is shot.

Drummond will live, and Lambert is placed in a private hospital until he recovers. Johnny sells Lambert a policy on the artifacts.

Notes:
- AKA "The archeologist who never should have left his tomb" or "The disappearance of Bruce Lambert".
- Edmond O'Brien drops the "Yours, uh Truly" ending.
- There is a promotion for O'Brien's newest movie, *D.O.A.*
- Roy Rowan is the announcer.
- Music is by Leith Stevens.

Producer: Jaime del Valle Writer: Paul Dudley, Gil Doud
Cast: Virginia Gregg, Jay Novello, Ed Begley, John Dehner, Pat McGeehan

Show:	**Bodyguard to the Late Robert W. Perry**
Show Date:	3/3/1950
Company:	**American Continental Life Insurance**
Agent:	**Mr. Gordon**
Exp. Acct:	**$463.00**

Synopsis: Johnny takes a night train to New York and cabs to Mr. Perry's New York City import office and arrives at exactly 9:00 a.m. Susan the receptionist buzzes him in and the office explodes. Perry had thought his life was in danger and now he is dead. Johnny gives the receptionist some water to drink as the occupants of the building stream in. Everyone is told to leave and Johnny explains to Susan that someone hooked up a bomb to the buzzer to kill Perry. Mr. Perry left last night and someone must have come in afterwards and rigged the bomb. Susan tells Johnny that his next appointment was to be with his partner Van Brooten, who came from Holland to pick up a check dissolving the partnership. Christine, the wife, was due later to finalize the upcoming divorce.

The fire department arrives and Johnny tells them someone will get burned when the cops arrive. The police arrive and conduct an investigation. At eleven, Van Brooten comes in to pick up the check. Johnny tells Van Brooten that Perry is dead, but Susan is confused. Susan gives Van Brooten the check and he leaves.

Johnny calls American Continental and tells Mr. Gordon what has happened. Johnny is told to stay on the case, and Mr. Gordon asks if the death could have been suicide. Johnny tells Gordon that trying to prove "suicide" to enable the suicide clause would require a "Santa" clause. Johnny will talk to the wife to see if fraud is involved.

Johnny cabs to the apartment of Christine Perry. Christine tells Johnny who he is and why he is there, and Johnny wonders about her motives. She tells Johnny that she knows very little about her husband's friends since she left him six months ago. She tells Johnny that last night she was with a friend, Al Donovan, at the Clover Club. Her husband was there also with Susan.

Al Donovan enters the apartment and tells Christine he is taking her out of there. Al takes a swing at Johnny after he starts asking questions. Al tells Christine that he was not with her at the club, and that she was supposed to be there with her husband talking about the divorce. Johnny listens from the floor as Christine and Al leave the apartment as the noon whistle blows outside. Johnny allows himself a full minute for lunch.

Johnny follows Al in a cab and after a car ride with Christine, she jumps out and Johnny follows Al to a police station. Johnny speaks with a police lieutenant and he tells Johnny that Al Donovan has made a full confession to bombing the office. Donovan told the police he was in love with Mrs. Perry and planted a bomb in the office. Johnny thinks he is trying to cover up something.

Johnny searches Perry's office and learns that Van Brooten was bald, and had been getting toupees from Perry for years. In the personnel files Johnny learns that Al Donovan was Perry's former bodyguard. Johnny also learns that

Susan the secretary had worked in a munitions plant during the war wiring bomb fuses.

Johnny goes to Susan's apartment and meets her when she comes in. Johnny tells her about Al's confession, but Susan thinks he is covering for Christine. Johnny mentions the Clover Club and Susan tells him that she was there with Perry. Mrs. Perry was there with a man Susan did not know, but Perry did. Susan tells Johnny that she has worked for Perry for four years. Johnny surprises her by telling her about her job wiring fuses. The doorbell rings, Susan answers the door and is shot. Susan is shot at five times and Johnny can find no one in the hallway. Susan is awake but sure that she will be arrested. She tells Johnny that the man in the office was a phony and she was shot because she was trying to blackmail him. Susan tells Johnny the man's name is Van Zandt and that he lives in the Marsden Hotel, and then she faints.

Johnny goes looking for the phony Van Brooten in the Marsden Hotel. Johnny cannot find any Dutch names, so he gets the rooms that the maids have not been able to make up and starts looking. Johnny finds pay dirt in room 427. Johnny gets the man out of the room by pulling the fire alarm. Johnny gets into the room and beats Van Zandt back into the room. Van Zandt tells Johnny that the real Van Brooten is drugged in the bedroom. Van Zandt had known Van Brooten in Antwerp and knew about the sale of the company. Van Zandt had drugged Perry's cocoa and set up the bomb in the office. Van Zandt did not know how Susan had known he was a phony. Johnny tells Van Zandt that Perry was sending his partner gray wigs, my red headed friend!

Johnny wires the insurance company that they will have to pay Christine, who was only guilty of trying to stay on the right side of a hot-tempered boyfriend. Christine had lied about the Clover Club not to fix herself an alibi, but to keep Al Donovan from learning that she had been out with the real Van Brooten who was trying to convince her not to divorce his friend Perry. Johnny expenses the fine of one hundred dollars for setting off the false alarm.

Notes:
- The program will move to Tuesday evening at a new time.
- Molly Goldberg's invitation to fun in the Bronx is now on Saturday night.
- The Red Cross is your protection   please support it by adding a quarter over what you gave last year.
- This program was performed as *The Robert Perry Case* on 3/4/1949.
- Roy Rowan is the announcer.
- Music is by Leith Stevens.

Producer: Jaime del Valle   Writer: Paul Dudley, Gil Doud
Cast: Walter Burke, Jeanne Bates, Joseph DuVal, Ted de Corsia, Joyce McCluskey, Raymond Burr

Show:	**Alec Jefferson, the Youthful Millionaire**
Show Date:	3/7/1950
Company:	**Great Corinthian Life Insurance Company**
Agent:	**Bob Douglas**
Exp. Acct:	**$711.00**

Synopsis: Bob Douglas calls Johnny and asks how quickly Johnny can leave for California. Johnny tells him right away, as his big toe needs defrosting. Bob tells Johnny that Alec Jefferson has disappeared, and it might be murder. Johnny tells Bob that he will have to pack two shirts, as looking for one man in a big state like California can be murder.

Johnny travels to Los Angeles, California to look for a missing millionaire, Alex Jefferson. Johnny goes to Rebel Wildcatters, Inc. and meets Mars Flaherty, Jefferson's partner. Mars has been looking for Alex but he has turned up nothing. Mars tells Johnny that he is wasting his time and money. Mars tells Johnny that Great Corinthian was the executor of Jefferson's trust, and had financed the venture. It was Jefferson's money and Mars' brains. Johnny is told that Jefferson had irritated many on the site with too much money and too many of other men's women. He was last seen one week ago.

Johnny tries to talk to the oilfield workers, but they tell him nothing. Johnny goes to Jefferson's apartment on Sunset Strip. Inside, the color scheme is "hangover green". There are loosely strewn women's clothes lying around and a loosely strewn woman in the bedroom who Johnny discovers is Jefferson's wife Ada. Johnny makes coffee and they talk. She tells Johnny that she needs money and has been waiting for a week. She knows Flaherty, as she used to be his girlfriend. She had reported Alex missing and has no idea why he has gone.

Johnny leaves and notices someone watching him from across the street. Johnny uses the old "slow walk-away, quick turn" routine to get close to the car. Johnny tells the driver that he looks like an old friend. Johnny slugs the driver and takes him to an empty house in the suburbs to search his wallet. The man is Phil Wilkins, a private detective. When Phil wakes up, he tells Johnny that he was watching the girl, and he knows who Johnny is. Phil tells Johnny that Flaherty had him beaten up when he had tried to sell Flaherty some information on Alex. Phil tells Johnny that Flaherty and Jefferson have some sort of queer deal. The papers are in the safe and he has the combination.

Johnny goes to the office with Wilkins. They get into the office, get the agreement from the safe and leave. In the car they find Flaherty in the back seat with a gun. Flaherty tells Phil to drive to his house as Jefferson is there, quite dead!

On the way, Flaherty tells Johnny that he was out all day, but has no witnesses. He is sure that someone has planted the body there to frame him. At Flaherty's house, Johnny looks at the body, and finds an earring beside it. Flaherty recognizes it as one he had bought for Ada. Flaherty tells Johnny that he had married Ada in Mexico in 1945. She had taken Alex to Mexico and married him without divorcing Flaherty.

Flaherty, Phil and Johnny go to Ada's apartment and confront her. She says she never got any earrings from Flaherty and they are not going to pin anything on her. Johnny accuses her of marrying both men so that she could collect in case one died. Ada struggles with Johnny and he calls the police. After reporting to the police that he has a murderer, Johnny slugs Flaherty. He tells everyone that Flaherty is the murderer. In the struggle with Ada, Johnny had noticed that she did not have pierced ears. The earrings that Flaherty said he bought were for pierced ears.

The police investigation finds no fingerprints on the firewood used to kill Alex, but they do find splinters under Flaherty's fingernails.

Notes:
- AKA "How I got a wildcat oil operation by the tail", or "The Youthful Millionaire".
- AKA "How they were drilling for oil, but what they struck was me."
- There is a promotion for O'Brien's new movie, *D.O.A.*
- Johnny expenses a pair of gold earrings engraved "To Olga, with love". Olga San Juan was the wife of Edmond O'Brien.
- Roy Rowan is the announcer.
- Music is by Leith Stevens.

Producer:	Jaime del Valle	**Writer:** Paul Dudley, Gil Doud	
Cast:	Michael Ann Barrett, Ed Max, Tony Barrett		

◆ ❖ ◆

Show:	**The Eighty-Five Little Minks**
Show Date:	**3/14/1950**
Company:	**Mutual Liability Company**
Agent:	**Ed Bonner**
Exp. Acct:	**$384.16**

Synopsis: Ed Bonner calls Johnny very early in the morning and tells him to get up and get his gumshoes on. Ed has $300,000 coverage on Elwood Faver's fur department. Now he does not have a fur department, as 85 mink coats have been stolen.

While in Boston, Massachusetts, Johnny is assigned to the theft of 85 mink coats from the Elwood Faver Department Store. Johnny arrives at the store by cab just in time to see the night watchman, Kronen, loaded into an ambulance. Inside the store, Johnny meets Lt. Delaney and reviews the case. Johnny is told that someone broke into the store, opened the safe with the combination, removed the furs and shot the night watchman. Dmitri Stroganoff, head of the fur department, and a very agitated man, reported the theft. Stroganoff just knew something would happen that day, and it did.

When Stroganoff meets Johnny, his spirits lighten. Johnny has his $300,000, yes? Johnny tells him that he is only an investigator. Stroganoff tells Johnny that the "Insurance company always says two words, PAY PREMIUM. Now I have two words, PAY STROGANOFF!" Stroganoff then gives 23 pages of statement to the police: at 8:45 Stroganoff discovered the theft, called Mr. Favor and then the police. Stroganoff tells them that no one had the combination except himself.

While Johnny and Delaney are talking over lunch (ham sandwiches and a beer) a call comes in that the night watchman has died without saying anything. Johnny then finds out that there was another watchman in the store, Al Reedy. Johnny goes to talk to Reedy. He tells Johnny that he had been on duty all night. He sat in his office and was listening to the radio all-night and heard nothing and knows nothing. Now leave him alone.

Johnny checks Reedy's personnel record and finds nothing. Then on a hunch, Johnny goes to the Middleton Safe Company to talk to the owner about the safe. Johnny finds the owner, Mr. Middleton, standing in a new safe that will be shipped to South America the next day. Johnny is told that no one could open the safe without the combination. Based on the serial number of the safe, D4536, only Middleton, Mr. Danner the chief engineer and Stroganoff knew the combination. Johnny asks to talk to Danner, but he cannot, as Danner is dead.

Back at his hotel, Delaney meets Johnny. He tells Johnny that the police have found a body in the Charles River that had been shot with the same .32 used to kill the night watchman. After a fruitless night at police headquarters, Johnny gets three hours sleep before Ed Bonner calls. Johnny tells him he is working hard on the case but Bonner is adamant about getting the case settled and Johnny sounds rattled. Johnny gets ready to leave and is met at the door by Stroganoff, who tells Johnny that one of the mink coats has been mailed to the store in a dirty cardboard box! At the store Johnny searches the coat and finds a ticket stub for the "Country Club Dance". A call to the country club uncovers a familiar name on the list of attendees, Patricia Reedy.

Johnny goes to see her, and Johnny tells her that he had seen her at the dance and how nice she looked in the mink coat. Her father interrupts and takes Johnny outside to talk. Reedy reiterates to Johnny that he did not help with the robbery and that he has a record. He tells Johnny that after serving time, he got married and had a daughter. His wife died and he is trying to help his daughter to have a nice life. He had borrowed the mink coat for the dance and had returned it. He tells Johnny that he had borrowed other things and told Patricia that the company let him borrow things. Johnny shocks him by telling him that he believes him and will forget the incident for the time being. Reedy is really shocked. On the way out, Reedy tells Johnny that the man the police found in the river was Ted Grey.

Johnny goes to the store and checks the personnel records. Johnny discovers that Grey had worked for the store two weeks earlier and was fired for insubordination. Johnny goes to Grey's apartment and finds nothing except 14 phone numbers written on the wall next to the phone. Johnny calls each one of the numbers and call number 8 hits the jackpot. Johnny calls Delaney and tells him where he is going. Johnny then goes to the Middleton Safe Company as he had recognized the voice of Mr. Middleton on call number 8. Inside the plant, Middleton shoots at Johnny. Middleton offers Johnny $100,000 to not turn him in, but Johnny declines the offer. Johnny asks if Middleton is using the same .32 he used to kill Grey, and Middleton tells Johnny "No, I have a Luger this time. A Luger with a special sight!" He tells Johnny that he had shot Grey because Grey had reported that there were 85 minks in the vault, but only took out 84, so he was cheating Middleton. Middleton fires again, but the special sight is of no use. Johnny is shot in the shoulder and Middleton is mortally wounded. Before he dies, Middleton tells Johnny that the furs are in the vault heading for South America.

At dinner the next night with Patricia Reedy, Johnny gets a frantic call from Ed Bonner. One of the minks has been stolen! Johnny reassures Ed that it will show up in the mail the next day, and then tells Patricia "You look lovely in mink." Johnny stays in Boston a few more days, sightseeing, until Patricia's eyes start saying marriage!

Notes:
- Johnny is shot for the first time.
- This story was done as *The Templeton Matter*, broadcast on 2/10/1957. The names and business are changed, but the plot is the same.
- The announcer urges the audience to complete their income tax forms by March 15th.
- Music is by Leith Stevens.

| Producer: | Jaime del Valle | Writer: | E. Jack Neuman, John Michael Hayes |

Cast: Harry Bartell, Joseph Kearns, Hans Conried, William Johnstone, Howard McNear, Gloria Blondell

◆ ❖ ◆

Show: **The Man Who Wrote Himself to Death**
Show Date: **3/21/1950**
Company: **Britannia Casualty and Life**
Agent:
Exp. Acct: **$635.24**

Synopsis: Miss Raimey calls Johnny from Britannia's legal department. Johnny asks if a murderer is executed, does the policy pay off? She has never seen that happen, but Johnny tells her to put on her make up. It is likely to happen any minute.

Johnny goes to Chicago, Illinois to look into the arrest of Stuart Palmer, who is insured for $100,000. The beneficiary is Neal Beasley.

Johnny goes to see Stuart in Jail. Stuart tells Johnny that he does not want his help and that no one recognizes his greatness. Lt. Kerrigan tells Johnny that Stuart was present when a wino was killed and Stuart was holding a cue like the one used to kill the man. Palmer tells Johnny that he hangs out in the west-end area to get background for his material — he writes crime stuff.

Johnny goes to see Stuart's wife, Marion. Her response is "why go after him. He is not guilty of anything bad". When Johnny tells her that Stuart has been arrested for murder, she says his lawyer Mr. Martin will spring him. Johnny is told that Stuart used to write for the radio, but he quit to write a play about crime. Now he lives with his subjects. She is sure that Stuart is going to get his play produced. With no money coming in, Johnny wonders how Stuart can afford so much insurance.

Johnny goes to see George Michealkoff, Stuart's former agent. He tells Johnny that Palmer is crazy, too artsy. And his play? It is probably sitting in the bottom of Halstein's desk. Want to read a copy? He tells Johnny that so far Palmer has been bailed out twice and is washed up. The problems all started with Neal Beasley, who Johnny has heard of.

Based on a tip from a wino named Roscoe, Johnny goes to the west-end to look for Beasley and finds him in the Atomic Tavern. Johnny finds Beasley and tells him why he is there. According to Beasley, Palmer is a good man, but fate gets everyone. Johnny sees Palmer enter and then leave when Palmer spots Johnny. Johnny chases Palmer and as he turns a corner, Palmer turns and shoots, killing a newsboy.

Johnny chases Palmer but loses him after a block. Johnny is looking for a phone when Kerrigan shows up, Johnny tells the whole story. But why Palmer would shoot at Johnny is the $100,000 question. A general alert is issued for Palmer.

Johnny calls the local agent for Britannia and tells him to cancel Palmer's policy as quickly as possible but is told that the agent can't do anything until tomorrow. The agent will call Hartford tonight and see what he can do. Johnny then goes to see Mrs. Palmer to tell her the news, but she will not believe him. Johnny is sure that he wants the police to kill him so that she can get the insurance. The phone rings and it is Stuart, who hangs up. Then the police show up.

Johnny tells Kerrigan what he knows and Kerrigan is sure that they will have to stop Palmer with a gun. Johnny then goes back to see Beasley who knows where Palmer is but won't tell. Beasley also tells Johnny that Palmer had offered him $10,000 to help him, but he does not want the money. Beasley reluctantly agrees to take Johnny to Palmer. When they get to the room where Palmer is, Palmer tells Beasley "Good work. Bring him in quickly." What kind of plot is this Johnny wonders? Inside Palmer tells Johnny that Beasley helped him plan the whole thing, but Johnny won't be around to tell anybody. When Johnny tells him that his policy has been cancelled, Palmer says that he still plans to go on.

The police show up and have Palmer's wife with them. She comes in and begs Palmer to give up and that she is not interested in the money. Palmer rejects her plea, goes out shooting and is killed by the police.

The policy is not cancelled in time, but Johnny is sure that the lawyers will find a way out. Beasley is in jail for sixty days for attempted insurance fraud. Johnny almost forgets to mention that Mrs. Palmer notified him that Stuart's play will be produced on Broadway.

Notes:
- AKA "Stuart Palmer, Writer".
- This program has only the dramatic portion because announcements and music would be edited in later by the production staff.
- This program contains a mid-program commercial for the *Bing Crosby Program* on Wednesday with Mildred Bailey and Clifton Webb.
- Roy Rowan is the announcer.
- Music is by Leith Stevens.
- There is a promotion for D.O.A.

Producer:	Jaime del Valle	Writer:	Gil Doud, David Ellis
Cast:	Lurene Tuttle, Lawrence Dobkin, Bill Bouchey, Bill Grey, Jack Kruschen, Herb Butterfield		

◆ ❖ ◆

Show: **The Village Scene**
Show Date: **3/28/1950**
Company: **Bay State Bonding and Liability Company**
Agent: **Doug Strand**
Exp. Acct: **$68.30**

Synopsis: Doug Strand calls and has a big bonding case for Johnny in Boston. Johnny tells Doug that he is already working on a case in Hartford, also bonded. Doug tells Johnny that a picture insured for $250,000 has just been stolen.

This case took place in Boston, Massachusetts, but turned out to be no tea party.

Johnny travels by car to Boston, to look into the theft of "The Village Scene" painted by Peiter Brueghel. The painting was stolen from the Maudan Gallery and is insured for $250,000. At the gallery, Johnny meets with Teresa Maudan, the owner's daughter. Teresa tells Johnny that Caesar Ritto, a local art appreciator, owns the painting. She is upset because she had urged Ritto to show the picture.

Mr. Maudan comes in and tells Johnny that he is discouraged because the police do not know anything about art. If the picture is not found, he will be forced to close the gallery and move to start over again. The gallery is his life and he had brought most of the work from Salzburg after the Anschluss. He also shows Johnny the window the thief had come in through.

Mr. Maudan has offered a $5,000 reward, but Mr. Ritto does not seem to care. He has also tried to protect his daughter from Ritto.

Johnny goes to talk to Sgt. Himes of the police. Sgt. Himes is glad to have Johnny on the case and the police are glad for Johnny's help. This case seems to be different and the police are looking for the picture's frame too.

Johnny is told that Ritto is supposedly a liquor distributor who made his money in the black market during the war. Ritto was also up before the Senate for buying contracts. Johnny mentions that fraud charges against Ritto might be easier to prove than finding the picture. Johnny goes to Ritto's house on Beacon Hill where the butler admits him. Johnny meets Lily Swanson, the girlfriend of Ritto who wonders if Johnny is the friend Ritto has been sitting up with. She warns Johnny about Teresa (she is poison) and is tired of Ritto. He wants refinement now, when he used to be interested in burlesque houses and going out to visit sick friends at night. Ritto comes in, there are words between them and Lilly slaps him and leaves.

Johnny talks to Ritto who seems to have an answer for everything. When Johnny tells him that there is a clause that requires prior notice before moving the picture, Ritto says he will find another clause that will nullify that one.

Johnny leaves and watches Ritto's house. A "long, cold time later" Johnny sees Ritto leave, and then Lily goes out and Johnny follows her. It is obvious that she is going to the gallery, so Johnny tries to beat her there. Johnny gets to the back window just in time to hear a woman scream and 3 shots. Johnny goes in to find Ritto alone with two bullet holes in him.

Johnny calls an ambulance and the police and asks Ritto what happened, but Ritto says nothing other than the gallery is where he meets Teresa. After talking to the police and saying nothing incriminating, Johnny goes to see Lily, who only asks if Ritto is dead. Johnny tells Lily that he knows she went to the gallery, but Lily said she was going to see what Ritto and Teresa were up to, but she changed her mind. Johnny continues to question her while he searches the house for the painting but finds nothing.

Johnny goes to the Maudan residence where he talks to Teresa while her father is in his studio. Teresa Tells Johnny that Ritto is her fiancé. She was there when Ritto was shot, but Ritto had told her to leave. She is marrying Ritto because she is tired of being the daughter of a poor man. Ritto is going to be rich and she wants to be a rich man's wife. Teresa's father comes in and is very distraught over what he just heard.

The next morning Sgt. Hines calls to say that the paining had been returned for the reward. On the way to the gallery, Johnny ponders: why was the painting stolen in the frame, why did Maudan not mention that he was an artist, why Ritto knew nothing about art but was not upset, why Maudan offered a reward but was a poor man. Was it a diversion because he knew he did not have to pay the reward?

At the gallery, Johnny finds Maudan and two pictures, the original and a copy. Maudan tells Johnny that he faked the theft as an act of love for his daughter. He hoped he could hold on to Teresa with the money, but he fears it is too late. Ritto comes in and sees the duplicate and gets angry. Maudan accuses him of bringing shame to his daughter and the family, then he shoots Ritto. Teresa comes in from the car and cries. She tells Johnny that Ritto knew the copy was being made. He knew her father was going to give the copy to Ritto and sell the original, but he did not care. Maudan is turned over to the police.

"The next time anyone assigns me to find a masterpiece, my expense account will be a masterpiece of overstatement!

Notes:
- AKA "The Missing Masterpiece".
- The Anschluss was the annexation of western Austria by Hitler.
- Johnny mentions having tickets for *South Pacific*.
- There is new music at the close of the program.
- There is a promotion for *D.O.A.*
- Roy Rowan is the announcer.
- Music is by Leith Stevens.

Producer:	Jaime del Valle	Writer: Paul Dudley, Gil Doud
Cast:	Tyler McVey, Charles McGraw, Walter Burke, Lillian Buyeff, Robert Griffin, James Nusser, Joan Banks	

• ❖ •

Show:	The Big Red Schoolhouse
Show Date:	4/4/1950
Company:	Great Chesapeake Fidelity Insurance Guarantee
Agent:	Paul McGraw
Exp. Acct:	$3,227.00

Synopsis: A man calls Johnny and tells him he has $500 for him. Johnny guesses that the mystery voice is Julius Caesar, but it is Western Union assigning Johnny to go to Manhattan, Nebraska and get a room in the Cheyenne Hotel. He is to investigate building irregularities. The Western Union man tells Johnny that he was stationed in Manhattan during the war. It makes a Texas army camp look like the promised land.

Johnny travels to Manhattan, Nebraska and arrives to a fire at the new school building. A man named Pancho Gonzales tells Johnny that he helped build the school, but it burned down in 16 minutes. Johnny helps the townspeople put out the fire and then goes to the Cheyenne Hotel where he receives a call from Paul McGraw. Johnny updates Paul on the big fire, and Paul asks if Johnny has been contacted by Joe Stankovitch — he is the man who reported that the new high school is in bad shape. Johnny has to tell Paul that the high school is where the fire was. Johnny is to contact Stankovitch. Johnny asks the desk clerk for a phone book, but he tells Johnny that he knows everybody in town. When Johnny asks about Stankovitch, he is told that he is in the morgue — his body was found in the ruins of the school.

Johnny goes to find out what he can, and on the way back to the hotel he sees four men beating up another man. Johnny breaks up the fight and the man tells Johnny that he is Bill Garrett, the architect of the school. Garrett tells Johnny that he had designed the school. The city agreed to build it and Garrett was sent to study at the Sorbonne in Paris. When he returned, the building exterior was his, but the interior was made up as they went along.

Johnny goes to see the builder, "Big Jim" Madden. Johnny finds an angry crowd is at his home. Johnny uses his ID to get past the guards and into the house. Johnny meets Madden who tells him that the city construction committee saw no reason for the boiler explosion. Madden tells Johnny that the janitor was drunk and did not watch the boilers. Johnny is told that the city will rebuild the school from the Insurance money. Madden gives Johnny 50 pages of building specifications for him to review.

Johnny goes to see Mike de Guerra, the building inspector. Vivian de Guerra is there dressed in a negligee and nursing a drink, but there is no sign of Mike. After Johnny notes signs of his absence, Vivian admits that Mike had left three months earlier.

Johnny then calls the insurance company's head office and reports that everything about the case is rotten. McGraw tells Johnny that he is sending eight additional agents to help Johnny.

Back in his hotel room, a man walks into the room and collapses with three bullet holes in him. Johnny searches the body and discovers that it is Mike de Guerra. Johnny takes the body to the morgue. The police hold Johnny overnight until the hotel staff finally concurs that de Guerra came into the hotel already wounded.

Back in the hotel, Johnny meets with the nine agents who have arrived. Johnny briefs them on the case, and tells them not to push anyone around, but not to be pushed around. Carl and Chip are to go after de Guerra's background and finances, etc. Rob and Tip are to find out about Madden. Paddy and Ralph are to look into the janitor Stankovitch. Rocky and Jerry look into everything else.

Later that morning the mayor comes in and talks to Johnny about the deplorable situation. He tells Johnny that the city will give its complete cooperation. The mayor outlines the history of the school project, but nothing new is learned. Johnny asks the mayor about the purchase orders for the school. The mayor does not know where they are, but he will look for them. He also tells Johnny that the city will file a claim for the insurance.

Johnny receives a call from Carl who has learned that de Guerra had made four $1,000 deposits, but his salary is only $7,000. Johnny goes to see Mrs. de Guerra who is now wearing a slinky black mourning dress and a poor mourning act. She tells Johnny that she did not know where the money came from, but it went for other women. Now without a husband and no insurance, she needs help. Johnny agrees to get her a $2,000 policy for the right information. She tells Johnny that the money came from Universal Rock Company, which is owned by Madden's brother. Mike had come back to ask Madden for more money and had gotten shot for his efforts.

On the way back to the hotel Johnny runs into Bill Garrett. He tells Johnny about a law he believes exists that says that a citizen may commit a crime to prevent a bigger crime. Bill tells Johnny that he had gotten his former secretary to steal a file from the mayor's office. The file was a folder containing the purchase orders for the school. Johnny mails the file to the insurance company for protection. Johnny goes to see the mayor and calls him a liar because he had the purchase orders. The mayor tells Johnny that he was going to go after Madden but did not know how. Johnny tells him that the insurance will never be paid and that the mayor should give himself up to the police.

Back at the hotel, Johnny gets more information from two witnesses. Later three tough guys walk into his room and suggest that he go with them. Johnny is escorted from the hotel but is met outside by his investigators who take care of the tough guys. After being slapped around, they tell Johnny that Madden had ordered them to take Johnny to the rock company.

Johnny and the boys go to Universal Rock and surround the main building. Johnny goes in with K. G. and there are shots, and Jim Madden falls down the stairs dead. Johnny and K. G. go in to see Mrs. De Guerra shoot the mayor. Johnny disarms her and calls an ambulance. As the mayor dies, he tells Johnny that the whole plot was his idea. He and Madden had made over $100,000 on the deal. De Guerra had wanted more money to keep quiet so the mayor had him killed. As the mayor dies, he asks, "Why is there always a falling out among thieves?"

Notes:
- The script title page does not include "The Story of" in the title.
- There is a promotion for *D.O.A.*
- In the program, Paul McGraw tells Johnny that he is sending eight agents to assist Johnny. When the men arrive, Johnny lists nine men: Ralph Haycraft, Carl Royal, Chip Hanigan, Paddy Phillips, Rocky Androsano, Jerry Katay, Tip Miller, Rob Corniel and K. G. Peterson. When assignments are given, K. G. Peterson is not listed.
- The announcer, Roy Rowan, errs on Waterman's name, calling him "Willer".
- Music is by Leith Stevens.
- This program was also done as *The Clinton Matter*, broadcast on 3/12 through 3/16/1956 with Bob Bailey.

Producer:	Jaime del Valle	Writer:	E. Jack Neuman, John Michael Hayes
Cast:	Vic Perrin, Elliott Reid, Hy Averback, Clayton Post, William Conrad, Virginia Gregg, Willard Waterman		

• ❖ •

Show: The Dead First-Helpers
Show Date: 4/11/1950
Company: Great Industrial Assurance Corporation
Agent: Bill Hudson
Exp. Acct: $520.25

Synopsis: Bill Hudson calls and tells Johnny that there have been a lot of accidental deaths at the Cornell Steel plant in Pittsburgh, and it looks like murder to him. Johnny will bring his sweat shirt and asks when the next plane is to "Smokesville".

Johnny travels to Pittsburgh, Pennsylvania to look into a series of five murders at the Cornell Steel Company. At the Cornell offices, Johnny meets Joel Barrett, the manager. Johnny learns that all of the dead men were first-helpers. Barnett explains that each melter-foreman is responsible for several furnaces and has a first-helper on each furnace. The first-helper has a second-helper and they have cinder-snaps. There was no common denominator in the accidents, except that each of the men was a senior worker who knew and followed the rules.

Johnny hires on as a cinder-snap and goes to work, and boy does he work! Johnny gets to know Andre, who enjoys showing him the ropes. "Remember the rules and you will be OK" Johnny is told. Andre tells Johnny that the men who were killed were careless.

Johnny meets Joe Poland, who is a gruff man. To Joe, Johnny looks like an office type. When Johnny mentions Kirk Brody, the last man killed, Joe tells him that Kirk was his friend. Johnny meets Fred, who is another first-helper, but he worries about his family and wonders when he will get his blue slip or have an accident. Fred knows that the other men were killed.

Johnny goes to Brody's cold-water flat to see his widow. She tells Johnny that she knew something was going to happen and warned her husband to be careful. She knows her husband was murdered, as all the men are worried about their jobs. She tells Johnny that he should go talk to Barrett.

At the office, Johnny tells Barrett of the rising tensions and the men's fright. Barrett tells Johnny that all the killed men were alone when they were killed. Johnny looks at the employment records. Johnny tells Barrett that he had discovered that each of the men was alone when killed, that they were killed by seniority, that Barrett had posted a memo saying there would be layoffs by seniority but that Barrett knew the company was not laying men off. Barrett says that his job is to boost productivity.

Johnny goes to Mike and tells him he is with the insurance company and warns him that, as the senior man, he is next. Later that evening, Mike is cleaning his furnace when a huge man dressed in an asbestos suit attacks him and throws him off of the furnace killing him.

Johnny chases the killer but only gets a fall and a safety lecture from the plant manager. Johnny gets the key to the locker room from the main office and searches the lockers. In Mike's locker Johnny only finds a wallet and a picture. In Andre's locker Johnny finds the asbestos suit, complete with a tear in the arm. Joe Poland comes in sick and tells Johnny that Andre is on furnace #10. Joe tells Johnny that he saw Andre wearing the suit, and that he does not like Andre. Johnny puts the suit in the office and goes to find Andre. Johnny finds Andre who invites Johnny home for some good French food. Johnny goes with Andre and meets his wife. Andre throws Johnny out when Johnny tells him that he found the suit in his locker.

Johnny goes to the office and takes the seniority list and goes to get some sleep. Johnny goes to his room and before going to sleep Johnny notices that Andre's name is next, so Johnny goes to see him. When he gets there, Andre is dead and Andre's wife tells Johnny that a big man had killed him and the suit was a plant.

Johnny takes a cab back to Barrett's office. Johnny blames himself to

Andre's death and gets Joe Poland's address, as he is next on the list. Johnny and Barrett go to Joe's flat, but his wife says that Joe is not home. Johnny searches the flat but finds nothing. The wife says that Barrett is to blame for everything and spits on him.

On the way out, Barrett expounds his management theory on Johnny: Men work better under pressure. If Johnny worked as a supervisor in a steel plant for 10 days, he would know that. Johnny calls the police and goes to find Joe in the plant. Johnny finds Joe on furnace #12 cleaning the furnace. Joe knows that he is on the top of the seniority list now, and no one is going to take that from him. Joe tells Johnny that he will get a raise now. No one can take his job from him. As Joe moves to grab Johnny he shoots Joe four times. Finally, Joe grabs Johnny's throat and Johnny fires one last time into the heart and Joe falls into the molten steel and disappears.

At the funeral they bury a block of steel in place of Poland's body and Joe's wife calls Barrett a murderer. Johnny's last action is to have Barrett removed as supervisor.

Notes:
- There is a lot of unverifiable slang used in the steel industry here.
- The mid-program commercial is for the *Burns and Allen Show.*
- Roy Rowan is the announcer, who promotes *D.O.A.*
- Music is by Leith Stevens.

Producer:	Jaime del Valle	Writer:	Gil Doud, David Ellis
Cast:	Joe Forte, Junius Matthews, Jack Petruzzi, Raymond Burr, Jack Kruschen, Kay Stuart, Peggy Webber		

◆ ❖ ◆

Show:	**The Story of the Ten-O-Eight**
Show Date:	**4/18/1950**
Company:	**Shipper's Indemnity**
Agent:	**Harry Poulden**
Exp. Acct:	**$312.00**

Synopsis: Harry Poulden calls and tells Johnny to take a plane to Buffalo. They have a blanket policy on the Atlantic Central Railroad, and a train car has been robbed. Get up there — and watch your expense account!

Johnny goes to Buffalo, New York to look into a boxcar robbery on the Atlantic Central Railroad.

In Buffalo, Johnny meets Eef Grimms, a "cinder bull" for the railroad. Eef tells Johnny "The Atlantic Central hustles six gully jumpers a day up to Rochester. Five hours after the 10:08 leaves here last night, she jerks up at Batavia so the clowns can water her down. That's when the donigan notices one of our brownies is busted open and half the jig is gone. So right away he wangdoodles a copperbuster up the line." Johnny seems to understand that the brakeman found the boxcar open and called ahead to the telegraph operator.

The boxcar in question had a mixed cargo and the bookkeepers are trying to determine what was in it. The train only stopped for the water, and for a passenger train to pass it. The yard workers had seen a blond woman hanging around asking questions claiming she was a reporter, but Eef had checked and none of the papers had a reporter named Ruth Smith.

Johnny guesses that the crooks followed the train in a truck and picked up merchandise thrown from the train along the road. Grimms is impressed that Johnny pretty much has it figured out. Now, to find the merchandise.

Johnny and Grimms go out looking for evidence in Grimms' army surplus jeep.

Along a road beside the right of way, they find a number of tire tracks indicating someone was going towards the tracks. At a shanty they find a man named Bogardus who had seen a yellow truck with no writing on it, which had headed back to Buffalo.

Johnny and Grimms go back to town and start looking for the truck. Johnny is called by Eef, who tells Johnny that the police have found the truck wrecked in a ravine. The driver, Rick Blakey, lives long enough to tell Johnny to look for Jake. Jake had slugged him and run him into the gully. As Eef and his crew stack the cargo, Johnny finds a card for a bar with a message, "Jake 8:00 Tuesday. He's always there".

Johnny goes to the Horseshoe Bar and Grill, and after bribing the bartender with a five spot to signal if Jake comes in. The bartender recognizes Johnny as a cop, and Johnny waits. Later the bartender leaves, and Johnny follows him and finds him hanging up the phone. He tells Johnny that Jake had just called looking for his glasses. He tells Johnny that Jake will be in his room, #210 at the Embassy Hotel. Johnny goes to the hotel but there is no room #210. On the way out, Johnny is "escorted" to an alley where Johnny meets a tall well-dressed man — Jake. Jake asks Johnny why he is looking for him. Jake's accomplice named Trench slugs Johnny and frisks him.

When Johnny wakes up, he goes and finds the bartender and slaps him around for setting Johnny up. Johnny finds out that Jake is Jake Samuels and that he has a partner named Trench, but he does not know where Jake lives.

Tired and groggy, Johnny gets a room in the Imperial Hotel. As soon as he checks in, Grimms comes to his room. The cargo has been checked and the only thing missing is a barrel of jeweler's rouge worth $247 being shipped to Boston by Ralph Morton, who runs a jewelry shop. It was being sent to Michael Adelson in Boston. Next morning Johnny rents a car and drives to Morton's store. On the way in, Johnny notices a man watching from across the street. In the shop Johnny finds Morton and a snappy blond woman dusting the counters. When Johnny mentions that the rouge was stolen, Morton drops the item he is working on. Morton tells Johnny that he did ship the rouge. The woman, Andrea, drops something when Johnny says that the thieves are guilty of murder. Morton tells Johnny that his rouge is a special formula liked by the man in Boston who designs jewelry.

Johnny leaves and approaches the man across the street who then leaves.

Johnny follows him to a drug store where the man is eating a butterscotch sundae. Johnny learns that the man is Ben Sanchez, a private detective. Ben thinks that Morton is a fence for jewels stolen from the Arcadia Company, where $250,000 in jewels was stolen. Ben tells Johnny that Morton has a record but he can't prove he is guilty of fencing anything, even though he lives in an $85,000 house.

The blond leaves the store and Johnny follows her to a nondescript house. As he is standing in front of the house, the same man from the night before puts a gun in his back, takes Johnny's gun and tells him to go in. Inside the house Johnny hears a woman and a man are arguing over money. Then an angry Jake comes in with the girl from the store. Johnny tells Jake what he is working on, and the girl is the one he saw in Morton's shop. The girl is angry because Jake owes her $45,000 for the $300,000 in jewelry. Jake tells her to leave and Trench insults her. She opens the door, turns and shoots Trench twice with an automatic. She tells Jake she wants the money now, but he tells Andrea that he does not have it. Johnny convinces the girl that if she gives him her gun, he will try to square it with the police. The alternative is the gun or a murder rap. She gives in and gives Johnny her gun. The police are called and they take over. Jake had hired Andrea to get information about Morton for $50,000, which she never got. Morton was shipping the Arcadia jewels to Boston in the barrel of rouge, which the police recovered. Expenses include a new foam rubber seat for Eef's jeep.

Notes:
- This program has only the dramatic portion because announcements and music would be edited in later by the production staff.
- Johnny is charged 50¢ for a drink.
- There is a lot of colorful railroad slang.
- This program contains a commercial for *The Bing Crosby Program* on Wednesday.
- Roy Rowan is the announcer, who promotes *D.O.A.*
- Music is by Leith Stevens.

Producer:	Jaime del Valle	Writer:	E. Jack Neuman, John Michael Hayes
Cast:	Ted de Corsia, Pat McGeehan, John Dehner, Harold Dryanforth, Bill Bouchey, Jeanne Bates, Clayton Post		

◆ ❖ ◆

Show: **Pearl Carrasa**
Show Date: 4/25/1950
Company: **Piedmont Mutual Life Insurance Company**
Agent: **Bob Case**
Exp. Acct: **$712.55**

Synopsis: Bob Case calls Johnny to tell him that a girl pulled from the East River was a policyholder. Johnny tells Bob to go to the police to find their killer. Bob tells Johnny that they know who killed her, and he is being executed right after midnight. Bob wants to know about the victim.

Johnny drives to Sing Sing Prison and talks to Marty Pruitt in his cell on death row where Marty is playing solitaire. Marty is Pearl Carrasa's murderer. He tells Johnny that he was paid $5,000 to kill Pearl, but he refuses to tell Johnny anything about who hired him. Marty tells Johnny to leave this case alone as it is an ungodly mess.

Johnny goes to the New York City police and speaks with Lt. Goldberg about the case. The only thing he can add is Pearl's last address on the east side. Johnny goes to the boarding house and talks to the manager who tells Johnny that Pearl had no visitors and received no mail. She only went out twice a day for about an hour. Johnny spends the rest of the day looking for a possible post office box within half an hour of the boarding house. The next day Johnny finds a grocery store with a mail drop, and a letter for Pearl Carrasa forwarded from the Rambeau Club in Las Vegas. Johnny calls Bob Case and gets authorization to travel to Las Vegas.

Johnny flies to Las Vegas, Nevada and to the Club Rambeau where Johnny strikes up a conversation with a girl at the bar. When Johnny mentions Pearl's name, she suddenly has to get back to work. Johnny asks the bartender about Pearl and is escorted back to the office of Peter Baron, who sports a red scar across his face.

When Johnny mentions that he is looking for Mrs. Carrasa, Baron gets really aggravated. After a few minutes of verbal sparring, Baron tells "Mike" to take Johnny to see Mrs. Carrasa. On the way out the door, four other men join Johnny and Mike and they beat Johnny. When Johnny wakes up, Baron wants to know how Johnny knows Pearl. Johnny tells Baron about the policy and goes unconscious.

After a visit to a doctor and a two-day rest, the girl Johnny met in the bar visits Johnny in his room. She tells Johnny that she is scared to death but does tell Johnny to tell Pearl never to come back. When Johnny tells her that Pearl is dead, she tells Johnny that the casino is really a front for drugs brought up from Mexico. She leaves Johnny to catch a bus out of town. As Johnny looks out the window, the girl is shot in the doorway of the bus.

Johnny gets to the girl's body just ahead of a deputy sheriff and tells him what happened. Johnny gives the deputy his ID and tells him about the case. The deputy tells Johnny that he knows that Pearl had gotten involved with Pete Baron and left town. Johnny is told that the police have been watching Baron, and that the Carrasa family is one of the finest names in town. They have been suspected of involvement in drugs but they have no evidence.

Johnny takes a cab to the Carrasa estate and is escorted to the library by the butler. In the library, Johnny tells Mr. Carrasa about Pearl, and he is saddened to hear of Pearl's death. Mrs. Carrasa rushes in worrying about whether the palms have been watered for the music club meeting tonight. When Johnny tells Mrs. Carrasa of Pearl's death, she is not sorry. Pearl had brought shame on the family by bringing her "friends" to the house. Why, she actually wanted to marry one of them! Johnny can take the check back, she does not want it. Johnny leaves the insurance papers and leaves the house.

On the way out of the house, Johnny sees Baron drive in. Johnny goes to the sheriff and tells what he saw. They both go back out to the estate. The butler is arrested at the front door to keep him quiet. As they enter the library, Baron is telling Mr. and Mrs. Carrasa about the murder of Pearl, who knew too much and was going to tell. Baron tells Mr. Carrasa "things like this happen". Mr. Carrasa retorts, "things like THIS happen", pulls a gun and shoots Baron. When the police take the gun from him, Mr. Carrasa tells them that everything was his wife's fault. He had a tile business after the war, but she wanted more. Nice clothes, nice houses and nice friends and sophistication! When Pearl brought a nice boy in, she humiliated the boy and then told Pearl to get out of the house. Mrs. Carrasa had gotten involved with Baron to get money and that lead to involvement with drugs. She had involved herself with the very people she wanted to avoid. Johnny takes the check and leaves. Johnny thinks the check should be used to clean up the respectable slums, but that is not his problem.

Notes:
- There is a lot of interesting background chatter in the casino when Johnny comes in and on the way to Peter's office.
- This program contains a mid-program commercial for *The Burns and Allen Program* on Wednesday.
- Roy Rowan is the announcer.
- Music is by Leith Stevens.
- The announcer gives a promotion for *D.O.A.*

Producer:	Jaime del Valle	Writer:	Gil Doud, Davis Ellis
Cast:	Hy Averback, Joseph Kearns, William Johnstone, William Conrad, Martha Wentworth, Sarah Selby, Virginia Gregg, Howard McNear		

♦ ❖ ♦

Show: **The Able Tackett Matter**
Show Date: 5/2/1950
Company: **Corinthian Life Insurance Company**
Agent: **Mr. House**
Exp. Acct: **$4,075.80**

Synopsis: Johnny is called by Mrs. Tackett, and she agrees to see Johnny that afternoon. She has a right to know if her husband is dead.

Johnny goes to the New York City apartment of Mrs. Tackett, where he is welcomed to the sounds of recorded tribal drum music. Johnny tells Mrs. Tackett that he is going to British North Borneo to look for her husband, who has not written for 5 years. Mrs. Tackett tells Johnny that her husband had last written that he was lost and was trying to find his purpose in life. Johnny tells her that he is probably looking for a dead man, but she insists that Able is alive, maybe he has just stopped writing. Johnny reminds her that if Able is dead, she gets $750,000 in insurance. But at 24, she wants to believe that he is still alive.

Johnny travels to the Philippines and gets on a cargo ship as "super cargo". At dinner, the captain asks why Johnny is going to Borneo. Johnny tells him that he is looking for a man no one has probably heard of, Able Tackett. "TACKETT!" screams the captain. The captain tells Johnny that everyone in South Asia knows the name of Tackett. He lifts his shirt to show Johnny a scar across his chest, inflicted by Able Tackett. "Something happens to men out here", the captain tells Johnny. Bursts of temper usually follow the mention of Tackett's name.

In Sandakan, Borneo, Johnny looks up the secretary to the Assistant District Manager who describes Tackett as a fabulous fellow, a man of mystery who is looking for something but who is probably dead. He can arrange for Johnny to go inland the next day on a supply lorry.

Johnny meets a woman named Inez who knows Tackett. Her husband is dying of fever, but she knows Tackett is alive and can get Johnny to him. The woman's husband dies, and she visits Johnny in his hotel room. She tells Johnny that she knows who sent supplies to Tackett just a month ago, Johnny reluctantly accepts her offer.

At a trading post, Johnny meets a man named George Brown, who has been trading there for 10 years. For $500 he can take Johnny to Tackett, but he will kill Tackett when he finds him. Brown had a good and peaceful trading relationship with the Dayak headhunters, but Tackett had gone in and upset the peace.

Johnny discovers that in the jungle, conversation is a waste of breath. On the first night, Johnny tells Brown that he did not want to take Inez along, but she insisted. Brown tells Johnny that Tackett is a troublemaker and is always stirring up the natives. Inez tells Johnny that Tackett had never talked to her about his wife, and that the trouble Tackett had in Manila was because the locals thought he was afraid of them.

On the 3rd day, they find the body of a native who had been killed by headhunters and left on the trail as a warning. On the whole trip, Inez, Brown and Johnny are all at odds over what they will do to Tackett. Inez loves him, Brown wants to kill him and Johnny wants prove he is alive so that he can go home to his wife.

Finally, on the 6th day, in a driving rain, they arrive at the small village of Longwye in Dutch Borneo. There is no sign of life in the village. As they make their way to the shack of Able Tackett, the drums of the Dayak Mamapalu, or "return from hunting" ceremony start. At the shack, Johnny and Brown both enter to find Able Tackett dead. Tackett had been killed by the headhunters. There is no positive ID, but the body is presumed to be Tackett.

Back in New York Johnny confronts Mrs. Tackett with the news of her husband's death, "He died from fever" Johnny tells her. Johnny tells her to go to the probate court and have him declared dead based, on the evidence he has. She declines insisting that Able is alive somewhere and could have changed his identity. Johnny leaves a "young woman slowly dying".

On this trip, Johnny relates that "I became an expert on pure unadulterated frustration!"

Notes:
- This program has only the dramatic portion because announcements and music would be edited in later by the production staff.
- This program contains a mid-program commercial for *You Bet Your Life* with Groucho Marx.
- British North Borneo is now Malaya.
- Dutch Borneo became part of Indonesia.
- The Dayak are the indigenous peoples of the area and were headhunters.
- Roy Rowan is the announcer and he gives a promotion for *D.O.A.*
- Music is by Leith Stevens.

Producer:	Jaime del Valle	Writer:	Gil Doud, Davis Ellis
Cast:	Ben Wright, Maria Palmer, Tudor Owen, Raul Chavez, Chris Kraft, Dan O'Herlihy		

◆ ❖ ◆

Show:	**The Harold Trandem Matter**
Show Date:	**5/9/1950**
Company:	**Clayson Mutual Assurance Co**
Agent:	**Jack Barton**
Exp. Acct:	**$736.82**

Synopsis: Jack Barton calls and gives Johnny the policy number 245-7809. Los Angeles, amount $1,150,000 straight life, beneficiary Mabel Trandem, insurer is Harold Trandem. There is no official problem, but the company is unhappy to hear that here has been an attempt on Mr. Trandem's life. Johnny is to go out unofficially to make sure that Trandem is OK.

Johnny travels to the Bel Aire, California mansion of Trandem and is escorted to the terrace. A scowling Mr. Trandem tells Johnny that he has taken precautions and does not need Johnny's help. While Trandem is talking to Johnny, he is shot and killed. The staff and bodyguard come in and everyone accuses Johnny. The bodyguard tells Johnny that he will get fired for letting Trandem get shot, so why don't they exchange information. Johnny relates that the only thing he saw was a puff of blue smoke from the bushes. The police are called and they only find some bent twigs and nothing else.

After the police leave, Johnny talks to Mabel, the wife. He tells her that the last word Trandem had said was "Lilah" and Johnny wants to know who she was. Mabel tells Johnny that Lilah Whinig was all Trandem ever talked about. When Johnny reassures her that the killing will not prevent her from collecting on the policy, Mabel is glad, as the money is the only thing he left her and the Jessie Frederica Mission. She tells Johnny that she had been a waitress until

Trandem met her. She had plenty of everything, but she still hated him. The closer you came to him, the more you hated him, Johnny is told. Mabel said she was going to get a small apartment and a couple of Siamese cats, as she has always wanted a cat.

Johnny goes to Lilah's apartment but no one answers. Johnny looks through the window and sees Lilah on the floor with a .38 caliber hole in her temple. The police are called and spend their time going over Trandem's love letters to Lilah. The phone rings and the police answer. It is from the Jessie Frederica Mission — the boys miss Lilah. Will she be coming down soon? Not likely is the answer.

Johnny goes to the rescue mission and talks to Miss Frederica, who mistakes Johnny for a client, even though he is pretty clean. Johnny tells her of the two murders and arranges to hang around and talk to the boys. Johnny spends his afternoon talking with a lot of confused old men. Johnny strikes up a conversation with "Little Ben" who knew Trandem. Ben knew Trandem, and he had given Ben tips in the market, but he had lost it all. But Trandem had worked his way back up from the bottom. Ben points to one man at the mission who hated Trandem and Lilah more than everyone else, Bill Sanderson. Trandem and Sanderson were partners, but Trandem had cheated him out of his brokerage business and sent Sanderson to skid row.

Johnny goes to get some dinner and finds Little Ben dead upon his return. Sanderson then approaches Johnny and takes him from the mission at knifepoint. In an old storefront, Sanderson tries to work Johnny over but Johnny eventually gets the upper hand. When Johnny confronts Sanderson with the killings of Trandem and Lilah, he manages to escape. Johnny calls the police and then goes back to talk to Mabel.

Max the bodyguard meets Johnny and tells Johnny that he has been fired. Max spins a wild story to Johnny, who is skeptical. Johnny agrees to let him tag along "on the swindle sheet". Johnny finds Mabel with a new cat and she tells Johnny that she does not know Sanderson. When Johnny sees a letter from Sanderson and plane tickets for 6:00, she pulls a gun and tells Johnny that Sanderson had killed Trandem for her. She tells Johnny that she should have married him first. Mabel does not believe Johnny when he tells her that Sanderson has killed Lilah and Ben. She locks Johnny in the library and leaves.

Johnny calls Max, who was taking a nap and fires him! Johnny runs out in time to see Mabel driving away. Johnny calls the police and advises them of what is happening. Johnny notes that there are too many cab rides on his expense report and asks they can send a car for him and take him to the airport. Lt. Binselli and Johnny wait at the gate but they do not show up. Johnny notes he felt "like Drew Pearson when his predictions come true." Johnny and Binselli then go to a roadblock south of Capistrano and wait. After dark, a car breaks through the roadblock and Johnny and Binselli give chase. Johnny manages to shoot out a tire with a rifle and the car crashes killing both Sanderson and Mabel.

After a week, Johnny gets ready to leave. He visits Miss Frederica at the mission and gives her a gift in the form of a check for $1,150,000. The mission had been the second beneficiary of the policy.

Notes:
- Roy Rowan is the announcer.
- Music is by Leith Stevens.
- This program contains a mid-program commercial for *Doctor Christian*, a program written by the audience.
- Edmond O'Brien may soon be seen in the Columbia Pictures production *The Los Angeles Story*. A check of *The International Movie Database* does not list this movie. Martin Gramms Jr. has determined that the movie was renamed to *711 Ocean Drive*.
- The insurance policy would be worth about $116,700,000 in 2017 dollars.
- Drew Pearson was a political muckraker during the 1940's and 50's.
- Johnny makes a reference that there are too many cab rides on his expense account.

Producer: Jaime del Valle   Writer: Gil Doud, Davis Ellis
Cast: Eda Reiss Merin, Ed Max, Gloria Blondell, James Eagles, Junius Matthews, Raymond Burr, Ted Osborne

• ❖ •

Show: The Sidney Rykoff Matter
Show Date: 5/16/1950
Company: East Coast Underwriters Association of America
Agent: Edward Holly
Exp. Acct: $982.28

Synopsis: Edward Holly calls Johnny. Johnny is told that East Coast has a policy on Sidney Rykoff who is a pugilist and who has been kidnapped and Holly has received a ransom note.

Johnny goes to see Mr. Holly who tells Johnny that Rykoff will die in seven hours at midnight if the $25,000 in ransom is not paid. This is a delicate matter and the police have not been called. Rykoff has a policy for $100,000, so the payoff is an easy decision for the company. Johnny gets the money, a list of serial numbers and charters a plane to Kansas City, Kansas. Over Ohio, the plane runs into a storm, and the pilot wants to land. Johnny tells him there will be a dead man in the morning if he does not get to Kansas City.

Johnny arrives in Kansas City at 11:40 and goes to the designated place in a local cemetery and is met by a man. Johnny gives the money to the man and is told he will be told where Rykoff is.

The next morning Johnny goes to the Southern Athletic club, Rykoff's "headquarters" and talks to Madill, his manager who says that Rykoff is probably out drunk somewhere. Johnny is told that Rykoff likes to drink bourbon and milk when he is in training. Rykoff has a good right-cross but has not been doing too good lately. His wife is a nice person but can be a demon. She bosses Rykoff around. If Rykoff loses, he sleeps in the hall.

On the way out, Al Barsumian approaches Johnny. Al tells Johnny that it is not time for Rykoff's binge. Rykoff's next binge is not due until September. Al tells Johnny that he handles bets for the fighters.

Johnny goes to see the wife and tells her that her husband has been kidnapped. She tells Johnny that Rykoff comes in whenever he feels like it. Johnny asks who knew of the $100,000 policy, and only his manager Madill, and her knew about it. She tells Johnny that she does not hang around with losers and did not arrange to kidnap Sidney. A man named Mickey Snell comes in and Mrs. Rykoff yells at him for losing a fight. She backs him out of the apartment and reaches for a wrought iron candlestick on the mantle but Mickey runs. Johnny leaves and follows Mickey to a bar. Mickey tells Johnny that he knows Rykoff and had been beaten by him a couple of times. Mickey tells Johnny that Rykoff was winning now. Johnny arranges to meet Mickey at his hotel later.

Johnny goes outside and waits to follow Mickey. Mickey comes out and at a street corner, a car runs Mickey down. Johnny tells the police what he saw, and the story about Rykoff. The police search Mickey's pockets and find only his ID and a lot of cash. Johnny looks at one of the bills, and it is a fifty from the ransom money.

Johnny reviews the evidence and considers that Mickey died either because of Al Barsumian's gambling ventures, the insurance held by Madill, or the old "kidnap yourself and collect the ransom" racket, the latter being the most probable. The next morning Johnny walks to Rykoff's apartment and confronts the wife with the kidnapping plan. She tells Johnny that she is tired of hearing about Rykoff. Rykoff had a lousy contract with Madill, so there was no way to win much. Johnny tells her that she is in debt and needs money so maybe she faked the kidnapping, wrote the ransom note and would collect twice.

The police show up and tell her that Rykoff's body has been found on the highway. There is little reaction in her face as she gets the news. She tells Johnny that she feels like she did when she got paroled for burglary and "a couple of other things". She did not know if Rykoff loved her or hated her, but he fought when she taunted him.

Johnny goes to the morgue and looks at the body and learns that the cause of death was a heavy instrument to his head.

The next morning, Johnny gets an early call from Al Barsumian asking him to come over immediately. Johnny goes to Al's place, where Johnny is taken to the basement and shown a gold trophy with caked blood on it, hidden in a box of ashes. Al tells Johnny that he was cleaning the furnace when he found it. Johnny asks Al if he made up the plan for a cover and tells him to call the police. Al pulls a gun instead. On the way up the steps, Johnny elbows the light switch and ducks as Al shoots at him. Johnny over powers Al and leaves him out cold on the floor. Johnny picks up the trophy and heads to Rykoff's apartment.

Johnny should have called the police and left town, but he had to resolve the insurance and the ransom money.

The door is open when he gets there and the wife is talking to someone with a familiar voice. Johnny goes down the street and calls the police and tells them to give him five minutes. Johnny sneaks into the apartment, places the trophy in its clean spot on the mantle and lights a cigarette. The wife comes in and Johnny suggests that there is something different in the room and points to the mantle. She sees the trophy and tells Johnny that no one is going to stop them. Mrs. Rykoff tries to hit Johnny, but he overpowers her. The man comes back and so do the police.

The wife confesses that she had killed Rykoff in an argument and had Garry hide the body. They sent in the ransom note and Garry collected the ransom. Garry also put the trophy in Barsumian's basement.

The police also raid Barsumian and shut down his gambling operation.

Notes:
- This program has only the dramatic portion because announcements and music would be edited in later by the production staff.
- The mid-program commercial is for *Burns and Allen*.
- Roy Rowan is the announcer.
- Music is by Leith Stevens.
- Edmund O'Brien's upcoming new movie *The Los Angeles Story*.

Producer: Jaime del Valle   Writer: Gil Doud, Davis Ellis
Cast: Howard McNear, Howard Culver, Walter Burke, John McIntire, Bill Grey, Jeanette Nolan

♦ ❖ ♦

Show: **The Earl Chadwick Matter**
Show Date: **5/23/1950**
Company: **Tri-State Life Insurance Company**
Agent: **Leland Scarf**
Exp. Acct: **$1,575.30**

Synopsis: The Ambassador Travel Agency calls and confirms Johnny's travel arrangements to travel to Bermuda on Pan American flight 134 from LaGuardia. The agent asks Johnny if he is going on vacation and Johnny tells her he is going there to look up a dead man.

Johnny goes to the Tri-state office to hear the story of a woman who has seen Earl Chadwick. Earl had embezzled $30,000 and disappeared in 1945. His wrecked boat was found and he was presumed drowned. Earl was declared dead in 1947. Johnny meets Mrs. Marshall, who had just been to Hamilton, Bermuda. Mrs. Marshall knew Earl and saw him in a bar (they were slumming) in Hamilton. She talked to him but he denied being Earl. Mrs. Marshall found out that Earl was using the name of George Brewster. Johnny is told that Chadwick's wife Grace had remarried to a business associate of Chadwick.

Johnny goes to Bermuda and checks in with the local police. Johnny learns from the chief inspector that the Brewster character is clean. Johnny goes to his hotel and memorizes the picture of Chadwick. That night Johnny goes to the bar where Chadwick was last seen. After several hours, the man comes in. Johnny takes him to his table and explains why he is there. Brewster tells Johnny about meeting some old fat dame who thought she knew him and agrees to meet Johnny at noon the next day at his house.

Johnny goes to the address and a woman answers the door. George is not there, but she lets him in, and Johnny looks over the papers left there. Brewster comes back and admits that he is Earl Chadwick and agrees to go back to Johnny's hotel, where he outlines the whole story. He had embezzled $10,000 and given the money to his wife, who was supposed to meet him in Mexico City after the insurance policy had been paid. But, she never showed up. Chadwick is now ready to go back to the states.

Johnny and Earl fly to New York and go to the home of his former wife Grace, and her husband Harold Anderson. Grace and Harold deny that the man with Johnny is Earl. Johnny leaves and asks about proof of his identity, but Earl has destroyed most of his records. Johnny tells Earl to go to his former dentist and get a full set of x-rays. Earl tells Johnny that he can be trusted but, just to be sure, Johnny hires a detective named Landreau to follow Earl.

Later Johnny goes to see the dentist, Dr. Homer Fields who gets Earl's old x-rays and compares them to the ones just taken and there is no match. Johnny questions the dentist about possible robberies of the records or misfiling but to no avail. Johnny asks where someone would go to get a set of x-rays. Dr. Fields tells Johnny that a dentist would only give x-rays to someone if they were their own. Johnny thanks him and leaves.

Johnny then goes in search of a paper trail for Earl at the hall of records and the police and finds nothing. Johnny checks with Landreau who reports that Earl had gotten wise to him. He followed Chadwick and saw him purchase a gun at a pawnshop. Johnny goes to the Anderson's hoping Earl is not there. The Anderson's are sure that someone has discovered the details of the case and is impersonating Earl. The man knows too much, Johnny says, to be an impostor. Johnny tells them that Earl has only made one mistake. Earl admits to taking $10,000 but $30,000 was taken.

Johnny goes back to the hotel and finds Earl there with the gun. He tells Johnny that he was scared, and being Brewster was getting dull. Johnny takes the gun away from him. Johnny tells Earl that the x-rays did not match and he is sure that Anderson had switched them. Landreau calls and Johnny arranges for him to get a fake driver's license for $500. Johnny has Landreau call Anderson and tell him he has proof that Earl is alive and the proof is for sale. Anderson arranges to come to the office. Anderson arrives at 11:30 as Johnny and Earl watch from the back room. Anderson agrees to pay Landreau $15,000 for the license. Anderson has $1,500 with him and reaches for the money only to pull a gun. Johnny rushes out and Anderson kills Earl. The police are called and the Armstrong's give their statement confessing their crime. The wife had convinced Earl to steal the $10,000 and Harold had taken an additional $20,000. Johnny is not proud if his part, but he was paid to find a dead man.

Notes:
- Music is by Leith Stevens.
- Roy Rowan is the announcer.
- Edmund O'Brien's upcoming new movie *The Los Angeles Story*.

Producer:	Jaime del Valle	Writer:	Gil Doud, Davis Ellis
Cast:	Lillian Buyeff, Tudor Owen, Virginia Gregg, Walter Burke, John Dehner, Ben Wright, Ted Osborne		

◆ ❖ ◆

Show:	**The Port-au-Prince Matter**
Show Date:	**5/30/1950**
Company:	**American Federated Life Insurance Company**
Agent:	**Harvard Huntington**
Exp. Acct:	**$424.70**

Synopsis: Dr. Colby calls and he tells Johnny that he is behind on his shots and needs a booster for diphtheria, small pox, typhoid, cholera and, if he can find room, tetanus. Johnny asks where he is going to get the shots, as it is a long flight to Haiti, and the plane seats are uncomfortable, at best.

Johnny is called, just as he is about to go to see the movie *Detective Story*, to the home of Mr. Harvard Huntington. Harvey tells Johnny that Ralph Gordon, the black sheep scion of the wealthy Hartford Gordon's, is insured for $150,000. Ralph is on his boat in Haiti and is dying of, and this is pure nonsense, of a voodoo curse. Harvey got his information from Ralph's older brother Thomas, who is a doctor and also in Haiti.

Johnny flies to Port-au-Prince, Haiti, buys some tropical clothes, and goes in search of someone to help find Gordon's boat. In a bar Johnny runs into Cap Regan, who tells Johnny that he has been there since before repeal, courtesy of a couple of prohibition agents. Cap tells Johnny that he can, for a fee, row Johnny out to Gordon's boat. Johnny tells Cap that he is with an insurance company. Cap tells Johnny that Gordon has been here for two months, and everyone on the crew has left. Gordon was always drunk and the crew refused to sail with him. Johnny is shown the boat and Cap tells him it is as filthy as a scow.

At the boat, Johnny is met by a woman in a pair of clam diggers and an off-shoulder tee shirt. The woman tells Johnny that she is Edwina, Ralph's wife. When Johnny explains why he is there and asks to see Ralph, she agrees and takes Johnny below. Johnny only gets as far as the cabin door where he is met by abusive shouts and cries for more wine. Johnny mentions the curse and Edwina tells Johnny that a man called Papa Luar had put a curse on Ralph after he cursed at him. Edwina knows Thomas and they hate each other. Edwina gets angry when Johnny suggests she is after the money and the ship's bosun invites Johnny to leave.

Johnny goes to see Thomas Gordon at the Hotel Francois, and Thomas agrees that the voodoo curse is trash and requires only a susceptible mind. Thomas tells Johnny that Ralph is only looking for escape through alcohol. "Let me know what you learn" are the reassuring words of the good doctor as Johnny leaves.

In a gathering storm, Johnny and Cap Regan go in search of Papa Luar and find him in a hut in a cane field. Johnny goes down a path to Papa Luar. Inside the hut Papa Luar tells Johnny that Gordon will die tonight in the wind and rain, and his magic is the key. When Johnny doubts his magic, he throws something into the fire that causes Johnny to stagger out of the hut gasping for breath and nearly passing out. When Johnny recovers he goes into the hut and finds small pieces of photographic film. Johnny notes that film made of cellulose and nitrates put out nitric oxide and nitrogen dioxide when burned. A combination that would meet the demands of any gas chamber.

Johnny and Cap go back to the yacht in a gathering storm. On the boat, Johnny overhears Edwina talking to the bosun. When he comes on deck Johnny knocks him out. Johnny then accuses Edwina of plotting with Papa Luar and the bosun to kill Ralph, which she denies. Edwina tells Johnny that she is tired of her husband drinking himself to death and is only plotting to divorce Ralph and marry the bosun.

Johnny and Edwina lock up the bosun and they both go back to Papa Luar where he tells Johnny that he does not know who Edwina is. Johnny confronts him with the film scam. When threatened with the police, he admits a that a man put him up to the phony curse. Papa tells Johnny that the man needs the storm so that the portholes on the boat will be closed. The man had also given Papa the film to use on Johnny. Edwina tells Johnny that she cooks the only food on the boat, and champagne is brought onto the boat. Johnny goes to the local liquor shop learns that a case of champagne has just been sent to the boat, packed in dry ice. A call to Thomas confirms that dry ice in a closed cabin could asphyxiate a drunken man. Johnny tells him to send for a pulmotor. If it is not too late, maybe he can use it.

Johnny finds Regan and Johnny gets him to row out to the boat in the storm. When they near the boat, Regan is shot in the leg and Johnny decides to swim for the boat. When Johnny gets to the boat, dear brother Thomas is holding a rifle on Johnny! The bosun pushes Thomas off of the boat, and Johnny breaks down the door to Ralph's cabin and carries him up to fresh air. Johnny gives Ralph artificial respiration to save a policyholder.

Thomas goes to jail (he wanted control of the family fortune, not Ralph's insurance). Ralph and Regan go to the hospital. Johnny buys a bottle of voodoo perfume for Edwina. Hopefully she will use it on her husband.

Notes:
- This program is essentially the same script as the Charles Russell version of *Haiti Adventure Matter* broadcast on 12/17/1949, but without his wise cracks.

- The Cap Regan character speaks with a British accent.
- The voodoo shaman is called Papa Luar.
- A pulmotor is an ambulance with a special respiration unit on it.
- This program contains a mid-program commercial for *The Groucho Marx Program* on Wednesday.
- *Detective Story* is a 1951 movie starring Kirk Douglas and directed by William Wyler.
- Roy Rowan is the announcer and promotes O'Brien's upcoming movie *711 Ocean Drive*.
- Music is by Leith Stevens.

Producer:	Jaime del Valle	Writer:	Gil Doud, Davis Ellis
Cast:	Willard Waterman, Earl Lee, Ted de Corsia, Charlotte Lawrence, Lou Krugman, Byron Kane, Dick Ryan, Clayton Post		

◆ ❖ ◆

Show: **The Caligio Diamond Matter**
Show Date: 6/8/1950
Company: **Inter-Commercial Insurance Companies of America**
Agent: **Henry Glacen**
Exp. Acct: **$65.34**

Synopsis: Henry Glacen calls to ask Johnny if he has heard of the Caligio Diamond. Henry tells Johnny that the $200,000 Caligio diamond is missing. The owner, Mr. Benson was found murdered the previous evening.

Johnny goes to the Benson residence in Hartford, Connecticut and meets with the daughter, Betty. She tells Johnny that her father had purchased the diamond in Italy three years earlier in Italy for $200,000. Johnny is told that the stone has a strange history as all of its owners have died violently. She tells Johnny that she was out with her fiancé until 3:00 a.m. and found her father in the library when she came home. Her father kept the stone in his safe. Only her father, her mother and the family attorney, Mr. Corrigan, who has free access to the house, knew the combination.

Johnny goes to meet with Mr. Corrigan. During a brief discussion interrupted by phone calls, Johnny learns that Benson and Corrigan had been schoolmates and had last seen him two weeks earlier. Mrs. Benson arrives and Johnny is escorted out the rear office door, but he stays to listen. "Darling, you look lovely in black" he tells Mrs. Benson as he kisses her and Johnny listens. Johnny hears that Corrigan is divorcing his wife and they will go to Bermuda when they get married. Johnny tries to leave but trips on the carpet and is caught by Corrigan and Mrs. Benson. After some "small talk" about ethics, Johnny agrees to keep the meeting from the police, for the time being.

On the street Johnny is stopped by a man, who offers him information. The man pulls a gun and tells Johnny to get into a car and then slugs him. Johnny wakes up in his torn-up apartment with both his head and the phone ringing. Henry Glacen wants an update, but all he gets is a request for a doctor from

Johnny who passes out. Henry comes over and tells Johnny that he does not want the police called. Johnny feels that the man who slugged him is looking for something.

Betty calls to say that the police have found the gun that killed her father, in her purse!

Johnny gets to police headquarters and meets with Lt. Parnell, an old buddy, who is on the case. Johnny is told that Corrigan is on the way, and that Betty's prints are all over the gun, but she knows nothing about it. She tells Johnny that she has not used that purse for a long time. Corrigan and Bob Gorman, the fiancé, show up and everyone starts questioning everyone else's motives. When asked of Corrigan had visited with Mrs. Benson, he claims the fifth amendment.

Johnny leaves and goes to Corrigan's apartment and finds an IOU from Benson for $2,000. He goes to Bob Gorman's apartment and finds a bill from a detective agency. Johnny then goes to police headquarters and finds a picture of a tall, thin man with a well-trimmed moustache.

Back at his apartment, Johnny finds a tall, thin man with a well-trimmed moustache drinking his bourbon ("This is lousy bourbon!"). The man wants the diamond and starts to leave. After the man tries to shoot Johnny, he slaps him around to find out what his angle is, but his story changes several times. Originally, he worked for Corrigan, and then Mrs. Benson and finally he tells Johnny that he works for the Gorman Detective Agency. Johnny tells him that his name is Vic, and that Gorman had hired him to get the stone, but when he got there it was gone and Benson was dead. Vic had slugged Johnny because he thought that Johnny had the diamond.

Johnny calls Bob Gorman and asks him to come over. When Bob gets there Johnny tells him that he had just talked to his employee Vic Hastings. Bob denies hiring Bob but admits that he hired Hastings to find the stone, because he wanted it. He had crashed a party to case the house but ended up falling for Betty. Gorman pulls a gun and excuses himself. Johnny calls Parnell and asks him to arrest Bob Gorman. Johnny goes back to the Benson house and confronts Mrs. Benson. She tells Johnny that she knows who has the diamond. She tells Johnny that Gorman had a violent temper. Johnny accuses her of framing Betty with the gun when Corrigan shows up. Johnny overpowers Corrigan takes him to the police.

Johnny states that this case hinged on a big guess that paid off. Mrs. Benson and Corrigan confess to the robbery. The police get Gorman and Hastings. Betty will probably be looking for a new boyfriend. As for the expense account, "that's pretty cheap."

Notes:
- **At the end there is a statement that "I told them my guess and with the authority of an Illinois judge they swallowed it". This is either an obscure axiom or a scripting error as the case takes place in Hartford.**

- Roy Rowan is the announcer and gives a promotion for O'Brien's upcoming movie 711 Ocean Drive.
- Music is by Leith Stevens.

Producer:	Jaime del Valle	Writer:	Gil Doud, Davis Ellis
Cast:	Wally Maher, Jane Webb, William Johnstone, Virginia Gregg, Stacy Harris, Bill Bouchey, Harry Bartell		

♦ ❖ ♦

Show:	**The Arrowcraft Matter**
Show Date:	**6/15/1950**
Company:	**Grand East Life & Liability Insurance Company**
Agent:	**Millard Snell**
Exp. Acct:	**$940.20**

Synopsis: Mr. Snell's secretary calls Johnny about the policies on the three missing Arrowcraft cruisers. In the past two weeks, three boats have sunk with no survivors. The next of kin are each suing for a million dollars.

Johnny flies to Los Angeles, California, rents a car and drives to Newport Beach where Mr. Snell has chartered a boat. They are going out to find the latest boat to be hit. Snell tells Johnny that another boat has been lost. So far that is four boats that have been lost with eleven fatalities and only seven bodies have been recovered.

At dawn they find the boat awash in the ocean swells. Johnny goes aboard and finds the body of a young girl floating face down in the cabin. Johnny examines the boat and the body, which has a strange bruise behind the ear. The body is taken to the charter boat and they head back. Snell is upset at finding the girl. Johnny tells Snell that he boat was registered to Chester McNeal.

After talking to the police, Johnny goes to talk to Dr. Seyne at the morgue. Johnny is told that the girl was Antonia Caruso, who was identified by her mother. Johnny mentions the bruise and the doctor agrees that a gun might have caused the bruise, and her hair braids might have softened the blow. Johnny wonders if she might have been thrown overboard and been alive and climbed back into the boat and died. Without the permission of the family there would be no autopsy.

Johnny goes to see the girl's mother, who is deeply upset. She tells Johnny that Antonia was going to marry Chester McNeal, whose father owned the boat. Chester loved her and she had worked hard to make sure that Antonia had what her parents didn't.

Back at the hotel, Snell is white-faced. Johnny learns that Fred Crocker, the local Arrowcraft agent has been killed in a hit-and-run accident. The papers relate that the Arrowcraft office had been ransacked earlier that day.

Johnny goes to the Arrowcraft office and looks through the papers for a list of customers, which is missing. Johnny is sure that someone is looking for something and killing people in the process. Johnny thinks that Crocker was in the office when it was searched and killed later.

Johnny throws a little party for members of the local press and gets them to print a story based on what he thinks is happening. The next day the story runs, along with one about a night watchman who is in the hospital after catching a prowler on an Arrowcraft boat. At the jail, Johnny questions the prowler, Jerry La Barber, but he is a hard character and says nothing to Johnny, besides his lawyer is on the way. Johnny is sure that La Barber is hiding something.

Johnny is able to contact two Arrowcraft owners and searches their boats and finds nothing. Johnny and Snell head back to the hotel with a bottle of Cognac to mourn the death of the night watchman.

Later, a woman calls Johnny from a phone booth and wants Johnny to meet her at a bar in Long Beach. She has something to say. Johnny carefully goes to the bar and is met by a man with a gun who escorts him outside to a car where the girl, Gwen, is driving. They drive to a secluded area where Gwen tells her story. Johnny is told that a man named George Masterson runs a chain of furniture stores, which is a front for the Mafia. She has written down everything she knows and told Masterson that the letter was hidden on an Arrowcraft boat. She feels that all the deaths are her fault because she just picked the Arrowcraft name out of the air. She did not go the police because she has a record.

Gwen gives the letter to Johnny and drives away. Johnny gets a hotel room, and reads the letter, the hottest document in California! The next morning Johnny mails the letter to the FBI. Johnny then goes to Masterson's office and beats him for the death of the boating victims, and then calls the police.

The FBI puts Gwen in protective custody. The crime ring is broken, and so far, the D.A. has 75 counts against Masterson.

Notes:
- This is the first program for the Wrigley gum manufacturers, who sponsors the program for several years.
- Edmond O'Brien can soon be seen in *711 Ocean Drive*.
- Bob Stevenson is the announcer.
- Music is by Leith Stevens.

Producer:	Jaime del Valle Writer: Gil Doud, Davis Ellis
Cast:	Howard McNear, Jeanne Bates, Clayton Post, Harry Bartell, Hy Averback, John McIntire, Jeanette Nolan

◆ ❖ ◆

Show:	**The London Matter**
Show Date:	6/22/1950
Company:	**Treasury Department, Bureau of Narcotics**
Agent:	**Mark Nelson**
Exp. Acct:	**$1,580.20**

Synopsis: Mark Nelson calls to ask Johnny to assist the Treasury Department with a smuggling ring. Johnny goes to the Commonwealth Hotel and gets the details from Mark. The Feds have allowed a shipment of drugs from India to enter the country via Seattle, and then on to Beverly Hills to the home of the actress Dorothy Rivers and her director-husband Broderick Green. Now, they are going to London, England to make a picture and their trunks are the only things that have left the house. Only one person, Lorraine Miller the confidential secretary, is going with the trunks, the other servants having been discharged.

Johnny goes on board the boat and gets final instructions from Mark. Johnny is told that Inspector Finch of Scotland Yard will meet him in England. The ship's detective, Clarence Dorn, has been told Johnny would contact him. Also, Lorraine Miller's brother is on the boat traveling under the name Miles Fanning.

Johnny meets the hazel-eyed, auburn-haired Lorraine and explains why he is there. When she tells Johnny how exciting his job must be, he tells her that "I once met a pig named Rollo who had eaten a diamond bracelet." They arrange to have drinks and dinner in her suite that night. After dinner they are talking when a porthole suddenly opens and Johnny sees a man's face. Johnny is told that the man he saw was her ex-husband and he will have to leave and not see her any more on the boat.

Johnny goes to see the ship's detective and asks him to keep an eye on Fanning. Johnny will check back with him every night. For five nights Johnny has to deal with watching the passengers.

On the night before docking, Lorraine comes to see Johnny and apologizes for her behavior. The phone rings and Dorn reports to Johnny that Lorraine and Fanning had met after dinner. Johnny tells Lorraine that the call was a request for a fourth at bridge. Lorraine leaves and Johnny pours himself a long drink. As soon as he tastes the drink Johnny knows he has been drugged.

Johnny wakes up to the voices of a doctor and another man who turns out to be Inspector Finch. Johnny tells them that Lorraine probably drugged the whiskey while he was on the phone. Finch tells Johnny that everyone is off the boat. The trunks were taken to their destination and will be unpacked by Scotland Yard agents. Also, Fanning is being followed.

Finch takes Johnny to his flat to recover. That afternoon a call comes in and the police report to Finch that the trunks are empty of drugs. Johnny and Finch go to the Yard to get the names of possible purchasers for the drugs. Mark Nelson calls and Johnny updates him on the lack of drugs in the trunks. Mark will call the states to double check that the drugs actually left.

A call comes in with the news that the constable following Fanning has been shot. Finch issues Johnny a gun to replace his, which he left on the boat, and they head to Fanning's flat to find Dorn dead. The police officer tells Johnny and Finch that Fanning was carrying a portmanteau when he left. Johnny surmised that Dorn had carried the drugs off the ship, taken them to Fanning and argued over the split and Fanning shot him.

Johnny and Finch go to Lorraine's flat but she is not there. They wait for a while and she shows up. Johnny confronts her that he knows who Fanning is. She breaks down and tells Johnny that her brother came back a different man after the war and was always in trouble. She tells Johnny that Fanning is on his way to Tangiers. Johnny and Finch get the name of the ship and head there. After ensuring that the crew is off the boat, the police go aboard, and in the usual hail of bullets Fanning is killed and the drugs recovered. Johnny arranges that Fanning's is the only name that will hit the papers.

Notes:
- Detective Dorn is wearing "Congress Gaiters"- elastic-sided low boots.
- Rollo the pig was in the Charles Russell program *Out of the Fire, Into the Frying Pan* broadcast on 8/21/49.
- RadioGOLDINdex notes that Tudor Owen and Ben Wright play double parts in this show.
- Edmond O'Brien can soon be seen in *711 Ocean Drive*.
- Bob Stevenson is the announcer.
- Music is by Leith Stevens.

Producer:	Jaime del Valle	Writer:	Gil Doud, Davis Ellis
Cast:	Wally Maher, Virginia Gregg, Herb Butterfield, Dan O'Herlihy, Tudor Owen, Ben Wright, Alec Harper		

◆ ❖ ◆

Show: The Barbara James Matter
Show Date: 6/29/1950
Company: Monarch Life Insurance Company
Agent: Frank Gaber
Exp. Acct: $344.59

Synopsis: Frank Gaber calls and asks if Johnny is free for a week. Mrs. Martin James has disappeared in Denver. Her husband is a wealthy contractor and she is insured for $200,000. Johnny hopes she is not dead, but Frank tells him the police say there is little possibility of anything else.

Johnny flies to Denver, Colorado to look into the disappearance of Mrs. Barbara James. Johnny meets with Detective Lt. Harrison and gets the details of the case. Mr. James is 50 and had married Barbara, who is 28, three years ago in Reno. Mrs. James' first husband was under contract to a movie studio. Mr. James had given her everything she wanted to keep her happy. She was reported missing 6 weeks ago and there has been no trace of her since.

Johnny goes to James mansion and meets a very old looking Martin James. James tells Johnny that he does not know why she ran off. She married him for money and he married her for her youth. James tells Johnny that he had come home one night and quarreled with her. She left and has not been seen since. James does not know any of her friends, but maybe Johnny should talk to Bennett at the Yellow Bird Café and Nightclub. James always felt that Bennett was the first one on her list. James tells Johnny "if you find her, tell her she need not come back".

Johnny goes to see Bennett at the Yellow Bird café, a blue lighted night spot. Bennett tells Johnny that he does not know where she is. Bennett tells Johnny that he had been seeing her at one time, but she gave him the brush.

"I hope you find her dead". Johnny talks to a girl at the dice tables. She confirms that Barbara had given Bennett the brush. She also tells Johnny that Bennett started his place with money he borrowed from Barbara. She also tells Johnny that Barbara's first husband, Fred Vogel, is in town. Bennett stops Johnny and asks him what the girl told him. Johnny mentions the husband and tells Bennett not to fire the girl.

Johnny goes to Vogel's hotel and follows him into his room at 3 a.m. Vogel tells Johnny that he has not seen Barbara for over three years. Vogel tells Johnny that he had gone to New York to make money and she was gone when he came home. Vogel has been in town for two months. Vogel tells Johnny that he came to town to see Barbara but he was afraid to see her, now he can't leave until she is found.

Next morning Harrison calls to report that Dorothy Weller, a dice girl from the Yellow Bird, was found on the highway — she had been shot four times. Johnny and Harrison go to the apartment of the girl. In the girl's closet Johnny and Harrison find a lot of expensive clothes. A call to the store where they were sold, Martin Rifling, tells Harrison that Dorothy had made over $3,000 in purchases and paid the bill herself.

Johnny goes to see Bennett again and accuses him of killing Dorothy because she was blackmailing him over Barbara James. Bennett tells Johnny that he and Barbara were going to run off, and Dorothy was sent to tell Barbara where to meet him. Johnny accuses Bennett of paying money to Dorothy to keep quiet about him and Barbara and suspects that someone was paying Dorothy to keep quiet about what happened at the James house.

Johnny goes back to the James place and demands the truth. By the swimming pool, Johnny tells James that he came home to find Barbara packing to leave with Bennett, and Dorothy was with her. When Johnny tells James that Dorothy is dead, he admits that he came home to find Barbara packing. There was a big fight, and he was paying Dorothy to keep quiet about the quarrel. Johnny and the police now focus on murder and search the estate several times over the next three weeks, with James following along and smiling.

Johnny is looking on the patio one day when Mr. Dolf comes up and asks to clean the pool. Dolf tells Johnny that he had designed and built the pool. It is made of steel and gunnite, a real quality job. He had started on May 23 and sprayed the gunnite on May 26. Mr. James wanted the pool filled in 10 days, but Dolf told him that gunnite needed 28 days to cure. So, on the 25th, when Barbara disappeared, the pool was just a hole in the ground! Johnny shocks Dolf by telling him to dig up the pool! James laughs at Johnny and his police order and tells Johnny that he will have his job. When the bottom of the pool is dug up, Dolf finds a loose area underneath. Johnny and Harrison dig in the loose soil and find a grave. James tries to run away and holds Johnny at bay with a gun. Johnny takes the gun away from him and tells Harrison that James will not need a new swimming pool.

Martin James had buried by Barbara James under the pool. It was a good tomb. Made to last a lifetime, but it was not deep enough.

Notes:
- Gunnite is a fine-grained cement which is applied under pressure from a spray gun.
- Bob Stevenson is the announcer and promotes *711 Ocean Drive*.
- Music is by Leith Stevens.

Producer:	Jaime del Valle Writer: Gil Doud, Davis Ellis
Cast:	Howard McNear, Parley Baer, Jack Moyles, Jean Spaulding, Jay Novello, Stacy Harris

❖

Show:	The Belo-Horizonte Railroad
Show Date:	7/6/1950
Company:	Swanson Industrial Insurance Corporation
Agent:	George Donnelly
Exp. Acct:	$1,492.54

Synopsis: George Donnelly calls and tells Johnny that they are having engine trouble. Swanson has a substantial policy on the Belo-Horizonte Railroad, but losses have been extensive. They have conflicting reports and it is either insurance fraud or murder. Johnny tells him that with his luck, it is probably both.

Johnny travels to Rio de Janeiro, Brazil, to look into a series of accidents on the Belo-Horizonte Railroad. In Rio, Johnny meets with Benjamin Hulley, president of the railroad, who is in the hospital. Hulley tells Johnny that there have been four accidents which have killed 20 people. One set of reports says they were accidents, and one that says sabotage. Johnny is told that the railroad hauls manganese, and Peter Yaradan is the main competition. Yaradan has offered to buy Hulley out, and has spread rumors, but Hulley tells Johnny that he will never sell. Johnny arranges to investigate, and Hulley arranges for a car and driver.

Johnny is assigned a driver named Sica, who tells Johnny who he is and why he is there — but he will not find anything. Sica tells Johnny that he is not really a driver, he is a poet. Sica takes Johnny to meet with Henry Mayers, who had filed the accident reports. His wife tells Johnny that Henry knew nothing about the busted pins. Henry comes in and tells Johnny that he knew the pins were sawed but let the locomotives go out anyway. He was scared and reported the wreck as an accident. Another man saw them too and let the train out, but Johnny will have to find out who that man was.

Johnny goes back to the hotel and waits, while playing Monopoly with Sica. Henry Meyers calls and tells Johnny to come back as he is ready to talk. Johnny goes back to find Meyers has been shot. Before he dies, he tells Johnny "Go to Vervita." Johnny tells Mrs. Meyers that Henry is dead and she rushes in screaming that she knew they would get him. While Johnny is talking to Meyer's wife about who Vervita is, a man with a gun comes to take them all to Mr. Yaradan. Yaradan holds a gun on Johnny and suggests that he should take a rest to help his investigation. Yaradan tells Johnny that all the stories Hulley tells about him are false. Yaradan suggests that Johnny should work for Yaradan, as the wages would be better while he was still alive. Johnny pulls a lamp over on Yaradan, jumps from a window and runs to the hotel.

Johnny writes up an account of what he knows so far and leaves it with the notary in the San Carlos Hotel and sends a series of telegrams. Johnny then goes back to Yaradan and demands the release of Mrs. Meyers and his driver. Johnny tells Yaradan that he will have a report sent to the police if he is not back at the hotel in two hours with the others. He also wants an apology and information: who is Vervita? Yaradan tells Johnny that the railroad has been on the verge of bankruptcy for two years and that he has offered to buy it from Hulley. Yaradan could use the railroad to consolidate his hold on the manganese fields and be a rich man. Yaradan tells Johnny that Hulley is sabotaging his own railroad. Yaradan offers $10,000 for Johnny not to file the report, but Johnny declines and they all leave.

Johnny learns from Mrs. Meyers that there was one survivor of the crashes, a man named Vervita. He is living in the mountains and only she knows where he is. Vervita was a fireman and saw someone pull a hand switch that put two locomotives on the same track. Johnny and Sica take a locomotive to the area and then walk to the cabin of Vervita. Mr. Vervita tells Johnny that Meyers was the one who pulled the wheel pins. Vervita is throwing Johnny out when he is shot. Johnny runs after the shooter, but he gets to the locomotive, overpowers the engineer and leaves. The locomotive is moving too fast and derails on a curve and crashes down an embankment. Johnny and Sica go over the wreckage and find a wallet. Inside is a card for the "Railway Engineers of South America", issued to Benjamin J. Hulley.

Johnny finds the car Hulley had driven to the cabin. Hulley is suspected to have hired Meyer's killer but there is no proof. The railroad is in receivership but still hauling manganese, and Yaradan was forced out of the country by public resentment at Johnny's report. Johnny notes that this case had him stumped right up to train time.

Notes:
- Bob Stevenson is the announcer and promotes *711 Ocean Drive*.
- Music is by Leith Stevens.

Producer:	Jaime del Valle	Writer:	Gil Doud, Davis Ellis
Cast:	Bob Griffin, Francis X. Bushman, Anthony Barrett, Martha Wentworth, Joseph DuVal, Jack Kruschen, Ted de Corsia		

◆ ❖ ◆

Show: **The Calgary Matter**
Show Date: 7/13/1950
Company: **Alliance Bonding Company**
Agent: **Mr. Matthews**
Exp. Acct: **$1,180.00**

Synopsis: Johnny gets a mysterious call from "Johnny Doe" about a $300,000 payroll robbery at Calgary Products in Camden. If he is interested, check the

Alliance Bonding office in New York and be home at 10:00 the next night.

Johnny goes to the Manhattan offices of Alliance Bonding to speak with Mr. Matthews, who admits that there had been a robbery at Calgary which had been kept quiet, due to similarities with another unsolved crime, the Brink robbery. Johnny gets the details on the robbery and Matthews gives Johnny clearance to work on the case.

That night Johnny gets a call from Philadelphia at 10:05 and the operator puts the call through. A girl tells Johnny not to call the police. She tells Johnny that a friend of the man who called Johnny wants to surrender to the New Jersey D.A. If you are interested, go the Branford Hotel in Bridgeport, Connecticut and check in as Charles Randall from Boston, you will be contacted.

Johnny goes to the hotel, located on the waterfront, and checks in. Johnny is met by a man who tells him to leave only his car keys in the room and to come with him. The man tells Johnny that he is only helping someone out. They crisscross the area to make sure that Johnny has not been followed, and head towards Long Island. They drive down a dirt road and arrive at a cabin where a young girl meets Johnny. She tells Johnny that the man had decided to leave, as it was not best to meet yet. Johnny complains about a plot out of "Dime Detective", but the girl gives him a case containing money from the robbery. She tells Johnny that the man wants to turn state's evidence and that he wants immunity and protection. Johnny says it will take two days to see what he can arrange, but immunity is never offered. They will call Johnny daily at 10:00 p.m.

Johnny goes to Trenton and talks to the District Attorney. Johnny is told that immunity is out of the question, but protection can be arranged. Johnny drives home and waits. On the second day he gets a call from Boston instructing him to meet in a rural area north of Boston. Johnny is told that he is being followed but can lose them. Johnny is given instructions and drives to the area. Later that night a man who introduces himself as Gannett meets him. Gannett is not armed and agrees to the terms offered by the DA, and they drive to Trenton watching for tails, but that is not the problem. When Johnny and Gannett get out of the car, Gannett yells "Al! No! Al, don't!" and is shot six times from the crowd. Later the police identify Gannett as Professor Arnold Gannett, LLD, Professor of Law at Russell University in New Haven!

Johnny now knows that the police have been looking in the wrong place! Johnny goes back to the cabin on Long Island Sound and meets the man from the hotel. Johnny tells him that Gannett is dead, and Johnny is told that the girl is Gannett's wife. Johnny wakes the girl and tells her of Arnold's death. She cries and tells Johnny that she does not know who killed him. Johnny learns that the other man is Earl Becker, a gardener at the University who knew Gannett and fished with him. Gannett told him that he was involved in the robbery, and that Gannett asked him to help him surrender. Mrs. Gannett tells Johnny that Gannett taught criminal psychology. His class had been discussing the Brink robbery and Gannett had a theory that it had been done by non-criminals. The theory grew into an obsession with him. He pulled the

Calgary job to prove his theory. His classes number in the 100's but there is a list at his home.

Johnny, Earl, and the girl drive to the Gannett home in New Haven, Connecticut, trying to beat the police. Johnny searches the files and finds a list or 100 names from the 1949–50 class, but there is one name that Johnny wants. Johnny slips out when the police arrive and goes to visit a particular name.

Johnny meets with Mr. Matthews of Alliance Bonding. His son Albert is packing for a canoe trip to Vermont. Johnny confronts Albert with the facts and he confesses to being involved, along with two other law students. Albert had used information from his father's insurance files to get the details.

Johnny wonders how many other crimes are committed by respectable people the police will not suspect.

Notes:
- Johnny's phone number is "STanley 3469".
- *Dime Detective* was a "pulp fiction" detective magazine which ran from 1931 to 1952.
- Johnny's car is a green coupe.
- Bob Stevenson is the announcer and promotes *711 Ocean Drive*.
- Music is by Leith Stevens.

Producer:	Jaime del Valle	Writer:	Gil Doud, Davis Ellis
Cast:	Ted Osborne, Florence Lake, Bill Bouchey, Virginia Gregg, John Dehner, Terry Kilburn		

◆ ❖ ◆

Show: **The Henry J. Unger Matter**
Show Date: 7/20/1950
Company: **Associated Insurance Companies of New England**
Agent: **Calvin Porter**
Exp. Acct: **$50.39**

Synopsis: Cal Porter calls to warn Johnny that Henry J. Unger is out of prison and looking for Johnny there in Hartford, Connecticut. Cal wants Johnny on the payroll to look into Unger for them.

Johnny sends a night letter to the prison asking for details. The doorbell rings, and Johnny opens the door to find Eileen Kennedy. She comes in and Johnny makes her a drink. Eileen is a former girlfriend and their conversation is polite but tense. She asks why Johnny sent her a telegram asking her to come here at 7:30? Johnny tells her that he did not send her a telegram. The doorbell rings, and Johnny opens the door to find Henry J. Unger and another man, Ferdie, who invite themselves in. Eileen tries to leave but is prevented from doing so by Unger. Ferdie ties Johnny to a chair, his sleeve is pulled up, and Ferdie sticks a needle into a "nice big blue bulgy vein" on his right arm and Johnny goes out.

When Johnny wakes up, he has a terrible hangover, his gun is in his hand, and Eileen is dead on the carpet. Johnny checks his gun, which has been fired twice, and his watch, which says 10:20 p.m. — three hours since Unger had come. Johnny hears the maid yelling that he had killed her and calling for the police. Johnny staggers out of the apartment and makes his way to the home office of a friend, Dr. Norwich. The doctor takes a blood sample, a gastric analysis and suggests that Johnny had been injected with alcohol. Dr. Norwich tells Johnny that the injection could have been self-inflicted, and a good attorney could prove that. Johnny gets a "Swiss bath" of ice-cold water, some vitamins and coffee to sober up.

Johnny goes to the Last Chance Café to talk to an informant who tells Johnny, for twenty-five dollars, that Unger comes there daily. Unger walks in and Johnny confronts him. Johnny asks him if it was revenge. Unger says that Johnny will never be able to find any proof, as it was a perfect crime. Johnny pulls his gun to force a written confession but police Lt. Sawyer puts him under arrest for the murder of Eileen Kennedy.

At the jail a lawyer is called for Johnny, who recounts what happens to Sawyer, but cannot prove anything. Sawyer tells Johnny that Eileen was shot twice, and that gastric analysis showed she had alcohol in her system. The bullets match the gun Sawyer took from him, a .38 automatic. Johnny's lawyer, Joseph P. Harris talks to Johnny and they discuss the case. Johnny is unable to provide anything that will prove he is innocent. Johnny is told that it will be a tough one.

At the trial, The State of Connecticut vs. John Dollar, Dr. Norwich testifies about the levels of alcohol in Johnny's blood and stomach. Rochelle Haberstan, Eileen's roommate, confirms that Eileen and Johnny were friends two years ago, and were going to get married. She testifies that Eileen had gotten a telegram and hoped that Johnny would not ask her to marry him. Harvey Sawyer testifies that a search of the apartment found four empty liquor bottles, each with a few drops left in them. Johnny is curious, as he only saw three bottles! Against his attorney's wishes Johnny asks to be put on the stand.

Johnny says that he can prove he is innocent. After recounting the testimony about the bottles, Johnny points out that a man who empties 3.5 quarts of liquor in less than 3 hours would not be able to put a hypo in the right arm with his left hand. Johnny relates that only Unger had a motive to cause him harm. Johnny tells the jury that the next witness, the elevator operator, will testify that Unger and Ferdie came to his apartment. At hearing this, Unger panics and bolts, but is caught by the police. Ferdie confesses and Unger is booked. Too bad there is no elevator in his building.

Notes:
- Eileen notes Johnny has gotten rid of a Rodin statue   probably "The Thinker"
- Eileen and Johnny were almost married.
- Johnny's gun is a .38 automatic, but he opens the breech and sees it has been fired twice. I have verified that you must either check the clip for missing rounds or count shell casings. You cannot tell just by looking

- at the breech.
- Johnny lives at 390 Pearl Street in Hartford.
- Bob Stevenson is the announcer and promotes *711 Ocean Drive*.
- Music is by Leith Stevens.

Producer:	Jaime del Valle	Writer:	Gil Doud, Davis Ellis
Cast:	Raymond Burr, William Conrad, Lou Krugman, Jeanne Bates, Sidney Miller, Mary Shipp, Parley Baer, Herb Butterfield		

◆ ❖ ◆

Show: **The Blood River Matter**
Show Date: 8/3/1950
Company: **Tri-State Life & Casualty Company**
Agent:
Exp. Acct: $740.00

Synopsis: Johnny gets a call from Blood River. Deputy Tom Grey tells Johnny that there is no transportation from Divide, so he will pick Johnny up. Colburn has not recovered and may not live until tomorrow.

Johnny travels to Blood River, via Parkinson and Divide, to investigate the shooting of a policyholder, Max Colburn. There is a $50,000 policy to be split between the son Frank and the daughter Mary. When Johnny arrives in Parkinson, he is called to the local hospital where Mr. Colburn has been moved. The deputy sheriff, Tom Grey, tells Johnny that Colburn had been shot four times with a .45. Johnny learns that the hired woman Millie had found him. She said a man had come to the door and asked for a meal. Mr. Colburn had sent the man away, but the man had shot him. He was moved to the hospital to get better treatment. Johnny and Tom go into the room with the children to wait. Max is described as a huge man, who was a legend in the area. His son Frank is a big man also. At 6:15 that evening, Max finally dies. The doctor tells Tom that being shot at point-blank range, he really did not have a chance. Max was a fine man, and the doctor hopes they find the killer. Frank yells at Tom for bringing Max to the hospital and spending too much time with Mary.

Johnny goes to Blood River, a small town deep in a valley between two tall mountains. The next morning Johnny and Tom go to the Colburn ranch to interview the hired woman named Millie. Duke, the barking dog, meets them and then Millie lets them in. Millie recounts to Johnny how a man had come to the door after dinner and asked for food. She had gone to the sitting room to tell Mr. Colburn, who went to the kitchen, yelled at the man who then shot Mr. Colburn. Millie would be able to recognize the man, who had a coat with a newspaper in the pocket. Johnny is told that Randy, the other hired man, had come from the bunkhouse, but he saw nothing. "Frankie, I mean Mr. Colburn" was out working and got back later. Tom tells Johnny that Millie never quite grew up inside. Tom tells Johnny that they had found the gun, wrapped in a newspaper. Johnny and Tom start to leave when a man, George Baxter, rides up. Baxter tells Johnny that the posse has found Elmer Brice and they are taking him to the jail. Tom tells Johnny that Brice was a hired man who Max Colburn had fired after he killed a colt.

When Johnny and Tom get back to the jail, a mob is starting to form. Millie comes in and identifies Brice as the killer. Brice is brought in and proclaims his innocence. He admits going to the ranch, but only to get a meal. After all, Colburn owed him that, after ruining his reputation over the accidental death of the colt. Besides, he never owned a gun. Baxter comes back and the mob is angry. There are shots, and Tom and Johnny try to move Brice to a more secure location, but the crowd overpowers them.

Later Tom and Johnny find Brice's body hanging from a bridge outside of town. Tom tells Johnny that Max was special, as he was going to divide up his land and sell it at reasonable prices to his neighbors. Johnny hands Tom a receipt for Brice's belongings signed by George Baxter. Tom tells Johnny that Brice could not read. Johnny wonders why he was carrying a newspaper if he could not read it. Or did he learn to read, and not to write?" Tom goes to Parkinson to report to the authorities and Johnny goes back to the Colburn ranch. On the way Johnny is stopped by a group of men who tell Johnny that Brice must have hung himself. Johnny confronts them with Brice's innocence.

At the ranch Johnny talks to Frank, who tells Johnny that everyone should have a trial, referencing Brice's lynching. Mary screams that Frank had killed his father and runs out crying, to go to the sheriff. Frank explains that he had angrily told his father to kill himself or he would. The argument was over the father's plan to divide up the ranch and sell it to his neighbors. Besides, he was out riding fences when the shooting happened. Frank tells Johnny that he is going to lay low for a while and Johnny tries to stop him. Millie comes in with a gun and tells Frank that he has to kill Johnny. She tells Frank that she lied and that she had killed his father for him. She had killed Max after Brice had left. She did it all for Frank. When Frank tells Millie they are finished, she shoots him twice, and Johnny takes the gun.

Frank will survive, Millie is in jail, and there was no fraud, so the policy will be paid.

Notes:
- **Bob Stevenson is the announcer and promotes *711 Ocean Drive*.**
- **Music is by Leith Stevens.**

Producer:	Jaime del Valle	Writer:	Gil Doud
Cast:	William Conrad, Virginia Gregg, Junius Matthews, Sammie Hill, Clayton Post, Tyler McVey, Dave Light, Howard Culver		

Show:	**The Hartford Alliance Matter**
Show Date:	8/10/1950
Company:	Cosmopolitan All-Risk Insurance Company
Agent:	Barton Keefe
Exp. Acct:	$180.00

Synopsis: Johnny is called by Barton Keefe about a building fire there in Hartford, Connecticut. The man who set the fire has been caught, and Barton wants Johnny to talk to him.

Johnny takes a cab to the Hartford Alliance building where he meets Barton, who tells Johnny that Clarence Pickett, who has an office on the third floor, owns the building. A police officer had caught a boy running from the building.

Johnny goes to police headquarters and meets Sgt. Broderick, who tells Johnny that the boy they are holding will say nothing. The boy admits to Johnny that he set the fire and wants what is coming to him. He wants no trial, and tells the police to just put him away. He is a clean-cut boy with clean hands and fingernails, not a troublemaker type. When the police take a snapshot, the boy goes ballistic and is put in his cell.

Johnny goes to the city offices and looks into Pickett's finances, which are not good. Pickett has been losing money in the stock market. Johnny finds Pickett at the fire scene and he tells Johnny that his office is right over where the fire started. Johnny tells Pickett what he has learned and Pickett gets angry. Pickett does not want to go to the police and identify the boy, but relents when Johnny threatens to get a court order.

At the jail, the boy tells Johnny and Broderick that Pickett paid him $50 to start the fire and owes him another $50. Pickett gets mad and walks out saying he never paid anyone to do anything. The police psychiatrist thinks that maybe the boy saw Pickett's picture in the paper. He is well bred and educated, but something is eating at him. Johnny wonders if the boy had a loan that he could not pay back.

Johnny goes to the ruins and talks to a workman who is trying to get a safe out of the loan company office on the first floor, but there is another one just like it that fell from the employment office on the second floor. As they are working to remove the safe, someone pushes debris down on them from one of the upper floors, injuring the workman.

Johnny talks to Barton and tells him of the accident and Barton tells Johnny that the workman is unconscious in the hospital. Johnny goes back to the jail and talks to the boy and tells him that he lied about Pickett and that there's something in the building he wants, but the boy will say nothing. Johnny then gets a lead on the boy's identity from Pine Orchard, Connecticut.

Johnny goes to the resort town of Pine Orchard and talks to Mrs. Landry, who recognizes the boy as Billy Brandon. The family is from Chicago but has an estate in Pine Orchard. The father is in Florida fishing right now. Johnny is told that Mr. Meeks, the gardener, told Mrs. Landry that the maid had just gone and left the house open. She thinks that the maid had come from the Hartford

Alliance Employment Agency that is located in the building that burned.

Back in Hartford, Johnny checks the files for the maid, Belle Muir, but finds nothing. A check is made on Benjamin Price who owns the employment agency and they find a lot! Johnny learns that Price has a record for fraud.

Johnny learns that the workman has died, so now it is arson and murder. Johnny goes to see Belle Muir who tells Johnny that she had worked for the agency for about a year. She left the Brandon estate because no one was there. She is surprised about Billy, as he was such a nice boy. She is surprised that Price has a record. On the way out, Johnny pauses at the door and hears Belle make a call. "He was here." started the conversation. Johnny goes to see Price who tells Johnny that Bell is going to marry him and that she has nothing to say. Johnny says he saw Price in the building, and he will get him for murder, but Price denies being there.

Billy's father, a big defense attorney in Chicago, shows up at the jail and after beating around the bush and a claim of blackmail by Johnny, Mr. Brandon comes out with the truth. Mr. Brandon tells Johnny that Billy had been involved in a traffic accident in Chicago that killed a woman. Mr. Brandon admits that he had bought off the only witness and Billy was acquitted. The maid had overheard a conversation with the witness and told someone. The father had made a payment to a man, and he can recognize him. They all go to Price's apartment with a warrant and the father fingers him as the man he paid the money to. The police arrest Price after a brief struggle. The policy will be paid. The son is charged with arson and the father is put out of business. Price and Bell are charged with fraud and murder.

Notes:
- Bob Stevenson is the announcer and promotes *711 Ocean Drive*.
- Music is by Leith Stevens.

Producer:	Jaime del Valle	Writer:	Gil Doud
Cast:	Hy Averback, Ken Christy, Raymond Burr, Gil Stratton Jr, Howard McNear, Ted Osborne, Peggy Webber		

♦ ❖ ♦

Show: The Mickey McQueen Matter
Show Date: 8/17/1950
Company: Hartford Police Department
Agent:
Exp. Acct: $0.00

Synopsis: Johnny's old friend Mickey McQueen, an old-style Irish cop in Hartford, Connecticut calls him and wants to talk.

Mickey comes to Johnny's apartment at 2:00 in the morning, but just can't say what he wants to say. Mickey tells Johnny that he is being moved to a desk job, but there is "murder being planned and being done" but no one can stop it. Mickey leaves and the next day Johnny goes to Mickey's apartment. Johnny is met by a distraught woman who points Johnny to a small door, a closet containing Mickey's uniforms and a dead Mickey McQueen, hanging from the clothes pole with his belt. The woman is Mickey's wife Thelma. She is young and attractive, with natural platinum blond hair. She tells Johnny that she was leaving Mickey and had come back to get her clothes. He was a kind and wonderful person, with not an enemy in the world. She tells Johnny that she had met Mickey after his wife had died. Johnny tells her that he thinks Mickey was murdered. A search of the apartment finds nothing, so Johnny calls the police and leaves.

That night Johnny follows Mickey's beat and talks to his friends. At the Cedrick Hotel, Johnny talks to the house detective, Ned Martin. Johnny tells him about Mickey's visit and Ned tells Johnny that he had talked to Mickey last night and he seemed down about his new desk job. Ned tells Johnny that Mickey's wife, Thelma Weaver, had done time in Joliet. Ned tells Johnny to drop the case, but Johnny wants to know more. If you want to find out more, see Fred Ku at the Calcutta Club, but don't tell him I sent you adds Ned.

Johnny goes to see Fred Ku, who is half oriental. Johnny feels he could retire from 10% of the bail posted by the customers in the bar. Fred takes Johnny to the office and tells Johnny that Mickey was a nice guy and that he did not take payoffs, and that he left Fred alone. Fred tells Johnny that he did not know Mickey's wife. Fred is called out of the office and Johnny looks around for another exit. The door opens and Thelma comes in and points a Colt .25 revolver at Johnny when he mentions Thelma Weaver.

Johnny throws ink on Thelma and is able to get the gun away from Thelma and tells her he knows of her past. She tells Johnny she had met Mickey after his first wife had died. She tells Johnny that she got out of prison and gave her friends in Chicago the slip. Mickey had arrested her for vagrancy and came back the next day to bail her out. She had used Mickey's soft side to get information for her friends from Chicago, who are outside in the bar. Mickey was being transferred to the police arsenal, and the boys wanted the keys. They wanted explosives for a jewel robbery at the Marquart Building. Roy Weaver, her husband had threatened to tell Mickey she was a bigamist unless Mickey helped him. She tells Johnny that Roy had taken the keys from Mickey and then Roy killed Mickey. Johnny tries to leave, but Roy comes in and objects. Roy thanks Thelma for warning him. Johnny is taken to an old wine cellar and slugged.

When Johnny wakes up, he discovers he is in an old wine cellar filled with burglary tools. Johnny figures out the situation and tries to find a way out. When the door opens, he fakes being unconscious and hears the men take out the tools to the cars where Fred has the explosives from the arsenal. After the men leave with Thelma, Johnny tries to force his way out. Johnny hears the door open and Ned Martin is there. He tells Johnny that a woman had called to say Johnny was locked in the bar and something was going to happen. Johnny tells Ned what is planned and Ned takes Johnny to the area of the Marquart Building, where Johnny sees the cars being unloaded. Johnny sees Thelma walking towards him. Roy calls to her and she turns and fires into the first car, igniting the cordite powder, which explodes. Thelma is shot, but she turns on the ground and hits the second car, which explodes.

Johnny gets to her in time for her to say that Mickey would be proud of her. She tells Johnny that they cannot send her back to Joliet, and then she dies. Ray Weaver lives long enough to sign a confession that he killed Mickey McQueen.

Notes:
- The program opens with an announcement that the *Hallmark Playhouse* will return at this hour on September 7th.
- *Phillip Marlowe* will now be heard on Friday nights along with *Up for Parole* and *Songs for Sale*.
- Bob Stevenson is the announcer and promotes *711 Ocean Drive*.
- Music is by Leith Stevens.

Producer:	Jaime del Valle	**Writer:**	Gil Doud
Cast:	William Conrad, Virginia Gregg, Ben Wright, Jim Nusser, Dan O'Herlihy		

◆ ❖ ◆

Show: The Trans-Pacific Import Export Company, South China Branch
Show Date: 8/24/1950
Company: Corinthian Liability & Risk
Agent: Al Harper
Exp. Acct: $3,544.00

Synopsis: Al Harper at Corinthian has a job for Johnny, but he won't like it. However, the commission will be big. The policy is for $250,000 and Johnny will have to travel to Hong Kong. Johnny is not scared yet. The policyholders are people they have had trouble with before. "Remember the Trans Pacific Import Export outfit?" "Yeah, I sent flowers to the widow." Johnny tells Al he is scared, but he will take a crack at it.

Johnny flies to Hong Kong, which is in turmoil. At the American Consul, Johnny meets Miss Vedras, secretary to the Consul, Mr. Grover. Johnny meets with Grover and after some small talk over the turmoil of war and a review of the case, Grover agrees to help Johnny with letters of introduction and phone calls. Johnny tells him that the previous case was settled because the investigator was killed.

Johnny arranges to get a room at a hotel owned by Miss Vedras' Portuguese father. The room is stark, but Miss Vedras comes to visit. Johnny offers her a cigarette or scotch, and she informs Johnny that he is being followed. Johnny is told where to look and spots the man outside. She stays only a few minutes, but long enough to tell Johnny about a love song being sung outside, and that she is looking for an American to take her out of China. She hates it here and is very impatient. She has no Portuguese relatives to help her.

The next day Johnny goes to see William Meadow, owner of Trans-Pacific. Mr. Meadow is clearly aggravated at the insurance company and is on the defensive, which infers guilt to Johnny. After Johnny is thrown out, he spends the rest of the day looking for former employees to get their stories. After an interview with the accountant, Franklin Abbott, and two others, the case is starting to form. When Johnny gets back to his hotel, Miss Vedras is waiting for him again in his room. She stays and they talk.

The next day Johnny speaks with a fire brigade supervisor, who tells Johnny that the fire was definitely set, and that timing devices were used. They give Johnny pictures and statements that he has photocopied and sent to Hartford. On the way back to the hotel, his tail is missing, but Johnny finds him in his room with a police badge and Miss Vedras dead on the floor.

Johnny tells the constable that she had gotten to the room before Johnny and someone thought her shadow on the blinds was his. The constable tells Johnny that he had been following him at the orders of Mr. Grover at the Consul.

A confused and distraught Johnny is driven to the police Superintendent Clyde's office to give his statement. He tells Clyde that he is convinced that Will Meadow had the girl killed and wants him arrested. Johnny goes to see Mr. Grover with his escort Constable Craine, and Grover tells Johnny that he knows about Vedras. Johnny tells Grover that Vedras is dead because of him, and that this case has been bad on his nerves. Johnny is sure that Vedras was killed because the killers thought she was Johnny.

After leaving by the back door to lose his tail, Johnny walks back to the hotel, puts his automatic in his pocket, and goes to Will Meadow's home. The houseboy tells Johnny that Meadow is not home. Johnny convinces him to tell Johnny where Meadow is. Johnny gets the location, a cottage on Repulse Bay. Johnny calls the police and tells them to meet him at the cottage. At the cottage, the police arrive as Johnny calls out to Meadow, who is surprised to see him. Johnny wants him to go back to town and they exchange shots and Meadows is killed. The police say that by shooting first, Meadow admitted guilt and allowed Johnny to defend himself. "Nothing good came out of this assignment except saving your company some money it didn't know it had."

Notes:
- There are two versions of this program. One dated 8/22/50 is the dramatic portion only, the other is dated 8/24/50 which has both music and dramatic portions. There is no script available to verify the dates.
- This program was used as the audition for Gerald Mohr and John Lund.
- Another reference to an automatic handgun.
- During the early 1950s there was a great deal of angst over a possible war in China between the Red Army and the Nationalists.
- This program contains a commercial for *Phillip Marlow* and *Songs for Sale* in the middle of the program.
- Roy Rowan is the announcer and promotes *711 Ocean Drive.*

- Music is by Leith Stevens.
- *The Hollywood Theater* follows this program.
- There is an announcement for the need for blood donations for the Red Cross.

Producer:	Jaime del Valle	Writer:	Gil Doud, Davis Ellis
Cast:	Tudor Owen, Lillian Buyeff, Hy Averback, Robert Griffin, Hal March, Dan O'Herlihy		

♦ ❖ ♦

Show:	The Virginia Beach Matter
Show Date:	8/31/1950
Company:	East Coast Underwriters
Agent:	Carl Brewster
Exp. Acct:	$855.75

Synopsis: Carl Brewster calls Johnny about a bodyguard case. Miss Janice Browning, who is living in Virginia Beach, Virginia, was engaged to Mark Robeson. Robeson was arrested for robbery and will be released from the state prison in Richmond tomorrow. He has promised to kill her.

Johnny cabs to Carl's office and learns about the case. Johnny reviews what he knows and tells Carl that Janice probably deserves what she gets. Johnny is told that the husband was sent up for robbery. Janice is penniless, but has a policy, therefore Johnny has been assigned to watch her. Carl has met Janice, and it will not be an unpleasant assignment.

Johnny travels to Virginia Beach and arrives at Janice's beach cottage house where Johnny is met by Betty the maid, a honey blond in shorts and a halter-top. Betty was not told about any investigator coming, but lets him in. When Johnny tells Betty that he thought Janice was penniless, which is why Johnny was hired, Betty knows nothing of her finances. She has done ok, though. She is out right now with George Masters.

At 5:00 p.m. Janice and George come home. Janice sends Betty to the beach and talks to Johnny. She tells Johnny that she really did not know what else to do. She last saw her fiancé six months ago and told him she was finished with him. Robeson told her that he would kill her when he got out. Johnny tells her to cancel their evening plans, and they all settle down for a long night.

Around 11:00 Betty comes out of her bedroom and talks to Johnny. She tells Johnny that she had not gone to the beach but had searched Janice's room. She found a wedding picture dated 1947. Shots ring out and Janice screams. Johnny runs outside and finds Mark Robeson standing by the window firing an empty .38 Police Special. Mark tells Johnny that he will not go back to the hospital as Johnny looks like a doctor. He is not going back. Mark tries to strangle Johnny but stops and disappears into the night.

Johnny goes in and confronts Janice with the things Mark had said. Johnny asks why she had set Betty up as a patsy. Janice tells Johnny that using Betty was George's idea, as was telling the story about Mark getting out of jail. She had tried to get detectives and the police to handle the case, but not one wanted to touch it. Going to the insurance company, she tells Johnny, was George's idea. She also tells Johnny that Mark was her husband and has been in a mental hospital in Pennsylvania but had escaped.

After talking to Janice, Johnny decides not to drop the case. Johnny calls Dr. Becker, who had treated Mark. He agrees to come over and calms Janice and talks to Johnny about Robeson's condition. Johnny is told that Mark is insanely jealous and will probably come back.

Janice calls George, but he does not answer the phone. Johnny borrows the doctor's car, and they drive to George's house where there is a light on, but no one answers the door. Johnny and Janice go in and find George strangled in his study, with a .38 lying on the desk, the same gun Mark had used earlier. The police are called and Johnny takes Janice back to the cottage and Dr. Becker sedates her.

The next morning, Janice tells Johnny that she was in love with George, and that Mark knew George. She had borrowed from the insurance policy to pay for Mark's hospital bills. Betty screams and tells Johnny that Mark is back, but there is no trace of him outside. That afternoon Betty is put on a bus for New York. Johnny goes to George's house and a deputy lets him look through the papers in the desk. In a ledger, Johnny finds an entry for a $20,000 loan to Janice. Johnny also notes a $5,000 loan against the policy in April. Johnny leaves and makes a call to the insurance company and they tell Johnny that the policy is for $50,000 and George is the sole beneficiary.

Johnny meets with the doctor and they develop a plan to deal with Mark. That afternoon Johnny parades Janice around in her bathing suit to lure Mark. Later she sits in front of a window. After that, Johnny waits outside. Finally, at 10:30 Mark shows up. Johnny stops him and tells Mark, "I am George Masters", but Mark tells Johnny that it was his fault that she was not in the room. Johnny walks into the light and mark recognizes him as a doctor. Mark tells Johnny that Masters is dead and he will not go back to the hospital. He grabs for Johnny, but this time Johnny is able to slug him. Johnny had figured out that Masters had given Mark the gun and told him to shoot Janice, but he had made a mistake and fired into the wrong room. When Mark came back he killed George because he had made him make a mistake.

Notes:
- This is a variation on *Bodyguard to Anne Connelly*, broadcast on 12/3/49. The names and location are changed and there are minor changes in the plot.
- The expense report includes $500 as payment for deceit.
- Bob Stevenson is the announcer.
- Music is by Leith Stevens.

Producer: Jaime del Valle   Writer: Gil Doud
Cast: Howard McNear, Bob Sweeney, Virginia Gregg, Jeanne Bates, Hy Averback

Show:	The Howard Caldwell Matter
Show Date:	9/30/1950
Company:	Britannia Life Insurance Company
Agent:	Mr. Nathan
Exp. Acct:	$1,050.00

Synopsis: Mrs. Caldwell calls to tell Johnny that her son is dead, she feels it as only a mother could. Johnny tells her that the insurance company must act on fact, not intuition.

Johnny goes to the Caldwell country estate. Johnny relates that Mrs. Caldwell was the answer to the question of why boys left home. She tells Johnny that she made Howard share everything. At age 23, he left for San Francisco and was studying to be an artist. He had met some people and enrolled in a school, the Orlando School of Art. Johnny is told that Howard wrote to say that it was better he not come home, and he will never see his mother again. He wrote that he is not mentally equipped for life.

Johnny calls Mr. Nathan of the insurance company. Nathan tells Johnny that Mrs. Caldwell's lawyer told her to call the insurance company. Johnny is told that there is a $200,000 policy on Howard.

Johnny goes to San Francisco, California and goes to Howard's last known address where the manager opens the apartment. Johnny finds Howard's clothes are still there. The manager tells Johnny that he knows none of Howard's friends. Johnny searches the apartment and only finds mail from his mother, and a collection of match folders with dates. Johnny also finds a folder of sketches of a beautiful woman.

Johnny goes to the art school where Mrs. Orlando tells Johnny that Howard had stopped coming to class. Johnny shows her the sketches, and she confirms that they are Howard's work, but she does not know who the model is.

Johnny visits the bars on a list he made from the matchbook covers, most not worth remembering. At "The Stop Sign" Johnny asks for Howard. The bartender does not know Howard, or the girl in the picture. However, a man in the bar knows Howard Caldwell. Johnny goes outside with him and gets into a car and meets another man, and they drive off. They tell Johnny that they have been waiting for someone to show up. They tell Johnny to drop the matter, as it is for the best. Then they take Johnny to his hotel.

Early the next morning, a phone call tells Johnny to buy an Examiner and look at the headlines. Johnny gets a paper and finds the headline: "Syndicate head found slain in auto trunk — Benjamin Miller western gang chief found dead." Johnny reads the article and learns that Miller was found in an abandoned car. On page four Johnny sees a picture of Nora Rush, with an address in Los Angeles, the girl Howard had drawn.

Johnny catches a United Airlines flight to Los Angeles and goes to Nora's Ardmore Street address. When he gets there Nora is still in her robe. She tells Johnny that she knows why he is there. She tells Johnny that she does not know where Howard is and cries. Johnny searches the house and finds a picture of Howard. Johnny tells Nora that he saw the sketches, and that a few other people have seen them. "How could he have been so stupid?" she tells Johnny. There had been nothing to link them together. She tells Johnny that Howard had killed Miller with her gun. Nora explains that she was going with Miller after she came from Chicago. She met Howard at a party and there was just something about him. They would meet in bars and then go to her place where he sketched her. Ben Miller saw him meet her and Ben hit her. Howard got angry and killed him and Howard had help moving and hiding Miller's body. Everything was OK until Johnny came. Johnny asks Nora why two friends would help? She tells Johnny that no one wanted Howard to take a wrap for killing Miller. She does not know where Howard is, and her brothers are flying in and will be there by noon.

After noon, Nora's brother Al arrives. Johnny tells Al that he will not call the police until they talk. Al tells Johnny that Nora fell for Howard. Ben stirred up mud about her past and Howard killed him. Johnny thinks it makes more sense if they were protecting their sister. Al agrees to take Johnny to Howard.

They drive to an apartment and Johnny knocks on the door. Johnny opens the door to find an empty apartment. Johnny slugs Al and goes back to Nora's house.

Howard is there in the bedroom, lying on the bed crying. Howard is glad that Johnny came. He tells Johnny that Nora didn't want me, just my name and money. Howard admits he killed Miller. He tells Johnny that he has lived with low class people and started to think like them. This was the first thing he has done by himself. Howard tells Johnny that Nora says he is a snob. Johnny turns Howard in for murder and the others as accessories.

Notes:
- Johnny takes United Airlines.
- There is a promotion for O'Brien's new movie *War Path*
- Roy Rowan is the announcer.
- Music is by Wilbur Hatch.

Producer:	Jaime del Valle Writer: Gil Doud
Cast:	Lurene Tuttle, John McIntire, Bob Sweeney, Hy Averback, John Dehner, Jeanette Bates, Jeanette Nolan

❖

Show:	**The Richard Splain Matter**
Show Date:	**10/7/1950**
Company:	**Corinthian Life & Liability Insurance Company**
Agent:	**Bruce Harvard**
Exp. Acct:	**$375.00**

Synopsis: Bruce Hardwick calls and has a case for Johnny. A policy was found at the scene of a murder without a body. Bruce wants Johnny to investigate.

Johnny travels to New York City and is met by homicide Sgt. Burns at the apartment of Richard Splain. Johnny looks through the apartment and Burns tells Johnny that Richard Splain rents it. There are signs of a violent struggle, but no one heard anything. Johnny finds part of a ship model and tells Burns that he will talk to Splain's wife and beneficiary.

Johnny goes to the apartment of Splain's wife Clara, a dumpy blonde. She tells Johnny that they had split up. A man named Mark Barnes knocks on the door and comes in and is protective of Clara. Johnny explains she is the beneficiary of a $35,000 policy. She tells Johnny that Splain was either in port or at sea, as he was a ship's carpenter. Mark tells Johnny that Splain would not call his wife when he came home. They want a divorce, but lawyers cost money. Clara tells Johnny that maybe Splain is not dead but someone else was killed.

Johnny goes back to Splain's flat. Burns is gone so Johnny tells the guard that he is working with Burns to get in. Inside Johnny finds Splain's ships papers, and his last ship was the Tangier. Johnny also finds a small address book. Johnny copies names until there is a knock on the door and a man enters. The man tells Johnny that he thought Splain was in. The man acts panicky but does not know where Splain is. He tells Johnny that he liked to talk about foreign places with Splain. Johnny pays him $10 for talking. Johnny then tails the man to his apartment where the name on the door is Paul Krell. Johnny calls Burns and updates him. Burns tells Johnny that he has gone to Splain's ship but did not get anything. Burns will call Johnny if anything turns up.

Next morning the phone rings. It is Clara Splain, and she must see Johnny immediately. She tells Johnny that the police have arrested Mark, and Splain's body has been found. She tells Johnny that Mark told the police nothing, but Mark could not prove where he was. She tells Johnny that she left Dick because he smuggled dope in model ships, and it is important to tell Johnny now.

Johnny ponders the ship models, Krell as a possible user, and the address book. Back at the apartment the police are there along with the body of Paul Krell who has been beaten. Johnny chides Burns for not calling and a nasty Burns threatens to arrest Johnny for meddling by sneaking in to the apartment earlier. Johnny tells him that he only came for the name of the ship. Burns tells Johnny that the only change to the apartment was an open drawer with a torn envelope in it. Johnny leaves before he locks horns with Burns, as the address book is gone. Johnny keeps quiet about the book and meeting Krell.

Johnny goes to Mrs. Splain and asks if she knows Krell, and she does not. Johnny asks Clara where Mark was last night and she tells Johnny that Mark was with her. She asks Johnny why she would tell him about the narcotics if the story were not true. Clara shows Johnny a model and opens a hidden compartment. She tells Johnny that she does not know who Splain's customers were.

Johnny goes to Krell's apartment and learns Krell was just a friend. Johnny goes to the next name on the list, Mr. Kentner. He does not know Splain but gives himself away when Johnny tells him Splain is dead. "That's bad" replies Kentner. He admits to Johnny that he bought ships models. He last saw Splain a week ago and had met him through a friend.

The next two stops uncovered nothing. Johnny goes to see Francine Wells and her father opens the door, as Francine was expecting Fred. Johnny tells him that it is important to talk to her and he lets Johnny in. Francine tells Johnny that he must have come to the wrong place, as she has never heard of Splain. When told Splain sold narcotics, she is shocked. Johnny tells her he is trying to find out who killed Splain and she admits she saw Splain last week. She was introduced to him by a friend and bought narcotics from him. Johnny shows her the list but she does not know anyone in it. Johnny gives her a business card and leaves.

Other visits give similar results, the people bought drugs from Splain. Johnny visits J. L. Tucker who knew Splain's wife and tells Johnny that she was shilling for Splain. Johnny calls Clara and she tells Johnny that Tucker had called and was looking for someone, so she told him about Dick. She was stiff and did not know what she was doing.

After dinner and drinks, Johnny meets Francine Wells on his hotel floor. She tells Johnny that she was no angel. After a party in Pennsylvania, someone got drugs, and that was the start. Now it has ended. She killed Splain. She tells Johnny that she went to Splain without money and he laughed, so she beat him. She cannot go on as she killed Krell also. Haven't I done enough?

Johnny calls on Mr. Wells. Johnny is looking for evidence, an address book. Mr. Wells admits that Francine confessed to cover him. He saw her and learned the truth and he killed Splain to protect her.

Notes:
- There is a promotion for O'Brien's new movie *War Path*.
- Bob Stevenson is the announcer.
- Music is by Wilbur Hatch.

| Producer: | Jaime del Valle | Writer: | Gil Doud |

Cast: Herb Butterfield, Raymond Burr, Howard McNear, Joe Gilbert, Bill Bouchey, Barry Kroger, Mary Lansing

◆ ❖ ◆

Show: **The Yankee Pride Matter**
Show Date: 10/14/1950
Company: **Tri-State Insurance Company**
Agent: **Carl Bush**
Exp. Acct: $2,686.00

Synopsis: Carl Bush calls and offers Johnny a fat commission in Singapore. The policy is for $300,000 and mechanical breakdowns are holding up a cargo ship.

Johnny goes to the Tri-State office and talks to Carl. Johnny is told that maritime insurance is a risky business. Johnny knows about bad bets — he bet on Notre Dame last Saturday. Johnny is told that the *Yankee Pride* has a cargo of tin bound for a West Coast defense plant. There is a time clause on deliveries, and Tri-State loses 2% per day on $300,000 if the ship does not sail before next week. Johnny is told that Vincent Ells is the local agent. Carl tells Johnny that he will send a bouquet of bourbon to his plane.

Johnny flies to Singapore and goes to the Tri-State office and talks to Ells, who tells Johnny that the unexpected is commonplace in Asia. Johnny is told that this could be a dangerous mission, as another adjuster has been killed. The agent was Chinese so the police aren't too concerned. He had gone to the *Yankee Pride* and never arrived. Death is not rare here in Singapore. Johnny is told the investigator has a brother and Johnny gets the address. Ells warns Johnny to proceed with caution.

Johnny goes to the ship and meets with the chief engineer who has malaria. Johnny tells him why he is there. The chief tells Johnny that a bearing is being flown in from Hong Kong. Sabotage is not likely as bearings go, and generators fail all the time. The chief tells Johnny that he will talk to the captain, so come back tomorrow.

Johnny goes to see the brother of the dead agent. The rickshaw driver waits and Johnny goes to the door. The man will not talk about his brother but lets Johnny in after Johnny tells him why he is there. Johnny is told that his brother was killed for his job or some other reason. He does not want to die and knows nothing. A man came here before the police did and warned him not to talk to police. He was an Englishman who works for someone else. His brother's last words were about a woman. There was always a new woman. She is Malayan and he did not mention her to the stranger. Johnny is told that the girl, Randee, works in a bar and there is where his brother met her. "Leave and do not come back" Johnny is told. As Johnny leaves, shots ring out and the brother is shot, but Johnny does not go back.

Johnny goes to the bar on Malabar Street after being unable to find a phone to report the shooting. The bar is crowded and Johnny orders a Scotch and asks for the girl. The bartender tells him to sit at a table and the girl comes to serve him. Johnny tells her that a friend told him about her. She tells Johnny that she learned English from a missionary school. She tells Johnny that the agent, Koo Fu Soon was no friend. She did not want to meet him again, as he made a fool of himself, as he was lonely. Are you lonely? Come to my house after work.

Johnny goes to her house and she does not lie about not knowing that Koo Fu Soon is dead. She tells Johnny that he is in trouble. As she mixes a drink, a man breaks in and tells Johnny that he is going for a ride. Johnny tries to fight and is knocked unconscious.

When Johnny wakes up he is in a mansion where he is introduced to the "Major". Johnny is told "You will accomplish nothing until I allow you to." Johnny is told that the chief engineer will move the ship on his order, and that the ship is going to Mexico. The Major tells Johnny that "One can buy anything, including petty official signatures, as the Major has power." He will let Johnny go on with his work, as Johnny is a harmless pipsqueak. Johnny is told to tell the insurance company that the Major will cover their losses. Two men, named Earl and Roy, take Johnny to his hotel. Johnny had seen the man's name, "Major Ralph Dixon" on an envelope, and he is a power-mad man.

Next day Johnny calls Ells and asks, "Who is Dixon?" as he claims to be behind the problems with ship. Johnny tells Ells to look into the ship's papers and Dixon's visa and to check customs. Johnny will start at the other end, as he knows his way around the bottom.

Johnny goes back to Randee and tells her there is going to be trouble. He will turn her in and no one will believe her. She tells of people who are afraid of an invasion and are sending their gold out of the area. The Major is in charge of shipping the gold out on ships. There is an estimated $100 million in gold being shipped. She tells Johnny that Mr. Ells is as greedy as everyone else, and he has been bought. If Johnny is wise, he will get out.

Johnny goes to Ells' home where there is no answer at the door. In a window Johnny sees Ells, dead with a pistol in his hand. Johnny goes to the hotel and gets his automatic and heads to the Major's place. Johnny forces his way in and tells the Major that Ells is dead. The Major tells Johnny that "He was weak and did not appreciate the Major's strength." Johnny tells him that there is only one way to stop the Major, to kill him, as he is a man of influence only in his own mind. Johnny is going to take him to the police as he knows about the gold and will stop the scheme. The Major only replies that he is late for a meeting at the club and starts to leave. As he walks out of the room laughing, Johnny shoots the Major. The police arrive and arrest the Major. The gold is seized when it arrives. The *Yankee Pride* will sail only two days late.

Notes:
- Another reference to an automatic handgun.
- This is the first time Johnny acts preemptively.
- There is a promotion for O'Brien's new movie *War Path*.
- This program was scheduled for 7/9/1952 but was preempted by the Democratic National Convention.
- Bob Stevenson is the announcer.
- Music is by Alexander Courage.

Producer:	Jaime del Valle	Writer:	Gil Doud
Cast:	Virginia Gregg, Bob Sweeney, Tutor Owen, William Johnstone, Wally Maher, Jack Kruschen, Ben Wright		

◆ ❖ ◆

Show:	**The Jack Madigan Matter**
Show Date:	**10/21/1950**
Company:	**Strool Bail Bond**
Agent:	**Manny Strool**
Exp. Acct:	**$2,720.00**

Synopsis: Manny Strool calls Johnny. He needs Johnny to save him $50,000. He provided bail for two witnesses who then disappeared, and Manny wants to talk to Johnny.

Johnny phones New York to check on Manny Strool's reputation, which is good enough for the courts. Manny tells Johnny that Jack Madigan forced him to put up the bond. Madigan wanted the men out on bond and now they have disappeared. Manny came to Johnny because the police don't care and detectives can be bought. Manny was referred to Johnny by his insurance contacts. Manny has learned that Johnny is honest, but tends to pad the expense account, but who doesn't. Manny gives Johnny the details on Nippy Bruno and Max Kraus. Johnny wants a $2,500 retainer before starting.

The check comes the next day, so Johnny goes to New York City. Johnny entertains a reporter friend and asks about Madigan. Johnny learns that much has been written about Madigan, and people have disappeared before.

Johnny takes a cab to the house of Nippy Bruno's sister, Vivian Brown, an actress. A man answers the door and announces Johnny. Vivian tells Johnny that he has come to the wrong place, as she has not seen Nippy in years. The man, who is called "Red", pulls a gun and Johnny is searched. Vivian and Johnny sit and wait until Jack Madigan arrives. Johnny tells Madigan that he did not expect to find Madigan and the sister of a witness together. Madigan apologizes for the gun and tells Johnny that his reputation is ill deserved. He wants the men to testify. He has decided to tell all, he is tired and is going straight. Johnny declines an offer of money from Madigan to stop snooping.

Johnny leaves, gets a cab, and sees Red watching him from a window. After making sure the cab is not followed, Johnny goes to Max Kraus' apartment, only to find that Red is there. He tells Johnny that he is Max Kraus. He tells Johnny that he has to do something with Johnny, so he takes him outside and heads for a car but is gunned down in the alley. Johnny leaves the scene because the dead man is not Max Krauss. Johnny goes to Manny Strool who tells Johnny that the phony description of Kraus was a mistake.

Johnny calls Vivian, who tells Johnny that Jack had left after he got a phone call. She wants Johnny to come up. Johnny takes a chance and walks to the apartment where she answers the door and lets him in. Johnny searches the apartment and finds no one there. Vivian tells Johnny that she wanted to tell him where Nippy is, and that she is involved too. Jack knew things would happen and he told Vivian that he will have the government eating out of his hand. She is ratting on Madigan because he cared only for himself. He is the one that wanted Max Kraus killed. Vivian had called Nippy at his hotel earlier, but now there is no answer. Vivian tells Johnny that Nippy is in a hotel on Lexington Avenue. Johnny takes Vivian to his hotel room for safety, and then goes to Madigan's address and sees the police in front of the building and a body in the sidewalk, Jack Madigan's body.

Johnny goes back to his hotel room and tells Vivian that Jack is dead. Johnny wants Vivian to go to the police, as she needs protection, but she won't go, as they would love to blame her. "It is easier to be rotten." she tells Johnny. Vivian then tells Johnny that she will give him Nippy. They go back to her apartment, and Nippy is there. Johnny tries to talk Nippy into giving up, but Nippy tries to kill Vivian and Johnny slugs him. Johnny calls the police and Vivian is held as an accessory.

Johnny talks to Strool and tells him not to make bail for her. Johnny tells Manny that he will never work for him again, and wait till you see my expense account! The expenses include an item for $2,500 in miscellaneous expenses, and Johnny is holding the retaining fee until this matter is settled.

Notes:
- This is an adaptation of *Witness, Witness, Who's Got the Witness*, broadcast on 10/22/1949 with Charles Russell and *The Tom Hickman Matter* on 8/13/52 with Edmond O'Brien. The names are different. For instance, in this case, one of the witnesses, Max Kraus, is the name of the Bail-bondsman who hires Johnny.
- There is a promotion for O'Brien's new movie *War Path*.
- Dan Cubberly is the announcer.
- Music is by Wilbur Hatch.
- *Sing it Again* is next, and the prize is $5,000.

Producer:	Jaime del Valle	Writer:	Gil Doud
Cast:	Sidney Miller, John Dehner, Clayton Post, Jeanette Nolan, John McIntire		

♦ ❖ ♦

Show:	**The Joan Sebastian Matter**
Show Date:	**10/28/1950**
Company:	**Corinthian Life Insurance Company**
Agent:	**Mr. Semplan**
Exp. Acct:	**$356.75**

Synopsis: Johnny calls Boston and gets the name of the police contact for the Joan Sebastian case from Mr. Semplan and is told to see Lt. De Rosa. Johnny asks if the police have a theory yet and is told they do not. So, it is either murder or suicide.

Johnny rents a car and drives to the Boston, Massachusetts police headquarters. Johnny meets Lt. De Rosa and tells him that the insurance company is nervous about a possible suicide case. Johnny tells De Rosa that the girl's mother is the beneficiary and is an invalid. Johnny leans that the mother has taken up with an old boyfriend. De Rosa tells Johnny that the girl was found in shallow water near a bridge, and it did not look like a typical suicide. The bridge was too low, and a suicide never does it without taking off their coat and shoes, and her purse is missing. She was 21 years old and pretty. Johnny is told that the inquest will be in two days. Johnny tells De Rosa that he wants to dig up his own background information.

Johnny goes to the site where the body was found. Johnny notes that the placement of the body indicates she was going towards Boston, not away from town. Johnny goes to Joan's apartment and talks to Mary O'Neal, Joan's roommate. Joan tells Johnny that Joan's death is a great shock. She never thought she would do anything like this. She tells Johnny that she expected some trouble, as Joan lived too fast after her mother went into the hospital. There were just too many men. One boyfriend is Harold Correy, who is a truck driver for North American Van Lines. Mary tells Johnny that Joan saw other men when he was gone. Johnny asks to look at Joan's things and Mary takes him to Joan's room. Johnny goes through a locked dresser with nothing but clothes, expensive perfume and jewelry, and a key with a heart-shaped head. Johnny keeps the key, as he wants to find out who made it.

Johnny calls North American Van Lines and is told that Correy is out of town and is due back at 3 a.m. Johnny calls Joan's employer and goes to see Mr. Hollis at his home, where Johnny meets Mrs. Hollis. Mr. Hollis tells Johnny that he knew nothing of Joan's private life, as he had no right to know, but he did know of Joan's invalid mother. Johnny tells Hollis that he thinks there was only one man, not many. Johnny asks for the names of Joan's coworkers and Hollis tells Johnny he will get the names of the co-workers if Johnny will call in the morning.

Johnny goes to see Correy at 10:30. Johnny tells Correy that the case looks like murder. Correy tells Johnny that Joan would never kill herself. Correy tells Johnny that he left Wednesday morning on a run, and Johnny suggests that he could have killed Joan before he left. Correy gets angry and tells Johnny that he wanted to marry Joan and throws him out.

Johnny calls De Rosa and learns that the cause of death has been ruled suicide, as the autopsy says Joan died of carbon monoxide poisoning. De Rosa thinks that someone probably moved her body to avoid embarrassment. Johnny goes to see De Rosa to read the autopsy report, which points to car exhaust but also shows a severe concussion. Johnny shows De Rosa the key and asks if he can find out where it was made.

Johnny goes to see Paul Anderson, the boyfriend of Joan's mother. Paul tells Johnny that the mother was 17 when Joan was born. He met Joan first, and realized she was an opportunist. He did what he could for the mother and did not send her to a home to get her out of the way. Paul does not know anything about a gold key but tells Johnny that Joan was heading for a bad end with no one to blame but herself.

Johnny goes to see Correy and talks to him in a nearby café. Correy tells Johnny that he is going out again, as he cannot take the pressure any more. Johnny talks to six of Joan's co-workers and finds nothing. Johnny goes to De Rosa and learns that the police have found the goldsmith who made the key. Johnny goes to talk to him, and he is positive, as it has his mark on it, "CF" for Cedrick Frost. Frost does not know for whom he made it for but searches his records and finds a gold key made in March for J. E. Carter. The gold key was made from a key to a cottage and was a surprise for his wife. Johnny tells De Rosa about the cottage, but De Rosa cannot assign men to search cabins in the area, as it is a county responsibility. Johnny searches real estate companies in the area and on the 3rd day he hits pay dirt. Johnny finds an agent who remembers renting a cottage to J. E. Carter in March. Johnny and the agent go to cottage, where Johnny sees tire tracks in a lean-to garage, and a stained rug, among other things inside. On the way out, Johnny locks the cottage door with the gold key.

Johnny goes to Mr. Hollis and tells him that he thought he would get away with it. He had rented the cottage and bought the key for Joan. Hollis admits that he was infatuated with Joan and wanted to break it off. Joan left the cottage and committed suicide in his car. Johnny tells him of the bloodstains and Hollis agrees to go to the police. When Hollis asks Johnny what had convinced him, Johnny tells Hollis that he had found a *Wall Street Journal* addressed to Hollis in the cottage. Mrs. Hollis comes in and tells Johnny that she killed Joan. She had gone to the cottage and waited inside, killed the girl, and carried her to the car.

Remarks: "I don't know what sticklers the Massachusetts courts of law are, but Joan Sebastian was not killed by the wronged wife. She was unconscious but alive when Hollis put her into the car trunk. She died there by carbon monoxide."

Notes:
- There is a promotion for O'Brien's new movie *War Path*.
- This story will be done twice by John Lund, once on 3/6/53 and again on 7/20/54 as *The Jeanne Maxwell Matter*.
- Dan Cubberly is the announcer.
- Music is by Wilbur Hatch.

Producer: Jaime del Valle   Writer: Gil Doud
Cast: Virginia Gregg, Howard McNear, Virginia Eiler, Wally Maher, John Stephenson, William Johnstone, Raymond Burr

♦ ❖ ♦

Show: **The Queen Anne Pistols Matter**
Show Date: 11/4/1950
Company: Tri-State Insurance Company
Agent: William Carter
Exp. Acct: $365.35

Synopsis: William Carter calls Johnny and tells him that the idiot cousin of a company vice president has sold a $15,000 policy on a pair of antique pistols for a trip from New York to Boston. Carter wants Johnny to see that the pistols are delivered, as someone has tried to steal them twice.

Johnny goes to the Tri-State office and meets Leonard Bonny, who has been injured. Bonny tells Johnny that he was attacked in Liverpool before boarding a ship, and in New York. Neither time did he have the pistols with him. Johnny sees the pistols in a leather box, two graceful flintlocks with a faint name etched on them. The pistols are going to Arthur Worthing of 272 Medford Street in Boston. Johnny is to deliver them, and Bonney will wait in Hartford.

Johnny takes a plane to Boston, Massachusetts and goes to the office of Arthur Worthing, who is happy to see the package. Worthing tells Johnny that James Freeman Norwhich made the pistols in 1705. They were fashioned during Queen Anne's rule, and have had a colorful history. These guns have caused many murders, and many murdered for them. The insurance policy is in force until Johnny delivers them to the purchaser, who is Mr. or Mrs. Jack Rawlins

Bride. Johnny is to deliver the pistols to them and tell them that Bonny or Worthing will contact them.

Johnny goes to the Bride address and gives the package to Mrs. Bride who screams when she sees it. Mr. Bride comes in and tells her that he will take care of the matter. Johnny is told that he will not a get signature from him. Bride asks if Bonny is here in America, and who Worthing is. Bride tells Johnny to get out with his fake form and pistols. "Your bluff won't work." he tells Johnny. Johnny goes back to Worthing, but the shop is empty and for rent.

Johnny sends a telegram to Tri-State and goes back to his apartment where the phone is ringing. Johnny tells Mr. Carter that Bride had called the pistols blackmail. Carter tells Johnny that he cannot find Bonny. Johnny tells Carter that he wants no part of this matter. Later Johnny looks over the pistols and decides that they are nothing worth $20,000. The engraved name on the pistols was "Bride" and the date is 1704. What was it all about?

Next morning Johnny gives the pistols to Tri-State and starts on another case. That night the Bride's butler meets Johnny at his apartment. He wants the pistols and does not like the story that they are in the Tri-State vault. As Johnny is told "Please get them in the morning", he is hit with a needle and collapses.

Johnny wakes up to the voice of Bonny. It is after 9:00 p.m. and Johnny sees that his apartment is torn up and Bonny's arm is no longer in a sling but filled with a Webley automatic. Bonney mumbles about the problem being Worthing's fault. Johnny and Bonny go to see Worthing in a shabby hotel in Boston. "We are in a mess as the pistols are locked up at the insurance company" Bonny tells Worthing. Worthing tells Bonny that the pistols are not important now. They have served their purpose. Now the plan is to blackmail the Brides to keep secret a two-year-old murder.

Bonny calls the Brides and leaves. The Brides arrive an hour later and meet with Worthing. Worthing tells that the pistols are locked up and cannot be delivered. Worthing tells the group that the Brides had their uncle, the Duke of Pembroke, murdered. The estate went to the Brides and the other relatives just nibbled at the edges. Worthing and Bonny will keep quiet about a murder in October 8,1948 when a killer hired by the Brides killed the Duke. The theft of the pistols was the motive. Bonny is where proof of guilt lies and he might need more money someday. Mr. Bride will pay $5,000 to Bonny at their house, the rest later. Mrs. Bride is hysterical and wants to go to the police, as too many people know what happened.

After the Brides leave, Worthing has his own plans for Johnny, who jumps him and overpowers him. Worthing is searched and his wallet has no ID. In the lining of his coat is a card: "Arthur P. Worthing, CID, Scotland Yard".

Worthing wakes up and tells Johnny that he was posing as a blackmailer. The scheme is intricate, but he obtained the Bride's confession with Johnny as a witness. The trial in England got no information, so Worthing had to turn criminal. Johnny is told that Bonny was hired to kill the Duke. If they kill Bonny, they will confess to the other murder. Worthing tells Johnny that the Duke was

Worthing's friend. Worthing calls the police and Johnny goes to the Bride's home with Worthing. Johnny hears angry voices in the library as the police take their positions. Inside Bonny is shot and the police rush in. The Inspector got what he wanted: Bonny is killed and the Brides are arrested. Expense account item #6 is $150 for miscellaneous items. You have to admit I deserve something for what I went through!

Notes:
- Webley pistols were manufactured in Great Britain.
- There is a freedom of worship commercial to support your church.
- Edmond O'Brien's latest film is *War Path*.
- Bob LeMond is the announcer.
- Music is by Wilbur Hatch.

Producer:	Jaime del Valle Writer: Gil Doud
Cast:	Ben Wright, William Conrad, Dick Ryan, Jeanette Nolan, Dan O'Herlihy, Tyler McVey

◆ ❖ ◆

Show:	**The Adam Kegg Matter**
Show Date:	**11/11/1950**
Company:	**Grand East All Risk Insurance Company**
Agent:	**Al Begney**
Exp. Acct:	**$230.40**

Synopsis: Al Begney calls and Johnny asks him what or who he insured that he should not have, or are you inviting me to dinner? Johnny tells him that he gets three types of phone calls: social, business and people who want money, creditors or otherwise. Al tells Johnny that the jewels from the Kegg burglary are insured for $120,000. Are you free? Unemployed yes, but not free.

Johnny travels to New York City to see Al Begney. They go together to see Mr. Kegg, who is a Broadway angel and an unlikable person. Mrs. Kegg answers the door and shows Johnny a newspaper that was left at their door with a note "see page 3 col 2". Johnny sees an antihistamine ad that has been changed to read "His time stops at sign on your cold cash insist at his time." The price has been changed to $98,000. There are instructions to go to a phone booth in Montclair, New Jersey at Maple & 7th, 10:30 tomorrow. Begney tells Johnny to pursue the ransom offer, but Kegg wants nothing to do with it. Johnny is told that the Keggs were out for the evening and the jewels were in a locked box in a locked drawer. Johnny talks to Danny, the bellboy operator. Danny tells Johnny that he has been in the apartment and put out the paper every morning but today. Danny tells Johnny that he lives in Queens, and that the maid lives in Montclair, but she has just resigned.

Johnny talks to the police who have found only some smudged fingerprints, and they are canvassing the known fences.

Johnny rents a car and goes to Montclair. At a phone booth near a bowling alley a car double-parks and Johnny is told to get into the car and not to cause trouble. Johnny tells the man that the ransom money is to be paid by the insurance company. Johnny tells the man he is staying at the Hotel Langley and walks back to his car.

Johnny visits Millicent Weaver the maid. She tells Johnny that she told the police she quit for personal reasons. She has a personal code of ethics. She also knew the location of Jewels.

Back at the hotel, there is a message for Johnny to meet a girl in booth #1 in the bar. Johnny goes to the bar and meets Mrs. Kegg, who is scared. She tells Johnny that Danny the bellboy has been killed, and she has to talk. She cries and tells Johnny her story. She is not feeling sorry for herself but is afraid of what her husband will make of it. She tells Johnny that Danny was killed by a hit-and-run driver. She relates that she only had the privilege of wearing the jewels until Kegg divorces her, which is in the works. She admits that Adam will rant and rave over this and she goes home.

The police did not print Danny's death in the paper. Johnny gets a phone call from Hartford. Al Begney tells Johnny that Kegg wants to drop the whole matter. Johnny tells Al he can't do it as it will look like they pulled off rather than uncover a murder.

Johnny goes to see Kegg and asks why he wants the investigation dropped. Are you afraid of what will come to the surface, that you might have faked the robbery? That Danny knew the setup and you killed him? Johnny tells Kegg that the investigation can't be dropped and Kegg tells him to go ahead if he insists.

Johnny goes to the police and tells them of the meeting in Montclair. Johnny also learns that Danny's death was an accident, and that the driver, a Miss Linquist from Florida, has given herself up. Johnny calls Tri-State to give up the case.

There is a knock, and Mrs. Kegg is at his door. She tells Johnny that she knows a man in Montclair. His name is Stanley Griffin, and she used to date him. He is a musician and lives in the village. Johnny goes to visit Stanley who tells Johnny that the stuff is in his apartment, and that he will make a statement in front of Kegg. Stanley opens a suitcase and gets the jewels.

At the Kegg apartment, Stanley gives the jewels to Mr. Kegg. He tells him that Mrs. Kegg was going to share the profits and will now will share the blame. Griffin leaves to give a statement to the police. He tells them that he did it to get her away from Kegg, but she threw him out so he made it look like she helped him. He was drunk and crazy and wanted to see her in prison with him.

This whole matter was no more than a cloud of smoke. The death was inconvenient, and it was a rare type of burglary, done for revenge by a jilted man.

Notes:
- **This story was done by Edmond O'Brien as *The Sidney Mann Matter* on 8/6/52.**
- **Edmond O'Brien's latest film is *War Path*.**

- Dan Cubberly is the announcer.
- Music is by Wilbur Hatch.

Producer:	Jaime del Valle	Writer:	Gil Doud
Cast:	Stacy Harris, Lamont Johnson, Jeanette Nolan, Jack Moyles, Hy Averback, Paula Victor, Raymond Burr		

♦ ❖ ♦

Show:	**The Nora Falkner Matter**
Show Date:	**11/18/1950**
Company:	**Great Eastern Life Insurance Company**
Agent:	**Jim Morris**
Exp. Acct:	**$1,120.40**

Synopsis: Jim Morris calls and asks, "Are you working on a case?" "Bonded Kentucky yes, but not insurance" answers Johnny. Jim tells Johnny that a woman in California wants to buy $200,000 in insurance, but the agent thinks she is holding back. Jim has decided to investigate.

Johnny travels to the Los Angeles, California office of Great Eastern to see Mr. Snyder, who gives Johnny the Faulkner folder. The husband is the beneficiary and Mrs. Faulkner would pay 6 months' premiums in advance, but she wanted to know when the policy is in effect.

Johnny goes to the house and talks to the neighbors who give varying accounts of Faulkner, who lives with her husband and mother-in-law. At the Falkner house, Johnny meets the mother in-law who has iron gray hair and is losing the battle to stay young. "Who is she seeing in Las Vegas?" Johnny is asked. "You're not the detective? You're not from the agency?" She tries to cover by telling Johnny that it is just a little game she plays. She tells Johnny that she knows nothing of a policy, but Nora does not tell her everything, and she is clever. Nora is always maneuvering to get her husband's affections. Johnny is told that Nora rushed Anthony into marriage in 1942, and while he was in the army, she partied. Andrew comes in and tells Johnny that he does not know of an insurance policy. Nora has not said anything to him, but he never knew what Nora is thinking. She relies on a psychic, Madam Starr.

Johnny goes to visit the psychic. Johnny asks her why Nora is so anxious to buy insurance. "Who are you?" she asks Johnny. "You mean you don't know?" chuckles Johnny. She tells Johnny that she only offers Nora advice, and that she is not a psychic. Nora has been coming for advice and she tries to help. Nora has been under severe mental strain the last few years. She wanted more tangible protection for her life. Everyone has reasons for protection. Johnny is told that Nora is in the Flamingo Hotel in Las Vegas.

Johnny flies to Las Vegas, Nevada on a Western Airlines excursion coach. Johnny goes to the Flamingo Hotel and checks in. When he mentions Mrs. Faulkner to the clerk, the sheriff is called. Johnny is told that she has been poisoned and is in the hospital. Johnny shows his ID and deputy sheriff Wood tells Johnny of the poisoning. Johnny is told that she is too ill to talk and is with her personal doctor. The sheriff has talked to the mother, and she fainted.

Johnny goes to the hospital room, and Dr. Brooks tells Johnny that Nora is resting, but Nora tells Johnny that she could not stand it any longer and took some poison and destroyed the remains. Johnny thinks the story sounds phony. Johnny tells Nora that her life is very unhappy and that she is lying to protect someone. Dr. Brook tells Johnny that there is a vitamin tonic called Hadacol in Nora's hotel room, and it might be the source of the poison.

They go to the room and Dr. Brooks accidently drops the bottle in the sink. The sheriff scoops up some and puts it in a container. In the lobby Johnny meets the managers of the hotel, Max Lewis and Nev Gilbert. The sheriff tells Johnny that the boys will take care of him. Johnny goes to the bar with Max who tells Johnny that he knows nothing of Nora. Max talks to Joe Rosenberg, the credit manager, who tells Johnny that he had signed for a $500 check, which limits the amount of checks cashed.

Andrew and his mother show up after midnight and are told Nora will recover, and the mother is so relieved.

Later that night Johnny is reading in bed when the phone rings. The sheriff tells Johnny that he is back at the hospital and Nora has been shot.

Johnny goes to the hospital and learns that Nora is dead but had named her husband before she died. Johnny is told that Dr. Brook was out for coffee when Nora's husband came in. The doctor tells Johnny that Andrew had threatened to kill her and said that no one would suspect him because he loved her. Nora wanted a motive, so she bought the insurance. Dr. Brooks did not know everything until that night. She told him that Andrew's mother had driven her to it and that she wanted to give him another chance. Anthony had come in briefly the day before and flew back. He arranged the poison when she would not go back with him. Andrew was a deranged war casualty and Nora was terrified of him yet defended him. The sheriff has a search underway and will call for some more men.

Johnny and the sheriff wait, as Las Vegas is a bad place to get away from. There is only one road in and one road out, and the sheriff has roadblocks on both. The roads end somewhere, so they wait for a radio report. The desert is a tough place and the sheriff gives some local color. A railroad section house calls with a sighting. When Johnny and the deputy get there, Anthony is hiding in a culvert. Both ends are covered and Johnny calls into the culvert. Anthony shoots once, then five more shots. The sheriff fires 11 times and then there is no answer. The sheriff asks who carried his life insurance.

The son was guilty in fact. Now the mother must start life alone knowing the guilt was hers.

Notes:
- **Johnny drinks rye and soda.**
- **Johnny notes to seatmate on the plane to Las Vegas that he used to like to fish but there is not much time for it now. He is always going to start.**
- There is a promotion for Western Airlines.
- **Hadacol was a patent medicine sold as a vitamin supplement with over 10% alcohol.**

- The sheriff tells Johnny that an old prospector was hit in the face with a drop of water and it took a bucket of sand to wake him up, and the old story about it being so hot a starving coyote was chasing a rabbit and they were both walking. Later it will be so hot that Andrew will crawl onto the electric chair to cool off.
- Edmond O'Brien's latest film is *War Path*.
- Dan Cubberly is the announcer.
- Music is by Wilbur Hatch.

Producer:	Jaime del Valle	Writer:	Gil Doud
Cast:	Parley Baer, Jeanette Nolan, Herb Butterfield, Lee Patrick, John Dehner, Tim Graham, Virginia Gregg, Wilms Herbert, Vic Perrin, Clayton Post		

♦ ❖ ♦

Show:	**The Woodward Manila Matter**
Show Date:	**11/25/1950**
Company:	**Columbia All Risk Insurance Company**
Agent:	**Ralph Weedon**
Exp. Acct:	**$3,940.00**

Synopsis: Ralph Weedon calls to tell Johnny that the take from the burglary is $75,000 and that an American clerk named Blake has disappeared.

Johnny goes to Manila, Philippines to investigate a burglary and is met by Floyd McDonald and Irving Morgan of the Woodward Hardware Company who take him directly to the office. Johnny is told that the safe was found open on Monday morning with $75,000 missing. The U. S. headquarters required them to keep the money on hand for monthly shipments home. Floyd and Irving disagree over Dan Blake the clerk. Floyd trusts him and Irving feel he is guilty. He has been missing four days, but it is easy to drop out of site in the area.

Johnny goes to his hotel and orders a pitcher of gimlets while he waits for his luggage. Later Johnny goes to the police and talks to Sgt. Malvar who is not looking for Dan Blake. He has captured the thief, a local man named Miguel, who cannot tell where he was that night, and was robbing another store last night. Johnny talks to Miguel and he tells Johnny that he does not have the money. If he had money, then why would he steal 5 pesos? Johnny thinks it is easier for Malvar to grill Miguel than look for the real person.

Johnny goes to the Woodward office and meets Charlotte Page, the niece of the owner. She shows Johnny the office layout, and Johnny tells her that it looks bad for Dan. She tells Johnny that she saw him occasionally and knows of no problems. Johnny is shown the office safe, which is under a rug in the office. Everyone trusted Dan, but he did not know the combination. Johnny gets Dan's address from payroll records and goes to Dan's room. From the contents of the room, Johnny learns that Dan was a student of the Philippines and traveled widely there.

Johnny goes to the police and tells Malvar of Dan's travels in the islands. Malvar tells Johnny that Dan has been found and taken aboard a ship. He was shot many times and is dead. The ship captain knows it is Dan because the man had mentioned his name before he died. Johnny calls Floyd but he is out so Johnny tells Charlotte to tell Floyd to come and look at the body. Charlotte is saddened to hear that Dan is dead. Later, Floyd and Johnny go to look at the body and Floyd confirms that it is Dan. They are told that Dan was found in a dugout in Tayabas Bay. Captain Kovah, the captain of an inter-island schooner found him. He was alive for a while but the money was not found on him.

Floyd and Johnny rent a boat to find Kovah, and find his boat, the *Sea Nymph* to be a wreck. They go onto the boat and talk to Kovah who tells them that Malvar thinks that Kovah has the money and that he had better give it to him. Kovah tells Johnny that he found the man in a dug-out Morro craft. He lived 15-20 minutes and said little. Kovah gets angry, as the police are getting papers to search his boat. Kovah tells Johnny that plenty could have happened on the way to Tayabas Bay, as the Huks would do anything for money.

Johnny and Floyd leave the boat, and Johnny is not sure of Kovah, as he may be lying. Later, Johnny sees in Malvar's report that the crew says that Dan said nothing, as the Huks had killed him. Johnny learns from Malvar that McDonald is deep in debt, so maybe he used Dan as a patsy, as there is no reason for Dan to have done it. Malvar tells Johnny that it is not wise to question McDonald, as he is a man of honor.

Johnny goes to see Irving Morgan, who tells Johnny that he has heard that the money is gone, as Floyd had said so. Irving also tells Johnny that the Huks can be handy to have around. "How much do you know of McDonald's personal life?" asks Johnny. "Does he owe you money?" Irving tells Johnny that Floyd is not the kind of man to do such a thing. Floyd has dinner at the Merchants Club every day, so question him at home, as Irving wants to stay away from this thing.

Johnny goes to see Floyd at his home, and a man comes out of the front door, Kovah. "Forget you saw me" he tells Johnny as he runs away. Johnny goes to the house and meets Charlotte, who tells Johnny that Kovah had come to see her and hit her because he wanted the money. She tells Johnny that she had the money and was holding it for Dan. They wanted to get away to have a life of their own.

Johnny calls Malvar and meets him at the harbor police, and they go out after Kovah. Malvar tells Johnny the police doctor says Dan was choked to death. They find Kovah 30 minutes after leaving. The police open up with a machine gun, and Kovah fires back, hitting a searchlight. Kovah's crew turns on him and he shoots them. The police machine gun cuts Kovah down, and Johnny goes aboard to find the money.

Charlotte was arrested but the money did not add up to the amount claimed.

Notes:
- The Huks, or Hukbalahaps were native people who rebelled against the government after WWII.

- The Moro were a group of Malay Muslims still active today.
- This program was done as *The Woodward Manila Matter* by John Lund on 6/29/54.
- Dan Cubberly is the announcer.
- Music is by Wilbur Hatch.
- Edmond O'Brien's new movie is *War Path*.

Producer:	Jaime del Valle	Writer:	Gil Doud
Cast:	William Conrad, Lillian Buyeff, Robert Griffin, William Johnstone, Hy Averback, Jack Kruschen		

♦ ❖ ♦

Show: **The Blackburn Matter**
Show Date: **12/16/1950**
Company: **Plymouth Insurance Company**
Agent: **Bob Hall**
Exp. Acct: **$345.75**

Synopsis: Bob Hall calls to tell Johnny that Gene Reimer, another investigator, and a friend of Johnny's has been killed in Charleston, South Carolina, and that his wife was with him. Johnny accepts the case, noting that "You cannot hunt for trouble without finding some." Johnny is told that Gene Reimer was looking into the death of Leland Blackburn who was bludgeoned to death in his study.

In Charleston, Johnny goes to see Gene's wife Barbara, who was an old flame of Johnny's before she married Gene. She tells Johnny that Gene had made her come, that he beat her, and that he had found out about a man she was seeing. She said she would like to have killed Gene for the things he had done.

Johnny goes to the police and meets Lt. Simms, who tells Johnny that Blackburn was killed in his home, that he was a stock broker, that his wallet was empty, and that the family has refused an autopsy. The police will force an autopsy and will have a report in a couple of days. Johnny is told that Gene was found in an alley near Magazine Street, shot three times with a .32, but Blackburn would have never set foot in that part of town.

Johnny goes to the Blackburn home and meets with Mrs. Blackburn, and the son Roland. Johnny is told that the Blackburns are a fine old southern family whose name must not be dragged into murder. Roland suspects a plot and wants his father's killers punished. Mrs. Blackburn tells Johnny that she was in bed at the other end of the house. Roland had gone to the kitchen and found Leland, who was a charitable, honest and pious man. She tells Johnny that she hopes to join him soon. Johnny calls Simms to pass on the statement of Roland and his suspicion he knows more. Simms tells Johnny that he had checked their finances and they were fine.

Back at his hotel Johnny is met by the house detective, Hal Brand. He tells Johnny that he had been paid by Gene to watch his wife, and that she had a visitor named George Richards just before Gene was shot. Richards has gone back to New York.

Johnny goes to Barbara and tells her he is angry that she lied. She tells Johnny that she did not know George was coming. She told him to leave, and that no one would find out. She tells Johnny that neither she nor George killed Gene. Right now, Johnny tells her, you need witnesses or the police will arrest you. Johnny searches for alibis for George but gets nowhere.

Johnny goes to see Simms and is told that he is in real trouble for not telling them about Gene's troubles with his wife. Johnny tells Simms that Gene had a mean streak, and that she was a friend. Also, all the evidence is circumstantial. Johnny wonders if Richards had set up a phone meeting to kill George? Barbara is brought in for questioning. The autopsy report comes in and discloses that Blackburn was a narcotics user.

Johnny goes to see Mrs. Blackburn and tells her of the required autopsy and the results. She tells Johnny that they thought they were doing the right thing, but Gene had found out. Blackburn had been buying from two men named Miller and Stone, who were blackmailing him. They had come to force him to buy more drugs, and then they killed him. Johnny is told that Gene had gone to meet the men and was killed.

Johnny gets the address and decides to go there alone. Johnny forces his way into the apartment and ends up shooting Miller as he runs out. Miller talks to the police and Stone is caught.

Back in Hartford, Barbara calls, but Johnny says he is on another case and has to earn a living. Goodbye.

Personal note: Cops, private or otherwise, should never marry. They are away from home too much and leave too many widows.

Notes:
- Johnny says he learned the business as a Pinkerton Agent.
- The script title page does not include the first name "Leland".
- Johnny references carrying an automatic.
- Dan Cubberly is the announcer.
- Music is by Wilbur Hatch.
- Edmond O'Brien's new movie is *War Path*.

Producer:	Jaime del Valle	Writer:	Gil Doud
Cast:	John Dehner, Jim Nusser, Jeanette Nolan, Georgia Ellis, John McIntire, Lawrence Dobkin		

♦ ❖ ♦

Show:	The Montevideo Matter
Show Date:	12/23/1950
Company:	Washingtonian Insurance Company
Agent:	Bill Brandon
Exp. Acct:	$1,650.00

Synopsis: Bill Brandon calls Johnny and tells him that an English woman has been found dead in South America. The London Investment Group wants Johnny to investigate the death.

Johnny flies to Montevideo, Uruguay and gets a room at the Hotel Madrid. Johnny then meets with Inspector Alcira and learns that Mrs. Madeline Furness has been killed. Her husband Roger owns a meatpacking plant, and their son Keith lives with them. The killing was four days ago, and the gardener, Ramon del Gado, found the body. Mrs. Furness was killed with a blast from a shotgun.

Johnny goes to the Furness home where Ramon is working. He tells Johnny that "she was a bad woman and he was a bad man". Johnny meets Keith, who is a stepson. He tells Johnny that his father did not kill her for the £5,000 insurance, and that Madeline was a schemer. Johnny is shown a picture of Madeline, who is a much younger woman. Keith tells Johnny that he goes to school in England, and that the body was found between their home and the house of Jack Strong, their neighbor.

Johnny meets with Mrs. Strong, who is in a wheelchair. She tells Johnny that there was a division between Madeline and her stepson. Johnny notes that Roger Furness must have found out about his wife's escapades with Mr. Strong. Everyone heard the gunshot, and money probably was the motive.

Johnny meets Mr. Furness, and he tells Johnny that he needs the money from the insurance. He admits that he knew about his wife and Strong. Keith comes in and tells Johnny that he killed his stepmother. Keith is arrested and jailed, but under questioning he is unsure of the facts.

Johnny goes to the Strong residence and sees Mrs. Strong walking outside the house. Once inside she is in the wheelchair again. She tells Johnny that she hurt her back in a hunting accident and is not supposed to walk. She admits to Johnny that she knew about her husband and Madeline. Mr. Strong comes in and attacks Johnny, who slugs him. Johnny goes to see Mr. Furness and accuses him of hiding behind his son's confession. On the way out, Furness is shot at the front door. Alcira later tells Johnny that del Gado is a common name, but they are looking for Ramon. Later he is arrested and admits to the killings. He tells the police that they killed his grandson with their automobile after his daughter had died.

Notes:
- This program is repeated on 7/23/1950 and 9/3/1952.
- The announcer is Dan Cubberly.
- Music is by Wilbur Hatch.
- Edmond O'Brien's next film is *War Path*.
- Story information obtained from the KNX Collection in the Thousand Oaks Library.

Producer: Jaime del Valle   Writer: Gil Doud
Cast: Ben Wright, Terry Kilburn, Lillian Buyeff, Jay Novello, Lou Krugman, Tudor Owen

Show: The Rudy Valentine Matter
Show Date: 12/30/1950
Company: County Court, Kings County
Agent:
Exp. Acct: $10.85

Synopsis: Rudy calls Johnny from Leavenworth prison in 1950, and reminds Johnny that he sent Rudy to prison, along with his wife and lawyer. Rudy is ready to settle up now.

Johnny goes to New York City and is almost hit by a car. A witness tells Johnny that the streets are not safe with all the drunk drivers. Johnny goes to the police and talks to Sgt. Foss who searches the records. Johnny learns that Rudy was convicted of robbing a delicatessen and was identified by the owner. Later the gun and money were found in his room. Rudy had been arrested for auto theft in 1939, and assault in 1940. He was 17 at the time. Johnny gets the address and goes to read the trial transcript. Johnny learns that the attorney was William P. Capper, who is now a successful lawyer. Johnny goes to see Capper and talks to him. Johnny is told that Rudy has also contacted Capper, but he calls it just talk.

Johnny goes to his hotel and wires the prison. The prison officials tell Johnny that Rudy got mail from Sybil Miller on 16th Street. Johnny goes to see Sybil and asks for Rudy, but she tells Johnny that he is not there. Johnny tells her of the threats and she tells Johnny that Rudy had promised to forget about the past. Sybil tells Johnny that Rudy has gone to Buffalo. Johnny goes to see Rudy's brother Anthony at a news-cigar stand he runs. Johnny meets Rudy's wife Pat, and Anthony tells Johnny that Rudy has not contacted them, but he will send Rudy's wife out of town for protection. Johnny gets a telegram from the prison that tells him that Rudy had spent time in the mental ward and had attempted suicide but is all right now. Johnny is then called by Rudy's wife, who tells him that Tony has been killed by Rudy.

Johnny goes to the apartment and meets Lt. Maxwell who tells Johnny that they have picked up Rudy's wife Pat. Johnny tells him that he has no description for Rudy.

Sybil comes to Johnny's hotel and tells Johnny about Tony. She argues with Johnny and accuses him of planting the gun. She tells Johnny that only a framed man would kill his brother and gives Johnny a description of Rudy. Johnny calls Capper and learns that he is on his way to Florida. Johnny goes to his hotel and meets Rudy at his door. Rudy tells Johnny that he has talked to Sybil, and that they did not kill Tony. Rudy tells Johnny that he went to Buffalo to look for a job and was driving a blue 1939 Plymouth coupe (Not the car that almost ran Johnny down). Rudy tells Johnny that his lawyer was responsible for putting the money in his room. Johnny convinces Rudy to give himself up to the police.

Johnny goes to see Pat and discovers that she is dead. Johnny goes to Capper's apartment and tells him that he was paid to throw the case and calls him an ambulance chaser. Capper tries to bribe Johnny, and then pulls a gun.

Remarks: "As I said at the outset, I do not expect the County Court, Part One to honor this statement. It would be fair and equitable to work out payment for a witness. It looks like I made that position again at Capper's forthcoming murder trial, and for me it'll be a waste of time. I know he is guilty."

Notes:
- The announcer is Dick Cutting.
- Music is by Wilbur Hatch.
- Story information obtained from the KNX Collection in the Thousand Oaks Library.

Producer: Jaime del Valle   Writer: Gil Doud
Cast: Sidney Miller, William Johnstone, Jack Moyles, Jeanette Nolan, Joseph Kearns, Clayton Post, Tom Hanley, Bill James

❖ ❖ ❖

Show: **The Adolph Schoman Matter**
Show Date: **1/6/1951**
Company: **Corinthian All-Risk Insurance Company**
Agent: **Harold Warner**
Exp. Acct: **$150.80**

Synopsis: The secretary for Harold Warner calls, and Mr. Warner wants to meet Johnny for lunch to talk about a policyholder in Allentown, Pennsylvania who was poisoned.

Johnny meets with Harold and is told that Adolph Schoman was in the steel and concrete business in Pennsylvania. Schoman held $150,000 in personal insurance and $200,000 with the company as beneficiary. The family also includes his wife Amelia, and children Eric, Max and Gertrude. Schoman was 80 and known to run the house like a factory and died last night.

Johnny goes to Allentown and meets with Mrs. Schoman who tells Johnny that her husband was an invalid and had cancer, which had been kept from the public. Johnny is told that he did not kill himself, that would be a sign of defeat. The children have no ambition and just hang around for the money, and the local doctor, Dr. Buchholtz has an office in town.

Johnny goes to see Dr. Buchholtz and is told that Adolph was a fool. Gertrude is an old maid, Max is an alcoholic and Eric is in an unsuccessful marriage with Betty Elliot, a model or working girl, which is below the family standards.

Johnny goes to see Betty, but she does not want to talk other than to tell Johnny that she does not live with Eric because he is a slave to the family. Betty thinks that the mother killed Adolph. At the inquest it is determined that an alkaloid poison was admitted by someone, and that there was an abrasion on his hand.

Johnny meets with the children and none of them remembers hearing anything. While they are talking Amelia screams and Johnny rushes upstairs to find poison in a glass of water. Amelia is ok, but Johnny calls the doctor. When Dr. Buchholtz arrives, Johnny gives him the glass, which he says contains belladrine. Amelia tells Johnny that she does not want the police called. When Johnny insists, he is told to leave, and takes the glass with him. On the way out, Max tells Johnny that Betty is pregnant. Johnny goes to talk to Betty, who tells him that Eric is to be disinherited. Johnny goes back to Amelia and tells her that she killed her husband because he wanted to disinherit Eric because of Betty and the child.

Notes:
- The announcer is Dick Cutting.
- Music is by Wilbur Hatch.
- This story was done by Edmond O'Brien as *The Amelia Harwell Matter* on 7/2/52, with a reversal of victims.
- Story information obtained from the KNX Collection in the Thousand Oaks Library.

Producer: Jaime del Valle   Writer: Gil Doud
Cast: Virginia Gregg, Joseph DuVal, Jeanette Nolan, Dick Ryan, Francis X. Bushman, Stacy Harris, Edgar Barrier

◆ ❖ ◆

Show: **The Port-O-Call Matter**
Show Date: **1/13/1951**
Company: **Great Eastern Insurance Company**
Agent: **Bob Radin**
Exp. Acct: **$450.60**

Synopsis: Bob Radin calls and Johnny is told to drop his current assignment. There has been a series of robberies in San Francisco. Bob wants Johnny to get right on it.

Johnny goes to San Francisco, California and meets Lt. Clark who tells Johnny about the four robberies at the Port-O-Call Savings and Loan. The first was at 9:15, the last at 10:55. The same group of 8-10 men, who appeared to wear makeup, did all of the jobs, and only one person talked and used a falsetto voice. So far, the take is $47,000. Johnny is told that the police are searching the usual places, so Johnny and Clark can only wait.

At 5:00 p.m. a call comes from missing persons that a Mrs. Geyer has reported her husband missing. Johnny and Clark talk to Mrs. Geyer, who tells them that her husband drives a cab and has not had an accident, and that she has three kids and a roomer. Johnny tells her of the robberies, and he is told that her husband would never get involved in a robbery. She leaves and the police put a tail on her. Johnny wonders if the robbers could have used a cab.

Johnny talks to the cab company drivers and discovers that a driver, Mike Landini is missing. Johnny goes to see Landini's apartment manager and looks through the apartment but learns nothing.

The next day a body is found. Mrs. Geyer is called in and is very upset, but it is not her husband. Johnny follows her to her home and asks why she is so upset. She tells Johnny that she had never seen a body before. Back at police headquarters, Mr. Prince from the bank tells Johnny and Clark that he remembers seeing a man with a manicure and a ring. Johnny remembers that the body had a manicure and is missing a ring. The police report in that no one has seen Mrs. Geyer, but they have not seen the roomer either, and Johnny wonders where he is. The police get two neighbors to identify the body as Mrs. Geyer's roomer. Johnny goes to the Geyer home with Clark. They search the room and hit pay dirt, drawings of the bank branches and a list of names. Mrs. Geyer tells Johnny that the roomer is named Ted Grace, was a salesman, got no mail, but had phone calls from the same man, and hung out at the Furlong Bar.

Johnny goes to the bar, orders a rye and soda, and asks the bartender for Ted, or Tony. The bartender tells Johnny that he knows no one by those names. On the way out, an old man calls the bartender "Tony". Johnny doubles back and watches Tony make a phone call. Johnny calls Clark and they confront Tony. Under pressure he admits to participating in the robberies and tells them that the organizers were 3 ex-cons from the east. Tony knew there would be trouble when the killing started. Tony gives Clark the name of the motor court where the three men are.

Clark and Johnny join other officers at the motor court in a rainstorm. Clark is shot going up to the door and two of the robbers die in a hail of bullets. Clark dies on the way to the hospital. It is probably not important, but the gunfight showed up on page two of the papers, the storm got page one.

Notes:
- Johnny is drinking rye and soda.
- Edmond O'Brien's new movie is *War Path*.
- Dick Cutting is the announcer.
- Music Direction is by Wilbur Hatch.

Producer:	Jaime del Valle	Writer:	Gil Doud
Cast:	Howard McNear, Ed Begley, Hy Averback, Jim Nusser, Virginia Gregg, Janet Scott		

◆ ❖ ◆

Show:	**The David Rockey Matter**
Show Date:	**1/20/1951**
Company:	**Britannia Life Insurance Company**
Agent:	
Exp. Acct:	**$840.75**

Synopsis: Miss Beale, the travel agent calls Johnny with his travel arrangements: National Airlines to New Orleans then Pan American to Managua, Nicaragua and a train to San Juan del Sur, Nicaragua. Why not make round trip reservations she asks, I'm not always sure I will come home from these trips Johnny replies.

Johnny goes to New York and gets information on David Rockey from the Maritime Union Hiring Hall. Johnny tells them that David had missed his ship and was unaccounted for. When asked why Johnny is going to all this trouble, Johnny tells them that David just became a millionaire.

Johnny flies to San Juan del Sur and meets with Mr. Wahl of the shipping line. Wahl tells Johnny to go back to Hartford, as Rocky is in jail for murder for knifing a man in a drunken brawl. When asked why the shipping company had not reported it, Wahl says one must be careful not to annoy the Guardia. Johnny discovers the Guardia were formed by the US Army and are a force to be dealt with carefully.

Johnny goes to see Rockey in the jail where Sergeant Ortega says that Rockey cannot be seen. Why? Because I say he is guilty, now leave! Johnny threatens to go to the American Counsel and is allowed ten minutes. The cell has no lights so Johnny uses a match for a light while David holds his ID. Johnny tells David that his adoptive father, Titus Morgan has died and left him $1.5 Million and $50,000 in insurance. David tells Johnny that he does not remember what happened that night. He was drinking with friends and remembers nothing. He tells Johnny that he liked Emiliano Sagasa and had no reason to kill him. He was with Emiliano, his wife Misha, a girl named Alicia and his coworkers Dave Light and Chris Binstead. David tells Johnny that he wishes he had stayed home with his adoptive family. Johnny thinks David is innocent, as there is no motive and the knife has not been found. Johnny sends a wire to Hartford and requests that a lawyer be sent to represent David.

Johnny meets with Misha Sagasa, who is an attractive girl who likes Americans because they always bring her presents, and that made her husband angry. She did not see the killing, as she was outside with Alicia. She tells Johnny that she heard talking and then Chris came out and said, "Dave killed Emiliano". Johnny wonders if he could he have meant Dave Light? Johnny tells Misha of David's inheritance and how he must learn the truth.

Johnny goes to see Chris Binstead. He tells Johnny that he saw Misha wake David up, some words were said and David killed Emiliano with a knife. Johnny goes back to the hotel and there is a message from Wahl telling him that Misha has been looking for Johnny and wants to see him immediately.

Johnny goes to Misha who tells Johnny that she has found the knife, which the Guardia had not even looked for. She tells Johnny that she just was thinking about it and looked behind a chest and there it was. Johnny takes the knife and tells Misha not to tell anyone anything about this.

Johnny charters a plane and takes the knife and his wallet to be processed for fingerprints. Later Johnny goes to see David Rockey, who tells of his being adopted and how he just did not fit into the high-society life of this adoptive father, so he just left. Later, Johnny learns that a lawyer is on the way and that the report on the prints is back, so he goes to the only place he can go. Johnny goes to see David and tells him that the prints on the knife were his, he had murdered Emiliano Sagasa.

The lawyer thinks there is a good change at a second-degree murder plea. But $1.5 million is worth waiting for.

Notes:
- The insurance and estate are worth over $14,500,000 in 2017 dollars definitely worth waiting for.
- Edmond O'Brien's new movie is *The Redhead and the Cowboy*.
- Dick Cutting is the announcer.
- Music is by Wilbur Hatch.

Producer: Jaime del Valle   Writer: Gil Doud
Cast: Lillian Buyeff, William Conrad, Jack Moyles, Tyler McVey, Edgar Barrier, Jay Novello

♦ ❖ ♦

Show: **The Weldon Bragg Matter**
Show Date: **1/27/1951**
Company: **Financial Surety**
Agent: **Jim Waldo**
Exp. Acct: **$65.80**

Synopsis: Jim Waldo calls Johnny and tells him that it still looks bad, and Dr. Bragg is still unconscious and the hospital is only admitting the police.

Johnny goes to the Redlands Hospital in Hartford, Connecticut, but the guard will not let Johnny in, and will only tell him that Dr. Bragg has been shot.

Johnny goes to Bragg's house and meets Lt. Gregory who tells Johnny that Bragg was in the study and was shot twice, and the gun was not an automatic. Mrs. Bragg was upstairs and heard the shots.

The next day Johnny goes to the hospital with Gregory and they are told that Bragg is dying. They go into the room to get a death-bed statement, and Bragg asks if Ethel is there. They leave and Johnny tells Gregory that Mrs. Bragg is named Gwen, and Ethel Johnson is the nurse.

Johnny goes to see Mrs. Bragg, and she asks Johnny if her husband asked for "her" and admits that she has lost her husband a long time ago. Johnny goes to see Nurse Ethel Johnson who tells Johnny that she loved the doctor, but his wife refused to give him a divorce. Ethel shows Johnny a letter from a psychiatric patient whose wife died in an operation and accuses Bragg of killing her.

Johnny visits Gregory and tells him about the letter. Gregory tells Johnny that his younger brother Floyd is the man who wrote the letter. Gregory tells Johnny that he tries to be a good cop and will arrest his brother if necessary. The ballistics report comes in and Bragg was shot three times by a .32 revolver from a distance of seven feet.

Johnny goes to see Mrs. Bragg and she denies what Johnny tells her about the divorce. Johnny searches the study and finds the accounts are in arrears, another patient had died in an operation, and the doctor had been sued but won the case.

Johnny goes to see Floyd at his job, but he is not there. Later that night Johnny finds Floyd at home and tells him about the letter. Floyd wants to confess to keep his brother out of trouble. Johnny tells Gregory about the conversation the next day. Johnny goes to the doctor's office the next day with Sgt. Bell and finds a box with .32 caliber shells inside of it. Johnny calls Gregory and arranges to meet him at his office. Johnny and Gregory go to see Ethel to confront her about the ammunition and Mrs. Bragg's denial of a divorce request. Ethel gets the gun and tries to shoot herself and fires once after Johnny grabs the gun. She admits that she had gone to see Bragg and had argued with him. She followed him and shot him in his study.

Notes:
- The announcer is Dick Cutting.
- Music is by Lud Gluskin.
- Edmond O'Brien's next movie is *The Redhead and the Cowboy*.
- Story information obtained from the KNX Collection in the Thousand Oaks Library.

Producer:	Jaime del Valle Writer: Gil Doud
Cast:	Howard McNear, Bill Bouchey, William Conrad, Lee Patrick, Stanley Farrer, Virginia Gregg, Clayton Post, Wilms Herbert, Jim Nusser

◆ ❖ ◆

Show:	**The Monopoly Matter**
Show Date:	**2/3/1951**
Company:	**Corinthian All-Risk Insurance Company**
Agent:	**Mr. Brandt**
Exp. Acct:	**$63.80**

Synopsis: Mr. Brandt calls about a fire but there are no details. It is the Monopoly Club in Waterbury.

Johnny rents a car and drives to Waterbury, Connecticut. The fire department is still on the site as Johnny arrives. Later the fire is under control and Johnny talks to the fire inspector, Captain McReady. The fire started inside, and the building is less than five years old and is licensed for public use. The alarm came in at 11:00 a.m. The owner has gone home. The firemen find proof of arson — a Molotov cocktail.

Johnny goes to see the owner, Gerald Hobson. He was at the site but his nerves got the best of him, so he went home. Thank goodness for the insurance. They specialize in the game Monopoly, harmless entertainment for the factory workers. Johnny asks about gambling, but Hobson denies anything. Johnny tells him that gambling debts could cause someone to burn the building. Hobson tells Johnny that a man had come by last week and made him pay for protection — he paid $100 and told the police who found nothing.

Johnny goes to see McReady about the possibility of extortion. Sgt. Winnick from the police arrives and they talk about Hobson. The police had gone to see

Hobson, but no one else had reported anything. They thought a transient had taken Hobson.

Johnny goes back to Hobson to tell him that he is under suspicion for setting the fire. His story of the protection racket did not hold up. Johnny is not as cautious as the police. Johnny tells Hobson he has looked into his finances and Hobson gets angry. He is in need of $18,000 and the insurance would help. Johnny goes back to Hartford and gets a call from Winnick the next morning. Winnick tells Johnny that Hobson's story is on the level — there was another protection racket try this morning and a shooting at a bowling alley.

Johnny drives back to Waterbury and meets Winnick at the bowling alley. The dead man was a bystander. The owner, Mr. Wrobleski is upset. He shot the man when they told him he was a foreigner and had to pay to work in the city. Carl came in and one of the men shot Carl. Wrobleski shot the other man and the shooter got away. The wounded man is Paul Loner from Chicago. The police are searching for the other man.

Johnny and Winnick go to the hospital to talk to Loner, who has little to say. Johnny tells him that he talked while he was unconscious but he does not believe them and is not going to talk. They found a gun but Loner says it is not his. Winnick says Wrobleski told them Loner was alone, to get information. He had a partner but does not know his name. To trick Loner, Winnick blurts out Bert Lucas' name and Loner is tricked into admitting Bert was his partner. Mr. Hobson comes in and Johnny apologizes for suspecting him. Hobson does not recognize Loner. Loner says both of them torched the Monopoly club because Hobson went to the police. They should have taken $500.

On the way out, a nurse has a call from Loner's wife. Johnny tells her that Paul is all right. She is just down the street. She will meet him downstairs so she will not have to talk to anyone. She knew something bad would happen. The wife tells Johnny that Bert Lucas was with Paul. She knows where Bert is. He is at the place they burned down, and he knows he killed the man at the bowling alley.

Johnny gets Winnick and they go to the Monopoly Club. The police go in with their Thompsons and look for Bert. They call for Lucas and are shot at, wounding an officer in the stomach. Lights are brought into the building and Lucas tries to run but is cut down.

Notes:
- The announcer is **Dick Cutting.**
- Music is by **Wilbur Hatch.**
- This is the same story broadcast with John Lund on 12/1/1953, but with a different cast.
- Story information obtained from the KNX Collection in the Thousand Oaks Library.

Producer: Jaime del Valle   **Writer:**   Gil Doud
Cast: Sammie Hill, Joseph DuVal, Tony Barrett, Parley Baer,

Herb Butterfield, Ted Osborne, Howard Culver, Kay Stewart

♦ ❖ ♦

Show:	**The Lloyd Hammerly Matter**
Show Date:	2/10/1951
Company:	Great Eastern Insurance Company
Agent:	
Exp. Acct:	$2,350.00

Synopsis: Johnny calls Frank to cancel dinner and tells him that he is going to Port Moresby, New Guinea. A man killed in 1942 has been seen alive.

Johnny flies to San Francisco and goes to the *SS Hanford Star* to talk to the first officer, Mr. Carlson. Johnny tells Carlson that he heard about him writing to the Hammerly family about Lloyd. Carlson tells Johnny that he had trained with Lloyd and had gone to the south Pacific with him in 1942, and Hammerly was his navigator. Carlson was sick one day and did not fly a mission to Gona where the plane was shot down and Lloyd was killed. Carlson tells Johnny that he saw Lloyd at the Canberra bar in Port Moresby. He recognized the slouch of his shoulders and called his name. The man turned and looked and walked away. Carlson asked the bartender, who was named Felix, who the man was, and he was given the name Bill Meadows.

Johnny flies to Port Moresby, gets a room in a Chinese hotel, and goes to the Canberra Bar. The bartender tells Johnny that Felix is dead, and that Bill Meadow owns a flying company, Papua Lines. Johnny goes to the office and learns that Bill is on a flight to Wau and will be back the next day. Johnny goes to the local police and talks to Constable Staire, who does not know Meadow, and tells Johnny that men's pasts do not matter there.

Johnny goes to see Mrs. Meadow and tells her why he is there. She tells Johnny that she does not know anyone named Hammerly, and that the story scares her. She tells Johnny that she met Bill four years ago, and they have a son he insisted on naming Lloyd.

The next day Johnny meets Bill Meadow, and half of his face is scarred from burns. Bill tells Johnny that "so it happened", referring to being recognized. Bill tells Johnny that he has been a coward for not going home. He asks Johnny about his family, and Johnny tells him that his father died 2 years ago. Bill asks Johnny to meet him later at his home. Johnny wires the insurance company about the meeting and about Felix being dead.

Johnny goes to meet with Bill and his wife and Bill tells Johnny that he flew on A-20's during the war, and on his last flight, the plane was shot down near a group of whites trying to escape the Japanese. They helped nurse Lloyd back to health, and after the war he picked a new name and bought new identity papers. Bill asks what will happen, and Johnny tells him that the insurance company will probably ask for their money back from the family. Johnny is not sure what the Army will want to do, and that he will not take Bill back with him. Bill tells Johnny that he will not go back. Johnny tells him about Felix the bartender being killed and leaves.

Johnny goes to his hotel and is attacked and shot at three times. Johnny wakes up in the hospital to the voice of Staire. Johnny is told that he was shot and hit with one bullet. Some natives have been arrested, and one had Felix's watch.

The next morning Johnny and Staire go to see Meadow, but he is not home, and has gone on a flight in monsoon weather. They rush to the airfield and the radioman is in contact with the plane, which is coming back from Wewak. Johnny and Staire watch as the plane fails to clear a hill and crashes attempting to land, killing Bill and his wife.

Notes:
- The announcer is Dick Cutting.
- Music is by Wilbur Hatch.
- Johnny is shot for the 2nd time.
- The A-20 "Havoc" was a twin-engine light-bomber/intruder built by Douglas.
- Edmond O'Brien's next movie is *The Redhead and the Cowboy*.
- Story information obtained from the KNX Collection in the Thousand Oaks Library.

Producer: Jaime del Valle Writer: Gil Doud
Cast: Jack Kruschen, Dave Young, Dan O'Herlihy, Francis X. Bushman, Virginia Gregg, Barton Yarborough

♦ ❖ ♦

Show: **The Vivian Fair Matter**
Show Date: 2/17/1951
Company: **Plymouth Insurance Company**
Agent:
Exp. Acct: $150.00

Synopsis: Johnny is called by a man with a tip for the police. He tells Johnny that an insurance company stands to lose $12,000 on a fur coat. Check with Carl Schmidt the jeweler and Oscar Minch the dressmaker in the Bronx. Johnny is also told to check with homicide and ask about Van Courtland Park.

Johnny calls homicide and is told to come immediately. Johnny goes to New York City and meets with Lt. Maguire and tells him about the call. Johnny is shown the file on a body that was found by a truck driver. There were no labels in the clothes and the shoes and purse were missing. Johnny calls the insurance company and gets a list of 14 names.

Johnny goes to see both Schmidt and Minch, and neither of them knows anything. Johnny goes back to the police and learns that the body has been identified by Mrs. Kaley as her sister, Vivian Fair. She tells Johnny that her sister always had men troubles and did not know right from wrong. Johnny calls the insurance company and learns that a policy had been issued in 1949 for a fur coat and two bracelets. Johnny goes to the apartment of Vivian and finds it a mess. Johnny finds a pair of shoes by the sofa, and there is a bloodstain on the heel. Johnny also finds a book that outlines her social life and blackmail. Johnny also finds a ledger book for a loan to her brother-in-law Vincent Kaley.

Johnny goes to see Mrs. Kaley. While he is there Maguire breaks in to search the apartment and asks Johnny about Vincent. Johnny is told that Vincent killed Vivian because she laughed at him, and that Vivian did not want him around because he was a cheap moocher.

Johnny goes to see Mr. Schmidt again, and after searching his records find a sale for a sapphire pendant, which Johnny forwards to Maguire. Johnny goes to his hotel and gets a message from the anonymous caller, who has seen the papers. He tells Johnny that Vincent did not kill Vivian. Johnny is told to meet the caller at a fruit stand on 59th street.

Johnny goes and buys a paper and sees a story about a wife killing her husband. Johnny meets with Vincent Kaley, and he knows who killed Vivian. Vincent tells Johnny that he had lost his job as a machinist and had borrowed money from Vivian, who loved to laugh at people who had to borrow money. She told Vincent to go away and bragged to him about her insurance. He had told some men named Lester and Jerry about the insurance and gave them a key to the apartment. Lester and Jerry waited for Vivian in her apartment, and she hit Lester during the robbery. Vincent was supposed to get part of the money and gives Johnny their address. Johnny takes Vincent to the police, and they go to the address for the men. The police find Lester in the apartment, and he blames Jerry for killing Vivian.

Notes:
- The announcer is Dick Cutting.
- Music is by Wilbur Hatch.
- Story information obtained from the KNX Collection in the Thousand Oaks Library.

Producer:	Jaime del Valle	Writer:	Gil Doud
Cast:	Stacy Harris, Wally Maher, Sidney Miller, Jeanne Bates		

♦ ❖ ♦

Show: The Jarvis Wilder Matter
Show Date: 2/24/1951
Company: Britannia Life Insurance Company
Agent:
Exp. Acct: $540.00

Synopsis: Johnny calls Mr. Mitchell Kendle, the defense attorney for Alma Wilder, to tell him that he is coming to look into the murder but the insurance is not a factor.

Johnny goes to Farmington, New Mexico where the newspaper is reporting that the grand jury is ready to indict Alma for murdering her husband. Mr. Kendle tells Johnny that Alma has confessed, and that he was hoping for a self-defense and temporary insanity plea. Johnny tells Kendle that Alma gets no insurance. Kendle tells Johnny to be careful if he goes to the ranch, as the

Wilders are the most hated people in this area for two generations. Russell, the twin of Jarvis, has all of Jarvis' bad qualities.

Johnny goes to the Wilder ranch and talks to an old ranch-hand. After gaining his confidence, the hand tells Johnny that Alma didn't shoot anyone. He had heard Jarvis yelling. When he came out of his cabin, he saw Alma lying on the ground on her belly with the gun beside Jarvis.

Johnny goes to see the police for details of the shooting. Johnny then visits Alma, who is 24. She tells Johnny that Jarvis was a cruel man. She is happy in jail, the happiest she has been in three years. She wants to forget her past life. Johnny asks if someone killed Jarvis for her, but she tells Johnny that she has no friends, and was not allowed out of the house. "Now leave me alone" she tells Johnny.

Johnny goes to see Kendle and asks why a woman would stay with a man she hated. Kendle tells Johnny that she had left once before, and Jarvis had beaten her. Johnny tells Kendall of his theory and Kendle is interested. Johnny goes to the police and they are interested. They agree to perform a paraffin test and to do tests on the rifle.

Johnny goes to see Russell Wilder, who tells Johnny to get out. Johnny tells Russell that he came to investigate the insurance claim and was told there were no problems. Russell gets belligerent when Johnny tells Russell that he killed Jarvis. Why were you out at 11 p.m.? What did you have to gain? Russell tells Johnny that he saw her kill Jarvis, and that he does pretty much what he thinks ought to be done.

Johnny goes to see Alma again and asks her about the night of the killing. She tells Johnny that she was trying to leave and had taken a rifle with her. Jarvis caught her and she shot him. Johnny is suspicious, as Johnny asks her about the rifle, and she does not even know how to cock the rifle. Johnny is then summoned to see the chief deputy. He tells Johnny that in looking at the murder weapon, they have found dirt in the butt plate. He also tells Johnny that the coroner's report also showed teeth marks on Jarvis' arm. They tested a similar rifle and got dirt into its butt plate. Johnny confronts Alma with a story that she was trying to leave and Jarvis tried to stop her. She bit him, and the rifle dropped to the ground and went off. She finally admits to Johnny that his theory is what really happened. She wants to stay in jail, as Russell said that if the police did not convict her, he would kill her, and Russell always does what he says he will do.

Alma is losing her freedom but spending it in a hospital where she is expected to recover.

Notes:
- Edmond O'Brien's new movie is *The Redhead and the Cowboy.*
- Dick Cutting is the announcer.
- Music is by Wilbur Hatch.

Producer: Jaime del Valle   Writer: Gil Doud

Cast:	Parley Baer, Tim Graham, William Conrad, Herb Butterfield, Mary Lansing

♦ ❖ ♦

Show:	**The Celia Woodstock Matter**
Show Date:	**3/3/1951**
Company:	**Washingtonian Life Insurance Company**
Agent:	**Sam Miller**
Exp. Acct:	**$73.60**

Synopsis: Captain Lyle Woodstock returns Johnny's call. Woodstock tells Johnny that there is no trouble with his wife's disappearance. At least not yet.

Johnny rents a car and drives to Bridgeport, Connecticut to meet with Captain Lyle Woodstock — captain only because he owns a 64-foot schooner. Lyle tells Johnny that he has discharged the servants and had lied to Mr. Miller about fearing for his wife's life. He had wasted money on a detective, David Slater, to follow his wife and asked the insurance company for help. Woodstock gives Johnny a folder about his wife, who is 27. He met her in Mexico and married her. They both like adventure. Woodstock is suspicious, as Celia has been seeing too much of Dr. Masterson in town. She sees him three times a week but she seems very healthy. Now she had disappeared.

Johnny goes to see Slater, who tells Johnny of the doctor visits and of losing her on a train to New York City after she took $2,000 from the bank. Slater had overheard a phone conversation with a man named Sprague. Johnny decides to tell Woodstock he is dropping the case as he gave up chasing wives a long time ago.

At the Woodstock house, a nervous man with a gun meets Johnny at the door. Johnny is locked in a closet and the man leaves. Johnny breaks out of the closet and finds Celia Woodstock shot on the floor. Johnny tries to call the police but the phone is dead, so he calls the police from a neighboring house. The police arrive and take Celia to the hospital. Johnny tells his story to Lt. Al Jester. Johnny remembers the man carrying a cheap nickel-plated .32. The police find another body upstairs and Johnny goes up stairs with Jester.

In a bedroom they find Capt. Woodstock with a .38 beside him. He has been shot in the back. Johnny gets a hotel room and the next day he talks to Dr. Masterson's former nurse, Janet Squire. Janet tells Johnny that she did not know of any romantic involvement between Dr. Masterson and Celia Woodstock, nor does she know a man named Sprague.

Johnny checks in with Jester and learns nothing. Johnny goes to see Dr. Masterson who wants his name kept out of the papers. He tells Johnny that Celia came to him for a sinus condition. She seemed satisfied with her husband and looked forward to a trip to South America. He tells Johnny that during one visit, Mrs. Woodstock became hysterical when the receptionist mentioned a call for "Mrs. Emile Sprague". Johnny reports in to Jester and learns that Celia was shot with a .38, Lyle by a .32, and there is no sign of Sprague.

Around midnight Celia recovers consciousness and at 3 a.m. talks to Johnny and Jester. She tells them that she was in the house when Emile killed

Woodstock and that she is really Mrs. Sprague. She married Lyle in Mexico and Emile found out and wanted money. She met him in New York and gave him the $2,000. Then he followed her to Bridgeport and forced her to take him to see Lyle. Lyle shot her and Sprague shot Lyle. Emile has an apartment on Commerce Street.

Johnny and Jester go to the apartment around 3:30 a.m. and surround it. Johnny sees Sprague watching them from the window as they go in. Johnny calls on a pay phone and urges Sprague to surrender. He tells Johnny that he shot Woodstock because he thought Celia was dead. Sprague runs from the apartment shooting and is killed.

I understand that the lawyers are now working to kick the bigamist wife out of the estate. I doubt that the insurance company has a chance of doing the same with the insurance money.

Notes:
- Edmond O'Brien's new movie is *The Redhead and the Cowboy.*
- The script page for this program lists Raymond Burr, but he is announced as Ray Hartman in the credits at the end of the program. See the notes in the next program, *The Stanley Springs Matter.*
- Dick Cutting is the announcer.
- Music is by Wilbur Hatch.
- *My Favorite Husband* is previewed.
- *Vaughn Monroe* is on next.

Producer:	Jaime del Valle	Writer:	Gil Doud
Cast:	Francis X. Bushman, Jim Nusser, Ted Osborne, Lurene Tuttle, William Johnstone, Tudor Owen, Ray Hartman		

♦ ❖ ♦

Show:	**The Stanley Springs Matter**
Show Date:	3/10/1951
Company:	**Financial Surety**
Agent:	**Ed Best**
Exp. Acct:	$0.00

Synopsis: Ed Best from Financial Surety calls about a problem with a cotton plant they own in the southwest. Someone says that illegal activities are being carried on.

Johnny cabs to "Insurance Row" and meets Mr. Best. Financial Surety has received an anonymous letter about illegal shipments. While it may be a crank, they do not want to go to the feds without evidence.

Johnny travels by plane, train and bus to get to Stanley Springs, a dusty depression in the desert. Johnny checks into the only hotel and is immediately approached by a girl named Ann Salvar. She lives in the hotel and wants to talk. Johnny thinks her curiosity might be a good way to check out strangers. Johnny tells her that he is in town researching a magazine article.

Johnny goes to the Stanley Springs office and meets Norman Staiger the manager. Staiger tells Johnny that they are a small outfit, just like others, and that there is a lot of work to do this week, so Johnny will have to talk to people after hours. Staiger introduces Mr. Phillips, the chief clerk, and Mr. Childs, the shipping clerk. Phillips is surprised when he meets Johnny and Staiger sees it.

Childs takes Johnny to the loading dock to watch bales being loaded. When Johnny returns Phillips is gone, and he is told that he went home sick. "Maybe he worries too much. You might want to go see him, he might be sicker than you think" Staiger tells Johnny.

Johnny goes to Phillips' house but no one answers. Johnny enters and sees a picture of Ann on the coffee table. That night, Johnny goes to hear Ann entertain and asks about Phillips. She tells Johnny to go away and she will see him at 4:00AM when she is off. Later she comes to Johnny's room and asks Johnny who he really is. When Johnny asks if she were expecting someone from the east, she tells Johnny that Phillips had smuggled a letter out of town. She tells Johnny that Staiger is smuggling narcotics, that Phillips found out, and Staiger would not let him leave town. She knows about it, and she cannot leave town either. Johnny tells her that he will call the Feds, but Ann tells him that there is only one phone in town, and it is in Staiger's office.

Johnny goes out and is met by Childs and another man. Childs tells Johnny that he saw Phillips come home last night around 9:00. Johnny goes to Phillips' home and finds him there with a .38 in his hand and a hole in his temple and another faint clue. The deputy sheriff is called and the body is taken out and the room examined. Johnny goes to see Ann and tells her of Phillips death. He tells Ann to stay in his room and let no one in. Johnny walks towards the bus depot followed by two men who are ready to keep him off a bus.

After breakfast, Johnny goes to the office and tells Staiger that Phillips was not a suicide. Johnny tells him that he had smelled chloroform. Johnny tells Staiger that they both know that Phillips was chloroformed and that someone put the gun in his hand and helped him pull the trigger. Staiger is told that he has been sitting on a good thing for a long time, and the town is a front for his operation, but he cannot control Johnny. Staiger tells Johnny to keep his empty accusations to himself. When Johnny tries to use the phone, he is beaten and told it is for employees only.

Johnny goes to the hotel room and Ann fixes his wounds. When asked why she is so calm, she tells Johnny that she has been afraid of many other things. She leaves and Johnny never sees her again.

Johnny goes to the office with his automatic. Childs is there and Johnny threatens to kill him if he does not tell him where Ann is. Childs says he does not know, so Johnny asks for Staiger. Johnny threatens again to kill him and Childs takes Johnny to Staiger in one of the warehouses. Staiger tells Johnny he is in trouble for beating Childs. He does not know where Ann is and is tired of Johnny's nonsense and walks off. Johnny shoots Staiger and wounds him to stop him from leaving. Johnny asks Childs to take him to the sheriff, as he wants to be arrested.

Johnny gets a lawyer, Ann is found alive and the Feds come to investigate. His expense account is not complete, as he is mailing it from jail.

Notes:
- The program announces special guest "Yours Truly, Olga San Juan" who was a radio and movie star of the 40's and 50's where she was typically cast as a gorgeous Latina spitfire. She was also married to Edmond O'Brien at the time.
- The script title page lists Raymond Burr as Norman Staiger, but there is a penciled notation "always Ray Hartman for R. Burr".
- Edmond O'Brien's new movie is *The Redhead and the Cowboy*.
- Dick Cutting is the announcer.
- Music is by Wilbur Hatch.

Producer:	Jaime del Valle	Writer:	Gil Doud
Cast:	Ray Hartman, William Conrad, Herb Butterfield, Olga San Juan		

• ❖ •

Show: **The Emil Lovett Matter**
Show Date: 3/17/1951
Company: **Columbia All-Risk**
Agent:
Exp. Acct: $93.45

Synopsis: Johnny is called by Sgt. Wybeck, who tells Johnny that the widow is still too sick to see. The girl is with her mother, a great motive for suicide.

Johnny goes to New York City and meets the mother-in-law of Emil Lovett, Mrs. Mueler, who is with Wybeck. Johnny learns that Emil has a criminal record. She tells Wybeck that Emil was a fence and shows Johnny and Wybeck where Emil was shot three times in the back while in his pajamas. The police find $500 in the bedroom, and a bolt of cloth. They wonder how Emil got that much money working in a poultry store for $35 a week.

Johnny goes to see Mrs. Mueler, who tells Johnny that she is ashamed of Emil. He was a thief and she did not talk to him. Johnny meets a "chunky brunette" wearing a negligee and mules who is Emil's wife Lila. Mrs. Mueler leaves, and Lila tells Johnny that she did not know her husband too well. He had brought the cloth to make curtains from, and always seems to have money. She tells Johnny that she was told to go for a walk just before Emil was killed, and a neighbor told her of the killing.

The police report showed that no one heard the shots that night. The parole board knew that Emil had met Rose DeLancey, and her boyfriend Frank is brought in. He tells the police that he knew Emil, but denies killing him, even though he was seeing Rose. The police identify the bolt of cloth as coming from a robbery, which confirms that Emil was a fence.

Johnny goes to see Rose and she tells Johnny that she has known Emil for six years and denies going with Frank. Johnny rushes to Lila's apartment where he meets Wybeck, who tells him that two hoodlums broke in and one was shot and has been taken to the hospital. Lila is questioned, but does not know the men, who wanted to know who killed Emil. Her mother-in-law was shopping at the time. The police decide to take Lila in. Johnny goes to the jail to talk to Joseph Maschiano in his cell. Joe has a record, and tells Johnny that he did not kill Emil, and tells Johnny to see his lawyer, Charles Hagan.

Johnny goes to see Hagan, who accuses the police of going by the regulations to solve the murder. He tells Johnny that Joe and his associate were doing their own investigation, and that if Emil were a fence, his customers would not kill him. Johnny tells Wybeck and he tells Johnny that there have been a number of robberies on the east side, but there has been little progress, and a good fence is the reason. Johnny goes back to see Joe, and he tells Johnny that Emil was an important man, and the boys miss him. Johnny visits Lila in jail, and Mrs. Mueler yells at her. Johnny tells Lila that she killed Emil, and she admits that she shot him with his own gun. She shot him because she just got sick of him.

Notes:
- The announcer is Dick Cutting.
- Music is by Wilbur Hatch.
- Story information obtained from the KNX Collection in the Thousand Oaks Library.

Producer:	Jaime del Valle	Writer:	Gil Doud
Cast:	William Conrad, Jeanette Nolan, Mary Lansing, Herb Butterfield, Jack Moyles		

• ❖ •

Show:	**The Byron Hayes Matter**
Show Date:	**3/24/1951**
Company:	**Corinthian All Risk Insurance Company**
Agent:	
Exp. Acct:	**$180.80**

Synopsis: Johnny gets a call from a man who has information about the Byron Hayes killing. The caller is Roy Corona, the chief suspect, and he wants to talk. A friend will tell Johnny where he is to go and what he needs to do to be picked up.

Johnny goes to New York City to work on the Byron Hayes murder, but there is little information to go on. Johnny gets a call from Roy Corona who wants to talk. Roy tells Johnny where he is to be picked up, and Johnny goes out to wait.

A car picks up Johnny and he is taken to meet Roy. Roy tells Johnny that he is the natural suspect because his girlfriend was seeing Byron when he got out of prison. He has witnesses, but they are all ex-cons too, and the police would not believe him. Roy tells Johnny that he was waiting outside her apartment and overheard Byron telling Rita that he could no longer pay her, and that he was not going to see her anymore. Roy is sure that she was blackmailing him. He left the apartment and she shot him. Johnny agrees not to tell the police yet.

Johnny goes to see Rita Cobb, who tells Johnny that she only knew Byron casually. He was just an acquaintance.

Johnny goes to see Mrs. Hayes, who is adamant that her husband was much too upright and respectable to have been seeing her and was not paying her. Rita was lying.

Johnny goes to Rita and asks why she is withholding information. She says she only met Hayes once or twice. Johnny asks her about Arnold Smith and Earl French, who also were her "friends". Was she blackmailing them too, Johnny asks. She tells Johnny that she was afraid to tell about the others. Johnny leaves and calls Rita from the corner and, as suspected, her phone is busy as she is warning someone.

Later Johnny gets a call from Earl Fischer in his hotel room. Earl wants to talk to Johnny confidentially. He tells Johnny that Rita had threatened him, and he must look after his reputation.

Johnny leaves to meet Earl at a bar and is shot at as he exits the hotel. A police patrolman takes Johnny's statement and Lt. Middleton arrives. Johnny tells him of the lead from Rita and tells Middleton that he must keep his source confidential. Johnny has no proof that Fischer tried to shoot him, so Middleton goes to arrest Rita. Johnny calls the bar but the bartender does not know an Earl Fischer.

Johnny goes to the Hayes residence and gets tough with Mrs. Hayes. She seems to be worried more with her reputation than her dead husband. Johnny suggests that maybe she shot him. Mrs. Hayes finally admits to knowing about Rita and the blackmail. She tells Johnny that she thinks the death is her fault, as she was over righteous and forced Byron to go to Rita. She tells Johnny that a man had come to her and told her about Rita and she confronted Byron with the information. She gives Johnny a perfect description of Roy Corona!

Johnny tells Middleton of the conversation and they question Rita. She calls the money she got "loans". Byron had come by for a visit and after he left she heard shots. She came out and found him in the hallway. Johnny tells her that they have proof of blackmail and are going to charge her with murder.

Later Johnny gets a call from Roy and he admits that he killed Hayes and wants to give up. Come and get me before I change my mind.

Johnny calls Middleton and they go to the location where Roy is. There is an exchange of gunfire, but Roy is not killed. Roy tells Johnny that he started the whole thing when he got out of prison and found out Rita was seeing other men. He wanted to frame her but Johnny tells Roy that Rita has confessed and the murder weapon was found in her apartment.

Johnny reports that Earl Fischer was brought in for questioning and released, but Johnny saw his wife, and Mr. Fisher is a condemned man.

Notes:
- Edmond O'Brien's new movie is *The Redhead and the Cowboy*.
- There is a mid-program commercial for *Gang Busters*.
- Dick Cutting is the announcer.
- Music is by Wilbur Hatch.

Producer:	Jaime del Valle Writer: Gil Doud
Cast:	Jim Nusser, Lee Patrick, Jeanne Bates, Ed Begley, Jack Moyles

◆ ❖ ◆

Show:	The Jackie Cleaver Matter
Show Date:	3/31/1951
Company:	Sierra All-Risk
Agent:	Carl Mason
Exp. Acct:	$280.00

Synopsis: Carl Mason from Sierra All-Risk calls Johnny and asks him to assist in looking for a policy beneficiary who has disappeared. Carl got a letter from the client last week and does not understand why she has disappeared so quickly.

Johnny meets Carl Mason, who tells Johnny about the death of Howard Shumaker, who had left a $40,000 policy to Jackie Cleaver, his ex-wife. Mason's last letters from Jackie came from Manchester, New Hampshire. Now she has disappeared.

Johnny rents a car and drives to the address in Manchester, which is a convalescent home. The manager, Mr. Forslund, tells Johnny that Jackie has moved out, and that she probably is in Middleton. She had no visitors and got checks from California twice a month.

Johnny gets an address from the local post office and drives to Middleton where she has moved out of the ratty hotel she was staying in. The manager thinks she went to New Haven and mentions also getting alimony checks from California. On the way out, a little man tells Johnny that he can help Johnny find Jackie, as she is a friend and maybe she does not want to be found. He will call Johnny the next day.

Johnny calls Mason from his apartment to tell about the man he met, and that he thinks Jackie is on the run. As soon as Johnny hangs up, there is a knock on the door. At the door is the man with a friend named Bert who invite themselves in and ask Johnny about Mason. The small man, who is named Happy, finds Mason's card and as Johnny tries to get it back is slugged. Johnny is told to stop looking for Jackie, as there is going to be trouble. Bert leaves to go to the hotel to see Mason while Happy waits, and then leaves after 25 minutes. Johnny goes to the hotel and finds a dead man in the bathroom, Bert! The police are called and Lt. Schiller gets Johnny's story and "encourages" Johnny to continue with his investigation.

Johnny wires a detective agency in California for information on Mason and Jackie, and then goes back to the hotel in Middleton to find more about Happy.

The desk clerk tells Johnny that his name is Snell Chapman, and that he has a girlfriend there in the hotel. Johnny is told that Snell hangs out at a couple bars in the area. Johnny tells the manager to have Happy call if she sees him, and starts visiting the bars.

At the first one, Johnny orders a dark rum and gets no information from the bar tender. On the way out, Happy meets Johnny in the parking lot. He knows that Bert is dead, but he can get Johnny in touch with Jackie. Johnny tells him that the police want to talk to Jackie too. Happy will call Johnny the next morning.

In the morning Johnny gets a reply from the agency in California. Mason is a disbarred lawyer who worked for a syndicate on the west coast, and Jackie was the star witness who helped break up the syndicate. Mason calls Johnny and wants to give up. He tells Johnny that he killed Bert in self-defense and needs Johnny's testimony. Johnny agrees to meet him after noon. Happy calls and agrees to meet Johnny at Schiller's office at 11:30.

Johnny meets Happy and Jackie at Schiller's office. She is surprised that they know what they do, as her testimony was supposed to have been kept quiet. She also tells them that her lawyer in Los Angeles sends the money as part of her testimony agreement.

Later, Johnny goes to meet Mason at a drug store. Mason tells Johnny that Jackie talked because she was a plant from the rival syndicate who moved in after the first one was broken up. They leave for the police and Happy meets them on the street and kills Mason. Happy is arrested and the police are looking for Jackie.

Since Mason was not associated with Sierra, Johnny hardly expects them to pay his expenses, but hopes they will learn what goes on behind their back.

Notes:
- Edmond O'Brien's new movie is *War Path*.
- This program was originally scheduled to air on December 9, 1950, but was pre-empted by the Hollywood Gold Cup horse race.
- The reference to *War Path* indicates that this program was the original version of the program as in the previous program, O'Brien's latest movie is *The Redhead and the Cowboy*.
- Dan Cubberly is the announcer.
- Music is by Wilbur Hatch.

Producer:	Jaime del Valle	Writer:	Gil Doud
Cast:	Ed Begley, Dick Ryan, Mary Lansing, Sidney Miller, Tim Graham, Virginia Gregg, Hy Averback, Jim Nusser		

Show: The Edward French Matter
Show Date: 4/7/1951
Company: Tri-State Insurance Group
Agent:
Exp. Acct: $2739.50

Synopsis: Mrs. French calls and Johnny advises her that the insurance company has authorized him to look for her son Edward French in the Malay States.

Johnny travels to Chicago to speak with Mrs. French. Johnny learns that Edward had left the states to manage a tea plantation with his English wife. The tea was sold to the Jewel Tea Company. On a trip to Singapore, Edward had disappeared. Johnny is looking into the matter for Tri-State.

Johnny travels for a week to get to the Singapore tea merchant Mr. Neeps, who tells Johnny that French had been there and had left after one day. Johnny is told not to worry, as French is impulsive and does things people tell him not to.

Johnny takes an armored train to Raub, Malaysia and is met by an armored jeep for the trip to the police. Johnny learns that Constable Whitlow, who had filed the report, has been killed in an attack by the bandits. Constable Downs advises Johnny that the bandits have just attacked the neighboring plantation owned by Mr. Stewart. Downs thinks that kidnapping may be the cause of French's disappearance, as the vehicle is missing and the body had not been found, and that is most unusual.

Johnny takes the armored police jeep to the French plantation and notes the well-armed enclosure. Johnny meets Mrs. French. As she is explaining that Edward had driven to Singapore, gunfire erupts. Keith Stewart arrives, fleeting glances are exchanged with Mrs. French, and a warning is given for an impending attack that night. Johnny is told to spend the night. Unable to sleep, Johnny goes to the veranda and overhears Keith and Mrs. French talking and there is no doubt they are involved in a plot concerning Edward. The attack comes and Johnny is given a Thompson sub-machine gun and joins in fighting off the 100 insurgents.

Johnny goes to Constable Downs and asks him to call a meeting of all the plantation owners so that he can talk to Mrs. Stewart alone. The meeting is called and Johnny goes to speak with Mrs. Stewart, who is a frail fever-wracked woman who knows of her husband's affair with Mrs. French. She tells Johnny that any future plans Keith might have will concern her, unless he kills her first, and sometimes she wishes he would. She does tell Johnny that her husband was gone for some time a month ago, when Edward disappeared.

Johnny goes to the French plantation and is met by Keith, who knows he has been to see his wife, but warns Johnny that she makes up things in her fevers. Johnny tells him of overhearing the conversation on the veranda. Mrs. French comes in and denies Keith's involvement and says the natives killed her husband. Johnny tells them that the police are searching for alibis and Keith admits he had met French on the road and shot him.

Johnny takes his gun and they go back to the Stewart plantation and are met by a man — Edward French! French tells Johnny and Keith that he had stayed alive after Keith had shot him. Now Keith will die, and he shoots Keith 6 times.

French had made his way to a local hospital where he had recovered anonymously. Now he is being held for murder.

Notes:
- Jewel Tea was a Chicago based tea company.
- Edmond O'Brien's new movie is *The Redhead and the Cowboy*.
- Dan Cubberly is the announcer.
- Music is by Wilbur Hatch.

Producer: Jaime del Valle   Writer: Gil Doud
Cast: Jeanette Nolan, John McIntire, Tudor Owen, Maria Palmer, Dan O'Herlihy

◆ ❖ ◆

Show: **The Mickey McQueen Matter**
Show Date: 4/14/1951
Company: **Hartford Police Department**
Agent:
Exp. Acct: $0.00

Synopsis: Johnny's old friend Mickey McQueen, an old-style Irish cop in Hartford, Connecticut calls him and wants to talk.

Mickey comes to Johnny's apartment at 2:00 in the morning, but just can't say what he wants to. Mickey tells Johnny that he is being moved to a desk job, but there is "murder being planned and being done" but no one can stop it. Mickey leaves and the next day Johnny goes to Mickey's apartment.

Johnny is met by a distraught woman who points Johnny to a small door, a closet containing Mickey's uniforms and a dead Mickey McQueen, hanging from the clothes pole with his belt. The woman is Mickey's wife Thelma. She is young and attractive, with natural platinum blond hair. She tells Johnny that she was leaving Mickey and had come back to get her clothes. He was a kind and wonderful person, with not an enemy in the world. She tells Johnny that she had met Mickey after his wife had died. Johnny tells her that he thinks Mickey was murdered. A search of the apartment finds nothing, so Johnny calls the police and leaves.

That night Johnny follows Mickey's beat and talks to his friends. At the Cedrick Hotel, Johnny talks to the house detective, Ned Martin. Johnny tells him about Mickey's visit and Ned tells Johnny that he had talked to Mickey last night and he seemed down about his new desk job. Ned tells Johnny that Mickey's wife, Thelma Weaver, had done time in Joliet. Ned tells Johnny to drop the case, but Johnny wants to know more. If you want to find out more, see Fred Ku at the Calcutta Club, but don't tell him I sent you adds Ned.

Johnny goes to see Fred Ku, who is half oriental. Johnny feels he could retire from 10% of the bail posted by the customers in the bar. Fred takes Johnny to the office and tells Johnny that Mickey was a nice guy and that he did not take payoffs, and that he left Fred alone. Fred tells Johnny that he did not know Mickey's wife. Fred is called out of the office and Johnny looks around for another exit. The door opens and Thelma comes in and points a Colt .25 revolver at Johnny when he mentions Thelma Weaver.

Johnny throws ink on Thelma and is able to get the gun away from Thelma and tells her he knows of her past. She tells Johnny she had met Mickey after his first wife had died. She tells Johnny that she got out of prison and gave her friends in Chicago the slip. Mickey had arrested her for vagrancy and came back the next day to bail her out. She had used Mickey's soft side to get information for her friends from Chicago, who are outside in the bar. Mickey was being transferred to the police arsenal, and the boys wanted the keys. They wanted explosives for a jewel robbery at the Marquart Building. Roy Weaver, her husband had threatened to tell Mickey she was a bigamist unless Mickey helped him. She tells Johnny that Roy had taken the keys from Mickey and then Roy killed Mickey. Johnny tries to leave, but Roy comes in and objects. Roy thanks Thelma for warning him. Johnny is taken to an old wine cellar and slugged.

When Johnny wakes up he discovers he is in an old wine cellar filled with burglary tools. Johnny figures out the situation and tries to find a way out. When the door opens, he fakes being unconscious and hears the men take out the tools to the cars where Fred has the explosives from the arsenal.

After the men leave with Thelma, Johnny tries to force his way out. Johnny hears the door open and Ned Martin is there. He tells Johnny that a woman had called to say Johnny was locked in the bar and something was going to happen. Johnny tells Ned what is planned and Ned takes Johnny to the area of the Marquart Building, where Johnny sees the cars being unloaded. Johnny sees Thelma walking towards him. Roy calls to her and she turns and fires into the first car, igniting the cordite powder, which explodes. Thelma is shot, but she turns on the ground and hits the second car, which explodes.

Johnny gets to her in time for her to say that Mickey would be proud of her. She tells Johnny that they cannot send her back to Joliet, and then she dies. Ray Weaver lives long enough to sign a confession that he killed Mickey McQueen.

Notes:
- This is a repeat of the 8/17/50 program. The program is essentially the same script with minor changes in the small talk and descriptive language. The background music in the bar is different. Some cast members are different.
- **Once again, Raymond Burr is named as Ray Hartman in the credits.**
- **Edmond O'Brien's new movie is *The Redhead and the Cowboy*.**
- **Dick Cutting is the announcer.**
- **Music is by Wilbur Hatch.**

Producer:	Jaime del Valle	Writer:	Gil Doud
Cast:	William Conrad, Martha Wentworth, Herb Butterfield, Jack Moyles, Ray Hartman		

• ❖ •

Show: The Willard South Matter
Show Date: 4/21/1951
Company: Great Eastern Insurance Company
Agent:
Exp. Acct: $373.00

Synopsis: Lou Krager calls Johnny and tells him that the boat belonging to Willard South has been found. It was empty and there were signs of trouble. Lou will meet Johnny at the police dock.

Johnny goes to Charlotte Amalie, Virgin Islands to investigate the disappearance of Willard and Georgina South. Johnny meets with Lou Krager who tells Johnny that the boat was found with no one on board. Johnny meets Officer Shoy who is investigating the case and he shows Johnny a bullet in the woodwork and bloodstains on the deck indicating that maybe someone pushed them overboard. Johnny is told that a lot of people disliked Mr. South, especially men whose wives were involved with Willard. Shoy shows Johnny a cut rope used to trail a dinghy, and Lou confirms that South always trailed a small skiff behind the boat.

Johnny goes to see Willard South's foster-mother but meets his brother Paul, who lives in Florida. The brother tells Johnny that he had been out searching as well. Johnny mentions Willard's bad reputation and is told that Willard had a lot of enemies. Johnny is told that the trip was a special occasion so that Georgina would talk to Willard. Mrs. South arrives and tells Johnny that she has come to expect bad things from Willard. She is sorry for Georgina because she let her marry Willard, who is a beast.

Johnny meets Celeste Robertson who was seen with Willard recently. She tells Johnny that she is on the island getting a divorce. She admits that she has spent some time with him over the past several weeks but had nothing to do with any murder or anything else.

After the Coast Guard planes and boats come back from searching for the small skiff, a radio report is received that Georgina South has been found alive. Johnny and Shoy go to meet the boat that found Georgina. Captain Bracken tells Shoy and Johnny that he found the skiff with her in it, and that she is going directly to Doctor Gar. Bracken tells them that she had seen her husband shot and thrown overboard.

The next day, Johnny and Shoy go to see Georgina South. She is able to recount how she and Willard had left for Calibra and were stopped by a boat claiming that they had run out of gas. A man from the boat came on board and shot Willard. The other man robbed her and threw Willard overboard. Georgina was set adrift in the skiff. The doctor tells Johnny that Georgina is in good shape because she had shelter and water in the skiff. Shoy agrees to wire the prisons in Puerto Rico to check for escapees who might have killed Willard.

Johnny goes to the waterfront to look at the boats again and is stopped by Captain Bracken and Johnny tells him about the possibility of escaped prisoners doing the job. Bracken tells Johnny that it would be fitting if convicts had killed Willard. Johnny examines both boats and finds nothing.

After Shoy gets a reply to his wire, Johnny decides to use the lack of clues as a weapon. Johnny goes to see Lou Krager and asks why he was so quick to help, and Lou tells him that the thought that Johnny needed help and offered it. Johnny tells Lou that he had showed him a cut line on the boat, but the line on the skiff was not cut. Why? You were able to find her when the Coast Guard could not because you knew where she was. Johnny tells him that a doctor will be there to prove that Georgina did not spend three days adrift. Krager gets angry and Bracken has to break up the fight.

Johnny goes to see Georgina at home. Mrs. South tries to protect her, but Johnny accuses her of knowing the truth like everyone else does. Johnny tells her that she should have known she could not have gotten away with it, as there were too many mistakes made. Mrs. South tells Johnny that both of her sons were adopted but Willard was a beast, the worst of heredity and environment. She tells Johnny that she is the murderer, and she had to kill Willard before he destroyed everyone!

Johnny thinks the confession is a fake, but it turns out to be true. There was a lot of conspiracy involved, and the trial will be very interesting.

Notes:
- The closing credits on this broadcast give the actors and their roles: Irene Hubbard is Evangela, Jan Miner is Georgina, Gilbert Mack is Lou, Fran Lafferty is Celeste, Ed Latimer is Sam, Maurice Tarplin is Shoy, Bernard Lenrow is the Doctor. Other actors on the script title page include Staats Cotsworth. All of these actors are based in New York City.
- The script title page for this program notes that the dramatic portion was taped in New York on 4/15/51   a week before broadcast.
- The mid-program commercial is for *Sing It Again*.
- There is a public service announcement about the dangers of forest fires.
- Edmond O'Brien's new movie is *The Redhead and the Cowboy*.
- Olin Tice is the New York announcer.
- Jimmy Mathews is the Hollywood announcer.
- Music is by Wilbur Hatch.

Producer: Jaime del Valle   Writer: Gil Doud
Cast: Irene Hubbard, Jan Miner, Gilbert Mack, Fran Lafferty, Ed Latimer, Maurice Tarplin, Bernard Lenrow, Staats Cotsworth

Show: The Month-End Raid Matter
Show Date: 4/28/1951
Company: Columbia All Risk Insurance Company
Agent:
Exp. Acct: $396.50

Synopsis: Lt. Arneson calls and tells Johnny that he can come down to the hospital whenever Johnny is ready. The driver is not going to live, and the loss is almost $250,000, and very little of the cash was marked.

Johnny goes to Kansas City, Missouri to investigate the $250,000 robbery of an armored car used by the Andover Department Stores. Johnny learns that the receipts from a three-day sale were being picked up when the armored car was robbed. One guard is killed and the driver, Carl Biller, is wounded and expected to die.

Johnny meets Arneson in the hospital and he tells Johnny that the wounded men were shot in cold blood, which means they might have known their killers. Two cars were used in the robbery to box-in the truck in a loading zone. The robbery division has heard rumors of a gang forming in town. While talking to Arneson, Johnny learns that the driver has died.

Johnny talks to Mrs. Biller in the hospital. She tells Johnny that she knew something would happen, what with all that money. Johnny notes that the robbers had shot the guards in cold blood, so maybe they did it to silence men who knew them. She knows of no reason why Carl would have been involved in a robbery. Johnny tells Arneson about the interview, and he decides to send two officers to watch her.

The next day, Johnny and Arneson meet with Emil "The Count" Ordoff, an informant. Emil tells Arneson that he has heard about a gang moving in from Chicago but knows nothing about the Andover job. Emil knows only about men named Pinky, Ross, Shorty and "The Mick". Emil does not want to tell more, as he might get shot too. Arneson is sure the money is in town and sends a wire to Chicago asking for information.

After learning more about the case, Johnny goes to see Mrs. Biller again, and asks her about Betty Claire and why her husband was seeing the wife of a known criminal who just got out of prison. She tells Johnny that she was going to tell the police about her. She had written to the bonding company warning them. She tells Johnny that her husband had seen Betty after her husband had been paroled. She tells Johnny that Carl did not come home the night before the robbery and had come home only to change clothes. Mrs. Biller hopes Betty gets hurt like she has been hurt.

Johnny and Arneson go to the apartment of Betty Claire. There is no answer at the door so they unlock the door and find Betty, choked to death in the kitchen.

There are signs of a struggle and a newspaper in the apartment indicates that Betty had died after Carl Biller. Later that day, the police find a body in a garage in the East Bottom area. The body has a receipt for a package, which is claimed by the police, and contains $15,000. Johnny, Emil and Arneson go to the morgue and Emil recognizes the body as Earl Norworth, a known criminal in Kansas City. Arneson tells Emil that he might have been bought and gives Emil until 10:30 to find out what he can from the streets.

The police sweep the city and the jails fill. A known associate of Arnold Claire, is brought in and he tells Johnny and Arneson that Claire is trying to go straight and is looking for a job and was not involved. The man tells them that he was with Claire and Betty until 2 a.m. before the robbery and that Billers was not there, which is different from what Mrs. Biller had said. A delivery boy can verify that there were only three people there. The man does not know about Betty being killed and tells Arneson that Claire is staying in a shack by the river. As they get ready to leave, Arneson is told that Emil has been killed. Arneson is going to miss him, as he was a good honest stoolie.

A check of the delivery boy confirms that only three people were in the apartment that night. Arneson, Stone and Johnny go to the shack to pick up Claire. Claire is taken without a fight and blames Stone for ratting on him and Stone tells Claire that he has gotten him involved in a murder. Claire admits that he had been trying to go straight, but he had killed his wife. He had killed her because she was involved in the robbery. Mrs. Biller had called him the night her husband died and told him that Betty had planned the job so that he would be blamed and go back to prison. So, he went to see her and killed her. Claire knows one man who was in the robbery, and names him to the police.

That man leads to another and that one to another until the gang is located in a house. Johnny learns that one of the men from Chicago, Ross Degnen, killed the guard only because he was high on narcotics. The police surround the house as the men try to escape in a car. There is a shoot-out and the gang members are killed, and all but $2,000 of the money is recovered.

Remarks: Johnny talked to Mrs. Biller and learned that she had talked to Arnold Claire and told him that Betty had set up the robbery, and she got her revenge — murder. The company owes Mrs. Biller a debt of gratitude, because when that broke, everything broke.

Notes:
- The mid-program commercial is for *Sing It Again*.
- Edmond O'Brien's new movie is *The Redhead and the Cowboy*.
- Dick Cutting is the announcer.
- Music is by Wilbur Hatch.
- There is a public service announcement about the dangers of house fires.

Producer: Jaime del Valle   Writer: Gil Doud
Cast: Herb Butterfield, Joseph DuVal, Virginia Gregg, Sidney Miller, Peter Leeds, Edgar Barrier

Show:	**The Virginia Towne Matter**
Show Date:	**5/5/1951**
Company:	**Plymouth Insurance Company**
Agent:	
Exp. Acct:	**$0.00**

Synopsis: Roy Underwood calls and tells Johnny to come over and he will tell where the stolen jewels are and who stole them.

Johnny goes to New York City, gets a room at the Hotel Bentley, and meets with Roy Underwood in the midst of a party where Johnny is interrupted by a particularly drunken girl. Johnny gives Underwood a list of the stolen jewels and is told that the description of the jewels is correct. Underwood tells Johnny that Virginia Towne stole them. She was at a party in the apartment and he saw her leave with them. He did not call police so he could allow her to think twice. The jewels were in a dresser drawer. She put them on, he told her to take them off and she refused. Johnny gets the address for Francis Adams, a friend of Virginia's.

Johnny goes to the apartment of Francis and meets Virginia at the door. She tells Johnny that the jewels were not stolen, as he gave the jewelry to her. Johnny tells her that without proof of ownership, the jewels belong to the insurer, who is Roy Underhill. She must give them back or Underhill will go to the police. She tells Johnny that she cannot give them all back as she has sold a bracelet at a low price to get money to live and needs $1,500 to cover the price. She tells Johnny that she had told Underwood she didn't want to see him anymore and he laughed at her.

Phil Kelly, a friend of Virginia's comes in and his hands clench as he hears the story. He tells Johnny that Underwood had put Virginia in shows using his influence. He had enjoyed her until he tired of her. Phil then tells Johnny that he stole the jewels to cover for her. Johnny does not want to see her arrested, so he tells Virginia that he will stall Underwood for two days. That is the best he can do and will check back tomorrow.

The next day Johnny checks in, and Phil is out raising money. On the third day, Virginia tells Johnny that the bracelet has been cut up, so they cannot get it back. She tells Johnny, "The next time I see you, you won't be my friend, just another man with some evidence", and wants to go out for a drink.

Next day Johnny goes to see Underwood, with the jewels. The missing piece is listed for $2,400, and Underwood signs the claim form. "I cannot afford to be taken advantage of by every young thing that happens along" he tells Johnny.

Johnny gives his report to the police and goes to his hotel to pack. Lt. Brinker comes to his room and tells Johnny that the jewels are missing again, and that Underwood has been shot to death in his apartment.

Johnny is told that Alice Breen, the drunken woman at the first party, had heard screaming and entered the apartment and found Underwood dead. She is being held as a material witness. Johnny goes over his story to the police and wonders if Virginia Towne could have re-stolen the jewels. Brinker tells Johnny that Underwood was ruthless in getting rid of women. The police allow Johnny to work alone in getting the facts from Virginia, even though the police know that Johnny had found Virginia before his report said he did.

Johnny goes to the apartment and both Virginia and Francis are gone. Johnny finds Phil, and he has not heard of the killing and does not know the whereabouts of Francis or Virginia. He tells Johnny that maybe she is looking for Johnny.

Phil takes Johnny to Virginia, in a room near the waterfront. Johnny tells Virginia that Phil brought him and tells her that Underwood is dead. She tells Johnny that she is hiding because she did not want to be arrested. She came here to hide from Underwood. "You have lied to me, and I believed them because I wanted to" Johnny tells her. Johnny tells Virginia that the police learned that Underwood bought all of the pieces at an auction last year. Johnny tells her that the jeweler says he told you he was going to cut up the bracelet. "I gave you three days, and now I am in trouble. I must clear myself with the police by taking you in." Johnny takes Virginia to the police in Phil's cab.

Brinker questions Virginia for two hours and then releases Breen. When Johnny leaves he sees Phil outside the police station. Johnny asks him to take him to his hotel, and Phil tells him that he knows she did not do it, as she told him with her eyes. Phil tells Johnny that he killed Underwood. He knew the family and she is a good girl. Johnny tells Phil that the police have the jewels, as Virginia had told them where she took them after she killed him.

Johnny directs the insurance company to send the expense check to Charles Hagen, attorney for the defense in the case of the People vs. Virginia Towne.

Notes:
- There are two version of this program, one with the dramatic portion only, and one with both drama and music.
- This program contains amid-program commercial for *Sing It Again*.
- There is a trailer at the end talking about the threats of communism and the need to buy Defense Bonds.
- Edmond O'Brien's new movie is *The Redhead and the Cowboy*.
- Dan Cubberly is the announcer.
- Music is by Wilbur Hatch.

Producer:	Jaime del Valle	**Writer:**	Gil Doud
Cast:	Ramsey Hill, Jean Wood, Virginia Gregg, Jack Moyles, Ed Begley		

Show:	The Marie Meadows Matter
Show Date:	5/12/1951
Company:	Washingtonian Insurance Company
Agent:	Bill Brandon
Exp. Acct:	$110.40

Synopsis: Bill Brandon calls Johnny about a double murder in Boston, a girl, and her mother. Bill heard about it on the radio, and there is a $50,000 policy that is a week old.

Johnny drives to Boston, Massachusetts and goes to the scene of the murder. The police and the bodies are still there. Johnny meets Sgt. Foley who tells him that the girl was stabbed twice, and her mother was strangled. The other daughter, Celia, found the bodies, and is the second beneficiary on the policy.

Johnny goes to talk to Celia, who is 24, and meets her husband Peter. Peter tells Johnny that Marie liked to hurt people. Irwin Dodge, who works for the phone company, is one of those. Johnny calls a number of other men and finds out that Marie had been involved with Peter also. Johnny calls Foley and learns that the mother was a sculptress, and that Marie was a model. Johnny goes to see Irwin Lodge, and he tells Johnny that her mother was always pushing her, and that her father had been thrown out of the house because he was not good enough for them. Irwin tells Johnny that the father works in a leather shop. Also, Peter married Celia to be near Marie.

Johnny goes to Marie's apartment and the doors are locked. A neighbor tells Johnny that Marie came in around 1:30 that morning. Johnny goes to see the father, Chester Meadows, and learns nothing. Johnny goes to see Foley and learns that Marie had been married to Mark Feedler for three days, and that Mark has skipped town.

The next day Feedler is captured by the police. He tells them that he loves his wife and had dinner with her that night. They had kept the marriage a secret from Marie's mother. He had been out of town looking at a cabin. Mark is released, and Johnny thinks that the mother killed Marie when she found out she had married. The autopsy report gives a sharp triangular weapon as the cause of death.

Johnny goes to the leather shop, and then to a hotel looking for Mr. Meadows. Johnny finds him, but he does not want to talk. Johnny calls the police and he is taken to a hospital to sober up. Johnny goes to see Celia who tells Johnny that her father could not have killed Marie or her mother, and that she and Peter had been at home with friends.

Johnny goes to the apartment with Foley and tells him that the case rests on who could get into the locked apartment. Johnny spots a tree outside and remembers that Dodge works for the phone company. Johnny goes to see Dodge and tells him about cleat marks on the tree outside the apartment. He throws his lines-man cleats at Johnny and tries to run, but Johnny stops him and he confesses to killing Marie and her mother.

Notes:
- The announcer is Dan Cubberly.
- Music is by Wilbur Hatch.
- Story information obtained from the KNX Collection in the Thousand Oaks Library.

Producer:	Jaime del Valle	Writer:	Gil Doud

Cast: Pat McGeehan, Ted Osborne, Robert North, Jeanne Bates, Herb Butterfield, William Johnstone

♦ ❖ ♦

Show: The Jane Doe Matter
Show Date: 5/19/1951
Company: New York Police Department
Agent:
Exp. Acct: $0.00

Synopsis: Lt. William Sexton of the New York police calls Johnny. He wants Johnny to come down and identify a "Jane Doe" who was found in Central Park with Johnny's name and phone number in her pocket.

Johnny goes to New York City, and goes to the morgue, but cannot identify the body. Over lunch Johnny thinks that he might know the girl but cannot remember from where.

Johnny meets with Sexton who tells Johnny that the body was found at 8:30 in Central Park by a delivery truck. She had been killed by a blunt instrument and thrown from a car. Johnny sees the note and recognizes his handwriting.

Johnny goes home and searches his files and finds eight cases that might be relevant. Johnny starts calling the names for the cases, and the fifth name was Sybil Miller. Johnny calls the apartment but is told that Sybil is married and has moved to Kansas or Nebraska. Johnny asks if she was a friend of Rudy Valentine. The manager remembers that a girl visited there two weeks ago and Mr. Koesler talked to her.

Johnny goes back to New York and talks to Mr. Koesler. He remembers seeing the girl but does not know her name. He does remember that she wore a waitress' uniform with "IB" on it.

Johnny starts a search of restaurants and goes to Inez's Basement Bar and Grill where he talks to Munsey and Burke who are hesitant to talk until Johnny mentions murder, then they tell Johnny that "they did it". Johnny is attacked and knocked out.

Johnny wakes up in Central Park and goes to his hotel where he gets fixed up, and then goes to see Sexton and tells him about the bar. Johnny is told that an apartment manager has identified the girl as Margaret Nelson. The manager told the police that the girl was not working and came from the middle west. Johnny and Sexton go to see the manager, Mr. Brimley, and he tells them that the girl came to town recently.

Johnny and Sexton go to the bar and see Burke who tells them that they have not had a waitress for three months, and her name was Mary Keats.

Johnny asks him who they were and he admits that Mary was selling drugs for Munsey and sold up to $15,000 a night. She left and the buyer, who is named Noland, killed her. Burke tells Johnny that Brimley also bought drugs from her also. Munsey comes in, sees the police, runs away and is shot three times.

Notes:
- The announcer is Dick Cutting.
- Music is by Wilbur Hatch.
- Story information obtained from the KNX Collection in the Thousand Oaks Library.

Producer: Jaime del Valle Writer: Gil Doud
Cast: Raymond Burr, Virginia Gregg, Howard McNear, Peter Leeds, Tudor Owen, Jim Nusser

◆ ❖ ◆

Show: **The Lillis Bond Matter**
Show Date: **5/26/1951**
Company: **Great Northern Bonding & Surety**
Agent:
Exp. Acct: **$308.90**

Synopsis: Pat Shade, a private detective working for the bank, calls Johnny. He tells Johnny that he knows Lillis, and he is a nice kid. Pat wants to know if Johnny wants to get together and compare notes. Johnny has no notes, but he will be glad to pick Pat's brain.

Johnny goes to Chicago, Illinois to look into the disappearance of a bank messenger and $80,000. Johnny meets Pat Shade, a detective who works for the bank. Pat knew Henry Lillis and thought he was a bright kid. He had a good reputation because he was bonded. His father had died some years ago and Henry has worked to help support his mother.

Johnny goes to see Mrs. Lillis, who is an attractive woman of forty. She tells Johnny that she knows the police suspect her son, but she is sure that Henry did not do it. She relates that she has not tried to meddle in her son's life, and let Henry work out his own life. She knew few of Henry's friends except for Raymond Lockhart, who works at a gas station.

Johnny goes to talk to Ray and he tells Johnny that he knew Henry and that Henry had a temper at times. Ray tells Johnny that Henry had a girlfriend who had a car, and that she was a "used dish". She had a strange name, but Ray cannot remember it, but her father worked at the bank. "Was the last name Shade?" asks Johnny. Yeah, that's it. Lillian Shade was her name.

Johnny meets with Pat Shade again. Johnny tells Pat that he has not told the police about Lillian yet. Pat tells Johnny that his daughter is away visiting friends somewhere. Pat tells Johnny that she was no good, just like her mother, and had started running around at thirteen. Pat tells Johnny that he did not know that she was seeing Henry. Pat thanks Johnny and tells him he will tell Sgt. Dyer immediately.

Next morning Dyer calls Johnny to tell him that Henry Lillis has turned himself in. Dyer tells Johnny that Henry told them that he had had a fight with an accomplice named Saunders, had hitchhiked into town to surrender and is in the hospital.

Johnny and Dyer go to see Henry in the hospital. Henry tells Johnny that he had pulled the robbery with Lillian Shade and gone to a house in Lake Bluff with Lillian. He tells Johnny that her father had warned him about her once, but he ignored him. He relates that he had met Lillian and they were in the same boat, as they both wanted the things they did not have. She told Henry that she would not marry him unless he was rich. She also told Henry that she had blackmailed some man to get the money for the car. She was always talking about the money Henry carried, so she waited for four days until Henry had a big delivery and then disappeared to the house in Lake Bluff. Later a man named Red Sanders, or maybe it was Saunders, showed up and Lillian told Henry that she was just using him, and told Henry to leave. Henry had a fight with the man and left without any of the money. He had to hitchhike into town, but only a minister would pick him up because of his torn clothes.

The police issue and APB for the man and Lillian Shade. Johnny and Dyer go to the house in Lake Bluff and find a car parked to the side of the house. Johnny and Dyer go in and find evidence of a fight and Lillian Shade in the kitchen, dead. The lab boys are called and Johnny goes to see Pat Shade to follow an idea.

Pat tells Johnny that after he talked to Johnny, he got drunk in the hotel bar. He went home and does not remember anything. When Johnny asks Pat about where he went, and tells Pat that Lillian is dead, Pat is afraid Johnny is trying to accuse him of doing it. Pat tells Johnny that he was so drunk that if he did kill Lillian, he would not remember it.

Johnny goes to see Dyer and reads the lab report. There is only one place to go. In the hospital, Johnny confronts Henry with the lack of car prints from Red Sander's car. There was only one set of car tracks, Lillian's. After being confronted with the facts, Henry admits that she had become scared and wanted to take the money back. He lost his temper and killed her because he thought she was faking, but she wasn't. In his next statement, Henry tells the police where he buried the money, so the company will not lose. But that is more than you can say for the two parents involved, either the deserving or the undeserving.

Notes:
- This program has only the dramatic portion because announcements and music would be edited in later by the production staff.
- In the opening, Edmond O'Brien tells Pat Shade that he will "pick up your brain" and the whole cast roars in laughter causing the director to restart the program.
- Johnny mentions that he has an extra bottle of whiskey in his bag.
- Edmond O'Brien's new movie is *War Path*.
- Bob LeMond is the announcer but the script title page lists Dick Cutting.

- Music is by Wilbur Hatch.

Producer:	Jaime del Valle	Writer:	Gil Doud
Cast:	Herb Butterfield, Jeanette Nolan, Tony Barrett, Tim Graham, Gil Stratton Jr.		

♦ ❖ ♦

Show: **The Soderbury, Maine Matter**
Show Date: 6/2/1951
Company: **Britannia Life Insurance Company**
Agent:
Exp. Acct: **$84.90**

Synopsis: Edward Wightman calls Johnny to assist in the investigation of Mr. Soderbury's murder. Johnny wants to talk with Ed as he was riding with Mr. Soderbury when he was killed. Ed tells Johnny that he has just left constable Remmen, and he has found the place from which the shots were fired. Ed arranges to meet Johnny in front of his hotel.

Johnny goes to Soderbury, Maine, a small New England village, to investigate the murder of the town's leading citizen, George Soderbury. Ed Wightman tells Johnny that there was a celebration in town to mark the reopening of a World War II factory. Wightman tells Johnny the factory was originally built to handle government contracts during World War II, and that the town's people are against the influx of outsiders and their ways. Fathers do not have their sons to work the farms and daughters marry outsiders. During the parade Mr. Soderbury was shot. The deputy sheriff Fred Remmen has found the place where the shots came from, the roof of a store that has stairs in the back. In the parade Mr. Soderbury was in the first car with the windows opened. Remmen comes from the roof and tells Johnny that there are a lot of excellent marksmen in the town. The prime suspect is Ben Sutherlin who lost his oldest son in an accident at the plant and has another son who will be sixteen soon.

Johnny learns that the Soderbury family has controlled the town for three generations but is not well liked. The sole survivor of the family is George's younger sister Beth. Johnny and Remmen go to see Ben Sutherlin, who is not home. His wife tells Johnny and Fred that he left last night and that she will not tell them where he is as she is keeping a trust. Remmen is sure that Ben has left and not gone through town, so he knows where he went. Remmen calls the county authorities and arranges for the body to be picked up for the autopsy.

Johnny goes to see Beth Soderbury that evening and meets Lawrence Taft there. Lawrence leaves and Beth tells Johnny that she was educated in England and does not feel like part of the town. George, her brother, was not famous for making friends, but he knew that what he was doing was forcing change on the townspeople. Johnny asks about Ben Sutherlin, and she knows that Ben is angry.

As they are talking Beth's dog "The General Scott" starts barking and shots ring out. Johnny goes to investigate and finds that dog has been wounded and that the whole village has turned out. Johnny calls Remmen and a search of the area turns up nothing so Johnny goes to his hotel.

On the way Remmen tells Johnny that Ed Wightman came when the factory opened and that Taft was an orphan who was raised by George Soderbury. He was a smart man who worked in the factory but was not happy. He was thick with Beth and would kill himself before he would harm George. Wightman was an outsider brought in to work in the factory.

Next day the county picks up the body and the state police bring in Ben Southerland. Ben tells Johnny and Fred that he heard of George's death when the police stopped him. Ben tells Johnny and Fred that he had taken his son to work on a farm away from the factory, and then went out to get drunk for the first time in twenty years and had a fight with some men in Brighton.

All but forty of the town's people have been checked by Fred and Johnny when the county reports that George had been shot with a .250/3000 caliber rifle. Four people are identified who own that type of rifle, including Ben Sutherland. The rifles are tested, and the results show that the murder weapon was not among them.

Johnny requests that Remmen hold a meeting with Ed Wightman, Lawrence Taft and Beth Soderbury on some pretense while Johnny looks for something. Johnny takes less than an hour to find some torn clothes and another rifle in a closet and then he goes to the killer. Johnny meets with Beth and tells her that Lawrence is the killer. Beth calls Lawrence and Johnny tells him he has found the torn clothes and the gun. Johnny tells Lawrence that he was outside listening when the dog barked and he shot it. Johnny tells Lawrence that he was an important man the last time the factory opened, but he has been left out this time. Lawrence admits that he had tried to kill Ed Wightman for Beth. He was ashamed that Ed Wightman had been brought in and that people were laughing at him. He had tried to shoot Ed but missed and killed George — his dearest friend to whom he owes everything.

Johnny relates that Beth was right when she told Johnny that anyone with generations of background in an insular village like that takes a chance when he comes out, to say nothing of a half-generation Hartfordian when he goes in.

Notes:
- This program is missing the music, which was to be added later.
- Edmond O'Brien's new movie is *War Path*.
- Bob LeMond is the announcer.
- Music is by Wilbur Hatch.

Producer: Jaime del Valle **Writer:** Gil Doud
Cast: Robert North, Howard McNear, Virginia Gregg, Larry Thor, Sammie Hill, Herb Butterfield, David Light

Show:	**The George Farmer Matter**
Show Date:	**6/9/1951**
Company:	**Great Eastern Life Insurance Company**
Agent:	**Mr. Mitchell**
Exp. Acct:	**$33.65**

Synopsis: Mr. Mitchell calls Johnny at 5:30 a.m. and tells Johnny to be in the New York office when it opens. George Farmer has burned to death and the wife has put in for a $100,000 double indemnity claim.

Johnny drives to New York City and meets with the Great Eastern manager who tells Johnny that Mr. Mitchell must have been sure that Johnny would take the case. Johnny tells him that Mr. Mitchell is familiar with Johnny's bank account. Johnny is told that George Farmer was on vacation at the Sportsman's Retreat when he was burned to death in a fire. His wife has filed a claim for $100,000.

Dr. William Evans, an insurance doctor calls with important news, so Johnny rushes to his office. Outside the Equitable Building, Johnny meets Dr. Evans who is on the sidewalk where he had jumped from his office. Johnny is taken to see Lt. Briggs when he tells the officers on the street the name of the body: "I made a guess. Evans had called his office on an insurance matter. Who pushed him?" Johnny asks Briggs. Briggs tells Johnny that Evans was seen coming out of the window feet first.

Johnny goes to see Mrs. Farmer. She tells Johnny that she has already talked to the insurance investigator and that she does not know a Dr. Evans, or who sold the policy to her husband. Johnny leaves and finds who sold the policy. Johnny then takes the subway to the home of Martin Ames where his wife is crying. She tells Johnny that her husband has just been in an automobile accident and is in the hospital.

Johnny rushes to the hospital with Mrs. Ames and meets Briggs there. While Mrs. Ames waits for the doctor to come, Briggs tells Johnny that Ames was involved in a hit-and-run accident and is dead. Briggs tells Johnny that before he died, Ames told the police that a car had run him off the road.

Johnny and Briggs go to Mrs. Farmer again and ask her why two men who knew her husband were dead? She tells them that she did not know either of the men. When asked why she did not go to the Catskills this year with her husband, she tells them that she had gone there for fifteen years and was tired of it. She tells Johnny that her husband had smoked in bed occasionally, but she had already told the investigator that, and Johnny should talk to her attorney. She tells Johnny that she is entitled to the money. Johnny leaves and suggests to Briggs that they drive up to the Sportsman's Lodge to find out how Mrs. Farmer knew that an investigator has been up there already.

Johnny and Briggs drive to the Sportsman's Retreat and speak with the foreman, a man named Pop Sloan. Pop offers them breakfast and tells them that the same people stay there every year. Mr. Phillips owns the resort and will be here that afternoon. Briggs remarks to Johnny about how beautiful it is here and Johnny reminds him that "his soul is showing". Pop tells Johnny that everyone is out fishing and that Mr. Farmer usually brought his wife with him. If she had come this year, she might have saved him. Everyone had hiked up to Willow Peak when the fire broke out, but Farmer did not go as he had trouble with his legs. Doc Combs has looked at the body and is out fishing now.

Later that morning Mr. Phillips the owner arrives from the city. Phillips tells Johnny that he was on his way to the lodge when the fire broke out. He knew Farmer, who was a quiet man. He had started a small fire two years ago but his wife had saved him. Farmer usually stayed for his whole vacation and was very stingy.

Dr. Combs comes in and tells Johnny that he knew Farmer and had identified the body by finding the broken wrist. "What broken wrist?" Johnny asks. George Farmer had broken his right wrist just a week before he came up to the lodge. Johnny has Briggs call the precinct to find out when and where the wrist was treated. Johnny thinks he can prove that Farmer was murdered.

The police call back and Johnny learns that Farmer broke his wrist on the 26th, and that it was treated at the Olive Hospital. Johnny is told that Farmer got to the lodge on the fourth and died on the eleventh. However, the policy went into effect on the 22nd, and the first claim was for the death, not the broken wrist. Johnny and Briggs go back to talk to Mrs. Farmer.

Johnny and Briggs confront Mrs. Farmer with what they know. She tells Johnny that her husband did not have a broken wrist when he bought the policy and broke the wrist later. She tells Johnny that she had come to the insurance doctor with her husband and Johnny reminds her that she did not know Dr. Evans. Briggs tells her the signature on the policy does not match the one on his driver's license.

Mrs. Farmer screams at Johnny to leave as he tells her how she sent someone else in to take the physical and forged her husband's name, so who helped you? Mr. Phillips comes in with his gun and removes all doubt about who helped her. There is a gunfight, and Philips is killed. Mrs. Farmer tells Johnny that she and Phillips had fallen in love but he had planned the whole thing. Phillips had gone to Dr. Evans for the physical and Ames had sold him the policy and he killed them both. Mrs. Farmer will probably get second-degree for complicity, and the insurance company can cancel the policy.

Notes:
- Dick Cutting is the announcer.
- Music is by Wilbur Hatch.
- Edmond O'Brien's new movie is *War Path*.
- Starting tomorrow, Guy Lombardo is replacing Jack Benny for the summer, and Mario Lanza is replacing Edgar Bergen and Charlie McCarthy.

Producer: Jaime del Valle   Writer: Blake Edwards
Cast: Hy Averback, John McIntire, Herb Butterfield,
              Harry Lang, Jeanette Nolan, Virginia Gregg

Show:	**The Arthur Boldrick Matter**
Show Date:	**6/16/1951**
Company:	**Corinthian All-Risk Insurance Company**
Agent:	
Exp. Acct:	**$77.30**

Synopsis: Dr. Karfe calls Johnny and advises him that Arthur Boldrick is lucky to be alive. Johnny can see Boldrick later that evening. Sgt. Wright hopes that Boldrick will talk to Johnny, as he is not the police.

Johnny goes to the Emergency Hospital in Hartford, Connecticut to talk to Arthur Boldrick who tells Johnny he was shot by a man in the alley behind his garage and cannot remember what he looked like. Arthur thinks that the man was after his car keys, and when Arthur pushed him, the man panicked and shot him. Arthur cannot give a good description of the man and asks Johnny if his wife can come to see him, as he sure wants to see his wife.

Johnny goes to the police and gives Sgt. Wright his report about a man in blue work clothes or overalls with a small caliber gun. Johnny goes to see Mrs. Velma Boldrick who lives in an area called "an older part of town" rather than a slum. Velma Boldrick shows Johnny where the shooting took place and tells Johnny that she heard shouting and ran outside but saw no one. Johnny is sure that the neighbors should have seen something at that time of the evening.

A neighbor, Will Wheeler, comes over and chides Johnny for bothering Velma. Will tells Johnny what he knows and relates to Johnny that theirs is a rotten neighborhood with rotten people. Johnny mentions that the wounds are aggravating an injury to a lung obtained in the war.

Johnny goes to see Wright and meets Mrs. Cole who tells them that she was working in her garden and saw a tan or brown car driving up the alley at the time of the shooting. She thought the car was backfiring but learned later it was gunfire. Wright tells Johnny that so far nothing fits, almost everyone saw nothing and one person sees a car.

Johnny goes to see Arthur with Wright and accuses Arthur of protecting someone. They tell Arthur of the conflicting evidence and Arthur finally admits to them that he was seeing his ex-wife without telling anyone. He was hurting her husband, his wife and the neighbors. Arthur has a relapse and is near death.

Johnny and Wright go to see Anna, the ex-wife, and Thomas Hood her husband. Wright tells her that Arthur told them that her husband had shot him. Johnny is told that Thomas is out of town on business and left at four. Since Boldrick was shot at five thirty he had left in plenty of time to shoot Arthur. Johnny is also told that Thomas has a tan sedan. Anna begs Johnny not to tell her husband about them, as he does not know anything. Anna will not tell Johnny where Thomas is, as she does not want him to find out about them.

Johnny and Wright go back to the hospital and learn that Arthur had given a deathbed statement naming Thomas as the shooter. Johnny goes back to see Velma to tell her of the statement, and the neighbor Will is there. Will is told about the statement and is surprised that Thomas Hood would kill Arthur. Will does not know if Velma knows about the first wife.

Back at police headquarters, a Mr. Mandel comes in to say that he might have been the car in the alley. He was delivering a repaired radio in the area and drove down the alley on the way home. He did not hear any shots as the alley is bumpy, and his car has a lot of loose bolts and is very noisy.

Johnny and Wright go to see Velma after reviewing the facts. She tells Johnny that she knows Arthur has died and only knew about the affair when Will had told her that day. After a few well-placed accusations by Johnny, Velma breaks down and admits she shot Arthur. He was going to see Anna and had told Velma where he was going. She tells Johnny that Will had lied and admits that she went outside and shot him.

Johnny thinks that Velma will get a "widows special" for second-degree murder and will be out in two years. So, the insurance company will have that long to figure out how to cancel the policy.

Notes:
- Edmond O'Brien's new movie is *War Path*.
- Johnny Dollar is moving to Wednesday next week at 9:00.
- Dick Cutting is the announcer.
- Music is by Wilbur Hatch.

Producer:	Jaime del Valle	Writer:	Gil Doud
Cast:	Edgar Barrier, Parley Baer, Jeanette Nolan, John McIntire, Wally Maher, Virginia Gregg, Jeanne Bates, Harry Lang		

◆ ❖ ◆

Show: The Malcolm Wish, M.D. Matter
Show Date: 6/20/1951
Company: Washingtonian Life Insurance Company
Agent:
Exp. Acct: $577.40

Synopsis: Mrs. Wish calls to ask about her husband's disappearance. She is quite frightened, and Johnny sets up an appointment to see her.

Johnny goes to San Francisco, California and calls on Mrs. Wish. Cecil, the daughter of Dr. Wish, meets Johnny at the door. She tells Johnny that she has something to talk with him about but has to meet Johnny somewhere. They agree to meet at the Hotel Cleveland coffee shop at noon. In the morning room, Mrs. Wish tells Johnny that her husband had received an emergency call at 9:00 p.m. and rushed out without telling her where he was going, and that he would be back in an hour. She has called Dr. Huber, Malcomb's business partner for a list of his patients.

Johnny takes a cable car to meet with Dr. Huber who has noticed a change in Doctor Wish over the past several months. Johnny is told that Dr. Wish is fifty-two and seems tired and not satisfied with life. Dr. Huber says it may be amnesia but probably not. Dr. Huber will provide Johnny the list of Dr. Wish's patients in the afternoon.

Johnny goes to his hotel to meet with Cecil but she had left a message saying that she could not make it and Johnny could call her after two. When Johnny leaves the hotel, he notices a blond man tailing him. Johnny goes to meet Lt. Hughes and the man follows. Hughes has no information for Johnny and can only wait. Hughes knows nothing of the man tailing Johnny and suggests that Johnny leave him on the hook. Johnny takes a roundabout trip to Dr. Huber's office and the man is still with him. Johnny goes back to his hotel and calls Cecil. She apologizes for not meeting Johnny and agrees to meet Johnny in his room at 8:30 that night. Johnny tells her he will call the police if she does not show. Johnny spends the rest of the afternoon visiting the doctor's patients to lead the tail away from the hotel.

That evening Johnny returns to his hotel to find Hughes at his door, and no Cecil. Hughes tells Johnny that the hat and shoes of Dr. Wish had been found with a suicide note on the Golden Gate bridge.

Johnny leaves to go to the Wish residence and notes that the tail is gone. Johnny and Hughes confront Mrs. Wish with the news. She tells Johnny that they had been a happy couple, and maybe she had been blind. Johnny talks to Cecil about what she knows. She tells Johnny that her father has reached that "dangerous age" and had been seeing another woman named Ann Movius. Cecil has talked to her anonymously and she seemed to be a nice person. Cecil knows nothing about the man who was following Johnny. Cecil gives Johnny the address for Ann Movius and Johnny and Hughes go there and find no one there.

Inside they find a suit coat with dried blood and a label from Carson City, Nevada. In the bedroom they find surgical dressings soaked with blood, a sales slip for a coat and shirt and a Nevada newspaper. The headlines covered a trio who had robbed a bookie and one of whom was shot. Johnny talks to the neighbors and the manager, none of whom knew Ann, or had seen an injured man.

Johnny goes back to see Hughes and learns that the man tailing Johnny was named Ned Ring, a criminal from Carson City. The Nevada police have a record for Alan Movius. An alert is sent out and Ned is captured at the airport. At police headquarters Ned is questioned. Johnny tells him that he had followed Johnny all day, but Ned denies it. After Ned is told what Johnny and Hughes knows Ned realizes his cohorts have abandoned him, he tells Johnny that Alan Movius is the one who was shot. They had shot the bookie and fled to San Francisco where one of the men, Alan Movius had a sister who knew a doctor. They tricked the doctor to come over and were holding him. Johnny gets a description of the others when a call comes in from Petaluma. A pharmacist there was suspicious of a prescription he had been given for sedatives. Dr. A. Wish had written the prescription.

Johnny and Hughes drive to Petaluma and locate the criminals at a motel. When they knock on the door, Dr. Wish answers, and tells them that the others are in the bedroom dead. He tells Johnny that he had poisoned them with the prescription he had obtained for Alan Movius. Dr. Wish then collapses from the same drug and is rushed to a hospital and is saved. Not only is Dr. Wish a three-time murderer, but it is premeditated as well.

Notes:
- Music is now provided by Eddie Dunstedter at the organ.
- The mid-program program is for George Raft as *Rocky Jordan*.
- Some catalogs list this program as *The Malcom Wish, Maryland Matter*, but the M.D. is correctly referenced as Medical Doctor.
- Edmond O'Brien's new movie is *War Path*.
- Dan Cubberly is the announcer.

Producer:	Jaime del Valle	Writer:	Gil Doud
Cast:	Jeanette Nolan, Virginia Gregg, Ray Hartman, Bill Bouchey, Tony Barrett, Lou Krugman		

♦ ❖ ♦

Show: **The Hatchet House Theft Matter**
Show Date: **6/27/1951**
Company: **Financial Surety Company**
Agent:
Exp. Acct: **$1,182.75**

Synopsis: Inspector Sailors from Scotland Yard calls Johnny to advise him that Inspector Findley is ill, and that he has taken over the Scott Jewel case. Sailors asks if Johnny has been brought in because the Yard's reputation has fallen since the Stone of Scone was stolen. Perhaps he and Johnny will have better luck.

Johnny goes to London, England and meets with Inspector Sailors who tells Johnny that Inspector Finch was very complementary about his work. Johnny is told that Mrs. Scott was staying at a house in Surrey and had a number of jewels stolen during a party. Johnny tells Sailors that Mrs. King has been known to be selling her jewels lately at below market prices. Johnny learns that Mrs. King has been seen with a man named Norman King. The loss of these jewels is around $100,000.

Johnny is driven to Hatchet House in Surrey to see Mrs. Scott but is told that she is out. Garret the butler tells Johnny that he has worked there for a long time and only "genuine" people were at the party. The maid, Millie Hankey, comes in and tells Johnny that the jewels were not the only scandal there, as Mrs. Scott has talked derisively of her former husband and that Mr. King is a slimy leech. She is only a working girl who knows right from wrong, and will be getting married soon, maybe next month. While Johnny is waiting in the library, Mrs. Scott calls the butler and says she will be in London at the Claridge Hotel for the night, so Johnny returns to Scotland Yard and updates Sailors.

Sailors recounts Inspector Finch's report that they should look into collusion between King and Millie, and Johnny calls New York to check on Norman King.

Johnny goes to see Mrs. Scott at her hotel. She tells Johnny that she suspects one of the servants, as things got pretty confused after 11:00 p.m. Johnny tells Mrs. Scott that Norman King has a record for forgery and stealing from rich old women and that he has disappeared. Mrs. Scott tells Johnny that she and King are the same types of people. They know what they want, and they want money.

Later that night Sailors calls to report that one of the jewels was found at a murder site in Limehouse. Johnny and Sailors drive to the scene where the body of George Kinsey is in a grubby room in a grubby part of town. He had been beaten and was found by a bootblack who owed him money. A brooch found in the room is identified as one of Mrs. Scott's. A woman named Gloria Stokes comes into the room and tells them that she had come in to see Kinsey and is taken in for questioning. Johnny learns that Gloria is married to Leonard Stokes and has not seen him in three days and went to see Leonard to see if he knew where her husband was. She knew Kinsey and he was no good and her husband spent too much time with him. When told of the robbery, she tells them her husband was not involved as he doesn't have the brains.

Johnny goes to Hatchett House to meet Mrs. Scott, who apologizes for letting Johnny see a part of her last night that she does not like. She tells Johnny that Norman is on a boat to New York. He left because he thought his record would come out, so he left before he was asked to leave. Johnny shows her a picture of Kinsey and Stoker, and she recognizes neither. Mrs. Scott tells Johnny that he doesn't like her, but Johnny tells Mrs. Scott "your physical part does not match up with a mental apparatus that deserves it" and she slaps him. The servants are shown the pictures and Garrett thinks he might have seen one of the men. Sailors questions the people in the village and finds a few who recognize Kinsey.

Back in London, Sailors gets a report that Leonard Stokes is on a train. Johnny and Sailors board the train and locate Stokes. Stokes admits that he did not kill George. He tells Johnny that George had picked him up and taken him to Seven Oaks and he waited outside Hatchet House while Kinsey went in to see a friend, a gardener. Kinsey came back and showed him the jewels on the way back to London. Kinsey had only taken one of them to give to someone. Later a police report shows that lip rouge was found on Kinsey's body, so Johnny and Sailors go to see Millie. Millie admits that she left the door open for Kinsey. He had promised to marry her and when she went to see him in London, he had told her to get lost so she killed him. He had called her a "stupid country girl", so she killed him.

The jewels are recovered, Millie is arrested and Mrs. Scott departs for the Isle of Capri.

Notes:
- The Stone of Scone, or the Coronation Stone was housed in Westminster Abbey and stolen by Scottish nationalists in 1950.
- The mid-program commercial is for Suspense, which will air the program *The Secret of Dr. Walter's Private Life.*
- Edmond O'Brien's new movie is *War Path.*

- Dan Cubberly is the announcer.
- Music is by Eddie Dunstedter.

Producer:	Jaime del Valle	Writer:	Gil Doud
Cast:	John McIntire, Ben Wright, Tudor Owen, Jeanette Nolan, Virginia Gregg		

◆ ❖ ◆

Show: The Alonzo Chapman Matter
Show Date: 7/4/1951
Company: Tristate Insurance Group
Agent:
Exp. Acct: $672.08

Synopsis: Lt. Schock calls Johnny to ask who Johnny is, and what his involvement is with the Alonzo Chapman killing. Johnny tells him he is working on the case for the insurance company. Johnny tells Schock that he heard about the case last night and got there that morning.

Johnny goes to Los Angeles, California, meets with Shock and is updated on the case. Johnny is told that Chapman had met a girl in a bar. They had stayed for a while and then left and were walking down the alley to her car when he was shot but not robbed. The girl, Norma Sale, had told the police that she had met Chapman that night.

Johnny goes to see Norma with Shock. Norma tells Johnny that she vaguely remembers last night. She relates how she had met Chapman in the bar, and they were just talking. He asked her to go to dinner with him, so they left and walked down the alley, as her car was closer that way. Norma tells Johnny that she has no boyfriend who would have been jealous. They were just walking down the alley and a man jumped from behind a trash box and shot him. Norma is not sure she would recognize the shooter.

Shock writes the Cleveland police for more information on Chapman. Johnny talks to the bartender in the bar. He remembers Chapman letting the girl have his chair at the bar, as it was crowded at that hour. They moved to a booth after a while and then left.

Johnny goes back to see Shock who tells Johnny that Mrs. Chapman is in town and might have a motive.

Johnny goes to see Norma's roommate and confirms that she has no boyfriend.

Johnny goes to see Mrs. Chapman who tells Johnny that she is not fond of her husband. He was attractive to women and knew it. She knew that something like this would happen, and now it has.

Johnny goes back to see Shock and tells him of the conversation. Shock tells Johnny that he has learned that Mrs. Chapman was seeing a man named Nicholson who has left Cleveland and has not been seen since.

Johnny and Shock go to see Mrs. Chapman and confront her with the information on Nicholson. She admits to seeing him and tells Johnny that they had a lot in common. She last saw him on Wednesday of last week. Johnny asks if he could have killed her husband, but she denies that she had told Nicholson where her husband was when he called her on Friday. She does admit that she and Nicholson had fought over her not pushing her husband for a divorce and gives Shock a picture of Nicholson.

Johnny takes the picture to the bartender and a bargirl, neither of which recognize Nicholson. Johnny takes the picture to Norma, and she thinks maybe it might be the shooter, but she is not sure.

Later that day, Nicholson is no longer a suspect. The Ohio police have found his body in his car. He had been drunk and had a fatal accident.

Johnny finds a vital clue in the newspaper. Max Gerber, a local mobster, had been staying at the same hotel as Chapman and was shot the previous night. Johnny goes to the morgue to see Gerber, and then visits Norma. He confronts Norma with the facts that she had left work sick the afternoon of the shooting and that she had never been to that bar before. Johnny asks Norma if she was paid to meet Chapman. Johnny shows Norma pictures of Alonzo Chapman and Max Gerber. She tells Johnny that she thinks that they are pictures of the same man. She then panics and admits that some men had said that they wanted her to distract Gerber as he owed them some money. She was hired because she was young and blonde. They only wanted money from him.

The second murder was a gangland rubout planned with a young blond as bait, the first murder was a mistake. The moral is that companies shouldn't hire salesmen, women shouldn't marry them and young blondes should stay away from them, but confidentially some of my best friends are insurance salesmen.

Notes:
- Edmond O'Brien's new movie is *War Path*.
- Johnny Dollar moves to 9:30 next Wednesday.
- Dick Cutting is the announcer.
- Music is by Eddie Dunstedter.

Producer:	Jaime del Valle	Writer:	Gil Doud
Cast:	John McIntire, Hy Averback, Harry Lang, Jeanette Nolan, Virginia Gregg		

♦ ❖ ♦

Show: **The Fair-Way Matter**
Show Date: 7/11/1951
Company: **Columbia All Risk Insurance Company**
Agent: **Sam Harris**
Exp. Acct: **$0.00**

Synopsis: Sam Harris calls to alert Johnny of a Fair-Way Airlines plane crash in Hartford, Connecticut. Sam is sure that a bomb caused the accident, and thirteen people were killed. The company wants to place responsibility and do whatever it can. Contact the airline representative Mr. Reed.

Johnny goes to the scene of the crash. The plane had been airborne less than a minute when it exploded and destroyed two houses on the ground killing at least 6 people. Johnny meets a hysterical Carl Reed of the airline who is talking to an equally hysterical Mrs. Goodhue about a daughter she fears was on the plane. The daughter was on the plane, but she has not been told yet. Carl tells Johnny that the explosion was in the tail of the plane, that the CAB is on the way, and that the state police are in charge of the investigation.

Johnny goes to find Captain Jim Lenhart of the state police in the hangar where the bodies are being collected. They wonder if the crash was murder with a motive, suicide or just a maniac.

The next day Johnny learns that nitroglycerine was the explosive. A tip to the police brings in Wilbur Wheeler, a maintenance worker for the airlines for questioning. Wilber is very nervous and asks what the police have on him. He admits that he had been in love with Shirley Goodhue, a stewardess, and had fought with a copilot when Wilbur learned that Shirley was going to marry him instead. Wilbur had threatened the copilot and his plane and knew that made him a suspect. He had heard of the crash on the radio and came back to work to help out. After questioning he is released and a police tail is placed on him.

Johnny relates that on the list of dead passengers, one man named Rupert Stone could not be located because of bogus information. Johnny and Lenhart go to visit a Mrs. Graham who is distraught over the loss of her husband. She tells Johnny and Lenhart that her husband had gone to Boston to visit his brother's grave, as he was a religious man. On the way out, Jim calls this case a rotten mess and admits that he could not ask Mrs. Graham if her husband's cancer could had caused him to commit suicide. They leave to go have a drink but are interrupted with the news that the explosive was found to have been in a first aid box in the rear of the airplane.

Wilbur Wheeler is brought in for more questioning. After a very nervous interview, Wilbur tells Lenhart that he has worked for the airlines for a year and a half yet does not know about the first aid kit carried on by Miss Goodhue. Wilbur denied knowing anything about the nitroglycerine. Wilbur is held for a lie detector test and an interview with the police psychologist. Johnny and Jim search Wilbur's room and find no radio, which Wilbur said he had listened to, and no newspapers are found.

On the next day the lie detector test proves negative and the psychologist says that Wilbur has a severe guilt complex. Carl Reed calls to report that another stewardess named Alice Turner is missing and a search of her apartment uncovers her shot dead. Johnny and Lenhart go to the apartment and Carl tells them that she was originally scheduled to fly on the plane that crashed but had switched at the last minute with Shirley Goodhue. Johnny is told that the stewardesses often switched flights among themselves. It seems now that the case against Wilbur is not very sound. Johnny and Lenhart go to visit Mrs. Goodhue and learn nothing new other than Shirley was called shortly before the flight and that one of the girls was sick. They are told that there were six girls in Hartford who swapped flights if one was sick. Johnny and Lenhart talk to the other girls and learn nothing.

On the way home, Johnny is met by a man named Moran in the hallway of his apartment and he wants to talk. Moran tells Johnny that he knew Alice and that he was to blame for the accident. Moran tells Johnny that a man named Arthur Church was using Alice as a courier for drugs, which were carried in the first aid kit. She wanted out, and Moran was hiding her. Alice had arranged a meeting with the Feds and Church had found out and killed her. Moran warned her to stay hidden and she had gotten Shirley to take her flight. Moran also tells Johnny that Church had hidden the explosives on the plane in Alice's kit, which was kept at the airport and picked up by Shirley.

Johnny and Lenhart go to Church's apartment with Moran. Moran goes in and calls for Church, but he opens fire and kills Moran, and Lenhart kills Church.

The expense account total is $25.95, but the total is hardly important compared with the losses of others so, just forget it.

Notes:
- This program is repeated by John Lund on 1/5/1954.
- The CAB, or Civil Aeronautics Board, was the forerunner of the FAA.
- *The Front Page* comedy is on the *Broadway Playhouse* tomorrow night
- There is a public service announcement for Defense Bonds at the end of the program.
- Ray Hartman is listed as a cast member at the end of the program, but the script title page lists him as Raymond Burr.
- Edmond O'Brien's new movie is *War Path*.
- Dan Cubberly is the announcer.
- Music is by Eddie Dunstedter.

Producer:	Jaime del Valle	Writer:	Gil Doud
Cast:	Peter Leeds, Ray Hartman, Martha Wentworth, Bill Bouchey, Vic Perrin, Virginia Gregg		

◆ ❖ ◆

Show:	**The Neal Breer Matter**
Show Date:	**7/18/1951**
Company:	**Great Eastern Insurance Company**
Agent:	
Exp. Acct:	**$556.70**

Synopsis: Dr. Hamill, the local coroner calls, and Johnny wants to talk to him. Dr. Hamill is convinced that the Breer death was from natural causes. Johnny tells him he has a letter that has raised doubts.

Johnny flies to a city not to be disclosed by the insurance company. Johnny goes to visit Dr. Henry Richards, the man who wrote the letter about Neal Breer. Johnny is told that Breer, who was 26, was a part owner of a service station with Westley Birtcher. Neal started having convulsions and supposedly died of a heart attack. Dr. Richards confirms that Neal had a heart condition, but bismine could also have caused the symptoms. Dr. Richards has reviewed the records, and Johnny tells him he will order an autopsy. Johnny goes to see the coroner about the autopsy and is told that he relies on the opinions of the doctors, and that Johnny will have to go to the family for permission to do an exhumation and autopsy.

Johnny develops the background of Neal Breer and is told to leave the case alone. Johnny goes to the widow, who is shocked at the suggestion of an autopsy. Johnny goes to see Neal's father, and he will not order the autopsy. Johnny goes to his hotel and has had a number of calls from a hysterical man. Johnny asks Hazel, the operator, to listen in if the man calls again. Later the man, who refuses to identify himself calls Johnny and tells him to stop the investigation and leave town. Johnny is causing trouble and will be hurt if he continues. After the man hangs up, Johnny calls the hotel operator who tells Johnny that she heard the man threaten him, and Johnny asks her to get Dr. Hammil's home phone number.

Johnny goes to see Dr. Hamill who tells Johnny that a toxicologist is on the way, and that the body will be ready for them. After the tests, the cause of death is found to be bismine.

Johnny calls Dr. Richards, and Johnny tells him he should be happy about the results: Neal Breer was killed with bismine. He tells Johnny that he does not know where to get bismine.

Johnny goes to see Neal's father who tells Johnny that he was not happy when his son eloped with that girl. The business partner had told him that Neal was down-in-the-mouth lately.

Johnny goes to see Wesley Bircher who tells Johnny that Neal had seemed to lose interest in things. Everyone was surprised at the marriage because the wife was so strong willed. She threw herself at Neal after her boyfriend went away to medical school. The old boyfriend was Alan Richards, the son of Dr. Richards.

Johnny gets the details of the day Neal died, and then goes to see Mrs. Breer. She denies murdering Neal and tells Johnny that she did not love him. Johnny tells her that Alan had called to warn him, and she tells Johnny that she had asked for a divorce and Neal refused. It was then that Alan decided to poison him. The rest of it I gave to the police, the fact that the uncommon poison was available to a medical student and was administered by way of a vacuum bottle of coffee. After that, I left town.

Remarks: I hope the company will understand my not going back to Dr. Richards. A doctor in doubt about a death certificate calling on the interested insurance company for confidential help is a splendid idea. But in this case, the doctor's son was an accomplice to murder.

Notes:
- This program opens with an aircheck from WBBM-FM, Chicago.
- The commercials are for Wrigley's Spearmint Gum.
- While Johnny is in his hotel room, he is listening to the radio, which is playing a public service announcement for the Woman's Army Corps (WAC).
- Edmond O'Brien's new movie is *War Path*.
- The announcer is Bob Stevenson.
- Music is by Eddie Dunstedter.

Producer:	Jaime del Valle		Writer:	Gil Doud
Cast:	Ralph Moody, Edgar Barrier, Joseph DuVal, Jeanne Bates, Mary Shipp, Tony Barrett, Peter Leeds			

Show: The Blind Item Matter
Show Date: 7/25/1951
Company:
Agent:
Exp. Acct: $1,074.00

Synopsis: The first half of this program is missing, but it takes place in Santa Barbara, California.

Johnny tells Madelon that her husband hired the detective. She tells Johnny that she loved Keith and did not kill her husband and does not own a gun. Johnny is told that her husband knew about Keith but would not give her freedom. The police arrive and Johnny goes back to his hotel. On the way Johnny spots a cab with a blond in it. Johnny follows her into the bar and is paged by Ed Belasco who tells Johnny that Keith has been arrested. Ed arranges to meet Johnny at the Harbor Pier.

Johnny goes to the pier where Belasco tells Johnny he can name the killer for $2,000, saving the insurance company $100,000. Johnny agrees to pay $1,000, and just as Belasco tells Johnny that the killer is John Forsyth, Mrs. Ridgeley's first husband, he is shot. Johnny takes his .38 and sees a man by a building. Johnny shoots and the man starts running.

Johnny goes to see Madelon and spots blood on the floor. She tells Johnny that the house boy cut his finger. Johnny tells her about Belasco and the private detective. She tells Johnny that her husband lives in Santa Barbara, but she has not seen him in fifteen years. As they are talking Forrest Graham comes in bleeding and tells Johnny that he had changed his name when he moved. Graham jells Johnny that he planted the blind item to make Ridgeley jealous and hired Belasco. Madelon hooked up with the piano player and he was sent to the cabin to ask for her freedom. Graham tells Johnny that he killed Ridgeley and collapses.

Remarks: Graham was John Forsyth all right, and he's lying in the morgue beside Belasco. Between them I don't think they'll be able to think of six pallbearers. Keith Tucker was released and Mrs. Ridgeley is being arraigned and will probably get her share for complicity. If you feel charitable on Christmas, just think of how much money I saved you."

Notes:
- This script is incomplete.
- Music is by Eddie Dunstedter.
- Edmund O'Brien's next film is *War Path*.
- Story information obtained from the KNX Collection in the Thousand Oaks Library.

Producer:	Jaime del Valle		Writer:	Blake Edwards, Dick Quine
Cast:	Hy Averback, Jack Moyles, Jack Kruschen, Virginia Gregg, Ted Osborne			

• ❖ •

Show: **The Horace Lockhart Matter**
Show Date: 8/1/1951
Company: **Washingtonian Life Insurance Company**
Agent:
Exp. Acct: $583.85

Synopsis: Bruce Yule, the attorney for the Lockhart estate calls Johnny. He wants to arrange a meeting to discuss how to solve a $200,000 question. Mr. Yule still does not know who died first.

Johnny travels from Santa Barbara to Los Angeles, California to work on a new case. The Lockharts had been killed early Monday morning in an auto accident on the Pacific Coast Highway. The police had received a call about the accident from an all-night garage. Yule needs Johnny to find the girl who reported the accident to the operator of the garage, as $200,000 rests on who died first, the husband or the wife. Johnny and Bruce agree to place information ads in the papers to ask the girl to contact them.

Johnny rents a car and drives to the garage. The owner, Mr. Gallagher, tells Johnny that a girl rushed in, woke him up, and told him there was an accident and then disappeared. Gallagher cannot remember exactly what she said even when Johnny tells him why it is so important. Johnny explains that the Lockharts were co-beneficiaries of the life insurance policy, and each had left a different second beneficiary. So, who was alive last would matter to the two beneficiaries. Gallagher remembers that the girl had blue eyes, wore very heavy makeup, maybe stage makeup, had a headscarf, bare legs and high heels and had headed back towards Los Angeles.

Johnny drives to the scene of the accident and finds a sheer drop-off to the beach. Johnny drives to the sheriff's office and a look at the photos, which tells him that the driver must have fallen asleep.

Johnny goes to the Lockhart mansion to meet the two beneficiaries, who have never met. Michael Adams, 27, of Seattle is the son of Mrs. Lockhart and is not used to being around money. Gail, 23, was the daughter of Mr. Lockhart and totally upset by Michael's insensitivity. Michael tells Johnny that he knows that he is an outsider, but $200,000! Wow!

Yule and Johnny agree to post a $1,000 reward for information leading to the girl. After seven days an apartment manager calls Yule with information and Johnny goes to see her. She tells Johnny that one of her tenants, Susan Lee, had moved out Monday, with a month's rent paid. She was a "specialty dancer" and had told the manager that she would come for her mail. Johnny looks through the mail and finds a bill from a photographer. A visit to the shop yields a picture of Susan Lee.

Yule is convinced by Johnny to leave the ads running for a while. Johnny drives to the Santa Monica club where Susan worked. The manager, Mr. Coberly, tells Johnny that Susan has just dropped out of sight. He had read about the accident but cannot understand why she was headed towards Los Angeles, as she got off her last show at 12:45 a.m. and the accident was at 2:00 a.m. Coberly tells Johnny that a girl named Lameen Dunne had picked up Susan's last paycheck.

Johnny gets the address and goes to see Lameen. She tells Johnny that Susan has made her promise not to talk, but something happened that night, and it was probably over the man that she married. Lameen tells Johnny that Susan had married a man named Philip Roberts in Mexico. He traveled a lot and she would meet him in a cabin several times a week. Susan came here that morning and told Lameen that she had to get out of town. Lameen tells Johnny that Susan also used to get flowers from a "masher" in San Diego and never read the cards. Lameen tells Johnny that she had brought the flowers home on Sunday and read the card, which said "As usual, if you ever need me."

Johnny gets the card with the florist's name and goes to San Diego and gets an address from the florist. Johnny visits the address and finds a hysterical Susan. She tells Johnny that she has read about the reward in the papers and cries about not killing him, that she was going to meet him but another car was there. She heard a woman's voice say that he was his wife and call him Carl and then there were shots. But she left and did not kill him. You are trying to trick me. I do not care what she says.

Johnny takes Susan to the police who go to the cabin and find a man and a woman shot to death. The man was a bigamist and his wife had found out and killed him and herself. Susan had seen the accident and tried to help but there was nothing to do. Johnny goes to see the beneficiaries and Yule tells them that Susan had testified that Mrs. Lockhart was still alive when Susan saw her. Michael is ecstatic. $200,000 for being born to the right mother!

Johnny remarks that in his opinion, the money went to the wrong person.

Notes:
- Commercials are for Wrigley's Spearmint gum.
- Edmond O'Brien's new movie is *War Path*.
- Bob Stevenson is the announcer.
- Music is by Eddie Dunstedter.

Producer:	Jaime del Valle	Writer:	Gil Doud
Cast:	Howard McNear, Hy Averback, Barbara Whiting, David Young, Virginia Gregg, Eddie Marr, Mary Jane Croft		

Show:	**The Morgan Fry Matter**
Show Date:	**8/8/1951**
Company:	**Britannia Life Insurance Company**
Agent:	
Exp. Acct:	**$136.65**

Synopsis: Lt. Barbe calls Johnny and tells him that Mrs. Fry was sent home after she identified the body. Come on down and get the details.

Johnny goes to Boston, Massachusetts where he learns that the body of Morgan Fry had been found in the Harbor after being there two days. The only clues were special shoes that were traced to a chiropodist. Mrs. Fry thought her husband was on Wall Street. Robbery is ruled out as the body was shot too many times. The policy is for $125,000, split between the wife ($50,000) and the company ($75,000).

Johnny goes to see Mrs. Fry, who tells Johnny that she last saw her husband three days ago, and that he would often go away for several days. On the way out the maid, Millie, tells Johnny that when Mrs. Fry went to Detroit recently, Mr. Fry had a woman in the house. Johnny goes to talk to Joseph Miller, the partner of Fry. He tells Johnny that he thought Fry was going to take the 5:40 train to New York, and that another woman was impossible. He does remember the secretary telling him that a woman had called for Fry.

Johnny calls Barbe and is told that he has learned nothing. Barbe receives a call and learns that Mrs. Fry has swallowed some pills, and the maid had called the police.

Johnny goes to the Fry home and talks to Millie who tells Johnny that Mrs. Fry came into the kitchen and said "what have I done?". Johnny goes to the hospital and Mrs. Fry tells him that she found out about the "other" woman and felt cheated. The woman had called and told her about the affair. She said that Morgan had told her to tell her if anything happened to him because he had been making illegal investments.

Johnny and Barbe go to see Miller, who is ready to talk. Miller tells them that he and his family have been threatened also. Miller tells them that they had invested some money in an organization that was building a racetrack in Nevada. The next investment was to buy some gambling equipment. The man they dealt with was Ernest Nebbie. Fry was killed when he discovered that the money was really used to buy narcotics. A man named Phillip Dean called after the killing and Miller gives them the address.

Johnny and Barbe go to see Dean, who denies killing Fry, but is ready to go to the police. Dean goes into his room to get his things and tries to run away but is shot outside by the police. Dean is saved in the hospital, and the woman was never found.

Notes:
- The announcer is Bob Stevenson.
- Music is by Eddie Dunstedter.

- Story information obtained from the KNX Collection in the Thousand Oaks Library.

Producer:	Jaime del Valle	Writer:	Gil Doud
Cast:	William Conrad, Edith Tackna, Virginia Gregg, Ted Osborne, Larry Thor		

♦ ❖ ♦

Show: The Lucky Costa Matter
Show Date: 8/15/1951
Company: NYPD Homicide
Agent:
Exp. Acct: $0.00

Synopsis: Louise Costa calls Johnny and tells him that something is wrong. Lucky is working on a case, and she has not heard from him for over a week. Can I talk to you?

Johnny details the case of Frank "Lucky" Costa. Johnny meets with Louise, who is hesitant to talk. She tells Johnny that Lucky has changed, something a wife can see, and that the change has been going on for a month. She thinks Lucky is involved with another woman, as he has made her think that he was hiding something. Supposedly Lucky is in San Francisco working on a divorce case. Louise asks Johnny to look into the matter for her.

Johnny goes to see Frank's brother Joe in Hartford, Connecticut. Joe tells Johnny that he had talked to Lucky for the last time a month ago. Joe asks Johnny if Lucky ever told him about his first wife, or his prison time. Joe tells Johnny that Lucky spent over a year in prison for grand theft over some furs he stole for his first wife, some 12 years ago. Johnny is told that the first wife, Hazel Macky, had called Lucky about a month ago. He was going to see her, so Joe called it quits as a brother. Joe tells Johnny that Hazel is in New York.

Johnny goes to New York City to see Hazel, and she tells Johnny that she does not know where Lucky is now, but he is working on a case for her. She tells Johnny that she needed a bodyguard and called Lucky. She tells Johnny that she had changed her mind about an old boyfriend and needed a bodyguard as the man, George Meyers, had told her he would get her. So, Lucky is looking for George for her. Johnny is told that when this is over, Lucky can go back to his wife.

Johnny does not tell Lucky's wife for two days. On the third day, George Meyers is found shot dead, shot by an "unknown assailant". Johnny calls Joe and visits him at lunch to tell him of the case. Joe is told that Lucky was supposed to guard Hazel from Meyers, but now it comes out that $200,000 is still missing from the robbery twelve years earlier, and Johnny thinks that maybe Hazel knows where it is. Johnny tells Joe that he must go to police with the news to stay clean with the police. After all, Louise started it he tells Joe, who walks off angry. "What a sour racket" Johnny mutters to himself.

Johnny goes back to New York and goes to see Hazel. She tells Johnny that Lucky is gone, and that he had killed George Meyers. She tells Johnny that

George had followed her to Lucky's hotel. George was waiting in the lobby and pulled a gun on them when they left and Lucky shot him. Johnny tells her that his theory is that Lucky agreed to kill Meyers for a share of the $200,000 and asks Hazel where the gun is. "Did you hire a detective as a ploy to kill George and hide behind his license?" Johnny asks Hazel, but she tells Johnny that she knows nothing about the money. Johnny tells Hazel that he will call the police as they can hold her as a material witness.

The police are called, and Lt. Carl Belder takes Hazel in, and the apartment is searched. Johnny finds a check stub that shows that Lucky had been paid for one week. The phone rings, and it is Lucky. He asks Johnny what he is doing there, and is where Hazel? Johnny asks Lucky to come in and talk, but he does not want to meet anywhere and hangs up. Belder tells Johnny that the exits to New York are covered. Lucky's clothes are still in the hotel, so there is no idea what Lucky will do.

Johnny goes to police headquarters where Hazel keeps to her story, a well-rehearsed statement that the police cannot prove otherwise.

Three days later, Joe calls Johnny from Hartford and wants to talk. Johnny goes to see Joe who invites him in. He tells Johnny that he is no better than a rat now. Lucky had called him and needs money. Joe told Lucky to call back tonight after 7:00 and Johnny will talk to him.

The call comes in and Johnny agrees to meet Lucky at 10:00 the next night. When Johnny meets Lucky, he tells Johnny that he needs money. Lucky tells Johnny that Hazel double-crossed him and used Johnny to set up the double-cross. She had only told Lucky about Johnny being there after he had killed Meyers. He tells Johnny that he knew how she was. Now he is lost, with no options and there is no way out now. Johnny starts to leave and Lucky pulls a gun. Johnny tells Lucky to use it. Johnny walks out and Lucky does not shoot. The police go in and Lucky is killed in a gunfight. Johnny records that his confession is useless, and that the police cannot charge Hazel, but you should bring her in and grill her until she talks.

Notes:
- **Johnny notes that 5 years ago he and Lucky worked for a big detective agency.**
- **Edmond O'Brien's new movie is** *War Path*.
- **Bob Stevenson is the announcer.**
- **Music is by Eddie Dunstedter.**

Producer: Jaime del Valle   **Writer:** Gil Doud
Cast: Virginia Gregg, Gloria Blondell, Hy Averback, Peter Leeds, Sidney Miller

Show: The Cumberland Theft Matter
Show Date: 8/22/1951
Company: Corinthian All-Risk Insurance Company
Agent:
Exp. Acct: $834.75

Synopsis: Deputy sheriff Dunlap calls Johnny to tell him that the inventory of the Cumberland Theft amount is up to $85,000. Johnny is also told that the Cumberland's maid will be coming back late tonight from Los Angeles.

Johnny travels to San Climente, California, and gets a room at the hotel. Johnny then goes to the bus station with deputy Dunlap to meet the maid. Johnny is told that thefts are rare in the area, and that the Cumberland's moved from Cincinnati when he retired. Mrs. Cumberland had inherited the jewels from her mother. Johnny meets Mabel Winder when the bus arrives and they go to the Cumberland home where Mabel is told of the robbery. Mabel tells Johnny that nothing unusual happened the night before. The only people who came to the house the next day were the mailman and James Dawes from the Abbott Dairy, but he never came into the house. Mabel denies stealing the jewels and tells Johnny that she went to Los Angeles to visit a friend and missed the regular bus because there were too many people. Johnny learns that the jewels were in a metal box, and Mrs. Cumberland had not worn them for a long time.

Johnny goes to the local docks to meet Mr. Cumberland, who is just returning from a fishing trip with three albacore tunas. Mr. Cumberland is not upset about the loss and assures Johnny that Mabel could not have taken them. Johnny calls the bus company and learns that the busses were not crowded, like Mabel had said. Johnny goes to see Mabel with deputy Dunlap, and she denies everything. Johnny even tells her about a son born during World War I that she gave away. Mabel finally admits taking the jewels and hiding them because her son needed money.

Johnny goes to Los Angeles and learns that Mabel's son, Randolph Ord, was born in Duluth in 1914 and was known by the police. Johnny meets Sgt. Maine who tells him that Ord is wanted for murder and was last seen in Omaha where he committed an armed robbery. Johnny talks to Mabel in the jail, and she tells Johnny about her son and how his grandparents had told him about her. He had written to her, and she had stolen for him and was proud of it.

Ord's accomplice, Jack Wilson, is arrested and is questioned by Maine. He admits to being in the bus station to find a locker. He got the key from Ord, whose mother had mailed it to him. Wilson tells Johnny that Ord is in Glendale. Johnny goes to the address, but Ord is gone. Johnny goes to the bus station and spots Ord. Johnny chases him and Ord is shot twice.

Notes:
- The announcer is Dan Cubberly.
- Music is by Eddie Dunstedter.

- Story information obtained from the KNX Collection in the Thousand Oaks Library.

Producer:	Jaime del Valle
Writer:	Gil Doud
Cast:	Parley Baer, Virginia Gregg, Howard McNear, John Stephenson, Larry Thor

◆ ❖ ◆

Show: The Leland Case Matter
Show Date: 8/29/1951
Company: Tri-State Insurance Group
Agent:
Exp. Acct: $496.13

Synopsis: Mrs. Case calls Johnny about the disappearance of her husband. Johnny tells her that he is with the insurance company, and Johnny wants to talk to her.

Johnny goes to New York City to meet Mrs. Case and stops at the police Missing Persons office and meets with Sgt. Dulco. Johnny tells Dulco that the previous Mrs. Case had reportedly tried to kill Mr. Case, but nothing was proved. Johnny is told that the current Mrs. Case reported him missing. He is 47 and owns a state-wide chain of grocery stores, Case Inc. Nothing is missing from the apartment or from his bachelor apartment at the office. Dulco relates there are a lot of missing person cases because of the world conditions. Johnny is told that the current wife is much younger than Mr. Case, and is very attractive.

Johnny goes to see Mrs. Case, and she is afraid of the reasons why her husband would have disappeared. She tells Johnny that she reported him missing on impulse and hates the all stories in the papers. She tells Johnny that they have a normal marriage. She had called her lawyer, Paul Frater, and he told her not to worry. She tells Johnny that she did not know any of her husband's business associates. She thinks they are holding back information and is angry and confused and does not know what to do. She accuses Johnny of thinking that she married Leland for his money, but she didn't.

Johnny goes to see Paul Frater. "Now add an insurance company tagging along with the suspicious grasping wife" Johnny is told. Johnny is told that it would be best if everyone left him alone. Mr. Case needed a rest and is probably in the country. Frater tells Johnny that he would not tell Johnny if he knew where Mr. Case was. Frater tells Johnny that he will talk to the wife when he gives her the divorce papers. She may have been happy, but Leland was not. There have always been scheming women, and Mrs. Case is a cheap upstate beauty contest type with only a high school education. Is there no way to stop this idiocy? Johnny talks to Leland's other friends and retraced his last steps to no avail.

Two days later Mrs. Case calls Johnny and she must see him as soon as possible. She tells Johnny that a man has called and demanded money. She is told that Leland is OK but they must have $10,000. She has until noon tomorrow to get the money. A man will call her to tell where to deliver the money. Johnny convinces Mrs. Case to work with the police to get to the men who have her husband.

The next day Johnny alerts Dulco while Mrs. Case gets the money. At 11:30 the phone rings. Johnny listens on the phone as the man agrees to the $8,600 that Mrs. Case has been able to get. Mrs. Case is told to take the money in a newspaper to a bus stop, and that a man will meet her at 11:50. They leave for the drop spot. Mrs. Case goes to the bus stop and a man asks her for her paper. Johnny grabs for the man and slugs him.

Dulco has the man, Eugene Lawson, and is checking out his address. Johnny questions Lawson and he does not know anything about Case. He tells Johnny and Dulco that he was just trying to get money from the wife. He had seen the article in the paper and tailed her, and there is nothing more. Lawson is told the FBI is on the way over, and Johnny starts to feel that Case is dead. The police go to Lawson's address and find an empty apartment.

On the next day, Johnny gets a call from Dulco who tells him about a call he had received from a hospital in White Plains. They have a man who meets Case's description.

Johnny and Dulco drive to the hospital and meet the patient who calls himself by the name "White". Johnny brings a picture that positively identifies the man as Leland Case, but the man does not know who he is. White recognizes the pictures as being of him. White tells Johnny that he only remembers getting off a train in White Plains and being attacked by men on the railroad tracks who took everything he has. Johnny tells White of his background and White remembers nothing.

White goes back to New York with Johnny and Dulco and meets Frater and Mrs. Case. There is no show of recognition by White of anyone there. Also, White knows nothing of running a large business. Johnny and Dulco leave White with his wife and Frater and White tells Johnny that he thinks he will be OK. On the way out, Johnny thinks he saw a wink from White. But then again, the light was not too good.

Notes:
- This program has only the dramatic portion because announcements and music would be edited in later by the production staff.
- Based on the script title page, the music is by Eddie Dunstedter.
- Dan Cubberly is the announcer.

Producer: Jaime del Valle   Writer: Gil Doud
Cast: Howard McNear, Parley Baer, Virginia Gregg, Larry Thor, John Stephenson

Show: The Rum Barrel Matter
Show Date: 9/12/1951
Company: Plymouth Life Insurance Company
Agent:
Exp. Acct: $43.55

Synopsis: Johnny calls Detective Walter Kirk to report a shooting. Johnny is told that it was part of a liquor store robbery and the owner was killed.

Johnny meets with Hartford, Connecticut Det. Kirk and tells about the cab ride and seeing a man shot. Kirk tells Johnny that the owner said the men were carrying water pistols, and that $300 was taken, but $500 was left in the cash drawer. Johnny goes to talk to Mr. Mueler, a quiet man who tells Johnny that a real gun was held on him. He let the man out, and then shot him at the door, but he was not the one with the money. Johnny gets a description of the others and learns that the victim had a tattoo on his left arm.

Later Johnny gets a photo of the tattoo and starts looking for the artist. Johnny goes to Bridgeport and talks to the owners of the tattoo parlors there and finds nothing.

Johnny then goes to Providence where a man recognizes the technique as that of Ron Curci in Boston.

Johnny drives to Boston and meets with Curci who remembers giving the tattoo to a man with two brothers who all got the same one. Johnny calls Kirk who is not in. Johnny learns that he is investigating another shooting at the Rum Barrel Liquor store.

Johnny goes to the store and learns that Mr. Mueler was shot, and that the shooter emptied the gun in him. Mr. Landry, the partner of Mueler arrives and Johnny asks him why Mueler shot the robber. He tells Johnny that Mueler wanted someone to try because he did not like being pushed around.

Johnny and Kirk go to see Mrs. Kline, who was a witness to the shooting. She tells Johnny that Mueler had laughed about the killing. A man came in and called Mueler by name, made him sit in the floor, and shot him. The next day Kirk is called by a Thomas Magill, who knows the killer. Johnny and Kirk go to see Magill, who admits to shooting Mueler. He tells Johnny that he and his brothers robbed the store to get money to send to their sister, who is in a hospital in Colorado. They came in with water pistols and Mueler said he was covered by insurance and begged them to take the money. When they were leaving he shot their brother David on the way out.

Johnny thinks that the confession was false, but he does verify that the sister is in the hospital.

Notes:
- The announcer is Dan Cubberly.
- Music is by Eddie Dunstedter.
- Story information obtained from the KNX Collection in the Thousand Oaks Library.

Producer:	Jaime del Valle Writer: Gil Doud
Cast:	William Conrad, Ted de Corsia, Edgar Barrier, Herb Butterfield, Virginia Gregg, Hy Averback

◆ ❖ ◆

Show:	**The Cuban Jewel Matter**
Show Date:	9/19/1951
Company:	**Intercontinental Indemnity & Bonding Company**
Agent:	**Roger Stern**
Exp. Acct:	**$708.83**

Synopsis: Roger Stern calls Johnny about a job. Bring a suitcase with summer clothes, you are going to Cuba.

Johnny goes to New York to meet with Stern. Johnny is told that Mrs. Lenore Carter had $800,000 in jewels stolen three months ago and now the insurance company must pay off. William Karnes, who was in on the robbery knows where the jewels are. The police in Havana are holding him for extradition on federal charges. Johnny is told that the insurance company wants to know where the jewels are before Karnes is put away. Johnny is to find out where the jewels are before Karnes is extradited. Also, there is a bonus if you succeed.

Johnny goes to Havana, Cuba and goes to the jail to meet with Karnes. Johnny poses as a reporter to get into the jail and question Karnes about the jewels. While Johnny is in the cell with Karnes, a man comes in with the police chief held at knifepoint and kills the guard, opens the cell and Karnes leaves. "A friend sent me", the man tells Karnes. The man with the knife apparently knows who Johnny is and tells him to leave too.

Johnny follows Karnes to a dark cantina and asks the barkeeper where Karnes is. The bartender does not like Johnny, so Johnny pulls his gun and suddenly the bartender remembers that Karnes went to see Maria. Johnny goes upstairs to Maria's room, and Johnny describes her as a good reason to uphold the good neighbor policy anywhere. Maria tells Johnny that she does not know where Karnes went and tells Johnny to leave. Johnny offers her a $300 bonus for information, and she gives Johnny an address to go to. Johnny has to check to see if his hair is on fire as he leaves.

Johnny goes to #3 Avenida Porfidio, breaks down the door as quietly as possible, and finds Karnes diving for a dresser drawer. Johnny points his .38 at Karnes and asks him where the jewels are. Karnes offers to make a deal, but Johnny only wants the jewels, so Karnes tells Johnny they are in a bedpost. The man with the knife comes in and thanks Karnes for telling him where the jewels are. He takes the jewels and Johnny's gun. The man tells Karnes that a friend told him to let Karnes out but he decided to take the jewels. The man leaves and Karnes hits Johnny with a metal bedpost.

When Johnny wakes it is night, and all seems lost. He goes to his hotel and calls Mr. Stern to update him. Johnny tells Stern that he wants the name of the person who gave the tip to Stern, but he cannot divulge that information. As Johnny is talking, the police show up with Sgt. Evans of the NYPD who wants to know who let Karnes out. Evans wants the story, so Johnny tells him why he is there, except for Maria and the jewels. Evans tells Johnny that he will call New York and Johnny is told to stay put.

After talking to Evans, Johnny goes to see Maria. She is singing and points to her room with her eyes. Johnny goes up to her room, and Maria comes up and makes herself comfortable. After some small talk she tells Johnny that Karnes came there three months ago, and he was "the best one around" and always seemed to have money. She tells Johnny that she was the only one Karnes spent time with. Johnny describes the man with the knife, but she does not remember seeing the man. As they are talking there is a knock at the door and Evans comes in and he wants to talk to Johnny.

On the way outside Evans tells Johnny that Intercontinental did not hire Johnny, and that Stern is out of town. Evans wants to arrest Johnny, but Johnny spots Karnes by the door. They follow Karnes and Evans is shot. Johnny follows Karnes and Johnny wounds him. Karnes finally runs out of ammunition as Johnny gets to him. Karnes tells Johnny that his fellow thief in the Carter job got him out, Roger Stern. Karnes dies and Johnny goes after Stern.

Johnny calls the airport for arriving flights from New York, and one is due in an hour. Johnny goes to the airport and waits for Stern's flight in a cab. Sterns catches a cab and is followed by Johnny to a building. Johnny breaks in and hears the man with the knife trying to convince Stern that he does not have the jewels. Roger Stern gives the man the old "count to ten before he shoots" routine and at ten the man tells Roger that the jewels are in his hat. Johnny interrupts the argument and the man throws a knife and kills Stern. Johnny shoots the man and the Jewels are found in a leather bag in his hat.

The final story is that Stern needed money and had given Karnes the combination to the safe but Karnes cheated Stern. Roger found him in Havana and hired Johnny. Johnny has saved intercontinental $800,000 and Roger Stern was an employee of the company when he hired Johnny, so please pay the bonus promised by Stern. If it takes longer than two weeks send it to the Cantina el Gallo where he is going for vacation.

Notes:
- Johnny is carrying a .38 revolver.
- Tomorrow night is *The FBI in Peace and War*.
- Edmond O'Brien's new movie is *War Path*.
- Dan Cubberly is the announcer.
- Music is by Eddie Dunstedter.

Producer: Jaime del Valle   Writer: Blake Edwards
Cast: Ted Osborne, Jack Kruschen, Barney Phillips, Nestor Paiva, Lillian Buyeff, Stacy Harris

Show: The Protection Matter
Show Date: 9/26/1951
Company: Columbia All-Risk Insurance Company
Agent: Phillip Martin
Exp. Acct: $101.92

Synopsis: A call comes in from Phillip Martin about Mr. Bennie Waxman who owns a deli that burned. It happened last night and it was arson. Come on down.

Johnny goes to New York City and Mr. Waxman's apartment. The police are there and Waxman tells Lt. Parkinson that he did not commit arson. Parkinson tells Johnny that an incendiary device was used. Johnny tells Parkinson that the Insurance was for $20,000, and Parkinson tells Waxman that he will not get the money. Parkinson tells Johnny that they are sure he is guilty and are pressing him hard, as a man died in the fire. Waxman tells Johnny that Waxman makes a good living but only has $600 in the bank. Waxman tells Johnny that he gave $5,000 to his daughter who they cannot find. Waxman tells Johnny and Parkinson that she is on a vacation and that he does not want the insurance money. Parkinson leaves and Johnny talks to Waxman. He tells Johnny that he cannot prove that he is innocent. Johnny asks him what he is afraid of, and Waxman claims he is only nervous. Johnny tells Waxman that the $5,000 excuse is pretty weak. Johnny leaves and thinks about the case. Johnny is sure that Waxman is scared, but of what?

Johnny goes to the 15th precinct, and Parkinson is in his office. Over a cup of coffee, they discuss the case. Parkinson admits that Waxman did not start the fire and that he is riding him to get information on a well-controlled protection racket. Parkinson tells Johnny that he is scaring Waxman to try and get information from his friends. Parkinson thinks that maybe the daughter was kidnapped, but Waxman has been beaten up and is not the type to pay protection. Why would he burn the store if he paid the $5,000 to the racket? As they are talking Parkinson gets a phone call from Angeleno Jusseppi, who wants to talk.

Johnny and Parkinson go the deli and talk to Angie and he tells them that he has evidence that Waxman did not burn the store. "Them guys who collect the money each week did it" he tells Parkinson. Angie freezes up and Johnny spots two men crossing the street. The men come in and tell Angie that they want the envelope. Parkinson recognizes one of the men named "Red" and is shot. Johnny shoots the men and Parkinson tells Johnny that the man with the red hair was named Dillon and worked for Dutch Fischer and then dies.

When the police arrive, Johnny explains what had happened to officer Brenners, who offers Angie protection. Brenners tells Johnny that the other owners are threatened. Angie tells Johnny that the men have his daughter but Angie wants no more trouble, as he must think of the others. Angie relents and tells Johnny and Brenners that the men took Waxman's daughter because he would not pay. Angie is told that the store was a lesson to the others after Waxman paid the $5,000 to get his daughter back. Angie tells Johnny that she is supposed to be freed tonight.

Johnny looks at mug shots and gets Dillon's record, and he is a bad boy. From the records Johnny learns that Dutch Fischer is still in prison. The FBI calls and they identify the other man as Lou Fleischman, who went up on a robbery charge with Dillon. Brenners checks the files and finds that a fourth man, George Biulotti is related to the other three. Biulotti's record is pulled and Brenners recognizes him as George Bivens, a reputable nightclub owner who is clean. Johnny goes to see Bivens at the Yellow Parrot, and slugs Ziggy to get into Bivens' office. Johnny tells Bivens that Dillon and Fleishman and Parkinson are dead. Johnny tells him about the jobs Bivens had worked with them. As Bivens tries to throw Johnny out a fight ensues and Johnny beats Bivens until he gets the information he wants. Johnny calls the police to pick up Bivens three minutes later.

Johnny then goes to a warehouse to meet Brenners. They enter through a window and find an office where two men are holding the girl. Brenners creates a diversion to get the men out of the office and there is a gunfight that kills the two men. Johnny and Brenners free the girl and she is taken to her father. The storeowners are planning the biggest block party since the Boston tea caper.

Make sure the next simple insurance fire is simple. I don't mind helping people out occasionally, but I'm too old and too under paid to go back to being a boy scout.

Notes:
- A new time is announced for next week Saturday, October 6.
- There is a public service announcement to support the Crusade for Freedom.
- The Virgil Akins — Freddie Dawson fight follows the program.
- The script page lists Hy Averback and Raymond Burr. Burr is announced as Ray Hartman, and Averback is replaced by Joel Samuels but the voice is Averback's.
- Dan Cubberly is the announcer.
- Music is by Eddie Dunstedter.
- Edmond O'Brien's new movie is *War Path*.

Producer:	Jaime del Valle	Writer:	Blake Edwards
Cast:	Joel Samuels, William Conrad, Sidney Miller, Jay Novello, Ray Hartman		

◆ ❖ ◆

Show: The Douglas Taylor Matter
Show Date: 10/6/1951
Company: Great Eastern Insurance Company
Agent: Mr. Nibley
Exp. Acct: $181.20

Synopsis: Lt. Rees from homicide calls Johnny and asks if he hired a detective named Douglas Taylor? He was found dead this morning. Come down and answer a few questions.

Johnny goes to the Hartford, Connecticut police headquarters and meets with Rees who tells Johnny that they do not know where or when Taylor was killed as his body was dumbed down by the freight yards. His wife told the police that he was working for Johnny. Johnny tells Rees that he cannot answer questions about the case because it will jeopardize a case worth $500,000, but Rees wants all the information. Johnny tells him that two men are suspected of insurance fraud and Taylor was tailing one of them. Johnny tells Rees that he knew Doug for about two years and knew of no troubles with his wife. Rees tells Johnny that the money is enough to hold Johnny on, but he is told to leave and Johnny knows that he is being followed.

Johnny calls Mr. Nibley at the insurance company and is told to drop the arson case he is working on. Johnny tells Nibley that Taylor's wife probably knows nothing about the case, but Johnny will check with her.

Johnny goes to see Mrs. Taylor and he tells her that Doug was not killed because of the case he was working on for Johnny. She tells Johnny that Doug was a police officer for 12 years, and she has been waiting for this day for 19 years. She is glad Johnny came by. She tells Johnny that Doug never talked about cases or any trouble. Johnny asks about another woman, and she tells him that she suspected Doug but never found out anything. She tells Johnny that Henry Varner, his ex-partner, is a hotel detective at the Hotel Millard.

As they are talking Rees arrives and jumps all over Johnny for rehearsing a story with Mrs. Taylor. Rees tells Johnny that Doug's office has been torn apart by someone looking for something. Rees tells Johnny to get the case cleared up, or he will put him out of business.

Johnny goes to see Henry Varner, who saw Doug last week. He seemed fed up over something and had said that there was going to be a change. He talked of going away, without his wife, who Varner describes as a jealous creep. He has no idea what the change was going to be. Varner tells Johnny that she could be capable of killing Doug, as she was strange.

Johnny goes back to the Taylor home and sees the lights go on. Johnny knocks at the door and a man with a gun opens the door. The man tells Johnny that he had hit Mrs. Taylor in the bedroom and tells Johnny that Doug was too filthy to stay alive and too dirty rotten to live. He leaves and shoots as Johnny tries to follow. Johnny holds back and realizes that he was young and out of his head with fear. The plain-clothes man following Johnny was nowhere to be found and Doug's killer disappears into the night.

Mrs. Taylor was OK but hysterical, and the police are called. She tells Johnny that the man was going to kill her, and that he said Doug had ruined two lives and that he had killed him. She tells Johnny that she has never seen the man before. Johnny is sure the man is the same one that broke into Doug's office.

When Rees arrives, Johnny tells him that he had not tried to lose the tail and what had happened. Johnny gives Rees a description of the boy, including the Smith and Wesson .38 with a black rubber grip, and a class ring on his hand. Rees accuses Johnny of firing the shots, but Johnny tells him he is not carrying his gun. Rees accuses Johnny of hiding the gun, but Johnny tells him he is being an ass, and to stop riding his badge so that they can work together on the case. Johnny tells him that it is obvious that Doug had something on the shooter. Rees tells Johnny that they had gone through Doug's house and office and had found nothing.

The next day Johnny sees his name in the papers as an investigator whose involvement is not clear. That night the boy comes to Johnny's apartment. He tells Johnny that Doug had brought Johnny in for protection. He had told Doug that he could not pay anymore and that he wants the file Doug has on him. Johnny tells the boy he believes him and tries to reason with him. The boy says that Johnny had come to Doug's apartment and that his name was in the paper, so he must have the file. The boy starts to leave and the door buzzes, but it is just a delivery boy. Johnny tries to get the boy to give himself to the police, but the boy is really nervous and will not give up, as he would rather die instead. He has to protect the family. The boy tells Johnny that his father had hired Doug to investigate the boy two years ago, and Doug had been blackmailing the family ever since. Johnny leaves the apartment with the boy and the police stop him on the street. Shots are fired and the boy is cut down with a submachine gun.

The father, Judge Bardette and the family was hit by scandal, which is what the boy was trying to stop.

Notes:
- The mid-program commercial is for *Our Miss Brooks* and *The Edgar Bergen and Charlie McCarty Show*, which return tomorrow night.
- There is a public service announcement for CARE and food given to the families of Yugoslavia.
- Once again, Raymond Burr is announced as Ray Hartman.
- This program was modified and done by John Lund as *The Singapore Arson Matter* on 11/28/52.
- Edmond O'Brien's next movie is *Silver City*.
- Dick Cutting is the announcer.
- Music is by Wilbur Hatch.

Producer:	Jaime del Valle	Writer:	Gil Doud
Cast:	Ray Hartman, Joseph Kearns, Edgar Barrier, Jeanette Nolan, Hy Averback		

◆ ❖ ◆

Show: **The Millard Ward Matter**
Show Date: **10/13/1951**
Company: **Plymouth Life Insurance Company**
Agent: **Willard Dunhill**
Exp. Acct: **$419.95**

Synopsis: Willard Dunhill calls from Plymouth Life Insurance Company and has an assignment for Johnny. A policyholder named Millard Ward was killed on a ship and there is a possibility of fraud. The ship is due in New Orleans tomorrow, and Willard wants Johnny to look into the case.

Johnny goes to New Orleans, Louisiana and meets the "Death Ship". Johnny goes on board with Lt. Tracy and meets the chief mate, Mr. Edward Donovan. Johnny is told that Louis Rodnick is in the brig and the knife is in the body. Johnny is told that Rodnick would say nothing. Donovan tells Johnny that Ward and Rodnick were working together and Ward's body was found in the forepeak.

Johnny looks at the murder site and is told that the knife was kept in the forepeak for opening paint cans. Donovan tells Johnny and Tracy that there had been bad blood between Ward and Rodnick. Johnny meets with Rodnick and he denies killing Ward or having anything to do with Ward's wife. He tells Johnny that he hardly knew Ward's wife and had met her once when he was sick and missed a trip. Rodnick tells Johnny that Ward was alive when he left the locker.

Tracy questions Rodnick and gets the same story. Johnny and Tracy talk to the crew, who tell him that Ward and Rodnick hated each other. Johnny and Tracy talk to Ward's wife, who tells them that Rodnick did not kill Ward, and that there was nothing going on between her and Rodnick. She tells them that she does not have too many friends and that she hates New Orleans and is sick and tired of Ward and did not leave him, as he would not last too much longer. As they leave, Mrs. Ward is told to come to the inquest the next day. Johnny then visits the two bars Rodnick hung out in and several people remember seeing Rodnick with Mrs. Ward, and one person tells Johnny he saw them leave separately, but never together.

At the coroner's inquiry, Herbert Massey tells the court that Ward and Rodnick were working together, and that he had found the body. Massey had gone to the forepeak to get Ward and found him with a knife in him and no pulse. The autopsy is read and said that the death might have been a suicide. Johnny goes to see Rodnick and he tells Johnny that he killed Ward in self-defense. Rodnick tells Johnny that Ward had always given him hard assignments and was riding him, so he killed him. Rodnick tells Johnny that Ward was trying to hit him with a paint can, so he killed in self-defense. Johnny suggests that Rodnick work on his story and hire a new lawyer.

Johnny and Tracy go to the ship and talk to Massey. They tell Massey that they need more evidence, so they go over what happened. Massey tells them that he noticed nothing out of usual in the forepeak and that there was no can of paint rolling around. Also, there were no signs of a struggle in the forepeak. Massey tells them that maybe everyone assumes Rodnick was the killer because of the bad blood. Johnny asks Massey who did kill him, and after talking over all aspects of the case, Massey thinks they are trying to blame him.

Johnny and Tracy go back to headquarters and Massey is investigated, but there is nothing on Massey, nothing on anyone. Johnny goes to see Rodnick and applies some pressure by accusing him of lying. Tracy tells Rodnick that the self-defense plea was the best thing that his lawyer could come up with. They make him think that Ward's wife had told them something about using him to kill Ward. Rodnick admits that Mrs. Ward was the one who begged him to kill Ward so they could leave New Orleans and live elsewhere. He was alone with Ward and had to do something, so he stabbed him.

There are no remarks as it was a clear case of attempted insurance fraud.

Notes:
- The forepeak is that part of a ship formed by the angle of the bow.
- *The Vaughn Monroe Show* returns tonight.
- Dan Cubberly is the announcer.
- Music is by Wilbur Hatch.
- Edmond O'Brien's next movie is *Silver City*.

Producer:	Jaime del Valle Writer: Gil Doud
Cast:	Sidney Miller, Barton Yarborough, William Conrad, Hy Averback, Jeanne Bates

♦ ❖ ♦

Show:	**The Janet Abbe Matter**
Show Date:	**10/20/1951**
Company:	**Columbia All-Risk**
Agent:	**Bob Rudd**
Exp. Acct:	**$2,796.00**

Synopsis: Bob Rudd from Columbia All-Risk calls Johnny and asks him to go to Malaysia and offers Johnny a bonus on this case. Johnny is told that an American woman and her daughter were killed there. The woman was the wife of an American planter. Her father got a letter hinting that the truth had been hidden.

Johnny goes to see Bob, who has a letter from Mrs. Abbe's father. He has information from the British authorities that the cause of death was from rebel gunfire. There is a $100,000 policy involved with the daughter as the beneficiary, and the husband as the second beneficiary. Johnny meets with Mr. Stevenson, Mrs. Abbe's father, who has the letter from the authorities in the area.

Johnny flies to Singapore and then on to Penang, Malaysia where he shows Constable Lamb the letter. Johnny is told that the plantations are under attack in that area, and that Mrs. Abbe was killed during an attack. The next day Johnny takes a train to meet Constable Rutherford who is not convinced that the husband killed his wife and daughter. Johnny is shown the official reports, written by the planters, of the attack by the Liberation Army. Johnny compares the handwriting of all the planters to the letter and does not find a match. Johnny goes to the plantation and is attacked on the way, but Johnny is sure that the attack was set up to scare him away. A rescue party arrives and Johnny meets two of the local planters, Gerrish and Sterley.

Johnny arranges to go to the Abbe plantation with Gerrish, and Johnny tells him that he knows that he did not get all of the records, and that one was missing. Gerrish is most uncooperative and will not tell Johnny who the missing planter is. Johnny ends up slugging Gerrish and is taken back to Constable Rutherford, but he is out with the troops who have gone to the Abbe plantation.

Gerrish drives Johnny to the Abbe plantation, where Abbe is a drunken wreck. Johnny gets into the compound and talks to Abbe, who admits killing his wife and daughter. Abbe tells Johnny that the rebels had taken Sterley's wife, and she was found later. All of the other planters took an oath to kill their wives rather than let them be taken by the rebels. He tells Johnny that the rebels were inside the house, which was on fire. He shot his wife and daughter but did not have to, because a rescue party arrived. The rebel attack starts, and Johnny notes that murder was committed, but without criminal intent. Johnny did not report that Abbe was found dead after the rebel attack.

Notes:
- The announcer is Dick Cutting.
- Music is by Wilbur Hatch.
- Story information obtained from the KNX Collection in the Thousand Oaks Library.

Producer:	Jaime del Valle	Writer:	Gil Doud
Cast:	Jack Kruschen, Barney Phillips, Lillian Buyeff, Nestor Paiva, Ted Osborne, Stacy Harris, Dan Cubberly		

• ❖ •

Show:	**The Tolhurst Theft Matter**
Show Date:	**10/27/1951**
Company:	**Tri-State Insurance Group**
Agent:	**Jim Madison**
Exp. Acct:	**$77.60**

Synopsis: Jim Madison at Tri-State calls Johnny about the Tolhurst fur theft. Johnny is told that a woman has called Jim about the case but does not want the police called. She wants a call back by three o'clock. Jim wants Johnny to talk to the woman and is willing to work without the police and will cut corners if Johnny will.

Johnny relates the origins of the Tolhurst theft, which occurred when three men entered a fur store at gunpoint and took $50,000 in cash. The police followed the getaway cars, and a gunfight ensued, but the men escaped.

Johnny goes to the Tri-State office to take the anonymous phone call. Johnny talks to the woman, and he tells her that the money is more important than having someone arrested and is willing to work without the police. The caller knows where one of the men is hiding. The man is at the Standing Hotel in Boston using the name Taft, and he is desperate.

Johnny drives to Boston, Massachusetts and follows the man named Taft into his room where the man pulls a gun. Johnny shows Taft his identification but Taft tells Johnny that Allen Less hired Johnny to find him. Johnny explains that he only wants the money and will help him to get a break. Johnny tries to convince him to tell what he knows, but to no avail. Johnny tells the man that he has been double-crossed and Taft slugs Johnny and locks him in the closet.

When Johnny wakes up, he searches the room, which is empty, and calls Tri-State and reports the events. Johnny tells Jim Madison that he wants to look into the money angle at the fur store, as there was too much money on hand.

Johnny goes to see Mr. Tolhurst the next morning and asks about the money. Tolhurst tells Johnny that most fur purchases are made in cash to make beautiful women more beautiful. And, there are many more rich men than there are beautiful wives, as opposed to women, that is. So, if wifey does not get the coat, she does not want to find a check paying for one, or the fur would fly, literally. Tolhurst tells Johnny that if the name of one of the purchasers were to become known it could endanger national security and be talked about on the floor of the Senate. Johnny is told that he has no record to indicate who bought the coats, even though it might endanger the insurance claim.

Johnny goes to his apartment and the girl from the previous day is calling and she is hurt. Johnny goes to her address and the girl tells Johnny that they beat her because they think she has the money, but she does not have it. They want to know where Fred Serrell (Taft) is. The girl tells Johnny that Fred has the money. He is at an auto court on the way to Boston, the Oak Springs Motel. She tells Johnny that her name is Virginia Cowley and she knows nothing of the robbery. Fred had left his car there and had told her after the robbery that there was big trouble. Johnny tells her he will have to call the police to stay out of trouble.

Johnny calls the police and tells his story but is still in trouble. Johnny drives to the motel and meets Lt. Crockett. Inside the cottage there are two bodies but Serrell is not one of them. He updates Crockett about the anonymous call and they go back to headquarters to talk. Johnny gives him all he knows, but Crockett wants Johnny to drop the case and to go home and brush up on police work!

Risking his license, Johnny visits the Cowley apartment and gets an address for Serrell in Princeton, so Johnny goes there. At the address, the landlord tells Johnny that Serrell is out of town. Johnny asks to get in to the apartment to leave a note, and the landlord tells Johnny that he can talk to Serrell's roommate, a man named Hacker who is there. Johnny talks to Hacker he had heard from Serrell a couple days ago because he needed money. Johnny tells Hacker about the robbery and Hacker knows Al Hudson and Les Vernick, two of Serrell's friends. Hacker confirms that Serrell had written to him using the name Taft. Johnny is told that Serrell's mother has a farm nearby in Tarrington. Johnny searches the room and then goes to the mother's farm after stopping by his apartment to pick up a pocket gun.

At the farm Johnny talks to the hired hand. He knows about the robbery and has sent Mrs. Serrell to town to keep the news from her. Johnny is told that Serrell will not come here, and that Mrs. Serrell is blind and nearly deaf. The hand tells Johnny that Serrell has not been back in three years, and that the neighbors had told him to leave, as he is bad. His mother thinks that Fred is in Australia in the hardware business, and no one will tell her otherwise.

Back in Harford the newspapers have the story and there are questions in Johnny's mind. The motel was close to where the car was abandoned so Johnny goes to the site and finds the car. Johnny calls Crockett and asks for assistance. Crockett will see what he can do, and Johnny waits for someone to come back to the car. At sunset, Serrell comes back and Johnny tells him that he cannot get away. Serrell tells Johnny that the money is buried there and Serrell offers him a share. As Serrell searches hysterically for the money, Johnny slugs him and takes his gun.

The police finally find the money so the company is not out. Johnny and Crockett get together, so Johnny is not out, and the girl was nothing. Serrell lost his mind over money, and Tolhurst did not lose the universal customer, the wealthy American husband.

Notes:
- Virginia Colley lived at 5860 Stoddard Street, Apt 12. There is a 5860 Stoddard Avenue today in Hartford.
- There is a public service announcement to buy Defense Bonds.
- This program was performed as *The Eighty-Five Little Minks*, on 3/14/1950. The names and business are changed, but the plot is the same.
- Dan Cubberly is the announcer.
- Music is by Wilbur Hatch.
- Edmond O'Brien's next movie is *Silver City*.

Producer:	Jaime del Valle	Writer:	Gil Doud
Cast:	Parley Baer, Virginia Gregg, Stacy Harris, Bob Sweeney, Herb Butterfield, Clayton Post, Howard McNear		

• ❖ •

Show: **The Hannibal Murphy Matter**
Show Date: 11/3/1951
Company: **Plymouth Insurance Company**
Agent:
Exp. Acct: $734.40

Synopsis: Inspector Trabert returns Johnny's call about the accidental death of Hannibal Murphy. Johnny is told that Mr. Murphy's death was not accidental. There was a bullet hole in his head.

Johnny goes to Kingston, Jamaica and checks into the Myrtleback Hotel, and then goes to meet Inspector Trabert. Johnny is told that Murphy has a wife, a brother and a stepdaughter staying at his cottage, and that the brother and stepdaughter had been visiting him here. Based on the bullet wound, Trabert has ruled out suicide. Johnny and Trabert go to see the Murphys, who are described as a family spoiled by money, and who could be hated by a lot of people. Johnny is shown the scene of the murder, which is a rocky beach below a cliff where a local boy found the body while fishing. Trabert tells Johnny that there are no signs of a struggle and it is confusing as to how the murder happened.

Johnny goes to the Murphy cottage where Johnny is met by Felice, the daughter of Mrs. Murphy. Felice tells Johnny that the death was not an accident. Johnny tells her that there will be all sorts of questions, but she is not worried even though she hated him, as he was rotten. Mrs. Murphy comes in and slaps Felice, who has been a "difficult child" and sends her to her room. Johnny is told that the brother, Paul, is out making arrangements. Mrs. Murphy tells Johnny that she knows of no one who would want to kill her husband, and that they do not go out much. She tells Johnny that Hannibal said he was just going to take a walk, as he was not sleepy. Mrs. Murphy tells Johnny that Felice is not guilty, but that she is a poor unbalanced girl full of warped hatreds and misunderstandings and that Felice will say things about Hannibal and me.

Johnny leaves and finds Felice outside on the bridal path. She tells Johnny that she is mixed up and thinks that Hannibal is stealing her mother from her. She tells Johnny that she is glad Hannibal is dead. Johnny tells her that he understands the problems of being a stepchild these days, as it is more commonplace.

Johnny tells Trabert about the conversations, and he calls Paul Murphy into his office to talk to him that afternoon. Paul tells them that he had gone to bed and Hannibal went for a walk. Hannibal had said nothing about meeting anyone. Trabert notes that a .25 caliber pistol was used at close range, so someone was with him or followed him, and robbery is not a motive. Paul has no additional information to give. A few minutes later Paul phones the inspector and asks for an ambulance as Felice has cut her wrists in a suicide attempt.

Johnny goes to the Murphy residence and speaks with Dr. Gurley who tells Johnny that Felice needs a good psychiatrist. Johnny speaks with Felice who tells Johnny that her mother and Paul killed Hannibal. Felice tells Johnny that last summer her mother had tired of Hannibal and had wanted a divorce. Felice tells Johnny and the Inspector that her parents had argued and Paul and Hannibal left. Later she heard a shot at 11:15. She tells them that Paul came back a few minutes later. She tells Johnny and the Trabert that she has always hated her mother and wants to be taken away from here, as she is afraid. The Trabert arranges for Felice to be taken to a police hospital and repeats her statement.

Trabert receives a call from a sporting goods storeowner, Mr. Innes, who tells him that a man tried to sell him a .25 caliber Webley pistol. Innes describes the man, who is English. Trabert goes to arrest Paul and Mrs. Murphy who deny the story told by Felice. Mrs. Murphy tells Inspector Trabert that Felice had lied and that she thinks that Felice killed Hannibal.

Mrs. Murphy and Paul are taken in, although Trabert tells Johnny that he has no alternative. Johnny goes to the hospital where Felice tells Johnny that she is alone now. She insists to Johnny that she told the truth. Johnny recounts her story detail by detail, but she sticks to it.

Johnny prepares to leave, but Trabert calls and reports that the gun from the store is the murder weapon, and it has been traced to a local criminal, Roy Church. Johnny talks to Church who tells Johnny that Paul was going to pay him 500 pounds to kill Hannibal but welshed on the deal after being paid 100 pounds. He needed money, which is why he sold the pistol. He was supposed to have taken the wallet but Hannibal fell over the cliff. So, Felice really did not see anything.

Johnny invites Trabert to come up and work a simple Hartford murder sometime, as it would do him good.

Notes:
- Later this evening *Gang Busters* tracks the perfect crime.
- The announcers are Dan Cubberly and Dick Cutting.
- Music is by Wilbur Hatch.
- Edmond O'Brien's next movie is *Silver City*.

Producer: Jaime del Valle   Writer: Gil Doud
Cast: Eric Snowden, Virginia Gregg, Jeanette Nolan, Ben Wright, Charles Davis, Dan O'Herlihy

♦ ❖ ♦

Show: **The Birdy Baskerville Matter**
Show Date: **11/10/1951**
Company: **Columbia All-Risk Insurance Company**
Agent: **Phillip Martin**
Exp. Acct: **$137.27**

Synopsis: Phillip Martin calls and has a job for Johnny. Carl Baskerville wants to change his beneficiary to a charity, as his brother is trying to kill him. Phil wants Johnny to be a bodyguard, and the policy is for half a million. Phil has looked at the records and Carl had sent his brother William to prison and he was released last week.

Johnny goes to the Long Island, New York mansion of Carl Baskerville where Collins, Mr. Baskerville's personal secretary, meets Johnny at the door. Collins is 6' 9" and is described by Johnny as "the tallest man I have ever seen". Johnny is taken to see Mr. Baskerville, who is in the garden feeding the birds, and he encourages Johnny to join him (here birdie, birdie!). Mr. Baskerville outlines to Johnny how he has retired after working his entire life to be successful. He tells Johnny that his brother William had been caught stealing $100,000 from the company and Mr. Baskerville was forced to prosecute him. William was to inherit Mr. Baskerville's entire estate, but now he must change the beneficiary as William has sent a letter threatening to kill him. Johnny is told that, after William has a chance to calm down, Mr. Baskerville will put him back in the will. Johnny is also told William had a girlfriend, Virginia Carter, who lives in Greenwich Village.

Johnny walks out to get a cab and hears shots. Johnny runs back to the garden and Mr. Baskerville is dead, with a bullet in his heart. Collins comes running out and tells Johnny that he had seen William with a gun. Johnny goes into the house to call the police. While talking to Lt. Brenners, Johnny realizes he has made a fatal mistake. He goes out to the body and discovers the letter is gone.

Johnny goes to Greenwich Village to visit Virginia Carter. At the door Johnny gets the quickest scalding in history, as Johnny is met by a lovely woman wearing "something thin enough to make a silkworm hang himself". Johnny is invited in, and sits in a very dark living room and has a very hot conversation with Miss

Carter. She tells Johnny that she knew William, and that he had shown her a good time. All of her men show her a good time. Johnny spends several hours with her trying to look at her photo album of her men. Finally, she shows Johnny a picture of William and tells Johnny that he used to play the saxophone. Johnny leaves and is almost rundown by a car.

At the musician's union, Johnny learns William has renewed his card, and is having his mail sent to a swing joint on 52nd street. Johnny cabs to the club and a piano player tells Johnny that William was there but just got up and left around 4:30. For a $5 bribe, Johnny gets William's address. Johnny goes to the address and gets no answer at the door. Johnny is curious enough about noises inside the apartment to open the door to find William swinging from a noose. Johnny is suspicious when he puts the chair under William's feet and they do not touch — he is dangling above the chair. The phone rings and Johnny answers it to hear Virginia's voice. Johnny hangs up and goes back to visit her.

Virginia lets Johnny in and makes a mistake by greeting Johnny by name. "Who told you my name?" he asks. After telling her what Johnny suspects, Virginia admits that she had been seeing Collins. She tells Johnny that William and Collins had stolen the money, but only William got caught. Collins had faked the letter to Mr. Baskerville to frame William. As they are talking shots ring out and Virginia is killed.

Johnny fires 6 times at Collins and hits him. Before he dies, Collins tells Johnny that he had used Johnny as a witness to frame William, whom he had killed to avoid splitting the money. He had called Virginia and told her to tell Johnny everything so that he could find William and arrange the suicide. Before he dies, Collins says it should be raining, as it is too nice of a night to die.

At the end, Johnny notes that murder isn't so bad. A ride in any New York cab makes a killing look like a Sunday School taffy pull.

Notes:
- **Edmond O'Brien asks listeners to donate blood for the Korean War campaign.**
- **The announcers are Dan Cubberly and Dick Cutting.**
- **Music is by Wilbur Hatch.**
- **Edmond O'Brien's next movie is *Silver City*.**
- **A program of the same title is broadcast on 3/10/1953.**

Producer:	Jaime del Valle	**Writer:**	Blake Edwards
Cast:	Stacy Harris, Bill Bouchey, Howard McNear, Sidney Miller, Virginia Gregg		

Show:	**The Merrill Kent Matter**
Show Date:	**11/17/1951**
Company:	**Washingtonian Life Insurance Company**
Agent:	**Mr. Lavery**
Exp. Acct:	**$378.40**

Synopsis: Mr. Lavery calls and asks if Johnny is ready for an assignment. Johnny is to go to a small town near Gallop to look into the death of Merrill Kent. Kent was thought to have died from an accident, but the police have information that leads them to think it was murder. Johnny is told he will have to arrange for an autopsy when he gets there, as Lavery wants to know if Kent was murdered or not.

Johnny travels to Fort Scott, New Mexico where Johnny meets deputy York, the local police department. York tells Johnny that he received a phone call that could not be traced. The caller disguised her voice and told York that Kent had been murdered. Johnny is told that Kent was killed when his horse fell and then dragged him back to his home. York calls the death bad luck. Johnny gets the name of the local physician, Doctor Snyder, and is not sure that York is happy about him being there.

Johnny visits Dr. Snyder and is met by his nurse, Mrs. Snyder. Johnny meets Dr. Snyder and tells him about the phone call, and Dr. Snyder calls it preposterous. Johnny tells him that he must ask questions and Dr. Snyder tells Johnny that he had been called to the ranch and Kent was dead when he got there. The body was on the ground, and Johnny asks if he could prove that Kent had been in the saddle. Dr. Snyder did not examine the boot or the ankle, as the body was covered with a blanket. Dr. Snyder tells Johnny that Kent had died from multiple fractures to the skull caused by an accident. Johnny tells him that he will order an autopsy, and that a sister from Seattle is on her way in case they need her authority. On the way out, Johnny hears a woman crying hysterically inside.

Johnny goes back to York's office and learns that Kent was often away on business, and Mrs. Kent did not go with him. York tells Johnny that the people in town are his friends, and he does not want anyone to turn out to be a killer, especially Maxine Kent, who is loved by everyone in the area.

Johnny goes to the Kent ranch and Mrs. Kent, a beautiful woman in her mid-twenties, meets Johnny at the driveway. She knows who Johnny is, as her brother had called her. She asks Johnny how she can order an autopsy so soon, and Johnny tells her all she has to do is to sign a paper. She tells Johnny she wants to do what is right.

Johnny goes back to York's office, and is told to go to Dr. Snyder's office and see York there. Mrs. Snyder has killed herself and left a letter claiming she was the caller. Johnny meets York who tells Johnny that Snyder had found his wife and that the letter claims that the call was based on false suspicions about Dr. Snyder and Mrs. Kent. Johnny reads the note, which outlines the suspicions that turned out to be baseless. Having no happiness in her future, it ended with her begging for her husband's forgiveness.

Johnny talks to Dr. Snyder who tells Johnny that he is in love with Maxine Kent but could not divorce his wife unless he were prepared to leave town, which he cannot do. He had broken off the affair and lied to his wife about it. When Merrill was killed, it fueled the doubts held by this wife and drove her crazy. Johnny asks why he said, "killed", and Snyder tells Johnny that his motives are public now and being wrong does not help.

Dr. Snyder tells Johnny that he was in his office when Kent was killed, and his wife had gone out to shop. Johnny tells him that the widow is authorizing the autopsy, and Snyder has nothing else to say. The deputies arrive and Snyder is put in jail.

After answering their questions, Johnny goes to the Kent ranch and meets Maxine's brother who tells Johnny that she has gone to Santa Fe. Johnny asks when she left and he tells Johnny that it was before Mrs. Snyder killed herself. Johnny tells him he should get his signals straight as Johnny was talking to her then. Johnny is told that Maxine flew apart when she heard about Mrs. Snyder and ran off to Santa Fe. Johnny is told that Maxine had nothing to do with Merrill's death as he was there when the horse dragged him in, and he took the foot out of the stirrup. Johnny learns that Dr. Snyder had not been to the ranch for several weeks, after Maxine made him stop. The last time was two weeks ago. He tells Johnny that he was the only one who knew where Merrill was going. Johnny tells him he will have Maxine picked up by the police, and the brother asks him to wait until morning.

The next day Mrs. Kent returns and signs the autopsy forms. The body is exhumed and the coroner's report is "Death by misadventure at the hands of person or persons unknown." Dr. Snyder and his wife's body are taken to the county seat and Johnny goes over all the evidence with York.

Johnny then goes back to the Kent ranch and asks Maxine why she ran out and is told that she just lost her head. Johnny tells her that the death was ruled accidental. Johnny and the deputy had gone out to the area where Merrill had gone and found a rifle he had fired, and where the horse had fallen and dragged him back. Maxine is happy that it is all over, that they believe her now.

Remarks: I'm sorry about the happy ending and the fact that everybody told the truth and that nobody was a criminal, and that the insurance claim is as good as New Mexico gold.

Notes:
- This program contains a commercial for the *Gang Busters* program, *The Talkative Boy.*
- Music is by Wilbur Hatch.
- Edmond O'Brien will soon be seen in the paramount production *Silver City.*
- The announcer is Dick Cutting.
- Edmond O'Brien talks about the duty of all citizens to provide blood for the soldiers involved in the Koran War.
- The script for this program lists Raymond Burr in the cast, but the announcer lists Ray Hartman.

Producer:	Jaime del Valle	Writer:	Gil Doud
Cast:	Ray Hartman, Joseph Kearns, Jeanette Nolan, Edgar Barrier, Virginia Gregg, Hy Averback		

♦ ❖ ♦

Show: **The Youngstown Credit Group Matter**
Show Date: **12/8/1951**
Company: **Columbia All-Risk Insurance Company**
Agent:
Exp. Acct: **$195.20**

Synopsis: Sgt. Biggin calls for Chief Allen to update Johnny on the robbery. Johnny is told that one victim has died and another one can be questioned shortly. Johnny tells Biggin that the take on the robbery is up to $48,000. Johnny is told that he can come over for the questioning.

Johnny goes to Youngstown, Ohio to work on a payroll robbery. Johnny is told by Biggin that the Youngstown Credit Group is a Savings and Loan set up to provide a check cashing service to plants in the Youngstown area. One of the trips was interrupted by a robbery. Both drivers of the car were thrown from it, and one has died.

Johnny and Chief Edward J. Allen, who had forced the Purple Gang out of Youngstown, go to the hospital to question Charley Watson. Johnny asks Allen why he is involved personally, and the Chief tells Johnny that "he has not gotten used to not being a sergeant". Charley tells Johnny that a car had been following them, and it had forced them off the road. Their car, a blue 1948 Plymouth, was taken and they were thrown from it while the car was in motion. Johnny is told that a number of people were familiar with the routine, and Charley gives a list of twelve names that the police check out.

Johnny goes to visit the widow of George Enfield, the man who died. She tells Johnny that she knows nothing and is worried about what to tell the kids and how to pay the bills. She did not know any of George's friends, and only knew that he went bowling a lot at the Highpoint Lanes.

Johnny is worried that the group will break up and the money will disappear. Later that night a tip comes in to the police. A farmer had seen a suspicious car, so Johnny and Allen go to visit the man. He tells them that he saw a blue car pull into a nearby dirt road where it was met by another car. Four men got out and drove back towards town. Johnny goes to the dirt road and finds the car, and a stain is found on the floor. The car is driven to police headquarters where the stain is confirmed to be blood.

The next day, the autopsy on George Enfield shows that he had been beaten, raising the suspicion that he knew who killed him. Johnny and Allen revisit Charley Watson, who can add only that he was begging for his life, yet George had said nothing. Johnny goes back to see Mrs. Enfield, who shows Johnny a railroad ticket to California. She tells Johnny that she knew something was wrong, as George had been out late every night for the past two weeks. She tells Johnny that she had called the bowling alley, but George had not been there for three days. She also remembers George talking to a man named Carl at the bowling alleys. She wonders why her husband would buy a ticket to California unless he was going to run away.

Johnny calls the police and a known criminal, Carl Huffman, is brought in. The reminds Carl that he has had problems with the law before and tells him to cooperate. Johnny tells Carl that he has been seen with George Enfield and asks if he was planning the robbery. During the questioning, Johnny tells him there is a witness to the car exchange. When Johnny tells Carl that his prints are on a piece of pipe found on the highway, Carl slips up and admits he was in on the robbery. Carl tells the that Bill Loyeck and Verne Clark were also involved, but it was Enfield's idea. Carl also implicates the Thayer brothers, who are back in town. Johnny is told that the Thayers were involved and were the ones who did the killing, as they did not like Enfield. They are back now, and are staying at their former hangout, the Tuxedo Club.

The police send men to watch the Tuxedo Club, and plans are made to pick up the Thayers at dusk. On the way Johnny is told all about the Thayers. Loyeck and Clark are picked up and they corroborate Carl's story. The police surround the club and the Thayer brothers try to escape but are forced back. The police, Allen and Johnny go to get them at 4:30, and the Thayers are killed in a hail of submachine gun fire.

The money was recovered for the most part, and the insurance company got the services of Edward J. Allen.

Notes:
- The following obituary is from the Congressional Record of 10/25/1990: Edward Joseph Allen was born November 13, 1907, in Erie, PA. He grew up in that southwestern Pennsylvania city and, on May 26, 1937, he married his hometown sweetheart, Dorothy Mae Davenport. They were blessed with two children and six grandchildren. Ed began his career as a patrolman in Erie and later worked with the FBI during World War II to assist Federal agents on investigations concerning sabotage, espionage, and subversion. After the war, he attended the FBI National Academy and in 1948 became police chief of Youngstown, OH. In Youngstown, Eddie teamed with a reform-minded mayor to drive the Mafia influence from that city. His efforts won him national recognition and Youngstown the "All-American City" Award in 1950. Later, in 1963, he published a book, "The Merchants of Menace", which analyzed Mafia activity in the United States.
- It is too bad that Rep. Dornan of California, who entered the above, did not know his geography, as Erie is in northwestern Pennsylvania.
- The Purple Gang was a real organization operated out of Detroit.
- Edmond O'Brien can be seen in the paramount production *Silver City*.
- Dick Cutting is the announcer.
- Music is by Wilbur Hatch.
- There is a public service announcement to give blood to assist in the Korean War.

Producer:	Jaime del Valle	**Writer:**	Gil Doud
Cast:	Ed Begley, William Johnstone, Parley Baer, Virginia Gregg, Tim Graham, Stacy Harris		

♦ ❖ ♦

Show: **The Paul Barberis Matter**
Show Date: **12/15/1951**
Company: **Britannia Insurance Company**
Agent: **Ad Meyers**
Exp. Acct: **$160.30**

Synopsis: Ad Meyers calls Johnny about the newspaper story on the disappearance of Paul Barberis, under somewhat mysterious circumstances. Johnny is told to go to the country place in Tylerville, which is where the maid called the police from.

Johnny drives to Tylerville, Connecticut, and meets Capt. Slack who tells Johnny that the house was all torn up, but there was no body, the car was gone and there were signs of a beating. Mrs. Barberis is coming up from New York later that day. Johnny is told that Paul Barberis was about 40, a successful criminal lawyer in Waterbury who is divorced and remarried. The wife called the house two days earlier and nothing seemed amiss. Paul Barberis also had come to the cabin unexpectedly. When the wife arrives, Slack tells her that someone was killed in the cabin, and that she is not to touch anything.

Johnny talks to the maid, who thinks that Mr. Barberis is dead. Johnny goes to Waterbury and talks to Andrew Proust, the partner of Barberis. Proust has no reason to think that Paul had killed anyone.

Johnny goes back to Tylerville and learns that two blankets are missing from the house, and that Barberis' car was the only one to have been there. Slack gets a call from a man in New Haven who might know something. Johnny goes to meet Mr. Taggert, who tells him that Phillip Ryan runs a service station in the area, and that his wife was killed and Barberis got the killer, a man named Hibson, off. Taggert is sure that Ryan is the one who killed Barberis.

Johnny and Slack go to see Ryan, who is expecting the police and leaves with them. Ryan is questioned and his confession seems sound. He tells Johnny that he was lured to the house and beat Barberis because he was out of his mind. Later the empty car belonging to Barberis is found in a quarry. The quarry is searched and Johnny goes back to Tylerville.

Johnny talks to Ryan's father who tells Johnny that Phillip was a good boy who got upset after the trial. Johnny and Slack return to the quarry, which is being pumped out. The maid comes there and tells Johnny that she heard Mrs. Barberis call for Phillip.

Johnny and Slack go back to talk to Ryan and go over his story. He tells them that he met Paul Barberis inside the house. He had a key and was supposed to meet Mrs. Barberis there. Johnny talks to Mrs. Barberis and tells her about Ryan's confession. She tells Johnny that she met Ryan at the trial and realized that her husband had no heart. She kept seeing Phillip and was supposed to be there but the husband found out. Phillips was supposed to leave if she did not arrive, and he didn't.

Notes:
- The announcer is Dan Cubberly.
- Music is by Wilbur Hatch.
- Story information obtained from the KNX Collection in the Thousand Oaks Library.

Producer:	Jaime del Valle Writer: Gil Doud
Cast:	Howard McNear, Raymond Burr, Jeanne Bates, Jeanette Nolan, Herb Butterfield, Peter Leeds

◆ ❖ ◆

Show:	**The Maynard Collins Matter**
Show Date:	**12/22/1951**
Company:	**Athena Life & Casualty Company**
Agent:	**Ed Grimm**
Exp. Acct:	**$310.00**

Synopsis: Johnny is called by Ed Grimm, who tells Johnny that Maynard Collins was found dead in Colorado Springs, but they think he was dead before the accident. The beneficiary is Delia Collins.

Johnny flies to Colorado Springs, Colorado and meets with Lt. Anders. Johnny is told that the Collins car went off the side of Canyon Road about 10:00 p.m., but Collins had been dead for about 2 hours, and had a severe blow to his head. His wife was at the theater in Pueblo at the time.

Johnny and Anders drive to Manitou Springs and talk to the neighbor, Mr. Pinkert, who tells them that he heard the crash. Johnny and Anders go to talk to Mrs. Collins and meet Ralph Turner, her nephew, and Ralph's mother Ada. Their story is that after dinner they went to a movie and Ralph drove them and then went bowling. Maynard did not go because he was supposed to play cards with Mr. Pinkert, but that was called off at the last minute. Johnny is told that Ralph and Maynard are very close, and that the car was left at the house.

Johnny verifies that Ralph was at a bowling alley from 7:15 to 10:15. Johnny talks to Mr. Pinkert, who tells them that he was home alone, and that he liked Maynard, but that Maynard and Delia always argued about money.

Johnny goes to police headquarters where Clint Bingham comes in and tells them that Maynard had called him around 7:30 about a flat tire. Clint went out and fixed it around 8:00. There was no one home, so he just fixed the flat and left. He tells Johnny that he heard a noise in the brush that sounded like someone running towards the Pinkert house. Anders tells Clint that Maynard was killed in the brush. A call comes in and Mr. Pinkert has been hit by a car and is in the hospital.

Johnny and Anders go to talk to Pinkert who tells them that he knew that Clint was at the house and thought he was running away, but he did not see him. Pinkert suggests that Johnny talk to Delia.

Johnny goes to see Delia and tells her about the talk of a fight. She tells Johnny that Maynard was paying for Ralph's college bills, but he found out that

Ralph was not really trying and would not pay anymore. Supposedly the Dean has not told Ralph yet.

Johnny goes to the hospital and learns that the murder weapon was a tire iron. Johnny is called by Dean Michener, who tells Johnny that Ralph did know that his uncle was removing him from the school because his secretary had told Ralph.

Johnny tells Anders and goes to the bowling alley and talks to the pin-girl who tells Johnny that she left the alley at 10:00. However, the alley was closed between 7:45 and 8:15 because that is her dinner break.

Johnny goes to the jail and Ralph admits knowing about the school. Ralph is told that his prints are on the tire iron and he confesses to walking to the house. He heard a car coming and left and then came back. He knew about Maynard and other women and he was bothering his mother, so he had to kill him.

Notes:
- The announcers are Dan Cubberly and Dick Cutting.
- Music is by Wilbur Hatch.
- Story information obtained from the KNX Collection in the Thousand Oaks Library.

Producer:	Jaime del Valle	Writer:	Kathleen Hite
Cast:	Ed Begley, Gil Stratton Jr, Jeanette Nolan, Virginia Gregg, Howard McNear, Hy Averback		

• ❖ •

Show: **The Alma Scott Matter**
Show Date: **12/29/1951**
Company: **Columbia All-Risk Insurance Company**
Agent:
Exp. Acct: **$572.00**

Synopsis: Alan Swain calls Johnny and wants to talk about the Alma Scott murder. He says he did not kill her and wants to talk. Johnny tells Alan he will meet him alone to talk.

Johnny goes to San Francisco, California to investigate the murder of Alma Scott. The police are looking for Alan Swain, who witnesses reported seeing leaving the apartment after the shots were fired. Johnny looks for Alan Swain for two days before Swain contacts him.

Johnny waits in front of a photography shop until a woman contacts Johnny and takes him in a cab to a café near the beach. The woman walks Johnny to the beach where he meets Alan Swain. Alan tells Johnny that he knows he is doing everything wrong and should have gone to the police, but he cannot prove he did not kill Alma. Alan tells Johnny that he and Alma were going to fly to Mexico to be married and then live in Los Angeles. Alan tells Johnny that the reservations are under the name A. J. Hall on CalMexico Airlines. He had used false names because Alma said that there might be people who would be looking for them. Alan tells Johnny that Alma had called him to say that certain people did not want her to leave and that she had changed her mind about going to

Mexico and hung up. Alan tells Johnny that he went to the apartment, heard shouting and a gunshot and then ran out. Alan tells Johnny that he has no idea who was in the apartment.

Alan leaves and the woman, who is Alan's sister Helen, takes Johnny to the café and they order drinks. Johnny asks Helen if the killer could have been a woman, as Alma had left a policy to a half-sister that cannot be found. Helen tells Johnny that Alma was a bad woman who was using Alan for something, and that Alan had no business being mixed up with her. Helen tells Johnny that Alma had previously been seeing a man named Walter Helm. Helen admits that she had tipped Helms to the marriage plans, but her plans to get Alan away from Alma are not working out. She leaves and Johnny goes to his hotel.

The next day Johnny visits the Scott apartment and talks to the witnesses. After interviewing all of them, their story of seeing only Swain in the hallway is full of holes, as no one was looking for another possible person in the hallway.

Johnny goes back to his hotel and is met by Walter Helm. Walter tells Johnny that he was a friend of Alma's and wants to get the killer. Walter reassures Johnny that the newspapers have told Johnny the wrong side of him, and that he is really sure that Swain is the killer. Walter tells Johnny that he had found out about Alma leaving with Alan and had paid her $15,000 to stay. But the check he gave her seems to be missing. Walter tells Johnny that he had given Alma a .32 caliber pistol registered to Walter that seems to be missing. Walter tells Johnny that he wants to "hire" Johnny, but Johnny says that it would be unethical to work for a suspect. Finally, Helm tells Johnny that he is going to offer a $20,000 reward for information.

The reward hits the newspapers and Alan calls Johnny about the reward scheme. Johnny tells him to give himself up, as the witnesses are not sure now of what they saw, but Alan is hesitant and must talk to Helen. Lt. Halloran of the police calls to tell Johnny that he has a confession from Helen.

Johnny goes to meet Halloran and tells him that he had met Alan and Helen but did not have enough to call the police. Halloran tells Johnny that the comment he had made to Helen about a woman killer had made her think Johnny had something on her, so she turned herself in.

Johnny talks to Helen in jail and she tells him that she never thought she would do it, and says she worked for 10 years in burlesque to support Alan. She tells Johnny that she killed Alma when she heard that she and Alan were going to Mexico. Helen had a .32 and shot Alma, waited until everyone left and went out the back door.

Halloran comes to the cell to tell Johnny that there has been a shooting at Walter Helm's home. Johnny goes there with Halloran and they find both Helms and Alan Swain shot. Alan tells Johnny that Helms took Alma away from him. Johnny talks to Helms who admits that he heard the shots while standing at the door and admits that he killed her. Alma was going to leave and he could not buy her back so he stopped her the only way he knew. No one was going to take her away.

Remarks: I was wrong from the beginning. I'm not making excuses for it, but I wasn't as far wrong as the sister. If her false confession had ended it, she wouldn't have taken the rap for her brother, who she thought was guilty, but for Walter Helm she was afraid was innocent. It only proves again that you have to watch the words that go above your signature.

Notes:
- Johnny drinks rye and soda.
- The mid-program commercial is for *The Edgar Bergen Show* tomorrow night.
- John Lund also did this program on 6/16/1953 as *The Emil Carter Matter*. The characters are reversed and the plot slightly different.
- Dan Cubberly and Dick Cutting the announcers.

Producer:	Jaime del Valle	Writer: Gil Doud
Cast:	Jack Moyles, Virginia Gregg, Jeanette Nolan, Herb Butterfield, Hy Averback, Harry Lang	

♦ ❖ ♦

Show: **The Glen English Matter**
Show Date: **1/5/1952**
Company: **Hartford Police**
Agent:
Exp. Acct: **$0.00**

Synopsis: This is a personal case based on Johnny's involvement with Glen English. Johnny has known Glen since 1947, and his wife even longer. Glen had studied under the GI Bill and opened a law office in Hartford, Connecticut in 1949. Johnny had occasionally used Glen for legal services and Glen had used Johnny.

Glen had called Johnny at 10:30 one night and had asked Johnny to photostat a statement, and told Johnny that he might stop by later, or he will see him in the morning. Johnny read of Glen's death in paper the next morning.

Johnny goes to see Glen's widow, Donna. Johnny looks through Glen's papers and finds nothing. Donna tells Johnny that Glen had called her from his office to say that he would be home late, so she went to a movie. She is sad that she will never see him again and wonders what will she do? Donna tells Johnny that she is going to stay with Glen's mother for a while.

Johnny goes to the office and talks to Glen's secretary. She tells Johnny that she had left at 5:00, and that Glen was working late for a new client. Johnny tells her that he will take care of her salary through the next month and looks through the office and finds nothing.

Johnny goes to see Lt. Dolger at police headquarters. Dolger tells Johnny that there is not enough evidence to launch a murder investigation. Johnny tells Dolger about the evidence Glen had mentioned, and Johnny thinks that Glen was killed on the way over to see him. Johnny tells Dolger that there is no reason for Glen to be at the intersection where he was killed, except that he was on his way to see Johnny.

Johnny gets the police reports and the autopsy report details that there were multiple fractures and internal injuries. Glen's personal effects tell nothing, only a supposition that he was killed.

Johnny goes to see Dr. Ramsey about the autopsy. Dr. Ramsey tells Johnny that a car struck Glen, and the internal injuries indicate that the car was driven fast.

Johnny looks at photos of the accident scene and finds nothing. Johnny turns down a case and goes to look at the accident scene to see if there is anything there.

Johnny goes back to see Donna who is OK now and staying with Glen's mother. Johnny asks her about the new client and she tells Johnny that Glen had been working late for the past two weeks. She tells Johnny that she remembers that their last conversation was a one-sided one and that she had lost her temper.

Johnny gets the key to her apartment and searches it. While Johnny is there, the phone rings and Johnny answers. The caller is a man who is calling to talk to Donna. The man wants to tell her that her husband was murdered, on account of something he told Glen. Johnny is told to go see Warren Kelly, he is the one that had English killed. After Johnny agrees to pursue the case and the man, whose name is Bruno, agrees to meet Johnny at Caruso's Cafe.

Johnny goes to the café and buys a drink (bourbon and soda, $.60). The bartender directs Johnny to a rear upstairs storeroom where Johnny meets Bruno Vick who apologizes to Johnny for getting Glen killed. Bruno tells Johnny that Glen was going to meet with a notary when three men killed him. Bruno tells Johnny that Warren Kelly is a syndicate boss who is using a contracting company for a front. Kelly killed Ed Waters, who was standing in his way. Bruno tells Johnny that he had helped bury the body, and that Kelly is searching for Bruno all over the country. Bruno tells Johnny that he had told Kelly that he was finished running, and he had gone to talk to Glen for advice instead of the District Attorney. Bruno takes Johnny to the window and shows Johnny the men who are watching him, Nat Reiner and Alex Shaw, so he cannot go to the police.

Johnny goes to call the police so Bruno can give up, but Dolger is not in. As Johnny is on the phone, Bruno sneaks by him and goes outside. Bruno confronts Nat and Alex and there is gunfire. Bruno is killed and Reiner is wounded.

Dolger shows up and Johnny tells him what happened, that Bruno came out knowing he was going to die. The police find a letter for the District Attorney in Reiner's pocket. The letter tells the details of the Waters killing and Glen's death.

Reiner is taken to the hospital and after a back operation, Johnny talks to Reiner and tells him that he had talked under the anesthetic and told the police everything. Johnny tells him that he knows where Kelly is and where Waters is buried and convinces Reiner to tell him about the accident. Reiner tells Johnny that they had followed Glen and Shaw had beat him and faked the hit and run accident after they took the letter.

Dolger and Johnny go to Alex Shaw's apartment, located in a "sore spot of a building". Johnny and Dolger break in the door and see Shaw running across the roof. The police open up and Shaw is killed in a hail of submachine gun fire.

If Johnny had been a better friend, he would have walked halfway to meet Glen.

Notes:
- The mid-program commercial for the new program, *The People Act*.
- Edmond O'Brien can be seen in the paramount production *Silver City*.
- Dan Cubberly and Dick Cutting are the announcers.
- Music is by Wilbur Hatch.

Producer:	Jaime del Valle Writer: Gil Doud
Cast:	Jeanette Nolan, Jim Nusser, Jeanne Bates, Wally Maher, Jay Novello, Edgar Barrier, William Conrad

◆ ❖ ◆

Show: **The Baxter Matter**
Show Date: 1/12/1952
Company: **Great Eastern Life Insurance Company**
Agent: **Luther Bishop**
Exp. Acct: **$324.10**

Synopsis: Luther Bishop calls Johnny and tells him that William Baxter has been killed. Baxter was thrown from this horse in McAlester, Oklahoma where he and his brothers are ranchers. Clay Baxter is in New York, and he does not think that it was an accident. Johnny is to go to the Sheridan Hotel to talk to Clay.

Johnny goes to New York and meets Clay at the Sheridan Hotel. Clay tells Johnny that his brother was not killed in an accident because he was too good of a horseman and knew how to fall. Bill's wife will inherit the ranch, which is worth between 8-10 million. Johnny and Clay go for drinks and then leave for Oklahoma City and then on to McAlester, Oklahoma.

In McAlester, Johnny meets Sheriff Billings who tells Johnny that Bill's horse had limped back to the ranch after the accident, and that Luke and Jake Tolliver, who are miners, found the body. Johnny is told that Bill and Clay did not get along, and that Clay bought his ranch after Bill got married. Johnny takes a shower and finds the sheriff feeding his catfish in the swimming pool.

Johnny and Billings go to the Baxter ranch and Johnny meets Wilma Baxter. Wilma invites Johnny to dinner, but Clay tells her that Johnny is with him. Wilma tells Johnny that she was in town all day on the day of the accident.

Johnny takes an agonizing horseback ride to the location of the accident. Johnny is shown the rock that Baxter's head hit and asks if an impression was taken, which it was not. The sheriff digs up the rock, and Johnny goes back to the ranch and meets Frank Kerry, the ranch foremen. Johnny is shown the horse Baxter rode, and notices a swollen hip that looks like it is infected.

Johnny goes back to town and meets with the coroner and gives him the rock. The rock is compared to the wound and it does not match, so Johnny wants an autopsy performed.

Johnny and Clay ride out to the Tolliver silver mine and are shot at as they approach. They yell back and forth at each other and Johnny finally gets to go up to the mine alone. The Tolliver brothers confirm that they found the body, and that Baxter was dead when they found him. They tell Johnny that they have saved their money and want to buy some insurance.

Johnny manages to leave a half-hour later. Clay lifts Johnny onto his horse and is then shot. Clay's horse runs off, and Johnny is forced to follow him until the horse stops, and Johnny falls off his horse.

Clay is taken to the doctor and was only grazed, but Johnny is very sore. Johnny learns that William Baxter did not die from the fracture, but from a long thin instrument that went under his eye and into his brain. Someone then jabbed the horse to make it look like an accident.

Johnny goes to the Baxter ranch with a pair of surgical probes he borrowed from the doctor. Johnny goes into the stable and finds what he is looking for. Wilma finds Johnny in the stable and he tells her that William was killed by a woman's murder weapon, a hatpin. Johnny tells Wilma that the Tollivers saw the murder.

Johnny goes back to the Tolliver's mine and tells them about Wilma. Johnny remembers a case in New York where a woman hit a man and then stabbed him with a hatpin. Johnny remembers that a woman planned it, a man did it and they both disappeared. Johnny sets up a trap in the mine with a set of dummies sitting at a table. Later Frank comes in and shoots at the dummies, and the Tollivers get the drop on Frank. Johnny ends up in a fight with Frank, who finally tells Johnny that Wilma had promised him a share of the ranch. Kelly is tuned in to the sheriff and admits that Wilma is wanted in New York.

Notes:
- The announcers are Dan Cubberly and Dick Cutting.
- Music is by Wilbur Hatch.
- Story information obtained from the KNX Collection in the Thousand Oaks Library.

Producer:	Jaime del Valle	Writer:	Blake Edwards
Cast:	Howard McNear, Jim Backus, Herb Butterfield, Virginia Gregg, Bob Sweeney, Sidney Miller, Lou Krugman, Dave Light		

♦ ❖ ♦

Show:	The Amelia Harwell Matter
Show Date:	7/2/1952
Company:	Corinthian All-Risk Insurance Company
Agent:	George Parker
Exp. Acct:	$122.35

Synopsis: George Parker calls Johnny looking for an investigator. Mrs. Thomas Harwell has been poisoned on Cape Cod.

Johnny goes to Parker's office and learns that the Harwells are textile heirs, and Mrs. Harwell heads the business. So far there are no details on the poison. Johnny is told that Mrs. Harwell was a domineering person who had $350,000 in total coverage.

Johnny rents a car and drives to Cape Cod, Massachusetts. The mansion is described as massive. Johnny talks with Thomas Harwell, the widower, and he tells Johnny that he is used to blunt talk. Johnny is told that Mrs. Harwell was an invalid and had little time left. She despised weakness and never told Thomas if she was in pain. Thomas tells Johnny that he does not approve of the children, as they are a rich woman's children, as he was not allowed to father them. Johnny is told that the servants are above suspicion. They are common people and therefore good. Thomas tells Johnny that Dr. Stevens is the family physician.

Johnny visits Dr. Stevens who wishes him success. He tells Johnny that Amelia had cancer and could have had an operation, but she would take advice from no one. Now, Thomas is passing from slavery to freedom. Dr. Stevens describes the daughter Maxine as a bitter old maid at 33, the son Dexter is 32 and an alcoholic who has just entered into an unsuccessful marriage. Johnny is told that Amelia could only have lived 2-3 months at most, and that a mercy killing is a possibility. Johnny is told that the poison is unknown and that an inquest will be held this afternoon. Johnny is told that Dexter is married to Gretchen Nielsen, a photographer with a small business there in town, and that she is below their standards.

Johnny visits Gretchen that evening and introduces himself, and she talks to Johnny reluctantly. She tells Johnny that she heard from the butler about the death. She is not living with Dexter, she tells Johnny, because she was thought of as a fortune hunter, and Dexter is a slave to the family. She thought their relationship would drag Dexter from the family, but he was tied to mother's money. Gretchen tells Johnny that Dexter would never kill his mother and that she thinks Thomas did it. Mrs. Harwell was in pain and frightened. Thomas knew it and wanted to help. Also, Gretchen tells Johnny that Mrs. Harwell had made a lot of mistakes.

Johnny calls Dr. Stevens and learns the cause of death was a non-alkaloid poison, one unusual for suicide.

Johnny goes to the Harwell residence and asks to see the children. Johnny meets with them and tells them that the poison used was not a pleasant one. Dexter is talking to Johnny when Thomas cries out in pain. Johnny rushes upstairs to find Thomas barely conscious as he points to a glass of poisoned water. There is no reaction from the children and Dr. Stevens is called.

After a short time, Thomas is all right as he only took a sip of the water. He wonders who would do this as he is not ready to follow Amelia. Johnny takes the glass out of the room as Dr. Stevens arrives. The glass has a lot of poison and Dr. Stevens thinks that it is probably canadine. Thomas tells Dr. Stevens that it is unnecessary to report this to the police. Johnny notices that there are marks on Thomas' throat, like he was strangled. Johnny tells Thomas, who is feeling better, that he must report this to the police. Thomas asks Johnny, for the sake of the family why must he report this to the police, as the results were harmless. Thomas tells Johnny that the servants will be fired in the morning. Johnny is adamant about reporting the incident and is told to leave when Johnny says he is calling in the police.

On the way out, the children are in the library. Johnny asks why Thomas does not want to report this, and Dexter points a finger at Maxine about his marriage and a baby on the way. Maxine says Dexter stayed because mother would disinherit him. Johnny leaves to give the glass to the police.

Johnny visits Gretchen and tells her of the second poisoning. Johnny hints about the baby and about being disinherited. Gretchen tells Johnny that Thomas was trying to help them, and not even Dexter had suspected. Thomas probably approved of the marriage and Thomas kept the marriage from Amelia, who found out and then died.

Johnny calls Dr. Stevens and then goes to the Harwell estate. He tells Thomas that he can spare Dexter from a murder charge. Johnny speaks to Thomas alone and tells him that the police are ready to charge Dexter, but you killed your wife. You gave her the water and she tried to scratch you when you tried to keep her quiet. Thomas admits doing it. He tells Johnny that he had many mistakes and wants to help the grandchild. He hoped Amelia would approve but she asked for a lawyer, so he killed her.

Notes:
- Commercials are for Wrigley's Spearmint gum.
- Music is provided by Eddie Dunstedter on the Organ.
- This program was done by Edmond O'Brien as *The Adolph Schoman Matter* on 1/6/51.
- The announcer is Charles Lyon.
- Edmond O'Brien's newest movie is *The Turning Point*.
- This is the last of the available digital Edmond O'Brien series.

Producer:	Jaime del Valle Writer: Gil Doud
Cast:	Vic Perrin, John McIntire, Herb Butterfield, Jeanette Nolan, Virginia Gregg, Peter Leeds

♦ ❖ ♦

Show:	**The Henry Page Matter**
Show Date:	7/16/1952
Company:	Hartford Police Bunko Squad
Agent:	
Exp. Acct:	$53.00

Synopsis: Hank Page from Page's Printing calls Johnny. He has something that he wants Johnny to look at. Johnny relates that he had used Hank to print his stationary.

Johnny goes to the bar in Hartford, Connecticut where they had arranged to meet and Johnny sees Hank run down by a car. Johnny rushes to the body, and Hank gives Johnny a silver cigarette case and tells him to hide it. Hank mentions something about the inside and his wife and then dies.

Johnny gives his statement to the police and then goes to the morgue. The police call the death natural causes, which Johnny questions, but will have to wait for the autopsy.

Johnny goes to see Mrs. Page and gives her the personal effects. She knew that Hank was going to meet with Johnny, and also tells Johnny that Hank had a heart condition. Johnny asks about the black eye Hank had, and she tells Johnny that Hank had fainted and fallen at home.

Johnny goes to a café and looks at the cigarette case, which contains foreign cigarettes and a 100 Florin note. Johnny goes to the office of Van Pelt and Meisner, Commercial Agents, and asks about the currency. Mr. Van Pelt tells Johnny that the cigarettes are his favorites, "Schiesswassers", and that the currency is worth $53.00. Johnny exchanges the note and Van Pelt offers Johnny $500 for the case. When Johnny refuses to sell it, Van Pelt gets angry and tells Johnny to leave, calling him a graverobber.

Johnny goes to eat and as a car approaches, Johnny is shot at. Johnny wakes up to find a bruise on his chest where the cigarette case had stopped the bullet. Johnny calls the police and is told that the plates on the car belong to Van Pelt.

Johnny goes to Van Pelt's apartment and finds Mrs. Page there. She tells Johnny that Van Pelt had called her, and that she knows nothing about the case. After waiting for an hour, Johnny searches the apartment and finds Van Pelt dead in the bedroom. Mrs. Page tells Johnny that she knew all of her husband's friends, but not much about his partner. She did know that Hank had met Soules in reform school, where they learned the printing business. Johnny searches her purse and then calls the police and leaves her locked in the bedroom.

Johnny goes to Page's print shop where a man tells Johnny that Soules is not there. Johnny asks to come in and the man gets angry. Johnny finally gets in and fights with the man, who is knocked out, along with his accomplice. Johnny finds the press, which is being used to print 100 Florin notes. Johnny grabs the case and some notes and goes to see Soules who tells Johnny that he was worried about the books because Hank had fired the printers two weeks earlier. Johnny accuses Soules of working for Van Pelt, and Soules pulls a gun on Johnny. Johnny gets the gun and Soules admits everything and is taken to the police.

Notes:
- The announcer is Charles Lyon.
- Music is by Eddie Dunstedter.
- Story information obtained from the KNX Collection in the Thousand Oaks Library.

Producer: Jaime del Valle   Writer: Gil Doud
Cast: Hy Averback, Howard McNear, Harry Lang, Virginia Gregg, Edgar Barrier, Jim Nusser

Show:	**The New Bedford Morgue Matter**
Show Date:	7/30/1952
Company:	City of New Bedford Police Department
Agent:	
Exp. Acct:	$213.30

Synopsis: Johnny is called by the New Bedford police. They have an unidentified body in the morgue. The police found Johnny's business card in her pocket.

Johnny goes to New Bedford, Massachusetts and meets Sgt. Quill who tells Johnny that the girl was a suicide. Her shoes are missing, and she only had a cheap religious medal. Johnny searches for religious supply houses and finds one that sold that particular medal. Johnny is told that it was sold ten years ago to a confirmation class at St. Dismas. Johnny goes to St. Dismas and meets with Father Ames who gives Johnny a list of the 10 girls from the 1946 class.

Johnny goes to see a Mrs. Starza, who tells Johnny that her daughter Julia is gone, but the missing girl is not her daughter and tells him to leave. Johnny is suspicious and leaves but sneaks back in and hears Mrs. Starza being consoled by a man she calls Carl. He tells her that he will take care of Julia by taking her to Chicago. Mrs. Starza wants to see Julia but is shot by someone.

Johnny searches the house and finds a union card and a photo on a dresser. A friend of Julia's comes to the house and tells Johnny that Julia worked at the Apex Fish Company. She started cleaning fish and moved up fast and became the secretary to Carl Hall. Tonia tells Johnny that Julia had some sort of problem, so she had given Julia Johnny's business card that she found in a bathroom at the train station one day. Tonia tells Johnny that Julia's boyfriend is Joe Gorelli.

Johnny goes to see Joe on his boat *The Julia*. Joe tells Johnny that Carl Hall made his money as a rumrunner, and then bought some fishing boats.

Johnny goes to see Carl Hall who admits that he knew Julia, and hated Joe. Carl tells Johnny that he had given Julia a fur coat for finding a smuggler on one of the boats. Johnny mentions the body in the morgue, and about Carl telling her mother that Julia would be taken to Chicago, and Carl laughs at Johnny. Johnny slugs Carl and then Joe comes in and kills Carl. Joe tells Johnny that he had killed Julia because he thought he was losing her to Carl.

Notes:
- The announcer is Charles Lyon.
- Music is by Eddie Dunstedter.
- Edmond O'Brien's next film is *This is Dynamite*.
- Story information obtained from the KNX Collection in the Thousand Oaks Library.

Producer:	Jaime del Valle	Writer:	Gil Doud
Cast:	Jack Moyles, John McIntire, Francis X. Bushman, Jeanette Nolan, Bob Sweeney		

◆ ❖ ◆

Show: **The Sidney Mann Matter**
Show Date: **8/6/1952**
Company: **Grand East All-Risk Insurance Company**
Agent: **Dave Robinson**
Exp. Acct: **$188.00**
Synopsis: This is the same story as *The Adam Kegg Matter*, with minor changes to the details and the names. The case takes place in New York City.

Notes:
- This story was done as *The Adam Kegg Matter* by Edmond O'Brian on 11/11/50.
- The announcer is Charles Lyon.
- Music is by Eddie Dunstedter.
- Story information obtained from the KNX Collection in the Thousand Oaks Library.

Producer: Jaime del Valle   Writer: Gil Doud
Cast: William Johnstone, Virginia Gregg, Hans Conried, Eddie Firestone, Elliott Reid, Jeanette Nolan

◆ ❖ ◆

Show: **The Tom Hickman Matter**
Show Date: **8/13/1952**
Company: **Maurie Strand Bail Bond**
Agent: **Maurie Strand**
Exp. Acct: **$2,204.06**
Synopsis: This is the same story as *Witness, Witness, Who's Got the Witness* and *The Jack Madigan Matter* with minor changes to the names.
The case takes place in New York City

Notes:
- The announcer is Charles Lyon.
- Music is by Eddie Dunstedter.
- Story information obtained from the KNX Collection in the Thousand Oaks Library.

Producer: Jaime del Valle   Writer: Gil Doud
Cast: Sidney Miller, Tony Barrett, Raymond Burr, Gloria Blondell, John McIntire

Show:	**The Edith Maxwell Matter**
Show Date:	8/20/1952
Company:	Dr. Ludwig Goya
Agent:	
Exp. Acct:	$0.00

Synopsis: Johnny is called by Miss Crane from Dr. Goya's office in Hartford, Connecticut. The doctor needs a detective and asked her to call Johnny.

Johnny goes to meet Dr. Goya, who is a psychiatrist, and who was a suspect in the Denov murder case. Dr. Goya tells Johnny that her physician had referred Mrs. Maxwell to him. She has told Dr. Goya that she saw a person in the street, her daughter-in-law Edith, who was accused of killing her son, Carter Maxwell. Mrs. Maxwell arrives and tells Johnny that he resembles the boyfriend of her daughter-in-law, who was jilted by the man. She tells Johnny about a dream she had about the murder weapon, and that Johnny is to protect her from Edith. Johnny is to go to her apartment on the pretext of having her sign some papers.

Johnny goes to the newspapers to review the case and learns that Carter Maxwell was the heir to a large fortune and was found stabbed. His wife was accused, but her mother-in-law Mrs. Maxwell refused to testify to the grand jury.

Johnny goes to visit Edith Maxwell, who tells Johnny about being seen on the street, and about the breakdown of Mrs. Maxwell. Edith tells Johnny how much he resembles her boyfriend and they have 2 black velvet cocktails while they talk. Johnny takes Edith to dinner and then to a ball game.

The next day Johnny learns that Mrs. Maxwell is in a nursing home and takes another case in Boston. When Johnny comes back he goes to see Edith with flowers. Edith reads Johnny a confession to the killing.

Johnny goes to see Dr. Goya and quits the case. While they are talking there are screams and Mrs. Maxwell comes in with a .32 and accuses Dr. Goya of sending her to an insane asylum. She tells Johnny that she has shot Edith.

Johnny rushes to Edith's apartment where he finds her shot. Edith tells Johnny that she has to save Mrs. Maxwell and get rid of the knife. Johnny reads the confession, which relates that Edith had found the body of her husband and was found holding the knife but could not remember anything else.

Johnny goes to Dr. Goya with the confession and wants him to analyze it, but he tells Johnny that Mrs. Maxwell is in a home. Johnny goes to the hospital to take Edith home, and stays with her while she recovers. Johnny and Edith have an argument and Johnny leaves. Johnny then reads in the papers that Carter Maxwell had committed suicide and that Edith had been trying to protect Mrs. Maxwell from the truth. Johnny arranges to meet Edith in a bar.

Notes:
- The announcer is Charles Lyon.
- Music is by Eddie Dunstedter.
- This story is confusing, as there are two women named Maxwell: Mrs. Maxwell, and Edith Maxwell.

- Story information obtained from the KNX Collection in the Thousand Oaks Library.

Producer:	Jaime del Valle Writer: Gil Doud
Cast:	Virginia Gregg, Joseph Kearns, Lee Patrick

◆ ❖ ◆

Show: **The Yankee Pride Matter**
Show Date: **8/27/1952**
Company: **Tri-State Insurance Company**
Agent: **Carl Bush**
Exp. Acct: **$2,686.00**

Synopsis: Carl Bush calls and offers Johnny a fat commission in Singapore. The policy is for $300,000 and mechanical breakdowns are holding up a cargo ship.

Johnny goes to the Tri-State office and talks to Carl. Johnny is told that Maritime Insurance is a risky business. Johnny knows about bad bets — he bet on Notre Dame last Saturday. Johnny is told that the *Yankee Pride* has a cargo of tin bound for a West Coast defense plant. There is a time clause on deliveries, and Tri-State loses 2% per day on $300,000 if the ship does not sail before next week. Johnny is told that Vincent Ells is the local agent. Carl tells Johnny that he will send a bouquet of bourbon to his plane.

Johnny flies to Singapore and goes to the Tri-State office and talks to Ells, who tells Johnny that the unexpected is commonplace in Asia. Johnny is told that this could be a dangerous mission, as another adjuster has been killed. The agent was Chinese so the police aren't too concerned. He had gone to the *Yankee Pride* and never arrived. Death is not rare here in Singapore. Johnny is told the investigator has a brother and Johnny gets the address. Ells warns Johnny to proceed with caution.

Johnny goes to the ship and meets with the chief engineer who has malaria. Johnny tells him why he is there. The chief tells Johnny that a bearing is being flown in from Hong Kong. Sabotage is not likely as bearings go, and generators fail all the time. The chief tells Johnny that he will talk to the captain, so come back tomorrow.

Johnny goes to see the brother of the dead agent. The rickshaw driver waits and Johnny goes to the door. The man will not talk about his brother but lets Johnny in after Johnny tells him why he is there. Johnny is told that his brother was killed for his job or some other reason. He does not want to die and knows nothing. A man came here before police did and warned him not to talk to police. He was an Englishman who works for someone else. His brother's last words were about a woman. There was always a new woman. She is Malayan and he did not mention her to the stranger. Johnny is told that the girl, Randee works in a bar and there is where his brother met her. "Leave and do not come back" Johnny is told. On the way out, shots are fired and the brother is shot, but Johnny does not go back.

Johnny goes to the bar on Malabar Street after being unable to find a phone to report the shooting. The bar is crowded and Johnny orders a scotch and asks for the girl. The bartender tells him to sit at a table and the girl comes to serve him. Johnny tells her that a friend told him about her. She tells Johnny that she learned English from a missionary school. She tells Johnny that the agent, Koo Fu Soon was no friend. She did not want to meet him again, as he made fool of himself, as he was lonely. Are you lonely? Come to my house after work.

Johnny goes to her house and she does not lie about not knowing that Koo Fu Soon is dead. She tells Johnny that he is in trouble. As she mixes a drink, a man breaks in and tells Johnny that he is going for a ride. Johnny tries to fight and is knocked unconscious.

When Johnny wakes up, he is in a mansion where he is introduced to the "Major". Johnny is told "You will accomplish nothing until I allow you to". Johnny is told that the chief engineer will move the ship on his order, and that the ship is going to Mexico. The Major tells Johnny that "one can buy anything, including petty official signatures, as the Major has power." He will let Johnny go on with his work, as Johnny is a harmless pipsqueak. Johnny is told to tell the insurance company that the Major will cover their losses. Two men, named Earl and Roy, take Johnny to his hotel. Johnny had seen the man's name, "Major Ralph Dixon" on an envelope, and he is a power-mad man.

Next day Johnny calls Ells and asks, "Who is Dixon?" as he claims to be behind the problems with the ship. Johnny tells Ells to look into the ship's papers and Dixon's visa and to check customs. Johnny will start at the other end, as he knows his way around the bottom.

Johnny goes back to Randee and tells her there is going to be trouble. He will turn her in and no one will believe her. She tells of people who are afraid of an invasion and are sending their gold out of the area. The Major is in charge of shipping the gold out on ships. There is an estimated $100 million in gold being shipped. She tells Johnny that Mr. Ells is as greedy as everyone else, and he has been bought. If Johnny is wise, he will get out.

Johnny goes to Ells' home where there is no answer at the door. In a window Johnny sees Els, dead with a pistol in his hand.

Johnny goes to the hotel and gets his automatic and heads to the Major's place. Johnny forces his way in and tells the Major that Ells is dead. The Major tells Johnny that "he was weak and did not appreciate the Major's strength." Johnny tells him that there is only one way to stop the Major, to kill him, as he is a man of influence only in his own mind. Johnny is going to take him to the police as he knows about the gold and will stop the scheme. The Major only replies that he is late for a meeting at the club and starts to leave. As he walks out of the room laughing, Johnny shoots the Major. The police arrive and arrest the Major. The gold is seized when it arrives. The Yankee Pride will sail only two days late.

Notes:
- This is a repeat of *The Yankee Pride Matter*, broadcast on 10/14/1950.
- This program was scheduled for 7/9/1952 but was preempted by the Democratic National Convention.

- The announcer is Dan Cubberly.
- Music is by Eddie Dunstedter.
- *The Line-Up* is announced for next week at this time, but the program did not start until 9/10/52.
- Story information obtained from the KNX Collection in the Thousand Oaks Library.

Producer:	Jaime del Valle Writer: Gil Doud
Cast	William Johnstone, Eric Snowden, Jack Kruschen, Ben Wright, Virginia Gregg

◆ ❖ ◆

Show:	**The Montevideo Matter**
Show Date:	9/3/1952
Company:	**Washingtonian Insurance Company**
Agent:	**Bill Brandon**
Exp. Acct:	**$1,650.00**

Synopsis: Bill Brandon calls Johnny and tells him that an English woman has been found dead in South America. The London Investment Group wants Johnny to investigate the death.

Johnny flies to Montevideo, Uruguay and gets a room at the Hotel Madrid. Johnny then meets with Inspector Alcira and learns that Mrs. Madeline Furness has been killed. Her husband Roger owns a meatpacking plant, and their son Keith lives with them. The killing was four days ago, and the gardener, Ramon del Gado found the body. Mrs. Furness was killed with a blast from a shotgun.

Johnny goes to the Furness home where Ramon is working. He tells Johnny that "she was a bad woman and he was a bad man". Johnny meets Keith, who is a stepson. He tells Johnny that his father did not kill her for the £5,000 insurance, and that Madeline was a schemer. Johnny is shown a picture of Madeline, who is a much younger woman. Keith tells Johnny that he goes to school in England, and that the body was found between their home and the house of Jack Strong, their neighbor.

Johnny meets with Mrs. Strong, who is in a wheelchair. She tells Johnny that there was a division between Madeline and her stepson. Johnny notes that Roger Furness must have found out about his wife's escapades with Mr. Strong. Everyone heard the gunshot, and money probably was the motive.

Johnny meets Mr. Furness, and he tells Johnny that he needs the money from the insurance. He admits that he knew about his wife and Strong. Keith comes in and tells Johnny that he killed his stepmother. Keith is arrested and jailed, but under questioning he is unsure of the facts.

Johnny goes to the Strong residence and sees Mrs. Strong walking outside the house. Once inside she is in the wheelchair again. She tells Johnny that she hurt her back in a hunting accident and is not supposed to walk. She admits to Johnny that she knew about her husband and Madeline. Mr. Strong comes in and attacks Johnny, who slugs him.

Johnny goes to see Mr. Furness and accuses him of hiding behind his son's confession. On the way out, Furness is shot at the front door. Alcira later tells Johnny that del Gado is a common name, but they are looking for Ramon. Later he is arrested and admits to the killings. He tells the police that they killed his grandson with their automobile after his daughter had died.

Notes:
- This is a repeat of *The Montevideo Matter*, broadcast on 7/23/1952 and 12/23/1950.
- The announcer is Dan Cubberly.
- Music is by Eddie Dunstedter.
- Story information obtained from the KNX Collection in the Thousand Oaks Library.

Producer: Jaime del Valle Writer: Gil Doud
Cast: Bob Griffin, Jay Novello, Hy Averback, Jeanette Nolan, John McIntire, William Johnstone

John Lund

John Lund (1911–1992) was the third Johnny Dollar.

The initial episodes present Johnny Dollar as a bland, calm and boring person. Part of the problem with this Johnny Dollar, is not the acting ability of John Lund, but the softness of his voice.

John Lund was a successful radio and motion picture actor, with at least 28 movies to his credit. John was able to convey the character, but his voice was too soft, especially after listening to Edmond O'Brien.

John Lund started out in Summer Stock theater, moved to Broadway and then to Hollywood where he appeared in over 25 films. Lund appeared in over 150 radio programs, including his stint as Johnny Dollar. Lund died in 1992.

The following are the Johnny Dollar programs performed by John Lund.

◆ ❖ ◆

Show: The Singapore Arson Matter
Show Date: 11/28/1952
Company: Great East Insurance Company
Agent:
Exp. Acct: $2,112.10

Synopsis: Inspector Brand calls Johnny to advise him that George Douglas is dead.

Johnny travels to Singapore and hires George Douglas to help investigate a case of Arson at a rubber firm, and George has been killed. Johnny meets with Inspector Barnes, who tells Johnny that George's body was found on the docks, but he was killed elsewhere, and his wife identified the body. Johnny cannot tell Inspector Barnes about the case, and leaves with the feeling that he is being followed.

Johnny calls on Mr. Sawyer the local agent, updates him and tells him that the case is on hold. Johnny visits the widow who tells Johnny that she has been waiting for someone to kill George, and that there was no "other" woman. She tells Johnny to talk to a good friend of George's, Henry Veller, who is the detective at the Hotel Raffles. Inspector Barnes arrives and accuses Johnny of conspiring with the widow. Johnny leaves and goes to see Veller, who is described as a sleazy detective. Veller tells Johnny that he met George in the war and that George had mentioned that there would be a change in his life soon. Veller also describes George's wife as the jealous type.

Johnny goes to see Mrs. Douglas and a man meets Johnny at the door. The man pulls Johnny in at gunpoint and tells Johnny that he hit Mrs. Douglas because she is too filthy to live. The man leaves and Johnny finds Mrs. Douglas in the bedroom. She tells Johnny that the man had said he killed George and was looking for something. Johnny calls Barnes and when he arrives, Johnny gives him a description of the man, including the Webley automatic he carried. Barnes tells Johnny that he had searched George's office and had not found anything.

Johnny goes to his hotel room and the man is there, and he turns out to be a young man and tells Johnny that he wants his file. Johnny tells him that he only hired George, but the boy tells Johnny that George had been blackmailing him for two years, and that his father had hired George. Johnny suggests that Veller may have the file, and the boy hits Johnny and leaves.

Johnny calls Barnes and they go to the Hotel Raffles, but Veller has resigned and is leaving on a ship that night, and the boy had gone to find him. Johnny and the go to the ship The Eastern Traveler and arrest Veller. Veller tells Johnny that George had given him an envelope to hold about Max Childress. Barnes is surprised because Mr. Childress is a very important man in the Customs Bureau.

Johnny and Veller leave the ship to try and lure Max. Max stops Johnny and Veller and tells them that he wants the envelope. Barnes calls for him to surrender and Max is shot.

Notes:
- The announcer is Dan Cubberly.
- Music is by Eddie Dunstedter.
- This story was done earlier as *The Douglas Taylor Matter*, broadcast on 10/6/1951. The introduction seems to be the case mentioned in *The Trans-Pacific* audition programs.
- Story information obtained from the KNX Collection in the Thousand Oaks Library.

Producer: Jaime del Valle   Writer: Gil Doud

Cast:	John McIntire, Eric Snowden, Jeanette Nolan, Jay Novello, James McCallion

◆ ❖ ◆

Show:	**The James Clayton Matter**
Show Date:	**12/5/1952**
Company:	**New York Mutual**
Agent:	**Chet Graham**
Exp. Acct:	**$56.35**

Synopsis: Chet Graham of New York Mutual calls. Chet has to go to California for a week. Can you watch the office for me for a couple days? Johnny can live in Chet's apartment and Chet will even give Johnny his tickets to "Wish You Were Here", and his girlfriend. Chet will call Johnny from California.

This account tells what is not in the papers. Johnny goes to Chet's New York office and is visited by Miss Jane Stebbins, who is Dr. Clayton's nurse. Johnny is told Dr. Clayton would like to talk to him in his office, as he is very busy. Johnny is told that the Doctor is acting strangely and has cancelled all outside calls.

She cries and they go to the office of Dr. Clayton who meets Johnny with a .32 Iver Johnson pistol. Jane goes to lunch and Dr. Clayton explains to Johnny that his life has been threatened and that he cannot even load the gun. Dr. Clayton can't go to the police, as it is a delicate matter. Dr. Clayton tells Johnny that a patient, Florence Harmon, is suffering from a marriage to her erratic husband Benjamin, and Dr. Clayton had advised her to divorce him. Dr. Clayton had talked to Mr. Harmon about the health of his wife, but he attacked him and threatened his life. Dr. Clayton tells Johnny that If he talks to him, Mr. Harmon might listen. Johnny tells Dr. Clayton to call the police and Dr. Clayton asks Johnny to talk to Mr. Harmon, for Mrs. Harmon's benefit.

Johnny goes to see the Harmons and Benjamin opens the door with a gun. Harmon slugs Johnny and leaves. Mrs. Harmon explains to Johnny about her husband. She tells Johnny that he attacked her doctor and is mad and liable to do anything.

Johnny goes back to Dr. Clayton's office and Sgt. Tom Bassman is there. Dr. Clayton and Nurse Stebbins are not there, and Johnny explains the situation. Nurse Stebbins returns and finds a note from Dr. Clayton saying that he is on an emergency call, but she does not recognize the address, which is in the warehouse district.

Johnny and Bassman go to the address and find the Clayton's car. A search of the area finds Dr. Clayton's body. The police question the neighbors, and two people in the area heard the shots and Mr. Harmon had been seen near a bar in the area and is suspected of luring the doctor there and killing him.

Later that night, Johnny bribes the night watchman to get into Dr. Clayton's office. Johnny is told that the police had been there earlier and had found Dr. Clayton's emergency kit. Johnny searches the files, and the patients went from "Abbott to Zybowski." In the files Johnny learns that Mrs. Harmon was never a patient, but Mr. Harmon was.

Johnny goes to see Nurse Stebbins at her small apartment and she is upset about the doctor. She tells Johnny that she had worked for Dr. Clayton for five years. "Who was he going to marry?" Johnny asks, "because the honeymoon has already been planned." Johnny tells her that the doctor had made reservations on the *Ile de France* for April. She tells Johnny that she does not know anything about them. She tells Johnny that Mrs. Harmon was Dr. Clayton's friend, and they had met when Mr. Harmon was a patient. He came in several times and then stopped, but Dr. Clayton had been seeing Mrs. Harmon all this time. She tells Johnny that the police had told her about Mr. Harmon's threats. Johnny tells Nurse Stebbins that the wrong man was killed.

Johnny goes back to see Mrs. Harmon and Johnny accuses her of using him as a witness for Dr. Clayton in killing her husband. She screams at Johnny that her husband did kill the doctor and throws him out.

Johnny calls Bassman from his hotel and explains what he has learned. While Johnny is on the phone, Benjamin Harmon comes into his room with a gun and tells him to hang up. He tells Johnny that he had followed him from his house and wants to know where his law office is. He tells Johnny that Dr. Clayton had called him and told him that a lawyer named Dollar was working on a divorce case for him. He tells Johnny that he did not kill Dr. Clayton. Harmon gets mad and goes for Johnny but Johnny overpowers him and discovers that the gun has not been fired. Harmon tells Johnny that he did not see Clayton and that he was out getting mad and drinking by the docks. He had called Clayton from a bar and told him where to meet him, but Clayton never showed, so he left and heard on the radio that he was wanted. He tells Johnny that Florence had other friends and it would have been too much for him to let her go. He tells Johnny that he is not well and only has a year to live. "They could have waited," he cries to Johnny. Johnny gives him a sleeping pill and confirms what Harmon told him.

Johnny goes to Nurse Stebbin's apartment. She tells Johnny that she fell in love with the doctor and knew he was lying and that he was a manipulative man. She tells Johnny that she had followed the doctor and pleaded with him. There was a struggle and the gun went off. Johnny tells her she can prove self-defense, but she tells Johnny that she cannot get off, as she killed Mrs. Harmon an hour ago.

Johnny tells Chet that he did not see his girl, and did not see the musical, he just sat there for three days. Do not call me for a long, long time, if you call at all.

Notes:
- Chet tells Johnny he can use tickets to *Wish You Were Here* which opened June 25, 1952 at the Imperial Theatre (New York) and ran for 598 performances.
- Music is by Eddie Dunstedter.
- Dan Cubberly is the announcer.
- John Lund's current movie is *Just Across the Street*.
- The *Ile de France* was a luxury ocean liner   soon to be replaced with

trans-Atlantic jet travel. The French liner was known for luxury first-class service.
- This program was also done by Bob Bailey as *The Shepherd Matter*, broadcast on 4/16 through 4/20/1956.

Producer:	Jaime del Valle	Writer:	E. Jack Neuman
Cast:	Virginia Gregg, Vic Perrin, Joseph Kearns, John McIntire, Jeanette Nolan		

◆ ❖ ◆

Show:	**The Elliot Champion Matter**
Show Date:	**12/12/1952**
Company:	**Great Eastern Fire & Casualty**
Agent:	**Don Vickers**
Exp. Acct:	**$516.54**

Synopsis: Don Vickers calls and asks Johnny to go to California with him. An office building has burned up and it looks like arson.

Johnny goes to New York to meet Don Vickers and they fly to Los Angeles, California. Don fills Johnny in on Elliot Champion, who is a self-made man who is very aggressive. Johnny is told that Ives has called and told Don that the building was burned, and that Champion is in financial trouble. Johnny is being brought in for protection, along with Vickers and Ives, against Champion who has never been beaten.

In Los Angeles, Johnny and Don check into the Statler. The next morning, they check in with Norman Ives who tells them that a man was seen loitering in the area of the building, and the description matches Elliot Champion. A newsboy told Norman that he saw a man go behind the building just before the fire started. Johnny is told that the fire was an amateur job and that the setter is not a firebug either. Someone moved five gallons of gasoline into the building that night. Johnny is told that Champion has not been told of these events. Johnny, Don and Norman go over the ruins that day and look at suspects that night.

The next morning Johnny goes to Champion's office where he meets Mildred Champion, who was beautiful but poorly dressed. Johnny asks to see Mr. Champion who yells at Mildred on the intercom. Mildred tells Johnny that he is nice today as Johnny goes in to see Mr. Champion, who knows why Johnny is there. Johnny tells him it is arson and Champion tells Johnny that Joseph Harrison is out of prison and that he had sworn he would get Champion for sending him to jail five years ago for theft. Champion is certain that Harrison did it. Champion tells Johnny that he saw the story in the papers and that the claim will be paid after the facts are in. Johnny leaves and reviews the trial to substantiate the story. The witnesses identify Harrison and an APB is issued.

Johnny goes to see Mr. Engle, who was Harrison's attorney. Johnny tells Engle that he wants to find Harrison, who has been identified as the man who set the fire. Engle tells Johnny that Harrison was a nice kid but everything was against him. Champion could have let him off, but he poured it on. Johnny tells him that it looks like Harrison is trying to get even with Champion. Engle has not heard from Harrison, so Johnny leaves. Later that afternoon two more witnesses identify Harrison as the man. At 5:00 Mildred calls Johnny and tells him that she knows where Joe is and to meet her at her house in an hour. At 5:30 Champion's lawyer calls and tells Johnny that they will sue if the insurance company does not pay immediately. At 5:38 Norman Ives calls to say that Champion was shot ten minutes ago and is dead.

Johnny goes to the house and sees Champion, shot in the head with a .38, and the police are looking for Harrison. Vickers and Ives arrive and show Johnny proof that Mildred Champion had married Harrison a month before the trial. Now Mildred has disappeared. Johnny had a definite opinion of Mildred but it was wrong.

Johnny goes to see Engle again and tells him of Champion's death. Engle tells Johnny that he knew that Mildred was married to Harrison. Johnny tells Engle that Champion was not too good at paying his taxes, but Engle can only tell Johnny that a wife cannot testify against her husband, but everyone else testified against Harrison. Engle feels that Champion was framing Harrison with embezzlement to cover the tax problems. Joe was a nice boy and Engle hopes no one ever finds him. But later that day Joe is found in the county hospital, in the morgue. Harrison had contracted tuberculosis in San Quentin and died of it in the hospital.

Don Vickers calls Johnny and tells him that a man had sold gasoline to a girl who looked like Mildred Champion. Johnny goes to Engle and tells him about Joe. Johnny asks Engle. "Did you help Champion frame Joe?", and Engle tells Johnny that he did not. There is a knock at the door and it is Mildred. Johnny tells Engle to hide and shots are fired through the door. Johnny chases after her and shoots her in her car. Johnny gets to the car and she tells Johnny that she wanted to kill Engle, who had helped her uncle. She tells Johnny that she had talked to Joe in prison and thought that Engle had helped to frame him. She had waited five years, only to have Joe die. She tells Johnny that she is not pretty and that no one looked twice at her, but Joe cared and she is dead inside.

Johnny expenses $85.00 that he pampered himself with to help forget Mildred talking about her lover.

Notes:
- Music by Eddie Dunstedter.
- Dan Cubberly is the announcer.
- There is a public service announcement about Travelers Aid at the end of the program.
- This program was combined with *The Upjohn Matter* performed on 9/19/1954, and was done by Bob Bailey as *The Bennet Matter*, broadcast 2/20/1956 through 2/24/1956.

Producer: Jaime del Valle   Writer: E. Jack Neuman

Cast: Eddie Marr, Joseph DuVal, Joyce McCluskey, Francis X. Bushman, Herb Butterfield

• ❖ •

Show: **The New Cambridge Matter**
Show Date: **12/19/1952**
Company: **New England Mutual Trust & Casualty**
Agent: **Dave Taylor**
Exp. Acct: **$125.00**

Synopsis: This is the same story as *The Plantagent Matter* broadcast on 3/5 through 3/9/1956, and takes place in New Cambridge, Massachusetts. The names change but the plot is the same.

Notes:
- The announcer is Dan Cubberly.
- Music is by Eddie Dunstedter.
- This is the first instance where a future Johnny Dollar (Bob Bailey) plays a role with the current Johnny Dollar.
- Story information obtained from the KNX Collection in the Thousand Oaks Library.

Producer: Jaime del Valle   Writer: E. Jack Neuman
Cast: Edgar Barrier, Joyce Manners, Robert Bailey, Bill Bouchey, Jeanne Bates

• ❖ •

Show: **The Walter Patterson Matter**
Show Date: **12/26/1952**
Company: **Delaware Mutual Life Insurance Company**
Agent: **Mr. Elgins**
Exp. Acct: **$610.13**

Synopsis: Mr. Elgins calls and asks Johnny to look into a claim. The case involves a $40,000 policy on Mr. Patterson, who died in 1947, but a friend says he is still alive.

Johnny goes to Wilmington, Delaware and the office of Mr. Elgins. Johnny is told that many people see someone who is dead, but they turn out to be misidentifications. Two weeks ago, Mrs. Virginia Collier stopped in Tucson and saw Walter Patterson in a Hotel bar and spoke to him. He told Mrs. Collier that his name was Yohler and that he was born in Tucson, Mr. Elgins has contacted the Tucson police who have reported that Yohler had not bought property there until 1947. Mrs. Collier remembered Patterson's limp, and Yohler has one too. Patterson went to Amherst but Yohler said he went to Notre Dame, but that did not check out. Johnny gets copies of the paperwork on the policies. Johnny is told that Patterson was killed in a rented plane in April of 1947 and that his body was never found. Patterson was declared dead and the claim check was issued then. Gloria Ann Patterson is the beneficiary. Mr. Brennan, the family lawyer, got copies of fingerprints and personal papers. Johnny is told that Mrs. Patterson put the money in the bank, and does not know about the sighting.

Johnny spends the day getting more information at the airport and from Lt. James Creightson of the Coast Guard, who had conducted the search. Johnny learns that an unreported rescue is possible, but not likely.

Johnny goes to Tucson, Arizona sure that he will only find a lot of desert sunshine. Johnny gets a motel room and looks up Sgt. Tyler at the police department. Johnny fills in Tyler as to why he is there. Johnny is told that no one knew Yohler until five years ago and that Yohler does not work, but always has money. Johnny is told that Will Yohler does not seem to be hiding from anyone.

Johnny visits Yohler and tells him that he is running down the Collier conversation, but Yohler does not remember it. Johnny shows Yohler a picture of Patterson, and he admits that there is some resemblance. Yohler tells Johnny that he was not in the army and he said that he did not go to Notre Dame and that he told the woman anything to get rid of her. Yohler tells Johnny that he went to Tulane and starts getting nervous. He tells Johnny that he has lived in several cities and was married once in 1944, but Johnny notes that he seemed uncomfortable. Yohler offers to get a birth certificate and other papers for Johnny that afternoon. Johnny asks for a set of fingerprints to prove Yohler is not Walter Patterson and he agrees to give Johnny the prints.

The fingerprints do not match those given to Johnny, so Johnny makes reservations to return home. Yohler calls Johnny and wants to talk and Johnny arranges to meet him at the Arizona Inn. Yohler does not show, so Johnny cabs to the house. The front door is open and Johnny calls the police. Johnny tells Tyler that Yohler is dead, and that he had been beaten.

The police come and examine the house, which showed signs of a violent struggle. Tyler asks Johnny to stick around so that Johnny can help him find a killer, as someone heard or saw something. Three witnesses are found, and one, Mrs. Lucas, tells Johnny that she took a walk that evening and went past Yohler's house and saw him talking to a man who was larger than Yohler with a tweed topcoat, his hat in his hand and red hair. He was there also when she came back.

An APB is issued and the cab companies checked. One cab recorded a man who came in on a plane from the east and used the name Roger Bales. Johnny calls Mr. Elgins and reports in, and as he is talking Tyler comes in with a wire. Johnny tells him that the war department has come back with a set of fingerprints that match. Mr. Elgins wants to call Brennan, who had supplied the prints, but Johnny tells him not to call Brennan, as he will handle it.

Johnny returns to Wilmington and goes to see Brennan and is met by Mrs. Patterson who tells Johnny that Mr. Brennan is sick. Mrs. Patterson goes upstairs to get Brennan and then starts to leave. When Johnny explains to Brennan why he is there, Brennan tells her to stay. Brennan tells Johnny and Gloria that he had gone to see Walter and had been in a fight with him. Brennan tells Johnny that he will tell this once, and the story will be different in court.

Brennan tells them that Walt did not die in the crash but was picked up by a fishing boat and taken to Charleston, South Carolina. Walt had called and had the idea to disappear. Walt hated Gloria and wanted a divorce. Walt had told Brennan that he could have Gloria for a price: $25,000 a year, which Brennan could afford. Walt just wanted to be away from everything. Johnny tells Gloria that Walt is dead now, really dead. Brennan tells Gloria that he had fought with Walt and killed him. Brennan claims that Walt was going to tell the truth and claim amnesia. It took Gloria five years to decide to marry Brennan and one lousy afternoon for Walter to come back.

It will be up to the courts to prove if Brennan killed Walter Patterson. Johnny is sure Mrs. Patterson is innocent.

Notes:
- The mid-program commercial is for the program *Theater of Today* on Saturday afternoons.
- Music by Eddie Dunstedter.
- Dan Cubberly is the announcer.
- This program was done by Bob Bailey as *The Chesapeake Fraud Matter*, broadcast on 10/17 thru 10/21/1955.

Producer:	Jaime del Valle	Writer:	E. Jack Neuman
Cast:	Fred MacKaye, Herb Butterfield, Stacy Harris, Virginia Gregg, Jeanette Nolan, John McIntire		

◆ ❖ ◆

Show:	**The Baltimore Matter**
Show Date:	**1/2/1953**
Company:	**All-States Insurance Company**
Agent:	**Don Freed**
Exp. Acct:	**$294.60**

Synopsis: Orin Vance calls and reminds Johnny that he had sent Orin to Ossining seven years ago for the Zeeman Case. Orin wants to do Johnny a favor, and maybe they can work out something. Orin asks Johnny to help him make some honest money.

A call to Sing Sing Prison tells Johnny that Orin Vance has been released as a model prisoner. Orin arrives at Johnny's apartment, and Orin asks not to be treated like a con. He tells Johnny that his wife would not let him in the house and told him to get a job or she'll divorce him, so he needs a stake to start a business. Orin asks if Johnny remembers the Towner Loan case in Baltimore, the million-dollar theft that was never solved. Orin can help Johnny solve it for half the reward. Orin tells Johnny that he knows two of the six men who did it and gives Johnny one of the stolen bills.

Johnny calls Don Freed, who verifies the serial number. Johnny explains the circumstances, learns that there is a $10,000 reward and gets approval from Don to work on the case. Orin tells Johnny that he got the bill from Leonard Torpe in New York. Orin had met Torpe in New York yesterday and

Torpe had showed him a stack of money he could not spend. Orin notes that Torpe was pretty drunk at the time. Orin had looked up the robbery and Torpe fits the description of one of the men. The other man is Harold King who lives in Reno. Orin leaves and will call Johnny in two days.

Johnny follows Orin to the main business section where he buys a ticket to New York. Johnny calls Pete Florian, a detective friend, and asks him to tag along to make sure no one tries to kill Vance.

Johnny takes a plane to New York and meets police Lt. Randall. Johnny asks Randall for a search warrant of Torpe's apartment. Johnny looks at the mug shots that show Torpe has a long record, and Randall wires Reno to ask them to hold on to Harold King. Johnny and Randall go to the apartment but they learn that Torpe had moved out the previous morning.

Johnny goes to his hotel and gets a call from Pete who tells Johnny that Vance is in a place at 680 155th street. Johnny cabs to meet Pete and learns that Vance has had visitors, and one of them is Torpe. Johnny and Pete go into the building and knock on the door. Johnny asks for Orrin Vance and Torpe opens the door and tells Johnny that there is no one named Vance there. Johnny forces the door open and shots are fired and Johnny hears the voice of a man dying.

Johnny is shot twice and is operated on at the police emergency hospital for two .38 gunshot wounds, one in the neck and one in the shoulder. Randall visits at the hospital two days later and tells Johnny that Pete was killed. Johnny explains how he had hired Pete and about Vance being the tipster. Randall tells Johnny that Pete had been shot four times but killed Torpe. Vance is in the hospital and the other man got away. Johnny tells Randall that he was trying to push into the room and everything got fuzzy. Johnny is told that the other man had stolen a car that was found with no prints.

Later Vance is able to speak and tells Johnny that the other man was Harold King who wanted to know what Vance had done with the $10 Torpe gave him. Vance tells Johnny that he has reward money coming, so he is not going to die.

Two days later Johnny goes to his hotel by ambulance and gets a phone call from a woman who asks if he is interested in finding Harold King. The caller is Melva King. She tells Johnny to meet her at Schraft's Restaurant on 42nd and Broadway, and that she will know Johnny by his pictures in the newspapers.

Johnny goes to the restaurant and meets Melva. She asks about the reward for the Baltimore job and is told she will only get half if she turns in Harry. She tells Johnny that Harry was in on the robbery but she was not involved. She wants a letter from the insurance company promising legal assistance if she gets in trouble. She tells Johnny that Harry has $45,000 that he cannot spend as all they got out of the robbery was marked bills. Johnny tells her he will call the insurance company and she agrees to call him in an hour.

Melva leaves and gets into a cab. Johnny starts to follow her when Randall picks him up and they follow her in his car. Randall surmises that she is offering

Harold to Johnny for the reward. Randall tells Johnny that he had a man following Johnny and that Melva King was from a rich family in Minnesota and got disinherited.

Johnny and Randall follow the cab to a train station in Bucks County and Melva makes a call but not to Johnny. Randall thinks that she is working both sides to see who will pay the most. Randall shows Johnny her file that has 16 arrests. A green caddy pulls up and Melva talks to the men for a while.

Randall orders a pickup and they follow Melva to a motor court. Melva comes out of the room with Harold King, who is wounded. Harold threatens to kill everyone and Johnny and Randall try to reason with him. Harold tells them that she had been bargaining with both sides while he was unconscious. Harry shoots Melva and Randall shoots Harold.

Remarks: The two men Melva had contacted were part of the six robbers and were arrested and told all. Johnny thinks that Vance deserves half of the reward. He thinks Pete Florian's widow deserves the other half.

Notes:
- The mid-program commercial is for US Defense Bonds and the payroll savings plan.
- Johnny is shot for the 3rd time.
- The script title page lists "Leonard Foley" as a character, but in the program the name is changed to "Leonard Torpe".
- This story and *The Rochester Theft Matter* were combined as *The Todd Matter* done by Bob Bailey and broadcast on 1/9 through 1/13/1956.
- Dan Cubberly is the announcer.
- Music is by Eddie Dunstedter.

Producer:	Jaime del Valle	Writer:	E. Jack Neuman
Cast:	Tony Barrett, Joseph DuVal, Clayton Post, John McIntire, Jeanette Nolan		

♦ ❖ ♦

Show: **The Thelma Ibsen Matter**
Show Date: **1/9/1953**
Company: **Eastern Life & Trust Company**
Agent: **Milton DeFranco**
Exp. Acct: **$84.15**

Synopsis: Milton DeFranco calls about a policy with a beneficiary they can't find. She is missing.

Johnny goes to Milton's office by bus. Milton tells Johnny that the deceased was John Linden who sold newspapers in front of the Metropolitan building. He had purchased two policies in 1940, and the beneficiary is Thelma Ibsen, who was 10 at the time. He bought them because he wanted to do something nice for a little girl. Johnny is told that Thelma Ibsen must be 23-24 now, and that Linden only saw her that one day.

Johnny goes to her local address at 113 Brainbridge in Hartford, Connecticut, but she had moved and had lived with an aunt after her parents died in an auto accident. Johnny visits a former work site and learns that Thelma just left one day and never came back. Johnny is told that maybe she went to New York and that Thelma was nice but she had plans of her own. She only talked of meeting someone nice and getting married.

Johnny visits the apartment hotel where Thelma had lived, and she had checked out in December of 1950. Johnny finds a picture in her high school yearbook and a driver's license went into Johnny's file. Two days later, the coworkers are re-questioned and one remembers Floyd Thurnball in New York.

Johnny travels to New York City and searches the phone books for Floyd Thurnball. The right one was #5 on the list. He tells Johnny that he had met Thelma in an office and that she had come to New York with him to be married. On December 24, 1950 she walked out of his car at a gas station, and he has heard nothing since. Floyd tells Johnny that Thelma was kind, sweet, and gentle and that he had only known her for three weeks. Floyd thinks Thelma was frightened of life and that he offered her the happiness she longed for but she was immature. Floyd tells Johnny that he has not tried to find her. She walked away from the car of her own free will with $2,300 taken from his wallet. "She had to steal it like a common thief." Floyd tells Johnny. Johnny leaves and notes that Floyd was the second elderly man in her life.

Johnny rents a car and checks out Floyd's story. At the gas station Earl Camden remembers Thelma leaving the car and the man waiting for her. Johnny talks to Floyd's sister Edna, who also corroborates the story and tells Johnny that Thelma left all her clothes there.

In New York, the police have a record of her being arrested for disturbing the peace, so Johnny goes there and learns that Thelma had moved. The landlady was talkative and told Johnny that Thelma always had parties and had men visiting her.

Johnny goes back to city hall and looks up the arrest record and gets the names of the others Thelma was arrested with. Johnny talks to a man named Unger, who gives Johnny an address, so Johnny goes there.

The manager of the building rings her room but no one answers, but he knows she is in. Johnny goes to the apartment on the 15th floor and the door is open. Johnny enters and finds Thelma standing on the window ledge, ready to jump.

Johnny goes in and Thelma tells Johnny that she is going to jump but asks Johnny how he knows her name. Johnny tells her that he knows her, but Thelma does not believe him. Johnny tells her of the picture in the school annual. The manager comes to the apartment and is shocked, so Johnny whispers for him to call the police. She knows that police will try to stop her but they won't, she will jump anyway. She sees a crowd and knows they want her to jump because no one wants to help her.

Johnny mentions that Floyd cared for her, but she tells Johnny that she is no good to anyone. She tells Johnny to tell Floyd that she meant to send the money back. Footsteps are heard in the hallway and Thelma shouts hysterically to close the door. She tells Johnny that for the first time she knows exactly what to do and how to do it and that she should have died with her parents.

Johnny tells her about the man who bought the policies and how he cared for her. She remembers him and talking about growing up, and that he had told her that she would be a lovely woman. Johnny tells her that he left her $1,000 and shows her the papers. Thelma starts to cry about the "poor old man".

Johnny expenses $3.50 for martinis. This was Johnny's first and hopefully last experience with an intended suicide, but the doctors say she will recover in time.

Notes:
- This program was merged with *The Emily Braddock Matter* and done by Bob Bailey as *The Broderick Matter*, broadcast 11/14 through 11/18/1956.
- The announcer is Dan Cubberly.
- Music is by Eddie Dunstedter.
- John Lund's current movie is *Just Across the Street*.

| Producer: | Jaime del Valle | Writer: | E. Jack Neuman |
| Cast: | Tom Tully, Jeanette Nolan, John McIntire, Joseph Kearns, Virginia Gregg | | |

❖

Show:	**The Starlet Matter**
Show Date:	**1/16/1953**
Company:	**Twin State Insurance Company**
Agent:	**Ken Ralston**
Exp. Acct:	**$366.05**

Synopsis: Ken Ralston calls Johnny from Kansas City, Missouri. Johnny is told that Phil Gardner is an agent in Hollywood who needs help. Gardner is "up to here" in starlets and one of his starlets is insured for $50,000 but her life has been threatened. Johnny asks about the commission and is told it is fat. Johnny loves Hollywood.

Johnny goes to Hollywood, California out of LaGuardia on flight 601. At the Sunset Ruxton Hotel Johnny flirts with an old friend, Judy the telephone operator.

Johnny goes to see Phil Gardner and is directed to the Chez Scotty restaurant across the street. Phil shows Johnny a picture of Toby Drake who Phil says will be a star. Phil tells Johnny that someone wants to murder Toby, and Phil does not want that kind of publicity. A phone is brought to the table and Phil learns that Toby is dead. Phil tells Johnny that her boyfriend called so he would be the first to know.

Toby drives Johnny in his jaguar, with the top down, to Toby's apartment. On the couch is her body with a silk stocking around her neck and Det. Kosca, who asks Johnny and Phil about how they found out. Phil recounts the story to Kosca and Phil tells Johnny to find out who did it. "Well, well, a little bulge there" says Kosca as he notices Johnny's gun. In the bedroom is the boyfriend

Roy Fulton, crying about Toby. Johnny talks to Roy and he tells Johnny that he had come to pick up Toby for a date, found the body and called the agent and the police. Roy tells Johnny that she should have been more careful, as she was too beautiful.

Johnny goes to his hotel and Judy tells Johnny that he has a message: "First Toby, then Stella Martin, you can't stop it Dollar". Judy tells Johnny that a man had called, left the message and hung up. Johnny calls Phil, but there is no answer so, Judy tells Johnny to call Hollywood Casting.

Johnny goes there and gets an address for Stella Martin in Westchester. Johnny goes to Stella's address and a man opens the door. Johnny forces his way in and the man slugs Johnny and knocks him out. Johnny wakes up to find Stella in the bathroom in a silk negligee and a black silk stocking around her neck.

Johnny recognizes Stella from a few b-grade movies. Kosca knocks on the door and Johnny tells him what happened. Kosca tells Johnny the police got a phone call about the girl. Johnny tells Kosca about the message and the man, who was about seven-feet tall. Kosca finds a note in Stella's hand: "There will be another one tomorrow, Dollar". Kosca gets angry with Johnny and throws him out of the house.

The next day Phil calls Johnny and he is accusative of Johnny's lack of protection so Johnny roughs him up a little to get information from Phil about a possible cover-up. Phil tells Johnny that Stella was just a pickup from Dorcas' drive-in restaurant three months ago. Johnny goes to the drive-in and talks to the manager Mel Dorcas. Johnny talks to Mel who remembers Toby and Stella. When Johnny mentions there might be a third murder, Mel mentions Peggy Brian, who was a close friend of theirs, and came to work with them in Toby's car. Mel gives Johnny her address in North Hollywood.

Johnny visits Peggy, who comes to the door hysterical and tells Johnny to go away. She wants to kill Johnny before he can kill her. Johnny takes her gun away and calms her down and tells her that he is there to help. She tells Johnny about a woman who was killed in an auto accident. Toby, Stella and Peggy had been on a trip to Oregon three years ago and had an accident in which a woman hit them and died. The police said it was not their fault and let them go.

Johnny decides to take Peggy out shopping, and to Ocean Park to take her mind off of the matter. Johnny calls the Hotel, Roy Fulton and Phil Gardner to let them know of his plans.

Johnny takes Peggy shopping and buys her a new dress. Then they go to the amusement park where Peggy figures out what Johnny is doing. In the fun house, Peggy is having a good time until she sees a tall man. Johnny sends Peggy into a spinning barrel and the man attacks Johnny. Johnny drags him out and he tells Johnny he followed him to be able to get at the killer. The man tells Johnny that Stella was dead when he got there.

Peggy screams and there is a man in the mirror. It is Roy Fulton with a gun. Roy shoots at them and Johnny shoots and hits him. Roy walks towards Johnny and then collapses. Roy tells Johnny that they killed his wife and then dies.

Johnny tells Ken Ralston to pay Phil Gardner face value of the policy. At least he kept one of the three girls alive, which is luckier than you usually get in Hollywood.

Notes:
- Dan Cubberly is the announcer.
- Music is by Eddie Dunstedter.
- John Lund's current movie is *Just Across the Street*.
- According to the script, the writers for this episode are Fargo Epstein and Daphne Fenster, but Morton Fine and David Friedkin are credited on the program. Possibly these are pseudonyms.
- Raymond Burr is back to his real name now.

Producer: Jaime del Valle
Writer: Morton Fine, David Friedkin
Cast: Raymond Burr, Dick Ryan, John McIntire, Sidney Miller, Vic Perrin, Virginia Gregg, Jeanette Nolan

♦ ❖ ♦

Show: **The Marigold Matter**
Show Date: **1/23/1953**
Company: **Marigold Police Department**
Agent: **Walt Younger**
Exp. Acct: **$4.00**

Synopsis: Johnny receives a call from Lt. Walt Younger of the Marigold police. Walt tells Johnny that Joe Hickey was killed last night — shot to death. Can you come up?

Johnny takes a bus to Marigold, Connecticut and meets Walt and Sgt. Cherry. Walt tells Johnny that Joe was found murdered. Johnny tells Walt that Joe did some work for him in Hartford years ago. Walt gives Johnny a letter addressed to him that was found on Joe's body. Johnny reads the letter, which refers to some strange things happening. Johnny tells Walt that he has not heard from Joe for two years. Walt offers to let Johnny get involved to assist them.

Johnny and Walt go to the site of the murder where the car was found by the side of the road, with no footprints in the snow. Walt tells Johnny that there was no sign of robbery so maybe it was revenge for a loan or something. Walt tells Johnny that Joe was shot at close range, so he must have trusted whoever did it. Johnny is told that Joes' wife was the last person to see him.

Johnny visits Joe's wife Pat, who thanks Johnny for coming. She tells Johnny that they were having problems and that she was thinking about divorce. She tells Johnny that she was home alone at the time of the shooting and that she did not do it.

Johnny goes to Joe's office and talks to Vivian Asher, who worked for Joe. She tells Johnny that he would find Joe's enemies and that she liked Joe, but there was no romance. She tells Johnny that she did not kill him and has witnesses. She agrees to go through the files to look for possible enemies.

Later Johnny gets the list, which has thirty-five names and addresses. Walt and Johnny interview the people on the list, and they all seemed to hate Joe for pressing them for loan payments, but not enough to kill him.

At the Shamrock Bar and Grill, Johnny meets Jim Tiel who knew Joe and calls him a bum. He tells Johnny that Joe was a lousy shark who tried to get money from him for a loan Jim paid off months ago. He tells Johnny that Joe came back later to say it was a mistake, but loan companies don't make mistakes. Johnny wonders about the bookkeeping error.

Johnny visits Vivian who tells him that Tiel was not on the list, as the list was not complete. Vivian tells Johnny that she had made a mistake and told Joe about it. Johnny asks to see the files, but Vivian tells Johnny to get a search warrant to see the files.

Johnny goes to see Walt about the warrant, but Walt is out. Johnny asks Cherry to get him a search warrant but he tells Johnny that it will take a day or so. Johnny also gives Cherry an ashtray with fingerprints that he wants checked, as Johnny thinks she might have a background. Walt comes in and they go back to the murder site as Walt thinks someone made a mistake, as the body fell in the wrong place. As they look at the site, five shots ring out and Johnny and Walt drop to the snow. Johnny senses that they have already talked to the killer of Joe Hickey.

The shots came from the road and Johnny hears a car drive away and notices that Walt has been shot twice. Johnny uses his tie to stop the flow of blood in Walt's leg. "At least exhibit "A" is in his leg" Walt tells Johnny. Johnny takes Walt to the hospital in Hartford and then drives to Joe's office.

In Vivian's desk Johnny finds the reason for her not wanting him to look around. Johnny visits Vivian and tells her that he is doing things his way. Johnny shows her $8,000 in delinquent loans recommended by her. She tells Johnny that she got scared and hid them. She tells Johnny that Joe had let her write loans and she made some mistakes. Johnny leaves and watches outside as she makes a phone call. Johnny watches the house for a while, but nothing happens.

The next day, Johnny interviews some of the names on the list of bad loans, and they all have receipts for the payments. At the police office, Cherry has a report on Vivian from Kansas City. It outlines six arrests and a conviction for both car theft and shoplifting, and she is still wanted in Denver for grand larceny. Cherry tells Johnny that she is well liked in town but Johnny mentions the bad loans and the payments she pocketed. Cherry thinks that she must have shot Joe when he found out.

Johnny and Cherry go to arrest Vivian. Cherry tells Johnny that he will take no chances as they knock on the door. Vivian opens the door and screams "Cherry" as Cherry tries to shoot her. Johnny slugs Cherry and Vivian tells Johnny that Cherry was a policeman in Denver and was blackmailing her to keep from being sent back. She tells Johnny that Cherry had shot Joe when he found out. Vivian tells Johnny that she only wanted to live there and be left alone as Johnny takes her to the police.

Cherry had been a policeman in Denver but was discharged for "conduct unbecoming an officer". The bullets came from his service revolver. Cherry was booked for murder with Vivian as an accomplice.

Notes:
- There is a CBS commercial at the end for *Gang Busters* and a CBS spot which says: "America now listens to 105 million radio sets and listens most to the CBS Radio Network".
- Dan Cubberly is the announcer.
- Music is by Eddie Dunstedter.
- John Lund's current movie is *Just Across the Street.*

Producer: Jaime del Valle   Writer: E. Jack Neuman
Cast: Parley Baer, Howard Culver, Vivi Janiss, Virginia Gregg, James Nusser

◆ ❖ ◆

Show: **The Kay Bellamy Matter**
Show Date: **1/30/1953**
Company: **Hemispheric Insurance Company**
Agent: **Bert Welch**
Exp. Acct: **$135.40**

Synopsis: Bert Welch calls about going to Broadway to see a theatrical agent named Lou Waltham. Lou has an insurance application for Kay Bellamy for a two-million-dollar policy, but the application does not check out.

Johnny goes to New York City and then to Lou Waltham's sound-proof office. Lou tells Johnny that Kay Bellamy is a valuable hunk of talent and that she needs coverage. Johnny tells Lou that he needs more information for the application, so Lou tells Johnny that Kay was a stripper two-years ago and now she is making $2,000 a week on radio, but she will not let her picture taken, not even for movies. Lou tells Johnny that Kay disappears between radio programs and works in burlesque as "Dawn Laviya". Maybe you can talk to her. She is in Boston now.

Johnny flies to Boston, Massachusetts and finds her theater. Johnny goes backstage and sees Dawn dancing with the chorus. Dawn walks backstage and Johnny calls her Kay Bellamy. She tells Johnny that is not her name. She walks away and a man named Kroll tells Johnny to leave. Kroll knows who Johnny is and why he is there and tells Johnny to tell Lou that Dawn does not need insurance. Kroll promises a personal hunting license from the boss if Johnny comes back. Johnny now realizes that Kay is taking orders from someone.

At a nearby café Johnny sits next to Lorene, a dancer. She tells Johnny that Lutzy Lazario, the dance manager, is always giving her a hard time. Just as she starts to tell Johnny about Kay's boyfriend, her ride comes and she leaves. Johnny goes to sit with Lutzy and a dancer named Valerie and tells them that he is scouting for Lou Waltham for dancers for a Broadway play. Suddenly they are interested. Valerie tells Johnny that Dawn can get a lot of money just by marrying her boyfriend, Martin Bayard Cullen III, who is big money. Johnny recognizes the name as "connections with a capitol "C".

Johnny gets a hotel room, and that night he watches the Dawn Laviya show as she takes off all the law would allow. At noon Johnny is awakened by a knock at his door. It is Kay Bellamy. She tells Johnny that she started out in burlesque and likes it. She tells Johnny that Lou cannot insure her unless she wants him to. As they are talking, the phone rings and Burt Welch tells Johnny that Lou is dead. He has been shot to death.

Johnny returns to New York and goes to Lou's office where Charlie Dyer and the police lab boys are at work. Johnny asks Charlie to let him look through a file drawer for the file on Kay Bellamy. Charlie opens the drawer and Johnny looks at her file and her contract was a dilly, as it allows nothing that would allow people to see her face. The file photo shows her always wearing a hat or veil. Johnny finds one picture that was taken in Mexico, and on her hand, was a wedding ring. Back to Boston!

Johnny meets Valerie on the plane and she tells Johnny that she came to meet with Lou Waltham but did not see him. She knows nothing about the murder and won't tell Johnny which plane she took this morning to come to New York.

Johnny goes to see Martin Cullen and asks him about Dawn. Johnny tells him that she is involved in a murder and he tells Johnny that Kay has been working him for a favor. Martin admits to Johnny that her uncle Fred is in the penitentiary and she wanted him to be moved east for the family. Johnny tells Martin that her real name is Kay Bellamy and that Fred is probably her husband. Johnny tells Martin that Fred Bellamy was involved in a robbery where a woman drove the getaway car. Martin tells Johnny that she does not like public places and that he must have been taken in. When Martin tells Johnny that Fred is on a train coming east, Johnny tells him to call Washington as he thinks someone will try to spring Fred. Lou must have found out the same things, muses Johnny.

On the way out, Kroll meets Johnny, who is ushered into a car and is told to drive. Johnny tells Kroll that he guesses the rest of the gang is going to meet Fred. Johnny drives really fast and tries to run into a truck but Kroll panics and jumps out of the car right into the truck.

Johnny drives back to Kay's theater and asks her if she is tired of running. She tells Johnny that she knows Fred is not going to be snatched as Martin had called her. She tells Johnny that she is glad it is over. She tells Johnny that Fred had had her watched to keep her in line. Johnny is going to call the police but she tells Johnny that she has already called them.

Johnny goes to see Lutzy and asks for Valerie. He tells Johnny that Valerie is in with the manager, Mr. Kroll. Johnny surprises Valerie and he tells her that she has lost a boyfriend. Johnny tells her that she and Kroll had trailed Johnny to New York and had killed Waltham. She tells Johnny that she only went with Kroll and had heard them arguing and then heard a shot in the office. Johnny accuses her of lying, as the office is sound proof. Valerie pulls a gun and Johnny takes it from her and calls the police.

Lou was never insured and the Kay Bellamy policy was never issued. They do not need to worry about the "missed appearances" clause of her current contract, as she will be missing them for about ten years. The only loss is Johnny's expense account. Johnny notes that he did not expense the pass to the Burlesque Review provided by Lou Waltham, nor the transportation back from Cullen's home, as that was provided by Kroll.

Notes:
- The script title page lists Lou's last name as "Waters" instead of "Waltham".
- The announcer is Dan Cubberly.
- Music is by Eddie Dunstedter.
- John Lund's current movie is *Just Across the Street*.

Producer:	Jaime del Valle	Writer:	Joel Murcott
Cast:	Raymond Burr, Gloria Blondell, Sandra Gould, Benny Rubin, Jay Novello, Jeanne Bates, Hy Averback		

◆ ❖ ◆

Show: **The Chicago Fraud Matter**
Show Date: **2/6/1953**
Company: **Columbia Accident & Life Insurance Company**
Agent: **Niles Hartley**
Exp. Acct: **$219.77**

Synopsis: Niles Hartley calls Johnny about a broker who wrote a $50,000 policy on Mr. Lane. Mr. Lane has died, he starved to death. Get on an airplane.

Johnny flies to Chicago, Illinois and checks in with Niles, who tells Johnny that a letter has been sent to the Insurance Commission advising them that payment is going to be held up pending a routine investigation. The sister of Mr. Lane, Lydia Staley has also called about payment on the policy. Niles tells Johnny that she has some trust funds for income but is upset. Johnny is told that Lane died on the street and was going to be buried by the city until he was identified. A routine post mortem had been done, and when Niles had checked out the body, it had all sorts of physical problems. Johnny wonders how Lane could have passed the insurance physical done by Dr. Unger.

Johnny goes to see Unger and tells him that he wants information on Christopher Lane. Johnny examines the files and asks Unger if he signed the letter and if the notes in the file are his. Johnny tells Unger that he had pronounced Lane physically sound, but he died two days ago. Unger tells Johnny that if Lane had no heart problem he could have developed one. Johnny tells Unger that Lane died of malnutrition, and Unger cannot explain it, nor can he explain the old heart lesions. Johnny looks at the file copies and asks Unger to go to the morgue. Unger and Johnny go to the morgue but Unger does not recognize Lane. Johnny has all of Unger's employees do the same, and no one recognizes Lane.

Johnny talks to the employees in Lane's apartment, and the elevator operator recognizes the body. She tells Johnny that she had seen him stoned a hundred times and that he was crazy. She tells Johnny that Lane got up at 10:00 a.m. and went out to get groceries and booze. The janitor, the maid, the doorman and the main desk clerk confirm that Lane had at least 18 months of heavy drinking.

Johnny goes to see the sister Lydia, who is foul tempered and wants to be paid. Johnny tells her that the investigation is for her benefit as well. She tells Johnny that she had not seen Chris for a year and was on good terms with Chris. She tells Johnny that she is widowed and has no children. Her attorney has told her to sue immediately. Johnny tells her to tell her lawyers that by dying on a public street the insurance company has learned that he could not have passed the exam. Johnny tells her that Christopher never took the exam. They are going to find out what happened, but based on the facts, we'd love you to sue us.

Johnny arranges for Lydia to be watched and goes to visit Mr. Rutherford, the agent who wrote the policy. Rutherford is surprised to hear from Johnny, who confirms that he has checked on Rutherford's 17-year record. Rutherford tells Johnny that he had been looking for a home in Wilmette, and Lane was the agent. Lane was in the real estate business and had a comfortable income from a trust and did not really work too hard. Lane had bought the policy from Rutherford sometime later. Rutherford tells Johnny that Lane was just a client who looked fine. Rutherford tells Johnny that he knows Unger slightly and had used him professionally. Johnny tells Rutherford that Lane died from malnutrition due to alcoholism.

Johnny calls Niles and learns that Lydia is fighting back and that the body has been cremated. Johnny tells Rutherford that he is in trouble, as he would have to have known about the drinking problem if he really had known Lane, and that he is the logical party for collusion. Rutherford slugs Johnny and runs out. Johnny calls Niles and then heads for Lydia's.

Johnny heads for Lydia's place and tells her about Rutherford. Johnny tells her that Rutherford had realized he has just ruined his whole life, but she tells Johnny that she does not know anyone by that name. Johnny questions her about the physical and she is adamant that her brother took the physical.

Niles has a warrant issued for Rutherford, and two days later Rutherford is still missing. Rutherford finally calls Johnny and he tells Rutherford that only Johnny and Niles know about the case. Johnny tells Rutherford that if he makes a statement Johnny might be able to get him off. Johnny arranges to meet Rutherford in 15 minutes.

Johnny meets Rutherford and Rutherford is pale and shaken. Johnny buys coffee and donuts and Rutherford tells Johnny that he met Lydia Staley right after his wife had died. He was interested in her and asked her to marry him, but she just laughed at him as he was not exciting to her. She told Rutherford that she wanted money and needed $50,000 in cash. Lydia told him about her brother, so Rutherford paid a man to take the physical. Rutherford wanted to cancel the policy, but she was holding the fraud over his head. Johnny tells him to make a statement and the charges will be dropped. Rutherford makes the statement and Johnny arranges for the chares to be dropped and Rutherford leaves town.

Before Johnny leaves town he goes to Lydia's apartment to have a release signed. At the door Johnny hears shots and breaks in the door to find Lydia shot. Johnny puts her on the couch and follows a trail of blood to the fire escape. Johnny follows Rutherford to the roof as he fires several times. Johnny gets to the roof and shoots. Johnny runs up and Rutherford tells him that Lydia had laughed at him and that she was planning to run away with someone else and told him that she had just used him. Rutherford and Lydia both died of their wounds.

Notes:
- This program was done by Bob Bailey as *The Lansing Fraud Matter*, broadcast on 12/12 through 12/16/1955.
- John Lund's current movie is *Just Across the Street*.
- Dan Cubberly is the announcer.
- Music is by Eddie Dunstedter.

Producer:	Jaime del Valle	Writer:	E. Jack Neuman
Cast:	Jack Moyles, Edgar Barrier, Peggy Webber, Mary Lansing, John McIntire		

◆ ❖ ◆

Show: **The Lancer Jewelry Matter**
Show Date: 2/13/1953
Company: Allied Adjustment Bureau
Agent: Pat Corbett
Exp. Acct: $70.25

Synopsis: Johnny is called by Pat Corbett who tells him that the Lancer jewelry store in Trenton has been robbed, and the Cummings Casualty wants a full report.

Johnny goes to Trenton, New Jersey, gets a hotel room and goes to see Sgt. Ralls who tells Johnny that the robbery occurred at 10:30 Saturday. A man and woman were looking at wedding rings and robbed the store. They took everything, which included $1,500 in jewels and a bank deposit for $830. The girl was about 21, and the man was older, about 35. There have been several other robberies in Jersey City, Buffalo and New York with similar modus operandi. A girl matching the description has been picked up and the police are holding her.

Johnny goes to the bank and examines the records for the jewelry company and suspects fraud because the bank deposit was too large. Johnny goes to Mr. Lancer and wants an inventory done. He admits that the girl did the robbery, but the cash was only $265.

Johnny reports the information to the insurance company and gets a call about another similar robbery. Johnny goes to the jail and talks to the suspect, Lena Roberts. He tells her that she has been identified in two robberies and offers to help her for information. She tells Johnny that the man was Paul

Handley, alias Edward Chamberlain. She tells Johnny that she met Paul at a correctional farm four months ago and describes the robberies to Johnny and tells him that Paul was going to go to South America. She tells Johnny that they have a stolen 1949 Mercury convertible. Johnny learns that Paul has a record for robbery and contributing to the delinquency of minors.

Johnny goes to a woman who he believes is Paul's mother, but she tells Johnny nothing, and he decides to stake out the apartment. Johnny watches the apartment from a bar across the street and sees a former accomplice named Thelma Warton. Johnny talks to her and she has not seen Paul for several days. Johnny calls the insurance company and is told to come home. Johnny goes to the airport and there are shots out front and Johnny spots Handley and follows him into the airport. Handley is confronted and shot and the jewels are found in a bag.

Notes:
- The announcer is Dan Cubberly.
- Music is by Eddie Dunstedter.
- This is the second appearance of a future Johnny Dollar   Bob Bailey in a program, but a digital program does not exist.
- This is the first reference to an "Adjustment Bureau" to settle claims.
- Story information obtained from the KNX Collection in the Thousand Oaks Library.

Producer: Jaime del Valle   Writer: E. Jack Neuman
Cast: Clayton Post, Bob Bailey, Jim Nusser, Parley Baer, Virginia Gregg, Martha Wentworth

♦ ❖ ♦

Show: **The Latourette Matter**
Show Date: **2/20/1953**
Company: **National Underwriters**
Agent:
Exp. Acct: **$219.50**

Synopsis: Lt. Dan Mapes calls and Johnny tells him that he is investigating for the Insurance Company. Johnny tells Mapes that he knew Thompson. Enjoy the weather he tells Johnny, you won't enjoy the case.

Johnny flies to Denver, Colorado. He had been there in 1947, but Denver has changed. Johnny rents an Avis car and goes to the Cosmopolitan Hotel. At 9:00 Johnny calls Bessie Thompson in the hotel and she tells Johnny to be careful, as everyone involved with this case has seems to die.

Johnny buys breakfast (on him) and talks to Bessie. She tells Johnny that she has buried her husband here and will go home. She is 32 and attractive, and maybe someone, well you know. She tells Johnny that the coroner said that Tommy was drunk and walked out on the highway. She asks Johnny if Tommy drank a lot, and Johnny tells her that he never saw him do anything, and that he loved her. Bessie tells Johnny that he had called and said that he was coming home, but he was killed. She knows Tommy was murdered, it was not a hit-and-run. She is sure that he had found something on Latourette. Johnny tells her that he is there to wrap up the details, and Bessie tells Johnny that Tommy's last report is missing. She is sure that he had something and was killed. Bessie tells Johnny that Tommy is in Crown Hill Cemetery, and Johnny tells her that he will send flowers.

Johnny meets Mapes and reads the police report. Johnny learns that the fire was reported at 2 a.m. and Mrs. Latourette's body was found in the ashes. The arson men reported that a cigarette had started the fire. Johnny also learns that Tommy had not been in the tavern where he was hit. Johnny asks why was he on Golden Road then? So far there is nothing to tie his death to Latourette. But Latourette will collect $80,000 in property insurance and there is $17,000 in life insurance to be collected. Mapes tells Johnny that Latourette was bowling when it happened, had a good home life and is OK financially. The police want whoever ran Tommy down.

Johnny reads all the reports, which outline a story of tragedy, violence and death. That evening Johnny goes to see Mr. Latourette and sees a man through the window that does not move. Johnny knocks and a boy talks to Johnny through the door and tells him that Mr. Latourette is out until tomorrow. Johnny asks to leave some papers, and the boy tells him to leave the papers under the door. Johnny is sure the voice was strained.

Johnny opens the door and the boy has a shotgun and Johnny finds Latourette dead and the boy is almost crying as Johnny talks to him. Johnny tells the boy who he is, and the boy is unsure of that to do as his gun has more work to do. The boy tells Johnny that "he killed a man and a woman. He killed Thompson, he ran over him because Thompson found out about his ladylove and Latourette burned his mother in a fire so they could be together. He'll see that they get together real soon!" The man is his father.

Bruce Latourette was young and scared. Bruce tells Johnny to turn around but Johnny won't. Bruce tells Johnny that his father had his mother killed and that the police do not know about Evelyn, but he is going to kill her. Bruce runs out and into his car and drives away.

Johnny calls the police and gives them the license plate number for Bruce's car. Mapes arrives and tells Johnny that Bruce has not been picked up yet. "And who is Evelyn" he asks. Mapes and Johnny talk to the neighbors and learn nothing.

At 10:15 a girl comes in to see Mapes. Dorothy Kelly tells Mapes and Johnny that she has information about Bruce, and that she heard about it on the radio. She tells them that they go to school together, and Bruce has been talking about his mother and has been depressed. Bruce had told Dorothy that "they killed her". She also tells them that Bruce had said that his father had been seeing a woman named Evelyn for a long time and that Evelyn had set fire to the store and killed his mother. Bruce had told all of this to a man named Thompson, and he was killed too. But Bruce did not tell her who Evelyn was, only that she is a skiing instructor somewhere and that Bruce had met her once.

Later a store manager identifies Evelyn Warder as a ski instructor. Mapes and Johnny go to visit her and she tells them that she does not know Frank Latourette, even after Johnny tells her Frank is dead. "Are you talking to everyone named Evelyn?" she asks.

Johnny and Mapes leave but are suspicious and watch the house. Johnny would like to sleep but there are too many things to think about as this case stinks! Suddenly they see Bruce's car and walk towards it. They call out to Bruce and he shoots at them. Bruce tells them to stay out of the way as he is going to kill her. He calls to Evelyn and tells her she killed his mother. Mapes tells Bruce to put the gun down. Bruce shoots and the police open fire and Bruce is hit.

Evelyn is charged with murder and arson. Bruce dies three hours later. Evelyn gives a confession to the fire and tells the police that it was her idea. She had a key and went into the store, saw Mrs. Latourette sleeping and set a trashcan on fire. She tells them that Frank had never talked about a divorce and that the boy had told Thompson about them. Thompson followed them to the tavern and she was driving her car and ran him down. Frank did not have the nerve to do it. He had money but no nerve.

Notes:
- The Avis Rental car is $12.50, about $115 in 2017 dollars.
- Dan Cubberly is the announcer.
- Music is by Eddie Dunstedter.
- There is a Crown Hill Cemetery in Jefferson County, near Denver.

Producer: Jaime del Valle   Writer: E. Jack Neuman
Cast: Eddie Firestone, John McIntire, Jeanette Nolan, Virginia Gregg, Sammie Hill

◆ ❖ ◆

Show: The Underwood Matter
Show Date: 2/27/1953
Company: Allied Adjustment Bureau
Agent: Red Eagan
Exp. Acct: $491.50

Synopsis: Red Eagan calls and tells Johnny that Mary just had twins. Come on down to my office for two cigars and bring a suitcase. Red tells Johnny that he has a dead client named Underwood in Rexford, Wyoming. They do not know if it was murder, suicide or an accident. It looks like all three.

Red explains they are in the same old spot, not being a friend for looking into the claim. The widow was called and hung up on Red. Underwood fell from the 4th floor of a hotel, and the policy is $25,000 double indemnity. Underwood also was a major stockholder of the local newspaper. Red tells Johnny to go to the inquest and make sure things are handled right.

Johnny travels by plane, train and bus to Rexford and attends the inquest.

The widow, Alyce, testifies that she last saw her husband at the hotel that day, and only stayed a few minutes. They called her at 3:00 and told her of the accident. She had gone to talk with him about their divorce. He was in good health and had been drinking lightly. Johnny notes that the widow was 30, with New York clothes, Tiffany rings, and Paris perfume and there was no emotion in her voice. The verdict was death by a fall.

Johnny wires the news to Red and goes to see Sgt. Hannon for the death certificate and the coroner's report. Hannon tells Johnny that the insurance company is stuck for $50,000. Johnny is told that Mrs. Underwood was raised here and went to school in the east. Mr. Underwood was rich and was old enough to be her father and he had raised her since she was 14. Hannon tells Johnny that she was going to get a lot of alimony, so there was no reason to kill him. Also, Ray was not the suicide type.

Johnny sends a report to Hartford and then gets a phone call from Red, who tells Johnny that the agent in Cheyenne had told him that Underwood wanted to change the beneficiary. But, on the morning he died, Underwood changed his mind.

Johnny goes to see Mrs. Underwood and asks her about the beneficiary change. Johnny is told that Mr. Underwood had moved out of the house a month ago and that they had had a bitter argument. It was a ridiculous thing and his impulse was to cancel the insurance policy. She tells Johnny that they did not get along, but they made up the day he died. She thinks that the fall was probably due to the argument. Johnny tells her that it seems hard to believe, based on past experience. She tells Johnny that she has told him the truth.

Johnny re-interviews the people in the hotel and then goes to see Hannon. Johnny tells him that he has learned that there was no liquor in the room, and that the hotel staff told him that Ray left a call for 11:30 and then called the insurance agent. There was no liquor in the room, but Mrs. Underwood had testified that he had been drinking. Maybe she made it up. Where did he get the drink, if he had one?

Johnny is sure that there is a problem now. Johnny calls Red Eagan and explains that he should cancel the claim and let her sue. Johnny tells Red that she was ready for everyone but you, so she did not know how to handle him when he called. Red is unsure about holding up the claim. Johnny bases his reasoning on instinct, statistics and experience. A young woman and an old rich husband make for trouble. Now she has everything. Johnny wants to file charges for suspected murder. Johnny reminds Red that Underwood did not have a drink, so someone helped her by pushing him out the window.

Johnny meets with Hannon and he tells Johnny that Mrs. Underwood is now unsure of the drink, and that the police will start looking for evidence. Johnny goes back to the ranch where a servant tells Johnny that Mrs. Underwood would frequently take trips out of town. He tells Johnny that she would take a small suitcase and the Cadillac, which would come back covered with mud and ice. Mr. Underwood complained about the trips and told her that she should not visit that man. The servant has known Mrs. Underwood for 13 years and had seen her grow up. He was sort of surprised when they married. She was a friend before they married and later they did not seem to be friends. The servant tells Johnny that he will probably be fired for talking like that, but the house is not the same anymore.

A complaint against Mrs. Underwood is issued but not served because the names of three men were uncovered. Only one of the men, a man named Tyler, was nearby, on a ranch, 80 miles away. Johnny and Hannon go to see him.

Tyler tells Johnny and Hannon that the Underwoods were both his friends and that he was not seeing Mrs. Underwood on the sly. He tells them that he was in Rexford in December for some shopping. Hannon wants to talk to the hired hands and Tyler asks if any action has been taken yet. When told a complaint is ready to be issued, Tyler tells them that Alyce's father was a drunk and that Underwood did everything for her, as she needed love. Tyler tells them that he had been seeing her. Tyler tells them that his people would lie for him, but he cannot let her be arrested for something he did. Tyler tells them that he killed Ray Underwood. Tyler had gone to see him and had gone in the back entrance of the hotel. Ray had called Tyler the night before and was sore. Tyler went to talk but Ray would not let him. Ray swung at him and Tyler pushed him away and he went out the window. That's all.

Notes:
- This program was done by Bob Bailey as *The Henderson Matter*, broadcast on 11/28 through 12/2/1955.
- Red's cigars cost $3.69 a box, so Johnny tells Red to buy him a drink instead.
- The mid-program commercial is for *City Hospital* on CBS on Saturday afternoons.
- Dan Cubberly is the announcer.
- Music by Eddie Dunstedter.

Producer:	Jaime del Valle	Writer:	E. Jack Neuman
Cast:	Ted Bliss, Jeanette Nolan, Joseph DuVal, John McIntire, Dick Ryan		

♦ ❖ ♦

Show: The Jeanne Maxwell Matter
Show Date: 3/6/1953
Company: Corinthian Life Insurance Company
Agent: Mr. Semplan
Exp. Acct: $266.85

Synopsis: Johnny calls Mr. Semplan in Boston and gets the name of the police contact for the Jeanne Maxwell case. Johnny asks Semplan if the case is murder or suicide?

Johnny rents a car and drives to the Boston, Massachusetts police headquarters. Johnny tells Lt. De Rosa that the insurance company is nervous about a possible suicide case. The girl's mother is the beneficiary and is an invalid. De Rosa tells Johnny that the mother has taken up with an old boyfriend. De Rosa tells Johnny that the girl was found in shallow water near a bridge and that it did not look like suicide. The bridge was too low, and a suicide never does it without taking off their coat and shoes, and her purse was missing. She was 21 years old and very pretty. The inquest will be in two days. Johnny tells De Rosa that he wants to dig up his own background information.

Johnny goes to the site where the body was found, and placement of the body indicates that she was going towards Boston, not away. Johnny goes to Jeanne's apartment and talks to Mary O'Neal, Jeanne's roommate. Mary tells Johnny that it is a great shock to her, and that she never thought Jeanne would do this. She expected trouble as Joan lived too fast after her mother went into the hospital. There were just too many men. One is Harold Cory, who is a truck driver for Seaboard Trucking Company. Mary tells Johnny that Jeanne saw other men when he was gone. Johnny wants to look at her things, and he goes through a locked dresser that contains nothing but clothes, perfume and jewelry, and a gold house key with a heart-shaped head. Johnny keeps the key, as he wants to find out who made it.

Johnny calls Seaboard Trucking Company and is told that Cory is out of town and due back at 3 a.m. Johnny calls Jeanne's employer and goes to see Mr. Hollis at home, where Johnny also meets Mrs. Hollis. Johnny tells Mr. and Mrs. Hollis that he suspects murder, as Jeanne did not do any of the things suicides typically do. Mr. Hollis tells Johnny that he knew nothing of Jeanne's private life, as he had no right to know, but he did know of the invalid mother. Johnny thinks there was only one man with enough money to buy her expensive things. Johnny asks about co-workers and Mr. Hollis will get them for Johnny if he will call in the morning.

Johnny goes to see Cory at 10:30 the next morning. Johnny tells Cory that it looks like murder. Cory tells Johnny that she would never kill herself. Cory tells Johnny that he last saw her on Tuesday and left Wednesday morning on a run and Johnny mentions that he could have done it before he left. Cory says he wanted to marry Jeanne and throws Johnny out.

Johnny calls De Rosa who tells Johnny that the cause of death is suicide, as the autopsy says she died of carbon monoxide poisoning. She killed herself and someone probably moved the body to avoid embarrassment.

Johnny goes to see De Rosa and reads the autopsy report, which points to car exhaust, but also shows a severe concussion. Johnny is convinced that Jeanne was killed. Johnny shows De Rosa the key and asks if he can find where it was made. De Rosa tells Johnny he will do what he can.

Johnny goes to see Paul Anderson, the boyfriend of the mother. Paul tells Johnny that the mother was 17 when Jeanne was born. He met Jeanne first and realized she was a cheap opportunist. He did what he could for the mother and did not send her to a home to get her out of the way. Paul does not know anything about a gold key and says that he knew very little about Jeanne.

Johnny goes to Mary's apartment and she cannot remember anything additional. She tells Johnny that Jeanne had never mentioned Paul Anderson to her, and that she never knew how Jeanne was able to put her mother in a nursing home.

Johnny goes to the Seaboard office and follows Cory to a restaurant. He tells Johnny that he is going out again, as he cannot take any more. Johnny talks to six of Jeanne's co-workers and finds nothing.

The police find the goldsmith who made the key and Johnny talks to him. The jeweler remembers that a councilman's wife had come in the same day. The gold key was made for a J. E. Carter. It was made for a cottage on the bay. Johnny tells De Rosa about the cottage but De Rosa cannot assign men to search cabins in the area, as it is county responsibility. Johnny searches real estate offices and on the 3rd day hits pay dirt. An agent rented a cottage to J. E. Carter and the rent was paid by cashier's check since May. They go to cottage where Johnny looks through the cottage and locks it with the gold key.

Johnny goes to Mr. Hollis and tells him "you thought you would get away with it." Johnny tells him that he had rented the cottage and bought the key. Hollis admitted he was infatuated with Jeanne and wanted to break it off. Jeanne left and committed suicide in the car. Johnny tells Hollis it was not suicide and Hollis agrees to go to the police. Mrs. Hollis comes in and tells Johnny that she had found out about them. She went out and waited and caught them and killed the girl and carried her to the car. "What have I done?" moans Mr. Hollis.

Notes:
- Edmond O'Brien did this program as *The Joan Sebastian Matter* on 10/28/1950.
- North American Van Lines is the Seaboard Trucking Company in this version.
- The conversation with the jeweler is omitted and replaced with a discussion with the realtor.
- The expenses are less: $266.85 versus $356.75.
- The vital clue, a *Wall Street Journal* with Mr. Hollis' name is not mentioned in this version.
- John Lund's current movie is *Just Across the Street*.
- Dan Cubberly is the announcer.
- Music is by Eddie Dunstedter.

Producer: Jaime del Valle   Writer: Gil Doud
Cast: Jeanette Nolan, Howard McNear, Barney Phillips, Ted de Corsia, Virginia Gregg, John McIntire, Dick Ryan

♦ ❖ ♦

Show:	**The Birdy Baskerville Matter**
Show Date:	3/10/1953
Company:	**Columbia All-Risk Insurance Company**
Agent:	**Phillip Martin**
Exp. Acct:	**$137.27**

Synopsis: Phillip Martin calls and has a job for Johnny. Carl Baskerville wants to change his beneficiary to a charity, as his brother is trying to kill him. Phil wants Johnny to be a bodyguard, and the policy is for half a million. Phil has looked at the records and Carl had sent his brother William to prison and he was released last week.

Johnny goes to the Long Island, New York mansion of Carl Baskerville where Collins, Mr. Baskerville's personal secretary, meets Johnny at the door. Collins is 6' 9", and is described by Johnny as "the tallest man I have ever seen". Johnny is taken to see Mr. Baskerville, who is in the garden feeding the birds, and he encourages Johnny to join him (here birdie, birdie!). Mr. Baskerville outlines to Johnny how he has retired after working his entire life to be successful. He tells Johnny that his brother William had been caught stealing $100,000 from the company and Mr. Baskerville was forced to prosecute him. William was to inherit Mr. Baskerville's entire estate, but now he must change the beneficiary as William has sent a letter threatening to kill him. Johnny is told that, after William has a chance to calm down, Mr. Baskerville will put him back in the will. Johnny is also told William had a girlfriend, Virginia Carter, who lives in Greenwich Village.

Johnny walks out to get a cab and hears shots. Johnny runs back to the garden and Mr. Baskerville is dead, with a bullet in his heart. Collins comes running out and tells Johnny that he had seen William with a gun. Johnny goes into the house to call the police. While talking to Lt. Brenners, Johnny realizes he has made a fatal mistake. He goes out to the body and discovers the letter is gone.

Johnny goes to Greenwich Village to visit Virginia Carter. At the door Johnny gets the quickest scalding in history, as Johnny is met by a lovely woman wearing "something thin enough to make a silkworm hang himself". Johnny is invited in and sits in a very dark living room and has a very hot conversation with Miss Carter. She tells Johnny that she knew William, and that he had shown her a good time. All of her men show her a good time. Johnny spends several hours with her trying to look at her photo album of her men. Finally, she shows Johnny a picture of William and tells Johnny that he used to play the saxophone. Johnny leaves and is almost rundown by a car.

At the musician's union, Johnny learns William has renewed his card, and is having his mail sent to a swing joint on 52nd street. Johnny cabs to the club and a piano player tells Johnny that William was there but just got up and left around 4:30. For a $5 bribe, Johnny gets William's address.

Johnny goes to the address and gets no answer at the door. Johnny is curious enough about noises inside the apartment to open the door to find William swinging from a noose. Johnny is suspicious when he puts the chair under

William's feet and they do not touch. He is dangling above the chair. The phone rings and Johnny answers it to hear Virginia's voice.

Johnny hangs up and goes back to visit her. Virginia lets Johnny in and makes a mistake by greeting Johnny by name. "Who told you my name?" he asks. After telling her what Johnny suspects, Virginia admits that she had been seeing Collins. She tells Johnny that William and Collins had stolen the money, but only William got caught. Collins had faked the letter to Mr. Baskerville to frame William. As they are talking, shots ring out and Virginia is killed. Johnny fires 6 times at Collins and hits him. Before he dies, Collins tells Johnny that he had used him as a witness to frame William, whom he had killed to avoid splitting the money. He had called Virginia and told her to tell Johnny everything so that he could find William and arrange the suicide. Before he dies, Collins says it should be raining, as it is too nice of a night to die.

At the end, Johnny notes that murder isn't so bad. A ride in any New York cab makes a killing look like a Sunday School taffy pull.

Notes:
- This is the same as the 11/10/1951 program, except for cast changes.
- The announcer is Charles Lyon.
- Music is by Eddie Dunstedter.
- Story information obtained from the KNX Collection in the Thousand Oaks Library.

Producer: Jaime del Valle   Writer: Blake Edwards
Cast: Stacy Harris, John McIntire, Howard McNear, Sidney Miller, Jeanette Nolan

◆ ❖ ◆

Show: The King's Necklace Matter
Show Date: 3/17/1953
Company: Eastern Indemnity & Insurance Company
Agent: Marty Fenton
Exp. Acct: $348.60

Synopsis: Marty Fenton calls Johnny with poetry: "A king there was with his premium paid even as you and I. But he sold his soul for a pot of gold, for rubies and diamonds precious and old, even as you and I." Marty needs help and will meet Johnny at the airport in Miami. There is a king and $250,000 in stones involved.

Johnny goes to Miami, Florida and meets Marty Fenton who briefs him on the case. Johnny is told that King Rawlings is a retired businessman who has a policy on a necklace and someone has attempted to steal the necklace from his safe. The policy renewal is coming up and Rawlings is in financial trouble. Johnny is to go to Los Ba os Island, the personal island of Rawlings, complete with a collection of, uh people.

Johnny takes a charter plane to the island and it met on the beach by a girl, Nita Valdez. She tells Johnny that she heard him land, and that she has been busy sunbathing. "You have come to see the King about the attempted theft?" she asks and tells Johnny that everyone on the island is a suspect. She tells Johnny not to be concerned about the necklace, because if it is stolen, King will know who did it. Nita tells Johnny that everyone stays for the same reason, money, but she will explain later as Johnny will understand when he meets King. She tells Johnny that she sunbathes there every day at the same time.

Johnny describes the King residence as a Moorish castle. Once inside, Timothy Harley, King's personal secretary escorts Johnny to the study. "You are here about the necklace? Did Miss Valdez say anything?" Johnny is asked. King Rawlings comes in and Johnny tells him he is there because he is an investigator. Rawlings shows Johnny a substantial safe with scratches on the door. Rawlings tells Johnny that he suspects either Harley or Nita Valdez as they love money and hate him. The safe is opened and Johnny looks at the necklace and tells Rawlings that it is paste, fake jewels. Rawlings has no explanation as the necklace was appraised when the policy was written and no one has the combination to the safe. "I am insured. You have to prove fraud" Rawlings sneers at Johnny.

Johnny calls Marty and updates him, and then Johnny goes outside to find Nita on the veranda, wearing a clinging silk gown. Johnny wonders if she looks better in the dress or the sun suit? Johnny tells Nita that Rawlings has confirmed that she hates him, and Nita tells Johnny that King acquires people, uses them, and casts them off. But it is easier to stay. She tells Johnny that she is not surprised the necklace is gone, and that he took it. Tim Harley calls to Johnny and asks him if it is true that the necklace is gone. Tim tells Johnny that "I wonder if that could account for it. Mr. Rawlings is on the second-floor landing. I think he is dead."

Johnny goes to the second floor where Rawlings is "stone cold dead".

Three hours later Marty arrives with Capt. Fuentes of the Havana police. Fuentes tells everyone that they cannot leave, as murder might be more important than robbery. Johnny tells Fuentes of the afternoon's activity and Marty is concerned about the jewelry. Fuentes has Rawling's body flown to Havana and then questions everyone, learning nothing. Johnny goes to Harley's room to talk, and he tells Johnny that Rawlings has a will, in the safe. Johnny asks about a copy of the will and is told that Señor Chavez might have one in Havana. Johnny spots his half-filled suitcase and asks him why he is leaving. Harley tells Johnny that his employment is terminated and why should Fuentes object. Johnny spots a package in the suitcase and opens it to find money, in crisp $100 bills. Harley tells Johnny that he saved it while working for Rawlings.

Later that night Johnny is smoking a cigarette on the veranda when shots ring out. Johnny fires back into the jungle and waits for Fuentes. Fifteen minutes later, Fuentes finds empty shell casings, and discovers that Harley is gone. At the boathouse, Fuentes discovers that there is a speedboat missing.

Johnny and Marty go to Havana, to meet with Señor Chavez about the will. Johnny wants to know if Nita or Timothy were named as heirs and is told that the will only names charities and public organizations. Chavez also tells Johnny that the rumors of financial ruin are false. On the way to the police, Chavez stops Johnny in the hallway with a phone call. Fuentes tells Johnny that Rawlings had died of natural causes and that Harley has been found dead with the combination to the safe in his pocket.

Johnny flies back to Miami with Marty. Johnny tells Marty that he is sure the necklace will show up, because it is in your briefcase. Johnny tells Marty that he had figured it all the time, and that all the loopholes had closed, and there was no other reason. Johnny reminds Marty that Rawlings had told Johnny that Marty had made the safe and supervised its installation, and that the copy of the necklace was too good. Johnny tells Marty that he had given Harley the combination and he made the switch. That is what the money was for, a payoff. Marty tells Johnny that he should have shot him on the veranda, but he tells Johnny that he never could out shoot Johnny.

With all deference to his chosen profession, sometimes this is a lousy business.

Notes:
- In Spanish, "Los Ba os" is "the bathroom".
- Commercials are for Wrigley's Spearmint Gum.
- Music by Milton Charles.
- Charles Lyon is the announcer.

Producer: Jaime del Valle   Writer: Sidney Marshall
Cast: Jack Moyles, Lillian Buyeff, Tom Tully, Howard McNear, Nestor Paiva, Don Diamond

◆ ❖ ◆

Show: **The Syndicate Matter**
Show Date: 3/24/1953
Company: **Employee Cooperative Group Insurance Company**
Agent: **Wilbur Runyon**
Exp. Acct: **$236.04**

Synopsis: Wilbur Runyon calls Johnny and apologizes for missing Johnny at the airport. He tells Johnny that he hopes the head office is not mad at him for sending for Johnny. Johnny tells him that four murders put a different light on things.

Johnny goes to Dallas, Texas and contacts Mr. Runyon, who tells Johnny that there is little more to know. There have been four murders at the new oil fields, and the men all had been beaten to death, maybe by the same person. Johnny is told that the wife always benefited as the company paid the premiums for the workers. Mrs. Gonzales is due in to pick up the check. She was unaware of the insurance and is due to have a baby soon. Johnny also learns that all of the workers had been new to the fields.

Mrs. Gonzales arrives and tells Johnny that her husband did not have a lot of money and worked hard, even when he was injured. There was some accident at the well and he had marks all over him. Runyon tells Johnny that another woman had mentioned the same thing. Johnny goes to get a job at the oil field, as there are four openings.

Johnny goes to Tupella, Texas and gets a job at the oil field and immediately meets Bull Farrell, the straw boss. Johnny tells Bull that he has not worked for a long time. Bull tells Johnny that if he needs money, to let him know. Johnny notes that Bull was friendly, too friendly.

Johnny goes to the payroll office and asks for an advance on his job, and the clerk tells him to see Bull Farrell. On the way out, Bull is waiting for Johnny and directs him to Frankie Roebling, who helps guys along, with a little interest. See him in room 12 at the Tupella Hotel tonight.

Johnny goes to the hotel, and Frankie is waiting for him. Frankie gives Johnny $20 and tells him that he expects $30 back on Friday. Johnny takes the money and asks about a loan form. Don't worry Frankie tells Johnny, he will remember. On payday, Johnny gets his $32 pay envelope and Bull reminds him that Frankie will want to see him. That night Johnny goes to the hotel where over fifty men are paying money to Frankie. Johnny asks Frankie for more time, and Frankie gives Johnny until next payday, when Johnny will owe $40. Don't be a tough guy Johnny is told, or you might soften up by next payday.

Johnny goes to the bars and tries to talk to the other men. Willie Prescott sits down and wants to talk. Willie tells Johnny that Roebling and Farrell were talking, and if you do not pay up, you will be roughed up. He tells Johnny that a couple of guys have died here, and that most of the guys have families and can't make ends meet.

On the walk to the rooming house a girl stops Johnny and asks for help with a butane tank. Several hours later Johnny wakes up after a beating and goes to his rooming house where he passes out again. Bull Farrell visits Johnny the next morning and tells him he should not have gotten drunk. Johnny accuses Farrell of having him beaten, but Farrell denies it and tells Johnny that Prescott is in the hospital. Also, Frankie likes Johnny so Johnny will be back at work.

Johnny sees a doctor and then goes to see the sheriff and explains the situation. Johnny asks him to suppose that you got Roebling trying to beat someone. He expects Johnny to pay next Thursday, and I'll be the pigeon. You arrest them and they will talk.

On payday, Johnny goes to Roebling's room to tell him he cannot pay. He will pay the $20 next week but Frankie makes the other $20 a gift. While Johnny walks to his room, Bull drives up in a car and he wants to take Johnny to a party. The boys in the car get out and start to beat Johnny until the sheriff shows up. The sheriff tells Johnny that he has put the men who owe Roebling money in protective custody and they have talked. Bull Farrell and the men who tried to beat Johnny are arrested, but do not talk.

Outside the jail, Roebling is nervous because he does not know what is going on. Johnny suggests that the sheriff have a guard tell Roebling that Farrell is going to be worked over tonight. Your deputy will be there and they can fake a beating behind the window shades. Then you will fake a confession.

What Roebling thinks is going on is what is important. Farrell is brought in and signs a denial paper.

Outside Roebling thinks that Farrell has signed a statement and bolts, and the sheriff goes after him. Roebling is arrested in his hotel room, and the syndicate is broken.

Johnny does not include his incidentals and miscellaneous as his oil well earnings covered them, proving that he lives within his means.

Notes:
- Charles Lyon is the announcer.
- Music is by Eddie Dunstedter.

Producer:	Jaime del Valle
Writer:	Joel Murcott
Cast:	Joseph Kearns, Lillian Buyeff, John McIntire, Stacy Harris, Tom Tully, Virginia Gregg, Parley Baer, Hy Averback

◆ ❖ ◆

Show:	The Lester James Matter
Show Date:	3/31/1953
Company:	Continental Adjustment Bureau
Agent:	Ed Talbot
Exp. Acct:	$151.22

Synopsis: Ed Talbot calls Johnny and asks him to come on down and work on a case for Corinthian Liability. They have a policy covering the Wallace Cottons & Company. There is a $4,185 shortage in the books, and they know who did it, a bookkeeper named Lester James. Your job is to figure out what he did with the money.

Johnny goes to New York City, checks in at the New Westin and then goes to the 17th precinct jail where Sgt. Mangone lets Johnny into meet Lester James, who does not want to be talked to. He tells Johnny that he knows what will happen in court. Johnny tells him that he wants to know what Lester did with the money, and that recovery of the money will affect what happens in court. James has never been in trouble before but just will not tell Johnny what he did with the money.

Johnny describes James as young, dark and tall, not the kind of man Johnny expected to meet. Johnny goes to James' apartment and speaks with the manager, Mrs. Anastasia Denovitch. She tells Johnny that James has no friends and that he never causes trouble. James has no girlfriend and has lived there 5-6 years. Johnny looks through the apartment, a grimy threadbare efficiency apartment. Johnny talks to the local merchants who remember James as a nice person who never had any money.

Johnny goes back to see Mangone after the hearing, at which nothing was said. Johnny is told that James has posted his own bail and will leave that evening. After James is released, Johnny follows him to the Empress Theater, and then to his apartment. Johnny knocks on the apartment door, but James does not answer. Johnny breaks down the door and takes James out of the gas-filled apartment. An ambulance is called and James is taken to the hospital.

After dinner Johnny goes back to the Empress Theater and talks to the doorman. After Johnny gives him a description of James, the doorman tells Johnny that he comes there to see Margie Cooke, who sings here. She is gone for the evening but the doorman calls Margie for Johnny, to see if she will talk to him.

Johnny goes to see Margie Cooke and explains why he is there. She tells Johnny that she knows the James name, and Johnny asks why James has been seeing her. She tells Johnny that she saw him once. He has given her a number of gifts, some expensive, and he also has sent orchids to her every night for about three months. She relates to Johnny that she had gotten a card from him, then the gifts started coming. She saw him once but did not go out with him as he was different and had no poise or sophistication. Johnny tells her that James had stolen the money to buy the gifts for her, but he was just a name to her. Johnny tells her that she was something more to him.

Johnny tracks down the gifts and their value totaling $2,780. Johnny tracks down reservations at expensive restaurants where the meal was never eaten that total $835. The florist bills totaled $680. The total was $4,295.

Johnny visits James at the hospital and tells him what he has learned. James is angry that Margie knows what he did. Johnny still has $410 to track down and shows James a list of what he has found. James tells Johnny that he saw her at the office where she was modeling some clothes and he thought money would attract her to him. Johnny suggests that he should have just called her and asked her to have a beer with him — it might have worked.

Margie Cook calls and Johnny tells her that James will probably go to prison, as most of the gifts are non-redeemable. After all the gifts were returned, Lester still owes $2,500. Margie offers to pay the difference for him, as he was the first man who was willing to go out on a limb for her.

James comes to trial, and thanks to Margie, he might get a suspended sentence.

Notes:
- This program was done by Bob Bailey as *The Forbes Matter*, broadcast on 12/26 through 12/30/1955.
- There seems to be an accounting error here. The loss was reported as $4,185, and Johnny is able to account for $4,295, $110 more than was stolen.
- Music by Milton Charles.
- Charles Lyon is the announcer.

Producer: Jaime del Valle   Writer: E. Jack Neuman
Cast: Peter Leeds, William Conrad, William Johnstone, Virginia Gregg, Clayton Post, Howard McNear

Show:	**The Enoch Arden Matter**
Show Date:	4/7/1953
Company:	**Hemispheric Life Insurance Company**
Agent:	Henry Grant
Exp. Acct:	$1,879.80

Synopsis: Henry Grant calls and tells Johnny to look at page one in the paper. Johnny is on page four and his second donut but turns back to see the picture of Mrs. Frank Loring and information about the Enoch Arden divorce decree for the husband who has been missing for seven years and is legally dead. Henry tells Johnny that Frank Loring was insured for $250,000, and now they have to pay off within ten days. Henry tells Johnny that he got a phone call from a nurse in Boston who saw Frank recently.

Johnny goes to Henry's office and goes over the details of the case. Miss. Ruth Beloin arrives, and she tells Johnny that she worked for a doctor in New York ten years ago, and now works in Boston. She thinks she saw Frank Loring in Boston two weeks ago at the clinic, where he wanted to be vaccinated and gave his name as Michael Walsh. He was going abroad, so she gave him the shots. When she saw the article in the paper his name came to her, as ten years ago Frank had been a patient. Johnny is told that Loring was a character actor who was good at accents and appearances. Henry tells Johnny that a man named Walsh sailed to Chile yesterday on the SS Castile.

Johnny goes to see Mrs. Loring, and a party is in full swing. Freddie tells Johnny that Mrs. Loring is happy as she is getting $250,000 because her husband is dead, and that she is going to Chile. Johnny finds Marsha Loring in the kitchen and tells her that they a common friend: Michael Walsh from Boston. Marsha drops a knife and yells at Johnny to get out. Freddie tries to interfere and Johnny is slugged with a bottle and wakes up in the basement. Johnny has breakfast, wires Henry to hold up payment of the claim pending his investigation and then flies to Colon, Panama Canal Zone.

The *SS Castile* is in port, and Johnny goes on board to Walsh's cabin, but a steward tells Johnny that Walsh has left the ship after he had gotten a wire last night. Johnny realizes that Walsh is not going to be easy to find.

On the street, a man with a gun stops Johnny and tells him that "Jose wants a gift." Johnny offers Jose his watch and slugs Jose as he takes it off. Johnny then asks Jose how he could get out of Panama without notice if the police were after him. Jose tells Johnny that in Porto Bayo there is a bar called "The Geisha Girl" run by Mr. Kamamoto who is very good at making people disappear.

Johnny takes a taxi to Porto Bayo and finds the Geisha Girl Café. Inside, a man with a cockney accent talks to Johnny and asks if he is in trouble. He tells Johnny that Kamamoto is in the storeroom. Johnny goes to the dark storeroom, where a voice speaks and someone knocks Johnny out.

Johnny comes to in a room with two men and Mr. Kamamoto, who tells Johnny that he had the exact amount of money in his wallet to pay for passage, over a thousand dollars. They are on a boat, the Okira Matsu, and will sail shortly for somewhere in South America. Johnny is told that he will be untied when they reach their destination, and that he is hot cargo and that they want to be able to get rid of the hot cargo if stopped by the police.

Johnny is sure that Kamamoto knows who he is, as his ID was in his wallet. Jose comes into the cabin where Johnny is tied up and tells Johnny that they do not want him to finish the trip, and that there are three other passengers on board. Johnny asks Jose to untie him and give him a gun. Jose unties Johnny and he goes out to the main cabin to find the Lorings and Freddie. He tells Frank Loring that he will not get the money, as Freddie will do anything Marsha wants him to do. Freddie loves Marsha and she will probably have him kill you. Marsha tells Johnny that she had been using Freddie, and that he is an idiot.

Kamamoto comes in and has Johnny's gun. Johnny tries to bargain with Kamamoto. Loring is paying Kamamoto $5,000 and lies to Kamamoto by telling him that the policy is for $25,000 and that Kamamoto can have it all. Johnny tells Kamamoto that he can go the whole $250,000 and the bidding goes on to see who will pay Kamamoto the most.

Frank and Kamamoto suddenly fire at the same time and Kamamoto is killed. Frank then kills Marsha and Freddie. Jose is in the doorway with Kamamoto's gun and tells Frank that he will kill him. Frank gives Johnny his gun and tells Johnny that he is hit, and that the whole idea was hers. He had hidden out like a dog, and she had come to Boston to see him occasionally at first then rarely. Johnny tells Frank that Marsha never was the lonely type.

Notes:
- Milton Charles provided the music on this episode.
- Charles Lyon is the announcer.
- The title of this story comes from what some states call Enoch Arden laws which allow a man or woman to get a divorce after a spouse has been gone for a specific period, typically 7 years. These laws were probably based on the character Enoch Arden, in a poem by Tennyson.

Producer:	Jaime del Valle	Writer:	Joel Murcott
Cast:	Stacy Harris, Mary Jane Croft, Howard McNear, John McIntire, Elliott Reid, Sidney Miller, Jeanette Nolan		

♦ ❖ ♦

Show:	**The Madison Matter**
Show Date:	4/14/1953
Company:	**International Insurance Corporation**
Agent:	**Paul Dupree**
Exp. Acct:	**$525.39**

Synopsis: Paul Dupree calls Johnny and asks him to come to his office to meet a girl. She is very pretty and very interesting and has just told Paul the most interesting story he has ever heard. She just told Paul that she was dead. Johnny tells Paul he better come over.

Johnny goes to the International building to see Paul Dupree where Johnny meets Mrs. Walker. She tells Johnny that she is legally dead, and that her husband Dr. Frank Madison has collected on her $10,000 policy. Her real name is Thelma Madison. Dr. Madison lives in Los Angeles and filed a death claim in 1951, and a Dr. Reed signed the Death Certificate. Thelma tells Johnny that a Wanda Thompson had come into the office and was ill. She was taken in and had heart failure in the examination room. In her pocket Frank found an address in Jersey City and called, but the mother had just died. And they were told that Wanda was the only family. She tells Johnny that Frank said that they were in luck and he used Wanda's body to be Thelma's. Dr. Reed was used to sign the death certificate because he had never met Thelma. Also, she tells Johnny that Frank needed money. Thelma went to New York and Frank was supposed to meet her there. Frank wrote for a while and stopped and never came. Johnny asks Thelma if she can she prove who she is, but she tells Johnny that she has never been finger printed. Johnny gets list of friends in Los Angeles, and Thelma tells Johnny that she works as a lab assistant in New York. She never got any of the money and is willing to sign a statement even though she can be held criminally liable for fraud. A statement is prepared and signed by Thelma.

Johnny goes to New York City and visits Thelma's apartment. The manager tells Johnny that she is a good tenant. Johnny looks around and finds nothing.

Johnny goes to visit Mr. Platt at Thelma's office, and her work story checks. Johnny calls Hartford to tell Paul that her story checks out. Paul tells Johnny that the coroner in New Jersey confirms that Mabel Thompson died there, and that Wanda the daughter was not found.

Johnny goes to Los Angeles, California and gets a room at the Statler. Johnny gets a package of pictures and prints for Thelma Walker, rents a car and starts looking.

Johnny visits a Mrs. Quincy who is shown the pictures and she knows her as Thelma Madison who died a year ago. She was Dr. Madison's receptionist. She tells Johnny that there was no funeral as the body was cremated.

Johnny goes to the police, who have a missing-persons report on Wanda Thompson that was filed by Anthony Rexford. Johnny goes to visit Rexford and he tells Johnny that he knew Wanda and had filed the missing-persons report. He tells Johnny that he had met her in a restaurant and they went to a movie. Then she just disappeared. He last saw her on June 5th, his birthday. He tells Johnny that Wanda did not drink, she just disappeared. Johnny is told that Wanda had come here for her health, as she had a heart problem, but nothing serious. Her doctor was Dr. Madison. Johnny checks with the phone company, but they find no record of a call to Jersey City by Dr. Madison.

Johnny goes to see Dr. Madison and asks him about Wanda Thompson. He tells Johnny that there is nothing in his files, but Johnny tells him that she supposedly came to see him several times. He tells Johnny that is wife was the receptionist but she was not too efficient, and that she is dead. Johnny tells Dr. Madison why he is there, and that he had talked to Thelma Madison about how Wanda had died there and how they had collected the insurance. Johnny shows him a picture of Thelma but he tells Johnny nothing, then he tells Johnny that he has never seen her. Johnny tells Dr. Madison that he has the whole story, but Frank has nothing to say.

Johnny prefers charges and Frank is arrested but he will not talk to anyone about the charges. A wire is sent to Paul Dupree to bring Thelma to Los Angeles, and she arrives the next day. Johnny asks Thelma about her statement about Wanda coming in and dying of a heart condition, and that Wanda had never seen Frank before. Johnny tells her that the call to New Jersey was never placed. Johnny tells Thelma that Wanda was a patient, and that most of the things in her statement are true, some do not make sense, that the case is too good to be real. Johnny tells Thelma that she had planned a premeditated murder, didn't you? Thelma admits that Frank knew about Wanda's condition, and that she had come in to help her sleep, so he took her to the examining room and then claimed that she had died of a heart attack, but she saw a hypodermic on the stand and had given her something. He had it all planned. He called Dr. Reed and told him it was Thelma. She had overheard it and left that night. She is glad it is all over now.

Notes:
- Charles Lyon is the announcer.
- Music by Eddie Dunstedter.
- This story was done by Bob Bailey as *The McClain Matter*, broadcast on 2/6 through 2/10/1956.

Producer: Jaime del Valle   Writer: E. Jack Neuman
Cast: Joseph Kearns, Lillian Buyeff, Parley Baer, Virginia Gregg, Tom Tully, John McIntire

♦ ❖ ♦

Show: **The Dameron Matter**
Show Date: **4/21/1953**
Company: **Federal Underwriters Inc.**
Agent:
Exp. Acct: **$551.10**

Synopsis: Lt. Joe Benson returns Johnny's call and Johnny tells him that he is working on the $65,000 National Savings and Loan holdup. Johnny is told that the night watchman has just died. Better come on down.

Johnny goes to San Francisco, California 10 hours after news of the holdup hit Hartford, and Benson tells Johnny that Bernie Manners, who was one of the four who pulled the job, has just been picked up. Johnny is told that Manners is a two-time loser with 25 arrests, but he only had $2.40 on him.

Johnny is taken to see Bernie, but he tells Johnny that he knows nothing, and was in his room sleeping. Bernie tells Johnny and Benson that he had been driving a truck but was fired. After several hours of questioning Bernie still has nothing to say. Benson tells Bernie that he has a statement from the watchman that says Bernie was one of the men. Bernie still has nothing to say for several more hours.

The phone rings, and Benson is told that the crime lab has found $20,000 in Bernie's car. Bernie finally tells the police that Eddie Page and Jack Ivers and a man named "Chick" are the others who were involved, and that Chick had planned the whole thing. Bernie does not know where they are now. Bernie just drove his car and dropped them at the Fairmont. Bernie tells them that Chick shot the guard for no reason, he just shot him in the back. Bernie gives the police a description and a check of the files uncovers 23 likely suspects.

The next day Johnny learns that the bullets that killed the watchman were from a .45 Colt automatic revolver. Johnny also learns that Ivers was recently released from San Quentin for auto theft, but he had not been seen at his rooming house for two days. Page is a two-time loser for armed robbery and is wanted in Denver. He has a sister in Eureka, and the police are talking to her.

Johnny talks to the bank auditors and learns that the total is $68,000. Johnny speaks to Hartford and they agree to suspend the insurance claim pending recovery of the money.

Johnny calls Benson, and he has a lead on Page. Johnny cabs to an address on Claire Street where Page's sister had been writing to him. They enter the building and Benson poses as a deliveryman and Page is confronted. Page shoots but no one is hit and Page is arrested.

Back at headquarters Johnny is told that Page has said nothing, but the police found $15,000 in Page's apartment. Page tells the police nothing about Chick or anyone else. Johnny and Benson eat and then return to questioning Page.

At 10:00 p.m. a drug store operator calls with a tip. Johnny and Benson go to the store and talk to Mr. Smith, who has read about the robbery and has found a bill wrapper on the floor. Johnny is told that a man dropped it about twenty minutes ago. Johnny is told that the man bought three bottles of scotch and other things and paid with a fifty and then Smith saw him go across the street to the Alden Hotel. Smith sees the man leaving the hotel and Benson recognizes him as Jack Ivers. Johnny calls to Ivers and he runs down the alley. Ivers shoots at Johnny and runs down the alley and jumps a fence and goes into an apartment house. Johnny calls to him and there is an exchange of gunfire and Ivers is killed.

Ivers is searched and $12,000 is found in a money beJohnny and Benson go to the hotel and learn that there is a second man in Iver's room, and he is still there. Benson knocks and then pushes the door open. A man is there "as drunk as you can get."

The man was Chester "Chick" Dameron of Toledo, Ohio who had a 17-year criminal record. 99.39% of the money was recovered. Pretty good for Federal Underwriters.

Notes:
- There are two versions of this program. One version is a network version with an aircheck from WBBM. The other version is an AFRTS program

with a story at the end about housekeeping and the Department of the Interior.
- This is totally irrelevant to the book, but my first job out of the military was with the National Savings and Trust Company in Washington, DC. I was taken back in time the first time I heard this episode and the name of the S&L.
- Charles Lyon is the announcer.
- Music by Eddie Dunstedter.

Producer:	Jaime del Valle	Writer:	E. Jack Neuman
Cast:	William Johnstone, Clayton Post, William Conrad, Peter Leeds, Howard McNear		

♦ ❖ ♦

Show: **The San Antonio Matter**
Show Date: 4/28/1953
Company: **Great Eastern Fidelity & Life Insurance Company**
Agent: **Ed Quigley**
Exp. Acct: **$573.49**

Synopsis: Ed Quigley calls Johnny and asks "Are you free?" Johnny tells him "If you mean am I available, yes". Ed asks Johnny if he remembers Mark San Antonio the bootlegger? Someone shot him and there is a trust setup for his daughter. The company wants a full report.

Johnny flies to St Petersburg, Florida to find rainy weather. Johnny gets a room at the St. Petersburg Hotel and contacts Lt. Benjamin and tells him of the need for a full report. Johnny is told that Mark San Antonio has a big place outside of town, was quiet and stayed out of trouble. San Antonio had called that morning to report two prowlers and a prowl car was sent out, but the two men had disappeared. The police investigated and found nothing. The cook had made breakfast for him and found him dead, shot twice from a Luger. The cook just worked there during the day. Johnny is told that Mark just spent his days painting pictures, pretty good ones too. He also listened to music, heavy stuff.

Benjamin thinks San Antonio must have stepped on toes running booze in New York but seemed to have gentled up. Johnny is told that San Antonio paid cash for his house and got a bank statement from New York every month. The lab is still working on the evidence. Johnny is told that San Antonio's daughter and the cook are at the house. The daughter, Edith Randall, had been living with an aunt and did not know Mark was her father until the insurance company told her. Johnny has dinner and talks to Ed about the trust fund.

Johnny cabs to the San Antonio house and meets Mrs. Olson the cook, who tells Johnny that she does not want to talk that day, as it has been a hard day. She also tells Johnny that Miss Randall is upset and cannot talk. Edith comes in and she wants to talk to Johnny. Johnny describes Edith as tall and dark-eyed with a happy mouth. She tells Johnny that she wants to find out more about Mr. San Antonio.

Johnny tells Edith about her father and she learns that she is the daughter of a racketeer. She is 26 and just before she was born her father was on trial for tax evasion. He had set up a trust that reverts to her. It amounts to $50,000. She offers Johnny a drink and they talk about Mark and his activities. She tells Johnny that she was reared far from the San Antonio name. She does not know how long she will be there, or why she came. She has not seen her father yet, but she has seen his life style. She feels much better about him and wants to know why and who killed Mark. Johnny leaves with a warm feeling.

The next morning Johnny talks to Mrs. Olson the cook and learns nothing new. Johnny talks with Benjamin, and he tells Johnny that there are other developments. Johnny is told that Mark's old partner, Jimmy Palalicci, was shot in Newark with a Luger, the same gun that shot San Antonio. So now the case now widens as information is gathered on Mark and Jimmy.

A day later Johnny goes to see Edith. She tells Johnny that someone has been after her, a reporter who wants a story, and that even Hollywood has called and she is frightened. Edith and Johnny walk out of the house and shots ring out. Johnny pulls his gun and there is no one there. Edith cries out and dies in his arms.

Johnny stumbles down to the road and sees a car leaving. Johnny shoots and the car crashes. Johnny runs to the car where one man gets out and the other man is dead. Mrs. Olson runs up and is told to call the police. The man tells Johnny that he is Giuseppe Rico, and that the other man was his brother Giovanni. The man wants to die rather than talk to Johnny. Johnny puts his gun to Giuseppe's temple and almost uses his last bullet to shoot Giuseppe but Johnny faints from a shoulder wound.

Benjamin is there when Johnny wakes up in the hospital. Johnny tells him what happened and learns the Rico's gun is the same one that killed San Antonio. Johnny is told that the Rico's are from New York and the police are looking for information. They flew in to town just to get San Antonio and his daughter. Then Johnny learns that Giuseppe Rico has died.

At police headquarters, Johnny learns the Rico boys were naturalized citizens but their father is missing. He was due to be naturalized soon and the immigration people are looking for him. That night Benjamin calls and tells Johnny that Pietro Rico has come in to claim the bodies.

Johnny goes to talk to him, and the old man knows that Johnny killed his sons but he will not talk. Johnny learns that Mark San Antonio's will discloses that Mark San Antonio's wife's maiden name was Rico. Johnny goes to the old man and tells him that his daughter had a daughter. The man tells Johnny that they all had to die, as they were all bad. Pietro tells Johnny that Mark had taken his daughter from Italy and that Palalicci helped him. Since that time, he has lived only to destroy them all. The daughter had to die as good does not come from a bad man. It was a vendetta.

Pietro Rico was turned over to the immigration officials.

Notes:
- There are two versions of this program. One version is an AFRTS program with a story about Presidential Succession. The other version is a network program with commercials for Wrigley's Spearmint Gum.
- Johnny is shot for the 4th time.
- This program was done by Bob Bailey as *The Valentine Matter*, broadcast on 10/31 through 11/4/1955.
- Charles Lyon is the announcer.
- Music by Eddie Dunstedter.

Producer:	Jaime del Valle	Writer:	E. Jack Neuman
Cast:	John McIntire, Joseph Kearns, Jeanette Nolan, Virginia Gregg, Jay Novello		

◆ ❖ ◆

Show: **The Blackmail Matter**
Show Date: 5/5/1953
Company: **National All-Risk Insurance Company**
Agent: **Phillip Shaw**
Exp. Acct: **$22.68**

Synopsis: Philip Shaw calls Johnny and tells him that Dale Martin is insured with National, and that a man was killed in his gym this morning. The police are there right now so you better get over there. Johnny agrees to go but tells Phil that he does not take off his shirt.

Johnny takes a cab to the gym at 1084 6th Avenue in Hartford, Connecticut. A nervous Dale Martin is there and a police officer tells Johnny that the coroner is due soon. Johnny gets a review of the events, and Dale tells Johnny that Mr. Royal was found in the locker room, and his neck looked broken. There were three assistants and three customers in the gym at the time. Johnny is taken to the rubdown room to look at the body and it is not a very pretty sight. Lt. Nathan, an old friend, arrives with the coroner and everyone in the gym was kept busy. Johnny tells Nathan that maybe someone was rubbing his neck and got carried away.

The police question the men in the gym and there are three prosperous clients, three assistants and six denials. Johnny learns that Bernie Carrol was working with Royal. He tells Johnny that he had sent Royal to the showers and started to work on another customer. Martin tells Johnny that he was just checking on supplies in the locker room. Jack Olsen tells Johnny that he went back to the locker room several times for coffee, and chalk for his hands, as he is new there. Johnny Morgan tells Johnny that he had been past the locker room too. Everyone goes to the police precinct to sign statements and are released.

Johnny goes home with Dale Martin, who offers Johnny some carrot juice. Dale tells Johnny that Royal had been coming there for over a year and that he had a lot of money. Johnny gets a phone call from Nathan and learns that Royal had a record for blackmail and a safe deposit box key in his suit.

Martin gives Johnny the address for Royal and Johnny meets Nathan there and they search the apartment. Johnny finds an appointment book that has Barbara Carrol's name in it several times.

Johnny goes to see Barbara Carrol, who lives with her brother Bernie and Jack Olsen. She tells Johnny that she had been out with Royal several times but he had mentioned nothing. Johnny notices a picture on the piano, and Barbara tells Johnny that it is Jack's father. Bernie had asked Jack to move in with them as he was living in a horrible place.

Outside the temperature is 90, and the case is going nowhere. Johnny tells Nathan that the man in the picture looks familiar, so Johnny goes to the morgue to look at pictures.

At the newspaper office Johnny gets what he wants. Back at police headquarters, Nathan tells Johnny that he has the contents of the safety deposit box, and that Royal was blackmailing a number of people. Nathan has evidence and a list of names. Johnny tells Nathan that the picture of Jack's father was of a prominent banker named William Barrett, who had jumped from a building. Barrett's name is on the list, so Royal had been blackmailing him.

Johnny and Nathan go to get Jack Olsen. At the Carrol apartment, Johnny and Nathan see Olsen getting into a cab, so they follow it across town to Long Island where the cab drives up to a sanitarium.

They follow Jack inside and talk to the manager. "Which one of you is the patient?" she asks. Dr. Feder comes out and they explain to him why they are there and he asks "Which one of you is the patient?" Nathan is told that Jack is seeing his mother, and her illness is related to her husband's suicide. The shock had driven her to a breakdown.

Nathan drives back to see Dale Martin and Johnny arranges for a visit to the gym the next day and asks Martin to make sure that Jack works on Johnny.

After a vigorous workout, Johnny gets a rub down from Jack Olsen and talks to him. Johnny mentions the picture and asks Jack about his mother, and he tells Johnny that she is dead. Johnny tells Jack that Royal was a blackmailer and tells Jack that his theory that someone in the gym hated him and killed him because he was blackmailing someone else.

As Jack is massaging Johnny's neck, Johnny asks Jack to suppose that the killer found Royal alone and killed him because he was blackmailing someone close to the killer who could not take it and committed suicide. Johnny suggests to him that he was blackmailing Jack's father and he could not take it and killed himself because he could not pay anymore. Jack finally tells Johnny that he killed Royal.

He finishes the massage and goes to the police. Nathan arrests Jack Olsen and gets a complete statement. Johnny has a drink with Dale Martin but can only see Jack Barrett.

Johnny goes to his office and has a fifth of very dry gin that Dale helps him finish. Johnny finally takes a very long drive in the country by himself.

Notes:
- Charles Lyon is the announcer.
- This is a network program with commercials for Wrigley's Spearmint Gum.
- Music is by Milton Charles.
- In this story, Johnny mentions going to his office rather than his apartment.

Producer:	Jaime del Valle	Writer:	Blake Edwards
Cast:	Edgar Barrier, Hy Averback, Hal March, Tony Barrett, Virginia Gregg, Jim Nusser		

• ❖ •

Show: **The Rochester Theft Matter**
Show Date: 5/12/1953
Company: Allied Adjustment Bureau
Agent:
Exp. Acct: $155.42

Synopsis: Johnny receives a collect call from Sgt. Papish, who works in the robbery detail, and he has instructions to call Johnny. They have found a mink coat that was stolen six months ago in the Jacoby case in Rochester. Johnny is told that the girl has said nothing as she is in the hospital with two bullet holes in her.

Johnny goes to New York City and goes to the New Westin and then to the police where he meets Papish. Johnny tells Papish that it has been six months since the Rochester theft. Johnny is told that the coat is in the crime lab, and that the girl has no prints on file.

Papish tells Johnny that the police received a complaint at three this morning and the girl was found in the doorway shot twice. A lady across the street told the police that she saw a car drive up and drop the girl off, but it could be any man in any car. The coat was the only clue, although she was wearing a ring that is unrelated. Johnny tells Papish that the claim has been paid off. The phone rings, and Papish is told that the girl is Eileen Maddon.

Papish and Johnny go to the address, which is a nice apartment in a nice area. Johnny meets Walters of the crime lab, and he tells Johnny that he has not found anything. Johnny and Papish meet Mrs. Stromberg from across the hall and she tells them that she met Eileen five months ago, and that her family lives in California. Eileen has several boyfriends, and one of her friends, Bill, has a car like the one seen the night before. He drives a black Cadillac. Bill is described as big and in his mid-thirties. Mrs. Stromberg tells Johnny that Bill would give Eileen gifts from time-to-time.

Johnny and Papish go to the hospital and the doctor gives them two minutes with her. In the room Eileen mumbles "Bill" and tells them that Bill shot her and then she dies at 3:35 p.m.

Johnny goes back to the apartment where the police find letters from her father, and a picture signed "Love Bill" in a closet. The police lab reports that Eileen was shot with a Colt .45 automatic, model 1911. Mrs. Stromberg returns and identifies the picture as the Bill who drives the Cadillac.

Papish gets a call and learns that Eileen had been married in 1951 to Bill Powers and is divorced. Johnny and Papish go to visit Bill Powers and they tell him of Eileen's death. He is stunned and tells them that he saw her just last week. Papish tells Bill that she was wearing a stolen mink coat. Papish tells Johnny that he noticed the black 1951 Cadillac convertible in the driveway, but he is not the same Bill in the picture.

They all go to the morgue to identify the body. Bill tells Johnny that their marriage failed for all the stupid reasons. Johnny wants to prove that she did not steal the coat, and Bill Powers tells Johnny that he knows about Bill Chambers. Papish shows Bill the picture and he tells Papish that it is Bill Chambers, but he does not know where Chambers lives or works. Bill tells Papish that Chambers wanted to marry her but she did not want to. Bill Powers tells them that he had bought a Cadillac because Chambers had one.

The police search their files and there are 24 William Chambers there and none were identified as Bill. The pawnshop detail turns up three more articles from the Jacoby robbery, and the description of the man matches Chambers. The Cadillac is found in a used car lot that morning. Johnny talks to the manager who tells him that the man was nervous and wanted a quick sale. The car provides prints for a William Carlson, who has several aliases and 14 arrests with two convictions for car theft.

As the search area widens more stolen property appears in pawnshops. Johnny and Papish go to the address provided in the last sale and find a William Courtney there. He is frisked and admits being Carlson and tells Papish that he let them find him. He tells them that he did not mean to kill Eileen, and that he will not talk down town. He tells Papish that he has been doing OK with house robberies, and that he met Eileen and they went out several times. He met her the other night, gave her the coat and asked her to marry him. She did not want the coat and said she was going to marry her ex-husband. Then he got mad and shot her. He got tired of running and started unloading the goods. Chambers collapses and tells them that he took some poison when they knocked on the door. Papish gives Chambers an antidote that saves his life.

The remaining Jacoby property and other items were found in the apartment and were impounded.

Notes:
- There are two versions of this program. One version is an AFRTS program that contains a story about the Air Force Academy cadets, and a story about President John Adams. The other program is a network program with commercials for Wrigley's Spearmint Gum.
- This story and *The Baltimore Matter* were combined as *The Todd Matter* done by Bob Bailey and broadcast on 1/9 through 1/13/1956.
- Eddie Dunstedter provides the music.
- Charles Lyon is the announcer.

Producer:	Jaime del Valle Writer: E. Jack Neuman
Cast:	William Johnstone, Jim Nusser, Virginia Gregg, John McIntire, Jeanette Nolan, Vic Perrin

◆ ❖ ◆

Show:	**The Emily Braddock Matter**
Show Date:	5/19/1953
Company:	Baltimore Liability & Trust
Agent:	Frank Preston
Exp. Acct:	$738.32

Synopsis: Johnny is called by Frank Preston and told that there is a bad check artist on the loose on the West Coast. So far, she has taken $4,500.

Johnny flies to Santa Barbara, California and meets Sgt. Lopez, and then goes to the hotel where the latest check was cashed. Mr. Sheridan tells Johnny that the woman came into the hotel, asked for him by name and acted as if she knew him. She told him that she had just been divorced and ran up a bill for $813.

Johnny goes to see Lopez and then calls Frank, who tells him that the woman has just struck in Malibu. Johnny goes to the sheriff's office in Malibu and meets Pell, who tells Johnny that a local man had just driven her to town.

Johnny goes to talk to Mr. Garland who tells Johnny that the woman was recovering from the loss of a child, and he had driven her to the Beverly Glen Hotel, and then to a bar in town.

Johnny drives into Los Angeles and goes to the bar, but the bartender has not seen any woman meeting the description. Johnny goes to the hotel and the luggage has not been claimed yet.

The next day the police have identified the woman as Emily Miles Braddock, who has a sister named Elaine in Los Angeles. Johnny goes to see the sister, who is crippled. Emily came to see her the day before to borrow money from Elaine. She is living on the county and is bitter that Emily has not cared for her but hopes that Johnny never finds her.

Johnny gets a photo of Emily and takes it to Garland who tells Johnny that the photo is of Emily, and that she is in a small hotel in Santa Monica under the name Evelyn Brady. Johnny calls Pell and they go to the dingy hotel and find Emily. She claims that there is a mistake, but they arrest her.

Emily Braddock was held at the Malibu sheriff's office and refused to admit any part of some 16 counts filed against her. Johnny is called to her cell before he leaves, and she tells him that they could have been friends, but she asks how Johnny got Garland to tell on her, and Johnny tells her that he only told Garland what she is — a thief and a crook and he told Johnny where to find her. She tells Johnny that she is not in court yet, but Johnny tells her that she is just as bad and just as dumb as the worst of them. She tells Johnny "stinking cops, you never give up! Stinking cop!"

Emily Braddock goes to trial next month and Johnny will not be there, but six clients of Baltimore Liability will be.

Remarks: The next time I go after a check artist, I hope it isn't a good-looking woman who feels that there is no one in the world that she can't dominate. This last one scared me, even if she was behind bars.

Notes:
- This program is an aircheck of WBBM, Chicago.
- The announcer is Charles Lyon.
- Music is by Milton Charles.
- This story was merged with *The Thelma Ibsen Matter* and became *The Broderick Matter*, broadcast on 11/14 through 11/18/1955.

Producer: Jaime del Valle Writer: E. Jack Neuman
Cast: James McCallion, John McIntire, William Conrad, Stacy Harris, Jeanette Nolan, Joan Banks

• ❖ •

Show: **The Brisbane Fraud Matter**
Show Date: **5/26/1953**
Company: **Cosmopolitan Bonding & Insurance Corporation**
Agent:
Exp. Acct: **$286.20**

Synopsis: Charlie Pantella calls from missing persons and asks if Johnny called about Mr. Brisbane. Johnny tells him he is an investigator for the bonding company and heard about the disappearance from an insurance broker who was one of Brisbane's clients. They have no leads, and Sgt. Pantella invites Johnny to go with him to talk to Mrs. Brisbane.

Johnny flies to Detroit, Michigan, and uses an attorney to issue a writ to impound the records of Brisbane's business, but the police got to them first. Sgt. Pantella tells Johnny that he has not gotten a lot of information, and that the D. A. is working on the books.

Johnny and Pantella go to talk to Mrs. Brisbane and she tells them that she last saw her husband two days earlier at breakfast. Pantella tells her that he had not gone to his office and she tells him that Mr. Brisbane likes to take the bus to work. Johnny asks about enemies, but she tells Johnny that she knows of no one, and that he never discussed business at home, as that was a rule. They have been married for almost 18 years, and she can think of no reason for him to run out. She tells Johnny that she had been out for dinner two days in a row and assumed that her husband was asleep in his room.

On Thursday, she called the office and learned he had not been there for two days and called the police. The maid told her that she had not made his bed for two days. She also tells Johnny that Mr. Brisbane would often not go to the office and would stay at home reading and writing in his study. Mrs. Brisbane does not know if anything is missing from her husband's bedroom, but the servants would know. She tells Johnny that he would have a cocktail, but was not a drunk, and that Dr. L. D. Wainer is the family doctor.

Johnny questions the servants and learns that Brisbane was a man of careful and precise habits. The study and bedroom are inspected, and it seems

Brisbane took only the clothes on his back. Johnny interviews the office staff, but nothing is learned.

The District Attorney reports that the business is healthy, and Dr. Wainer reports that Brisbane was in excellent health, for a man in his condition and circumstance. Johnny is told that Brisbane knew how to relax and had tried his hand at writing occasionally. Brisbane had had a complete physical recently and was in excellent physical and mental health, and no one had noticed any signs of amnesia. Dr. Wainer tells Johnny that he had met Brisbane socially and that Hugh Brisbane has quite a head on his shoulders. Dr. Wainer relates that Brisbane had the ability to quote the classics, and remembers him quoting a Greek, Callicles. He was so impressed he looked up the quotation and shows it to Johnny. The quote: "But if there were a man that had sufficient force, he would shake off and break through and escape from all this. He would trample underfoot all our formulas and spells and charms, and all our laws that are against nature. The slave would rise in rebellion and be lord over us and the light of natural justice would shine forth." This was quoted to Dr. Wainer on Monday, the day before Brisbane disappeared.

Brisbane's disappearance was complete and final until the District Attorney's men find that $5,000 was taken from the savings account.

Johnny and Pantella visit the bank and talk to the teller, Mr. Cook, who shows them the withdrawal slip and recognizes Brisbane's picture. Cook tells them that Brisbane had taken out large amounts of money before, and that he took this money in large bills and put the money is a small bag. Cook tells Johnny that Brisbane was in no hurry when he left, like he had no place to go. Johnny verifies that Brisbane had not left home with the bag, and all the transportation exits are watched.

Pantella gets a call from a bar, and the bartender tells him that Brisbane had been there Tuesday night. Johnny and Pantella go to talk to the bartender and he recognizes a picture of Brisbane and tells Johnny and Pantella that Brisbane stayed in the bar until 2 a.m. He was on the phone long distance and Brisbane had asked for $20 in quarters.

Johnny contacts the phone company, and a search of their records indicates a call was made to Kenneth Temple in San Francisco. Johnny tries to reach Temple but is not able to get him on the phone. Johnny vaguely recognizes the name but cannot place it.

Johnny and Pantella to go to the Brisbane home and ask Mrs. Brisbane if she knows the name Temple, but she does not know anyone by that name. She tells Johnny that she had been to San Francisco along with her husband two years ago.

Pantella gets a call from Mr. Temple, who tells him that Hugh Brisbane is there. Hugh talks to his wife and then to Pantella. Mrs. Brisbane tells Johnny that Hugh had told her that he was leaving her and everyone else. He was going to take a long sea trip with Temple and would not be back for a year, if he ever came back. He wrote it all in a letter that she should get today. She tells Johnny that she cannot understand why he would want to leave, and that he should have talked to her about it. Johnny tells her that maybe he did, but his doctor was the only one he met who ever listened to him.

"It was true. Hugh Brisbane had just walked out one day and had no intention of coming back for a long, long time. And as far as the police were concerned, there was no way to stop him. As far as we are concerned, we will have to sit on that $25,000 bond and hope that he'll come back to Detroit some day when he gets whatever it is out of his system. There is nothing we can do either."

Notes:
- This is an AFRTS program that contains a story about the jamming of radio signals.
- This story was done by Bob Bailey as the five-part story *The Callicles Matter*, broadcast on 4/30 through 5/4/1956.
- Quoted from "Gorgias" by Plato, circa 380 BCE.
- Charles Lyon is the announcer.
- Music by Eddie Dunstedter.

Producer: Jaime del Valle   Writer: E. Jack Neuman
Cast: Jay Novello, Jeanette Nolan, John McIntire, Joseph Kearns, Virginia Gregg

♦ ❖ ♦

Show: **The Costain Matter**
Show Date: **6/2/1953**
Company: **Federal Insurance & Claims Adjusters**
Agent: **Shelly Thomas**
Exp. Acct: **$227.50**

Synopsis: Shelly Thomas calls and asks Johnny if he would like to work on a case for him in Toledo. Someone has taken $12,482.16 in stolen merchandise. Shelly just wants a factual account of the thefts.

Johnny goes to Toledo, Ohio to investigate 37 stolen merchandise claims, likely a shoplifting ring.

Johnny meets with Lt. Sturges and tells him that he is investigating for the insurance companies. Johnny is told that the Maumee Dress Shop reported a coat and dress missing, then three days later the M'Ladies Shoppe reported a theft. Then more came in, and the last one was just two days ago. The merchandise is usually expensive and always women's clothes in size 10, and none of the articles have been sold.

Johnny goes to see Sgt. Grace Beidler, a policewoman who tells Johnny that this thief has good and exclusive taste. Grace thinks that based on the color of the clothes, the woman recipient has green eyes and short red hair. The choice of clothes colors and cosmetics lead them to the conclusion that the thief's eyes are green, and that the hats are designed for a woman with short hair. Johnny asks Grace "what if someone is doing it for a woman?" Johnny is told that it is impossible to watch all the stores, so they are checking all of the beauty salons for well-dressed redheads. Johnny spends a day and a half studying the reports and agrees with Beidler.

Sturges calls Johnny about a lead and they meet at Cole's Apparel. A clerk there tells Johnny and Sturges that she saw a woman wearing a green suede coat that had been stolen a month ago. She saw the woman at the cafeteria across the street and is sure the coat is the one. The woman she saw had dark hair and wore glasses. She got suspicious and left in a cab.

At the cab company Johnny and Sturges check the cab records and get an address for the fare. They go to the apartment building and the manager recognizes the coat as belonging to Miss Lillian Jones, who just moved in two days ago. They go upstairs and Sturges knocks, and the woman answers the door and they go in. The woman denies stealing the coat and tells Johnny that she had her lunch in her apartment. She also denies even having a green suede coat.

Sturges takes her down town where he discovers that she has a record, one arrest for grand theft a year ago but no conviction. The clerk and cabby identify Miss Jones and Sturges searches the apartment. Lillian will not talk and wants to call a lawyer. Later the police return with the coat they found in a hamper. It was positively identified as the stolen coat. Lillian finally admits to stealing the coat from the Costain home while she was working there as a domestic.

Johnny and Sturges meet with Mr. Costain at his home and tell him about Lillian Jones and the coat. Mr. Costain knows nothing of the coat. He tells Johnny that he had let Miss Jones go, as she did not work out. Johnny is told that Mrs. Costain died last February. Mr. Costain agrees to come in the next day to identify the coat. On the way out, Johnny mentions a photograph of a woman with red hair and green eyes. A check of the neighborhood reveals that the Costains had been there less than a year and had lived in Detroit before that. Johnny learns that Mrs. Costain had died of a heart condition.

At police headquarters, Costain calls and changes his story and wants to see Johnny and Sturges. Johnny and Sturges return to the house where Mr. Costain tells them that he has had a problem with servants and had filed an insurance claim for the coat, which Mrs. Costain had bought before she died. Johnny notes that the coat was stolen after Mrs. Costain died. Mr. Costain tells him that his wife is not dead, and that she will come back and he will have all these beautiful things for her.

He tells Johnny that when she went away, he would go out and walk through the stores and would steal the things she liked. He had denied her the things she loves, so now he has made it up to her by stealing the things she liked. He tells Johnny that everything is in her bedroom.

Notes:
- This is an AFRTS program with a musical selection the end.
- Charles Lyon is the announcer.
- Music by Milton Charles.

Producer:	Jaime del Valle
Writer:	E. Jack Neuman
Cast:	Hal March, Hy Averback, Edgar Barrier, Virginia Gregg, Mary Lansing, Peggy Webber

◆ ❖ ◆

Show:	**The Oklahoma Red Matter**
Show Date:	6/9/1953
Company:	Universal Adjusters
Agent:	Frank Ahern
Exp. Acct:	$286.45

Synopsis: Frank Ahern at Universal Adjusters calls and wants Johnny to go to Kentucky to look at a horse which Mr. Calgore has insured for $65,000. The horse was injured and had to be destroyed.

Johnny goes to Lexington, Kentucky and gets a room at the Southern Hotel. Johnny then goes to the Calgore business office where he learns that Mr. Monroe is no longer at the company and that he will have to see Mr. Calgore. Johnny calls the farm and is told that Mr. Calgore is out.

Johnny goes to see Dr. Pierce, the veterinarian. Pierce tells Johnny the horse was injured by a piece of equipment and injured his leg, and Calgore had the horse destroyed and cremated on the premises. Johnny is told that there are no x-rays and that Pierce had advised Calgore to have the animal destroyed. Pierce tells Johnny that Calgore took his word, and asks why he won't.

Johnny mails the medical report to a veterinarian in Cleveland and drives to the Calgore farm. Lucy Calgore meets Johnny at the door and is sad about the horse. She tells Johnny that the horse was not injured. Calgore comes in and slaps Lucy. He tells Johnny that Lucy gets hysterical whenever he shoots a horse. Calgore thinks Johnny is going behind his back by going to Pierce. Johnny tells him that the claim will not be paid until he finishes his report. Calgore tells Johnny that he fired Monroe for filing the claim so soon. Johnny tells Calgore that he went to Pierce because that was the logical place to start.

Calgore tells Johnny that he is not afraid of Johnny or the insurance company, but Johnny tells him that so far, the information is not in Calgore's favor. Calgore tells Johnny that the horse was scared by a mouse, reared back into the machinery and was injured. The trainer, Jim Knight has been fired, and that no one else was there. Calgore tells Johnny that accidents happen and that he gets rid of the animals as soon as possible. Calgore calls Abbott the butler and tells him to throw Johnny out.

Johnny talks to the horse handlers and gets Jim Knight's address in Baltimore. Johnny meets Lucy near the stables and she is more reluctant to talk. She tells Johnny that Red was the best horse they have had in several years.

Johnny checks on Calgore's finances and wires Hartford and Jim Knight in Baltimore. Later, Johnny gets a call from Mrs. Knight who tells Johnny that her son is at the Calgore Farm. Johnny tells her that he left the farm and she tells Johnny that he has not come home. That is not like Jimmy, maybe there is something wrong. Now Johnny is suspicious.

After returning to the farm, Abbott shows Johnny the room where Knight stayed, and tells him that no one saw Jim leave. Abbott tells Johnny that Lucy had driven him around, so maybe she knows where he is.

Johnny talks with Lucy again and she tells Johnny that she had been arguing with father for weeks and had used Johnny to get back at him. Lucy tells Johnny that she had been seeing Jim Knight and that her father did not like it. She tells Johnny that she had been looking for an excuse and thinks that maybe her father is mad. She tells Johnny that she does not know where Jim is. Lucy tells Johnny that the Calgores have always been angry people but that her father has not been himself lately. She tells Johnny that he once bought a new car and wrecked it when there was a small problem. She is in love with Jim Knight, and always has been.

Back at the farm Johnny talks with the hands. Later Frank Ahern calls to say that Calgore's finances are good, and that Calgore has not threatened to sue, so maybe he does not have a just claim.

Johnny visits Pierce again and tells him the claim is being denied. Johnny has checked Pierce out and does not believe his story. Johnny tells Pierce that Calgore will have to sue and produce Jim Knight, and that means that Pierce will be required to testify.

Pierce tells Johnny that he has been Calgore's friend for 18 years and that Calgore asked him to lie for him. He tells Johnny that Red was dead when he got there, and that Red was not the horse they thought he was and Calgore just shot him and Knight saw it. Pierce thinks Calgore is losing his mind.

Johnny drives back to the farm and Abbott opens the door and tells Johnny that this is not a good time to be there. Lucy tells Johnny that father is not in a good mood and that she has been crying because she cannot please him. Calgore walks in and yells at Johnny to take his hands off of Lucy or he will kill him too, and then he hits Lucy with his cane and walks out.

Johnny calls the sheriff and goes to the stables. Calgore tells Johnny to go away and warns him that he has a shotgun. Johnny tells Calgore that Pierce has talked to him. Calgore tells Johnny that he will shoot the whole bunch and shoots at Johnny. Johnny fires back and hits Calgore.

As he dies, Calgore tells Johnny that he shot Knight and his body is under the floor of the stable. Calgore asks Johnny "I'm not crazy, am I?" and then dies.

Notes:
- This is an AFRTS program that contains a story about the Attorney General.
- This was done by Bob Bailey as *The Duke Red Matter*, performed on 1/23 through 1/27/1956
- Charles Lyon is the announcer.
- Music by Milton Charles.

Producer:	Jaime del Valle	Writer:	E. Jack Neuman
Cast:	Jean Howell, Dave Young, John McIntire, Peter Leeds, Parley Baer, Roy Glenn, Jeanette Nolan		

Show:	**The Emil Carter Matter**
Show Date:	6/16/1953
Company:	**Columbia All-Risk Insurance Company**
Agent:	
Exp. Acct:	$572.00

Synopsis: A woman calls and asks Johnny about the Emil Carter killing. She is Janice Lait and she wants to talk. She tells Johnny that she did not kill Carter.

Johnny goes to Los Angeles, California where the police are searching for Janice Lait, who had been seen running from Emil's door after shots were fired. Johnny is looking for Emil's brother Frank, the beneficiary.

Johnny cabs to the harbor in San Pedro and waits to be met in front of a sporting goods shop. A man asks Johnny for a match and takes Johnny to the girl in a cab. On the way, the man is quiet and bored. Near the beach, the man takes Johnny to Janice who is waiting in a car.

Johnny tells Janice that he knows she is a former dancer who got involved with Emil. Johnny tells her that she is doing all the wrong things typical of a scared killer. She tells Johnny that she was in the hallway and heard the shots and then ran. She wants to tell Johnny about her side of the story.

She tells Johnny that she and Emil were going to leave town and live in South America. They had reservations in a different name, as there were friends who would not want him to leave. That night he called and told Janice that he had changed his mind about marrying her. She went to the apartment and heard voices inside, and then shots and she ran. Johnny tells Janice that he will not tell the police as they will not believe him.

The man and Johnny walk to a café and the man, who Johnny guesses is Janice's brother Frank, asks Johnny why a man would have killed Carter. Johnny tells him that the insurance company wanted that question answered, and about the insurance policy on his brother.

Frank tells Johnny that Emil Carter was married to a common law wife and was paying her $1,500 a month to keep the secret. Frank had tipped the wife that Emil was leaving for Mexico, and that Janice did not know about the wife. He tells Johnny that he did not think that Janice would go rushing up to the apartment. Johnny learns that the woman's name is Hazel Carter. Johnny goes to his hotel after deciding that what he learned was too weak to give to the police.

The next day Johnny talks to the residents of the apartment building and learns about the greatest hindrance to investigation, the average eyewitness.

Mr. Samuel Nelson is a composite of the tenants. He tells Johnny that he came out and saw Mrs. Roberts in the hallway. He looked to the rear and saw Mrs. Robinson and heard someone running towards the front. Mrs. Roberts said nothing, but Johnny tells him that she said she did. Now everyone is confused about what they saw, and no one can swear to having seen Janice being in the hallway. Johnny mentions a second woman, but Mr. Nelson is confused about what he saw.

Johnny talks to Lt. Scott at homicide, and he is not sure of Johnny's evidence. Johnny tells Lt. Scott that he is not sure that Janice is innocent and is only thinking of the insurance angle. Scott tells Johnny that he has questioned Carter's wife and other relatives.

At his hotel, Hazel Carter is waiting for Johnny in the bar. She tells Johnny that they have a common problem. She tells Johnny that Janice's brother called her and told her that she is a suspect, and she wants to get rid of the suspicion. She wants to know about how to offer a reward for information.

In Johnny's room, Hazel tells him that she is relieved that the brother had gotten the news out about their relationship. With him gone, there is nothing. She loved Emil and talked to him when she heard he was leaving. She tells Johnny that Emil had enemies. She wants to offer $5,000 to Johnny to help, and he suggests that she go to the papers.

The next day the reward hits the papers and Janice calls Johnny and asks him about the reward and whether it is a trick. She tells Johnny that her brother had told her about Hazel last night. She tells Johnny that the police will have to find her, and that she will not give up, as she has to think.

Scott calls Johnny and tells him that he has a confession from Janice Lait's brother. Johnny tells Scott about meeting Janice at the beach and that the discussion with the brother was nothing. Scott tells Johnny that when Johnny mentioned the angle of a man killing Emil, Frank thought Johnny had something on him, so when the reward hit the papers, he gave up.

Johnny goes to visit Frank in his cell, and Frank tells Johnny that he never thought he would go so far as to murder Emil. Frank had been shilling for Janice for ten years. When he found out Emil was taking her out of the country, Frank went to talk to him. They argued about Janice, Carter laughed at him so he shot him. He stayed in the apartment until the crowd left and went out the back door, but Johnny finds a lot of errors in his statement.

Scott comes in to tell Johnny about a shooting between two women at Hazel Carter's apartment. Johnny and Scott go to the apartment. The doctor tells them that both are still alive. Johnny talks with Janice, who tells Johnny that she hopes she killed Hazel. Johnny tells her that Frank had tried to save her so she knew that Hazel must have done it. Johnny talks to Hazel who admits killing Emil because he was going away with Janice.

Johnny was wrong from the beginning. Frank took the wrap for Janice because he thought Hazel was innocent.

Notes:
- This program was performed as *The Alma Scott Matter* by Edmond O'Brien on 12/29/1951.
- Charles Lyon is the announcer.
- Music by Eddie Dunstedter.

Producer: Jaime del Valle **Writer:** Gil Doud

Cast:	Mary Jane Croft, Hal March, Hy Averback, Frank Nelson, Mary Lansing

• ❖ •

Show:	The Jonathan Bellows Matter
Show Date:	6/23/1953
Company:	Intercontinental Indemnity & Bonding Corporation
Agent:	Roger Stern
Exp. Acct:	$208.60

Synopsis: Roger Stern calls and tells Johnny that someone has tried to kill Jonathan Bellows, the industrialist. He is insured for $500,000. Go look into it, his wife Edith is expecting you.

Johnny drives to New York City and meets with Mrs. Edith Bellows. She tells Johnny that her husband was shot at in his garden. Edith tells Johnny that he is sixty-three and does not like meddlers, and the police are meddlers. Edith tells Johnny that she is mildly concerned, and Johnny tells her that the insurance company is very concerned. Johnny is told that Edith is wife number three, and that Bellows has a son, Ralph.

Edith drives Johnny to the upstate mansion in the station wagon. At the mansion, Johnny meets Ralph who tells Johnny that his father is in the library with Professor Wilt. Ralph is sure that this father will blow a fuse at Johnny's being there. Ralph tells Johnny that his father is a tough, bigoted and unreasonable man, and that he likes making him blow a fuse.

Johnny meets Bellows who is playing chess with the professor. Bellows objects to the insurance company sending a meddler and tells Johnny to get out or he will have Johnny fired. Johnny gets tough and tells Bellows to sit down. Johnny reminds him that the insurance company has an interest in his life, and if there is no investigation, he will call the insurance company and tell them to cancel his policy. Johnny tells him that if he tries to get tough with Johnny again, he will turn him over his knee to give him the spankings he missed as a child. Suddenly Bellows softens and wants to talk to Johnny alone.

Bellows shows Johnny a letter that threatens his life and tells him "you will pay for Ashantay". Bellows tells Johnny that he had been involved in a mining operation in Africa thirty years ago, and that his partner Frank Victor had been killed in a cave-in after an argument, and that he was cleared of any guilt. Bellows has told Johnny this because he has decided to trust Johnny. Johnny asks if Frank is still alive, or is it blackmail, or a scare tactic? Bellows tells Johnny to take the station wagon back to town and stay in the Park Avenue apartment.

Johnny arrives at the apartment to a bellman that is charged with looking after Johnny's every need. Johnny calls Roger Stern and requests more information on the family, Professor Wilt and the servants. Later Johnny gets a call from Bellows, or is it Bellows? The voice tells Johnny to go to a bar and pick up a package and bring it to him.

Johnny goes to the bar, picks up the package and drives it to the mansion. At the mansion, Ralph is out and Edith is leaving. Johnny goes to the library where Bellows tells Johnny that he knows nothing about a package, and then suddenly remembers that he does. As Bellows is opening the package, Johnny goes to phone a company physician when Ralph comes in. As Johnny is explaining about the package there is a massive explosion, and Bellows is killed — there was a bomb in the package.

Johnny drives back to the bar and looks for the bartender, who has gone home. The current bartender gives Johnny the address of Earl Phillips, who lives on East 157th street.

Johnny goes to the apartment and gets no answer at the door. Johnny gets the landlady, "who is four years older than Grant's tomb" to open the door where Johnny finds Ernie stabbed to death. Johnny spots a trail of blood leading to a closet and convinces the landlady to call the police. "Go down the police and call the stairs" she repeats on the way out, scared to death.

Johnny opens the door and finds the man with the knife, Professor Wilt. They struggle and Professor Wilt is shot. Before he dies, Professor Wilt tells Johnny that he had once been a carnival worker and learned hypnosis. He eventually became a psychoanalyst and met Bellows through his wife. It was a good setup. When he learned of the Ashantay incident, Edith came up with the idea to get rid of him. The phone call was done under hypnosis and the opening of the package was a post-hypnotic suggestion. Wilt dies before the police arrive.

Mrs. Bellows is arrested and Johnny gives his story to the police.

Notes:
- This is an AFRTS program with a story about keeping time, and a story about the presidency of Chester A. Arthur.
- Roger Stern was the agent for Intercontinental Indemnity & Bonding Company in *The Cuban Jewel Matter*, but he was killed in that story. Roger Stern also appears in several stories after this one. See the Reports section for the stories.
- Music by Eddie Dunstedter.
- Charles Lyon is the announcer.

Producer: Jaime del Valle Writer: Blake Edwards
Cast: Clayton Post, Virginia Gregg, Tony Barrett, Ralph Moody, Howard McNear, Martha Wentworth

◆ ❖ ◆

Show: **The Jones Matter**
Show Date: 6/30/1953
Company: **Concourse Mutual Life Insurance Company**
Agent: **George Dean**
Exp. Acct: **$418.40**

Synopsis: George Dean calls and asks Johnny how he would like to go to Las Vegas? George tells Johnny that Lili L'Seur has just had a $30,000 diamond necklace stolen. She still has the same two bad habits, gambling and collecting young men.

Johnny flies to Las Vegas, Nevada, checks into the Flamingo Hotel and goes to see Lili at her hotel. Lili is with Eddie Lawson when he gets there. When Johnny tells Lili why he is there, she is puzzled. Oh, the necklace! She is afraid that Johnny is going to ask all sorts of embarrassing questions. She would love to talk to Johnny, but Buck and Devastator are waiting for her. Eddie explains to Johnny that Buck is her riding instructor, and Devastator is her horse. Eddie tells Johnny that he is going to marry Lili. Johnny is told to come to the hotel after the show, everyone involved will be there.

Johnny drives to the Lazy J Ranch and talks to Buck, who has no idea of what happened. He tells Johnny that he was there with Miss Jo, Joan Drake, who had wanted to meet Lili. Joan and Lili had gone to change clothes and came back. Then he heard Lili scream that her rocks were gone. That is about all. Buck has something else to tell Johnny, and he guesses that Buck is going to marry Lili.

Johnny talks to Marshall Kimberly and gets the story of the theft. It seems that Lili, Eddie, Joan and Buck (who is from Los Angeles, not Texas by the way) were on the terrace when the jewels disappeared. Joan is from the east and is a floor manager at the "Billion Dollar Club". Johnny mentions the slot machine in the Marshall's office and puts in a dollar and loses. Johnny is told that the slot machine is rigged to lose and that the proceeds go to the local orphanage.

Johnny goes to talk to Joan Drake. While Joan is playing and losing at roulette, Johnny leans that she was born to rich parents and went to a swank eastern college. Her father was involved with another woman. When everyone found out, his clients left him, his wife divorced him and he committed suicide after the other woman jilted him. Johnny asks Joan why an educated woman like her is working in Las Vegas for $50 per week and hanging out with Lili. Joan tells Johnny that Vegas has the glamour and glitter that she was used to.

Later that night after Lily's show, everyone is there at the pool terrace. Lili tells Johnny that she had worn the necklace for her show and after changing clothes with Joan, she had put it in a handkerchief by her chair and it vanished. Johnny tells her that the insurance company will want more, so she tells Johnny that she had played the slot machine and won a jackpot, and that Joan was sitting there too. They were all in bathing suits, so it was hard to hide anything. Buck and Eddie walk up to Lili and argue over who will walk Lili to her next show.

Later that night, Joan calls and asks Johnny if the insurance company will deal for information. Johnny tells her that he must check. She also tells Johnny that her real name is Jones, and that her father was Jonathan Vanderlay Jones and that Lili was named in his divorce as the other woman.

Johnny and Joan eat dinner and Johnny wonders if Joan is out for revenge or knows who and how the necklace was stolen. After the show, Lili tells Johnny that she wants to drop the claim. Johnny asks Lili who did it, or whom she thinks did it. Johnny runs through the likely suspects are, and that he is curious now.

After Lili leaves the marshal pages Johnny and is told that Kimberly has found Joan Drake in a parking lot — dead. Johnny goes to the scene and finds Joan, beaten in a car belonging to Buck. Her hands are rusty and greasy and the car radiator is still warm. Johnny tells Kimberly that Joan had called and wanted to deal, so maybe she did know who did it, and died trying to prove it.

Johnny goes to the pool and examines it. He wraps his room key into a handkerchief, and throws it in, and watches it float down into the drain at the deep end. Johnny goes to the pump house, shuts down the pump, and uses a brand-new wrench to open the suction tank where he finds his room key and the necklace.

On his way back out, the lights go out and someone pushes Johnny into the pool and swims toward him. Johnny uses the wrench to hit the swimmer. Kimberly arrives and they pull Eddie Lawson from the pool. Johnny tells Kimberly that Eddie had taken the necklace, and that Joan had found out where it was and died for her efforts.

Johnny goes to see Lili and gives her the necklace. Johnny tells her that Joan is dead and that Eddie killed her. She tells Johnny that she really meant no harm to anyone. Lili tells Johnny that the necklace was given to her by someone with the initials "JVJ", but they really do not mean anything to her.

Johnny notes the policy is coming up for renewal and advises against it, as Lili is a bad risk.

Notes:
- Charles Lyon is the announcer.
- Music by Eddie Dunstedter.

Producer:	Jaime del Valle Writer: Les Crutchfield
Cast:	Ken Christy, Mary Lansing, Vic Perrin, Hal March, Parley Baer, Virginia Gregg

♦ ❖ ♦

Show:	**The Bishop Blackmail Matter**
Show Date:	**7/7/1953**
Company:	**National All-Risk Insurance Company**
Agent:	**Phillip Shaw**
Exp. Acct:	**$46.35**

Synopsis: Johnny is called by Phillip Shaw and told that Mrs. Bishop has been found dead. She was with Tony Grayson, a known blackmailer. It looks like Grayson killed her and then shot himself. She has a $32,000 policy with the husband as the beneficiary.

Johnny goes to New York City and talks to Mr. Bishop in his apartment, and he tells Johnny that he knew that his wife was being blackmailed. He got a phone call from a friend of Tony's who told him that the blackmail would continue. Johnny is told that Mrs. Bishop was wild in her youth and that the man has some letters she wrote and he wants $100,000. Johnny also is told that Mrs. Bishop had all of the money in the family.

Johnny goes to the 5th precinct and meets Lt. Beck who tells Johnny that Bishop has been married for three years. Johnny also sees some photos of the murder scene and is told that the friend of Tony Grayson is a wino named Wilbur Truitt. Johnny calls Mr. Bishop and tells him about Truitt and then goes to the Parrot Club and finds Wilbur.

For the price of a bottle, Johnny is told that Grayson has a friend named Leo Fink. Wilbur gives Johnny the address and tells him that he is the second person to ask him for that information that day.

Johnny goes to Fink's address and finds Beck there. Leo Fink is dead and the room has been torn up and it looks like the killer used the fire escape. Johnny asks Beck about a glass in the pictures and is told that it had prints from Grayson's right hand.

Johnny goes to see Mr. Bishop and tells him about the death of Fink, but Bishop has an alibi. Johnny goes back to talk to Beck who tells Johnny that Wilbur will not talk about who else asked him for the address. Johnny is told that the paraffin tests showed that Grayson did not fire the gun, but Mrs. Bishop did. Johnny thinks that Mrs. Bishop killed Grayson and someone she trusted took the gun and killed her.

Johnny goes back to the Parrot Club and for another bottle learns that the other man was Louie Crabb, an assassin who just walked in the door. Johnny hits Crabb with a bottle and Wilbur is shot. When Crabb wakes up he tells Johnny that he was paid by a "John Jones" to kill Fink, and will be paid tonight on the ferry, and was supposed to wear a carnation in his lapel.

Johnny goes to the ferry that night with a carnation in his lapel and spots Mr. Bishop. Johnny tells him that he hired Crabb to kill Leo and killed his wife for her money. Bishop hits Johnny and runs, but Johnny shoots him. Bishop admits to killing his wife. He found the letters and gave them to Grayson and was splitting the blackmail.

Notes:
- The announcer is Charles Lyon.
- Music is by Eddie Dunstedter.
- Story information obtained from the KNX Collection in the Thousand Oaks Library.

Producer:	Jaime del Valle	Writer:	Blake Edwards
Cast:	John Stephenson, William Johnstone, Jack Moyles, Herb Butterfield		

◆ ❖ ◆

Show: The Shayne Bombing Matter
Show Date: 7/14/1953
Company: Columbia All-Risk Insurance Company
Agent:
Exp. Acct: $123.70
Synopsis: The introduction to this program is missing.

Johnny goes to New York City to get the information on David Shayne and meets with Lt. Will Stevens, an old friend. Johnny is told that David's brother is being held, as he mailed the box and it came from California. Charles swears that he did not do it and they were very close. Johnny reminds Stevens that Cain and Abel were close also. Stevens tells Johnny that there does not seem to be a motive in the case. After his lawyer showed up, Charles hushed up and will not talk. David was a factory foreman at Bishop and Harding and was active in union affairs.

Johnny talks to Charles Shayne in his cell and tells him that he is investigating his brother's death. Charles tells Johnny that he did not send in the bomb. He tells Johnny that the package came from California, where he was working in a shipyard for eight months. Johnny is told to look at the police report if he wants more answers. Johnny asks why he came back to New York, and Charley tells Johnny that he quit and came back to New York because he did not like the job.

Johnny goes to the hospital to see Mrs. Shayne. Johnny tells her that Charles is OK. She tells Johnny that she made a mistake telling the police that Charles sent the package, as he did not do it. She feels that David must have been wrong. She tells Johnny that they were in the kitchen, and that the package was delivered to the factory addressed to David. He came home and told her that the package was from Charles.

Johnny then goes to see Mary Shayne, David's sister, who is also in the hospital. She is sedated, but she tells Johnny that Charles did not do it, as he was helping David. She tells Johnny that Charles knows who sent the package and that David was making speeches against the Workers Protective Association and Charles was helping David in California. A man named Wagner called David all the time, and he is a lawyer. David also told someone at the factory that Charles was helping him. It was Ralph Pryor who he sometimes ate dinner with. On the way out, a sidewalk photographer takes Johnny's picture.

Johnny takes a cab to the factory and talks to Ralph Pryor. Ralph tells Johnny that Shayne was a good friend and that he had worked there for six years. He tells Johnny that he had said goodbye to David when he left work yesterday. Ralph tells Johnny that the mail comes in from the mailroom and that the foreman usually sends someone from the floor to get it. Johnny goes to the mailroom and there had been a heavy package for David, and that someone picked it up. Johnny calls Stevens and tells him that David did not send the package. Stevens agrees, as the contents were high-grade dynamite. Johnny asks Stevens to pick up Ralph Pryor and to hold him as long as possible.

Johnny waits outside the plant until Pryor is picked up. Johnny then goes to see Stevens and tells him that Charles was doing undercover work on the WPA. Stevens tells Johnny that the WPA is an extortion ring that muscles in on the local unions and forces people to pay up. The FBI has been working for over a year on busting it. Johnny is told that Pryor will not talk and Johnny wants to see who bails him out. Stevens tells Johnny that John Wagner also came to see Charles. If Wagner is involved, he probably threatened Charles.

Johnny tells Stevens that if Charles was working with his brother, then Wagner probably threatened his family with another bomb to keep Charles quiet. So, if the bomb was sent from within the factory, someone else is involved. As they are talking Stevens is told that Wagner has come in to see his client, Ralph Pryor.

Johnny spots Wagner, who was wearing blue suit, homburg and spats. When Wagner leaves, Johnny follows him in a cab to a waterfront dive. Johnny goes in and asks the bartender about Wagner. When Johnny asks where the back door goes, the bartender tells "Mr. Dollar" to go back there with him, as Johnny is expected. Johnny wants to make a call first but the bartender has a gun and takes Johnny back to see Wagner.

Behind the backroom is an office with Mr. Wagner who tells Johnny that he is in serious trouble. Johnny is told that the photographer had taken his picture, and that they looked him up and found out who he is. Johnny is told that Al will take him out and take care of him. Johnny confirms with Wagner that Pryor knew the package was coming and that they had switched the contents with the dynamite. David thought there were important papers in the package. Their people knew of the package and alerted them.

A buzzer warns of trouble out front. Al shoves Johnny out the back door as Stevens comes in with Pryor. Al turns to shoot Stevens, who shoots Al first. Wagner goes out the window and Johnny chases him. Johnny tackles Wagner and knocks him out. When Stevens yells at Johnny for taking a risk, Johnny tells him "You gotta be crazy to be a hero".

Wagner was the head of the WPA and Pryor worked for him. When David told Pryor of Charles' work, Pryor told Wagner, who had him substitute the dynamite when the papers showed up. Wagner had sprung Pryor, and Stevens had followed Pryor to Wagner's just in time to save Johnny.

Notes:
- Charles Lyon is the announcer.
- Music by Eddie Dunstedter.

Producer:	Jaime del Valle	Writer:	Blake Edwards
Cast:	Junius Matthews, Frank Nelson, Clayton Post, Virginia Gregg, Mary Lansing, Sammie Hill, Jim Nusser		

♦ ❖ ♦

Show: The Black Doll Matter
Show Date: 7/21/1953
Company: National All-Risk Insurance Company
Agent: Phillip Shaw
Exp. Acct: $467.60

Synopsis: Phillip Shaw calls Johnny about a shooting in Los Angeles. The victim was Miss Judith Thompson. Johnny is told to get the details at the office before he flies to Los Angeles.

Johnny flies to Los Angeles, California and goes to the Wentworth Hotel.

Johnny meets Lt. Brickford and learns that Miss Thompson was shot once with a .38 and the police have talked to witnesses, and so far, there is no real reason for the killing. Johnny is told that there is a new boyfriend, named William Karns, who works for Timpkin Aircraft as a test pilot. Also, Miss Thompson was shot in her apartment and the boyfriend is a former military pilot. The police are sure that she went out that evening, but they do not know where.

Johnny and Brickford go to talk to Bill Karns at the Timpkin Aircraft plant. Johnny and Brickford meet with Mr. Timpkin and tell him why they are there. They are told that Bill is getting ready to take up a new airplane so Johnny and Brickford go out and watch the tests, and they are impressive.

After the plane lands, they go to the office and Brickford tells Bill that Judith is dead. Bill tells Brickford that he had stayed home on the night of the killing, and then he changes his mind. He tells Johnny that he is married and separated, but he was lonesome and took Judy out that night.

Bill tells Johnny that they went to the beach and played the concessions on the pier, and nothing unusual happened. Bill tells Johnny that he had split with his wife over his job. Bill really loves his wife and does not want his name in the papers.

Johnny and Brickford leave and on the way out, Bill runs after them to tell them he almost had a fight with a man running the shooting gallery on the pier. He had won a big black doll and Judy wanted it and he had to almost fight the man to get it for her. Bill tells them that Judy took the doll home, along with a lot of other trinkets. After they pull away, Brickford tells Johnny that the doll was missing when they searched the apartment, but that the trinkets were there.

Johnny and Brickford go to the apartment of the dead girl where they find the trinkets on the dresser, but there is no black doll. Johnny and Brickford go back to talk to Bill Karns at his apartment before they head for the pier. Bill tells them that he is positive that Judy took the doll home. Bill confirms that the argument was over the doll, and that Judy took it home with her. Bill agrees to go with Johnny and Brickford to the pier to identify the man he had argued with after he is told that the doll is missing.

After dinner, they all drive to the amusement pier and look for the shooting gallery. Johnny spots a black doll on the top shelf and Johnny shoots out all the targets and wins the doll. Brickford asks the man running the stand, whose name is Virgil Wellman, who was running the stand three nights ago. Brickford is told that a man named Charlie Gilbert was running the stand that night, but that he quit last night. Johnny and Brickford question Virgil and learn that he had never met Charlie until three weeks ago when he hired him, but that he had a bad temper. Brickman is sure that he has seen Virgil somewhere, and takes the doll to have it examined.

Later that night the phone rings and Brickford tells Johnny that a man has been pulled from the ocean. There was no identification, but he looks the way Gilbert had been described. Also, Johnny is told that Virgil Wellman, who is really Virgil Sheldon, has a record of narcotics arrests and has served five years.

Johnny goes to city hall and meets Brickford and goes over the information Brickford has. Bill Carnes arrives and identifies the man who was pulled from the ocean as the man he argued with. Johnny learns that the man has been identified by his prints as Charles Sidney, alias Sidney Gilbert and Charles Gilbert, and that Gilbert was wanted by the FBI.

Johnny and Brickford go back to the pier to talk to Virgil, but the gallery is closed, so they look around. Johnny tells Brickford that the doll Bill had won probably had something in it and was supposed to be picked up by a particular party, but Karns got there first. Johnny hears a boat pull up to the landing, and Johnny sees two men pass a crate off to two men on the landing. Johnny sees Virgil and another man bring the crate up to the pier. Brickford calls to Virgil to stop, there is shooting and Virgil is wounded and the other man is killed. Brickford opens the crate and it is full of black dolls, all stuffed with drugs.

Virgil tells Johnny about a plan to pass the dolls off to a pickup man on a certain night each week. Bill had won the doll, so Virgil had to go after it. Judith found Virgil searching her apartment, and he killed her. Virgil shot Charlie because Bill could identify him.

Johnny gets to take his doll home with him. It looks awful but makes a fair ashtray.

Notes:
- This is an AFRTS program that contains a story article about signal jamming, and a story about the presidency of George Washington.
- Charles Lyon is the announcer.
- Music by Eddie Dunstedter.

Producer:	Jaime del Valle	**Writer:**	Blake Edwards
Cast:	Dick Ryan, William Johnstone, Frank Nelson, Hy Averback, Bill James, Tom Hanley		

♦ ❖ ♦

Show: The James Forbes Matter
Show Date: 7/28/1953
Company: Intercontinental Indemnity & Bonding Corporation
Agent: Roger Stern
Exp. Acct: $148.48

Synopsis: Roger Stern calls Johnny about James Forbes who was killed last night. It looks like and accident, but it might not be. Johnny will come to the office and get the details.

Johnny goes to New York City to meet with Roger Stern and then registers at the Madison Hotel. Johnny goes to talk with Lt. Arthur Parkhill. Johnny is told that Mr. Forbes fell over a 110-foot cliff, and it looks like an accident. There is no motive, but there is a wife and lots of money and $500,000 in insurance. Johnny is also told that Mr. Forbes often took long walks and fell over a cliff. Financially he was doing well, and there was no suicide note.

Johnny rents a car and goes to Long Island, New York to meet Mrs. Forbes. The butler tells Johnny that she is seeing no one. Johnny tells the butler who he is, and the butler then tells Johnny that Mrs. Forbes will see him, she forgot to tell the butler. Johnny tells her that the investigation is a routine matter. She tells Johnny that Mr. Forbes left right after dinner about 9:00 just like any other night, and the police found him. She was worried when he did not return and called William, her butler. William looked for him and then called the police, who found the body the next morning. Johnny wants to see the spot where Forbes died and William takes him there.

William tells Johnny that he has been working for the Forbes for ten years, and that theirs was a good marriage. At the shore, Johnny sees the cliff where Forbes fell. It was foggy, William tells Johnny. Williams tells Johnny that he is not convinced that it was an accident. This morning he felt different. He tells Johnny that Mr. Forbes knew the area, but little things have happened. Mrs. Forbes has made calls, affectionate calls, but not to Mr. Forbes. Also, whenever Mr. Forbes left on business, Mrs. Forbes went to town and returned only the day before Mr. Forbes would return. Williams tells Johnny that once the person she was in town visiting, Mrs. Weatherwax, came to the house, and she told William that she had not seen Mrs. Forbes for a long time. Williams did not think about it at the time, but he just has to tell someone. Johnny asks William to call him if Mrs. Forbes gets anymore of the calls.

Johnny goes to his hotel and updates Parkhill. Later William calls and tells Johnny that Mrs. Forbes has received a call. She just left and was going to the city. Johnny is told that he can intercept her at the George Washington bridge. She is driving the gray Cadillac sedan, with license plate 6A31593.

Johnny drives to the bridge and follows Mrs. Forbes south into the city. At 41st and 5th Avenue, a man gets into her car, and for an hour she drives and talks to the passenger. At 11:30 the man gets out at 108th street and throws her a kiss. Johnny parks and follows the man to Apartment 1D where the name on the door is Roger Phillips.

Johnny calls Parkhill, who tells Johnny that he will check on the name. While Johnny is talking, a cab pulls up and Phillips gets into it.

Johnny follows Phillips to the waterfront and the Blue Toad Saloon. Johnny follows Phillips into the one-room saloon and sees another man sitting with Phillips. A girl comes to Johnny's table and asks Johnny to buy her some champagne. She tells Johnny that he is too nice for this joint.

She is Jane, and Johnny looks like a "Mike" to her and asks Johnny whom he is watching. She tells Johnny that the tall handsome man just passed Timmy a bundle of money. She tells Johnny that the police know Timmy, and he is a bad boy with no friends.

Phillips leaves and Johnny goes to his car and waits for Timmy to come out. Johnny follows Timmy to the Bayview Hotel and calls Parkhill and gives him the name. Johnny is told that Timmy Collins is an assassin and that he has an old forgery rap. Johnny is told that Phillips is a socialite playboy. Phillips comes from Cleveland, and so does Collins. Johnny is told that the police will stake out the hotel.

Next morning Parkhill tells Johnny that Phillips left Cleveland owing Collins a lot of gambling debts. Parkhill thinks that Timmy probably met Forbes and gave him a shove. Johnny suggests that Mrs. Forbes fell for Phillips and they plotted to have him killed. So, Phillips makes a deal with Timmy to do the job for a big payoff. Parkhill will check with the banks, and Johnny will go to see Phillips to see it he will take some bait.

Johnny goes to Phillip's apartment and tells him that he wants to talk about Mrs. Forbes, the one who picked you up last night and gave you money. Johnny tells Phillips that he is in big trouble. Johnny tells him that he knows about Cleveland and Timmy. Johnny leaves Phillips to wonder. Johnny waits for Phillips to make some calls and then calls William. He tells Johnny that Mrs. Forbes is going to meet the same man by the cliffs. Phillips took the bait.

Johnny calls Parkhill who tells Johnny that Phillips had called Collins and told him that Johnny was on to them. Johnny is told that Mrs. Forbes has withdrawn $10,000 from the bank.

Parkhill picks up Johnny and they drive to Long Island and go to the cliffs. Johnny spots Mrs. Forbes walking, and they stop her. Johnny and Parkhill tell her that they know all about who killed her husband and how he was killed. Johnny tells her that now they are going to kill you. Johnny and Parkhill tell Mrs. Forbes that they know all about the meeting last night, but Mrs. Forbes does not believe them.

Johnny and Parkhill hide their car and let Mrs. Forbes find out for herself. Phillips and Collins arrive and try to run her down. Parkhill shoots and the car crashes.

They were going to kill her. Mrs. Forbes tells Johnny everything.

Notes:
- Charles Lyon is the announcer.
- Music by Eddie Dunstedter.

Producer:	Jaime del Valle	Writer:	Blake Edwards
Cast:	Larry Thor, Jack Moyles, Mary Jane Croft, Jean Howell, Robert Griffin		

◆ ❖ ◆

Show: The Voodoo Matter
Show Date: 8/4/1953
Company: International Insurance & Bonding Company
Agent: Nelson Price
Exp. Acct: $461.40

Synopsis: Nelson Price calls Johnny with a job in the West Indies, near St. Leger, Haiti. Claude Shelton has a big policy on his farm and is having trouble.

Johnny goes to Port-au-Prince, Haiti and gets a hotel room where Claude Sheldon shows up, per arrangements. Sheldon is sick and tells Johnny that there has been more trouble. He tells Johnny that he is a farmer and has been doing well until several months ago. Since then, there has been a fire in the cane fields, dead cattle, and several farmers have died. Now he is sick from a voodoo curse. There is nothing wrong with him physically, and a local doctor examined him and his wife and found nothing wrong. He tells Johnny that after getting ill, Sheldon received a very low offer from a local banker acting for Arthur Cotswold, who is the richest planter in the area, and the other farmers got the same offer. Sheldon collapses and Johnny takes him to the hospital where he dies. An autopsy is ordered and Johnny heads for the Sheldon Farm in St. Leger.

At the Sheldon farm there are natives and drums, and Johnny senses that something is wrong. At the door is a 7-foot, 300-pound native named Bimba. Bimba knows who Johnny is, and that Sheldon is dead. Bimba tells Johnny that the drums are for Madam. She is dead and the natives are her friends. She died at the same time as her husband. Bad Voodoo, Johnny is told. Bimba tells Johnny that Cotswold is a big man, and that the drums are good voodoo for the Sheldons.

Bimba takes Johnny on horseback to see the local police, Inspector Georges. Georges tells Johnny that Cotswold is very prominent, and it is better not to bother him, as he has a violent temper. Georges hopes Johnny will not find anything wrong as he is not going to look for trouble. Inspector Georges tells Johnny that he is the law, but that he prefers the middle of the road.

Bimba tells Johnny that Georges said to forget about Cotswold, but he thinks Johnny will do what he wants, as Johnny is not afraid. As Johnny and Bimba go to see Cotswold, drums are starting again and Bimba sings something. He tells Johnny that today is papa dambala.

At the Cotswold mansion Bimba tells Johnny to watch Mr. Joscelyn, as he is a bad man. At the door, Joscelyn lets Johnny in and tells him that Cotswold is expecting him. Cotswold knows why Johnny is here and tells Johnny that the farmers are suspicious and think he is responsible. He tells Johnny that he tried to help Sheldon and that he wants his land. He tells Johnny that none of his cattle are sick and that he wants the land and will do away with the sick cattle. His advice to Johnny is to go home and leave well enough alone. He is not a patient man so heed his advice and do not persist. Johnny tells Cotswold that he is paid to persist.

Johnny gets an idea and sends Bimba on to the farm, as he goes back to town and talks to Georges who has the autopsy report. Johnny learns that Sheldon died of brucellosis, or Bang's Disease. Johnny tells Georges that he is going to look for the cause of the infection, as only the cattle of the small farmers are infected. Johnny tells Georges to issue a search warrant, or he will have him held as a material witness. Johnny tells Georges that he has a plan. Bimba and his friends will help by setting a fire to get Cotswold out of the house. Georges agrees to help, reluctantly, as long as it is a harmless fire.

Johnny goes to the Sheldon farm and there is a crowd outside the house, and Johnny senses that something is wrong. Inside the house, Bimba is lying on the floor almost dead. He has been stabbed in the back. He tells Johnny that he has talked to his friends and they will help. Johnny tells Bimba that he will stay until Bimba dies. There is a voodoo burial ceremony, complete with pigeons, dead chickens, cornmeal, fire and chants. Suddenly Bimba's body sits up and then falls back.

Johnny and the Georges go to Cotswold's and wait for the fire to start. When the house is empty, they go in to search and find nothing. In the barn Georges finds a hypo and a bottle which he will take to be analyzed.

Cotswold appears and stops them while Jocelyn searches them. Georges tells Cotswold that he has a search warrant, but Cotswold tells him it is useless, and that they have made a serious mistake. Cotswold tells Johnny that the hypodermic was used to infect the cattle, but they will never tell anyone. Cotswold confirms to Johnny that Joscelyn had killed Bimba.

Jocelyn walks them out towards the fields when Cotswold screams in terror from the house. In the house they find Cotswold on the floor of the study with a broken neck, and a ghostly image that looks like Bimba. Joscelyn shoots at Bimba 6 times but Bimba crushes Joscelyn.

Johnny does not want to know what happened, he only wants to get back to Hartford and relax in a tub of hot mud. It looked like Bimba. Maybe it was. The natives did not find it unusual as Cotswold was a bad man, and Bimba came back to kill him. Johnny tells it just the way he saw it. Or am I?

Johnny can be contacted at the Greenbrier rest home, 3rd mud pie from the left.

Notes:
- Dambala (or Damballah-Wedo) is a serpent spirit of the local regions of Haiti.
- Brucellosis or Bang's Disease, is an infectious disease of farm animals that is sometimes transmitted to humans. In humans the disease is also known as undulant fever, Mediterranean fever, or Malta fever. In susceptible animals, primarily cattle, swine, and goats, brucellosis causes infertility and death.
- Charles Lyon is the announcer.
- Music by Eddie Dunstedter.

Producer: Jaime del Valle   Writer: Blake Edwards
Cast: Tudor Owen, Parley Baer, Roy Glenn, Ben Wright, William Conrad, Jester Hairston

❖

Show: The Nancy Shaw Matter
Show Date: 8/11/1953
Company: Columbia All-Risk Insurance Company
Agent: Phillip Martin
Exp. Acct: $604.65

Synopsis: Phillip Martin calls Johnny with a job. Miss Nancy Shaw the actress is insured and has just had $100,000 in jewels stolen. Johnny offers to waive his expense account just to work with Nancy Shaw — just kidding!

Johnny flies to Los Angeles, California and drives to Santa Monica to meet with Sgt. James Dodd. Dodd tells Johnny that there have been three other robberies, all with the same M.O. Johnny gets a list of the stolen items and is told that Miss Shaw was robbed on the maid's night off. Johnny tells Dodd that he will visit Miss Shaw and is told that she lives at 913 at the Artist Colony in Malibu. Dodd will call the guard to tell him to let Johnny in. Dodd tells Johnny that the thief probably parked on the highway and worked his way into the house.

Johnny drives to Malibu and is allowed into the colony and drives to Miss Shaw's house. Bernice the maid takes Johnny to Nancy, who is wearing a white sun suit that almost makes Johnny's hair catch on fire.

Johnny has a gin and tonic with Nancy and there is small talk about Johnny and his job. Johnny goes over the list of stolen items and gets a confirmation from Nancy. Nancy suggests that they go out and sit on the beach and tells Johnny that there are plenty of swimming trunks in the guesthouse. Nancy meets Johnny on the beach in a red bathing suit. When Nancy teases Johnny about his lack of a suntan, Johnny tells her "I'm not white, just pearl gray".

They sit on the beach and there is talk of sandcastles and dreams unfulfilled. Dave Asher, Nancy's fiancé, comes to the beach and is miffed at Nancy and tells Johnny to leave, but Johnny tells him to leave. Dave tells Johnny that he has some private matters to settle, but Nancy tells Dave to leave. Dave tells Nancy that he is going to end the relationship and he leaves. Nancy tells Johnny that she should have dropped him sooner, as Dave is just a rich young man. She tells Johnny that Dave was with her on the night of the robbery. As they leave the beach, Nancy asks Johnny to take her to a party that night.

At the party, Johnny and Nancy go outside to talk by the pool, and Johnny muses that being with Nancy is very nice. Nancy asks Johnny to kiss her and he does, and that was nice too. As they get ready to leave the party, Dave walks up to Johnny and wants to talk to him. David tells Johnny that he does not like Johnny, or glamour-gal Nancy, so Johnny slugs Dave and he falls into the pool.

Back on the beach they talk and Johnny finally leaves at sunrise. At 4:00 p.m. Dodd calls Johnny and tells him that he made the front page by putting David Asher in the pool. Dodd tells Johnny that he has been checking on Dave, and no one has heard of him, but he does have money. But three months ago, David was broke.

Johnny goes to see Nancy and Bernice tells Johnny that Nancy is not in and that she is seeing no one. Johnny notices that Bernice has been crying, so Johnny runs up to Nancy's bedroom. Johnny goes in and discovers that Nancy has been beaten. Nancy tells Johnny that the doctor is on his way, but Nancy will not tell Johnny who did it. Johnny gives Nancy a sleeping pill and goes to talk to Bernice who tells Johnny that it was Dave Asher who beat her. Bernice also tells Johnny that she found a diamond on the floor after Dave left.

Johnny calls Dodd and asks if the stone is on the list. Johnny is told that there was a ring with a large diamond on the list and Johnny tells Dodd about the beating. Bernice tells Johnny that Nancy and Dave had visited all the people who were robbed just before the robberies occurred. Johnny gets the address for Dave and arranges to meet Dodd there.

Before Dodd arrives, Johnny slugs his way into the apartment and breaks Dave's nose. Dave tells Johnny that he had bought the ring from some man. Johnny slugs him again and Dave admits that he was casing the houses when he went with Nancy, and that Stanley Fisher was the man who actually stole the jewelry. Dave tells Johnny that Fisher lives at the Shelton Hotel and that he has the rest of the loot. Dave tells Johnny that he beat up Nancy because he got mad at her. Dodd comes in and tells Johnny that they know about Fisher. Dodd takes care of Dave, and Johnny goes back to Nancy.

After things are wrapped up, Johnny visits Nancy and tells her that he will come back and visit her on his next case in California. Nancy tells Johnny that she will rob every house in California to make that happen. Nancy kisses Johnny, who asks "Are you sure my hair is not on fire?"

Notes:
- Charles Lyon is the announcer.
- Music by Eddie Dunstedter.
- The M.O. modus operandi is one's method or style of operation.

Producer:	Jaime del Valle	Writer:	Blake Edwards
Cast:	Mary Jane Croft, Thelma Johnson, Peter Leeds, Vic Perrin		

♦ ❖ ♦

Show: The Isabelle James Matter
Show Date: 8/18/1953
Company: National Life & Casualty Insurance Company
Agent: Don Maynard
Exp. Acct: $335.04

Synopsis: Don Maynard calls and tells Johnny that Isabelle James was murdered in Tulsa, Oklahoma. Johnny will come to the office to get the details.

Johnny goes to Tulsa, Oklahoma after getting the information on the case. At the police department Johnny meets Capt. Clifford Kissig, who would like to help Johnny, but he is stumped. Kissig tells Johnny that there have been four killings in three weeks, and Isabelle James is the latest. Johnny is told that there are no clues or witnesses, that the killing all took place in deserted areas, and that the lab thinks the killer is using a razor. Johnny is told that Dawson, Isabelle's hometown is not too far away, and Kissig tells Johnny that he had found the insurance papers. Johnny is told that her uncle, the beneficiary, is just a poor farmer who can use the money. Johnny tells Kissig that he will be there until the killer is found.

Johnny drives to the farm of Morley Parrish, who is in his late fifties and suspicious of Johnny. Morley invites Johnny in when he mentions the money from the insurance. Morley opens a jug of homemade whiskey and offers it to

Johnny. Johnny takes a sip and almost chokes. Morley apologizes because he did not shake the jug to make it smoother, sort of.

Morley tells Johnny that he thinks the man who killed the others also killed Isabelle. She had run off to Tulsa and visited Morley occasionally. Morley tells Johnny that she never wrote and said nothing on her last visit. Morley offers Johnny more whiskey and after a polite refusal, Morley tells Johnny that he has to finish the jug once he opens it.

Back at his hotel, Kissig calls Johnny to tell Johnny that they have a suspect. The police have a man who was following a girl. She screamed and called the police and when they got there they found that the man was carrying a straight razor. Johnny goes to see Kissig and is told that the man, Alvin Storey has said nothing. He told the police that he was just carrying the razor while he was out for a walk.

Johnny and Kissig interrogate Alvin for some time and Alvin tells them he was on the way to a show downtown, but Kissig tells Alvin that he was going in the wrong direction.

Kissig and Johnny have coffee and discuss Alvin. Kissig tells Johnny that it is hard to tell, as men make mistakes when they are scared. The phone rings, and Kissig learns that Alvin has just confessed.

Johnny relates that Alvin looked tired but relieved as he tells his story. He admits that he killed all of the girls. He does not know why he killed them he just wanted to. He used to dream about killing women. The first one he killed on Garvey Boulevard on the 11th. But Alvin tells Johnny and Kissig that there were only three girls, not four. Alvin knows the names of the girls he killed, and Isabelle is not one of them. He read about her in the paper but he did not do it.

The next day Johnny gets a wakeup call and is told that Morley Parrish is waiting for him in the lobby. Johnny dresses and goes to talk to Morley, who tells Johnny that he has come to talk about his niece. He tells Johnny that he wants the insurance money to buy some land. Johnny tells Morley that he will not get the money until he is finished with the investigation, and that the same man may not have killed Isabelle.

Johnny tells Morley that the razor used on the other girls was a different razor than the one that was used on Isabelle. Johnny tells Morley the he wants him to get his money but has to wait until the killer is caught with the same razor that killed his niece. Morley leaves and Johnny tells him he will get the money when he is convinced that the killer has changed razors.

Johnny calls Kissig, and Cliff tells him that Storey killed all the girls but James. Johnny tells Kissig about the story he told to Morley, who Johnny thinks killed Isabelle for the insurance money. Johnny tells Kissig that he had not told Morley that Storey had been arrested. Johnny thinks Morley will go out and try to kill someone to prove the killer has changed razors, and that he has to go to the farm to get the razor.

Kissig and Johnny drive to Morley's farm and wait for him to come home for his razor. As Johnny watches from Kissig's car, Morley comes home and then leaves. Johnny stops him and Morley tells Johnny that he has business and that he is in a hurry. Johnny tells him that he will give him a ride, but Morley declines, and Johnny tells him that he is walking, but he does not want a ride. Johnny asks Morley for the razor and Morley tells Johnny that he killed Isabel. Morley tells Johnny that he sure could have used the money. He thought he had it all figured out, but you sure can't beat those scientific police methods. Morley is told that the state will take care of the farm and Morley wants Johnny to take the jug behind the stove so it will not be wasted on a stranger.

Morley gives his story to the police and confirms Johnny's suspicions.

Notes:
- This program is called *The Kimball Matter* on the script title page.
- Charles Lyon is the announcer for the opening of the program.
- Music by Eddie Dunstedter.

Producer:	Jaime del Valle	Writer:	Blake Edwards
Cast:	Parley Baer, Howard McNear, Joseph DuVal, Clayton Post		

◆ ❖ ◆

Show: The Nelson Matter
Show Date: 8/25/1953
Company: Columbia All-Risk Insurance Company
Agent: Phillip Martin
Exp. Acct: $301.01

Synopsis: Phillip Martin calls Johnny with a job. Carl Nelson has been shot and the beneficiary Maude Gilkerson has disappeared.

Johnny goes to New York City and goes to see Lt. Korchack who asks Johnny how much insurance "The Frog" has. Korchack explains to Johnny that Nelson got the nickname because he looked like one. Korchack tells Johnny that he thinks that Carl's wife Maude knows about the killing. Johnny is told that Nelson was a hood with a record and that he had been associated with Ellis Hartje, a big gangster. Johnny tells Korchack that he has a "source" for information on how to find Maude.

Johnny cabs to skid row and the Het's Hilarity to talk to Wilbur Truitt. Wilber has missed his friend "Bucko" and laments his financial downturn. He tells Johnny that he used to make fifty cents a day. Johnny asks for the location of Maude Gilkerson and tells Wilbur that she might be worth two bottles. Johnny tells Wilbur to tell Maude that she has $10,000 coming from Carl Nelson's insurance.

Later that afternoon Wilbur calls Johnny at his hotel and tells him that Maude is not happy. She is hiding and wants to make a deal. She wants enough money to leave the country in exchange for information that is worth it.

Johnny starts to go out and is met at the door by Ernie and Goon, who invite themselves in. They want to talk about why Johnny is in town. After some rough stuff, they tell Johnny to lay off the Nelson killing, or the police will investigate the Dollar killing.

Johnny goes to Maude's address and meets her. Johnny wants to know what information she has, and Maude wants all the money and tells Johnny that she must leave as soon as possible as she does not want to die. She tells Johnny that she needs $500. Johnny gives her $200 and she tells him that Carl had been working for Hartje for a year and was worried about getting hit on the head. She tells Johnny that Carl knew a lot, and had collected enough evidence to put Hartje away, and Maude has the evidence. Johnny tells her that he will get the rest of the money in an hour and Maude gives him the key to a locker in Grand Central Station.

As Johnny walks back towards town, he sees a car following him. Johnny spots a blind beggar man and puts the key into his cup. Goon stops Johnny and puts him in the car and Bert asks Johnny what Maude had told him.

Johnny is stripped and searched and then taken to an apartment building to meet Ellis Hartje. Ellis tells Johnny that he is running things, so Johnny better cooperate. Hartje tells Johnny that he wants the information Maude has, and Johnny tells him that he only talked to her about the insurance. The phone rings and on the phone, Ernie tells Hartje that Maude had given Johnny a key.

Bert and Goon take Johnny to a warehouse in the bowery and beat him to find out where the key is. After a long beating Goon is distracted by a phone call and Johnny over powers him and then takes out Bert. Johnny takes Bert's gun and car and heads back to the blind beggar. Johnny gives the beggar some money to buy the key back.

Johnny goes to Korchack and updates him on what has happened. Korchack arranges to have Bert and Goon picked up. Johnny tells Korchack that Ernie and Frank were the ones sent to Maude's place, and Korchack arranges to have them picked up. Korchack tells Johnny that Maude was pulled from the river an hour ago.

Johnny and Korchack go to Grand Central Station and open the locker. Inside there is a package and Korchack is shot at. In the ensuing gunfight, Bert and Goon are killed and Korchack is wounded.

After a visit to the hospital, Johnny and Korchack go to the Hartje penthouse with a squad of men where Hartje shoots through the door. The police go in shooting and Hartje is killed.

Notes:
- This is the second Blake Edwards story where the character Wilbur Truitt appears.
- Charles Lyon is the announcer.
- Music by Eddie Dunstedter.

Producer:	Jaime del Valle	Writer:	Blake Edwards
Cast:	Victor Rodman, Joseph Kearns, Herb Butterfield, Jim Nusser, James McCallion, Martha Wentworth, William Conrad		

Show: The Stanley Price Matter
Show Date: 9/1/1953
Company: World Insurance & Indemnity Company
Agent: Handley Conrad
Exp. Acct: $113.40

Synopsis: Handley Conrad calls and asks if Johnny can take a job. Handley tells Johnny that the New York police have confiscated $100,000 in jewels found in the water pipe beneath the sink of a murdered man named Wells. A client in Europe was robbed three months ago, and Handley thinks these are the same jewels, but they are not in their settings, and some have been re-cut. The police are holding Mrs. Wells who claims that the jewels are hers but does not know how they got into the water pipes. So, Johnny has to prove that the jewels are stolen.

Johnny trains to New York City and goes to see Capt. Fred Dee of the robbery detail. Fred tells Johnny of the call from Stanley Price telling them about the jewels. There was a shot and the line went dead. When they got there, they found Robert Wells dead. The wife has been released due to lack of evidence.

Fred tells Johnny that Wells had just returned from Europe. Stanley Price is a small-time hood who has been making book lately. Mrs. Wells went back to the apartment and Fred is having the apartment watched. Johnny tells Fred he has a friend who knows all about the bookmakers in the area, but Johnny will not tell Fred his name.

Johnny gets a room, rents a car and drives to the Greenwich Village home of Henri DuValle, an abstract painter. Johnny finally gets Henri to open the door and Johnny asks him if he knows Stanley Price. Johnny offers $25 and Henri finally remembers that Price owes him $11.80, but he still does not know where he is. Price was in the fish business as he had brought Henri two halibut he had caught from his boat. The boat was kept at a place called Schooner Landing.

Johnny drives to the waterfront and Schooner Landing where an old man tells Johnny that he knows Stanley Price, but he has not seen him lately and owes him money. The man tells Johnny that Price was not a fisherman and did not know anything about running a boat even though he had a commercial fishing license.

Johnny goes to the Bureau of Licenses and finds one with a picture of Price on it. Johnny then goes to see Mrs. Wells and shows her the picture of Price whom she had seen visit her husband. Johnny tells her about the call from Price and his interest in the case. Mrs. Wells is anxious to help straighten Johnny's curly hair, but Johnny opts to leave.

Johnny goes to his hotel and is met by a man with a gun who wants the picture of Price. Johnny gives the man the license and counts to twenty as he leaves, and then Johnny calls Henri and then goes to see Fred.

Johnny tells Fred that it was important to the insurance company to prove the jewels were stolen in a short period of time, before they would have to turn them over to Mrs. Wells. Johnny has a hunch that it if he turns the jewels over to Mrs. Wells the case will open up very quickly. Johnny knows that only three people knew where he was staying: Mr. Conrad, Fred and Mrs. Wells. Fred is sure that Mrs. Wells told Price where Johnny was. Johnny tells him that Price has not paid Henri his $11.80, so it was not Price that held him up.

Johnny tells Fred that Well's boat from Europe landed last Wednesday while Price was out fishing. When Wells arrived, Price went out fishing for two hours, came back and disappeared. Then, Wells has a sink full of jewels he had dropped overboard for Price to pick up. But Johnny is not sure who killed Wells in his own apartment. The whole thing had to be planned by someone who knew when Wells would return, namely Mrs. Wells.

Johnny goes to the morgue to look at Wells and Johnny tells Fred that the body is not Wells, but Stanley Price. Johnny asks Fred to let him take the jewels to Mrs. Wells, as a representative of insurance company. Johnny gets the jewels and goes to the apartment followed by two police officers.

Johnny is let in and gives her the jewels, with no strings attached. Mrs. Wells is puzzled why Johnny is mixed up in this case, and he tells her that the insurance company thinks the jewels are stolen, but Mrs. Wells is not convinced. She tells Johnny it is too easy and she tells Johnny she thinks he is trying to trap her, then someone knocks Johnny out.

Johnny wakes up alone in the apartment and goes out to look for the police who are gone. Johnny calls Fred who tells Johnny that the police are following Mrs. Wells and Johnny tells him that she is a decoy, leading them away from Mr. Wells who left by the back door. Johnny tells Fred to meet him at Schooner's Landing.

Johnny goes to the landing where the old man tells Johnny that Price's boat has been gassed up and is ready to leave. Johnny runs to the boat and jumps on to see Mr. and Mrs. Wells. Johnny is held at gunpoint as Wells takes the boat out.

Mrs. Wells takes the wheel and Johnny tells Mr. Wells he knows who he is. Wells tells Johnny that he killed Price because he wanted a larger cut and was calling the police. He had put the jewels in the pipe and hoped the police would not find them. A Coast Guard boat approaches and Wells tells Johnny to get on the bow. Johnny grabs a life preserver and slugs Wells with it, but not before he shoots Mrs. Wells. Johnny stops the boat for the police.

Johnny buys a good dinner for $8.75 and gets a good night's sleep.

Notes:
- Charles Lyon is the announcer.
- Music by Eddie Dunstedter.

Producer:	Jaime del Valle	Writer:	Blake Edwards
Cast:	John Stephenson, Kenny Delmar, Jay Novello, Howard McNear, Mary Shipp		

Show:	**The Lester Matson Matter**
Show Date:	**9/8/1953**
Company:	**Columbia All-Risk Insurance Company**
Agent:	**Phillip James**
Exp. Acct:	**$154.50**

Synopsis: Phillip James calls about an arson case. Lester Matson's plastics plant has burned and there was $700,000 in insurance. The police have found evidence of arson.

Johnny trains to New York City and rents a car. Lt. Ridgeway updates Johnny and tells him that arson definitely was involved and that high-octane fuel in a ten-gallon can was used. Ridgeway tells Johnny that he has a lead on Lester Matson, who was at a party with his daughter that night, but he acted funny. Ridgeway has talked to Matson, but he acted scared, like he was hiding something. Johnny tells Ridgeway that the insurance coverage will not cover the actual losses in the fire.

Johnny goes to see Lester Matson in New Jersey, and Christine Matson meets Johnny in the library and Johnny tells her why he is there. She tells Johnny that she has been playing tennis, and Johnny tells her that he used to play a little, but not anymore. Mr. Matson comes in and they talk. Matson tells Johnny that the police have investigated the fire, that he was at a party with Christine and that he found out about the fire when he came home. Matson is sure that the fire was an accident but does not like the idea of a fire being started intentionally. He worries about what might have happened if it had started during the day.

Johnny tells him that a pyromaniac does not target plants during the day. Matson tells Johnny that he has two more plants, so he hopes he is not an exception to the rule. Matson agrees to give Johnny as much information as he can. Johnny senses that the idea of a pyromaniac eases Matson's uneasiness as he tells Johnny what he can.

Johnny calls Ridgeway from his hotel. Johnny tells him of the firebug angle and the change in Matson's attitude. Johnny thinks that Matson may know who started the fire. Johnny tells Ridgeway that he thinks that maybe the daughter started the fire. He tells Ridgeway that he has met her, and he is still smoldering.

At 4:30, Johnny is in the bar "freshening up" when he is paged to the hotel phone. Christine tells Johnny that she called to talk, but she must be discrete. If certain parties saw her talking to Johnny, her father's life would be in danger. Johnny agrees to meet her in a cab.

Johnny meets Christine's cab and gets in. As they drive around, she tells Johnny that her father is being blackmailed and knows who burned the plant. She tells Johnny that two men had demanded a percentage of the business and protection, and they burned the plant to make their point. Her father did not tell the police because of her. The man had threatened to do something worse if he talked, and her father is afraid they meant Christine. She wants Johnny to help without making a big issue of it. She tells Johnny that her father had told her all of the details when she saw him upset. She tells Johnny that he would rather lose everything than lose her. Johnny tells her to drive to the house so he can talk to her father.

At the Matson home, Christine tells her father that she has told Johnny everything, and that Johnny will not bring in the police unless it is necessary. Matson tells Johnny that Christine does not realize how foolish she is, and that he must think of his family as the men will do anything. He tells Johnny that there is no alternative, and they will continue to bleed him dry and will kill Christine if he does not pay. Christine tells her father that the blackmail will kill him as it is taking his freedom and will ruin him.

Johnny tells Matson that the men have effectively kidnapped his business from him, and that he has a job to do and will do it. A shot is fired through a window in the study and Matson is hit. Johnny runs outside as Christine calls the doctor and hears a car starting in the front of the house. Johnny runs to the front of the house, sees the car pull away and shoots. Johnny tells a frantic Christine to stay with her father until the doctor comes.

Johnny walks to the car, which is wrapped around an oak tree. Johnny sees a man halfway through the windshield and bleeding. Another man surprises Johnny, takes his gun, and walks him up to the garage to get another car with a gun in his back. He knows Johnny is an insurance man, so Johnny will be his insurance.

They walk to the garage and a car drives up. When the man turns to look, Johnny slugs him and tells the doctor to go to the house where his patient is.

Lester Matson lives, and the men were identified as Ernie Starbuck and Stan Cole. Ernie was dead in the car and Stan went to prison for life.

On the way home Johnny stops to see Christine. He agrees to have a drink with her and ends up taking the late train home.

Notes:
- Charles Lyon is the announcer.
- Eddie Dunstedter provides the music.
- This is an AFRTS program that contains a story about the State Department, and a story about the presidency of Andrew Jackson.

Producer: Jaime del Valle   Writer: Blake Edwards
Cast: John Larch, Hal March, Lillian Buyeff, William Johnstone

• ❖ •

Show: The Oscar Clark Matter
Show Date: 9/15/1953
Company: National Life & Casualty Insurance Company
Agent: Don Maynard
Exp. Acct: $168.59

Synopsis: Don Maynard calls Johnny and tells him that Oscar Clark is being held for a hit-and-run and the woman he hit was hurt. Clark has a $200,000 policy and did not know that he hit anything. Clark is also a wealthy man with influence.

Johnny goes to Miami, Florida and meets with Lt. Eddy who tells Johnny that Lucille Best is from Chicago and lives in a hotel. She has a broken leg and a back injury. She was found on the highway and requested her physician, Dr. Hawley. She told the police that she had a flat tire and a car hit her when she got out. She got the tag number and the car belongs to Oscar Clark.

Clark's car has a dent and blood stains, and Clark was booked on a 318. He admitted to the police that he stopped at the Red Mill Tavern and had one drink and left at 7:20.

Johnny goes to see Oscar Clark who denies everything and claims he is being framed. Johnny goes to see Dr. Hawley and he tells Johnny that Lucille is doing OK, except for the fractured leg and a back injury. He tells Johnny that Lucille came to Florida for her health and her doctor recommended him to her. He also tells Johnny that Lucille has hired a lawyer.

Johnny looks at the x-rays and goes to his hotel where he is called by Eddy who tells him that the lab has made a discovery that proves Lucille is a liar. Johnny goes to see Eddy and he tells Johnny that a metal object was used to dent the fender, and that the glass from a headlight is missing. Also, the blood on the car was smeared on with a rag.

Johnny goes to see Clark and tells him of the new discoveries. Clark tells Johnny that he left his car with an attendant when he went into the tavern. When he left, his car was at the far end of the parking lot. Johnny wonders if the car could have been damaged there.

Johnny goes to the Red Mill and talks to the bartender who tells Johnny that the valet is Sammy, a jockey who hurt his back in a racing accident. Johnny is told that Sammy was healed by Dr. Jones, who is no longer practicing.

Johnny leaves and waits for Sammy to leave and then follows him to a small house. Johnny goes in and talks to Sammy, who admits that Hawley thought up the idea. Hawley had fixed up Sammy's back and he dented the car to pay his bill. They picked Clark because he was rich and Hawley broke the girl's leg.

Dr. Hawley walks in and shoots Sammy. He tells Johnny that he is going to have an accident. Eddy comes in and disarms Hawley. Eddy tells Johnny that they had staked out both Hawley and Sammy.

Notes:
- The announcer is Charles Lyon.
- Music is by Eddie Dunstedter.
- Story information obtained from the KNX Collection in the Thousand Oaks Library.

Producer:	Jaime del Valle	Writer:	Blake Edwards
Cast:	Tom Tully, Barney Phillips, Francis X. Bushman, Parley Baer, Joan Miller, Sam Edwards		

Show:	**The William Post Matter**
Show Date:	**9/22/1953**
Company:	**Columbia All-Risk Insurance Company**
Agent:	**Ray Kemper**
Exp. Acct:	**$87.05**

Synopsis: Ray Kemper calls and tells Johnny that Mrs. William Post has been killed. Her body was found by a detective named Sax and her attorney George Simon. The husband is suspected of killing her.

Johnny goes to New York City and meets Lt. Roseman at the 5th precinct. Johnny is told that Teresa Post was found stabbed four times, gagged and robbed. Sax and Simon had appointments at the time, and her jewels and a cloth coat are missing. The Posts had argued and separated, and she had filed for divorce over her husband's cheating, based on evidence obtained by Sax. A mink coat was left in the closet and the husband was with Jane Hughes at the time.

Johnny goes to meet Sax, who tells Johnny that it is easy to find a husband with another woman and that Post made the mistake of leaving the fur coat.

Johnny goes to see George Simon who tells Johnny that he met Sax at the apartment and had been in his office all day.

Johnny goes to talk to Jane Hughes, and she is a real dish! At first, she tells Johnny to leave thinking he is a reporter. Finally, she tells Johnny that she was with Post all afternoon. Bill Post comes in and tells Johnny to leave.

Johnny goes to the apartment and meets Pete the janitor, who is singing to himself. Johnny has to pay Pete a $20 bribe to get into the apartment, where he finds nothing. On the way out, Pete tells Johnny that he does not like Mrs. Post.

Johnny goes to his hotel and gets a call from Roseman who tells Johnny that the cloth coat has been pawned. Johnny goes to the pawnshop and the owner tells Johnny that the man who hocked the coat was singing to himself.

Johnny goes back to Pete and he denies pawning the coat. Pete is taken in and put in a line-up and is identified by the pawnshop owner. Pete tells Johnny that Mrs. Post gave him the coat. Johnny convinces Roseman to let Pete loose.

Johnny goes to see Jane again and tells her and Post that Pete killed his wife, but he needs their help to trap him. Johnny wants Jane to dress up like Mrs. Post and go to the apartment and call Pete to complain about the plumbing.

Johnny and Jane go to the apartment where she buzzes Pete to fix the plumbing. Pete comes up to the apartment and tells Jane that she is dead. He killed her once and will kill her again.

Johnny stops Pete and the jewels are found in a paint bucket in the basement. Pete admits that he was robbing the apartment when she came in, so he had to kill her. Pete did not take the mink coat because he thought that the cloth coat was prettier.

Notes:
- The announcer is Charles Lyon.
- Music is by Eddie Dunstedter.
- Ray Kemper is the name of the sound man for this program.
- This program contains a scene reminiscent of *The Line-Up* complete with the introduction to *The Line-Up* theme. Most of the actors were *Line-Up* regulars.

Producer:	Jaime del Valle	Writer:	Blake Edwards
Cast:	Jack Moyles, William Johnstone, Benny Rubin, Charles Davis, Mary Jane Croft, Hy Averback, Howard McNear		

♦ ❖ ♦

Show: **The Amita Buddha Matter**
Show Date: 9/29/1953
Company: **World Insurance & Indemnity Company**
Agent: **Hanley Conrad**
Exp. Acct: **$527.15**

Synopsis: Hanley Conrad calls and asks if Johnny is employed. Johnny is available, so Hanley tells him to go to Los Angeles, where William McEdwards was killed in a house fire.

Johnny flies to Los Angeles, California, rents a car and goes to see C. H. Anderson, Chief of Police in Beverly Hills. Anderson tells Johnny that Lt. Hankins received the call and went to the fire where he found William McEdwards burned to death in his bedroom. The autopsy showed that McEdwards had been stabbed and beaten. For the time being the murder angle is to be kept confidential.

Johnny goes to Encino to talk to McEdward's wife, Pat. She tells Johnny that she had been visiting friends in Pasadena, and to leave an old Chinese Buddha with Charley Willkins. Her father-in-law got the Buddha while he was in Korea and gave it to them. Her father-in-law is a production executive for a movie studio, and she knew of nothing unusual that day.

Johnny goes to his hotel and makes an appointment to see John McEdwards, William's father. When Johnny gets to the house there is a tall metal fence with four Great Danes behind it. McEdwards quiets the dogs and lets Johnny into the house. McEdwards tells Johnny that the dogs are named Samson, Delilah, Cleopatra and The Duchess. They are good dogs but very protective. Johnny is told that a friend had a man break into his house and their Great Dane caught the man and broke his neck. Johnny is told that Bill was a wonderful son and it is hard for John to deal with the loss.

He tells Johnny that he had been in Korea for three months working on a movie and was digging a small dam when he found the Buddha in a box. He decided to give it to Bill and Pat when he came back. Johnny learns that Bill was pretty solid but settled down when he met Pat and had bought the insurance. The dogs start barking again and Pat comes in. She tells Johnny and her father-in-law that Chief Anderson had called and told her that Bill had been murdered. Johnny wonders if the Buddha is involved somehow.

Johnny drives to Encino to talk to Charles Willkins about the Buddha. After a brief history of the Buddha, Charles thinks that this is the original Amita Buddha of Contemplation, from 200 BC, and estimates that it is worth at least $150,000 and probably $500,000.

Johnny drives back to Beverly Hills to talk to chief Anderson who tells Johnny that the Buddha is the first lead they have. Bill had no enemies, so who knew of the Buddha? Anderson will check the studio and steamship and airlines, and Johnny will go back to talk to McEdwards.

Johnny drives to the McEdwards home and talks to McEdwards in the kitchen for about an hour about the case. The phone rings, and McEdwards comes back looking shaken. He tells Johnny that a man on the phone said that he had Pat and that she was OK. McEdwards was told to get the Buddha and tell no one or there will be trouble. McEdwards agrees to let Johnny follow him to Charles Willkins' home to get the Buddha.

On the way back, Johnny parks out of sight and they walk into the house where Pat is waiting for them along with two men. Alan Sutker and Don Roache tell McEdwards that they are there for the Buddha. McEdwards explains that Johnny was a friend who just happened to be there when the call came. "Too bad for your friend", Sutker tells him, and then explains that he had been tracking the Buddha for a long time and had buried it after a man named Woo Sung died, under "mysterious circumstances". Sutker tells then that he had waited in Tokyo until the war was over but McEdwards got there first. Now he wants the Buddha.

McEdwards wants to know which one of them killed his son, and Sutker tells him that Roache had burgled the house to get the Buddha, but Bill caught him in the act and he resisted, so he was killed. He tells McEdwards that it is of no difference that he knows this, as he will not be around to tell anyone. Sutker tells them to go out and get into his car.

Outside McEdwards punches Roache, who hits him with his gun, driving the dogs in the pen crazy. Samson jumps the fence, followed by the others, who attack Roache and Sutker. After the melee, Roache is dead with a broken neck, and Sutker is crying for a doctor. McEdwards tells Johnny that the end was appropriate, as Samson was Bill's dog.

Notes:
- Charles Lyon is the announcer.
- Music by Eddie Dunstedter.
- Sound man Bill James is credited with the sound of Sampson barking.

Producer:	Jaime del Valle	Writer:	Blake Edwards
Cast:	James Nusser, John Stephenson, Jeanette Nolan, Sammie Hill, Herb Butterfield, Bill James, Robert Griffin, Edgar Barrier		

❖

Show: The Alfred Chambers Matter
Show Date: 10/6/1953
Company: Columbia All-Risk Insurance Company
Agent: Phillip Martin
Exp. Acct: $114.05

Synopsis: Phillip Martin calls and has a job for Johnny. Phillip insures Mr. Alfred Chambers of Pittsburgh, who was shot to death yesterday, and it looks like murder. Chambers had rented a cabin on Les Cheneaux Island, about 30 miles south of Sault Ste. Marie, Michigan where the wife found him shot through the chest in the cabin. Johnny will leave in the morning

Johnny flies to Sault Ste. Marie, Michigan and cabs to the police department and meets Capt. George Lane. Johnny is told that Chambers had rented the Forrester cabin and spent three days alone before his wife arrived. Mr. Schoenberg took her to the island where she found her husband shot through the chest. There are no suspects and Mrs. Chambers told the police that she had separated from her husband a week before he came to the island and that Chambers had been dead for fourteen hours.

Lane and Johnny travel to the island and Johnny learns that Chambers was shot outside the cabin and crawled inside, that the cabin does not have electricity, though others on the island do, and that Chambers had rented a boat to get on and off the island. Also, the coroner discovered that Chamber's shoes were still damp, and that he had been in the water with his clothes on.

Lane thinks Chambers was shot while he was on the docks, fell in the water and waded to shore and was shot about five in the afternoon, four hours before darkness. Lane tells Johnny that Chambers was shot by a .22 long rifle, and that the mud on his shoes matches the mud down by the docks. Johnny and Lane agree that it was probably someone on the island who shot Chambers.

Johnny drives Lane's car to the hotel to talk to Mrs. Chambers, who tells Johnny that this is her first visit to the island. She knew that her husband had been seeing another woman, and they had decided to separate but did not because of the publicity, her husband is in the steel business and they have two children. She had seen the girl once and tells Johnny that her name is Jane Elkins who also lives in Pittsburgh.

Before this she would not have cared about the girl, but because of the children it matters. She had come to the island to talk with her husband one last time. She tells Johnny that she has thought about killing her husband but cannot think of anyone else who would. The phone rings and Mrs. Chambers tells someone to come right up. She asks Johnny to stay as the phone call was from Jane.

Jane Elkins comes to Mrs. Chamber's room and is introduced to Johnny. She tells them that she was never in love with Mr. Chambers and had no idea he was coming here. She tells Johnny that she came up with her fiancé a week ago. Jane does not know where she was when Chambers was shot but saw him last on Tuesday. Jane's fiancé Charles Weatherwax knows about her and

Chambers and did not take it too well. Jane tells Johnny that on Tuesday she went back to the house and that Charles was out on a boat. Jane tells Mrs. Chambers how sorry she is and leaves to attend a cocktail party for her at the Weatherwaxes.

Johnny gets a room and updates Lane, who will check on Jane. Johnny decides to crash the party and rents a ride on Schoenberg's boat. Johnny spots Jane and goes to talk to her. Jane threatens to have Johnny thrown out until Johnny asks her if she wants to talk to the police instead. Jane tells Johnny that Charles got back about 6:30 on the night Chambers was shot.

Charles walks up and tells Johnny to leave and Johnny now knows that Charles is jealous and violent. Jane tells Charles that Johnny is an investigator and Johnny asks Charles where he was yesterday, and if he owns a .22 rifle. Johnny tells Charles that the bullet can be traced to the rifle it was fired from — it's called ballistics. "Isn't science wonderful?" Johnny asks and leaves.

Johnny leaves but watches the Weatherwax docks. Ten minutes later Charles takes a boat to a spot 300 yards off the shore and dives into the water. Johnny rushes to the boat as Charles surfaces, pulls his gun and asks what kind of fish Charles is after. Back on the dock Johnny takes Charles to the house and asks what he was looking for. Charles tells Johnny that he did not kill Chambers but he was with him when he was killed. He had gone there to tell him to stay away from Jane and was standing on the dock when there was a shot and Chambers fell into the water. Charles thought he was dead and left in a panic. Charles remembered he had a .22 in the boat and threw it overboard.

When Johnny had mentioned ballistics, Charles realized he had thrown away the one piece of evidence that would clear him so he came back to find it. Johnny tells Charles he does not believe him and Charles tackles Johnny and takes his gun and points it at Johnny's head. Johnny wrestles with him, gets the gun away from him and asks Charles why he did not fire when he had the chance. Charles tells Johnny that he is not the shooting type.

Charles tells Johnny that the story he told is true, and Johnny believes him this time. Johnny is sure that if Charles did not shoot Chambers, Jane did, as she had motive, opportunity and no alibi. Charles admits that he killed Chambers and did not know that Jane had broken up with him. Chambers got nasty and Charles shot him. As they are talking a shot rings out and they run to investigate.

In a small cove they find a boat and a small boy with a .22 rifle. The boy greets them and tells Charles that he lives on Fire Island and was hunting squirrels. The boy had come there on Tuesday and got two squirrels. Johnny tells him "that's not all you got, sonny."

Well that's the way things work out sometimes. You think you have a cold-blooded murder on your hands and it turns out to be a young kid who shouldn't have been given a gun on his birthday.

The .22 was checked by the ballistics department and proved to be the one that fired the fatal shot. At the inquest the jury returned a verdict of accidental manslaughter. However, it is doubtful that young Jimmy Bishop will ever want another gun as long as he lives.

Notes:
- Charles Lyon is the announcer.
- Music by Eddie Dunstedter.

Producer:	Jaime del Valle	Writer:	Blake Edwards
Cast:	Hal March, Marvin Miller, Jeanette Nolan, Jane Webb, Richard Beals		

◆ ❖ ◆

Show: **The Phillip Morey Matter**
Show Date: **10/13/1953**
Company: **National Life & Casualty Insurance Company**
Agent: **Don Maynard**
Exp. Acct: **$99.38**

Synopsis: Don Maynard calls and asks Johnny to go to New York City, where Morley Productions is in trouble because Phil Morley has had a breakdown. Go see what you can do.

Johnny goes to New York City and meets with Milton Gradke, the producer, who is very concerned with Phil's condition. Johnny is told that Phil is very sick, and that his doctor, Charles Ewing, told Milton that Phil had had a breakdown caused by something personal. Johnny is told that he cannot see Phil, as he is too sick, so go talk to the doctor.

Johnny goes to see Phil Morley at his apartment but is met at the door by a man who will not let him in. Phil staggers into the room, and it is clear to Johnny that Phil has had a "90 proof breakdown" and is drunk. Phil tells Johnny that he does not want insurance as he is a lousy risk, and to go away. Phil tells Johnny that he will stay drunk "until they have another blue snow".

Johnny goes to his hotel for a drink and is met in the bar by the man in the apartment, who introduces himself as Richard Long, the writer and director on the program. Richard swears to Johnny that Phil had only started drinking the night before after a call from his wife's lawyer to let him know she was divorcing him. Johnny tells Richard that he will have to report that to the insurance company. Johnny knows that Phil has lost other contracts for drinking and has had several wives take him to the cleaners.

Richard tells Johnny that the current wife, Janet, is going to do the same as all the other wives, namely to take him for everything she can get. Johnny is told that she got whatever she asked for from Phil, just like everyone else because Phil is a nice guy who cannot say no. When the lawyer called last night, Phil went for the bottle. Richard tells Johnny that Janet is a real tramp, but she played him for what he could get, and there were no witnesses.

Johnny goes to see Janet at her apartment. On the way up, Johnny meets a man rushing out of the elevator. Johnny wonders "Now who is that man? I know him from somewhere." Janet meets Johnny at the door, and he tells her why he is there. Janet tells Johnny that Phil has been drunk for over a month, and that she tried to help him. Besides, she tells Johnny, Phil has lots of money and he can afford a dozen more ex-wives. And as for Richard Long, he is just jealous.

Janet mixes Johnny a glass of bourbon and water and they talk. When Johnny tells Janet that he recognizes her from a picture he saw once, she shows him a photo album of her pictures, which curdles his drink, but tells Johnny that Janet is up to no good. In one of the pictures Johnny sees the man he saw leaving the building and the name comes back to him.

Johnny leaves and goes back to talk to Richard Long at this hotel. Johnny tells Richard about the man he saw, who is named Eugene Sweet. Johnny tells Richard that Sweet had been convicted of forgery in California, and Johnny had worked on the case. Johnny explains that Sweet would introduce a young woman to a rich older man, and after the wedding, Sweet would forge checks and then the girl would divorce the old man and get a nice payoff. Johnny guesses that they are probably doing the same thing to Phil. Richard tells Johnny that a man named Swift introduced Janet to Phil, but the description of Swift matches that of Sweet, so Johnny and Richard go back to see Janet.

When Johnny and Richard get to the apartment, they see Swift going in. While waiting for the elevator, Milton Gradke comes down and is very upset. He tells Johnny and Richard that Phil got away from him, and that he has a gun and is probably is upstairs.

When Johnny and Richard get to Janet's floor, the apartment door is open and Phil is threatening Janet and Swift. Johnny is able to talk the gun away from Phil, the police are called and Janet and Swift confess. They had fleeced Phil out of over $300,000 in forged checks and had taken advantage of his spending habits.

Notes:
- Charles Lyon is the announcer.
- Music by Eddie Dunstedter.

Producer:	Jaime del Valle	Writer:	Blake Edwards
Cast:	Joseph DuVal, Sidney Miller, Hy Averback, William Johnstone, Jeanette Nolan		

♦ ❖ ♦

Show: **The Allen Saxton Matter**
Show Date: **10/20/1953**
Company: **Great Eastern Life Insurance Company**
Agent: **Stanley Mitchell**
Exp. Acct: **$119.93**

Synopsis: Stanley Mitchell calls and tells Johnny to go to New York and see Allen Saxton. He has recently returned from Europe with a "priceless" painting and has applied for insurance on it. Several experts claim it is a fake, and Saxon is angry because he paid $200,000 for the picture.

Johnny goes to New York City, rents a car and drives to the Saxton home in New Jersey. Saxton, who has a bad cough, tells Johnny that he had paid $200,000 for the painting in Paris, and that he was told that it was supposed to be a genuine Marchaux, and that the dealer, Rene Francois, was one of the most respected in Paris. Then a guy named Lippert tells Saxton it is a fake.

As Allen takes Johnny to see the picture, Allen's daughter Barbara comes in, and starts rolling her eyes at Johnny. Johnny looks at the picture and calls it "uh, beautiful". Allen tells Johnny that Rene Francois is in town until the painting is authenticated. Barbara wants Johnny to stay for dinner, and Allen tells Johnny to leave, as Barbara is spoiled and Allen wants to save Johnny, as he is too nice a guy. At the door Barbara throws a vase at her father and almost hits him.

Johnny goes back to his hotel to wait for the experts to analyze the painting. Johnny calls some numbers in his black book when there is a knock at the door and Barbara comes in. She apologizes for arguing with her father and tells Johnny that she is hungry and wants Johnny to take her to dinner.

After $22.78 for dinner Johnny takes Barbara home. Johnny comments that Barbara made Delilah look like a girl scout. After telling Barbara he will not marry her, Johnny takes her to the open front door, deposits her in the foyer and heads for the car. Barbara screams and Johnny runs in to find Allen in the library with a bloody head.

After calming Barbara, Allen tells Johnny that he had heard a noise, went down stairs and saw a man stealing the picture. The man hit him with a flashlight and cut the picture out of the frame and ran. "She didn't get you drunk and marry her, did you?" asks Allen. Allen asks Johnny if he would marry Barbara for her money. Johnny answers "No, I would marry her for your money." Allen laughs and starts to worry for his picture again.

The police are called and Johnny goes back to his hotel to call the Paris office of the Insurance Company and asks the manager, Howard Gilbert, to check up on Rene Francois' departure from Paris, as he was not due in New York until that day.

Johnny drives to the apartment of an old friend, Henri for information. Henri tells Johnny that only his landlord or a vampire would go to such extremes to be there at that hour. After slipping some money under the door, Johnny is let in and tells Henri why he is there. Johnny tells him about Saxton and the theft of the painting, and Henri denies that he would steal the picture as he could paint something better for less than $200,000. After paying a series of small bribes to cover his back rent and an overdue deli bill, Henri tells Johnny to go to the Shelton Arms Hotel and see Gasten Chambrez, who just arrived from Paris yesterday.

Johnny goes to the hotel and has a message from Howard Gilbert telling Johnny that Rene Francois left Paris that day and is due in New York that afternoon.

Johnny drives to the Shelton Arms and knocks on the door of Chambrez's room. Johnny invites himself in with a fake message from Francois and convinces Chambrez to talk. After a convincing smack on the jaw, Chambrez admits that Rene Francois had paid him $10,000 to steal the painting, which is under the pillow on the sofa. Rene Francois wanted the painting back because there was evidence that the picture was a fake and he feared for his reputation.

Johnny takes Chambrez to the police, and Rene is picked up at the airport. Rene tells the police that he hired Chamberlay to take the painting because he had discovered that there was a possibility that the painting was a fake, and he wanted to protect his business.

Johnny goes to see Saxton, who is happy that he has his $200,000 back. Johnny tells Allen that he will have to pay the $85 Johnny paid in bribes. Barbara has a bad hangover but is ready to go back to Hartford with Johnny. Johnny tells her no. He is an insurance man and knows a bad risk when he sees one — him.

Notes:
- Charles Lyon is the announcer.
- Music by Eddie Dunstedter.

Producer:	Jaime del Valle	Writer:	Blake Edwards
Cast:	Edgar Barrier, Hal March, Virginia Gregg, Jay Novello		

◆ ❖ ◆

Show: **The Howard Arnold Matter**
Show Date: **10/27/1953**
Company: **World Insurance & Indemnity Company**
Agent: **Hanley Conrad**
Exp. Acct: **$123.66**

Synopsis: Hanley Conrad calls. Howard Arnold, the attorney for the gangster George Castro, is insured and they do not want anything to happen to him. He called and is worried and needs protection. Hanley told him to go to the police, but they would do nothing unless Arnold exposed Castro.

Johnny goes to New York City and calls Howard Arnold. Arnold is not home, so Johnny leaves a message to call him at the Ellsworth Hotel. Johnny calls Arnold's office and he is not there either.

At 7:00 p.m. Howard Arnold comes to Johnny's hotel room. He tells Johnny that he has not been to the office or home in several days. Howard relates to Johnny that he has had a falling out with George Castro the gangster. Howard was his attorney and he knows too much and Castro is afraid he will talk. Howard tells Johnny that their relationship has snapped and that Castro will try to liquidate him. Johnny tells Howard that he is there to stop that, but George tells him that just keeping Castro's boys away is not very practical. Howard wants Johnny to keep something for him, an envelope with information about Castro. Johnny is to hold on to it for a couple hours and then will give it back to Arnold after he makes some arrangements. Johnny hides the envelope under a dresser drawer and goes out for dinner.

Johnny eats and comes back to his room to find Marty Fleet waiting for him. Marty wants the envelope but Johnny plays dumb. Marty slugs Johnny and then tears the room apart. When Johnny wakes up, the room is torn apart but the envelope is still there.

Johnny calls Arnold and suggests that he take the envelope back. Arnold gives Johnny instructions to go to an isolated place where he is to meet Howard to turn over the envelope.

Johnny rents a car and goes to the designated spot. As Johnny gives the envelope to Howard, Marty appears and wants the envelope. Howard offers Marty $15,000 but he only wants to slug Johnny for lying. When Johnny wakes up he discovers Howard's car in a ravine burning with a man in it.

Johnny flags down a car and calls the fire department and the police. When the police arrive, Johnny gives his story to Lt. David. Johnny cannot figure out how Fleet got there so quickly as he could not have followed Arnold, and he was there when Johnny arrived. Maybe it was Howard's wife.

George Castro is brought in for questioning and Mrs. Arnold identifies the body in the car based on a ring and watch. She is certain that the body is Howard's. She tells the police that Howard had not said where he was going or where he had been. You should see the people who Howard worked for. Johnny thinks that there is something odd, why Fleet only knocked Johnny out and did not kill him.

George Castro is brought in and is told about Howard. "It is such a shame" Castro tells them. Castro does not like David or Johnny and tells them that. Johnny tells Castro that Fleet killed Arnold, but Castro does not believe it. Suddenly Johnny thinks of something. Where is Fleet? David tells Castro that the politicians are not going to bail Castro out this time and Castro tells David that Fleet is in the Alton Arms Hotel. David arranges to get Fleet at the hotel, and Johnny goes to see Mrs. Arnold.

At Mrs. Arnold's home Johnny asks her about Howard and his job. She confirms to Johnny that Howard made a lot of money and that they were happy. Johnny asks her why this killing is so funny? Johnny tells her that Fleet was supposed to have killed Howard, but he did such a poor job of searching his room. Fleet met Howard and Johnny on the road but could not have followed Johnny to Howard. Someone told him where to meet us.

Johnny tells her that she had told the police that she did not know me, but on the phone the first time you said you knew me. Johnny tells her that he thinks that someone hired Fleet and wanted to use him to frame Castro. Johnny tells her that the "arrangements" Howard had made were mysterious. Maybe Howard arranged to have himself killed so you and he could leave the country. "The man in the car was Fleet, wasn't it?" Johnny tells her.

Howard comes into the room with a gun and tells Beth to take her car and follow him in Johnny's car. Johnny asks, and Howard tells Johnny that Fleet was in the car. They leave the house and walk to Johnny's car when a police car drives up. Howard is distracted and Johnny slugs him. David is promised an explanation in a nice loud saloon, on the expense account.

Howard and his wife are arrested and Johnny explains the whole story over drinks and dinner for David.

Notes:
- Charles Lyon is the announcer.
- Music by Eddie Dunstedter.

Producer:	Jaime del Valle	Writer:	Blake Edwards
Cast:	David Young, Jeanette Nolan, John McIntire, Hy Averback, Frank Nelson, William Conrad		

♦ ❖ ♦

Show: The Gino Gambona Matter
Show Date: 11/3/1953
Company: Intercontinental Bonding & Indemnity
Agent: Roger Stern
Exp. Acct: $112.07

Synopsis: Roger Stern calls Johnny with a job. Stern insures Barney Rico, a former gangster who has been a-number-one-citizen for the past seven years. The policy was for $100,000, and Rico was murdered yesterday. Johnny is to see Lt. Briggs at the seventh precinct for the details. Johnny will leave as soon as he can pack a bag.

Johnny trains to New York City and gets a room. Johnny arranges to meet Lt. Briggs over a lunch of corned beef. Briggs tells Johnny that he has no idea whom might have killed Rico, and that he used to work for the Gambona gang. Johnny tells Briggs that Rico's brother is the beneficiary. Johnny remembers that Rico was the one who testified against Gambona and had him sent back to Sicily. Gambona had also threatened to get even with Rico, who had owned a series of barbershops, and his brother Dave is scared stiff.

Johnny buys lunch and goes to see Dave Rico. Dave Rico's wife tells Johnny that Dave is not home, so Johnny cabs to the main barbershop. Johnny arrives after six and knocks on the door. Johnny is about to leave when he sees a man stagger inside the shop and collapse.

Johnny kicks in the door as the man collapses and Johnny hears him mumbles something. The man is Dave Rico, and he names Gambona as his killer. Johnny calls Briggs and tells him what has happened, but Art tells Johnny that Gambona is in Sicily, so maybe Dave meant the Gambona mob. Briggs will wire the authorities to make sure Gambona is still in Sicily.

Johnny goes back to the precinct and goes through the mug books to find the remaining members of Gambino's gang. One is a girl named Virginia Barrett, who sings at a club called the Pirates Den.

Johnny cabs to the club on East 34th street. Johnny tells a waiter he wants to talk to Virginia, and she joins him a few minutes later. Johnny asks her if she has heard from Gino lately, and she tells Johnny that Gino is in Sicily. Johnny tells her about Dave and Barney Rico, and she is unmoved, but walks away looking worried.

Johnny follows her backstage and is stopped by a large man who tells Johnny to go back outside and tries to slug him, but Johnny knocks him out. Johnny goes to the alley and sees Virginia jump into a cab.

Johnny follows her in another cab to an apartment building. Johnny rings the doorbells and fakes being a flower delivery boy to get in and goes to Virginia's apartment. The man from the club runs up the stairs and stops Johnny from knocking. Johnny tells him he is on a scavenger hunt, but the man can only guarantee Johnny some broken bones. Johnny knocks and Virginia lets Johnny and Marco in. Inside the apartment Johnny finds Gino Gambona.

Gino Gambona is sitting on a chair looking at Johnny. Marco shoves Johnny into a chair and Gino asks Johnny who he is, and Johnny tells him he is an investigator for the insurance company that insured Barney Rico. Gino tells him that the company does not have to pay off on anyone and asks how much insurance Johnny has. Gino tells Johnny that he saw him knocking on the door of the barbershop, and that he killed Dave because his name was Rico.

Gino tells Johnny that Marco was one of his boys from the old days, and that he came back to the country to get something. Gino tells Johnny that as soon as the police figure out he is in the country, he will be back and no one will have seen him. Marco is told to take Johnny for a drive by the river while he and Ginny go to pick up the stuff.

On the stairs a woman calls and distracts Marco, allowing Johnny to slug him. The woman was looking for someone with some flowers for her, and Johnny tells her he will personally buy her a whole acre of orchids.

Johnny goes back to the apartment but Gino and Ginny are gone. Johnny calls Briggs and they take Marco to the precinct and they interrogate him, but he says nothing. Finally, Marco gives in and tells Briggs that he was supposed to get ten-grand for smuggling Gambona into the states, and that Gino has some money stashed somewhere. Marco tells Johnny that he was supposed to meet them at Grand Central station by the oyster bar.

Johnny and Briggs rush to Grand Central and the area is staked out, but Gino and Ginny fail to show. Johnny is sure that Marco has already made arrangements to get Gambona out of the country and suspects a boat will be used. Johnny is sure that Gambona planned to get into the country, kill the Ricos, get the money and leave as quickly as possible.

Johnny and Briggs start to check all the boats that arrived within the past two days and are leaving for Italy that night. The schedules are checked and the Atlantic Star is scheduled to sail at 1:00 a.m. from Pier 16. Johnny and Briggs arrive at Pier 16 at 12:50 and go to see the captain on the bridge. Briggs arrests the captain and he tells Briggs that Gambona has signed on as a cook and is in the galley.

Briggs and Johnny go to stateroom D and force their way in and arrest Ginny. The boat is cleared and Johnny goes into the galley with his hand on his .38. Gino pushes the pots and pans over onto Johnny and tries to run out until Briggs shoots him.

Gino was dead. Virginia Barrett and Marco, full name Marco Dandoy, got five to ten years for their parts in the crime. The Captain of the Atlantic Star got two years and Briggs got a promotion. Johnny returned to Adelaide Jones with the flowers he had promised her, and all-in-all, everyone got just what was coming to them.

Notes:
- This is an AFRTS program that contains a story about children's games and the origins of the term "G-Men", and a story about coinage and American elections.
- The announcer is Charles Lyon.
- Music is by Eddie Dunstedter.

Producer:	Jaime del Valle Writer: Blake Edwards
Cast:	Peter Leeds, John McIntire, Virginia Gregg, Jay Novello, Jeanette Nolan, Clayton Post

♦ ❖ ♦

Show:	**The Bobby Foster Matter**
Show Date:	11/10/1953
Company:	**National Medical & Hospitalization Insurance Company**
Agent:	Walter Jackson
Exp. Acct:	$196.96

Synopsis: Walter Jackson calls and asks Johnny to conduct an investigation. Walter's company writes a group health and hospitalization policy at the Riggs Bearing Company in Riggs City, Florida. They have just received a claim for the son of an employee that involved an operation by a team of neurosurgeons and technicians flown in from Boston. Dr. Grant Howell, director of the hospital attached a report to the claim that needs investigation. Johnny is told not to spare any expense on this case. If the report is correct, there is a vicious racket spreading, a racket that victimizes children.

Johnny flies to Miami and takes a bus to Riggs City, Florida. Johnny gets a room and goes to see Dr. Howell who is expecting him. Nurse Flo Rogers tells Johnny that the doctor will give him the details. Johnny has a cigarette with Flo and she tells Johnny that the town is a little dull, and Johnny offers to fix that.

Johnny sees Dr. Howell and tells him that while the claim was rather high, they are not questioning his medical ability, but are interested in the attached report. Dr. Howell tells Johnny that the report should interest the whole country, because it is about a vicious, unscrupulous racket that is a potential child-killer that preys on panic and fear.

Dr. Howell takes Johnny to the hospital to see Bobby Foster. In the bed is a 5-year-old boy who is in a coma, with only a fair chance of recovery if he comes out of the coma, but he will be paralyzed if he does. Dr. Howell does not know who is behind the racket, the worst one he has seen in his 40 years of being a doctor. Dr. Howell tells Johnny that there was a polio scare in town and some children came down with similar symptoms. An expert was called in, but rumors of an epidemic spread through town.

The parents held a mass meeting to demand that Dr. Howell inject all the children with gamma globulin, but he refused because the treatment is hard to get unless there is a real epidemic. Dr. Howell was called to the Foster home last week, and Bobby had all the signs of a cerebral embolism, an air bubble in the blood veins. Dr. Howell called in the neurosurgeons because he was not skilled enough to do the operation. The air bubble was caused by criminal negligence during a hypodermic injection.

The needle marks were still on Bobby's arm, but Dr. Howell does not know who did it. He does know that other children were injected with no problems. The parents deny that the boy was treated by anyone, but they are lying. The child was sick and taken to a quack and given a shot they thought was gamma globulin. Johnny tells Dr. Howell he will go to visit the parents, but Dr. Howell tells Johnny that it will be a waste of time. They have another child, a girl, and Dr. Howell thinks that the girl has been threatened.

Johnny gets a list of names from Nurse Flo, who offers to help Johnny any way she can. Johnny arranges to meet Flo for dinner at a local bar and grill, as a civic duty.

Johnny cabs to the home of the Fosters, near the beach. Mrs. Foster answers the door and does not want to talk to Johnny. Johnny asks her about the injection, but she tells Johnny that Bobby did not have any shots and gets very upset. She tells Johnny that she cannot tell Johnny who gave Bobby the shot because of Margaret. Mr. Foster comes home and tells Johnny to leave. Johnny tells him he owes it to his son to talk to Johnny, but Foster knocks Johnny down.

Johnny goes to his room to shower and change clothes and then goes to the Tropics Cafe to meet Flo. Johnny tells her what happened at the Fosters and tells Flo that he is sure that the daughter's life has been threatened. Johnny tells her he will question all the parents the next day. Flo tells Johnny that she overheard the bartender tell a man where to take his child for an injection, but she could not hear where the man was told to go.

Johnny tells Flo to leave and goes to the bar and drinks himself into a dark mood with double bourbons. Johnny tells Mickey the bartender that he has something that no one can help him with. The bartender thinks it is woman trouble, but Johnny tells him that the kids are sick, and that is why he is there. The bartender tells Johnny that he can get him some gamma globulin and gives Johnny an address.

Johnny takes a cab to the address after getting some coffee to remove the chill from his spine. At 2 a.m. Johnny arrives at a deserted beach house. Johnny walks up the drive until a man calls him by name and tells him to stop.

Mr. Foster grabs Johnny and searches for Johnny's gun, which he is not carrying. Foster puts Johnny into his car and drives Johnny out of town. Foster stops at a long auto trailer and Johnny is taken inside to meet Flo who tells Johnny that the bartender is her husband. Flo offers to fix a drink and asks Johnny why he was not surprised to see her. Johnny tells Flo that Foster knew

Johnny's name when he went to see them, and that she and Dr. Howell were the only ones who knew he was in town.

Flo tells Johnny that she is keeping Foster's child for them, and his arrival called for drastic measures. She tells Johnny that Bobby's injection was an accident, and that Mickey had given him the shot. She tells Johnny that they charge $50 for each injection of colored water.

Mickey arrives and Johnny tells him that he knew they would want to talk to Johnny before he started talking to the other parents and learned their identity. Johnny tells Mickey that Flo plays a very convincing bachelor girl and talks too much. Johnny tells Mickey that Flo told him that he had killed the Foster girl.

Foster rushes in very angry and slugs Mickey, allowing Johnny to take Flo's gun. Foster wants the gun to kill Mickey but Johnny tells him that Margaret is really safe, and Flo tells him the same thing.

"This case deserves publicity, Mr. Jackson. Lots of it."

Notes:
- This is an AFRTS program that contains a story about Benjamin Franklin and his saying about death and taxes, and a story about President Buchannan.
- The announcer is Charles Lyon.
- Music is by Eddie Dunstedter.

Producer:	Jaime del Valle	Writer:	Don Sanford
Cast:	Frank Nelson, Mary Lansing, John McIntire, Jeanette Nolan, Tom Tully		

◆ ❖ ◆

Show: **The Nathan Gayles Matter**
Show Date: **11/17/1953**
Company: **Great Eastern Life Insurance Company**
Agent: **Mr. Bishop**
Exp. Acct: **$235.00**

Synopsis: Mr. Bishop calls and asks Johnny if he is free. Bishop tells Johnny that his company insures a New York City police officer by the name of Nathan Gayles, who was killed yesterday. Johnny remembers reading that Gayles was shot in his garage. Bishop tells Johnny to contact Gayle's partner, Sgt. Kemper of the 15th precinct.

Johnny trains to New York City and gets a room. Johnny calls Sgt. William Kemper and arranges to meet him. Kemper tells Johnny that Gayles had been after a hood named Bancroft who had gotten tired of the chase and let the word out he was going to kill Gayles. Kemper tells Johnny that Gayles had called in and told him he had something hot on Bancroft and wanted Kemper to meet him at his house. A stoolie named Virgil Cummins was supposed to give Gayles something that would fry Bancroft.

Kemper went to see Gayles and found him dead in his garage. A neighbor saw a man running away and identified him as Bancroft. But the neighbor changed his mind when Bancroft was put in a line-up. Probably someone had gotten to him and changed his mind for him. The man is scared stiff for his wife and four kids. Bancroft told the police that he was with his girlfriend, and the girl corroborated the story. Kemper went looking for Cummins and found him in his room strangled with a light cord. Now there is no evidence against Bancroft.

Johnny cabs to the Gayle home and talks to Evelyn Gayle and meets her two children. She has told the children their father is away on a trip. Evelyn tells Johnny that the day Nathan was killed was their seventh anniversary and that she expected him home around six. She was at the store when Nathan got home, and she saw the police and the ambulance when she got home. She had left the kids with their grandmother as she and Nathan were going out to dinner and see a show. She knows the neighbor George Fisher and had talked to him. She told him that he should talk to the police, and that hiding a killer is no way to protect his family. Johnny tells her he will talk to Fisher and leaves.

Johnny talks to Mrs. Fisher who refuses to tell Johnny where Mr. Fisher works. Johnny goes back to the hotel and calls Kemper and has lunch. Johnny meets Kemper in the hotel lobby and tells him that he wants to know where Mr. Fisher works. Kemper tells Johnny that Fisher was killed an hour ago by a hit-and-run while going to lunch with two coworkers. All three were hit, but only Fisher was killed. There was a witness who identified the car.

The police found the car later, and it had been reported stolen. Bancroft was with his girl at the time and had been at his hotel all morning. The witness said there was a man driving the car, and the police are searching for prints.

Kemper also tells Johnny that they had gotten a call from a jeweler who told them that Gayles had been looking at watches and had taken two of them home to let his wife decide which she wanted. The watches were missing when Kemper got there, and the car glove compartment was open and empty. The watches were expensive, and an alert is out for them. Kemper wants Johnny to try and find out if the girl, Betty Holmes, has one of the watches. Kemper tells Johnny that Betty is attractive and likes men with money. Kemper will get Bancroft out of the way, but only for a while.

Johnny changes hotels and becomes Johnny Dollar the Texas oilman, complete with accent and boots. Johnny goes to a fur store where Betty is shopping and he pretends he is buying a fur coat for momma. Johnny wants a full-length coat and the sales lady goes to get some, allowing Betty to talk to Johnny. She offers to help Johnny with the coats and he tells her he has mink upholstery in his car, a double length Cadillac with gold door handles. There are formal introductions and Johnny spends an hour looking at coats and orders two coats for momma.

Johnny arranges for dinner and goes to his hotel to tell Kemper what is going on. Kemper tells Johnny that the police will keep Bancroft held as long as possible and arranges a limo for Johnny to use.

That night the limo is waiting, complete with officer Danker as a chauffeur and Johnny takes Betty to "The 21" and spends $45.95 on dinner. Johnny avoids the nightlife of the clubs by going to Betty's apartment for a glass of hot milk, on his doctor's recommendation of course.

Johnny tells Betty that she is a nice girl who has everything she needs. Betty tells Johnny that she has everything but a man, and would like to get back to the farm, where she was raised. Johnny asks for the time, and Betty tells Johnny that she does not own a watch, so Johnny tells her he will buy her one, which earns him a great big kiss. Betty tells Johnny that he has a friend who has some watches he will sell wholesale and will arrange for him to visit Johnny at his hotel. Johnny asks Betty for a favor, "could I...have some more milk?"

Johnny meets Kemper at his room and he arranges for Bancroft to be released. The next Morning Johnny has breakfast with Kemper when Betty calls. She tells Johnny that the jeweler cannot come, but he gave the watches to her, and she will bring them by. Johnny is sure that Bancroft is playing it safe by not showing up.

Kemper hides when Betty arrives and shows Johnny the watches. The price for the watches is $500, and $700, wholesale. Johnny calls Kemper in and tells him that the watches are the one Gayles had. Betty pleads innocence until Kemper threatens Betty with jail.

She tells them that Bancroft went out the servant's entrance of the hotel when he went to murder Gayles. She also tells them that she stole the car that Bancroft had used to run down Fisher, but she had nothing to do with it.

Betty is taken away and tells Johnny "Thanks, you all."

Notes:
- This is an AFRTS program that contains a story about the great seal of the US, a story about the State Department.
- Dinner is about $420 in 2017 dollars.
- The watches are priced today at over $4,500 and $6,300. Pretty expensive watches for a policeman in the 1950's.
- Charles Lyon is the announcer.
- Music is by Eddie Dunstedter.

Producer:	Jaime del Valle	Writer:	Blake Edwards
Cast:	Jim Nusser, Jack Moyles, Jeanette Nolan, Mary Jane Croft		

Show:	**The Independent Diamond Traders Matter**
Show Date:	**11/24/1953**
Company:	**Atlas Indemnity Insurance Company**
Agent:	**Eric Carlson**
Exp. Acct:	**$64.20**

Synopsis: Eric Carlson calls Johnny with a job. Atlas Indemnity insures most of the independent diamond traders. They are the small dealers on the street in New York. Two thirds have cancelled policies and gone broke. Johnny is to see E. G. Moss, he is the president of the Independent Diamond Traders.

Johnny goes to New York City and phones Mr. Moss and makes an appointment. There is a light snow falling so Johnny indulges himself and walks to the office. At the Independent Diamond Traders office, a woman is talking with Moss. There is a brief argument followed by some minor passion and Moss agrees to get rid of Susan and meet the woman that night.

As the woman leaves by the back entrance, Johnny is caught eavesdropping by Susan, Moss' stepdaughter. Johnny and Moss talk about the situation and Moss tends to ramble on about how two thirds of the dealers have gone out of business, some after thirty years. He has given Mr. Carlson all the details, but Johnny tells Moss that he was to fill Johnny in. Moss tells Johnny that falling prices are driving the small traders out of business. The market is rigidly controlled, but someone has flooded the market lately. Johnny tells Moss he will start asking around the other diamond houses.

On the way out, Johnny asks Susan to bury the hatchet. She tells Johnny that Moss is crazy over that woman and they agree to call it a draw. Johnny checks into a small hotel near the diamond district.

Johnny goes to eat and comes back to his hotel where the desk clerk has a package for him. The clerk is "always on duty", but he does not know who delivered the package. In his room, Johnny opens the package to find a card from "Mona" and a pair of 10-carat diamonds. The phone rings and it is Mona. Johnny tells her that he has the package and is interested in the contents. Mona tells Johnny that she can help him, as she knows who is flooding the market. Mona wants Johnny to meet her at the Surf and Sand Club.

Johnny goes to the club on Long Island to meet Mona. Johnny waits at the bar until a red-headed Mona comes in. Johnny introduces himself and she takes Johnny out to her car for a drive. The car is a Mercedes Benz with a speedometer that goes up to 120 mph, and Mona wants to try it out, until Johnny turns off the ignition. She tells Johnny that she likes to act on impulse, and that she used the diamonds to make sure Johnny would keep the blind date. Mona tells Johnny that Captain Ledru will tell him everything. Ledru did not meet Johnny, as Ledru is wanted by the police.

Mona drives to a rundown cottage where the captain is, and Mona tells Ledru that Johnny was alone. Ledru tells Johnny that he is sailing tonight, and that he is the one dumping the diamonds, which he smuggles into the country. This is his last job, and Johnny is going to do one last delivery job for him. Johnny gives the diamonds back to Mona but Ledru pulls a gun. Ledru tells Johnny that the police are watching his client and Johnny must make a delivery for him. Ledru tells Johnny to get up so that he can convince Johnny, who expects a beating.

They go out back to a dock where there is a cabin cruiser. Onboard Johnny and Ledru meet Moss, who tells Johnny that he is disillusioned with Mona. Ledru tells Johnny that they will kill Moss if Johnny does not do what is asked. Johnny is left alone with Moss, who tells Johnny that Mona has led him on, but he overheard a plan. Johnny thinks there is no way out and there is no way he can get past the police at the delivery point.

Ledru comes back in, but Johnny is still not sure and wants to hear more before he decides. Ledru tells Johnny that he will phone the client and tell him who Johnny is, and that Johnny is interviewing all the merchants, etc. and he wants to meet with him. The police will know Johnny is on legitimate business and will let him alone. Johnny gets an envelope and is told to bring back another one. Ledru warns Johnny that if he tries to bring back the police, Ledru will sail with Moss.

Mona drives Johnny to a gas station where Johnny calls the client and arranges the meeting. Johnny takes a cab to the client, makes the delivery, gets the money and returns to Ledru.

The boat is pulling at the ropes and is ready to go when Johnny gets back to the boat. Johnny tells Ledru that he has the money papered to his body, as the client did not want him walking around with a package. Ledru reaches to get the bow rope and Johnny pushes him into the water and gets on the boat while Mona is running helplessly on the dock.

Johnny sets the wheel of the boat towards the center of the channel as Moss comes out with a gun. Moss tells Johnny that he, Ledru and Mona are all in it together, and that he did his part to get Johnny's cooperation. Everything was staged, and Susan knows nothing. Johnny takes the gun from Moss and slugs him.

Johnny calls the police from the boat and gives them a description of the Mercedes. The police catch them and they will be out of circulation for a long time.

Notes:
- Charles Lyon is the announcer.
- Music is by Eddie Dunstedter.

Producer:	Jaime del Valle	Writer:	Don Sanford
Cast:	Howard McNear, Parley Baer, Jeanette Nolan, Virginia Gregg, Dick Ryan, John McIntire		

◆ ❖ ◆

Show:	**The Monopoly Matter**
Show Date:	**12/1/1953**
Company:	**Corinthian All-Risk Insurance Company**
Agent:	**Mr. Brandt**
Exp. Acct:	**$62.20**

Synopsis: Mr. Brandt calls Johnny about a fire, but there are no details. The fire is at the Monopoly Club in Waterbury.

Johnny rents a car and drives to Waterbury, Connecticut. The fire department is still on the site as Johnny arrives. Later, after the fire is under control, Johnny talks to the fire inspector, Captain McReady, and is told that the fire started inside, that the building is less than five years old and is licensed for public use. The alarm came in at 11:00 a.m., and the owner has gone home. The firemen have found proof of arson, a Molotov cocktail.

Johnny goes to see the building owner, Gerald Hobson. He tells Johnny that he was at the site, but his nerves got the best of him so he went home. "Thank goodness for the insurance." he tells Johnny. Hobson tells Johnny that he specializes in the game Monopoly, a harmless entertainment for the factory workers. Johnny asks about gambling, but Hobson denies anything. Johnny tells him that gambling debts could cause someone to burn the building. Hobson tells Johnny that a man had come by last week and made him pay for protection. He paid the man $100 and told the police, but they found nothing.

Johnny goes to see McReady about the possibility of extortion. Sgt. Winnick from the police arrives and Johnny talks to him about Hobson. Winnick tells Johnny that the police had gone to see Hobson, but no one else had reported anything, so they thought a transient had taken Hobson for $100.

Johnny goes back to Hobson to tell him that he is under suspicion for setting the fire, as his story of the protection racket did not hold up. Johnny tells Hobson that he is not as cautious as the police and tells Hobson that he has looked into his finances and Hobson gets angry. Johnny tells Hobson that he is in need of $18,000 and the insurance would help.

Johnny goes back to Hartford and gets a call from Winnick the next morning. Winnick tells Johnny that Hobson's story is on the level, that there was another protection racket try this morning and there was a shooting at a bowling alley.

Johnny drives back to Waterbury and meets Winnick at the bowling alley. Johnny is told that the dead man was a bystander, and that the owner, Mr. Wrobleski is upset. Johnny is told that Wrobleski shot the man when they told him he was a foreigner and had to pay to work in the city. Wrobleski tells Johnny that Carl came in and one of the men shot Carl. Wrobleski shot the other man and the shooter got away. Johnny is told that the wounded man is Paul Loner from Chicago, and that the police are searching for the other man.

Johnny and Winnick go to the hospital to talk to Loner, who has little to say. Johnny tells him that he talked while he was unconscious but Loner does not believe him and is not going to talk. Johnny tells him that the police found a gun but Loner tells Johnny that it is not his. To get more information, Winnick tells Loner that Wrobleski told them Loner was alone. Loner tells them that he had a partner but does not know his name. To trick Loner, Winnick blurts out Bert Lucas' name and Loner is tricked into admitting Bert was his partner. Mr. Hobson comes in and Johnny apologizes for suspecting him. Hobson tells Johnny that he does not recognize Loner. Loner tells Johnny that he and Lucas had torched the Monopoly Club because Hobson had gone to the police. Loner comments that they should have taken $500.

On the way out, a nurse tells Johnny that she has a call for Johnny from Loner's wife. Johnny takes the call and tells her that Paul is all right. She is just down the street and will meet Johnny downstairs so she will not have to talk to anyone.

Johnny meets with the wife, and she tells Johnny that she knew something bad would happen. Johnny is told that Bert Lucas was with Paul, and she knows where Bert is. He is at the place they burned down, and he knows he killed the man at the bowling alley.

Johnny gets Winnick and they go to the Monopoly Club. The police go in with their Thompsons and look for Bert. They call for Lucas and are shot at, wounding an officer in the stomach. Lights are brought into the building and Lucas tries to run but is cut down.

Notes:
- This is the same program broadcast on 2/3/1951 by Edmond O'Brien, but with a different cast.
- The script title page lists ad libs by sound men Ray Kemper and Bill James.
- Charles Lyon is the announcer.
- Music is by Eddie Dunstedter.

Producer:	Jaime del Valle	Writer:	Gil Doud
Cast:	Sammie Hill, William Johnstone, Stacy Harris, Parley Baer, Howard McNear, Herb Butterfield, Jeanette Nolan, Joseph DuVal		

♦ ❖ ♦

Show:	**The Barton Baker Matter**
Show Date:	**12/8/1953**
Company:	**Universal Bonding & Indemnity Company**
Agent:	**Charlie Maxwell**
Exp. Acct:	**$604.15**

Synopsis: Charlie Maxwell calls and has a job for Johnny. In a rapid-fire delivery that prevents Johnny from talking, Charlie tells Johnny that he insured Mr. Frank Meadows who lives in Newport, California and that Meadows was killed last night. How long will it take for you to pack and catch a plane? Lookup Lt. Solomon of the Newport Police when you get there Johnny. Have a good trip. "Yeah, I'll try, Mr. Maxwell" Johnny is able to get in after Charlie hangs up.

Johnny flies to Los Angeles and rents a car for the drive to Newport, California where he meets with Lt. Solomon. Johnny learns that Frank Meadows ran a charter boat business. The police got a call about shots being fired, and when they got there, Frank had been shot three times, and two bullets were missing from his gun, so he shot it out with someone. Johnny is told that the prime suspect is Frank's partner, Dave Geller, who is missing. Solomon tells Johnny that there is no reason for the killing, and that Frank and Dave got along well, so maybe it was a woman. Frank has a wife, and Dave is single and Johnny is told that Mrs. Meadows is the kind who might cause a lot of trouble under the right circumstances.

Johnny goes to see Mrs. Meadows, and Johnny is inclined to agree with Solomon. She is very attractive, blond and tan, and probably in mourning, but Johnny doubts it even though the tight bathing suit was black. Johnny tells her that he was sent out to investigate the killing, and Mrs. Meadows asks how much the insurance was for. She is surprised when Johnny tells her it was $25,000, but Johnny tells her that she will not get the money until the investigation is complete and the deceased is buried. She tells Johnny that Frank was buried this morning at 8:00. Johnny asks her if she dumped him off of a surfboard and she gets indignant, but Johnny tells her he only gets like that when he sees someone so broken up.

She tells Johnny that her husband is dead and nothing will bring him back. She tells Johnny that Frank and Dave did not get along very well because they just disagreed over things. Frank had argued with Dave before their last trip, and when they came back, Solomon told her that Frank had been killed. She tells Johnny that they had gone fishing alone for yellowtail.

Johnny gets a room and calls Solomon, who tells Johnny where the boats is, and that there was no tuna on the boat when it came back. Johnny has dinner and drives to the landing where the boat, the Jay Belle, is tied up.

Johnny goes on board and enters the cabin and is stopped by a man with a gun. Johnny is told to turn on the lights, and the man tells Johnny that Baker must have sent him, because he knows all the cops in the area. Johnny tells the man who he is and why he is there. Geller takes Johnny's ID and gun and tells Johnny he must do something about him. He tells Johnny he did not kill Frank but will not tell him why he is hiding.

There are footsteps on the dock and Dave turns out the lights. Dave tells Johnny that if something happens to him, Johnny is to go to Bernie's garage and tell Bernie that Dave sent him, and to get the tool kit. Dave goes onto the deck and there are shots.

Johnny looks out of the cabin to see a tall, thin man in a white suit pointing a gun at him. The man tells Johnny that he is Barton W. Baker, and he is going to kill Johnny like he killed Dave.

Baker comes into the cabin and smiles at Johnny. Another man, Hank, asks Baker what to do with Dave, and Baker tells him to throw Dave in the water. Baker asks Johnny about the tool kit, but Johnny feigns ignorance. Hank is told to hit Johnny, which he does. Baker offers Johnny $10,000 for the toolkit. Johnny tells Baker who he is but that he cannot prove it, as his wallet is on Dave. Johnny is beaten until he faints, but Johnny does not pass on the information.

Johnny wakes up on the beach looking up at the moon. Johnny gets up and sees Mrs. Meadows walking down the beach. She takes Johnny back to her house and fixes his wounds. Johnny asks her about Baker and Hank, but she does not know either of them. Johnny tells her what happened and asks her if she knows about a tool kit at Bernie's. Johnny tells her to call Solomon and borrows her car.

Johnny drives to the garage and wakes up the attendant, who turns out to be Bernie. Johnny asks Bernie for the tool kit, but Bernie is hesitant to turn over the tool kit until Johnny tells him that Dave is dead, and that Solomon is on his way. Johnny tells Bernie he is an investigator and Bernie gets the box for him.

Johnny opens the lock with a crowbar while a car horn blows outside. Bernie goes outside, and Johnny finds nothing but new tools inside the box, all painted black except for one. Johnny scrapes some shavings off the handle and discovers the shavings are solid platinum.

Bernie comes back in with Baker and Hank. Hank takes Bernie out and Baker tells Johnny that he let him live so he could lead Baker to the tools. Johnny is told that Frank was supposed to pick Baker up and land, but Frank found out about the tools. Johnny asks if Baker is an alien, and Baker confirms that he is.

Baker tells Johnny that Dave and Frank had been paid to pick up Baker south of the border. Dave figured out what the tools were made of and forced him ashore and took the kit. Baker managed to phone his operatives in Los Angeles, who met the boat and killed Frank.

Shots ring out and Johnny hits Baker with the wrench. Solomon comes in and Johnny tells him that he owes Mrs. Meadows an apology. Johnny gives Solomon the wrench and tells him that Baker is going to have a very expensive headache.

"On the way over to my motel, I explained the events to Solomon, who did a little mumbling and shaking himself. Then after a fresh shower and a change of clothes I went over to Mrs. Meadows and expressed my most heartfelt thanks."

Johnny spends some time in Newport and sees Mrs. Meadows a few times but does not get much of a tan. Barton Baker comes up for trial on illegal entry, smuggling and three counts of espionage. I hope he enjoys his stay in the USA.

Notes:
- This is an AFRTS program that contains a story about the regulation of time in the US, and story about the presidency of Warren G. Harding.
- Charles Lyon is the announcer.
- Music is by Eddie Dunstedter.

Producer:	Jaime del Valle	Writer:	Blake Edwards
Cast:	Frank Nelson, Jim Nusser, Mary Lansing, Clayton Post, Edgar Barrier, Junius Matthews		

♦ ❖ ♦

Show:	**The Milk and Honey Matter**
Show Date:	**12/15/1953**
Company:	**Eastern Indemnity & Insurance Company**
Agent:	**Mr. Mitchell**
Exp. Acct:	**$1,480.20**

Synopsis: Johnny is awakened by Mitchell and asked what he knows about the land of milk and honey. Johnny complains about being called at 4:30 a.m., but Mitch tells Johnny that the sun has been up for three hours in Beirut, Lebanon and is shining brightly on a happy man named Bret Cunningham on a ship-wrecked yacht. Cunningham is happy to the tune of $90,000. Johnny does not blame him and starts to go back to sleep. Mitch tells Johnny that the yacht went down in clear weather and a calm sea. "Well I've always wondered what milk and honey taste like" replied Johnny.

Johnny flies to Beirut, Lebanon and gets a room at the Saint George Hotel and finds Bret Cunningham thirty-five minutes later in the Es Suweida, a swank casino. Chips and a brunette named Najda surround Cunningham at the roulette table. Johnny introduces himself and tells Cunningham that he wants to talk about the shipwreck. Cunningham asks for the insurance check but Johnny only has questions.

Cunningham tells Johnny that the boat hit a derelict and sank in less than three minutes. Johnny questions the story, but Cunningham tells Johnny that he will be in the casino when Johnny is ready to pay off.

Johnny goes to the harbor and talks to Commissioner Florot who tells Johnny about the wreck of the *Happy Times*. The story was confirmed in writing by one of the eight-man crew who survived the sinking. A gunboat went to the scene the next day, found the derelict and destroyed it and the yacht was detected in 70 fathoms of water.

Johnny learns that Cunningham was in route from Istanbul to Beirut and that he spends a lot of time here gambling, with a different girl on every trip. Johnny wonders why there were only two survivors out of a crew of eight. Johnny gets the name of the survivor, Casimir Andescu, and finds him on a narrow twisting street named El Akbad.

Johnny knocks and the door is opened and Johnny is told that it is feeding time for his birds, so Casimir cannot talk. Johnny tells Casimir who he is and Johnny is invited in. While he feeds the birds, Casimir tells Johnny that he takes one of his favorites with him on all his voyages. He tells Johnny the same story that Florot had told Johnny, but Johnny tells Casimir that he wants the real one. Casimir tells Johnny how poor he is, and that he only wants 10% of the claim. Johnny offers $500, but Casimir will tell him nothing.

Johnny leaves and sends a radiogram to the intelligence division of the police in Istanbul and goes back to the hotel. Cunningham calls Johnny and offers to sign a quitclaim for the wreck, so Johnny heads for the casino to meet with him.

Johnny is stopped by a police officer at the casino, and Johnny sees remains of an automobile accident. Johnny spots Florot and is told that Cunningham's car was just blown up by a bomb. Johnny tells Florot about the offer of the release, which only confuses the situation.

After a quick investigation by Florot, Johnny is driven back to his hotel where Najda is waiting for him in the lobby. She does not wince when Johnny tells her that Cunningham is dead. She tells Johnny that she likes something better than Cunningham or Johnny, money, $90,000 to be exact. Johnny tells her that the money will go to the estate and Najda tells Johnny that she is Mrs. Bret Cunningham.

Johnny calls Florot, who calls the casino manager who confirms the marriage. Johnny calls Istanbul and speaks with Chief Inspector Divrigi. He tells Johnny that they know that Cunningham's boat sailed on the 24th of November, but their problem is with the motor schooner the *El Hussein*, that was being towed by Cunningham's boat. They have no record of the owner, one Casimir Andescu.

Johnny goes back to see Andescu, but he has disappeared, complete with his birds. Johnny rents a motor launch, complete with skipper, winch and 100 fathoms of steel chain and grappling hooks.

Four hours later they arrive at the site of the wreck and start fishing. Two hours before sundown they hook something and are shot at from the shore as they try to pull it up.

Back in port, Johnny shows Florot their catch. It is the transom of a lifeboat with the name *El Hussein* on it.

A sunburned Johnny goes to see Najda and she asks for the insurance check. Johnny asks about Casimir and is told that he is a nothing. Johnny accuses her of fraud and murder and tells her that someone sank the *El Hussein* and then put in a claim for the yacht. Najda is ready to seduce Johnny, but Johnny tells her she cannot spend the money in prison.

Najda tells Johnny that Bret had lost $10,000 to Casimir in Istanbul and could not pay. Casimir did not like that, because he is a big-time gambler and businessman. It was Casimir who suggested sinking the *El Hussein* and splitting the money 50-50. However, Bret won a lot of money and wanted to pay off Casimir and keep the insurance money. The call to Johnny was to try and get a better deal from Casimir, but Casimir killed Cunningham. Casimir has taken the yacht to a small place called Kibati.

Johnny and Florot drive to Kibati and find the yacht in a small inlet, where it had been hastily disguised. Johnny finds Casimir on the boat with his birds, which Casimir tells Johnny need their sleep and object to the sound of guns. Casimir tells Johnny that Cunningham's fate was most just. Johnny tells him about being shot at, and Casimir tells him that refraction had ruined his aim.

Florot tells Casimir that he has enough to arrest him and tells Casimir to leave with him. Casimir starts to plead for his birds and shoots at Johnny and Florot. Casimir is killed and Johnny tells Florot that Casimir was right about one thing. The birds did object to the noise.

Incidental Remarks: I still would like to know what milk and honey taste like."

Notes:
- This is an AFRTS program that contains a story about housekeeping in the government, and a story about the presidency of Chester A. Arthur.
- The script spells Lillian Buyeff's name as "Byeff".
- Charles Lyon is the announcer.
- Music is by Eddie Dunstedter.

Producer:	Jaime del Valle	Writer:	Sidney Marshall
Cast:	Don Diamond, Ramsey Hill, Hal March, Lillian Buyeff, Ben Wright, Jay Novello		

Show: The Rudy Valentine Matter
Show Date: 12/22/1953
Company: County Court, Kings County
Agent:
Exp. Acct: $10.85

Synopsis: Rudy calls Johnny from Leavenworth prison in 1950, and reminds Johnny that he sent Rudy to prison, along with his wife and lawyer. Rudy is ready to settle up now.

Johnny goes to New York City and is almost hit by a car. A witness tells Johnny that the streets are not safe with all the drunk drivers.

Johnny goes to the police and talks to Sgt. Foss who searches the records. Johnny learns that Rudy was convicted of robbing a delicatessen and was identified by the owner. Later the gun and money were found in his room. Rudy had been arrested for auto theft in 1939, and assault in 1940. He was 17 at the time.

Johnny gets the address and goes to read the trial transcript. Johnny learns that the attorney was William P. Capper, who is now a successful lawyer. Johnny goes to see Capper and talks to him. Johnny is told that Rudy has also contacted Capper, but he calls it just talk.

Johnny goes to his hotel and wires the prison. The prison officials tell Johnny that Rudy got mail from Sybil Miller on 16th Street.

Johnny goes to see Sybil and asks for Rudy, but she tells Johnny that he is not there. Johnny tells her of the threats and she tells Johnny that Rudy had promised to forget about the past. Sybil tells Johnny that Rudy has gone to Buffalo.

Johnny goes to see Rudy's brother Anthony at a news-cigar stand he runs. Johnny meets Rudy's wife Pat, and Anthony tells Johnny that Rudy has not contacted them, but he will send Rudy's wife out of town for protection.

Johnny gets a telegram from the prison that tells him that Rudy had spent time in the mental ward and attempted suicide but is all right now. Johnny is then called by Rudy's wife, who tells him that Tony has been killed by Rudy.

Johnny goes to the apartment and meets Lt. Maxwell who tells Johnny that they have picked up Rudy's wife Pat. Johnny tells him that he has no description for Rudy.

Sybil comes to Johnny's hotel and tells Johnny about Tony. She argues with Johnny and accuses him of planting the gun. She tells Johnny that only a framed man would kill his brother and gives Johnny a description of Rudy. Johnny calls Capper and learns that he is on his way to Florida.

Johnny goes to his hotel and meets Rudy at his door. Rudy tells Johnny that he has talked to Sybil, and that they did not kill Tony. Rudy tells Johnny that he went to Buffalo to look for a job and was driving a blue 1939 Plymouth coupe (Not the car that almost ran Johnny down). Rudy tells Johnny that his lawyer was responsible for putting the money in his room. Johnny convinces Rudy to give himself up to the police.

Johnny goes to see Pat and discovers that she is dead. Johnny goes to Capper's apartment and tells him that he was paid to throw the case and calls him an ambulance chaser. Capper tries to bribe Johnny, and then pulls a gun.

Remarks: As I said at the outset, I do not expect the County Court, Part One to honor this statement. It would be fair and equitable to work out payment for a witness. It looks like I made that position again at Capper's forthcoming murder trial, and for me it'll be a waste of time. I know he is guilty."

Notes:
- This is the same story as the previous program from 12/30/1950, but with different cast members.
- The announcer is Charles Lyon.
- Music is by Eddie Dunstedter.
- Story information obtained from the KNX Collection in the Thousand Oaks Library.

Producer: Jaime del Valle   Writer: Gil Doud
Cast: Sidney Miller, William Johnstone, Jack Moyles, Jeanette Nolan, Joseph Kearns, Clayton Post, Tom Hanley, Bill James

♦ ❖ ♦

Show: The Ben Bryson Matter
Show Date: 12/29/1953
Company: Keystone Mutual Assurance Company
Agent: Ed Murphy
Exp. Acct: $823.82

Synopsis: Ed Murphy calls and he wants Johnny to come to his office. It is about Ben Bryson. Johnny tells Ed that it was too bad Ben died that way. Ed tells Johnny that Ed should have died a year sooner.

Johnny cabs to Ed's office where he tells Johnny how close he was to Ben and it was too bad that he missed the curve and crashed into the Pacific where the body was never found. Ed tells Johnny that the company had started getting complaints about unpaid claims they had settled previously. The company looked into the matter and discovered that Ben had embezzled $80,000 from his accounts. Ed gives Johnny a ticket for San Francisco, California, but Johnny wants to pass on this case. Ed tells Johnny he can't, as too many questions need to be answered. Johnny agrees to do it because Ben was his friend.

Johnny flies to San Francisco and gets a room at the Fairmont Hotel. Johnny cabs to Ben's apartment in the Franciscan Arms, a luxury building with a manager named Maurice, who has a real gardenia in his lapel. The manager, for $20, tells Johnny that Ben had been living there for six months and was a free spender. Mrs. Kern was a friend of Ben's and they were inseparable. Johnny wants to talk to her, but he is told that she is away. Maurice tells Johnny that it is a tragic coincidence that Mrs. Kern's husband also died in a tragic accident.

Johnny visits the bar and the bartender remembers Ben, who spent a lot of time there with Alvie Kern. He had been there with Alvie the night he died. Johnny realizes that he needs to talk to Alvie, as so far, he has nothing to go on.

Maurice calls Johnny two days later and for $20, he tells Johnny that Mrs. Kern has written to have her mail forwarded to Panama City.

Johnny flies to Panama City, Panama and is met by Captain Devano of the police. He tells Johnny that he received his radiogram and that Mrs. Kern is registered in a small hotel near the waterfront.

Johnny goes to the small hotel and speaks to Mrs. Kern, who only wants to forget about Ben after the horrible accident. She tells Johnny that they were going to get married and that she came to Panama to get away from the memories. Johnny mentions Ben's wealth and she is surprised, as she thought that Ben worked for an insurance company, and besides, her husband left her a lot of money. She was only married for ten months.

Johnny offers her a cigarette, but she does not smoke. Johnny walks through the apartment and asks her where the smoke came from that he smelled when he got there. Johnny starts to open a closet when Mrs. Kern turns out the lights and Johnny is hit on the head.

Johnny wakes up to find Alvie staring at him. She tells Johnny that she hit him, but Johnny tells her that he knows what is happening as only Ben Bryson shreds his cigarette butts like the ones in the ash tray. Johnny tells her that Ben Bryson hit him.

Johnny buys some aspirin, gives Ben's description to Devano and goes to bed. The next morning Johnny is met at breakfast by Mrs. Kern, who tells Johnny that Ben did not hit him, it was a friend of hers. She tells Johnny that Ben is dead, and she is the one who tore up the cigarette papers. Johnny is sure that Ben is still alive and it hurts hard to learn that he has been stealing. Now he is alive, and Johnny has to catch him and take him back.

Devano comes to see Johnny and tells him that they have found Ben. Johnny and Devano drive to the harbor where they are told that Ben is living on a boat there. Johnny goes onto the boat and Ben tells him to come on in and asks why it had to be him. Ben tells Johnny that Alvie was not supposed to come for six months. Ben tells Johnny that he stole the money for Alvie so that he could live her life style, and that they were going to go to South America to start again. Johnny asks Ben why she still has her apartment, but Ben tells Johnny that she has moved out. Ben pulls a gun and tells Johnny that he is going to go on and will kill Johnny if he needs to. Ben locks Johnny in the boat and drives away.

Devano finds Johnny and tells him that Ben was able to take the car because he was not paying attention. The police are alerted and after two hours Devano is called and told that Ben and Alvie have been found. They were driving on a mountain road, missed a curve and the car crashed into the ocean.

Johnny rents a boat and a diver and goes to the site of the accident. The diver goes down and reports that Alvie is dead, but Ben is not in the car. The same pattern, a crash and a missing body.

Johnny climbs up the rocks and finds Ben in a crevasse, broken and dying. Ben tells Johnny that it was just like they did in San Francisco, only real this time. Johnny tells Ben that Alvie is dead and Ben tells Johnny that he made her come with him. She told him that she did not love him and was only after his money. Ben tells Johnny that he would do the same thing again if he could. The money is in his coat and Ben tells Johnny to give it to Ed and dies.

Johnny encloses a cashier's check for the $72,652 recovered from Ben Bryson, embezzler.

Notes:
- This is an AFRTS program.
- This program was performed by Bob Bailey as *The Confidential Matter*, broadcast on 9/10 through 9/14/1956.
- Charles Lyon is the announcer.
- Music is by Eddie Dunstedter.

Producer: Jaime del Valle   Writer: Les Crutchfield
Cast: William Johnstone, Jack Edwards, Joseph DuVal, Lillian Buyeff, Jeanette Nolan, Tom Tully

• ❖ •

Show: **The Fair-Way Matter**
Show Date: **1/5/1954**
Company: **Columbia All-Risk Insurance Company**
Agent: **Sam Harris**
Exp. Acct: **$25.95**

Synopsis: Sam Harris calls to alert Johnny of a Fairway Airlines plane crash in Hartford, Connecticut. Sam is sure that a bomb caused the accident, and thirteen people were killed. The company wants to place responsibility and do whatever it can. Contact the airline representative Mr. Reed.

Johnny goes to the scene of the crash. The plane had been airborne less than a minute when it exploded and destroyed two houses on the ground killing at least 6 people. Johnny meets a hysterical Carl Reed of the airline who is talking to an equally hysterical Mrs. Goodhue about a daughter she fears was on the plane. The daughter was on the plane, but she has not been told yet. Carl tells Johnny that the explosion was in the tail of the plane, that the CAB is on the way, and that the State Police are in charge of the investigation.

Johnny goes to find Captain Jim Lenhart of the State Police in the hangar where the bodies are being collected. They wonder if the crash was murder with a motive, suicide or just a maniac.

The next day Johnny learns that nitroglycerine was the explosive. A tip to the police brings in Wilbur Wheeler, a maintenance worker for the airlines for questioning. Wilbur is very nervous and asks what the police have on him. He admits that he had been in love with Shirley Goodhue, a stewardess, and had fought with a copilot when Wilbur learned that Shirley was going to marry him instead. Wilbur had threatened the copilot and his plane and knew that made him a suspect. He had heard of the crash on the radio and came back to work to help out. After questioning he is released and a police tail is placed on him.

Johnny relates that on the list of dead passengers, one man named Rupert Stone could not be located because of bogus information.

Johnny and Lenhart go to visit a Mrs. Graham who is distraught over the loss of her husband. She tells Johnny and Lenhart that her husband had gone to Boston to visit his brother's grave, as he was a religious man. On the way out, Jim calls the case a rotten mess and admits that he could not ask Mrs. Graham if her husband's cancer could had caused him to commit suicide.

They leave to go have a drink but are interrupted with the news that the explosive was found to have been in a first aid box in the rear of the airplane.

Wilbur Wheeler is brought in for more questioning. After a very nervous interview Wilbur tells Lenhart that he has worked for the airlines for a year and a half yet does not know about the first aid kit carried on by Miss Goodhue. Wilbur denied knowing anything about the nitroglycerine. Wilbur is held for a lie detector test and an interview with the police psychologist. Johnny and Jim search Wilbur's room and find no radio, which Wilbur said he had listened to, and no newspapers are found.

On the next day the lie detector test proves negative and the psychologist says that Wilbur has a severe guilt complex. Carl Reed calls to report that another stewardess named Alice Turner is missing and a search of her apartment uncovered her shot dead.

Johnny and Lenhart go to the apartment and Carl tells them that she was originally scheduled to fly on the plane that crashed but had switched at the last minute with Shirley Goodhue. Johnny is told that the stewardesses often switched flights among themselves. It seems now that the case against Wilbur is not very sound.

Johnny and Lenhart go to visit Mrs. Goodhue and learn nothing new other than Shirley was called shortly before the flight and that one of the girls was sick. They are told that there were six girls in Hartford who swapped flights if one was sick. Johnny and Lenhart talk to the other girls and learn nothing.

On the way home, a man named Moran meets Johnny in the hallway of his apartment building, and Moran wants to talk. Moran tells Johnny that he knew Alice and that he was to blame for the accident. Moran tells Johnny that a man named Arthur Church was using Alice as a courier for drugs, which were carried in the first aid kit. She wanted out and Moran was hiding her. Alice had arranged a meeting with the Feds and Church had found out and killed her. Moran warned her to stay hidden and she had gotten Shirley to take her flight. Moran also tells Johnny that Church had hidden the explosives on the plane in Alice's kit, which was kept at the airport and picked up by Shirley.

Johnny and Lenhart go to Church's apartment with Moran. Moran goes in and calls for Church, but he opens fire and kills Moran, and Lenhart kills Church.

Notes:
- This is an AFRTS program that contains a story about the Post Office and rural routes and a story about the presidency of John Tyler.
- Cast information courtesy of Stewart Wright.
- Bill James is credited with the voice of Skipper the police dog.
- This program was performed as *The Fair-Way Matter* on 7/11/1951.
- Music is by Eddie Dunstedter.
- Charles Lyon is the announcer.

Producer: Jaime del Valle Writer: Gil Doud
Cast: Howard McNear, William Johnstone, Martha Wentworth, Ken Christy, Clayton Post, Mary Lansing, Bill James

• ❖ •

Show: The Celia Woodstock Matter
Show Date: 1/12/1954
Company: Washingtonian Life Insurance Company
Agent: Mr. Miller
Exp. Acct: $73.60

Synopsis: Captain Lyle Woodstock returns Johnny's call. Woodstock tells Johnny that there is no trouble with his wife's disappearance. At least not yet.

Johnny rents a car and drives to Bridgeport, Connecticut to meet with Captain Lyle Woodstock — captain only because he owns a 64-foot schooner. Lyle tells Johnny that he has discharged the servants and had lied to Mr. Miller about fearing for his wife's life. He had wasted money on a detective, David Slater, to follow his wife and asked the insurance company for help. Woodstock gives Johnny a folder about his wife, who is 27. He met her in Mexico and married her. They both like adventure. Woodstock is suspicious, as Celia has been seeing too much of Dr. Masterson in town. She sees him three times a week but she seems very healthy. Now she had disappeared.

Johnny goes to see Slater, who tells Johnny of the doctor visits and of losing her on a train to New York City after she took $2,000 from the bank. Slater had overheard a phone conversation with a man named Sprague. Johnny decides to tell Woodstock he is dropping the case as he gave up chasing wives a long time ago.

At the Woodstock house, a nervous man with a gun meets Johnny at the door. Johnny is locked in a closet and the man leaves. Johnny breaks out of the closet and finds Celia Woodstock shot on the floor. Johnny tries to call the police but the phone is dead, so he calls the police from a neighboring house. The police arrive and take Celia to the hospital. Johnny tells his story to Lt. Al Jester. Johnny remembers the man carrying a cheap nickel-plated .32. The police find another body upstairs and Johnny goes up with Jester.

In a bedroom they find Capt. Woodstock with a .38 beside him. He has been shot in the back. Johnny gets a hotel room and the next day he talks to Dr. Masterson's former nurse, Janet Squire. Janet tells Johnny that she did not know of any romantic involvement between Dr. Masterson and Celia

Woodstock, nor does she know a man named Sprague.

Johnny checks in with Jester and learns nothing. Johnny goes to see Dr. Masterson who wants his name kept out of the papers. He tells Johnny that Celia came to him for a sinus condition. She seemed satisfied with her husband and looked forward to a trip to South America. He tells Johnny that during one visit, Mrs. Woodstock became hysterical when the receptionist mentioned a call for "Mrs. Emile Sprague". Johnny reports in to Jester and learns that Celia was shot with a .38, Lyle by a .32, and there is no sign of Sprague.

Around midnight Celia recovers consciousness and at 3 a.m. talks to Johnny and Jester. She tells them that she was in the house when Emile killed Woodstock and that she is really Mrs. Sprague. She married Lyle in Mexico and Emile found out and wanted money. She met him in New York and gave him the $2,000. Then he followed her to Bridgeport and forced her to take him to see Lyle. Lyle shot her and Sprague shot Lyle. Emile has an apartment on Commerce Street.

Johnny and Jester go to the apartment around 3:30 a.m. and surround it. Johnny sees Sprague watching them from the window as they go in. Johnny calls on a pay phone and urges Sprague to surrender. He tells Johnny that he shot Woodstock because he thought Celia was dead. Sprague runs from the apartment shooting and is killed.

I understand that the lawyers are now working to kick the bigamist wife out of the estate. I doubt that the insurance company has a chance of doing the same with the insurance money.

Notes:
- This is an AFRTS program that contains a story about the Attorney General and a story about the presidency of James Madison.
- This program was performed by Edmond O'Brien on 3/3/1951 but with a different cast.
- Music is by Eddie Dunstedter.
- Charles Lyon is the announcer.

Producer:	Jaime del Valle	Writer:	Gil Doud
Cast:	Howard McNear, Victor Rodman, Ken Christy, Virginia Gregg, William Conrad, Edgar Barrier, Jim Nusser		

◆ ❖ ◆

Show: The Draminski Matter
Show Date: 1/19/1954
Company: Empire Insurance, Limited
Agent: Bill Gardner
Exp. Acct: $348.40

Synopsis: Bill Gardner calls Johnny and asks him how he likes Oysters Rockefeller. (Love 'em) And where do you find the best ones? (New Orleans, of course.) Good. There is a plane leaving at 4:30. Find out why a daffy client left the back door of her shop open and let someone walk out with $75,000 in furs. Her name is Princess Draminski — she is not a real princess, but you won't care. "All that and oysters too, Bill?", Johnny replies, I'm your boy.

Johnny flies to New Orleans and goes to the shop of Princess Draminski, located at the edge of the French Quarter. Johnny notes that the shop is between a used car lot and an herbal remedies shop. Johnny meets the Princess and she is glad for "it" to happen — for Johnny to fall in love with her, men always do. The Princess shows Johnny the rear door and tells him that sometimes she forgets to lock it — "I am a little careless." When Johnny starts to scold her, she tells him that she is only a woman, how can she do everything right?

Outside the door Johnny finds a dead-end alley — something unusual for a professional burglar. The Princess tells Johnny that "Honest Tom" has a car lot on the other side of the building at the end of the alley, and Professor Balderoff is on the other end. Back inside the shop Johnny hears a loud noise from the Professor's shop. Johnny is told that the Professor only makes the noise when a man is with the Princess — he has the jealousy and is madly in love with the Princess.

Johnny goes to visit the Professor and finds him in his back room. Johnny explains who he is and asks the Professor if he heard anything on the night of the robbery, but the Professor knows nothing and suggests that Johnny talk to Tony Mariaccio. The Princess barges in and yells for Johnny to stop killing the professor — she thinks Johnny has the jealousy and is there to kill the professor! Johnny reminds her that he is only there to find the uninsured furs, remember?

Johnny hears music outside and is told that it is Tony. The Princess calls him a troubadour of music, the Professor calls him "a pig of a pig of a pig" — a street beggar fed by a monkey! Johnny is told that Tony is madly in love with the Princess and brings her gifts, roses, caviar, perfumes. He has money from an uncle or cousin. She tells Johnny that Tony goes to the shop, but do not worry, she locked the door this time! She tells Johnny that Honest Tom watches the shop when she goes out. Honest Tom is in love with the Princess.

Johnny talks to Tony, but he works for pennies and knows nothing, but he is sad for the princess. Tony tells Johnny that his monkey really likes him because the monkey tries to pick Johnny's pocket. When Johnny asks how many pennies it take to buy caviar, Tony accuses Honest Tom of telling bad stories, because he is a big crook. Tony tells Johnny that he lives across the street over the antique shop. Tony tells Johnny to come to his room after it is dark.

Johnny talks to Honest Tom who is a fool for the girl — she has class, culture and royal blood. He tells Johnny that he loves to do things for her and is surprised that someone has not cleaned out the store. Johnny tells Tom what has happened, and he tells Johnny that he closed the car lot about 9:00 last night. While Tom tries to sell Johnny a car, he tells Johnny that the Professor is nuttier than a fruit cake

Johnny cabs to police headquarters and talks to the captain of the Safe and Loft Detail, who tells Johnny that the police have washed their hands of the case.

Johnny cabs back to the French Quarter and goes to Tony's room. Johnny knocks but no one answers — he only hears a whimpering sound inside the room. Johnny opens the door and the monkey jumps into Johnny's arms. Johnny turns on the light to find the monkey covered in blood just as someone turns off the light — the last thing Johnny remembers.

Johnny wakes up, turns on the light, and finds Tony on the floor, dead. Johnny runs to the Princess' shop to use the phone. Tom comes in to tell Johnny that he had seen him running across the street.

Johnny calls Lt. Lewis and updates him on what has happened. Both Tom and the Princess are shocked at Tony's death. The Princess tells Johnny that Tony had been there earlier that evening.

Lewis tells Johnny that Tony's death is not some pointless crime, and Johnny agrees. Johnny tells Lewis that he thinks Tony had some money, as he had been buying gifts for the Princess. Johnny is sure that Tony did not steal the furs but might have known who did and maybe tried some blackmail.

Johnny walks outside and looks at Tony's window and the line of sight angle and gets an idea. Johnny goes into the shop and asks about a trap door in the ceiling. Johnny finds the opening and climbs out on the roof where he looks straight across to Tony's window. Johnny looks at the skylight in the Professor's shop and sees nothing, but on the side of the car lot Johnny sees what he is looking for — a fire escape.

Johnny climbs down the fire escape and lands sprawling on the ground and rolls under a parked car. Johnny hears footsteps and tries to get to a set of ankles next to the car. Lewis calls out and Johnny warns him that Tony's killer is there. Lewis shines a light and Johnny grabs the ankles when he hears a gun shot.

Lt. Lewis handcuffs the shooter and Johnny tells him that the man is Honest om, the man who runs the car lot and stole the furs. He used the trap door to remove the furs and Tony saw him and tried to blackmail Tom. Johnny is told that the furs are in the trunk of a car on the lot.

Johnny tells Lewis he is late for a date and asks where the best place is for Oysters Rockefeller.

Remarks: Thanks for the oysters included in expense account item 3!

Notes:
- Music is by Eddie Dunstedter.
- Charles Lyon is the announcer.
- All commercial breaks are for Wrigley's Spearmint Gum.
- Cast and story information courtesy of Stewart Wright.

Producer: Jaime del Valle Writers: Les Crutchfield
Cast: Clayton Post, Lillian Buyeff, Robert Griffin, Hal March, Jay Novello

Show:	**The Beauregard Matter**
Show Date:	**1/26/1954**
Company:	**Plymouth Mutual Insurance Company**
Agent:	**Dave Brace**
Exp. Acct:	**$203.40**

Synopsis: Dave Brace calls and tells Johnny that sapphires are bad luck. Johnny tells Dave that black cats are bad luck too, but Dave tells Johnny that cats do not get stolen. Dave tells Johnny that the stones are worth $30,000 and mentions Benny Stark. Johnny remembers him as a jewel thief, and Dave tells Johnny that Benny called from Rockport, Illinois and wants to make a deal. The client is Ellen Beauregard, a big wheel in Rockport society. Dave has already made reservations and told Benny that Johnny is coming.

Johnny flies to Rockport, Illinois, gets a room at the Bleeker Hotel and waits for Benny Stark to call. Johnny is visited in his room by Jarrett Beauregard, the uncle of Ellen Beauregard. Jarrett tells Johnny that Ellen does not use the best judgment and Johnny tells Jarrett that thinks he will be able to recover the necklace. Jarrett tells Johnny that the necklace was an engagement present from Phil Avery, her fiancé.

Johnny gets a call from Benny, and he tells Johnny to go to the Pink Pigeon at 9:00. Benny tells Johnny that he has been double-crossed had has some information for him. Jarrett tells Johnny that Ellen is impulsive and leaves.

Johnny rents a car and calls on Ellen Beauregard. As Johnny walks to the house Johnny sees a man and the maid "engaged" in the sunroom. The maid answers the door, and she knows who Johnny is and goes to get Ellen. The man from the sunroom, who is Phil Avery, comes out and tells Johnny that he hopes that Johnny can recover the necklace, as the insurance will not cover the sentimental value.

Ellen meets Johnny and she tells him that Phil is impulsive but does not mean any harm. She shows Johnny the safe where the necklace was kept and tells Johnny that the house was empty when it was stolen. She warns Johnny that Uncle Jarrett means well but is a little vague.

As Johnny leaves he sees someone at the coach house. Johnny goes there to meet Lois the maid and takes some papers from her meant for the incinerator. A nervous Lois is called to the house and in the papers, Johnny finds a .32 revolver with one chamber fired. Ellen finds Johnny and tells him not to believe Lois, as she as caught her in all sorts of lies. Ellen has been planning to let her go, but Uncle Jarrett raised objections.

Johnny goes back to his hotel room and finds a man there who asks Johnny if he knows Benny Stark. The man is chief of police Cotton, and he tells Johnny that he found Johnny's name where Benny had written it down. Johnny tells Cotton why he is there and about the appointment later that night with Benny. Cotton tells Johnny that Stark was killed a few hours ago by a .32. Johnny gives him the gun he took from Lois and tells Cotton where he got it. Cotton recognizes the gun as belonging to Jarrett Beauregard.

Cotton tells Johnny that the family is not as wealthy as it used to be, but Jarrett seems to have a lot of money lately. Phil has been in Rockport for a couple years and is a civic leader.

There is a knock at the door and Cotton goes to the bathroom to listen as Lois comes in. She tells Johnny that she found the gun under her mattress and wants it back. Johnny tells her it is not that simple and calls Cotton into the room.

Johnny buys lunch for the president of the Central City Bank and learns that the Beauregards are aristocratic socially, but they are broke and mortgaged to the hilt. Jarrett seems to have a lot of money lately, probably borrowed from Phil Avery, a go-getter who has been elected to the bank's board of directors. He has several jobs and has had to postpone the wedding. Lois is a pretty little girl and what Johnny has heard is probably gossip.

Johnny goes to see Cotton, who is talking to Phil Avery. He tells Johnny that Lois is not involved with the theft or the murder. Cotton is going to search the house and Phil goes to see Lois. Johnny shows Cotton a photo of the necklace and asks if anyone in town could make a duplicate of it. Johnny is told that someone would have to go to Chicago for that. Cotton arranges for a local jeweler to give the Chicago police the technical information on the necklace.

Back in his room, Ellen calls Johnny and asks him to come to dinner. Johnny rents a car and drives to Ellen's. Johnny is about to play billiards with Phil when Cotton calls. He tells Johnny that the jeweler who made the copy has been located and that the client was a girl who fits the description of Ellen Beauregard. Johnny tells him that he has found the necklace and Cotton is on his way.

Uncle Jarrett tells Johnny that he has discovered the family secret and Johnny asks him to get Ellen and bring her to the billiards room. In the billiards room Johnny breaks the balls on the billiards table and tells Phil that Lois is only an innocent bystander, even though he found the necklace hidden in her room. Johnny tells Phil that the family is broke and looked at Phil as a way to get money, but Phil was playing the same game.

Johnny tells him that Ellen was the key to open any door in town and that he used his last money to buy the necklace. Then he saw the Beauregard's accounts at the bank and discovered they were even broker than he was, so he brought Benny Stark in. But Benny told Phil that the necklace was a fake and Phil thought Benny was trying to double cross him and killed him. Phil is told that Ellen sold the necklace a week after he gave it to her and had an imitation made, and Phil had taken the imitation necklace to Lois' room to frame her.

Phil pulls a gun on Johnny and when Ellen opens the door and distracts him, Johnny hits him with his pool cue. Johnny tells Ellen that Phil had had the safe broken into and then killed his partner. Johnny tells Ellen that she has committed fraud by submitting a claim on a necklace that she had already sold. Johnny is sure that the insurance company will prosecute, and that Cotton is on his way.

Notes:
- This is an AFRTS program that contains a story about the improvements in communication and changes in the Cabinet, and a story about the presidency of Teddy Roosevelt.
- This program was performed as the 6-part *The Kranesburg Matter*, broadcast on 8/24 through 8/31/1956.
- Cast information courtesy of Stewart Wright.
- Charles Lyon is the announcer.
- Music is by Eddie Dunstedter.

Producer: Jaime del Valle   Writers: Les Crutchfield
Cast: Howard McNear, Herb Butterfield, Ted de Corsia, Jane Webb, Lamont Johnson, Mary Jane Croft

♦ ❖ ♦

Show: **The Paul Gorrell Matter**
Show Date: 2/2/1954
Company: **Plymouth Insurance Company**
Agent: **George Post**
Exp. Acct: **$369.80**

Synopsis: George Post calls and asks about Johnny's trip to Arizona. Johnny tells George he was told to come out in a hurry and only knows that $100,000 was stolen and two guards were killed. George tells Johnny that if he is willing to take one of the biggest gambles in his life, they might be able to crack the case.

Johnny flies to Phoenix, Arizona and notes that the newspapers were reporting the death of an unidentified man who would later be part of Johnny's investigation. George has the newspaper on his desk and tells Johnny that the two guards were disarmed and killed to prevent identification of the robbers.

The man in the paper, Palovic, was the only other witness, and that Palovic was the other robber, but the newspapers and police do not know that. Palovic had called George to tell that he had split up with his partner, Paul Gorrell, as there was not supposed to be any shooting during the robbery, but Gorrell shot the guards in cold blood. Palovic told George he was on parole and would go back to jail for 20 years if he told the police.

He wanted the insurance company to stop Gorrell from enjoying the blood money and told George where Gorrell was and what his plans were. Gorrell is still in Phoenix, and Johnny thinks the case should be turned over to the police. George tells Johnny that Gorrell has mailed the money to someplace in or near Los Angeles. George tells Johnny that Gorrell has arranged to share a ride to Los Angeles, and Johnny figures he will be the third man in the car. Johnny is leery but accepts the case. Johnny realizes that if the insurance company involved the police, they would spend all their time pursuing Gorrell and not the money.

Johnny also realizes he is working behind the law's back, which he does not like. Johnny does not like the getaway method because Gorrell would be in charge, and Johnny could not risk taking a gun.

Johnny phones the driver, a Mr. Bovie, and he tells Johnny that he already has two men and a woman, and another passenger would be too many. Johnny arranges to come to his house, and if there is room, he will go.

The next morning Johnny goes to Bovie's house and Gorrell arrives and tells Bovie his partner will not be coming. Johnny is introduced and tells Gorrell he is from Connecticut. Johnny describes Gorrell as one who would be able to blend in anywhere. The woman, Miss Shelton, arrives and the car is loaded. Gorrell asks to drive and Johnny sits in the back with Shelton. Bovie gets nervous when Gorrell drives in the wrong direction, and Johnny wonders if he was trying to avoid roadblocks.

Johnny notices a green coupe following them as they pull out and Gorrell notices him looking around. Later that evening, in Blithe, California, the car overheats and Bovie looks for a mechanic who tells Bovie that the water pump is bad and that he cannot get one until morning. All of them start to walk to a motor court when the green coupe drives up beside them and Gorrell tries to get away from it. The car drives on, and Gorrell tells them he thought it was somebody he did not want to talk to, but Johnny noticed him mechanically reach for his automatic. Johnny is sure Gorrell is back to being an uncontrollable killer. Johnny wants to call the police, but he does not.

They get rooms and Gorrell comes to see Johnny and tells that he had gotten into trouble in Phoenix and wants Johnny to tell the others why he acted like he did. Gorrell tells Johnny that he only has six dollars and had lost his money in a poker game and had run out on the men in the game. Gorrell asks Johnny to help him straighten things out when he gets to Los Angeles.

In Los Angeles, Johnny goes with Gorrell to the Prince Hotel on Spring Street to pick up personal things he had shipped out before the trip. Gorrell tells Johnny that when he gets the suitcase he can pay off the guys following him. Gorrell offers Johnny $25 to pick up the suitcase for him. Johnny and Gorrell get rooms at the hotel and Johnny gets the receipt for the suitcase.

Johnny calls the police, tells them his story, and arranges to meet a plainclothes officer near the express office. Johnny meets Sgt. Mason, shows his ID, and tells why he is playing the case like he is. Johnny gets the suitcase and Mason follows Johnny into the hotel. Johnny knocks at the door but Gorrell does not answer. Johnny goes in, but Gorrell is gone. Johnny asks Mason to go with him to his room and open the suitcase, but Mason tells him he has no right to open someone's personal property and leaves.

Johnny checks the suitcase at a bus station and goes back to wait. Miss Shelton visits Johnny and tells him to pack up and get out of town because he is involved with some bad people as Gorrell is using him. She also tells Johnny that some men had come for Gorrell, the same ones in the green car. There is a knock at the door and Gorrell tells Johnny to let him in.

Gorrell has been shot and staggers into the room. Shelton tries to leave but Johnny wants answers. She tells Johnny that two men in Phoenix roped her into it and paid her $200 to go with Gorrell and follow him. She heard them talking about a robbery and killing and caught on to what was happening. They were the ones who pulled the robbery in Phoenix. There were four men who planned it, but Gorrell tried to take the money for himself. They also mentioned a phone call from a punk named Palovic. The men were trying to find out where the money was, and she figured that Johnny was the man who Gorrell told them had the suitcase.

Johnny calls Mason and the hospital. Fifteen minutes later Johnny opens the door to find two men with guns. Johnny tells them that Gorrell talked to him before he passed out. Johnny tells the man to look in the dresser for a claim check and the man gets it, but it does not have a name on it. There is another knock and Mason is at the door. Gorrell starts to mumble and Johnny slugs the man and lets Mason into the room. Johnny is told that Gorrell will probably not live to enjoy his money, and not to play lone-wolf on any more cases, but to level with the police.

Notes:
- This is an AFRTS program that contains a story about the patent and copyrights processed by the Department of Commerce, and a story about the presidency of Zachary Taylor.
- Charles Lyon is the announcer.
- Music is by Eddie Dunstedter.
- Cast information courtesy of Stewart Wright.

Producer: Jaime del Valle   Writer: Gil Doud
Cast: James McCallion, Parley Baer, Jack Edwards, Jane Webb, Jack Moyles, Tom Tully

♦ ❖ ♦

Show: The Harpooned Angler Matter
Show Date: 2/9/1954
Company: Washingtonian Life Insurance Company
Agent: Phillip Martin
Exp. Acct: $1,043.90

Synopsis: Phillip Martin calls and asks Johnny if he has his passport ready. Johnny asks "Where to now?" and Phil tells Johnny that he is going to a small town on the French Riviera called Cassis. Phil has a death claim on a policy for Arnold Bernier. The policy is for $75,000 and written thirty-three years ago. Johnny asks if Phil never expects his clients not to die, and Phil tells Johnny that Arnold died with a fishing spear through his back. Johnny will be ready in an hour.

Johnny flies to Cassis, France and rents a 1937 Maybach Victoria and breaks down twice.

Johnny gets to the office of Count Lazlo Andescu, who asks for the check and tells "my darling Mr. Dollar" that he is like a charge 'd affaires for the bereaved and the unfortunate. He tells Johnny that Bernier was involved in the latest and most ungentlemanly sport of skin diving. He had been down for an hour when someone went down and brought him up. Andescu considers the case closed and wants the check. When Johnny mentions that the widow might have killed Arnold, Andescu tells Johnny that she could never do such a thing.

Johnny goes to the Bernier villa and to meet the widow Magda Bernier, who tells Johnny that Arnold was a wonderful provider, but husband's death is of no importance to her and to get all of his future information from the local police.

Johnny meets Insp. Laniel, who tells Johnny that skin-diving was a fatalistic past time of Bernier, whose body was discovered by David North, an American scientist. North was returning to the surface and found Bernier's body inside a grotto with a spear through it. Laniel has no personal suspects and tells Johnny that Magda has no financial motivation, as Bernier was an immensely wealthy man. Bernier was retired and his attorney says his affairs are in perfect order and there were no personal enemies.

Johnny gets a call from David North, who wants to talk about the murder of Arnold Bernier. North tells Johnny to meet him in a café, and that he was told that Johnny was there by Magda, his future wife.

Johnny waits in the café for an hour when Andescu shows up and asks Johnny about the check. The murder is of no consequence now to Andescu as he knows who killed Bernier. It has to be David North, because he has provided the proof by his suicide. "Oh, did I forget to tell you? They are taking his body from the bottom of the gulf even now".

Johnny rushes to the beach where a boat is bringing the body to shore. Laniel orders North taken to a doctor and tells Johnny that North apparently went diving rather than keeping his appointment. He had been down for fifty minutes when the crew became concerned and found North in the same grotto where Bernier was found. North's aqualung was working, he had a scalp wound on his head and a fishing spear was found near him. Laniel tells Johnny that he has just found evidence that North killed Bernier, so a suicide would have closed the case.

Johnny goes to Laniel's office to wait for North to wake up. Laniel tells Johnny that North had run out of funds and Andescu saw an opportunity to make a commission and persuaded Bernier to loan North $2,000. Laniel thinks that North's getting friendly with Magda provided a reason to kill Bernier, save his ship, and get the girl. North will tell them if they are right when he wakes up.

Johnny goes to see Magda and she tells him that David worships her and would do anything for her, even murder. She tells Johnny that the talk of marriage was nothing and that she had been in the house all morning and seldom swims.

Johnny goes to check up on North but Laniel tells Johnny that North just died.

Johnny drives to Marseilles and is passed by a big limousine with Magda Bernier in it. Johnny drives to the home of Armond Gautier and is told to call his office. When Johnny tells Gautier that Magda is the number one suspect in Bernier's killing, he lets Johnny in. Gautier tells Johnny that Bernier had given Magda her own fortune, one she could not spend in a lifetime and the balance goes to charitable institutions. Johnny brings up North's youth, but Gautier tells Johnny that Magda would not give up her life style for a temporary amusement. Johnny tells Gautier that there is another man in her life, and that Gautier should have gotten rid of Magda's perfume before he let Johnny in.

Johnny goes back to Laniel and asks him to send a diver to the grotto, and he will have an answer to the murder. Laniel acts as the diver and goes down to the grotto. Forty-five minutes later Laniel surfaces and gives Johnny a small wooden box marked "Marine Specimens".

As Johnny looks at the contents of brown looking weeds, Andescu points a spear gun at Johnny's back. He tells Johnny that Laniel is at the entry of the grotto and will soon drown. Andescu says that Johnny figured out his drug smuggling plan too quickly. He tells Johnny that he buys the hashish in the Red Sea area for practically nothing with Bernier's money and transports it with North's ship and hides it in the grotto to sell when the time is right. Bernier found the warehouse so he had to kill him. North was going to get a box to show Johnny when he was killed. Johnny suddenly throws the box at Andescu.

"Things happened pretty fast just about then. The box hit Andescu in the chest, the spear missed me by slightly less than a hair, my fist hit Andescu's jaw, and he hit the water. Oh, a jolly good time was had by all, including Laniel. I managed to raise some help from the shore and get a diver down to him before his oxygen ran out.

Andescu wound up in the local jail where charges are being preferred against him now: two counts of homicide, two of attempted homicide and a slight case of drug smuggling. I did not see Magda Bernier again. I didn't think I could take any more of that. When you honor the death claim, send the check care of Armond Gautier, Marseilles."

Notes:
- This is an AFRTS program that contains a story about the weathermen in the Department of Commerce, and a story about the presidency of John Adams.
- The Maybach was a high-end automobile made in Germany from 1921 until 1940.
- Charles Lyon is the announcer.
- Music is by Eddie Dunstedter.

Producer: Jaime del Valle   Writer: Sidney Marshall
Cast: Howard Culver, Lawrence Dobkin, Virginia Gregg, Edgar Barrier, Lou Krugman

Show:	**The Uncut Canary Matter**
Show Date:	2/16/1954
Company:	**Eastern Indemnity & Insurance Company**
Agent:	**Mr. Harrison**
Exp. Acct:	**$373.85**

Synopsis: Mr. Harrison calls and wants Johnny to go to Beverly Hills to find an uncut canary, an uncut orange-yellow 89-carat diamond insured for $125,000 that has disappeared. Johnny tells Harrison that he'll see what he can do.

Johnny goes to Los Angeles, California and to the Johanna Jewelry store, the last resting place of the diamond. Johnny asks for Johanna and the manager tells Johnny that Madam Johanna is very tired. Johnny tells the manager, Mr. Carter, that if Johanna wants to file a claim, it will be on his time, not hers.

Johanna comes from her office and Johnny is shown to her office. She tells Johnny that she purchased the diamond in Rio over a year ago. She is taking her time planning the cutting of the diamond as one wrong move will shatter the stone and make it worthless. Her father learned that the hard way 25 years ago with a stone similar to the canary.

She tells Johnny that it was gone last night when she and Carter came to watch the stone being cut. She has two excellent cutters, Adolph Spiers and Hans Plesman, and they have been with her for over 30 years. All of them have the combination to the safe, but none of her employees would have stolen it. As she is talking, Adolph calls and tells her to send the police to his house and he will give them the uncut canary.

Johnny calls Chief Anderson of the Beverly Hills police, and Lt. Hankins comes to pick up Johnny. Johnny is told that the robbery chief is ill, so Hankins is on the case for the chief. Hankins tells Johnny that Johanna is always looking for a way to make a buck and that the canary is supposedly uncuttable, she bought it under the market price and has held it for over a year. There is also a rumor that Johanna also needs money.

At Adolph's house no one answers the door so Johnny and Hankins go out back and hear a car running in the closed garage. In the garage they find Adolph Spiers dead. While the police do their work, Johnny calls Johanna at her home and office, and then calls Mr. Carter, but no one is home at either number.

Johnny cabs to the apartment of Hans Plesman, the other diamond cutter. At the door Plesman wants the lenses he ordered from Albert. Johnny tells him who he is and wants to talk about the stone. When Plesman asks why Johnny did not question Adolph, Johnny tells him that Adolph is dead, and probably murdered. "Nonsense!" he tells Johnny. "He did not steal the stone, I did!" Plesman then clams up and will say nothing, even to the police.

At police headquarters, Hankins tells Johnny that they have little to hold Plesman on. The coroner calls and tells them that Adolph probably did not die of carbon monoxide poisoning.

Johnny cabs to Charles Carter's apartment where Carter is doing a head stand in his shorts. Carter tells Johnny that it is good for the internal organs.

Johnny wants to know where he was this evening, and Carter tells Johnny that he was at the beach exercising. Carter is not surprised that Adolph is dead, as he was in lousy shape. Johnny tells Carter that shape had nothing to do with it. Carter tells Johnny that Johanna was not with him, and that she is a gentle soul and the epitome of womanhood, and not one to be maligned. Carter also tells Johnny that he does the head stand twice a day for 30 minutes.

Johnny calls Hankins and is told that Plesman still refuses to talk. Over a cup of coffee, Johnny remembers the comment Plesman had made at his door, and Johnny checks the yellow pages, and calls the optician Albert Schoenbeck at home. Schoenbeck tells Johnny that he had made lenses for Johanna and her father, and that he had made lenses for a refractometer for Plesman. Schoenbeck explains to Johnny that a refractometer is used to measure the bending of light through a stone, which tells what type of stone is. He confirms Johnny's thoughts that it could also be used to spot imperfections in a stone.

Johnny cabs to Johanna's house and asks her about the rumors of financial problems. If they were true, Johnny tells her the insurance on an uncut or uncuttable diamond would help. She calls it nonsense and tells Johnny that he had better leave, as he has gone too far. Johnny mentions Adolph's murder and she tells Johnny that she does not know about it. Johnny tells her that someone took the stone from him or killed him to stop him from talking about who did. She calls that unbelievable, but Johnny tells her that it is not as unbelievable as the conversation she had with him after he had died. She tells Johnny that she knows about Hans and that her lawyer is arranging bail. She is not going to change her story of the phone call either.

Because it is too late to get a cab, Johnny walks back to town and thinks about the problem. It takes about an hour to get to a phone to call Hankins who tells Johnny that Plesman has been sprung and went home.

Johnny goes to Plesman's home and asks him if he has cut the stone yet. Plesman tells Johnny that he was just getting ready to and Johnny asks to watch with Johanna, who is also there. Plesman tells Johnny that Adolph would have smashed the stone, just as he did for Johanna's father 25 years ago, but that the refractometer will make the difference.

Plesman tells Johnny that he could not let Adolph do that to his Johanna, as he was going to give it to Johanna as a gift and had to stop him. Plesman takes the stone and instructs Johanna on how to cut the stone, and she splits it perfectly. Plesman tells Johnny that Adolph would have ground it to bits, and that he has saved her business.

Plesman starts to tell Johnny that once it is cut and polished...but he starts getting weak and lies down. Johanna tells Johnny that Plesman had called her to tell her that he had hidden the stone in her house and that he had killed Adolph. The stone will accomplish everything he wanted, but she would have rather smashed it than to have Plesman do what he did.

Notes:
- This is an AFRTS program that contains a story about the Secretary of State and a story about Abraham Lincoln.
- Chief Anderson and Lt. Hankins were also characters in *The Amita Buddha Matter*.
- Charles Lyon is the announcer.
- Music is by Eddie Dunstedter.

Producer:	Jaime del Valle	**Writer:**	Sidney Marshall
Cast:	William Johnstone, John Stephenson, Hal March, Virginia Gregg, Fritz Feld		

♦ ❖ ♦

Show: The Classified Killer Matter
Show Date: 2/23/1954
Company: Eastern Indemnity & Insurance Company
Agent: Ted Albright
Exp. Acct: $191.15

Synopsis: Ted Albright calls Johnny at 4:00 a.m. Frank Harvey has been murdered. Johnny will grab the first plane out.

Johnny goes to Chicago, Illinois and is met by Ted Albright and a winter blizzard. Ted tells Johnny that Frank was at the office until 6:45 and that a truck driver found his body out on Mannheim Road, and that he had been shot three times. Ted is really on edge as he tells Johnny that he had to drive back from Milwaukee with his wife and has had no sleep.

Johnny goes to see Lt. Franchetti who tells him that the bad weather will hold down crime, except for the rise in deaths from yacki-dak — antifreeze that the bums drain from car radiators and drink. It is really deadly. Johnny is told that Harvey was killed trying to sell his car, a 1953 Cadillac convertible, and that he had been running an ad in the papers. A garage mechanic had seen Harvey talking to a customer who drove off with him around 6:55. The truck driver found Harvey at 8:37 in a snow bank. Franchetti is sure that they should be able to identify the gun, and that an APB is out for the car, which is still missing.

A call comes in and Johnny goes with Franchetti to Mannheim Road where Harvey's car has been found. The owner of a beer and hamburger joint found the car in the parking lot and called the police. There are bloodstains all over the seat and a woman's compact on the floor.

Johnny goes back to the insurance office to talk to Ted Albright. Johnny asks him, since he was Frank's boss, did Frank have any girlfriends. Ted tells Johnny that he did not know of any, and that there were no recent claims either. Ted tells Johnny that Frank only had a $10,000 policy, with his mother as the beneficiary.

A man calls and wants to bargain for information on the killing. "You gotta make a living you know, what with the high cost of living". Johnny agrees to meet Mr. Taggert at the Biloxi Hotel at Wells and Grand.

Johnny cabs to the hotel and meets Mr. Taggert with $20 to help combat the high cost of living, which must have included garlic and bourbon. Taggert shows Johnny the register where a woman named Alma Carter had checked in, scared and frightened, and she had stains on her coat. She was listening to the news broadcasts all night and had asked Taggert to buy her a paper. The compact in the news suggested to Taggert that he better call the insurance company.

Johnny knocks on the door of room 14 and talks to Alma Carter. She asks Johnny why an insurance man would want to talk to a stranger in her room. Johnny tells her that they are not strangers, as he saw her picture on Ted Albright's desk, Mrs. Albright.

Mrs. Albright tells Johnny that she was with Frank Harvey last night. Frank was going to talk to a prospect and had asked her to come along, and that Ted thought she was in Milwaukee. Frank introduced the man, but she did not hear the name. The man asked Frank to drive out Mannheim Road to his house where the man asked him to stop, and then just shot Frank. She jumped out of the car ran and fainted by a shack. She got a lift to town and got a room at the hotel. She did not call the police because she was out with a man who was not her husband and involved in a murder. She just wanted to avoid scandal.

Johnny takes Mrs. Albright to Franchetti where she makes a statement and is held as a material witness and a pickup is ordered for Ted Albright. Johnny is told that the mechanic, Will Zeigler has looked at the mug books, but has not found any one.

Johnny goes to his hotel room and is called by Ted Albright. Ted is in the lobby and he wants to talk. Ted comes to Johnny's room and asks Johnny if he knows about his wife Alma. He tells Johnny that he had suspected she was seeing Frank, and that he went to Milwaukee to check on her story. Johnny tells Ted to turn himself in to the police, which Ted agrees to do.

Johnny goes to the garage to talk to Will Zeigler. Johnny tells him who he is and that he wants to ask questions. He tells Johnny that it was rough, he was standing right there when the man picked up Harvey. He tells Johnny that he had never seen the man before, and that he had never seen Ted Albright either. Zeigler tells Johnny that there was nothing strange about the man, so he must be a psycho.

He sees the ad, figures he will take the man out in country and kill him and steal the car. Zeigler tells Johnny that a car thief will take the car when no one is around, but this guy puts himself here where Zeigler can see him and does not back out when Harvey picks up the girl at the insurance building. Zeigler tells Johnny to tell Franchetti that one of those guys I picked out is a psycho.

Johnny goes back to talk to Alma and asks her what kind of work the man they picked up do? She tells Johnny that all they talked about was cars, and that there was a sweet odor, like nail polish remover about him.

Johnny cabs back to the garage and Zeigler is gone, so Johnny goes to his rooming house where Zeigler is getting clothes to take to the cleaners. Johnny wants to talk about the psycho theory, as Zeigler might be right. Johnny tells

Zeigler that he has another angle, the man may have had plans for the girl too. Zeigler shows Johnny a fancy $100 jacket and tells Johnny that there is nothing like nice clothes and a fancy car, and Harvey's car was a dreamboat! With a car like that and clothes like these he could really get the girls.

Johnny notes that there are a lot of clothes going to the cleaners, and asks Zeigler if it is hard to get the acetone out of your clothes? "Yeah, that stuff really clings" he tells Johnny. "That is what Mrs. Albright said." Johnny tells him. Zeigler tells Johnny that she is a classy dame. Johnny tells Zeigler that he knew he was the killer because of the remark about picking up the girl at the insurance company.

Zeigler tries to pull a gun and Johnny shoots at him. Zeigler says he always gets excited at the wrong time, like with the car. He ruined the upholstery and had to ditch the car.

Notes:
- This is an AFRTS program that contains a story about the Secretary of Health, Education and Welfare, a story about Franklin D. Roosevelt.
- Cast information courtesy of Stewart Wright.
- Charles Lyon is the announcer.
- This is the first appearance of a future Johnny Dollar Bob Bailey in a program for which a digital recording exists.
- Music is by Eddie Dunstedter.

Producer:	Jaime del Valle Writer: Sidney Marshall
Cast:	Bob Bailey, William Conrad, Junius Matthews, Virginia Gregg, Sidney Miller, Fred MacKaye

♦ ❖ ♦

Show:	**The Road-Test Matter**
Show Date:	3/2/1954
Company:	**Consolidated Indemnity Company**
Agent:	**Mr. King**
Exp. Acct:	**$217.40**

Synopsis: Mr. King calls from Consolidated Indemnity and tells Johnny that he has to do this job for him and he can't take no for an answer. Allied Motors has a new car that is crashing. Go out and find out what is happening.

Johnny flies to Detroit, Michigan and goes to the Allied Motors test track. Johnny has to talk his way through security and looks for Mr. McGregor. Johnny explains to McGregor why he is there and McGregor tells Johnny that he is testing the model three years out. He has been there for 25 years and this model makes a lot of changes. There have been three other crashes, but they have the best engineers working on the cars.

Johnny is taken to see the car and is told that they look sharp but have all fallen apart. The drivers have been told to give the car everything, but they are afraid. Johnny suspects a grudge but is told that there is no sign of sabotage. McGregor tells Johnny that the drivers are experienced but that the designers are new and that McGregor will leave the motives to Johnny.

Johnny gets the address of the last man who was killed and visits Mrs. Grace Johnson, who has a "for sale" sign on the front yard. She tells Johnny that she is moving, as there is no reason to stay. Johnny asks her if anyone would have wanted her husband out of the way, and she tells Johnny that they had not been getting along, so she turned to a friend and started thinking about getting Steve out of the way. She tells Johnny that the man has not been to see her since. The man is Joe Simmons — a former test driver.

Johnny confirms that Simmons had quit after Steve Johnson was killed, and that he had moved out of his rooming house. Johnny finds Simmons at a local bar and talks to him. Johnny asks Simmons for help and tells him about Mrs. Johnson.

Simmons tells Johnny that Steve was his friend and that Steve knew about his being with the wife. Simmons tells Johnny that he quit driving, as the car is not right. It handles like a dream, and then just goes apart. Johnny asks about bugs put in the cars or if a driver was in the way. Simmons tells Johnny that his hunch is bad because he cannot get to the cars because of security, and he would have to want to do it. Joe gets up to leave and Johnny tells him not to leave town.

Johnny goes to the hotel and calls McGregor who is not in. Lt. Farish meets Johnny in the hotel lobby and tells Johnny that he wants to talk about the case. Johnny tells of the possible involvement of Joe Simmons and Grace Johnson. Farish tells Johnny that there is a problem with his theory, Simmons no longer works at the plant and there has been another crackup. Farish tells Johnny that the police cannot get involved, so it is his baby. The police want Johnny to go to work driving the cars and that it is important. "Oh, the things I get involved in!" laments Johnny.

At the track McGregor is working on a wrecked car when Johnny asks about why the car went to pieces. Johnny asks to be put in driving a car. Johnny and McGregor go to his office and talk over a drink of scotch. Johnny is told that he will not be needed. McGregor lets Johnny listen to a memo telling the Allied executives that the design should be dropped in the interests of safety, and that they should return to the traditional means of designing cars. He tells Johnny that he will get the driving job if they do not accept the recommendation.

Johnny convinces the head office to continue the tests for one week, and goes to see the head designer, Ted Brand. They talk over something to drink, coffee. Ted is only 22 or 23 but is the chief designer. Ted tells Johnny that the car is perfect on paper and should handle like a dream. He also tells Johnny that the old guys just hate progress.

Johnny cabs to see McGregor after dinner. His wife answers the door and tells Johnny that he is not home and will probably stay the night at the plant because they are working him so hard. She would love to talk to Johnny and tells him that Ken loves his job and has turned down a pension. He works hard but has so much in his mind and wants to make one more showing before he quits. Johnny asks her not to tell McGregor that he was there. She tells Johnny that Ken had given a lifetime of loyalty, but is now outdated, so how would Johnny feel?

Farish calls Johnny and tells him that McGregor has been killed at the plant. Johnny goes to the plant and meets Farish who tells Johnny that there were signs of a struggle and Johnny tells him that McGregor had stayed the night. Farish tells Johnny that McGregor had left at midnight for an hour and that Simmons had left much earlier. Johnny goes to Kirby's Bar, but Simmons is not there.

Back at his hotel, a man who wants to talk about the car meets Johnny. He tells Johnny that he might be a stoolie, but he had nothing to do with the killing of McGregor. He tells Johnny that McGregor had picked up Simmons and brought him back to the plant and that Simmons and McGregor were in it together. They were worried about Johnny driving and Simmons had to talk McGregor into fixing the car so Johnny would get the business. Simmons was working for a stockholder who was kicked out of management when he was found to have been involved in the rackets. The man wanted to hurt the company and had the means to do it. McGregor was sore at being eased out and Simmons knew it and got the old man to go in deeper. Simmons killed him when he would not go further. The man tells Johnny that Simmons is expecting him at the Kearns Hotel and Johnny calls Farish.

Johnny meets Farish at the hotel and the man tells Farish that Simmons has a gun. The man goes into the room and Johnny and Farish follow him in. There are shots, and Simmons is killed.

The name of the stockholder has been submitted and the police are holding him. Johnny believes that he should be able to repay the claims paid by the company, from jail of course.

Notes:
- This is an AFRTS program that contains a story about children's games and the origins of the term "G-Men", and a story about President Taft.
- Charles Lyon is the announcer.
- Music is by Eddie Dunstedter.

Producer:	Jaime del Valle Writer: David Chandler
Cast:	Fred MacKaye, William Johnstone, Virginia Gregg, Ted Bliss, Clayton Post, Hy Averback, Eleanor Audley, Joseph Kearns

♦ ❖ ♦

Show: The Terrified Taun Matter
Show Date: 3/9/1954
Company: Washingtonian Life Insurance Company
Agent: Tom Benson
Exp. Acct: $2,296.45

Synopsis: Tom Benson calls and tells Johnny that a man and his wife, Harrison and Maida Langley, have two policies with double indemnity for $125,000 each. The underwriter has written to say that someone is trying to kill them. They live in Kuala Lumpur.

Johnny goes to Kuala Lumpur, Federated States of Malaya, gets a room at the Coliseum Hotel, and goes to see George Alistair, the local rubber tea broker. After Alistair's complaining about the climate, Johnny mentions the murder claim from Langley. Johnny is told that the whole thing is rubbish from a diseased mind, and that the jungle and terrorists have gotten to him. Johnny is told that the plantation is in territory held by the terrorists. Johnny is also told that no one in his or her right mind would live there, and that an investigation is a waste of time. Johnny asks Alistair why he stays if the hates the country so much and Alistair tells Johnny that he is making too much money to leave.

Johnny rents a 1949 armor-plated Ford and drives to the Sundown Rubber Plantation. The guard at the plantation tells Johnny to talk to tuan Crawford because tuan Langley is sick because his wife has disappeared. Johnny goes to Langely's house and walks in. Langley meets Johnny with a gun and accuses him of killing his wife and trying to kill him. Johnny shows Langley his ID and takes the .38 Webley from him, firing a shot in the process.

As Johnny fixes a drink, Langley reads the identification papers and finally believes that Johnny is there to help. Langley tells Johnny that he has been threatened by terrorists and has been helpless to stop it. Langley tells Johnny that Maida has disappeared and that is why he is upset. Crawford comes in to investigate the shots and accuses Johnny of being a vulture gathering for the feast. Crawford tells Johnny that he will take Johnny on a tour of the plantation. Langley tells Johnny that Crawford has been carrying on with his wife, and that he has a motive to kill him.

Johnny talks to Crawford about the situation and he tells Johnny that Langley gets threatening notes and phone calls, but no one ever sees them. Crawford tells Johnny that Langley has been carrying a gun everywhere and spying on Mrs. Langley and him, but there was nothing. Crawford shows Johnny some cut wire and cut trees and a bloody sleeve. Crawford thinks Langley faked the whole thing to get the insurance money on his wife as there is a $50,000 note coming due soon, and Langley needs the money.

Back at the house the servant Bandar tells Johnny that Langley has left for Kuala Lumpur after he received a telephone call. He left taking a .45 automatic with him and said something about giving Dollar something to investigate.

Johnny calls Alistair who confirms that he had called Langley about some rubber shipments. Alistair tells Johnny that he had mentioned Langley's wife casually and Alistair tells Johnny that he just finished having a drink with her at the Coliseum Hotel bar.

Johnny rushes back to town and goes to see Alistair, who tells Johnny that he has not seen Langley. Alistair tells Johnny that Maida claims that she was on a shopping trip. Johnny tells Alistair to call the police and asks him if he knows who holds the note on Langley's plantation. Alistair tells Johnny that he holds the note.

Johnny goes to Mrs. Langley's room and she tells Johnny that she thinks Harry is just in a lather over the plantation and all the work. She tells Johnny that she was there during the raid and was packing for her trip. Johnny tells her that Crawford and Langley say she disappeared. But she tells Johnny that Bandar and Harry knew she was coming to the hotel, and that Harry is going to meet her here. She tells Johnny that she was a former chorus cutie when she met Harry, and she is going to ask him to take her to Singapore.

Shots ring out and they fall to the floor. The shots came from another hotel room across the street, and Johnny rushes to the other hotel where the clerk says a man named Harrison Langley rented the room. Johnny goes back to Maida's room to discover that she is gone. Johnny contacts the police, who eventually decide to pick up Langley.

At the hotel bar Johnny sees Langley and goes to talk to him. Langley admits that he came there to kill her as they walk to a small garden where they talk. Langley tells Johnny that his wife no longer loves him, and that she and Crawford love each other and only want his money. They want Langley declared mentally incompetent to get the money. The threats and terrorist activity were a front, so he came here to kill her, as there is no other answer. He tells Johnny that he has walked the streets all afternoon thinking about the situation and that he should have gone and killed her.

Johnny takes his .45 and determines that it has not been fired. Johnny tells Langley to wait and makes three calls. Johnny learns that the bullets from Maida's room were from a .38, that Bandar admitted that Maida had told him to say that she had disappeared, that Crawford is in Kuala Lumpur and will return by midnight. Also, Johnny learns that Crawford took his gun and Langley's .38 Webley, and that the clerk at the hotel identified the man who checked in as Crawford.

Johnny drives back to the plantation with Langley and along the way he hears an explosion on the road. They come upon an armored car and find Crawford and Maida in the car. Crawford has the .38 and Johnny thinks that he was the target. Langley is bitter because Maida only wanted money but she schemed and connived to get it all, but she did not succeed. She was a tramp. Langley breaks down at last and cries for his wife.

Johnny could not prevent the loss of Maida Langley, but everyone seems to have lost something.

Notes:
- Although the script title uses the word "Taun", according to a former Indonesian co-worker, the local word for "sir" or "mister" is Tuan, not Taun.
- Charles Lyon is the announcer.
- Music is by Eddie Dunstedter.

Producer: Jaime del Valle Writer: Sidney Marshall
Cast: Howard McNear, Ben Wright, Jack Edwards, William Johnstone, Jack Moyles, Virginia Gregg

Show:	**The Berlin Matter**
Show Date:	3/16/1954
Company:	Camden Life & Fidelity Company, Ltd.
Agent:	Dave Hopkins
Exp. Acct:	$693.03

Synopsis: Dave Hopkins calls and asks if Johnny has a German visa, and Johnny tells him he sleeps with it under his pillow. Sam Harvey is a consulting engineer who has just upped his insurance to $50,000 and changed beneficiaries to a new wife. Now he is dead.

Johnny flies to Berlin, West Germany and checks in at the Waldenstern Hotel. Johnny then cabs to the police to meet with Lt. Wilhelm Meissner, who updates Johnny on the case. Johnny is told that Sam Harvey was found in the harbor and was identified by papers on his body. Johnny reviews the report and notes that his body was found in Spandau, in the British Zone, but Johnny thought he worked in the American Zone.

Meissner shows Johnny the map of Berlin, with Spandau in the British Zone, just above the French Zone. Meissner thinks that Harvey probably died in the French Zone and the river currents took him to Spandau. The area of the French Zone is rough, and Harvey is not the first person to be dumped in the river there. A friend of Harvey's, Paul Turner, made a positive identification, informed his wife in Vienna, and buried the body. Johnny buys Willie a beer and then goes to see Paul Turner.

Paul tells Johnny that he does not know who killed Sam, and that he probably went to the beer festival in the area, got drunk and fell into the river. Paul tells Johnny that he never mentioned insurance, but his wife is worth every penny of the insurance. She is in Vienna and will be here soon. Paul tells Johnny that there have been a lot of tears over Sam, so try to be gentle and polite. Paul is a German interpreter for the Army, a really nice job. Paul has a wire that says Elsa is over her illness and will be there at 18:00 tonight.

Paul and Johnny go to pick up Sam's wife at Tempelhof Airport. Paul tells Johnny that he will know her when he sees her, as they had palled around before Sam married her. They meet Elsa, who is confused about who Paul is. It has been a long time she tells Johnny.

Johnny tells Elsa why he is there. She tells Johnny that she was in Vienna when Sam died, and that she has to live there because of the refugee problems. Johnny goes to his hotel and has knockwurst and sauerkraut with black beer for dinner and 10 hours of sleep with no dreams.

The next morning Meissner calls and Johnny is told that there is a barge in the British Zone, "I vill send zee car, you vill get dressed and meet zee car and you vill come!" Johnny meets Meissner on the barge and Meissner's attitude goes from "Johnny" to "Herr Dollar".

On the barge is a dead man, Curt Hausman, captain-pilot of the barge. Under his arm is a letter he had started to write. Meissner translates the letter that says, "if you wish of Sam Harvey to know, come you to the barge". The letter is addressed to Johnny Dollar.

Meissner wants to know what Johnny said to Turner and Harvey's wife that caused the murder of the boat captain. Johnny is told that Hausman was a thief and a black-marketeer and a smuggler. He was also an eel, very slippery with no evidence to convict him when caught. Johnny notes that Hausman was found near the same area where Sam Harvey was found, so he must have known something and someone killed him. Captain Hausman has a friend named Mary Fuller, an American entertainer, who came to entertain the American troops and decided to stay. She works at a carnival at Zehlendorf.

Johnny and Meissner go to see Mary Fuller. Meissner tells Mary that Curt is dead and she starts to cry. Mary does not know why he would be writing a letter to Johnny. She does not know who killed Curt, but she knows that Sam owned the barge with Curt and was a thief with him. Sam worked as an engineer when the barge business was slow. Mary tells them that she knew his wife and was her shopper. Sam would give her money and she would buy goods in the French and British zones and send them to her. She shows Johnny a pair of pierced earrings. Sam had liked them and she bought some for his wife and then had her ears pierced. She also tells them that she does not know Paul Turner.

Johnny goes to Paul Turner and gets the address for Elsa. Johnny goes to apologize to her and to give her the papers for the insurance money. She tells Johnny that she will send them to Johnny by messenger. Johnny tells her that she is a very beautiful woman and asks her to put her hair up for him to see how she would look. Johnny tells her that she is beautiful with her hair that way. Johnny cabs back to Mary and asks for the wife's address in Vienna.

Johnny takes a plane to Vienna. A woman at the address Johnny got from Mary tells Johnny that Mrs. Harvey is dead, she died yesterday. She received a wire last week and it was given to the woman who took care of her, and that the woman arranged for the funeral when she died. Johnny guesses that this other woman moved out after she died. Yes, she did, the woman tells him.

Back in Berlin, Johnny goes back to see Elsa and Paul is there. Elsa has the papers and gives them to Johnny who tears them up and asks for her real name. Johnny tells Paul that he knows everything. Sam's wife was ill and Elsa had taken care of her. The tip-off was the pierced ears. Sam's real wife had them and Elsa did not. Johnny figures that Paul was in on Sam's murder to get in on the smuggling business. Paul tells him that Curt did not want Paul in on the deal and so Paul killed him. Paul pulls a gun but Johnny beats it away from him. Elsa tells Johnny that she has nothing, and even paid for the funeral, so she deserves something, as Vienna is not so nice. Johnny says she will have to talk to a nice guy named Willie.

Notes:
- This is an AFRTS program that contains a story about seals and fish the Great Seal and those that swim in the ocean, and a story about President Millard Fillmore.

- There is a very proper German clicking of heels every time Wilhelm makes a point.
- John Lund twice makes a slip and asks why Paul's wife has not shown up instead of Sam's wife.
- Charles Lyon is the announcer.
- Music is by Eddie Dunstedter.

Producer: Jaime del Valle   Writer: Morton Fine, David Friedkin
Cast: Benny Rubin, Edgar Barrier, Gerry Gaylor, Hal March, Virginia Gregg

♦ ❖ ♦

Show: **The Piney Corners Matter**
Show Date: 3/23/1954
Company: **Tri-State Assurance Company, Ltd**
Agent: **Bob Crale**
Exp. Acct: **$120.70**

Synopsis: Bob Crale from Tri-State tells Johnny that he has a letter about the killing of Martha Williams, "look close to home" it says. The letter is from anonymous in Piney Corners, Pennsylvania. Bob tells Johnny that Martha Williams died a month ago and the company is ready to pay off the $10,000 policy.

Johnny goes to Piney Corners, Pennsylvania and meets Jake Finley, the constable. Jake tells Johnny that he has no real facts and that it could have been hunters. But she was shot with a squirrel rifle notes Johnny. The police in Philadelphia could not identify the bullet and everyone here has one of those rifles Jake tells Johnny. Jake agrees to take Johnny out to see Ben Williams, but Johnny will have to pay for the gas as the town does not have much money.

Johnny and Jake drive to the farm and stop to talk to the Keelers, the neighbors. Mrs. Keeler knows that Johnny is with Tri-State. She tells Johnny that the Williams are good neighbors and that Martha had been an invalid after an operation last year. Mrs. Keeler tells Johnny that Ben has been hanging around a girl, a real flibbertigibbet. The girl is Flora Lane who works at the Inn. Johnny tells Mrs. Keeler that the company appreciated her letter and she asks Johnny how he knew it was her. Johnny tells her that he had guessed she had sent the letter.

Johnny and Jake examine the most likely place for the shot, right next to a survey marker for a highway that would have made the land worth something. Jake explains how Martha was sitting by the window and someone shot her and got away. Johnny asks if the girl in town is pretty and if Ben was seeing her beforehand. Jake tells Johnny that Ben eats most of his evening meals there. Martha would be an invalid as long as she lived, but Jake relates that Ben is not the type. Jake tells Johnny that Mrs. Keeler liked Martha but never really liked Ben, so don't pay too much attention to her.

Johnny and Jake walk down to the farmhouse and Tom Smith, the hired man, meets them at the door and tells them that Ben is not there. Johnny asks Tom where he was when Martha was killed and Tom gets real excited and tells

Johnny that he was nowhere near the place when Mrs. Williams was shot, and leaves. Jake tells Johnny that Tom tends to get excited and is not too long on brains. He is also a dead shot and never misses.

Jake and Johnny go back to town when Ben does not show up.

Johnny goes to the Piney Inn for dinner and meets the waitress, Flora Lane. Flora recommends the pot roast and Johnny asks to talk to her. She is surprised that Johnny found her so fast, she thought they would have a chance, as Ben would never have given her a minute while his wife was alive. "Doesn't being acquitted mean anything", she asks.

She thought that Johnny knew that four years ago she was a housekeeper in Chicago where the wife died. The police said that she wanted to marry the husband and tried her for murder, but she was acquitted.

Johnny finishes dinner and goes to see Jake and tells him that Flora had told Johnny the whole story. Johnny tells Jake that he thinks he could make a case against Ben. Jake tells Johnny that the farm is mortgaged to the hilt, and that Ira Keeler has a $7,500 note on the farm for a loan he had made to Ben to pay for the operation. However, the farm is only worth $4,500. Johnny asks if Ben has a squirrel rifle, but Jake says he only has a shotgun. Johnny tells Jake that he had noticed that the hooks on the mantle were made for a longer rifle and Jake remembers seeing one there, a long time ago.

Johnny and Jake go back out to see Ben, who is home. They go back to the kitchen, where the fire is warming the house and talk. They tell Ben that they want to talk about who killed Martha. Johnny tells Ben that he has an idea, but it is only an idea. Johnny tells Ben that it looks like he killed Martha, and Flora could be the reason. Johnny notes that Mrs. Keeler thinks Ben killed Martha, and what about your squirrel rifle? Ben tells Johnny that the squirrel rifle was stolen the week before Martha was killed. Martha knew who took it and had asked Ben not to report it. Only Mrs. Keeler and Tom were in the house that week, and Tom is crazy about guns.

Jake and Johnny go to the shack Tom uses and Tom stops them with a gun. Johnny asks to look at his gun and finds that it is a .22. Johnny asks Tom what he did with Ben William's rifle, and Tom tells Johnny that Ira Keeler gave him $3 for it three weeks ago, a week after Martha was shot. Tom tells Johnny that he would never hurt Mrs. Williams. Besides the gun has never been used as it has rust in the barrel.

Johnny takes Jake's car back to see Ira Keeler, and Mrs. Keeler meets Johnny at the door. She tells Johnny that the letter was a terrible thing to do, and that she does not hate Ben. She notes that a woman on a farm wants more than hard work, and Ben would not pay attention to her.

Johnny goes in to find Ira Keeler working on his books. Johnny asks Ira about Ben's squirrel gun and Ira replies that Tom probably stole it. Johnny tells him that it was stolen from Ben. Johnny looks at the rifle over the fireplace, and there is rust all over the breech and sees that the hooks on the mantle have been there for years. Johnny tells Ira that he knows who killed Martha.

Johnny relates that most people kill for hate or gain, and this one was done for gain. Johnny asks who benefits? Ben did at first, but someone would benefit more, someone who made a $7,500 loan out of kindness, something that was not in Ira's nature. Ira tells Johnny that it was not kindness, it was good business at the time.

If the road had gone through the farm would have been worth twice that amount. Johnny tells Ira that the hooks do not fit the rifle that is on it. Ira finishes the books and tells Johnny that farming involves risks and often mistakes. He knew he made a mistake as soon as he pulled the trigger and takes Johnny out to behind the barn where the rifle is buried.

Notes:
- This is an AFRTS program that contains a story about the Coast Guard, and a story about President Andrew Johnson.
- Charles Lyon is the announcer.
- Music is by Eddie Dunstedter.
- This program was performed by Bob Bailey as *The Shady Lane Matter*. on 7/9 through 7/13/1956.

Producer: Jaime del Valle   Writer: Les Crutchfield
Cast: Jess Kirkpatrick, Parley Baer, Ralph Moody, Mary Lansing, Sam Edwards, Virginia Gregg

• ❖ •

Show: **The Undried Fiddle Back Matter**
Show Date: **3/30/1954**
Company: **Eastern Indemnity Insurance Company**
Agent: **Tom Harrison**
Exp. Acct: **$480.30**

Synopsis: Johnny is called by Tom Harrison and told about Edward Colton, a lumber baron in Portland. There has been a $10,000 payroll robbery committed by his son, and he wants the money back in 48 hours.

Johnny flies to Portland, Oregon, and goes to the Colton Building where Mr. Colton wants action. Johnny is told that his son went to the bank to pick up the payroll money and just disappeared, he is sure of it. Colton only wants the money back.

Johnny goes to see the police and Det. Podlas tells Johnny that Colton got the money from the bank, got into a cab and disappeared. The payroll money was in $20's, $10's, and $5's and Colton had a black satchel that was chained to his waist. Podlas gets a phone call and Colton's body has been found.

Johnny goes to a lumber mill on the Willamette river where he meets Cam Rogers who tells Johnny that he was checking on the crossfire and fiddle back, which is a grain pattern used by violin makers. There were three logs in the kiln that the old man was going to use for a desk for his son. When he checked inside he found the body with the empty money bag. Cam is upset that the bloodstains have ruined the wood just like the son was ruined.

Johnny goes to visit the widow, and she knows that her husband is dead. She is sure that Eddie did not steal the money.

Johnny calls Podlas and is told that the cause of death was a concussion while erect, and that the cab company has been called.

Johnny goes to the cab company and finds the driver who took Colton to his home in the 900 block of Chestnut where Colton met his blond wife.

Johnny goes to the address on Chestnut and the resident, Francine Martin, is not at home.

Johnny rents a car and goes to see Mr. Colton who tells Johnny that he knows about Francine and calls her a hustler who used to be a clerk, but was fired 10 days ago. Johnny gets her personnel records and learns that she made a play for all the men in the office. Johnny also learns that her brother is Max Wilkowsky who is a cabby.

Johnny goes to the cab company and Max tells Johnny that Francine wanted the best out of life and was leaving for Mexico on payday.

Johnny follows Max home where Francine meets him. Johnny goes in and meets Francine who tells Johnny that Eddie was going to get a divorce, and that they were going to live in Mexico. She tells Johnny that Eddie took the money to the mill while she packed, and that she used to date Cam Rogers who was sure he would get her.

Johnny leaves to go to the police but finds Cam Rogers in the back seat of his car. Cam tells Johnny to drive to the mill and tells him that Eddie was supposed to end up in the river but the plant was busy, so he hid him in the kiln. Johnny causes the car to skid and Cam is thrown across the front seat. Later Johnny finds the money in the trunk of Cam's car.

Notes:
- The announcer is Charles Lyon.
- Music is by Eddie Dunstedter.
- Bill James is credited with the part of a crying baby.
- Story information obtained from the KNX Collection in the Thousand Oaks Library.

| Producer: | Jaime del Valle | Writer: | Sidney Marshall |

Cast: Clayton Post, Ralph Moody, Jack Moyles, William Conrad, Virginia Gregg, Mary Jane Croft, Bill James

♦ ❖ ♦

Show: **The Sulphur and Brimstone Matter**
Show Date: **4/6/1954**
Company: **Eastern Indemnity Insurance Company**
Agent: **Philip Martin**
Exp. Acct: **$585.60**

Synopsis: Phillip Martin calls and asks what Johnny knows about hydroelectric power dams. There is a completion clause on a project in Venezuela, and the project is in trouble and the company will lose $5,000 a day for delays. Asa Travers had wired about problems and was killed. "I wonder if coffee is any cheaper in Venezuela?" Johnny muses.

Johnny goes to Caracas, Venezuela and meets Señor Metarzza, Asa Travers' partner. They fly to the dam site in a Cessna piloted by Metarzza and he tells Johnny that he knows of no reason why Travers was killed, and that the federal police are on the case. The government is financing the dam and it is interested in the dam's completion. Metarzza admits that there have been problems with equipment and lost or stolen material, but he thinks that there are some dishonest men involved and maybe someone is trying to slow things down to get the project to run over the scheduled date.

At the work site Johnny goes to the construction office and runs into a young lady. Inside Johnny asks for Capt. Borros, and the straw boss Bill Anthony gives Johnny a hard time. Bill does not need anyone poking around slowing things down. He tells Johnny that Borros has gone to Travers' house, about 10 miles from here. Get a company jeep and driver, it will get you out of here. Johnny asks about the girl and Bill tells him that she was Filomena Travers, Asa Travers' widow. Johnny tells Bill that their business must have been real important as neither one had wiped the lipstick from their chins!

Johnny goes to the motor pool and gets Pedro to take him to Travers' home. Pedro knows why Johnny is there and he knows that when evil men bring evil things it will bring evil. He tells Johnny that the dam is evil, and that it is not right to change the course of a river. Travers was destroyed by his evil. At Travers' house Johnny hears shots coming from a barn.

In the barn is Filomena using her shooting gallery, and she is quite proficient. She tells Johnny that she is using a .38 on a .45 frame, but it is not the same gun that killed Asa. She tells Johnny that Borros has gone, but she knows why Johnny is there. She is not grief stricken either, as she always looks forward, not to the past. Metarzza arrives and tells Johnny that they must return to the dam as Borros has halted all work on the dam.

At the work site the equipment is idle and Borros is talking to Bill Anthony. Borros tells Johnny that he halted all work to stop irreparable damage to the site. Anthony was going to blast a passage to the river way and was using too much dynamite, and it would have caused a massive landslide. Borros has discovered that more than twice as much dynamite than is required has been used. Johnny and Borros start to go and check on the charges, but someone has set them off.

The investigation showed that the proper amount of dynamite, 25 cases, had been taken from the storehouse, and that the charges were set off by a crude firing device found in the woods over the site. The damage is not as great as was thought and can be bypassed. Metarzza tells Johnny that he is going to Caracas to talk to people who can countermand Borros' orders. Borros tells Johnny that he knows that there are always men who can be bought. There have been 8 men killed by accidents so far, and he stopped construction to save lives.

As Johnny prepares to eat at the mess hall that night, Mrs. Travers calls him. She is going to Caracas and wants Johnny to visit her there. She remembers that Asa had told her that the works of the devil always carry the odor of sulfur and brimstone, and that there is an old sulfur mine close to the location of the blast. Johnny asks Pedro about the mine and he knows that it is there but has not been worked for many years.

Pedro takes Johnny to the mine, and Pedro tells Johnny that there is evil in the mine. In the mine Johnny finds dynamite cases, some empty, some full. That explains where the extra dynamite came from. Behind the cases Johnny finds the body of Bill Anthony, and a gun with the initials "GM" on the butt. Johnny realizes that Getulio Metarzza is the owner of the construction company. Johnny tells Borros what he has uncovered, and they both leave for Caracas.

Johnny checks in to the Grand Palacio Hotel and notices that the sulfur dust from the mine had turned the silver coins in his pocket almost black. Johnny goes to the Hippodromo Nacional to see Filomena Travers, and she is surprised to see him there. Johnny notes the lack of grief in her voice and tells her about the sulfur mine, and that Borros is going to pick up Metarzza right now.

Filomena pays for her drink with a coin that is almost black. She tells Johnny that the coin had been given to her so that she could burn a candle for her husband and that Pedro de la Cuesta had given it to her.

Johnny finds Borros and they both go back to the construction site to find Pedro. When they arrive at the dam site, they see Pedro with a box of dynamite. Borros prepares to fire but Johnny asks to try to talk to Pedro, but Pedro warns Johnny off.

Pedro tells Johnny that the blast will prevent the evil, it will not stop the dam but it will be a sign from heaven. Pedro tells Johnny that the dam will drown his wife, who is buried in the valley where the dam would cover it. They wish to drown her grave to make filthy money, so how could he allow it.

Pedro tells Johnny that he killed Travers because he would not listen, and that Anthony had followed him to the mine.

Borros fires at Pedro to scare him and Johnny tackles Pedro. Borros tells Johnny that he did not hit Pedro, as he did not want to risk hitting the dynamite. Johnny muses that the dynamite could have gone off when he dropped the crate!

Notes:
- Charles Lyon is the announcer.
- Music is by Eddie Dunstedter.

Producer:	Jaime del Valle	**Writer:**	Sidney Marshall
Cast:	Howard Culver, Don Diamond, Lillian Buyeff, Jay Novello, Donald Lawton		

• ❖ •

Show: **The Magnolia and Honeysuckle Matter**
Show Date: **4/13/1954**
Company: **Eastern Fire & Casualty Company**
Agent: **Bill Randall**
Exp. Acct: **$176.45**

Synopsis: Bill Randall calls Johnny and boy, you are in luck to get away from all this rain and cold, basking in the magnolias and honeysuckle. You are going to Charleston, South Carolina. The Ambrose Cooper Paper Company caught fire and burned last night and it was the second fire in two years. It killed a secretary and cost us $100,000, unless you can prove it was arson. "Maybe the mint juleps are in bloom there too" muses Johnny.

Johnny goes to Charleston, South Carolina and rents a car to drive to the paper company where he meets with Lt. Hervey. Johnny is told that there is no question of arson, as the fire burned real fast up front. Hervey tells Johnny that Robert and Norman Cooper run the company for their mother, Alice. The floor in Norman's office shows signs of deep scorching, signs of an amateur. The night watchman found the fire and turned in the alarm at 4:17. He was burned trying to pull Felicia Farrell, Norman's secretary, out of the building. It does not make much sense, why was the girl there at 4 in the morning. Norman took her out last night but now has disappeared.

Johnny goes to visit Alice Cooper at her mansion, and Robert, her brother-in-law is there too. Robert thinks Johnny should be looking in the criminal part of Charleston and not here. Alice tells Johnny that Norman is away on a hunting trip, and that he left at midnight. Robert blurts out that Norman had nothing to do with the fire and Alice tells Johnny that he left at midnight to get to the hunting camp at dawn. Norman had taken Felicia to a company dance that night and had taken her home by eleven. She was an attractive girl, but not the type for Norman.

Johnny goes to the plant, but Hervey had gone. Johnny eats at a restaurant near the paper plant and the waiter tells Johnny that it was real pretty. He saw it last night because the night man was sick and he had to work for him. There was no one around except Horace Singleton the night watchman. He came into the restaurant and had been nipping and wanted some company. Horace was talking about how happy he would be when he retired. He always seemed to spend his money on booze. That was just before the fire started. The waiter tells Johnny that he never thought to tell that to the police.

Johnny gives the information to Hervey, and they drive to Horace's shack, which is on fire. They break in and find Horace's body with an empty bottle in his hand. At least he answered one question, he did not start the last fire as no liquor smells like gasoline.

Back at Hervey's office, they figure that the arsons are being used to cover up another crime. The coroner's report says that Felicia's lungs were not burned or seared, so she was asphyxiated before the fire started. Hervey gets a call that Norman Cooper has been picked up for speeding, and Felicia's hand bag and a couple of gasoline cans were in the trunk of his car.

Norman is brought in and is not upset. He tells Johnny and Hervey that he heard the news on the radio and sped back to town. He tells them that he had brought Felicia home around 11:45 and went home. She must have forgotten her purse in the car. He tells Johnny that he always carries gas in his car, in case he runs out on the road. Last night was the only time he had taken Felicia out, as his regular date, Marianne James, had stood him up. He tells Johnny that Felicia's regular boyfriend is his uncle, Robert Cooper, the man his mother is going to marry.

Johnny goes to talk to Marianne, but she is not home, and a neighbor tells Johnny that she works at a botanical garden in the area.

Johnny drives to the garden and gets on her guide boat to talk to her. Johnny tells her that he wants to cut the botanical talk. Johnny tells her who he is and wants to talk about Felicia Farrell. Marianne tells Johnny that the only thing she knows about Felicia is what she reads in the paper. Johnny tells her that Norman said she knows about Felicia, but she tells Johnny that Norman is a darlin' thing but gets the craziest ideas. She tells Johnny that she does not make enough money to buy the clothes necessary to see people like him.

Johnny suddenly "finds" some money in the boat and gives it to her and she suddenly becomes more talkative. of course, she knows Felicia, how silly to say she didn't. She was going to go to the dance with Norman but got a headache and asked Felicia to go for her. She had never gone with Norman before, and she never went out with Robert. One of them is lying, and it is not Marianne.

Johnny goes back to the hotel and calls Hervey, who has been checking the financial records. Hervey tells Johnny that Felicia had been making regular deposits for the past two years and there was a corresponding withdrawal in Robert's account. Also, Felicia has a safety deposit box, and Johnny joins Hervey to open it.

At the bank, Johnny learns that the box is owned jointly by Felicia and Marianne James, who had been in earlier that day. In the box is a marriage license issued the year before to Robert and Felicia. So, Felicia must have been blackmailing Robert who was planning to marry Mrs. Cooper. And, Robert probably killed the watchman when he caught him killing Felicia. Johnny thinks that Marianne was in today to get the marriage certificate to blackmail Robert with, and Robert may try to get her too.

Johnny drives to Marianne's place where Norman is waiting for Marianne to come home. Norman tells Johnny that she was going to meet someone at the garden after work, some sort of business arrangement.

Johnny and Hervey rush to the garden and find Robert's car in the parking lot with Marianne's. Johnny and Hervey search the grounds and hear screams and then shots.

Johnny shoots at and hits Robert and he throws his gun down. Robert tells Johnny that she should not have tried to blackmail me. There is nothing worse than blackmail. Johnny says Felicia could think of something worse!

Notes:
- This is an AFRTS program that contains a story about getting things done via the "do it yourself" plan, and a story about President Andrew Jackson.
- Charles Lyon is the announcer.
- Music is by Eddie Dunstedter.

Producer:	Jaime del Valle Writer: Sidney Marshall
Cast:	Hal March, Herb Butterfield, Lee Patrick, William Johnstone, Howard McNear, Virginia Gregg

◆ ❖ ◆

Show:	**The Nathan Swing Matter**
Show Date:	4/20/1954
Company:	**Great Eastern Life Insurance Company**
Agent:	**Mr. Mitchell**
Exp. Acct:	**$435.05**

Synopsis: Mr. Mitchell calls and Johnny tells him that he is completely available. Mitchell tells Johnny that Nathan Swing is insured, but his body was found in the Los Angeles harbor — someone shot him. Contact Sgt. Matthews.

Johnny goes to Los Angeles, California and meets Sgt. Matthews. Johnny is told that Nathan Swing had a record and had been shot once in the chest and once in the shoulder. A stoolie has told the police that some of Jimmy Dorando's boys had met with Swing, but Swing was a small-time crook. After the killing, the special investigator Dan Fletcher, who is after Dorando on vice matters, suddenly calls off the investigation. Dorando was supposed to appear tomorrow, but now "there is not enough evidence". Matthews tells Johnny that Fletcher is thought to be an honest man.

Johnny goes to meet with Daniel Fletcher, but he is not in the office that day. A call to Matthews gets Johnny Fletcher's home address.

Johnny goes to the house, which is in a very nice area, and the butler opens the door. Johnny introduces himself to Fletcher and tells him that he is there to talk about the murder of Nathan Swing. Johnny thought that Fletcher might know something about Swing. Fletcher tells Johnny to call him tomorrow, but Johnny tells him that he will see what Jimmy Dorando has to say, and Fletcher gets anxious. Fletcher tells Johnny that he knows about people who beat around the bush and throw their weight around. Fletcher threatens Johnny, saying that he will have his job, but Johnny tells him that he will stay on the case until his insurance company says to stop. Fletcher's daughter Mary comes, in and he tells her to go back to bed, she should not be up. She asks if it is about Jimmy and she starts crying and Fletcher tells Johnny to leave.

Johnny goes to his hotel and calls Matthews. Johnny asks for the address for Jimmy Dorando. Matthews tells Johnny that it will be better to go to his café later tonight, when some undercover officers can be there to watch out for Johnny. Johnny goes to the café and asks for Dorando.

Johnny gets a scotch and water and a muscle man named Tony approaches Johnny to ask why he wants to see Dorando. Johnny tells him it is about Nathan Swing and Johnny is taken to see Jimmy Dorado in his office. "What are you investigating?" asks Jimmy. Johnny tells him about the Swing murder and Jimmy tells Johnny that he does not know anything about Swing. Also, he does not like Johnny, so don't bother me anymore.

Johnny goes out of the office and starts to leave when he sees Mary Fletcher go back to Dorando's office. Johnny waits outside until she leaves.

She drives west and Johnny follows her to a deserted pier. She is trying to jump when Johnny pulls her back and takes her crying to her car to talk. Johnny tells her who he is and she tells him that he should have let her jump, as she does not want to talk about anything. She tells Johnny she only saw Nathan Swing once, the night she killed him.

Mary stops crying and admits to Johnny that she killed Swing, even though it will ruin her father. She had been seeing Jimmy for a long time, and her father found out when Jimmy told him. Jimmy told him that Mary had killed Swing, and to call off the investigation because Jimmy has the gun that Mary used. Swing had come in to talk to Jimmy about some sort of bet. There was an argument and Swing pulled a gun. Jimmy took it away and Swing went after Jimmy with a poker. She picked up the gun and shot Swing. Johnny tells her now that Dorando is in a better position now because he has the gun. Johnny tells her that he will try to get the gun away from Dorando. She can lie long enough for your father to prosecute him, and then you can talk to the police.

Johnny drives back to Dorando's café and tries to think of some way to get the gun. Johnny remembers an alley behind the café and a window in Jimmy's office. Johnny walks back to the window and hears Dorando and Tony talking until the window is shut. Johnny sees Jimmy take the gun from a safe, put it in a box and give it to Tony.

Johnny follows Tony to Union Station where he is about to put the box in a public locker. Johnny tries to get the gun and Tony runs shooting down the platform. Tony runs into a tunnel and Johnny hits him. Johnny gets the gun and calls Matthews.

Johnny gets Dorando's address in Beverly Hills and tells Matthews to meet him there. Johnny drives to Dorando's house and climbs the fence into the yard and tries to open the French doors to the study when the lights go out.

Dorando is there when Johnny wakes up and Johnny wants to know who hit him. Dorando tells Johnny that he is trespassing and that he could kill him. Dorando tells Johnny that he had found the box, but the gun is missing and Dorando figures that Johnny was the one that killed Tony. Johnny tries to fool Dorando and stall for time until the police get there. Dorando starts to shoot Johnny when Mary comes out with the gun. Dorando and Mary fire at the same time and Mary is hit. Mary tells Johnny that she is sorry she hit him. She had looked for him at the café and then came here. She got the gun and dies before telling Johnny any more.

Dorando is dead and Fletcher won't have to prosecute. After he buried his daughter, Fletcher closed his office and took a long vacation. Maybe it helped some, but I doubt it.

Notes:
- **This is an AFRTS program that contains a story about the US Post Office, and a story about President Calvin Coolidge.**
- **Charles Lyon is the announcer.**
- **Music is by Eddie Dunstedter.**

Producer:	Jaime del Valle Writer: Blake Edwards
Cast:	Clayton Post, Tim Graham, Dick Ryan, William Johnstone, Virginia Gregg, Jay Novello, David Young

♦ ❖ ♦

Show:	**The Frustrated Phoenix Matter**
Show Date:	4/27/1954
Company:	**Washingtonian Life Insurance Company**
Agent:	**Mr. Bradley**
Exp. Acct:	**$153.50**

Synopsis: Mr. Bradley calls and asks if Johnny has read any good books lately, specifically books by Martin Vaniberg? Martin has not written anything for twenty years but wanted to change the beneficiary of his $25,000 policy. The police are looking for his wife after Martin was killed.

Johnny goes to Chicago, Illinois, gets a room at the Sherman House and cabs to the offices of the newspaper to brush up on Vaniberg. The editor suggests Johnny talk to Richard Hanley, a critic and confidant of Vaniberg for 20 years. Vaniberg's wife would be a better source as Hanley was her first husband.

Johnny cabs to Hanley's apartment and Hanley offers to tell Johnny either about the man or the writer. Hanley tells Johnny that Vaniberg was a genius as a writer in the thirties, but he followed that with twenty years of desolate life. Hanley had tried to get Vaniberg to write again for many years, but the vows were many and the accomplishments few. Hanley also tells Johnny that he had not planned to give Vaniberg his wife, and Hanley has not seen either of them in five weeks. Johnny is told that Vaniberg had nothing, and there was no reason for anyone to kill him.

Johnny goes to see Lt. Worsak who tells Johnny that Vaniberg was shot in his apartment around 11 p.m. with a .25 Beretta. Nobody heard the shots, nobody saw anyone go in our out. Dalton Towler found the body at 3 a.m. this morning. Towler was working on some earth-shattering poems and wanted to show them to Vaniberg. The police found a portable typewriter in the apartment but no manuscript.

Johnny visits Dalton Towler in Newberry Park, talking to a pair of uninterested squirrels. Johnny introduces himself and wants to talk about Vaniberg. Towler tells Johnny that Vaniberg is the final degradation of genius. Towler tells Johnny that Martin Vaniberg is not dead, as a soul such as his will rise from his ashes and write again like the Phoenix. Johnny asks who would want to kill Vaniberg, and the answer is any of the hack writers of the world. Towler tells Johnny that the wife, Elaine, was a dedicated servant to Vaniberg, and that Towler had never considered the insurance as a motive. Towler tells Johnny that Elaine was typing a manuscript at Martin Hanley's apartment.

Johnny goes back to Hanley's apartment to ask about what Towler had told him. Hanley tells Johnny that he did not mention the manuscript because his attorney was out of town and he wanted to consult with him first. Hanley expects her tonight at eight and Johnny tells Hanley that he and Worsak will be there also. Hanley tells Johnny that Elaine had left at midnight, an hour after Martin was killed.

Johnny cabs to see Worsak and finds him running out into a car. Johnny is told that a woman has taken an overdose and is in the hospital with a signed Vaniberg book, and the police had found a .25 Beretta under her pillow.

At the hospital an intern tells Johnny and Worsak that the patient is 30, Caucasian, complains of an overdose, has normal vital signs, and her stomach has been pumped. Johnny notes that the signs do not point to an overdose and the intern agrees. In the room the woman is pleading for Martin Vaniberg to forgive her, as she did not mean to do it. She does not care who Johnny and Worsak are. Martin was her only true love and she worshiped him.

Worsak recognizes her as Dolly Darling, a stripper. Even so, she tells them that she loved Martin, and that they were secret lovers. Worsak mentions the laws against suicide and filing a false crime report and suddenly her agent Sammie Farwell is a rat, as it was his idea. He told her it would be a great gimmick and now she is going to get nothing out of it. Worsak tells her that she probably will get 30-90 days, depending on the judge.

Worsak confirms that the stunt had nothing to do with Vaniberg's murder. Johnny checks out most of Vaniberg's former haunts and ends up at Towler's apartment. Johnny asks Towler about the poems he rushed to Vaniberg. He tells Johnny that they were just drivel and that he had destroyed them. Johnny asks if he had destroyed Vaniberg's manuscript as well, but Towler tells Johnny that he had not found a manuscript. Towler tells Johnny that Vaniberg was writing under contract to someone. Towler had seen it and it was filth. He would have destroyed it but it was gone. When Elaine found out what he was doing she left him. Johnny mentions that the police looking for the manuscript, and Towler tells Johnny that if the material came out it would be worse than murder.

Johnny calls Worsak and learns that Elaine has been found, in the river. She has been shot as well and Hanley is in the hospital with a breakdown. Johnny's job is done but he is curious about the gun and the manuscript. If someone knew enough to use a Beretta in Dolly's stunt, before the police knew what kind of gun it was, maybe there is a motive there.

Johnny and Worsak go to visit Sammie Farwell to see if they can find that motive. In the hallway they hear shots and go in to find Towler in the office burning the manuscript, and Farwell dead in the other room and a Beretta on the desk. Towler tells Johnny that he knew there had been a serious disagreement between Vaniberg and Farwell over Farwell's attention to Elaine. Farwell ended up shooting Vaniberg and then Elaine. Towler did not go to the police because he was only interested in the manuscript. Towler was tipped to the identity of the killer by a friend after Johnny's visit. He came up and demanded the manuscript from Farwell and they fought over the gun. All in all, things have turned out quite well in Towler's opinion.

Notes:
- This is an AFRTS program that contains a story about the Agriculture Department, and a story about the presidency of Benjamin Harrison.
- Charles Lyon is the announcer.
- Music is by Eddie Dunstedter.

Producer:	Jaime del Valle Writer: Sidney Marshall
Cast:	Dan O'Herlihy, Ken Christy, Junius Matthews, William Conrad, Virginia Gregg

♦ ❖ ♦

Show:	**The Dan Frank Matter**
Show Date:	**5/4/1954**
Company:	**Commonwealth Mutual Assurance Company**
Agent:	**Jim Bates**
Exp. Acct:	**$194.90**

Synopsis: Jim Bates calls Johnny and asks "if a chief of police got killed, what would be the most likely reason for it?" Jim has a hunch on this one, because the chief is middle aged, shot with his own gun in his own house. The beneficiary is a twenty-seven-year-old wife of eight months, the $50,000 policy is seven months old, and the wife filed a claim within 24 hours of his death. Johnny thinks he had better look into it.

Johnny goes to the great lakes town Middleboro and the home of Dan Frank. Johnny meets Pete Parker, a reporter for the local paper who is a little drunk. Pete had just asked the wife about insurance, Dan had some and Laura will probably get it. Pete tells Johnny to watch himself as the town looks sleepy, but it is wide open, with rackets and everything. The chief gets $6,000 but look at his house and his wife...very expensive. Dan was involved all right.

Mrs. Frank meets Johnny and is surprised to learn that they are paying so promptly but gets angry when she learns Johnny is an investigator. She knows they are trying to get out of paying the policy. Laura shows Johnny where Dan fell and tells Johnny that there was a noise and Dan went down to investigate and was shot with his own gun. She tells Johnny that Dan had enemies because of his job. Johnny tells her that 24 hours is too quick to file a claim and Laura tells Johnny to talk to Max Beely.

Johnny meets Max Beely, who tells Johnny that he can prove that she did not kill Dan — he was there. He and Dan were going fishing, so he spent the night at the house. He heard someone in the hall and went out when Laura turned on the lights, and the shots rang out. Laura was standing next to her room when Dan was shot. Max makes a good alibi, as he is the city attorney. Max tells Johnny that Laura has a cash register inside of her and Dan found out too late. "So that is why he needed to get involved in the rackets?" asks Johnny. Max is caught off guard and agrees.

The city commissioner, Mr. Corbit, comes in and tells Johnny that Eddie Sales killed Dan because Dan had sent Sales to jail and Sales swore he would get even, and that Sales was paroled last week. Find Sales and you will find the key to the killing and the rackets Johnny is told.

Outside, Laura honks her car horn at Johnny, who confirms that Max gave her an alibi. She tells Johnny that she is ready to be friendly and cooperative. A car speeds by and shots are fired and Laura asks why someone would shoot at Johnny, but he thinks the shots were meant for Laura.

Johnny finds Pete in a bar and asks for more information about Laura. Pete tells Johnny that Laura is a four-star tramp, a former dancer and the former girlfriend of Eddie Sales. Pete tells Johnny that he is in love with Laura and that she was his girl before Eddie Sales. Pete notes that the gun was found beside Dan, and everyone assumed he was shot with it, but it took the police two days to find out Dan had been shot with his own gun. Pete gets a call from the office and learns there is a fire at Laura Frank's place and they cannot get inside.

At the scene of the fire Johnny and Pete can only watch as the house is destroyed. Laura is in a car with Max Beely and she is sure that someone is after her. She tells Johnny that she had taken a nap and woke up with the house in flames. Max notes that the house is insured as well, and Pete tells her that now all her assets are in cash. Johnny thinks it may be Eddie's work. There are shots and they see a man staggering out of the basement of the house — it is a badly burned Eddie Sales.

At the hospital, the doctor says the odds are against Eddie. Johnny cannot figure the shots, they came before he got out of the house. The phone rings, and Laura wants to talk to Johnny in the lunchroom across the street. Johnny tells Pete to stay there and goes to meet Laura, who asks Johnny if he thinks she is attractive. She asks Johnny to turn in his report so she can get the money. Johnny wants to know why she heard the noise, and why she sent Dan downstairs and why she turned on the lights making him a perfect target. Johnny is going to wait to see what Eddie says, and if he says nothing, she is in the clear. Laura offers Johnny $10,000 to file a positive report.

Pete comes into the lunchroom and tells Johnny that a fireman told him that the cellar door was padlocked from the outside, and that Eddie fired the shots to open the door. So maybe Eddie was supposed to die in the fire, right Laura? Pete asks Johnny what he wanted to see him about and Johnny tells Pete that he did not call him and they rush back to the hospital room.

Johnny realizes that Laura called him to get him out of the room. Inside, Johnny sees Beely coming out of the elevator because the commissioner called him. They go back to the room to find no policeman at the door and commissioner Corbit holding a pillow over Eddie Sale's face. Max is sure now that Corbit was in charge of the rackets, and Corbit pulls a gun.

When Johnny asks Corbit why he had Dan killed, Max tells Johnny that he and Dan were going fishing so that Dan could spill the beans about the rackets and Laura found out and tipped off Corbit. Eddie hid out in Laura's house and she locked him in. Corbit heads for a window and falls out. Laura comes in and tells Johnny that now there are no witnesses.

Johnny tells her that her insurance claim really is a confession. The claim says that they found Dan Frank shot with his own gun, but the police did not find out for two days. So how did you know, Mrs. Frank?

Notes:
- This is an AFRTS program that contains a story about the seal of the US and the swimming variety, and a story about the presidency of John Quincy Adams.
- Charles Lyon is the announcer.
- Music is by Eddie Dunstedter.
- This program was performed by Bob Bailey as *The Open Town Matter,* broadcast on 7/23 through 7/27/1956.

Producer:	Jaime del Valle	Writer:	Les Crutchfield
Cast:	Jim Nusser, Peter Leeds, Virginia Gregg, Joseph Kearns, Frank Nelson, Joseph DuVal		

♦ ❖ ♦

Show: **The Aromatic Cicatrix Matter**
Show Date: 5/11/1954
Company: **Eastern Maritime & Insurance Company**
Agent: **James Harrington**
Exp. Acct: **$196.10**

Synopsis: Johnny is called by James Harrington and told that the cabin cruiser of Thomas Bellamy exploded and he was killed, and there was a $10,000 policy. James notes that this is the second husband lost in a boating accident in three years.

Johnny goes to the British Colony of Bermuda and gets a room at the Bermudian Hotel. Johnny goes to Harrington's office, but it is closed so Johnny goes to see Inspector Brice who tells him that the explosion killed Bellamy and almost destroyed the boat, which was at the dock in St. George's harbor.

Johnny goes to the Bellamy residence where a young lady on a motor bike greets him. Betty Bellamy introduces herself and tells Johnny that "old poopsie" Harrington told her that he was coming. She tells Johnny that Thomas Bellamy was her stepfather, and that her father was killed the same way. She tells Johnny that Thomas was murdered, but not by his wife, and Betty suspects poopsie.

Johnny goes to the Bellamy perfume factory and meets Michael Forrest who tells Johnny that he heard Thomas and Harrington arguing about some trust agreements. Michael tells Johnny that Mrs. Bellamy and Mr. Harrington are in the lab. While they are talking there is an explosion and Harrington staggers out, and Johnny goes in to get Mrs. Bellamy. Harrington tells Johnny that Mrs. Bellamy had just lit a cigarette, but there was nothing in the lab that was flammable.

Johnny goes to the boat and meets Forrest, who tells Johnny that there was ether and benzene in the lab that Harrington had suggested as a new way to process the perfume.

Johnny goes to the police who tell Johnny that Mrs. Bellamy is ready to confess. Johnny goes to the hospital, but the doctors will not let him in. Johnny meets Dr. Randall who tells Johnny about a cicatrix, which is an internal scar.

Insp. Brice arrives and tells Johnny about a confession by Betty, and that the estate of £5,000 would go to Betty. Johnny goes to see Betty who tells Johnny that she wants to apologize to poopsie because her mother has just died, and Betty tells Johnny that she hated her mother.

Johnny goes back to see Dr. Randall who tells Johnny that the cicatrix was a mental scar on Betty caused by the death of her father and had caused her to go to a sanatorium. Johnny goes to Harrington's office and he tells Johnny that he had suggested the solvents, but there was no record of purchases. Harrington tells Johnny that he remembers the smell of ethyl oxide, which was not the same as medical ether, and that he had joked that Dr. Randall should be there.

Johnny goes to a chemist shop and gets the evidence he needs, that Miss Betty Bellamy was the purchaser.

Johnny calls Insp. Brice and learns that Betty is missing. Johnny eats dinner and finds Betty on the hotel terrace. Betty tells Johnny that she has found love, and that Mike had suggested coming to the hotel.

Brice arrives and tells Johnny that he will get Michael while Johnny occupies Betty until the doctor arrives.

Notes:
- The announcer is Charles Lyon.
- Music is by Eddie Dunstedter.
- Story information obtained from the KNX Collection in the Thousand Oaks Library.

Producer:	Jaime del Valle	Writer:	Sidney Marshall
Cast:	Ben Wright, Tudor Owen, Virginia Gregg, Hal March, Eric Snowden		

♦ ❖ ♦

Show: **The Bilked Baroness Matter**
Show Date: 5/18/1954
Company: Eastern Indemnity & Insurance Company
Agent: Ben Turner
Exp. Acct: $50.45

Synopsis: Ben Turner calls and asks Johnny how he likes hobnobbing around nobility. Johnny is going to meet Olga Zsarvas who had $100,000 in furs and jewelry stolen from her penthouse last night. A former photographer husband just filed for bankruptcy and she has been seen with him lately.

Johnny drives to New York City and the penthouse of the Baroness Zsarvas. Inside she tells Johnny that the maid is off and she is on the way out to a cocktail party. She has told the police everything and tells Johnny to see them. She relents and tells Johnny that she noticed the items missing at about

3:00 when she got home. She had some friends over, they went to a show and then to dinner and Thomas Bentley, her former husband brought her home. Now she really must go as good friends are irreplaceable, but the jewels are insured.

Johnny talks to the staff of the hotel and only learns that Olga's place is a gathering place for every screwball in New York.

Johnny goes to see Lt. Lewisson, who tells Johnny that it probably was an inside job. The only way in was with a key and whoever did it knew exactly where to go. Also, Olga gives out keys like trinkets, so it could have been anyone. Lewisson agrees with Johnny that no one could have gotten out with the furs without being seen. The doorman says that one of her friends, Vasili Udescu stayed behind and that he has a record for running a confidence game and shoplifting furs. Lewisson thinks that the case might be closed when they pick Vasili up. Johnny thinks that is not the case, as he has not had an easy case in three years and doubts that Lewisson has had one either.

Johnny goes to the studio of Thomas Bentley, where a photo shoot is underway. During a quick break Johnny introduces himself and is told to come back some other time. Johnny thinks that it is funny how he is in full operation when he is supposed to be broke. Bentley tells Johnny that there is no tie-in between the robbery and him. Olga always moves upwards and never would get involved in fraud to help out a former husband. He tells Johnny that he went to see her because he wanted a $20,000 loan from Olga, but she would not give it to him. So, the creditors are letting him run the shop until he gets the money to pay his bills.

A muscleman actor wants to talk about using a loincloth to show off his body. "The body of Hercules and the brain of a second-class ape" notes Bentley. Thomas asks if Johnny could offer a reward for the return of the goods, just out of curiosity.

Johnny calls Lewisson and learns that Udescu has been picked up with some the jewels in his apartment.

At Lewisson's office, Udescu is complaining about being treated like a common criminal and will sue them for every penny. Lewisson shows him some jewels that are covered by the policy. Udescu tells them that he was at the party last night and did not go out because he had seen the play and did not want to be bored and he knows nothing about the jewels. Johnny now has some of the jewels but still needs to find $87,000.

Johnny goes to the Plaza Hotel, and Tom Bentley calls to tell Johnny that he knows where the loot is.

Johnny calls Lewisson and goes to meet Bentley at his studio, but Lewisson is there already. Lewisson tells Johnny that Tom Bentley is in the back of the studio, dead, shot by the .357 magnum rifle lying next to him on the floor.

Johnny goes back to the office with Lewisson and meets Olga and the model he had seen earlier at Bentley's studio, Herta Werner. Olga is ready to sign a complaint when Herta reminds her of the secret cabinet in the den where she had placed the jewels during a taffy pull. She had forgotten about them and had included them in the list of items stolen. Poor, dear Vasili. Olga signs a statement about the jewels and leaves with Herta. Lewisson calls down stairs and there is nothing new on the killing, no prints and no witnesses.

Johnny cabs to the apartment of Herta Werner, who is expecting him. Johnny reminds her how she had batted her eyes at him at police headquarters and asks her how much she wants to give him information, and she wants $1,000, which will require a lot of information. The apartment is covered with pictures of Harley Townsend, the model Johnny had seen at the studio complaining about the loincloth. Harley is Herta's soon to be ex-husband. Herta tells Johnny that Harley has a key to Olga's apartment. He was at the party and left at 12:30 and came back at 1:30 with Tom Bentley.

Bentley had called today at 7:00 and Harley blew up. He said he would not settle for $10,000 when he could get $50,000. Harley told Bentley he had better wait for him and get over there, and he took some cartridges with him. She does not know where Harley is either.

Johnny cabs back to Lewisson and tells him of the conversation. Lewisson thinks that Bentley and Harley worked the job together, Bentley wants $20,000 to turn the stuff back in and Harley objects and kills him. Now they need to find Harley. Johnny thinks that maybe someone posing as a service man could have gotten upstairs, but the street was torn up for repairs, preventing a pickup and would not be fixed until today.

Johnny and Lewisson go to the building and check with the superintendent who tells them that the street is fixed and the service people are coming in regular now. There is a new laundry man there now. Maybe he will take something out as he probably is in the laundry room now.

Johnny and Lewisson go to the laundry room and find Harley pushing a laundry cart out. Lewisson calls out for Harley to stop but Harley pulls a gun and fires. Harley is shot and killed, and the furs and jewels are in the laundry cart.

They were kept in a storage room overnight. Johnny notes that they need to go to the shooting range more often, as one of the coats has a hole in the sleeve.

Notes:
- Charles Lyon is the announcer.
- Music is by Eddie Dunstedter.

Producer:	Jaime del Valle	Writer:	Sidney Marshall
Cast:	Hal March, Mary Lansing, Parley Baer, William Johnstone, Peter Leeds, Jay Novello, Virginia Gregg, Joseph DuVal		

Show:	**The Punctilious Firebug Matter**
Show Date:	**5/25/1954**
Company:	**Eastern Indemnity & Fire Company**
Agent:	**Jeff Connors**
Exp. Acct:	**$309.25**

Synopsis: Jeff Connors calls and asks Johnny to come to Dallas. There is a firebug on the loose and there have been four fires in four weeks. The claims total $95,000 so far. Come on down, there will be another one tonight, the firebug hits Tuesday nights.

Johnny goes to Dallas, Texas and meets with Jeff Connors who outlines the fires so far, with claims of $95,000. The fire starts every Tuesday at 11:00 p.m. Len Borchardt says that the bug may be in the insurance office, but there is no reason to suspect anyone. Jeff is sure he will lose his job if the fires do not stop. Lt. Borchardt calls and there has been another fire in an apartment building. Jeff realizes that the policy was just written that week.

Johnny and Jeff go to the site and meet Borchardt. There is not much to do until the building cools down in the morning. Johnny is told that a man in the building reported the fire, but he was trapped in the building and does not know his wife and kids died in the building. By 1:00 p.m. the only witness has died on the way to the hospital. Borchardt tells Johnny that he will find evidence of a candle fuse when they search the ashes. Borchardt suspects someone in the office and mentions that Jeff's personal problems are not keeping him from working. His wife has been sick and he recently lost a child in a house fire.

Johnny goes to the office and finds a woman there. She is Sally Martin, Jeff's secretary. She tells Johnny that she came by after a date to get some paperwork ready for Jeff. The papers are for the building that just burned. Sally suggests to Johnny that Jeff answer any more questions. Sally's date, Bill Trendler comes in and Sally relates the details of their date, but Bill seems to know nothing about it.

Later after a short nap Johnny has breakfast and meets with Borchardt, who tells Johnny that there was a 1953 Ford involved in a hit and run in the area of the fire last night, and it was registered to Jeff Connors. The report detailed how Connor's car was at the scene around 9:00 p.m. Johnny tells Borchardt that Jeff was driving a Plymouth Coupe when he picked him up at the airport. Borchardt tells Johnny that the police have issued an APB for Connors.

Johnny takes a cab to the Connors home. The wife tells Johnny that Jeff went to have his car fixed. Johnny tells her that he came to see her. She tells Johnny how Jeff fell apart when they lost their son. He bottled up his emotions and would not talk about it. He has been depressed since the recent fires and she suggested moving or sports. Jeff has been out on Tuesdays lately.

Johnny checks out the other fire locations and finds nothing. Johnny calls Borchardt and learns that Sally and Bill's story checks out. Bill Trendler used to work for Jeff, but quit to open a bowling alley.

Johnny goes to the bowling alley and talks to Bill about the fires. In his office, Johnny asks Bill about working for Jeff. Bill tells Johnny that he was just not a good insurance agent. He relates that Jeff came here occasionally, and he last saw him four weeks ago with Sally. Johnny is suspicious about Bill's story.

Johnny calls Sally from the hotel but she is not in. Borchardt calls and tells Johnny that they have found Jeff's car, in 12 feet of water. Johnny goes to the location and when the car is lifted from the river, there is no one in it. Borchardt drops Johnny off at the hotel and then Johnny goes to talk to the elevator man in Jeff's office. Johnny learns that Sally Martin had been there, and someone was waiting for her in a car.

Johnny cabs to Sally's apartment and pounds on the door. Sally lets Johnny in and Johnny asks her where Jeff is and Sally says she does not know where Jeff is. She tells Johnny that Mrs. Connors called last night. She usually calls on Tuesday's to get information on new policies but had called today and got the address for a new apartment policy. Johnny rushes to the apartment building and meets Borchardt. Sally's car is in the alley as they move in.

Johnny and Borchardt find Jeff in the car. He tells them that he wanted to handle this himself. He tells Johnny that he ditched the car to cover up the problem. Jeff tells Johnny that his wife is in the building, setting the fuse and Borchardt goes in to get her. Jeff tells Johnny that Sally is not involved. It does not make much sense that his wife is a firebug. She was such a lovely girl.

Johnny has seen fires burn everything, but this is the first time he has ever seen a fire burn the heart out of a man. He does not want to ever see that again.

Notes:
- **Charles Lyon is the announcer.**
- **Music is by Eddie Dunstedter.**

Producer:	Jaime del Valle	Writer:	Sidney Marshall
Cast:	Hal March, Barney Phillips, Jeanne Bates, Sam Edwards, Virginia Gregg, Jim Nusser		

◆ ❖ ◆

Show:	**The Temperamental Tote Board Matter**
Show Date:	6/1/1954
Company:	**Washingtonian Life Insurance Company**
Agent:	**Ben Gordon**
Exp. Acct:	**$354.95**

Synopsis: Ben Gordon calls Johnny with a strange case. Luis Alvarado has a $50,000 policy and owns a racetrack in Puerto Rico with his brother. He was found with a winning ticket on a long-shot in his hand and a .38 bullet hole in his chest.

Johnny goes to San Juan, Puerto Rico, checks in at the Carib Hilton, and meets Captain Cardenas. Capt. Cardenas tells Johnny that the insurance has nothing to do with his murder as Tony Randolph, the gambler, has been trying to buy the racetrack, but Luis threw him out. Luis was last seen at 6:00 p.m. and he was killed with a .38 at about 4:00 this morning. Tony has an alibi — he was asleep. The winning ticket was $72.00 to win, but it has no bearing on the murder. Cardenas tells Johnny that Luis and his brother Jose were very close. But so were Cain and Abel notes Johnny.

Johnny goes to the racetrack offices where he meets Maria Rodriguez, Jose's secretary. She was expecting Johnny and tells him that she has to work but also acts as hostess to special guests. She tells Johnny that she can meet him at 8:00 that night.

Johnny cabs to Tony Randolph's hotel and meets him. Tony admits to Johnny that he wanted to buy the racetrack, but the Alvarado boys are playing hard to get. As for the fight with Luis, well they were just clowning around. Tony does not know who killed Luis, he was a nice guy. Tony tells Johnny that he will use his connections to look into the murder for Johnny.

Johnny goes back to the track to meet with Jose but Cardenas is there and tells Johnny that Jose has been shot at his home. Johnny and Cardenas go to Jose's home and meet his son, Tomás. In the living room is a dead man with a .38 near his hand. He is Julio Mendoza, a former employee. Tomas tells Johnny that he heard angry voices and then heard his father cry out. Tomas brought his .45 Colt automatic to the room and Julio shot at him, so he shot Julio. Tomas tells Johnny that his father is unconscious and has a bad heart.

Johnny is told that Julio ran a pari-mutuel machine at the track and was fired by Luis for cheating. Johnny speculates that the pari-mutuel ticket under Julio's arm has something to do with it. The ticket was on the same horse as the ticket that was in Luis' hand.

Johnny goes to his hotel and eats. Cardenas calls and tells him that Julio's gun is the same one that killed Luis, so case closed. Later Tony Randolph calls Johnny to tell him that Mendoza is the wrong cookie. Someone has figured out how to beat the races. Go ask Jose Alvarado about it.

Johnny cabs to Maria's address and meets her in her swank apartment. She is dressed and ready to go. But Johnny wants to ask some questions about the pari-mutuel machines first. Maria tells Johnny that the pari-mutuel machine records each ticket and it places the total bets on the tote board. The system is automatic and fool-proof. The pari-mutuel system only pays out as much money as is bet, but $21,000 was bet on the fourth race and $26,000 has been paid out, all on $10 winning tickets. Maria tells Johnny that she saw the bookkeeper's totals last night after the track closed. Luis and Jose usually were the only ones to see the figures but she saw them because she stayed late. She tells Johnny that Tomas is in charge of the guards and security, and that Julio Mendoza ran a $10 machine.

Johnny cabs to Cardenas' office, but he is unimpressed with the information because the machine cannot be fixed and each ticket has a unique number punched on it.

Johnny borrows a car and goes to talk to Tony Randolph again. Johnny wants to know who Tony is gunning for to get Johnny off the hook. Johnny wants some professional advice: what if someone figures out how to beat the system and Luis found out and someone killed him.

Tony tells Johnny that in order to beat the system you could print your tickets. You could use the recorded numbers to print your own tickets with the tote board off.

Johnny goes back to Cardenas with his theory. Johnny learns that the head bookkeeper left after the seventh race for a personal matter and has been killed in an auto accident. Cardenas gets a phone call and learns that the gun found by Julio was registered to Jose Alvarado. Johnny calls Maria and asks to see her.

Cardenas and Johnny go to the racetrack and the watchman tells them that no one is there. They spot a light in the ticket office and Johnny figures that someone is running the machines by hand. The person in the office hears them and calls out. Cardenas yells "police" and there are shots. Tomas Alvarado is wounded and does not want to die at the track. Tomas confesses to the murder of Julio and Luis but recants after he learns he will live. Cardenas tells Johnny that he will take care of the unfinished business while Johnny goes to see Maria.

Johnny goes to see Maria to take care of his unfinished business. Johnny tells her of the events of the night and she tells Johnny that Tomas would have had everything if he had waited. Johnny tells her that there was probably some woman working with him. "What did you do with the tickets," Johnny asks her, "sell them to a fence?" Johnny tells her that she tipped her hand when she told Johnny that she had seen the bookkeeper's report, but she did not know that he had left early. Johnny drops her at the police station.

Jose was still too ill for visitors and Johnny did not get to see him. How can you give $50,000 in one hand and take away a son with the other?

Notes:
- This program has some problems with an echo that masks Maria's last name. On the script title page and in the body of the story it is Rodriguez, in the program it sounds like Rolsan.
- Charles Lyon is the announcer.
- Music is by Eddie Dunstedter.

Producer:	Jaime del Valle **Writer:** Sidney Marshall
Cast:	Hal March, Edgar Barrier, Don Diamond, Lillian Buyeff, Ted de Corsia

◆ ❖ ◆

Show:	The Sara Dearing Matter
Show Date:	6/8/1954
Company:	Federal Life Insurance Company
Agent:	Ed Gross
Exp. Acct:	$372.25

Synopsis: Ed Gross calls and wants Johnny to investigate the death of Sara Dearing, the silent movie actress who retired in the twenties and supposedly died in a fire. There is a rumor that she did not die from the fire, and her estate is the beneficiary of her policy.

Johnny flies to the Inglewood International Airport and drives to Palma, California. Johnny visits the Palma News and asks for the editor and runs into trouble, he is expecting a man and meets a woman, Maggie Lacey, and no, she does not need any printing supplies.

Johnny tells her that he wants some information on the article about Sara Dearing's death, and he tells her who he is and why he is looking into the death. Maggie tells Johnny that the coroner says she was burned to death, but Maggie found a medicine bottle in the ruins and the contents were for a very powerful medicine. She thinks that the two men who visited her caused the fire.

She tells Johnny that there are two men who visit her every year on her birthday, and Maggie took their picture last year. They left on the 6:20 bus and the fire started at 8:00. Maggie tells Johnny that Sara was a recluse and died broke. There was just enough money to pay Hilda Brauer, the maid.

Johnny visits Dan Cox, the sheriff, and Dan tells Johnny that the reports are unfounded. As for the drugs, they could have been purchased anywhere, and the two men are old friends who come every year, and no, I will not give you their names. Dan tells Johnny that Sara did not commit suicide and preferred solitude. As for her health, she was always in frail health. Also, the coroner felt that an autopsy was not needed, and Dan is also the coroner.

Johnny visits Hilda Brauer the maid, who is very upset. She tells Johnny that she had been to the movies and there was a fire when she came back. She tried to rescue Sara but could not. She knows nothing of the two men and cannot say any more, so go away. Dan Cox drives up and tells Johnny to leave them in peace and do not trespass on the property again. On the way out, Johnny notices that there are four photographs of the same man on a table.

Back at the newspaper office, Johnny asks Maggie for the picture of the two men, and one of the men is the man in the photos in Sara's house. Johnny borrows the photo and heads for the Hollywood Library. Johnny spends four hours looking through the standard casting directories and finds his man in the 1928 edition. His name was Neville Thomas. His agent was Matty Freeman. Johnny phones the artist's guild and discovers that Matty now runs a restaurant.

Johnny visits the restaurant and is met by Matty Freeman. Johnny shows Matty the photo and tells him that he has a witness to his being in Palma. He tells Johnny that he was in the business when Sara was acting. Johnny tells Matty that he has an opportunity to clear his name of suspicion, but Matty tells him that Sara died in a fire. Johnny wants to know where Neville is but Matty does not know where he is. When Johnny mentions getting police assistance, Matty tells him that Neville is in his office.

In the office Neville tells Johnny that Sara was a vixen and a temperamental woman. Neville last saw her when they made their final picture, but Johnny tells him he was there on the day she died. Neville admits he did visit occasionally, that Sara was in love with him but he only pitied her. He had read that she died in a fire, but Neville can prove he was in Matty's apartment at the time. Johnny realizes that their alibis are well rehearsed, and on the way out he sees Dan Cox talking to Matty.

Johnny gets a room in a hotel, takes a shower and takes a sleeping pill. Later the phone rings, and Maggie is calling. She has to see Johnny right away. She is in Hollywood and will meet Johnny in the lobby in five minutes.

When Maggie gets there Johnny is still half-asleep from the pill. Maggie has done some research on Sara Dearing and shows Johnny a picture of the people who will be receiving her estate: Hilda, Matty, Neville and Dan.

Johnny sends a wire and goes back to bed. Ed Gross calls Johnny about the wire and wants to know what is up. Ed tells Johnny that he has received a letter from the estate, and Dan Cox mailed it.

Johnny drives back to Palma and goes to see Hilda and finds out he is expected, as Dan Cox is there. Dan tells Johnny that Hilda is ill and cannot be disturbed. Johnny reads the picture caption and Dan tells him that Johnny probably thinks that the four of them killed Sara for the estate.

Dan tells Johnny that Sara was not murdered. She was dead when the fire started. Hilda came home, found the open bottle of sedatives and thought that Sara had committed suicide, so to protect her reputation, she set the fire to destroy the evidence.

Johnny is ready to report death by suicide, but Dan tells Johnny that there is more. After Matty and Neville had visited, Sara had another visitor, who is down the hall.

Johnny is introduced to Dr. James Harding, and he tells Johnny that he has broken up his first vacation in years. Dr. Harding tells Johnny that he was an old friend of Sara's and her doctor. He had stopped by on his way to the desert, and Sara was very ill and was dying and was in a great deal of pain. So, he administered the sedatives to ease her pain, and she died peacefully. Dr. Harding then went to Dan's office and left a death certificate on Dan's desk and left. Hilda returned and found the sedatives, and the rest you know.

Dan reported that Sara died in the fire so that he would not have to charge a dear old friend for arson. Hilda did set the fire, but do you think she committed a crime? Johnny says no, and leaves.

Notes:
- This is an AFRTS program that contains a story about the presidency of James Monroe, and a story about the State Department.
- Charles Lyon is the announcer.
- Music is by Eddie Dunstedter.

Producer: Jaime del Valle Writer: Don Sanford
Cast: Joseph DuVal, Lillian Buyeff, Tom Tully, Jeanette Nolan, Don Diamond, William Johnstone, Jack Edwards

Show:	**The Paterson Transport Matter**
Show Date:	6/15/1954
Company:	**Eastern Indemnity & Insurance Company**
Agent:	**Tom Benson**
Exp. Acct:	**$184.45**

Synopsis: Tom Benson wants Johnny to go to Kansas City as fast as possible, maybe he can stop a homicide. The Paterson Transportation Company has had a series of six robberies and beatings. The last driver is in the hospital.

Johnny flies to Kansas City, Missouri and is met by Walt Hendricks, VP of the Paterson Transport Company who outlines the events so far. Walt explains that the man will buy something C.O.D. and have it delivered to a vacant house and then beats the driver. The police have been riding with the drivers, but the last man got beaten in his own garage after coming home from a movie with his wife.

Johnny gets a room and a Paterson car for his use. Johnny talks to Lt. Herman about the robberies and learns that each one has either been at the farthest point in the route or the last stop on the route, like the robber is familiar with the routine of the drivers. He has gotten more violent with each robbery, and Herman thinks he must be a psycho. The description of the man notes a limp in the left leg. A look at the map shows that the robberies seem to form a rough circle. They know Milton Speers is next and are watching him. Herman hopes the man will try when the police are on a truck.

A report comes in about a Paterson truck involved in an accident where the driver was killed. The truck was in for repairs and was being test-driven by Milton Speers.

Johnny and Herman drive to the scene and learn that the truck suddenly veered into a parked car. The driver did not die from the impact, so maybe he had a heart attack. Johnny wonders why the truck was being test-driven on a residential street, and why it was going fast enough to cause skid marks before it crashed, and why it was Milton Speers.

Mrs. Robertson, a local woman, is upset and wants to talk to Herman. She tells him that the citizens need to be protected, as they cannot even park their cars on the street without drunk drivers hitting them. She tells Herman that she was in her apartment playing whist when the accident happened. The driver had to be drunk, because she saw one man walk away from the crash and go off limping down the street.

Johnny gets the driver's statements for all of the accidents and the driver who was beaten last night dies. Johnny meets Walt Hendricks, who tells Johnny that Milt had a perfect record. Johnny tells Walt that, according to the police, Speers was the next driver to be hit. Walt tells Johnny that Speer's truck broke down and he went out alone to test the truck. Counting Speers, every driver has been hit. Johnny gives 8-5 the robber will try something.

Johnny goes back to Herman's office and learns that Speers died from a .22 bullet in the brain. Herman gets a phone call from Mrs. Robertson who has just seen the man in the truck outside her apartment.

Johnny and Herman go and talk to Mrs. Robertson, who tells them that the same man she saw this morning was looking at her car. She is positive about the man because he was limping and wearing a gray suit and went into the bar at the corner.

In the bar, Johnny spots the man and they search him. The man is Gerald Wesley, and he tells Herman that he just got into town and was looking at the car out of curiosity. Herman takes Wesley down to the office and Wesley has nothing to say. He knows nothing about the robberies but had read about them in the papers and has just come from Folsom Prison in California. Herman wires Folsom and they verify that Wesley had been paroled the day before. Mrs. Robertson looks at a line-up and makes a perfect identification, of Sgt. Grayson.

Johnny goes back to the garage where Walt is looking for drivers. Johnny tells him that the man is familiar with the routine, so maybe money is the frosting and he has a grudge. Walt tells Johnny that the company has a good labor record, and he even called Mrs. Thompson his former secretary. She used to work for the company and was involved in a car accident and was crippled. She talked to her husband who knew about the company through her, but they could think of nothing. Mr. Thompson thought he knew the pattern and had warned Milt to be careful.

Johnny goes to the hotel and calls Tom Benson to have him look through the records on the Thompson accident. In forty-five minutes Tom calls back and tells Johnny that the Thompsons had been at a party at the company and Mr. Thompson had had too much to drink. On the way out, he drove into the wrong lane, and a delivery truck hit him. The driver was killed and Mrs. Thompson suffered two broken vertebrae. Mrs. Thompson gets a lifetime income of $100 a month and the husband just got out of the hospital.

Johnny visits the Thompsons and is met by a practical nurse and then talks to Mrs. Thompson who is very appreciative but still would like to be able to be up and about. Her husband Charlie just left, and he feels terrible about the drivers and has been so worried. He has wanted to ride along with the drivers and protect them. He has felt so protective ever since the accident. He is wonderfully forgiving. He told her that the robber would go from one driver to another. He is determined that nothing will happen. He is going to protect Mr. Hendricks.

Johnny calls the police and then calls Walt Hendricks but gets a busy signal. Johnny drives to the garage, but Walt is not in the office. Johnny goes to the garage and calls for Mr. Thompson only to be answered by shots which Johnny returns. Walt comes out of an office and they find Charlie Thompson dead. Johnny tells Walt that someone had to stop him.

Ballistics verified that Thompson's .22 Colt had killed Speers. Johnny talks to Mrs. Thompson, who somehow believes that her husband died a hero while capturing the bandit single-handed.

Notes:
- This is an AFRTS program that contains a story about the presidency of Grover Cleveland, and a story about the value of the word security
- The original title, according to the script tile page is *The Perilous Parcel Matter.*
- Charles Lyon is the announcer.
- Music is by Eddie Dunstedter.

Producer:	Jaime del Valle	Writer:	Sidney Marshall
Cast:	Clayton Post, Hal March, Ed Begley, Hy Averback, Jim Nusser, Lee Patrick, Virginia Gregg		

♦ ❖ ♦

Show: **The Arthur Boldrick Matter**
Show Date: 6/22/1954
Company: **Corinthian All Risk Insurance Company**
Agent:
Exp. Acct: **$77.30**

Synopsis: Dr. Karfe calls Johnny and advises him that Arthur Boldrick is lucky to be alive. Johnny can see Boldrick later that evening. Sgt. Wright hopes that Boldrick will talk to Johnny, as he is not the police.

Johnny goes to the Emergency Hospital in Hartford, Connecticut to talk to Arthur Boldrick who tells Johnny he was shot by a man in the alley behind his garage and cannot remember what he looked like. Arthur thinks that the man was after his car keys, and when Arthur pushed him, the man panicked and shot him. Arthur cannot give a good description of the man and asks Johnny if his wife can come to see him, as he sure wants to see his wife.

Johnny goes to the police and gives Sgt. Wright his report about a man in blue work clothes or overalls with a small caliber gun.

Johnny goes to see Mrs. Velma Boldrick who lives in an area called "an older part of town" rather than a slum. Velma Boldrick shows Johnny where the shooting took place and tells Johnny that she heard shouting and ran outside but saw no one. Johnny is sure that the neighbors should have seen something at that time of the evening.

A neighbor, Will Wheeler, comes over and chides Johnny for bothering Velma. Will tells Johnny what he knows and relates to Johnny that theirs is a rotten neighborhood with rotten people. Johnny mentions that the wounds are aggravating an injury to a lung obtained in the war.

Johnny goes to see Wright and meets Mrs. Cole who tells them that she was working in her garden and saw a tan or brown car driving up the alley at the time of the shooting. She though the car was backfiring but learned later it was gunfire. Wright tells Johnny that so far nothing fits, almost everyone saw nothing and one person sees a car.

Johnny goes to see Arthur with Wright and accuses Arthur of protecting someone. They tell Arthur of the conflicting evidence and Arthur finally admits to them that he was seeing his ex-wife without telling anyone. He was hurting her husband, his wife and the neighbors. Arthur has a relapse and is near death.

Johnny and Wright go to see Anna, the ex-wife, and Thomas Hood her husband. Wright tells her that Arthur told them that her husband had shot him. Johnny is told that Thomas is out of town on business and left at four. Since Boldrick was shot at five thirty he had left in plenty of time to shoot Arthur. Johnny is also told that Thomas has a tan sedan. Anna begs Johnny not to tell her husband about them, as he does not know anything. Anna will not tell Johnny where Thomas is, as she does not want him to find out about them.

Johnny and Wright go back at the hospital and learn that Arthur had given a deathbed statement naming Thomas as the shooter. Johnny goes back to see Velma to tell her of the statement, and the neighbor Will is there. Will is told about the statement and is surprised that Thomas Hood would kill Arthur. Will does not know if Velma knows about the first wife.

Back at police headquarters, a Mr. Mandel comes in to say that he might have been the car in the alley. He was delivering a repaired radio in the area and drove down the alley on the way home. He did not hear any shots as the alley is bumpy, and his car has a lot of loose bolts and is very noisy. Johnny and Wright go to see Velma after reviewing the facts. She tells Johnny that she knows Arthur has died and only knew about the affair when Will had told her that day.

After a few well-placed accusations by Johnny, Velma breaks down and admits she shot Arthur. He was going to see Anna and had told Velma where he was going. She tells Johnny that Will had lied and admits that she went outside and shot him.

Johnny thinks that Velma will get a "widows special" for second-degree murder and will be out in two years. So, the insurance company will have that long to figure out how to cancel the policy.

Notes:
- This program was performed on 6/16/1951, but with a different cast and crew.
- The announcer is Charles Lyon.
- Music is by Eddie Dunstedter.
- Story information obtained from the KNX Collection in the Thousand Oaks Library.

Producer: Jaime del Valle   Writer: Gil Doud
Cast: Lou Krugman, Parley Baer, Jeanette Nolan, Tom Tully, Frank Nelson, Mary Lansing, Virginia Gregg, Charles Calvert

◆ ❖ ◆

Show: The Woodward Manila Matter
Show Date: 6/29/1954
Company: Columbia All-Risk Insurance Company
Agent: Ralph Weadon
Exp. Acct: $2,611.80

Synopsis: Ralph Weedon calls to tell Johnny that the burglary take is about $55,000 and that an American clerk named Blake has disappeared. Johnny will be staying at the Hotel Tondo, and Ralph will contact him if he gets additional information.

Johnny flies to Manila, Philippines to investigate a burglary and is met by Floyd McDonald and Irving Morgan of the Woodward Hardware Company who take him directly to the office. McDonald tells Johnny that he had discovered the loss on Monday morning when he found the safe open. McDonald tells Johnny that the U. S. headquarters required them to keep the money on hand for monthly shipments home. The managers disagree over the clerk, Dan Blake. McDonald trusts Dan, and Morgan feels he is guilty as he had access to the office. Blake has been missing four days with no sign, but it is easy to drop out of site in the area.

In his room, Johnny orders gimlets and waits for his luggage as he watches the harbor area.

Johnny then goes to the police and talks to Sgt. Malvar who is not looking for Dan Blake. He has captured the thief, a local man named Miguel who is a professional thief. Miguel cannot tell the police where he was that night, and was caught robbing another store last night, but he does not have the money.

Johnny talks to Miguel who tells Johnny that he does not work and has two daughters who work in prison. He has no money, and if he did then why steal 5 pesos? Malvar tells Johnny that the daughters are out of prison and stay away because Miguel steals their money. Johnny thinks it is easier for Malvar to grill Miguel than look for the real thief.

Johnny goes to the Woodward office and meets Charlotte Page, the niece of the owner. She shows Johnny the office layout. Johnny tells her that it looks bad for Dan, but she cannot believe he did it. She tells Johnny that she saw him occasionally and knows of no problems. Johnny is shown the office safe under the rug in the office. Charlotte tells Johnny that everyone trusted Dan, but he did not know the combination.

Johnny gets Dan's address and goes to Dan's room. Johnny finds a good biography of Dan Blake from the things in his room and learns that he was in the Merchant Marine and had traveled in the Philippines.

Johnny goes to the police and tells Malvar of Dan's travels in the islands. Malvar tells Johnny that Dan has been found in a dugout and taken aboard a ship. He had been shot many times and is dead, but the money has not been found yet.

Malvar tells Johnny that the man was Dan Blake because he had told the ship captain his name before he died. Johnny calls McDonald to come and look at the body. McDonald and Johnny go to look at the body and confirm it is Dan. Johnny tells McDonald that Dan was found in a dugout in Tayabas Bay. He had been shot in the back four times when Captain Kovah, the captain of an inter-island schooner found him. He was alive for a while but no money was found.

McDonald takes Johnny to the docks where they rent a boat to find Captain Kovah. They locate the *Sea Nymph*, which is a wreck, and go aboard and talk to Captain Kovah. He tells Johnny that all Malvar says is that Kovah has the money and that he had better give it to him. Johnny tells Kovah that there is over $75,000 missing from the robbery.

Kovah tells Johnny that he found the man in a dugout, a Morro craft, and there was no money in it. He lived 15-20 minutes and said little. Kovah gets angry when Johnny questions him and tells Johnny that the police are getting papers to search the boat. Kovah tells Johnny that plenty could have happened on the way to Tayabas Bay, as the Huks would do anything for money.

Johnny leaves the boat and is not sure of Kovah, as he may be lying.

Later, Johnny sees Malvar's report and also learns that McDonald is deeply in debt. Johnny does not think it wise to question McDonald, so he goes to see Morgan, who tells Johnny that McDonald told him that the money is gone for good. Johnny tells him that the Huks can be a handy people to have around. Johnny asks how well he knows of McDonald's personal life, and Morgan tells Johnny they are friends and that he sees McDonald socially. Johnny asks Morgan if McDonald owes him money too, as McDonald owes a lot of money to a lot of people. Johnny asks if McDonald could have stolen the money and Morgan is sure that he is not the kind of man to do such a thing. Morgan tells Johnny that McDonald usually has dinner at the Merchants Club and Johnny leaves to question McDonald at home. Morgan wants to stay away from this thing.

At McDonald's home, Johnny sees Kovah running out of the front door. "Forget you saw me" he says as he runs. Johnny tries to stop him but he gets away.

Johnny goes to the house and meets Charlotte. She tells Johnny that Kovah had been there with her and that he hit her and demanded the money, so she gave it to him. She had the money and was holding it for Dan, who kept calling her name while he died. She tells Johnny that they wanted to get away to have a life of their own.

Johnny calls Malvar and meets him at the harbor police and they go out after Kovah. Malvar tells Johnny that the police doctor says Dan was choked to death by Kovah to learn about the money.

Johnny and Malvar find Kovah after 30 minutes and the police open up with a machine gun. Kovah fires back and hits a searchlight. Kovah's crew turns on him and he shoots them. The police machine gun cuts him down.

Notes:
- See the original program of 11/25/1950 for comments on the local natives

- This is an AFRTS program that contains a story about the weather department, and a story about the presidency of Theodore Roosevelt.
- This program was performed as *The Woodward Manila Matter* by Edmond O'Brien on 11/25/1950.
- The announcer is Charles Lyon.
- Music is by Eddie Dunstedter.

Producer:	Jaime del Valle	Writer:	Gil Doud
Cast:	Ed Begley, Lillian Buyeff, Jay Novello, Berry Kroeger, Joseph Kearns, Don Diamond		

◆ ❖ ◆

Show: **The Jan Breughel Matter**
Show Date: 7/6/1954
Company: **Eastern Indemnity & Insurance Company**
Agent: **Tom Leslie**
Exp. Acct: **$135.85**

Synopsis: Tom Leslie is sending Johnny a check for $25,000 to buy a painting in Detroit. It is called *The River* and was painted by Jan Breughel. It was stolen eleven years ago. Johnny does not like paying for stolen property, but the company does not want to take a $125,000 loss. Johnny will do it but he won't like it.

Johnny flies to Detroit, Michigan and cabs from the Statler Hotel to the Masterson Gallery. A nervous man named Merwin Hacker, the general factotum, meets Johnny. Hacker takes Johnny to Masterson's office where he is expected. Masterson thinks that being a go-between is novel. He tells Johnny that a man came in and wanted a painting appraised, and it was the Breughel. Masterson tried to detain him but he left.

Yesterday he called back to offer Masterson a commission to get the insurance company here today at four o'clock. It is 2:30 now, so you have time to figure out how to capture the man. Johnny tells Masterson that the statute of limitations has run out, and there is nothing he can do to the man. But it is worth it to get a masterpiece back into the world.

Johnny cabs to the police and meets Lt. Griswold who gets the case file for the original robbery, but the file has nothing to say. Griswold thinks that Selena Jeffers, the daughter of the owner, was involved. She was 18 at the time and had fallen in love with the painting, but he could not prove it. Johnny does not want to make the deal but will have to.

Johnny goes back to the gallery and the phone rings at 4:00. Johnny is told to go to 2135 N. DeVersey and have the cash with him. Johnny tells the man that he is going to bring an expert and the man says to bring anyone Johnny wants.

Johnny goes to the Jeffers estate and talks to Selena. Johnny asks if she wants to buy the picture, but she has no interest. Johnny asks her to go along to identify the picture, and to help identify the man if possible. She agrees to go with him.

The next day Johnny cashes the check and goes to the apartment on DeVersey. The name on the door was Eddie Travers. Johnny has the money and wants to see the painting. Selena is positive that the painting is real, so Johnny gives the money to Eddie, who starts to count it while Selena leaves. Eddie cannot figure the insurance companies, why should they care? Johnny takes the painting to Masterson and then goes to his hotel.

Johnny goes to the airport to leave and is stopped by Merwin Hacker. Johnny tells Hacker that he took the painting to the gallery and Hacker tells Johnny that he thinks the painting is a forgery. Hacker drives Johnny back to the gallery and shows Johnny the painting. Hacker tells Johnny that he was preparing the painting for storage and was nervous and his hand slipped. He shows Johnny a paint chip. Under the paint chip there is a different type of paint. Johnny asks about local experts on art forgery and Hacker refers him to Steven Durwood.

Johnny calls Griswold and he orders a pick up on Eddie Travers. Steven Durwood looks at the picture and tells Johnny to come back in an hour.

Johnny goes to see Selena and tells her of the forgery. She offers Johnny a drink and she tells him more is involved. The painting was her childhood image of perfection, but there is no proof that the picture is the same. If it was the one that was stolen, she will pay the $125,000 to the insurance company.

Back at Durwood's studio, he is at a loss. The painting is a genuine 17th century painting in appearance, but the flecks of paint on the flowers are strange, as only on the flowers is there modern paint. Steven tells Johnny that some forgers use an electric oven to age a painting and maybe the forger slipped up and left a clip on that corner. Griswold calls and tells Johnny that they have Eddie Travers.

Johnny cabs to police headquarters and Eddie has little to say. Johnny tells him that he could be held for fraud and bunco for selling a fake painting, and that is worth 10 to 20 years. "Yeah, the job seemed too easy" Eddie tells them. He tells Johnny that the man who hired him is Merwin Hacker. Johnny calls the gallery and Hacker has gone for the day.

Johnny and Griswold go to Hacker's house, which is on a farm. In the barn is a workshop for making forgeries. In the back they find Hacker dead. Johnny takes the painting to the gallery and gives it to Masterson, who tells Johnny that Hacker had been there for 15 years. Johnny tells Masterson that Hacker had been forging paintings, but not passing them, he is the one who did that.

Johnny tells Masterson that Hacker disclosed the forgery because he found out you were shortchanging him. Masterson admits that he stole the painting from Selena Jeffers because it was the first one they had made and the paint had started to chip.

Too bad your detective work is for nothing because of the statute of limitations Masterson tells Johnny. Johnny tells him that Hacker is dead and there is no limitation on murder. A paraffin test shows Masterson had fired a gun and Travers identifies him as Merwin Hacker.

Notes:
- This is an AFRTS program that contains a story about time and the Department of Commerce, and a story about the presidency of Franklin Pierce.
- The original title of this story on the script title page was *The Flowering Judas Matter.*
- Music is by Eddie Dunstedter.
- Charles Lyon is the announcer.

Producer:	Jaime del Valle Writer: Sidney Marshall
Cast:	Parley Baer, Howard McNear, William Johnstone, Jack Moyles, Hal March, Virginia Gregg

❖

Show:	**The Carboniferous Dolomite Matter**
Show Date:	**7/13/1954**
Company:	**Eastern Indemnity & Insurance Company**
Agent:	**Bill Wesley**
Exp. Acct:	**$2,074.05**

Synopsis: Bill Wesley calls and asks Johnny what he knows about oil wells, and Johnny tells him that he would not mind owning one. Bill has a policy on the Van Oosterhaut Oil Company equipment, and they have lost $60,000 in equipment and Pieter Oosterhaut wants an investigator.

Johnny flies to the Van Oosterhaut Oil Company in Madan, Sumatra and meets with Pieter Van Oosterhaut who tells Johnny that he is a gambler and that he needs Johnny to keep the game honest. He tells Johnny that a landslide has destroyed his rigging equipment and that the explosion was set. Other things have happened as well, and there is no doubt that sabotage is involved. The local authorities sent a man to investigate, but he is against Pieter too. Pieter wants Johnny to stay for three weeks until his drilling permit expires.

Johnny gets a room and calls the government offices and then goes for dinner. A lovely young woman helps him with the menu. Her name is Fredrika Reynolds, Pieter's daughter. She wants Johnny to convince Pieter to accept the insurance money, because her husband is an oilman and he says there is no oil there. She tells Johnny that there are always accidents, maybe these were due to old equipment. Johnny tells her that Pieter has a stronger case. She tells Johnny that a man's life is worth more than $60,000, that her father has a weak heart, and Johnny could lose his life too. Johnny has Sambal Goreng for dinner.

Johnny goes to bed early but Inspector Pajak calls on Johnny and asks for his gun. The magazine is full and the gun is clean. Pajak tells Johnny that he had gone to Pieter's office and had called his office. "What caliber killed Pieter" Johnny asks. "It was a .38, the same caliber as yours. But how did you know?" asks Pajak. "Intuition" Johnny tells him. Johnny and Insp. Pajak go to the oil shack and Pieter's body is there. Johnny learns that

Fredrika had told the inspector that Johnny was the last person to see Pieter. Pajak asks if there is anything different in the office, and Johnny only notes some metal canisters. Pajak tells Johnny that they came in after Johnny left. They are well borings and indicate that the well is dry. Pajak tells Johnny that Fredrika is distraught from the news of her father and is going to leave Madan. Johnny tells Pajak he will stay to find out why Pieter was murdered.

Johnny gets a call from Don Reynolds, who wants to see Johnny. Don knows who shot Van Oosterhaut. Reynolds comes in seven minutes later and tells Johnny that he does not want the inspector involved. Johnny is told that Sunga Tabaran is a wildcatter, and Pieter had tangled with him over some oil leases. Pieter won and Sunga said he would get even. He came back about the time of the sabotage and Sunga was Pajak's expert. They had a fight the other day, and Sunga is in Madan now.

Johnny goes to see Sunga Tabaran in a small bungalow. Johnny introduces himself and wants to talk, but Sunga tells Johnny it is too early. Johnny tells him that murder is not particular about the hours it keeps. Johnny notes that it is dawn yet he is dressed and asks about the argument with Van Oosterhaut. Sunga tells Johnny that he is looking around and trying to judge him, but he will disappoint Johnny. On the way out, Johnny says to extend his condolences to Fredrika — her purse is on the table.

Johnny leaves and wonders why is Fredrika there? Johnny takes a rickshaw to Pieter's office and then to the hotel. Inspector Pajak meets Johnny in the lobby and warns him not to interfere in internal affairs.

Johnny goes to the shop of Herr DeGroot and shows him part of an oil sample. DeGroot knows that they are from Van Oosterhaut's well because they are specimens of carboniferous dolomite, which is a great signifier of oil 100-500 feet below the surface. Don Reynolds has been bringing them in regularly, so why did he not tell Pieter?

Johnny calls Reynolds and Sunga, but they are both out. Johnny calls the airport and the controller tells him that both Reynolds and Sunga have left for the oil fields and that Reynolds came in twice last night.

Johnny goes to Pajak and tells him that the evidence adds up to murder. Reynolds knew that Pieter would hit oil so he tried to stall Pieter until the permit would run out and then drill himself. Pieter must have found out and Reynolds killed him. Fredrika went with Sunga to the oil field to confirm her suspicions and Reynolds followed them.

Johnny and Pajak rent a plane and go to the drilling area, and there is no one around when they arrive. Johnny spots Reynolds with a nitroglycerine tube in his hand and realizes that he is going to shoot the well. He tells Johnny that he is going to try to blast through some rock. Johnny tells Reynolds to drop the nitro or he will shoot.

Reynolds runs to the well and Johnny shoots the nitro tube in Reynolds hand, causing it to explode and kill Reynolds. Pajak is ready to arrest Johnny until he sees Fredrika and Sunga tied up in the tool shed and realizes that Reynolds was going to kill them.

The trip home did not seem half as long as the walk to the tool shed to see it Sunga and Fredrika were alive. They were.

Notes:
- This is an AFRTS program that contains a story about housekeeping within the government, and a story about taxes.
- Music is by Eddie Dunstedter.
- Charles Lyon is the announcer.
- Johnny is carrying a .38 automatic.

Producer:	Jaime del Valle	Writer:	Sidney Marshall
Cast:	Hal March, Edgar Barrier, Virginia Gregg, Jay Novello, Hy Averback, Marvin Miller		

♦ ❖ ♦

Show:	**The Jeanne Maxwell Matter**
Show Date:	7/20/1954
Company:	**Corinthian Life Insurance Company**
Agent:	**Mr. Semplan**
Exp. Acct:	**$265.85**

Synopsis: Johnny calls Mr. Semplan in Boston and gets the name of the police contact for the Joan Sebastian case. Johnny asks Semplan if the case is murder or suicide.

Johnny rents a car and drives to the Boston, Massachusetts police headquarters. Johnny tells Lt. De Rosa that the insurance company is nervous about a possible suicide case and that the girl's mother is the beneficiary and is an invalid. De Rosa tells Johnny that the mother has taken up with an old boyfriend. De Rosa tells Johnny that the girl was found in shallow water near a bridge and that it did not look like suicide. The bridge was too low, and a suicide never does it without taking off their coat and shoes, and her purse was missing. She was 21 years old and very pretty. The inquest will be in two days. Johnny wants to dig up his own background information.

Johnny goes to the site where the body was found, and placement of the body indicates she going towards Boston, not away.

Johnny goes to Jeanne's apartment and talks to Mary O'Neal, Jeanne's roommate. Mary tells Johnny that it is a great shock and that she never thought Jeanne would do this. She expected trouble as Jeanne lived too fast after her mother went into the hospital — there were too many men. One is Harold Cory, who is a truck driver for Seaboard Trucking Company. Jeanne saw other men when he was gone. Johnny wants to look at her things and he goes through a locked dresser that contains nothing but clothes, perfume and jewelry, and a gold house key with a heart-shaped head. Johnny keeps the key, as he wants to find out who made it.

Johnny calls Seaboard Trucking Company and is told that Cory is out of town and due back at 3 a.m. Johnny calls Jeanne's employer and goes to see Mr. Hollis at his home where Johnny also meets Mrs. Hollis. Johnny tells Mr.

and Mrs. Hollis that he suspects murder, as Jeanne did not do any of the things suicides normally do. Mr. Hollis tells Johnny that he knew nothing of Jeanne's private life, as he had no right to know, but he knew of the invalid mother. Johnny thinks there was only one man with enough money to buy expensive things. Hollis tells Johnny that he will get the names of Jeanne's co-workers if Johnny will call in the morning.

Johnny goes to see Cory at 10:30 and he tells Cory that it looks like murder. Cory tells Johnny that she would never kill herself. He last saw her Tuesday and left Wednesday morning on a run and Johnny tells Cory that he could have done it before he left. Cory tells Johnny that he wanted to marry Jeanne and throws Johnny out.

Johnny calls De Rosa, who tells Johnny the cause of death is suicide. The autopsy says she died of carbon monoxide poisoning. She killed herself and someone probably moved the body to avoid embarrassment.

Johnny goes to see De Rosa and to see the autopsy report which points to car exhaust but also shows a severe concussion. Johnny is still convinced that Jeanne was killed. Johnny shows De Rosa the key and asks if he can find where it was made and De Rosa tells Johnny he will do what he can.

Johnny goes to see Paul Anderson, the boyfriend of the mother. Paul tells Johnny that the mother was 17 when Jeanne was born. He met Jeanne first and realized she was a cheap opportunist. He did what he could for the mother and did not send her to a home to get her out of the way. Paul does not know anything about the gold the key and tells Johnny that he knew very little about Jeanne.

Johnny goes to Mary's apartment and she cannot remember anything additional. She tells Johnny that Jeanne had never mentioned Paul Anderson to her, and that she never knew how Jeanne was able to put her mother in a nursing home. Johnny talks to six of Jeanne's co-workers and finds nothing.

The police find a goldsmith who made the key. Johnny talks to him. The Jeweler remembers that a councilman's wife came in the same day. The gold key was made for a man named Carter. It was made for a cottage on the bay.

Johnny tells De Rosa about the cottage but De Rosa cannot assign men to search cabins in the area, as it is county responsibility. Johnny searches real estate offices and on the 3rd day hits pay dirt. An agent remembers renting a cottage to J.E. Carter and the rent has been paid by cashier's check since May. They go to the cottage where Johnny looks through the cottage. On the way out, Johnny locks the door with the gold key.

Johnny goes to Mr. Hollis and tells him he thought he would get away with it. Johnny tells Hollis that he rented cottage and bought the key and killed Jeanne. Hollis admitted he was infatuated with Jeanne and wanted to break it off. Jeanne left and committed suicide in the car. Johnny tells Hollis it was not suicide and Hollis agrees to go to the police. Mrs. Hollis comes in and tells Johnny that she had lost her husband and had found out about them. She went out and waited and caught them and killed the girl and carried her to the car.

Remarks: "I don't know what sticklers the Massachusetts courts of law are, but Jeanne Maxwell was not killed by the wronged wife. She was unconscious but alive when Hollis put her into the car trunk. She died there by carbon monoxide."

Notes:
- This is an AFRTS program that contains a story about the presidency of James Monroe, and a story about the functions of the various Departments of the government.
- This is a repeat of the program of 3/6/1953, but with minor modifications and a different cast.
- *The Joan Sebastian Matter* on 10/28/50.
- The announcer is Charles Lyon.
- Music is by Eddie Dunstedter.

Producer:	Jaime del Valle	Writer:	Gil Doud
Cast:	Parley Baer, Howard McNear, Virginia Gregg, Hal March, William Johnstone, Jack Moyles		

♦ ❖ ♦

Show:	**The Radioactive Gold Matter**
Show Date:	**7/27/1954**
Company:	**Corinthian Insurance Company**
Agent:	**Ed Trask**
Exp. Acct:	**$165.45**

Synopsis: Ed Trask calls and wants Johnny to go to the Washington Research Hospital in South Bend. There has been a robbery and $150 worth of gold isotope has been stolen.

Johnny goes to South Bend, Indiana and cabs to the hospital where Dr. Reid McKinlock is in charge. Johnny is told that the missing gold is a lethal weapon as it is highly radioactive and is used in treating tumors. It is stored in glass vials in lead boxes in a safe. There were only four ounces, and other materials in the vault were worth much more. The gold had been used the day before and was found missing this morning and the box had been left behind. Nurse Doris Florea tells Johnny that it was her fault. She checks the vault and locks it, at least she thinks she locked it. The vault was open this morning so she forgot to lock it.

Johnny goes to police headquarters and sees Lt. Aridos, where the police are trying to close the details. There have been no leads from the staff and the news media have been notified. Johnny gets a list of the hospital staff and heads back to the hospital.

Aridos stops Johnny and tells him that they have a lead, and they head to a pawnshop owner who thinks he has the gold. The man, Mr. Parker is glad to see the police. He knows it is the right stuff as a man came in with three ounces of gold leaf he said he got from his office windows. The gold is in the back office and Parker will not get near "that atomic bomb stuff". Parker tells

Johnny that the man brought it to the shop in an envelope. While Aridos gets a lead box, Johnny gets the address of the seller. Parker tells Johnny that he would go to the hospital to get checked, but a man must make a buck.

Johnny and Aridos head to the hospital to see Dr. McKinlock, who is working with Steve Wrojack, who has a suspected malignancy, when they get there. Dr. McKinlock gets a Geiger counter and the gold is not radioactive.

Johnny gets a hotel room and is called in the middle of the night. Dr. McKinlock wants him to come in to the hospital. Doris Florea is hysterical and thinks she is dying from radiation poisoning.

Johnny arrives at the hospital and Dr. McKinlock tells Johnny how she came in and was crying, so the night doctor called him in. She has some radioactive exposure, but it is too early to tell. They go in and ask her what she is guilty of and she tells Johnny that she is careless and incompetent and that she exposed herself to the radioactivity night after night. She tells them that she has been shortcutting the safety procedures, but she did not take the gold. She is only guilty of leaving the gold in the treatment room where anyone could take it.

Johnny tells Aridos the good news and Johnny is told that every crank in town is calling the police.

Johnny goes to the hospital and continues the questioning. Dr. McKinlock comes in and tells Johnny about finding radioactivity in the hallway. They follow the signals from the Geiger counter and find a rubbish cart in a closet. Johnny calls Aridos with the names of orderlies and other staff who are brought to the hospital for testing, but none of the staff show any signs of contamination.

Johnny goes to the hotel and Aridos calls and wants to pick him up. An eight-year-old boy was found playing with a bottle from the hospital with traces of gold in it.

At the hospital, the boy's mother, Mrs. Thatcher, tells Johnny that Bobby was playing in the back yard. She had gone out to get him, saw the bottle and brought him into the hospital. Bobby told her that he found the bottle in the next-door neighbor's yard. Mr. and Mrs. Wrojack the neighbors are having a 50th anniversary party tonight. A check of the hospital records show that Mr. Wrojack was there on the day of the theft.

Johnny and Aridos go to visit Wrojack, who tells them that it is too bad that they find out tonight, on their anniversary. They go to the workshop to talk. Mr. Wrojack knows that they are after the gold. He has it in the workshop and tells Johnny that he had used the rubbish cart to get it out of the building. Mr. Wrojack took it to make a ring for him and his wife Anna. After fifty years she deserves something nice for her golden anniversary. Mr. Wrojack knows it was wrong, but he did what he had to do to make a gift for Anna. Mr. Wrojack does not read in English so he does not know about the news, but he will pay back the hospital.

Notes:
- According to the script title page, the original title was *The Golden Ring Matter.*

- Charles Lyons is the announcer.
- Music is by Eddie Dunstedter.

Producer:	Jaime del Valle	Writer:	Sidney Marshall
Cast:	Lou Merrill, Joseph Kearns, Jeanne Bates, Hy Averback, Howard McNear, Mary Jane Croft		

♦ ❖ ♦

Show: **The Hampton Line Matter**
Show Date: 8/3/1954
Company: **Worldwide Maritime & Insurance Company**
Agent: **Jack Loring**
Exp. Acct: **$158.55**

Synopsis: Jack Loring calls about an easy job. All Johnny has to do is to fly to Sault Ste. Marie, sit back and look important and watch the Coast Guard do all the work. Jack tells Johnny that a man named Carl Richards set off a bomb on the ore boat *Hampton Queen* and the damage is about $56,000. Johnny is needed as a formality.

Johnny flies to Sault Ste. Marie, Michigan and meets Coast Guard Commander Winters. Johnny tells Winters that he understands Carl Richards is the main suspect. Johnny is told that Richards operates a supply boat and had called on the *Hampton Queen* yesterday at 13:00. Richards came up the Jacobs ladder himself, went below and then left. The explosion happened later and an engine room hand saw Richards in the room where the explosion took place. When the supply boat landed, Richards was not there. Elsa Richards, the daughter, does not know what happened to her father and has dared the Coast Guard to charge her. Winters wonders what the motive was, as Richards has an excellent reputation.

Johnny goes to the Richards supply boat and Miss Elsa Richards stops him. She tells Johnny that she has nothing to say to him because he is not interested in the truth. Johnny notes the odd cargo and asks Elsa about the blasting powder.

Johnny goes to the Shoreview Hotel and finds Capt. Torgeson, who does not know where Richards is. Capt. Torgeson knows that Richards is not responsible for the blast, because he has known him for 25 years. Nor does he know why Richards went below decks. Johnny is told that the blast went off in an empty storage locker, but if they wanted to do some real damage, the engines were nearby. Capt. Torgeson tells Johnny that Richards has never said a bad word or cheated anyone, so Johnny asks why Richards disappeared.

Back at the Coast Guard a report comes in from the station in Three Harbors. A man tried to sneak aboard a Hampton Lines boat there and was shot. The man was Carl Richards.

Johnny and Winters pick up Elsa and they fly to Three Harbors. Johnny, Elsa and Winters meet the man who shot Richards, and Elsa goes in alone to be with her father. Bill Fraser tells Johnny that he was standing the night watch and saw the dinghy under the stern. He haled it and got shot at, so he shot back and got a lucky shot. Fraser tells Johnny that the dinghy was carrying blasting powder. Fraser tells Johnny that Three Harbors is the closest port to Canada, so maybe Richards was going there. Winters gets a call and another Hampton boat has had an explosion.

Johnny and Winters go to Parisian Island, and go aboard the James K. where the skipper, Capt. Hartzell, shows them the damage that looks just like what was done on the *Hampton Queen*. The blast looks like it came from inside the central pipe in the ceiling.

In the morning Johnny calls Winters and learns that the Richards inquest is finished, the verdict was justifiable homicide, and the funeral is this afternoon. Johnny requests an autopsy and then Johnny searches the supply boat and finds nothing.

Johnny gets a call from Jack Loring who learns that another boat is damaged. Loring tells Johnny that he has had all the boats tied up for the time being. Johnny tells him to cancel the order for 24 hours. Johnny calls the hospital and there is no report on the autopsy.

At the dry dock, Johnny sees Captain Hartzell who tells Johnny that he has not seen Richards for three weeks. Johnny asks Hartzell for a crew list and gets a list from the Hampton Queen and takes the information he was looking for to Winters. On each list, there is a substitute sailor for Bill Fraser.

Johnny calls Three Harbors and learns that Richards died from drowning, not from gunshots. Also, Fraser has shipped off on another boat and Elsa is on the supply boat heading out.

Johnny and Winters take a plane out to intercept them. Johnny tells Winters that he had a hunch and the booby traps tipped him off. If Fraser were bringing in contraband the booby traps would be perfect to cover up anything that was discovered. And they only needed one in-bound trip to get the goods. Richards probably was covering for his daughter by destroying the evidence and they killed him. Nice people!

Johnny and Winter board the Agnes Hampton to look for Fraser. Near the engine room Fraser tells them to go above decks. He laughs and tells them he will sink the ship, as he has a real charge this time. Fraser taunts Johnny to take him. Fraser tells Johnny that he has a Bangalore torpedo and can set it off from anywhere on the boat. Johnny tries to get close enough to jump him while Winters stalls for time by telling Fraser that Elsa is going to Canada without him.

Johnny is able to jump Fraser and knock him unconscious. Johnny tells Winters that Fraser had gotten to the pipe before Johnny hit him, but the bomb was a dud. Elsa Richards had run out on Fraser and was picked up by the Canadian authorities.

Notes:
- This is an AFRTS program that contains a story about the collection of taxes, and a story about the presidency of Abraham Lincoln.
- The script title page notes that the previous title was *The Nefarious Supply Boat Matter.*

- The Bangalore torpedo was used as a means of exploding booby traps and barricades left over from the Boer and Russo-Japanese Wars.
- The cast credits are given as: Jim Nusser is Jack Loring, Hy Averback is Commander Winters, Lee Patrick is Elsa Richards, Ed Begley is Capt. Torgeson, Clayton Post is Capt. Hartzell, Hal March is Bill Fraser.
- Charles Lyons is the announcer.
- Music is by Eddie Dunstedter.
- This is the last available digital program with John Lund.

Producer:	Jaime del Valle	Writer:	Sidney Marshall
Cast:	Jim Nusser, Hy Averback, Lee Patrick, Ed Begley, Clayton Post, Hal March		

♦ ❖ ♦

Show: **The Sarah Martin Matter**
Show Date: 8/10/1954
Company: **Washingtonian Life Insurance Company**
Agent: **Ed Reynolds**
Exp. Acct: **$318.05**

Synopsis: Ed Reynolds calls Johnny and asks him to go to Milwaukee and check out Joe Martin. His business has gone to pot, there are shortages in his accounts, and he has separated from his wife who Joe had said was trying to kill him.

Johnny flies to Milwaukee, Wisconsin and is paged at the airport. Johnny answers the page and is met by police Lt. Hanks who tells Johnny that Joe Martin is dead.

Johnny goes to Joe's home at Whitefish Bay and learns that Joe was killed the previous night by two shots from a .32. His stepdaughter Hazel Martin had discovered Joe less than an hour ago. Hazel tells Johnny that she did not live at the house, and that her mother killed Joe. Hazel tells Johnny that she came to the area to visit a client and decided to stop by and visit her dad, who she had last seen two months ago. Hazel tells Johnny that Joe had made her the beneficiary of the $65,000 policy and claims that her mother tried to kill Joe after they separated by starting a fire at his house.

Johnny goes to the Schroeder Hotel and is called by Mrs. Sarah Martin who tells Johnny that she has some information. Johnny goes to the Juneau Hotel to meet Mrs. Martin and is told that she had called the office and was told about Joe, and that Johnny was investigating. Sarah tells Johnny that they had been estranged for a year, and that she had made enemies of all their friends. Sarah tells Johnny that she was at Lake Geneva and had been at a movie when Joe was killed and has proof. Sarah tells Johnny that she has a Smith and Wesson .32, so Johnny takes her to the police.

At the police department, Johnny meets a Mr. Everett Norvell who tells Johnny that he killed Joe Martin. Everett tells Johnny that he was an insurance salesman and that Joe owed him money. They had fought and Everett stabbed Joe. Everett wants to talk to the reporters and get photographed, but Johnny calls him a "Confessin' Sam".

Johnny goes to Joe's office and hires a CPA to go over the books. Johnny also talks to the secretary, Esther Buchwald. Esther tells Johnny that Joe was a fool to get involved with those two harpies, and that he had no enemies. Lt. Hanks calls Johnny, and he tells Johnny that there has been a gas heater explosion at the cabin in Lake Geneva.

Johnny goes to the cabin where a .32 was found in the rubbish. The gun is the murder weapon and was registered to Joe.

Johnny goes back to the office and the CPA has found a $20,000 shortage in the books. Joe has lunch with Hazel and tells her about the gun. Hazel tells Johnny that Joe had not used the gun in three years and had given it to the boyfriend of his secretary, Everett Norvell.

Johnny goes to the office and talks to Esther who tells Johnny that Everett had juggled the books, and that Joe had found out. Esther tells Johnny that she is an old maid and Everett was the only man who paid any attention to her. Johnny calls the police and Everett is arrested.

Notes:
- The announcer is Charles Lyon.
- Music is by Eddie Dunstedter.
- Story information obtained from the KNX Collection in the Thousand Oaks Library.

Producer:	Jaime del Valle Writer: Sidney Marshall
Cast:	Jay Novello, John McIntire, Howard McNear, Virginia Gregg, Mary Jane Croft, Jeanne Cagney, Lou Merrill

♦ ❖ ♦

Show:	**The Hamilton Payroll Matter**
Show Date:	**9/5/1954**
Company:	**Corinthian Insurance Company**
Agent:	**Bill Fedderson**
Exp. Acct:	**$417.65**

Synopsis: Bill Fedderson calls Johnny and asks if he remembers the Hamilton Payroll Robbery two and a half years ago. The robbers wore Halloween masks and got away with $85,000. Bill tells Johnny that the money has turned up in Tijuana. See Captain Reyes for details.

Johnny goes to Tijuana, Mexico, gets a room at the Reforma Hotel and goes to see Reyes who tells Johnny that three bills have been traced to the area, all 20's. Señora Rosa Fuentes runs a quinta and made the deposit, which was made from the rental money. Currently there are five Americans staying there. The guests include a Miss Jamison from Kansas City, Mr. Haines and his wife from Los Angeles, and Mr. Burke and Mr. Behrens from New York.

Johnny goes to the quinta acting as a tourist and meets the Haines, who tell Johnny that they are on their honeymoon. Johnny meets Burke, who Johnny recognizes as a New York numbers racket member named Callenti. Burke tells

Johnny that he is on vacation and invites Johnny to go to the jai alai games with him.

Johnny gets a room and meets Dorothy Jamison who knows that Johnny is an insurance investigator, because Burke had told her. Johnny goes to update Reyes and learns that Behrens has been found shot to death by a .38. Johnny is told that Behrens was a Patterson New York police officer. Reyes gets a call and learns that another $20 has surfaced at the jai alai fronton, and it was passed by Mrs. Haines.

Johnny goes to the fronton and talks to the cashier, Louis Campos who tells Johnny that he works at a bank and knows how to spot wanted currency. Johnny watches a jai alai match and Burke comes in and Johnny tells him about the robbery. Burke bets Johnny $20 that a certain player will win the match, and Johnny wins the bet. Burke pays Johnny with a $20 and the bill is clean. Johnny updates Reyes and learns that the Haines are clean.

Johnny goes to the quinta and searches the rooms and finds nothing. Johnny has a drink with Dorothy who tells Johnny that Mr. Haines is interested in why Johnny is there. Reyes arrives and tells Johnny that Mr. Haines has been killed. He was found near where Behrens was found and was shot six times. His wife was found nearby and taken to the hospital.

Johnny goes to the hospital and Mrs. Haines tells Johnny that she and her husband were robbed and everything they had was taken except her rings. She admits that she only had two bills left, and her husband had told her that he might go to prison because she took the money from his wallet to play at the fronton. She also tells Johnny that the man who robbed them bragged about killing Behrens.

Johnny finds a receipt for a package at the post office and finds a package with the rest of the money.

Notes:
- The announcer is Charles Lyon.
- Music is by Eddie Dunstedter.
- Story information obtained from the KNX Collection in the Thousand Oaks Library.

Producer:	Jaime del Valle	Writer:	Sidney Marshall
Cast:	Lou Krugman, Don Diamond, Virginia Gregg, Jim Backus, Hans Conried, Mary Jane Croft		

◆ ❖ ◆

Show: The Great Bannock Race Matter
Show Date: 9/12/1954
Company: Seaboard Mutual Life Insurance Company
Agent: Bill Blake
Exp. Acct: $1,207.90

Synopsis: Bill Blake calls and asks Johnny if he wants to go to Scotland. The village of Roxburgh has a race called the Bannock Race. Miss Elsie McCleod won this year and then died. She ate the bannock she had made and died of poison. Bill wants Johnny to find out if she was married.

Johnny flies to Roxburgh, Scotland and goes to meet Inspector Michaels of Scotland Yard, who tells Johnny that there was no record of Miss McCleod ever being married. She was born in the village, became an actress and came back to run a curio shop. Insp.

Michaels tells Johnny that the bannocks have to do with the Battle of Culloden where Prince Charlie was defeated. The bannock is an oatcake and every year the village holds a race to see who can make theirs the quickest. This year Elsie won and ate her bannock and died after the Earl of Roxstane handed the bannock to her. Elsie has a cousin who is her next of kin, and he is running the shop now.

Johnny goes to visit the Earl of Roxstane who calls the thought of marriage nonsense. While talking, the Earl's fiancée Alice Merrick comes in and tells Johnny that at their engagement party, Elsie said in an odd manner that she would have to present her husband.

Johnny goes to the shop and meets Alfred, who tells Johnny that he saw the race and tells Johnny that there were stoves at one end of the town, and Roxstane was at the other. The contestants made their batter at home. Johnny inspects the living room, and Alfred is nervous, so Johnny calls for Michaels.

The inspector arrives and he and Johnny remove a number of bank passbooks from different banks in different cities. Michaels suspects that they were from blackmail. Johnny is told that Lord Roxstane is really Henry Claridge, and that his title is inherited.

Johnny flies to the town of Frontignan in the south of France and spots Miss Merrick there. Johnny goes to see Pierre le Blanc, a collector of theater programs where Johnny finds a program from 1940 for the play "Gay Lady Gay" where Elsie had a role. Johnny goes to a local photographer and meets Miss Merrick again. Johnny tells her that he has proof that Elsie had married Henry in 1940. Alice tells Johnny that Henry feared Elsie.

Johnny goes back to Roxstane and he tries to bribe Johnny and tells him that he and Elsie were only married for two days and never saw her again until he got the title. He tells Johnny that Elsie tried to blackmail him, but he did not kill her.

Johnny goes to see Alfred and tells him that he will not inherit Elsie's money. Johnny goes to see Michaels and they go see the Earl and Alice and tell them that he cannot give the insurance money because Roxstane is a suspect.

While they are talking shots are heard and the bullets come through the curtains. The police arrest Alfred and Johnny tells him that he killed Elsie. He tells Alfred that he made two batches of bannocks and the inspector can prove it by the crumbs in his pockets.

Notes:
- **The announcer is Charles Lyon.**
- **Music is by Eddie Dunstedter.**

- Story information obtained from the KNX Collection in the Thousand Oaks Library.

Producer:	Jaime del Valle	Writer:	Gibson Scott Fox

Cast: Howard McNear, John McIntire, Lou Merrill, Virginia Gregg, Alex Harford, Jay Novello

♦ ❖ ♦

Show: **The Upjohn Matter**
Show Date: 9/19/1954
Company: **Continental Fire & Casualty Company**
Agent: **Matt Brandon**
Exp. Acct: **$293.65**

Synopsis: Matt Brandon calls Johnny from St. Louis and is in court with the Upjohn Printing Company case. Johnny is told that Tierney was in the building on the night of the fire and there has been a lot of expert testimony by the attorney Eggleston. Johnny will come out to testify.

Johnny flies to St. Louis, Missouri and goes to the courtroom. Johnny is called to testify and tells the court that he has been an investigator for seven years, had spent four years in the Army Air Corps, and was a member of the New York Police Department. Johnny also has a number of letters of reliability from the insurance companies he has represented. Johnny testifies that he was called in to investigate a fire at the Upjohn Printing Company and found evidence of celluloid and paraffin wicks. Johnny states that Pat Tierney improvised the method and that he had ink from the plant on his clothes. The case is closed and goes to the jury.

Johnny goes to talk to Tierney and gives him the option of talking to him, or hoping on the jury. Johnny really wants Upjohn, who paid Tierney to set the fire. Johnny wants Tierney to tell the court he was hired. Tierney refuses to cooperate with Johnny.

The jury comes back and Tierney is found guilty. On the way out, Tierney calls to Johnny that he wants to talk. Johnny talks to Tierney in his cell and he tells Johnny that he was paid $2,500 by Upjohn, and that he contacted Upjohn through a friend. Tierney changes his story to Johnny several times, and Johnny reminds him that his sanity has been proven. Tierney finally admits that he met Upjohn in a bar a month before the fire. He knew that Upjohn was in financial trouble and got $3,500, which he has hidden in a can in a vacant lot. Johnny goes to the police and Upjohn is arrested.

Notes:
- The announcer is Charles Lyon.
- Music is by Eddie Dunstedter.
- This story was merged with *The Elliot Champion Matter* to become *The Bennet Matter* performed by Bob Bailey and broadcast on 2/20 through 2/24/1956.

- Story information obtained from the KNX Collection in the Thousand Oaks Library.

Producer: Jaime del Valle   Writer: E. Jack Neuman
Cast: Joseph DuVal, Joseph Kearns, John McIntire, Jay Novello, Bob Sweeney

Bob Bailey

Bob Bailey (1913–1983) was the fourth actor to portray Johnny Dollar, but to millions of old time radio fans, there is only one Johnny Dollar.

After a lapse of almost a year and a month, veteran producer/director Jack Johnstone was brought in to resurrect the character of Johnny Dollar back to the CBS audience with the voice of Bob Bailey.

From the first broadcast, listeners could tell that something was different. Not only was the format of the program different, with one 15-minute episode each weekday, but Bob Bailey was able to infuse energy into the character. Bob Bailey was a real person infusing his personality into the program.

Bob had come to Johnny Dollar after a long and successful run as George Valentine in *Let George Do It*. Bob had a long history of acting, starting at age two in a play his actor parents were appearing in.

Bob played Johnny Dollar until 1960, when CBS moved the program to New York. Bob continued to write for television, but eventually he dropped out of sight, lost to the world and even to his family for over ten years. Bob had a problem with alcohol, but eventually recovered and was working in a rehabilitation facility when he was stricken with a stroke.

During Bob's acting career, he appeared in over 20 movies and short films, and over 700 radio programs, including his stint as Johnny Dollar. Bob died in 1983.

The following are the Bob Bailey Johnny Dollar programs.

Show: The Macormack Matter
Company: Allied Casualty & Insurance Company
Agent: Ed Barth
Synopsis:
Episode 1   Show Date: 10/3/1955

Father Taggert calls Johnny from Sing Sing. Michael Kearns wants Johnny to talk to Michael, as he is dying.

Allied did not authorize the investigation but you will probably pay it. Johnny goes to Sing Sing Prison and visits Michael Kearns in the infirmary. Johnny had put Mike in prison, and now he is very sick and has to be awakened.

Mike is glad to see Johnny and tells him that Johnny was the best insurance cop. Prison is a lousy place to die and Mike was thinking about his life. He had a wife once and has to do something for her. Mike asks Johnny if he would pick up some clean, easy money for him.

He tells Johnny that he roomed with Joe Panning, who has been paroled. He put in his time, but he had something waiting for him outside, money. Joe yelled "Macormack" in his sleep, and a guy named Macormack was robbed a couple years back for $100,000 and Joe was in on it. There must be a reward out for it. Look into it and get the reward and send half to my old lady.

Mike dies and Johnny heads to New York City and goes to the police to look at the Macormack files. The case is open and unsolved so Johnny calls Frank Porter of Allied and asks for information on the Macormack robbery. Johnny learns that there is a $7500 reward on the case.

Johnny gets a mug shot for Joe Panning and his address from the parole officer. Johnny goes to see Joe and tells him about Mike. Johnny asks if he can buy Joe a drink and they talk. Johnny starts to think that another man was involved in the Macormack case.

Johnny wants to go to Long Island and see a friend and asks Joe to go along. When Johnny mentions Julian Macormack, Joe gets suspicious and goes back to his room. Johnny goes back to the hotel the next morning and Joe has gone.

Tomorrow, there is living proof that a pretty girl can be just as dangerous as, well, a pretty girl.

Episode 2   Show Date: 10/4/1955

Frank Porter calls with the information on the Macormack case and Johnny tells Frank about the tip on Joe. Frank tells Johnny not to bother Julian Macormack as it could be dangerous.

Johnny rents a car and drives to the Macormack mansion where Julian is packing for a trip to Europe. Johnny tells Macormack who he is and about the lead on the jewelry. Johnny tells him that he may have a clue. Macormack tells Johnny that they had just returned from their honeymoon and the safe was opened, not cracked. Only he knows the combination.

The police and insurance company were called and Frank Porter worked very hard to collect. Macormack did not get much as he had violated the policy and collected only $20,000 on the jewelry, which was an heirloom. Johnny tells Macormack of the tip on Joe Panning and thinks that Mrs. Macormack will be glad to see the jewelry again.

Johnny leaves and thinks that Macormack is scared of him. Johnny has lunch at Walgreens and then goes to the Allied office and meets Frank Porter. Frank shows Johnny pictures of the jewelry and hopes he has better luck. Frank gives Jules Martin as the police contact. Frank tells Johnny that someone just picked the safe and got clean away. The hardest part is that none of the goods has surfaced. Maybe the guy still has it and we can only wait. Just let me know when you find something.

Johnny goes to the parole office and Panning has not called in. Johnny goes back to the police and pulls Panning's file. A police clerk tells Johnny that he had already given Johnny the address. Did you forget?

Johnny rushes to the Allen Hotel and runs into a woman in a sable coat who tries to run past Johnny with a gun in her hand. Johnny reaches for the gun and she hits him. Johnny follows her to the street and loses her. The desk clerk saw no one but tells Johnny that Joe is out.

Johnny borrows a passkey to open Joe's room but it is already open. Joe's clothes were there and the room has been searched and trashed. Johnny gets a drink and thinks. Mike's tip was really good.

Tomorrow, a slight case of mayhem when the right guy turns up in the wrong place.

Episode 3   Show Date: 10/5/1955
Lt. Jules Martin returns Johnny's call and Johnny tells him that he wants to talk about the Macormack job.

Johnny buys drinks for Martin after looking at Panning's room. A pickup is ordered for Panning and Johnny relates how he got involved and how the case is working out. Johnny describes the woman and her gun, but she could be anyone. Martin recalls that Macormack was kind of strange. He will call Johnny when Panning is picked up.

After two days, there is no news on Panning. Johnny checks the files on Panning again and finds the name of an ex-wife, Iris Carter. Vital Statistics gives a general description that could match the woman who hit him.

Johnny goes to the last address and asks the manager for Iris. She tells Johnny that she knew both Iris and Joe but does not know where she is, but she used to work in a bookstore nearby. Johnny gets a description of Iris and goes looking for the bookstore where the owner tells Johnny that Iris had worked there and does not know where to find her.

At the Showboat restaurant, the manager remembers Iris' boyfriend and his work address at a nearby club. Johnny goes to the club and talks to the trumpet player, Jack Lang. Johnny asks about Iris and her ex-husband. Jack tells Johnny that she and Joe were all washed up and she might have gone back to Ohio, she was sick of losers. Jack shows Johnny a picture, and it is the girl who Johnny saw outside of Panning's apartment.

Johnny checks with Martin and nothing has turned up. Martin tells Johnny that Julian Macormack had complained about Johnny. Martin gets a call and Joe Panning has been found, in the harbor. He had been shot and his feet burnt.

Tomorrow, a phase of this case that should be called the talking corpse. Believe me, this one said plenty.

Episode 4   Show Date: 10/6/1955
Frank Porter calls and Johnny tells him that Panning has been found. Johnny asks Frank to help him find Joe's wife, and Frank wants to come over and get the facts.

Johnny hires a secretary to record the events for Allied, the police and himself, and gives a copy to Frank Porter. Johnny is sure that he will find the goods as he cannot see a small-time crook pulling a big-time jewel robbery. Frank tells Johnny that he feels he is not helping a bit, so be careful if you keep on this case.

Johnny goes to see Lt. Martin and reads the medical report on Panning. The Medical Examiner says that Joe had been dead 48 hours and shot twice with a .25 at close range. Johnny feels that Iris seems to be the key to opening the case, and that maybe Joe was ambushed. Martin tells him that the burns on Joe's feet indicate he was not ambushed and was dead when the feet were burned. Johnny thinks that the burns were a cover up and maybe the searched room was to throw me off.

A witness, Edmond Thompson comes in and tells Martin that he had seen a guy dumped in the water. It was against the will of god and the laws of nature. Edmond was on a vacant lot and saw a long black car with a lot of chrome pull up to the water and a man dumped the body into the water. Then Edmond prayed. The car was a coupe and the man had the devil's face.

Johnny goes to his hotel where Jack Lang has called with a tip. Johnny goes to the Al-Mar theater in the Bronx. Johnny asks for Iris Carter and a gruff doorman gives him a hard time until a girl named Gloria Ward tells Johnny that she knows Iris. Johnny tells Gloria that Joe is dead and she tells Johnny that Iris is a good girl and married to a nice guy. She lives in Long Island and her name is Iris Macormack.

Johnny almost has it figured but is shot at in the alley behind the theater as he is leaving. Johnny is hit, and the long black coupe with all the chrome got away.

Tomorrow, the end of the trail for a .38 slug.

Episode 5   Show Date: 10/7/1955
Johnny calls Ed Barth at Allied Casualty and tells him he has been shot but is OK. He reviews the case and tells Ed that Mrs. Macormack is Mrs. Panning. Johnny gets the go ahead to continue, as it is better that Johnny is shot than Frank Porter.

Johnny buys a bottle of scotch, for medicinal purposes, and then goes back to the alley and gets the .38 slugs out of a telephone pole.

Johnny goes to Long Island and checks the garage and finds a 1955 Cadillac and a Jaguar there. At the house, Mrs. Macormack opens the door and does not want Johnny to come in, but he does.

Johnny tells her that Joe is dead, and she cries. Johnny tells her that she had helped Joe rob the safe, and she tells Johnny that Joe made her do it. She went to see him because he had wanted money, but Joe was not there. She has not seen Joe, and she loves her husband. Joe came around after the honeymoon and threatened to tell the husband about her past and she opened the safe for him.

Julian comes into the room with a gun and tells Johnny that Iris is innocent as far as he is concerned. The jewels are hers to do with as she chooses. Julian offers Johnny money for him to go away. Johnny tells him that he has already tried to kill him once and hits him, as the safety on the .38 is on. Johnny takes the gun and there is cosmoline in the barrel. It had never been fired.

Johnny cabs to Queens and Frank Porter's apartment. Johnny waits in the lobby for Frank to come home but the manager does not like people loitering in his exclusive building. Johnny gives him a little bribe and gets into the luxury apartment.

Frank shows up thirty minutes later and is not surprised that Johnny is there. Johnny tells him what he has learned and compliments Frank on his apartment, as they cost money.

Johnny tells him that Julian offered Johnny money, so he had experience doing it. It was Frank that had called the parole office and had killed Joe.

Frank tells Johnny that when he was brought in to the Macormack case Frank recognized Iris and confused the clues. He tipped the cops and framed Joe. Frank offers to buy Johnny but he refuses.

Frank collapses and tells Johnny that he had hit him twice at the theater. Frank dies.

Johnny locates Joe's wife in Iowa, and she accepts half the reward.

"Remarks: Gee Whiz!"

Exp. Acct: $265.91

Notes:
- Johnny is complimented for tipping his hat in episode 3.
- Johnny is shot for the 5th time in Episode 4   the first time for Bob Bailey.
- Cosmoline is a fairly thin, soft, grease-like material used to protect machined materials.
- John Dawson is an alias for E. Jack Neuman.
- Johnny never mentions that he earned himself half of the $7,500.
- All of the 5-part episodes were taped on the same day, usually between 9:00 and 3:00. The time would vary over the life of the 5-part programs.
- Roy Rowan is the announcer.
- According to the script, music direction is by Rick Marino.

Producer:	Jack Johnstone	Writer:	John Dawson
Cast:	Mary Jane Croft, Virginia Gregg, Marvin Miller, Forrest Lewis, Frank Gerstle, Herb Butterfield, Herb Ellis, Tony Barrett, Ken Christy, Jack Kruschen, Junius Matthews		

♦ ❖ ♦

Show:	**The Molly K Matter**
Company:	**Marine & Maritime Casualty, Ltd.**
Agent:	**Dave Borger**
Synopsis:	
Episode 1	Show Date: 10/10/1955

Dave Borger calls and he is in mourning for *Molly K*, she is insured for $500,000 and sank 20 miles off of the Golden Gate bridge. Fly out and take a look and don't get killed.

Johnny goes to San Francisco, California and lands at mid-morning. The *Molly K* had disappeared just 36 hours earlier.

Johnny gets a room and meets with the Harbor Master, Tim O'Rourke, who is presiding at an inquiry. The presidings are informal and disclose that the *Molly K* left at 10:12 for Yokohama with a grain cargo, and Edgar Brawley is the captain. At 10:38 the pilot was dropped and the fog was medium-to-dense. At 12:49 the Coast Guard got the first distress signal.

Lt. Cmdr. Barton Fields takes the stand and relates that five minutes after the first SOS, there was a second SOS. Several boats were launched and two crewmen are missing. Johnny studies the teletype messages and listens to the other testimony. The seeds of suspicion are small but grow.

Capt. Brawley takes the stand and relates that the pilot was dropped and then they hit a submerged derelict. His story is the same as the other stories, everything was normal after they dropped the pilot. All the normal precautions were taken because of the fog. Capt. Brawley felt the ship hit the derelict, surveyed the damage and got everyone top side and gave the abandon ship order.

Johnny asks if he can ask a few questions and asks why there was no mention of the first sailing a week earlier when a cargo fire caused them to go back to port? An insurance claim was filed and then later cancelled. Brawley retorts that he had to get under way to keep from losing money. He does not know what started the fire. Bill Mack discovered the fire, and Mack is missing.

Johnny asks how he saw the derelict in the fog as the Coast Guard found nothing when there was no fog. Mr. Hawkins says it felt like a blast. Hawkins objects and does not want to get involved in anything. Johnny thinks that an explosion caused the ship to sink and Johnny will find out who did it. Murder is involved.

After the hearing, Johnny walks the Embarcadero and thinks about how the men in the hearing room were scared.

Tomorrow, a strange girl, and a strange threat, and a promise that is stranger than both.

Episode 2   Show Date: 10/11/1955
A girl calls Johnny and tells him that he does not know her, but he will soon. Molly K was her mother. Meet me at 9:00, pier 29.

Johnny eats after covering all the usual sources Johnny then cabs to pier 29, with Alcatraz in the background. Just short of the Brawley Shipping office where a light is burning, Johnny gets that old feeling he has had before in the Orinoco jungle, in the Casbah of Algiers, London's Soho, and in Suez, that there was someone watching him.

Johnny opens the office door and a man stops him with a gun. The man tells Johnny to turn around and Johnny obliges and then the man slugs him. He knows it is Johnny, and he is as tough as they say.

The door opens and a girl comes out. She tells Dean to leave and invites Johnny in. The office is plush and cozy and they talk, sparring-type talk. After two scotches, she tells Johnny that she is Ellen Brawley, Capt. Brawley's daughter. Dean Sutton is an exporter she knows, but he is not normally so jealous. It was his cargo on the *Molly K*. She is a free agent and has no obligation to Dean.

She mentions the hearing and Johnny tells her that there are some things that do not add up. There is a big mortgage on the *Molly K* and her father could have made out well from the insurance. Johnny tells Ellen that Lu Tang, Shanghai Lu, holds the mortgage and that Lu owns a nightclub in Chinatown. Johnny knows Lu Tang, and she is quite a girl.

Ellen tells Johnny that her father had no part in sinking the *Molly K*. Ellen hopes they would be friends and kisses him. That's pretty friendly, but the papers say you are engaged to Dean Sutton.

Johnny leaves, and the fog is thicker. On the way out, Johnny is stopped by Mr. Hawkins. He tells Johnny that he was scared, and there is something strange going on. There are some things that have not been brought out yet. Hawkins tells Johnny that the Chinese steward Benny Wong did not drown.

Bennie is shot at, but the bullet may have been meant for Johnny!

Tomorrow, a dead man can tell a tale. It all depends on how he died.

Episode 3   Show Date: 10/12/1955
Lu Tang calls Johnny and tells him that it has been a long time. Johnny tells her that he has to get rid of a drunk and will meet her later. She will do anything for Johnny. He wants her to find Benny Wong. Oh, it is too bad Johnny is here for the *Molly K*.

Johnny gets Hawkins drunk and asks him if Mack had a girl. Someone shot at you to keep you quiet. Hawkins tells Johnny that the crew thinks the ship was sunk on purpose. The first fire was discovered by Bill Mack, and Brawley hit him and told him not to spread rumors. On the second trip, Mack slipped into the hold and had not come back out when the explosion went off in the forward hold. Hawkins does not remember seeing Benny either. Capt. Brawley had hired Benny himself. Mack was dead before the ship sank, as someone had cut his throat.

Hawkins sees Brawley come in and Brawley complains about Hawkin's company. Johnny tells Brawley that there is a lot against him. So, do not go spending the insurance money yet. Brawley tells Johnny that he even has tried to turn his daughter and Dean Sutton against him. Johnny tells him that he is in this up to his neck, and Brawley slugs him. Johnny hits Brawley and leaves him on the floor and Johnny notices that Brawley is carrying a gun.

Johnny goes to see Lu Tang, who is wise, shrewd, and alert. She is a mysterious woman, and the most beautiful woman Johnny has ever known. Johnny remembers last year in Paris and Lu Tang wants to marry Johnny right now. Johnny tells her that he has been mad for her for years.

Lu tells Johnny that she did not sink the *Molly K*, nor has she found Benny yet. She had a stake in the boat, and it was a sound business deal that was insured. The wheat cargo belonging to Dean Sutton was a good investment.

A young man comes in and Lu talks to him. She asks if Johnny would send her to jail if she were involved, and of course he would. She tells Johnny that she is not part of the deal. If it was sunk, Johnny thinks an explosion did it. Lu tells Johnny that Benny Wong was a demolition sergeant in the war and an expert on explosives.

Tomorrow a double cross and a double play, and a lovely girl forces the jealous sea to give up it's dead.

Episode 4   Show Date: 10/13/1955
Dan McKay of the harbor police calls, and Johnny is told that he under arrest for assault and battery, etc. Capt. Brawley has signed a complaint, but Johnny has witnesses. Dan is serious and wants Johnny to come down and talk about it.

Johnny cabs to the harbor police and talks to Dan McKay, an old friend who tells Johnny that the charges were probably filed to slow him down. Dan thinks Johnny has a strong and circumstantial case, but there are a lot of unsolved crimes in the bay. Dan tells Johnny that the human element is a good thing to work on. Brawley is a tough man but not a crook. Even under pressure he will act according to type, and a knife is not his nature.

Johnny thinks Brawley was strapped for cash and hauled the cargo on contingency. He got scared off and withdrew his claim. On the second trip, Benny probably killed Mack when he was caught snooping around.

The phone rings, and the call is for Johnny. Lu Tang tells Johnny what he needed to know. Johnny asks Dan to come and talk to the man that blew up the Molly K.

They cab to the Fa Song Fish Company where Benny is hold up armed, scared and dangerous. At the warehouse, they go to a back room and open the back door. They burst in and Dean Sutton is there. They find Benny dead in a corner, shot three times. Dean says he did not shoot Benny, but that he got a phone call to meet someone there about the *Molly K*, a man.

Johnny discovers that Benny has been dead for hours and was shot with a .45, and Johnny remembers that Brawley was carrying a .45.

Johnny goes to his hotel room to wait. There is a knock at the door and it is

Ellen. She asks if her father had been there. She tells Johnny that she is scared and lonely. Her father was furious last night and left.

The phone rings, and Johnny is told that Brawley was picked up and denies everything. But his gun has been fired and the bullets match the bullets in Benny. Johnny does not tell Ellen about her father because Johnny is suspicious and uncomfortable. It is Ellen's perfume, he smelled it in the room where Benny was murdered.

Tomorrow, a deadly rendezvous in the fog shrouded waterfront, and an explosion that rocked the city, the payoff!

Episode 5   Show Date: 10/14/1955
Lu calls and tells Johnny that the grain prices in Tokyo fell three weeks ago and are holding steady. So that is what caused the *Molly K* to sink. Lu tells Johnny to come over later and tell her anything, especially about a certain night in Paris.

Johnny calls Hartford and New York and then cabs to Dan's office where Brawley will not talk. Johnny tells Dan that Brawley is innocent. Johnny tells Dan that Brawley has the money in the bank to pay the mortgage on his ship. The cargo was insured by another company for top market value, and the market broke four days before the ship sank. The shipper now gets full price for the cargo. Brawley was in the middle trying to protect his daughter. Dan issues a bulletin to pick up Dean Sutton. Dan tells Johnny to call if he finds him before we do.

Johnny leaves and walks through the fog. At pier 29 Johnny sees a small boat which does not belong there. Johnny goes on board and hears nothing. Johnny opens the hatch and freezes as the boat shifts to expose a booby trap.

Johnny goes to the Brawley office and knocks. The door opens and Ellen is there. She tells Johnny that she has tried to find Dean and is trying to find a way to help her father. She tells Johnny that Dean owns a boat, and Johnny tells her that it is tied up near here. Johnny tells her that Dean had hired Benny Wong to get the insurance money, and that her father is in the clear. Ellen cries and Johnny holds her. Johnny breathes in and smells the perfume.

The puzzle is solved but he feels the gun in his side. She tells Johnny that she is a dead shot, ask Benny Wong. Johnny realizes it had to be Ellen, that it was her idea, as Dean was too weak. She tells Johnny that he is too honest and Johnny figures that Ellen is clever enough to get rid of Dean too.

Johnny hears Dean walk in and Johnny edges back to the door. They tell Johnny that they are going to build a fire for him. Dean walks between them and Johnny drags Dean outside.

The railing breaks loose and they end up in the water while Ellen is firing blindly. Johnny drags Dean under the water and finally breaks free, but Dean did not come up for two days.

Johnny gets out of the water but Ellen is gone and Dan McKay runs up and tells Johnny that he saw a girl running to the cruiser. Johnny yells at Ellen to stop but she gets on and the bomb goes off. It was not meant for Johnny, it was rigged by Dean to get her in a double-cross.

The company will have to pay off on this one. The sea has taken Capt. Brawley's boat, his wife and his daughter.

Exp. Acct: $547.60

Notes:
- Only the script title page for episode 1 spells the ship "The Molly K." with a period.
- Roy Rowan is the announcer.
- According to the script, music direction is by Rick Marino.

| Producer: | Jack Johnstone | Writer: | Les Crutchfield |

Cast: Virginia Gregg, Peter Leeds, Barney Phillips, Vic Perrin, James McCallion, Hy Averback

♦ ❖ ♦

Show: **The Chesapeake Fraud Matter**
Company: **Universal Adjustment Bureau**
Agent: **Pat Kelleher**
Synopsis:
Episode 1   Show Date: 10/17/1955

Pat Kelleher calls from Baltimore. John Reardon died in 1950 and the policy was paid off, and Eastern wants them to look into the matter. Reardon was seen two days ago.

Johnny goes to Baltimore, Maryland and arrives at Friendship International Airport and meets Pat. Johnny has investigated a lot of alive-but-dead reports. When the chairman of the board of Eastern Fidelity sees someone, we investigate. The $10,000 policy was issued in 1944 with the wife as beneficiary. Reardon was lost in a boating accident. Only Reardon was not found. Atlantic States Ltd. held the policy on the boat. The courts declared him dead after three years and paid $20,000. Mrs. Reardon is a nice person who does not need money. She waited for a month because she was upset and did not need the money.

Johnny visits Mr. Paul Coombs, the Eastern Fidelity chairman of the board, who is glad Johnny is working on the case. John was a close friend of his and was a fine man, you will know how to handle him. Coombs saw Reardon at the Brown Palace Hotel in Denver, he said his name was Frank Bowers and had lived in Toledo, gone to Ohio University and was a mining engineer. Coombs just let the conversation drop, but everything about Frank Bowers pointed to Reardon. Coombs is hesitant when Johnny says he is going to visit Mrs. Reardon. Johnny is worried that maybe John was not as fine as you thought.

Johnny has dinner with Pat and is troubled over the case. Johnny is going to start with Mrs. Reardon and, who knows how he will handle it. Pat notices Mrs. Reardon at the bar and Johnny goes to introduce himself. Johnny tells Elizabeth that he knew John and asks how he is. He is apologetic to learn he had been dead that long. Johnny was sure he met them in Denver three years ago. Mrs. Reardon invites Johnny out for a drink, and do not mention her husband's name again.

Tomorrow a little talk to a widow who may not be a widow at all, and a strong feeling that a smile can sometimes be more dangerous than a gun.

Episode 2   Show Date: 10/18/1955
Pat calls and asks about Mrs. Reardon. Johnny found out she is upset and invited me for cocktails.

Johnny calls George Handley, a P. I. and asks him to get information on Reardon. Johnny calls Mrs. Reardon and he is expected at 7:00 p.m. She is sorry for yelling at him last night. She was shocked at John's death and it disturbs her, but it is good to know he is dead. Johnny tells her that he is an investigator and almost tells why he is there. She tells Johnny that they had been married for four years, and he had given her all she needed. She was nineteen and not really grown up. She loved him, but Johnny is not convinced. She is not sure he loved her. They started not getting along and she started drinking.

Hugh Brian comes in and is introduced to Johnny. Brian tells Johnny that he must have never met Mrs. Reardon or you would not have started drinking with her. Brian is the Reardon attorney and tells Johnny he is just leaving. You never knew John Reardon and just picked her up. Good-bye Mr. Dollar.

Johnny spends several days investigating the boating accident and meets with Lt. Jack Halverson. Jack tells Johnny that the report told all the facts. The people who took the boat out did not know what they were doing. If the body was in the bay, we would have found it.

Johnny goes to visit Mrs. Reardon and Brian is there. Johnny tells Brian that he is working on a case about her husband being alive. Brian is told of the meeting with Coombs and Johnny is going to investigate. Brian says that his being alive would be wonderful for her and apologizes for thinking Johnny is a playboy after her. Brian agrees to get vital statistics on John Reardon.

Johnny gets a call from Elizabeth who tells him to drop the case, and then hangs up.

Tomorrow at trip to Denver and a look at a man whose gun makes it pretty emphatic he does not want to be looked at.

Episode 3   Show Date: 10/19/1955
Hugh Brian calls and he has the information on Reardon. Johnny wants the information and will meet him in an hour.

Johnny gets a telegram from Denver, and there is little evidence that Bowers is really Reardon. Johnny wires back and tells him Johnny will be there. Johnny sees Brian and he has the necessary documents for Johnny. Johnny explains the fraud aspects of the case to Brian. Johnny gets a picture, physical data, marriage license, fingerprints, etc.

Johnny leaves for Denver, Colorado. Johnny rents a car and meets with George Handley. George has little to say about Bowers — he has an office but only goes there occasionally. He gets money from a New York bank, and has a nice bank account. He does not go with anyone and has a lot of friends. He came to Denver in 1951 from Toledo. Bowers does not seem to be hiding from anyone. George looks at the picture and it matches Bowers. George continues working on background details.

Johnny visits Bowers and he tells Bowers he is making an investigation from Baltimore. Johnny reminds him of the meeting with Coombs and Bowers does not remember it. Johnny shows him the picture and he does resemble the man in the picture. Johnny asks him about going to Ohio State, but Bowers says he could have told him anything, he went to Carnegie Tech. Bowers has lived in a lot of places and was married once in 1942. Bowers starts to get uncomfortable. Johnny asks for a set of fingerprints and they go to George's office and take Bower's prints.

George notes that the prints do not match. Bowers is not Reardon. Johnny tells George to stay on the case.

Tomorrow another man comes to Denver. He doesn't check in to a hotel or carry luggage, at least not much luggage — just a .38 Colt.

Episode 4   Show Date: 10/20/1955
Western union calls with a wire from Baltimore about the information sent. Come home, your expenses are too high. Johnny wires that fingerprints do not lie but people do.

Johnny is trying to prove that John Reardon is still alive but the evidence points otherwise, but Johnny is not convinced.

Johnny meets with George, and he is watching Bower's house, but nothing will change. Johnny thinks the situation over and his stubborn ness — Frank Bowers was too cooperative.

Frank calls and asks how he made out with the fingerprints, he was curious. Johnny offers to meet him for a drink. Johnny figures him for being over confidant.

Bowers comes in, followed by George. Johnny asks Bowers what he should do? Johnny tells him he is too nice about too many things. Johnny says Bowers matches the book on him, but Johnny does not believe him. Johnny calls him a liar and Bowers wants to hit Johnny but leaves to make a phone call for a date.

Frank comes back and he does not have a date for the night. Frank gets mad and rushes out.

George tells Johnny that Frank had called Baltimore. Johnny follows Frank out and they encourage each other to go to Baltimore. They walk to Frank's car and Johnny is slugged and Frank drives off. Johnny goes to his room and waits for a call.

Next morning George calls and tells Johnny that Frank had gone home. Johnny wires Frank's fingerprints to Washington. George reports in that Franks is nervous.

Johnny goes to Frank's house to meet George. There is a man in Frank's house and they prepare to go in. The man leaves, there are shots, and George is hit. Johnny can only lay there as he does not have a gun.

Tomorrow proof that an insurance case is one thing, the murder of a pal is something else. Tomorrow, the windup.

Episode 5   Show Date: 10/21/1955
The operator calls and Pat is on the phone. Johnny tells Pat that Bowers was killed, as was George. Johnny wants to find out who killed George.

Johnny talks with the police. Lt. O'Neal talks to Johnny about the case and George's involvement. O'Neal tells Johnny that a big man with a topcoat was at Bowers' house and that he shot George and Bowers. Johnny had excited Bowers and he had called Baltimore. The police tell Johnny to be careful next time. Someone must have seen something. Three different people give the police information on the case. Bowers had let the man in and argued with him.

A neighbor tells Johnny that the man was taller and had a tweed coat, she would recognize him anywhere. O'Neal turns up a cab fare that had picked up a fare at the airport.

Johnny calls Pat in Baltimore and tells him that a man named Orrin Williams was the man who killed Bowers. O'Neal gives Johnny a wire from Washington. The prints Johnny had proved that Bowers was John Reardon. The prints Johnny had come from Brian. O'Neal says Bowers was trying to call Brian in Baltimore.

Johnny flies back to Baltimore and goes to Brian's residence. Ellen opens the door and Johnny wants to tell Ellen and Hugh something. Ellen tells Johnny that she had married Hugh Brian this morning.

Hugh comes downstairs and Johnny tells him things were not OK. Johnny tells him the police will be there to see him. He tells Ellen to listen as he tells Johnny that he will only tell this once, and it will be different in court.

Hugh tells them that he had gone to Denver to see John, who had been living there. John had been picked up by a fishing boat and was taken to Charleston. John had called Hugh and they arranged for John to disappear. It was John's idea. He was in debt and wanted out, it was his chance to get away from the things he hated. John told Hugh he could have Elizabeth for a price, $25,000 a year, which Hugh could afford.

And then along came Johnny Dollar. Johnny tells them that John Reardon is dead — shot to death by Hugh Brian. Hugh tells them that Frank/John had called and told Hugh he was going to tell Johnny everything, so he went out and shot him. It took Elizabeth five years to decide to marry Hugh and one day for John to decide to come back.

Exp. Acct: $1,124.98

Notes:
- This program was done as *The Walter Patterson Matter* by John Lund on 12/26/1952.
- Friendship is now the Baltimore/Washington International Thurgood Marshal Airport.
- Roy Rowan is the announcer.

- According to the script, music direction is by Rick Marino.

Producer:	Jack Johnstone Writer: John Dawson
Cast:	Jeanne Bates, D. J. Thompson, Hy Averback, Will Wright, John Dehner, Tony Barrett, Paul Dubov, Forrest Lewis

♦ ❖ ♦

Show: The Alvin Summers Matter
Company: Northeast Fidelity & Bonding
Agent: Fred Wilkins
Synopsis:
Episode 1   Show Date: 10/24/1955
Fred Wilkins calls Johnny with a case. Alvin Summers had embezzled $75,000 and Fred just got a call from Santa Tomas, Mexico from a man who has information about Summers.

Johnny flies to Santa Tomas and gets a room in the better hotel in town. Benito, the desk clerk, grabs his bag and becomes the bellboy. He tells Johnny that his cousin has a fishing boat, and he will show Johnny the sights for a small fee. In the room, Benito turns on the overhead fan and looks out the balcony. You can see the ocean, if you stand on the rail and look around the building. Johnny asks if anyone has been asking for him just as the balcony door slams shut because of the fan and surprises Johnny. Benito thinks Johnny is jumpy. Benito has never heard the name Summers. It is hard to think in the heat, but a $5 bill helps Benito's memory. Benito tells Johnny that he has seen the man and Johnny tells him he might have a few more bills for him.

As Johnny is resting and there is a knock at the door, and E.K. Carson wants to see Johnny. As soon as he saw Johnny, he knew he was an American and wants to get Johnny into cribbage game. Carson is the regional salesman for the Hold-Tight Zipper Company. Carson really wants to talk as he is really lonely. "We can talk and play a game of cribbage" he tells Johnny.

Johnny goes to the cantina next door and meets a girl there. Gloria talks to Johnny about the guitar player and notes there is no one listening to him. She picked a great spot for a vacation, at least it was until now. Johnny notes an American watching him and then the man leaves. Gloria is going to her hotel and Johnny will meet her there on the terrace in half an hour. Johnny thinks she wants more than his manly charms.

In his room, Johnny finds the man from the bar, but with a gun. He searches Johnny, takes his gun and wants to know who Johnny is. Johnny tries to talk to him but the man hits him. He knows why Johnny is here. He will hate it here, and hits Johnny again. "Leave now or leave never" he tells Johnny.

Tomorrow, a threesome on a moon lit beach. A girl, me and a man with a knife.

Episode 2   Show Date: 10/25/1955
Gloria calls and Johnny tells her about the man in the bar. Gloria wants to nurse Johnny on the terrace. Johnny gets a doctor to sew him up and then goes to meet Gloria.

At the Playa del Mar Hotel, Johnny meets Gloria on the terrace. He tells her what happened in the room, and that he will find out what it is about. Gloria tells Johnny that the place is less boring now. Gloria suspects Johnny is not in town on vacation as he is not the Santa Tomas type. She tells Johnny that he came here to find or meet someone. Maybe she was looking for Johnny or vice versa.

The flamenco singer is singing, so they walk down to the beach. Johnny sees Benito and he tells Johnny that a friend of his worked for the man in the picture as a house boy and told him where the house is in the jungle. Benito will take him there at midnight. Benito tells Johnny that he should not have come to the Playa del Mar, he will spend all of Benito's money.

Johnny runs into Carson on the way back to meet Gloria on the path to the beach where her scarf looks bigger than her bathing suit. Johnny gets some swimming trunks and they head for the water. They sit under the cliff and talk.

Johnny spots two men walking on the beach, and one is the man from the bar, and he has a friend with a machete. Johnny and Gloria hide behind the rocks until the men leave. Gloria is afraid Johnny is in some sort of trouble. She is afraid for Johnny and kisses him.

It is almost midnight, so Johnny goes to his room. The balcony door is open and someone is out there. It is Benito, dead from a cut throat.

Tomorrow, there are some people you do not want to meet in a dark alley. But sometimes it cannot be helped.

Episode 3   Show Date: 10/26/1955
Lt. Gomez calls and Johnny tells him he had been making funeral arrangements. Benito was found in your room. Let's discuss the matter further.

Johnny pays for the funeral and burial of Benito and goes to visit Gomez. Johnny tells Gomez that it was obvious that Benito died of knife wounds, but Johnny tells him what happened. But Gomez wants to know what is behind the killing, but Johnny has an alibi and had no reason to kill Benito.

Johnny gives Gomez his card and tells why he is in Santa Tomas. Johnny tells Gomez that Benito was going to take Johnny to the Summers house that night. Johnny tells Gomez about Carson and the man in his room.

Johnny is told that the man is Señor Krause, but Gomez does not know much about him. Sgt. Romero comes in and verifies Johnny's alibi with Gloria and tells Johnny that Carson has been arrested for disturbing the peace.

Johnny and Gomez talk to Carson, who tells them he was just having some fun, he had grabbed the serape of one of the dancers and chased her and broke a guitar. He was just trying to have some fun. Carson is told he will have to pay a fine and damages, and Johnny is sure he will expense it. Gomez tells Johnny that before the Playa del Mar was built, the town used to be a haven for undesirables from the states. Johnny tells Gomez that Gloria says she is on vacation, and Gomez tells Johnny that she has been in town for several months. Gomez warns Johnny to be careful and not to take the law in his own hands.

Gloria meets Johnny outside the police office and tells Johnny she heard about Benito. Johnny sees someone following them across the street. It is Krause. Johnny goes down an alley and tells Gloria to go to her hotel. Johnny waits for Krause and slugs him. Johnny beats him and wants to know why he is following Johnny.

Krause thinks Johnny is in Mexico to take him back to the states. Johnny is sure that Krause is wanted and tells Krause that he is not a cop and puts his lights out. Johnny goes to his room and hears someone there, so he goes in through the balcony to find Gloria going through his bags.

Tomorrow, how to fall into a trap in one easy lesson.

Episode 4   Show Date: 10/27/1955

Johnny finds Gloria in his room and Johnny tells her she was acting. She can explain, but Johnny does not want to be number two on the list of people killed in his room.

Johnny adds the expenses for entertaining Gloria Harris after he caught her searching the room. She is probably tied up with the Summers matter. She tells Johnny she is stranded because she has no passport. She has been drifting for a year and came to Santa Tomas because other fugitives were here. She was just trying to find out why Johnny is here.

Gloria tells Johnny that if he can help her get a passport, she can help him. She knows that Johnny is here about Alvin Summers because she read the report in his brief case, and she has met Alvin Summers. Johnny must know someone who has an extra passport for a price.

She tells Johnny that she will take him to see Alvin. She met him a couple months ago and had dinner there. Gloria tells Johnny that she only lied about one thing, why she was here. Everything else she meant.

Gloria leaves and Johnny thinks about the case and then decides to go to meet her. The phone rings, and Fred tells Johnny that Alvin called again this morning and wants to know if someone is coming down.

There is a knock at the door and it is Lt. Gomez, who is angry that Kraus had been beaten. Do not take the law into your hands. Johnny tells Gomez that he has to do things on his own because Gomez only has two men. Lt. Gomez is afraid he will have to attend Johnny's funeral too.

Johnny and Gloria walk down the beach and go past the path to Summers house and work their way back to the path in case someone is watching. Johnny hears someone tailing them. Gloria walks on and Johnny circles toward the sound. Johnny trips and the man disappears.

They approach the house and Johnny opens the door, but there is no one there. It looks like he has not been there for several days and there are signs of two people being in the house. Maybe he is dead. Johnny tells Gloria to talk as he goes back outside to catch who ever there was out there.

Suddenly there is a gun in his back and a voice tells him to drop his gun and do not turn around. Any move might be your last.

Tomorrow, how to find out what you have been looking for the hard way.

Episode 5   Show Date: 10/28/1955
Johnny tells the voice his name. The voice tells Johnny not to move or it will be his last.

Johnny figures his life is worth 2 cents now. The man wants to talk to him. The man tells Johnny to be in his room in one hour and then disappears.

Gloria comes out and the man is gone. Johnny tells Gloria that he did not find anything. She is worried about her passport and tells Johnny that her imagination is working overtime as she thinks someone is watching her. Johnny is sure that the voice is the man who called.

Back at his hotel, Johnny sees Carson checking out, because half the world is waiting to get zipped up! Carson wants Johnny to keep the events of the previous night quiet, and Johnny assures him that his secret is safe. Carson tells Johnny that he will look him up in the states.

When Johnny gets to his room, the phone is ringing, but no one is there. There is a voice in his room that tells Johnny that he has searched the room. The voice is Alvin Summers. He had made the calls and is ready to give up.

Johnny turns on the fan as Summers starts to talk and the balcony door slams shut so Johnny turns the fan off. Alvin tells Johnny that his deal went real sour and he spent his time hiding instead of having a good time. Every shadow is someone following him. So, he called the bonding company to send an investigator. Johnny tells Alvin to come home and bring the money, which Alvin tells Johnny amounts to $60,000 and is in a safe deposit box in Mexico City, because he had to be careful. Alvin tells Johnny that he had come to search his room and saw Benito come in, but he did not kill him. Alvin had kept under cover so they would not find him, the man who arranged for him to come here and the woman who helped him.

Gloria comes in with a gun and wants the safe deposit key. She had found out that Summers was going to turn himself in but he disappeared and she used Johnny to find him. Gloria invites Johnny to come with her, but he wants no part of it.

There are shots from the balcony and Gloria is dead. Carson comes in and tells Summers that he had crossed him. He tells Johnny that he had to kill Benito.

Johnny turns on the fan as Carson talks, he needs some air. When the door slams Carson wheels, Johnny knocks the lamp over and shoots Carson. Johnny tells Summers to call the police and Johnny tells Carson he finally got Johnny into a game and he lost.

Johnny takes Alvin back with him to the states. He wonders if Gloria meant what she said, not that it matters.

    Exp. Acct: $923.00

Notes:
- Roy Rowan is the announcer.
- According to the script, music direction is by Rick Marino.

Producer:	Jack Johnstone Writer: Robert Ryf
Cast:	Virginia Gregg, Marvin Miller, Don Diamond, Tony Barrett, Parley Baer

♦ ❖ ♦

Show:	**The Valentine Matter**
Company:	**New Britain Insurance Company**
Agent:	**Roy Vickers**
Synopsis:	
Episode 1	**Show Date: 10/31/1955**

Roy Vickers calls and tells Johnny that a bellhop has robbed a safe in a New Orleans hotel. A diamond necklace is the property of a client. Look into it for us.

Johnny goes to New Orleans, Louisiana where the police have wrapped up the case with all the goods recovered. Johnny reports the results and looks for something to do.

Johnny finds a bar and runs into a rugged old man. Johnny recognizes the man as a prohibition era figurehead. Johnny sits down and introduces himself to Mr. Valentine and buys him a drink. Valentine pegs Johnny for a cop but Johnny tells him he is an insurance investigator but once was a cop.

Valentine has been in New Orleans for three months and no one has recognized him. Valentine tells Johnny about his days violating the Volstead Act and that he wants to live a nice quiet life and is flattered that Johnny recognized him. Johnny agrees that he will not tell the police or anyone that Valentine had the dinner Johnny would buy for him at Jimmy Moran's. After dinner, they listen to some jazz and drink sazaracks.

The next day as Johnny prepares to leave he is given a message from Inspector De Baca of the police, who wants Johnny to come to his office to talk to him.

De Baca asks Johnny about Dan Valentine and his evening with him. Johnny is told that the police have been watching Valentine and they want to know if Johnny had any business with him. Valentine has no visitors and lives alone, and you are his first visitor.

The phone rings, and De Baca is told that Dan Valentine has been shot. A newspaper boy found him and a neighbor carried him in.

They go to the scene and Johnny tells Dan that the police had called him in. Dan tells Johnny that he shot himself cleaning his gun and asks Johnny to phone a private hospital for him. Dan is operated on and Johnny waits for him to wake up.

De Baca tells Johnny that he is sticking around to make sure Dan is OK because Dan is quite a man. Dan wakes up and thanks Johnny for his help. Dan insists that he shot himself, but Johnny encourages him to go to the police. Dan tells Johnny that he will handle things himself.

Johnny cabs to the airport, is delayed for five hours until his plane is fixed. Johnny gets a call from Roy Vickers in Hartford. Johnny tells Roy about the incident with Dan. Roy tells Johnny that New Britain carries a $50,000 policy on Dan, so look into it. Okay, Roy!

Tomorrow all the king's men, that could be the New Orleans police force, try to keep one man alive. And they almost do it.

Episode 2**Show Date:****11/1/1955**
Insp. De Baca calls and Johnny tells him that he has been assigned to look into the Valentine matter. Johnny is told that Dan has said nothing, and only Dan can keep himself alive.

Johnny requests a copy of the insurance policy and beneficiary information. Johnny meets with De Baca and tells him the insurance company wants a separate report. They want to make sure the policy is not being broken. Johnny thinks that, unofficially, the company wants Dan to stay alive. De Baca tells Johnny that Valentine has lived quietly, but now you meet him and he is shot. "Are you a bad-news boy?" Johnny is asked.

Johnny tells De Baca he is wrong and De Baca gives Johnny a very thick folder on Dan Valentine, his long and sorted history, prison on tax evasion and a wife and daughter. De Baca brings in a witness to the shooting, Willy Blakley. Willy was driving a milk truck and saw Valentine walking. A black car approached with two men and Valentine stopped and looked at the car and smiled a sad smile. Willy would not recognize the men again. When Valentine stopped, Willy heard two noises, "Whack!" and Valentine fell down. Willy was scared and left. De Baca thinks the noises were from a silenced gun.

Johnny visits Dan but he can have no visitors, as he is weak. A woman comes in to see Dan and Johnny follows her. She gets into a cab and Johnny follows her in a cab. He goes to her room and introduces himself to Mrs. Anne Valentine.

Johnny tells her who he is, and she tells Johnny that she has not been called by that name in many years, in the hotel she is Anne Ward. Johnny tells her that he wants to keep Dan alive, just like she does. She tells Johnny that she has not seen or contacted Dan in thirteen years, and his daughter knows nothing of her father. Her daughter thinks that she is on vacation. Dan wanted her not to contact him as he was ashamed of what his reputation would do to her. Johnny is sure that there is something to worry about.

Johnny eats and gets a package from Hartford, checks with De Baca and goes to the hospital where Johnny gets the run around. Johnny learns that Dan has disappeared from the hospital. A nurse tells Johnny to find Mr. Valentine if you want to keep him alive. Johnny is worried about Dan taking care of the matter himself, even if it kills him.

Tomorrow, what happens to a 30-year-old grudge when somebody explains it with bullets.

Episode 3**Show Date:****11/2/1955**
Ann Ward calls and asks Johnny if he has heard from Dan. She is worried he will die. Johnny tells her that he has not told the police she is in town. Ann wants Johnny to come over and talk.

Johnny meets with Mrs. Valentine and she is very worried about Dan. She does not know where Dan is and thinks he might have wanted to see somebody. Johnny asks why Dan came to New Orleans to live. She tells Johnny that he did not want to interfere with their lives. She has no answers to any of Johnny's other questions. Ann tells Johnny that a man named Conrad Webster lives in the area, and he had done legal work for Dan in the old days. Johnny remembers that he had seen the name on Dan's insurance policy. Dan might have gone to him for help. Johnny will try to find Webster and maybe Dan.

Johnny locates Webster in a crummy duplex on Gentile Street and wants to talk. Johnny has a bonded gift for him. After a long pull at the bottle, Johnny tells Webster that he is looking for a man, Dan Valentine, a friend of his. Webster tells Johnny he is not a friend of Dan's, as he does not look like an ex-prisoner. Dan is not there and he does not know where to contact him. Johnny is told that his concern is a pressing irritation to Webster. Johnny tells Webster that he is a friend, but Webster tells him that all of Dan's friends are gone. Dan should have never lived in that age, he was an explorer. Webster has not the strength to be anyone's friend and he bids Johnny goodnight.

Johnny goes to his hotel and the next morning the papers are full of the story, including the news of Dan's wife and daughter. Johnny calls Anne and apologizes for the events. She is going call her daughter and tell her. Johnny suggests she change hotels and names.

Johnny calls De Baca, and Dan is still missing and the two men are still unidentified. Johnny goes to the Roosevelt Hotel to see Mrs. Ward and De Baca is there. Johnny is told that Dan had come in, gone to her room and then left with Mrs. Valentine. That evening De Baca and Johnny go to a small hotel where they find Mr. and Mrs. Valentine, dead.

Tomorrow, proof that the murder of Dan Valentine and his wife are not the only murders to be solved.

Episode 4   Show Date: 11/3/1955

Roy Vickers calls and asks Johnny about Valentine. Johnny tells Roy he could not find him, let alone keep him alive. Roy has just talked with the daughter. Johnny is told to do what he can, as Roy needs a full report.

Johnny and De Baca eat dinner and discuss the case. Two men with dark suits was the description of the men who killed the Valentines. The job was a professional one and Valentine knew them. Valentine saw his wife was in town and Ann just got in the way. Johnny thinks it has something to do with his family. If Dan was expecting trouble from his enemies, he would have carried a gun.

De Baca tells Johnny that Dan had spent most of his time painting and listening to music. De Baca tells Johnny to have Webster visit him. as he is missing.

Johnny learns that the bullets were from an Italian pistol, a Rombero of 37.5 caliber, so far untraced.

Johnny goes to the Valentine house and meets the cook, Mrs. Iacino. She tells Johnny that it has been a hard day, what with the police and Miss Ward. Teresa comes in and wants to talk to Johnny, and Johnny finds Teresa to be a beautiful girl. Teresa wants to know about her father but Johnny cannot tell her much.

Johnny tells her that Dan had thought about her by the things he did. When she was young, Dan had set up a trust for her, which has paid for her education. Now that he is dead, she gets the trust. She tells Johnny that she hardly knew her father but is very upset about her mother's death and cries. Johnny comforts her and they talk.

They talk about Dan's paintings that look like Italian landscapes. Johnny is told that Teresa's mother came from Italy. Teresa tells Johnny that she wants to see Johnny again. Johnny leaves and goes back the next day to talk to Mrs. Iacino.

Johnny helps with the funeral arrangements and goes back to work with De Baca. The police have found Webster by Lake Pontchartrain, shot to death by the same gun that killed Valentine.

Johnny goes to see Teresa who is frantic. She tells Johnny that she has been hounded by the press and by a Hollywood agent. Johnny realizes that she has grown to love her father. They walk outside and shots are fired. Terry is shot and dies as Johnny reaches for his gun, but no one is there.

Tomorrow a sober lesson on how long, how far and how deadly one man's hate can be.

Episode 5   Show Date: 11/4/1955
De Baca calls and Johnny tells him what happened. Johnny checks his gun and goes looking for the killers.

After Teresa is shot, Johnny staggers down the driveway and sees a car pulling away. Johnny shoots twice at the car and is shot at twice. The car crashes, and Johnny runs towards it and pulls a wounded man from the car, but there is also a dead man in the car. The man's name is Sisto, and he wants a doctor. Johnny threatens to kill him if he does not talk.

De Baca arrives and he takes Johnny's gun. Johnny tells De Baca that he should have killed him, he wanted to kill him. Johnny waits while the body of Teresa is taken away. Johnny and De Baca discuss the events and Sisto has told the police nothing. De Baca had found papers that identify the men as Sisto and Darvy Chianti from New York. Johnny and De Baca cannot figure things out and then learns that Sisto has died.

Johnny goes to the Valentine house and Mrs. Iacino is there. She knows nothing of the Chianti brothers. Dan had given her a thousand dollars and he was a nice man who had been forgiven. Johnny looks at the paintings and goes back to see De Baca who tells Johnny that the New York police have reported that the Chianti brothers came to America at age 18, were naturalized citizens with no records. The father was due to be processed soon, but he has disappeared.

Johnny tries to sleep when De Baca calls and tells Johnny that Mr. Chianti has come to get his sons at the morgue. De Baca and Johnny talk to the man. He knows the boys had killed the others but will not say much other than he is still alive.

Johnny appears before a coroner's jury and is cleared of all charges.

Johnny visits Pietro Chianti and tells him that Ann Valentine was his daughter and that Johnny has a copy of the marriage license from New York. Pietro tells him that Teresa and the others had to die because they were all bad. He had ordered it. He was the father. Only bad can come from a bad man.

Dan had taken his daughter from his village in Italy many years ago, and Webster had helped. He lived to find Valentine and kill everyone involved. It was a vendetta. He was a bad man who did bad things.

Johnny leaves New Orleans and has had enough of the town.

"Remarks: Whenever I close my eyes, I can see a lovely girl standing at the bottom of a long curving stairway, smiling because I am in the room. That's all."

Exp. Acct: $1,290.38

Notes:
- This story was done as *The San Antonio Matter*, broadcast on 4/28/1953.
- The Volstead Act, passed in 1919, enforced prohibition under the 18th amendment to the Constitution.
- The sazarack is the quintessential New Orleans cocktail of French brandy mixed with his secret blend of bitters, a drop of water and a bit of sugar.
- Jimmy Moran's is a famous New Orleans restaurant.
- Roy Rowan is the announcer.
- According to the script, music direction is by Rick Marino.

Producer:	Jack Johnstone	Writer:	John Dawson
Cast:	Lillian Buyeff, Betty Lou Gerson, Barney Phillips, Will Wright, Forrest Lewis, Marvin Miller, Jay Novello, Jack Moyles		

♦ ❖ ♦

Show: The Lorko Diamond's Matter
Company: Transworld Fidelity Company
Agent: Ben Tyler
Synopsis:
Episode 1   **Show Date:**   **11/7/1955**

Ben Tyler calls and asks Johnny to go to Algiers. Lorko Diamonds has just lost courier with a briefcase full of diamonds in Algiers, and the briefcase is missing.

Johnny goes to Algiers, Algeria in North Africa. The easy trip was ended when Johnny lands and talks to Inspector Marcus of the Algerian police, who trusts special investigators and is sure Johnny will catch the criminals in a matter of hours. But Johnny feels a "cold wind" from the inspector.

Johnny follows Marcus to his office where a man from the local diamond firm is waiting to give Johnny the details. Johnny is sure nothing escapes the inspector, except the diamonds. Marcus tells Johnny that the officials in Paris say that Pierre "goofed". Jan Zeindorf is very excitable about the diamonds, as Africa is for barbarians.

Johnny is told that the courier had worked for Lorko for 15 years and that he never had heart failure before. Paul Gruber, the courier, was unexpectedly taken ill on the plane and died in the police clinic, and the autopsy is this afternoon. The briefcase was given to the customs property man, Andre Jordine who was busy and did not have time to place the briefcase in the vault immediately. A few minutes later Marcus heard shots. Marcus discovered that Jordine had been shot and the diamonds were gone.

Marcus found out what was in the briefcase two hours later — $100,000 worth of diamonds in various settings. They were being sent to Countess Maria D'Atolia, a beautiful, sleek, chic woman. She may be the only one who knew the diamonds were coming. Johnny is told that Jordine will recover, and Zeindorf is still very nervous.

Johnny talks to the plane crew and the airport staff. Johnny thinks that maybe Jordine might be the man.

Johnny goes to the hospital and visits Jordine and tells him who he is. Jordine tells Johnny that he was working in the files, turned around to see a tall, thin man with a gun. He ordered him to turn around and then the man hit him and took the briefcase. He fumbled for his gun and fired a shot. He did not know what was in the briefcase. Johnny examines the wound and tells Jordine that he is lucky to be alive. Jordine knows the Countess and she is so... The pet theory is limping now and Jordine is not the suspect.

Marcus meets Johnny in the hospital and asks, with a smile, how Johnny is doing. Not good is the answer. Marcus tells Johnny that the autopsy is in and the courier died of poison. The courier was poisoned on the plane by someone who knew what he was carrying, and that was the Countess D'Atolia.

Tomorrow, a lovely woman lies beautifully and a sinister whisper drifts out of the Casbah.

Episode 2   Show Date: 11/8/1955
The Countess D'Atolia calls Johnny, and she is at her residence. "Did you think I would just run over to see you?", she asks. Johnny tells her that he wants to talk to her about the diamonds. I'll be there at 8:00.

At dinner, Johnny is met by Insp. Marcus, who would love to have a glass of his favorite brandy. Insp. Marcus is still working on the man who sat next to the courier. Insp. Marcus is amazed that Johnny has not solved the case yet. He suggests Johnny change his plans to question the Countess, but Johnny thinks she is in this up to her neck. Johnny thinks she has every one hypnotized by her charm, and that an accomplice could have helped her kill the courier. When Johnny asks if Insp. Marcus is the man, he tells Johnny that he wonders what he would do if the countess asked him to kill someone.

The American consulate calls with some information and then Johnny goes to see the Countess who opens the door and is surprised that he came. Johnny tells her that we either play "cat-and-mouse" or do you turn yourself in now? As Johnny explains why he thinks she is involved, she asks for a cigarette and tells Johnny she expected him to be annoying but not insulting. You are under the idea I had something to do with the theft. Johnny has more than one reason as she is the only one who knew of the diamonds.

She tells Johnny that dozens of her friends knew the diamonds were coming, but Johnny shows a letter telling exactly when they were coming and instructions not to tell anyone. She tells Johnny that she had told a girl she had met at a party, and Insp. Marcus was there. Johnny tells her that her title is inherited and she has moved around since the end of the war. She is well known and gets a long on her title and her looks but is flat broke. Yet she orders diamonds on approval. So how were you going to pay for them?

She throws an ashtray at Johnny and tells him to leave, and then she cries. Johnny holds her and kisses her and tells her it was a sudden impulse. But he still thinks she is guilty.

Suddenly Johnny tells her to douse the cigarette and open the windows as he heads for the kitchen to find all of the gas jets open. Johnny breaks the windows and turns off the gas. In a closet Johnny finds the body of Zeindorf, who seems to be a little bit dead.

Tomorrow, a desperate fight in an Algiers alley, a killer is named, and a lovely lady confesses her shame.

Episode 3   Show Date: 11/9/1955
The Countess' phone rings and then goes dead. The Countess tells Johnny that she knows nothing about Zeindorf. The Countess gives Zeindorf some smelling salts to wake him up. She tells Johnny that Zeindorf knew some things and he will tell Johnny.

Johnny buys smelling salts for Zeindorf and scotch for himself. Zeindorf wakes up and tells Johnny that he was there because no one has found the diamonds, so he came himself. He was hiding and waiting for everyone to go to sleep but he does not know who turned on the gas. The Countess tells Johnny that her maid is not here, that she left when Johnny got there. She hired the woman through and agency, and she lives in the Casbah. Zeindorf gets ready to leave and Johnny tells him that the diamond people normally investigate their clients so why did you send diamonds to someone who is broke.

The Countess tells Johnny that she was not really the client. Someone else would actually pay for the diamonds, up to $20,000. The man is Charles Barrett. He has been in Algiers for about three months and lives on a yacht. Zeindorf has a letter from Barrett promising to pay for the diamonds up to $20,000 in exchange for considerations, they are an engagement present. The Countess is sorry Johnny kissed her as Barrett is an overbearing spoiled little boy. She tells Johnny that she has few other options. Johnny tells her she is not he first woman to marry for money. "Who said anything about marriage?", she asks. So far both suspects are off the hook.

As Johnny takes a car to the yacht of Charles Barrett he notices an English car following him. The car matches speeds with him and Johnny tells the driver to block the road so he can talk to the driver. "Let's hope we have seen the same movies" muses Johnny.

Johnny runs back to the car and a big beefy man comes out fighting. Johnny knocks him out and searches him as Insp. Marcus drives up. Insp. Marcus tells Johnny the man is Charles Barrett. Insp. Marcus was following him and, by the way, Marcus enjoyed the fisticuffs, but Johnny's footwork was just so-so.

Marcus tells Johnny that a man named Bobo sat next to the courier, and they shared a bottle of wine. Bobo is well known in the Casbah and can be hired. Marcus has not tried to pick him up, as police in the Casbah makes people disappear. Also, Marcus tells Johnny that Jordine has disappeared.

Marcus tells Johnny that he has bugged the countess' apartment and their conversation was most interesting. Johnny calls Marcus a rat. But not to worry, Marcus tells him, he is the soul of discretion, and a Frenchman!

Johnny notes that the Casbah had been mentioned twice that night. He has questions, and the trail leads to the Casbah.

Tomorrow, a bungling fool, a tightening net and a violent death in a crooked alley in the Casbah.

Episode 4   Show Date: 11/10/1955
Abdul calls Johnny and tells him that he has a little business and Johnny is looking for him. Abdul runs an employment agency and he hired the countess's maid. Johnny will pay Abdul $10 for the address.

Johnny pays $15 to Abdul for the address of a girl named Chatta, who Johnny thinks was the one who turned on the gas. In his hotel room, Johnny puts a gun in his pocket as there is a knock at the door. It is Charlie Barrett who apologizes for the fight. Johnny wants to know what he wants. Charlie tells Johnny that he is in the meat business, he cans the squeal. Charlie wants to talk man-to-man. He has a claim on the countess and has bought things for her. They had a fight last week when he told her she had to stop "ginnyflipping" around with other men, and that made her mad. The fight was before the diamonds were shipped here, and he cannot forget about her. Johnny tells Charles he was in the apartment for business. Charles tells Johnny that he is someone in the States, but Johnny slugs him and calls room service to drag him out to the hall.

Johnny goes to the Casbah and walks through the streets, and people stop talking as he passes by. Johnny goes to the address Abdul gave him, which was a coffeehouse. Johnny goes in and asks for Chatta and is told to sit down. Johnny sits and drinks coffee and waits.

Finally, a man sits with him. The man knows how to find Chatta, as she is his wife, and he is Bobo, the man that killed the courier. He tells Johnny that he only gave him some wine but maybe it was a bad vintage. Bobo wants to talk of diamonds. It is possible Chatta turned on the gas but Bobo wants to talk of diamonds. Bobo tells Johnny that the company would like to get the diamonds back and Bobo asks about making a deal. Bobo can lead him to their location and he has at least 30 men in the room to protect him if Johnny tries anything. Johnny tells Bobo he does not make deals with killers.

A voice warns of the police and Bobo disappears. Insp. Marcus comes in to find an empty coffeehouse. Johnny tells Insp. Marcus that he had had a gun on Bobo and that Marcus has goofed. There are shots outside and they run out and search the area.

Johnny finds Bobo in an alley, shot three times in the back. Bobo tells Johnny that a 12-foot-tall dragon shot him to protect his honor. Bobo admits that he attacked Jordine and dies.

Marcus comes up and they look at the short stocky body of Bobo. Johnny tells Marcus that he knows the whole story, the whole filthy rotten story.

Tomorrow, the odds are set, the last chip is down, and it is the last spin of the wheel, and death is the croupier.

Episode 5   Show Date: 11/11/1955

The Countess calls and tells Johnny that she is being followed. She is in a coffeehouse on the waterfront. Johnny tells her that everything was set up, now she has to stay there.

Johnny cabs to the waterfront to go to the Countess. Insp. Marcus had set a trap, but she left before he got there. The street is dark and Johnny enters the Marrakech coffeehouse. She tells Johnny that she was visiting a friend, Charlie. Johnny tells her of the conversation with Charlie, and she tells Johnny that she knew he would come around. Johnny tells her the facts just seem to point to her. Johnny asks about Charlie, and she is not sure that she will marry him. Charlie had given her his car, and someone had followed her.

As they leave, shots ring out and Johnny runs for a curb to draw their fire. Johnny fires back and a man runs away and into a car. Johnny gets in Charlie's car and they follow the other car.

Johnny follows the car and finally has to stop when the other car misses a turn, rolls down a hill and explodes. Johnny sees the driver of the car before it explodes. Johnny tells the Countess that now that she knows that she is safe, that the other driver, Jordine, will not talk as he was the only one left, and oh, Maria did not know about Bobo, he is dead too.

The plan was to make sure that the courier died, so that the briefcase would go to Jordine. But Bobo was a tough cookie. He attacked Jordine but tried to kill him but Andre got to his gun. Andre got the idea for a double cross and went after Bobo in the Casbah and killed him. Now Insp. Marcus is at her apartment waiting for Andre to appear. Why did both Andre and Bobo try to kill her unless she was in on it? She tries the charm routine, but it fails. Johnny tells her she is rotten and leaves the Countess to walk back to town.

Johnny goes to the Customs Property office with Marcus who opens the safe that contains the briefcase with the diamonds...so beautiful. Johnny knew that Andre was lying because he described his assailant as tall and thin, but Bobo was short and stocky, so Andre had lied. The diamonds were in the vault where Andre had access to them. Insp. Marcus will probably not do anything to the Countess, as she would cry and the court would blame him.

"Social Item. To be circulated widely. The Countess Maria D'Atolia was married yesterday to C. K Barrett, a big tycoon in the meat business. The

happy couple will make their home in Chicago. All companies in that area who may be asked to underwrite insurance on the life of C. K. Barrett — DON'T!"
Exp. Acct: $1,214.60

Notes:
- The Casbah is the old section of most North African towns.
- In the cast line-up at the end of episode 5, C. K. Barrett is listed as a cast member, but he is a character in the story. The script title page for episode 4 lists Gerald Mohr as C. K. Barrett.
- Roy Rowan is the announcer.
- Musical supervision is by Amerigo Marino.

Producer:	Jack Johnstone	Writer:	Les Crutchfield
Cast:	Lillian Buyeff, Jack Moyles, Vic Perrin, Gerald Mohr, Lawrence Dobkin, Forrest Lewis, Jay Novello		

◆ ❖ ◆

Show: **The Broderick Matter**
Company: **Eastern Trust Insurance Company**
Agent: **Robert Steel**
Synopsis:
Episode 1   Show Date: 11/14/1955

Mr. Steele calls. The Universal Adjustment Bureau suggested that he call Johnny. They need help paying the beneficiary of a policy as she has disappeared.

Johnny takes a bus to the Hartford, Connecticut office of Robert Steele. The policyholder was John Smith, he was malnourished and had two policies for $1,500 and the beneficiary was Lorraine Broderick. John Smith made his payments on time every month but he was broke and sold newspapers for a living. Lorraine was eleven at the time and just stopped by to talk to him one day. Smith asked an agent to help him do something for a nice little girl. It has hard for him to make the payments, so let's hope that Lorraine deserves the insurance.

Johnny goes to the last known address of Lorraine and learns that the parents were killed in 1948 and Lorraine had moved out.

Johnny goes to a high school in the area and speaks to Sister Mary Regina. Johnny tells her he is looking for Lorraine Broderick, who possibly went to school there. She looks in the files and she did attend the school and there is an address for a guardian uncle. Sister Mary remembers Lorraine, who had the face of an angel. Johnny tells her about the insurance policies and the Sister gets an annual and shows Johnny a picture of Lorraine.

Johnny goes to the address of the uncle, but he had died, and Lorraine had moved. Johnny learns that Lorraine had worked for a dentist after that. Johnny calls Mr. Steel and asks for help in tracking the agencies that hire for dentists. Johnny also tries to locate Lorraine through former students.

Johnny gets the name of Dr. David Pollard who had hired Lorraine. Johnny talks to Dr. Pollard and he asks Johnny how she is. Lorraine had not worked there for several years and he does not have an address for her. She quit suddenly and never came back. Dr. Pollard goes with Johnny for a drink and tells him that she was a sweet girl, but there was something about her and she had plans of her own. Many men were used by her and knew it. She was out to take people for what she could get. She is rotten, plain rotten.

Tomorrow, the expense goes way up. Yeah, it takes money to prove how wrong one man can be.

Episode 2   Show Date: 11/15/1955

Carl Walden calls Johnny. Lorraine used to live in his apartment building. She moved out with no forwarding address. Carl does not think she wants to be found.

Johnny gets photographs of Lorraine from the high school photographer. Carl Walden tells Johnny that she had pulled out in the middle of the night and probably went to New York. She had walked out on some doctor who probably had it really bad for her. There was another guy too, a big man with gray hair, a homburg and a Cadillac, but he never came around again after she moved out.

Johnny places ads in the New York papers and checks with Cadillac dealers in the area. After five days Johnny gets a call from Lorraine in New York. She wants to know what Johnny wants. The line is suddenly switched and a Mr. Dameron is on the phone. He tells Johnny that he knows Lorraine.

Johnny goes to New York City and meets Mr. William Dameron. Dameron is the president of the Union Brokerage Company. Dameron knew Lorraine and asks for Johnny's credentials. Johnny tells Dameron about the policies and his efforts to find Lorraine. Dameron does not know where she is. She came to New York with him and they were going to be married even though he only knew her a week.

He was taking her to a party and stopped for gas. Lorraine got out of the car and disappeared. She was staying with Dameron's sister and left her clothes there. Dameron thinks that Lorraine was frightened of life. He thought he could offer her the security she longed for, but she was too immature. Dameron tells Johnny that he waited for her to return but she never came back. She just got out and left for her own reasons.

Dameron gives Johnny the location of the gas station and Johnny tells him that the others had told him the truth, so why would she leave on Christmas Eve with no clothes or plans. "How much did she take?" Johnny asks. Dameron tells Johnny she took $6,500 from his wallet and notes that "there is no fool like an old fool, is there?"

Tomorrow, when the trail really gets hot and goes right down on a police blotter.

Episode 3   Show Date: 11/16/1955

Bob Steel calls, and Johnny tells him he has not found Lorraine. "Do you want to go on?" asks Johnny. Steel says yes. Johnny thinks John Smith left money to a nice little girl, and he is trying to find a woman who is not so nice anymore.

Johnny goes to the gas station and talks to the man who was on duty. Edward Quinlan remembers her. She just got out and walked down the street. He felt sorry for the guy. Johnny talks to Dameron's sister who verifies his story.

Johnny requests a missing-persons investigation and learns that she had been booked under an alias on drunk and disorderly charges. Johnny goes to the address on the record but Lorraine had moved. The landlady tells Johnny Lorraine was always having parties and had lots of men around.

Johnny rechecks the court record for those arrested with her. One of the men tells Johnny that he saw her at an apartment building in Manhattan.

Johnny checks with the manager of the apartment building and learns that there was a Lorraine Bradley there four months ago, and the picture matches. She had written a bad check and the police are looking for her. The police records for Lorraine Bradley show five warrants in New York, Chicago, and San Francisco. Three days ago, she had passed a bad check in Santa Barbara. Johnny calls Mr. steel and gets permission to travel to the coast.

Johnny travels to Santa Barbara, California and talks to the operator of a hotel who is chagrined about being taken. Mr. Harrington tells Johnny that she was the best at getting what she wanted. She was there for four days and had the best of everything and paid for the $813 bill with a bad check. Johnny asks why she would check in alone, and Mr. Harrington tells Johnny that she had become friends with others in the hotel.

She came in a cab and called for the manager and pretended she knew him. She said she had just been divorced and was coming from Lake Tahoe. Mr. Harrington checked the address and there was a Robert Bradley in Beverly Hills, but Mr. Harrington learned that Mr. Bradley was in Europe with his wife and family. The bill showed no phone calls and the check was a blank one.

Johnny meets with Sgt. Martin, who tells Johnny that the same woman has passed bad checks all over the area. Johnny interviews the others who had taken the bad checks, and the story is the same.

Johnny calls Mr. Steel and he tells Johnny that Lorraine has just hit in Malibu Beach.

Tomorrow, a long look at what seven years can do to a woman's life.

Episode 4   Show Date: 11/17/1955

Deputy King from the Malibu Sheriff calls Johnny and he tells Johnny that he wants Lorraine, and Johnny tells King that they both want Lorraine. King is expecting some action, come on over.

Johnny travels to Malibu Beach and meets with King who tells Johnny that Lorraine was in the local inn, using the name Bradley. She hung out with Joe Tappan, who had driven her down town that morning. Tappan lives in the artist colony. A call comes in and Tappan is home, so King and Johnny drive out to see Joe Tappan.

Johnny and King stun Joe with the news that Lorraine is a phony. The picture matches and Joe tells Johnny that he thought he knew her when he met her at the Seaside Inn four days ago, but there must be some explanation. He dropped her bags at the Beverly Glen hotel and then took her to a bar to meet her lawyer. She was dressed in a black dress and a mink stole. The story she gave was that a baby had died and drove her away from her husband, and Joe believed her. Joe tells Johnny to try believing in people for a change.

Johnny drives to Hollywood and the luggage is still in the hotel. The lobby is watched and Johnny and King go to the Topper Club, but the bartender has not seen the woman there today.

The luggage is not claimed that day and so Johnny goes to see Joe Tappan again and tells him that Joe did not hear what Johnny told him. Johnny tells Joe the whole story, and that there was no baby. Johnny tells Joe that he has to find her to stop her and Joe is involved. "Where is she?" Johnny demands.

Joe tells Johnny that she is at the Wentmore Hotel under the name Evelyn Brady. She had called Joe an hour ago and told Joe she loved him. What kind of crazy world is this?

Johnny goes to room 1302 in the Wentmore Hotel. Johnny finds the door open and knocks. He goes in and finds a woman on the ledge ready to jump.

Tomorrow, the end of the trail for me, and for Lorraine Broderick.

Episode 5   Show Date: 11/18/1955
The desk clerk calls, and Johnny tells him to call the police. Lorraine tells Johnny it will do no good, as she is going to jump.

Lorraine tells Johnny to back off, she is going to jump. Johnny tries to calm her and offers her his coat. She asks Johnny how he knows her name. Johnny tells her of the high school picture and she wants to see his face and tells Johnny that he is not from Hartford, and she never knew him.

The room clerk comes up and Lorraine screams, and Johnny tells him to call the police. She tells Johnny that she wants the police and a big crowd for when she jumps. She sees a crowd gathering. Johnny tells her that if she dies it will make him afraid to die. She is not afraid to jump she tells Johnny. Johnny tells her that she was afraid to love any of the men she had been involved with. Johnny tells her he wants to help her.

She asks Johnny why everyone died and left her alone. Johnny tells her that Mr. Dameron still loves her, but she does not love him. She says she is no good and never has been. She tells Johnny to tell Dameron she meant to send the money back.

Someone runs in and she screams to get out and close the door. She finally knows what she wants to do, and that is to jump. She tells Johnny that she should have died with her parents. Johnny tells her that old John Smith had faith in her, and it meant a lot to him. She remembers buying a paper from him and talking to him that one day. Johnny tells her he had bought the policies for her. Johnny shows her the check and his identification papers. Lorraine cries over that poor old man.

It was Johnny's first and hopefully last experience with a suicide. Johnny returns the check, as Lorraine is not a responsible person, but the psychiatrist says she will be OK in time. Mr. Dameron is called and comes to Los Angeles, Joe Tappan has hired an attorney and the insurance company wants restitution rather than prosecution.

Exp. Acct: $1,132.14

Notes:
- This program is a combination of *The Thelma Ibsen Matter*, broadcast on 1/09/1953, with parts of *The Emily Braddock Matter*, broadcast on 5/19/1953.
- *The Cronin Matter* is announced for next week.
- In a CBS memo in the Thousand Oaks Library, the order of the programs was changed with *The Amy Bradshaw Matter* being aired next, and *The Cronin Matter* listed as "TBA".
- Roy Rowan is the announcer.
- Musical supervision is by Amerigo Marino.

Producer: Jack Johnstone   Writer: John Dawson
Cast: Eleanor Audley, Barbara Eiler, Virginia Gregg, Carleton Young, Harry Bartell, Herb Ellis, John Dehner, Marvin Miller, Tony Barrett, Frank Gerstle, Chester Stratton, Lawrence Dobkin

♦ ❖ ♦

Show: **The Amy Bradshaw Matter**
Company: **Northwest Indemnity Alliance**
Agent: **George Atkins**
Synopsis:
Episode 1   **Show Date:**   **11/21/1955**

George Atkins calls Johnny about going to New York City. Someone is trying to kill the actress Amy Bradshaw.

Johnny goes to New York City and visits the Criterion Theater where he meets David Coleman, the director. Johnny is told that the play has been running for 22 weeks, but last night Amy got a note that made her upset, and her performance is suffering. Johnny tells David that these notes are usually harmless, and maybe someone is using the note as a cover.

Johnny talks to Amy after the show and he is impressed with her but she thinks Johnny is wasting his time. Johnny suggests talking over a drink but she has a date. What about tomorrow?

Mike Pomeroy, her agent, comes in and leaves when he sees Johnny and the offer of the drink is taken up by Amy. She asks Johnny to leave by a different door to avoid a man who was waiting for her, Porter Cain.

Johnny and Amy talk over drinks. She tells Johnny that she has been acting for a long time and she usually gets what she wants. Johnny tells Amy that he thinks that the letter is more than a crank. She tells Johnny that last night she went for a walk and was pushed out into traffic. It was probably just a fluke, but she wonders if someone might hate her. Johnny asks of it could have come from a friend, and Amy tells him that her few friends are good ones. Amy tells Johnny that the beneficiary of her policy is William York, her husband from whom she is separated.

Johnny takes Amy home and sees a man waiting in a car. Johnny watches the car and sees Mike Pomeroy go into the building. Johnny sees another man watching too.

Tomorrow, the Criterion Theater and a third act curtain that wasn't in the script.

Episode 2   Show Date: 11/22/1955
Al Sintella, NYPD calls and Johnny tells him about the threat to kill Amy.

Johnny cabs to see Det. Lt. Sintella about the actress. Johnny shows Lt. Sintella the note and tells him about the push into traffic. Sintella smells a publicity stunt and thinks Johnny is stage-struck. Johnny tells Sintella that the suspects are the director, the producer, her agent, and a man named Porter Cain and her husband, who is the beneficiary.

Johnny goes to see Porter Cain at noon and he is still eating breakfast. Over coffee and Chopin, Porter tells Johnny that Amy is his career. She is a hobby, and he is a collector of things, one-of-a-kind things. He shows Johnny a signet ring supposedly owned by the Medici's and the only one in existence. He is going to add Amy to his collection, in time, and he has time.

Johnny cabs to the theater that evening and hears Mike Pomeroy tell Amy about his plans for Sheila, so don't make her look bad. When Mike leaves Johnny goes to see Amy. She thinks that her making mistakes over the note is silly.

Mike meets Johnny when he leaves and Johnny tells him about the note. Mike thinks that the note is nothing and Johnny should mind his own business.

After the program, Johnny talks to Cain who is going to talk to Amy later. Johnny tells him that he has a date with Amy and Cain leaves. Johnny goes in after everyone has left and Amy screams. Amy tells Johnny that a sandbag had almost hit her. Johnny investigates the catwalk and goes back to Amy. She is scared that someone really is trying to kill her.

Tomorrow, a man steps onto the stage from out of the past and into a role he does not want to play.

Episode 3   Show Date: 11/23/1955
Lt. Sintella calls and Johnny tells him what happened last night. Sintella tells Johnny that maybe his hunch is right. He tells Johnny that the husband is living in Greenwich Village.

Johnny cabs to the address of Bill York, Amy's husband. The address is a rooming house. Bill tells Johnny that Amy always wanted to apologize for him. He is an artist, what more could he ask for. Johnny says he has not read any of Bill's books, and Bill tells him that no one else has either. He is living the unfettered life of an artist and lives comfortably in hock. He has written a manuscript that Mr. Pomeroy is holding in hock. Bill has not seen Amy in months.

Johnny goes to see Emory Taylor, the producer, who is out. His wife Dora is sweet and comfortable behind the bar in the apartment. Dora tells Johnny that she would like to kill Amy because Emory was working too hard for her. She tells Johnny that Coleman was in love with Amy, and she does not want Emory to fall either. Cain is not the type to be hurt by Amy.

Johnny meets Pomeroy in a bar and he tells Johnny to mind his own business. Johnny tells him about meeting with York and he tells Johnny that he paid Bill to stay away from Amy. He has a play lined up and wants his money. Bill could work in television but Bill thinks he is too good for that. The new play will star Sheila Mitchell.

After the show, Johnny takes Amy home and again he spots the man on the street. Johnny gets behind the man and discovers that it is Bill York.

Tomorrow, I find I have even more of a reason for keeping Amy alive than I had realized.

Episode 4   Show Date: 11/24/1955
Lt. Sintella calls and Johnny tells him to come to his hotel room. He has Bill York there and he has plenty to tell them.

Johnny "invites" Bill York to his hotel room. Sintella arrives and Bill asks them why he would kill Amy. They tell Bill about the insurance money and the debt to Pomeroy. Bill tells them that he had opportunity but not motive. Amy always got what she wanted and Bill had always been a failure. Bill admits he would watch her once in a while, but that is all.

Bill goes down stairs with an officer and Johnny tells Sintella what he has been up to. Sintella chastises Johnny for breaking the rules and he still believes that Johnny is smitten with Amy.

Johnny thinks about what Sintella says and goes to Amy's apartment to see if he is right. She tells Johnny that she has noticed the police guard, and she is glad Johnny is there.

There is a phone call, and Amy tells Porter Cain that something is out of the question. Amy tells Johnny that she is glad he is there and kisses him. She is sorry and apologizes for putting him into her life. The clock is ticking but it still is affecting her life by her getting older. Johnny decides not to see Amy after the case is closed.

Johnny visits Porter Cain and he tells Johnny that he had hoped he would meet Johnny again. Porter tells Johnny that when he gets Amy, his collection will be complete. He tells Johnny that he has always gotten anything he wanted, except for a lollypop he wanted when he was nine. He could not get that, so he smashed it.

Tomorrow, well it's the wind up, and a pretty rough one.

Episode 5   Show Date: 11/25/1955
Amy calls and is frantic. She is in her dressing room. She tells Johnny that she knows who is trying to killer. Please hurry.

Johnny cabs to the theater and sees a figure in the distance. In the dark theater, Johnny hears shots and runs to Amy's room where he finds Mike Pomeroy dead. Amy tells Johnny that someone outside the room had shot Mike, so Johnny runs out to search and calls Lt. Sintella.

In Amy's dressing room, she tells Johnny that Mike had called and wanted her to meet him in her dressing room. They were talking and a hand appeared in the door. Mike saw it and ran to protect her and was shot. He fell against the door causing the gun to fall in the dressing room. The hand had a large signet ring on it, Porter Cain's signet ring.

Sintella arrives and Amy relates her story to him and an order to pick up Porter Cain is issued. At police headquarters, Cain is unaware that Pomeroy is dead. He admits he had called Amy and asked her to meet him. He saw her leave and followed her to the theater, but did not go in. Johnny tells him that his motive was to kill her if he could not have her.

Johnny takes Amy home and she is very quiet. The phone rings and Sintella calls. Suddenly Johnny feels old, tired, and sick. Johnny tells her that the gun had no fingerprints on it. Johnny tells Amy that she killed him and faked the attempts on her life.

She tells Johnny that she loved Mike but he was drifting away from her. She felt dead so the she faked the attempts, after all, she is a very good actress. As Amy goes out into the hall to meet the police, she asks Johnny not to forget her. Amy does not look back, and Johnny is glad.

"Remarks: Amy repeated her confession to Lt. Sintella, her case is coming up soon. Sweet case. Well, tomorrow is another day, so they tell me."

Exp. Acct: $185.20

Notes:
- This program is noted for the special "Giant Animal" offer.
- Roy Rowan is the announcer.
- Musical supervision is by Amerigo Marino.

Producer:	Jack Johnstone	Writer:	Robert Ryf
Cast:	Virginia Gregg, Florence Wolcott, Don Diamond, Larry Thor, Vic Perrin, Carleton Young		

◆ ❖ ◆

Show: The Henderson Matter
Company: Paramount Insurance Adjusters
Agent: Tim Connors
Synopsis:
Episode 1   Show Date: 11/28/1955

Tim Connors calls and tells Johnny that he is a father. Come to the office and get a cigar...and bring a suitcase. In Culver Montana Mr. Henderson is dead. It was either murder, suicide, an accident, or all three.

Johnny buys a map and tries to find Culver, Montana and then goes to Tim Connors office (the cigars cost $2.00 a box — don't smoke it). The Henderson heirs think that the insurance company is trying to cheat them for looking into the death. The claim is for $25,000. George Henderson, a rancher, fell from a hotel window and there was no inquest. Connors has phoned the sheriff and he will help. Tim called the widow and she hung up on him.

Johnny goes to Great Falls and trains to Culver, an ugly, dingy town. Johnny gets a room in the Butte Hotel, the only hotel, and meets Eef Holton, the sheriff, who brings a bottle to help warm things up. They have a drink and Eef tells Johnny that he is visiting "unofficially", and Johnny will have to go it alone in town. Culver is a small, tight community and there are people who do not care about the details that bother the insurance companies or the people who dig up details. Eef tells Johnny that the funeral is at three. Eef likes Johnny, he is all right because he does not ask questions until he has one to ask.

Johnny goes to the cemetery for the funeral with Eef, who points out Pauline Henderson to Johnny, who is amazed that she is only 26 and George was 52. Johnny tells Eef he will ask for a coroner's inquest just from seeing her.

Tomorrow, I find out how hard it is to believe what I see, and I see plenty.

Episode 2   Show Date: 11/29/1955
Eef calls Johnny about his filing for the inquest. The coroner left it up to Eef, and the mayor will probably have to OK it. You have stirred up trouble and it will find you.

Johnny sits and waits until Mayor Newton visits Johnny about the inquest request. He tells Johnny that George's death was a blow to the community but Johnny replies that only half a dozen people were at the funeral. The mayor tells Johnny that an inquest would only prove George fell out of a window. Their police force is small and it would cost a lot of money. Johnny tells the mayor that he wants proof it was an accident, he wants an inquest.

Johnny meets with Eef for coffee and is told that the inquest is on for tomorrow. Johnny notes that Eef will not have time to do anything, and Johnny suspects someone is trying to stop the inquest.

At the inquest the next day, the doctor testifies that George died of a broken neck. The maid testifies that she saw Mr. Henderson the morning of the accident and that Mrs. Henderson was in the lobby, but she does not know if she went up. Everyone else had the same vague story.

Mrs. Henderson testifies that she last saw George on Thursday when she went to see him around noon at the hotel. She was at the dentist when she heard the news. She went to talk to George about their divorce, which they had decided on a month ago. Mrs. Henderson does not think he was upset over the discussion, and she thinks he had a drink while they were talking.

Johnny notes the New York clothes, the Paris perfume, the Tiffany jewelry and a Riviera look on Mrs. Henderson. The verdict comes in fifteen minutes, accidental death. Mayor Newton gloats over the results and Johnny tells him he will send a report saying that the inquest was a sham and that now people will be more relaxed and get careless.

Tomorrow, people do get careless all over Culver, Montana.

Episode 3   Show Date: 11/30/1955
Eef calls and Johnny tells him that he is ready to go to work, so help me move around the city. Eef says the case is closed officially but he will help, as it needs investigating.

Johnny wires Tim Connors and tells him he is not satisfied with the inquest and is staying. The operator wishes him luck.

Johnny mails the report to Connors and then Mr. Porter, the manager, comes to his room to tell Johnny that he must give up his room as they are "all filled up". It is a sort of convention. Johnny smells a rat and forces him to back down. "Go back to 'no one' and tell 'them' I am staying put and call the police if you want" Johnny tells him.

Johnny tells Eef about the manager and Eef calls it stupid. Johnny tells Eef that the company is out $50,000 now. Eef tells Johnny that Mrs. Henderson is a local girl, Pauline Underwood. She went to school in the east and spent time in Europe. Everyone knew that they were not getting along. George raised Pauline since she was fourteen and he was good to her and her father worked for George. Eef tells Johnny that she has no reason to kill him, as she was getting a generous settlement. Eef does not think it was suicide. Johnny asks who owns the hotel and Eef tells him it is Noah Baxter.

Johnny asks Eef to look into all of Pauline's friends. Johnny wonders why Mrs. Henderson has not hired a lawyer to sue for the money, and Eef wonders too.

Tim wires Johnny to go see Mr. Thurber, an insurance agent in Great Falls. Johnny drives to Great Falls and Thurber tells Johnny that he had been out hunting and heard of the death yesterday. Two days before he left, Henderson wanted to change the beneficiary on his policy to Matilda Knickerbocker. It was just a name to put in.

Then Henderson called back to say that he had changed his mind. He called on the same day he died, just after noon. Thurber knew both of the Hendersons and tells Johnny he wished he was married to Mrs. Henderson. George was just the opposite of Pauline. Thurber thinks she married George for his money and would have killed for it.

Tomorrow the whole affair becomes a town issue, and I become the town goat.

Bob Bailey closes this program with the following: "Incidentally, let me take a moment to say thanks for the many kind letters you have sent. We appreciate them more than you know and I only wish it were possible to answer them all personally. Again, thank you."

Episode 4   Show Date: 12/1/1955
Mrs. Henderson calls and Johnny tells her he wants to come out this afternoon. She tells Johnny that she will meet him at the Big Horn Lodge at 4:00.

Johnny buys galoshes because of the 14 inches of new snow. Johnny tells Eef that he might have to leave, as the company wants him to come home. Johnny borrows Eef's car for the drive to the lodge. Eef tells Johnny that he has looked for some friends of Pauline's but has found nothing yet. Johnny tells Eef of his meeting with Mrs. Henderson. "Don't let her rang-dangle you" Eef tells Johnny.

As Johnny passes the cemetery, he sees a car, and an old woman is standing at the Henderson grave. Johnny stops and introduces himself to Mattie Knickerbocker, the schoolteacher in the town.

She tells Johnny that George was a wonderful man to her, and she will miss him, and Johnny tells her that he knew George too. Mattie comments on George's laugh and Johnny agrees. She tells Johnny that she did not come to the funeral because she did not think she could bear it. She notes the birds in the snow and how wonderful they are.

She tells Johnny that she knows who Johnny is, and asks if it was curiosity that made him stop. Johnny thinks that Mattie was the first person to talk to him frankly.

Johnny meets Pauline and orders Pernod for Pauline and bourbon for himself. Johnny tells her about meeting Thurber and Mattie, and the call to ignore the change. Johnny asks if something happened in the room.

She tells Johnny that they had agreed on the divorce and that she would have a generous settlement. They met one day and had a bitter argument and George's response was to cancel her out of the insurance. They had met to apologize for the argument. Johnny tells her that it is unusual for a man to leave an ex-wife as a beneficiary. She also tells Johnny that she preferred to talk to him at the lodge rather than at her home.

That evening Johnny rereads the inquest testimony and goes to see Eef the next morning. In the personal effects there is no mention of a bottle, and no one brought him any, yet he had a drink before breakfast. Mrs. Henderson said that he had a drink before and while she was there.

Johnny thinks that she put that in to make everyone believe George was tipsy. So, where did he get the drink? "That is a pretty good question son." Eef tell Johnny.

Tomorrow the wind up. Yeah, the whole case blows sky high.

Episode 5   Show Date: 12/2/1955

Johnny gets a call from Hartford and Tim asks Johnny about his wire asking to deny liability to Mrs. Henderson. Johnny has proof that Henderson did not have a drink. Tim is on his way out.

Eef promises Johnny a reinvestigation of the facts. Tim meets Johnny and tells him they should move in now, and that Henderson had not been drinking. Johnny tells Tim that Mrs. Henderson was ready for the inquiry, and she was ready for me, but she was not ready for you and that is why she hung up.

Johnny has three things to go on, instinct, experience and statistics. Mrs. Henderson married an older man and would have everything in her favor. Johnny pushes to have charges filed and Tim says they need more evidence.

Eef and Johnny go over the notes and Mrs. Henderson tells Johnny and Eef that she might have been mistaken. Eef tells Johnny that they need to find who helped her pull this off, and Mrs. Henderson's background is searched.

Johnny and Eef drive out the Henderson ranch where a servant tells them that Mrs. Henderson would take trips in the Cadillac, and Mr. Henderson would argue with her about meeting "that man". She had watched Pauline grow up and was surprised when they married as she was different. She fit in, but was different.

Eef's deputies uncover three men who knew Mrs. Henderson, one is Noah Baxter. Eef and Johnny drive to the Baxter ranch and speak with him. He denies seeing Mrs. Henderson on the sly as they were both good friends. Baxter was on the ranch when George died and was last in town three weeks ago. Johnny asks if they can talk to the help, and Baxter admits that she would come occasionally to talk. Baxter tells them that she did not kill George, because she loved him.

Baxter then tells them he lied, that there was something between them. She would come to cry on his shoulder, because George wanted to divorce her and marry Mattie Knickerbocker. Baxter wanted Pauline but she wanted to be married to George.

Baxter went to see George to tell him to go back to Pauline. He tells Johnny that his hired-help would lie for him. He drove into town and went to George's room, just after Pauline left. George was mad and swung at him once and Baxter shoved him and he went out the window. He had killed him.

We still had to pay double indemnity. Mattie, Pauline and Noah will pay another way, with the hurt that comes to nice people.

Exp. Acct: $802.50

Notes:
- This story was done as *The Underwood Matter*, broadcast on 2/27/1953.
- Those irritating inflatable animals again! But for only two episodes.
- Roy Rowan is the announcer.
- Musical supervision is by Amerigo Marino.

Producer:	Jack Johnstone	Writer:	John Dawson
Cast:	Lillian Buyeff, Irene Tedrow, D. J. Thompson, Herb Ellis, Marvin Miller, Forrest Lewis, Bob Bruce, Russ Thorson		

♦ ❖ ♦

Show: **The Cronin Matter**
Company: **Surety Mutual and Trust Company**
Agent: **Joe Parker**
Synopsis:
Episode 1   **Show Date:**   **12/5/1955**

Joe Parker calls Johnny about a gorgeous doll named Dolly McClain who married Barnaby Cronin. He gave her the "Circle of Fire" necklace worth $500,000. Dolly is coming out of seclusion, giving a party and is going to wear the necklace. We have a problem.

Johnny goes to the New York City apartment of Dolly McLain to discuss the necklace. She tells Johnny that she has been hibernating since Barnaby died.

Johnny also meets Sylvia Blake, a friend of Dolly's. She asks Johnny if he is "the Johnny Dollar", and that she would not want to be in his shoes for a million dollars, for a half a million, maybe. Sylvia is a writer who wrote about Dolly's necklace once.

Dolly invites Johnny to the party and Johnny tells her that Joe Parker is really worried about the necklace. She tells Johnny that she wants no detectives at the party. Barnaby gave her the necklace at a party a long time ago, and she wore the necklace then and was perfectly safe. He was running two railroads and a bank at the time. Dolly relents because she likes Johnny and wants him at the party where hundreds are invited to her home in the Adirondacks.

Sylvia tells Dolly that she has a visitor and pours a drink for Johnny. The guest is named Shorty Webber who Johnny recognizes from Broadway, and Shorty has an invitation. Sylvia tells Johnny that Shorty is a freeloader whereas Johnny is working his way.

Johnny accuses Sylvia of once writing a story about the necklace and its attempted theft and Sylvia tells Johnny that someone will steal the necklace. Johnny tells her that maybe it will be Sylvia Blake as she has written stories about all the famous jewel thefts for the past fifty years. She tells Johnny that the jewels are like her, beautiful and brittle.

Johnny looks for Dolly and finds Shorty Webber searching the mail of her desk. Johnny takes Shorty's .38 snub-nose, "it belongs to a friend" he tells Johnny. Shorty tells Johnny that Dolly is an old friend, and that he wanted to marry her once. Shorty tells Johnny that Dolly does not know he has served time for jewel theft, but he is looking out for Dolly, and he knows how word gets around.

Dolly comes in and Johnny tells her that he and Shorty have a mutual friend, a prison warden. Dolly is sure that Shorty was doing a benefit for the prisoners.

Shorty leaves and so does Johnny, but not before Dolly tells Johnny that she has had a premonition. She is old and feels that something awful will happen to her.

Tomorrow, a man who is afraid of his shadow, a girl who is afraid of nothing, and a stranger who strikes in the dark.

Episode 2   Show Date: 12/6/1955
Jason Prell calls Johnny and wants to talk to him immediately. Prell manages Dolly's trust accounts and he wants to talk before the train leaves. He tells Johnny not to get the necklace, to leave it where it is. Prell tells Johnny that he is worried about Mrs. Cronin's sanity.

Johnny cabs to the newspaper office to look at the morgue files on Dolly, who was a dancer and social butterfly in the 20's. Barnaby Cronin married her and the necklace is mentioned. Barnaby dies and then Dolly went into seclusion.

Johnny cabs to the railway station to find the train and meets JPrell, who is an old friend and has managed Dolly's business affairs. Prell knows how Dolly has gone downhill and this party is a bad idea. Prell wants Johnny to point out to Dolly how dangerous this party idea is.

Prell is sure that she has burned herself out. She believes in people and lives in a dream world. Most of her friends were trying to use her, and he and Barnaby tried to protect her. Prell is sure that the necklace will be stolen. Prell tells Johnny that the capitol in the trusts is adequate but the necklace is her own property. Her belief in the past keeps her alive. Prell wants Johnny to call the bank and tell them not to deliver the necklace, but Johnny tells him he has it on him. "Heaven help us all" replies Prell.

The train pulls out but only six people are there, Johnny, Dolly, Sylvia, Prell, Shorty and a newcomer Laura Dean who knows who Johnny is: he is there to protect the necklace. She tells Johnny that Mrs. Cronin had sent an invitation to her aunt, who had died, so Dolly said to come.

Laura dodges the question of who her aunt was. She only tells Johnny that Dolly and her aunt were the Siamese Twins. Johnny then makes the connection to Fritzy Morel. Johnny did not know her, but Laura says that she loved to party. Johnny knows that Laura is a liar, because Fritzy Morel had died with no relatives.

Prell rushes in and tells Johnny that Dolly is ill and he rushes to her stateroom. Dolly tells Johnny that it is just nerves and she is OK now and has some tablets to take. Dolly asks about the necklace and shows Johnny a letter that she wants him to sign and keep. Johnny reads it and the letter gives the necklace to Sylvia Blake. "Do not tell her, as it will be years before she gets it" she tells Johnny. Dolly is sure that her old friends went on ahead and will meet her at the house.

Johnny goes to his stateroom and catches a glint of light and is hit on the head and the leather case with the necklace is gone.

Tomorrow, an old love and an old hate and violence breaks out at midnight.

Episode 3   Show Date: 12/7/1955

Dr. Bigby calls Johnny and Johnny wants him to come to the Cronin place. Bigby tells Johnny that he is very busy and cannot come out. If Johnny is a friend of Dolly's, take her back to New York City now, before it is too late.

Johnny cabs to Wells Falls, New York, the local town and looks for the doctor, but cannot find him. Johnny finds the pharmacist, but he cannot fill the prescription for Dolly. Johnny goes back to the house and gives the cab to Prell, so he can go to Tupper Lake to get the prescription filled.

Johnny looks for Miss Atherton the housekeeper and she notes a storm is brewing. She knew Barnaby, and he was just another man. But Dolly was always worshipping someone. Dolly was born and raised in the village and Miss Atherton worked with her. Dolly got Barnaby to spend a fortune to build the summerhouse. Dolly has been generous by keeping her on when the house is closed.

She tells Johnny that Bigby is the coroner and had lost his medical license ten years ago and is a drunk. Ask Bigby about his statements, he would know.

She tells Johnny that Dolly has come home to die and knows it. Barnaby came back to die here too, on a stormy night like tonight. He was alone when he died and Bigby could not get here because of the storm.

Johnny notes that the house seemed out of sorts with the events, all dressed up with nowhere to go. Prell brings back the medicine, and the dinner is served. Shorty teaches Laura some dance steps and Johnny watches the rain. Sylvia notes the thunderstorm makes for a perfect setting.

Sylvia asks Johnny about the cut on his head and he tells her it was a sudden stop on the train. Sylvia suggests that someone got the necklace, but Johnny says nothing. Sylvia hopes that someone got the necklace, and Johnny tells her she will be sorry for saying that someday. She suggests that they smooch for excitement and Johnny obliges.

Shorty asks why everyone is gathered together, and Johnny tells him it was Dolly's suggestion. Shorty tells Johnny that he has been in love with Dolly for 35 years and would die for her. Dolly had arranged for Johnny to show everyone the necklace and they are all mesmerized by it. Prell's face goes white and Johnny tells Prell that he had taken the necklace from the case and Prell bolts. Johnny goes after him and the electricity goes out.

Tomorrow, a white lie, a bullet from the darkness and death comes in from the rain.

Episode 4   Show Date: 12/8/1955
The phone rings but the call to the sheriff is cut off. Johnny believes that the wires were cut. A shot comes in through the window and Johnny goes out to get Prell.

Johnny is shot at as he and Shorty go outside where Prell is shooting blindly. Shorty stays with Johnny because he cares for Dolly. Johnny spots Prell and circles around to his location. Johnny notes that Prell knows Johnny had him pegged. Johnny tells Prell to drop his gun and something happens and there is a shot and Prell is dead. Johnny tells Shorty that Dolly is going to be hurt by what is happening.

Johnny changes clothes, retrieves the necklace and checks in with Dolly. Dolly is glad that Laura Dean is there, she is such a nice girl. Dolly thought she heard shots, but Johnny tells her it was thunder. She tells Johnny that she had good friends and good times and Barnaby, who she worshipped. He never did a wrong thing in his life. And Jason Prell has been such a good friend. She tells Johnny that she grew up in Wells Falls. Barnaby died here and she has come back. Dolly asks to see the necklace and he puts it on her and then she goes to sleep. "Good night dancing darling" Johnny tells her.

The next morning Johnny fixes some coffee and ponders the situation. He wonders how he will tell Dolly that Barnaby was as big of a crook as Prell was. Laura comes into the kitchen and talks to Johnny. She mentions the shooting and Johnny ignores it.

Johnny tells her that she is lying about being the niece of Fritzy Morel. Johnny tells her that Fritzy did not have a niece. Laura tells Johnny that Fritzy lived in the same rooming house and when the invitation came she just decided to go.

Miss Atherton comes in with a grim and strange look. She announces that Mrs. Cronin is dead.

Tomorrow, the questions and answers for the living and the dead. The final payoff and fate itself pays the last trump.

Episode 5   Show Date: 12/9/1955
Dr. Bigby calls and Johnny tells him to come out, as they need a coroner. Johnny is calling from the forestry station and tells Dr. Bigby that Prell and Mrs. Cronin are dead. Mrs. Cronin was murdered.

Johnny gets a ride back from the forestry station and waits for Dr. Bigby. Maybe Dolly was better off now, he wonders. Sylvia comes in and has a cup of coffee. Johnny tells her that Jason Prell is dead, and so is Dolly. Johnny gives Sylvia the necklace and tells her of the will. Johnny tells her that it is fake, worth $300 to $400 dollars. It has been in the vault and was broken up long ago, and Prell probably was in on it. He had complete control of her trusts and was stealing her blind. Barnaby had disposed of the necklace and did not tell her. He was pretty shady after he teamed up with Prell.

Miss Atherton announces Bigby, and she tells Johnny not to believe him, as he is a chronic drunk. Johnny tells Sylvia that Dolly thought she was giving Sylvia the real necklace. She is glad it is a copy and will always remember that she thought it was real, like her world.

Bigby was another man under Dolly's spell and tells Johnny that everybody loved her. Johnny thinks that Jason Prell killed her because Prell got a prescription filled and the contents of the bottle are different. Bigby thinks he knows what the pills are.

Bigby tells Johnny that he had been drinking when Barnaby died. He called it a heart attack, but Barnaby was poisoned. He knew he was wrong and turned to the bottle. Barnaby would come up to see "her" every couple of weeks and everyone knew it.

Miss Atherton comes in and Johnny asks her why she did it. She tells Johnny that she killed Barnaby when he told her that he was breaking off their affair. She just changed the pills in the bottle, it was so easy. She asks Johnny to call the sheriff.

Bigby tells Johnny that he had substituted the poison with sugar pills after Barnaby died and Miss Atherton had given them to Dolly. So, Mrs. Cronin died of natural causes.

"Remarks: The insurance angle here seems a little muddy. Premiums were paid for years on an item that didn't exist, and yet no claim was filed and none will be. So, well, I leave it to the legal eagles. Me, I am beat and tired and a little sad. I have come out of this with a kind of nostalgia for a time and place I never even knew. And I am halfway in love with a girl back in that time and place, a girl I have never seen. Oh, sure, I know it is a dream world and a dream girl and none of it exists. But it's too bad. I wish it did because she must have been

a honey, a real sweet heart, a dancing darling."
Exp. Acct: $263.30

Notes:
- Roy Rowan is the announcer.
- Musical supervision is by Amerigo Marino.

Producer: Jack Johnstone   Writer: Les Crutchfield
Cast: Virginia Gregg, Shirley Mitchell, Vivi Janiss, Barbara Fuller,
               Benny Rubin, John Dehner, Parley Baer

◆ ❖ ◆

Show: **The Lansing Fraud Matter**
Company: **Universal Adjustment Bureau**
Agent: **Jim Carter**
Synopsis:
Episode 1   Show Date: 12/12/1955

Jim Carter calls from the Universal Adjustment Bureau, he is going to Tucson where James Lansing was insured for $50,000 and died two days ago, he starved to death. Johnny will meet Jim at the airport.

Johnny flies to Tucson, Arizona with Jim Carter. Jim tells Johnny that he has advised the state insurance commission that they are holding up payment. They will be there before the letters arrive and have room to investigate, but they need to work fast, as the commission will start asking questions fast.

James Lansing's sister Arlene Kennedy has asked about the payment and she was told it would be a day or two, but she could be rough. She has some money and influence in the area and is upset.

James Lansing died on the street with no identification. The police did a post mortem and the county was going to bury him, but Jim had the coroner hold the body. Jim thought it might not be Lansing at all. The post mortem showed chronic heart condition, lung history and debility. He took a physical before the policy was issued and was OK when it was issued. So how did he get in that condition in two years? They will go to see Dr. Mahood, the examining physician first. "Hey, cute stewardess" Jim remarks to Johnny. Johnny and Jim get back to business and they study the files.

In Tucson, Johnny checks into the Pioneer Hotel and goes to see Sgt. Younger who filed the DOA report. Sgt. Younger tells Johnny that the man was found dead on the street. There was no identification so the coroner performed an autopsy. They had a print match based on a traffic arrest. The sister identified the body. He had been dead an hour before he was found. Younger tells Johnny that death was natural causes and they will have to pay off. Johnny tells Sgt. Younger that he has to be sure they insured the right man.

Johnny calls Jim who has the history on Dr. Mahood. Johnny visits the office and talks with Mahood. Johnny tells him that in 1953 he examined a man we need information on, but Mahood does not remember him. He thinks he signed the exam form and the notes look like his. Johnny tells him that the forms pronounced him sound, but he died two days ago. Mahood thinks he could have developed a heart condition since the exam.

Johnny tells him that Lansing died of malnutrition. It could not have been overlooked and the coroner says he had been sick for several years. Mahood cannot explain any of the problems but tells Johnny that the nurse will find the exam forms for him tomorrow. Johnny wants them first thing and is riding him hard!

Tomorrow, $50,000 is a good price for a killing. Most anybody will listen for that kind of money.

Episode 2   Show Date: 12/13/1955
Dr. Mahood calls about the report forms he sent. Johnny tells him that the forms do not straighten things out. You have to come to the morgue with me to identify Lansing.

Johnny tells Jim about going to take Mahood to the morgue. Jim tells Johnny that the doctor is OK financially. Too bad that Lansing died on the street. Johnny tells Jim that they do not have to be careful. Call the state people and tell them we do not think this is legitimate and see who yells.

Johnny takes Mahood to the morgue to see the body and he tells Johnny that he only examines whoever the insurance agent sends over. Mahood tells Johnny to call his attorney for any further questions. He does not remember seeing Lansing and cannot determine if the body was the man he examined. Johnny has the doctor's staff examine the body as well, with no results.

Johnny tells Jim that the doctor is too angry over this, so Johnny is going to Lansing's address. The apartment manager is willing to look at Lansing's body at the morgue and she recognizes him. She has seen him drunk many times. He would get up at 10 and buy some groceries and booze and drink all day. He was fried by noon for years.

He tried to sell real estate and always had the money to pay his rent. Johnny wonders how he had money to buy booze and insurance. Johnny spends time gathering information on Lansing and determines that he had been drinking heavily for 18 months.

Jim tells Johnny that Lansing had lived in Los Angeles and was fired for drinking on the job, and Mrs. Kennedy is upset at the investigation. Johnny is told that Hillary Franks sold the policy and has been in business for 17 years. Johnny is sure that only Arlene Kennedy would benefit and would need expert help to get the papers signed and the physicals taken. If Franks did something wrong, he will be looking for us. Jim checks the cylinders of a .38 and tells Johnny to carry it.

Tomorrow, there is a bit of excitement when a pair of thieves start a falling out. Matter of fact, a lot of excitement.

Episode 3   Show Date: 12/14/1955
Mrs. Kennedy returns Johnny's call and he tells her that he is investigating James Lansing's death. She tells Johnny to call her lawyer. Johnny tells her he wants to talk to her, and she hangs up.

Johnny rents a car and drives to Mrs. Kennedy's house. Mrs. Kennedy does not want to talk to Johnny and tells him to leave. Now! She tells Johnny that Jim drank himself to death, now pay me. It is cut and dry. Johnny tells her it is not and tells her of the results of the autopsy. They will have to discredit one or the other and will not pay until the matter is cleared up. She wants to know what Johnny wants.

She finally tells Johnny that she was on good terms with Jim and he left her his insurance. Jim had spent his trust money long ago. Her attorneys have told her to sue.

Johnny tells her that Jim died on the street, and that is what caused us to investigate. She tells Johnny that Jim came to her the day after he took the exam, and he was fine. Johnny tells her they think someone else took the exam. Sue us if you want, but we will meet you in court.

Johnny and Jim have lunch and discuss Mrs. Kennedy. Jim tells Johnny that the commission wants us to act discretely and promptly. Jim also tells Johnny that her husband, a lawyer, died five years ago and left her some insurance. She has some income from an oil company and could use the money. Johnny has started on Franks, who Mrs. Kennedy has probably called.

Johnny reads Hillary Franks' file and the phone rings. It is Franks. He tells Johnny that Mrs. Kennedy has called and Johnny goes to his office where Johnny and Franks discuss the matter.

Franks was surprised to hear from them, and Johnny tells him that he feels Mrs. Kennedy is involved in a fraud. Johnny tells Franks about Lansing and Franks tells him that he was interested in a house at one time and Lansing was the agent. He managed to sell Lansing the policy sometime later. Lansing had a small income and did not remain in the real estate business. He was just a client and looked fine to him and does not recall if he drank.

Johnny tells Franks that Lansing was an alcoholic. Franks also had never met Mrs. Kennedy. Johnny tells Franks he will leave, and Franks should think about what they talked about, and Johnny will want some better answers.

Johnny notes that Franks was a bad, unprepared and awkward liar and Johnny is going to get him. But Franks did not know what to do about it.

Tomorrow, a bad liar turns into a pretty good gunman.

Episode 4   Show Date: 12/15/1955

Jim Carter calls about Franks, who Johnny thinks is doing everything wrong. Mrs. Kennedy is fighting back and her lawyers have filed suit and the body has been cremated. Johnny is going back to see Franks.

Johnny composes a letter to the insurance commission and gives copies of the examinations and statements.

Johnny drives back to Franks' office and asks if he wants to make a statement. Franks tells Johnny that he only sold a policy and does not know Mrs. Kennedy. Johnny tells him that he arranged for someone else to take the physical. Franks tells Johnny that he only knows Dr. Mahood slightly and sent Lansing to him just like any other policy.

Franks resents Johnny's insinuations and Johnny tells him that Franks is relying on his reputation. When Johnny tells Franks that he is going to swear out a warrant for him and Mrs. Kennedy, Franks hits him with a paperweight and runs from the office.

Jim comes in and Johnny tells him what happened. Johnny wants a statement from Franks and tells Jim that he will not run far, as Franks does not know how to run.

Johnny goes to see Mrs. Kennedy and tells her about Franks telling everything to him. Johnny tells her that Franks had helped her. He will not run far, and he will realize his life is ruined and he will blame you and probably wants to kill you, so do we talk? She tells Johnny that she had nothing to do with Jim taking out the insurance and that Johnny cannot prove any of the things he is saying.

Jim and Johnny watch Franks' office and the Kennedy home. Jim has called in the police and a warrant has been issued. Jim thinks maybe Frank's went to Mexico, but Johnny thinks he will think things out and call him.

The next day Johnny goes to Frank's office and talks to the receptionist Maria. She has worked for Franks for 12 years and does not believe any of the things they are saying. Johnny tells her where he is staying and tells her to have Franks call Johnny if he calls her.

At 11:00 p.m. Franks calls and wants to explain things so he can pass it on to the home office. Johnny tells him that the insurance company does not want to prosecute. Franks tells Johnny to meet him at the San Javier Mission and come alone — he has a gun.

Tomorrow, $50,000 worth of murder.

Episode 5   Show Date: 12/16/1955

Jim calls Johnny and he tells Jim about going to meet Franks. If Johnny gets a statement, he will try to have the charges dropped.

Johnny cabs to the Mission to meet Franks. The cabby is leery of dropping Johnny off when he sees a man by the bell tower.

Johnny meets Franks who has a .38 and is wearing the same clothes. Johnny tells Franks that Jim Carter will help have the charges dropped if they get a statement from him. They are on his side if he will help them.

Franks tells Johnny that he met Arlene Kennedy after his wife died, and he became interested in her. They dated and he asked her to marry him, but she laughed at him and told him he was boring. She only wanted money from life and laughed at him. She knew they could have lived comfortably but she wanted travel and clothes and would not marry him unless they could live the way she wanted. She wanted $50,000 in cash.

When her brother came to Tucson, he only had a year to live and so she paid for his apartment and booze and made Franks buy a nice fat policy on him. It was an investment because he was going to die. Franks paid a man $100 to take the physical for Lansing and then waited for Lansing to die. It was too late then, but he wanted out but couldn't. She thought he was weak.

After the policy was issued she talked less about marriage. She made it clear she was innocent and Franks had done everything.

Johnny takes Franks to town where he signs a statement. The police are called and the charges dropped and the insurance company agrees to waive prosecution. Franks says he will close his office and move away.

Franks leaves and Mrs. Kennedy withdraws her claims. Johnny stops by to see Mrs. Kennedy to get the papers signed and there are shots. Johnny breaks down the door and finds Mrs. Kennedy shot.

There are bloodstains leading to the back and Johnny trails Franks to a ledge where he shoots at Johnny. Johnny shoots twice and Franks is hit. He tells Johnny that he came back to see her and she laughed at him. She was going to run away with someone else and had just used him.

Mrs. Kennedy is dead when the police arrive and Franks dies on the way to the hospital.

Exp. Acct: $1,121.13

Notes:
- This story was done as *The Chicago Fraud Matter*, broadcast on 2/6/1953.
- In Episode 4 Howard McNear slips on Mahood's name and calls him Maherb.
- Roy Rowan is the announcer.
- Musical supervision is by Amerigo Marino.

Producer: Jack Johnstone   Writer: John Dawson
Cast: Mary Jane Croft, Vivi Janiss, Jeanne Tatum, Hy Averback, Barney Phillips, Russell Thorson, Howard McNear

• ❖ •

Show: **The Nick Shurn Matter**
Company: Tri-Mutual Insurance, Ltd.
Agent: Don Wilkins
Synopsis:
Episode 1   **Show Date:**   **12/19/1955**

Don Wilkins calls and tells Johnny that Mel Priker got himself killed last night. Johnny tells Don that Priker "was born to be murdered". Don tells Johnny that Tri-Mutual has a $100,000 policy on him and Nick Shurn is the beneficiary and is being held by the police. There is one witness, but she has disappeared. Maybe some of Nick Shurn's boys have found her. Go check it out.

Johnny goes to New York City and meets with Lt. Ed Rafferty, who is complaining about shoplifters and his son's desire for a motor bike. Rafferty tells Johnny that Nick killed Priker, but they will not be able to prove it. Rafferty thinks that Mel and Nick were partners in the nightclub and Priker was killed there when they were arguing about money. Shots were heard around midnight and the cleaning crew found him at 3:00 AM, shot with his own gun. Shurn was found at another club with Benny Stark. He had been at a shooting range earlier so the paraffin test was positive.

Miss Kathleen O'Dare, the hatcheck girl was seen leaving at the time of the shots but denies it. Later the cab driver changed his story too. Rafferty does not think that Nick got to her. She just went home, packed, took her daughter and disappeared. Johnny thanks Rafferty and tells him to call Ralph Sterner about the motor bike.

Johnny walks out and finds Nick Shurn and Benny out front. Nick reminds Johnny that he was cleared of the charges in their last meeting. Nick invites Johnny for a ride and but Johnny declines, so Nick tells Benny to go for a walk.

Johnny talks to Nick and tells him that he is on the Priker case. Nick offers to let Johnny go to Vegas for a month with $10,000 if he just says the word. Johnny tells Nick that even if he does not make an insurance claim, Johnny will investigate. Nick tells Johnny that he did not kill Priker. Johnny is worried for Kathleen with Nick around and tells Nick he going to tag him.

Johnny goes to the rooming house of Kathleen and searches her rooms and finds nothing. On the way out of the building, Johnny makes a contribution to Santa and is met by Benny, who tells Johnny that some friends want to talk to him. Johnny fakes Benny out with the "two cops on the steps" routine and slugs him. Santa gets the contents of Benny's wallet, $500.

Tomorrow, an old lady with a broken arm, a shivering girl and bullets in the snow.

Episode 2   Show Date: 12/20/1955

Mrs. Gottler calls Johnny about Kathleen, and he tells her that he wants to help Kathleen. That's want the other man said, the one that broke her good right arm.

Johnny cabs to the rooming house and meets Mrs. Gottler who is holding a gun. Johnny convinces her to put the gun down, and Johnny offers to help wrap her packages as they talk.

One package is a muffler for a nephew over in Brooklyn. They have those terrible winters over there. Johnny says it will be warmer this year because they won the pennant.

Mrs. Gottler tells Johnny that Benny broke her arm to find out where Kathy is. Johnny asks where she is and Mrs. Gottler tells Johnny that she left in the middle of the night. She was everyone's favorite, so good luck to finding her. Johnny tells her that she helped Kathleen pack, so where did she go? You had a sample of what the others will do. Kathleen would not tell her where she was going to protect Mrs. Gottler.

Mrs. Gottler gives Johnny a picture of Kathleen and he notices a photographer's name on the picture, Branberry, Michigan. Johnny kisses Mrs. Gottler and she mumbles "Mr. Dollar! MR. DOLLAR!"

Johnny travels to Branberry, Michigan, a lumber village where there is a foot of new snow on the ground. The town is very quiet about giving out information. Johnny talks to the operator who asks him questions and tells Johnny that Kathleen lives in New York. Everyone was keeping quiet about Kathleen.

Johnny talks to the deputy, Dan Martin, who wants to know who Johnny is. Johnny tells Dan that Kathleen is a witness to a murder. Dan tells Johnny that he has been in love with Kathleen since grade school and would die for her. Johnny tells Dan that they are not helping by hiding her. He knows the men who are after her and they don't play games. Dan tells her that he does not know what Kathleen is afraid of.

Johnny drives to mill #4 to see Mike O'Dare and comments on the beauty of the village at dusk. Mike knows who Johnny is, and the answer is "no". Johnny cannot hurt her if he cannot find her. They hear a car drive up to the mill, and Benny Stark gets out. Benny shoots at Johnny and then drives away. They have found her.

Tomorrow, a lonely vigil in the snow, a killer prowls the night and a lovely lady vanishes.

Episode 3   Show Date: 12/21/1955

Dan Martin calls and Johnny tells him that Benny is in town. He shot at Johnny and is headed towards town. Dan tells Johnny to block the turnoff and he will have 20 men with deer rifles blocking the roads within a half hour.

Mike and Johnny block the road turnoff with a bottle of applejack, "the best thing to happen to an apple". Mike asks Johnny about what Kathleen is running from as she was scared and came home for help. Johnny tells Mike that he is not sure if she is mixed up in the murder, but he must talk to her. Mike tells Johnny that they will help protect her and fight to stop Johnny from taking her back.

A car drives up, and it is a local man, Ted Perkins, and Mike waves him through. Mike tells Johnny that people mind their business here. After two hours Johnny only sees three cars and a truck full of Christmas trees, but no Benny. As the temperature drops and the wind comes up, Mike tells Johnny that a blizzard is in the offing, maybe tomorrow. Mike tells Johnny that Kathleen never hurt anyone, and now people are looking for her to kill her, it does not make sense. Johnny notes another time when men were looking for a child to kill him.

A car approaches with relief from Dan. Johnny is told that Benny had been seen and broke through a shootout. Johnny tells Mike that Benny would never run, he would do his job to kill Kathleen.

Mike and Johnny go to town and Johnny looks through the parked cars for Benny's car. Johnny finds a car alongside a building, Benny's car. Johnny approaches but the car is empty.

Mike takes Johnny to Dan Martin's house, where Kathy is. Dan tells Johnny that Benny has taken a different car. Johnny asks Mike to wake up Kathy, and Dan tells Johnny to be easy on her. She had left town because she and Dan had argued. She went to New York and married some guy who left her. She belongs here. Mike comes down and tells Johnny and Dan that she has disappeared.

Tomorrow, a little girl who believes in Santa Claus, a big girl who believes in very little, and both of them facing death.

Episode 4   Show Date: 12/22/1955
Mike calls Johnny and he tells Mike that no one has seen Kathleen or Benny. Mike tells Johnny that Dan has found nothing either, we must find her, maybe Benny got her. Johnny tells Mike to pray.

Johnny buys gas for the county truck and picks up Mike. Johnny tells Mike that Benny has not found Kathy because she took your car, her clothes and a rifle. Kathy knew about the roadblock and how to get around them. She is in the area, so where would she go to hide out? Mike thinks of Pine Lake Road, it dead-ends at the lake and there are cabins beyond the end of the trail.

Johnny gets a lantern and batteries and they drive to Pine Lake. There are car tracks in the road and Johnny spots Mike's car in the trees. The car is empty and cold and there are footprints heading up the trail. Johnny tells Mike to go for help as Johnny follows the trail. Johnny sends Mike away so he would not know about the other car hidden in the snow, the one stolen by Benny Stark.

Johnny goes up the trail following the footsteps. After almost two hours the trail disappears and the cold starts to take over and Johnny becomes disoriented. Johnny's light hits Benny beside a tree and there are shots.

Johnny shoots back and stumbles on without a light. Johnny becomes lost and hears music in the woods. Johnny recognizes it as the cold and fatigue leading to a permanent sleep. Johnny moves toward the music, which becomes louder. Johnny calls out and sees a blaze of light and a girl with golden hair and a rifle.

Johnny warms up and moves away from the stove only when his shirt starts to smoke. Kathy tells Johnny that she and her daughter are ok, and have plenty of supplies. Johnny tells her that he just guessed where she was.

Johnny tells Kathleen about Mrs. Gottler, and about Benny Stark, who is dead in the snow.

Tomorrow, the show down. Victory, and then disaster when a visitor to the little town of Branberry turns out to be death.

Episode 5   Show Date: 12/23/1955
Johnny Dollar is my name, j-o-h-n-n-y d-o-l-l-a-r. "That's not right. You forgot to capitalize" Jill tells Johnny. My name is J-i-l-l O-'-D-a-r-e. Is my mother pretty? Why don't you marry her so I can have a daddy?

Johnny gets a million-dollar feeling being with Kathleen and Jill. It is 4 a.m. and the storm is worse, so Jill is sent to bed. Kathleen tells Johnny that Jill is great little girl and the only thing Kathleen did right.

She knows why Johnny came, he wants her to come back. She tells Johnny that she heard nothing and did not see or hear anything. Johnny tells her that Nick will send someone else. She tells Johnny that she is not wide-eyed about Nick, she had a legitimate job and Nick is crazy about Jill. Johnny tells her she is letting the people in town down. The city has made a coward of her. Johnny tells her that she is scared, and that will make you do things you do not want to do. You have to fight the fear, do it for Jill, teach her courage.

Kathleen finally tells Johnny that Nick and Mel were arguing. Mel yelled out and there were shots. She ran to the office and Nick was there with a gun. He told me to get out and keep quiet if I wanted to live. Kathleen agrees to make a statement and Johnny tells her he will stand by her. Kathleen and Jill sleep in Johnny's arms — that was the million-dollar feeling.

Mike and the rescue party arrive the next day and they go to town for the Christmas Eve program. Mike and Jill go in early and Kathy and Johnny arrive late and sit in the back.

After 10 minutes another man comes in, Nick Shurn. Nick checks Johnny for a gun, and Johnny is not armed. Nick tells them to ease outside, or he will kill Kathy.

Outside Mike gives Johnny a bag and tells Johnny "don't uncork it until you are ready for some serious business". Jill runs outside and wants to see Uncle Nick. Dan comes outside and Nick is forced to pick up Jill as Johnny takes Nick's gun.

Johnny and Kathleen walk and he tells her that Jill saved Nick's life. Mike had slipped him a gun in the paper bag, and he had Nick covered. Johnny tells Kathleen that she showed a lot of courage, and she mentions another man who had courage 2,000 years ago.

"Remarks: Merry Christmas! Merry Christmas to all of you from all of us on the program. And God bless you."

Exp. Acct: $486.20

Notes:
- This is the first Bob Bailey Johnny Dollar Christmas program.
- Roy Rowan is the announcer.
- Musical supervision is by Amerigo Marino.

Producer:	Jack Johnstone Writer: Les Crutchfield
Cast:	Virginia Gregg, Peggy Webber, Don Diamond, Ben Wright, Jack Kruschen, Barney Phillips, Sam Edwards, Ken Christy

◆ ❖ ◆

Show:	**The Forbes Matter**
Company:	**Continental Adjustment Bureau**
Agent:	**Mr. Turner**
Synopsis:	
Episode 1	**Show Date: 12/26/1955**

Pauline Morris calls for Mr. Turner. How would you like to handle a case for us while you are on vacation in New York City? There is practically no commission but Johnny will do it for Pauline, if he will go to dinner with him at the Crystal Room.

Johnny meets Pauline for dinner and gets the details on the case. Century Styles has filed a claim through their insurance company, Eastern Delaware. The auditors have found a deficit of $4,285, and your contact is Mr. Robert Elliott.

Johnny travels to New York City, gets a room at the New Westin hotel, calls Mr. Elliott, and then goes to the Century Styles office. Mr. Elliott is colorfully dressed and Johnny admires the, um, merchandise, real and inanimate. The auditors have left a report of their findings. Elliott is the creator of "Patsy's Things", a thankless task, and the loss is devastating. The company operates on a shoestring and the loss is stopping a major show. A "ruthless brigand pussyfooted off with the money", Elliott tells Johnny. The auditors simply found the shortage.

Johnny goes to his hotel and reads the auditor's report, which points to an inside job. Johnny meets with the auditor and learns that the loss is legitimate. Johnny is told that Sheldon Forbes, who is still on the payroll at Century, handled the books containing the theft.

Johnny goes to the District Attorney to explain the case and then goes to talk to Forbes.

Johnny meets with Forbes, who is just an average type person. Johnny tells Forbes who he is and why he is talking to him. Johnny shows Forbes the books but he says nothing. Forbes admits to stealing the money, but he cannot give the money back as he does not have it and wants Johnny to take him to jail.

What makes a man steal? Everybody's tried to answer that question at one time or another. Tomorrow I'll take a crack at it.

Episode 2   Show Date: 12/27/1955

Robert Elliott calls and tells Johnny that he feels terrible. He is at the District Attorney's office and they want him to sign a complaint. Elliott is worried about the claim, and Johnny tells him that the check is on the way now. Johnny is not finished, as he has to recover the money.

Johnny gets a rental car and drives to the police where Johnny is told that Forbes is being held in the central jail.

Johnny drives to the office of Edward Gumby, Attorney. Gumby is the court appointed attorney for Forbes and Johnny explains who he is. Johnny wants to recover the money rather than prosecute. Gumby has not talked to Forbes yet, although he knows that Forbes was married and widowed after the war. Gumby tells Johnny that the money is probably in an old sock, as that is the way these cases go. Later the police tell Johnny that there is no evidence of the money in Forbes' apartment or car.

Johnny visits Forbes in jail, but Forbes does not want to talk to anyone. Johnny tells Forbes that he has to recover the money and wants to help him. Forbes thinks that 3-12 years in jail is worth the money he took. Forbes will tell Johnny nothing about what he did with the money. Johnny tells him he will track down what happened with the money.

Johnny checks Forbes' files and meets Gumby in the jail. Gumby tells Johnny that there is not much to say. Forbes wants to plead guilty and take his medicine, but he is not a criminal. The court would listen to a mercy plea, but Forbes wants to plead guilty. Gumby calls Forbes a calendar job, born between two wars interspersed with a depression in the middle.

Tomorrow, a sudden twist in the case that throws all the usual theories right out the window. The unexpected.

Episode 3   Show Date: 12/28/1955
Ed Gumby calls Johnny and tells him that the hearing is set for this afternoon, but it will just be a formality. Sentencing will be at the end of the week. Gumby will try to get Forbes to return the money and Johnny is going to find out where the money went.

Johnny eats lunch with Mr. Haven of the Century Styles accounting department. Johnny tells Haven that Forbes will probably go to prison. Haven has no idea why Forbes took the money. Everyone in the office is upset and Forbes did not go with any of the girls in the office. Havens remembers a change in Forbes' nature in the last six weeks, he was more anxious. Johnny goes to the Century office and talks to the staff about Forbes.

Johnny goes to Forbes' apartment and talks to Mrs. Anastasia Kanopka, the manager. Johnny asks about Forbes, but she is hesitant to say anything other than Forbes had no visitors and did not cause trouble. He has no girlfriends and worked very hard. He is a poor fellow who just thinks and paints and listens to music. She gives Johnny the keys and Johnny searches the dismal apartment, but there is nothing worth $4,285 in the apartment. Johnny looks at Forbes' 1946 Ford and finds nothing.

Johnny eats at a local diner and learns that the local people knew him.

Johnny goes to the jail and meets Gumby there. The hearing was held and Forbes would say nothing, so sentencing is Friday. Gumby tells Johnny that Forbes will be released on bail at 8:00 that night.

When Forbes leaves, Johnny follows him to the Empress Theater. Johnny then follows Forbes to his apartment and goes in 15 minutes later. Johnny smells gas and breaks down the door, breaks a window and drags Forbes out.

Tomorrow, a switch in the case that starts a real chase and a race against time.

Episode 4   Show Date: 12/29/1955
The police operator calls and tells Johnny that the ambulance is on the way.

Johnny calls an ambulance and the interns try to revive Forbes, who is barely alive, but a hypodermic shot brings him around and he is taken to Belleview hospital. The police question Johnny and then he goes to the station house to sign a statement.

Johnny then goes to the Empress Theater and talks to Frank the doorman about Forbes' visit earlier. The doorman remembers Forbes, he comes there to see Betsy Walker. He comes asking to see her, but she never sees him. She has gone home, and the doorman will not give Johnny an address or phone number, so Johnny asks him to call Betsy for him.

Johnny goes to Betsy Walker's apartment and meets her and tells her why he is there. She knows Forbes' name but not him. She met him once and he is quite impossible. She tells Johnny that Forbes' had given her a number of presents, expensive presents. Forbes would also send her orchids at the theater. She got a card asking her to go to dinner, then the orchids and then the gifts. She gave some of the gifts away.

When she did meet him, he was unsophisticated and un-poised. Johnny tells her that Forbes had stolen the money to buy the gifts and tried to kill himself. Apparently, you meant something to him.

Tomorrow, proof the $4,285 worth of unrequited love can spell three years of prison. But sometimes there is an angle, in this case a rather startling one.

Episode 5   Show Date: 12/30/1955
Betsy calls Johnny and she will see him in an hour to inventory the gifts. She tells Johnny that she does not mind giving the gifts back.

Johnny travels around New York recapping the value of the gifts bought by Sheldon Forbes for Betsy Walker, total $2,780 bought with stolen money. Johnny also tracks down a series of restaurants where $835 was spent on meals never eaten. $670 was also spent on flowers sent to Betsy. Total amount spent equals total amount stolen.

Johnny visits Forbes in the hospital and tells him about Betsy Walker and the gifts. Neither Johnny nor Betsy think that the ordeal is funny. Johnny has taken the gifts back and Johnny asks Forbes to sign an inventory report. Forbes signs the document and tells Johnny that all it means to him is dollars and cents.

Forbes tells Johnny that Betsy was a model during a showing at the office and he saw her there in a black dress, and he had never seen anyone like her. He tracked down her name and thought that the money would give him a way to meet her. He was going to give the money back. There was no other alternative, as he had nothing else to give. She makes more in an hour than he made in a week. Johnny is convinced that Forbes was guilty of love at first sight.

Johnny wires the insurance company that the recovered goods comes to about $2,500 and then meets Betsy in the lobby of his hotel. Over a drink, Johnny tells her that Forbes will be sentenced on Monday. Betsy is upset about the whole thing and asks Johnny what would happen if she paid the other $2,000? Johnny tells her it would be up to the court. "He did all these things for me" she tells Johnny.

She tells Johnny that she is not much of an actress or singer, but he is the first man she has ever known who would go out on a limb for a girl, and she was that girl. "That poor stupid wonderful dumbbell does not belong in jail" she tells Johnny. Johnny kisses her and thanks her for renewing his faith in mankind.

"Remarks: She got Forbes to change his plea. She paid back the additional money. He comes to trial next week. He might get a suspended sentence."

Exp. Acct: $363.51

Notes:
- This story was done as *The Lester James Matter*, broadcast on 3/31/1953.
- The Waldorf, The Stork Club and "The 21" are mentioned   all are very expensive New York restaurants of the time.

- Roy Rowan is the announcer.
- Musical supervision is by Amerigo Marino.
- Next Week's program is a trip south of the border with romance and trouble. This could be *The Flight Six Matter*, which is aired on 1/30/1956, but it was not taped until 1/22/1956.

Producer:	Jack Johnstone	Writer:	John Dawson
Cast:	Lillian Buyeff, Sandra Gould, Jack Edwards, Herb Ellis, James McCallion, Parley Baer, John Stephenson, Howard McNear, Bob Bruce, Junius Matthews		

♦ ❖ ♦

Show: **The Caylin Matter**
Company: **Trinity Mutual Insurance Company, Ltd.**
Agent: **Walt Albright**
Synopsis:
Episode 1 **Show Date:** **1/2/1956**

Walt Albright calls and tells Johnny that he has asthma, again. Whenever Walt gets suspicious, he gets asthma. Eddie Caylin died yesterday under mysterious circumstances, with a $5,000 policy issued just 6 weeks ago at the wife's request. The beneficiary is the widow.

Johnny goes to Los Angeles, California and is met at the airport by Presley Welsh, the local agent. Johnny is daring and expenses a cup of coffee for Welsh.

Welsh tells Johnny that he knew better than to write the policy and that Caylin had laughed at the retirement benefits, but Mrs. Caylin was very serious. Welsh only saw Caylin twice and no claim has been filed yet.

Johnny gets a room at the Beverly Wilshire Hotel and then goes to the police. Johnny meets Det. Sgt. Reynosa and is told that the case facts do not add up. A call was received at 4:20 a.m. for a car that appeared to have burned from an accident, but the upholstery seemed to have been soaked with gasoline. The body was burned but there were some personal effects that were used to identify Eddie Caylin. The police found a locked door and signs of a fight at his home, but the wife was away at a friend's cabin, alone.

Johnny is told that Eddie Caylin was a "promoter", a small-time agent, bookie and gambler. He was in a poker game with Topo Leenly and supposedly won $60,000. The police had Leenly in for questioning, but he told them he had never heard of Caylin. Reynosa thinks this case is hokey and murder, but quien sabe, who knows.

Johnny gets the address for Mrs. Caylin and has a hunch about the door lock. Johnny goes to the apartment of Mrs. Caylin and a man exits the apartment and comes out. It is Mr. Welsh. He tells Johnny that he got a wire from Hartford and the claim has been filed for double indemnity and Mrs. Caylin wants immediate payment. Johnny tells him that the policy probably will not be paid at all.

Tomorrow, a lovely girl lies, cries and crosses her heart and hopes to die and a killer fires from the dark.

Episode 2   Show Date: 1/3/1956
Johnny meets Mrs. Caylin and tells her why he is there. She tells Johnny that she has a right to file a claim. Johnny asks her how many keys are there to the front door? The number will hang someone.

Johnny tells Mrs. Caylin that he does not have a name yet, but she will be smart to answer his questions, but she asks Johnny to leave when he tries to question her. She changes her mind and tells him to stay. She tells Johnny that Eddie hung out at the Eloinaise and the Brass Monkey bars. She goes to change and tells Johnny to pour himself a drink. Johnny braces himself for a lovely woman.

Twenty minutes later she comes back in dressed for "a special evening in". Johnny makes her a scotch and soda and asks her how Eddie died. She tells Johnny that Eddie had a lot of friends and no enemies. A good friend was Pete Steimer, who has also disappeared. The others drift in and out based on Eddie's finances. He also had a lot of women, mostly dancers and strippers. She tells Johnny that she did not kill him and does not know if she loves him. She could have killed him at times and loved him at others.

She went to Lake Arrowhead after a fight and heard of the accident on the radio. She identified a wallet, a watch and a ring but not the body. She feels that Eddie is not dead. She thinks that Eddie won some money from that Topo Leenly character. She would never know, as Eddie never spent money at home, but only where it would show. She tells Johnny that she had to dress herself up so that she could feel anything and gave the wrong impression. Johnny apologizes for coming in with the wrong impression. She tells Johnny that her name is Lila.

Johnny sees a man outside and hears a sound in the next terrace. Johnny goes out and is attacked and a shot is fired. Johnny kicks the man and tells Lila to call Sgt. Reynosa. The man is big and stocky and the name in the wallet is Topo Leenly.

Tomorrow, we meet a Latin doll from Santa Monica, an erudite bartender and a terpsichorean ecdysiast and they are all in the cast.

Episode 3   Show Date: 1/4/1956
Sgt. Reynosa calls Johnny and tells him that Topo is not scared and says that Johnny jumped him. He claims he was calling on a girl friend who gave him the wrong address. Johnny tells Reynosa that Topo is scared and maybe he will lead us to Eddie Caylin. Reynosa tells Johnny that Eddie is downtown on a slab. "Wanna Bet?"

Johnny is following a hunch about the locked door. Johnny cabs to the Café Eloinaise, a seedy bar on Santa Monica Blvd. The hostess has a beautifully rounded, um, Latin accent. She is Pepita, and Johnny buys her a drink. Johnny asks about meeting her after work, but she cannot, as she lives with her mother. Johnny gives her $10 for information on Eddie.

She tells Johnny that she last saw him on Thursday, before he was killed. Eddie told her he loved her, bought a drink and borrowed the money to pay for it. He was in the bar for an hour with Pete, but no one has seen him either. Eddie did not seem worried or scared. Every girl was Eddie's girl, but only one girl in each bar. Pepita tells Johnny that at the Brass Money there are some strippers, and Eddie has a big thing with one of them. Her name is Marty Midnight. Pepita tells Johnny that she is off at 1:00 AM, but Johnny does not want to bother her mother. "My mother lives in Havana, Cuba", exclaims Pepita.

Johnny cabs to the Brass Monkey Inn, which is a very lively place. Johnny talks to the bartender about the seven-girl chorus line called the Pleiades. The bartender tells Johnny that he reads a lot and has a system. He reads the dictionary and has read it twice and is back up to "J".

Johnny gives him a twenty for a drink and asks for information on Marty Midnight. The bartender tells Johnny that she has not been around since Eddie died. The bartender tells Johnny that Marty moved after she took up with Eddie, and Pete has not been around either. Another guy who worked for Topo Leenly, Mike Kelso disappeared that night too. Topo comes in all the time. Say, are you the guy that broke his arm? Have a drink!

Johnny is told that Topo met Eddie at the bar and the bartender told Eddie to stay out of the card game. Johnny recounts how it could have happened but there are too many loose ends.

Someone yells "police" and the bartender thinks the place is being raided. The raid turns out to be Reynosa who is looking for Marty Midnight. He tells Johnny that a man was found dead in her apartment. It was Eddie Caylin.

Tomorrow, a stakeout, a manhunt, and a tired intern breaking his heart to keep life in a broken body.

Episode 4   Show Date: 1/5/1956
Johnny answers the phone and Lila is calling for Sgt. Reynosa. Johnny tells her that he is at Marty Midnight's. Eddie is dead now in Marty's apartment.

Johnny and Reynosa go to the apartment of Marty Midnight and watch Eddie Caylin's body loaded into the ambulance. Reynosa wants to know why Johnny knew Caylin was alive. Johnny tells him about his hunch about the locked door. If it had a night latch or spring lock it would be obvious. The evidence of the fight meant that someone would have to get out fast, and who else but Eddie would stop to lock the door, out of habit.

Johnny thinks that Eddie won the money and went home, so Topo sent Mike Kelso to get the money back, and Kelso ended up getting killed. Eddie put the body in the car and burned it with Pete Steiner's help. The jewelry was a plant. Eddie, Pete and Marty were going to leave the country, but now Marty and Pete are gone. Topo is out of jail now, so it could be him.

The doorbell rings and a woman named Jeanette Dubois comes in. She had called the police about the shooting. She did not give her name because she was afraid of being implicated, but a friend said she must go to the police.

She tells Johnny that she heard shots, the door opened and a girl came out, a girl with long black hair. She wore a white raincoat, wiped something and threw it in the door and ran down the street. Miss Dubois then went home and called the police.

Johnny tells Reynosa he is surprised about Marty, and then shots rings out. A man had been surprised and shot at the police and ran into the woods around Griffith Park. The police surround the area and Johnny and Reynosa go in to search. Shots are fired and the man is hit. It turns out to be Pete Steimer.

Johnny goes to the hospital to wait for Steimer to wake up. Pete wakes up and asks for Eddie. "He should be here", Pete tells him. "Eddie always runs out and leaves someone else to face the music", Pete says and dies.

Tomorrow, a quarry run to earth, a strange alibi, and a shocking twist at the windup.

Episode 5   Show Date: 1/6/1956

Sgt. Reynosa calls Johnny at the hospital and Johnny tells him Pete is dead. Reynosa has Marty Midnight with a ticket to San Diego in her coat pocket.

Johnny cabs to police headquarters to help interrogate Marty. During the questioning, Marty says nothing except to ask for a lawyer. Reynosa tells her he will call her folks and she starts to talk.

She tells Reynosa that she did not know that Eddie was married at first, but he said that he was getting a divorce. Eddie killed Kelso in self-defense and they were going to go to Mexico. She was going to go back to her folks and did not know that Eddie is dead. She thought they were after Pete at her apartment. Johnny and Reynosa talk outside and agree this case is strange. Reynosa is sure the killer is Marty.

Johnny goes to see Lila to tell her what has happened. Lila is waiting for Johnny and fixes him some coffee. Johnny tells her that Marty was arrested, and Lila feels sorry for her. She had four years of Eddie lying, and wonders why she went through it.

Reynosa calls and tells Johnny that the paraffin test was negative and that Marty was not wearing a raincoat when she was picked up. Johnny tells him to come to Lila's place. Lila has black hair and Johnny goes to the closet and finds her damp white raincoat with smudges on it.

Johnny tells Lila to give him the facts. She tells Johnny that she wondered if Eddie was alive, so she went to Marty's apartment and forced her way in. She fought with Eddie and he pulled a gun on her, it was self-defense.

"Remarks: So, the question still stands. Why do they do it? Why do girls go blind when the Eddie Caylin's walk in? You might ask a strip-teaser down in San Diego. But do not look for her under the name Marty Midnight. She is Jean Luanne Jagline now, a quiet kid. Lives at home with her folks."

Exp. Acct: $596.85

Notes:
- **Terpsichorean: of or relating to dancing.**
- **Ecdysiast: Strip teaser.**

- The Pleiades, or "Seven Sisters" (or Subaru in Japanese) is an open cluster of stars in the constellation "Taurus the Bull", typically visible in the winter in North America.
- Roy Rowan is the announcer.
- Musical supervision is by Amerigo Marino.

Producer:	Jack Johnstone	Writer:	Les Crutchfield
Cast:	Virginia Gregg, Lucille Meredith, Alma Lawton, Gloria Blondell, Howard McNear, Harry Bartell, Peter Leeds, Byron Kane		

◆ ❖ ◆

Show: The Todd Matter
Company: Four State Insurance Company
Agent: Don Freed
Synopsis:
Episode 1 **Show Date:** 1/9/1956

Orin Vance calls and tells Johnny that he had sent Orin to Ossining, but he will do Johnny a favor. He has information about the Todd case, which cost your company $75,000.

Johnny calls Don Freed to discuss the Todd Burglary and requests information on the stolen goods. Johnny goes to the International Adjustment Bureau to look at the case involving Vance.

Orin Vance comes to Johnny's apartment and asks not to be treated like a con. He tells Johnny that even his wife will not let him in the house unless he gets a job. Vance needs a stake, and offers Johnny information on the robbery, specifically the serial number of a mink coat from Zellerbachs. Johnny calls Four State who tells him that the numbers match and that there is a $5,000 reward. Vance wants a check for $2,500 and will leave for Indiana in a couple hours.

Johnny gives Orin the check and gets the name of Gloria Tierney in New York City. Johnny goes to the airport to see Vance off and flies to New York City. Johnny checks in at the New Westin hotel and then with the police, where Gloria has no record.

Johnny goes to the apartment of Gloria Tierney, but she is not in, so he checks with the manager, Mrs. Stromberg and leaves his name. Johnny watches the building for three hours and sees no one.

Gloria calls Johnny at midnight. She tells Johnny that she will be leaving town in the morning and tells Johnny to come over now. Johnny gets there in less than 15 minutes but the apartment is dark and locked. The manager tells Johnny that Gloria was waiting in the hallway and that Gloria looked worried and she had been wearing her mink coat.

Johnny goes outside and there is no one there. Johnny then sees a woman weaving as she crosses the street. Johnny runs up to her and the girl is Gloria, and she has been beaten. A 1955 Cadillac pulls up and Gloria is shot three times and falls into Johnny's arms as Mrs. Stromberg goes inside to call the police.

Tomorrow, the same old business of murder, but with a brand-new twist.

Episode 2   Show Date: 1/10/1956
Sgt. Dan Mapes calls about Johnny's statement. He wants Johnny to come to headquarters.

Johnny wires Don Freed about the events and asks him to hire counsel for him, and then he goes to see Mapes.

Johnny tells Mapes why he was at the apartment and what happened. Johnny tells Mapes about the mink coat, which the police have as stolen property. Gloria is still in critical condition. Mapes tells Johnny that Gloria had nothing else from the robbery, only the coat. Johnny tells Mapes that he cannot tell him about the tip he got about the coat. Mapes threatens to hold him, but Johnny tells him that an attorney is on the way over to see that he is treated nice.

Johnny and Mapes go to the apartment house and talk to Mrs. Stromberg. She tells them that Gloria had moved in a year ago and was a quiet girl. She did not work, but always paid her rent on time with a check. Gloria has a family in California. She had a few boyfriends but Mrs. Stromberg had never seen the car.

Mapes gets rough with Mrs. Stromberg and then she remembers seeing the car there before, and the driver was Bill "something" who is tall and dark and well-dressed. He was in his mid-thirties and came several times a week. Bill seemed to have money and clothes and gave Gloria the mink coat and other small gifts but no jewelry. She really did not talk about a lot of things, she was just a nice innocent girl. Mapes calls the office and learns Gloria is dying.

Tomorrow, I take some lessons from a good policeman on how to find out what has to be found out.

Episode 3   Show Date: 1/11/1956
Dr. King calls and there has been no change in Gloria's condition. He tells Johnny and Sgt. Mapes to come over to the hospital.

Johnny and Mapes arrive at the hospital and Dr. King tells them that they can have only two minutes. A priest is in the room and Gloria is barely conscious. Mapes asks Gloria her name and condition and she only says that Bill shot her. Gloria relapses and then dies without telling anything.

Johnny and Mapes have a drink and discuss the case. They agree that Gloria was not the type of girl to have a stolen mink coat. Mapes comments that "Boy, this whiskey is really bad. Two more doubles please bartender!" Mapes tells Johnny that he is really glad to have Johnny working on the case. Johnny tells Mapes that he really could have gone for Gloria.

At the apartment, Mapes finds letters from the family in California and a picture from Bill. The lab reports that the bullets came from a .45 Colt. Mrs. Stromberg comes in and identifies the man in the picture as Bill. The phone rings, and Mapes asks Mrs. Stromberg if Gloria had ever mentioned being married. Mapes tells Johnny that Gloria was married and divorced from William Powers who has no record.

Johnny and Mapes drive to see Powers and tell him about Gloria. Powers is upset and tells them that he saw her last week. Powers does not know anything about a mink coat. Powers is not the man in the picture but he has a 1955 Cadillac Coupe de Ville.

Tomorrow, well you find one killer and you find them all, and then you have to start all over again.

Episode 4   Show Date: 1/12/1956
Johnny gets a call from Don Freed, who is worried about his expenses. Johnny tells Don that Gloria had the coat but Johnny knows nothing else. Johnny gets kind of upset and Don tells Johnny that he is a real man-eater today!

Bill Powers goes to the morgue and then they all have coffee. Powers tells Johnny and Sgt. Mapes that he does not believe Gloria was wearing a stolen coat. Powers had been seeing Gloria regularly, and knew about Bill Chambers. Sgt. Mapes shows him the picture and Powers identifies it as Bill Chambers. Powers tells Johnny that he was going out with Gloria and had asked her to marry him. Powers tells them that he and Gloria had broken up for all the stupid reasons and were going to be remarried. She did not want to marry Chambers. She told Powers two days ago she would remarry him. He had bought a Cadillac just like Bill's to influence her.

A check finds 24 names like Bill Chambers, but none matched the description. Later two pieces of jewelry from the robbery show up in a pawn shop and the description of the seller matches that of Chambers, but the addresses were phony.

A call comes in to Mapes and the Cadillac has been sold in the Bronx. The car lot manager gives a description and prints are taken from the car and a check gives seven aliases and a record of car thefts for one William Charles.

The check continues, and more jewelry shows up. Johnny wires Four States with an update, and then a call comes in about Bill Charles from a woman.

Johnny cabs to Schraft's Restaurant to meet the caller. She asks Johnny about the reward and Johnny tells her she will only get half of the reward. She tells Johnny that she also wants legal protection and Johnny tells her he will work on it. The woman tells Johnny that she is Melva Charles, the wife of Bill Charles, and that she will meet Johnny again in two hours.

Johnny follows her out of the restaurant and Mapes picks him up and they follow her. Johnny outlines the discussion and Mapes tells Johnny that he had been followed. Mapes tells Johnny that Melva had been born to a wealthy family but has been in trouble all her life. They stop at an apartment building and go into the door. Shots are fired and Johnny is hit.

Tomorrow, well there are times when $75,000 worth of stealing isn't worth a plugged nickel.

Episode 5   Show Date: 1/13/1956
Johnny is barely able to answer the phone in his room at the hospital. Sgt. Mapes tells Johnny that he had been shot twice but is luckier than Gloria.

Johnny bribes an orderly to buy him breakfast and Mapes comes in to visit. Johnny tells him that the last thing he remembers is being shot. Johnny is told that Melva got it, Charles shoved a butcher knife in her back for trying to sell him out. A man in the hallway was shot three times and a woman on the street was injured. Charles opened fire and Mapes shot back. Charles is upstairs in critical condition. Mapes gives Johnny a book of poetry to read.

The story is in the paper the next day and Charles' gun is the one that killed Gloria, but no jewelry was found. Mapes brings a wheelchair and Johnny goes up to see Charles. Charles tells Johnny and Mapes that he did not mean to kill Gloria. He had been doing OK with burglary jobs and had met Gloria through a mutual friend and wanted to marry her, but she wanted to marry someone else, so he got mad and shot her. Charles will not tell Johnny about the goods from the Todd robbery and dies without saying anything.

Johnny recovers after three more days and visits Mapes. They both wonder about the Todd jewelry. Johnny visits Mrs. Stromberg and she gives Mapes a shot of bourbon. Johnny asks her about the night Gloria was killed, and how she said, "you'd have her call me". Johnny tells her "You sent her out so Charles could take care of her and were waiting for me in the hall because you knew I was an insurance investigator". Charles would not tell Johnny who introduced him, but Johnny tells Mrs. Stromberg that it was her, and that she is keeping the goods.

Johnny tells her that Melva would sell him for $2,500 but did not know where the jewels are. When Johnny tells her to go with him to see Mapes, she tries to buy Johnny, but he wants her behind bars.

The house is searched and the goods are found behind a cement block in the basement. The recovery was 90%, but lives were lost in the process.

Exp. Acct: $1,095.00

Notes:
- This story was done as *The Rochester Theft Matter*, broadcast on 5/12/1953.
- This story is interesting. It incorporates parts of two other stories by E. Jack Neuman, *The Baltimore Matter* and *The Rochester Theft Matter*. The basic story is from *The Rochester Matter*, but the ending comes from *The Baltimore Matter.*
- Johnny is shot for the 6th time.
- Roy Rowan is the announcer.
- Musical supervision is by Amerigo Marino.

Producer:	Jack Johnstone	Writer:	John Dawson
Cast:	Vivi Janiss, Barbara Fuller, Shirley Mitchell, Lawrence Dobkin, Frank Gerstle, Marvin Miller		

Show: The Ricardo Amerigo Matter
Company: Philadelphia Mutual Liability & Casualty Company
Agent: Harry Branson
Synopsis:
Episode 1   Show Date: 1/16/1956

Harry Branson calls from Philadelphia and asks Johnny what he knows about violins. An Amati, insured for $30,000 has been stolen.

Johnny trains to Philadelphia, Pennsylvania, checks in at the Belleview Stratford and then cabs to see Harry "old sober sides" Branson.

Harry tells Johnny that two policies had been issued, one for the violin and one for the owner. Ricardo Amerigo was a world-famous virtuoso, but he has disappeared and the violin is gone. The Port Morris police think he might have drown in an accident. Ricardo was going to the shore, crashed through a guardrail and disappeared in a tidal creek.

Johnny cabs to the office of Peter Corbin, the booking agent and "benuficiary" of the policy. Peter tells Johnny that he brought Amerigo to this country and kept him on top while he was working, but now he is working on a bottle and is not playing. Ricardo is in debt up to his ears so Peter took out the insurance for himself and the violin, but Peter has had to pay for the last few premiums. Peter gets upset when Johnny infers that he would be the most likely suspect and throws Johnny out. Peter takes a swing at Johnny but Johnny decks him.

Johnny calls Harry, who has been called by the Port Morris police, there is evidence of murder.

Johnny goes to South Vineland to see Ad Boles, an old friend, retired investigator, and general know-it-all. Ad knows that Johnny is on the Amerigo case. Ad had contacted Barney Peters of the Port Morris police and learned about the next of kin and knew Branson would call Johnny. Ad had shown them where the steering arm had been cut, and Ad suspects Pete Corbin, as he is the most likely person because the car had been kept in Corbin's garage. Ad thinks that Pete only let Ricardo drive when he was drunk to get the insurance. Johnny bets his commission and expense account that Corbin is not the guilty party.

Ad offers to fly Johnny to Port Morris in his private plane. Johnny calls Harry to learn that Pete Corbin has disappeared.

Tomorrow, a soggy day in a soggy south Jersey swamp, and a discovery almost too good to be true.

Episode 2   Show Date: 1/17/1956

Sgt. Peters calls about Ad and Johnny coming over. Sgt. Peters tells Johnny that Pete Corbin is there, but he cannot hold him. He might be gunning for you.

Johnny and Ad Boles fly to Port Morris in Ad's plane, weaving through the air in the process. Ad is positive that Pete is the suspect.

In Port Morris, Johnny and Ad meet Sgt. Peters and they drive to the site of the accident. On the way, Johnny learns the tide was on the way out at the time of the accident.

A car approaches driving too fast and Johnny spots Pete Corbin driving it, but the road is too narrow for them to turn around and follow.

At the bridge, Johnny examines the site and spots a bird's nest with a fiddle case resting on it. Johnny wades into the black muck and pulls the case out and then struggles to make it back to the bridge.

In the car, Johnny has the violin and finds a piece of a shirt with Amerigo's initials fastened to the case. Ad is now sure that Corbin is the suspect as he had the best opportunity. Pete staged the accident so that a deputy would see it happen, but where is the body? Sgt. Peters agrees that the case is too easy to blame on Corbin but Ad reminds Johnny to send him the check when he finds Corbin guilty.

Johnny takes a bus back to Philadelphia with the violin. Johnny calls Harry Branson and tells him that he has the violin, and Harry comes over to get it. In Johnny's room, Harry opens the case and the violin turns out to not be the right fiddle, maybe?

Tomorrow, the results of a poker game, and believe me there are times when the cards can really be stacked against you.

Episode 3   Show Date: 1/18/1956

Pete Corbin returns Johnny's call. Johnny asks if Pete can explain what he was doing in Port Morris yesterday. Johnny tells Pete that he is on his way over to see him.

Johnny buys new clothes and Harry agrees to take the violin to an expert for an examination. Forresto Cherneglario, or whatever it is, is the man who identified the violin for the policy. Johnny confirms that the car had been tampered with and that there is no body. Harry tells Johnny that Ad Boles called and Harry tends to agree with him.

Forresto Cherniarro (I knew that was it) arrives and pronounces that the violin is the Amati. All of the details of the violin verify that the violin is the Amati, including the label. Johnny tells Forresto that a fiddle player at the hotel says it could be a fake, but Forresto sells good violins, some of his sell for $65, so he knows. Harry tells Johnny that a representative of the Wurlitzer Collection had verified it. Johnny takes the violin and leaves.

Johnny goes to see Pete Corbin and shows him the violin and tells him that it was just where he planted it. Johnny thinks that putting the shirt there was too much. Corbin denies planting the violin and tells Johnny that he was just looking for Ricardo when he was in Port Morris. Pete tells Johnny that he is also "the executive" of Ricardo's will, so why would he leave a fiddle in the swamp.

When Johnny tells Pete that the car had been tampered with, he is shocked and wants to know "who done it". Pete identifies the violin and Johnny tells him that the accident was a motive for repayment of the money Ricardo owed. Johnny thinks that pinning the case on Pete is wrong, he is not smart enough to do it, and will play it that way until he proves otherwise.

Pete tells Johnny that at the time of the accident he was at Willie Elliott's playing poker with Jerry Goldsmith, a composer, conductor and piano player, and Eric Snowden, a fiddle maker. Johnny gets the addresses and Pete tells Johnny that Snowden was the only man Ricardo would let touch the violin. Johnny calls the poker pals to arrange for Johnny to visit them.

Tomorrow, a trio of musicians. The question, which one's story was playing a little flat?

Episode 4　　Show Date:　　1/19/1956
A man calls Johnny about the investigation. The caller tells him it is no gag and hangs up.

Johnny goes to all of the bars frequented by Ricardo and learns nothing. At the Hangover Club, Johnny is told that Ricardo would buy a few drinks and just get plastered until a friend would drag him out. Too bad he was so far gone.

Johnny cabs to the home of William Elliott who tells Johnny that he had known Ricardo for years. When Johnny goes to see Jerry Goldsmith, he takes the Amati.

Johnny tells him he is an investigator and Jerry spots the case. He admits to Johnny that he had coveted the violin and wanted it more than anything, but not enough to kill for it. Jerry tells Johnny that Ricardo only had four friends and none would have killed him. Jerry looks at the violin and it is the Amati. Jerry plays it but it does not have the sound he is used to. It looks like the Amati but is sounds wrong.

Johnny cabs to Eric Snowden's violin shop on a side street amid the downtown area. Snowden immediately recognizes the violin case. Snowden locks the front door and takes the violin up to his second-floor workroom to examine it.

Johnny notices that the shop is full of tools and violins and hacksaws, including one with axle grease on it. Snowden verifies that the violin is Ricardo's. Johnny tells Eric that someone else had said that the sound was not quite right. Snowden looks closely and tells Johnny that the violin must have been tampered with.

Someone pounds at the door and while Snowden goes downstairs Johnny looks around the shop and accidentally knocks open a cabinet with a violin in it, an exact duplicate of the Amati.

Tomorrow, well it's a wind up, but a windup with a real twist.

Episode 5　　Show Date:　　1/20/1956
Harry Branson calls Johnny and wonders about where Ricardo is. What if the violin was an imitation? It may be a phony.

Johnny finds a duplicate violin by accident and switches them while Snowden is gone.

Johnny takes the violin and arranges to come back later before Snowden can make any adjustments to it. When Johnny leaves the shop a flowerpot almost hits him and Snowden apologizes from the window above.

Johnny calls Harry to have the police watch Snowden and goes to Jerry Goldsmith's. Johnny has Goldsmith play the violin again and the sound is back! That violin is the Amati.

Johnny cabs to Harry's office and then to Erick Snowden's office. Johnny tells Snowden that the flowerpot had come from the third floor of the building. Johnny takes him back up to the second-floor workroom and shows him the violin and asks if it is the Amati.

After Snowden says it is, Johnny tells him to open the cabinet and Snowden tells him to leave. Johnny tells Snowden that he had found the copy and Snowden tells him that the loss of the Amati would be too great, so when Ricardo disappeared he made a copy and switched it.

A door opens and Ricardo Amerigo comes in. He tells Johnny that the car wreck and the duplicate fiddle were his idea. He wanted the fiddle to come back after he disappeared so that it could be played by someone else. The insurance was his last chance to payback Pete and his other friends. Only Eric knew of the plans. Would you buy me a drink before you call in the police?

"Remarks: No insurance payment necessary on either the Amati or the man. And I guess he really was a man, more than he knew. What the courts will do about him and about Eric Snowden, well the courts will do. And I am glad I have to have no part of it. You know, it's funny. Somehow, I think I have a little better appreciation of music now then...ah well."

Exp. Acct: $182.65

Notes:
- Andrea Amati made matched sets, or consorts of instruments during the 1560's and 1570's.
- The title character is a play on the name of the music director, Amerigo Marino.
- Musical supervisor and violinist, Amerigo Marino.
- During the credits for parts 1-4 Sam Dawson is credited as the writer. In the final episode, Roy Rowan credits Jack Johnstone with writing this week's story.
- The script title pages list "Jack and Sam Dawson" as the writers.
- This is the first time Bob Bailey mentions a commission.
- Bob flubs "Elliott's name in episode 4, calling him Elliert.
- The Wurlitzer Collection is a 19th century chamber music collection at the University of Cincinnati.
- In the story, Jerry goldsmith is mentioned. The late award-winning composer Jerry Goldsmith was an employee of CBS radio in the 1950's and could have known Jack Johnstone, who had a habit of writing friends and coworkers into the scripts. The Willie Elliott could possibly be a reference to William "Wild Bill" Elliott, but I cannot confirm that.

Producer: Jack Johnstone   Writer: Sam Dawson
Cast: Harry Bartell, Lawrence Dobkin, Vic Perrin, Barney Phillips, Forrest Lewis, Eric Snowden, Herb Vigran, James McCallion

Show: The Duke Red Matter
Company: Universal Adjustment Bureau
Agent: Niles Pearson
Synopsis:
Episode 1   Show Date: 1/23/1956

Niles Pearson calls and tells Johnny that he is worried about $65,000 worth of horseflesh. The horse Duke Red, who won the Futurity last year, was insured and had been destroyed.

Johnny goes to San Francisco and then to San Pietro, California. Johnny goes to the Abbott Stables office and asks for Mr. Abbott, and Johnny is told he is always at the ranch and that Mr. Monroe, the business manager who filed the claim three days ago, is no longer with the company. Mr. Abbott has fired him. The secretary Judy calls the ranch and is told that Mr. Abbott out for the day. Johnny asks where Mr. Monroe is, but is told that he has moved out of town.

Johnny rents a 1940 Terraplane and drives to the office of Dr. James Gorry, the local Veterinarian. Gorry knows that Abbott and Monroe had quarreled and tells Johnny that Duke Red was worth more than $65,000 as Gorry takes care of all of Abbott's stock.

He tells Johnny that Duke Red had stumbled up against a tractor and cut his hamstring. A report was made and Gorry shows Johnny the report. Johnny spots that the carcass was cremated that night and is told that Ben Abbott wanted it that way. There are also no x-rays to prove the injury. Gorry tells Johnny that it would have been wrong to not destroy the animal and that there was no use in consulting with another vet. Only Ben Abbott was there when the accident happened.

Johnny tells Gorry that he needs more than a report to substantiate the claim. Gorry tells Johnny he has been in business for 30 years, but Johnny tells him that he cannot take any one's word, so Gorry tells Johnny to leave. Johnny drives back to town and wonders why Gorry had not taken photos.

Johnny checks on Gorry with Judy, secretary in Abbott's office and she tells him that Gorry is a fixture here and is the best vet in the area. Johnny asks Judy to dinner and she accepts. She tells Johnny that she has worked for Mr. Abbott for a year and a half and that Monroe and Abbott had quarreled, and she wondered about it. Judy sees Mr. Monroe at the bar. Johnny stops him as he is leaving and Monroe tells him to talk to Mr. Abbott. Monroe is leaving town now, and it was not his horse. Monroe tells Johnny to let Abbott handle is own dirty business.

Tomorrow, there is proof that things are as just about as wrong in this case, and as dangerous, as they can get.

Episode 2   Show Date: 1/24/1956

The operator calls with a call from Mr. Pearson. Mr. Person got the wire to hold up the claim. Johnny tells him that the case is all wrong and something is cockeyed.

Johnny sends Dr. Gorry's report to a veterinary service in Cleveland and then drives to the Abbott farm.

Johnny is met at the door by the butler who tries to find Mr. Abbott. A girl and an old man enter the room arguing and ignoring Johnny. She wants to live her life and he tells her she will do as he tells her. They leave and then the girl comes back in.

The girl tells Johnny that her father does not approve of her company. Johnny introduces himself, and the girl tells Johnny that she is Terry Abbott, Ben's daughter. She knows that Johnny is there about Duke Red.

She tells Johnny that Red was a great horse and would have won a lot of money. Red was the only horse worth anything and he was not injured.

Ben Abbott comes in and he tells her to go to her room. She tells him it was murder, and Ben slaps her. Ben explains to Johnny that she always gets upset when an animal is destroyed. Ben tells Johnny that Gorry had called and Johnny tells him that he needs to go to everyone. Ben does not like Johnny sneaking around and tells Johnny that he does not know what he is doing. Ben tells Johnny that Monroe filed the claim too soon and that he was going to wait until the excitement died down. Losing that animal also caused a morale problem at the ranch.

Johnny tells Ben that they will pay when they are satisfied the circumstances were proper, and that they are not satisfied now. Johnny tells Ben he will get his information from whom ever he needs to in order to complete his investigation.

In frustration, Ben tells Johnny that the horse was coming back from a training session and was scared by something, reared back into the tractor and cut his Achilles tendon. Gorry said the horse did not have a chance, so Ben shot him. Johnny wants to talk to the trainer, Tom Warner, but Ben has fired him and he is gone as he knew better than to stay around. There was no one else around at the time. Ben tells Johnny that accidents happen, and he deals with them and the insurance company cannot tell him how to run his farm. Terry did not see the accident. Ben calls Cully, the butler, and tells him to throw Johnny out if he ever comes back.

Johnny leaves and Cully stops him and apologizes for Mr. Abbott and tells Johnny that he is just not himself. Johnny tells Cully that he thinks Ben is losing his mind and Cully agrees with him.

Tomorrow, the whole case starts to fall apart like a man full of bullet wounds, which is just about the case.

Episode 3   Show Date: 1/25/1956

Johnny receives a call in the stable office from Terry, where Cully had told her to call him. Did you believe all those things I told you? I'll be right down.

Terry meets Johnny in the stable office with a disdainful pout. She tells Johnny that he is so sure of himself although he knows nothing. Johnny tells her the only thing he knows about horses is that Duke Red is dead. Terry is very evasive about the things she had said earlier and has been upset lately.

She tells Johnny that Duke Red was the best horse they had ever had, and that the accident has turned everyone upside down. Johnny asks what Monroe meant about the "dirty business and where Tom Warner is. Terry tells Johnny that Warner is in Baltimore.

Johnny drives to town and gets Tom Warner's address. Johnny sends a wire to Niles Pearson for a run down on Ben Abbott's finances and then a wire to Tom Warner.

At the local bank, Johnny asks about Ben Abbott's credit. The manager, Dale O'Ryan, gets the file and tells Johnny that there will be nothing to find in Ben's finances as $65,000 is small change to him, and that Terry runs him a couple thousand or so a month.

Johnny reviews the folder and finds nothing unusual. The only questionable item is a check to Mr. Monroe marked "bonus" considering that they had argued. There is also an outstanding salary for Tom Warner. Johnny wonders why doesn't he kick?

A check at the Abbott office showed no forwarding address for Tom Warner. At dinner Johnny receives a call from Baltimore. Tom Warner's father tells Johnny that Tom is in San Pietro, California. He is not at home, he is at Mr. Abbott's farm.

Tomorrow, well sometimes a dead man can answer a lot of questions.

Episode 4   Show Date: 1/26/1956
The operator calls with a call from Niles Pearson. Johnny is told that Mr. Abbott does not need money, but no one knows what happened to Tom Warner. Abbott's claim has been filed for a week but he has not threatened to sue.

Johnny suspects that the death of Duke Red did not happen as reported. Johnny drives to the Abbott Ranch and Cully meets him at the door. Johnny asks for Tom Warner, but no one knows where he is.

Cully takes Johnny to the stable and lets Johnny search the room used by Tom Warner, but the room is bare. Cully tells Johnny that no one saw Warner leave. Tom had a lot of friends and the others on the farm have talked. Tom was a good horse trainer and did not have a temper. Tom could even handle Mr. Abbott.

Cully tells Johnny that Mr. Abbott has had a hard time since his wife died, he seems to have troubles at time. He really counted on Duke Red, and the other horses were no match. Warner did not have a car, so maybe Miss Terry drove him out. She used to drive Tom around and Mr. Abbott disapproved of it.

Johnny talks to the others on the farm, and they were grumbling and complaining. Johnny goes to the house to see Mr. Abbott but meets Terry, who is ready to see Johnny tossed out on his ear. Johnny asks if she is mad at Tom Warner for leaving and not saying good bye. She tells Johnny that the argument on the first day was over Tom. She had said the things she did to try and get even at her father, to put him in a bad light. They had argued over Tom Warner for weeks.

She tells Johnny that she had seen a lot of Tom after her mother and brother were killed in a car crash. Her father blamed the accident on Tom. Terry ask

Johnny "do you think he is mad? The Abbott's are an angry people." Terry tells Johnny that her father seems as though he is on the edge of something.

Two years ago, he bought a new car and crashed it when something minor went wrong. Tom never got angry, and he would sit with her and read while she was doing things. If he had said goodbye, she would have left with him, and he knew it.

Johnny meets constable Polk and tells him about the claim on the horse. Johnny asks for assistance in finding Tom Warner and Johnny fills out a missing person's report.

Tomorrow, well it all hinges on a decent man who knows he is loved and never says goodbye.

Episode 5   Show Date: 1/27/1956

Dr. Gorry returns Johnny's call and he does not want to talk to him. Johnny says that he has reason to not believe what Gorry told him. Johnny tells him that the matter with Tom Warner is in the hands of the police and Gorry relents and agrees to talk to Johnny.

Johnny buys breakfast for constable Polk and is told that there is little Polk can do with a small police force. Polk is going to talk to Mr. Abbott and then they will plan.

Johnny calls Hartford and has a man check for Tom Warner in Baltimore and then goes to see Gorry.

Johnny tells Gorry that the head office is ready to close the case and not pay the claim. Gorry tells Johnny that Abbott did not want to file the claim and fired Monroe. Abbott blamed the accident on Warner and fired him. Abbott hated Warner because he was seeing Terry. Johnny would hate to see Gorry get the book. Abbott will have to prove his case and he cannot, and Gorry would have to go to court too.

Gorry tells Johnny that he has been Abbott's friend for 20 years. The horse was dead when he got there and Ben had just shot him and swore Gorry to silence. The horse was not what Abbott had hoped for and would not run, or could not run. Tom Warner had seen Abbott shoot the horse. Abbott gave Tom some money and told him to go away. Gorry seems to think that Ben is losing his mind. Johnny asks why did Abbott pay Monroe and not Warner? Gorry tells Johnny that Ben said he did pay Warner.

Johnny drives to the farm and Cully opens the door and asks Johnny to come back later. Constable Polk was there earlier and Mr. Abbott is awful mad.

Terry comes in, and even in the darkened house Johnny can see that her father has beaten Terry. Ben comes in with a cane and beats Terry and Johnny while ranting about killing another man already.

Johnny calls constable Polk and tells him what happened and searches the grounds for Ben. Johnny hears a disturbance in the stables and Ben shouts at Johnny to leave. Johnny tells him he knows about Gorry lying and tells him to throw down the shotgun. Johnny tells him he is smashing his whole life.

Ben fires and Johnny shoots back. Ben tells Johnny that Warner is buried under the floor of the stable. Warner had seen him shoot Duke and told him he was crazy. "I'm not crazy, am I Dollar?" Ben dies and the police find Warner's body buried where Ben said it was.

Exp. Acct: $802.65

Notes:
- This story was done as *The Oklahoma Red Matter*, broadcast on 6/9/1953.
- A CBS memo in the Thousand Oak Library notes that *The Duke Red Matter* was formerly titled *The Abbott Matter*.
- Johnny gives his height as not quite 6' 1".
- The Terraplane was made by the Hudson Automobile Company.
- Roy Rowan is the announcer.
- Music supervision is by Amerigo Marino.

Producer: Jack Johnstone   Writer: John Dawson
Cast: Barbara Fuller, Barbara Eiler, Herb Butterfield, John Stephenson, Parley Baer, Will Wright, Bob Bruce, Forrest Lewis

◆ ❖ ◆

Show: **The Flight Six Matter**
Company: **Guarantee Transport Insurance Company**
Agent: **Pete Cardley**
Synopsis:
Episode 1   Show Date: 1/30/1956

Pete Cardley calls Johnny about an air crash in Mexico. The plane crashed in the mountains and Pete is stuck for $75,000. Somebody meant for it to crash.

Johnny flies to Mexico City, Mexico and finally finds the office of the Inspector General of Civil Air Transport. Inside is Mack Macklin, and Irishman from Chicago. Mack gives Johnny the information on the crash.

There were no survivors and the plane did not catch fire. A crew is working on the crash site now. The crash probably was sabotage. Some Indians were watching the plane and the tail blew off and the plane crashed. Mack is questioning the ground crew and checking on the passengers and crew. There were three flight insurance policies issued and Johnny has the names. There was no cargo on the plane so the crash was aimed at a passenger.

A man enters the office demanding information on the crash. He is Ramon Delagos and one of the passengers was Maria Delagos, his wife. Ramon is saddened that she is dead. She had just come to visit him and was returning home. Marie's brother, Don Serrano, is staying at the Hotel Reje but he and Ramon are not on speaking terms. Ramon is staying at the Monte Casino and Mack tells him that he will be notified when the bodies are brought in. Mack tells Johnny that Ramon is an exporter from Cuba, but the brother is the beneficiary if the policy. Mack guarantees Johnny complete cooperation.

Johnny rides up to the crash site in a jeep. On the site are the Mexican army searchers and some silent Indians.

Gino Romero meets Johnny and tells him that a single explosion caused the crash and they have found many pieces of the plane. The baggage is totally destroyed and burned but the seats are not burned. The clothes smell of dynamite and small pieces of the dynamite casings have been found.

Drums start beating as the bodies are taken out and Johnny notices a young blond woman. Gino tells Johnny that she is a daredevil, one who is always looking for adventure. Her name is Marvel Terrence. Johnny recognizes that Marvel Terrence is the beneficiary of two of the insurance policies.

Tomorrow, a fighting girl, and a lucky break, and then murder evens the score.

Episode 2   Show Date: 1/31/1956

Johnny receives a radio call from Mack for Gino. Johnny tells Mack that nothing is new. Mack tells Johnny that a baggage handler named Ramirez was acting strange. He had one suitcase that he would let no one touch. Johnny tells Mack that he is about to tangle with a tiger.

Johnny senses that Marvel Terrence is a real tiger, as Gino had suggested. She was watching the bodies being removed with cool dispatch.

Johnny introduces himself and she is annoyed and tells him to run along. She tells Johnny that she came up because she had friends on the plane, "so beat it buster". Johnny wonders how she will spend the $50,000 from the passengers Palmer and Roarke. She does not know about the insurance policies and it is a surprise as Ed and Jim were her friends.

An aggravated man tells Johnny that he brought her up, but not to be pushed around by a morbid publicity seeker. Marvel tells the man that Johnny is an investigator, and about the insurance.

The man is Bill Blakely and he is very angry that Johnny wants to know why he is there. Bill tells Johnny that he was a partner of the two men who were killed on the plane and is annoyed that Johnny accuses him of killing Ed and Jim to get the business. Marvel had known them for several months, they were just friends, it was just a game.

She tells Johnny that she is a wealthy orphan who just drifts around and plays the game. She is at the Hotel Monte Casino and could teach Johnny the game. She tells Johnny that she knows Ramon Delagos and Johnny asks "didn't you know his wife was on the plane". She tells Johnny that she did not know he had a wife. See me and I will straighten out your ideas. She tells Johnny that she had reservations on the plane and cancelled at the last minute. She cancelled because Bill talked her out of going.

Johnny and Gino head back to town and talk about Marvel and her game. If she is guilty, Johnny will pin it on her. Gino does not think she is guilty, she is very rich. Gino tells Johnny that Blakely is making a road and they all worked and played together. They were all after Marvel, and in their warehouse, there is much dynamite.

Johnny gets a room at the Del Prado and meets Mack Macklin in the bar. During drinks, dinner and more drinks, Mack tells Johnny he has been in

Mexico for seven years but would like to see Chicago again and that he was last there in 1932. He tells Johnny that he flew on the wrong side of a war once and cannot go back. Mack gets a phone call and learns that Ramirez has been killed.

Tomorrow a bereaved-relative lies, a frustrated lover comes up fighting, and a lovely lady in the case just vanishes.

Episode 3   Show Date: 2/1/1956
Don Serrano calls Johnny and Johnny recognizes him as Marie Delagos' brother. Don Serrano has some information on the crash. He knows it was the evil work of a diabolical maniac, the product of the warped mind of a scheming worthless unspeakable dog, a sneaking, money-hungry snake, a scurrilous unprincipled...Don Serrano come on up!

Johnny buys breakfast for himself and Don Serrano, a classic Spanish gentleman full of hate who speaks of the duello, the honorable way to resolve these issues. Johnny tells him that Ramon Delagos was in Mexico to pursue his business, and Don Serrano tells Johnny that Ramon's business was women with money. Johnny tells Don Serrano that Maria had come to meet her husband and found out about Marvel Terrace, and you bought her a ticket on flight 6.

Don Serrano tells Johnny that Ramon always lied to her and was only interested in her wealth. Half of the estate goes to Ramon and the other reverts to Don Serrano. Don Serrano had managed the estate before Ramon got involved. Maria was a pious woman who could not divorce Ramon. They had not seen Ramon, but Ramon knew of the flight. Who else would have been so vile as to put explosives on the plane. Do you doubt me?

Don Serrano knows Marvel Terrace and he thought she was going on the plane too, but he saw her talking to an American. Johnny asks why Maria took out the insurance and left him the insurance and Don Serrano tells Johnny that it was just a whim. Johnny tells Don Serrano that he would also benefit from the crash. Don Serrano wants to kill Johnny but Johnny tells Don Serrano that he is always looking to kill people and tells him to leave.

Johnny checks out a number of leads and finds nothing. Maria, Palmer and Roarke seem to be the center of the case for which there are four suspects, Ramon, Don Serrano, Marvel and Bill Blakely.

Johnny calls Marvel and sets up a lunch date, which she does not keep. Johnny goes to her hotel and the desk clerk starts to call her room and then remembers she had checked out at 11:00.

After lunch Johnny runs into Ramon Delagos and asks him about Marvel Terrence, but he knows nothing of her plans. Johnny tells Ramon that Don Serrano had blamed him, but Ramon tells him that Don Serrano is only interested in money. Maria knew about Marvel and accepted it but Don Serrano hated him because he lost control of Maria's money. Johnny calls Don Serrano, Blakely, and Ramon's hotel to learn that they have all checked out, with no forwarding addresses.

Tomorrow a rendezvous in a tropic port. And a lot of things come together, like romance, desire, and death.

Episode 4   Show Date: 2/2/1956

Gino calls Johnny and he has tracked the four suspects to Acapulco. Gino has reservations on flight six for himself and Johnny.

Johnny and Gino fly to Acapulco, Mexico. Gino has called his contacts and has the hotels for the suspects. Marvel and Blakely are at the Hotel Los Flamingo, Ramon is at the Hotel Caleta and Don Serrano is at the Club de Pesca.

Johnny and Gino go to the Los Flamingo, as Johnny thinks Marvel is at the heart of the case. Johnny finds Marvel on the terrace by the cliffs and she is not surprised to find him here. Johnny does not want to have a social chat and Marvel is aware that Johnny knows her type, which scares her.

She tells Johnny that she wants to be buried at sunset. She has no relatives and is lonely with only a large trust fund to spend. She has no confessions to make and can only guess who caused the accident, as she doesn't know. She tells Johnny that she does not remember seeing Ramon or Don Serrano at the airport and that Ramon had met Bill and they hated each other. Johnny tells her that the others have followed her to Acapulco. Marvel wants Johnny to take her to dinner and dancing, and she goes to change.

Johnny calls Don Serrano and Ramon, who were not in. Johnny wants to see Bill but he knocks on Johnny's door. Johnny has a gun on him because he had seen Blakely listening outside his door. Bill knows he is under suspicion as he now owns the business and has a warehouse full of dynamite. Johnny mentions that he forgot Marvel, but Bill says it would not make sense to bomb the plane, as she had a reservation on it and only changed her mind at the last minute. Bill tells Johnny that he talked her out of the flight, but not because it was going to explode.

Johnny enjoys a pleasant evening with Marvel and takes her back to her room. Later that night Johnny hears screaming and meets Gino in the hallway. They go to Marvel's room to find the door open and Marvel's slippers by a broken guardrail on the cliffs. They go down to the beach and find Marvel dead on the beach, alone and lonely.

Tomorrow, a desperate killer is cornered and strikes back in a deadly counter-attack, final showdown!

Episode 5   Show Date: 2/3/1956

Mac Macklin calls Johnny and Johnny tells Mack that he is following the suspects. Johnny tells Mack that Marvel was going to help, but he and Gino had just pulled Marvel from the surf. It was murder.

Johnny calls Mack with the news of Marvel's death. Gino comes rushing in and tells Johnny that the police have blocked the grounds. They run out and search the brush, the only place where someone can hide. They hear someone moving and quietly move in.

Johnny corners Don Serrano, who tells Johnny that he was looking for Ramon, who was not in his room. He thought that Ramon was at Marvel's room. Don Serrano tells Johnny that he went there to kill Ramon.

Don Serrano is turned over to the police and then they search Bill Blakely's room where the bed has been slept in. Johnny opens Bill's suitcase and inside they find an open box of .38 cartridges.

Johnny and Gino rush to the Hotel Caleta with the police. In room 34 they call for Ramon and Bill Blakely opens the door. He gives Johnny his gun and tells him that Ramon has not shown up. Marvel had told Bill that Ramon had followed her and that she was scared of him. She was a great kid.

Outside they hear shots and run after Ramon. The police block the beach and Johnny and Gino go after him. Gino spots a boat and thinks Ramon is near it. They split up and Ramon surprises Johnny behind the boat. Ramon tells Johnny to push the boat into the water and they row out across the bay.

Johnny splashes an oar and Ramon almost hits him. Ramon admits killing Maria to get to Marvel. Marvel told him she was suspicious and was falling in love with Johnny, which made him crazy. They hear a police launch start up. Ramon turns to look and Johnny clubs him with an oar. The police pick him up but Ramon tries to take over the police boat and is killed.

"Remarks: I will never see another sunset now without thinking of her, somewhere out beyond it. I hope she does not feel alone anymore."

Exp. Acct: $608.10

Notes:
- Roy Rowan is the announcer.
- Musical supervision is by Amerigo Marino.

Producer: Jack Johnstone Writer: Les Crutchfield
Cast: Virginia Gregg, Ben Wright, Edgar Barrier, Don Diamond, Russ Thorson, Jack Moyles

♦ ❖ ♦

Show: **The McClain Matter**
Company: **Tri-State Insurance Underwriters**
Agent: **Don Taylor**
Synopsis:
Episode 1   Show Date: 2/6/1956

Don Taylor from Tri-State calls. Don asks Johnny if he wants to come to his office and meet a pretty girl? She just told me the most interesting thing I have ever heard. She told me that she was dead.

Johnny cabs to Don Taylor's office to meet a pretty well-dressed woman in her late twenties. Don wants Mrs. McClain to talk to Johnny alone, as she has a most unusual story. Johnny tells her he is an investigator for whoever will hire him.

She tells Johnny that she is legally dead and that her husband collected on her $10,000 insurance policy. Her husband is Dr. David McClain, and he lives in Los Angeles.

She was the receptionist when a patient came in off the street that was sick. He took her into an examining room and she had a heart attack and died. He told Mrs. McClain what had happened and they searched her to see who she was. Her name was Teresa Corbit from Jersey City. They called the address and discovered that the woman's mother had died and the frantic apartment manager was trying to locate Teresa. The manager told Dave that Teresa was the only living relative. Then Dave said we are in luck. The girl had no relative and no one would know that they would use her body.

Dave called Dr. Reed from next door and she hid. Dave told Dr. Reed that the body was his wife. They tried to revive her but they knew it was too late. Reed signed a death certificate and she was buried two days later. When Johnny asks why Reed did not know her if she was the receptionist, she tells Johnny that Reed was new and that they had never met.

She stayed in a hotel and then went to Palm Springs. Dave collected the insurance and she came to New York. Dave was going to close his practice and come to New York. He wrote saying he was on his way and then stopped writing.

Johnny asks what she wants them to do and she tells Johnny that she has been thinking about the matter for two years and does not want to get anyone in trouble. It sounds fantastic but it is the truth. It is good to tell it to someone after all this time.

She tells Johnny that the whole thing was Dave's idea. She has been working in a lab in New York under the name of Patricia Kennedy. She can prove who she is in Los Angeles and can give Johnny a list of people who can identify her. She tells Johnny that Dave was badly in debt and needed money, and this seemed like a good way to get it. Teresa Corbit had nobody, and she does not know who Dave contacted.

She came to Hartford because the insurance company has been robbed. "What about you?" Johnny asks, "He did everything, didn't he?" She tells Johnny that she read in a Los Angeles paper that Dave is going to get married in June.

Johnny tells Don to get the legal staff to get a statement ready. Johnny asks if she is aware that, if the story is true, she and her husband can be criminally charged. She says yes and cries.

Tomorrow, some well thought out lies, well, believe it or not, they come true.

Episode 2   Show Date: 2/7/1956

Don Taylor calls and asks what they should do now. Johnny tells him they need more facts. She has not told them the truth.

Johnny lunches with Don Taylor, who thinks they should act. Johnny recounts the whole story and how today she says she is tired of waiting. Johnny says there are holes, too many holes. Why did the doctor just decide on the trick at the last minute? Mrs. McClain was the receptionist but she allowed the woman to see the doctor without getting a name. Doctors will always get a name and address unless they know you. Everything she has said needs to be verified.

Don has checked on the policy and the facts check. The death certificate gives the cause as coronary thrombosis and all the other details seem to check. Johnny is worried about all the things she didn't say.

Johnny goes to New York City and cabs to Mrs. McClain's apartment. The manager tells Johnny that she is a good tenant and has few friends. The manager is suspicious but lets Johnny look around the apartment. Johnny then goes to the medical lab where her story also checks out. Johnny calls Don and he tells Johnny that a Mrs. Corbit had died, and that the county buried the body.

Johnny flies to Los Angeles, California and sleeps. That afternoon Johnny gets a package of information from Don and rents a car. Johnny checks the addresses provided, but only the last one checks out.

A Mrs. Henderson lets Johnny in and Johnny shows her a picture that is really familiar, it is Doris McClain, she died a year or so ago very suddenly. She knew Doris for about 5 years and worked with her. She tells Johnny that she read of the death in the papers, and she wants to know what this is all about. She tells Johnny that Dave probably got over it, so why didn't you go to Dr. McClain? "I'm going to call him" Johnny tells her.

Johnny calls Don Taylor and asks for a private eye to watch Mrs. Henderson, someone might want to kill her.

Tomorrow, a bit of information about a girl who had a date to die, that's right.

Episode 3   Show Date: 2/8/1956
Vic Wade calls Johnny and he knows where Theresa Corbett is.

Johnny goes to see Wade, who shows him a statement they have. They got a request from the boyfriend named George Riley, but they never learned much.

Johnny goes to see Riley who admits that the police have been following him. He tells Johnny that he met Teresa in a restaurant and last saw her on January 19th, her birthday. George had gone to the police and mentioned her mother to them. Johnny tells him that Teresa is dead and is buried in Los Angeles.

Johnny goes back to see Wade and he tells Johnny that they did not know about her heart condition, and that there is no record of a phone call to New Jersey from the doctor's office. Johnny is sure that Teresa's doctor was Dr. McClain.

Episode 4   Show Date: 2/9/1956
Johnny gets a call from the desk, which connects him with Dr. McClain, who thinks Johnny is crazy. Johnny wants to see him and the doctor tells Johnny that he will call the police if he comes over. Well, get busy, I am on my way.

When Johnny goes to buy gas, George Riley stops him. They drive out and he tells Johnny that he was thinking about Terri. The police came to see him and they are going to exhume the body. "It will be her, won't it?" he asks Johnny.

George wants to get his hands on the bird that killed her. George was going to marry Terri and she just walked out. Now you tell me that she was killed, but what about me? Why is she dead? That doctor just took her and buried her, what is his name? Johnny tells him that he will know soon enough as Johnny will find out what happened.

Johnny drives to the offices of Dr. McClain and he tells Johnny that he was intrigued by the call. Johnny asks if Pauline Henderson called him, and Johnny tells him that he had seen Mrs. Henderson because she would recognize his wife. McClain is baffled at Johnny and wants to know what he wants.

Johnny tells him about the investigation of Teresa Corbit in 1954, but he does not remember it. McClain searches the files but there is no record of Teresa.

Johnny tells him that Teresa had come to see him several times, but McClain tells Johnny his wife was his receptionist, but she was not very good. Johnny tells him that not having a file makes him suspicious. Johnny tells McClain about Mrs. McClain coming in and making the statement and that she is very much alive and he has witnesses. The doctor has nothing to say.

Johnny prefers charges against McClain and he is arrested but refuses to talk. Johnny wires Don with the events and Don wires back to tell Johnny that he is on the way out with Mrs. McClain. Johnny learns that the coroner has exhumed the body and identified it as Teresa Corbit.

Johnny visits McClain one last time and tells him that his wife will be there the next day and that he wants a statement. Johnny suggests he pleads guilty, but McClain says he will never get him into court.

The next morning McClain is released on bail, which worries Johnny.

Johnny drives out to an address in the Pacific Palisades and hears shots as he walks into the building. Johnny shoots at the man as he runs out and then walks to George Riley, who tells Johnny that he has shot McClain. He did it for Terri, his girl.

Tomorrow, a brand new, or rather startling statement from Mrs. McClain, without lies.

Episode 5   Show Date: 2/10/1956
Don Taylor calls and Johnny tells him that Dr. McClain has been shot. He is alive but barely. Don tells Johnny that he will meet him at the hospital.

Johnny rents a tape recorder and goes to McClain's room to meet Don. Johnny tells Don that Riley is being held for assault with intent to kill.

Don and Johnny go to the room and McClain asks why the recorder is there. Johnny tells him that he wants a statement. McClain tells Johnny that he will talk later, and they leave.

McClain recovers within a week and a trial date is set. Johnny tells Don that there is still more to it, he is not satisfied. Riley and Teresa are the ones who are suffering. Don flies home and Johnny wraps up the details.

Johnny goes to interview Mrs. McClain again in the jail. She is expecting a three-year sentence, which is not too long. Johnny tells her they have enough to charge conspiracy. Johnny reads to her from her statement about Teresa Corbit coming into the office and having never met her before and about the call to New Jersey. Johnny tells her that the phone company has no record of a call being billed. She accuses Johnny of calling her a liar.

Johnny tells her that he had found out that Teresa Corbit was a patient of McClain, but she is adamant that she did not know her. Johnny tells her that the story was too real, it could not have happened as explained. Johnny tells her that she knew Teresa's history and that Teresa Corbit had only one living relative. She was a patsy right from the beginning, wasn't she?

Mrs. McClain admits that Teresa had come in with a telegram about her mother dying and was upset. She asked for something to help her sleep and Dave mentioned her case being terminal, but she was not that sick. Dave went back to the examination room and she just waited. He buzzed her and when she went in to the room, Teresa was dead. She knew what he had done when she went in because there was a hypodermic on the table. They had not talked about it, but he had it all planned out.

She left town that night and Dave said he would take care of anything. He said he killed her and that she would go to the gas chamber with him if she said anything. She told the story about the phone call to get back at him. She is glad it is all over.

"Remarks: Murder charges have been filed against the McClains, and they stand trial next month. George Riley received three years and a suspended sentence for assault with a deadly weapon. I was wrong about practically everything in this case. All the lies came true, but so did the facts."

Exp. Acct: $768.60

Notes:
- This story was done as *The Madison Matter*, broadcast on 4/14/1953.
- Roy Rowan is the announcer.
- Musical supervision is by Amerigo Marino.

Producer:	Jack Johnstone	Writer:	John Dawson
Cast:	Lucille Meredith, Betty Lou Gerson, John Stephenson, Bob Bruce, Vic Perrin, Tony Barrett, Herb Ellis		

♦ ❖ ♦

Show: **The Cui Bono Matter**
Company: **Surety Mutual Insurance Ltd.**
Agent: **Don Hancock**
Synopsis:
Episode 1   **Show Date:**   **2/13/1956**

Don Hancock calls and asks Johnny "cui bono", who benefits. Don tells Johnny that a little doll named Luanne Parker in Greenpass, Virginia does, to the tune of $100,000 double indemnity. She admits to shooting her stepfather twice with a .38. The coroner is going to call it an unavoidable accident. Seems "lil' ol' Magnolia blossom" thought papa was a prowler. I think you should put yourself on the payroll.

Johnny trains to Greenpass, Virginia, three miles from the railroad station. Johnny takes Jake Deegley's cab to the hotel. Jake tells Johnny that this is a one-horse town, just one of everything, including one county attorney, who was Dan Parker, the deceased, who had been elected five times. Johnny asks if Dan had any enemies and Jake tells him that Luanne just took him for a prowler. When Johnny asks if Luanne is well liked, Jake tells him that he and his seventeen-year-old grandson and everyone else in town are in love with Luanne. She loved her stepfather and did everything with him. Dan was well-to-do, but not rich. Jake tells Johnny to be careful about doing his job, or he will get a lot of trouble.

Johnny checks into the hotel and goes to see sheriff Jim Peterson in the local poolroom. Sheriff Peterson calls it an accident and Johnny tells him it is a routine investigation. Sheriff Peterson tells Johnny that Dan's stepdaughter killed him.

Dan had been to Richmond and was walking back to town. Jake was at the Happy Holler and Dan was not expected. Dan came back early and there was no one to meet him. He took a shortcut across the terrace and hit a chair that woke up Luanne. When she heard him fumble in the lock and come up the stairs, she fired twice and killed him. She shot him in the dark. Dan taught her to shoot, and she was real good. There were some prowlers and Luanne had heard noises before. Mary Jackson the housekeeper was there and she told the same story. Luanne was real close to her father and was broke up about it. She did what she thought was right and will regret it for the rest of her life.

Sheriff Peterson tells Johnny to look all he wants, but the answer will come out the same. When Johnny tells sheriff Peterson he wants to attend the inquest, Johnny is told that it was this morning and the verdict was death by misadventure with no recommendation for prosecution. Sheriff Peterson warns Johnny to walk easy.

Johnny looks over the transcript and there was nothing suspect. She was a good student and everyone in town loved her, but cui bono?

Tomorrow, beauty is as beauty does, and an idol is found to be made of flesh and blood.

Episode 2   Show Date: 2/14/1956

Tom Bates, the acting county attorney calls. Johnny wants to talk about the case and will come right over.

Johnny reads the local paper about the death of Dan Parker, but it did not mention that Luanne stood to get $100,000. Johnny meets with Tom Bates and Johnny convinces Tom that he has the legal resources to make it real hot for him.

Tom thinks Johnny is trying to muddy things up and get out of paying the insurance. Tom tells Johnny that there was no hint of suspicion in the inquest, but not much of anything else either. Johnny traps Tom into admitting he is in love with Luanne. Johnny insists that he has not accused Luanne of anything. Johnny only wants the total story of how Dan died.

Tom tells Johnny that he had worked for Dan for three years and got along well with Dan. Dan approved of his relationship with Luanne over the, uh, others, but she is not ready to settle down. Dan had no enemies, but he was too easy sometimes. Tom is going to press some issues, like the Happy Hollow Roadhouse, run by Sammie Drake, who should be run out of town. Luanne knows Drake, but everyone knows everyone here. Luanne was a dead shot and can outshoot everyone in the county. No paraffin test was done because she admits to firing the gun. Johnny asks Tom "cui bono"? Maybe someone else will benefit. Maybe someone used her.

Johnny rents the taxi and talks to various people around town and learns that Luanne was a smart, sweet, all-American girl.

Johnny goes to meet Luanne and is met by Mary Jackson. She tells Johnny that Luanne is staying with Dr. Prayley and his wife. Johnny would like to talk to Mary also. He explains why he is there and learns that Mary had raised Luanne.

She shows Johnny the house and where the shooting took place. She tells Johnny that when she heard the shots she turned on the lights and Luanne ripped off his tie, but he was gone. Mary tells Johnny that she makes $95 a month, that Dan has a nice new house and bought Luanne a new car last year, but he only made $5,000 a year. With all this they were still arguing.

Mary tells Johnny that Luanne and Dan had argued about Sammy, who put ideas in her head. Luanne was a restless one, and he put crazy notions of going to New York into her head. That was the only thing Dan refused her. He told her that she would have to do it over his dead body.

Tomorrow the net tightens, a rat runs for cover, then the whole thing blows wide open.

Episode 3   Show Date: 2/15/1956
Tom Bates calls and Doc Prayley said you had been threatening him. Johnny only told him he would get a court order if necessary to talk to Luanne. Tom warns Johnny and Johnny warns Tom that he will talk to Luanne one way or another.

Johnny goes to the Happy Hollow Road House and muses over the case on the way there. In the roadhouse, Johnny finds a bar and jukebox and maybe a game in the back. Sammy Drake talks to Johnny (what's the word Mack) and Johnny replies "save your money and buy booze".

Sammie tells Johnny that it is rough, and Johnny tells him that it will be rougher with a new County Attorney and Sammy asks, "what's the pitch Mitch?" Johnny tells Sammy who he is and Sammy tells him to "tie me up and mail me off!" Johnny wants to know about Dan's death but Sammy tells him "you're out of luck Chuck, I don't know nothing about nothing from nothing, see what I mean?" Sammy is sure that Bates is after him because his doll has been here.

Sammy tells him to come into the office and asks "what did you say your name was, buzz?" and Johnny tells him "Johnny Dollar, rhymes with collar". Sammy pours a drink and tells Johnny that the food is good here. Sammy cannot see any reason to worry about Johnny and tells him that no one had anything to do with killing Dan. Dan was his fix in the town, so why would he kill him? Sammy will pitch the sheriff but does not think he will play.

Sammy tells Johnny that Tom has "the drooling goose" over Luanne and did not like her hanging around him. Sammy did not like it either, she was too spoiled and thought she could do whatever she wanted. Dan did not like it but could not do anything. Sammy did not put any ideas about New York in her mind, she came in with them. She was busting her braces to get to the action. She has the whole town fooled, except for me. She is smart and colder than a fish and Sammy is tough, but he is scared of her.

Johnny has dinner and cabs to the railroad station and talks to the stationmaster. He was on duty when Dan Parker came back. Dan came in on the #8 and spoke with him. He tells Johnny that there was some fellow with him that Dan met on the train. They talked and the man got back on the train. When the train pulled out, the man said he would be seeing Dan. Dan called home but got a busy signal and had to walk home.

Tomorrow, a tense interview, a subtle attack by a shrewd and dangerous opponent and complete surrender.

Episode 4   Show Date: 2/16/1956
Tom Bates calls and Tom does not want to fight Johnny and tells him that Luanne will be available at 2:00. You will go out with me and interview her while I am there.

Johnny eats a late breakfast and waits for Tom Bates to pick him up. On the way to the Parker house, Tom tells Johnny to give up and stop trying to break the claim. Tom has blocked every move Johnny has made.

Johnny tells Tom that all the company wants is the facts, so, what is the real reason for your actions. Maybe you know she is guilty and are covering up for her, or maybe she is covering up for you. Cui bono applies to you. You get Dan's job, you can run Sammy Drake out of town, and if you marry Luanne, you will get the insurance!

Luanne opens the door and Johnny is introduced to her. She tells Johnny that she feels fine now and has thought about what daddy would say. She is going to try to live her life for the future. Tom tells her that Johnny is trying to trick her to cheat her out of the policy, but Luanne tells Tom to leave and they talk alone.

Johnny tells her what he has learned, and that only one person has said anything against you, and she knows that it was Sammy Drake. She tells Johnny that she saw right through him and she played along with him and Sammy took her seriously. She likes people and has had a wonderful life. She tells Johnny that going to New York was her only argument with her father.

Luanne tells Johnny what had happened that night. After midnight something woke her and she saw a prowler out the window. She tried to get to the phone downstairs but heard someone at the door. She got the gun and heard someone in the house, so she shot without considering. She heard him fall and she turned on the light and saw it was daddy.

Johnny asks why the phone was busy when Dan called at the depot. She says that the phone is usually off the hook at night. She asks Mary if the phone was off the hook and she says it was. Johnny thanks her and leaves.

One way or another she was quite a girl, either she was an innocent girl or a cold-blooded killer.

Tomorrow, one slip of fate, and then the avalanche, and a wind up that will raise the hair on the back of your neck.

Episode 5   Show Date: 2/17/1956
Sheriff Peterson calls and asks Johnny about his talk with Luanne. Johnny tells him he is going back tomorrow and is sure the company will pay when the claim is filed. This is the first report that has ended with a question mark.

Johnny gets a 20-page report notarized and the case comes down to did she know she was shooting at her father.

Johnny goes to the Happy Hollow for dinner to kill an evening. Sammy meets him ("Well wrap me up and mail me south, here's that Dollar man again") and buys Johnny a scotch. Johnny tells Sammy he is going back and Luanne will probably get the money. "Bang, bang and the little lady wins a prize. She was really shooting for new shoes that night." Johnny sees sheriff Peterson come in, just in time. Sammy tells Johnny that sheriff Peterson is going to replace Dan Parker in protecting him.

A man asks Johnny to have a drink with him and asks what line Johnny is in. He is in "ladies ready-to-wear". He believes in living while you can. It can happen to anyone, like a guy named Parker he met on the train. You never know. Johnny asks the man if he had talked to Dan Parker.

The man tells Johnny that they talked about his daughter, and Dan wanted him to meet her. Dan expected his daughter to be there and tried to call her at the station but could not get her, so he got back on the train. He shows Johnny his tie and takes him outside. He tells Johnny that Parker was wearing one, and he liked it so Dan gave him one. His daughter had given him three just the week before. In the shadows the man shows Johnny his tie, which glows in the dark.

Johnny goes back to Luanne's and he returns her loaded gun, and places it on the table. Johnny tells her he was planning to leave and asks her if she likes his necktie, it is just like the one her father was wearing. Johnny bought it from the man in the bar. It was a great setup, what with him wearing a tie that glowed in the dark. The tie he gave to a stranger is going to hang you.

Luanne turns off the lights and fires at Johnny three times. The sheriff comes in and tells Luanne that the gun was loaded with blanks. Johnny gets up and Luanne screams that she was tricked, and sheriff Peterson takes her to the jail.

"Remarks: When you gave me this assignment Don, you asked a question, a phrase in Latin: cui bono? Who benefits? So here is your answer: nobody."
    Exp. Acct: $382.65

Notes:
- This story is the one that is most commonly misspelled in catalogs and books. The correct spelling of the Latin phrase is "cui bono".
- Roy Rowan is the announcer.
- Musical supervision is by Amerigo Marino.

Producer:	Jack Johnstone Writer: Les Crutchfield
Cast:	D. J. Thompson, Mary Jane Croft, Forrest Lewis, Byron Kane, Russell Thorson, Sam Edwards, Dal McKennon, Howard McNear

◆ ❖ ◆

Show:	The Bennet Matter
Company:	Four State Fire Insurance Corporation
Agent:	Andrew Cord
Synopsis:	
Episode 1	Show Date: 2/20/1956

Andrew Cord calls and asks Johnny if he wants to go to San Francisco. Andrew tells Johnny that five companies have issued $100,000 each in fire insurance for a builder named Arnold Bennet, and his last project has burned to the ground. The total coverage is $500,000 and the experts say the fire is phony.

Johnny flies to San Francisco, California with Andrew Cord, and on the plane, he learns that Bennet is a man who is the last of his kind, a man of many jobs and not one to let things stop him from getting what he wants. He has made Time and Life several times and has done well. Andrew tells Johnny that he does not like Bennet, maybe it is because of his roughshod nature.

Andrew's man in San Francisco believes that the fire was arson, and we have to prove it. Four State and National Fire Underwriters will be the only company investigating this.

Andrew tells Johnny that Bennet is in financial trouble with his taxes, and the fire is an out. Bill Underwood is the arson man in San Francisco. Bill will handle the fire, Andrew the finances and Johnny will handle Bennet. Tony is a little scared of Bennet, as no one has ever beaten him.

Johnny gets a room at the Fairmont Hotel and goes to the fire site with Andy to meet Bill, who tells them that the watchman remembers seeing a man around the site, as did three witnesses, but the police have no matches in their files. The newsboy remembers seeing the man catch a bus shortly before the fire began.

Bennet has been out and does not like us snooping around the site. Bill is positive that it was set, it burnt too fast and too well. Amateurs mess up a fire, a bug sticks around and brags, but this one just disappeared. Bill tells Johnny to watch his step with Bennet, he does not care about anyone. Johnny attends a lineup for the three witnesses, but no one is identified.

Next day Johnny goes to Bennet's office and meets Elizabeth Bennet, the niece of Arnold Bennet. Johnny tells her he is with the insurance company and she buzzes Arnold, who is a real pain.

Bennet asks Johnny in and knows why he is there. Bennet tells Johnny the fire was deliberate and that Tony Midas set the fire. Get him and you get the arsonist. Midas worked for him once and was caught stealing money and was sent to prison. He is the one you want. Bennet knows his enemies and friends, so don't waste his time. Tony Midas has just been released from prison.

Bennet thinks that the insurance people are a bunch of hacks, now get busy! Johnny notes that he is paid very well to find out what he needs to find out, but sometimes it is not enough money.

Johnny reviews the trial of Tony Midas, and eventually the witnesses agree that Tony Midas was the man they saw, and the police issue and APB. Elizabeth Bennet calls Johnny and tells him that she will help Johnny find Tony. Come to my house in an hour. Then Bennet's lawyers call and threaten a law suit. On the way to Elizabeth's Johnny meets Andy Card in a police car and they rush to Bennet's house. Andy tells Johnny that someone has shot Arnold Bennet.

Tomorrow, the trail gets so rough a couple of people just fall off dead.

Episode 2   Show Date: 2/21/1956
Bill Underwood calls and Johnny tells him that Bennet has been shot. Bill tells Johnny that he has proof that the fire was set.

Bennet is taken to the hospital and given a 50-50 chance. Johnny thinks that the evidence is against Midas, even though he was in prison with a professional burner. Andy tells Johnny that Tony Midas is married to Elizabeth Bennet. Johnny tells Andy about the meeting with Elizabeth, and the address where she lives is the house where Bennet was shot.

Johnny goes to meet with Mr. Engle, the attorney who represented Tony Midas. Johnny tells him about the evidence of the arson and Engle tells Johnny that Bennet poured on the heat during the trial. Tony said he was framed, but there was no way he could win. Tony has not contacted Engle, but he would like to see him if he contacts Johnny.

Johnny wants to know the real issues. What about the tax problems, and the relationship with his niece? Johnny thinks Engle can tell the real story. Engle personally thinks that Bennet framed Tony to cover the tax shortages. Tony had no experience and probably was used. Engle hopes Johnny never finds Tony or Elizabeth.

But Johnny finds Tony Midas, in the county hospital, just before he is taken to the morgue. Tony had died of TB in the county hospital.

Tony turns out not to be the suspect and attention focuses on Arnold Bennet.

Bill Underwood comes in with news. George Foley is in town. Foley is the best wick-and-celluloid man in the country if you want a building burnt down. The police spotted him in the hospital lobby trying to get to Arnold Bennet and he was tracked to an address on Barengo Street.

Johnny, Bill and Andy rush to the address and talk to the police. They think Foley is trying to get money from Bennet for burning the building. Johnny decides to shake up Foley and they go it to talk to him.

Johnny knocks, the door opens and there is shooting. Johnny and the others are OK and they take Foley out.

Tomorrow, we have an arsonist right in the palm of their hands, with very surprising results.

Episode 3   Show Date: 2/22/1956
Andy calls Johnny and the police have been talking to Foley all night, but he will not talk. They need to link Foley to Bennet and Johnny has an idea.

Johnny and Andy meet for a drink and they discuss the case. First it was Tony, now Foley, but who shot Arnold, the niece? She has a reason and Johnny wants to deal with her and offer her legal assistance.

Johnny cabs to Marty Engle's office and tells him to lock his door. Johnny tells him that Midas is dead and wants to know what Engle has done. Johnny wants to know if he helped Bennet frame Tony, but Engle denies it. Johnny tells him that Elizabeth probably shot Bennet and she might be out to get you.

There is a knock at the door and it is Elizabeth Bennet. Johnny tells Engle to hide and shots are fired. She runs out and Johnny shoots at her car stopping it. Johnny goes to Elizabeth who wants to know if she killed Engle who she blames for killing Tony.

She tells Johnny that Arnold stole money and framed Tony. She knows he hired George Foley and tried to blame it on Tony. She knew Tony was dying the last time she saw him. She shot Bennet and tried to kill Engle. They killed Tony when they sent him to prison. She waited for five years to hold him and now he is dead, but what can we do now. She tells Johnny that nobody even looked at her until Tony, and now he is dead and she wants to die.

The police finally arrive and Johnny tells them there is no problem. Elizabeth is taken to the jail where she makes a statement about Foley, shooting Bennet and trying to shoot Engle.

Johnny meets Engle in the jail and Engle tells Johnny that he is not going to press charges and wants to defend Elizabeth. Andy comes in and tells Johnny that they are going to go after Foley. Andy tells Johnny that the insurance company will pay for Elizabeth's legal fees.

Johnny catches a flight home at midnight but Andy Card calls the next morning and wants Johnny back in San Francisco. Jake Eggelston is going to defend George Foley. Johnny remembers Andy's words that he would never get Bennet and gets the first plane out.

Tomorrow, a fight against a strong man and one of the cleverest lawyers in the country. Join us in court!

Episode 4   Show Date: 2/23/1956
Andy calls Johnny in his hotel and tells Johnny that they still have not connected Bennet to Foley. The defense attorney is really slick.

Johnny flies back to San Francisco and goes to the court building. The case is going well, but Foley will not talk.

The court calls Johnny as a witness. The District Attorney questions him and Johnny tells him he has been an investigator for 10 years or more, was in the Marine Corps for four years and was a Detective Sergeant 2nd grade for the New York Police. He has numerous letters of reliability from 13 insurance companies and adjustment bureaus and his police record.

He was hired to conduct an investigation of the Bennet building fire. They determined it was arson based on the evidence. The method used was determined to be a woolen wick soaked with paraffin in a bag of celluloid. Johnny testifies that Foley had improvised the method and has used that method in several fires. Foley also had tried to contact Arnold Bennet and there was evidence on Foley's clothes to prove he was in the building. Johnny also testifies that Elizabeth Bennet told him that her uncle had hired Foley.

Eggelston questions all of Johnny's testimony and requests that his testimony be stricken. Johnny goes to the Judge and asks to see Foley in jail with his attorney.

In the jail, Johnny tells Foley that he will give him a break if he cooperates. The jury will throw the book at Foley, but they want Bennet. Tell them Bennet hired you and plead for mercy and save five years on the sentence. Foley risks going with the jury and tells Johnny he would like to kill him when he is set free.

Tomorrow, a verdict in and out of a courtroom. The wind up.

Episode 5   Show Date: 2/24/1956
Andy calls and Johnny tells him about meeting with Foley. Andy tells Johnny that the jury is coming back in.

Johnny calls the hospital and learns that Bennet is recovering. The jury comes in and they give the verdict: guilty as charged. Foley calls for Johnny to see him, as he has some things to tell him.

Johnny goes to see Foley with Andy and he wants information. Johnny tells Foley that Bennet is in the hospital and Foley is in jail. Johnny tells him that they can get Bennet, and his conviction is the lever. Foley hates Bennet getting away with things.

Foley tells them that Bennet hired him and paid him $2,500 to burn the building and that he could blame Tony Midas. A friend told him to contact Bennet and he called him. Bennet wanted the building burned and offered him $1,000. They haggled and settled on $2,500. Bennet left the money at the check stand in the bus terminal. Foley went to see Bennet to shake him down for more money. Foley finally admits meeting Bennet in his car on Market Street on the night the building was torched. Johnny doubts Foley's story and continues questioning him.

Johnny returns the next day to continue questioning Foley. Foley finally admits Bennet met him and paid him after the building was on fire. All this was done on one night. Johnny feels Foley is trying to make him question his sanity. Andy brings in the medical findings and Johnny tells him he is sane.

Foley finally breaks down and admits he met Bennet a month before the fire. He knew Bennet was in trouble and would need a fire. Foley made the proposition and Bennet liked the idea. Bennet paid Foley $3,500 and he did the job, and Foley buried the money in a can in a vacant lot and will take Johnny there.

"Foley is sentenced and Bennet is charged, but he dies in the hospital. In a way, you can still say that no one ever beat Arnold Bennet. He beat himself."

Exp. Acct: $1,140.37

Notes:
- This story was done as *The Elliot Champion Matter*, broadcast on 12/12/1952 with elements of *The Upjohn Matter*, broadcast on 9/19/1954.
- Johnny Dollar's history: 10 years plus as an investigator, 4 years in the Marines, Detective Sgt. 2nd Grade, NYPD.
- Roy Rowan is the announcer.
- Musical supervision is by Amerigo Marino.

Producer:	Jack Johnstone	Writer:	John Dawson
Cast:	Lillian Buyeff, Stacy Harris, Chester Stratton, Will Wright, Marvin Miller, Hans Conried, Edgar Barrier, Parley Baer		

♦ ❖ ♦

Show: The Fathom-Five Matter
Company: Delta Liability
Agent: Ralph Steedler
Synopsis:
Episode 1   **Show Date:**   2/27/1956

Ralph Steedler calls and greets Johnny with poetry from the bard, "Full fathom five thy father lies, of his bones are coral made, those are pearls that were his eyes". Ralph has $75,000 in insurance lying at the bottom of the ocean, so they say. It happened in Miami Beach, check with the D. A. there. The insured was William Markey and the beneficiary his wife was.

Johnny goes to Miami, Florida to check in to the death of William Markey. At the district attorney's office, Barney Wilson is also confused. They are presuming that he is dead, but it has not been proved. Johnny knows little about the case.

The dead man is William Markey, who owned a consulting engineering firm in New York. They have been here a month and he was supposedly drowned two days ago. Barney tells Johnny that Markey came to bid on a job, and that he and brought his wife and a young fellow named Danny Haynes, a friend. They rented a house and three days ago Markey and Danny went fishing and rented the cruiser *Fathom-Five*.

They were anchored off a reef and were fishing from a dinghy. Danny took Markey back to the boat so he could fix breakfast, and later noticed that the boat was on fire. Danny could not get back on the boat and it sank a few minutes later. It was foggy and there were no other boats in the area, so Haynes rowed back to shore and reported the accident.

A salvage company is working on getting the boat up and the currents in the area are dangerous. It would be possible to swim back, and maybe Haynes was lying. Maybe the boat will be raised or the body will show up. Barney wants the body declared dead to charge Haynes with murder. Johnny gets the addresses for Mrs. Markey and Haynes.

Johnny wires Hartford for an investigation on Markey. Johnny cabs to talk to Danny Haynes. Danny tells Johnny that he has told the police the whole story, so go see them. Johnny tells Danny that Barney Wilson's mind is made up, but his is not.

Danny tells Johnny that he had worked with Markey for several years and they socialized some. Edna, um, Mrs. Markey suggested that Danny come along. Markey suggested that they stay and Danny was getting a free vacation. Markey and his wife were getting along OK. Markey suggested the fishing trip and he called Danny at 5:00 a.m. and they went out.

They went out to the reef and Markey went back to the boat to fix breakfast. Danny saw the flames through the fog, and the cruiser sank. Danny tells Johnny that the gasoline hotplate may have caused the fire as it was in bad shape.

Johnny asks if Markey could have committed suicide. Danny gets angry when Johnny suggests that maybe he and the wife were more than just friends.

Tomorrow, a lady weeps, a lover curses, and a strange grim relic is brought up from the sea.

Episode 2   Show Date: 2/28/1956
Barney Wilson calls and understands that Johnny has talked to Danny. Johnny bets 6 to 5 that Danny did not do it. Barney tells Johnny that the boat should be raised around 8:00, so meet him at the harbor police at 7:30.

Johnny cabs to the house of Mrs. Markey, who is a very beautiful woman. She is shocked over the death of her husband and does not know about the papers. Johnny tells her there are no papers, as he is an investigator and needs details from her. Johnny wants to know about her husband's mental attitude, and she gets huffy. Johnny needs the questions answered for the claims board.

She tells Johnny that Bill was not the type to kill himself. She offers Johnny a drink and Johnny fixes a scotch on the rocks and she tells him that they were very happy. She did not know anything of the finances and she had worked as a dancer. Her husband was all for Danny coming on the trip and did not show any resentment. She never saw any brooding from her husband. Danny only saw her as a friend.

Johnny tells her that her husband supposedly died, and the insurance company will not pay until the body is found, or Johnny finds sufficient evidence of death. The police are going to fight for an immediate court decision, but we will fight it. Johnny tells her that her husband either died from an accident, suicide or murder, but no insurance will be paid until one of the causes is proved.

Johnny leaves and notices a man watching the house. He drives off as Johnny approaches him. Johnny gets the last three numbers of the plate — 642.

Johnny cabs to the harbor police and meets Barney. They take a boat out to the wreck and Johnny tells him that he has not taken a position yet, but the insurance company will block any motions. Barney tells Johnny that the police found a shoe belonging to Markey on the beach. Johnny asks Barney to check the plate number he saw.

At the wreck site the boat is brought up and the hull is undamaged. Johnny and Barney both spot a solid column of water coming from the hull. Barney declares that the sea cocks were left opened. The boat was sunk deliberately and Markey was murdered.

Tomorrow, a photograph, a silver cup, a harried widow and the dead begin to stir with life.

Episode 3   Show Date: 2/29/1956
Barney calls and asks if Johnny is on an expense account. If so, how about buying me lunch? Barney tells Johnny that he has a lead on the car tags. They were bought by John Smith but the address was an empty lot.

Johnny buys lunch for Barney Wilson and they discuss the case and the lack of the body. Barney feels that it is an old story, two men go out and only one comes back and that spells murder. Barney feels that the Markeys took a liking to Danny who then took a liking to the wife. He made a nuisance of himself and then Markey noticed that Haynes needed straightening out.

He took him out to talk to him and Haynes knocked him out and threw Markey overboard and sank the boat and rowed ashore. Johnny feels the insurance is the key. Johnny is sure that it is fraud and Danny is the fall guy.

Johnny tells Barney that he got a long wire from New York and learns that Markey is in financial trouble and has been living too high. Johnny thinks Markey fired the boat, swam ashore and is waiting for the wife to collect the insurance. The wife is acting too tense and is afraid she will say the wrong thing. The harbormaster has told Johnny that it is 1-in-100 that the body would go out to sea. Johnny has also arranged for counsel to fight any court actions.

Johnny calls Mrs. Markey and asks for a photo of her husband. She does not think she has one but Johnny remembers seeing one on a table. Johnny sends a messenger out to pick up the photo and then goes to see "Truthful Tom", the dealer who sold the car to John Smith.

Tom is a typical used car salesman. Johnny tells him it looks like a car stolen from a friend, but Tom tells Johnny that he has papers on all his cars. Johnny tells him he is an investigator, but Tom is adamant about his honesty. Tom does not remember John Smith but remembers the car. The man paid cash, long-green mazoola. Johnny shows him a picture of Markey and Tom tells Johnny that he was the man who bought the car.

Johnny goes back to Mrs. Markey and returns the photo. Johnny tells her about the purchase of the car two weeks before his supposed death. Johnny tells her that it was not a smart scheme and that she must be pretty expensive to support and that she is one step away from prison.

If you file a claim, we will hit you with both barrels, so talk to your husband before you do anything. If you want to convince me, show me his body.

Tomorrow, a crazy kid in love, a right decision by a court and then the whole case smashed wide open.

Episode 4   Show Date: 3/1/1956
A call comes in for Johnny from Barney. He tells Johnny that the police are looking for the car and that the court will meet tomorrow at ten. See you there.

Johnny phones the insurance company legal department and then rejoins Mrs. Markey, who is nervous and pacing the floor. Johnny tells her that he has some facts to back up his ideas.

Johnny tells her that attempted fraud is not a scheme to get out of paying the policy. Johnny outlines that her husband is broke, that he saw a chance to pull a swindle with the policy and that they worked it out together. He bought a car and has a room somewhere and was waiting for a foggy day. You played Haynes along and your husband took the boat out, sank it, swam back to his car and drove off.

When she doubts that her husband, or any one could swim back to shore, Johnny tells her that his report included information that Markey is a champion swimmer. Johnny tells her that the proof will come if she files a claim. The doorbell rings and Johnny muses that he wants to end the case. Mrs. Markey returns and tells Johnny the doorbell was someone looking for an address.

Johnny leaves and determines that the visitor was someone she did not want Johnny to know about.

Johnny goes to see Danny Haynes, who tells Johnny that he was reading and had been there all evening. Danny tells Johnny that Mrs. Markey told him how Johnny talked to her, and she has had too much of that kind of trouble from Markey. She told him about it, and Danny almost felt like hitting Markey. Danny tells Johnny that if Markey is doing something, he is doing it alone. Mrs. Markey is a swell girl and he would die for her.

Johnny goes to the court and meets with a local attorney for the insurance company. The hearing is swift and informal, and the judge rules that requests for a ruling must be unquestionable, and the evidence indicates that William Markey is possibly still alive so the court will not declare William Markey dead.

Barney tells Johnny that he hates to see Danny get away with murder. Barney gets a message and tells Johnny that the coast patrol has just pulled a body from the ocean. A quick check of the prints showed it was William Markey.

Tomorrow, a dead man tells a tale, but not the tale he was meant to tell, and thereby hangs the windup.

Episode 5   Show Date: 3/2/1956

Barney calls and tells Johnny that he was over confident, and now has to apologize to Mrs. Markey. Barney tells Johnny not to be too hasty. Barney tells Johnny that he does not know what this case is. If you want to lose your mind, come over to the morgue.

Johnny cabs to the morgue to meet Barney and he shows Johnny the body and they are convinced it is Markey, but Johnny notices that the body does not show any signs of decomposition. The autopsy also showed that the body was only dead since last night and that Markey was alive after the sinking. He died of drowning, but the body was wearing two shoes. Also, Markey was drowned in fresh water. Barney wants to know who killed him and they both go to see Danny Haynes.

At Danny's room Johnny learns that Danny is not in and had been gone most of the day. The room is searched and nothing is found. Back in his room, Johnny gets a call from Barney. The car has been found in front of an apartment building. Barney picks up Johnny and they go to the apartment building.

The manager tells them that he rented an apartment two weeks ago to Mr. Jones who did not stay in the apartment for the first several nights. He went out last night and did not come back. A young friend brought the car back an hour ago and he is in the apartment now, packing Mr. Jones' clothes for a trip.

Barney and Johnny go up to the apartment and knock on the door. Barney calls to Danny and he shoots. They hear breaking glass and break in to find that Danny has run down the fire escape and shoots back at them. Barney warns Danny to surrender and after being shot at, Barney shoots him. "Well, he did say he would die for her, and it came to that."

Barney and Johnny drive to the Markey house, force their way in and find evidence of a struggle, water in the tub and a wet dressing gown in the closet.

Johnny goes to his hotel room and finds Mrs. Markey there. She tells Johnny that she heard that the police are looking for Danny and she wants to know what is happening. Johnny tells her to go to her house and talk to Wilson.

Johnny tells her it was her husband, not Haynes who came last night. Johnny gave her the idea to drown her husband and Danny helped her. She tells Johnny that she will get the best lawyer money can buy, but Johnny tells her there will be no money.

The policy was already void when she and Haynes killed her husband last night. It ended five days ago when he sank the boat. You lost your husband, your boyfriend your insurance claim and maybe your life.

"Remarks: You quoted a line of Shakespeare at the start of this case, Ralph: 'Full fathom five your father lies'. Well you are wrong. It turns out to be the widow who lies, and lies and lies."

Exp. Acct: $684.95

Notes:
- From the *Tempest*, Act I, scene ii: "Full fathom five thy father lies, of his bones are coral made, those are pearls that were his eyes: Nothing of him that doth fade, but doth suffer a sea-change into something rich and strange."
- Roy Rowan is the announcer.
- Musical supervision is by Amerigo Marino.

Producer: Jack Johnstone   Writer: Les Crutchfield
Cast: Mary Jane Croft, Barney Phillips, Carleton Young, Eleanor Audley, Sam Edwards, Shepard Menken, John Dehner

• ❖ •

Show: **The Plantagent Matter**
Company: **Eastern Seaboard Casualty Insurance Company**
Agent:
Synopsis:
Episode 1   Show Date: 3/5/1956
Mr. Costello from the Plantagent Hotel calls. Johnny tells him that he is coming to investigate the burglary at the hotel after the weather clears.

Johnny travels to Vicksburg, Virginia and then to the Plantagent Hotel where he learns that the case has been solved and the goods have been recovered. Johnny arranges for return travel and goes out for a walk. In the parking lot Johnny overhears a couple arguing, and the woman pleads for help. The man tells Johnny that the woman has had too much to drink and he tries to punch Johnny, who gets the best of him. The man walks off and tells Amy that he was only trying to beat some sense into her and leaves Amy and Johnny in the parking lot.

Amy starts to cry and tells Johnny she had only one drink. Johnny buys her a drink in the hotel and they talk. Johnny tries to tell a joke and she thanks him for not asking about her or her troubles and gets up to leave. Johnny helps her get a cab and tells her to call him if she needs any help.

The girl gets into the cab and suddenly gasps in pain. She says she didn't think he... and Johnny tells the cab to rush to the hospital.

The girl is taken into the emergency room and Johnny waits, and waits, and waits. Finally, the doctor asks Johnny to come to his office where there are two doctors and a nurse. Johnny tells the doctor what happened at the hotel and the doctor wants Johnny to complete some papers and tells Johnny that the girl is dead. Johnny is confused and asks, "under the circumstances, what would you do?"

Tomorrow, how can you help a dead girl. Somebody had to help her, and guess who?

Episode 2   Show Date: 3/6/1956
Johnny receives a call from Jim Aikens of the Vicksburg police. Jim is sending a car to pick him up. They have some questions to ask him and he tells Johnny that they have not identified her yet, she is just Jane Doe.

Johnny buys a paper and reads about the mysterious girl when Jim Aikens meets him in the lobby. Johnny tells him who he is and about the burglary case, and shows him his identification. Johnny tells Jim how he met the girl, and what happened. Johnny tells Jim that he does not know the girl's name or the man's name.

Johnny goes downtown with Aikens and gives him a statement. In the morgue, Johnny identifies the girl's body. Aikens asks about the girl and tells Johnny that no one seems to know the girl. All the girl's clothes were standard, and she is probably a local girl, but no one has reported her missing. Aikens tells Johnny that the girls' purse is missing and wonders why Johnny did not notice the man's car. Aikens gets a phone call and Johnny seems to be drawn to the dead girl.

Aikens tells Johnny that the lab had called and told him that a drug called perimythol killed her. It had been in her system for an hour before it killed her. Aikens thinks it was suicide, but Johnny disagrees.

Johnny packs and makes arrangements to leave. Johnny gets a drink and asks the bartender about the previous night, but he does not remember anything. Johnny tells him that a lady lost her purse, but none has been turned in. The bartender tells Johnny that the police had been in talking about the girl. Johnny searches the booth where he had sat and then goes to the parking lot. Johnny asks if a purse had been turned in, and then searches the lot and the attendant finds a purse under a car. Johnny looks into the green suede purse and finds no identification, but a .32 automatic that had been recently fired.

Tomorrow, a dead girl's .38 automatic comes to life.

Episode 3   Show Date: 3/7/1956

The operator calls with Johnny's call. Johnny calls the police and needs information about a gun. Johnny is told to come to the licensing division and bring the gun with him.

Johnny cabs to the city hall and gets the ownership information on the girl's gun. The serial number of the Colt .38 automatic is "JJJ-4769992 X". Johnny fills out a form and the clerk searches for the information. Johnny learns that the gun was purchased by the Piedmont Banking Service in 1950 and was licensed to Raymond W. O'Connell on Polk Street.

Johnny muses over talking to Lt. Aikens but rents a car and drives to the Polk street address. A woman expecting Paul meets Johnny at the door. Johnny asks for Raymond O'Connell and the woman asks him in. She is Terry O'Connell, Ray's widow, he died of pneumonia a year ago. She tells Johnny that a lot of his friends from the service come by to see him.

While they talk, Johnny sees a picture of the man he had met in the parking lot. Terry tells Johnny that he is Paul Dameron. She had met Paul after trying to kill herself, and they are going to be married. Terry asks Johnny to have dinner with her and Paul, but Johnny declines.

Johnny leaves and reads the paper with the girl's picture on the front page. Paul Dameron arrives and Johnny stops him on the sidewalk and asks who the girl in the parking lot was. Paul tells him the girl was Amy Durand and that she works in the same office he does. Terry is Amy's sister.

Johnny tells Paul of the drink and the trip to the hospital and Paul is shocked. Johnny shows him the paper and he tells Johnny that he did not think she was that desperate, he had no idea she would do it. Paul apologizes and asks Johnny to call him later.

Johnny takes the gun to Aikens, but he is away working on a homicide. Johnny is told that some guy named Belden was shot three times with a .38.

Tomorrow, information about the gun that blows the case sky high.

Episode 4   Show Date: 3/8/1956
Mr. Oldfield calls and Johnny tells him he needs an attorney. Johnny wants him to take a statement and give some advice.

Johnny buys coffee and waits for Samuel W. Oldfield, a local attorney. Mr. Oldfield arrives and Johnny tells him who he is, about the girl and about how he came into possession of the gun with three missing shells. Johnny tells him that he did not turn in the gun because he thought he could help the girl. Mr. Oldfield tells Johnny that a statement might help protect him. They go to the office and Johnny completes a statement.

Johnny goes to see Lt. Aikens and asks about the Belden case. Johnny is told that they are sure Belden was shot with a .38, and that Belden was an auditor who had found a shortage in the books of a textile wholesalers and the chief accountant is missing, Miss Amy Durand. Aikens thinks it is apparent that Amy killed the auditor, but Johnny does not want the case closed yet.

Johnny goes to see Terry O'Connell and she tells Johnny that her sister is dead and that Paul had gone to identify the body. Johnny tells her who he is and how he met Amy and took her to the hospital. Johnny got her address from the gun in Amy's purse.

Johnny tells her about the murder of Belden, and Terry recognizes the name. Johnny tells her that the police have the evidence to show that Amy stole $10,000 from the textile firm. They have evidence of suicide but Johnny wants to help Amy because she was not a thief or a suicidal type.

Terry tells Johnny that Amy saved her from a suicide attempt and was always kind and decent and good. Amy had introduced her to Paul and had bought things for her. She must have stolen the money for her.

Tomorrow, all the evidence comes true. A helpless dead girl gets her help.

Episode 5   Show Date: 3/9/1956
Paul Dameron calls and wants to talk to Johnny and thanks him for Amy and Mrs. O'Connell. He tells Johnny that the papers have connected her to Amy. Johnny tells Paul that he has the gun and cannot believe Amy would shoot a man and then take poison.

Johnny gets Sam Oldfield to prepare a statement and they go to the police to turn in the gun. Lt. Aikens gets the gun and the statement. After an hour, Aikens tells Johnny that the gun was the murder weapon, but Johnny did not need the lawyer, as no charges will be filed. He has the killer and the motive and the reason.

Mr. Oldfield leaves and Aikens talks to Johnny and tells him that there is a bottle of perimythol in Amy Durand's medicine cabinet. Aikens tells Johnny that he was a cop once and should have known better than to withhold evidence, and Aikens will not be so generous the next time Johnny comes to town.

Aikens gets a call and starts to leave and tells Johnny that Amy had a good motive. Paul Dameron meets them in the hallway and tells them that he and Amy were arguing and he had just discovered the shortage in the accounts, but not of killing the auditor. Paul offers Johnny a check for his kindness and Johnny refuses.

Aikens tells Johnny of finding a certified check in Amy's apartment from a New York bank. Johnny tells him that any reasonable bank or auditor would want restitution, so why kill the auditor with a check in her hand.

Johnny interviews people who had known the auditor and learns that he was the type who would have listened to Amy and accepted repayment. So why did she shoot him and then commit suicide?

Johnny goes to visit Dameron and tells him the case is not closed yet. Dameron tells Johnny that he did not know about the check. Johnny thinks that Amy borrowed the money to cover for someone else, you.

The auditor was smart and found out who took the money. He called you over to ask you about it and about repayment and you killed him. You fixed the papers to make it look like Amy stole the money. Amy was going to repay the money because you meant something to Terry, a woman who tried to kill herself once, and might do it again if she found out the man she was going to marry was a thief. You killed the auditor and then took Amy out and poisoned her. You could have fought me in the parking lot, but you had to get back and plant the poison in Amy's apartment.

Paul attacks Johnny and they fight. Johnny beats Paul and forces him to call the police.

Exp. Acct: $702.13

Notes:
- At the end of episode two there seems to be some confusion over the caliber of the girl's gun, first it is a .32, then a .38.
- Drinks are $1.00 each at the hotel bar.
- While this case is directed to the insurance company at the beginning, the later episodes are to Johnny, indicating that he is footing the bill on this one.
- This story was done as *The New Cambridge Matter*, broadcast on 12/19/1952 with John Lund. No recording of this program exists.
- Roy Rowan is the announcer.
- Musical supervision is by Amerigo Marino.

Producer: Jack Johnstone   Writer: John Dawson
Cast: Michael Ann Barrett, Jeanne Bates, Marvin Miller, Frank Gerstle, Lawrence Dobkin, Jack Kruschen, Ken Peters, Herb Butterfield

❖

Show: **The Clinton Matter**
Company: **United Adjustment Bureau**
Agent: **Al Davies**
Synopsis:

Episode 1   Show Date: 3/12/1956

John Dollar gets a Western Union message from the United Adjustment Bureau in New York, to proceed to the Northern Hotel in Clinton, Colorado ASAP. Building irregularities are suspected effecting several insurance companies. Johnny replies that he is on his way.

Johnny flies to Denver and then to Grand Junction where he rents a car and drives to Clinton, a sleepy mountain town. Johnny arrives as the school building is burning. Johnny assists in fighting the fire and then goes to his hotel where he has a message. Albert Davies calls and Johnny tells him of the fire. Al asks if Julian Osborne has contacted Johnny yet. He feels that the school building is in bad shape. Johnny tells Al that the school is what burned down.

Johnny checks the local phone directory for Julian Osborne. The desk clerk tells Johnny that Osborne had been burned to death in the fire. Johnny walks to the sheriff's office and meets Paul Daugherty, who is friendly until Johnny mentions Osborne. Johnny is told that Julian was the school janitor and Johnny tells the sheriff that Osborne had reported something wrong with the school to the insurance company. Daugherty tells Johnny that the body is in the morgue, but Osborne has no family or friends. He was the janitor of the school, and Florrie Hawkins hired him, and it is a bad night to go calling.

Johnny visits Miss Hawkins and she is thankful that school was not in session. Florie gets a phone call from the sheriff while Johnny is there and suddenly she cannot help Johnny and he must go, as she is tired. Johnny is sure the phone call wore her out and he tells her about the report of building problems. She tells Johnny that Julian probably imagined things. Johnny tells her that if the sheriff calls again, he is in the Northern Hotel.

Johnny calls Al Davies, updates him and is told to stay around. Johnny visits the school ruins, and on the way back to the hotel sees several men beating another man in an alley and Johnny chases them off. The man tells Johnny that he is David Baines and that he architected the school. The men beating him thought he was a bad architect.

Johnny takes him to his room and fixes him up and tells him why he is in town. Baines tells Johnny that he designed the building, and before the building was built, Roy Vickery sent him to Europe to study. Roy is the contractor who built the school, but you are wasting your time in Clinton. This is a tight, hot, mean little burg, and you will not find out anything here.

Tomorrow, there is a lot if information to be had in a town that will not talk. And there are times when the silence screams all over the place.

Episode 2   Show Date: 3/13/1956

David Baines calls Johnny and tells him that he is staying off the streets and advises Johnny to do the same. Johnny tells him that the town has filed a claim and Johnny must stay to investigate. Johnny tells David that he expects help from him.

Johnny wires Dodd and Company to request copies of the insurance policies. The newspaper blames the fire on overheated boilers.

Johnny visits the fire chief and is told that Julian passed out and the boilers exploded and that is that. He did not build the building and does not know why it spread, nor why the boilers were on when school was not in session. Johnny tells him he will get his information one way or another, but the chief cannot hear him.

Johnny and Baines have breakfast and Johnny asks for information and David tells him that the town is the playground of Vickery, Handley and Daugherty.

Vickery is a builder with a million dollars and a million Angeles. Fire chief Handley is a friend of Vickery and Daugherty keeps the law orderly for Vickery. Baines tells Johnny that the boilers had automatic shutoff mechanisms. They used the exterior plans Baines had drawn but made up the rest as they went along. Baines tells Johnny that a delegation of townspeople has gone out to get an explanation from Vickery.

Johnny goes to see Vickery and finds the police are guarding the house, and Daugherty warns Johnny to watch his step. Johnny wants to see Vickery and Daugherty tells him no one is seeing Vickery. Johnny shouts to the angry crowd that he is an investigator and is looking in to the fire and that the sheriff will not let him go in. Johnny asks Daugherty to let him in again, and he is let in.

Johnny meets Vickery, a big man in a blue suit who complements Johnny on how he handles the sheriff. Johnny wants to know about the building and Vickery tells Johnny that the civic building committee has just met and cannot find anything wrong, and that they will rebuild with the insurance money. Johnny asks for, and gets, a copy of the building specifications from Vickery.

Johnny and Baines go over the specifications, and they are just what Baines had specified. Johnny wants him to make a sworn statement, but Baines tells Johnny that Vickery would kill him. And they will kill Johnny if he goes too far.

Roy Vickery calls and Johnny tells him he thinks the specifications are fakes. Johnny tells him he will stay and Vickery tells him to get out of town, NOW!

Tomorrow, a lady who promises to love honor an obey a building inspector but wound up a widow.

Episode 3   Show Date: 3/14/1956

Florie Hawkins calls and wants to talk. She asks Johnny to meet her for cocktails at the Traders Inn, outside of town. She has heard of how he is not frightened of anyone, and she is sick of how things have been done.

Johnny buys dinner and waits for Florrie, who shows up late. She tells Johnny that she does not want to be seen by any of Daugherty's friends. He had called and warned her the night before. She tells Johnny that she knew Osborne had written the insurance company, and everyone knew the building was not up to specifications. She is willing to help Johnny.

Johnny is sure that if she and Baines will help, others will come forward as well. She knows that 1,400 students could have been in the school. Florrie suggests that the building inspector, Richard Hobb might help. He is a decent man and might help. Johnny tells Florrie to give him a statement and then to fly to Denver. She gives Johnny a statement at the Inn and then Johnny takes her to the airport.

Johnny wires a friend in Denver and asks him to watch over Florrie. Johnny calls Baines and asks for a statement and he agrees, but he will not hide in Denver. Baines gives Johnny the statement and Johnny mails it to himself at the hotel. Johnny calls Daugherty, Handley and Vickery about the statements, but they all laugh.

Johnny goes to the home of Richard Hobb, but he is not home, and his wife wants company. Johnny notices that she is slightly drunk and that Hobb has moved out, as there is nothing of his there, "When did he leave?" Johnny asks. She tells Johnny that he left during the fire. Johnny senses that she is scared and tells her to have Hobb contact him.

As Johnny is leaving Vickery drives up. "She is a lovely girl, isn't she?" Vickery tells Johnny. Johnny feels he has been ordered out of town because he was going to ask some embarrassing questions. Vickery tells Johnny that he should stop while he is ahead.

Johnny calls Al Davies and tells him that the case is a mess and that he cannot expect any help from the town. Al tells Johnny that he will send help. Johnny goes to bed and a man breaks through his door calling his name. When the man collapses, Johnny sees three bullet holes in Richard Hobb's body.

Tomorrow, the town of Clinton begins to fall apart, and it takes a lot of work to pick up the pieces.

Episode 4   Show Date: 3/15/1956

Al Davies calls and tells Johnny that help is on the way and should be there soon. Johnny tells Al of Richard Hobb's murder. Al tells Johnny to be careful until we get there.

As Johnny gets his breakfast sheriff Daugherty enters his room and asks for a cup of coffee. Daugherty tells Johnny that he almost held him for murder, but he is not getting anywhere. They want to find out all they can and asks Johnny "why do you think he came to your room?" Johnny tells him that maybe his conscious told him to come and talk about a substandard building. Daugherty tells Johnny to keep out of his way and he will keep out of Johnny's.

Two hours later Al Davies shows up with help: Toby O'Brien from Continental States Insurance, Rob Schwartz and the Mix twins from Columbia Adjustment, Todd Weaver fresh from a case for Canadian Adjusters, Lou Donniger and Thad Thomas from Chicago — all experienced investigators.

Johnny briefs everyone on the case and gives out assignments. Toby and Thad will look into Hobbs. Rob and Toby will look into Vickery. Jim and Al Mix will look into Julian Osborne. Lou will take fire chief Handley. Al will handle the Sheriff. Everyone else just spread out. Johnny wants statements and will offer protection to anyone who wants it. Don't push anyone, but don't be pushed around. Johnny knew the eight men would be conspicuous.

Johnny gets a call from a man and is told he wants to talk. Earl Kennedy will pick Johnny up down stairs. After ten minutes a car drives up with five men and Johnny gets in.

They drive out of town and Earl, the construction foreman on the school, introduces the men, most of who worked on the construction project and Frank Gibson the newspaper editor. They have seen the men Johnny brought into town are all willing to make statements. Earl can prove they shortchanged the town during construction, and Frank tells Johnny that the paper is at his disposal, as long as what he prints is the truth. The men are all willing to testify.

Johnny is told that Hobb had big ideas and played ball with Vickery, who was born in Clinton and has built most of the town. Johnny is told that Vickery is the only person who would have the purchase orders, but Johnny will not get them. Johnny and the men go to the newspaper office to give their statements.

Al Davies meets Johnny in his room and shows Johnny seven men outside the hotel. There is a knock at the door and Daugherty yells at Al for bringing in troublemakers. Al is told that the men outside are indignant citizens.

Daugherty wants Al's men withdrawn by sundown or they will suffer the consequences. Johnny tells Daugherty that his agents are armed and will not be intimidated. Johnny also demands that Daugherty resign by sundown or he will force him out of office. Johnny shows him the statements and Daugherty tries to attack Johnny and tells him "I'll kill you, Dollar!"

Tomorrow, the end and the beginning of Clinton, Colorado. It all happens when the smoke clears.

Episode 5   Show Date: 3/16/1956

Toby O'Brien calls and he has heard about the run-in with Daugherty. Toby has discovered that Hobb got paid off after his inspections to the amount of $20,000.

Johnny gets photocopies of the deposits to Hobb's account and Al tells him the town is running scared. Al is told to mail the photocopies to the home office.

Johnny drives to Hobb's house and the wife meets Johnny in a slinky black dress and a glass of bourbon. She is "broken up" but cannot cry about Richard.

She does not know about any money, but she suspects he spent it on other women. They both wanted more excitement than his salary could offer and she suspects that Vickery gave him the money.

She tells Johnny that she has no insurance and needs money if she is forced to leave because she talked. She wants a $2,000 endowment policy and Johnny tells her he will arrange it.

She tells Johnny that Richard got the money from the Clinton Gravel Company. He came back last night and told her that Vickery was going to make a patsy out of him and that he was going to see you. Johnny remembers that Vickery was outside the house when he left, and he might have killed Hobb himself.

Johnny goes to the hotel and meets Baines, who has a bottle of bourbon in his hand. He tells Johnny about a law that allows one crime to be committed to prevent another crime. He tells Johnny that he has committed two crimes. He dishonored his noble character by disappointing the trust of a young woman, and he engineered a theft, he is a Fagan. Under the guise of loving a young secretary eternally, he got Vickery's secretary to steal the original purchase orders from Roy Vickery's office.

Johnny mails the papers to a broker in Denver and 14 hours later Johnny gets a reply that the materials used were not passable, and the insurance company will not pay. Toby calls with two witnesses to Hobb's killing and tells Johnny that Vickery did it himself. In the afternoon newspaper is a story about the investigation naming Vickery, Daugherty and Hanley.

Johnny has a visit from deputy Eagan and several others who jump Johnny and take him outside. On the street, Johnny sees several of his agents coming and calls for help. They jump the deputies and take them to his room where Eagan tells Johnny that Vickery wanted him taken to the gravel plant.

Johnny drives to the gravel plant and sees several cars there. The exits are covered and Toby goes in with Johnny. They hear shots and run in and find Vickery shot and Handley dead. Toby spots Daugherty on the back stairs and Johnny follows him. While Toby gets the others to block the doors, Daugherty surprises Johnny and tells Johnny that he will kill him, but Toby rushes in and shoots Daugherty. Daugherty's last words are about the falling out among thieves. Vickery survives and is charged with 28 counts of murder and conspiracy.

Exp. Acct: $2,385.03

Notes:
- This story was done as *The Big Red School House*, broadcast on 4/4/1950.
- In episode 4, Al Davies tells the sheriff that he brought eight agents with him for a total of nine, but Johnny only lists seven in episode 3, which with Al makes eight. There was also a mix-up in the agent count in *The Big Red School House* story.
- In episode 2, the script credits Dick Ryan, Tom Hanley and Ray Kemper with ad libs.
- Roy Rowan is the announcer.
- Music supervision is by Amerigo Marino.

Producer: Jack Johnstone   Writer: John Dawson
Cast: Jeanette Nolan, Lucille Meredith, Carleton Young, Herb Ellis, Jack Petruzzi, Bob Bruce, Herb Butterfield, Paul Richards, Edgar Barrier, Russell Thorson, Jack Moyles, Frank Gerstle

♦ ❖ ♦

Show: **The Jolly Roger Fraud Matter**
Company: **Universal Adjustment Bureau**
Agent: **Pat McCracken**
Synopsis:
Episode 1   Show Date: 3/19/1956

Pat McCracken calls with a case, but Johnny is going out on vacation in La Jolla California. Pat tells Johnny that there is enough commission to pay for two vacations, just come down to my office. Okay (sucker).

Johnny cabs to Pat's office and prepares to argue his way out of the case. Pat is sure Johnny will solve the case in a couple days and will put the whole vacation on the old swindle sheet, plus there is the commission.

Pat tells Johnny that the Jolly Roger was insured for $460,000 and Bert Parker in San Diego has the details. He gave you the *Molly K Matter*, and that was quite profitable, wasn't it?

The boat is a floating palace with a wooden hull, which is why she burned to the water line and sank. Pat has told Bert that Johnny is on the way and has notified the Mexican authorities. Pat grabs Johnny's bags and tells him about the case on the way down the elevator. Pat tells Johnny that the diesel yacht *Jolly Roger* is owned by Paulus Zanagian, a former rum-runner, gun-runner, shipbuilder, and suspected spy in both wars. Johnny cannot argue with Pat, so he takes on the case.

Johnny lands in San Diego, California and is met by Jan Penny, Bert's secretary, who is going to work on the case with Johnny. Penny tells Johnny that Bert is in the hospital, the victim of a hit and run. Penny tells Johnny that Bert thinks he was hit deliberately.

Johnny visits Bert in the hospital and he tells Johnny that he knows he is dying and that he knows he was run down. Bert tells Johnny that he had gotten threatening calls about holding up the claims on the *Jolly Roger*. Bert tells Johnny to drop the case and is wracked with pain and dies three hours later.

Johnny takes Penny to Ray Kemper's Cat Club to help drown their sorrows. Penny tells Johnny that she came to California to be in pictures but did not like the life style and then she met Bert who hired her. She loved Bert for being a nice guy. Penny is glad that Johnny is a straight guy, like Bert. Johnny has two jobs now, the *Jolly Roger* and finding Bert's killer.

Johnny takes Penny home and stops by the police to check on the hit and run and learns nothing.

At his hotel, Johnny gets a phone call and Penny is hysterical. She tells Johnny that she was followed and she just got a threatening phone call. The caller told her that she will have an accident if she helps Johnny.

Tomorrow, well it may sound corny, but where there is smoke, there is fire.

Episode 2   Show Date: 3/20/1956

Jan Penny calls and tells Johnny about a threatening phone call. She was told that there will be two fatal accidents if they work on the Jolly Roger case.

This case is going to the Universal Adjustment Bureau now because Southwestern's agent has died.

Johnny goes to see Penny and she lets Johnny in and tells him that the voice on the phone was the same one that threatened Bert. She warns Johnny to be careful, as Zanagian is trying to get the claim processed. She tells Johnny that Bert did not want to insure the boat, but the two years of premiums were hard to turn down. Zanagian himself put in the claim and demanded immediate payment. Bert did not want to pay and they killed Bert, and now she is frightened. Johnny tells her to get some sleep while he sleeps on the sofa with his gun.

In the morning, Johnny goes to visit the police and Lt. Joe Franklin tells Johnny that they have not really learned anything.

Johnny then goes to see Zanagian, who knows about Bert. Zanagian knows everything Johnny has done and he is depending on Johnny to make prompt payment on the policy. He is looking out for Johnny and has a trusted man watching Johnny during his stay.

Zanagian tells Johnny that they were testing some new equipment when the ship sank. He will not bore Johnny with the details which Johnny will get from the Coast Guard. Zanagian tells Johnny that he must have settlement without delay so that he can leave immediately. He needs cash and is a most generous person.

Johnny tells him that a claim for $460,000 must be investigated, and the claims make the case suspicious. The offer of a bribe does not help. So, sit back and wait to see if you get the money at all. Zanagian reminds Johnny of the accidents, but Johnny tells him he does not scare easily.

Johnny goes to the Coast Guard and talks to Lt. John Smith, who believes that Zanagian sunk the boat himself. They sent down divers but could see nothing. The crew was lost except for a cabin boy who was taken to a Mexican hospital. Smith offers Johnny his car so Johnny can drive to Tijuana to question the boy. Smith tells Johnny that both Holland and Switzerland have tied up Zanagian's funds.

As Johnny is leaving, Zanagian arrives and would offer Johnny a ride to Tijuana but, alas, he has just learned that the cabin boy has just died. What a pity.

Tomorrow, a dead man talks, and what he has to say isn't very pleasant, for it all adds up to just one good solid threat to yours truly, Johnny Dollar.

Episode 3   Show Date: 3/21/1956

The operator returns Johnny's call to Dr. Hernandez in the hospital. Johnny is told that the cabin boy just died but under mysterious circumstance. He said things that you must know.

Johnny calls the hospital in Tijuana from a pay phone and then talks to Lt. Smith. Johnny relates what the doctor said and asks Lt. Smith to get him a rental car delivered to the hotel. Lt. Smith is sure that Zanagian needs money to get to Europe and get the impounded funds.

Johnny gets a rental car and drives to Tijuana, always watching for a tail. Johnny sees a variety of cars and trucks on the road, but no one tailing him.

Johnny arrives at the hospital and meets Dr. Hernandez. Johnny tells him about the Jolly Roger and how well Zanagian resembles a pirate. Dr. Hernandez tells Johnny that after the boy was brought in a man called and wanted to see him. They operated on the boy and the operation was successful. Dr. Hernandez set up a special nurse to watch the boy. She left the boy for a minute to tell how the doctors how well he was recovering and when she returned the boy was dead. Someone got into the room and killed him with a knitting needle.

The police were told but they are at a loss. The boy told Dr. Hernandez things that he wrote down. When Dr. Hernandez searches in his desk for the notes, they are gone. The boy had told Dr. Hernandez that he had seen a strange device brought on the ship. Only the captain had handled it, and it was taken to the engine room. The device looked like an alarm clock set for 2:35. Johnny wonders why, if the captain knew about it, why he would put it on board.

Dr. Hernandez tells Johnny that the captain was hit by a small mast and was unconscious. Johnny tells the doctor to let no one know he has talked to Johnny. Zanagian is after Johnny and will be after anyone who helps him.

Johnny calls the Coast Guard and learns that Lt. Smith is dead, from a hit and run accident an hour after Johnny left him. Johnny tells Dr. Hernandez to "watch your step, doctor".

Tomorrow, some real help from two close friends. You know, close enough to kill.

Episode 4   Show Date: 3/22/1956

Sgt. Franklin calls and he tells Johnny that he thinks the Jolly Roger was sunk. Johnny tells him that both Bert and Lt. Smith were killed and Jan Penny is helping him. Franklin tells Johnny that they are sending a man to watch Jan Penny. But what about you?

Johnny notes that he was really looking forward to skin diving, or investigating the girls in bikini bathing suits, but now he is looking into the sinking of a luxury yacht.

Johnny briefs Franklin about the boy, the time bomb, the falling mast and the impounded funds. Bert Parker did not last long after refusing to pay the claim, and Johnny has been threatened. Johnny is told that Tommy Golden will watch Jan Penny and Johnny asks about the hit and run of Lt. Smith.

Franklin tells Johnny that the car was a black Buick sedan, a '54 or '55, with no plates. Franklin is that sure Zanagian is behind this and Johnny wonders if Franklin is working for him. Franklin notes that Zanagian usually has helpers but they have not been able to spot them. Johnny tells Franklin about the men in Zanagian's room and learns that they have been tailed. When Johnny tells Franklin that he is going to go see Jan, Franklin tells Johnny that Jan Penny drives a black Buick.

Johnny goes to Jan's apartment and she is worried about Johnny. She had taken a cab to the office and no one bothered her there, but she feels she is being followed. Jan urges Johnny to back out of the case, but Johnny will not do it, it is his job to take risks.

Jan breaks down and they have a drink and talk. Johnny wonders why he cannot relax and enjoy the situation with Jan. Johnny tells her he is going to the police and she tells Johnny to take her car, an old black Buick with a new paint job. She tells Johnny that she took a cab that morning so they would not mar the new paint job.

Johnny goes to the garage and notices the new paint job and the partially open hood. Johnny opens the hood and finds a bomb wired to the ignition.

Tomorrow, the wind up, where the obvious becomes only too obvious.

Episode 5   Show Date: 3/23/1956
Johnny calls Jan and wonders why she is surprised. Johnny tells her that he changed his mind and will be back after taking a walk. She tells him to take a drive, but she does not want to go along with him.

Johnny calls Jan and does not tell her of the bomb. Johnny goes back upstairs and hears her talking to someone on the phone.

Johnny calls Sgt. Franklin from the lobby and tells him what he has just heard, and that he is going to lay it all out to Jan. Johnny goes back upstairs and tells Jan to sit down while he tells her about the open hood and the bomb and why she did not hear an explosion. Jan plays dumb and worries about the threats.

Zanagian and Artiz come in via the service entrance with a gun drawn. "How awkward to take the service entrance" Zanagian tells Johnny. Zanagian takes Johnny's gun and Johnny tries to hit Artiz. Zanagian wants to talk about why Johnny suspects Jan of complicity.

Johnny tells him that apart from the threatening phone calls that only Jan received, Zanagian had someone follow Johnny. Zanagian tells Johnny that Jan and Artiz are his only staff. Johnny knows how to dodge a tail, and Artiz says that Johnny is too good.

Zanagian calls Johnny an intelligent man, and only Jan could provide the information he has, and Jan did a good job on Bert and Lt. Smith. Johnny gets angry and Artiz holds him back.

Zanagian tells Johnny about the millions impounded in Europe. Jan tells Johnny that Zanagian's friends are well paid for their efforts. All Johnny has to do is approve the claim and he will get more than money, like Jan for example. "Work with me or I will eliminate you." Johnny asks Artiz to lower his gun and Johnny asks how Zanagian knows Johnny will not double-cross him.

Johnny tells Zanagian the he has good news for him, he has just given a confession to Sgt. Franklin. Johnny slugs Artiz who fires and falls to the floor when Franklin comes in with reinforcements. Franklin tells Johnny that he knew that the phone call was being listened to. But Zanagian is dead, shot by Artiz. Jan pleads with Johnny to listen to her, but Johnny can only tell her to "shut up!".

"The fabulous crooked empire of Paulus Zanagian is kaput, the same way it happens when every man who tries to break the rules of international law and order. You might almost call it death by his own hand, though of course little Artiz will be made to pay for it. Jan, same thing I guess. Why do they do it?"

Exp. Acct: $523.23

Notes:
- Pat McCracken makes the first of many appearances.
- In episode 5, Johnny addresses the expense account to the "Universal Adjusters Bureau".
- In episode 1, Pat notes that Bert Parker had assigned Johnny *The Molly K Matter* case, but the original program names Dave Borger and a different insurance company, Marine & Maritime Casualty Ltd.
- This is the first of many programs written by Jack Johnstone.
- The expense total is really a subtotal, pending what Johnny spends on vacation.
- The announcer is Roy Rowan.
- Musical supervision is by Amerigo Marino.
- Ray Kemper is a CBS soundman.

Producer: Jack Johnstone **Writer:** Jack Johnstone
Cast: Virginia Gregg, Forrest Lewis, Paul Frees, Jay Novello, Harry Bartell, Don Diamond, Vic Perrin

◆ ❖ ◆

Show: **The LaMarr Matter**
Company: **Universal Adjustment Bureau**
Agent: **Pat McCracken**
Synopsis:
Episode 1   **Show Date:**   **3/26/1956**

Pat McCracken calls Johnny and asks about Johnny's vacation, which is on the expense account for the Jolly Roger Matter. Johnny asks Pat about approval to work on the LaMarr case. This is a case that will make your hair curl!

Johnny is on vacation and enjoying the beach in La Jolla where he is staying at the El Crescenta, alone except for Vonnie LaMarr, who thinks Johnny runs a filling station. Johnny has told her that his rich uncle left him some money for a vacation.

She is really a wonderful girl who he met after clearing up the Jolly Roger Matter. Vonnie was waiting for her father to arrive, but he had to delay the trip at the last minute. A telegram arrived for Vonnie and her father had delayed his trip because of doctor's orders. He just had a checkup with Tri-Mutual Insurance.

She senses something is wrong and Johnny lets her call home from his cottage. She tells Johnny that daddy is OK and she tells daddy all about Johnny. Mr. LaMarr tells Vonnie that he just had indigestion, and they go back to the dining room. That was three days ago.

Vonnie starts talking about love at first sight and Johnny gets a little nervous. Vonnie senses that Johnny does not run a filling station and he tells her that he might be a social bum. She tells Johnny that she has had her share of worthless fops, all trying to get into the LaMarr name. She tells Johnny she is waiting for someone like Johnny as they snuggle on the beach.

Pedro arrives and he has telegrams for Johnny and Vonnie. Vonnie's is from the family doctor, her father has died. Johnny makes reservations for her to return home, and then calls Pat McCracken who had sent his wire. Pat wants him to stop in South Bend, Indiana and look into the death of Thomas Rene LaMarr, insured for $1.5 million. They think it is murder.

Tomorrow, a set of circumstances arise that are enough to keep a man from trusting even himself.

Episode 2   Show Date: 3/27/1956
The operator calls with Pat McCracken's call. Johnny tells Pat that the he is leaving for South Bend with Vonnie LaMarr. She does not know that they think it is murder.

This starts the LaMarr case expenses. Johnny tells Pat that Vonnie is on vacation in La Jolla and no claim has been filed yet. Pat tells Johnny that he knew of LaMarr's death through Tri-Mutual's agent, Lawrence Comstock, who is a close friend of Mr. LaMarr. Comstock had been staying at LaMarr's house and had called the doctor when LaMarr collapsed. Comstock called Pat and specifically asked for Johnny. Johnny tells Pat that he does not want Vonnie to know he is investigating the case.

Johnny checks with Vonnie and he tells her he is going to go home with her, to help out. She is thankful that Johnny is so wonderful. Even with Vonnie, Johnny has to suspect everyone in this case, with a million and a half on the line.

On the plane, Johnny tells Vonnie he will be staying in South Bend and has contacted a business friend there, and she is very inquisitive over what Johnny does for a living. Vonnie has wired home to Harrison the butler, and Edward Wilson her father's doctor.

The plane lands in Chicago and they take a cab to the LaMarr home in South Bend. The large household staff meets Johnny and Vonnie at the door and Vonnie tells Harrison that Johnny is to be allowed in at any time.

Johnny cabs back to Chicago to talk with Larry Comstock. Larry tells Johnny that he thinks that LaMarr was murdered. He had known LaMarr for years and had written all of his policies. LaMarr's company had just been bought out and he was getting ready to retire and take care of Vonnie, his adopted daughter.

Johnny tells Larry that he knows Vonnie. Larry tells Johnny that in all the years he has known LaMarr, there are things in Vonnie's past that no one but he knew. Larry tells Johnny that Dr. Wilson examined LaMarr, and he was in excellent health. Larry suspects the man who could benefit by LaMarr's death, the man Vonnie is really in love with.

Tomorrow, some stuff I didn't want to hear, but I had to.

Episode 3   Show Date: 3/28/1956
Vonnie calls and asks Johnny to come to the house. She asks if Johnny's business is related to her father's death. "Do you too think he was murdered?" she asks Johnny.

Johnny talks to Larry Comstock, who tells Johnny that he and Dr. Wilson were the only friends Thomas LaMarr had. They enjoyed the same things and belonged to the same clubs. LaMarr was in excellent health, which is why he was allowed to increase his insurance, for his adopted daughter.

Larry and Dr. Wilson were at the LaMarr house that Friday night and they played three-handed pinochle. That night young Walter Marcin, LaMarr's personal secretary was there. They played golf Saturday and just relaxed on Sunday. They quit playing cards just before midnight and went to bed. LaMarr said he might need a sleeping pill, which Larry knew were only sugar pills. Larry heard a crash, ran up to his bathroom and saw LaMarr on the floor.

Ed was called and he suspected some rare poison. Samples of the pills were sent to Chicago and Washington. Walter Marcin is LaMarr's personal secretary and has been married to Vonnie for over a year. LaMarr's will leaves all of his assets to the corporation, except for the insurance, which goes to Vonnie. The only way someone could benefit was to be married to Vonnie.

Larry knows that Marcin has something on Vonnie. Walter Marcin handled all of LaMarr's investments and made it clear that he wanted to take his place at the company, but LaMarr would not allow it. LaMarr knew some of the transactions Marcin had made were not really moral and that Marcin would use the company for personal gain if given the chance. Larry is sure that Marcin poisoned LaMarr.

Johnny asks "what if Vonnie had something to do with it?" and wonders why she wanted Johnny if she was already married. Why did she know where Johnny was, why did she get him under her spell? Larry tells Johnny that he is striking out because he is hurt, but do not let it affect your judgement.

Tomorrow, well it doesn't take long to find out what has to be done on this case because the turning point in the thing comes straight to me, and with a vengeance.

Episode 4   Show Date: 3/29/1956

Dr. Wilson calls Johnny and tells him that Larry had asked him to call. Dr. Wilson has just left the police autopsy surgeon and Thomas LaMarr definitely had been poisoned. Johnny tells Dr. Wilson that he is in the LaMarr will, which is a shot in the dark. Johnny is on his way to see him.

So far, the evidence seems to point to Walter Marcin, married to Vonnie without LaMarr's knowledge.

Johnny meets with Dr. Wilson, who has heard of Johnny through Larry Comstock. Johnny took a shot at guessing that he and Larry are beneficiaries, and would therefore have a reason to cause LaMarr's death. Johnny is also aware that Vonnie is married to Marcin.

Dr. Wilson tells Johnny that after the death of her mother, Vonnie got involved in gambling through her "friends" and became deeply in debt. Marcin found out and told her he would pay off her debts if she married him. He quietly used the profits of LaMarr's investments to pay off her debts. She was upset over the death of her mother and was desperate. Dr. Wilson tells Johnny that he too is upset. He and Larry are beneficiaries, but only in a minor way. Johnny apologizes for his suspicions.

Dr. Wilson tells Johnny that LaMarr died from a poison called pyradameron, which causes the heart to burst and leaves no residue. Dr. Wilson only found evidence, a strange coloration, on LaMarr's tongue. It is strange, as the last known source, a small island off of Greece, died out many years ago, and the Greek government had burned all of the known plants and seeds. The poison could have been mixed with the pills, but there was no evidence of the poison on them.

Johnny follows a hunch and goes to the library closest to the LaMarr home, and only finds a reference to the plant "Blephara Purpurus Kelandus".

Johnny goes to the main library in Chicago, where the librarian is an expert on rare drugs and poisons. He has read about pyradameron in a mystery, "The Case of the Yellow Lipped Monster". The plant is extinct now for many years and is really deadly. It is in the book "Flora Exotica Mediterranean" which turns up missing when he searches for it. He is sure that it was there yesterday, and it is never taken out without his knowledge as there is no other book which would cover the plant.

Johnny cabs back to the LaMarr home and talks to Harrison. Johnny is told that Vonnie and Marcin are out making funeral arrangements and Vonnie had indicated she would travel and settle down elsewhere. The staff will probably find employment elsewhere. Harrison tells Johnny that Marcin lives in the house. Johnny finally tells Harrison who he is and asks to see Marcin's room.

Harrison is sure that Marcin had been a clever scheming young man planning to take over the corporation and had tried once to marry Vonnie. But he has changed. Harrison had overheard conversations between Marcin and LaMarr where LaMarr confronted Marcin with is activities and his prison record for embezzlement. But even then, LaMarr was ready to give him a second chance and Marcin changed his ways. Johnny finds a book in Marcin's room — "Flora Exotica Mediterranean".

Tomorrow the windup, and a switch that will make your head spin.

Episode 5   Show Date: 3/30/1956

Larry Comstock calls and Johnny asks about the results of the police crime lab. Larry tells Johnny that they found evidence of the poison on LaMarr's toothbrush. Johnny tells Larry to send the police, he almost has the case wrapped up.

Johnny recounts the case and how the clues seem to point to Walter Marcin, and the book he found in Marcin's room.

Marcin catches Johnny in his room, and Johnny shows him his identification, and tells why he is there. Johnny comments on the book he found about the poison pyradameron. Marcin tells Johnny he got the book in the library but did not kill LaMarr. Johnny tells Marcin about his secret marriage to Vonnie, the stock deals and killing Thomas LaMarr. Walter tells Johnny that he was married to Vonnie, and that he had tried to get a place in the company by showing LaMarr how clever he was, but LaMarr gave him a second chance and he has changed now.

Walter tells him that he and Vonnie are divorced, she mailed him the papers from Reno before she went to La Jolla. Walter had taken the book to try and figure out where the poison had come from, knowing suspicion would fall on him. They had been out and Harrison told them that Johnny was there and wanted to talk to Vonnie. Walter had come upstairs, and Vonnie had gone somewhere in the house. Marcin tells Johnny that they were only married on paper, in spite of their secrets. She has been drinking and is more deeply in debt now than before. Suddenly Walter senses that maybe Vonnie is involved.

The pyradameron plant is extinct, but Marcin wonders if Dimitri, the Greek gardener might know something. Before going to the gardener's cottage, Johnny checks with Harrison, phones Larry who is out, and then calls the librarian, who tells Johnny that the book had been checked out once by "LaVon LaMarr".

Marcin and Johnny go out to meet with Dimitri. Johnny asks Dimitri if he had ever seen a flower like the one in the book. Dimitri had seen them in the old country and he had kept some seeds that Vonnie had planted in her secret garden. Vonnie had sent Dimitri a toiletries case from California and shows it to Johnny. Johnny notices a yellow tint on the toothbrush and Walter remembers that LaMarr had gotten one also.

They walk to Vonnie's secret garden to find Vonnie digging with a shovel. She is "burying her garden of things she had grown for daddy". Johnny pulls up the pyradameron plant and Vonnie tries to attack him. Walter and Johnny subdue her as she screams and tries to buy off Johnny.

"Believe me, this is one case I wish I had never seen. Oh sure, you, the company are all right, you will not have to pay off a million and a half in insurance: your gain. But me, I've lost something. Faith. Faith and...I'm sick over the whole thing. Expense account, I'll add it up later. Right now, I'm going out and get roaring... get some flowers, some clean flowers and just sit and look at them."

Exp. Acct: $0.00

Notes:
- Both the plant "Blephara Purpurus Kelandus" and pyradameron are fictitious.
- Virginia Gregg must clear her voice in episode 1.
- Roy Rowan is the announcer.
- Musical supervision is by Amerigo Marino.

Producer: Jack Johnstone   Writer: Jack Johnstone
Cast: Virginia Gregg, Harry Bartell, Lawrence Dobkin, Eric Snowden, Howard McNear, John Dehner, Jeanne Tatum, Joseph Kearns, Paul Richards, Jack Moyles

Show: The Salt City Matter
Company: Samuel Ruben & Associates
Agent: Samuel Ruben
Synopsis:
Episode 1   Show Date: 4/2/1956

Sam Ruben calls and Johnny complains about having to hock his watch on his last job for Sam in Hong Kong. Sam needs help with Ed Julian. ED JULIAN! So long Sam, call the police. Sam is calling Johnny because he cannot call the police.

Johnny knows the name Ed Julian, as does every policeman in the country. Johnny goes to see Sam Ruben, who would like to have Johnny on his payroll. Johnny tells him that Ed Julian is a well-known criminal. Sam has a $50,000 insurance policy on Ed Julian but nothing has happened to Ed yet.

The policy was issued a month ago, and Sam knows Julian was a bad risk. Julian is in San Francisco, and Sam wants Johnny to go to Julian and ask him to cancel the policy. Johnny knows that there is no way that he can approach Julian, what Sam really wants is for Johnny to watch Ed until Sam can figure out how to cancel the policy. Sam tells Johnny that he has heard through the grapevine that some on Ed's old friends are gathering in San Francisco, the kind who would like to kill him. Sam tells Johnny that an agent in San Francisco had sold a policy to Edwardo Saccavetti, and she only found out later who he was and sent Sam a wire. Johnny negotiates with Sam for expenses and a $2,500 commission.

Johnny flies to San Francisco, California and gets a room at the Fairmont Hotel. Johnny cabs to the address of Ed Julian on Nob Hill, where Johnny interviews a policeman who tells Johnny that Mr. Saccavetti moved out a week ago with his wife and their clothes. Johnny is troubled when he finds a listing for Edward Julian Enterprises in the phone book. Johnny calls the number and asks for Mr. Julian, and is told that he is not there, and is not ever expected back.

Johnny goes to the address and walks in to find a man there and asks for Julian. The man tells Johnny that he wants to find Julian too. He is Ray Gumby, Julian's lawyer. Gumby pours Johnny a drink and tells Johnny that the enterprises were not much, but they have all been sold. Johnny wants to find Julian to protect him, but Gumby tells Johnny that he has been left holding the sack. He hopes to get Julian served so he can be put in jail. Gumby was a fool to accept Julian as a client. Johnny suggests they work together to keep Julian safe. Gumby gives Johnny a subpoena for Ed Julian and agrees to pay Johnny $200 if he can serve it.

Tomorrow, that's when I begin to find a myth can be stranger than fiction.

Episode 2   Show Date: 4/3/1956

Johnny goes to see Insp. Walsh and updates him on Julian, who is out of town. Johnny tells him that the town is full of thugs and about his arrangement with Gumby.

Johnny goes to see the local agent, who is named Eleanor. She fixes Johnny a cup of black coffee while he tells her why he is there. She tells Johnny that she met Julian in a restaurant and his wife Lorraine was with him. They had dinner and she sold him the policy, in spite of the fact that Julian made a pass at her. She also tells Johnny that she knew Lorraine from high school.

Johnny has dinner and Eleanor tells Johnny about Jim Reno, and mentions Chili Winters from Chicago, Lollovitch and Pachaki from Detroit and Fritzie Chrysler and Turkey Johnson from Toledo, all gangsters. She tells Johnny that it is too bad about Lorraine.

After dinner, Johnny is called by a man named Wade who tells him that Julian is at the Skyline Apartments. Johnny goes to the apartment and runs into Swifty, who Johnny knows as a hood.

Johnny asks about Julian and Luke walks up and Johnny is beaten and put in a cab and sent to a Turkish bath.

Episode 3   Show Date: 4/4/1956

Johnny calls the Skyline Apartments and Johnny tells the clerk that he was slugged there last night. Tell the guys that hit me I am on the way over.

Johnny gets two stitches and then calls the world's prettiest insurance broker in San Francisco, Eleanor Stover. Johnny goes to see Eleanor and tells her that he had a run-in with two of Ed Julian's hoods and that he is trying to issue a subpoena to get him into court.

Johnny then cabs to the Skyline Apartments where Johnny calls "Swifty" and asks about his partner. Luke comes over and they ridicule Johnny, who asks them what floor Julian is on. When they try to stop Johnny, he pulls his gun and pistol-whips them.

Johnny goes to the fourth floor where a woman opens the door and Johnny finds that Ed Julian is gone. She tells Johnny that he is taking a chance being there. The woman is Ed's wife, Lorraine and Johnny tells her that Eleanor Stover was a friend of hers ten years ago in school. Lorraine does not expect Ed to come back but Johnny wants to wait.

She asks about Swifty and Luke, Johnny tells her that Swifty and Luke were glad to see him come up. She is upset when she sees the stitches in Johnny's head. Johnny tells her he is trying to protect Ed, but she has no idea where he is. She tells Johnny that the others came from the east, and Ed was talking with Chilly Winters and then they left. She did not like Chilly's looks and she tells Johnny to leave, or Ed will kill her.

Johnny goes to look up the record on Chilly Winters, which is long and ugly. Johnny goes back to his room and the Skyline desk clerk is waiting for him.

He tells Johnny that he needs every penny, and that he knows that Johnny is not a thug, but he knows where Julian is. Johnny gives him some money and the man tells Johnny that Ed Julian is in Salt City for a big meeting.

Johnny gets a map of California and finds Salt City, 300 miles away. Johnny calls on Ed Gumby, and he knows that Salt City is a company town and that

Johnny should not go there. Johnny is sure that something big, just out of touch is going to happen.

Johnny buys a train ticket to Salt City and finds a yellow grimy little town around a yellow grimy smelter. Johnny wants a cab to the smelter works, but the cabby will not take him there. A hobo tells Johnny that Salt city is the end of the line. He has left twice never wanting to come back. This place is a dump somebody made and forgot about. Johnny senses nothing but a feeling that "it is going to happen here".

Tomorrow, well maybe I was psychic or something, because tomorrow is when that feeling, that hunch turns into action.

Episode 4   Show Date: 4/5/1956
Johnny gets a call through to San Francisco and talks to Ed Gumby and tells him that things look terrible. Johnny should be back tonight if he is lucky. There is not much law enforcement here, but Johnny will serve Ed if he can.

Johnny checks his bag and walks to the Salt City Bar and Grill, where a girl named Connie talks to him. She does not blame Johnny for not wanting to leave soon and stops talking when Mr. Reno comes in.

Johnny recognizes Reno from the Landry murder case in Baltimore in 1950. He tells Johnny that he is Jim Reno, and that he runs the restaurant. He suggests that Johnny have the stew and tells Connie to fix it. Reno tells Johnny that Ed Julian is at the smelter and Reno offers to call Johnny a cab, he owns the Taxi company also.

Johnny finishes his coffee and then rides out to the smelter works. Johnny spots Ed Julian and another man in a room sitting on chairs. They were not dead, but kind of in-between, like Johnny before he passes out.

Johnny wakes up to see a man who tells him why he is there, and that Ed Julian does not need anything. Reno tells Johnny that Ed did not want you to protect him, and you got into an argument. You pulled your gun and shot Ed and Chilly Winters, like this, and Reno shoots them. The police here only need your gun and you will be arraigned and tried right here in Salt City. You walked right into it.

Johnny jumps up and slugs Reno and manages to hit him with a lamp. Johnny walks back to town and goes to the Bar and Grill. Johnny finds Connie and tells her what happened and goes over the events of the morning with her. Johnny gives her $350 to buy a car and hides in her room while she gets a car. She packs and they drive to San Francisco.

Johnny calls the police and they tell him he is wanted for murder, and Johnny tells them he can explain it if they give him time. Johnny goes to Ed Gumby's office and then to his home where Ed opens the door with two bullet holes in his neck. Ed tells Johnny that Swifty and Luke did it an hour ago and then Gumby dies and Johnny wonders why people are dying where ever he goes. It was that same old feeling.

It winds up tomorrow, the whys and wherefores, love and hate, the usual ingredients for big explosions.

Episode 5   Show Date: 4/6/1956

Johnny is called by Eleanor and he tells her that he is wanted for murder and needs help. She tells Johnny that she will meet him on fisherman's wharf in her blue 1952 Ford convertible.

Johnny cabs to Fisherman's Wharf and is tired after two days of lost sleep. Eleanor drives up and he gets into her car and she drives off. Johnny will tell her what happened and asks her to go to Inspector Dan Walsh and tell him what he is going to tell her. Johnny tells her about Ed Gumby and the plan to get Ed Julian into jail to keep him out of trouble. Johnny tells of the trip to Salt City and Jim Reno's involvement and about Ed Gumby being shot. Eleanor takes Johnny to her office where Johnny sleeps.

Johnny goes to see the desk clerk at his apartment and tells him about the men he has seen killed, and how the clerk took a chance to come to see Johnny, but your kind does not take chances.

Johnny forces the man to tell him that Mr. Julian told him to tell all of them to make it difficult for Johnny. Then he sent a letter telling him where to send Johnny and then Johnny knocks the clerk out.

Johnny calls Eleanor to tell the police to pick up the desk clerk, and Swifty and Luke too.

Johnny goes to the Skyline Apartments to see Mrs. Julian. She tells Johnny that she did not expect to see him and he better leave before Ed gets there. Johnny tells her that Chilly and Ed are dead, and that she has been double-crossed. Johnny tells her that they wanted Chilly out of the way and that Jim Reno is in command. Ed had told her to get Johnny to go to Salt City.

Johnny asks her to sign a statement on how Ed Julian and Jim Reno planned to get rid of Chilly Winters and how Ed took Chilly to Salt City with him. About how he knew that Ed Gumby had a subpoena, and how Johnny would end up in Salt City and be a patsy for the killing of Chilly. Only Jim Reno decided he would be better off with them dead.

She tells Johnny that Ed Gumby knew all about the enterprises and they killed him. Jim Reno comes in and tells Johnny that he needs to go back to Salt City, and that Lorraine has $50,000 coming to her now. Reno knew that Johnny would be there, and he wants Johnny to go back to Salt City to talk to the police. Johnny slugs Reno, and Lorraine is shot. She asks Johnny to tell her she looks like a nice girl, and then she dies.

Johnny gets a lawyer to help explain what had happened and goes back to Hartford, after a long good bye to Eleanor. Johnny tells her that he will be back when the trial starts.

Exp. Acct: $3,262.00

Notes:
- The content for episode 2 was obtained from the script on file in the KNX Collection at the Thousand Oaks Library.
- Roy Rowan is the announcer.
- Musical supervision is by Amerigo Marino.

Producer:	Jack Johnstone	Writer:	John Dawson
Cast:	Barbara Fuller, Jeanne Tatum, Barbara Eiler, Lawrence Dobkin, Dick Ryan, Jack Edwards, Barney Phillips, Junius Matthews, Tony Barrett		

◆ ❖ ◆

Show: **The Laird Douglas Douglas of Heatherscote Matter**
Company: **Philadelphia Liability & Casualty Company**
Agent: **Harry Branson**
Synopsis:

Episode 1   Show Date: 4/9/1956

Harry Branson calls Johnny and tells him that he has a very important case. Laird Douglas Douglas of Heatherscote. "Can you come and see me, there is a nice retainer, expenses and commission if anything happens. Come by plane, this is urgent" Harry tells Johnny.

Johnny flies to Philadelphia, Pennsylvania and stays at the Benjamin Franklin, a nice hotel. Johnny is debating taking a shower when Harry calls and tells Johnny to come to his office immediately, this is an emergency due to the time issue.

Johnny takes his .38 Colt and goes to see Harry, who Johnny finds waiting on the sidewalk. Harry tells Johnny that "we have a serious problem with Laird Douglas Douglas of Heatherscote. He is in my office now, with Mrs. Peter Malcolm Kelly Van Piten. She insists you to act as his bodyguard, as she is aware of your work on the Ricardo Amerigo case and she is a very big policyholder".

Harry tells Johnny that the Laird has a $5,000 policy, a short life expectancy and that he is four years old. Harry is positive that the life of Laird Douglas Douglas is in danger. Johnny is told he has an expense account equal to his retainer of $750 a week. Johnny is told his services will only be required until the Laird appears at Bala Cynwyd.

Harry walks Johnny into his 13th floor office to meet Mrs. Van Piten and the Laird, who is asleep in Harry's office. They enter Harry's office to meet the Laird — who is a dog that goes after Johnny's leg.

Here's our star to tell you about tomorrow's intriguing...well tomorrows episode: Tomorrow, well I've handled some pretty doggy cases in my time, but never as a pooch's bodyguard. But suddenly this one starts to smell much too strongly of murder.

Episode 2   Show Date: 4/10/1956

Johnny is called by Ray Roland, and Johnny tells Ray that he may need his help. Let's have lunch. Have you met his Lairdship? "Yeah, I know" Ray tells Johnny.

Johnny buys a new pair of pants and recounts the case. At the introduction the Laird goes for Johnny's leg and tears up his pants as Harry reminds Johnny of the retainer and expense account. Mrs. Van Piten gives Johnny $150 to replace his trousers and a biscuit for the Laird. Johnny gives the biscuit to the Laird, who is now Johnny's best friend.

Mrs. Van Piten wants Johnny to stay at her place. When Johnny tells her that he is not sure about the case, she ups the retainer to $1,000 a week, and "the Laird, a Scotty, excuse me, a Scottish Terrier", is now Johnny's best friend.

Mrs. Van Piten tells Johnny that Bala Cynwyd is a dog show that the Laird must win, and he will unless someone interferes. Someone might try to dope him as it has been tried before, once last year and a few weeks ago. Mrs. Van Piten tells Johnny that Harrison R. Kenworthy will not get away with it, but she will not divulge any names. Johnny must watch over the Laird until he wins the show.

Johnny "talks over" the case and tells Harry he is doing this only for the money. Johnny asks about Kenworthy, who owns a Kerry Blue Terrier, Lady O'Diddies Rollamar Meen, who Johnny will just call Mimi.

Ray Roland arrives and Ray tells Johnny that Bala Cynwyd is the biggest dog show in the country and that Kenworthy owns Mimi, who is a champion dog. And, Mimi is the better dog. Ray tells Johnny that Kenworthy is loaded and is in love with Mrs. Van Piten, but she will not marry him until the Laird beats Mimi in the dog show, but Kenworthy would never allow that. It is deadly serious to them, it is all pride.

Last year the dog was poisoned and saved at the last minute. Mrs. Van Piten did not know it was poison. Johnny believes them, and the finger points to Kenworthy, but Ray tells Johnny that he and the police do not feel the same way. Ray urges Johnny to duck out on this case. Kenworthy is not guilty because on each occasion Mrs. Van Piten had a bodyguard who was murdered. Still want the case Johnny?

Tomorrow, well the joke is no longer a joke, especially when a killer trains his sights on me.

Episode 3   Show Date: 4/11/1956

Lt. Steve Howard from the police calls and Johnny asks him about a murder at the dog show last year. Johnny asks Howard if he wants to look at the setup for an attempted murder — his.

Johnny cabs to his hotel from Harry's office and his dog of an assignment. Howard arrives in Johnny's room and Johnny shows him his handbag, which is now locked. Johnny tells Howard that it was open when he left, and there was no sign of the maid in the room. Johnny had picked up the bag and it weighed too much, almost twenty pounds. Johnny shows Howard where a window had been pried open. Howard decides to call the office.

Johnny buys a new pair of pants and calls Mrs. Van Piten to advise of a delay. "Oh, have a couple of suits made and charge them to me" she tells Johnny. Johnny cabs to the police office and learns that his suitcase had explosives in it which would have gone off if he had opened it. Johnny was suspicious because of the previous deaths of bodyguards, but Howard thinks that there is more to it.

Mrs. Van Piten's whole life revolves around the dog, and it would kill her if he died. She is a remnant of a fast dying class of very rich people who control others with their money, which is power. Howard has no idea who would be trying to kill her. She only has one living relative, a nephew Warren Staley, but the police can find nothing on him.

Johnny cabs to "The Maples" in Germantown where the Van Pitens live. The butler takes Johnny to the reading room, where Mrs. Van Piten and "Douggie" await him. Mrs. Van Piten asks Johnny to please call him Douglas, as Doug is such a common name.

She takes Johnny to his suite, and on the way there they meet Warren Staley, her nephew. Warren takes Johnny to his suite and gives him the tour, including the rooms for Douglas and Mademoiselle Poireau, the dog's governess. Johnny talks to Warren, who makes scotch and sodas for them in Johnny's room. He tells Johnny that he will be a very rich man when his aunt dies, but he wants to try and stand on his own two feet.

He is the only member of the empire left and he will survive to keep control of East Moreland Oil from Harrison Kenworthy with whom there has been a battle over control for years. Kenworthy has a son, Ronald, who is a good friend of Warren's.

Warren fixes himself a second drink, and Johnny asks him about the rivalry and the attempts on the dog. Kenworthy should be the primary suspect, and you should be suspect number two. Warren starts to stammer, and then complains of not being able to breathe, collapses and dies.

Tomorrow, things and people finally begin to line up on the case, just well enough for it to blow sky high.

Episode 4   Show Date: 4/12/1956
Lt. Howard calls and Johnny has been ordered confined to his room because he is the only one trust worthy enough to not destroy evidence.

Johnny calls the police and they arrive almost immediately. Johnny showers and shaves while waiting for Howard and the lab boys to arrive. When they get there, Johnny explains what happened.

Mrs. Van Piten rushes in hysterical with Ronald Kenworthy, who blames Johnny for the death. Ronald tells Johnny that he had been there for 45 minutes and was talking to Mrs. Van Piten and was on his way to see Warren. Ronald takes Mrs. Van Piten out, and Johnny tells Howard that Warren was also concerned, and was going to tell him whom he suspected when he died. The police doctor tells them that the poison was penorphic acid, the same poison used on the dog and the previous bodyguards.

Johnny tells Howard that Warren had poured a drink from a bottle, and Johnny notices that the bottles have been switched. Johnny and Howard go into the dog's rooms and then to the room of Mademoiselle Poireau, who is caught dressing and screams. Howard apologizes and tells her to get dressed and assigns a guard to her.

Howard tells Johnny that he goofed and allowed someone to switch the bottles while he showered. Johnny tells Howard he goofed too, by smudging any prints on the doorknobs. Howard would peg this on Johnny, except for his reputation.

Johnny and Howard go downstairs and listen to the questioning of the household staff, which turns up nothing. Johnny has a lot of suspicions, which includes everyone, but there is no evidence.

The police search the house well into the evening and find nothing. Johnny stays with Mrs. Van Piten, who holds up rather well. She tells Johnny that Warren meant a lot to her. Johnny asks her about Warren being the sole heir of the family, and that Warren told Johnny that Kenworthy and his son would acquire the Oil Company holdings if he married Mrs. Van Piten.

Johnny is sure that now there is only one person who would benefit: Ronald Kenworthy. Suddenly Ronald appears and tells Johnny that he has said enough, too much for his health.

Tomorrow, all cards are laid on the table and believe me, the deck proved to have been stacked right from the beginning. Tomorrow, the windup.

Episode 5   Show Date: 4/13/1956
Ron Kenworthy calls and Johnny tells him that he is on his way over to see him. Ron tells Johnny to call the police as Johnny had accused Ron of killing Warren before Johnny threw him out of Mrs. Van Piten's house.

Mrs. Van Piten agrees that the attempt was really on Johnny's life, and he tells her of the attempt in the hotel. She agrees that Ronald stands to inherit the entire empire. "Ronald, who pretended to love me, and was Warren's best friend".

Johnny has no evidence, but she tells Johnny that she will help him get the evidence and Ronald will pay, and no one will stand in her way. She tells Johnny to shoot first, as Ron is a cornered rat.

Johnny walks to the Kenworthy estate and passes the garage where he sees Andy LeForte, a clever second story man who would do anything for money. He reasons that Andy could have planted the bomb and the poison.

Johnny goes to the gatekeeper's cottage and calls the police. The gatekeeper tells Johnny that Andy had been there about a year or so. Johnny talks to Lt. Howard and then goes to the Kenworthy mansion.

Ronald is upset about being thrown out and tells Johnny that Warren really wanted nothing of the estate and that she hated him for it. Ron tells Johnny that he and his father have been planning to dissipate their estate to benefit others. Ron will benefit, but he will have to work at it, he will be a man.

Johnny goes back to see Mrs. Van Piten and tells her about seeing Andy LeForte. Johnny tells her that he should have gotten wise sooner.

He recounts her pledge to marry Kenworthy, but the real reason was to get access to his assets. When she realized that her dog was not ready to beat the Kenworthy dog, she ordered the murder of the handlers. She learned of the disposal of the Kenworthy assets and that Warren wanted to do the same. She had also learned from Ray Roland that her dog did not have a chance so she would not let it compete.

She had someone booby trap Johnny's bags to get rid of him, and she killed Warren, which got another obstacle out of the way. Mrs. Van Piten offers Johnny money and then reaches for a gun. "Wouldn't it be easier if I just gave you $100,000, or $200,000?" she asks Johnny.

Andy LeForte comes in with a gun drawn and tells Johnny to get up, and Mrs. Van Piten tells him to do it now. Johnny tells Andy that she will kill him as he is shooting Johnny. Lt. Howard shoots Andy and Mrs. Van Piten tries to talk her way out of the situation, but Howard tells her to SHUT UP!

"Remarks: I'm glad I am poor."

Exp. Acct: $1,113.40

Notes:
- A Kerry Blue Terrier is any of an Irish breed of medium-sized terriers with a long squarish head, deep chest, and silky bluish coat.
- In an interview, Jack Johnstone said that he owns a Kerry Blue Terrier named "Lady O'Diddies Rollamar Meen".
- A Scottish Terrier is any of an old Scottish breed of terrier that has short legs, a large head with small erect ears and a powerful muzzle, a broad deep chest, and a very hard coat of wiry hair.
- Penorphic acid is a fictitious substance.
- Roy Rowan is the announcer.
- Musical supervision is by Amerigo Marino.

Producer:	Jack Johnstone	Writer:	Jack Johnstone
Cast:	Jeanette Nolan, Harry Bartell, Byron Kane, Jack Kruschen, Bill James, James McCallion, Ken Christy, Dick Ryan, Bert Holland, Jack Edwards, Hy Averback, Roy Rowan		

◆ ❖ ◆

Show:	The Shepherd Matter
Company:	Richard Porter
Agent:	Richard Porter
Synopsis:	
Episode 1	Show Date: 4/16/1956

Johnny receives a call from Dick Porter, a broker who wants to hire him. Porter has a client who is buying too much insurance, like he is getting ready to die.

Johnny flies to Providence, Rhode Island and has a drink with Dick Porter. Johnny is told that Dr. Shepherd called two days ago and asked about straight life insurance rates and bought an additional $80,000, for a total of $100,000. He is not married, and his mother is the beneficiary.

Porter is working on the paperwork, and he wants Johnny to look into him. He has a good practice in the area and lives over the office. Porter is suspicious because the doctor called him. Or he could be the one person in 100 who values insurance.

Johnny rents a car and collects information on Dr. Shepherd. Johnny learns that he is in good financial shape and belongs to several clubs.

Johnny goes to the office and asks to see the doctor. The nurse tells Johnny that the doctor is out, but Johnny tells her that he just saw him walk in. Johnny tells the nurse, Miss Corrine Streeter, that he wants to see the doctor and gives her his card. She tells Johnny that the doctor is seeing no one and has been acting strangely.

Johnny looks into the office, and sees the doctor holding a .32 automatic with the safety off. The doctor takes Johnny's credentials, and then apologizes to Johnny about the gun. He tells Johnny that he is very nervous and tells the nurse to leave early and lock up. Johnny has Dr. Shepherd set the safety and they go into the office to talk.

Johnny tells him that Mr. Porter had asked him to look into the policy, but the gun indicates he is in trouble. The doctor tells Johnny that a homicidal maniac has threatened his life. He would go to the police but a patient's welfare is involved.

Several months ago, he treated a woman named Forbes who was mentally distraught. He talked to her and discovered that her problem is her husband. He told her to move out and divorce the husband, as it would be the best thing to do. Dr. Shepherd explained the situation to the husband and he ranted and raved and attacked him. Johnny tells him that he should have called the police. Dr. Shepherd tells Johnny that the insurance was to care for his mother, in case something happened to him. Johnny tells Dr. Shepherd that he does not believe him.

Tomorrow, the Shepherd Matter becomes a matter even the police cannot handle.

Episode 2   Show Date: 4/17/1956

Dick Porter calls and Johnny tells him that Dr. Shepherd has been threatened and Johnny thinks he is a liar.

Johnny buys aspirin for Dick Porter and suggests that the policy might not be a good idea. Johnny tells Dick about the call to Dr. Shepherd who Johnny thinks is nuts or very clever, so Dick asks Johnny to stay in town for a few days.

Johnny goes to Dr. Shepherd's office where Miss Streeter is upset and asks if Johnny is the reason why the doctor is carrying a gun. Johnny is buzzed into the office and asks Dr. Shepherd if he wants to change his story. He tells Johnny that he still must be careful of Mrs. Forbes' condition. Johnny tells him to prefer charges, but Shepherd must be careful.

He tells Johnny that he could approach Paul Forbes and talk to him. Shepherd offers to pay Johnny to speak to Forbes but Johnny tells him he was going to anyway.

Johnny drives to the Forbes home in a very nice neighborhood. A man opens the door and hits Johnny with a gun and runs away. The butler, Upton, runs out and asks where Mr. Forbes is. Johnny tells Upton that Forbes hit him. Mrs. Forbes tells Upton to call the doctor and get the first aid supplies.

Johnny tells Mrs. Forbes who he is and Upton gives Johnny a drink while Mrs. Forbes apologizes for her husband's temper. Mrs. Forbes tells Johnny that he has attacked her physician and now him, he is mad, but Johnny notices a black eye on Mrs. Forbes. Upton is talking to Johnny as he regains consciousness.

Upton tells Johnny that he had fainted and that Forbes did attack Dr. Shepherd and Mrs. Forbes. This is an unhappy house.

Dr. Shepherd arrives and Johnny asks for an aspirin. Dr. Shepherd tells Johnny that he will prefer charges against Forbes and sends Mrs. Forbes upstairs. Dr. Shepherd tells Johnny to come to his office and calls the police.

Johnny leaves and thinks maybe he should not have left. He might have saved a life.

Tomorrow, well the big lie is as true as little green apples. Join us when I bite into one and spit out a bullet.

Episode 3   Show Date: 4/18/1956
Miss Streeter calls and she tells Johnny to come in for a head x-ray. The doctor is out right now and is most insistent.

Johnny takes a cab to see Dick Porter and they have a drink. Porter thinks that Johnny is finished, but Johnny wonders why he was hired. The doctor explained the reasons for the insurance, but not to Johnny's satisfaction.

Johnny tells about Forbes and the threats and that Johnny went to see Forbes this morning and was attacked. He was given first aid while the family apologized for Forbes' behavior. Johnny still thinks that Dr. Shepherd's story is still leaky.

The family said that Forbes had threatened Shepherd, but Shepherd lies. His reason for not calling the police and his description of Forbes as a homicidal maniac that Johnny could reason with. And why would Forbes hit him? Someone must have put someone up to it. Mrs. Forbes seemed ok, but she had been hit too.

Johnny cabs to the office for the x-ray which is done by Miss Streeter. Johnny asks Miss Streeter if she is in love with Shepherd, but she dodges the question and Johnny asks her "He is a liar, isn't he?" Johnny wonders why she did not ask who the friend was that hit him.

Johnny drives to the home of Clara Shepherd. Johnny introduces himself, and she tells Johnny that her son must be up to something. She has not seen or talked to him in three years and he does not think much of her as a mother. "Is it too early for a cocktail?" she asks Johnny.

She tells Johnny that she has told her friends that her son is successful and cares for her, and she feels that Johnny is nice to his mother. If she did get money from Charles it would make for a tax problem. Johnny has a martini with her and leaves at 4:00.

Johnny goes to Shepherd's office and officer Phil Crosby is there. Crosby tells Johnny that no one knows where the doctor is, and they need to get a signature on a complaint. Miss Streeter then finds a note about an emergency on Putnam Street.

Johnny tells Crosby that Forbes is really angry and they drive to the area of the emergency, which turns out to be a vacant lot. Johnny spots the doctor's car and Crosby calls for assistance. Johnny waits and Crosby drives up and tells Johnny that a report is out on Dr. Shepherd. Two blocks away they find the body of Dr. Shepherd.

Tomorrow, a liar is still lying even though he is dead. Tune in tomorrow and I'll tell you all about it.

Episode 4   Show Date: 4/19/1956
Officer Crosby calls Johnny to come down town, to room 203, City Hall. He wants a better story about Paul Forbes.

Johnny buys a paper and reads of Dr. Shepherd's murder. It appeared that Forbes lured the doctor out and killed him.

Johnny visits Crosby and several other police officers and Dick Porter. Johnny tells them how he had been hired and how Forbes had hit him and how he distrusted Dr. Shepherd. Crosby asks why Dr. Shepherd went out on an emergency and did not carry his bag and did not have the .32 you saw him with.

Johnny suggests that someone Dr. Shepherd knew and trusted lured him out. Crosby recounts all of Forbes' activities, yet Johnny still says the doctor is lying. Johnny is told that the police are looking for Forbes and they will find him.

Johnny goes to the morgue and meets Corrine Streeter. Johnny tells her that the police think Forbes killed the doctor. She wants to know why Johnny is not out helping find Forbes. She tells Johnny that she loved Doctor Shepherd more than her whole life and Johnny feels he has just heard the first truth in two days.

Johnny thinks about the case over dinner and drives to the office of Dr. Shepherd and bribes the guard to let him in. The guard tells Johnny that the police had just left, and they found the emergency bag. Johnny searches the office and finds no records for Mrs. Forbes, but he does find a record for Mr. Forbes.

Johnny goes to the apartment of Corrine Streeter, who has just gotten home. Johnny asks her who Dr. Shepherd was going to marry because he had made reservations on the *Ile de France* for June.

She tells Johnny that Mrs. Forbes was the only person the doctor has seen socially in the past year. Mr. Forbes came for a year and then stopped and went to another doctor in Baltimore. Johnny asks why he was brought into the case, and he suggests the wrong man was killed that night.

Johnny goes to visit Mrs. Forbes and tells her that he had been brought in to the case by the large purchase of insurance, so that he would be there to back up a self-defense plea. Johnny tells her that she and Dr. Shepherd were going to France. Her husband killed her boyfriend just like he said he would, but you have lost your doctor. She screams at Johnny to get out, and he goes to his hotel.

Johnny calls officer Crosby and tells him what he thinks happened and how it backfired. Johnny tells him that Forbes was supposed to die. While he is talking, Johnny is told to hang up by Paul Forbes, who has a gun, and is blazing mad.

Tomorrow, I find out how hard it is to kill a lie. Sometimes you have to kill it twice.

Episode 5   Show Date: 4/20/1956
The hotel operator calls and Johnny tells her he was cut off, but he wants to sleep and tells her to take a message if anyone calls. Forbes tells Johnny to stay quiet or he will shoot, and Johnny tells him he is crazy.

Forbes visits Johnny at seven in the morning. He saw Johnny at his house and followed him. Forbes wants to talk and he asks where Johnny's home is and where he practices. He asks if Johnny is licensed to practice law in Rhode Island.

Johnny tells Forbes that he is an insurance investigator looking into insurance for Dr. Shepherd. Forbes tells Johnny that Dr. Shepherd called him and said a lawyer named Dollar was coming over to talk about a divorce. Johnny now knows why Dr. Shepherd called him, and Forbes tells Johnny that he did not kill Shepherd. He is sure that Johnny is in on it to get his wife away from him and starts to beat Johnny, but Johnny overpowers him.

Forbes looks lifeless and Johnny pours a couple of drinks and gives Forbes one and tells him to talk. Johnny sees that the gun has not been fired and Forbes tells Johnny that he does not know where he was when Shepherd was shot. After he hit Johnny he drove to Shepherd's office to see him, and then back to his house and then just drove around.

He got some sandwiches and some drinks. He called Shepherd around 5 or 6 and wanted to meet him and talk to him. Forbes did not see Shepherd because he never showed up. He drove around and heard on the radio he was wanted for murder.

Forbes tells Johnny that Pauline had always had other friends, and he really needed her this year. She wanted a divorce but he would not give it to her. He needed her, and she knew he would be gone soon. He has leukemia and will be dead within a year. Johnny gives Forbes some sleeping pills and calls the clinic in Baltimore, and they confirm the leukemia.

Johnny drives to see Corrine Streeter, who is expecting him. She tells Johnny that it is an old story. She applied for a job and fell in love with the boss. She knew that the doctor was plotting to get rid of Forbes and had heard the doctor call Forbes and tell him a lawyer was coming over. She was there when he got the call and followed him. She pleaded and fought with him and the gun went off.

Johnny tells her that it was self-defense, but she tells him she cannot get off. She has just killed Mrs. Forbes.

Johnny tells Porter to call someone else if he ever needs a policy investigated.
Exp. Acct: $485.00

Notes:
- This story was done as *The James Clayton Matter*, broadcast on 12/5/1952.

- The *Ile de France* was a luxury ocean liner soon to be replaced with trans-Atlantic jet travel. The French liner was known for luxury first-class service.
- Roy Rowan is the announcer.
- Musical supervision is by Amerigo Marino.

Producer:	Jack Johnstone	Writer:	John Dawson
Cast:	Jeanne Bates, Virginia Gregg, Russell Thorson, Parley Baer, Herb Ellis, Barney Phillips, Lawrence Dobkin		

♦ ❖ ♦

Show: The Lonely Hearts Matter
Company: Northwest Surety Company
Agent: Dave Elwood
Synopsis:
Episode 1   **Show Date:**   4/23/1956

Dave Elwood calls and asks if Johnny is free. Dave tells Johnny to come over and meet a nice girl. Johnny mentions lonely hearts and Dave jumps. Dave tells Johnny that if the girl is telling the truth, it may mean murder.

Johnny cabs to the office of Dave Elwood and he tells Johnny about Norma Wells, who has just flown in from Chicago. Her father died suddenly three days ago of acute enteritis and he had a $50,000 term-life policy written five months ago. The beneficiary is his second wife Mabel Burke, who he married six months ago. Norma thinks that Mabel killed him. He had met Mabel through a lonely-hearts club.

Johnny talks to Norma who is very nervous. Johnny has Dave send out for some food while Norma tells Johnny that Mabel is strange, fuzzy around the edges. Not batty, but strange. Mabel would never let Norma be alone with her father. Norma is sure that she is not having a father fixation, but she was not suspicious until the night he died. Norma has a trust fund and some bonds, but the policy was Mabel's idea. She started talking about insurance the week they were married.

Her father was taken ill and Mabel would not allow him to call Norma, and she called her doctor, who has refused to sign a death certificate. Norma went to her father's doctor who suggested she come to the insurance company because the cause of death was questionable. Norma tells Johnny that he had met Mabel through a club of some sort.

Breakfast is brought in and Johnny tells Dave that the case needs looking into. Johnny will have Norma order an autopsy, but he will not bet that Norma is telling the truth.

Johnny and Norma fly to Chicago, Illinois where Johnny learns that an autopsy has been ordered but is being held pending a court order.

Johnny cabs to the Rendezvous Club and meets a lovely receptionist. Johnny asks how he can join the club and she tells Johnny that none of the women in the club are under 45. They will take his application and put the information in the bulletin. Johnny tells her he is looking for a friend named

Jonathan Wells, and she suspects that Johnny is with the police.

Johnny starts looking for the files and Johnny puts her on top of her desk when she complains. Johnny then enters a room where a cigar is still burning in the ashtray. Johnny learns that the receptionist is Fanny Tetler, who has worked there for a year. Johnny asks about a file on Mabel Burke and Fanny tells Johnny that Mabel owns the club.

Tomorrow, another day, another husband, another death, and a sweet little old lady rocks and smiles.

Episode 2   Show Date: 4/24/1956
Max Lancer calls from the District Attorney's office. He tells Johnny that the autopsy is still in progress. The family doctor thinks Norma is suffering from temporary hysteria and he was not serious in suggesting the insurance company. The death may have caused her to imagine things.

Johnny eats and muses over the facts. Maybe it was hysterical suspicion. Norma knocks on his hotel door and she is scared and wonders if she is crazy. She had gone to sign the authorization for the autopsy and went home. The phone rang and no one was on the line. Then she hears footstep outside her door, but no one was there. Then the phone rang again and no one there, so she came to see Johnny.

Johnny tells her that he can do nothing until the autopsy results come in. Johnny tells Norma that Mabel owns the club. Johnny mentions the cigar and Norma tells him that Burton Creely, Mabel's nephew, smokes cigars. He moved in with them right after the wedding and he is the reason she moved out as he was always after her. She does not think he works, but just sponges off of Mabel. Her father got along with Burton, but he was different around him. Johnny tells her to stay put and goes to see Mabel Wells.

Mrs. Wells opens the door and Johnny introduces himself. She tells Johnny that he is mistaken, Mr. Morningly is her agent. Johnny tells her he is from the main office and has some questions. She tells Johnny that she thinks death is a doorway to a much greater life. Norma used to live here, but she moved out.

Mabel offers Johnny some tea and cookies and tells him that Jonathan always had tea and cookies every afternoon at 4:00. That's how she won him, with cookies and cakes. She had been so lonely when she met Jonathan. Mr. Walter Maberly Burke had died two years earlier of acute indigestion. She started the club because she was lonely and Burton suggested she start the business, that's how she met Jonathan. But Burton actually runs the club. She will have to move soon and all she has is the insurance and the worst luck with husbands.

Johnny goes to his hotel and meets Max Lancer in the lobby, and he has his hat in his hands. Max tells Johnny that the autopsy showed that Jonathan Wells died of ground glass, so it is murder after all. Johnny asks Max to check on the death of Walter Maberly Burke in St. Louis.

Tomorrow, a strange attack, a scared girl, a hunt in the dark, and thirteen knots make a noose.

Episode 3   Show Date: 4/25/1956
Johnny gets a call from Dave Elwood and tells him about the autopsy report. Dave will stop the claim, which was filed that day. Johnny asks for the Mutual Records Service to check on Walter Burke's records. Dave calls her "Murdering Mabel", but Johnny tells him she is just a sweet old lady who has bad luck with husbands.

Johnny buys dinner for Norma and they eat in his room. Johnny is sure that Norma is right now. The autopsy report gives Johnny a green light to move forward now. Johnny is not sure that Mabel is the one who did it. Johnny tells Norma that Max Lancer had called the room, but she did not answer, and she tells Johnny that she was there.

Johnny and Norma cab to her apartment through a busy city. At her apartment the door is open, but she remembers locking it. Johnny goes in and finds no one there, but the apartment has been searched, someone was looking for something.

Norma looks through the apartment and fixes some coffee. She fixes hers with cream and sugar, which Johnny thinks looks funny. Johnny looks at the sugar, and finds ground glass in the sugar.

Johnny calls Max and arranges for a policewoman to escort Norma to a hotel. Johnny cabs to the Wells residence and asks for Burton and is told that he is not there.

Johnny goes to the club and opens the unlocked front door where he finds Creely with a gun. Johnny tells him the safety is on and takes it away from him. Creely tells Johnny that he is breaking in, so Johnny tells him to call the police.

Johnny tells Creely who he is, and about leaving the office the other day. Creely gives an excuse about thinking Johnny was a bill collector, and then that he was late for an appointment. He saw no necessity for talking to Johnny, as his aunt could tell him everything. When asked if he went to see Norma, Creely tells Johnny that Norma is a smug self-satisfied little phony.

Johnny tells Burton about finding the ground glass, the same thing that killed Jonathan Wells. Creely is amazed that Wells was killed. Who would do it, he was such a nice guy and never quarreled with anyone. Burton tells Johnny that he only tried to be friendly with Norma and is engaged to Miss Tetler. He has a heart condition and runs the club.

Creely gets excited when Johnny tells him that Mabel is a suspect. "Have you considered Norma as a suspect?" asks Creely. "Yes, I have." Johnny tells him.

Tomorrow, another murder comes to light, another link in a long chain, and an old lady weeps for the lost years.

Episode 4   Show Date: 4/26/1956
Dave Elwood calls and gives Johnny an update. Johnny is told that Walter Burke died and left Mabel $50,000. Johnny wonders if there had been husbands before Walter.

Johnny is visited by Max and he tells Johnny that he had been a guest of Mabel all night and wants to see Nora now. Johnny updates him on Mabel's husbands.

Nora arrives with her guard and Max tells Johnny that Gertie the guard used to beat up the men she arrested and had to be transferred.

Johnny goes to see Mabel who rattles on about Max and her husband. When Johnny tells her about the ground glass, she calls that ridiculous and tells Johnny that her husband would have known. She tells Johnny that one's death is written in the stars, and that astrology is as real as reincarnation.

Johnny receives a call from Max who tells Johnny that Walter Burke died of ground glass. Johnny hangs up just as Mabel collapses in pain.

Episode 5   Show Date: 4/27/1956
Max Lancer calls Johnny and asks how Mabel is. Johnny tells Max that it was ground glass, the same as her husband. Johnny tells Max that they were only going on suspicion about the insurance. Johnny thinks someone tried to murder her.

Johnny waits at the hospital for Mabel to recover. He had tagged her as a murderer, and now she has the key.

Johnny meets Burton Creely in the hallway and tells him she is weaker now. He wonders who would do such a thing. There had been no visitors to the house and she had always been a lonely person. Creely tells Johnny that the police think she killed Jonathan and then tried to kill herself. Norma walks up and Creely leaves.

Johnny tells her about Mabel's condition and she tells Johnny that Mabel is too mean to die. Norma thinks maybe she did it for remorse or is insane.

A nurse tells Johnny that Mabel wants to see him. Johnny and Norma go into the room, and Creely comes in a few moments later. Mabel is smiling weakly and tells Johnny that she is ready to die. She tells Burton to straighten his tie and is happy to see Norma there.

Mabel tells Johnny that she has been thinking, and that death is just a doorway. She tells Johnny that she did not kill Jonathan, and Johnny tells her he knew that. She had been puzzling over who did kill him and she has decided to tell Johnny. She chides Burton for giving her a box of chocolates that morning. She can understand why he did it. She tells Johnny to take Burton and give him a good talking to, he must not go around...and then she dies.

Burton pulls a gun and holds Norma as a hostage as he locks Johnny in a closet. Johnny finally breaks out and calls the desk only to learn that a man has stolen an ambulance.

Johnny meets Max downstairs and they follow the ambulance to signs of a crash. A man yells that there is a man with a gun in the woods.

Johnny goes into the woods and glimpses Burton and tells him to give up. Johnny has his gun at his side and cannot aim it. Norma pulls away from Burton and Johnny takes a chance and shoots. Johnny runs up and discovers that Norma is OK, but Burton is dead, shot in the heart.

"Remarks: A heart with a bullet hole in it, there is a real lonely heart."
Exp. Acct: $416.40

Notes:
- The content for episode 4 was obtained from the script on file in the KNX Collection of the Thousand Oaks Library.
- Ground glass is used as a murder weapon in this story, and in *The Fatal Filet Matter*. There are several articles on the internet that dispel the effectiveness of ground glass as a murder weapon. But it does make for a good story.
- Roy Rowan is the announcer.
- Music supervision is by Amerigo Marino.

Producer: Jack Johnstone Writer: Les Crutchfield
Cast: Lucille Meredith, Mary Jane Croft, Virginia Gregg, Herb Ellis, Howard McNear, Stacy Harris

◆ ❖ ◆

Show: **The Callicles Matter**
Company: **Eastern Casualty & Trust Company**
Agent: **Dave Blaine**
Synopsis:
Episode 1   Show Date: 4/30/1956

Robert Ekker calls Johnny about an appointment with Mr. Parsons. Johnny wants to talk about David Parsons, who is missing. Johnny is told that Mr. Parsons Sr. is home ill today. Come to the office and I will arrange to take you out there. Johnny does not want to be any trouble, but Ekker tells Johnny that there would be more trouble if he did not come to the office.

Johnny flies to Los Angeles, California and meets Robert Ekker at Parsons Stocks and Bonds. Ekker asks why Johnny thinks David Parsons is missing. They do not know where he is, but he is not missing. Johnny tells Ekker that David has not been seen for ten days, and that is missing. Ekker tells Johnny that when talking about David with his father, do not use the word missing as Mr. Parsons Sr. is very adamant about some matters.

Johnny tells Ekker that David Parsons is insured for $100,000 and has access to large amounts of stocks and bonds, and that is why the insurance company is interested. Ekker tells Johnny that David Parsons is worth over a million dollars.

Johnny finds copies of the insurance policies on Ekker's desk and tells Ekker that he has looked up the answers to the questions Johnny had just asked him.

Johnny and Ekker drive to the home of David Parsons Sr. in a new 1956 Studebaker Golden Hawk, and Ekker avoids all talk of David Parsons Jr. In the home, Mrs. Parsons greets Johnny and tells him he is not supposed to meet her. The matter will be handled from "upstairs" as her father in-law feels he has extraordinary powers in this matter. Mr. Parsons screams for Ekker and Mrs. Parsons leaves.

Ekker and Johnny go to Mr. Parsons' bedroom where Mr. Parsons is in bed. Parsons demands Johnny's ID and yells at Ekker to call Boston and check on

Johnny. Johnny tells him that his ID is real and he can call him at his hotel. Johnny thought Mr. Parsons could straighten things out, but it appears Johnny will have to go to someone else. Johnny tells Parsons that he must find out about the situation, and Parsons tells Johnny he will break him in half if he tries.

Ekker is told to leave and Johnny is told he has five minutes. Johnny tells Parsons he has five minutes, ten minutes or a million minutes if he needs them. Johnny has a report that Parsons' son has been missing for ten days, one of David's clients reported it. Parsons says "bah" to Johnny and gets really mad when Johnny asks if he has had an audit. Ekker is called and told to throw Johnny out, but Johnny tells Parsons that he has Ekker by 25 pounds. Ekker tells Johnny he will wait downstairs.

Parsons relents and tells Johnny that David had left a week ago Tuesday, and they have heard nothing, and that the police have not been called. They are waiting to hear from David. Parsons has not looked to see if anything is missing and tells Johnny that he will post $100,000 in cash if necessary. Parsons does not want the matter in the papers. Johnny tells him that he cannot transfer liability, and you better fix it so I can talk to Mrs. Parsons. Johnny leaves the bedroom as Parson is looking for something to throw.

Johnny meets Mrs. Parsons at the front door and he tells her he wants her to file a missing person's report. She tells Johnny to come see her at 2:00. Ekker tells Johnny to be careful, as Johnny is Parsons' kind, his dish of meat.

Johnny ignores Ekker's comment, and compares Parsons to Svengali and Rasputin, but Parson is not in the same class with them, but he should have guessed it. Ekker was trying to tell me, but I would not listen.

Tomorrow, some more facts on how the earth swallowed a man.

Episode 2   Show Date: 5/1/1956
Mrs. David Parsons calls Johnny and asks if she can pick him up at his hotel. If her father in-law knew she was meeting him, he would probably kill her.

Johnny calls Dave Blain and explains the case so far, and how Parsons Sr. tried to throw him out. Dorothy Parsons picks up Johnny and he comments on how it looks as though she is going on a picnic. She is going to drive to the ocean, and tells Johnny to stop looking glum. She suggests going to lunch to talk.

She stops the car and they walk along the beach. She tells Johnny that she married David when she was 18 and has been married for 14 years. They live well and David is successful, but Johnny notices that she does not talk about missing David, and he does not believe her. Why does no one want to talk about this, he wonders.

Dorothy tells Johnny that she last saw David on Tuesday at breakfast, he ate and left for work. She called later and he had not come in to the office. Tuesday night she was out with friends and came in late and did not look in David's bedroom. On Wednesday, Ekker called and asked to speak with David, who was not at the office. She then called David's father, who said he would handle things. He hinted that David might have gone off with someone because he had gone off several times before and said nothing when he came back.

She tells Johnny that David is brilliant and impeccable and a devoted husband. Johnny asks her if she expected Johnny to make love to her and she says "yes, why?" She thinks she is attractive and Johnny asks why she stalled him all afternoon. Johnny asks why she told him she would call the police and then changed her mind. She tells Johnny that she wants to go home.

While Dorothy makes a phone call at a gas station, Johnny watches southern California roll by. Dorothy tells Johnny that she had called home and Johnny tells her he is going to the police. She tells him that there is no need, as David has come home.

They start to drive to the Parsons home and there is a crash, Johnny is shaken up and Dorothy is dead.

Tomorrow, trouble comes early and stays late.

Episode 3   Show Date: 5/2/1956
Dave Blaine calls and wonders why Johnny is in the hospital. Johnny tells of meeting with Dorothy and the accident. Parsons is back, and he will wrap it up. She was a nice person, and he saw her die.

Johnny gets a sedative at the hospital and wakes up screaming "Look Out!". Sister Amadea tells Johnny to go to sleep, but Johnny wants to talk about it. He tells her about the case and what he had learned. It was a strange afternoon, he could have fallen in love with her. He tells her he never gets used to things like this and goes back to sleep.

The next day Johnny buys a paper and reads of the accident, an unidentified woman was killed. No names, no details. Ekker visits Johnny in his hotel room and tells him that Mr. Parsons Sr. is concerned about him, and young Parsons is upset over his wife.

Johnny settles up his hotel bill, buys plane tickets and goes to the Parsons home. Parsons still has a vile temper and blames Johnny for Dorothy's accident. Johnny helps himself to Parsons' whiskey, and then meets David Parsons, who is not what Johnny expected. He did not look like a broker.

David tells Johnny that he rode a freighter up to Seattle, he just wanted to be alone and think and decided not to tell anyone. Johnny asks David to sign some reports and Johnny asks the name of the ship, which David says was the Loreen B, a lumber ship. Johnny checks back into his hotel, cancels his plane reservations and calls Ekker, who is not in.

Johnny rents a car and drives to Ekker's apartment and waits for him. Ekker comes in, and leaves with Johnny following right behind him to the Parkway Funeral Home. After waiting a few minutes, Johnny goes in to see Ekker looking at the body of Mrs. Parsons.

Johnny asks Ekker who she is, because she is not Mrs. Parsons. Ekker tells Johnny that the girl is Ellen Myers, his fiancé. She was a special girl, and he loved her and she would do anything for him. Parsons had blown up and she volunteered to mislead Johnny.

The "David Parsons" is just someone the old man hired, he has 23 detectives looking for the real David. Parsons wants it kept quiet because there is a merger in the offing and he wants David clean and unsullied when the merger is complete.

Johnny tells Ekker that he was wise to the fake David because he was not broken up, and because he was a bad actor. He also gave some bad answers to being on a ship. Ekker tells Johnny he will help him.

Tomorrow, we find out that Callicles was a Greek, maybe the greatest one of them all.

Episode 4   Show Date: 5/3/1956
The operator calls with Johnny's number, and Johnny tells Parsons that he is still looking for his son. Johnny has two signatures that constitute a witness forgery. I'd be willing to call a lawyer and see what kind of noise I can make. I'll be there in 20 minutes.

Johnny hires an attorney to impound the records of the brokerage house and gives him the forged reports.

Johnny drives to see Parsons and tells him that he did not believe either of the actors. "You have botched up everything. You tried to drive me off the trail" he tells Parsons. Johnny gets the name of the detectives, Universal Operators, and Mr. Underwood as the detective Parsons had hired, but they have gotten no leads.

Johnny tells Parsons that he has started the process of an audit and Parsons goes ballistic. Johnny is told that the real Mrs. Parsons has been sent to Palm Springs and Johnny tells Parsons to call her, get her up here and let her know that he will talk to her at 2:00.

Johnny drives to Underwood's office and gets a report on what they have done. Johnny fires Underwood and tells him that Parsons would confirm it. After lunch, Johnny drives to the home of David Parsons and speaks to the real Mrs. Parsons.

She tells Johnny that she was the last person to see David, on the 13th. He had not packed any clothes and he has no enemies, but he never discussed the office at home. They have been married 18 years and have never talked of divorce. The office thinks he is on a business trip.

They entertained and traveled and enjoyed their life. He liked to read and write and fancied himself a scholar of literature. David was not a drunk and was in good health and had a quiet personality.

She tells Johnny that she has been seeing some friends in Palm Springs. Johnny is getting mad and tells her to file a missing person's report, as she may have fooled around too long. The police arrive and interview everyone. The District Attorney negates Johnny's court order and starts their own audit.

Johnny visits David's physician, Dr. Warner, and tells him about David being missing. Johnny is told that David was in excellent health for a man in his position. David knew how to escape from his father and had no mental problems. They played golf and the Parsons seemed happy.

He had talked to David informally once, and he could quote the classics. One time he just stared off into the distance and quoted Callicles: "But if there were a man who had sufficient force, he would shake off and break through and escape from all this. He would trample under foot all our formulas and spells and charms, and all our laws, which are against nature. The slave would rise in rebellion and be lord over us and the light of natural justice would shine forth." He quoted it the day before he disappeared.

The answer is with a Greek who lived two thousand years ago. Tomorrow, we'll find it.

Episode 5   Show Date: 5/4/1956
David Parsons Sr. calls Johnny and tells him that the papers are full of David's disappearance. Johnny ask if he wants him to give the papers the other half of the story, about arranging for people to impersonate your son.

Johnny buys the newspaper and reads about the story. He calls Parsons later and tells Parsons that he should have called the police earlier. The District Attorney has impounded the books, and $5,000 is missing from David's personal account, it was withdrawn on the morning he disappeared. Parsons tells Johnny that David means nothing to him, the only reason he wants him back is to complete the merger.

Johnny goes with officer Jerry Ingle to interview a bank teller who has the withdrawal slip. The teller tells Johnny that Parsons came up and gave him the slip. He was a little surprised, but Parsons has withdrawn large amounts before, and Parsons asked for it in $100s and $50s. The teller tells them that Parsons was not in a hurry that morning, like he did not care what direction he went in. Other Angeles are investigated, and Parsons is spotted all over the area.

Johnny locates a bartender who remembers seeing Parsons there. He did not talk to anyone and was making a long-distance call and had asked for $20 in quarters. Parsons had asked him if he knew Callicles. Johnny tells Ingle that Callicles was a poet and the bartender tells them he thought he was a bookie.

Ingle checks with the phone company and learns that a call had been placed to Kenneth Temple in San Francisco. Johnny calls and gets no answer at the number, and then drives to the Parsons' home.

Mrs. Parsons does not know who Temple is and is getting upset as the phone rings with a call for officer Ingle. Mr. Temple is on the phone and Temple says that Parsons is with him now. Mrs. Parsons talks to David, who asks if she remembers the times he had asked her to talk to him. About all the time she was too busy with other things. David tells her that this is the end of things for them, and for father too. Tell him that. Tell him the merger is all his. His anger does not worry me anymore. He is going away with Temple. He is shipping out on Temple's boat and will not be coming back. Johnny asks about Callicles. So, you found out, and he repeats the verses.

The police close their case and the insurance company will have to sit on the $100,000 bond and hope David Parsons comes back.

"Remarks: 'Why didn't he talk about these things to me?' Mrs. Parsons asked. I told her he did but no one ever listened. She didn't understand that either."
Exp. Acct: $1,100.59

Notes:
- Grigory Yefimovich Rasputin (1872-1916) was a Russian mystic and court figure with a pervasive influence over the imperial family.
- Svengali was a maleficent hypnotist in the novel *Trilby* (1894) by George du Maurier.
- One night in the hospital: $14.95 ($135 in 2017 dollars)   not a bad deal.
- The quote is from Plato's *Gorgias*: The speech of Callicles is from "convention" and "nature". Technically the references in the program should have been to Plato, not to Callicles.
- This story was done as *The Brisbane Fraud Matter*, broadcast on 5/23/1953.
- Virginia Gregg was in both versions of this story.
- Roy Rowan is the announcer.
- Music supervision is by Amerigo Marino.

Producer: Jack Johnstone   Writer: John Dawson
Cast: Virginia Gregg, Harry Bartell, Lillian Buyeff, Will Wright, Jeanne Bates, Carleton Young, Lawrence Dobkin, Bert Holland, Marvin Miller, Herb Vigran

• ❖ •

Show: The Silver Blue Matter
Company: Mono-Guarantee Insurance Company
Agent: Ralph Dean
Synopsis:
Episode 1   Show Date: 5/7/1956

Ralph Dean calls and tells Johnny that his wife wants to kill him. She wants a mink coat but he cannot afford one. Yesterday he lost 80 silver blue mink coats in Los Angeles and she wants to know why he can pay for 80 minks and not buy her one. Johnny tells him to buy her flowers and Ralph tells him he did, and they went into the disposal. So now what do I do?

Johnny flies to Los Angeles, California and meets Lt. Ramon Garcia at the airport. Johnny is told that there is a man dying in the hospital that Johnny needs to talk to, the night watchman who saw the thieves, they were just kids, a gang.

Johnny and Garcia rush to the hospital and wait for the night watchman to wake up. Johnny learns that the guard is Albert Crismun, who has no family, and was beaten by the gang members. He worked in a warehouse district. The police check the area regularly, and the kids hit 3 minutes after the police went by. The kids only know minks and passed up Chinchilla coats worth twice as much.

Crismun's partner was on his rounds and was slugged, and no one saw anything. Crismun wakes up and asks for water and asks who Johnny and Garcia are. He tells them the kids came with a telegram, he opened the door and one of them hit him. The kid was 18 or 19, dark skinned with a dark jacket. Crismun says he would recognize one of them, he had a mark on his arm and then he loses consciousness. Garcia tells Johnny that in that neighborhood there are 50,000 kids in who fit that description.

Johnny talks with the owner of the furs and then goes to the warehouse and inspects it. Like the police, Johnny finds nothing. Garcia tells Johnny that he grew up in the area, and it is a backwash of society. The residents are not on their side, they always are against the police. There are gangs there, and some of them are pretty rough.

They probably used the lunchroom across the street to case the warehouse. Red Wellers is the owner and Johnny is told that he might be able to get something from him. Garcia tells Johnny to remember that Crismun may die before he makes any deals.

Johnny meets with Red Wellers and he knows Johnny is working on the fur case. Red knows nothing and tells Johnny that the only people in the diner were old men with long beards. Johnny tells him that Crismun is dying, and gives him his hotel, just in case.

Tomorrow, fear stalks the streets, closing the mouths of a sullen and suspicious people, terrifying a lonely girl and bringing death in a dusty alley.

Episode 2   Show Date: 5/8/1956

Red Wellers calls Johnny and asks what will happen if he talks. Red tells Johnny that he will need money to move if he talks, and Johnny tells him he can take care of it.

Johnny calls Lt. Garcia at the hospital and learns that Crismun is still unconscious. Johnny waits for Wellers to arrive, but he does not show.

Johnny cabs to the warehouse and the area is deserted. Johnny goes to the diner and there is a girl working there.

Johnny asks about the boss and is told that he is not there. Johnny gets Red's address but the girl tells Johnny that Red was going out somewhere. Johnny tells her that he is working on the theft of the furs and she drops the silverware. She tells Johnny that she is Carla Monte and lives in the area and has worked there for a year. Carla tells Johnny that kids do hang out there, but she does not know any of their names, and Johnny recognizes that she is plainly scared.

Johnny tells Carla why she is scared and tries to convince her to talk, but she tells Johnny that he does not have to live here, and maybe the mobs have already taken over here. Johnny tells her that only a small minority turns to crime, but she cannot tell him anything.

On the way out, Carla asks Johnny if someone knew someone who could help, could he keep him or her out of it? Johnny tells her that he can be lenient, and she decides to trust him. She knows someone who might be involved, her brother Eddie.

Johnny cabs to Carla's apartment and then to a drive-in and then to a pool hall looking for Eddie. Carla tells Johnny that Eddie should not hang out there, but they have no parents and he will not listen to a sister.

They spot Eddie and she introduces Johnny. Carla wants Eddie to talk to him, and Johnny tells Eddie that he wants to talk. Johnny asks if Eddie knows anything about the robbery and Eddie tells Johnny that he "don't know nothin' about nothin'" and leaves.

Johnny calls Garcia and learns that Eddie was involved in the robbery. Johnny tells Carla that Red Wellers has been found dead in an alley.

Tomorrow, a lonely broken-hearted girl, a blood-stained shirt, and a fight with a cornered rat.

Episode 3   Show Date: 5/9/1956
Lt. Garcia calls Johnny just as he has finished his breakfast. Garcia demands that Johnny come to headquarters, he wants to know more about Eddie Monte.

Johnny cabs to Garcia's office and they talk about the case. Garcia apologizes for yelling at Johnny and tells him that the chief was on his back. Garcia wants to know how Eddie figures in, as he has a record for petty crimes.

Johnny tells him the things he learned from Carla and how he went to see Eddie. She suspected Eddie and asked Johnny to help keep Eddie out of trouble.

Garcia tells Johnny that Red was killed for trying to talk about the kids using the diner for a lookout spot. Johnny feels that Carla is a nice girl, and is special, in spite of everything. Garcia tells Johnny that he knows what Johnny is talking about. He had a sister who was special, but she ended up in prison.

The police have been checking fences with no results so Johnny cabs to the diner to see Carla. The diner is closed, so Johnny walks to Carla's apartment, where the door is locked.

Carla lets Johnny in and tells him that Eddie did not come home last night. Johnny asks for two drinks and makes her take one to relax. Johnny tells Carla that the police are looking for Eddie in connection with Red Wellers' murder. They think Eddie is a member of the gang. Carla tells Johnny that Eddie was out all night and did not come home until morning.

Just as Johnny asks to look through Eddies' room he comes home. Carla tells Eddie to give himself up, and Eddie tells Carla that she sold him out because his friends told him the police were looking for him. Johnny starts to call the police and Eddie pulls a gun.

Johnny is told to back off and Carla is told to pack some clothes for him. Carla tells Eddie a police car has just pulled up. Eddie threatens to kill Carla, and then runs out the door.

Tomorrow, a police net tightens and traps a frightened rat, a boy sobs in a jail cell, and an innocent man dies in his sleep.

Episode 4   Show Date: 5/10/1956
Lt. Garcia calls and Johnny tells him that the police are still there, but Eddie got away. Johnny tells him that he is looking for the furs, not Eddie. Johnny is

told that the police are looking for Eddie's friends on the list.

Johnny feels like 2 cents and looks out the window. Johnny surveys the slums, which have fostered Eddie and so many others and Carla blames herself for Eddie's problems. Johnny tells her she did the best she could. Carla asks why Johnny did not use his gun to kill Eddie, and he does not know why.

Johnny looks though Eddie's room and plays a record to keep him company. Johnny finds nothing but a lot of photos of hotrods. Johnny finds a recent photo of a hotrod with Eddie beside it. Obviously, it is his, but Carla does not know that he owns one. Johnny thinks Eddie might have used the truck to carry the furs, and that Eddie is the leader of the gang.

Johnny cabs to Garcia's office and learns two of Eddie's friends have been picked up, but one had an alibi. Johnny shows him the photos of the truck and the license plate. Garcia does not recognize the background and he agrees to have copies made.

Johnny and Garcia question Mario Santores, who has a record for possession of stolen goods, and he claims that he was framed and does not know anything. Johnny tells him that Eddie Monte remembers a lot about what he and Mario did and who was involved, but Mario has not heard of the robbery. Mario starts to stumble and admits he heard of the robbery. Johnny tells him that Eddie told about Mario stabbing Red Wellers and Mario tells him that Eddie lied to them. Mario agrees to tell them the truth.

Tomorrow, a cautious search, an ambush, bullets and tears, and the end is violence

Episode 5   Show Date: 5/11/1956

Carla calls Johnny in Lt. Garcia's office, and he tells her that the police have picked up Mario, who has just made a statement and that Mario says that Eddie planned everything. She tells Johnny that she is coming to headquarters as she wants to be there if Eddie is brought in.

Johnny reads Mario's statement, and thinks he was telling the truth about Eddie buying the truck and organizing the robbery. Crismun's remark about a boy with a mark on his arm matches the mark on Mario's arm. Mario also told them that Chuey Marel killed Wellers, and that no one knows where Eddie took the furs. So far Eddie is only guilty of the robbery, and Garcia is glad for Carla.

Garcia gets a call and learns Chuey Martel has been picked up, and that Crismun has died. Now Eddie is wanted for murder. Johnny rents a car and searches the area with Carla looking for the area in the photograph.

In an alley, Carla spots the fence and shack in the photos. Johnny tells Carla to call the police from a nearby house and then walks to the shack in the near darkness.

Johnny finds Eddie's truck behind the shack with the furs, and Eddie is there with a gun. Eddie knows about Crismun, and Johnny urges him to give up, as Carla is with him. Eddie is going to kill Johnny, and Johnny keeps talking to him about Carla, and what he is doing to her.

Carla calls for Johnny just as Garcia runs up to the shack. Johnny tells

Garcia that Eddie has jumped the fence and is running across the railroad yard. Garcia and Johnny chase after him as Eddie is trying to outrun a train, but he does not make it. Garcia tells Johnny that "there must be better ways to die."

"Remarks: Well, I guess Carla made the remarks for me. 'I don't know Johnny. Those 80 fur coats, they will go back into stock now and they will be sold to women who will wear them to parties and dances and night clubs, and they will be happy in them and they will never know about Eddie or me or what happened here tonight.'"

Exp. Acct: $541.25

Notes:
- Roy Rowan is the announcer.
- Music supervision is by Amerigo Marino.

Producer: Jack Johnstone   Writer: Les Crutchfield
Cast: Lucille Meredith, Edgar Barrier, Vic Perrin, Jack Kruschen, Tommy Cook, Richard Crenna

♦ ❖ ♦

Show: **The Medium, Well Done Matter**
Company: **Universal Adjustment Bureau**
Agent: **Pat McCracken**
Synopsis:
Episode 1   Show Date: 5/14/1956

Pat McCracken calls and asks if Johnny has had his fortune told. Johnny tells Pat that he has, a fortuneteller, Madam GaGa told him he would become an insurance investigator and it has stuck. Pat asks how Johnny would like to try his hand as a psychic investigator.

Johnny cabs to Pat's office and he does not know what type of case this will turn out to be. Pat tells Johnny that Tommy Green in New York has a young, badly spoiled (Johnny loves 'em that way) client named Carol Sharpe who is a playgirl and has a $110,000 policy with the family as beneficiaries. She just requested Tommy to change the beneficiary to a man named Tony Ricardo and a Madam Celia something. Tommy had another client turn up dead after making a medium the beneficiary.

Johnny travels to Tommy Green's office in New York City, and Tommy outlines the case. Tommy tells Johnny that spiritualism is a recognized religion, but there are charlatans, and one had bilked his mother when he was a kid. Madam Celia Morgana Morgana is the one in this case. Tommy has not changed the beneficiary yet, but he cannot stall too much longer. Tony sounds like a play-boy, but Tommy does not know much about him.

Johnny cabs to the Bell Towers on the East River and inquires about a small apartment for a few days. Johnny is told that there is a five-room penthouse available for $1,500 a month. Johnny shows the manager his card and asks for something near Miss Sharpe. She is not in trouble and Johnny does not want her to know he is there. There is a two-room apartment on floor 10 available at $325 per week, one week in advance.

Johnny calls an old buddy, Randy Singer, and Johnny wants to meet with him. Johnny orders a bottle of scotch and when Randy gets there he tells Johnny that Carol Sharpe is loaded and throws her money around at the clubs. Randy also knows Madam Celia Morgana Morgana, he has chased her all over the island of Manhattan. She sees the past, the future and right into your pocket book, and is operating in Jersey now. She operates with class. She goes into a trance and makes with the voices. She claims the trances cause great agony of body and mind and tells of her medical bills and the clients pay. At each séance she tells them just a little and has them hanging, and if you come back next week she will tell you more. Randy tells Johnny that he will see if he can dig up a séance to show him what goes on. There are dozens, hundreds to choose from. Randy had handled the case Tommy Green told him about. Johnny asks Randy to run a make on Tony Ricardo.

Johnny ponders how to meet Carol Sharpe and the phone rings. Randy has setup a date with a medium for tonight. Randy can write a book on Ricardo. Make sure you meet him first and carry a gun.

Tomorrow, well sometimes the best laid plans can take a terrible beating when a lovely girl steps into the picture.

Episode 2   Show Date: 5/15/1956

Randy calls and tells Johnny that he has nothing new on Tony Ricardo, just look out for him. Randy is working on setting up a séance and will call Johnny.

Johnny talks with Tommy Green and wonders what will happen if Madam Celia turns out to be OK? Johnny tells Tommy that Randy had hinted that Tony was not legitimate. Tommy is sure that Celia is a fraud.

Johnny tells him that he is staying at the same apartment building and asks Tony to find out how the family in Pennsylvania is doing. Get the local newspaper to run a fake news story or something, editors love to talk.

Johnny cabs back to the apartment and runs into Carol in the elevator. Johnny acts spacey and tells her that he must be psychic. He cannot believe it. He used to have a dream as a kid about a girl named Carol, and she looks just like the girl in the dream. Johnny apologizes and tells her he must have just imagined it.

Carol tells Johnny that he had a veridical dream, a "truth dream", a psychic experience. Johnny tells her that he does not believe in that, but she tells him that there are thousands of cases on record. Johnny apologizes again and goes to his apartment.

Johnny notices that Carol saw which apartment he went into. Fifteen minutes later Carol calls and tells Johnny that she wants to talk to Johnny about his dream. She got his name from the desk clerk. When she tells Johnny her name is Carol, they arrange to meet for drinks later.

Randy calls and tells Johnny that he has a séance set up for tonight. Meet me around seven at headquarters.

Johnny and a well-dressed Carol meet in the cocktail lounge and Johnny tells her she probably thinks he was just trying to pick her up. Johnny orders sherry and bitters for Carol and VO over ice for himself. Carol talks about the dream Johnny had and she tells him that the only way he could have known her was through a psychic experience. Johnny almost tells Carol who he is, but the waiter interrupts and saves him.

Carol tells Johnny about Madam Morgana Morgana and the messages she has received. Carol begs Johnny to go to see Madam Morgana Morgana with her. Johnny agrees and Carol agrees to set up a meeting for tomorrow.

Johnny stops by his room before going to see Randy, and there is a note under his door, "If you value your life you will stay away from Carole Sharpe."

Tomorrow, I find out a thing or two about a killer and about a medium not so well done.

Episode 3   Show Date: 5/16/1956
Tony Ricardo calls and asks if Johnny has received his note. Tony is anxious when Johnny tells him the police will be interested in it. Tony wants to see Johnny and leaves his phone number, Sunrise 3-9970.

Johnny cabs to the 18th precinct where he tells Randy about meeting Carole and the dream story and going to see Madam Morgana Morgana tomorrow.

Randy shows Johnny the file on Tony Ricardo, who has a record a mile long. Johnny tells Randy that the man he talked to was much younger than the man in the file. Randy remembers that Tony has some kids, including Anthony Jr., a Rutgers graduate.

Johnny and Randy cab to the location of the séance and are met at the door by a tall dark man who takes them in to the temple, an old dining room with a table and chairs. After a flash of light and a puff of smoke, the medium, Madam Clarabelle, appears in the room wearing an old bed sheet, a turban and the faint odor of gin. Each person is asked to put something personal on a tray, and Johnny puts in his watch.

They all join hands to form a flux, and her assistant Hemmingway passes among them asking for $5.00. The medium asks for "Votan" to join them, and there is a knocking on the floor. A ring is picked up and she sees clothing and sewing machines. She picks up Johnny's watch and sees tall buildings and sees Tri-Mutual and Universal Adjustment, and papers with "policy" written on them. I have many things to tell you.

She picks up Randy's badge and yells "A COP!" and the séance is over. Hemmingway bolts out the door, but Randy holds on to Madam Clarabelle and she tells Randy that all the money goes to charity.

Johnny asks how she knew so much about him, and she tells him that Hemmingway (that bum!) asked where you came from, and Hartford is known for insurance. The clothing maker called from a hotel, so she called the hotel back and got his address in Woodbine, New Jersey. There is nothing there but farms and clothes factories, and he was not a farmer. It was so easy.

Johnny goes back to his hotel and Randy tells Johnny that Madam Morgana

Morgana will not be so easy to expose, if you can expose her.

Tomorrow, the medium, well-done appears.

Episode 4   Show Date: 5/17/1956
Carole calls Johnny and tells him that she has made the arrangements for the séance to night at eight. Carole agrees to have dinner with Johnny at six.

Johnny meets Tony Ricardo whose father was a well-known gangster. Tony apologizes for the threatening note and tells Johnny that he is concerned about the spiritualist who is influencing Carole. Johnny tells him that he knows that Tony is going to be named as a beneficiary, but Tony tells Johnny that it was Madam Morgana's idea. When Johnny tells him that the dream sorry was made up, Tony is speechless.

Johnny tells him that he is an investigator and is meeting with the medium to try and prove that she is a fraud. Tony is afraid that Carol will change her policy and turn up dead. Tony briefs Johnny on how Madam Morgana Morgana conducts her meetings.

Johnny calls Tommy and he tells Johnny that the family is doing fine in Mauch Chunk, Pennsylvania. The mother and two brothers will not have to work for a living. Dave is the bad sheep, and tears around the country in a sports car and is somewhere here in New York now.

Johnny calls Randy and asks him to find David Sharpe, no description, staying somewhere here in the city. Call me when you find him.

Johnny cabs to a camera shop and buys a small camera, special film and very special flash bulbs.

Randy calls back and tells Johnny that they have located David Sharpe, it was just dumb luck. He is staying not too far from Johnny, and Johnny asks Randy to put a tail on him.

Johnny has dinner with Carol but is preoccupied. They take a cab to Union City and go to the house where Madam Morgana Morgana is. Madam Morgana Morgana, a plain woman welcomes them by name, and takes them inside. Johnny tells the woman that he doesn't think that he is psychic, but they thought his brother Richard was. The woman has a strange feeling about Richard, as that name has been on her mind all day.

Johnny meets the others in the circle and the séance begins. Johnny flicks a lighter, and is told he can smoke, but Johnny says it is just a nervous habit. Johnny notes some metal horns on the floor, through which the voices of the spirits come. Johnny flicks his lighter, and Carol tells him not to light it.

Madam Morgana Morgana writhes as if in pain and the séance begins. Carol hears a voice of her father and he talks to her, as Johnny takes pictures with his camera. The voice tells Carol to always do what he instructs her to do.

A voice calls "John", and Johnny calls for "Dick", his brother. Johnny carries on a brief conversation with Dick about things only a brother would know. Amazing! But Johnny notes that he never had a brother.

Johnny plays it straight and even stays around afterwards but cannot wait to develop the infrared film in the camera at the police labs.

Tomorrow, the wind up, and a bit of heartbreak for a very chastened girl.

Episode 5   Show Date: 5/18/1956
Carol calls and tells Johnny that he was so quiet on the way back last night. Carol tells him she paid $100 for the session. Johnny asks her to meet him for breakfast.

Johnny calls Randy and asks about the film and the tail. Randy tells Johnny that David was in the area of the séance last night. Johnny calls Mauch Chunk and talks to the local newspaper editor about the family, especially Dave.

At breakfast, Johnny tells Carole that he wants to see Madam Morgana Morgana again, today. Johnny mentions that Carol has a brother, David, and she tells Johnny that he is not really a brother. Her mother took him in, but she would rather not talk about it. Her father allowed it, but David's father had been a criminal, and his father was before him. Her father left money to him, but it was never enough.

When Carol asks how Johnny knows these things, he tells her who he is and why he is there. She tells Johnny that she hates him, and he tells her that he is sure that Madam Morgana Morgana is a fraud. Johnny tells Carol to call Tony and to meet him at the 18th precinct.

Johnny and Randy look at the pictures he took, and they are revealing. Carol and Tony arrive, and Johnny shows them the pictures. Carol sees Madam Morgana Morgana moving the trumpets with a rod. She also sees a tube coming from a trumpet where a man could whisper into it. Johnny shows the trumpet in front of him and tells Carol that the story of the brother was made up. Randy tells Carol about the fraudulent medium who could tell Johnny much more. Johnny reminds her of what he was able to find out about her, and Johnny asks if Tony was in with her. Randy tells Johnny that David is on the move again.

Johnny and the others take a cab to the house of Madam Morgana Morgana, and Johnny notices a Studebaker Golden Hawk with Pennsylvania tags parked in the back. Carole recognizes it as David's car. Randy stays out front while Johnny rings the bell and Madam Morgana Morgana opens the door, and Johnny invites himself in, with the others.

Johnny tells her that she will never have another séance, the monkey business is over. Johnny shows her the pictures and tells her about the camera he used. She tells Johnny that she was not doing anything malicious. Carol has money, as do the others who come to her. She tells Johnny that the insurance was not her idea.

Johnny asks where David is, and he comes into the room. David knows all about Johnny. Tony realizes that putting him as a beneficiary would send the police after him, allowing the others to get out of town.

The lights go out, and there are shots, and a fight breaks out, only Johnny ends up beating on Randy, and Tony had grabbed David when the lights went out. Randy tells Johnny that he had sneaked in the back door and took over when he saw what was going on.

"Well, what happens to David Sharpe and Madam Morgana Morgana is up to the courts. It's a cinch she is out of the ghost rackets for a while, a long while. And of course, Carol did make a change in her policy, to cut off David. Oh, and if you don't mind, I'll hang on to that tricky little camera and stuff, in case I run into another medium, well done."

Exp. Acct: $892.90

Notes:
- According to the script title page this story is called *The Medium, Well Done Matter*, not *The Matter of the Medium, Well Done.*
- Randy Singer makes the first of many appearances as Johnny's long-time friend.
- One has to wonder at the tongue-in-cheek use of the name Clarabelle, at a time when the *Howdy Doody Show* was on television with a clown of the same name.
- Jack Johnstone mentioned in a taped interview that he had done a lot of investigations into psychic phenomenon for another radio program called *Somebody Knows.*
- This is the second reference to a Studebaker Golden Hawk, a really classy classic car which cost around $3,000 — about $27,000 in 2017 dollars.
- Roy Rowan is the announcer.
- Music supervision is by Amerigo Marino.

Producer: Jack Johnstone   Writer: Jack Johnstone
Cast: Virginia Gregg, Lawrence Dobkin, Lurene Tuttle, Harry Bartell, Eleanor Audley, Joseph Kearns, Herb Vigran, Junius Matthews, Tony Barrett, Sam Edwards

◆ ❖ ◆

Show: **The Tears of Night Matter**
Company: **Universal Adjustment Bureau**
Agent: **Hilary Fuchs**
Synopsis:
Episode 1   Show Date: 5/21/1956

Hilary Fuchs returns Johnny's call. Johnny tells him that he is reviewing a claim from Mrs. Wendover and asks why she let a $50,000 policy lay around for two years before making a claim.

Johnny travels to Miami, Florida, and calls Hilary Fuchs the next morning. Fuchs is a CPA and is surprised that Johnny came all the way to Florida to handle the claim. Fuchs tells Johnny that Mrs. Wendover had hired him to get her affairs in order, as the treasury folks were after her for back taxes. Noah Wendover died two years ago last April 14. Johnny tells Fuchs that the insurance company did not know about the death until the claim was filed.

Johnny is told that the Wendovers had taken some friends out on their boat and Wendover developed appendicitis and died before they made port. Mrs.

Wendover is a little wacky, or insane. The Wendovers were crazy for each other, and spent money like crazy, and they had it to spend. Now Mrs. Wendover has met someone and she is coming out of her grief. All the papers on my desk are hers and the policy was the first thing Hillary discovered, that and $90,000 in un-cashed dividend checks.

Hillary is tired of looking at the papers and leaves to play golf. Hillary tells Johnny that Mrs. Wendover has about $950,000 in the bank, so she is not trying to cheat the company.

Johnny verifies the death certificate and starts looking through the papers on the desk. Johnny leaves and goes to his hotel. Fuchs calls him and tells Johnny that Mrs. Wendover is having a fit.

Johnny cabs to the office and sees a 1956 Cadillac at the curb with a purse on the front seat, a mink stole on over the back of the seat and the keys in the ignition. The car is registered to Mrs. Wendover.

Johnny goes in and learns that Fuchs had some papers for her to sign and told her about Johnny, and she blew up, she is right on the edge.

Johnny meets Mrs. Wendover, who could be 16 or 36, with bright black eyes. Johnny tells her he is there to verify the facts. She knows her husband is dead, she saw him die.

She asks Johnny if she will get the money and Johnny presumes she will be paid. Her dad owned an insurance company once. "Would one of the men sitting at desks write "OK" on the policy if they knew about me?" she asks.

Johnny asks why an adjuster would question the claim. She tells Johnny that she is indolent and irresponsible, and a curse. Noah died, and her father died, and her brother died, no one lives around her. As Mrs. Wendover goes out to her car Fuchs tells Johnny that her brother died in Korea, and her father had a heart attack.

Johnny rushes out to drive her home. Johnny listens to his heart beating, and it never lets him down. It always does that when trouble is around. Mrs. Wendover asks Johnny, "Mr. Dollar, do you think he'll will die too?"

Tomorrow, right out in the broad daylight, I have a look at the tears of night.

Episode 2   Show Date: 5/22/1956
Hilary Fuchs calls Johnny to make sure that Mrs. Wendover is OK. Johnny tells him that she is scared and thinks she is responsible for the death of her father, brother and husband. Johnny tells him that she said someone else would die.

At Mrs. Wendover's apartment, Johnny is fixed a drink. Mrs. Wendover tells Johnny that he is probably worried about the claim, and that she had handled things badly. She wanted to talk to Johnny to tell him of the curse.

She tells Johnny that her father died of a heart attack, her brother in Korea, and her husband on the boat. But she still feels that she is a curse. Johnny asks who she was talking about on the ride back, but she does not remember riding in the car, she blanks out at times, and has seen a psychiatrist for it.

Johnny asks who "he" is and she tells him that he is Teddy Martin. She will marry him, when he asks her. He is like Johnny and does not believe in a curse, he makes her laugh. Johnny tells her to marry this guy, and she kisses him and thanks him for talking to her. J. Dollar — oracle. Johnny is still bothered by the curse.

Johnny goes to see Fuchs and tells him that he is filing his report recommending payment of the claim and is flying back tonight. Johnny types up his report and calls for plane reservations and waits for the airlines to call him back.

A man walks into the office and tells him that Costigan wants to see him. Johnny tells him he has the wrong man, but the man points his gun at Johnny and Johnny twists the man's arm and takes his gun. Johnny asks if the man is Sam Costigan from Chicago, the one they kicked out a few years ago. The man, Frank Scanlon, tells Johnny that Costigan wants to see Fuchs about the Wendover dame. Johnny gives him his gun, tells Frank to behave himself, and tells him to take him to Costigan.

Johnny goes out to a black Packard and is driven out to see Costigan. Johnny describes Frankie as a punk who is too obvious.

Johnny is taken to a well-lit mansion where a man named Feely opens the door and takes Johnny into the house, which is now a casino. Frankie takes Johnny upstairs and puts the .38 into his ribs and Johnny tells him he is going to be in trouble, but Frankie is looking forward to dealing with him.

Tomorrow, there is a curse that goes with the Wendover name, goes where ever it is.

Episode 3   Show Date: 5/23/1956
The phone rings, and Johnny answers and says "Johnny Dollar" and Frankie takes it from him and asks what he is up to. Johnny walks into the room and says "Hello Sam." to which Sam Costigan replies "Johnny, Johnny Dollar!" Frankie is surprised that Johnny is not Hilary Fuchs and Sam tells Frankie to leave.

Sam sits behind his desk staring at Johnny as he relates why he is in Florida and how Frankie had brought him to the casino. Sam tells Johnny he is doing ok, but the profit is not the same as in the old days. Frankie is a punk, but the best he can find.

Johnny tells Sam about the claim, and Sam shows him a necklace called The Tears of Night. Mrs. Wendover left it with Sam last week when she was here with Teddy, she is a little screwy. She sent Sam a check for $5,000 and wants Johnny to take the diamonds back to her. Johnny tells Sam he can act, but cannot lie. Sam tells Johnny the check bounced. Johnny tells him she cannot write a check without Fuchs to countersign it.

Sam tells Johnny that she had called and wanted the necklace back or she would call the cops. Sam tells Johnny to take the ice back to Mrs. Wendover and he will take the loss and show Johnny a good time at the casino. Johnny takes the necklace, but tells Sam that he will not come back, he does not trust Sam. Johnny leaves and sees Feely wiping his face in the casino.

Johnny calls a cab and goes to see Mrs. Wendover, who is expecting Teddy when she opens the door. Johnny is looking at her throat as she tells Johnny that she must call Teddy and slams the door. Johnny notes that the dress Mrs.

Wendover was completed with The Tears of Night, the same necklace that is in his pocket.

Johnny opens the case to see label for "The House of Mortuis" inside and a phone number. Johnny calls the number and arranges for a meeting.

Johnny cabs to the Sandy Beach hotel to meet Hannibal Mortuis and shows him the necklace. Mortuis is taken aback and asks how Johnny came to have it. Johnny tells him about Mrs. Wendover, who Mortuis calls "a lovely body propelled by a ridiculous mind. Such conduct!". Mortuis is sure that the necklace is real, and shows Johnny how well the diamonds are mounted, an incomparable masterpiece worth $10,000 but Wendover paid $25,000 for it.

When Johnny tells him he saw another one, Mortuis tells Johnny that it must be a fake. This requires an artist, and I am that artist. A copy could get by the unpracticed eye, to a layman. "Latet in angius herba" — that is Latin. All Johnny tells him that all he knows is "Agricola" — a snake in the grass. Mortuis is gratified to see his work.

Johnny asks if she had mentioned a curse, and Johnny tells him he is only a friend in a way, off and on, and Mortuis laughs. Mortuis notes that the fog is coming in, and it is dark, so maybe Johnny should leave the necklace in his safe, but Johnny declines the offer and leaves. Mortuis leaves him with "Omnia Mortuis bonun vocal est" — "all speak well of Mortuis".

Johnny notes that the fog had come in so Johnny gets some wrapping paper and stamps from the night clerk and calls a cab. When the cab arrives, Johnny mails the necklace to himself at his hotel. He does not think the two hoods following him saw him mail the package as he gets into a cab and is followed to this hotel.

Tomorrow, and the old curse comes up with an old-fashioned flourish.

Episode 4   Show Date: 5/24/1956
Johnny makes a call to Hilary Fuchs and asks him to come to his hotel. Johnny tells Fuchs that some of Costigan's boys are here and might want to use him for target practice.

Johnny gets a bottle of scotch as Fuchs arrives. Johnny asks what he knows about the necklace, but Fuchs tells Johnny that he has never heard of it.

Johnny relates the case so far, including Costigan and the necklace and Mortuis. Johnny asks Fuchs who made the necklace she was wearing, but he knows nothing. Johnny shows him the hoods outside and Hilary tells him to call the police. Johnny knows that Mrs. Wendover needs help, which is why he is staying.

Johnny takes Fuchs' car keys and tells Fuchs to stay in his room. Johnny drives to Elise Wendover's apartment where Toby and Feely are waiting for him. "Got a match, Dollar?" they taunt him, but Johnny remains silent. They go through his pockets and then work him over when he tells them he does not have the necklace.

Johnny remembers trying to wake up and has a very bad dream.

At 6:00 a.m. Johnny wakes up and goes to Mrs. Wendover's apartment, where he finds her sitting in front of a window laughing with the phone in her hand. She tells Johnny that he has met some people who told them a lot about her. Did they tell you about Teddy Davis? She cried when Noah died, and when her brother died, and when Daddy died, but I must not cry anymore. Teddy asked me to marry him, and he is not interested in my money and he is such a good painter.

She mumbles about Mr. Costigan and becomes hysterical. She thinks all they live for is money. Johnny turns on the lights to find Feely and Toby on the floor dead.

Tomorrow, the tears of night come home.

Episode 5   Show Date: 5/25/1956
Teddy calls for Elise and Johnny tells Teddy who he is, and that there have been two murders and that Elise is going to need him. Teddy will come right over.

The police arrive and Lt. Brady thinks Johnny is crazy and calls Hilary Fuchs to back up his story. Teddy arrives with a doctor and a lawyer and Elise is taken to a private hospital. Powder tests prove that Elise did not kill Toby and Feely.

Teddy returns and talks to Johnny and is thankful for his involvement. Brady suspects Johnny and Teddy offers Johnny his lawyer. Brady tells Teddy to scram and asks for Johnny's buzzer. Johnny tells Brady why he is in town and about the curse. Teddy interrupts and Brady tells him "I am going to pop you in the cooler if you interrupt again!"

Johnny tells Brady about Costigan and the necklace, and how Mrs. Wendover was wearing the necklace. He relates the beating and finding the bodies in the room. Johnny tells Brady that he has been an investigator for 14 years. Brady tells Johnny he knows that Johnny is not involved, and that Costigan was shot earlier.

Johnny goes back to his hotel room to find Mortuis there. Mortuis apologies for the actions of Toby and Feely. He is impressed by the ingenious way Johnny used the post office to protect the necklace. Mortuis declines a drink and he tells Johnny that they will wait for the mail. Johnny wants to know about the double-cross, but Mortuis tells him it is a triple-cross.

Scanlon asked him to duplicate the necklace and was going to double-cross Costigan. Costigan found out and Scanlon killed him. Scanlon then killed Feely and Toby with Mortuis' help and took them to Mrs. Wendover's apartment, such a crude touch. It would help keep her from complaining about a fake necklace to the police. Scanlon is also dead, but what is one more murder today? Mortuis tells Johnny that the police will find Scanlon in Mortuis' hotel room.

Mortuis tells Johnny that the Tears of Night are really worth $100,000. Mortuis wants to live out his remaining years, and the necklace will help him live like a king! Vene, vidi, vici! And then, a whimpering end: Requiescat in pace! Mortuis is going to turn the necklace into cash and will have spent the money before the police catch him.

There is a knock at the door, and Scanlon comes in and shoots Mortuis and Mortuis kills Scanlon, again. "De Mortuis nil nisi bonum", "Speak well of the dead" Mortuis tells Johnny and dies as Johnny calls the police. Mrs. Wendover will recover.

"Remarks: I'll stand for the last two days of expense myself, I didn't have any business sticking my nose in the jewelry end of it. But if you make me pay for them, don't ever try to hire me again."

Exp. Acct: $405.16

Notes:
- Musical supervision is by Amerigo Marino and Carl Fortina.
- Roy Rowan is the announcer.

Producer: Jack Johnstone   Writer: John Dawson
Cast: Virginia Gregg, Vic Perrin, Jack Kruschen, Jay Novello, William Conrad, Frank Gerstle, Marvin Miller, Will Wright

♦ ❖ ♦

Show: **The Matter of Reasonable Doubt**
Company: **Americon Northern Trust Company**
Agent: **Ben Guardley**
Synopsis:
Episode 1   Show Date: 5/28/1956

Ben Guardley calls and tells Johnny to save his money, the money he will get from this case. He has a crazy one. The case is a trust arrangement with a cumulative endowment insurance rider for up to a half million. Mrs. Ezra Gramely is leaving the money to her granddaughter Susan. She owns the Flintrock Ranch in Nevada. Jonas Parks started the deal and got cold feet. Parks thinks the old lady is crazy. Maybe Jonas is crazy.

Johnny travels to Las Vegas, Nevada and checks out Jonas Parks, who is in excellent financial shape and scrupulously honest. Johnny rents a "drive-it-yourself" hired car and drives the 23.6 miles to Flintrock to meet with Jonas Parks. Jonas is glad Johnny is there as the day has been odd, with rain clouds over the river. Jonas chides Johnny for acting interested in desert storms, and Johnny tells him he was sizing him up. Johnny has determined that Jonas is not crazy, and Jonas says he was checking Johnny out.

Jonas tells Johnny that he started the trust arrangement, and that there is something wrong at the ranch. He has a hunch and brought Johnny out on that hunch.

Mrs. Gramely is a widow who runs the ranch. Her son and his wife lived there and did most of the work. They were killed three years ago, and now the ranch is going to their daughter, Susan. Walter Gramely, her nephew, manages the ranch.

Mrs. Gramely came to town and sprung the idea of the trust on her own.

She wanted the ranch transferred to Susan within three years. Walter came in and was told what was happening, and Walter said she would never go through with it.

Jonas visited the ranch, and she told him to continue working on the deal. Now, Walter will not allow anyone on the ranch. Walter thinks that she is losing her mind and wants to keep it quiet. Jonas suggests that Johnny tell them he is an investigator with the Cattleman's Association.

Johnny drives to the ranch and stalls the car a short distance from the ranch, the old "out of gas" trick. While walking to the ranch, Johnny is caught in a rainstorm, but continues walking.

A shot rings out and Johnny sees a man on a horse coming towards him. Johnny hides and then gets the drop on him and tells him to drop the rifle. The man tells Johnny that he is trespassing and the ranch is missing cattle. Johnny tells his story about being from the Cattleman's Association and asks to see Mrs. Gramely but is told that he cannot see her.

The man tells Johnny to go to his car and he will send some gasoline, and then get out and stay out as he will not miss the next time.

Johnny walks back to the car and a station wagon approaches and Susan Gramely introduces herself and tries to pour gas into the tank, but she spots that the tank is full.

She tells Johnny that he is not with the Cattleman's Association, he is there to dig up the past and what is going to happen. Susan thinks that is fine and dandy. She loved her dad, and she knew what he did when he got angry.

She tells Johnny he is the type that smashes ahead to find out things, but be careful, you are smashing into a bomb.

Tomorrow, the dead past speaks in a musty morgue, or tries to, and a living lady gets cozy, or tries to, really tries to.

Episode 2   Show Date: 5/29/1956

Jonas Parks calls and Johnny tells him he was rained on, shot at and threatened and out-smarted by a sixteen-year-old girl, and he still has not seen Mrs. Gramely. He is giving up for tonight and is warming his bones over a triple brandy. Johnny asks about the accident and Jonas tells him to go see Will Conners. He runs the paper, tell him I sent you. And be careful.

Johnny buys a bottle of brandy and takes it to his room to warm up, and muse over the case.

Next morning Johnny visits Will Conners at the paper. Johnny introduces himself and Will Connors tells Johnny that Jonas told him to answer any questions. Will asks if there is a story in what Johnny is doing, and asks for a scoop if there is, it would do him good, so Johnny promises him the story.

Johnny asks for anything he has on Mrs. Gramely and the ranch. Will has noticed that there is something funny going on out there as Walter acts as scared as she does. Susan is strange, but not one to be scared. Walter's fancy wife is too much for him, and she is scared also.

Johnny asks about the accident, and Will offers to get the morgue files. He tells Johnny it had been raining and the accident happened on the road to the ranch. There had been an argument and Hilda grabbed her car to come to town. Ed ran out in his car too, it was a habit when he got mad. Mary went with him and they came upon Hilda's car in the road and hit it and were killed, but Hilda was not in the car. Johnny reads the files and learns nothing.

Susan meets Johnny in the newspaper office, and notices Johnny is reading about the accident. She tells Johnny that he is not an investigator for the Cattleman's Association because Aunt Hilda had called the Cattleman's Association and they told her they never heard of you, and Mr. Parks did not know you either, but he was lying. Susan tells Johnny that she will set up a meeting for Johnny to see her grandmother and call him at the hotel, the Carman Manor.

Back in his hotel room, there is a knock at Johnny's door and Hilda Gramely is there. Johnny notices a nice cigarette case and she tells Johnny that it was a gift, she is always getting gifts. Johnny asks her about a wedding ring and she tells Johnny that it is around somewhere. Johnny pours her a brandy and she tells Johnny that she likes all sorts of gifts, money, and most of all excitement. Johnny tells her he has no money, and never gives gifts. "You have brandy, so pour us a drink, and we'll talk...about excitement".

Tomorrow, a worried old lady shows her mettle, a gambler shows his hand, and the game gets tense, tight, and a little bit frightening.

Episode 3   Show Date: 5/30/1956

Susan calls and Johnny says hello to "Mr. Wilson". Susan tells him that her grandmother will be expecting him, and suspects that Hilda is there. "Has she made her pitch yet?" Susan asks Johnny and tells him that Uncle Walter will kill her someday. Johnny calls a taxi for Hilda and does not expense the six brandies she had.

Johnny drives to the ranch and meets Mrs. Gramely. "Susan is a brash little flibbertigibbet, and I love her." she tells Johnny. Johnny tells her about the trust arrangement and why he is there. She tells Johnny that she did not know that Jonas was there earlier. Johnny tells her that Jonas thought she was losing her mind and was working in her best interests. She calls Johnny a presumptuous whelp and wishes she were thirty years younger.

The last few months have been hard, but she denies that anything is wrong. Johnny tells her that she has stopped going to town and having visitors and backed down on the trust arrangement. She tells Johnny that she had discovered that Walter and Hilda were stealing her blind and have cut the ground out from under her. Walter found out, and stopped the trust plans, but Hilda was behind it.

Johnny tells her that Hilda must have planned the accident and Walter went along with it. Mrs. Gramely is shocked to learn that her son had been murdered.

Susan tells Johnny that grandma will be OK, but she knows now that Walter and Hilda killed her parents. Susan knows that Walter gambles, and gambles and gambles, mostly at the Lead Balloon Club. It is the only club that will take his IOU's. Deuce McCoy runs the club. Hilda spent the rest. She is what is called a luxury dame. Susan does not know any of Hilda's boyfriends, but she is a cool operator.

Johnny visits Deuce McCoy at the Lead Balloon and wants to talk about Walter Gramely, who is there at the club gambling. Johnny is told that Walter is not into Deuce now, but he does buy off his IOU's. Johnny tells Deuce that Walter may be doing time for embezzlement soon. Deuce plays stupid when Johnny asks if he knows Walter's wife. Johnny notices a cigarette case on his desk and Deuce does not know who it belongs to, but Johnny does, it belongs to Hilda.

Tomorrow, the pressure hits the top and the whole mess starts to crack.

Episode 4   Show Date: 5/31/1956

Susan calls and asks why Johnny is not out there, on the old Boulder cut-off. Johnny's friend had told her to meet Johnny on the road, and she called the hotel on a whim. Johnny tells her to come straight to his hotel, fast, while you are still alive.

Johnny had expected results, but not that quickly. He had told Deuce McCoy who he was and what he wanted and was surprised that the news was out so quickly. Johnny is sure that Susan would have been killed.

Susan arrives at the hotel and Johnny lets her in to his room and she tells Johnny that no one followed her, and everyone was out at the ranch. Walter did not call her, and she did not recognize the voice. Johnny tells her that the phone call was not a joke.

Johnny tells Susan about the plans for the trust, and that her grandmother is still in charge. Her grandmother was scared to say anything. Susan tells Johnny that Grandma is in better spirits than in months. Johnny is not sure who is behind the phone call, but Jonas and Will Conners also knew about the trust. Johnny asks Susan if she is scared, which she is not. Johnny tells her to stay in the room, and do not let anyone in.

Johnny goes to the newspaper office and talks to Will Conners who hopes Johnny might have a scoop for him. "Are you getting close to the "deneweyment"? You know, when the detective closes the case?" Will asks. Will tells Johnny that Deuce runs the casino for a syndicate, but he lets women get in the way. Johnny asks Will to go watch over Susan in his hotel. Will warns Johnny that Deuce packs a gun all the time.

At the Lead Balloon Johnny goes to Deuce's office and walks in to find a very drunken woman named Nicki in the office. Johnny starts to go through Deuce's desk and asks if Nicki is in it too, and she pegs Johnny for the FBI. She gets real mad when Johnny asks about Hilda. She tells Johnny that Walter was here earlier, and Deuce left after they talked and he made a phone call. Johnny tells her that Deuce is not coming back, he is in a jam.

Tomorrow, I tag the pitch too late and a runner gets home. The score one to nothing, in favor of death.

Episode 5   Show Date: 6/1/1956
Mrs. Gramely calls and Johnny tells her that he had told Walter that he had to put her on the phone or Johnny would come there with the police. She tells Johnny that she told Walter to not let him talk to her. She has decided not to set up the trust. Johnny tells her that he is coming to the ranch.

Johnny buys coffee for Nicki and ponders the call from Mrs. Gramely. Maybe Jonas was right about her sanity. Nicki tells Johnny that things were all right with Deuce before Hilda got there and that she will get Hilda if it is the last thing she does. Johnny tells her about the plot on Susan by Deuce to kill her. Nicki tells Johnny that it was Hilda's idea. Johnny tells her that Deuce is probably on the run, and the police will get him.

Johnny drives to the ranch and Walter meets Johnny at the door. Johnny wants to hear Mrs. Gramely tell him to leave, and he tells Walter to get out of the way. Mrs. Gramely enters the room, and Johnny walks them to the living room, where Hilda is listening.

Mrs. Gramely tells Johnny that there is no case now, so please leave. She tells Johnny that her son was killed in an accident.

The phone rings, and Walter gives the phone to Johnny. Will Conners tells Johnny that Deuce was caught at the airport and is in jail, and Johnny tells the others. Johnny tells them that Deuce will talk.

Johnny tells Mrs. Gramely that Susan has been in his hotel room. Mrs. Gramely tells Johnny that Walter and Hilda had told her that Deuce had Susan, and Walter pulls a gun on Johnny.

Hilda tries to think, and Walter tells her that she has thought for ten years and look at the mess they are in. Walter tells her that Deuce was at the airport because he was running out on them. Nicki walks in and tells them that Hilda is a real brain. Nicki is not afraid of Walter's gun and she tells Walter that the money he lost at the table was going right back to Hilda via Deuce after hours. Hilda denies it, but Walter shoots her, and gives the gun to Johnny.

Johnny tells Mrs. Gramely to call the police, and Walter tells Johnny that killing her was the first big thing he has done in ten years that Hilda did not plan.

"Remarks: Nicki wonders why Hilda was running around when she already had a man of her own, her husband. Of course, he didn't amount to much, but not many men do. What did she expect to find in this world? Pearls in all her oysters? A turkey in her soup?"

Exp. Acct: $596.45

Notes:
- Musical supervision is by Amerigo Marino and Carl Fortina.
- A denouement is the final outcome of the main dramatic complication in a literary work.
- Roy Rowan is the announcer.

Producer: Jack Johnstone   Writer: Les Crutchfield

Cast:	Susan Whitney, Richard Crenna, Jeanette Nolan, Forrest Lewis, Inge Adams, Paul Richards, Jeanne Tatum

◆ ❖ ◆

Show:	The Indestructible Mike Matter
Company:	Lakeside Life & Casualty Insurance Company
Agent:	Peter Branson

Synopsis:

Episode 1   Show Date: 6/4/1956

Pat McCracken calls. "Oh no, what have you got for me this time? The last case you gave me was that phony spiritualist case which is still haunting me. And the Laird Douglas Douglas of Heatherscote case about drove me out of my mind" Johnny tells Pat. "Well you made money on them, didn't you?" Pat asks.

Johnny cabs to see Pat McCracken and Pat starts buttering him up immediately. A friend in New York, Peter Branson, the brother of Harry Branson, needs a favor. But Pete is different, believe me.

Johnny goes to Peter's New York City office and Peter is Harry's twin in all ways. Peter tells Johnny that Michael Jeremiah Flynn is a bum, with a $50,000 policy. The policy is only two months old, and his office assistant had issued the policy. Flynn passed a physical somehow and paid the premium in cash. The address is the Glad Hands Mission, down in the Bowery.

Pete is worried about what happened before. Four times this same type of policy has been issued, and fraud was involved. A derelict is insured by a gangster, then collects when the policyholder is killed. The beneficiary on this one is John Wesley Cosgrave.

Johnny reviews the folder and gets a room at the Brakley, a dingy hotel and buys some old clothes. Johnny visits the Glad Hands Mission/flophouse and is greeted by Daddy Bill, who invites Johnny to attend the meeting tonight. Johnny tells him that he is looking for Mike Flynn. Johnny is told that Mike is staying there and is a big contributor who has taken the pledge — many times. Johnny concocts a story for Daddy Bill and learns about the mission residents, except for Mike. The quartet starts rehearsing and Johnny is asked to join in, as he has a wonderful voice.

Johnny takes a nap in the mission and wakes up to see a man staggering into the mission. It is Mike Flynn. Mike collapses and Johnny sees why, there are two bullet holes in his chest. Someone wants to collect on Mike.

Tomorrow, well, tomorrow there is proof that life is a very tenacious thing, even in the broken body of a Bowery bum.

Episode 2   Show Date: 6/5/1956

Peter calls about Johnny's message, and Johnny tells him that Mike was shot, but should pull through, and Johnny wants to talk to Mike before going to see the beneficiary.

Johnny cabs to see Mike Flynn in a room at the mission. Mike thanks Johnny for helping him, and Johnny looks at the holes where the bullets just went through him. Mike shows Johnny a stab wound he got last week.

Mike tells Johnny that he was shot down near his "private place" where he goes to drink. Mike tells Johnny that Daddy Bill wants Mike to stay there in the mission. Mike pulls out a bottle of his special mix, sterno and alcohol, and tells Johnny that he has been drinking it for years. Mike tells Johnny that he collapsed because he had overindulged, but please don't tell Daddy Bill.

Mike tells Johnny that he was walking back to the mission and a car passed and there was a stinging feeling in his side. He is sure that the men in the car were probably just arguing about something. Johnny tells Mike who he is and that he is there to save his life.

Mike is so pleased that Mr. Cosgrave offered to buy him insurance. Cosgrave helps the mission because he came to the mission when he was young and Daddy Bill helped him, so he gives food, money and jobs to the brothers. Mike does not know what type of jobs, because the men never come back.

Johnny tells Mike that the accidents were part of a scam to collect the insurance. Mike tells Johnny that he gets the money for the insurance in an envelope at the mission, but yesterday's envelope did not come. Mike gets up and they go downstairs and Mike tells Johnny he will take him to his private place.

Downstairs Mike spots his envelope with $20 in it, and he has a package. Inside are two bottles, one for him and one for Johnny. Johnny takes Mike to his room and tells him not to let anyone in, and not to leave.

Johnny cabs to the 18th precinct and talks to Randy Singer while the lab boys look at the bottle. Johnny asks Randy to look into Cosgrave.

Johnny gets a report on the liquor bottle and there are no prints on it, but the seal was broken and the bottle has wood alcohol in it. Johnny rushes to the mission and runs to Mike's room and breaks in to see Mike lying across the bed, moaning about the hangover he will have.

Tomorrow, the would-be beneficiary of Mike turns out to be a very interesting and dangerous man.

Episode 3   Show Date: 6/6/1956
Johnny calls John Cosgrave, and he tells Johnny that he has been expecting the call. Johnny tells Cosgrave that he is interested in why he is insuring a Bowery bum.

Johnny cabs to see Randy Singer and tells him that Mike is OK, and happy. Johnny tells Randy about the stab wound and the shots and Randy calls him "Indestructible Mike"! Randy tells Johnny that Cosgrave is a well-known gangster with a subsidiary of Murder Inc. He was last picked up in 1948, but no one can prove he is involved in the rackets, and that he is listed as "retired". All the witnesses against him seem to disappear or are killed.

Johnny cabs to Cosgrave's apartment, which his expensively and tastefully appointed. Cosgrave is well-built and well-dressed. Cosgrave shows Johnny a Picasso and a Salvador Dali and tells Johnny that he must have only the best.

Cosgrave tells Johnny that he was born in a poor area and received a meager education from criminals. He visited the mission one night and was helped, so he has tried to help the inhabitants from time to time.

Cosgrave slips when Johnny asks him what type of jobs he has provided and asks Johnny "What business is it..." Cosgrave tells Johnny that Mike had wanted to own life insurance so he bought it for him. Johnny asks "Dutchy" where his money comes from and Cosgrave slips back into his former attitude.

He admits making millions in the past but those days are over, he pocketed the profits and that is why he is retired. Thanks to some unexplained rub-outs he has managed to stay clean with the law. Johnny refuses to believe that Cosgrave would pass up an opportunity to make a quick buck, at Mike Flynn's expense.

Cosgrave tells Johnny not to try and pin anything on him if Mike dies. Cosgrave apologizes for not offering Johnny a drink and pours him a 25-year-old Scotch. Johnny leaves with a feeling he is being followed.

Johnny cabs to his hotel and Mike is still there. Mike did not eat the food Johnny had left him because he had nothing to drink with the food, it was so dry. Johnny takes Mike out for lunch, and only one drink. Johnny wonders if Daddy Bill is involved with Cosgrave.

After lunch Johnny and Mike walk back to the mission on the back streets where a truck swerves and hits Mike. Johnny tells a bystander to call an ambulance, but the man tells Johnny that it is too late.

Tomorrow, somebody's going to have to pay for what is happening here, yes that's a promise.

Episode 4   Show Date: 6/7/1956
Randy calls Johnny at Bellevue hospital. Johnny tells Randy that Mike is still alive, but Johnny is not sure he will survive this one. The first precinct boys are working on the truck, and Johnny asks Randy to check with them and get some history on the Glad Hands Mission.

Johnny is sure that Cosgrave is behind the accidents to Mike as he waits in the hospital. Johnny gets a phone call from Cosgrave, he tells Johnny that he knows about a lot of things that do not get into the papers. "Dutchy", Cosgrave tells Johnny that he had nothing to do with it. Johnny tells him that he was there and tells Cosgrave he might have seen the driver of the truck.

Johnny waits some more and is allowed to see Mike around midnight. Mike is lying in bed smiling from ear-to-ear. He will be OK, and is impressed with the room, and the nurses, they are so nice. And it smells so nice here, he has not even seen a bed bug! Johnny turns off the light and tells Mike that he will be back in the morning, but Mike needs something to help him sleep. Johnny sneaks Mike three fingers of whisky into his water glass.

Johnny cabs to his hotel room thankful that Mike is alive. Johnny gets a call the next morning from Randy and tells him that Mike is OK. Johnny learns that the truck has been found, but the driver, Lefty Skillman, was found in the East River.

Randy tells Johnny that the flophouse building was built in 1901 as a piano store, then a grocery store, a clothing store, a speakeasy, and a saloon. In 1944 William Grover Larson took over the lease.

Johnny spots the lie Cosgrave told about getting help there as a kid, before the mission was opened. The owner of the speakeasy was Larson also. Johnny feels that Larson was the front man for Cosgrave. He is now using the flophouse to get his thugs, who are never seen again. Johnny hears someone outside his room, opens the door and is knocked out.

Johnny wakes up to the voice of Randy and strange meaningless sounds. Johnny wakes up in the hospital and realizes what had happened and is put to sleep.

Mike calls to Johnny and he wakes up in Mike's room. Mike tells Johnny that Randy had told Mike that Johnny has to be careful, they are out to get him too.

Tomorrow, well old Mike may have been indestructible, I knew by now that I wasn't. So tomorrow the windup, it had to be while I was still alive.

Episode 5   Show Date: 6/8/1956
Johnny is called by Randy, and Johnny thanks him for his help. Johnny tells Randy that he is going to the mission to settle things with Daddy Bill. And he has his gun.

Johnny and Mike check out of the hospital and cab to the hotel. Mike is put in a room on the fifth floor. Johnny picks up his .38 and heads to the mission, walking the last few blocks.

The mission is empty when Johnny gets there and he waits in a back office. A man walks in and tells Daddy Bill he is ready but realizes that Johnny isn't Daddy Bill.

He tells Johnny that his name is Emery, and that he rode the rods in from Ohio, and boy was he in a jam there. Daddy Bill promised him that the police would not find him, and he has a job for him to get him out of the country. Emery tells Johnny that Daddy Bill left a package for Mike or Johnny that contains liquor. Johnny does not want to open the package, and Emery tells Johnny that Mike always shares his stuff with Lefty Skillman. Johnny recognizes the name, Lefty was driving the truck that hit Mike. Johnny senses the package does not gurgle.

Johnny tells Emery that he is going to the Waldorf, and that Mike is recovering in room 203 at the Brakley Hotel. Johnny tells Emery to tell Daddy Bill to call him at the Waldorf.

Johnny calls Randy and then cabs to the 18th precinct. Johnny asks Randy to register him at the Waldorf, and then cabs to his room at the Brakley. Johnny tells the desk clerk to tell anyone looking for Mike that he is in room 203.

Johnny spills some whisky in his room and checks in on Mike with a bottle. Johnny makes him promise to stay in the room and goes back to the second floor. Johnny leaves the door unlocked and waits.

The phone rings, and Randy tells Johnny that the package was a bomb. Johnny hangs up and gets into the bed as he hears footsteps. There is a knock at the door and Daddy Bill is outside and comes in with Cosgrave. Daddy Bill is sure that Johnny is at the Waldorf, and just as Cosgrave tells him he will do it himself, Mike knocks on the door and calls for Johnny.

Cosgrave tells Johnny to get up and takes his gun and then opens the door to let Mike in. The door bursts open and there are shots as Randy comes in with Mike. Mike ends up is sitting on Daddy Bill, despondent that the bottle he hit him with is broken. Daddy Bill complains about Cosgrave hanging things on others and shoots Cosgrave, killing him.

"The world will be a bit better without Dutchy Gordon, alias J. Wesley Cosgrave. And of course, the courts will take care of Daddy Bill Larkin, plenty. Mike, Indestructible Mike, well he will probably out-live the rest of us. I hope I can get down to see him now and then, talk over our great adventure together."

Exp. Acct: $1,126.50

Notes:
- Wood alcohol, or methyl alcohol, or methanol, is the simplest of all the alcohols. It was formerly made by the destructive distillation of wood. When taken internally, by either drinking the liquid or inhaling the vapors, methanol is extremely poisonous.
- In the 1930's Lucky Luciano, and Meyer Lansky successfully unified the great criminal gangs into a vast national crime syndicate with a board of directors of organized crime and an enforcement arm that was to become known as Murder Incorporated.
- In 2014, the program *American Experience* told the story of *Iron Mike* Malloy, a bowery wino who was poisoned   several times   so that the benefactors of an insurance policy could collect. This story is so similar to *Indestructible Mike* that I wonder if Jack Johnstone   who was working in New York when this event took place   used this real-life event as a source for this story.
- Johnny references the "Glad Hand Mission" in episode 1, and Cosgrave calls it the "Helping Hand Rescue Mission" in episode 3.
- Musical supervision is by Amerigo Marino and Carl Fortina.
- The announcer is Roy Rowan.
- Johnny notes the use of a .38.
- The Waldorf refers to the Waldorf-Astoria, one of New York's more expensive hotels at the time.

Producer: Jack Johnstone   Writer: Jack Johnstone
Cast: Howard McNear, Lawrence Dobkin, Harry Bartell, Herb Vigran, Alan Reed, Roy Glenn

◆ ❖ ◆

Show: **The Laughing Matter**
Company: **Union States Casualty Company**
Agent: **Ed Renzer**
Synopsis:
Episode 1   **Show Date:**   **6/11/1956**

Ed Renzer calls and tells Johnny that his plane for Ensenada leaves in two hours. Charley Burton is down there, the big Nightclub/TV star, "Good old loveable Charlie". Someone has threatened to kill him and he has $500,000 in insurance.

Johnny travels to San Diego and then to Ensenada, Mexico and the plush Balboa Hotel. Johnny comments on the two towns: the tourist Ensenada and the poor working-class section of warehouses, packing plants and slums.

Frank Maltz, the executive producer meets Johnny and tells him that he has not called the police because Charlie would object because he has had crank letters before. Frank tells Johnny that Charley found a note yesterday under the door, and Charley tore it up. It said "Only the gods are immortal, Burton. You will never leave Ensenada alive." Nothing has happened since the note. Frank tells Johnny that he has to form his own conclusions on who would want to kill Charley. Johnny is told to talk to the others, Gloria Dale is the feminine lead and gorgeous, and Al Schriber is a newcomer with a real talent. Frank thinks that someone in the family wrote the note and that is why he sent for Johnny. Frank hates Charley's guts, and he wants to make sure that if Burton is killed that justice is done, and the killer caught.

Johnny goes out to meet Gloria Dale, a lovely girl. Johnny tells her why he is there and she tells Johnny that everyone has heard of the note from Charley and his ingratitude that someone should pull such a practical joke. Gloria thinks anyone who knows him might have written it. She sticks around because she has a contract, as is the situation with Frank.

Al Schriber joins Gloria and his reaction is "Happy Days! So, that earthworm is really insured? Maybe the advertisers are out to kill him to make a profit." Al tells Johnny that he would not try to kill Charley.

As Johnny savors a drink on the terrace, he sees a man move towards the terrace and argue fiercely with a girl. The man sees Johnny and flees. The girl was a maid at the hotel. The man had been heading towards Charley Burton's room.

Tomorrow, the great man condescends and shivers a little too, and a girl's hidden hate is blacker than the sea-wet rocks she vents it on.

Episode 2   Show Date: 6/12/1956
Charley Burton calls Johnny, who is glad that he is out of seclusion. Charley tells Johnny that he does not need protection, but Johnny tells him that the insurance company does not agree. Are you going to talk, or do I call the insurance company and your sponsors? I'll see you in an hour.

Johnny cabs to the office of the police and asks for a run-down on Valina Morales, the hotel maid. Capt. Parral tells Johnny he will call him later.

Johnny calls on Charley Burton. Johnny asks for a double scotch on the rocks and Charley calls room service, and then cancels the order when Johnny will not give his room number. Charley tells Johnny that he will not tolerate that highhanded behavior from a hireling, but Johnny tells him he is not Charley's hireling. Johnny tells him he does not like Charley, and there is nothing he can do about it. Charley tells Johnny that he likes him, he is uninhibited. Johnny tells Charley that everyone seems to have the same bad opinion of him.

Charley recounts all of the shortcomings of his costars and how he had taken them from the bottom. He does not take the threat seriously and tells Johnny that not one of the cast has a reason to kill him. Charley tells Johnny that those who complain the most do not lead to murder, and Johnny agrees. Charley tells Johnny that the note was a joke. Johnny asks about the maid and Charley remembers her, she is utterly charming. Johnny reminds him that her husband might not like Charley's attitude.

Johnny walks down to the beach and finds Gloria with a bottle and shares a glass with her. She tells Johnny that she sent Al off to bed. She likes him, but there is no click. She is trying to forget the emptiness and the hate for Charley Burton.

She tells Johnny that she was leaving the show last year and was about to be married to a man named Jerry, and Charley was furious. She got a note from Jerry saying they were through, and then he went on a hunting trip to Canada. She signed a new contract and then learned that a crooked detective had told Jerry about a faked private life, and that Charley Burton was behind it. She could not fight Charley because Jerry was killed on the way back from the trip. She hates Charley but has no nerves, so she drinks.

Johnny is awakened in the night by a gunshot and Charley Burton banging on his door. He tells Johnny that someone has shot at him through the window of his room, someone is out to kill him.

Tomorrow, a thickening web, clinging and sticky. But one of the flies pulls free by using a gun.

Episode 3   Show Date: 6/13/1956

Capt. Parral calls Johnny and Johnny tells him about the shooting. "Before you get here, see if you can find Frank Maltz" Johnny tells Parral and he tells Johnny that he will make the "APC". No Johnny corrects him, "it is an APB". "What is this APB?" Parral asks.

Johnny buys coffee and tries to wake up. In Burton's room, Parral asks where Charley is, and Johnny tells him he has moved rooms and is scared. Johnny relates how Charley was asleep and how the shot broke the window and landed over his head. He ran to Johnny's room and a search was made, but Johnny saw no one. Johnny tells Parral that any of the staff could have fired the shot.

Johnny tells Parral who the others are, and Johnny tells him that all of them hate Charley. Parral is still looking for Valina, but she is not at home and her husband is missing. The phone rings, and Parral answers and tells Johnny that Frank has been found in a cantina in town.

Johnny cabs to the cantina and finds Frank Maltz wrapped around a bottle. Frank tells Johnny he has been there forever. It is a crossroads for two different worlds, and they are all dead. He is not really drunk and has been in every bar in town.

Johnny asks where he was at 12:40 when Burton was shot at. Frank tells Johnny that he has not been back to the hotel since he left at 10:00. Frank tells Johnny that he hangs around Burton to help someone else, Al Schriber. Frank tells Johnny that it will be his show next year if he can hang on because the sponsors are tired of Charley. Frank is married and tells Johnny that his wife is in a sanitarium, paralyzed. That is why he has to stay on with Charley. When the hate gets too much, he goes to visit his wife.

Johnny leaves and is met on the street by Parral, who tells Johnny that the maid has come home, and they rush to the house. Parral questions her about Charley and learns that he had been bothering her. When Johnny had seen him, her husband was going to see Charley, but she has not seen him since.

Tomorrow, death tries once more, and this time doesn't miss, but death you know, is blind.

Episode 4   Show Date: 6/14/1956
Charley Burton calls and tells Johnny that he is still alive. Johnny tells him that he may be good old loveable Charley to others, but he is a pain in the neck to Johnny. "Your sponsor may think you are worth $500,000, but my price on you is three cents" Johnny tells him.

Johnny recounts how everyone around Charley Burton hates him, and about the attempt to shoot him last night.

Johnny meets Frank at breakfast and he apologizes for making a fool of himself last light, but Johnny asks when that was. Johnny tells him about talking to the maid, and the others seem to be off the hook. Johnny tells how her husband had come out to the hotel and that the police are looking for him.

Al Schriber meets them and he is going to go swimming before "old blubber tummy" gets up. Frank reminds him about the schedule for today, a slapstick desert island scene.

Al describes the scene and the punch line about a cousin in congress. Johnny is told that Charley has all the good lines in this scene. Charley walks up and gives Al a hard time and Al tells Charley that if he fires him, he could have another show in no time. Frank and Charley argue over Al's talent and Charley tells him he has always looked out for the welfare of his coworkers. Johnny tells him that he does not want to see Charley killed, that would mean he loused up, but Johnny takes pride in his work.

Johnny tells Charley that the husband of the maid, Nacho Morales, is looking for him. "That native girl is married?", Charley asks. Charley tells Frank and Al that he is carrying them. He decides to trade roles, he will take Al's role, and allow him to change any line, and Frank jumps at the opportunity. Frank tells Johnny that the note was written in English, but Valina and her husband only speak Spanish.

The scene is set up at the end of the bay, and Johnny goes to watch. The last scene is re-filmed, and Al drinks from a glass of fake wine and collapses and dies.

Tomorrow, a frantic game of musical chairs, with every player desperate, because the loser in this game gets the electric chair.

Episode 5   Show Date: 6/15/1956
Charley calls for Capt. Parral and Johnny answers. He tells Johnny that it might have been him who was killed. Johnny knows he is there to protect Charley because someone was crazy enough to insure him.

Johnny buys a beer for Parral and waits for night. Parral tells Johnny that Al was poisoned with "much cyanide". Johnny thinks that the wrong man was killed. Parral wonders about Nacho, who has disappeared, but they will find him.

Johnny cabs to the hotel and meets Gloria, who asks about what happened to Al. They go in to the bar and she asks about Charley and Al changing roles. What irony, Charley goes for the maid and Al gets killed.

Johnny reminds her that the Morales do not speak English, and that the note was written in English. Johnny gets a call from Parral and learns that Nacho has been picked up. Johnny tells Gloria that she did not know that Al was going to drink from the bottle, not Charley.

Johnny goes to see Nacho Morales, who is a small man with gnarled hands. Johnny and Parral go in and question him. Nacho tells Parral that he had been hiding on a boat because he had seen Charley fire the shot himself.

Johnny goes to Charley and tells him that Nacho has been caught. "He should be beaten, that is the only way to make that kind talk" Charley tells Johnny. Johnny tells Charley that he killed Al Scriber, and wrote the letter and fired the shot at himself, and that the argument that day was phony.

Charley pulls a gun on Johnny and tells him that he will not be tagged for killing Al. Parral comes in and tells Charley to drop his gun, but Charley tries to shoot anyway and Parral kills him. Too bad Charley could not have seen the look on his face, a comedian would have appreciated it, why he would have died laughing.

"Remarks: Re policy on Charles Z. Burton, deceased. Refer Clause 34, sub paragraph C, 'if the insured dies while committing a felony, this policy is null and void'. The superior court of Baja, California rules that Charley was killed while resisting arrest and committing and assault with a deadly weapon. So, you can keep your half a million bucks."

Exp. Acct: $791.55

Notes:
- On several occasions, Johnny is told he should go into television, but his standard reply is "I'll wait until it is perfected".
- The announcer is Roy Rowan.
- Musical supervision is by Amerigo Marino and Carl Fortina.

Producer:	Jack Johnstone	Writer:	Les Crutchfield
Cast:	Virginia Gregg, John Dehner, Lucille Meredith, Lawrence Dobkin, Gil Stratton, Harry Bartell, Don Diamond		

• ❖ •

Show: **The Pearling Matter**
Company: **Eastern Liability & Trust Company**
Agent: **Morton Scotman**
Synopsis:
Episode 1   **Show Date:**   **6/18/1956**

Morton Scotman calls and he wants Johnny to see him. Morton tells Johnny that David Pearling was supposedly killed in a boating accident several days ago, but he is still very much alive.

Johnny tells Mr. Scotman that he is reading about Mr. Pearling now in the newspaper, but the papers will never have all the story.

Johnny meets Mr. Scotman and tags him as a meticulous man, who turns out to be Vice President and Chairman of the Board of Eastern Liability. Johnny tells Scotman that he has handled several other cases, the last being the San Antonio case. He tells Scotman that he usually works through an adjusting agency. Scotman tells Johnny that this idea was his own, and only one other person knows about it. The board may not approve what he is going to suggest.

David Pearling is still alive, and the story will be retracted. The boat did explode, but he was a not on it. Pearling is well regarded in financial circles, and the report of his death affected several commodities on the New York Exchange, companies in which he holds varying positions. A report of his death could allow people to make money with little risk.

Scotman wants Johnny to find out if the situation has been taken advantage of. Johnny thinks that this case is not in his line, but Scotman thinks it is. Eastern Liability has considerable investments in some of those commodities, and Scotman wants to know if they have been cheated or are about to be cheated. Johnny has dinner with Scotman, who provides him with financial information on the companies.

Johnny flies to Key West, Florida and goes to meet Mr. Peyton, the editor of the local paper. Johnny asks him about the story on Pearling and is told they are running a retraction today.

Peyton calls for Gracie Edwards and then tells Johnny that the story was a mistake. Pearling had been here for a week or ten days of fishing and rented a boat. The boat was coming back for fueling and blew up. Pearling could not be found and was presumed lost. It turns out that Pearling was sleeping in his room when it happened and took a train back that afternoon.

Johnny asks to see the reporter. Johnny is told that she had been at the dock when the boat caught fire and that Gracie has been a reporter for several years.

Gracie, a short stocky redhead comes in and Johnny tells her who he is. Johnny gives the Eastern Liability Company as his current employer and suggests that they go to lunch. Gracie tells Johnny that she did what every cub reporter would do, she turned in a story without checking the facts.

Johnny is worried about Gracie being on the docks and is told that it is more or less her beat. She likes to see the boats come back in the afternoon. Johnny suggests they go to the docks and look at the boats.

They cab to the docks and Gracie points out where the boat *The Outwatcher* blew up. She had been there an hour or so and phoned in her story just before three. Johnny thinks it is funny that she saw the boat in trouble and immediately phoned in her story and Johnny asks where she phoned it in from, as there are no phones there. Gracie tells Johnny she took a cab into town.

Johnny then asks where her sunburn is, every redhead burns in an hour when the sun is like this. Gracie does not like the questions, but Johnny tells her he has to find out from her what happened. If he has to, he will talk to the adjuster who worked the insurance claim on the boat.

Johnny tells her she is a good reporter and would have checked her facts. She tells Johnny that somebody paid her to file the story. Mr. Pearling paid her to print the story that he was dead.

Tomorrow, the affairs of Wall Street follow the current trend in cheating and mayhem.

Episode 2   Show Date: 6/19/1956

Johnny calls Mr. Scotman and tells him about Pearling paying someone to print the story. Johnny will meet Scotman at Idyllwild airport.

Johnny flies to New York City and meets Mr. Scotman in the airport coffee shop. Johnny tells him that the reporter was paid $100 in cash to print the story, but she would deny it. If the story would affect the market, it would probably happen today and Pearling would probably take advantage of brisk trading over the report. If it does happen, Scotman would probably report it to the stock exchange.

They cab to Wall Street and watch the action, but there was is no manipulation. The question is, why did Pearling pay the reporter? There is a reason, and Johnny wants to find out why.

Johnny buys lunch for Scotman and checks into the New Westin and rents a car.

Johnny drives to the Pearling estate and is met at the door by a young woman. Mrs. Pearling tells Johnny that Mr. Pearling is not there. Johnny tells her to tell Mr. Pearling that he has just come from Key West and has spoken with a reporter there.

Mr. Pearling comes to the door and tells Johnny that his wife told him to throw Johnny out. Johnny tells him he is 10 pounds lighter but 15 years younger. Johnny asks him why he paid Gracie Edwards to print the story, but he tells Johnny that there is no way to prove he paid the girl. Johnny tells him that Eastern Liability thought he was trying to fix the market. Pearling tells him only that he paid the reporter and the boatman in cash for his own reason.

Johnny realizes that a man does not tell someone to leave, he invites him in and lies to him. So, Johnny drives back to the hotel and waits.

Later the phone rings and Celia Pearling calls from the lobby. She apologizes and asks Johnny if he is a sensation seeker. Johnny tells her that she knows who he is because she has checked on him and knew where to find him. She asks if Johnny is going to continue with the matter, and Johnny tells her that he believes that the answers David gave were unsatisfactory. She is sure that the issue was a personal one and does not matter.

Johnny buys her a drink (bourbon and water) and she finally opens up. She tells Johnny that they have a daughter named Eugenia, and she is the reason for the story. They are capable of many things, but not child rearing.

Genie got sick of having too much money and no attention and left town.

She left a note saying that they would never see her again. They have no idea where she has gone and miss her.

They have hired the Aimwell agency to try and find her. They thought that a story about David's death might cause her to call them, but they have not heard from her.

Tomorrow, the trap is all baited and guess who walks in.

Episode 3   Show Date: 6/20/1956
The operator calls Johnny with a call from Aimwell detectives. Johnny asks Mr. Aimwell about the Pearling case and he hangs up.

Johnny cabs to the offices of the Aimwell Detective Agency and meets with Niles Aimwell. Niles tells Johnny that he does not know what Johnny is talking about, so please leave.

Johnny tells him that he knows they are working for the Pearlings and shows Niles his identification and license. Johnny tells him about the newspaper story and the reporter who was paid to print the story and the effort to contact the daughter. Johnny tells Niles he has had time to talk to the Pearlings, and he might lose them as a client. Johnny might want to see the operator's report on the case.

Niles has the secretary call the Pearlings and tells Johnny what they have done so far. They thought they had her located in several cities but they missed her. She is probably traveling alone, and five men have been on this case for 11 months to the day, with no luck, and Niles is one of them.

Johnny apologizes for riding him so hard. Mrs. Pearling calls and Niles tells Johnny that he will cooperate with him. Johnny gets the files and an offer of a bottle of cold beer. The file is complete, but Johnny gets nothing from it.

Johnny meets with Scotman and updates him on the missing daughter. Scotman is relieved that there was no manipulation and closes the case.

Johnny goes to pack, and then realizes he does not believe anybody or anything because there is money in it. Johnny thinks in the bar, and then goes to see Mr. Scotman.

Johnny asks him how the case strikes him and the answer is "neat". Johnny thinks it is too neat. Scotman is sure now that Pearling was not the type of man who would try to manipulate the market. Johnny wonders why the police were not brought in. Johnny is sure that Pearling is lying when he says he wants his daughter back at home. Scotman tells Johnny to continue with the case.

Johnny visits Aimwell to tell him that they will be seeing a lot of each other. Aimwell tells Johnny that Pearling had told him to contact Johnny. Niles comments on the picture of Pearling's daughter, about how lucky he would be to be with her. Niles does not blame Johnny for wanting to meet her. Niles shows Johnny a wire. She has been located in New Orleans.

Tomorrow, well once you get in on a joke, you do what they tell you, you go along with the gag.

Episode 4   Show Date: 6/21/1956

Dave Pearling calls and wants to talk to Johnny. He tells Johnny that Aimwell has reported that Johnny is looking into his private affairs. He should be annoyed but is not. He will be home all day.

Johnny calls Scotman and he thinks that Johnny should check it out, so Johnny drives to the Pearling home.

Johnny is met by a private detective who offers Johnny a drink. He is Brad Copeland, one of Niles Aimwell's operatives, and he tells Johnny that Niles is in conference with Mr. Pearling. Johnny does not believe what he has said, and Brad tells him he is the one who found the girl.

Johnny tells him about the story and Brad tells Johnny he got a phone call from a man telling him where the girl was. He checked it out, and she is the girl. Niles and David come into the room and Niles leaves with Brad.

David tells Johnny he is the most competent man he has seen, and that he has just fired Aimwell. He wants Genie to come home and wants Johnny to persuade her to come home. Johnny tells him he was going to anyway. He had not made a move to do anything, and she was found too soon after Johnny got involved.

Johnny leaves for New Orleans, Louisiana and checks into the Roosevelt Hotel. At the desk, Johnny sees a large man smile when the desk clerk calls his name for the bellboy.

The man tells Johnny that they thought he would never get there, and the rest of the boys are in room 810. The Delta Cotton Growers are going to have a good time at this convention.

The man leaves and Johnny asks the desk clerk about the convention and is told that it was held last month, and that there is no room 810. Johnny made the man play out the game and neither knows the other. Johnny wants to know who the man is because of the .38 under his left arm.

Johnny eats and goes to the address on Ursuline Street. A blond opens the door and Johnny asks about Genie Pearling. The girl tells Johnny that she is Janice Floyd, a roommate. Janice leads Johnny to a room containing a coffin with a girl in it. Janice tells Johnny that the girl is Genie, and that she died of leukemia. Johnny tells her that he is an investigator and Janice tells him that there have been others there looking for her and throws Johnny out.

Johnny gets a copy of the death certificate and the medical report and makes a show of checking out. The blond man is in the lobby and at the airport.

Johnny eludes him and follows him back to the Ursuline address. Johnny stops the man on the street and confronts him. The man tells Johnny to go back to New York and walks away. Johnny remembers that there is money in this case, plain old money.

Tomorrow, there is still money in it. More money than it takes to save a life.

Episode 5   Show Date: 6/22/1956

Janice Floyd calls Johnny and is concerned that he does not believe that Genie is dead. She had been through an ordeal lately and if he is going to interfere, she will call the police.

Johnny writes to Mr. Scotman and encloses the documents and tells of Janice's behavior.

Johnny calls Janice and tells her she is being taken. He is there to find Genie Pearling and wants to talk. She tells him to see her tonight.

Johnny walks to the apartment and the blond man slugs Johnny in a dark part of the street. A cabby finds Johnny at midnight and thinks he is drunk.

The cabby takes Johnny to Janice's address and he knocks on the door. Janice lets him in and he sees that she is packing. Johnny asks if the big blond man is part of the reason. Johnny tells her that the man had come here to talk to her and that he had slugged Johnny. Johnny tells her that he carries a gun, and he is surprised.

Johnny tells her that the girl who died was not Genie Pearling, and if necessary he will have the body exhumed. She tells Johnny that she is Genie Pearling and it was Janice Floyd that died. She figures that if she switched identities, her family would not bother her anymore. That was Al Britt's idea, Al saw to it that Janice had her identity.

She hates her family and wants her own life. She is going to marry Al. Johnny tells her that she is worth $100,000, an irrevocable trust she gets when she becomes 25. It would go to her father if she were dead.

She realizes that Al had been paid to make love to her and arrange the switch. Al breaks in, and she tells Al she knows about him, and tells him to leave.

Johnny talks with her and she is not sure what she wants to do. Johnny gets ready to leave and is met by Al Britt, who wants to talk.

He tells Johnny that he really messed it up with him and Genie, and he is leaving town. Johnny tells Al that she does not like her father, and he does not like him, and what he will do if she goes back. Al tells Johnny that her father had hired him to find her, and he had planned the switch, but did not know about the trust fund. But Al made a mistake and fell in love with her. Funny how things work out.

Johnny stops by the apartment on the way to the airport. She is not going to New York, and does not want to talk to Al. She cries over what he did, but she loves him. Johnny tells her to talk to him the next time he calls. You may not have a mother or father, but you have him. I'd take him if I were you.

"Remarks: She took him. They were married in Tampa this morning"

Exp. Acct: $714.35

Notes:
- Mr. Scotman tells Johnny that he had worked for them on the San Antonio Matter. When John Lund did *The San Antonio Matter*, he worked for Great Eastern Fidelity & Life Insurance Company, not the Eastern Liability & Trust noted in this case. When Bob Bailey did the story as *The Valentine Matter*, he worked for New Britain Insurance Company. All versions of the story were written by E. Jack Neuman, and John Dawson (aka E. Jack Neuman).
- Roy Rowan is the announcer.

- Musical supervision is by Amerigo Marino and Carl Fortina.

Producer:	Jack Johnstone	Writer:	John Dawson
Cast:	Mary Jane Croft, Forrest Lewis, Jeanette Nolan, Russell Thorson, Michael Ann Barrett, Jack Petruzzi, Barbara Fuller, Herb Ellis, Marvin Miller		

◆ ❖ ◆

Show: The Long Shot Matter
Company: National Underwriters Association
Agent: Jim Darryl
Synopsis:
Episode 1 **Show Date:** 6/25/1956

Jim Darryl calls and welcomes Johnny to Hollywood. Jim tells Johnny that he wrote up the Palmquist policy, $100,000 double indemnity on both the doctor and his wife. Johnny tells Jim that National Underwriters is worried about the double indemnity clause, because Johnny has an anonymous letter saying that someone is going to collect.

Johnny flies to Hollywood, California and stays at the Beverly Hilton.

Johnny cabs to the offices of Darryl and Clark and meets Jim Darryl, who is shaving and watching passersby and making checkmarks on a list. He tells Johnny that he counts Bermuda shorts and his partner counts gray suits, the loser buys lunch.

Johnny shows Jim the letter about the policy. Jim tells Johnny that Palmquist is an old-line family, a doctor and a hunter. The wife is an invalid, and there is a son, Eric, who lives with them and is the beneficiary of the policy.

Johnny walks to the Palmquist office and is met by the receptionist, Steffi Lund. Johnny is told that the doctor is not in, and Johnny tells her he will come back at five.

Johnny rents a car and drives to the Palmquist home. Johnny knocks at the door and no one answers. In the back Johnny finds a woman in a wheelchair, pouring whiskey from a bottle. She tells Johnny that it is not a medicine, and that her husband thinks it is a sign of weakness, then she drops the glass and asks Johnny to wheel her into the house. Johnny notices a boy watching them from a window.

Johnny asks her some questions, but she does not answer. Suddenly she seems to awaken when Eric enters the room. Eric offers to show Johnny out, and the woman seems to go back into her lethargic state. "You are a good son Paul" she tells Eric.

Johnny asks Erick how he manages to go from Eric to Paul, and he tells Johnny that she is not insane. Paul was an older brother who died three years ago, and that is part of the reason she is like that.

Johnny goes to visit Lt. Berry at homicide and shows him the note, which goes to the lab. Johnny visits Dr. Palmquist at 5:00, but he is not there as he had cancelled all of his appointments. The nurse offers Johnny an appointment for the next day.

Johnny visits a drive-in theater and has dinner and a double feature and then goes to his hotel where he runs into Jim Darryl who tells Johnny that someone killed Mrs. Palmquist a couple of hours ago.

Tomorrow, variations on an old theme. You pays your money and you takes your choice, but no matter how you pick it, it comes out murder.

Episode 2   Show Date: 6/26/1956
Lt. Berry calls and tells Johnny that he has been busy. Come on down and I will introduce you to the killer.

Johnny rushes to police headquarters where Berry tells Johnny that they got a call from Palmquist around 9:00 last night. The police got there and found a Colt .38 and the doctor holding a rifle on the man.

The doctor had been on a house call and when he got home he saw a man through the window holding a gun on Mrs. Palmquist. He snuck in to the house and got behind the man, who became rattled and shot Mrs. Palmquist. Dr. Palmquist then hit the man with a paperweight.

Johnny is suspicious, but there is evidence that the man broke in, and the gun was his. Berry checked on the patient, and she is a real looker, Mrs. Laura Considine. She backs up the story completely. The killer is an ex-con with a record of small stuff who has a really wild story.

Johnny meets with the suspect, Lonnie Miller, a tall erect man, who does not look like a killer, but more like a Victorian antimacassar who did not look like a prowler. Johnny tells Lonnie who he is, and he tells Johnny that the police did not believe him.

He tells Johnny that he is nearly 60, and has done nearly everything in the book, but has never killed anyone. Johnny tells him that the police seem to have evidence pointing to him.

Lonnie tells Johnny that he had just gotten out of jail and was hitchhiking when a man in a Cadillac gave him a ride. They stopped for coffee and then left and the car had a flat. Lonnie changed the flat, and the man told him to stay in town as he might have a job for him. He told Lonnie that his name was Carter.

He called last night and told me to come to his house at 9:00 to meet a man who had a job for him. The house was in the palisades. When he got there, he rang the bell and the door opened and he was hit on the head. When he came to, there was a dead woman on the floor, and Carter was holding a rifle on him. But the police called him Dr. Palmquist.

Johnny leaves Miller and talks to Berry who tells Johnny that the doctor is resting in the hospital and has not been told what Miller has said.

Johnny thinks about the case over lunch and a few martinis, and then goes to the hospital to meet Dr. Palmquist, who apologizes for being a bad advertisement for his profession. Johnny tells him he is investigating the insurance policy, and Palmquist tells Johnny that he should look for another climate, as California does not agree with him.

On the way out of the room, Johnny meets the most beautiful woman he has ever seen. Palmquist tells her she has the wrong room, but Johnny notices the initials on her purse, "LC" for Laura Considine. The doctor is ill, and the patient comes to visit! You cannot trust anyone these days.

Tomorrow, beauty may be skin deep, but fear goes a lot further down than that, sometime as far as death.

Episode 3   Show Date: 6/27/1956
Lt. Berry calls and tells Johnny that Dr. Palmquist has complained. He told Lt. Berry to keep unauthorized people away from him and to call his lawyer if they want anything. Meet me for lunch and I will try to sell you that we have the killer.

Johnny thinks there are too many Angeles to this case.

Johnny cabs to the Barkley for lunch with Berry but on the way out of his hotel Johnny sees Eric Palmquist and Steffi Lund in a white Cadillac. When they spot Johnny, they drive off.

Berry had ordered lunch and is unimpressed that Palmquist and Lund are an item. Berry does not like the smell of this case, but it is ex-con versus respected citizen, and Berry is watching everyone. Johnny is told that the nurse is a nice kid, that Eric gambles some and drinks, and that Laura Considine lives in Long Beach. Also, the lab report on the note shows that it is untraceable.

Johnny is paged for a phone call, Steffi Lund needs to talk to him. She will explain about the car. She wants Johnny to come to Dr. Palmquist's office, and hurry.

Johnny rushes to the office and gets a speeding ticket on the way. As the officer writes the ticket, Johnny notices that he is being followed.

At the office the man drives on, and Johnny goes upstairs. In the office Steffi asks what Johnny wants and tells him that she did not call him. But Johnny notices the signals in her eyes pointing to the other room. A voice tells Johnny to come into the office, and inside Johnny finds Eric Palmquist holding a .38.

Steffi is hysterical and tells Johnny that Eric is mad. Eric laughs because no one tells him what to do, and they are both afraid. Eric likes it when others are afraid and laughs. Eric suddenly has the same empty look that Mrs. Palmquist had, and he collapses.

Eric recovers in a few minutes, and Steffi tells Johnny that Eric will be all right. Steffi tells Johnny that Eric has circulatory lability, a form of extreme hypertension, enough to make him faint from fear. Eric is seeing a psychologist, and a cure will take a long time. Eric is scared of his father, the nice gentle healer, and her father-in-law. He is scared of his father and has kept the marriage a secret. Johnny is glad that he was too scared to shoot, otherwise he would be the primary suspect in the killing of his mother.

Johnny leaves with Steffi still upset and drives into the garage of his hotel. On the way to his room Johnny is hit by a man, the man who was following him. "You are in the wrong town punk, take the hint". Johnny does, he passes out.

Tomorrow, a study in reactions, three of them, one by a man who should know, one by a man do does not, an another by a bullet.

Episode 4   Show Date: 6/28/1956
Dr. Van Klauser returns Johnny's call. Johnny tells Klauser that he would like to see him today because he is running out of time. Johnny is told that he can come in at 11:00.

Johnny sees the hotel house medic and gets a checkup. Johnny then goes to meet Dr. Van Klauser at 11:00 and learns that Dr. Klauser is treating Eric Palmquist.

Johnny shows Klauser his ID and asks about circulatory lability. Johnny learns that it is a form of provoked hypertension, and very dangerous. It could cause a man to kill. Johnny calls for messages, and Lt. Berry wants to see him.

Johnny drives to see Lt. Berry and Johnny tells him about being hit. Berry tells Johnny that Lonnie has been identified as the buyer of the gun at a pawnshop, but Johnny is not convinced.

Johnny visits with Lonnie and asks him why he lied. Johnny wants to know why he bought the gun at a Burbank pawn shop, and that he had showed a driver's license at the time. Lonnie tells Johnny that his license is in his wallet in the property files. Johnny asks him to tell the story again.

Johnny checks the property folder, and there is no driver's license in it. Johnny buys an old newspaper that has photos of both Lonnie Miller and Dr. Palmquist.

Johnny then drives to Long Beach and finds the taco shop where Lonnie said he and Carter stopped. Johnny talks to Irving Gonzales, who tells Johnny that no one could pronounce his real name, Plutarco. Irving tells Johnny that he is looking for something, so ask the questions, as Irving can spot a cop.

Johnny shows him the pictures and he remembers reading about the case but tells Johnny that he would only be guessing. Johnny drives to see Laura Considine, but the drive is gated. As Johnny leaves he sees a car drive away from the house.

On the way back to the highway Johnny hears a shot and puts the car into the cliffs. Johnny wonders about how good a shot a man must be to put a bullet into a moving tire. Johnny remembers being warned about a man who always had time to go hunting, and who was an excellent shot, Dr. Palmquist.

Tomorrow, you want to hide something, put it in plain view. Only don't go overboard on the system if you are hiding a murder.

Episode 5   Show Date: 6/29/1956
Laura Considine calls, and Johnny tells her that she is the best friend a doctor can have. She tells Johnny that she has to talk to him and that she will meet him the hotel bar in an hour. Johnny tells her that the martinis will be waiting.

Johnny meets Mrs. Considine and Johnny reminds her of meeting him in Palmquist's hospital room. She tells Johnny that Victor's wife was a millstone around his neck, a woman in love with a bottle. And Eric is insane and hates his father. Eric gets a fortune by his mother's death, and yet Johnny is badgering Victor Palmquist. Johnny tells her that there is a lot of hate and there is usually a good reason for it.

Johnny rents a car and drives to the pawnshop in Burbank. Johnny asks Mr. Lerner about the gun sale, and he tells Johnny about the information written in the logbook. Johnny shows him the newspaper with the pictures, with Johnny's arm hiding part of the pictures. Lerner moves Johnny's arm and tells him that Miller bought the gun. Johnny tells him that he had to move his arm to tell which man had bought the gun.

Johnny rushes back to see Lt. Berry, who is out. Johnny talks to Lonnie, and asks him a few questions, and then meets with Berry. Johnny tells him that Palmquist and Miller are about the same size and color, and clothes can make a difference. If Palmquist wore work clothes to buy the gun, anyone would identify Miller as the killer. Johnny tells him that Palmquist arranged for the tire to go flat. When Miller changed the tire, Palmquist lifted the wallet, bought the gun and arranged the murder. Berry does not buy the story because Johnny still cannot find proof.

Steffi visits Johnny in his room and tells him that Erick has been drinking and ranting about Mrs. Considine and his father being a killer. She wants help. She tells Johnny that Eric is going to get a gun at home and then go to Mrs. Considine's to kill her.

Johnny and Steffi drive to Palmquist's house, and Johnny learns about him on the way. Steffi tells Johnny that the doctor is a tyrant who despises any form of weakness in his family. Paul was the favorite son and hunted with the doctor. Paul had a cold once and was humiliated into going hunting by his father. Paul ended up dying of pneumonia.

At the Palmquist house, Johnny finds Eric asleep on his bed. Dr. Palmquist comes home, so Johnny gets Steffi out of the house and then goes to the garage via a window to look at the trunk of the Cadillac.

Suddenly Palmquist is telling Johnny he should have asked about a key. Johnny tells him there is a tire with no puncture in the trunk, and Palmquist opens fire with a gun. Johnny manages to get off a shot as Berry comes in through the window. Berry tells Johnny that he did not like the look in Johnny's eye when he left and had him tailed. Johnny is told that "he is easier to tail than a trolley car."

Eric Palmquist admitted sending them the original warning note out of fear of his father. He never knew until the death of his mother that he was the beneficiary.

"Remarks: About Hollywood, let's call it the easterner's revenge: it's a nice place to visit, but I wouldn't want to live there."

Exp. Acct: $490.80

Notes:
- An antimacassar is a cover used to protect the back or arms of furniture.
- When Johnny visits the hotel doctor, he mentions a second wound, but Johnny was only hit once.

- Roy Rowan is the announcer.
- Musical supervision is by Amerigo Marino and Carl Fortina.

Producer:	Jack Johnstone Writer: Tony Barrett
Cast:	Virginia Gregg, Vic Perrin, Lillian Buyeff, Russell Thorson, James McCallion, Edgar Barrier, Don Diamond, Herb Butterfield

• ❖ •

Show:	**The Midas Touch Matter**
Company:	**Greater Southwest Insurance & Liability Company**
Agent:	**Jake Kessler**
Synopsis:	
Episode 1	**Show Date: 7/2/1956**

Pat McCracken calls and wants to know where Johnny has been. Johnny tells Pat that he has been buying fishing gear for a trip to New York and the Esopus or the Beaverkill for some trout. Pat suggests Lake Mohave in Arizona. Be the guest of Greater Southwest. There is a fish out there that might be worth three million bucks. "I'll be right over" Johnny tells Pat.

Johnny cabs to the office of Pat McCracken. Johnny is told that he had better be packed, as Pat has his tickets to Las Vegas. Take a car from there to Kingman and see Jake Kessler, the local agent. The case is the Midas Touch gold mine. With one to three million at stake, no one is going to quibble over your expense account. "Maybe I will take a look at those Lake Mohave bass" Johnny tells Pat. Johnny grabs some American Express Travelers Checks and heads for the airport.

Johnny gives a vivid description of the night sky in Las Vegas. Johnny gets a room at the Flamingo Hotel and incurs some "incidentals" at the casino. Next morning Johnny rents a car and drives to Kingman, Arizona.

Johnny drives to Jake's office, where Jake is dressed in cowboy attire. Jake has reserved a room for Johnny at Lake Mohave Resort, a nice place to stay. "Too bad you are not a fisherman" Jake tells Johnny. Johnny tells Jake he just happens to have brought a couple of rods and reels with him. "Good, Buster Favor will show you all the spots down there" Jake tells Johnny. Jake tells Johnny about the Midas Touch mine, which is in the area of Lake Mohave.

The mine was closed in the early thirties, but "Hard Luck" Dennis has been looking at the mine. He is a prospector and promoter who makes a fair living for himself and he had some trouble in Texas over some phony oil stock. He has been poking around looking for a strike and got a lease on the mine. The assay reports showed ore worth $1,100 a ton.

He needed some money for a pumping job, as Lake Mohave had raised the water levels and the mine was pretty deep. He went to the Haskell brothers, Ernie, Kevin and George, who were brokers out east and retired in the area. They got bored and bought the 2-Lazy-2 ranch and some cattle, and with Alex Bundy as foreman they did all right. All their insurance is with Jake, $500,000 a piece with double indemnity.

Dennis needed money and went to the Haskells, who wanted no part of it. He took them to the mine and let them take samples, and then they went in for $20,000 each. Three days ago, there was a cave-in and all three of the Haskells were killed. So, was it an accident or murder? Johnny is told that he will have to find Hard Luck Dennis. The wife of Kevin Haskell is the beneficiary of all three policies. The phone rings and Hard Luck Dennis is on the phone. He wants to see Johnny.

Tomorrow, I find that one of the fishermen who hangs around Lake Mohave is a character called death.

Episode 2   Show Date: 7/3/1956
Hard Luck Dennis calls and tells Johnny to come see him, and do not bring a gun. Meet me at three o'clock at the mine.

Johnny tells Jake about the phone call and that he will handle the matter himself, without help from the police. Jake feels that the mine was salted, but Captain Tad Harding of the police will prove it. He is at the mine now. Jake is positive that Dennis is guilty and salted the mine to get the money. "Well, if he is guilty, why would he call me?" asks Johnny. Jake agrees to not get anyone else involved.

Jake and Johnny go to see Tad Harding, who confirms Jake's story, and tells Johnny that there was no evidence of the mine having been salted. He learned that the cause of the cave in had been linked to a cable attached to a rock column that had been pulled out. Johnny tells Jake that now they need to find out who might have pulled the cable.

Johnny stalls Jake by going out to the resort to check in. On the way, Johnny finds the trail Dennis had described and follows it up to a shack. Johnny sees no sign of life at the shack.

Johnny sees a sudden movement that turns out to be a turtle. Inside the shack Dennis surprises Johnny. Dennis tells Johnny that he did not kill the Haskell boys, and Johnny agrees. Dennis tells Johnny that the town is against him, because the town liked the Haskells. Dennis knows that Capt. Harding had been to the mine. Dennis tells Johnny that the Haskells were murdered, but he did not kill them.

He had taken them to the mine, and while they were getting samples, he went out to investigate the sound of a car. Dennis looked outside the mine and something hit him and knocked him out. When he came to, the cave-in had happened and the Haskells were dead. Dennis hears a car coming up the road and Dennis turns to look at it. There is a shot, and Dennis is hit.

Tomorrow, the so called trackless desert yields a set of tracks that lead straight to, well if I told you, you would know, wouldn't you?

Episode 3   Show Date: 7/4/1956
Jake calls Johnny and Jake has been at the hospital. Johnny is told that Dennis may never talk as the bullet went right through his neck. Johnny tells Jake to call him when he can talk to Dennis. "In the meantime, I'm going to try

and snag me some of those Lake Mohave bass."

Johnny buys gas for the rental car and describes the resort area. Johnny gets Buster Favor, the general factotum of the resort to direct him to the Midas Touch mine.

Buster agrees to take Johnny there, and on the way, Johnny relates the facts of the case so far to Buster. Johnny is told that Dennis is a funny old character and was OK when he was prospecting, and when he could not make the big strike, he tried to find a sucker.

At the mine, Buster and Johnny use a flashlight to go into the mine. Buster finds a rattlesnake and uses a shovel handle to get the snake to strike and then snaps the snake like a whip. When Johnny ask if the snake could have been planted, Buster mentions the old scorpion in the monument trick used by prospectors to mark their claims.

Buster finds where the pillar has been picked at, and Johnny sees gold. Buster tells him that the only gold in the mine is in the pillars. Remove them and the mine collapses. Buster finds the winch and the steel rope. Buster tells Johnny that every ranch in the area has one, but this one does not belong in a mine.

Johnny takes a hard swing at a pillar in the mine, and starts a cave-in. Back at the resort Johnny is ready to go fishing, and Buster provides all the fixings. At the dock Johnny has a message to call Jake. Johnny calls Jake, who tells him that Dennis will recover and will only talk to Johnny.

Johnny drives to the hospital and sees Dennis who tells Johnny that "he" probably saw him poking around the mine, and figured Dennis recognized the winch, and tells Johnny that only Alex used the Union Standard model and that Alex was in love with Kevin Haskell's wife. Dennis tells Johnny that he will tell that to the court's if necessary and that Johnny is the only friend Dennis has.

Johnny talks to Jake to get directions to the 2-Lazy-2 ranch. Johnny suddenly changes the subject and rushes out the door, he is sure that someone was listening. Johnny is sure that it was Alex Bundy.

The chief calls Jake and tells him that Dennis is dead. Somebody climbed up the fire escape and killed Dennis with a bailing hook.

Tomorrow, the case is closed, and then it suddenly reopens with a bang from a .30-06 rifle.

Episode 4   Show Date: 7/5/1956
Buster calls Johnny and Johnny tells Buster that Dennis has been killed. Buster tells Johnny that he has found tire tracks at the miner's shack where Dennis was shot and more of the same tracks at the resort. Johnny is on his way.

Johnny buys gas at the sign of the flying red horse and meets Buster at an old wagon trail where Buster shows Johnny the tracks with the right front tire is almost worn smooth. Buster also found the same tracks at the shack. The trail ends up at the lake, so Buster suggests taking a boat to intercept the driver.

Buster and Johnny travel up the lake and notice a dust trail alongside the lake. Buster pulls in, and suddenly Johnny hears a noise. Johnny notices holes in the boat and they hear shots, someone is shooting at them. Buster pulls around a point and sees the dust heading back to the highway. Johnny tells Buster that he knows exactly where to look for the jeep that made the tracks.

Johnny and Buster head out to the 2-Lazy-2 ranch. Buster tells Johnny that the gun that was used to shoot at them was a long barreled .30-06, probably with a scope. Buster tells Johnny that Alex Bundy had drunk too much once and mouthed off about the rich millionaires and how he would help turn the worm. That is when the talk of him and Dora started.

At the ranch, Buster spots the jeep and Johnny drives by it so Buster can look at the tires. At the main house, Buster notices Johnny has a gun which Johnny describes as a ".38 lemon squeezer".

Dora opens the door and invites Buster and Johnny in. Buster introduces Johnny and Dora knows that he is there to investigate the mine accident. Johnny tells her about the evidence in the mine and the winch that came from this ranch. Dora wonders who would benefit here at the ranch? Johnny suggests that Alex Bundy would benefit by marrying into the family, he is interested in you isn't he.

Dora tells Johnny that he was interested in her, but she knew he was only interested in the ranch and knew that her husband was ill and did not have a long time.

Johnny tells Dora about someone killing Dennis and overhearing him tell Jake that he was going fishing. The man who did it was a crack shot and was driving a jeep. Dora tells Johnny that the jeep was gone that afternoon.

She offers to help and gives Johnny a high-powered hunting rifle. She tells Johnny that she was on the rifle team in college. Dora is about to give a gun to Buster when Alex yells at Dora about not telling him she was going to take the jeep. Suddenly Dora turns her gun on Johnny and tells him his gun is not loaded!

Tomorrow, well sometimes justice is done by strange and devious means.

Episode 5   Show Date: 7/6/1956
The phone rings, and Dora tells Johnny to answer it. Jake is on the phone and asks Johnny what he is doing there, as Dora has filed a claim. Johnny tells Jake he is looking at proof of murder right now. "Why don't you come on out here" he tells Jake as he throws the phone at Dora.

Proof of murder will save the insurance company $1.5 million. Now Alex has pointed the finger at Dora.

Buster pushes Dora who manages to crease Johnny's arm. As Buster starts to take the gun, Alex comes in with a gun.

Alex tells Johnny that Dora lied. She shot at Johnny by the lake, but he shot Dennis. He killed Dennis because he was going to talk, and he had to protect his neck. She was smarter than me and kept getting me in deeper and deeper. He got drunk once and told everyone he wanted the ranch. She heard about it and told him he could have the ranch with her. She plotted to get rid of her husband and kept him involved. He helped with the boats once when the

Haskells almost drowned. She told Dennis to take them to the mine. She would have killed me the way I killed Hard Luck.

Johnny tells him he is in too deep now. Alex tells them he is going to kill Dora. She grabs her rifle, but Alex kills her and runs out the door.

Johnny calls Jake to get the police to set up roadblocks as Buster looks for ammunition. Johnny and Buster drive out after Alex and follow him towards Davis Dam. At the top of a hill they see a police roadblock. Johnny heads towards Lake Mohave as a windstorm blows in.

At the resort, Ham Pratt tells Johnny that Alex took his boat out on the lake. Buster starts his boat and they follow Alex up the lake towards Nevada. As they ride the chop up the lake they finally start to catch up with Alex. As they pull up beside him Alex rams them with his boat.

That's really all there is to it, except that Ham had followed behind and picked up Buster and Johnny. Alex sank with his boat.

"Remarks: There is no question of course but that the Haskells had been murdered, no double indemnity. And Dora's little scheme to collect a cool three million, well it got her exactly what she deserved. Won't people like that ever learn?"

Exp. Acct: $978.35

Notes:
- This is the first of several appearances of Jake Kessler and the Lake Mohave Resort.
- Jack Johnstone related once in a taped interview, that he used to go fishing with his friend Robert Taylor at Lake Mohave Resort.
- My friend Bill Brooks, who knew Jack, told me that Buster and Ham were the actual owners of the resort.
- Jack Johnstone was married to a woman named Bundy and liked to use the names of his friends in his stories, so possibly Alex is a relative. Also, Jack used John Bundy as a pen name.
- The Esopus and Beaverkill are well known trout rivers in New York state.
- From 1886 to 1940, Smith and Wesson made a "Safety Hammerless" .38 revolver called a "lemon squeezer". It was popular with gamblers and detectives because it could be fired from inside a coat pocket. The term lemon-squeezer came from the grip-safety which required the user to hold it like a   well a lemon squeezer!
- Johnny is knicked, so I guess this counts as being shot for the seventh time.
- This is the first mention of American Express Traveler's Checks.
- The flying red horse is a veiled reference to Mobil Gasoline.
- Roy Rowan is the announcer.
- Musical supervision is by Amerigo Marino and Carl Fortina.

Producer: Jack Johnstone   Writer: Jack Johnstone
Cast: Virginia Gregg, Johnny Jacobs, Herb Butterfield, Parley Baer, Barney Phillips, Shepard Menken, Roland Winters

Show: The Shady Lane Matter
Company: Star Mutual Insurance Company
Agent: Pete Carlson
Synopsis:
Episode 1   **Show Date:**   **7/9/1956**

Pete Carlson calls, complaining to Johnny about working while the family is out on Cape Cod. Pete has a letter about the Bates murder that tells him to "look close to home". The signer was anonymous. The husband was the beneficiary, and the company is on the verge of paying the policy. Johnny agrees to go to Shady Lane, Vermont, if he can find it on the map.

Johnny travels to Shady Lane, Vermont, a small quiet town with one of everything, including Jed Bramler, the constable.

Johnny talks to Jed and is told that the killing is a mystery. The bullet was hand poured for an old-fashioned squirrel rifle. Ellen Bates was married and was shot in the heart. It could have been an accident, maybe a hunter who shot anything that moved, but hunters do not use old-fashioned rifles. Ellen Bates was a fine woman, but they have nothing to go on. There are no motives and no enemies.

The bullet was sent to New York, but the test results told them nothing and there are about 300 of that type of rifle in these parts. Ellen was sitting in front of her window and was shot. Johnny tells Jed that people are facts, and you can check on people. Maybe she saw something that made her dangerous to someone, or maybe someone would benefit from her death.

Johnny shows Jed the letter that was mailed from Shady Lane. Jed tells Johnny not to count on the letter too much. Ben Bates is the beneficiary, but Ben does not have the capacity for murder. Johnny wants to meet Ben and Jed agrees to drive him there, but Johnny will have to pay for gas as the town is kind of frugal with its money. Johnny wants to talk to the coroner, but that is Jed.

Johnny and Jed drive to the Bates farm. On the way, they stop and talk to Ben Preeny, Ben's neighbor.

Johnny is introduced to Mr. Preeny, who is building a stone fence. He tells Johnny that he plans ahead and builds right. Sarah Preeny is called out and Jed mentions the investigation of the murder. When Martin Preeny mentions that Johnny comes from Hartford, Sarah is surprised.

Martin tells Johnny about the operations that left Ellen an invalid. Sarah tells Johnny that Ben hardly took care of Ellen at all but spent time with that flibbertigibbet in town. Martin calls Sarah back and Johnny thanks Sarah for sending the letter. "How did you know?" she asks. Johnny tells her he was just guessing.

Tomorrow, of two who are not even accused, one confesses and one denies, and both very strangely.

Episode 2   **Show Date:**   **7/10/1956**

Johnny gets his call from Pete Carlson in Hartford. Johnny needs to know when the policy was written and Pete tells Johnny that it was about 4 years ago.

There is a policy on Ben Bates as well.

Johnny buys a newspaper and wonders about this case, there is no evidence, no witnesses, no motives or leads.

Jed takes Johnny up to the site where he thinks the shooting took place and Johnny notices the poor condition of the farmland. Jed tells Johnny that he had brought in dogs to search the area but found nothing. Johnny notices a stake and Jed tells him that it is a survey stake for a new highway that did not materialize. The highway could have made the farm worth something if the road had gone through here.

Jed shows Johnny where the shot must have come from and mentions that Ellen was not alone at the time. Mrs. Preeny was with her at the time but did not see anyone.

Johnny asks Jed about the gossip of Ben and the waitress and Jed tells him that Ben eats most of his evening meals there, and folks think that there is some interest growing between them. Johnny thinks that he would not be the first man to kill an invalid wife for a younger woman, but Jed tells Johnny that Ben was not like that. Jed also tells Johnny that Mrs. Preeny liked Ellen but did not like Ben for some reason. It is just her nature.

Johnny and Jed walk to the house and knock on the door. Grodie comes from behind the house and tells Jed that Ben is out, and Grodie does not know when he will be back. Jed introduces Johnny to Grodie Hawkins who does odd jobs, and Johnny asks if he was there the day Mrs. Bates was killed and he denies being there very loudly. Jed tells Johnny that Grodie gets kind of excited when blamed for things, and he is a dead shot, he never misses.

Johnny and Jed leave and return to town, where Johnny eats dinner at the Inn. Johnny asks the waitress if she is Millie Wells, and she tells Johnny that he works fast. She had hoped that she and Ben would have some time. She never thought about Ellen Bates while she was alive, and Ben never looked twice at her either. "Doesn't it mean anything if a person has been acquitted?" asks Millie. When Johnny asks of what, she replies murder, and then realizes that Johnny did not know what she was talking about. Johnny tells her she should tell him about it.

Tomorrow, a sudden twist, and a cool threat, a strange revelation, and the lies come thick and fast.

Episode 3   Show Date: 7/11/1956

Jed calls Johnny and asks for Millie, and Johnny tells him that she is crying at the moment. Jed tells Johnny that she is a nice woman, but Johnny tells him that everyone in town is nice to him.

Johnny buys dinner and Millie tells him that she and Ben never saw each other before his wife died, no matter what the people say. Millie tells Johnny that even being tried for murder brands a person for life. She tells Johnny that Ben has been coming in to eat here, and he knows about the trial. After Ellen died, he said that one day he would like to see more of her.

Millie tells Johnny that four years ago in Chicago, she had been working as a governess. The wife died under mysterious circumstances and she was accused of killing her to marry the husband.

Johnny stops by Jed's office and tells him that Millie has stopped crying. Jed tells Johnny that she had stopped by and told Jed about it on her first day in town. Johnny is convinced that a case exists against Ben.

Jed tells Johnny that the farm is mortgaged to the hilt and that Martin Preeny had loaned Ben $7,500 for Ellen's operations. The farm is only worth $4,500, so Ben feels obligated. The insurance policy would have released the pressure and still leave some money to marry Millie.

Johnny asks if Ben has a squirrel gun, and Jed tells Johnny he only has a shotgun. Johnny tells Jed that the shotgun was resting on a set of hooks designed for a different gun, a squirrel rifle. Jed seems to remember seeing a squirrel rifle there many years ago.

Johnny and Jed go back to the Bates farm and find Ben at home. Ben takes them to the kitchen and offers them some lemonade. Jed tells Ben that they are there to talk to him. Johnny thinks Ben might have killed Ellen, but Ben tells him he would never harm a hair on Ellen's head. Mrs. Preeny thinks he did it, and Ben tells them she is crazy.

When Jed asks about the squirrel rifle, Ben tells them it was stolen a week before Ellen was shot and he has not seen it since. Ellen thought she knew who took it, and Ellen asked him not to report it. The only people who were there at the house were Mrs. Preeny and Grodie. When Johnny asks if Grodie could have killed her, Jed tells Johnny that Grodie is a nice boy. Johnny asks if Jed cares if the murder victim is ever identified and Ben tells Johnny that Jed is Ellen's uncle. She was, "but it don't have no bearing".

Tomorrow, a slow net tightens and the fish turn frantic, and one of them is armed and dangerous, as deadly as a shark.

Episode 4   Show Date: 7/12/1956

The phone rings at Ben's house, but no one is there when Johnny answers it. Ben thinks that it probably was Millie Wells. Johnny tells Ben that she was tried for murder and your wife has been murdered and the town is talking, add up the facts, Ben.

Johnny still feels that Ben is the key to the case, but Jed tells Johnny that he is not the type. Johnny thinks that Jed is too close to everyone. Ben tells Johnny that he would never have killed his wife, and he is not involved with Millie. Ben explains about not reporting the missing rifle after the murder and Ellen's desire to not report it before the killing. She was going to talk to whoever took it but was killed before she could. Johnny asks Ben for a suspect, and he tells Johnny that Ellen had no enemies, and he would not kill her for the money.

Johnny and Jed drive back to town and go to the shack where Grodie lives in return for keeping an eye on the store. They walk back to the shack and Jed trips over a box. Grodie yells at them with a gun and tells them to stop until he has a light on them. Johnny asks to look at his gun and it turns out to be a .22.

Jed asks Grodie what he did with the rifle he took from Ben Bates' place. Grodie denies taking it, and Jed walks him back to the jail.

In the jail Jed tells Johnny that he knows Grodie, and he is lying about something. Jed tells Johnny that Ellen was the most liked person in the township, and Johnny still comes back to Ben as the guilty party. Johnny asks Jed how he and Ellen got along, and the answer is "just fine."

Grodie calls for Jed and they walk back to talk to Grodie. He tells them he did steal the gun and sold it to Martin Preeny to hang in his house. Preeny gave Grodie $4.00 for it about three weeks ago. When Johnny tells Grodie that he had the gun in his possession when Ellen was killed, he tells Johnny that the gun has never been fired, it has rust in the barrel.

Tomorrow, one domino tips, the whole stack tumbles, and the last man falls with a crash.

Episode 5   Show Date: 7/13/1956

Johnny is called by Mrs. Preeny and she wants to talk with him. Johnny tells her to come to his room but she could never do that, the town would talk. She tells Johnny that she has done a terrible thing and must confess.

Johnny and Mrs. Preeny meet in the lunch room where she tells Johnny that she did not do it, "That girl did not warm the teapot properly".

She tells Johnny that she did not want Martin to know she was meeting with Johnny and she tells Johnny about the letter. It was a terrible thing to do. The things she said about Ben were not true. She knows that Ben had nothing to do with killing Ellen. She also made up the things she said about Ben and Millie. Her husband is steady and reliable, but life on a farm is not easy for a woman, and sometimes they get silly notions. She wants a little warmth and understanding. But Ben Bates never even looked at her, and that is all she wanted.

Johnny walks to Jed's office and Grodie is still asleep. Johnny asks about picking up the gun from Martin, and Jed tells Johnny he can use the car, but it will cost him $3. Johnny jests about wondering how Jed made a living before he got there, and Jed tells Johnny that it was speeding tickets, but the new highway will end all that, as it misses the town completely. Johnny tells Jed that if it had come through the town, it would have saved Ellen Bates. Johnny tells Jed about the visit from Mrs. Preeny and Jed tells Johnny it was probably because Martin did not pay attention to her.

Johnny drives to the Preeny farm and Mrs. Preeny meets Johnny on the doorstep and tells him that she is on the way out. Johnny promises that he will not talk about, well you know.

Johnny goes in to see Martin, who is finishing his books, and Johnny asks him about the squirrel gun and tells him that Grodie had stolen it from Ben. Johnny inspects the gun, and it is all rusty. Johnny also notices the gun hooks, which had been there for years, and Johnny knows.

He knows who killed Ellen Bates. It was somebody who stood to profit more than Ben did. Somebody who loaned Ben $7,500 out of kindness, something not in your nature. But it was not kindness it was good business. Johnny asks where the rifle is that originally hung by the fireplace. Martin tells Johnny that there might not have been one, but Johnny tells him that the neighbors will remember.

Martin writes down the final figures in his journal and mentions that he had a good year last year. You take risks and sometimes you lose. He knew he made a mistake as soon as he pulled the trigger and takes Johnny out behind the barn where the rifle is buried.

Exp. Acct: $186.60

Notes:
- This story was done as *The Piney Corners Matter*, broadcast on 3/23/1954.
- Roy Rowan is the announcer.
- Musical supervision is by Amerigo Marino and Carl Fortina.

Producer:	Jack Johnstone	Writer:	Les Crutchfield
Cast:	Jeanette Nolan, Forrest Lewis, Shirley Mitchell, Will Wright, Bert Holland, John Dehner		

♦ ❖ ♦

Show: **The Star of Capetown Matter**
Company: **Tri-Eastern Indemnity Associates**
Agent: **Joe McNab**
Synopsis:
Episode 1   **Show Date:**   **7/16/1956**

Joe McNab calls Johnny about the star of Capetown, a diamond about the size of a jumbo olive. It is insured for $150,000. So far three men have been killed over it. The diamond is in Capetown, South Africa. Interested?

Johnny cabs to Joe McNab's office, and Joe is worried about Andrew Lanings Forbes III who is an international playboy who owns the diamond now. He treats it like a piece of costume jewelry and carts it around with him. The insurance company wants him to put it in permanent custody. Forbes is in a party-giving mood now, and they are worried.

Joe wants Johnny to talk to Forbes and convince him to let them take care of the diamond. Johnny is willing to take the case but is worried about the three men who have died over the diamond. Joe tells him not to worry, that was thirty years ago.

Johnny flies to Capetown, South Africa and cabs to the mansion of Mr. Forbes, which Forbes describes as "adequate". Forbes tells Johnny that it was unnecessary for the company to send him. Forbes offers to show Johnny the diamond and takes it from his jacket pocket. Forbes was expecting Johnny and decided to play a joke on him. Johnny looks at the diamond that he thinks is the size of a golf ball. Forbes takes Johnny to his bedroom and puts the diamond in a wall safe.

Johnny is concerned because the bedroom opens on to a terrace, so Forbes agrees to put the diamond in a bank vault the next morning. Forbes is giving a party for Agatha, his sister that night. She worries about him and is ashamed of what he is doing to the family name.

Johnny is invited to the party and asks Forbes for a guest list. Forbes tells him he has no idea who is going to show up.

Johnny stops by the local police office and gets Captain Van Tuyl to provide a guard for the party. Johnny goes back to the house for the party, which is well under way. Johnny meets a girl named Sheila, a friend of Forbes. She tells Johnny that she attends most of his parties.

Forbes walks up and welcomes Johnny and tells him that Agatha is not enjoying the party, and Forbes points her out. Forbes tells Johnny that she hates the party, Forbes and Sheila. A new arrival, Helen is pointed out by Sheila. Johnny wonders why Sheila keeps tagging along, and she tells Johnny that not going would not seem normal, and she wanders to the bar.

Johnny spots Forbes showing off the diamond as Agatha talks to him and he puts the diamond away. Forbes enjoys himself with Helen and goes onto the terrace.

After a while Johnny misses Forbes and looks for him on the terrace and then the bedroom where Forbes is on the floor with a knife in his ribs and no diamond.

Tomorrow, a girl who is exciting, beautiful and deadly.

Episode 2   Show Date: 7/17/1956
Lt. Van Tuyl of the police calls and tells Johnny that the diamond is still missing. He has a suspect — the whole party.

Johnny cabs to police headquarters and talks to Van Tuyl, who has nothing but questions. Johnny outlines his involvement in the case and the diamond. Johnny tells Van Tuyl that he was at the party the whole time and knew no one at the party. Johnny tells him about Agatha, Sheila and Helen, who was the last person Johnny saw with Forbes. Johnny tells Van Tuyl that there was no guest list. Johnny gets the mug shots of known jewel thieves and recognizes one of them, Julio Biac. Johnny thinks he was there but is not sure.

Johnny walks out for some fresh air and looks around the waterfront. Johnny spots the silhouette of a person on the roof of a building following him. Just in time, Johnny ducks as a roof tile crashes to the pavement. Johnny runs to the roof but sees no one.

Johnny goes to his hotel room and smells the scent of perfume. Sheila is in the room waiting for him and she wants to talk about last night. She tells Johnny that she left before it happened, she thinks. Johnny tells her she was sober enough to see Forbes and Helen leave, and to know that Johnny went to Forbes' room.

She tells Johnny that she had been watching and saw Helen leave the room with a bottle of perfume. That is always the first gift from Forbes to a new girlfriend. The perfume is called "Forever". She tells Johnny that she was waiting in the garden to talk to Forbes. She saw Johnny go into the bedroom and then left.

Johnny thinks that the only way for her to get off the Forbes merry-go-round was to kill him, but she tells Johnny she did not do it. Johnny suggests she go talk to Van Tuyl, and she tells Johnny that she is on her way there, as Van Tuyl had called her.

Johnny goes to the ship "Southern Empress" to see Agatha Forbes. She tells Johnny that Andrew had told her about him, but she is tired and does not want to talk. She will be in New York in a month, maybe she will be calm enough to talk then. Suddenly Johnny sees someone and breaks off the conversation.

Johnny sees a girl who looks like Helen and goes into the lounge looking for her but sees Julio Biac who was the bartender at the party. Julio runs down a passageway, but it dead-ends and Johnny has him trapped. Julio pulls a knife and lunges at Johnny who is able to subdue him.

Van Tuyl thanks Johnny for sending Biac ashore. Johnny tells him that Biac did not have the diamond, so the ship will have another passenger, Johnny!

Johnny gets a room from the purser and goes to the hotel to get his bags. In his room Johnny is slugged and recovers in time to see his ship steaming out of the harbor.

Tomorrow, I take a trip all right, a one-way trip.

Episode 3   Show Date: 7/18/1956
Lt. Van Tuyl calls and Johnny tells him about being slugged to keep him from sailing. Johnny feels the diamond is on the ship. Van Tuyl tells him that Biac's story agrees with Johnny's, but he swears he does not have the diamond. Johnny feels it was passed to someone on the ship, or he was chasing someone who had it. Van Tuyl will arrange for a helicopter to get Johnny to the ship.

Johnny gets a ride to the ship on a military helicopter with a throbbing head, still unsure the diamond is on the ship. Johnny lands on the ship and goes to his room. Johnny goes to the stateroom of Agatha, and Helen opens the door.

She leaves to go to her cabin, and Agatha agrees to talk to Johnny, as it is probably her duty as long as Johnny does not drag the Forbes name through the dirt. Johnny asks if there was a motive other than the diamond, but she had not thought of that. Johnny asks her if Sheila could have done it, but Agatha refuses to discuss her.

Johnny is surprised to find Helen in the stateroom, and Agatha tells Johnny that she is her traveling companion and that she is a thoroughly nice person. Agatha tells Johnny that Helen had decided to take the ship at the last moment and Agatha had hired her. Johnny tells her that Helen is suspect number one, and Agatha is surprised. Agatha tells Johnny that she will not file a claim until she gets to New York, which will give him time to find it, and the murderer.

Johnny goes to this stateroom and finds the door open. Inside is the same smell of perfume. Johnny remembers that Sheila has the perfume, and remembers it in his hotel room earlier, and thinks of Helen. In the hallway Johnny collides with a passenger, Ben Stacy, a loud-mouth who tells Johnny "See ya 'round, partner" as he walks away.

Johnny locks his door and goes for a martini. Johnny is sure it was Helen in his room, but then he spots Sheila at the bar. Johnny tells Sheila she took an interesting boat. She tells Johnny that there have been other women, but Andy always came back to her, so forget she is on board. Johnny is now sure that Helen is the prime suspect.

Johnny spots Helen, Agatha and Ben on the deck, and goes to talk. Helen leaves with a headache, and Ben tells Johnny that he and Forbes were the best of friends. He was not at the party but would have been there had he known what was going to happen. Ben tells Johnny that he can show them some really interesting places in Day-Kar (Dakar) and leaves.

Johnny asks Agatha if she knew Ben, but she tells Johnny that her brother had all sorts of strange friends he did not mention to her.

Johnny goes to his room, and sees that he has had a visitor, as the room is torn apart. Somebody figures that Johnny has the diamond now. Johnny has to get the diamond before Dakar, the end of the trail for him.

Tomorrow, my one good lead jumps ship, the hard way.

Episode 4   Show Date: 7/19/1956

The purser calls, and Johnny asks for a steward to fix his room. The purser tells Johnny that a cablegram had been sent to Julio Biac to meet him at the usual place in Dakar. The sender's name was Corner, but there is no one on board by that name. The purser is going to talk to the steward who delivered the message to the radio room.

Johnny tips the purser for the good news and now knows that Julio was not working alone.

Johnny starts for the purser's office and is met by Helen. She complains to Johnny about him tearing up her room. Johnny takes her to the bar to talk and she tells Johnny that she is so confused about people watching her. She tells Johnny that she did not know Forbes long, and that the party was strange. Forbes was interested in many people, and she did not encourage him. He gave her a bottle of perfume which Johnny tells is the usual first gift. She could not believe the news of his death nor his attitude about the diamond.

She made the trip suddenly to get away from Capetown, and Agatha is really a nice person. Before she goes back to work, Johnny asks her to a dance to be held that night.

Johnny walks her to Agatha's stateroom and Agatha tells Johnny that he is very suspicious. Johnny tells Agatha about the cablegram and she hopes the publicity will die down soon and wishes Andrew had met Helen sooner.

That night Helen and Johnny dance and go out on the deck to talk. Helen tells him that he seems so nice now, and he kisses her. Ben Stacy walks up laughing and Johnny gets miffed. Ben wants to set up a little shore party for Dakar tomorrow. Ben can show you some places you won't believe. Johnny agrees, and Stacy walks off.

The purser finds Johnny and tells him that the steward has disappeared. Johnny hears Helen screaming and goes to her. She tells Johnny that someone grabbed at her from behind a lifeboat and then ran off. Is she lying or telling the truth?

Johnny puts her in her cabin, and there is a "man overboard" call. The crew recovers the body, which turns out to be the missing steward. Johnny's one good lead is gone.

Tomorrow, I finally figure out the deal, only to find my opponent is holding all the aces.

Episode 5   Show Date: 7/20/1956

Ben Stacy calls Johnny to say they will be docking in an hour. That was some excitement last night wasn't it, about the steward falling overboard? Johnny tells Ben that he thinks he got pushed.

When the ship docks, Johnny goes to meet Ben, Helen and Agatha. Ben arrives and Agatha is going to stay on board.

Johnny and Helen get a good tour of Dakar from Ben. Ben directs Helen to a local shop and while Helen tries on clothes Johnny worries about her passing the diamond to someone. Ben disappears and Johnny goes to look for him only to be followed by a man with a knife.

In an alley, Ben pulls Johnny into a room and a man named Hassan follows Johnny inside. Ben tells Johnny that he is after him for the diamond. Johnny tells Ben that Biac knifed Forbes and Ben threw the steward over board. Ben had also been searching the rooms. Ben demands the diamond and Hassan starts beating Johnny to get it.

Ben tells Johnny that a friend owns the store Helen is in and if she has the diamond, she will get it from her. Ben tells Johnny that the only time Helen could have passed the diamond was last night on deck. Suddenly Johnny understands the case.

Ben leaves Johnny with Hassan and Johnny tries to talk to him. Johnny asks Hassan what Ben is giving him and tells Hassan that everyone who works for Ben ends up dead or in jail. That would never happen to you, would it? Johnny knows where the diamond is and Hassan can come with him.

As Hassan starts to think, Johnny slugs him and then goes after Ben, who comes back into the room. Johnny overpowers him and gets the police to hold Hassan and Ben.

Back on the ship Johnny visits Helen and thanks her for the snow job. Johnny asks her for the perfume bottle, smashes it and finds the diamond in the base. Agatha comes in with a gun and tells Johnny that she and Andrew had used Helen. Johnny asks Agatha why, and she asks Johnny if he knew how it felt to have someone drag the family name through the dirt?

The family is deeply in debt, but the will precludes the sale of the diamond. They had arranged for someone to sell the diamond and get the insurance. She had not planned on Andrew dying, and the creditors had started pressing her. Johnny tells her that she has failed to keep the name clean and is trapped. Are you going to brand it with murder? Johnny takes her gun and she tells Johnny she has failed all the way.

Johnny turns over the diamond to the authorities and Agatha is charged with insurance fraud. Julio Biac and Ben Stacy were indicted in the murder of Forbes.

"Remarks: About Agatha, I guess she did what she did because she thought the ends justified the means, which is one of the oldest sucker traps of them all. About Helen, well now that she is no longer a suspect, could be I'm no longer building up to a big letdown with her. At least it has not come yet, and I am still waiting. And the waiting is real pleasant."

Exp. Acct: $1,283.60

Notes:
- Bob Bailey gives a promo for the next episode, which describes *The Sea Legs Matter*. However, the next broadcast is *The Open Town Matter*.
- Dakar is the capital of Senegal.
- Roy Rowan is the announcer.
- Musical supervision is by Amerigo Marino.

Producer: Jack Johnstone   Writer: Robert Ryf
Cast: Jeanne Tatum, Virginia Gregg, Harry Bartell, Chester Stratton, Marvin Miller, D. J. Thompson, Tom Hanley, Ray Kemper

♦ ❖ ♦

Show: **The Open Town Matter**
Company: **Great Plaines Guaranty Company**
Agent: **Ralph Kearns**
Synopsis:
Episode 1   Show Date: 7/23/1956

Ralph Kearns calls and tells Johnny he is 52 and has married a 27-year-old woman, taken out a $50,000 insurance policy on a chief of police's salary with the wife as the beneficiary. Three days ago, you were shot to death and your wife filed a claim less than 24 hours later. What do you think? You have 56 minutes to catch the plane to Greensport, Missouri. And watch yourself, it is supposed to be a wide-open town.

Johnny travels to Greensport and the Townhouse Hotel where Johnny is met in the lobby by Averil P. Potzer, the local Great Plaines agent. Potzer tells Johnny that the wife wants her money and that she had asked for a claim form less than 13-hours after the chief was shot. Johnny calls her cold-blooded, but Potzer tells him that she is anything but cold-blooded, if you know what I mean, man-oh-man, WOW!

Johnny cabs to the home of Edward Blake, the dead sheriff. A tipsy man meets Johnny on the sidewalk and tells Johnny that he is a copper. Johnny tells him that he is in insurance, and the man says that is just what he had been asking the widow about and had just been thrown out of the house. He is Joe Craley, a reporter for the local paper. Johnny gives a "no comments" response to his questions about insurance.

Johnny asks Joe about where the action is in town, and Joe tells him he is pretty fast. Don't poke around, or you could get hurt. Johnny asks how the sheriff could afford a house in a nice area on this salary, and Joe tells him that his wife is even more expensive. Johnny asks Joe if the police chief was in on the gambling, and Joe gives him a "no comment". Johnny wants to talk to him later and Joe tells him to just look for "the alcoholic from the paper".

Johnny meets Mrs. Blake, and she is happy to see Johnny and did not think they would pay so quickly. Johnny tells her he is there to investigate the killing. She tells Johnny the company is trying to get out of paying, she knows how they operate.

Johnny tells her he wants more information, the details of the killing. She tells Johnny that her husband was shot to death with his own gun right here in his own house. Johnny asks for her to show him how it happened, and that there will be no payment until he is satisfied. She makes a quick pass at Johnny and then it is back to business.

She relates how her husband fell and his gun was lying right beside him. It was around 2:00 a.m. when she heard a noise and Ed went down to investigate. His gun was on the table. She went into the hall and heard shots. She ran downstairs and found him dead. The police say a prowler forced the lock. The police figure the man used the gun on the table. She does not know who the prowler was, but Ed had some enemies. Johnny asks if a friend could have done it.

Johnny notices a diamond-studded watch, the nice house and the new car, all on a policeman's salary, but she knows nothing about Ed's finances. Johnny asks if Ed was in on the rackets, and she asks Johnny if he wants a drink.

Johnny tells her that 24 hours is quick for a grief-stricken widow to file a claim, and she tells Johnny that she is not grief stricken. She tells Johnny to see Dave Sherman the city attorney to see if she is guilty. Then, if you are nice, I might even cooperate.

Tomorrow, a smash in the teeth loosens things up, and an airtight alibi gets air conditioned with bullets.

Episode 2   Show Date: 7/24/1956

Johnny gets a call from Dave Sherman. He has made the records available, but Johnny wants to talk to him personally. Martie Blake told me to talk to you. Dave tells Johnny that if he wants to light a fuse in this town, he will give Johnny some matches.

Johnny cabs to city hall to talk with Dave Sherman and notes that the newspaper headlines are calling for action. Johnny tells Dave that he has been to see Mrs. Blake already, and she is not grieving.

Dave tells Johnny that Ed had to make money after meeting Martie, he had to. Then she married him. Dave tells Johnny that he is on the wrong foot in this case. Johnny tells about her turning on her charms, and the scanty details she provided.

Dave tells Johnny that she is cold-blooded and used to be a dancer who lived by her wits. Dave tells Johnny that they were not alone, he was there with them. "Well, she has a good alibi" notes Johnny.

Dave tells Johnny that he was spending the night and that he and Ed were going fishing the next morning. He heard some noises and went out into the hall right after the shots were fired, and Martie was standing in her doorway. Dave tells them that he and Blake were not really good friends but their differences were not a motive for killing him. Johnny wonders if Martie was the motive, after all Dave is around her age.

Dave tells Johnny that she has a built-in jukebox and only plays if you put in money. Johnny tells him that Martie must have been the reason Blake got into the rackets, and Dave asks Johnny what makes him think that there are any rackets in town, and where he got his information.

Mayor Will Lyons comes in and Dave introduces Johnny. Johnny tells him his theory has just blown up. Johnny asks for the official theory and the mayor tells him that when they find Shorty Wells, they will have the killer. Wells had been put in jail by Blake, had sworn to get him, and is out on parole now but no one can find him.

When Johnny mentions rackets to the mayor gets flustered, but Dave tells him that Johnny knows. The mayor tells Johnny that there are rackets, but no one knows who is in charge. But find Shorty and the case will be closed.

On the way out of city hall Johnny is honked at by Martie Blake, who wants to talk to him. Johnny tells her that he has talked to Dave and asks why she did not tell him about Dave. She tells Johnny that he is not being nice. When Johnny mentions Shorty Wells, she tenses up.

There are shots from a speeding car, and Martie tells Johnny that someone is out to kill him. "How do you know they were not after you Mrs. Blake?" asks Johnny.

Tomorrow, an old flame and a new one, and two men get burned. One becomes an alcoholic, the other a human torch.

Episode 3   Show Date: 7/25/1956

Joe calls and asks how Johnny is making out? Johnny wants to talk, but Joe tells him not tonight, he is drunk and might talk too much. Johnny tells him about the shots, and Joe tells him to beat it. Greensport is a wide-open town.

Johnny cabs to the home of Will Lyons the mayor, to get right to the top of the story. Will and Johnny talk in the library and he tells Johnny that he had heard the shots. Will tells Johnny that the town is looking into the shooting matter, but there are no witnesses. Johnny tells him that he is not sure that he was the target, but he does not know why anyone would have wanted to kill Martie.

Will tells Johnny that there is a police guard at Martie's house now, and Johnny asks him if he can trust the officer, or anyone else for that matter? Will tells Johnny that every effort to carry out raids on the mob were unsuccessful. Dave and Will suspected that Ed was on the take, but never could find any evidence. Dave and Ed were not friendly at all, and his being there was odd, but Ed had asked him to go fishing. Everything Will can think of comes back to Shorty Wells. Johnny is doubtful about Shorty.

Will tells Johnny that Dave was really close to Martie before she married Ed. Johnny asks if Will can trust Dave Sherman, but he is not sure.

Johnny calls on Martie Blake, and she tells him to join the party — her. She comments on her bodyguard, and how he blushed and stammered when she asked him to come in for a drink, which Johnny fixes. Martie tells Johnny that he probably knows how to party, and he tells her he has a system.

First, he hooks up with the rackets so he can buy his wife all sorts of things, and Martie tells him to back off. Johnny tells her that the bullets were for her, so who would want to kill her? Did Dave really see the shooting or is he just giving you an alibi. Johnny asks where Shorty Wells is and she throws Johnny out.

Johnny goes looking for Joe Craley and finds him after three martinis. Johnny asks about Martie and Joe tells him that she hates champagne, but always orders it, and that she is a four-star tramp. She is the ex-girlfriend of Shorty Wells and Ed Blake took her away from him.

As for the police, some of them are useless. Like the ones who took two days to discover Ed had been shot with his own gun. Joe loves Martie, always has. She was his girl before Shorty Wells.

Tomorrow, a man with a gun, desperate, faces a blazing inferno and gambles for his life.

Episode 4   Show Date: 7/26/1956

Johnny gets a call from Joe and is told to hang on. There is a big story breaking, a fire at Martie Blake's house.

Johnny rushes to the fire at Martie Blake's house, which is fully involved in flames. Dave Sherman tells Johnny that he got there after the fire engines and that Martie is OK. The police guard was there but did not see how it started.

Dave and Johnny argue about Dave and Martie and their alibi, and the past boyfriends of Martie. Dave tells Johnny that Joe started drinking when she dumped him for Shorty Wells. When Dave found out that she was going with Shorty, he went after the rackets.

Johnny finds Martie in Dave's car, and she is scared. She agrees that someone is after her, why else burn her home. She does not know who though, maybe it was Shorty, to get even.

She tells Johnny that she was sleeping on the sofa and woke up with flames around her. Joe walks up and asks if Martie has confessed, and they argue back and forth. Joe tells Johnny that the house is insured against fire, and too bad the car didn't burn, or everything Martie had would be in cash.

Johnny hears shots and they see a man staggering out of the basement of the house. Joe and Johnny rush up to the man who is unconscious. It is Shorty Wells.

Johnny is in the hospital with Dave, waiting for Shorty Wells to recover. Dave is sure that the case is tied up with the rackets.

Dave takes a call and tells the mayor that Shorty may not recover. Shorty mumbles but says nothing. Joe comes in from filing his story on the fire. They wonder why Shorty was firing the shots. Shorty Wells is the only lead now, and if he dies they are beat.

Tomorrow, death strikes again, leashes out violently and mistakes its target, and a wide-open town blows sky high.

Episode 5   Show Date: 7/27/1956
The phone in the hospital room rings and Martie asks how Shorty is. She wants to talk to Johnny, she is ready to talk. She is at an all-night diner across from the hospital.

Johnny tells Dave about Martie and Joe will call Johnny if Shorty recovers. Joe reminds Dave about the mistake with the sheriff's gun and the botched raids. Johnny tells them to stay with Shorty while he goes to see Martie.

Martie asks Johnny if she is hard to take. She has an alibi and wants Johnny to convince the insurance company with a nice report. Johnny still wants some details as to why she heard the noise, she turned on the lights and she filed the claim. Johnny wants to wait for Shorty to recover but she offers Johnny $10,000 to file the report.

Joe comes in and tells Johnny that the basement door was padlocked on the outside and Shorty wells was shooting to get out of the basement. Johnny asks Martie if Shorty was supposed to die there.

Joe asks Johnny what he wanted and tells Johnny that the nurse had told him that Johnny had called. They rush back to the hospital and meet Dave leaving and he tells them that the mayor had called him.

They all go back up to the room to find that the police guard is gone. The door is open and Johnny walks in to find the mayor holding a pillow over Shorty's face, but Shorty is dead. The mayor tells Johnny that he was moving the pillow, and Dave tells him that he had suspected the mayor of being in on the rackets.

Will pulls a gun and tells them to back off. Johnny asks why he had Ed killed and Dave tells Johnny that Ed Blake was going to pull out of the rackets and tell him everything, that was the purpose of the fishing trip. Johnny figures that Martie tipped off the mayor, and Shorty was staying at Martie's house. They fight with the mayor and get his gun but the mayor throws himself out of the window. "Well, he got out of being prosecuted".

Johnny goes back to Martie at the diner. "Too bad, Johnny, you will have to pay off now. Shorty is dead and the mayor is dead — no witnesses" she tells Johnny.

Johnny tells her that there is one witness, her claim form, which is really a confession. It says "we found my husband's body at the foot of the stairs, that he had been shot and killed with his own gun". The claim was in the office within less than 24 hours of Ed's death. The police did not find out until two days later. Real neat confession, huh Martie?"

"Remarks: Martie Blake never was able to explain how she knew about that gun. She sure tried."

Exp. Acct: $516.20

Notes:
- This story was done as *The Dan Frank Matter*, broadcast on 5/4/1954.

- At the end of the program Bob thanks "all those who are so kind about writing and telling us how much you like Johnny Dollar. It's a very gratifying experience. It's encouragement to all of us who are involved in production of the program, well, we appreciate your letter more than you know. As always, I will try to answer you promptly, but sometime the mail does pile up. In any event, thanks. Thanks very much for writing."
- Roy Rowan is the announcer.
- Musical supervision is by Amerigo Marino.

Producer: Jack Johnstone Writer: Les Crutchfield
Cast: Jeanne Tatum, Paul Dubov, Joseph Kearns, Stacy Harris, Russell Thorson

◆ ❖ ◆

Show: The Sea Legs Matter
Company: Universal Adjustment Bureau
Agent: Pat McCracken
Synopsis:
Episode 1   **Show Date:**   **7/30/1956**

Didn't you tell me once you were a nut for fishing? This is Pat McCracken. "You know you spiked my plans to go fishing a couple of weeks ago, so what's on your mind?" Johnny asks Pat. "Big Fish, real big fish" is the answer. Did you ever hear of Douglas R. Lanphier, the millionaire sportsman, yachtsman and playboy? "Didn't I read somewhere?" asks Johnny. "Yeap, right on the bottom of the deep blue sea, and a $400,000 claim has been filed. You interested?" asks Pat. An expense account based on that will be a pleasure!

Johnny cabs to Pat's office where Pat has a hand full and head full of information. Mrs. Constance Lanphier has filed two claims. One is against Douglas' life policy for $250,000, and the other is $150,000 for the loss of the yacht. Lanphier was cruising along the coast of Central America in his boat *The Sea Legs*. The boat hit some rocks and sank, and he and the other crewman were lost. Two and a half years ago, Lanphier filed a claim for a boat lost in the same place, near the Baldero Islands off of Nicaragua. Mrs. Lanphier is at home on Long Island.

Johnny travels to Long Island, New York to visit Mrs. Lanphier. The cab driver tells Johnny that the estate has been sold off to cover their fast living. Johnny finds a manor house with new houses being built around it. Johnny rings the bell and Mrs. Lanphier greets him. Johnny tells her why he is there, and she tells Johnny that the initial shock has passed. She has problems, mostly financial and does not know how to describe what happened. She was along on the trip until the day it happened.

They were cruising slowly along the coast, in *The Sea Legs*, a motorsailer of 68 ft. Along the coast. Doug put in at San Juan del Paro, where the ship was built, but sandbars prevented entry so they went on to Bluefields. Doug had some radio work done and went out to sea to test the radio near the Baldero Islands. That is where *The Connie O.* was lost two years ago.

She told Doug not to go out there, because of the treacherous currents and rocks, but Doug had to go to prove a point. He blamed the loss of the other boat on poor seamanship and wanted to prove he could take a boat through there safely. His last words were that a rock had torn the bottom out. A search party was sent out but the bodies were never found. There was no time to put on life preservers.

Johnny tells her he will have to do an investigation, and she tells Johnny that she needs the money. Johnny asks her what her plans are, and she tells Johnny she is going to sell the property and move to Europe, alone.

She starts to imply that Johnny is trying to stop the claim and will tell her that Doug is still alive. The more she talked, the more Johnny is convinced that something is wrong with this case.

On the way back to town, the cabby tells Johnny that the Lanphiers were very close to each other, and he should know, he knows everything in Cutchogue.

Johnny goes back to New York City and arranges to fly to Managua, Nicaragua after clearing the trip with Pat McCracken and telling him that he smells a rat. Johnny asks Pat to have someone keep an eye on Mrs. Lanphier.

Johnny is a called later by Pat and is told that Randy Singer has been asked to keep an eye on her, but she has left town.

Johnny cabs to La Guardia Field when suddenly Mrs. Lanphier gets on board flight and sits next to Johnny.

Tomorrow, the seeds of suspicion really begin to sprout, with the help of one of the wildest characters I ever met.

Episode 2   Show Date: 7/31/1956
The operator gives Johnny his call to Pat McCracken, who has not found a trace of Connie Lanphier. Johnny tells Pat that he knows where she is, she was sitting right beside me on the plane.

Johnny buys dinner in Dallas for Connie and then they board a midnight plane to Nicaragua, where he learns nothing about the case. Connie cannot get over the coincidence of them going to Nicaragua at the same time, and she knows the country. Johnny is starting to feel very leery. Johnny wonders why she cares more about the lost boat than about the lost husband.

Johnny eventually gets to his hotel and is awakened at 6:00 a.m. by a man knocking on the door. Oscar Patrick Vladimir Poscaro lets himself into the room.

Call me Oscar, since we are working together. Oscar can get Johnny anything, for a cost. Breakfast arrives: orange juice, tomato juice, creamed chipped beef on toast, eggs benedict, lamb chops, scrambled eggs, little sausages, toast, honey, jam and coffee. If Oscar is to be of service, he must keep his strength up! No one else in Central America can get Johnny the kind of help Oscar can get him.

Oscar knows who Johnny is, and who has not heard of the "famous freelancing insurance instigator" with the lovely big fat expense account! Who is Oscar to not learn from such a great man? Johnny is about to haggle Oscar down to $20 per day, but Johnny finally tells Oscar he is not hired.

Oscar tells Johnny that he knows all about the boat and something crooked is going on with it. Oscar tells Johnny that he should go to Porto Gardo, and Oscar has a plane ready for his own personal use. Johnny wants to contact the authorities, but Oscar tells Johnny that it would be a waste of his time. Johnny wonders what his racket is and the answer is simple, money.

Oscar gives Johnny the address of a small airfield and goes through Johnny's pants looking for a small tip for bringing up breakfast.

Johnny goes to the police who tell Johnny that Oscar lives on American tourists and can be trusted implicitly, and he knows the country.

Johnny talks to Captain Ramirez at the coast guard, and he can tell Johnny nothing more. He suggests that Johnny get a pilot and guide for the Baldero Islands, and he can recommend one named Oscar Patrick Vladimir Poscaro!

Johnny cabs to the airfield where Oscar has a plane waiting for him. The plane usually costs $35 per day but Oscar has a special rate, only $45 a day, but it is a special rate because it includes Oscar.

Oscar tells Johnny that he is disappointed in Johnny because he told Mrs. Lanphier what he was doing. She came rushing out to the airfield, rented a plane and took off just a few minutes ago.

Tomorrow, the sea, the rocks, and dear old mother nature bring some pretty startling facts to light, and the case takes a sudden twist

Episode 3   Show Date: 8/1/1956

Johnny sends a ham radio call to Pat McCracken from the airplane because there is no phone in Porto Gardo. Johnny tells Pat that Mrs. Lanphier has disappeared, and that she has rented a small plane. Johnny tells Pat to watch her place in Long Island and call me if she comes back.

Johnny is sure that the claims are fraudulent but cannot tell why. Porto Gardo is the last place where *The Seal Legs* had been heard from, by a ham operator named Oscar Poscaro, who complains about cranking the generator for the call!

Oscar set up a transmitter in Porto Gardo because the authorities in Bluefields required him to have a license. Oscar does not have a pilot's license either, so Johnny tells him that he does and he will fly from now on.

Johnny goes to the plane to fly over the islands, and Oscar tells him that is why he is so "unvaluable", to guide Johnny to the islands, until Johnny tells him he can also look at the maps. "But Mr. Dollar, that wouldn't be fair!" complains Oscar.

Johnny flies over the islands and notes that they could be dangerous at night. Oscar tells Johnny that the boat went down at 10:21 a.m. on a clear day like today. Johnny notes the clear channel between the islands but there are no rocks. Oscar tells Johnny that only when the tide is changing is the channel dangerous.

Johnny spots a packing case and wants to follow it to see where the tides take it, but Oscar tells him it will end up on the beach in front of his house, that is how he got the lumber for his radio shack. Oscar tells Johnny that when *The Connie O.* sank, he got all sorts of things, but when *The Sea Legs* sank there was nothing.

Johnny lands the plane and cabs to the coast guard and talks to Captain Ramirez who tells Johnny that on the day in question the tide was just after neap, it was rising.

Johnny goes to the airfield and gets the plane again. Johnny flies south to San Juan del Paro, where Johnny sees a small plane at an airfield, it is the one Mrs. Lanphier rented.

Oscar lands the plane and Johnny sees a car cutting in front of them. Johnny tries to get the plane off the ground, but the car hits their landing gear and they crash.

Johnny hears a plane starting and realizes the other plane has taken off, and that he saw the man behind the wheel of the car, Douglas Lanphier.

Oscar and Johnny are OK, but the plane is totaled and Oscar tells Johnny that he also recognized Douglas Lanphier as well.

Tomorrow, the dark back streets of San Juan del Paro yield some valuable information, and a threat of sudden death. And believe me, it is not an idle threat.

Episode 4   Show Date: 8/2/1956
The operator calls Johnny and connects him to Pat McCracken. Pat has a man watching the Lanphier place, but she has not returned. The man had let himself in and answered the phone. It was the operator from San Juan del Paro with a call from a man on whom she has made a claim. Johnny tells Pat that Douglas is not dead, he tried to wreck their plane.

Johnny pays a man for a ride into town and Oscar comes in handy with the Indian dialects. The town has only a small number of boats and a few buildings.

Johnny and Oscar get rooms in the hotel and have a doctor look at them. American dollars go far here, unless Oscar gets a hold of them.

Johnny notes that on the flight in, he noticed several shipyards, and Oscar tells him that only one is still in operation. Johnny tells Oscar about the insurance claims on *The Connie O.* and that the ease of collection on the first one gave Lanphier ideas. He brought the second boat down and it disappeared, but Johnny does not think that the boat sank.

Johnny is sure that Constance was in the other plane. Also, she had told Johnny that she heard *The Sea Legs* go down, but Oscar had told Johnny that the radio just went dead. Johnny thinks that Lanphier probably brought the boat to a shipyard and had it rebuilt. Johnny also wants to find the other man on the boat, Ramon Gonzales, and he probably is still around, unless Lanphier killed him.

Johnny and Oscar go to the shipyard to look around. On the way, Johnny spots a man drinking beer in a saloon and thinks he might be Gonzales. Oscar might recognize him up close, so he goes in to look at the man.

Oscar makes small talk with the man, who gets angry with him and tells him to leave. Oscar runs out at knifepoint but is sure that the man is Gonzales.

Johnny and Oscar go to the shipyard and find *The Sea Legs* with new paint and fittings, a moved cabin and other changes, a good job of disguise. On the transom, Johnny can feel the old name under the new paint.

Johnny wants to go back to talk to Gonzales, but Oscar is afraid. Gonzales meets them in the shipyard with his knife, and Johnny manages to slug him.

Johnny wants to wake him up and talk to him, but Oscar is afraid he might have a friend. He does, Mrs. Lanphier with a gun pointed right at Johnny's back!

Tomorrow, sometimes when you wind up a case, things take a turn, a sudden switch that makes you wish you hadn't won.

Episode 5   Show Date: 8/3/1956

Captain Ramirez returns Johnny's call and Johnny tells him to bring a plane to San Juan del Paro, where he can make several arrests, one of them a killer.

Johnny calls Ramirez and recounts what has happened before that, the plane crash caused by Douglas Lanphier, finding *The Sea Legs* and Ramon Gonzales.

Connie Lanphier surprises Johnny as he is trying to wake up Gonzales. Connie tells Johnny that she knows Oscar, "that chiseling, money grabbing..." until Oscar interrupts her.

Johnny tells her that the disguise was good, and Connie tells Johnny that they would have gotten away without Oscar's help. She tells Johnny that they had to file the claims to get the money. Johnny tells her about the discrepancies in the story she told Johnny, and Connie warns Johnny as Gonzales tries to attack him with the knife.

Connie disappears and Oscar tells Johnny that he was looking out for him and did not see Connie leave. Johnny tells Oscar that he has proof that Douglas Lanphier is not dead and the boat was not lost. The case is closed except for a few details and Oscar is one of them.

Johnny tells Oscar that he could have stopped Connie because he is carrying a gun and Connie did not have one. Johnny tells Oscar that he now knows why Oscar stayed so close to him. Oscar tells Johnny that he was paid by the Lanphiers for some services, including his radio. That is why he knew about the wreck and could help Johnny.

Oscar tells Johnny that he was only trying to help, but Johnny tells Oscar that he only told Johnny what he would find out anyway. His real job was to keep Johnny away from Connie Lanphier when she came to find her husband.

Oscar complains about being called a crook, but Johnny tells him that he could have avoided the plane crash and had insisted that Johnny take his seat belt off while Oscar wore his, so that Oscar could be there to collect from Lanphier. Oscar let all this happen for money.

Oscar tells Johnny that he has always loved money but would not have let anyone kill Johnny. Oscar tells Johnny that Mr. Lanphier was responsible for the plot, and totally controlled his wife. Oscar tells Johnny that he is telling the truth, for once in his life, He was hoping that Johnny would pay more than the Lanphiers so that he could be on Johnny's side, the good side for once.

Oscar is ready to tell Johnny where Douglas Lanphier is when Lanphier walks in ready to kill Oscar for talking. Oscar reaches for his gun and they end up shooting each other.

Johnny calls Captain Ramirez and lets him take charge. Extradition procedures are under way for Connie, and Douglas' body is being taken to the states. Oscar's body? Johnny leaves some money with Ramirez for a decent burial.

"Remarks: I wonder what kind of a deal Oscar Patrick Vladimir Poscaro was able to make at the Pearly Gates, or where ever he was headed. And, you know something, I kind of hope it was a pretty…well I hope is wasn't too bad a deal."

Exp. Acct: $841.95

Notes:
- Johnny tells Oscar he has a pilot's license.
- Roy Rowan is the announcer.
- Musical supervision is by Amerigo Marino.
- During episode 4, Don Diamond plays Pat McCracken.

Producer:	Jack Johnstone Writer: Jack Johnstone
Cast:	Harry Bartell, Lawrence Dobkin, Virginia Gregg, Parley Baer, Don Diamond, Russell Thorson

◆ ❖ ◆

Show: **The Alder Matter**
Company: **Worldwide Mutual Insurance Company**
Agent: **Vic Kelly**
Synopsis:
Episode 1   Show Date: 8/6/1956

Vic Kelly calls and asks Johnny about his Spanish. You may have to be more than a linguist to unscramble this one. William Billy "Up again, down again" Alder the promoter, is up to his ears in Venezuelan oil, and is insured for $250,000, and has changed the beneficiary five times in a month. What does that mean? "It means I will be right over" Johnny tells Vic.

Johnny cabs to Vic Kelly's office, and he is worrying over the policy on Alder. Johnny knows Alder is a super salesman, who has been in a bunch of businesses. The policy is not outrageous given the oil he is pumping out of the ground. The changing of beneficiaries started a month ago. Johnny thinks that Alder is worried. Vic tells Johnny that the policy has a clause that allows us to investigate irregularities.

Johnny flies to Caracas, Venezuela and goes to visit the local police chief, Jefe Velasquez, who is apologizing about the lack of air conditioning in his office. "He is avoids talking about Alder so he will not give Johnny the bum cow". There is nothing to put your finger on. They seem like a nice family, but when you stay there for a while, you know something is wrong, just like an oil well which will blow up one day.

Johnny rents a car and drives to the huge and impressive Alder home. At the front door, Johnny sees a girl being kissed by a young man, who runs off when Johnny clears his throat. The girl tells Johnny that there is nothing her father can do to stop her from seeing Paul. Johnny tells her who he is and asks to see her father. She is Peggy Alder, and her father will be home in an hour. Johnny waits on the patio with a drink.

Mr. Alder arrives and is glad to see Johnny. He has read the policy and knows Johnny has the right to ask questions, but he does not have to answer. Johnny asks Alder what he is to do and Alder starts to waffle and will tell Johnny nothing. He asks Johnny to stay in the house and to keep him alive. Johnny senses that Alder is afraid.

Johnny is put in a guestroom, and at dinner he eats only with Mr. Alder and Peggy. Johnny is told that Mrs. Alder is in town with some guests, for the bullfights. Alder tells Peggy that she has disobeyed him by bringing Paul Kincaid here, and Peggy blames Johnny but her father tells her that the servants have eyes too.

Alder apologizes for embarrassing Johnny and tells him that Kincaid is an oilfield foreman, who will never have the chance to move up in the company or the family.

Alder and Johnny talk after dinner, but Johnny learns nothing. Suddenly there is a gunshot and a bullet misses Alder and Johnny rushes out to the jungle area where the shot came from.

Tomorrow, one man dances attendance, another dances death, and a woman calls the tune.

Episode 2   Show Date: 8/7/1956

The Caracas police operator calls and Jefe Velasquez asks Johnny how things are. Johnny tells him about the gunshot and asks to use the ballistics lab. Velasquez tells Johnny he should be worrying about the next bullet.

Johnny tips Natcho Gomez who had helped Johnny search the jungle for the gun. Natcho is very pleased that Johnny has given him the money. He was sure that Johnny would not find anything, but he is afraid for Johnny.

Johnny drives to Caracas and wonders about what Alder is up to. Johnny meets with Jefe Velasquez, gives him the bullet and then takes him to lunch, where Johnny is introduced to the Pisco Sour, "they do not solve the case for you, but they make you happy about being worried".

Jefe Velasquez asks if Johnny has met Mrs. Alder, and Johnny tells him she got home late. Also, Alder does not want Johnny to mention the shooting to any of the guests either.

The drinks arrive, and Jefe Velasquez tells Johnny to relax and take a sip. Very nice! Johnny asks why Jefe Velasquez is surprised that he had not met Mrs. Alder and he tells Johnny that Mrs. Alder does not object to being seen with a good-looking man.

Johnny goes back to the lab and learns only that the bullet came from a Luger.

Johnny drives back to the house, and notices a car in front of the house, which swerves and cuts him off. The driver gets out and asks Johnny if he knows who he is. Johnny tells him that he did not tell Alder about him, and Kincaid tells Johnny to stay away. Johnny thinks that maybe he is there to look for an empty Luger casing.

Johnny asks him how badly he wants to get into the family and Kincaid answers by trying to slug Johnny, and the fight is rough, but Johnny wins out (I better get in shape or take up accounting!).

Johnny goes in via the service entrance, and Natcho takes him upstairs and fixes his face. Natcho is amazed that Johnny won. Johnny asks about the music downstairs, and Natcho tells him that El Mantante, the matador is a guest in the house. The Alders really like the corrida, and El Mantante is giving a demonstration of the passes with the cape. You should go watch it, it is lovely. "Anybody ever ask the bull?" asks Johnny.

Johnny joins the guests, about six people clapping to the motions of El Mantante, but Alder and Peggy are showing disdain for him. Constance Alder introduces herself to Johnny and will introduce him to the others when the display is over. Johnny notices Mr. Alder glaring at his wife as she sits down.

Mrs. Alder moves from the room, and Johnny goes out to the patio and notices someone searching the grounds where the shot had come from the previous night. Johnny recognizes the searcher as Constance Alder.

Tomorrow, two sides of the same old yarn, and whichever side you choose you have to call it wrong.

Episode 3   Show Date: 8/8/1956
Constance Alder calls and asks if Johnny is OK. Why ask? Well, you did leave the living room. Yes, but you left too, and I was not bored. I wanted some air on the patio. You can see everything, the harbor, and the slope beside the patio and anyone who might be on it. Mrs. Alder wants to see Johnny in his car in a half hour.

Johnny wants to hear what she has to say and goes down stairs where Mr. Alder stops him and asks about the cuts on his face. Johnny tells Alder that Kincaid feels Johnny was hired to bust up the romance. Alder's only response is to call Kincaid an idiot.

Johnny tells him that he is fed up with Alder, "am I supposed to be a mind reader?" Johnny wants to know whom he is to protect Alder from. Someone has tried once so he must have some idea, but Alder clams up and will tell Johnny nothing. Johnny tells Alder that he could call the company and have his policy cancelled. Alder tells Johnny that the guests think Johnny is a friend from the states. Johnny asks which side Alder is on, his or his killer's.

Johnny goes to his car, forgets his keys and runs back in to get them. On the way, he runs into a woman who apologizes and runs off. Johnny gets his keys and notices that his wallet has been moved.

In the car, Mrs. Alder tells Johnny she knows who he is, and Johnny tells her never to search a pro's room, but she tells Johnny that she did not go into his room.

Johnny describes the woman he ran into, and is told that she is Doris Cole, a friend from the states. Her room is right next door to Johnny's.

Johnny asks what she was looking for in the jungle, and she asks him if he thinks she tried to shoot her husband. She tells Johnny that she was looking for some trace of the shooter, like a shell.

Johnny tells her that her statement was a mistake, because only an automatic ejects a shell, and she knew what type of gun was used. Mrs. Alder slaps Johnny and then apologizes. She tells Johnny that her husband told her who Johnny was.

Back at the house Johnny looks out on to the patio to see Mrs. Alder arguing with Mrs. Cole. There is a knock at the door and Mrs. Cole apologizes for being so abrupt with Johnny. Johnny senses that Mrs. Cole did not know about the social graces, and is then visited by Mrs. Alder, who did. Johnny is told that El Mantante is taking everyone to dinner tonight.

The night was a gourmet dinner, jai alai and nightclubs. El Mantante was a man who knew what had to be done and did them, and Mrs. Alder had her eyes on him all night. El Mantante asks Johnny why he is watching him and Mrs. Alder, and tells Johnny that he does not chase other men's wives.

Johnny asks him what he does when he is the pursued? He tells Johnny that acquisition is her game. Johnny tells him that he thought El Mantante was after the Alder fortune, but Johnny is told that El Mantante makes $10,000 for a Sunday afternoon's work. (Where does a fellow take bullfight lessons?)

Johnny watches the Alders dancing and then fakes a headache to get back to the house. Johnny searches Mrs. Cole's room and finds a passport for Dora Jansen and an unsigned letter from New York about the arrival of a ship, the Caribbean Star. Mrs. Cole apologizes for Johnny's headache and tells him that there is no aspirin in her room!

Tomorrow, motives for murder are like peanuts, once you start you can't stop. One difference though, a peanut won't kill you.

Episode 4   Show Date: 8/9/1956

Alder calls Johnny and thought he had rung Mrs. Cole's room. You got the right room, we were just discussing aspirin. Johnny is not going to arrest her, and tells her she had searched his room, and asks what she was looking for.

Johnny is not apologetic for searching Mrs. Cole's room and lying as the whole house is full of lies. Johnny buys a paper the next morning and sees that the Caribbean Star is due at noon.

Johnny drives to the oil field to see Alder who blows up when her tells of the passport belonging to Mrs. Cole. "How dare you search the room of a guest in my house?" Johnny asks who Mrs. Cole is and is told that she is "an old friend" and not a well woman. Johnny is sure that Alder knows who shot at him, and Alder asks if Johnny found anything else in the room.

Johnny goes to the cable office and wires Vic Kelly to ask for information on Doris Jansen/Cole, Passport #19B67943-11. Johnny tells the clerk that he will pick up the answer at the cable office.

Johnny goes to the arrival pier and hides behind a newspaper while watching the passengers. Johnny sees Doris Cole meet a man and follows them to a cheap hotel. Johnny asks the desk clerk about the man who just came in, and the desk clerk plays dumb. The clerk asks Johnny for money and Johnny pays

$10 for a name, Arthur Singer. Johnny goes to the room and listens to angry voices through the door.

Johnny goes to the cable office again and wires Vic for information on Arthur Singer. The cable clerk asks Johnny why his business partner is so angry. A man came in after you left and was worried about something in the message. She showed him the message and then he got angry. Johnny describes the man to her and asks her to send the answers to Alder's house where they can read them together.

Johnny goes to the office of the shipping lines and looks at the passenger list, which does not include Arthur Singer. Johnny goes back to his car and is attacked by a man as he gets into the car. Johnny overpowers the man and gives him to a policeman.

Jefe Velasquez tells Johnny that the man was a cheap hood, who does not know who hired him. He is lying but will not change his story.

Johnny asks to "talk" to him, but Jefe Velasquez does not allow it. Johnny asks Jefe Velasquez if he will follow the man if Johnny does not prefer charges, and Jefe Velasquez agrees.

Tomorrow, a puzzle never fits itself together, you've got to snoop, pry and juggle the pieces, and sometimes people get killed that way.

Episode 5   Show Date: 8/10/1956
Johnny is called by the cable office and they have the answer to his wires. Johnny will come and get them.

At the cable office Johnny gets nothing from Vic.

Johnny spots Mrs. Alder watching him on the street and buys her breakfast. She says little over breakfast, and Johnny tells her she knows why he is there. Johnny tells her that she has been the beneficiary twice and was looking for the gun and was following him, and she gets angry and leaves.

Johnny follows her to the hotel of Arthur Singer where she stays for a half an hour.

Johnny goes to see Jefe Velasquez and outlines the case and players to him. Johnny figures that Mrs. Alder, Mrs. Cole and Singer are in on something together, but not to kill Alder for the money. Alder is afraid of what they know and the shot was to warn him that they mean business. Johnny is going to do some acting, and Johnny and Jefe Velasquez lay out a plan.

At the airport, Johnny buys a plane ticket and goes to Alders office with the ticket. Johnny tells him he has had all he can take and is leaving at 6:00. He is going to recommend that the company cancel the policy.

Alder tells Johnny that the changing of beneficiaries was to get someone down here to protect him. He is in a jam and needs protection until it is over. Someone wants to kill him over a business deal. Alder will not tell him who, but Johnny tells Alder that the man is in town, and he is leaving.

Johnny goes back to the house, packs and says goodbye. He then drives to the airport, checks his bags and returns to Caracas and checks into a small hotel to wait.

Finally, the call comes and Jefe Velasquez tells Johnny to be patient. He will call him as soon as something happens, as he is watching everyone.

Jefe Velasquez calls again and will pick up Johnny. Velasquez tells Johnny that as soon as his plane left, Mrs. Cole picked up Singer and drove to the Alder house, but Alder saw them coming and drove to the oil fields, followed by the others.

Johnny and Jefe Velasquez drive to the oil field where Alder, Cole and Singer are in a work shack. Johnny sees Dora pointing a Luger at Alder and Singer pleading with her to not shoot. She tells Alder that her brother Arthur had rigged the books on Alder's last bankruptcy and had gone to jail for three years.

Alder pleads that he will make it right but needs time. Dora tells Alder that she had shot at Alder, and his bodyguard (Johnny) is on his way home, so now she is going to kill him.

Johnny rushes in and holds her at gunpoint. In a panic, she shoots Alder and runs outside but runs into a protective fence around an oil well. Johnny goes to Alder who tells him that he would have paid.

Alder tells Johnny that his wife only knew about it and her running around was to punish him, as he could not afford to complain as the case could be reopened

"Details: Billy Alder was rushed to the Caracas hospital, underwent some excellent surgery and, relax claims department, he is going to make it. As for the shady business tactics, that is out of my bailiwick, that is for the law boys."

Exp. Acct: $833.14

Notes:
- Jefe is the Spanish word for "chief".
- Roy Rowan is the announcer.
- Musical supervision is by Amerigo Marino.

Producer:	Jack Johnstone	Writer:	Tony Barrett
Cast:	Gil Stratton, Harry Bartell, Barbara Fuller, John Dehner, Virginia Gregg, Don Diamond, Vivi Janiss, Tony Barrett		

• ❖ •

Show: **The Crystal Lake Cabin Matter**
Company: **Amalgamated Life Associates**
Agent: **Tom Wilkins**
Synopsis:
Episode 1   **Show Date:**   **8/13/1956**

Tom Wilkens calls Johnny about a $50,000 policy on Edward Russell. Johnny has not heard of him, but no one else has either. His wife Leona in Denver has filed a missing person's report on him. Johnny thinks maybe he just got tired and Tom tells Johnny that Russell's car turned up in a storage garage with his luggage in it.

Johnny flies to Denver, Colorado and goes to visit Mrs. Russell who is very attractive. Johnny is expected and she tells him that she has told the police everything, and Johnny asks her to repeat it.

Johnny is told that Ed left to go to Boulder on real estate business, but he never got there. Johnny notes that the car was found in Colorado Springs, in the opposite direction.

Mrs. Russell tells Johnny that she has heard nothing from him in a week, and that he was impulsive but has no enemies. She hopes that he is in a hospital and cannot call. He had not been depressed and he was not the type to commit suicide. She tells Johnny that they were getting along OK.

She shows Johnny a brochure for Crystal Lake, a resort in the mountains. She does not think that Ed had ever been there. She tells Johnny that no amount of insurance money would make up for Ed.

Johnny looks at the brochure and rents a car to drive to Crystal Lake, Colorado. Johnny surveys the calm peaceful surroundings and the fishing possibilities.

Johnny visits Ansel Garrett, the local deputy. Johnny briefs Ansel about the case, and shows him a picture of Ed, who he remembers seeing. Ansel tells Johnny that he may be looking in the wrong place.

Russell came to ask about a man named "Bill", but there are several of them in town. Ansel saw him later in the bar talking to Betty Norton, a rich heiress who travels at a pretty good clip. Ansel tells Johnny to not go off half-cocked. Don't accuse until you find a body.

Johnny drives to the house of Betty Norton. She invites Johnny for a swim before she will talk to him so Johnny swims, and swims very hard to keep from freezing.

After the swim, Johnny asks her about Ed Russell. She does remember him, but does not know where he is. Betty asks what Johnny is doing with his time.

Back in his hotel room Ansel calls and tells Johnny that they have found Russell, he is dead.

Tomorrow, a cabin with a lovely view of a beautiful lake, a nice comfortable quiet spot for murder.

Episode 2   Show Date: 8/14/1956
Ansel calls and tells Johnny that Russell is dead. He was found in a cabin on the other side of the lake.

Johnny wires Tom Wilkins about the murder and goes to see Ansel. Johnny is told that a man named Bixby found the body. Ansel asks Johnny to recount the story he was told, and Johnny tells him about the business trip and the tears from Mrs. Russell. Johnny tells about talking to Betty and getting nothing.

Clarence Bixby comes in. He tells Johnny that the body was found in his cabin and the lock had been changed. He was going to sell the place, but no one will buy it now.

They drive to the cabin, and Bixby tells him that he had advertised the cabin, and a man named Putnam came up to look at it. Johnny sees where the lock had been pried off and Bixby shows him where the body was found. Bixby offers Johnny a cigar, and Johnny watches him tie the cigar wrapper into a knot, which is how Johnny feels.

Johnny goes back to town and calls Mrs. Russell. She will be coming up to confirm the identification. Johnny asks if she has heard of Clarence Bixby, but she has not.

Johnny calls the Denver police to have her checked on, but they already have and she is clean.

Johnny looks up Mr. Putnam in the hotel bar and he tells Johnny of going to the cabin. He had been looking for a cabin for a long time and wanted to buy Bixby's as a surprise for his wife. Putnam had never heard of Russell.

Johnny goes to the bartender and asks for a glass of I. W. Harper and soda. Johnny tells him it must have been quite a fight, referring to his black eye. He tells Johnny that he hit his head picking up a box.

Johnny tells him who he is and he tells Johnny that Russell had hit him. Russell was there with Miss Norton. She called him by his first name, and Russell got angry and asked if he had lived in Denver. They went outside and had a fight and Russell left. Russell was asking for trouble. The bartender tells Johnny that Russell left with Betty Norton.

Johnny goes out to think and walks along the lake. Johnny sees some movement and runs after it, but no one is there.

Tomorrow, a girl who lied, and a padlock that didn't.

Episode 3   Show Date: 8/15/1956

Betty Norton calls and she tells Johnny to come over. Johnny tells her that he wants to talk about murder.

Johnny drives out to see Betty Norton, who has the bourbon ready. Johnny wants to talk, but she wants to dance. Johnny tells about her meeting with Russell and tells her she lied.

She tells Johnny her father told her she could do whatever she wanted, as long as it stayed out of the newspapers. She tells about the fight, which was the reason for the lie. She took Russell to get some coffee, and Russell kept mumbling about someone named Bill. Hiram, the cab driver came in and told him that someone was looking for him, and they left. She never saw him again.

Johnny tries to call Hiram, but he does not answer. Johnny thinks he hears something outside and opens the door, but there is nothing there. Johnny tells Betty that maybe she killed Russell because he would not play things her way, but she tells Johnny that she can always find those who will play. She tells Johnny that he won't play, and she likes that, so stay for a few minutes. Johnny stays for a few minutes.

In the morning, Johnny tries to reach Hiram and then goes to see Ansel, who is talking to Bixby. Bixby asks Ansel to keep his cabin out of the papers, and Ansel agrees. Bixby offers cigars and leaves.

Johnny is told that Mrs. Russell has arrived and Johnny tells Ansel about meeting with Betty. Johnny wonders if Bixby is the killer, and Ansel wonders too, but Ansel has checked on him and found nothing. Johnny wonders about Putnam and asks Ansel to call Putnam's wife.

Johnny goes to visit Bill Jensen at the boathouse and asks him about Russell. Jensen does not remember seeing him and Johnny notices that the boats in the boat house are padlocked. Johnny notices that the locks on the boats are like the ones used at Bixby's cabin.

Johnny looks for Hiram, who is still not there. After dark Johnny goes back to look at the boats and sees that the locks are the same as on Bixby's cabin door and one is missing from one of the boats.

Suddenly Johnny is shot at and becomes trapped in the office at the boathouse.

Tomorrow, a shot in the dark that missed, and another that hit the bulls eye.

Episode 4   Show Date: 8/16/1956
Ansel Garrett calls, and Johnny tells him to come to Bill Jensen's boathouse. The killer has him trapped there.

Someone is stalking Johnny in the boathouse and has tried to break down the door. Ansel comes in and turns on the light to find Bill Jenson. He tells Ansel that he had come there because he thought there was a prowler. Bill mentions that he saw someone outside, but the person disappeared.

Johnny tells Ansel about the missing lock and shows him. Bill thinks someone stole the lock. Johnny outlines the case and mentions his padlock, and the shooting. Ansel tells Bill to come to the office, as Ansel wants to check his gun. After an hour of questioning, Bill tells them nothing new.

The phone rings and it is Mrs. Putnam. Ansel asks about the cabin and she tells him that she knows nothing about it. Johnny and Ansel question Putnam, and Ansel tells him that his wife does not know about him being there. Putnam tells him that he is in trouble, with his wife. He just wanted a place to get away from her once in a while.

Johnny and Ansel talk about the case and the lack of leads. Johnny and Ansel walk to Hiram's shed, but the car is gone. Johnny wants to buy Ansel a drink, and they walk to the hotel. Johnny mentions that the killer could be someone they do not know.

Mrs. Russell spots Johnny and tells him she is going home in the morning. Johnny asks her about who Bill might be, but she says that there is no connection with anyone at the lake to her husband.

Johnny looks for Ansel who is gone. Back in his room Johnny gets a phone call from Ansel. Hiram's body has been found in a ravine.

Tomorrow, the windup, the payoff. A payoff with illegal tender, hot lead.

Episode 5   Show Date: 8/17/1956
Ansel calls Johnny and tells him that when he looks for somebody, they end up dead. They just found Hiram's body in a ravine.

Johnny drives to the three-mile grade and meets Ansel who tells Johnny that the car and body are at the bottom of a ravine. It was no accident, there was a bullet hole in Hiram's head. Ansel suggests Betty Norton did it, but Johnny is still suspicious of Mrs. Russell. Johnny wonders why the body was placed in a cabin.

Johnny goes to Betty Norton's, but she has gone to Denver. Johnny calls the Denver police and asks for assistance in locating her. Johnny then goes to Hiram's rooming house and finds nothing.

Johnny finds Bill the bartender in the hallway. "Don't try to pin his murder on me" he tells Johnny. When Johnny asks how he knew Hiram was murdered, Bill tells him he got the news from a deputy.

Johnny goes back to the hotel and finds Bixby at the bar. Johnny tells Bixby that he can clean up the cabin now, but Bixby is not sure he will sell it. Johnny gets the key and goes to the cabin, where he searches for an hour and finds nothing.

Johnny goes to Mrs. Russell's room to say goodbye. She is leaving in the morning and will probably sell the house. Her lawyer is going to file a claim for her. Johnny spots something in the room that resolves all the issues.

Johnny asks if he can use the phone to call Ansel. Johnny asks about the new lead and fakes a positive response about a lab test. Johnny leaves and listens by the door as she makes a call. She leaves and walks along the lakeshore, with Johnny following behind.

Suddenly there is a gun barrel in his back — Bixby's gun barrel. Leona Russell walks back to Johnny and tells Bixby "I wanted to talk to you Bill, to warn you." Johnny tells him about the cigar wrapper in her room, and Bixby tells her that he should never have seen her. Johnny guesses that his middle name is William. Bixby tells him it is Wilford.

Johnny tells him he had lured Russell up to the lake and killed him and then killed Hiram so he could not talk. He then stole a pad lock to put suspicion on Bill Jansen. And poor little Mrs. Russell is in on it. Bixby tells her that this whole thing was her idea and he is getting out.

Bixby turns to Leona and Johnny lunges at him but too late as Bixby shoots Mrs. Russell. Johnny slugs Bixby, takes his gun and checks on Mrs. Russell, who is dead

"Remarks: About Bixby, in jail awaiting trial on three counts of murder, Edward Russell, Hiram, Leona Russell. About Leona, who had engineered the whole deal for a payoff, well she got paid off alright."

Exp. Acct: $423.00

Notes:
- The title of this story on the script title page is *The Crystal Lake Cabin Matter*, but in each episode the "Cabin" is dropped from the investigation title.
- For the promo for the next episode, Bob Bailey tells the audience "Next Week, beginning on Friday night, because I am sure you will want to listen to the Republican Convention Monday, Tuesday, Wednesday and Thursday of next week, a simple string of beads, and each bead on it a motive for murder." The next program is the 6-part *Kranesburg Matter*.
- Roy Rowan is the announcer.
- Musical supervision is by Amerigo Marino.

Producer:	Jack Johnstone	Writer:	Robert Ryf
Cast:	Richard Crenna, Charlotte Lawrence, Jeanne Tatum, Howard McNear, Forrest Lewis, Herb Ellis		

Show:	The Kranesburg Matter
Company:	Tri-State Guaranty Company
Agent:	Bob Lawder
Synopsis:	

Episode 1   Show Date: 8/24/1956

Bob Lawder calls Johnny and tells him that he has had a pearl necklace worth $20,000 stolen. Smiley Prell tells us he has the necklace and is in Kranesburg, Ohio and wants to negotiate. Melba Krane is the owner. You already have your reservations.

Johnny travels to Kranesburg, Ohio where he gets a room in the Krane Hotel and waits for Smiley Prell to call.

Johnny is visited in his room by Phineas Krane, the uncle of Melba Krane. He tells Johnny that he and Melba are the last two members of the Krane family, and that the necklace is the property of Melba. Phineas asks if Johnny is sure that the person who called him really was a man, could it have been a woman?

Phineas tells Johnny that he has met no strangers lately, and that this is a small town. Johnny asks what Krane has on his mind, is there something phony about the robbery? He tells Johnny that he only came to reassure Johnny that he would do anything Johnny requires to get the necklace.

Phineas tells Johnny that Melba is headstrong and does not use good judgement, and he wanted to let Johnny know what to expect, as she is very upset. The necklace was a gift from her fiancée, Dean Sellers. The important thing is the sentimental attachment to the necklace and beauty of it.

Johnny gets a call from "you know who. Meet me in the Green Lion bar in an hour and a half, and no cops". Phineas starts to leave and Johnny asks him to finish what he was saying, but Phineas tells him that Melba is impulsive at times and does not mean any harm.

Johnny rents a car and locates the Green Lion bar. Johnny then goes to the bank and talks to Milton Borkly, the president. Johnny asks Borkly for a financial status of the Krane family. Milton asks if Johnny looking for the company or the family.

The company is doing quite well. The family is the social leader of the town but they are flat broke. Their estate is mortgaged to the hilt, but Phineas has been walking around with a lot of money lately. Milton tells Johnny to have more than an idea before he talks to any of the Kranes. Milt has wondered how Phineas was getting his money and thinks that maybe he borrows it from Dean Sellers.

He is new in town and will be rich soon. He is so busy that he has had to postpone the wedding once. There are rumors, but we will skip them, you understand.

Johnny goes to the Green Lion bar and has two martinis while waiting for Smiley. He comes in late and only has a minute. Something has come up he has to straighten up. Smiley tells Johnny to meet him at 1412 N. Oak Street, room 6. "Meet me there at nine tonight. Someone is trying to give me the old double-cross. Meet me at nine and I will give you more than the beads".

Monday — a thief stalls for time — and old man lies desperately — and a strange girl whispers the dread word...murder.

Episode 2   Show Date: 8/27/1956

J. D. Bartlett calls back and she is the Tri-State agent in town. She yells at Johnny for not looking her up when he got into town but going to that bar instead. Johnny tells her he was going to meet the jewel thief there. Are you sure J. D. Bartlett is a woman? "You're the first man who ever doubted it" she tells Johnny.

Johnny thinks that this case is nutty and tells J. D. Bartlett that.

Smiley tells Johnny that he has to leave, and has things to do, something personal. Smiley tells him that Johnny knows he always works alone. Johnny tells Smiley that he does not have the necklace and is trying to pull a con. Smiley describes the pearls and their platinum mounts, an exact description. Meet me tonight, and no cops.

Johnny starts to leave and watches Smiley get into a cab. Johnny sees Phineas sitting in another cab watching Smiley. Johnny gets Krane out of the cab and takes him to his car. Phineas tells Johnny that he is wrong for thinking that he was watching that man. Krane tells Johnny that he was waiting to talk to Johnny about Melba. He thought he might have left a wrong impression about Melba as he was upset at the time.

Johnny tells Phineas that he wants to get the necklace back one way or another. Johnny tells him that he thought this was going to be a quick recovery, but it is not turning out that way.

Johnny goes to visit Miss J. D. Bartlett, the local agent. Call me "J. D." It makes me one of the boys. Johnny tells her of the various events and she tells Johnny that she only allowed the policy to be sold. She got Jim Markley to appraise the jewels and then issued the policy.

She tells Johnny that Melba had Dean Sellers hooked before his bags were unpacked. That skirt has the ethics of a boa constrictor and about as much personality as a face painted on an egg. Melba is more worried with the Krane name, but they are all broke. Phineas is a rare bird, but he would commit murder to protect the Krane name.

Tomorrow, when somebody kisses the wrong somebody, and somebody gets burnt up over it, and then a gun is found in the ashes ... Man, it's murder.

Episode 3   Show Date: 8/28/1956

Melba Krane calls Johnny. He tells her that he wants to talk to her about the theft, but she tells Johnny that she has talked to the local police. Johnny invites himself to come over in 45 minutes. He usually gets what he wants, but so does she.

Johnny walks to the Krane mansion while a storm gathers. Johnny sees a man in a suit and the maid in the sunroom, busy with each other. The maid answers the door and is excited when Johnny tells her who he is. Johnny asks if he interrupted her as she goes to get Miss Krane.

Johnny meets Dean Sellers in the lobby and he knows Johnny is the insurance guy. Johnny tells him he has no leads yet and is not sure that the man who contacted him has the necklace. Dean asks Johnny what happens if the necklace is recovered. Johnny tells him that if the claim has been paid, and the owner does not want to negotiate, the necklace will be sold. Dean hopes the necklace will be recovered soon.

Johnny mentions the scene in the sunroom, and Dean tells Johnny that appearances can be deceiving sometimes, and Melba is very understanding. Drop into my office if I can help.

Melba Krane comes in and tells Johnny that Dean is impulsive and headstrong. But he never means any harm by it. Johnny tells her that the same words were used to describe her.

Melba fixes scotch on the rocks and they talk about the robbery. "Here's to pearls, the frozen tears from the eyes of Allah", Johnny calls them. Johnny tells her that the man who told him that had just knifed someone for nine pearls.

Johnny tells her that he is not a cop, just interested in protecting the interests of the insurance company and looking for fraud. She asks about the thief, and Johnny tells her he does not know and that he might be trying to pull a fast one.

Johnny asks why she postponed the wedding, and she tells him it was Dean's idea. He has not called off the engagement and won't.

Johnny asks to see the safe the necklace was in, and it is behind a picture. It is an old safe, one easily opened. The robber must have gotten in with a key, while the house was empty. Johnny tells her he will meet with Smiley Prell tonight. Melba warns him about Uncle Phineas, he makes things up from time to time, he is eccentric.

Johnny walks to his car in the gathering dusk and sees Betty getting ready to burn a package in the incinerator. Johnny offers to help, but she objects and then runs off crying as Melba calls her. In the package is a .32 revolver with one chamber recently fired.

Tomorrow, a strange disappearance, a grim cry in the night, and a quarry is run to earth in room 413.

Episode 4   Show Date: 8/29/1956
Betty the maid calls Johnny and asks "Have you told anyone about it?" Johnny wants to know who used the gun and she tells Johnny she found the gun and does not know anything except that she is in trouble.

Johnny rushes to meet Smiley at 9:00 on the Oak Street address. Johnny goes to room 6 and knocks. The door is unlocked and Johnny rushes in to find Phineas Krane there.

Johnny tells him to sit, and Phineas can explain why he is there, alone. He came to ask questions of the man who lived there. He came here to talk to him about personal matters. He tells Johnny that he had followed him there one day. Johnny would understand if he could explain. Phineas is not scared of the threat to talk to the police, his grandfather founded the town, you know. Phineas had seen the man under unusual circumstances, before and after the robbery.

Johnny tries to link Phineas to insurance fraud, but he does not bite the bait. Johnny tells him that he will have to talk to someone, so think it over.

Johnny searches the room, finds nothing, and goes to his hotel to find a man there who asks Johnny about Smiley Prell. He is Ed Durham, the chief of police.

Johnny tells him who he is and about Smiley Prell. Durham tells Johnny that Prell has been shot dead. He was found in a back alley by the park.

When Durham tells Johnny that Prell was shot with a .32, Johnny goes to retrieve the gun from under the mattress, but Durham has already found it. Johnny tells how he got the gun and Durham recognizes the gun as one belonging to Phineas Krane.

Johnny asks about the Kranes, and Durham verifies the story told to him by the bank, including Phineas' sudden supply of cash.

Johnny asks about Dean Sellers, and Durham tells him nothing new. There is a knock at the door, and Betty is there. Durham goes into the bathroom, and Johnny lets Betty in. She asks Johnny for the gun. She tells Johnny she found the gun hidden in a drawer in her room at the Kranes and she was trying to get rid of it. Johnny calls Durham out of the bathroom.

Tomorrow, a castle crumbles, cupid goes to jail and a lovely iceberg thaws a bit.

Episode 5   Show Date: 8/30/1956

Dean Sellers calls. He wants to talk to Johnny but Johnny tells Dean that he is on the way out to jail with Betty. What! Was Betty there? Dean is concerned about Betty so Johnny will meet him in the bar in 5 minutes.

Johnny buys a drink for Dean Sellers, who is now concerned about Betty the maid. Dean tells Johnny that at first, he was just flirting with Betty, but has fallen in love with her. He delayed the wedding to Melba because he had too much work. He was not sure if he was going to ask her to return the pearls, but then they were stolen.

Johnny tells him that the man who stole the jewels was killed, but Betty had nothing to do with it, as someone is trying to frame her. Johnny tells Dean that the evidence is against her as she was found trying to destroy the gun, but most people would go to the police.

Johnny tells Dean that the safe was opened when Betty was gone, supposedly. Betty could have told Prell when she was gone. Johnny tells him that maybe she wanted a whole necklace, rather than part of the insurance. Dean tells Johnny that without the necklace, he does not have a case.

Johnny drives to the jail with the hunch that the case will turn out messy. Chief Durham tells Johnny that Betty wants to talk but will not change her story. She also did not know Prell, and the necklace has not been found.

Johnny tells Durham about Dean and Betty, and he agrees that maybe she is being framed, but by who. Johnny asks if a local jeweler could make a duplicate necklace, but there is no one here in town who could do it, maybe in Cincinnati.

Johnny really wants to know if anyone had gone to Cincinnati to have one made. Durham tells Johnny that maybe Jim Markley can call around and find out for us. Johnny also asks for a complete rundown on Dean Sellers.

Johnny goes to his hotel and there is a knock at the door, and Melba Krane wants to talk. Johnny offers her a cognac, and she wants a double.

She wants to make something clear to Johnny about Dean trying to protect Betty. Melba knows about the scene in the sunroom and tells Johnny that she has seen others. His alibis should not be given credence. After another double Cognac, she accuses Johnny of being on Betty's side, but Johnny tells her he is on the side of the insurance company. She asks if Johnny has seen Uncle Phineas, and Johnny tells her to sit down, they have not even started to talk.

Tomorrow, a bomb drops, the timid run for cover, and all is not as it seems, not even murder.

Episode 6   Show Date: 8/31/1956
Phineas Krane calls, and he is mad. He wants to talk to Johnny, as there have been a number of changes since last night. Johnny tells him to wait, as he is waiting for a call from the police. Phineas tells Johnny that he might tell Johnny what the police call would. You should have called last night, he might have made a deal.

Johnny calls Cincinnati, and then Cleveland and then waits for information. Finally, the calls come in and jackpot!

Johnny dives to the Krane estate and is met on the terrace by Phineas. He wants to talk to Johnny alone, while he is permitted to as it is too late to save things now. He tells Johnny that he was in Prell's room looking for the necklace and knew everything was over when he heard that Prell had been killed. In the beginning, he was in favor of what happened, and asks Johnny to be easy on her. There is no excuse for him and his niece, and they are looking for a soft way out.

Phineas was guessing that Prell had stolen the necklace. He had seen Prell hanging around and saw him talking to his employer. Melba comes to the terrace and tells Phineas to leave. Melba asks if Johnny had been pumping Phineas. Melba tells Johnny that Dean is in the billiards room and Johnny tells her he might have some vital information.

Melba asks what would happen if she withdrew the claim? Johnny tells her that the investigation would go on because the police are involved. Johnny tells Melba that the pearls were a gift of great sentimental value from Dean, who is broker than she is, and she is angry. Johnny tells her that he has a complete run down on her. Johnny asks to search Betty's room.

Johnny plays pool with Dean and tells him that Betty is innocent, even though Johnny has found the necklace in her room. Johnny tells him the Kranes are not so innocent. They are broke and used your interest in Melba to get cash. Johnny tells Dean that he was playing the same game and of how he milked his last wife in Florida of $150,000, of which only the necklace was left when you got here.

You broke off the wedding when you found out the Kranes were broke and used Betty as a pigeon. You used Prell to steal your investment, and when he told you the pearls were phony you accused him of a double-cross and killed him when he tried to deal with the insurance company.

Johnny tells Dean that Melba sold the necklace a month after you gave it to her, and she had a copy made, which you killed Smiley over. Dean pulls his gun and tells Johnny to drop the cue.

Melba comes in and Johnny slugs him with the pool cue. Johnny tells her that Dean had the pearls stolen and killed Prell. Johnny tells her that she filed a claim on a necklace she had already sold and will be prosecuted. You two were made for each other.

Johnny is sending the necklace under separate cover to the insurance company, with his sincere condolences.

Exp. Acct: $409.10

Notes:
- This story was done as *The Beauregard Matter*, broadcast on 1/26/1954.
- *The Kranesburg Matter* has been the subject of much discussion: was it six episodes or seven episodes? In 2005 Stewart Wright resolved the issue by reviewing the scripts on file in the KNX collection and determined that the endings on the first and second mp3 files in circulation have been changed to support an additional story. The details above have been changed to reflect the correct endings. Stewart's research was published in the August 2005 issue of *Radiogram*, published by SPERDVAC.
- The script for the second episode is called "Episode ONE-A", the final episode is called "Episode Five", probably adding to the confusion.
- Roy Rowan is the announcer.
- Music supervision is by Amerigo Marino.

Producer: Jack Johnstone Writer: Les Crutchfield
Cast: Howard McNear, Forrest Lewis, Paul Richards, Mary Jane Croft, Virginia Gregg, James McCallion, Shirley Mitchell, Russ Thorson

• ❖ •

Show: The Curse of Kamashek Matter
Company: Inter-Allied Life Insurance Company
Agent: Jimmy Sayer
Synopsis:
Episode 1   **Show Date:**   9/3/1956

Jimmy Sayer calls and tells Johnny that how he feels depends on Johnny. Have you heard of King Tut, and the curse on those who disturb his tomb? Wait until you hear of the curse of Kamashek.

Johnny cabs to the office to talk to Jim Sayer, who wants Johnny to visit Mr. Eric Turnbull, a very important client. He asked specifically for you. You handled the Parkinson case a couple years ago, and she was his sister. Johnny will take the case for the nice fee associated with it.

Johnny trains to Stamford, Connecticut and is driven to the Turnbull mansion, where a Studebaker Golden Hawk is parked in the drive. Haskins the driver-butler tells Johnny to go in, unless...

Johnny enters the house, which is classic Victorian mansion. An older man is shaking his fist at a young lady, who has angered him by calling him Uncle Eric. The girl, Dorothy, is told to leave and Johnny is offered a drink.

Turnbull asks Johnny to help him, as Johnny is a man he can trust because of the case of his sister and the fraudulent relatives Johnny was able to trap. The problem is Donald, the son of his sister.

All of Donald's money is tied up in a trust which Turnbull controls until Donald turns thirty. Donald has been living with him and is now 25. He does not work and has majored in archeology and Egyptology instead of business and finance.

Donald Cronin comes in and is introduced to Johnny. Donald tells them that he is going to Thebes to work on the tomb of Kamashek, a very important find. Turnbull is tired of Donald wasting his time and money on these wasteful expeditions. Johnny mentions a collection of Donald's artifacts from Yucatan, but Turnbull is adamant about exercising his rights to control the funds and tells Donald that he has to learn to increase the fortune, not squander it, and to protect the family name.

Donald tells him he is going, and there is nothing he can do to stop him, and he does not care if he is cut off. Donald leaves, for Egypt.

Johnny wonders why Turnbull is so protective about Donald's money when he has money of his own, and how does the girl figure in? Turnbull tells Johnny that there is another aspect to the case. Donald has insured himself for $100,000, half to the museum and half to Dorothy Harkness, his fiancée. Dorothy has been prodding Donald and is trying to engineer Donald's death.

Johnny is driven to the train station by Haskins, and meets Dorothy, who tells Johnny to call her because Donald is in danger from the curse of Kamashek.

Tomorrow, a little order starts to come out of the department of utter confusion and a promise of murder.

Episode 2   Show Date: 9/4/1956
Johnny calls Stamford and talks to Dorothy Harkness. She wants to talk about the trip Donald is taking. Johnny asks about the curse of Kamashek, and Dorothy tells him it means murder. Johnny catches the next train.

Johnny trains to the Stamford apartment of Dorothy Harkness. She knows who Johnny is and tells Johnny that Mr. Turnbull does strange things and that she and Mr. Turnbull do not get along too well. Donald wants to marry her, but she is not sure about it.

She wonders if he wants to marry her to get away from his uncle, and she is not interested in his money. Her father is the curator of the museum, who likes Donald for the money he is bringing into the museum. She tells Johnny that Donald is doing important things with his research and she is afraid of Donald getting hurt.

Turnbull wants to keep as much of Donald's money has possible. His uncle knows that the best way to get Donald to do something is to tell him he cannot do it. She tells Johnny that Donald is a bit of a child and does not think things through. She does not want Donald to go, as the curse will give his uncle an opportunity to do something to him.

Dorothy tells Johnny about the curse of King Tut and the mysterious deaths of those who participated in opening the tomb. Dorothy tells her that anyone who goes on one of these expeditions opens themselves up to murder. She is afraid that his uncle will kill Donald to protect the fortune.

She is happy with her financial situation and hates Johnny for bringing up the insurance she will get. She tells Johnny that on his last expedition a man caused some accidents that could have killed Donald and that Turnbull had hired the man behind Donald's back. "Remember what I have told you", she implores Johnny.

Johnny calls the Turnbull home and asks for Donald, but Turnbull sends the car for him. Turnbull tells Johnny that Donald will be leaving in a few days, and he has to let him go to protect his reputation in the eyes of his colleagues and the universities interested in his work. But Johnny will be going with him, there will be no expenses spared.

Trumbull has arranged for Johnny to get $5,000 in American Express Travelers Checks, and if you need more, wire me. Trumbull tells Johnny that on his last expedition a man had been hired by Dorothy Harkness to cause accidents.

Johnny is sure that somebody is lying, and somebody is going to try and kill Donald Cronin.

Tomorrow, suddenly the reason for a carefully planned murder becomes crystal clear, and a race against death becomes a race for my own life.

Episode 3   Show Date: 9/5/1956

The operator at the Explorers Club calls, and she tells Johnny that she cannot reach Mr. Cronin. Johnny tells her to leave a message for Donald, that I will meet him at the club.

Johnny trains to New York to pick up his travelers checks and the teller makes a remark that this transaction will close out the account.

Johnny cabs to the Explorers Club and leaves a message for Donald to sit tight. On the way out of the club, Johnny is stopped by Percival Thronghurst Scatterday. He heard Johnny asking for Donald and he is glad that Johnny is going with Donald to Egypt. It should be an important expedition if history is correct about Kamashek.

Percival asks if Johnny knows about the curse and warns Johnny to not be present when the inner sarcophagus is opened. There was a warning on the walls that whoever opened and touched the tomb of the king would die. Remember those who entered King Tut's tomb. Percival tells Johnny to take care of Donald, and himself. Percival tells Johnny that Donald is at his uncle's place in Stamford.

Johnny discounts the importance of Percival and cabs to Mr. Turnbull's stock brokerage and talks to David Wilt. Johnny overhears a conversation with Mr. Turnbull, which would bring his investment down to nothing. Johnny tells him that the conversation is now part of his investigation and is not to be told to Turnbull. So, Turnbull is not so wealthy after all.

Johnny calls Dorothy to tell her he is going to Egypt with Donald. If he calls, tell Donald to call me. Johnny cabs to the Turnbull estate and Turnbull is glad to see Johnny. He is worried because no one has heard from Donald.

Johnny tells him of his investigation into the financial condition, and Turnbull is really the one who will benefit from Donald's wealth. Turnbull tries to convince Johnny that he is not really broke.

The phone rings and Johnny answers and it is Percival, who tells Johnny that Donald has flown to Egypt. Turnbull puts on a dramatic appeal to protect Donald, and Johnny wishes he had been lying as two lives would have been saved.

Tomorrow, a flight into darkness, and when day has come there is blood on the desert sands.

Episode 4   Show Date: 9/6/1956
Dorothy calls and asks if Johnny has found Donald. Find him before his uncle kills him she begs Johnny. Johnny tells her that that Donald is on his way to Egypt, and that he will take the next plane.

Johnny goes to New York City and flies to Cairo, Egypt. Johnny talks to the other passengers, except for one man who pretends to sleep when Johnny wants to talk to him. But Johnny could see the man watching him when a seatmate used a makeup mirror.

When the plane lands in Paris, Johnny helps Caroline, his seatmate off the plane, arranges for a date in New York, and goes back to talk to the mysterious man, but the man grabs him in a hallway and tries to beat him.

Johnny overpowers him and wants to know who hired him. The man tells Johnny that Frederick Turnblow hired him and that he does a lot of strong-arm work for Turnblow. He paid the man to get Johnny out of the way. Johnny takes the man's passport and gets back to his plane when he is paged.

Eric Turnbull is calling him long distance, and tells Johnny to come back immediately, the case is closed as Donald is dead and the curse has been fulfilled. Johnny does not believe in the curse and wants to know about the thug he hired.

Suddenly Johnny realizes that the name of the man the thug gave was Frederick Turnblow, instead of Erick Turnbull, but they sound alike. Someone else instructed the thug to say that Eric Turnbull had hired him.

Johnny changes planes and calls the Egyptian authorities who tell him that the tomb had been ransacked, and only two people had touched the bones after they had been sprayed with a preservative, a native worker and Donald Cronin, who shipped the bones to his uncle. Both of the men have died mysteriously.

Only the men Donald brought, Carl Fortina and Walker Harkness, who is the son of the curator, have returned to the states. Johnny looks for the thug, who has disappeared.

On the flight back, Johnny tries to figure the angles on the case. Is it Eric Turnbull who opposed the trip, or Dorothy Harkness who would get the insurance, and her father who would benefit from the insurance, but how does Walter Harkness figure in to it?

Back in Stamford, Haskins opens the door and tells Johnny that Turnbull is broken up about Donald and has received a package which he is inspecting. Johnny rushes inside and Turnbull is dead

Tomorrow, the windup, and a sorry example of what the lust for money can do for nice people.

Episode 5   Show Date: 9/7/1956

"Dr. Sinclair returning your call, Stinky". Johnny asks Dr. Sinclair to assist on a case. Johnny thinks that two people have been poisoned, and he wants Leonard to help him prove it. If they were not poisoned, it was a curse.

Dr. Leonard Sinclair, an old school chum, is a noted toxicologist who works with the police. Johnny wants him to examine the bones to see if poison was involved.

Haskins tells Johnny that he had brought the package into the library, and Turnbull was dead when Johnny got there, and Johnny wants the police called later, and Johnny wonders how Haskins figures into the case.

Dr. Sinclair arrives with his portable laboratory. He looks at the body and determines that Turnbull has been poisoned. Len tells Johnny that it probably was a rare poison and brings in his lab equipment and some white mice. Len thinks that the poison was recent, not from the time of the pharaohs.

Johnny calls the coroner and then Dorothy, who is not home. Len tells Johnny that the poison was "curaba arcinium", which can be fatal if put on the skin in powdered form. Len tells Johnny that the solution must have been sprayed on the bones, and Johnny remembers that the doctors had told him that the bones had been sprayed in Egypt.

Dorothy and Walter Harkness arrive, and Johnny tells him he has been looking for Walter and asks if he wants to write his confession now. Johnny tells Dorothy that Donald was in love with her and made her a beneficiary if his insurance. Walter is working for the museum, which is depending on Donald's money, and is the other beneficiary. Eric was opposed to Donald's interest in the museum because in Donald's will he leaves the estate to the museum. No wonder Eric was worried and hated Dorothy. She was being used as a tool, and your father only wanted money for the museum.

Johnny tells Walter that he knows what killed Donald, just like he does. Johnny tells about the spraying of the bones, and the poison in the solution. Walter tells Johnny he sprayed the bones and washed his hands afterward as he was told to do. Walter is about to tell Johnny who prepared the solution, when Walter's father arrives. He is there to pick up the bones to take to the museum.

Johnny thought he would be there, and will give them to him, if he takes them out in his bare hands. He refuses, and Johnny tells him of the poison. He admits to the poison, and pulls a gun, but Len shoots him and kills him. Dr. Harkness just confirmed the results of his tests.

The museum will benefit, from the insurance and estate, without Dr. Adam Harkness.

Remarks: "Well, it doesn't mean a thing, I know. But I kinda wonder what I would have found if I have been assigned to investigate the deaths of the people who excavated some of those other old Egyptian tombs, tombs that had a curse on them. Heh, heh, heh. Interesting thought isn't it."

Exp. Acct: $985.00

Notes:
- After episode 4, Bob Bailey thanks the audience for the letters that are sent to the program. "So many come in everyday that it's become quite a chore to answer them, but you know something, I love it. As a matter of fact, your letters are appreciated by all of us who are involved in the production and presentation of the show, our director, the writers, and the various members of our cast, and our excellent technical crew. So please don't stop."
- The poison "curaba arcinium" is another Jack Johnstone invention.
- This is the third program to mention the Studebaker Golden Hawk. It makes you wonder if Jack Johnstone owned one at the time of the writing.
- Roy Rowan is the announcer.
- Musical supervision is by Amerigo Marino.

Producer: Jack Johnstone   Writer: Jack Johnstone
Cast: Paul Dubov, Alan Reed, Richard Crenna, Virginia Gregg, Ben Wright, Forrest Lewis, Eric Snowden, Barney Phillips, James McCallion, Les Tremayne

♦ ❖ ♦

Show: **The Confidential Matter**
Company: **Eternity Mutual Insurance Company**
Agent: **Mort Parkinson**
Synopsis:
Episode 1   Show Date: 9/10/1956

Mort Parkinson calls, and he feels bad. Mort wants Johnny to come over to his office and talk — this is confidential. It is about Ed Morgan. I know he was a good friend of yours, but it is too bad he did not die a year sooner.

Johnny cabs to Mort's office and they talk about the late Ed Morgan. Mort tells Johnny about working with Ed in the old Johnstone building, and its furnishings. Mort tells Johnny that he liked Ed Morgan, and thought of him as a son, and hired him, and watched him become chief adjuster for the West Coast, and then just like that, he drives his car off a cliff into the Pacific.

Mort shows Johnny a list of clients requesting settlements that Ed had marked paid. They sent and investigator and found that Ed's accounts had been doctored for some time. He had embezzled close to $80,000, but Johnny cannot believe it. Ed had a reputation of living like an old bachelor.

Mort wants Johnny to find out what happened, but Johnny wants out of the case. Mort tells Johnny that there are too many questions, and Johnny has to do it. Mort tells Johnny that he knew Ed, and it would be better if a friend looked into the matter, rather than a stranger. Johnny gives in and takes the case.

Johnny flies to San Francisco, California on prepaid tickets and goes to Ed Morgan's apartment at the Drakely Arms, a swank luxury apartment. The manager is only too glad to help Johnny, but there is little he can tell Johnny about Mr. Morgan. As Johnny offers him a crisp $20 to smooth the path, the manager gets a call from the Countess who wants a bucket of suds, just plain old beer, that she mixes with crème de menthe.

The manager tells Johnny that Morgan had lived there for six months, paid $1,200 a month, and was a free spender. Mr. Morgan had no visitors, and no friends in the building, except for Mrs. Barrett. The Countess calls again and her dog is thirsty too.

Johnny is told that Mr. Morgan and Mrs. Barrett were inseparable and that her husband had died early this year. Mr. Morgan moved in about six weeks after she moved in. He had met her when her husband died, something to do with the estate. Johnny wants to talk to Mrs. Barrett but she is not here, she is probably upset about having two deaths with tragic coincidences, her husband died in some sort of accident.

Tomorrow, the trail back into a man's past is a faint and twisting one, and at times it runs through quicksand.

Episode 2   Show Date: 9/11/1956
Mack Woodson calls from the claims company. He is working on the files, and $80,000 is missing. The looting was carried out very cleverly. Johnny wants to meet him in the office tomorrow.

Johnny gets a $1 martini (a heck of a belt for a buck) and thinks about the luxury apartment of Ed Morgan.

Johnny asks the bartender about Ed Morgan, who was an eager supplicant for his services. The bartender thought that Ed was too unrestrained for the Drakely, he was always running out to some gala nightspot, which Johnny notes was most unusual for Ed.

Johnny is told that Ed always came in with Nicki, Mrs. Barrett. They would stay for a drink and then go to the opera, or dinner. He was here on the night he died, and Mrs. Barrett was not upset at Ed's death.

Johnny cabs to the apartment of Lisa DuVal, Ed's secretary, who was Miss Bohemian at home and listens to progressive jazz. She tells Johnny that she lives that way as an antidote for the insurance business. She stayed because of Ed, he was wonderful to work for, until the last few months. He was always tense and under pressure. She used to see him occasionally to listen to music and talk, until the last few months. She thinks that maybe he was tense because of the money. "Or were you going to say, until she came along?" asks Johnny.

Lisa admits that she had been in love with Ed since she started but he never saw her. She is sorry that Johnny has to do what he is doing. Lisa has met Mrs. Barrett, who she compares to a vampire. She had come to the office with a life insurance claim on her husband who had just died. Ed just melted down and lay down at her feet. She came to Ed because of the double indemnity on the policy.

Johnny cabs to the office of Ed Morgan to see Mr. Woodson and learns that Ed was running hog wild. He would deposit checks from Hartford into a disbursement account, withdraw the cash as a disbursement, and have the checks come back to him, very clever, but he should have known that it would not last. The seeds of the collapse were the complaints from policyholders. Johnny is looking at a file folder on Mrs. Barrett, whose husband died in an accident, unless he was murdered.

Tomorrow, $80,000 and a beautiful girl, both missing. Then one of the two is found, and a bombshell explodes.

Episode 3   Show Date: 9/12/1956
Hector Nerkly calls from the Drakely Arms. Hector can give Johnny some information if he will come over. Johnny cannot find out anything in Ed's office, but he will be over in 30 minutes.

Johnny cabs to the Drakely Arms and Hector tells him that Mrs. Barrett can be contacted, but he wants to know why Johnny wants to talk to her. Hector asks to keep his name out of the matter, and tells him, after another $20, that Mrs. Barrett has requested that her mail be forwarded to American Express in Panama City, Panama.

Johnny sends a number of wires and then flies to Panama where Captain Garcia, of the Federal police tells Johnny that Mrs. Barrett (oh, what a lovely lady) has been located, and has not changed her name. She is at the Hotel Premeso, a small hotel on the waterfront usually used by sailors and fishermen.

Johnny rents a cab for the day, gets a room and goes to the Hotel Premeso, which is not the flophouse he expected. Johnny goes to the room of Mrs. Barrett, who is expecting a bellboy. Johnny tells her he wants to talk about Ed Morgan. Johnny tells her the reports about her were not exaggerated. She knows who Johnny is, as Ed had talked about him.

She tells Johnny that she is trying to forget the accident. Johnny asks her what time she left him. She tells Johnny that Ed had taken her to dinner, and then went to see a client. They were going to be married. She knew that Ed worked for an insurance company, and Johnny asks how he could afford to live the life style he did.

Johnny offers her a cigarette, but she tells him that she does not smoke. Johnny tells her he smelled smoke when he came, and searches for someone else. Johnny finds a man in the closet who knocks him down and runs out.

Johnny recovers and sees Nicki Barrett cowering along the wall, but the assailant is gone. Nicki tells Johnny that she hit him, but Johnny knows that only one person tears up his cigarette papers, Ed Morgan!

Tomorrow, a search for a dead man who intends to stay dead, and who is willing to kill to do it.

Episode 4   Show Date: 9/13/1956
Captain Garcia calls and Johnny tells him about being hit. Johnny tells him that Ed Morgan is here in Panama, and Garcia will have the police search for him.

Johnny wires Hartford advising them that the case has taken a new direction.

Mrs. Barrett meets Johnny the next morning at breakfast. Johnny offers her breakfast, fried fish and papaya, which she declines. Johnny tells her that he knows Ed Morgan was in the room the previous night, but she tells him he is wrong. She tells Johnny that it was a "friend" who hit him. He is married and should not have been there, which Johnny tells her is a snow-job. She tells Johnny that she learned to tear up cigarette papers from Ed. You were wrong, so why be stubborn. Johnny asks how much of the money she got, and she gets angry.

Johnny tells her that Ed was his friend and it hurt when he found out that Ed was stealing, and now he is alive and he has to take him back. She tells Johnny that she and Ed were going to be married, and that Ed had told her that Johnny was cold, hard and ruthless.

Captain Garcia arrives and meets Mrs. Barrett. "take a look, you may soon be arresting her for fraud" Johnny tells him. Captain Garcia tells Johnny that they have located Ed Morgan, so Johnny and Garcia drive to a small inlet away from town. Johnny is told that Ed is on one of the boats tied to the wharf. He has been there for about a month, living alone on the boat.

Johnny goes to the boat and calls for Ed, who tells him to come onboard. Ed asks why it had to be him, and Johnny asks why he did it. Ed tells Johnny that he would not understand, and that Nicki was with him all the way. She had always lived high, and he had to steal from the company to keep up with her. They decided to get out of the country, and he needed the money to get started.

When Ed tells Johnny that she had sold everything she had, Johnny tells him that she still has her apartment and everything else, he saw it.

Ed pulls a gun on Johnny, who asks if he would use it. Johnny lets him go, and he escapes while Garcia runs to the boat to check on Johnny.

Tomorrow, fate plays a devil's tune, collects a payment long overdue and the music ends on a scream.

Episode 5   Show Date: 9/14/1956
Captain Garcia calls and tells Johnny that they still have not found Ed Morgan. The entire police force is active alert! "Do you know where he is?" No, Señor.

Johnny cabs to Garcia's office and learns that so far Ed has escaped, even driving a stolen police car. Garcia tells Johnny that Morgan had taken the woman away just five minutes before the police got there. Johnny tells Garcia that Ed used to be his best friend, and that he only got involved after the monies were found missing.

Garcia gets a phone call and tells Johnny that Morgan has been sighted on a narrow shore-road. The car fell into the water and no bodies have been found.

Johnny rents a boat and diver with an old-fashioned diving suit and goes to the wreck sight. Johnny notices the cliff, and the similarity to the one in California. The diver comes up and tells Johnny that the car is a mess. The woman is inside the car, but the man is not there. Johnny knows that Ed would not kill Nicki and leave her there, so Johnny climbs the cliff face and finds Ed on a ledge.

Ed tells Johnny that they did not make it, and it is kind of funny, just like they did it in San Francisco, only for real. Ed knows he is dying, but it does not matter anymore. He made her come with him, and she got mad and told him the whole story. She only came down to get the rest of the money and told him that she did not love him.

Ed tells Johnny that if he could go back, he would do the same thing for Nicki. He came to get Nicki because he bought her and paid for her. Ed tells Johnny that the rest of the money is in his coat and asks Johnny to give it back to Mort. Ed asks Johnny to shake hands with him one more time but cannot find his hand and dies.

Johnny is sending, under separate cover by American Express, $62,112.30. "Remarks: No Mort, not on this one, Ed Morgan was my friend. The report stands."
Exp. Acct: $912.61

Notes:
- This story was done as *The Ben Bryson Matter*, broadcast on 12/29/1953.
- In part one, the manager remarks about the $20 tip Johnny gives, and Johnny tells him to "think of it as expense account item three."
- Hugh Brundage is the announcer.
- Musical supervision is by Amerigo Marino.

Producer:	Jack Johnstone	Writer:	Les Crutchfield
Cast:	Virginia Gregg, Jack Edwards, Russell Thorson, Shirley Mitchell, Stacy Harris, Bob Miller, Harry Bartell, Vic Perrin, Frank Gerstle		

◆ ❖ ◆

Show: **The Imperfect Alibi Matter**
Company: **Northeast indemnity Associates**
Agent: **Joe McNab**
Synopsis:
Episode 1   **Show Date:**   **9/17/1956**

Joe McNab calls and is not glad to talk to Johnny. Ever hear of Harvey Stone, the industrialist? He took over from his father. He has over $100,000 in insurance.

Last night a small object hit his windshield, it was a bullet.

Johnny cabs to Joe's office and is told about the case. Joe is not sure that the bullet was meant for Stone. His father had built up the business, and Harvey is running it now. He lives with his father and stepmother in West Chester County and has an apartment in town.

Harvey is running around with a singer named Helen Barrett, and his family is not pleased. He has one enemy, Dutch Krieger the gangster, who is putting on an act of going legitimate. Harvey was involved in a real estate deal, and when he found out Krieger was involved, he backed out, and Dutch will not forget something like that. The father and stepmother are the beneficiaries. Go down there and keep Harvey Stone alive.

Johnny travels to the Stone estate in Westchester County, New York and meets the very young Mrs. Daphne Stone, the wife of Mr. E. J. Stone who tells Johnny that Harvey will be back soon. Do not call him a stepson in front of him as he is very sensitive. Mr. Stone Sr. is in a wheel chair and will be here soon, he will not let anyone push him. No one seems to have any reason to believe that there is anyone after Harvey. Johnny mentions Helen Barrett and Daphne tells Johnny not to mention it to E. J.

Mr. Stone wheels in and tells Johnny that precautions are not necessary. Mr. Stone takes Johnny to see his orchids in the solarium as a pretext to talk. He asks Johnny about Harvey and the bullet, but Johnny has not made up his mind yet. E. J. tells Johnny that Harvey is a poor businessman who does everything wrong, except for Helen. Mr. Stone did the same thing and got Daphne from a chorus line, but Daphne disapproves.

Just as E. J. tells Johnny that he wants to kill Harvey sometimes, Harvey walks in. Daphne offers Harvey a drink, and he tells her "yes darling", which ruffles everyone's hackles. Daphne and E. J. leave and Harvey talks to Johnny about the company and Daphne. Harvey tells Johnny that his heart is not in the business.

Last night he was out driving his new sports car and heard a noise and then the windshield shattered. Harvey racked it up to some kid with a gun. Johnny asks him about Dutch Krieger and Harvey tells him that he could not associate the Stone name with a criminal. Harvey does not want to talk about Helen, he tells Johnny that there may not be a wedding.

Harvey offers to take Johnny to the train and while Johnny waits in the driveway he is beaten up.

Tomorrow, well look, you should never get into a card game with a professional gambler. He can deal you any card he wants, even the ace of spades, the death card.

Episode 2   Show Date: 9/18/1956

Joe McNab calls and Johnny updates him on the fight. Johnny tells Joe to take out a policy on him.

Johnny describes the workout he received and suspects Dutch Krieger was behind it.

Johnny goes to see Dutch, who is sitting at his desk flipping a coin. On the way in, Johnny spots his assailant in the club. Dutch admits to Johnny that he knows Stone, and Dutch reminds Johnny about a guy named Tonelli who cannot walk, but things change.

Johnny goes to see Helen Barrett at the club. She is worried about Harvey because of Dutch. She tells Johnny that their wedding has not been cancelled, just postponed because of family pressure.

Johnny goes to his hotel, and then to the financial district where he learns that the Stone Corporation is healthy financially.

Johnny goes back to his hotel and is called by Helen. Johnny has to come to Harvey's apartment, he is dead. Helen tells Johnny that Harvey had called and wanted to talk about the wedding. She went back home to pack while Harvey made reservations for Mexico. She came back and found Harvey dead.

Johnny calls Lt, Restelli and updates him and then goes to see Dutch, but he tells Johnny that he was at the club all night. On the way out, Johnny spots a picture of Daphne signed "To Dutchy with all my love".

Episode 3   Show Date: 9/19/1956
Joe Restelli from homicide calls about the Harvey Stone killing and tells Johnny that they are still holding Helen Barrett. Johnny has a hunch and is coming right over.

Johnny cabs to police headquarters to talk to Lt. Joe Restelli. Restelli tells Johnny that Harvey was shot in the forehead at close range with a .38 Smith & Wesson found beside the body, but there were no prints and Helen was wearing gloves. She was packing to elope with Harvey and found him dead when she came back. The coroner placed the death at 11:30 to 12:00.

Johnny tells Restelli that Harvey took over the Stone companies, and the father's wife was the same age as Harvey. Both the father and his wife were the policy beneficiaries. Johnny tells Restelli that he had gone to Dutch Krieger's office and saw a picture of Daphne there. Restelli thinks that maybe there was a question of whether the marriage would take place, and maybe Harvey was going to cut Helen out.

The phone rings and someone wants to see Restelli about the killing. The man comes in and tells them he is Alvin Gentry and he claims that he killed Harvey Stone. Stone was making a play for his girl, a hatcheck girl at Barney's. His girl was Doris and Stone was urging her to go away with him, so I killed him. He used a .45 colt and shot him in the chest. Restelli tells Gentry to leave and get his facts straight. Johnny calls Gentry a "Confessin' Sam", someone who confesses out of a sense of repressed feelings of guilt. As Johnny gets ready to go see Daphne, another call comes in from a man who slit Harvey's throat with a razor.

Johnny cabs to the Stone estate and sees E. J.'s wheelchair without him in it. Johnny spots E. J. in the solarium walking around his flowers. When E. J. spots Johnny he hobbles back to the chair.

Daphne comes in and is hesitant to talk. E. J. is acting bewildered. Johnny tells her that he saw E. J. walk, and she tells Johnny that he can do it for short periods.

Johnny tells her that he knows that she was fighting the marriage. She tells Johnny that Helen would not be able to keep the Stone name clean. Daphne had stopped an affair with his secretary Martha Winters.

Johnny tells her that E. J. had taken her from a chorus line, but Daphne tells Johnny that not all chorus girls are equal and that she has put her past behind her.

Johnny asks about the picture in Dutch Krieger's office, and is told that the picture was part of the past. Daphne tells Johnny that she has lost someone very dear to her because Harvey was a friend, a real friend.

Johnny goes to Helen's apartment and talks to the tenants. A woman remembers hearing Helen telling someone to quiet down. It was a friend of hers, Alvin Gentry.

Tomorrow, up pops an eyewitness and drives the final nail into the wrong coffin.

Episode 4   Show Date: 9/20/1956
Lt. Restelli calls back, and Johnny tells him about Alvin, he is a friend of Helen Barrett's. Johnny learned that Martha Winters was a friend of Harvey. Restelli tells Johnny that she is in his office.

Johnny cabs to Police headquarters again and meets Miss Winters. She lives in the same building as Harvey, as he used to work from his apartment.

The night of the murder she saw Helen walking towards Harvey's apartment at 11:30. Harvey was her friend, so she decided to tell the police. Johnny asks her about their marriage plans, and she tells Johnny that they had decided mutually to change their plans.

Johnny goes over the timings of the visits to Harvey's apartment by Helen. Johnny still has a hunch that Helen is innocent. Johnny tells Lt. Restelli that E. J. did not like the way Harvey was running the company, and the attention he paid to Daphne. Johnny tells Restelli that E. J. can also get out of his chair. And Daphne wants to protect the Stone name and the picture was part of her past. Johnny mulls over the case and still does not believe that Helen killed Harvey.

Johnny visits the supper club Alvin Gentry manages, and where Helen used to sing. Johnny asks why Alvin made the confession and why he lied about knowing Helen Barrett. He tells Johnny that he knows her and went to see her to ask her to come back to the club to sing. Alvin tells Johnny that Helen was with him at the time of the killing and will swear to it. Johnny is sure that Alvin is lying, but why?

Johnny checks up on Martha Winters and goes to her apartment. Johnny asks her about her statement and about calling off the marriage. Johnny tells her that he heard another story at the Stone office, which upsets her. Johnny tells her that Harvey called off the marriage and almost fired her.

Johnny tells her that she said she saw Helen at 11:30, but, where were you? She tells Johnny that she was standing at the front entrance of her apartment and Johnny tells her that she could not have seen Helen, as Helen came in the side entrance. Martha tells Johnny that it had to be her and admits that she lied. The trap about the side door pays off.

Tomorrow, the wind up. A gambler stakes his life on his hand and loses.

Episode 5 Show Date: 9/21/1956
Lt. Restelli calls and Johnny tells him that Martha had lied. Restelli tells Johnny that Daphne was in the city on the night of the murder.

Johnny cabs to the Stone estate to question Daphne. On the terrace, Johnny tells her that the investigation is not going well, that there are problems. Johnny tells her that she has been giving him incomplete answers. Johnny reminds her that she lied about E. J. being able to get out of his wheelchair. Johnny brings up Dutch, but that is part of her past too.

Johnny asks about her being in the city that night. She tells Johnny that she went in to talk to Harvey about Helen, to talk him out of marrying Helen. She was there from 9:00 to 10:00, and when she left he had decided not to elope with Helen. Daphne decided to stay in a hotel that night instead of coming home.

Johnny asks if that was the whole truth and she tells him that everything she has done has been to protect the Stone name. Johnny wonders what "everything" included?

Johnny goes back to the city and meets with Helen. Johnny tells about Martha's false statement and Alvin's confession. She tells Johnny that she liked Alvin but did not see him after meeting Harvey. She tells Johnny that Alvin was there a few minutes while she was packing and Johnny tells her Alvin swore she was with him during the murder.

Johnny talks with Restelli and is tired of show people, they act too good. Restelli feels Alvin is holding something back.

Johnny goes back to his room and mulls over the case and gets a weird little idea.

Johnny goes to Alvin's club and waits for the club to close. Alvin tells Johnny that he is tired of being a sucker and is withdrawing his statement about being with Helen. Johnny tells him that he is not a sucker, but a smart man trying to put a noose on Helen's neck.

Johnny tells him that love can turn to hate fast, and Alvin needed a good reason to do what he did, maybe losing Helen was that reason. He wanted Helen bad and killed Harvey and then made the false confession to frame Helen.

Alvin tells Johnny that he had found Helen standing over the body and tried to cover for her. Johnny tells him that his confession was correct, as the police had made a mistake, Harvey was killed with a .45 and Alvin blurts out that it was a Smith and Wesson .38. Johnny tells him that only the police, and the killer know that. Alvin runs from Johnny and takes a shot at him. Johnny shoots and hits Alvin in the shoulder.

Lt. Restelli arrives and takes Alvin to jail and arranges to release Helen.

"Remarks: Here I thought that Dutch Krieger was the gambler in the case. But that little game of winner take all that Gentry had been playing was just about the weirdest I have ever heard of. I thought about him up there in the death house at Sing Sing and realized that the big trouble with that kind of gamble that he was taking is that the loser's seat can get awfully hot."

Exp. Acct: $192.40

Notes:
- The details for episode 2 are taken from the script on file in the KNX collection at the Thousand Oaks Library.
- Roy Rowan is the announcer.
- Music supervision is by Amerigo Marino.

Producer: Jack Johnstone   Writer: Robert Ryf
Cast: Virginia Gregg, Tony Barrett, Shirley Mitchell, Will Wright, Chester Stratton, Ted de Corsia, Barney Phillips, Lillian Buyeff, Harry Bartell

◆ ❖ ◆

Show: The Meg's Palace Matter
Company: Inter-Coastal Maritime and Life Insurance Company
Agent: Byron Kay
Synopsis:
Episode 1   Show Date: 9/24/1956

Byron Kay calls and tells Johnny that things in Cod Harbor are terrible. Meg McCarthy runs an eating place and it may be murder, mayhem or whatever. I know it is Saturday but come on over and let's talk.

Johnny travels to Boston and meets with Byron Kay. Johnny is told that Meg's restaurant is insured for $15,000 and that Meg has $25,000 straight life on herself. Meg has been threatened and the restaurant has been set on fire once. Byron promises Johnny a day of fishing or he will double the expenses.

Johnny travels to Cod Harbor and Meg's Palace, a big disreputable place. Johnny goes to the back and hears a woman arguing, with a frying pan in her hand, at a man about his crew getting drunk and breaking up her place. The man runs from the kitchen with Meg throwing glassware at him. "Ain't he the darlingest man?" she tells Johnny.

Johnny finally gets a chance to introduce himself, but only after yelling at her about interrupting him. Meg is ranting on about how she is going to marry Billy, the man she just threw out, who is the beneficiary of her life insurance.

Johnny tells her why he is there, and she tells Johnny that Captain Billy Morgan is not one of those who are threatening her. There is a dozen who would like to see her place burnt, because she gives the men the most and best food. Meg tells Johnny that she is sleeping on the bar to protect herself.

Meg suspects Clem Harris, who runs the Silver Plate, who is too soft and polite and soft spoken. Then there is Ernie Turner who runs the Manor House Café next to the bait house. The third suspect is Tony Fortino, who runs

Irving's Chop Suey joint. They all are conniving because they will not sell out to her. Meg loves it when Johnny yells at her, which is often.

Johnny tells her that she has no evidence, but Meg is about to take him to see the site of a fire when the phone rings with a call for Johnny. "We know why you are here, Dollar. But you won't be here long, understand. Either you go quiet, the way you came, or you go out in a long wooden box, get it?" Johnny is told.

Tomorrow, well they say that darkness can cover a multitude of sins. It can also cover a strong man armed with a deadly weapon.

Episode 2   Show Date: 9/25/1956
Johnny is called by Byron Kay, who had trouble getting in touch with him. Johnny tells Byron that someone has threatened him and asks him to send some things to him, quietly at night, so no one knows it got here.

Johnny orders a batch of fire extinguishers from Byron. Johnny talks to the fishermen who direct him to the shack of Mr. Beasley, the chief of police, mayor and judge, all acting positions.

He tells Johnny that the town is really part of Barnsboro but has to be self-sufficient. Johnny tells Beasley about Meg's Palace and the insurance. Beasley has been told of the threats but has not done anything to look into it. He would look into it if anything serious happened. Beasley tells Johnny that he is the chief of police because he lost his boat and took the job. Johnny asks about the competitors to Meg, and Beasley tells him to go talk to them, but they do not like strangers messing around in their affairs.

Johnny walks back to the Palace and finds Capt. Morgan shouting at a group of men who are cleaning up the Palace. Capt. Morgan tells Johnny that Meg is cleaning Johnny's room, and Johnny wants to ask him some questions.

Johnny asks Capt. Morgan about being the beneficiary of the life insurance policy, and he explodes and wants to fight. Meg comes in and tells Capt. Morgan to get back to work and tells Johnny to go out fishing with Capt. Morgan in the morning and talk then.

Johnny walks outside for some fresh air and sees someone hunched over at the front of the building. Johnny is easing up on the person when the side door opens and someone slugs Johnny.

Tomorrow, a trip to sea on the *Lily Ann* that starts out like an ordinary fishing trip, but somewhere on board lurks a man with murder in his heart. And his next intended victim, me.

Episode 3   Show Date: 9/26/1956
Johnny receives a call from Tim Beasley, who wants to talk to him. Johnny tells him that all he got was a warning the last time they talked. Beasley tells Johnny that he was the one who picked him up and carried him inside. Johnny goes to talk to him.

So far there are no expenses on this case as Meg is providing him a room and food.

Johnny meets with Beasley, who has taken a change of heart and has
thought about how he had talked to Johnny. Beasley tells Johnny that the
locals usually try to settle things among themselves. He had gone to talk to
Johnny and heard the noise from a fight and found Johnny on the ground.

Johnny tells him that he heard the door open just before he was hit, so it
had to be someone on Billy's crew. Beasley tells him that no one on the crew
could have done it, but Johnny tells him someone did. Johnny tells him to look
into the owners of the other restaurants while he is out on the boat. He also
tells Beasley to check the handwriting on the threat letters while he is gone.

Johnny sleeps for a few hours and is awakened by Meg, who brings him some
coffee. Meg sees the wound on his head, and Johnny tells her what happened.
Johnny tells her that someone on the crew must have done it, but she hopes
he is wrong.

Johnny meets the crew for breakfast. There is Charlie, who is liked by all the
others, Montgomery, who is the engineer, and Ole, the first mate. After breakfast
the boat casts-off and heads out to sea.

Johnny watches the crew from the bow and wonders about the case and
how to trap one of them. Suddenly someone picks up Johnny and throws him
overboard and he is run over by the boat.

Tomorrow, the motives for arson and murder begin to take definite shape in
the form of a confession.

Episode 4   Show Date: 9/27/1956

Dr. Champion calls and tells Johnny that he had ordered Meg to keep him in
bed. Johnny was unconscious yesterday and Dr. Champion asks how Johnny
fell overboard. Johnny tells him he was pushed!

Johnny realizes he cannot walk on his leg with a splint on it, and Meg brings
him a plate of food. Johnny wants to get up, but Meg tells him to stay put, or
else. Johnny is told that Capt. Morgan is out fishing now, as he has to keep up
the payments on the boat.

Meg tells Johnny that the crew told her he had fallen overboard. She tells
Johnny that the crew had seen him standing on the bow, then heard him yell,
and then saw him in the water. Charlie was telling everyone he saw it all.

Johnny tells her that he was thrown overboard by someone. He is sure that
whoever threw him overboard did the other things too. Johnny asks if Beasley
had been there to get the notes, and Meg tells him that he has not been there.
Beasley has threatened to close her for violating town ordinances, so maybe
Tim Beasley and Tim Harris are working in cahoots.

Dr. Champion arrives and takes off the splint as it was there to make sure
that Johnny stayed in bed. Capt. Billy arrives and then the other crewmembers
to see how Johnny is. Johnny is told that Charlie did not come, as he was in
Barnsboro today picking up supplies and visiting a sister. Johnny stops Montgomery
and asks about Charlie and gets the address of his sister.

Johnny goes to see Beasley who is not there. A neighbor tells Johnny that
he is in Barnsboro.

Johnny rents an old truck and drives to Barnsboro. Johnny stops at the house of Charlie's sister and meets Charlie there. Charlie puts on an act about Johnny being OK, and Johnny sees that he is packing. Charlie tells Johnny he is tired of fishing.

Johnny asks why he did it, and Charlie tells him that "he" made him do it and that he had killed a man once and had escaped from a reformatory. He made Charley do these things so he would not go back to jail. Charlie tells Johnny he will go back with him. Charlie is ready to tell Johnny who "he" is when Charley is shot in the heart. Johnny sees a car disappearing down the road, and wonders for whom the shot was really intended.

Tomorrow, a killer strikes again, but one of his victims rises from the grave to strike back.

Episode 5   Show Date: 9/28/1956
Chief Walters from the Barnsboro police calls. Johnny tells him to get there fast to pick up a body.

Johnny calls the police and chief Walters comes to the house. Johnny leaves with the chief and Johnny tells him about the case and the various things which have happened. Johnny tells him that he has too many suspects. The chief has just seen Capt. Morgan in Barnsboro. Johnny tells him about Beasley, his cousin and the notes.

Back in Cod Harbor Johnny sees that the Palace is on fire, and the town is there fighting the flames with pumps from the various boats in the harbor. Chief Walters sees immediate evidence of arson, and Capt. Morgan is directing the effort to fight the fire.

Johnny notices that Meg is not there and gets chief Walters to lift him up into the front of the building so he can get to Meg's room, where she is found unconscious with a wound on her head. Johnny is able to get her out of the building.

Johnny wakes up, and Meg is tending to a burn on his arm. They are in Clem Harris' house, and she is grateful for Johnny saving her life. She tells Johnny that someone had hit her and left her in the building to burn.

Chief Walters comes in with Capt. Morgan, who is angry because he has been arrested. Johnny tells him that he is guilty of arson and murder, and that the insurance was the reason.

Johnny tells him that he had compared his handwriting with some other documents, and Morgan confesses. He tells Johnny that he needed money to save his boat. Meg goes ballistic because the boat is more important than her.

Meg tells Johnny that maybe she will move somewhere to get away from the town. She is Meg McCarthy and no man will get her down! If she were only younger and prettier...

Meg asks about the letters and Johnny tells her that he had faked it and had never seen any handwriting samples. Meg breaks down about Capt. Morgan as she really loved him.

The insurance will have to be paid on the building, and the courts will deal with Captain Billy.

Exp. Acct: $221.60

Notes:
- Roy Rowan is the announcer.
- Music supervision is by Amerigo Marino and Carl Fortina.

Producer: Jack Johnstone   Writer: Jack Johnstone
Cast: Virginia Gregg, Jack Kruschen, Byron Kane, Forrest Lewis, Bert Holland, Stan Jones, Bob Bruce, Austin Green, Harry Bartell

♦ ❖ ♦

Show: **The Picture Postcard Matter**
Company: **Global Casualty**
Agent: **Tom Wilkins**
Synopsis:
Episode 1   Show Date: 10/1/1956

Tom Wilkins calls and he has a $100,000 headache, uncut diamonds which have been stolen. There is a fat fee if you can recover them.

Johnny cabs to Tom Wilkins' office and is told that the diamonds were being taken from Zurich to Amsterdam and were stolen at the airport in Zurich. The courier had a briefcase that was cut off of his wrist during a fake fight. One of the men was described as stocky with a thick neck, not much help. Tom has a special delivery letter from a man named Sebastian that offers help for a reward. The letter has instructions for a meeting, and to use caution.

Johnny flies to Zurich, Switzerland and thinks about the case on the way.

Johnny gets a cab to go to the Hotel Pola and a woman gets into his cab thinking Johnny was someone else. The woman tells the driver to stop and she exits the cab after giving Johnny a big kiss. Johnny notices that the woman, Ilsa Schaeffer, had left her purse in the cab.

Johnny takes the purse to the cab office and then goes to the hotel. In the lobby a man stops Johnny with a gun in Johnny's ribs. They leave by the side entrance where Johnny is told to get into a car. The man is sure that Johnny has the diamonds. The woman did not leave the cab with her purse, so Johnny must have them. Johnny tells the man that the purse was empty, but to no avail.

Johnny tries to slug the man and is hurt by a passing cab, allowing the man and his car to disappear. Johnny calls Tom Wilkins and updates him on the events and the need for caution.

Johnny goes to his room and waits for a call from Sebastian. Later while Johnny reads a newspaper in the lobby a man sits down behind him. As Johnny starts to leave the man tells him to hide his face in the paper as they talk.

He is Sebastian and tells Johnny he can guarantee the return of the diamonds for $25,000. The man passes a postcard to Johnny signed by F. Greuner. The postcard is from the Kleibach Inn and is part of the solution.

Sebastian will provide proof tonight. His address is on an inner page of his newspaper, which Johnny is to get when he leaves.

That night Johnny goes to the address and knocks on the door, but no one answers. Johnny goes in and waits. Johnny hears a dripping faucet and goes to the bathroom to find Sebastian floating in the bathtub.

Tomorrow, a perfect stranger wants to get acquainted, and a beautiful girl asks me to go skiing. Trouble is, either or both of them could be trying to kill me.

Episode 2   Show Date: 10/2/1956
Inspector Honneger of the Zurich Police calls Johnny. He has no information about Sebastian, and Johnny tells him about the diamond robbery. The inspector tells Johnny that Sebastian was probably killed by a woman.

Johnny cabs to the police and meets with Insp. Honneger, who asks Johnny to provide the information he has. Johnny outlines the robbery, the letter and his meeting with Ilsa, the man in the lobby, and Sebastian.

Johnny thinks that Sebastian was a member of the outfit that stole the diamonds and would get more from returning the diamonds than by fencing them. Johnny shows Honneger the postcard and tells him that the card was part of the solution to finding the diamonds. Honneger tells Johnny that Sebastian was hit and drown, a technique used typically by women.

Johnny leaves for Kleibach, Switzerland and gets a room in the chalet-like Kleibach Inn. Johnny talks to the manager, Otto Friedrich about the post card.

Otto tells Johnny that it is not a good picture and that he does not sell them anymore. The village sells them though. Johnny asks about the name Sebastian, and F. Greuner, and Otto tells Johnny that he will ask around the village.

Johnny is visited in his room by Geoffrey Harris who is looking for a Johnny Dollar from London. He thought Johnny might be old "Bunny". Geoffrey and Johnny walk out and Johnny spots a friend at the bar.

Johnny goes over and sits down with Ilsa. She thanks Johnny for turning her purse to the cab company. Johnny asks if she had meant to pass something to him in the cab, but she plays ignorant. She is at the inn to go skiing and comes her often and invites Johnny to come skiing with her tomorrow.

Johnny goes to ask Otto about Ilsa and learns that this is her first visit. Johnny returns to the bar and tells Ilsa that he will ski with her tomorrow. Ilsa tells Johnny that they will ski the north slope, which some consider too dangerous. Johnny is sure that Ilsa will "take good care" of him.

Tomorrow, well, skiing is a strenuous sport, so is hunting. Put them together and it is liable to kill you.

Episode 3   Show Date: 10/3/1956
Otto calls with a phone call from Insp. Honneger who tells Johnny that there is no line on Sebastian's killer. Honneger tells Johnny that another postcard was sent to Sebastian, and he is sending it to Johnny. Johnny tells him that he is going skiing with Ilsa that morning.

Johnny rents ski equipment for $3.00 and goes to meet Ilsa. Johnny and Ilsa ride to the top and work their way down the mountain. Johnny notes that it has been 4 years since the last time he skied.

They stop on a ridge and Ilsa asks for a cigarette. Ilsa points out the Inn below and the coincidence of meeting Johnny at the Inn, and suddenly there are shots. Ilsa points to a hill and Johnny leads off towards the hill for cover. Johnny sees a cliff and they stop in time. Ilsa tells Johnny that she had forgotten about an avalanche that took out the slope. Johnny tells her that this is one coincidence too many.

Back at the inn, Johnny and Ilsa talk by the fire. Johnny tells her that she has to tell him what is going on. She tells Johnny that she knows Sebastian, but not about his murder. Sebastian was just a friend who had asked her to share the cab with Johnny and leave her purse in it. He told her that he was in trouble and needed her help. Ilsa tells Johnny that she is telling the truth about not knowing about the diamonds.

Johnny tells her about the possibility of Sebastian trying to double-cross his own people or another group trying to get to the diamonds. Ilsa tells Johnny that Sebastian told her to meet him there. Johnny describes the man in the lobby, but she does not know him. Ilsa describes a friend of Sebastian with a stocky thick neck named Breuner, but Johnny suggests it is Greuner.

Johnny asks about the Englishman Harris, but she does not know him. Ilsa goes to her room and Otto asks Johnny how the skiing was.

Johnny asks how he knows if a woman is lying, and Otto tells Johnny to believe what he wishes. Otto gives Johnny a letter and tells him that Mr. Harris was out climbing the rocks this morning. Johnny opens the letter and calls Insp. Honneger. The card came this morning and shows a small skier's shelter on the front. Johnny tells Honneger that he is going to the shelter to see if it is the hiding place of the diamonds.

Johnny starts up the trail to the shelter and sees someone going down the rocks towards the inn that looks like Harris. At the shelter, Johnny finds the contents all torn up.

Tomorrow, a third part of the key turns up in the form of a corpse.

Episode 4   Show Date: 10/4/1956

Insp. Honneger calls Johnny from the lobby of the inn. Johnny tells him that he found the shelter all torn up. Honneger tells Johnny that a man matching the description of the one who attacked him brought a ticket to Kleibach, so maybe the diamonds are here after all.

Johnny has coffee with Insp. Honneger and discusses the case. Johnny tells Honneger about the conversation with Ilsa about Sebastian, and Johnny tells him that after the robbery the gang split up, and Greuner was to hide the diamonds and get back to Sebastian with their location. Now Sebastian wants to double-cross them and another gang has moved in. Sebastian moved too slowly and was killed, and Greuner does not know that Sebastian is dead.

Johnny tells of the Englishman who likes to climb mountains and maybe Ilsa positioned him where Harris could shoot at them. Honneger will have the police watch the trains station and goes back to Zurich.

Johnny looks at the mountains from his balcony and sees the doors to Harris's room open. Johnny searches the room and finds a rifle in a closet that had been fired.

Johnny finds Otto and asks where Harris is, and is told that he left for the village before dinner. Johnny leaves and runs into Ilsa who wants to know what she must do to get Johnny to trust her.

Johnny and Ilsa go to the village to look for Harris. Johnny tells her about finding the rifle in Harris' closet. Johnny notices that someone is following them and goes into an alley. Ilsa is told to walk on while Johnny waits in a doorway.

Johnny listens to the man as he passes the alley and then hears Ilsa scream. Johnny runs to Ilsa and sees a man on the street. Ilsa tells Johnny that the man fell from the window, and that he is Sebastian's friend Greuner.

Tomorrow, the windup. I find out that some people will not hesitate to kill anyone who gets in their way. And that is not so good when the man in the way is me.

Episode 5   Show Date: 10/5/1956
Otto calls returning Johnny's call. Johnny tells Otto to look out for Harris and call him at the hotel in the village if he comes back. He has found Greuner, dead.

Johnny and Ilsa go to Greuner's room to look around. She tells Johnny that she heard Greuner scream when she came out of the alley. Johnny opens the room and finds nothing. Johnny hears a door being locked and breaks in and from the window sees a man running down the street, it is the man who jumped him in Zurich.

Johnny goes back to the inn and thinks about the case. Johnny shows Ilsa the two post cards, but they mean nothing. Johnny tells her of the connection between Sebastian and Greuner. Ilsa realizes that there might be a line between the two sites.

Geoffrey Harris comes in and asks how Johnny is enjoying his stay. Johnny tells him about being shot at and the killing in the village, and how Harris was in the vicinity both times. Johnny asks him about his rifle, but Harris tells Johnny he does not have one and does not like Johnny's attitude and leaves.

Ilsa is gone when Johnny goes back and Otto shows Johnny a postcard meant for Sebastian, which has a picture of the village square. Johnny goes to his room and looks at the cards. Johnny realizes that there might be some place where all three of the buildings in the pictures could be seen.

Johnny walks out and finds a small barn where he is able to see the inn, the shelter and the village square. Johnny enters the barn and finds a leather case. Johnny hears footsteps and jumps the man who comes in, the man from Zurich. He is Anton, who is trying to get the diamonds.

Johnny asks who Anton is working for and Otto comes in. Johnny realizes that Otto had shot at him and let Johnny lead him to the diamonds. Otto takes the diamonds from Anton, who is shot by Otto. Johnny slugs Otto and goes to Anton, who is wounded in the shoulder.

"Remarks: Otto and Anton were turned over to police Inspector Honneger, the diamonds are in safekeeping. About Otto, well, greed is one of the seven deadly sins. It sure turned out to be the deadliest one for Otto. About Ilsa, well, ah, please consider me available for any future assignments in Switzerland."

Exp. Acct: $1,723.00

Notes:
- Roy Rowan is the announcer.
- Music Supervision is by Amerigo Marino.

Producer: Jack Johnstone   Writer: Robert Ryf
Cast: Lucille Meredith, Vic Perrin, Forrest Lewis, Stan Jones, Ben Wright

• ❖ •

Show: **The Primrose Matter**
Company: **Mid-States Industrial Insurance Company**
Agent: **Brad Taylor**
Synopsis:
Episode 1   Show Date: 10/8/1956

Brad Taylor calls and Johnny asks if he has caught another chief accountant with his hand in the till. Brad tells Johnny that this is about the Kansas City payroll stickup. It was the Jipper Nitson gang. He was recognized in Phoenix and one of his boys was shot at a roadblock, but Jipper got away with the $100,000 payroll. Johnny agrees to go out and look for the money. Brad tells Johnny to be careful, they killed a state trooper at the roadblock.

Johnny travels to Tucson, Arizona and contacts Lt. Cal Mervin of the state police. Johnny is told that the police were caught off guard and four men got the drop on them. One man was shot and his body was thrown out of the car later. Nitson and two others got away, but Bledsoe was the one who was shot. One of them had a tommy gun and used it.

Mervin shows Johnny a map of the area, and the terrain is very rough. The Mexican authorities have told Mervin that the car has not gone to Nogales. Johnny is sure that they did not double back and are not in Mexico, so maybe they are still in the area. Johnny wonders if a civilian could stumble on them.

Johnny offers to act like a rock-hound to get information. Mervin tells Johnny to go to Dave Bright's place and he will set you up. Keep in touch so I can let you know when the gang has been picked up in Portland, or Montana.

Johnny equips himself to look like a prospector and goes to Jake's Bar and Grill to get information. Johnny buys a scotch for himself and Jake. Johnny tells Jake that he is out looking for uranium. Jake tells Johnny he knows most of the country and Johnny asks how to get back away from the highway and get lost.

Jake tells him that there is only road one that might fit the bill, the Santa Rosa Summit road which dead ends at Primrose Camp. Jake tells Johnny that the police have been looking for some robbers, but he is sure that they are in Mexico. The road is in good shape and goes up to about 6,000 ft.

The Primrose Camp is Pop Bardell's place. He runs a gas station and a store and has some cabins. He gets hunters and campers and prospectors as customers. He has a new helper, a nephew from Tulsa, but he did not have an Oklahoma accent. He was very closed-mouth as well. Jake asks Johnny what he is looking for, because he is the first city person to come out here with a shoulder holster and a gun.

Tomorrow, a talkative man freezes, a taciturn man thaws, but a dead man can't do either. All he can do is be dead.

Episode 2   Show Date: 10/9/1956
Lt. Mervin calls and Johnny tells him that he is checking in. Lt. Mervin recognizes the number as Jake's. Johnny tells him he is playing a lead and going into the Santa Rosa Mountains.

Johnny drives up to Primrose Camp and talks to Pop Bardell. Johnny asks if he can get a cabin from Pop, but Pop tells Johnny that the cabins are full. Johnny wants to prospect and is reassured that there are no cabins. Pop warns Johnny about the dangers of snakes and getting lost. Johnny tells the man that he will wait to talk to Pop, but the man says he is Pop. Johnny tells him that he is nowhere as talkative as Jake described him.

A man calls from the lunchroom and Pop hurries in. Johnny walks in to see the man, but Pop tells him that he cannot go in. The man comes out and asks if there is trouble. Johnny tells him he wants some cigarettes. The man asks what brand, and Johnny replies "Chesteroids" and is given a pack and told to pay Pop.

Johnny asks the man if he knows Clem Wilkie who is working on the new power plant in Tulsa, which is almost finished. Johnny drives off and notes that there is no new electric plant in Tulsa. Johnny drives to the end of the road and notes that no one had been there. Johnny is certain that the robbers are there.

Johnny walks back to the hill above the camp and watches with binoculars as two cars come and go. Johnny sees Pop and his wife but not their daughter or the nephew.

A prospector surprises Johnny and asks if he is watching someone. He recognizes Dave's clothes and knows Johnny is a city-slicker. Johnny asks if the man lives there, but he tells Johnny that he has been prospecting for three weeks and has seen no one. The man is Jed Marsh. He would stop by to talk to Pop but will skip it this time, and Johnny mentions the nephew. Jed tells him that Pop has no close relatives. Pop used to be a prospector and bought the camp to settle down. Jed asks Johnny to look at a wrecked and buried car for him.

Johnny goes to the car with Jed and opens the door to find a body inside. Johnny notes that the man had been shot and Johnny tells him that the state police killed him. Johnny tells Jed who he is, and who he is after. Johnny is sure that they are at Primrose Camp.

Tomorrow, a lion's den reluctantly opens its door to let a trusting victim step inside. And the victim, me.

Episode 3   Show Date: 10/10/1956
Johnny calls Lt. Mervin from a forest station phone. Johnny tells him that he has found the stolen car in the mountains with a dead man in it. Johnny tells him not to bring the police there, as something is wrong at Primrose Camp.

Johnny convinces Lt. Mervin to hold his men off for 24 hours. Johnny drives to Primrose Camp and asks if there is a vacancy, but all the cabins are dark. Pop tells him it is better if he goes to the crossroads. Johnny tells him he cannot drive, as the headlights are broken.

Johnny spots a station wagon and wants to borrow it, but Pop tells him he cannot. Pop asks Johnny what he is there looking for. Pop is very nervous about Johnny staying around there, but Johnny cannot leave.

The nephew walks up and asks what the trouble is, and Pop tells him that Johnny's lights are out. The man offers to let Johnny stay in cabin number 2. He would not want Johnny to go off and tell bad stories about them, as it might cause trouble.

Johnny pays for the room and Myra Bardell offers to fix him some food. She tells Johnny that the people who are renting the cabins are not eating there. She mentions her daughter and tells Johnny that she is not feeling well and starts to cry.

Johnny eats his breakfast and Myra tells Johnny that Pop cannot help himself. She tells him that they are in dangerous trouble but will not tell him what. The place is a powder keg, please leave and do not set it off.

Johnny goes to his cabin and finds Pop there with an oil lamp. Pop tells Johnny not to listen to the misses. She is just upset, you know how women are sometimes.

Johnny asks about his daughter and Pop tells Johnny that she is in Tucson. Johnny mentions the nephew and Pop tells Johnny that he has been there for a few weeks. Johnny confronts him with the things he knows, but Pop says nothing.

Johnny notes that a tire is missing from his jeep, and Pop tells him it went flat and will be fixed in the morning.

Tomorrow, a tightening noose. People held fast in the grip of fear. Then violence.

Episode 4   Show Date: 10/11/1956
Jed calls Johnny from the forest ranger phone. Johnny asks Jed to meet him on the road below Primrose Camp. Johnny tells him that there is trouble and it is tied into the robbery.

Johnny goes to meet Jed March at the ranger patrol phone. Suddenly the nephew is behind Johnny with a gun. The man takes Johnny's gun and slugs Johnny when he gets smart with him. Johnny tells him that Jed is coming to help him. Johnny tells him that he is not Pop's nephew and that he came east from Kansas City. Johnny recognizes him as Spade Keller, who worked with the Carzotti mob, and is now with Jipper Nitson.

Johnny tells him he has found their car and is now looking for the money. Now there is no one but him and Jipper to take the heat. Spade asks if the police know about the car, and Johnny plays dumb and insinuates that he and Jed are after the money. Spade asks Johnny what he is planning to do and then knocks Johnny unconscious.

Later that evening, when Johnny wakes up, Jed is being held by Spade. Jed is searched and Spade slaps him with his gun. Johnny tells Jed that Spade is jumpy. They tell Spade that one of them will jump him if he doesn't watch it. Johnny tells Jed that the gang has already killed three others.

They get up and spread out along the road to spread Spade's attention. Jed tells Spade that he is standing close to the rocks by the cliff, where the snakes are. There is the sound of a rattlesnake, Spade panics and falls over the cliff. Jed shows Johnny the rattles he has in his pocket. He tells Johnny that he uses them to spook tenderfeet.

Tomorrow, a lovely girl screams in terror as a cornered rat turns and fights back. Fights the way a rat fights.

Episode 5   Show Date: 10/12/1956
Lt. Mervin calls and Johnny tells him that he has another body for him, Spade Keller, who fell over a cliff. Johnny asks Lt. Mervin to hold off until noon. Johnny tells him that Jed will meet him in a green station wagon that they are going to steal.

Jed and Johnny go back to the camp and Jed steals the car and Johnny sees Pop Bardell come running out after it. Johnny meets him and asks if anything is wrong. Johnny tells Pop that maybe his nephew took the car.

Johnny tells him that the nephew seems to have taken over the place but Pop does not seem to be the kind to let anyone tell him what to do. Johnny tells Pop who he is and that he knows the gang is there. Johnny tells Pop that Spade Keller is dead and that Jed Marsh took the car to meet the police while Johnny tries to get Jipper. Pop tells Johnny that his daughter is in Tucson and will not take a chance.

Myra comes out and tells Pop that Johnny is right, they have to take the chance. Johnny tells them that he might be able to get to their daughter without harming her. Pop tells Johnny that Nipper is in a tunnel with their daughter.

Johnny gives Pop his wallet and gun and goes up the trail with his equipment. Johnny ignores the tunnel when he gets there and then finally goes in. Johnny is slugged in the tunnel and Jipper walks outside to check on things.

Johnny whispers to Jenny and tells her not to worry. She tells Johnny that the money is in the tunnel. Johnny tells her to get Jipper with his back turned to Johnny. Jipper comes in and tells her to leave Johnny alone. Jipper tells her that something is wrong.

Jenny lures him to her and Johnny gets up and hits him with a rock and takes his gun. Jenny tells Johnny that he killed Jipper but Johnny tells her the state probably will kill him.

"Remarks: The state eventually did, kill him I mean."

Exp. Acct: $914.15

Notes:
- Roy Rowan is the announcer.
- Music Supervision is by Amerigo Marino.

Producer: Jack Johnstone   Writer: Les Crutchfield
Cast: Marvin Miller, Junius Matthews, Herb Ellis, D. J. Thompson, Herb Butterfield, Tony Barrett, Barbara Eiler

♦ ❖ ♦

Show: The Phantom Chase Matter
Company: Universal Adjustment Bureau
Agent: Pat McCracken
Synopsis:
Episode 1   **Show Date:**   **10/15/1956**

Pat McCracken calls Johnny and he has $120,000 on his mind. Pat thinks that Thomas Chase, partner of a Wall Street investment firm, has the money. Pat thinks that Chase has embezzled the money, but he has jumped bail and disappeared.

Johnny cabs to Pat's office and they discuss the case. Johnny is told that Everson and Chase is a high-class operation. Mr. George Everson is the senior partner and a widower. Thomas Chase is the junior partner, and a former football player, an all-American type. Chase is married to Lola Chase, and she seems to be a really nice girl. The missing money is currency, checks and negotiable securities. Everson can give you more details on how it was pulled off. Everson is not sure that Chase is guilty, but Pat asks Johnny if an innocent man would jump bail.

Johnny goes to New York City and the office of Mr. Everson, who cannot believe that Tom did it.

Johnny is told that Tom became a partner 5 years ago. The firm has always maintained a fluid relationship with their customers, and a clever man could juggle figures. Tom had been managing some of the bigger accounts lately that were interested in long term growth. Everson discovered the missing money when a client decided to liquidate his account and the shortage was found.

An audit was conducted and the district attorney was brought in. Johnny gets the files and Everson shows Johnny where the documents recorded each transaction. Everson tells Johnny that Tom would not talk after arrested, and that Everson had arranged bail, which Tom jumped.

Everson had eaten dinner with them a week earlier and Lola told him that Tom was acting moody and preoccupied lately. Everson asks Johnny to find out why Tom did it.

Johnny arranges to have dinner with Lola Chase. Johnny notes that Lola is quite a dish. Lola tells Johnny that she thought she knew Tom, but apparently, she did not. He liked golf and sailing and had an extensive jazz collection and hi-fi setup.

She tells Johnny that Tom had become moody lately and stayed out late at night. They had planned a trip and he cancelled out and told her to go alone. She found out Tom had been arrested when she got back from Martha's Vineyard.

Johnny is visited by Mr. Everson in his hotel room. He shows Johnny a newspaper article about New Orleans jazz. In a picture of a jazz place is Tom Chase. Everson is sure that, based on the pose, the man is Tom Chase.

Yeah, on to New Orleans where the trail proves to be pretty cold but warms up fast.

Episode 2   Show Date: 10/16/1956
George Everson calls and tells Johnny that he may not be so sure about the picture. Johnny tells him that New Orleans would be a good place, given Tom's interest in jazz. My plane leaves in an hour.

Johnny goes to the airport and George Everson meets him there to tell him that if the trip is unfruitful, he will pay the expenses. Johnny goes over the facts of the case with Everson before leaving. Johnny asks about another woman, but George thinks that idea is not possible.

Johnny flies to New Orleans, Louisiana and heads for the Latin Quarter. Johnny locates Ace's Castle, the bar in the newspaper article and orders a scotch and soda. The bartender tells Johnny that this is not a tourist place, but for the locals who come to listen to Pops Harker and nurse their troubles.

Johnny shows him the picture and points to the man in the background. The bartender does not recognize the picture or the name Tom Chase. If he is on the street, Tom will come back.

Johnny goes to talk to Pops, who was just warming up. Johnny tells him he is looking for a man named Tom Chase, but Pops doesn't know the name. Pops would know the voice, but not the picture, as he is blind.

Johnny waits for several hours but nothing happens. At midnight Freddy Quintana sits down with Johnny and tells him that he should be glad to see him. It is his business to help people, when money is involved, and for a few bucks he can help Johnny find Tom Chase. Freddy describes Chase and Johnny tells Freddy to bring him there but he tells Johnny that Tom does not want to be found. He tells Johnny that Tom is going under the name Tom James, and that he will be back in an hour with proof. On the way out, Pops tells Johnny that Freddy was a bad one, he could tell from his voice.

Freddy returns with a letter he found in a trash can. The letter was written to Lola, and a comparison of handwriting Johnny had matches.

There is a little game of chance called dealer's choice. Fine, until the dealer gets dealt out, the hard way.

Episode 3   Show Date: 10/17/1956
Freddy calls Johnny and tells him that the deal is complicated and that Tom is

hiding again. Freddie tells Johnny to meet him at Ace's Castle at ten o'clock with the money.

Johnny calls Pat McCracken and gets his agreement for the $500 payoff to Freddy. Johnny calls Everson who is happy Johnny is making progress.

As Johnny waits for the meeting time, Lola Chase comes to his hotel room. She tells Johnny that George had told her about the phone call, and she decided to come there to be with Tom, if he is there. She might be able to talk to Tom.

Johnny tells her of the letter from Freddy, and she asks to see it. Lola reads the letter and wants to come with Johnny to meet Freddy.

Johnny and Lola eat dinner and then go to Ace's Castle. Lola comments to Johnny on his job and he tells her that sometimes he does not like it, like now. Johnny and Lola get a table at Ace's Castle and wait. Pop tells Johnny that he should stick to the good ones when Freddy comes in.

Freddy tells Johnny that he has Tom James waiting for him on the pretext Freddie is getting passage for him. Freddy gives Johnny an address and tells Johnny to meet him there at midnight. Lola asks to go with Johnny and he reluctantly agrees.

Johnny and Lola go to the rooming house and go into room 8. They walk in and the room is empty, so they wait. After 30 minutes Johnny takes Lola to her hotel and goes to Ace's Castle where Lt. LeFevre of the police sits down with Johnny and asks him why he is there. Johnny tells him about Freddy and tells LeFevre who he is. LeFevre takes Johnny to the alley in the back where Freddy Quintana is dead.

Somehow, I manage to parlay a scrap of burnt paper into a plane ticket for what almost turns out to be a one-way trip.

Episode 4   Show Date: 10/18/1956

Lt. LeFevre calls and tells Johnny that he needs to talk about his involvement with Freddy.

Johnny cabs to police headquarters and tells LeFevre about all the details of the case he is working on, and the events so far in New Orleans.

Johnny shows LeFevre the picture from the newspaper and tells him about meeting Freddy at Ace's Castle and the letter from the trash can. Johnny tells LeFevre about going to meet Freddy and finding him dead. LeFevre tells Johnny that Freddy was a really bad boy, and a lot of people would like to have killed him.

Johnny goes to tell the bad news to Lola and she wishes she could call off the investigation. Johnny is called by LeFevre, who has just located Tom James' room.

Johnny cabs to the rooming house and meets LeFevre there. The room is empty and there are some burnt papers in a trashcan. Johnny identifies the handwriting and finds a piece of envelope with the letterhead of "Everson and Chase" on the corner. LeFevre finds another scrap with the number "12, 23" on it.

Johnny goes to the rental agent and asks about the room rented to Tom James. The man tells Johnny that the rent was paid in advance, and that a friend rented the room for Mr. James. The agent would love to have a friend like that, "boy, what a woman!"

Johnny returns to Lola and tells her to go back to New York. Johnny tells Lola that it looks like Tom is not traveling alone now. Lola returns to New York, and Johnny mulls over the case and the numbers "12, 23". While Johnny reads through the paper he notices the harbor news. Maybe the numbers refer to a ship and its departure time!

It's about a trail that heats up, and a girl who doesn't exactly help to cool things off.

Episode 5   Show Date: 10/19/1956

Johnny is called by Lt. LeFevre and Johnny tells him of the new lead. Johnny tells him about the numbers and the harbor news article, and LeFevre tells Johnny that he will work on it.

Johnny cabs to LeFevre's office and learns that pier 23 is a busy place, but the police are working on getting more information. Johnny relates telling Lola about the woman, and her trip back to New York. Johnny tells LeFevre that he is glad he is single, based on the type of people he has to deal with.

LeFevre is called and gets information on a ship, "The Caribbean Star" that left pier 23 at midnight on the night James disappeared. It is bound for Trinidad via Havana and Haiti, and there is a passenger named James on the passenger list. Everson calls and Johnny tells him about the woman who rented the room.

Johnny flies to Port-au-Prince, Haiti and meets the Caribbean Star. Johnny goes to James' stateroom and he has to break in only to find an empty room. The purser arrives and tells Johnny that Mr. James got off in Havana. The purser tells Johnny that James had asked where the airline offices were. Johnny calls the Havana police and asks Lt. Escobar to check the airlines and find out where James went and call him back. Lt. Escobar calls Johnny two hours later and tells Johnny that James had purchased a ticket to Barbados.

Johnny flies to Bridgetown, Barbados and sees why Tom would want to come there. The island is bigger than Johnny thought. Johnny checks all the hotels for Tom and finds nothing.

While Johnny is thinking in the hotel bar, a girl asks if he is Johnny Dollar and joins him. She tells Johnny that she knows where Tom James is. Her name is Connie, and she tells Johnny that she is the one that rented the room and wants out. She wants money to get back to the states.

She tells Johnny that Tom will be at the Trade Winds Bar on the waterfront at 10:00. Johnny goes to the bar and sees Connie go in. Johnny realizes that he is being followed and chases the man into a warehouse where he is knocked out.

Next, a small fishing boat and a deserted island and a man waiting there for me. A man with a gun.

Notes:
- The cast for the first five episodes is given at the end of this week's programs.

Cast: Virginia Gregg, Michael Ann Barrett, Lawrence Dobkin, Forrest Lewis, Peter Leeds, Barney Phillips, Tony Barrett, Vic Perrin

Episode 6   Show Date: 10/22/1956
Connie calls Johnny and tells him she waited for him at the Trade Winds. Johnny tells her about getting slugged, but she knows nothing about it. She is in the lobby, and Johnny will be right down.

Johnny is ready to chuck the case for 2 cents when Connie does not show up. The desk clerk tells Johnny that he saw her leave after making a phone call. He had seen her with a large athletic man, who Johnny muses, could be Chase.

Johnny visits the local police and meets Inspector Whitsett. Johnny outlines the case to him and tells him where he has been so far. Johnny gives Whitsett a description of Connie and he agrees to look for her. Johnny tells of meeting Connie, and the meeting at the Trade Winds, but wonders why she left the hotel after calling him.

Back at the hotel, the desk clerk tells Johnny that Connie has not come back. Johnny tells him that he is going to the Trade Winds, and the clerk warns Johnny that it is in a dangerous part of town.

Johnny goes to the Trade Winds and buys a rum punch. Johnny spots Connie and goes out after her and finds her in the alley. She tells Johnny that she is not Chase's girlfriend, and she was trying to work something for herself. When Johnny talked about murder, she wanted to back out.

Connie tells Johnny that she met Chase in Barbados two days ago and heard that Johnny was looking for him. She wanted to set up Chase for money, she is broke and wants to get back to the states.

She tells Johnny that Chase had mentioned a friend who was coming and about a conversation with a fisherman on the wharf. Johnny takes her out to the docks and they look for the man Chase had talked to. Johnny talks to the man and learns that he took a passenger to Lagos Island. It is an island with an abandoned house, and the man took food with him. Johnny feels that it is on the up-and-up, or a big trap. He will have to go to Lagos Island to find out.

Getting to the island of Lagos, easy. Getting away from it in one piece, that is another story.

Episode 7   Show Date: 10/24/1956
Lola Chase calls Johnny from her hotel in Maresol Beach, Barbados. She had to come here, after all Tom is her husband. Johnny goes to see her.

Johnny cabs to Lola's hotel and meets her on the terrace. She tells Johnny that she has discovered that it hurts to get kicked in the face, but you get over it. Deep inside she knew it had to be another woman but she cannot be hurt anymore. Lola is there because she feels obligated to be there. Johnny tells her about the island and the girl who led him on. Johnny tells her he should be back by dark.

Johnny calls Everson who does not know that Lola is in Barbados. He will fly to Barbados and take her back with him. Johnny tells him that he might have located Chase and is going to go pick him up.

Johnny rents a power cruiser and goes to see Insp. Whitsett. Johnny tells him about the island, and Whitsett shows him the island on a chart. Both Johnny and Insp. Whitsett feel that this could still be a trap. Whitsett tells Johnny about the island and does not think that anyone would be there.

Johnny gives Insp. Whitsett his radio call letters, "6X3" and asks him to watch the fisherman he got the information from and to radio Johnny if the man goes out to sea.

Johnny gets the boat and sets course for the island. In the cabin, Johnny finds Lola, who has stowed away. She wants to be there when Johnny finds Tom. She does not want Tom or Johnny to get hurt. She has thought a lot about Johnny and maybe if things were different...

Johnny gets a call from Whitsett who tells Johnny that the fisherman left about 20 minutes after he did.

Johnny gets to the island and lands at the abandoned pier. Johnny and Lola walk towards the house through the undergrowth and are suddenly shot at. Johnny hides in a gully and works his way towards the shots. Lola is scared that Johnny has a gun and is afraid that Johnny might hurt Tom.

Lola notices that the next shots come from behind them, and Johnny realizes he has been suckered in to getting away from the boat. He rushes back to find the boat leaving with a man at the helm. Lola tells Johnny that it is Tom.

Next, a friend to the rescue, and an unfriendly phone call from a killer.

Episode 8   Show Date: 10/25/1956

Johnny Dollar, "boy genius", who lets Tom get his boat away from him. Tom is no dummy. Johnny tells Lola that they are alone on the island, and there is no way off.

Johnny tells Lola that they might be there quite a while. She asks Johnny to stop calling Tom her husband. Johnny wonders why Tom did not finish him off in the warehouse and did not kill him when he was shooting at him. Lola tells Johnny that in other circumstances she would not mind being there with Johnny.

Johnny builds a fire and goes to the house and finds some food. After eating they go back to the fire, build it up, and wait.

Johnny dozes off, and Lola wakes Johnny up when she sees a boat. Johnny realizes that it is a police boat with Whitsett on it. Johnny tells him what Chase had done, and Whitsett tells Johnny he had seen a boat heading back to Barbados.

Back in Bridgetown, Whitsett tells Johnny and Lola that George Everson is there waiting for them. Johnny spots the boat he had rented, and Whitsett starts watching the airlines and charter boats.

Johnny goes to talk to George Everson and updates him with what has happened. Everson still feels that Lola feels strongly about Tom, so maybe she could talk to him. He would tell Tom to give himself up and give back the money and work on restitution to their investors. Johnny tells him that Tom will not give himself in as he probably is the one who killed Freddy Quintana.

Johnny cabs to Whitsett's office and learns that Chase is still on the island. Whitsett tells Johnny that the island is big, and Chase could be anywhere. Whitsett gets a phone call and learns that a man answering Chase's description has just checked into a hotel. Johnny and Whitsett go to the hotel and enter the room with a passkey. The room is empty, and the window is open. Johnny just missed him again.

Johnny goes to his hotel and finds Tom Chase in his room. Tom takes his gun and Johnny asks why he did it. He tells Johnny that he did it for a woman, but that turned sour. He came to Johnny's room because he could not shake Johnny and is tired of running. It is the end of the line for Johnny.

Tomorrow, the pay off. But who gets paid off, and how and why? Well the answers to those questions surprise me plenty, and maybe they will you too.

Episode 9   Show Date: 10/26/1956

Johnny is called by Lola and Tom tells him to hang up. Lola realizes it is Tom, and she tells Johnny that she is coming over, but Johnny tells her not to. Tom has a gun and he means business.

Johnny figures his next expense item is for burial expenses. Tom asks him why Lola is involved in this. He tells Johnny that the girl turned sour and it is too late for anything. He cannot run and cannot take it anymore, and Tom slugs Johnny.

When Johnny wakes up, Lola and George are there. He tells them what happened and about Tom ranting wildly. Johnny wonders why Tom did not kill him. It is almost as if…oh skip it.

Johnny goes to see Insp. Whitsett and tells him what has happened. Whitsett gets a call for Johnny. Lola tells Johnny that Tom was just there in her cottage, and that he just drove off towards the mountains.

Johnny goes to the cottage and they get into a car and drive off towards where Tom had gone. She tells Johnny that Tom had just wanted to see her one more time before...

Johnny drives up to Tom's car, parked next to a cliff and tells Lola to stay in his car. Johnny climbs down and finds the body. Johnny drives Lola back to her hotel and calls Whitsett.

Johnny thinks about the case and Lola and himself who had come a long way for nothing. Johnny visits Whitsett the next day and learns the inquest verdict was suicide, and that the burial will be here in Barbados. Johnny does not have the money and the chances are not too good at finding it.

In Chase's pockets the police had found a book of matches. Johnny goes to the bar where the matches came from, searches the area and finds Tom Chase's last room, but the money is not there. Johnny compares the handwriting on the register, gets a few wild ideas, and calls Pat McCracken with a request for information. Pat calls back and gives Johnny the information he had asked for. Yep, Johnny had come all the way to Barbados, but the case was solved in New York.

Johnny calls Lola and George and tells them to meet him at Tom's grave. Johnny tells them that he has been a jerk for two weeks because he has been chasing a dead man. Johnny tells them that they engineered the whole deal with only two people.

Johnny tells Lola that she had gone to New Orleans and rented the room for Tom James instead of going to Cape Cod. Freddy's letter matched the handwriting given to him by George, but Freddie played his part well, only to be killed by Lola. Johnny tells them that they hired a man to lead Johnny on a merry chase, and all the while the real Tom Chase was dead in New York.

Johnny tells Everson that he is the one that juggled the books and killed the impostor. When Johnny tells him that the body will be exhumed, George pulls a gun on Johnny.

Johnny tells him that New York knows all about the case, and George tells Lola that the partnership is now dissolved. Both Johnny and Lola lunge for George, and Lola is shot in the arm. Johnny tells her that Tom had said nothing when he was arrested because he knew what she was up to, but he loved her too much and was willing to cover for her.

Everson and Lola are turned over to the authorities and Everson gives up the keys to a safe deposit box in New York, where the money had been all the time. He also showed Johnny the spot on Long Island where he and Lola had buried the body of Tom Chase.

"Remarks: Pat, the next time you call me for an assignment like this one, I hope you get a busy signal."

Exp. Acct: $1,723.00

Notes:
- The program which would have been aired on October 23 was preempted by a speech by Adlai Stevenson.
- The episodes for this program were recorded a week apart.
- Roy Rowan is the announcer.
- Music Supervision is by Amerigo Marino.

Producer: Jack Johnstone Writer: Robert Ryf
Cast: Michael Ann Barrett, Jack Edwards, Ben Wright, Virginia Gregg, Don Diamond, Forrest Lewis, Richard Crenna

◆ ❖ ◆

Show: **The Silent Queen Matter**
Company: **State Unity Life**
Agent: **Vic Carson**
Synopsis:
Episode 1 **Show Date:** **10/29/1956**

Vic Carson calls Johnny and has a job for him. His agent in Venice... "Venice, I'd love it! Soft nights along the canal..." Venice, California Johnny. Vic's agent there has reported the death of Bernard Slade in Ocean Park, which is right next door to Venice. He ran a penny arcade and body was found there, and this apartment was plastered with pictures of Mavis Gale, a silent screen star. The police reported that someone had drawn a question mark over each of her pictures, and she is the beneficiary of Slade's policy.

Johnny travels to Ocean Park, California and calls Sergeant McKay, who is at the amusement park. Johnny walks to the park and notices that the penny arcade is busy. Johnny asks for a dime's worth of pennies from a blond in the change booth and asks her about Barney Slade. Johnny tells her who he is and she tells Johnny that Barney was a real nice guy.

She tells Johnny that Barney did not have any enemies. His friends were everyone here along the pier, including her. The girl tells Johnny that she has never heard of Mavis Gale. She tells Johnny that McKay is in Barney's apartment and Johnny goes back to the room.

Johnny notes that the walls are covered with pictures of silent movie stars. Johnny goes out the back door to meet McKay who tells Johnny that the killer might have put the question marks on the pictures, and that some pictures are missing. Johnny asks if there was any missing money, and McKay tells Johnny that Twilah, the change girl, did not think so.

Twilah told McKay that Barney rarely let anyone into his apartment. Twilah found the body in the morning. Barney was shot twice with a .38, and the apartment was messed up. Barney typically used the back entrance, which was open when the body was found. Johnny notices the heavy bolt and chain on the door and tells McKay that Barney did not have to let someone in unless he wanted to. McKay tells Johnny that Barney was found in his pajamas and a robe so he probably got up to let someone in, but the place was off limits to all of his friends.

McKay is looking for a friend called "the preacher", who was seen with Barney by Sam Heckstram. Sam remembers seeing the preacher come out of Barney's room. Barney had told Sam that the preacher was a dear old friend.

Mavis Gale has been told and was upset, especially about the crayon marks. McKay did not know that she was the beneficiary of Slade's policy and tells Johnny that Mavis told him that she had never heard of Barney Slade.

Johnny calls Mavis Gale's home and then goes to the funeral home where Slade's friends are, and the manager tells Johnny that Mavis Gale is not there. The man at the funeral home knows most of the people along the pier but does not know anyone called "the preacher".

Johnny looks at the guest book and sees no one there who is a minister. Then Mavis Gale enters, a thin woman in a well-tailored suit. Johnny goes to talk to her and she turns towards him and collapses.

Johnny calls McKay and tells him that Gale has just identified Barney as a former husband, Tom Sanford, who was killed in a hunting accident, twenty-seven years earlier.

Tomorrow, a stagecoach ride. I get some lumps, and a surprise witness turns up.

Episode 2   Show Date: 10/30/1956
Sgt. McKay calls and Johnny tells him about Mavis Gale being married to Tom Sanford, who was killed 27 years ago. Mavis just identified Barney Slade as Tom Sanford. Mavis is still there, and Sgt. McKay is on his way over.

Johnny buys coffee for Mavis and walks outside. A man stops Johnny and asks about Mavis being Barney's wife. Mort, the manager thought he heard her say that. He learned who Johnny is from Twilah.

He is Frank Jessup, who runs the mermaid game on the pier. Frank tells Johnny that Barney never mentioned her to him, and she has never been to the arcade. Twilah has been there for 5 years, and Twyla liked Barney a lot. Barney mostly talked about fishing and pinochle, which they played several times a week. They played at Frank's place or Sam's boat.

McKay arrives and goes in to talk to Mavis, alone. Mavis comes out and they put her in her car and she leaves. McKay tells Johnny that Mavis was a good actress, and Johnny wonders if she still is.

Johnny gets a newspaper and goes to Mavis Gale's home. The papers tell all about the hunting accident when Tom Sanford was supposedly killed with a shotgun.

McKay drives out and tells Johnny that the doctor has ordered her to see no one. Johnny tells McKay that she and Tom had had a pretty stormy marriage. Johnny wonders if someone hired a man to kill Tom Sanford and then recently realized that the wrong man was killed, and this time he does the job himself.

McKay drives Johnny to his hotel and he wonders why Sanford put his ID on a dead man and then disappeared, and about the question marks on the pictures. Maybe Barney wondered if his wife hired someone to kill him, and used the question marks to draw attention to Gale.

Johnny travels to see an agent named Milo Martin, one of the men on the hunting trip. Johnny finds Milo on a ranch where a western movie is being filmed.

Milo has read about the killing in the paper and tells Johnny that finding the body of Tom was a horrible experience. Milo has no idea about why anyone would kill Tom, who was a client of his, as was Miss Gale.

Milo tells Johnny that Tom was a gambler and drank too much and was jealous, and they were fighting all the time. Of the men on the hunting trip, Francis Trevelian, a producer is still around, as is Jarvis Pockett.

Milo is called and invites Johnny to ride the stagecoach back to the ranch house. After a rough ride in the stagecoach, Johnny goes back to his hotel room where McKay calls him and tells him that there is a witness who saw Mavis at the arcade two nights before the murder.

Tomorrow, a bowl of lentil soup, and I almost end up in a cemetery.

Episode 3   Show Date: 10/31/1956
Vic Carson calls and he tells Johnny that things are opening up on the coast, and about Sanford and Slade being the same person. Johnny tells Vic about Mavis being at the arcade, and that he has not found out anything about the pictures. Johnny tells Vic that he is looking for "the preacher".

Johnny goes to the penny arcade and Twilah tells Johnny that she is sure that she saw Mavis Gale there. Mavis was just standing in the front door like she was waiting for someone, while Barney was helping Frank fix a machine. Mavis just waited and then left without seeing Barney.

Frank walks up and tells Twilah that they are going to the funeral home again that night. Johnny asks Twilah and Frank if they know any of the names of his suspects, but they do not know any of them, besides Sgt. McKay had already asked them.

Johnny goes out to try and find George Shelton and ends up at a bar. The bartender gets Johnny a glass of I. W. Harper and soda, and tells him that George has had it rough, and could not act in talking movies because of his voice. He was involved with an actress, Josephine Hinch, and it went sour.

The bartender gives Johnny and address for George in Glendale and tells Johnny that he misses the preacher also. For $5, Johnny learns that the preacher is Jarvis Pockett, who runs a rescue mission. Johnny also learns that George has been dead for a couple years.

Johnny goes to the mission and waits to talk to Pockett. After the residents sing a hymn, Johnny is caught in the rush and ends up with a bowl of soup.

Johnny meets with Jarvis Pockett in his office and he tells Johnny that he had seen Tom Sanford fighting with a man when the gun went off and the other man was killed. They all agreed it was best to let the world think that Tom was dead.

Pockett tells Johnny that he knows the name of the man who tried to kill Tom. Johnny thinks that the man who hired him knows the man's name also. Pockett tells Johnny that the man was Joe Fallon, who was Mavis Gale's personal chauffeur.

Tomorrow, audience with the queen, and a brush with a killer.

Episode 4   Show Date: 11/1/1956

Sgt. McKay calls Johnny in Barney's office. Johnny tells Sgt. McKay that he is there with Jarvis Pockett, using a key Barney had given him. Johnny tells Sgt. McKay about Joe Fallon, the chauffeur of Mavis Gale.

Pockett paces in Barney's office until Sgt. McKay arrives. Pockett is sure that the whole wall was covered with pictures and the missing ones were from a movie he made with Mavis and George Sheldon and Tom. The others were of Mavis and Tom. Johnny notes that none of the other pictures are of Tom Sanford, who had not changed too much. The question marks were to draw attention to Mavis. Maybe Barney left Mavis the money to repay Mavis for his actions earlier.

Pockett leaves and Johnny talks with McKay about the killing on the hunting trip, and how someone caught up with Tom living as Barney Slade. McKay gets a call from headquarters, they just got a call from Francis Trevelian. Mavis Gale is at his beach house and wants to talk to them.

Johnny and McKay drive to the beach house and meet Mavis and Trevelian in the den. McKay asks her why she told him that she did not know Slade. She tells McKay that she did not know it until she saw Tom in the funeral home. She tells him that she had gone to the arcade two nights before the murder. She was afraid that she would be involved deeper.

She had received a call that a dear old friend was in trouble and that she should go to the park, where the friend would meet her at 8:00, but no one came. Johnny asks if Joe Fallon means anything to her, and Trevelian explodes. She tells Johnny that she had fired Joe just after she and Tom were married.

Johnny tells her that they have learned that it was Joe who was killed, not Tom. Trevelian tells them that Fallon had been mentioned to him in a phone call about a business deal. Johnny is sure that the same man made the two phone calls.

Johnny goes to his hotel and tells McKay that the pictures bother him. Johnny walks to the amusement area and walks on into Venice.

Johnny hears a shot, and sees a man collapse on a bridge. Johnny gets to the man to find Pockett, who points to an area "over there". Johnny runs after a man and loses him in the darkness. Johnny hears footsteps and then is knocked out.

Tomorrow, a man who talked too much, and it killed him. Yeah, the payoff.

Episode 5   Show Date: 11/2/1956
Milo Martin calls Johnny and tells him that he has just read of Jarvis Pockett's murder and his being attacked. Milo mentions that he did get a message from someone about Joe Fallon. Johnny tells Milo that the caller will call back, as he is after blackmail.

Johnny cabs to see Sgt. McKay, who tells Johnny that Pockett was killed with two slugs from the same gun that killed Slade.

Johnny reviews the case to figure out where they are. Johnny tells McKay about the call to Martin and the probable blackmail. Pockett probably did some snooping and got himself killed.

Johnny and McKay go to the funeral for Tom Sanford/Barney Slade. Frank stops them and remarks about the nice funeral. Frank mentions how Mavis showed no tears at all.

Johnny goes back to his room and sleeps for a while. Johnny goes to Barney's room and knocks over a bottle from the table. Twilah comes in and tells Johnny that Barney had been sick and they took care of him at Frank's place. He had gotten sick playing cards and Doc Ferris was called.

Johnny goes to see Dr. Ferris who tells Johnny that Barney was very sick and was delirious at times, but Frank had stayed with him all night to tend to him.

Johnny cabs back to the amusement park and learns that Frank had gone home early. Johnny cabs to his apartment and is told that he has just left for a walk. Johnny follows him and sees a big Cadillac slow down and toss out a package. Frank gets the package and runs towards Johnny, who stops him.

Frank offers Johnny half the money and tells Johnny that Barney had told him about his past while he was sick. Frank tells Johnny that he went to Barney with a plan to blackmail the others, but he had to kill him. Johnny asks who gave Frank the money and Milo walks up with a gun and thanks Johnny for holding Frank.

Johnny tells Milo that Frank really does not have any proof that Milo had hired Fallon to kill Tom, but Milo tells Johnny that he could not take chances. Milo had hoped to get close to Mavis when Tom was out of the way, but she ignored him. Milo tells Frank that he will not talk and Frank runs away. Milo shoots Frank and Johnny belts Milo.

"Remarks: About Frank Jessup: he got his out there on the sand dunes for the murders of Tom Sanford and Jarvis Pockett. About Milo Martin: in jail awaiting trial for murder of the above-mentioned F. Jessup. About Mavis Gale: she is going to see to it that the good work at brother Pockett's rescue mission goes on and will donate $25,000 to the cause. Yeah, you guessed it, the insurance money."

Exp. Acct: $436.25

Notes:
- This is the last of the five-a-week episodes.
- At the end of this program, Bob Bailey tells the audience "I think you will be glad to know that beginning Sunday, instead of five times a week, we will be on the air only once a week, but with a complete half hour story. Remember, that's beginning this coming Sunday. So, join us, won't you?"
- George Shelton appears as a suspect without being mentioned previously.
- The announcer is Roy Rowan.
- Music Supervision is by Amerigo Marino.

Producer: Jack Johnstone Writer: Adrian Gendot
Cast: Paula Winslowe, Virginia Gregg, Vic Perrin, Paul Dubov, Frank Gerstle, John Dehner, Lawrence Dobkin, Chester Stratton

END OF VOLUME 1

Index

Numbers in **bold** indicate photographs.

"Able Tackett Matter, The" 115-117, 1259, 1301
"Adam Kegg Matter, The" 157-159, 253, 1264, 1288, 1302
Adams, Bill 1204
Adams, Inge 586
Adams, Mason 1091, 1092, 1115, 1157, 1159
"Adolph Schoman Matter, The" 167-168, 250, 1259, 1288, 1302, 1321
"Alder Matter, The" 629-634, 1285, 1311
"Alec Jefferson, the Youthful Millionaire" 100-101, 1265, 1301
"Alfred Chambers Matter, The" 340-342, 1257, 1305
"Alkali Mike Matter, The" 778-780, 1284, 1314
"All Too Easy Matter, The" 1200-1202, 1283, 1320
"All Wet Matter, The" 1124-1126, 1277, 1298-1299, 1319
"Allanmee Matter, The" 876-877, 1266, 1315, 1322
"Allen Saxton Matter, The" 343-345, 1265, 1305
Allen, Casey 1159, 1186, 1232
Allen, Lynn 59, 80
"Alma Scott Matter, The" 243-245, 313, 1257, 1288, 1303
"Alonzo Chapman Matter, The" 208-209, 1279, 1303
"Alvin Summers Matter, The" 448-452, 1272, 1307
"Alvin's Alfred Matter, The" 973-975, 1264, 1317

"Amelia Harwell Matter, The" 168, 248-250, 1259, 1288, 1303
American Experience 590
Ames, Marlene 84
"Amita Buddha Matter, The" 338-339, 380, 1284, 1305
"Amy Bradshaw Matter, The" 465-468, 1273, 1307
"Archeologist, The" 96-97, 1265, 1301
"Aromatic Cicatrix Matter, The" 403-404, 1262, 1305, 1322
"Arrowcraft Matter, The" 127-128, 1264, 1301
"Art for My Sake Matter, The" 1050-1051, 1270, 1296, 1318, 1323
"Arthur Boldrick Matter, The" 203-204, 415-416, 1259, 1303, 1306, 1322
Arthur, Jack 1212, 1225
Arvan, Jan 51
Audley, Eleanor 384, 465, 526, 576, 752, 765, 800, 824, 858, 885, 896, 985
Aurant, Dick 1238
Averback, Hy 24, 109, 115, 128, 140, 144, 145, 147, 159, 163, 169, 185, 202, 209, 214, 215, 218, 223, 226, 228, 230, 239, 243, 245, 251, 258, 277, 292, 303, 310, 314, 322, 338, 343, 347, 384, 415, 423, 427, 429, 444, 448, 481, 553, 1244
Avery, Gaylord 1184

"Back to the Back Matter, The" 1008-1010, 1258, 1317
"Backfire that Backfired Matter, The" 936-937, 1282, 1316

Backus, Jim 248, 431
"Bad One Matter, The" 4, 1037-1038, 1271, 1317
Baer, Parley 4, 21, 24, 48, 58, 60, 80, 84, 88, 96, 132, 137, 161, 173, 178, 204, 220, 221, 233, 241, 275, 280, 292, 297, 311, 317, 326, 330, 336, 355, 357, 375, 391, 406, 416, 421, 425, 452, 477, 489, 505, 522, 558, 609, 629, 687, 692, 696, 706, 728, 735, 769, 788, 798, 802, 819, 836, 845, 847, 872, 875, 880, 909, 914, 926, 995, 998, 1004, 1029
Bailey, Bob 3, 4, 5, 7, 9, 10, 13, 25, 27, 109, 263, 264, 265, 267, 269, 271, 279, 280, 284, 293, 297, 301, 304, 308, 311, 365, 382, 391, 403, 433, 435-1042, **435**, 1043, 1048, 1051, 1052, 1053, 1237, 1242, 1244, 1245-1250, 1251, 1253, 1254, 1255, 1258, 1260, 1261, 1262, 1263, 1264, 1266, 1267, 1268, 1269, 1270, 1271, 1272, 1273, 1274, 1275, 1276, 1277, 1278, 1279, 1280, 1281, 1282, 1283, 1284, 1285, 1296, 1306-1318
Bainter, Robert (aka Bailey, Bob) 792, 793
Baker, Fay 86
"Baldero Matter, The" 894-896, 1284, 1316
"Baltimore Matter, The" 8, 267-269, 304, 496, 1254, 1290, 1293, 1304
Banks, Joan 107, 306, 745, 945
"Barbara James Matter, The" 130-132, 1270, 1302
Barrett, Michael Ann 101, 530, 600, 674, 677
Barrett, Tony 101, 133, 173, 199, 206, 213, 253, 269, 303, 315, 440, 448, 452, 465, 513, 549, 576, 605, 634, 658, 670, 674, 692, 803, 807, 819, 876, 902, 932, 934, 977, 1000, 1242, 1244
Barrier, Edgar 52, 168, 171, 192, 204, 213, 223, 228, 239, 247, 251, 265, 279, 303, 310, 339, 345, 359, 368, 377, 389, 410, 423, 509, 522, 535, 571, 605, 711, 745, 817, 822, 824, 830, 849, 853, 900, 918, 949, 960, 1006, 1015
Bartell, Harry 24, 103, 127, 128, 465, 493, 500, 540, 544, 553, 567, 576, 590, 594, 619, 629, 634, 653, 658, 662, 692, 698, 702, 717, 720, 726, 741, 754, 756, 764, 769, 778, 780, 795, 796, 800, 815, 828, 833, 835, 844, 858, 863, 866, 877, 879, 892, 894, 898, 910, 914, 931, 938, 947, 951, 963, 967, 973, 978, 993, 998, 1003, 1012, 1015, 1024, 1026, 1040, 1042, 1242, 1244, 1245, 1250
"Barton Baker Matter, The" 357-359, 1283, 1305
"Basking Ridge Matter, The" 867-868, 1262, 1315, 1322
Bates, Jeanne 54, 92, 99, 113, 128, 137, 145, 147, 176, 184, 196, 204, 213, 230, 242, 247, 265, 277, 408, 427, 448, 530, 558, 567, 765
Bauer, Charita 1219
"Baxter Matter, The" 247-248, 1265, 1292, 1303, 1321
"Bayou Body Matter, The" 951-953, 1280, 1216
Bayz, Gus 853, 932, 1031, 1033
Beals, Richard 342, 696, 726, 853, 879, 900
"Beauregard Matter, The" 371-373, 644, 1275, 1289, 1305
Beck, Jackson 907, 1091, 1092, 1121, 1150, 1155, 1204, 1234
"Bee or Not to Bee Matter, The" 26, 1135-1138, 1282, 1319
Begley, Ed 24, 92, 97, 169, 184, 185, 194, 241, 243, 415, 419, 429
Behrens, Frank 1108
Belasco, Leon 812
Bell, Ralph 1046, 1077, 1078, 1087, 1098, 1165, 1173, 1186, 1197, 1219
"Belo-Horizonte Railroad, The" 132-133, 1278, 1302

"Ben Bryson Matter, The" 363-365, 653, 1269, 1288, 1305
"Bennet Matter, The" 3, 4, 264, 433, 518-522, 996, 1264, 1292, 1308-1309
Benson, Court 1121, 1123, 1130, 1131, 1146, 1161, 1169
"Berlin Matter, The" 387-389, 1256, 1305
Bernardi, Hershel 991, 1028
"Big Date Matter, The" 1053-1055, 1280, 1296, 1318
"Big H Matter, The" 10, 913, 914-915, 916, 920, 1163, 1266, 1316
"Big Red Schoolhouse, The" 107-109, 535, 1265, 1287, 1292, 1301
"Big Scoop Matter, The" 685-687, 1273, 1313
"Bilked Baroness Matter, The" 404-406, 1261, 1306
"Birdy Baskerville Matter, The" 235-236, 287-288, 1257, 1286, 1303, 1304, 1322
"Bishop Blackmail Matter, The" 317-318, 1271, 1304, 1322
"Black Doll Matter, The" 320-322, 1271, 1305
"Blackburn Matter, The" 163-164, 1275, 1302
"Blackmail Matter, The" 301-303, 1271, 1304
Blaine, Martin 1115, 1141, 1142, 1165, 1197
"Blind Item Matter, The" 213-214, 1303, 1321
"Blinker Matter, The" 842-844, 1278, 1315
Bliss, Ted 284, 384
Blondell, Gloria 103, 119, 218, 253, 277, 493
"Blood River Matter, The" 137-138, 1279, 1302
"Blooming Blossom Matter, The" 10, 702-704, 1267, 1313
"Blue Madonna Matter, The" 890-892, 932, 1263, 1315

"Blue Rock Matter, The" 9, 1176-1178, 1277, 1319
"Bobby Foster Matter, The" 349-351, 1271, 1305
"Bodyguard to Anne Connelly" 77-79, 145, 1255, 1287, 1301
"Bodyguard to the Late Robert W. Perry" 38, 98-99, 1255, 1287, 1301
Boland, Joseph 1227
Boles, Jim 1057, 1074, 1084, 1085, 1141, 1142, 1143, 1144
"Bolt Out of the Blue Matter, The" 927-928, 1264, 1316
"Boron 112 Matter, The" 796-798, 1263, 1314
Botzer, Allen 24, 50, 52, 761, 811
Bouchey, Bill 56, 62, 105, 113, 127, 135, 149, 172, 206, 211, 236, 265
"Brisbane Fraud Matter, The" 306-308, 567, 1260, 1288, 1304
"Broderick Matter, The" 271, 306, 461-465, 1262, 1288, 1307
Brown, Vanessa 88
Bruce, Bob 472, 489, 505, 513, 535, 662, 692, 717, 720, 757, 764, 831, 836, 844
Brundage, Hugh 653
"Buffalo Matter, The" 940-942, 1282, 1316
"Bum Steer Matter, The" 769-771, 1280, 1314
Burke, Walter 92, 99, 107, 121, 123
"Burma Red Matter, The" 1187-1189, 1271, 1319
"Burning Carr Matter, The" 689-692, 1217, 1280, 1313
"Burning Desire Matter, The" 961-963, 1282, 1316
Burns, Allan 1110
Burr, Raymond 99, 111, 119, 137, 140, 149, 155, 159, 179, 181, 188, 197, 211, 226, 228, 238, 242, 253, 273, 277, 700
Bushman, Francis X. 133, 168, 175, 179, 252, 265, 336
Butler, Daws 82, 1238

Butterfield, Herb 51, 65, 86, 105, 130, 137, 149, 161, 174, 178, 181, 182, 189, 192, 196, 199, 200, 202, 223, 233, 242, 245, 248, 250, 265, 267, 318, 331, 339, 357, 373, 397, 440, 505, 530, 535, 605, 609, 670, 704, 711, 720

Buyeff, Lillian 51, 94, 107, 123, 144, 163, 165, 171, 224, 231, 290, 292, 297, 335, 361, 365, 370, 394, 410, 412, 419, 456, 461, 472, 489, 522, 567, 605, 658, 711, 726, 777, 778, 819, 866, 890, 894, 945, 953, 1003, 1021, 1239, 1241, 1242, 1244

"Buyer and the Cellar Matter, The" 1126-1128, 1285, 1319

"Byron Hayes Matter, The" 182-184, 1259, 1302

Cabibbo, Joseph 1184, 1186, 1189, 1193, 1195, 1197

Cagney, Jeanne 430

"Calgary Matter, The" 7, 133-135, 1254, 1302

"Caligio Diamond Matter, The" 125-127, 1268, 1301

"Callicles Matter, The" 308, 562-567, 1260, 1288, 1310

Calvert, Charles 416

Camargo, Ralph 1046, 1061, 1075, 1076, 1119, 1184, 1191, 1208

Campanella, Frank 1169

Campbell, Patsy 1110

"Can't Be So Matter, The" 5, 1157-1159, 1285, 1319

Canel, Pat 1150, 1176

"Canned Canary Matter, The" 965, 998-1000, 1040, 1071, 1276, 1317

"Captain's Table Matter, The" 1082-1085, 1266, 1298, 1318

"Carboniferous Dolomite Matter, The" 5, 421-423, 1261, 1306

Carlson, Dean 1232

"Carmen Kringle Matter, The" 791-793, 1282, 1314

Carpenter, Cliff 1126, 1146, 1148, 1167, 1171

"Carson Arson Matter, The" 826-828, 1285, 1315

"Case of Barton Drake, The" 46-48, 1255, 1300

"Case of the Foxy Terrier, The" 1300, 1321

"Case of the Hundred Thousand Dollar Legs, The" 44-46, 1267, 1300

"Case of Trouble Matter, The" 691, 1215-1217, 1270, 1320

"Casque of Death Matter, The" 912-914, 1274, 1316

Cassar, Barbara 1123, 1146

"Cautious Celibate Matter, The" 904-905, 1263, 1316

"Caylin Matter, The" 489-493, 1279, 1308

"Celia Woodstock Matter, The" 178-179, 367-368, 1283, 1286, 1302, 1305

Chadwick, Bob 1025

Chandler, David 24, 384

Chandler, Freddy 1215

Charles, Milton 290, 293, 295, 303, 306, 309, 311

"Charmona Matter, The" 762-764, 1268, 1314

Chavez, Raul 117

"Chesapeake Fraud Matter, The" 267, 444-448, 1281, 1288, 1306

"Chicago Fraud Matter, The" 277-279, 481, 1257, 1291, 1304

Christy, Ken 82, 140, 317, 367, 368, 401, 440, 485, 553, 851

"Chuckanut Matter, The" 1111-1113, 1284, 1319

"Cinder Elmer Matter, The" 1146-1148, 1285, 1319

"Circus Animal Show Matter, The" 79-80, 1256, 1301

"Classified Killer Matter, The" 380-382, 1261, 1305

"Clever Chemist Matter, The" 715-717, 1275, 1313

"Clever Crook Matter, The" 1128, 1319, 1323

"Clinton Matter, The" 7, 109, 531-535, 1281, 1287, 1292, 1309
"Close Shave Matter, The" 869-870, 1282, 1315, 1322
"Clouded Crystal Matter, The" 892-893, 1279, 1315, 1323
Cole, Robert 1080
"Collector's Matter, The" 1006-1008, 1264, 1317
"Confederate Coinage Matter, The" 749-752, 1275, 1314
"Confidential Matter, The" 365, 649-653, 1262, 1288, 1312
Connors, Chuck 1244
Conrad, William 24, 30, 46, 65, 79, 80, 94, 109, 115, 137, 138, 142, 157, 163, 171, 172, 178, 181, 182, 189, 217, 223, 226, 230, 247, 293, 299, 306, 326, 331, 347, 368, 382, 392, 401, 581, 1238
Conried, Hans 103, 253, 431, 522, 713, 728, 747
Cook, Tommy 571
Corbett, Lois 56, 59, 685
"Costain Matter, The" 308-310, 1263, 1304
Cotsworth, Staats 190
Courage, Alexander 151
"Crater Lake Matter, The" 868-869, 1273, 1315, 1322
Creed, Don 1191
Crenna, Richard 30, 571, 586, 639, 649, 677, 726, 731, 747, 793, 942, 944, 983, 993, 1029, 1033
Croft, Mary Jane 215, 295, 314, 324, 328, 338, 353, 373, 392, 427, 430, 431, 440, 481, 518, 526, 562, 600, 644, 696, 737, 756, 764, 767
"Cronin Matter, The" 465, 472-477, 1277, 1307
Crowder, Connie 84
Crutchfield, Les 25, 317, 365, 370, 373, 391, 403, 444, 461, 477, 485, 493, 509, 518, 526, 562, 571, 585, 594, 614, 624, 644, 653, 670, 1288, 1289
"Crystal Lake Cabin Matter, The" 634-639, 1312

"Cuban Jewel Matter, The" 223-224, 315, 1268, 1303
Cubberly, Dan 153, 155, 159, 161, 163, 164, 165, 185, 187, 194, 196, 206, 208, 211, 219, 221, 222, 224, 226, 230, 231, 233, 235, 236, 242, 243, 245, 247, 248, 257, 258, 260, 262, 264, 265, 267, 269, 271, 273, 275, 277, 279, 280, 282, 284, 286, 687, 689, 692, 694, 695, 696, 697, 700, 702, 704, 706, 708, 710, 711, 713, 715, 717, 719, 720, 722, 724, 726, 728, 729, 731, 734, 735, 737, 739, 741, 743, 745, 747, 749, 751, 763, 765, 767, 769, 771, 773, 775, 776, 780, 782, 784, 787, 788, 790, 793, 794, 796, 798, 800, 801, 803, 805, 807, 809, 811, 812, 815, 817, 818, 821, 822, 824, 826, 828, 830, 831, 864, 865, 866, 868, 869, 870, 872, 873, 875, 876, 877, 879, 880, 882, 883, 885, 886, 888, 890, 891, 892, 894, 896, 898, 900, 902, 904, 905, 907, 909, 910, 912, 913, 915, 916, 918, 920, 922, 932, 934, 935, 943, 945, 947, 949, 951, 953, 954, 956, 958, 959, 961, 963, 964, 965, 967, 968, 1012, 1013, 1195, 1239, 1241, 1250
"Cui Bono Matter, The" 513-518, 1277, 1308
Culver, Howard 82, 121, 138, 174, 275, 377, 394
"Cumberland Theft Matter, The" 219-220, 1259, 1303, 1321
"Curley Waters Matter, The" 885-886, 1270, 1315, 1323
"Curse of Kamashek Matter, The" 27, 644-649, 1268, 1293, 1312
Cusick, Fred 1217
Cutting, Dick 167, 168, 169, 171, 172, 173, 175, 176, 177, 179, 181, 182, 184, 188, 192, 197, 198, 202, 204, 209, 228, 231, 235, 236, 238, 240, 243, 245, 247, 248

"Dameron Matter, The" 297-299, 1263, 1304
Damon, Les 1050
"Dan Frank Matter, The" 401-403, 623, 1257, 1289, 1305
Darnay, Toni 1126, 1133
"Date with Death Matter, The" 7, 886-888, 1270, 1315
"David Rockey Matter, The" 169-171, 1256, 1302
Davis, Charles 235, 338
Dawson, John 24, 439, 440, 448, 456, 465, 472, 481, 489, 496, 505, 513, 522, 530, 535, 549, 558, 567, 581, 599, 600, 685, 694, 702, 710, 719, 1287, 1288, 1289, 1290, 1291, 1292, 1293
Dawson, Sam 25, 500
de Corsia, Ted 92, 99, 113, 125, 133, 223, 286, 373, 410, 658
De Koven, Roger 1065, 1080, 1089, 1090, 1123
"Dead First-Helpers, The" 109-111, 1266, 1301
"Deadly Chain Matter, The" 928-929, 1071, 1258, 1316
"Deadly Crystal Matter, The" 916, 1048, 1230-1232, 1284, 1320
"Deadly Debt Matter, The" 1017-1019, 1280, 1317
"Deadly Doubt Matter, The" 876, 881-882, 1282, 1315
"Deadly Swamp Matter, The" 5, 986-987, 1275, 1317
"Death by Jet Matter, The" 1059-1061, 1296, 1318
"Death Takes a Working Day" 54-56, 90-92, 1265, 1286, 1300, 1301, 1321
"Deep Down Matter, The" 979-980, 1027, 1258, 1317
Deering, Olive 1232
Dehner, John 24, 49, 52, 58, 59, 77, 79, 92, 97, 113, 123, 135, 147, 153, 161, 164, 448, 465, 477, 526, 544, 594, 614, 634, 682, 685, 708, 710, 719, 729, 731, 734, 769, 790, 849, 998, 1026, 1245, 1250
del Valle, Jaime 25, 92, 94, 96, 97, 99, 101, 103, 105, 107, 109, 111, 113, 115, 117, 119, 121, 123, 125, 127, 128, 130, 132, 133, 135, 137, 138, 140, 142, 144, 145, 147, 149, 151, 153, 155, 157, 159, 161, 163, 164, 165, 167, 168, 169, 171, 172, 173, 175, 176, 177, 179, 181, 182, 184, 185, 187, 189, 190, 192, 194, 196, 197, 199, 200, 202, 204, 206, 208, 209, 211, 213, 214, 215, 217, 218, 220, 221, 223, 224, 226, 228, 230, 231, 233, 235, 236, 239, 241, 242, 243, 245, 247, 248, 250, 251, 252, 253, 255, 257, 258, 260, 263, 264, 265, 267, 269, 271, 273, 275, 277, 279, 280, 282, 284, 286, 288, 290, 292, 293, 295, 297, 299, 301, 303, 305, 306, 308, 310, 311, 313, 315, 317, 318, 320, 322, 324, 326, 328, 330, 331, 333, 335, 336, 338, 339, 342, 343, 345, 347, 349, 351, 353, 355, 357, 359, 361, 363, 365, 367, 368, 370, 373, 375, 377, 380, 382, 384, 386, 389, 391, 392, 394, 397, 399, 401, 403, 404, 406, 408, 410, 412, 415, 416, 419, 421, 423, 425, 427, 429, 430, 431, 433, 434, 1239, 1241
"Delectable Damsel Matter, The" 836-838, 1271, 1315
Delmar, Kenny 333
Demetrie, James 1157
Dendrick, Richard 1084, 1085
"Denver Disbursal Matter, The" 8, 815-817, 1274, 1314
"Department Store Swindle Matter, The" 82-84, 1267, 1301
"Desalles Matter, The" 700-702, 1258, 1313
"Diamond Dilemma Matter, The" 809-811, 1270, 1314
"Diamond Protector Matter, The" 36, 84-85, 1255, 1301, 1321
Diamond, Don 52, 77, 290, 361, 394, 410, 412, 419, 431, 452, 468, 485, 509, 540, 594, 605, 629, 634, 677, 830, 893, 847, 951, 963

"Dixon Murder Matter, The" 737-740, 1275, 1313
"Do It Yourself Matter, The" 1161-1163, 1266, 1319
Dobkin, Lawrence 24, 52, 54, 56, 59, 62, 64, 67, 71, 73, 75, 80, 86, 105, 164, 377, 461, 465, 496, 500, 530, 544, 549, 558, 567, 576, 590, 594, 629, 674, 682, 689, 696, 698, 700, 713, 726, 741, 747, 749, 756, 759, 767, 778, 782, 787, 790, 793, 795, 800, 807, 824, 830, 849, 851, 856, 857, 858, 861, 864, 866, 869, 870, 873, 876, 883, 896, 898, 900, 902, 907, 910, 918, 931, 936, 940, 942, 944, 949, 958, 960, 961, 963, 964, 970, 977, 1006, 1013, 1026, 1036, 1038, 1250
"Doninger Doninger Matter, The" 1223-1225, 1272, 1320
Donnelly, Bob 1135, 1137, 1138, 1278
"Doting Dowager Matter, The" 876, 882, 883-885, 1263, 1315
"Double Deal Matter, The" 1000, 1039-1040, 1274, 1317
"Double Exposure Matter, The" 984-985, 1270, 1317
"Double Identity Matter, The" 944-945, 947, 1282, 1316
"Double Trouble Matter, The" 870-872, 1279, 1315
"Double-Barreled Matter, The" 1128-1131, 1271, 1297, 1319
"Doubtful Dairy Matter, The" 767-769, 1281, 1314
Doud, Gil 24, 25, 34, 36, 38, 40, 42, 44, 46, 48, 49, 51, 52, 54, 56, 58, 59, 60, 62, 64, 65, 67, 69, 71, 73, 75, 77, 79, 80, 82, 84, 85, 86, 88, 92, 94, 96, 97, 99, 101, 105, 107, 111, 115, 117, 119, 121, 123, 125, 127, 128, 130, 132, 133, 135, 137, 138, 140, 142, 144, 145, 147, 149, 151, 153, 155, 157, 159, 161, 163, 164, 165, 167, 168, 169, 171, 172, 173, 175, 176, 177, 179, 181, 182, 184, 185, 187, 189, 190, 192, 194, 196, 197, 199, 200, 204, 206, 208, 209, 211, 213, 215, 217, 218, 220, 221, 223, 228, 230, 231, 233, 235, 239, 241, 242, 245, 247, 250, 251, 252, 253, 255, 257, 258, 260, 286, 313, 357, 363, 367, 368, 375, 416, 419, 425, 1238, 1242, 1244, 1286, 1287, 1288, 1289, 1290, 1291
"Douglas Taylor Matter, The" 226-228, 260, 1265, 1289, 1303
Douglas, Hugh 987, 1023
"Dr. Otto Schmedlich" 66-67, 1255, 1301
"Draminski Matter, The" 368-370, 1262, 1305, 1322
Draper, Margaret 1159
Dryanforth, Harold 113
Dryden, Robert 1055, 1057, 1058, 1059, 1067, 1072, 1074, 1076, 1082, 1087, 1089, 1090, 1094, 1096, 1098, 1101, 1113, 1119, 1130, 1131, 1135, 1137, 1138, 1148, 1152, 1153, 1171, 1176, 1191, 1197, 1227
Dubov, Paul 49, 51, 54, 58, 59, 60, 64, 67, 69, 71, 84, 86, 448, 624, 649, 682, 759, 769, 790, 811, 849, 882, 902, 907, 920, 922, 929, 938, 963, 1004, 1021, 1031, 1244
Dudley, Paul 25, 34, 36, 38, 40, 42, 44, 46, 48, 49, 51, 52, 54, 56, 58, 59, 60, 62, 64, 65, 67, 69, 71, 73, 75, 77, 79, 80, 82, 84, 85, 86, 88, 92, 94, 96, 97, 99, 101, 107, 1238, 1286, 1287
"Duke Red Matter, The" 311, 501-505, 1281, 1288, 1308
Duncan, Herb 1163, 1182, 1204, 1221
Dunstedter, Eddie 206, 208, 209, 211, 212, 213, 215, 216, 218, 219, 221, 222, 224, 226, 250, 251, 252, 253, 254, 257, 258, 260, 262, 264, 265, 267, 269, 271, 273, 275, 277, 279, 280, 282, 284, 286, 288, 292, 297, 299, 301, 304, 308, 313, 315, 317, 318, 320, 322, 324, 326, 328, 330, 331, 333, 335, 336, 338, 339, 342, 343, 345, 347, 349, 351, 353, 355, 357, 359, 361, 363, 365, 367, 368, 370, 373, 375, 377, 380, 382, 384, 386, 389, 391, 392, 394, 396, 398, 401, 403, 404, 406, 408,

410, 412, 415, 416, 419, 421, 423, 425, 427, 429, 430, 431, 432, 433, 1239, 1241
"Durango Laramie Matter, The" 807-809, 1263, 1314
DuVal, Joseph 99, 133, 168, 173, 192, 213, 265, 269, 284, 330, 343, 357, 365, 403, 406, 412, 434

Eagles, James 119
"Earl Chadwick Matter, The" 121-123, 1280, 1301
"Eastern Western Matter, The" 819-821, 1279, 1314
"Edith Maxwell Matter, The" 254-255, 1260, 1303, 1322
"Edward French Matter, The" 186-187, 1279, 1302
Edwards, Blake 24, 202, 214, 224, 226, 236, 248, 288, 303, 315, 318, 320, 322, 324, 326, 328, 330, 331, 333, 335, 336, 338, 339, 342, 343, 345, 347, 349, 353, 359, 399, 1286, 1292, 1293
Edwards, Jack 56, 60, 365, 375, 386, 412, 489, 549, 553, 653, 677, 700, 745, 759, 767, 771, 819, 828, 859, 870, 875, 890, 898, 910, 923, 966, 967, 1000, 1010, 1245, 1250
Edwards, Sam 24, 336, 391, 408, 485, 518, 526, 576, 715, 740, 747, 771, 773, 805, 831, 868, 872, 877, 885, 888, 909, 917, 925, 931, 936, 938, 943, 944, 953, 956, 964, 968, 971, 978, 987, 991, 1003, 1006, 1015, 1019, 1022, 1023, 1031, 1038
"Eighty-Five Little Minks, The" 8, 101-103, 233, 710, 1271, 1288, 1301
Eiler, Barbara 465, 505, 549, 670, 715
Eiler, Virginia 155
"Eleven O'Clock Matter, The" 798-800, 1262, 1314
"Ellen Dear Matter, The" 698-700, 991, 1237, 1245-1250, 1284, 1313, 1322
"Elliot Champion Matter, The" 263-265, 433, 522, 1265, 1292, 1304

Ellis, David 24, 88, 105, 111, 1287, 1290
Ellis, Georgia 52, 54, 60, 64, 67, 69, 84, 164
Ellis, Herb 440, 465, 472, 489, 513, 535, 558, 562, 600, 639, 670, 698, 704, 719, 722, 729, 752, 761, 778, 807, 812, 815, 964, 967, 1017, 1031
Ellison, Joan 1113
"Embarcadero Matter, The" 933-934, 1263, 1316
"Emil Carter Matter, The" 245, 312-314, 1257, 1288, 1304
"Emil Lovett Matter, The" 181-182, 1257, 1302, 1321
"Emily Braddock Matter, The" 271, 305-306, 465, 1256, 1288, 1304
"Empty Threat Matter, The" 1041-1042, 1264, 1318
"Enoch Arden Matter, The" 294-295, 1267, 1304
Epstein, Fargo 273
Eric, Elsbeth 1072, 1232
"Evaporated Clue Matter, The" 966-967, 1264, 1317
Everett, Ethel 1152, 1153, 1206, 1229
"Expiring Nickels and the Egyptian Jackpot, The" 4, 59-60, 1258, 1301

"Fair-Way Matter, The" 209-211, 365-367, 1257, 1257, 1286, 1303, 1305
"Fairweather Friend Matter, The" 902-904, 1263, 1316
"False Alarm Matter, The" 982-983, 1280, 1317
"Fancy Bridgework Matter, The" 953-954, 1280, 1316
Farrer, Stanley 172
"Fatal Filet Matter, The" 562, 909-910, 1258, 1316
"Fatal Switch Matter, The" 989-991, 1284, 1317
"Fathom-Five Matter, The" 522-526, 1260, 1309
Fein, Morton 273
Feld, Fritz 380

"Felicity Feline Matter, The" 743-745, 784, 1258, 1314
Fennelly, Parker 1106
Fenster, Daphne 273
Fernandez, Peter 907, 1234
"Fiddle Faddle Matter, The" 1106-1108, 1280, 1319
"Final Chapter Matter, The" 13-22
Fine, Morton 25, 273, 389
"Fire in Paradise Matter, The" 800-802, 1264, 1314, 1322
"Firebug Hunter Matter, The" 85-86, 1261, 1301, 1321
Firestone, Eddie 253, 282
"Fishing Boat Affair, The" 62-64, 1268, 1301
Fitzgerald, Neil 1225
"Five Down Matter, The" 1024-1026, 1071, 1276, 1317
"Flask of Death Matter, The" 1003-1004, 1283, 1317
"Flight Six Matter, The" 489, 505-509, 1266, 1308
"Forbes Matter, The" 293, 485-489, 1258, 1289, 1308
Forte, Joe 111
Fortina, Carl 581, 585, 590, 594, 600, 605, 609, 614, 662, 689
Foster, Roger 1189
"Four C's Matter, The" 1225-1227, 1266, 1320
"Four's a Crowd Matter, The" 1212-1215, 1277, 1320
Fox, Gibson Scott 24, 433
Francis, Eugene 1104, 1148, 1150, 1176, 1186
Francis, Ivor 1113, 1137, 1138, 1143, 1144, 1155, 1189, 1210, 1219
Frank, Carl 1055, 1072, 1074, 1123, 1128, 1130, 1131, 1232
Franklin, Paul 25, 715
"Frantic Fisherman Matter, The" 924-925, 1163, 1266, 1316
Frees, Paul 540, 1040
Friedkin, David 25, 273, 389

"Frisco Fire Matter, The" 900-902, 1266, 1316
"Froward Fisherman Matter, The" 834-835, 1191, 1258, 1315, 1322
"Frustrated Phoenix Matter, The" 399-401, 1283, 1305
Fuller, Barbara 477, 496, 505, 549, 600, 634
"Funny Money Matter, The" 741-743, 1263, 1314
"Further Buffalo Matter, The" 4, 942-944, 1282, 1316
Fussell, Sarah 1178

Galen, Hetty 1208, 1215
Garde, Betty 1155
Gaylor, Gerry 389
Gendot, Adrian 24, 682
"George Farmer Matter, The" 201-202, 1265, 1303
Gerson, Betty Lou 67, 79, 82, 456, 513, 1238
Gerstle, Frank 440, 465, 496, 530, 535, 581, 653, 682, 689, 704, 717, 747, 754, 756, 780, 798, 811, 817, 836, 838, 840, 842, 861, 868, 876, 880, 882, 910, 912, 923, 929, 934, 953, 954, 963, 970, 975, 977, 997, 1010, 1017, 1033, 1035, 1244
"Ghost to Ghost Matter, The" 830-831, 1277, 1315
Gibson, John 1208
Gilbert, Joe 149
Gillespie, Jean 1072
Gillian, Bill 1163, 1173
"Gino Gambona Matter, The" 347-349, 1268, 1305
"Glacier Ghost Matter, The" 728-729, 865, 1280, 1313, 1322
"Glen English Matter, The" 245-247, 1267, 1303
Glenn, Roy 24, 311, 326, 590, 694, 987
Gluskin, Lud 172
"Gold Rush Country Matter, The" 1319, 1323
"Gold Rush Matter, The" 1221-1223, 1266, 1320

"Golden Dream Matter, The" 1170-1171, 1266, 1319
"Golden Touch Matter, The" 710-711, 890, 1276, 1313, 1322
Goldsmith, Jerry 704
Gordon, Clark 73, 1238
Gorman, Tom 1121
Gould, Sandra 79, 277, 489, 985
Graham, Tim 82, 161, 178, 185, 199, 241, 399
"Grand Canyon Matter, The" 1184-1186, 1273, 1319
Grant, Bernard 1067, 1091, 1092, 1101, 1176
"Gravedigger's Spades, The" 94-96, 1271, 1301
Gray, Sam 1094, 1108, 1121, 1155, 1157, 1159, 1180, 1180, 1221, 1232
"Great Bannock Race Matter, The" 431-433, 1276, 1306, 1322
Green, Austin 662, 715, 737, 740, 765, 796
Green, Marty 1208
Gregg, Virginia 13, 24, 97, 109, 115, 123, 127, 130, 135, 138, 142, 145, 151, 155, 161, 168, 169, 172, 175, 185, 192, 194, 197, 200, 202, 204, 206, 208, 209, 211, 214, 215, 217, 218, 220, 221, 223, 233, 235, 236, 239, 241, 243, 245, 248, 250, 251, 253, 255, 257, 263, 267, 271, 273, 275, 280, 282, 286, 292, 293, 297, 301, 303, 305, 308, 310, 315, 317, 320, 345, 349, 355, 368, 377, 380, 382, 384, 386, 389, 391, 392, 397, 399, 401, 403, 404, 406, 408, 415, 416, 421, 423, 425, 430, 431, 433, 440, 444, 452, 465, 468, 477, 485, 493, 509, 540, 544, 558, 562, 567, 576, 581, 594, 605, 609, 619, 629, 634, 644, 649, 653, 658, 662, 674, 677, 682, 685, 687, 689, 692, 694, 700, 702, 708, 710, 711, 713, 717, 719, 720, 722, 724, 726, 728, 729, 731, 737, 741, 743, 745, 747, 749, 752, 754, 757, 761, 771, 773, 777, 778, 780, 782, 785, 787, 790, 802, 803, 807, 809, 817, 819, 821, 822, 828, 830, 831, 835, 838, 842, 847, 851, 855, 856, 861, 863, 864, 865, 866, 869, 872, 873, 875, 876, 877, 879, 880, 882, 883, 885, 896, 900, 902, 904, 905, 907, 910, 915, 917, 920, 922, 923, 926, 928, 929, 931, 932, 936, 937, 938, 940, 947, 949, 951, 953, 954, 956, 958, 963, 964, 966, 968, 971, 973, 975, 977, 978, 980, 983, 985, 989, 991, 993, 995, 997, 998, 1000, 1003, 1006, 1008, 1010, 1013, 1015, 1019, 1021, 1026, 1031, 1033, 1035, 1036, 1040, 1042, 1245, 1250
Grey, Bill 105, 121
Griffin, Robert 94, 107, 133, 144, 163, 258, 324, 339, 370, 1239, 1241
Griffis, William 1180
Griggs, John 1084, 1085, 1193
Grimes, Jack 907, 923, 1046, 1059, 1087, 1089, 1090, 1165, 1180, 1189, 1217, 1225, 1234
"Gruesome Spectacle Matter, The" 861-863, 940, 1280, 1315, 1323
"Guide to Murder Matter, The" 1142-1144, 1280, 1319

Haines, Hilda 1119
Haines, Larry 1055, 1077, 1078, 1080, 1082, 1116, 1157, 1212
"Hair Raising Matter, The" 873-875, 1071, 1144, 1277, 1315
Hairston, Jester 326
"Haiti Adventure Matter" 81-82, 124, 1255, 1287, 1301
Halop, Billy 826, 840, 866, 926
"Hamilton Payroll Matter, The" 430-431, 1259, 1306, 1322
"Hampton Line Matter, The" 427-429, 1284, 1306
"Hand of Providential Matter, The" 947-949, 1275, 1316
Hanley, Tom 167, 322, 363, 535, 619, 726, 729, 735, 809, 836, 873, 886, 905, 998, 1004, 1024, 1025, 1031, 1063
Hannes, Art 1046, 1055, 1057, 1059, 1061, 1065, 1067, 1074, 1075, 1077, 1080, 1082, 1084, 1086, 1092, 1094,

1096, 1097, 1101, 1104, 1106, 1108, 1113, 1121, 1123, 1126, 1128, 1130, 1133, 1135, 1137, 1139, 1141, 1144, 1146, 1152, 1156, 1157, 1159, 1161, 1165, 1167, 1169, 1178, 1182, 1186, 1193, 1195, 1197, 1202, 1204, 1206, 1208, 1210, 1214, 1219, 1221, 1225, 1227, 1229, 1232

"Hannibal Murphy Matter, The" 233-235, 1275, 1303

"Hapless Ham Matter, The" 963-964, 1262, 1316

"Hapless Hunter Matter, The" 787-788, 1278, 1314

Hardy, Joe 1210

Harford, Alex 433

"Harold Trandem Matter, The" 117-119, 1257, 1301

Harper, Alec 130

"Harpooned Angler Matter, The" 375-377, 1283, 1305

"Harried Heiress Matter, The" 1001-1003, 1046, 1072, 1176, 1268, 1317

Harris, Stacy 127, 132, 159, 168, 176, 224, 231, 233, 236, 241, 267, 288, 292, 295, 306, 357, 522, 562, 624, 653, 687, 706, 708, 710, 734, 741, 757, 815, 844, 909, 936, 966, 968, 973, 1000, 1015, 1019, 1924, 1033

Hartford Alliance Matter, The 139-140, 1259, 1302

Hartman, Ray (aka Raymond Burr) 179, 181, 188, 189, 206, 211, 226, 228, 238, 239

Hatch, Wilbur 64, 65, 67, 69, 71, 147, 149, 153, 155, 157, 159, 161, 163, 164, 165, 167, 168, 169, 171, 173, 175, 176, 177, 179, 181, 182, 184, 185, 187, 188, 190, 192, 194, 196, 197, 199, 200, 202, 204, 228, 230, 231, 233, 235, 236, 238, 240, 242, 243, 247, 248

"Hatchet House Theft Matter, The" 206-208, 1263, 1303

Hausner, Jerry 65, 873, 949, 995

Hayes, John Michael 24, 103, 109, 113, 710, 1287, 1288, 1292, 1293

"Heatherstone Players Matter, The" 745-747, 1272, 1314

"Henderson Matter, The" 284, 468-472, 1274, 1289, 1307

Hendrickson, Fred 25, 907, 1121, 1155, 1197, 1200, 1202, 1204, 1206, 1208, 1210, 1212, 1215, 1217, 1223, 1225, 1227, 1229, 1232, 1234

"Henry J. Unger Matter, The" 6, 135-137, 1255, 1302

"Henry Page Matter, The" 250-251, 1267, 1303, 1321

Herbert, Wilms 52, 161, 172

"Here Comes the Death of the Party" 48-49, 1275, 1300, 1321

Hill, Ramsey 194, 361

Hill, Sammie 58, 138, 173, 200, 282, 320, 339, 357

"Hired Homicide Matter, The" 956-958, 1281, 1316

Hite, Kathleen 24, 243

Hodge, Al 1189

Hodge, Kenny 1025, 1071

Holland, Bert 553, 567, 614, 662, 685, 713, 787, 886, 892, 951, 1019

Holland, Richard 1061, 1108, 1110, 1182

Holland, Tom 73, 856, 937

"Hollywood Matter, The" 718-719, 1271, 1313, 1322

"Hollywood Mystery Matter, The" 876, 879-880, 1261, 1315

Holmes, Wendell 1098

"Hood of Death Matter, The" 1202-1204, 1264, 1320

Hooper, Mary Ann 863, 864, 1002, 1070, 1072, 1159, 1161

"Hope to Die Matter, The" 783-785, 1263, 1314

"Horace Lockhart Matter, The" 214-215, 1283, 1303

Hosley, Pat 1159

"Hot Chocolates Matter, The" 1153-1155, 1278, 1319

"How I Turned a Luxury Liner into a Battleship" 58-59, 1274, 1300, 1321

"How Much Bourbon Can Flow Under the Bridgework?" 51-52, 1271, 1300, 1321
"Howard Arnold Matter, The" 345-347, 1284, 1305
"Howard Caldwell Matter, The" 146-147, 1256, 1302
Howard, Fred 77
Howell, Jean 311, 324
Hubbard, Irene 190
Huber, Ethel 907, 1046, 1055, 1057, 1059, 1061, 1065, 1067, 1071, 1074, 1075, 1078, 1080, 1082, 1085, 1087, 1089, 1092, 1094, 1096, 1097, 1101, 1104, 1106, 1108, 1110, 1113, 1115, 1116, 1119, 1121, 1123, 1126, 1128, 1131, 1133, 1135, 1137, 1140, 1142, 1144, 1146, 1148, 1150, 1152, 1157, 1159, 1161, 1163, 1165, 1167, 1169, 1171, 1173, 1176, 1178, 1180, 1182, 1184, 1186, 1189, 1191, 1193, 1195, 1197, 1202, 1204, 1206, 1208, 1210, 1212, 1214, 1217, 1219, 1221, 1227, 1229, 1232, 1234
Hughes, Gordon T. 25, 54, 56, 60, 62, 64, 65, 67, 69, 71, 73, 75, 77, 79, 84, 85, 86, 88

"Ideal Vacation Matter, The" 765-767, 1282, 1314
"Ike and Mike Matter, The" 1171-1173, 1281, 1319
"Imperfect Alibi Matter, The" 653-658, 687, 1273, 1312, 1322
"Imperfect Crime Matter, The" 1102-1104, 1277, 1318
"Impossible Murder Matter, The" 864-865, 1280, 1315, 1322
"Independent Diamond Traders Matter, The" 353-355, 1256, 1305
"Indestructible Mike Matter, The" 586-590, 1269, 1310
"Informer Matter, The" 8, 1076-1078, 1274, 1298, 1299, 1318
"Ingenuous Jeweler Matter, The" 795-796, 1274, 1314

"Isabelle James Matter, The" 328-330, 1271, 1305
"Island of Tin-Yutan, The" 5-6, 71-73, 1276, 1301
"Ivy Emerald Matter, The" 1178-1180, 1277, 1319

"J. P. D. Matter, The" 764-765, 1263, 1314
"Jack Madigan Matter, The" 69, 151-153, 253, 1277, 1287, 1302
"Jackie Cleaver Matter, The" 184-185, 1276, 1302
Jacobs, Johnny 609, 704
"James Clayton Matter, The" 261-263, 557, 1272, 1289, 1304
"James Forbes Matter, The" 322-324, 1268, 1305
James, Bill 167, 322, 339, 357, 363, 367, 392, 553, 696, 722, 745, 777, 793, 805, 836, 849, 853, 873, 886, 894, 904, 905, 932, 971, 998, 1004, 1024, 1025, 1031, 1033, 1062, 1063
James, John 729
"Jan Breughel Matter, The" 419-421, 1306
"Jane Doe Matter, The" 196-197, 1272, 1303, 1321
"Janet Abbe Matter, The" 230-231, 1257, 1303, 1321
Janiss, Vivi 49, 275, 477, 481, 496, 634, 692
Janney, Leon 1050, 1065, 1106, 1108, 1128, 1157, 1195, 1223
"Jarvis Wilder Matter, The" 176-178, 1256, 1302
"Jeanne Maxwell Matter, The" 155, 284-286, 423-425, 1259, 1289, 1304, 1306
Jerome, Edwin 811
"Jimmy Carter Matter, The" 898-900, 1254, 1316
"Joan Sebastian Matter, The" 153-155, 286, 425, 1259, 1289, 1302
"Johnson Payroll Matter, The" 859-861, 1282, 1315
Johnson, Lamont 159, 373

Johnson, Raymond Edward 1072, 1104, 1163, 1219
Johnson, Thelma 328
Johnstone, Doug 964, 965, 999, 1032, 1115, 1182, 1183
Johnstone, Jack 9, 10, 13, 15, 21, 24, 24, 25, 26, 435, 440, 444, 448, 452, 456, 461, 465, 468, 472, 477, 481, 485, 489, 493, 496, 500, 505, 509, 513, 518, 522, 526, 530, 535, 540, 544, 549, 553, 558, 562, 567, 571, 576, 581, 585, 590, 594, 600, 605, 609, 614, 619, 624, 629, 634, 639, 644, 649, 653, 658, 662, 666, 670, 677, 682, 685, 687, 689, 692, 694, 696, 697, 700, 702, 704, 706, 708, 710, 711, 713, 715, 717, 719, 720, 722, 724, 726, 728, 729, 731, 734, 735, 737, 740, 741, 743, 745, 747, 749, 752, 754, 756, 757, 759, 761, 763, 765, 767, 769, 770, 771, 773, 775, 776, 778, 780, 782, 785, 787, 788, 790, 793, 795, 796, 798, 800, 802, 803, 805, 807, 809, 811, 812, 815, 817, 819, 821, 822, 824, 826, 828, 830, 831, 833, 835, 836, 838, 839, 842, 844, 845, 847, 849, 851, 853, 855, 856, 858, 859, 861, 863, 864, 865, 866, 868, 869, 870, 872, 873, 875, 876, 877, 879, 880, 882, 883, 885, 886, 888, 890, 891, 893, 894, 896, 898, 900, 902, 904, 905, 907, 909, 910, 912, 913, 915, 917, 918, 920, 922, 923, 925, 926, 928, 929, 931, 932, 934, 935, 937, 938, 940, 942, 944, 945, 947, 949, 951, 953, 954, 956, 958, 959, 961, 963, 964, 965, 966, 967, 968, 970, 971, 972, 973, 975, 977, 978, 980, 982, 983, 985, 987, 989, 991, 993, 995, 997, 998, 1000, 1002, 1003, 1004, 1006, 1007, 1010, 1012, 1013, 1015, 1017, 1019, 1021, 1023, 1024, 1025, 1026, 1028, 1029, 1031, 1033, 1035, 1036, 1038, 1040, 1042, 1046, 1048, 1050, 1051, 1053, 1055, 1057, 1059, 1060, 1061, 1063, 1065, 1067, 1069, 1071, 1072, 1074, 1075, 1078, 1080, 1082, 1085, 1087, 1089, 1092, 1094, 1096, 1098, 1101, 1104, 1106, 1108, 1110, 1113, 1115, 1116, 1119, 1121, 1123, 1126, 1128, 1131, 1133, 1135, 1138, 1140, 1142, 1144, 1146, 1148, 1150, 1153, 1155, 1157, 1159, 1161, 1163, 1165, 1167, 1169, 1171, 1173, 1176, 1178, 1180, 1182, 1184, 1186, 1189, 1191, 1193, 1195, 1197, 1200, 1202, 1204, 1206, 1208, 1210, 1212, 1215, 1217, 1219, 1221, 1223, 1225, 1227, 1229, 1232, 1234, 1235, 1236, 1242, 1244, 1245, 1249, 1250, 1293, 1297
Johnstone, William 24, 79, 103, 115, 127, 151, 155, 163, 167, 179, 196, 241, 253, 257, 258, 293, 299, 305, 318, 322, 335, 338, 343, 357, 363, 365, 367, 380, 384, 386, 397, 399, 406, 412, 421, 425, 1239, 1241
"Jolly Roger Fraud Matter, The" 536-540, 1281, 1309
"Jonathan Bellows Matter, The" 314-315, 1268, 1304
"Jones Matter, The" 315-317, 1257, 1304
Jones, G. Stanley 696, 706, 722, 731, 743, 765, 773, 785, 798, 809, 885, 892, 904, 905, 912, 932, 934, 945, 947, 956, 968, 975, 1004, 1008, 1017, 1021, 1023, 1026, 1042
Jones, Stan 662, 666
Julian, Joseph 907, 1080, 1163, 1180, 1234
Juster, Evelyn 1104, 1133, 1229

Kane, Byron 24, 125, 493, 518, 553, 662, 724, 767, 775, 796, 828, 835, 892, 926
Kane, Michael 1150
"Kay Bellamy Matter, The" 275-277, 1267, 1304
Keane, Teri 1057, 1061, 1077, 1078, 1101, 1150, 1217, 1223
Kearns, Joseph 103, 115, 167, 228, 239, 255, 263, 271, 292, 297, 301, 308, 331, 363, 384, 403, 419, 427, 434, 544, 576, 624, 722, 735, 756, 767, 777, 796, 828, 831, 859, 863, 892, 915, 920, 970, 971, 1238, 1239, 1241

Keith, Richard 780, 1184, 1229
Kemper, Ray 338, 357, 535, 540, 619, 717
Kendrick, Richard 1113
Kern, David 1150
"Key to Crime Matter, The" 1137, 1234-1236, 1282, 1320
Kilburn, Terry 135, 165
"Killer Kin Matter, The" 1019-1021, 1264, 1217
"Killer's Brand Matter, The" 754-756, 1282, 1314
"Killer's List Matter, The" 817-819, 1268, 1314
King, Wally 1071
"King's Necklace Matter, The" 288-290, 1261, 1304
Kinsella, Walter 1227
"Kirbey Will Matter, The" 706-708, 1280, 1313
Kirkpatrick, Jess 96, 391
Kleeb, Helen 931
Kohl, Arthur 1115, 1135, 1159, 1186, 1221, 1229
Kolveg, Pinto 58
Kraft, Chris 117
Kramer, Bill 1165, 1210
Kramer, Mandel 3, 5, 10, 907, 1043, 1057, 1075, 1076, 1080, 1098, 1099-1236, **1099**, 1251, 1253, 1254, 1261, 1262, 1264, 1266, 1267, 1270, 1271, 1272, 1273, 1277, 1278, 1279, 1280, 1281, 1282, 1283, 1284, 1285, 1296, 1297, 1318-1320
"Kranesburg Matter, The" 373, 638, 639-644, 1279, 1289, 1312
Kroeger, Berry 419
Krugman, Lou 24, 51, 54, 125, 137, 165, 206, 248, 377, 416, 431
Kruschen, Jack 49, 51, 58, 105, 111, 133, 151, 163, 175, 214, 224, 231, 257, 440, 485, 530, 553, 571, 581, 662, 694, 698, 717, 734, 782, 793, 815, 826, 840, 859, 900, 938, 1000

Lafferty, Fran 190

"Laird Douglas Douglas of Heatherscote Matter, The" 549-553, 1274, 1309-1310
"Lake Mead Mystery Matter, The" 897-898, 1282, 1316
Lake, Florence 135
"LaMarr Matter, The" 540-544, 1071, 1281, 1309
"Lancer Jewelry Matter, The" 279-280, 1254, 1304, 1322
Lang, Harry 202, 204, 209, 245, 251
"Lansing Fraud Matter, The" 279, 477-481, 1281, 1291, 1307
Lansing, Mary 149, 178, 182, 185, 279, 310, 314, 317, 320, 351, 359, 367, 391, 406, 416
Larch, John 335
"Larson Arson Matter, The" 949-951, 1274, 1316
Latimer, Ed 190
"Latin Lovely Matter, The" 793-795, 1282, 1314
"Latourette Matter, The" 280-282, 1272, 1304
"Latrodectus Matter, The" 1085-1087, 1274, 1298, 1299, 1318
"Laughing Matter, The" 590-594, 1281, 1310-1311
Lawrence, Charlotte 125, 639, 706
Lawrence, Elizabeth 1091, 1092, 1130, 1131
Lawton, Alma 493
Lawton, Donald 394
Lazer, Joan 1206
Lead Audition 1244
Leader, Anton M. 25, 1238
Lee, Earl 125
Leeds, Peter 192, 197, 211, 213, 218, 242, 250, 293, 299, 311, 328, 349, 403, 406, 444, 493, 674, 710, 761, 780, 790, 817, 826, 869, 954, 985, 995, 997
"Leland Case Matter, The" 220-221, 1279, 1303
LeMond, Bob 157, 198, 200
Lenrow, Bernard 190, 1113

"Lester James Matter, The" 292-293, 488, 1258, 1289, 1304
"Lester Matson Matter, The" 334-335, 1257, 1305
"Leumas Matter, The" 937-938, 940, 1285, 1316
Lewis, Abby 1180, 1217
Lewis, Forrest 440, 448, 456, 461, 472, 500, 505, 518, 540, 586, 600, 614, 639, 644, 649, 662, 666, 674, 677, 689, 706, 708, 711, 715, 717, 728, 729, 734, 752, 757, 769, 771, 788, 793, 802, 803, 817, 828, 830, 831, 833, 835, 842, 845, 847, 853, 861, 864, 865, 866, 880, 883, 886, 890, 892, 900, 914, 920, 922, 925, 926, 932, 934, 937, 947, 960, 961, 966, 970, 977, 982, 997, 1000, 1003, 1004, 1008, 1010, 1012, 1015, 1026, 1028, 1031, 1035, 1038
"Life at Steak Matter, The" 918-920, 1258, 1316
Light, Dave 138, 170, 200, 248
"Lillis Bond Matter, The" 197-199, 1266, 1303
"Limping Liability Matter, The" 855-856, 1282, 1315, 1322
Lipton, Bill 1065, 1072, 1077, 1078, 1080, 1096, 1108, 1110, 1133, 1135, 1141, 1142, 1155, 1161, 1173, 1182, 1184, 1193, 1206, 1229
"Little Man Who Was There Matter, The" 938-940, 1282, 1316
"Little Man Who Wasn't All There, The" 69-71, 1283, 1301
"Lloyd Hammerly Matter, The" 8, 174-175, 1265, 1302, 1321
Lloyd, Rita 1115, 1161, 1195, 1221
"London Matter, The" 128-130, 1278, 1302
"Lone Wolf Matter, The" 1092-1094, 1277, 1318
"Lonely Hearts Matter, The" 558-562, 910, 1273, 1310, 1322
"Long Shot Matter, The" 600-605, 1272, 1311

"Look Before the Leap Matter, The" 27, 975-977, 1282, 1317
Lorde, Athena 1050, 1096
"Lorelei Matter, The" 1219-1221, 1277, 1320
"Lorko Diamonds Matter, The" 456-461, 1278, 1307
Lorring, Joan 1057, 1075, 1076, 1082, 1098
"Loss of Memory Matter, The" 734-735, 1258, 1313
"Lost by a Hair Matter, The" 929-931, 1285, 1316
"Love Shorn Matter, The" 875, 876, 882-883, 885, 1282, 1315, 1323
Lovett, Dorothy 62
"Low Tide Matter, The" 1099-1101, 1278, 1318
"Lucky 4 Matter, The" 849-851, 1280, 1315
"Lucky Costa Matter, The" 217-218, 1274, 1303
Lund, John 3, 10, 40, 143, 155, 163, 173, 211, 228, 245, 259-434, **259**, 447, 530, 599, 1043, 1237, 1238-1241, 1251, 1253, 1254, 1256, 1257, 1258, 1259, 1260, 1261, 1262, 1263, 1265, 1267, 1268, 1269, 1271, 1272, 1275, 1276, 1279, 1281, 1283, 1284, 1290, 1304-1306
"Lust for Gold Matter, The" 835, 1189-1191, 1282, 1319
Lynn, Rita 86
Lyon, Charles 250, 251, 252, 253, 254, 288, 290, 292, 293, 295, 297, 299, 301, 303, 304, 306, 308, 309, 311, 313, 315, 317, 318, 320, 322, 324, 326, 328, 330, 331, 332, 335, 336, 338, 339, 342, 343, 345, 347, 349, 351, 353, 354, 357, 359, 361, 363, 365, 367, 368, 370, 373, 375, 377, 380, 382, 384, 386, 389, 391, 392, 394, 396, 398, 401, 403, 404, 406, 408, 410, 412, 415, 416, 419, 421, 423, 425, 427, 429, 430, 431, 432, 433

MacDonald, Dan 1089
MacDonald, Edmond 64, 67, 86, 88

Macdonnell, Norman 25, 49, 51, 52, 58, 59
Mack, Gilbert 190, 1155, 1217
MacKaye, Fred 267, 382, 384
MacLaughlin, Don 1161
"Macormack Matter, The" 8, 436-440, 1254, 1306
"Mad Bomber Matter, The" 1144-1146, 1266, 1319
"Mad Hatter Matter, The" 704-706, 1263, 1213
"Madison Matter, The" 295-297, 513, 1269, 1291, 1304
"Magnanimous Matter, The" 1012-1013, 1282, 1317, 1323
"Magnolia and Honeysuckle Matter, The" 394-397, 1261, 1305
Maher, Wally 127, 130, 151, 155, 176, 204, 247
"Malcolm Wish, M.D. Matter, The" 204-206, 1283, 1303
"Malibu Mystery Matter, The" 856-858, 1284, 1315
"Man Who Waits Matter, The" 4, 7, 995-997, 1261, 1317
"Man Who Wrote Himself to Death, The" 103-105, 1256, 1301
Manners, Joyce 265
Manson, Allan 1096, 1104, 1106, 1123, 1152, 1153
March, Hal 65, 144, 303, 310, 314, 317, 335, 342, 345, 361, 370, 380, 389, 397, 404, 406, 408, 410, 415, 421, 423, 425, 429
"Marie Meadows Matter, The" 195-196, 1283, 1303, 1321
"Marigold Matter, The" 273-275, 1269, 1304
Marino, Amerigo 461, 465, 468, 472, 477, 481, 485, 489, 493, 496, 500, 505, 509, 513, 517, 522, 526, 530, 535, 540, 544, 548, 553, 558, 562, 567, 571, 576, 581, 585, 590, 594, 600, 605, 609, 614, 619, 624, 629, 634, 638, 644, 649, 653, 658, 662, 666, 670, 677, 682, 685, 687, 689, 692, 694, 696, 697, 700, 702, 706, 708, 710, 711, 713, 715, 717, 719, 720, 722, 724, 726, 728, 729, 731, 734, 735, 737, 739, 741, 743, 745, 747, 749, 751, 754, 1250
Marino, Rick 439, 444, 448, 451, 456
"Markham Matter, The" 683-685, 687, 1283, 1313
"Marley K Matter, The" 723-724, 1268, 1313, 1322
Marr, Eddie 215, 265
Marsh, Myra 62
Marshall, Sidney 25, 290, 361, 377, 380, 382, 386, 392, 394, 397, 401, 404, 406, 408, 410, 415, 421, 423, 427, 429, 430, 431
Martin, Ian 1065, 1143, 1144, 1210, 1225
"Mary Grace Matter, The" 773-775, 1270, 1314
"Mason-Dixon Mismatch Matter, The" 735-737, 1275, 1313
Mason, William 1046, 1057, 1135, 1169, 1178, 1180, 1219
Masterson, Paul 64, 65, 67, 69, 73, 77
Mathews, Jimmy 190
"Matter of Reasonable Doubt, The" 581-586, 1255, 1310
Matthews, Grace 1227
Matthews, Jim 923, 925, 926, 928, 929, 931, 937, 938, 940, 942, 943
Matthews, Junius 51, 58, 64, 111, 119, 138, 320, 359, 382, 401, 440, 489, 549, 576, 670, 692, 704, 731, 734, 749, 787, 793, 803, 809, 811, 824, 842, 855, 863, 875, 880, 882, 904, 936, 942, 944, 949, 956, 960, 964, 971, 1012, 1015, 1021
Max, Ed 69, 101, 119, 1238
Maxwell, Bob 907, 1234
"Maynard Collins Matter, The" 242-243, 1256, 1303, 1321
McCallion, James 261, 306, 331, 375, 444, 489, 500, 553, 605, 644, 649, 702, 710, 729, 795, 849, 865, 872, 873, 882, 886, 888, 904, 917, 928, 942, 944, 973, 982, 1010, 1017, 1021, 1033, 1038

"McClain Matter, The" 297, 509-513, 1279, 1291, 1308, 1322
McCluskey, Joyce 99, 265
McCrary, Karen 1210
McGeehan, Pat 97, 113, 196
McGrath, Paul 1189
McGraw, Charles 107
McIntire, John 24, 121, 128, 147, 153, 164, 187, 202, 204, 208, 209, 250, 252, 253, 258, 261, 263, 267, 269, 271, 273, 279, 282, 284, 286, 288, 292, 295, 297, 301, 305, 306, 308, 311, 347, 349, 351, 355, 430, 433, 434, 743, 809, 905
McKennon, Dal 518
McKenny, Bob 10, 946, 947, 1049, 1050, 1206
McLeod, Mercer 1189, 1277
McManus, Kenny 946, 947
McNear, Howard 21, 24, 26, 103, 115, 121, 128, 132, 140, 145, 149, 155, 169, 172, 197, 200, 215, 220, 221, 233, 236, 242, 243, 248, 251, 286, 288, 290, 293, 295, 299, 315, 330, 333, 338, 355, 357, 367, 368, 373, 386, 397, 421, 425, 427, 430, 433, 481, 489, 493, 518, 544, 562, 590, 639, 644, 696, 700, 704, 717, 722, 735, 745, 771, 782, 793, 803, 805, 835, 879, 896, 920, 929, 970, 975, 1013, 1023, 1026
McVey, Tyler 107, 138, 157, 171
Meader, Phil 1089, 1090
"Medium Rare Matter, The" 1130, 1131-1133, 1281, 1319
"Medium, Well Done Matter, The" 6, 571-576, 1133, 1281, 1310
"Meek Memorial Matter, The" 711-713, 1255, 1313
"Meg's Palace Matter, The" 658-662, 1268, 1312
"Mei-Ling Buddah Matter, The" 920, 920-922, 1128, 1285, 1316
"Melancholy Memory Matter, The" 724-726, 1275, 1313

"Melanie Carter Matter, The" 73-75, 1270, 1301
Menken, Shepard 526, 609, 715, 735, 856, 861
Meredith, Lucille 493, 513, 535, 562, 571, 594, 666, 711, 777, 795, 805, 845, 886, 888
Merin, Eda Reiss 119
"Merrill Kent Matter, The" 237-239, 1283, 1303
Merrill, Lou 427, 430, 433, 689, 798, 812, 815, 983, 993, 1024
"Merry Go Round Matter, The" 10, 969-970, 1282, 1317
Metz, Stuart 1115, 1116, 1119, 1148, 1212, 1217, 1223
"Michael Meany Mirage Matter, The" 729-731, 784, 1263, 1313
"Mickey McQueen Matter, The" 23, 140-142, 187-189, 1267, 1302
"Midas Touch Matter, The" 8, 605-609, 707, 1266, 1311
"Midnite Sun Matter, The" 4, 831-833, 1273, 1315
Milano, Frank 1227
"Milford Brooks III" 7, 9, 40-42, 1237-1238, 1260, 1267, 1286, 1300
"Milk and Honey Matter, The" 359-361, 1261, 1305
"Millard Ward Matter, The" 228-230, 1275, 1303
Miller, Bob 653
Miller, Joan 336
Miller, Marvin 342, 423, 440, 452, 456, 465, 472, 496, 522, 530, 567, 581, 600, 619, 670, 710, 713, 737, 761, 785, 811, 821, 855, 859, 883, 910, 914, 936, 958, 985, 993, 997, 1003, 1012, 1023, 1026
Miller, Sidney 69, 86, 137, 153, 167, 176, 185, 192, 218, 226, 230, 236, 248, 253, 273, 288, 295, 343, 363, 382
"Million Dollar Jewelry Matter, The" 1318, 1323
Mind in the Shadows 34

Miner, Jan 190
"Ming Toy Murphy Matter, The" 721-722, 1263, 1313
"Missing Chinese Stripper Matter, The" 87-88, 1255, 1301, 1321
"Missing Matter Matter, The" 863-864, 1282, 1315, 1322
"Missing Missile Matter, The" 10, 945-947, 1050, 1206, 1263, 1316
"Missing Mouse Matter, The" 694-696, 784, 1263, 1313
Mitchell, Shirley 477, 496, 614, 644, 653, 658, 708, 785, 790, 798, 851, 864, 875, 883, 893, 931, 983, 1006
Mitchen, Joan 694
"Mixed Blessing Matter, The" 1166-1167, 1285, 1319
"Model Picture Matter, The" 777-778, 1282, 1314
"Mohave Red Matter, The" 844-845, 1266, 1315
"Mohave Red Sequel Matter, The" 845-847, 1266, 1315
Mohr, Gerald 3, 143, 461, 1237, 1241-1244, 1253, 1254, 1259, 1290, 1306
"Molly K Matter, The" 440-444, 536, 540, 1269, 1306
"Monopoly Matter, The" 172-174, 355-357, 1259, 1286, 1302, 1305, 1321
"Monoxide Mystery Matter, The" 865-866, 1274, 1315, 1322
"Montevideo Matter, The" 164-165, 257-258, 1283, 1287, 1302, 1303, 1304, 1321, 1322, 1323
"Month-End Raid Matter, The" 191-192, 1257, 1303
"Monticello Mystery Matter, The" 1138-1140, 1267, 1319
Moody, Ralph 213, 315, 391, 392, 870, 875, 925, 928, 940, 964, 971, 978, 985, 989, 1042
"Moonshine Matter, The" 977-978, 987, 1275, 1317
"Moonshine Murder Matter, The" 719-720, 1275, 1313, 1322

"Morgan Fry Matter, The" 216-217, 1256, 1303, 1321
"Morning After Matter, The" 1072-1074, 1254, 1298, 1299, 1318
Morrison, Anne 49, 58
Mosley, Donald 902
Moyles, Jack 132, 159, 167, 171, 182, 184, 189, 194, 214, 245, 252, 279, 290, 318, 324, 338, 353, 363, 375, 386, 392, 421, 425, 456, 461, 509, 535, 544, 713, 805, 819, 821, 838, 856, 926, 985, 1017, 1021, 1244
Murcot, Joel 24, 277, 292, 295
"Murder Ain't Minor" 23, 52-54, 1269, 1300
"Murder is a Merry-Go-Round" 38-40, 1273, 1300
Myers, Marty 1208
"Mystery Gal Matter, The" 993-995, 1071, 1258, 1317

"Nancy Shaw Matter, The" 326-328, 1257, 1305
"Nathan Gayles Matter, The" 351-353, 1265, 1305
"Nathan Swing Matter, The" 397-399, 1265, 1305
"Neal Breer Matter, The" 211-213, 1265, 1303
"Negligent Nephew Matter, The" 908-909, 1254, 1316, 1323
"Nelson Matter, The" 330-331, 1257, 1305
Nelson, Frank 314, 320, 322, 347, 351, 359, 403, 416, 685, 694, 708, 715, 726, 737, 740, 761, 773, 775, 807, 809, 822, 826, 833, 883, 898, 907, 983
"Net of Circumstance Matter, The" 893-894, 1280, 1316
Neuman, E. Jack 24, 103, 109, 113, 263, 264, 265, 267, 269, 271, 275, 279, 280, 282, 284, 293, 297, 299, 301, 305, 306, 308, 310, 311, 434, 439, 496, 599, 710, 1239, 1241, 1242, 1244, 1287, 1288, 1289, 1290, 1291, 1292, 1293

"New Bedford Morgue Matter, The" 252, 1257, 1303, 1321
"New Cambridge Matter, The" 265-267, 530, 1272, 1289, 1292, 1304, 1322
"Newark Stockbroker Matter, The" 1318, 1323
"Nick Shurn Matter, The" 481-485, 1278, 1307-1308
"Night in Paris Matter, The" 931-932, 996, 1263, 1316
"No Matter Matter, The" 1227-1229, 1261, 1320
Nolan, Jeanette 121, 128, 147, 153, 157, 159, 161, 164, 167, 168, 182, 187, 199, 202, 204, 206, 208, 209, 228, 235, 239, 242, 243, 245, 247, 250, 252, 253, 258, 261, 263, 267, 269, 271, 273, 282, 284, 286, 288, 295, 301, 305, 306, 308, 311, 339, 342, 343, 347, 349, 351, 353, 355, 357, 363, 365, 412, 416, 535, 553, 586, 600, 614, 731, 737, 740, 741, 782
"Nora Falkner Matter, The" 159-161, 1265, 1302
North, Robert 196, 200
Novello, Jay 71, 84, 97, 132, 165, 171, 226, 247, 258, 261, 277, 301, 308, 333, 345, 349, 361, 370, 394, 399, 406, 419, 423, 430, 433, 434, 456, 461, 540, 581, 700, 719, 722, 1245, 1250
"Noxious Needle Matter, The" 853-855, 1285, 1315
"Nuclear Goof Matter, The" 967-968, 1264, 1317
"Nugget of Truth Matter, The" 1159-1161, 1281, 1319
Nusser, James 24, 69, 107, 142, 164, 169, 172, 179, 184, 185, 197, 247, 251, 275, 280, 303, 305, 320, 331, 339, 353, 359, 368, 403, 408, 415, 429

O'Brien, Edmond 3, 6, 7, 69, 89-258, **89**, 259, 286, 313, 357, 368, 419, 710, 1251, 1253, 1254, 1255, 1256, 1257, 1259, 1260, 1263, 1264, 1265, 1266, 1267, 1268, 1270, 1271, 1272, 1274, 1275, 1276, 1277, 1278, 1279, 1280, 1283, 1301-1304
O'Herlihy, Dan 117, 130, 142, 144, 157, 175, 187, 235, 401
Oates, Edward 1104, 1142
Ocko, Danny 1057, 1075, 1076
Ogilvie, Jack 1067
"Oklahoma Red Matter, The" 310-311, 505, 1281, 1288, 1304
Oland, Cliff 1223
"Old Fashioned Murder Matter, The" 1108-1110, 1277, 1319
"Oldest Gag Matter, The" 1217-1219, 1277, 1320
"One Most Wanted Matter, The" 872-873, 1279, 1315, 1322
"One of the Rottenest Rackets Matter" 1130, 1297
"One Too Many Matter, The" 1150-1153, 1261, 1319
"Only One Butt Matter, The" 922-923, 1261, 1316
"Open Town Matter, The" 27, 403, 619-624, 1266, 1289, 1311
Ortega, Santos 1059, 1094, 1101, 1108, 1130, 1131, 1184, 1189, 1225
Osborne, Reynold 1135, 1139, 1140, 1173, 1215, 1223
Osborne, Ted 119, 123, 135, 140, 174, 179, 196, 214, 217, 224, 231
"Oscar Clark Matter, The" 335-336, 1271, 1305, 1322
Otto, Walter 907, 1121, 1155, 1191, 1212, 1214, 1216, 1223, 1225, 1227, 1229, 1232, 1234
"Out of the Fire, Into the Frying Pan" 56-58, 130, 1259, 1300
Owen, Tudor 117, 123, 130, 144, 165, 179, 187, 197, 208, 326, 404

"P. O. Matter, The" 972-973, 1270, 1317
Paiva, Nestor 224, 231, 290
Palmer, Maria 117, 187
"Paradise Lost Matter, The" 4, 1013-1015, 1272, 1317

"Parakoff Policy, The" 9, 32-34, 1260, 1300
Parkhurst, Doug 1152, 1153
"Parley Barron Matter, The" 740-741, 1279, 1313
"Paterson Transport Matter, The" 413-415, 1261, 1306
Patrick, Lee 161, 172, 184, 255, 397, 415, 429
"Paul Barberis Matter, The" 241-242, 1256, 1303, 1321
"Paul Gorrell Matter, The" 373-375, 1275, 1305
"Pearl Carrasa" 113-115, 1275, 1301
"Pearling Matter, The" 594-600, 1261, 1290, 1311
Pearson, GeGe 71
"Peerless Fire Matter, The" 726-728, 1264, 1313
"Perilous Padre Matter, The" 1115-1116, 1281, 1319
"Perilous Parley Matter, The" 8, 875-876, 882, 885, 965, 1282, 1315, 1322
Perrin, Vic 24, 109, 161, 211, 250, 263, 273, 305, 317, 328, 444, 461, 468, 500, 513, 540, 571, 581, 605, 653, 666, 674, 682, 692, 698, 710, 720, 724, 752, 759, 764, 775, 777, 796, 802, 812, 815, 821, 822, 844, 849, 851, 856, 865, 872, 893, 894, 896, 902, 934, 940, 953, 954, 963, 978, 983, 987, 998, 1008, 1013, 1024, 1026, 1035, 1244
Peters, Ken 530
Petrie, George 1067
Petruzzi, Jack 111, 535, 600
"Phantom Chase Matter, The" 670-677, 1282, 1312-1313
"Philadelphia Miss Matter, The" 1113-1115, 1254, 1319
"Phillip Morey Matter, The" 342-343, 1305
Phillips, Barney 52, 224, 231, 286, 336, 408, 444, 456, 481, 485, 500, 526, 549, 558, 609, 649, 658, 674, 687, 700, 708, 726, 735, 741, 749, 756, 767, 817, 824, 833, 838, 845, 847,
857, 858, 869, 870, 890, 894, 925, 926, 937, 953, 954, 961, 966, 971, 997, 1006, 1019, 1028, 1029, 1040, 1244, 1245, 1250
"Phony Phone Matter, The" 991-993, 1148-1150, 1269, 1279, 1317, 1319
"Picture Postcard Matter, The" 9, 662-666, 1264, 1312
"Piney Corners Matter, The" 389-391, 614, 1279, 1289, 1305
"Planner Matter, The" 1061-1063, 1270, 1296, 1297, 1318, 1323
"Plantagent Matter, The" 265, 527-530, 1262, 1289, 1292, 1309
Polen, Nat 1067, 1152, 1153, 1197
"Poor Little Rich Girl Matter, The" 760-761, 1270, 1314
"Port-au-Prince Matter, The" 82, 123-125, 1287, 1301
"Port-O-Call Matter, The" 168-169, 1265, 1302
Post, Clayton 109, 113, 125, 128, 138, 153, 161, 167, 172, 233, 269, 280, 293, 299, 315, 320, 330, 349, 359, 363, 367, 370, 384, 392, 399, 415, 429
Powell, Dick 3, 7, 9, 42, 1237-1238, 1253, 1254, 1260, 1300
"Price of Fame Matter, The" 802-803, 932, 1264, 1314
Price, Vincent 802, 803
"Primrose Matter, The" 666-670, 1270, 1312
"Protection Matter, The" 6, 225-226, 1257, 1303
"Punctilious Firebug Matter, The" 407-408, 1261, 1306
"Purple Doll Matter, The" 1089, 1298, 1299, 1318, 1323

"Queen Anne Pistols Matter, The" 155-157, 1279, 1290, 1302
"Quiet Little Town in New Jersey Matter, The" 1319, 1323
Quine, Dick 214

"Racehorse Piledriver Matter, The" 64-65, 1269, 1301
"Radioactive Gold Matter, The" 425-427, 1259, 1306
Raeburn, Bryna 1178
Raskyn, Sam 1046, 1133, 1171, 1184, 1186, 1223
"Rasmusson Matter, The" 692-694, 1282, 1313
"Rat Pack Matter, The" 1087-1090, 1262, 1298, 1299, 1318
Readick, Bob 3, 29, 1043-1098, **1043**, 1251, 1253, 1254, 1258, 1260, 1262, 1264, 1266, 1270, 1273, 1274, 1277, 1278, 1280, 1281, 1283, 1284, 1285, 1296, 1297, 1318
"Real Smokey Matter, The" 1023-1024, 1274, 1317, 1323
"Really Gone Matter, The" 934-936, 940, 1282, 1316
"Recompense Matter, The" 1028-1029, 1280, 1317
"Red Mystery Matter, The" 960-961, 1282, 1316
Redfield, William 1077, 1078, 1089, 1090, 1094, 1128, 1139, 1140, 1150, 1173, 1212
"Redrock Matter, The" 997-998, 1266, 1317
Reed, Alan 590, 649, 719, 765, 809, 822, 824, 845, 847, 866, 876, 882, 902, 912, 923, 961
Reid, Elliott 94, 109, 253, 295
Repp, Guy 1072, 1123, 1133, 1155, 1165, 1186, 1221, 1229
"Rhymer Collection Matter, The" 1010-1012, 1271, 1317
"Ricardo Amerigo Matter, The" 497-500, 1274, 1308
Rice, Rosemary 1065, 1212, 1223
"Richard Splain Matter, The" 147-149, 1259, 1302
Richards, Paul 535, 544, 586, 644, 812
"Rilldo Matter, The" 1206-1208, 1279, 1320

"Ring of Death Matter, The" 1074-1076, 1277, 1298, 1318
"Road-Test Matter, The" 382-384, 1258, 1305
"Robert Perry Case, The" 36-38, 99, 1255, 1287, 1300, 1321
Robinson, Bartlett 855, 865, 894, 898, 902, 907, 914, 915, 925, 936, 942, 944, 947, 968, 982, 985, 1003, 1008, 1029
Robinson, Larry 1055, 1206, 1208, 1227
"Rochester Theft Matter, The" 269, 303-305, 496, 1254, 1290, 1293, 1304
Rodman, Victor 331, 368
"Rolling Stone Matter, The" 828-830, 1282, 1315
Ronson, Adele 1139, 140
Rose, Ralph 25, 80, 82
Rost, Elaine 1087
Rowan, Roy 54, 56, 58, 59, 60, 94, 96, 97, 99, 101, 105, 107, 109, 111, 113, 117, 119, 121, 123, 125, 127, 143, 147, 439, 444, 447, 451, 456, 461, 465, 468, 472, 477, 481, 485, 489, 493, 496, 500, 505, 509, 513, 517, 522, 526, 530, 535, 540, 544, 548, 553, 558, 562, 567, 571, 576, 581, 585, 590, 594, 599, 605, 609, 614, 619, 624, 629, 634, 638, 644, 649, 658, 662, 666, 670, 677, 682, 685, 831, 833, 835, 836, 838, 839, 842, 844, 845, 847, 849, 851, 853, 855, 856, 857, 859, 861, 863
"Royal Street Matter, The" 687-689, 1275, 1313
Rubin, Benny 277, 338, 389, 477
"Rudy Valentine Matter, The" 166-167, 362-363, 1260, 1286, 1302, 1305, 1321, 1322
Ruick, Melville 1169, 1212, 1225
"Rum Barrel Matter, The" 222-223, 1275, 1303, 1321
Russell, Charles 3, 6, 7, 31-88, **31**, 89, 124, 130, 153, 1251, 1253, 1254, 1255, 1256, 1258, 1259, 1261, 1263, 1265, 1267, 1268, 1269, 1270, 1271, 1273, 1274, 1275, 1280, 1283, 1300-1301

Ryan, Dick 96, 125, 157, 168, 185, 273, 284, 286, 322, 355, 399, 535, 549, 553
Ryan, Vic 62
Ryf, Robert 25, 452, 468, 619, 639, 658, 666, 677, 687, 756, 767, 778, 782, 790, 800, 807, 819

"Salkoff Sequel Matter, The" 813-815, 1141, 1280, 1314
"Salt City Matter, The" 545-549, 1276, 1291, 1309, 1322
Samuels, Joel 226
"San Antonio Matter, The" 8, 299-301, 456, 599, 1265, 1290, 1293, 1304
San Juan, Olga 101, 181
Sanford, Don 24, 351, 355, 412
Santoni, Renee 1232
Sanville, Richard 25, 34, 36, 38, 40, 42, 44, 46, 48
"Sara Dearing Matter, The" 410-412, 1306
"Sarah Martin Matter, The" 429-430, 1283, 1306, 1322
"Saturday Night Matter, The" 980-982, 1277, 1317
Schoskis, Michael 1212, 1214, 1223
Scott, Janet 169
"Sea Legs Matter, The" 4, 619, 624-629, 1282, 1311
"Search for Michelle Marsh, The" 31, 60-62, 1280, 1301
Seel, Charles 62
Selby, Sarah 115
Sewell, Bud 756, 757, 759, 761
Seymour, John 1110, 1217
"Shadow of a Doubt Matter, The" 1002, 1046, 1174-1176, 1283, 1319
"Shady Lane Matter, The" 391, 610-614, 1277, 1289, 1311
"Shankar Diamond Matter, The" 888-890, 1276, 1315
"Shayne Bombing Matter, The" 318-320, 1257, 1304
"Shepherd Matter, The" 263, 553-558, 1276, 1289, 1310
Sherwood, Madeline 1055, 1204

"Shifty Looker Matter, The" 1121-1123, 1264, 1319
Shipp, Mary 73, 96, 137, 213, 333, 1238
"Short Term Matter, The" 7, 9, 1057-1059, 1272, 1296, 1318
Shoskus, Mike 1155
Shue, Bob 1025
"Shy Beneficiary Matter, The" 5, 781-782, 1282, 1314
"Sick Chick Matter, The" 803-805, 1277, 1314
"Sidewinder Matter, The" 970-971, 1266, 1317
"Sidney Mann Matter, The" 158, 253, 1264, 1288, 1303, 1321
"Sidney Rykoff Matter, The" 119-121, 1260, 1301
"Silent Queen Matter, The" 677-682, 1277, 1313
"Silver Belle Matter, The" 771-773, 1263, 1314
"Silver Blue Matter, The" 567-571, 1271, 1310
"Silver Queen Matter, The" 987-989, 1317
Simes, Eugene 1155, 1223, 1225
Simons, Constance 1210, 1215, 1229
"Simple Simon Matter, The" 1084, 1090-1092, 1281, 1318
"Singapore Arson Matter, The" 228, 259-261, 1265, 1289, 1304, 1322
Singleton, Doris 52, 56, 65, 77
"Skidmore Matter, The" 965, 1182-1184, 1281, 1319
"Skimpy Matter, The" 8, 1210-1212, 1271, 1320
"Skull Canyon Mine, The" 75-77, 1274, 1301
"Slow Boat from China, The" 34-36, 85, 1274, 1300
Smith, Bill 1046, 1067, 1121, 1193, 1215
Smith, Charles B. 24, 689, 696, 706, 713, 722, 726, 731, 737, 740, 745, 752, 773
"Smoky Sleeper Matter, The" 7, 757-759, 1157, 1272, 1314
Smolen, Vivian 1227

Snowden, Eric 235, 257, 261, 404, 544, 649, 694, 754, 885, 890
"Soderbury, Maine Matter, The" 199-200, 1256, 1303
Solow, Larry 1232
Sommers, Jimsey 1182
Sonnenberg, Nellie 1119
Soule, Olan 989, 991
Spaulding, Jean 132
"Squared Circle Matter, The" 696-698, 1075, 1269, 1313
"SS Malay Trader, The" 92-94, 1268, 1301
"Stanley Price Matter, The" 332-333, 1284, 1305
"Stanley Springs Matter, The" 89, 179-181, 1263, 1302
Stanley, Robert 25, 830, 844, 861, 882
"Star of Capetown Matter, The" 4, 614-619, 699, 943, 1278, 1311
"Star of Hades Diamond, The" 36, 85
"Starlet Matter, The" 271-273, 1281, 1304
Stehli, Edgar 757, 865, 954, 1061, 1084, 1085, 1215, 1217
Stephenson, John 155, 220, 221, 318, 333, 339, 380, 489, 505, 513, 702, 728, 788, 980
Sterling, Bill 1050, 1065, 1074
Stevens, Jim 1072, 1121, 1148, 1161, 1176, 1193, 1195, 1217
Stevens, Leith 48, 49, 50, 52, 54, 56, 58, 59, 60, 62, 73, 77, 79, 80, 82, 84, 85, 86, 88, 92, 94, 96, 97, 99, 101, 103, 105, 107, 109, 111, 113, 115, 117, 119, 121, 123, 125, 127, 128, 130, 132, 133, 135, 137, 138, 140, 142, 144, 145
Stevenson, Bob 79, 80, 84, 85, 86, 88, 128, 130, 132, 133, 135, 137, 138, 140, 142, 145, 149, 151, 212, 215, 216, 218
Stewart, Kay 174
"Stock in Trade Matter, The" 1095, 1096-1098, 1285, 1318
"Stolen Portrait of the Duke of Massen, The" 42-44, 1263, 1300

"Stope of Death Matter, The" 1026-1028, 1281, 1317
"Story of the Ten-O-Eight, The" 111-113, 1276, 1301
Stratton Jr, Gil 140, 199, 243, 594, 634, 731, 757, 805, 826, 840, 898, 902, 940, 942, 944, 966, 973
Stratton, Chester 465, 522, 619, 658, 682, 711, 745, 749, 836, 838, 956, 964, 1023, 1035, 1040
Stuart, Kay 111
"Sudden Wealth Matter, The" 958-960, 1282, 1316
"Sulphur and Brimstone Matter, The" 392-394, 1261, 1305
Summers, Jocelyn 1176
"Sunny Dream Matter, The" 785-787, 1282, 1314
"Suntan Oil Matter, The" 10, 713-715, 1277, 1313
"Super Salesman Matter, The" 1035-1036, 1282, 1317
Sweeney, Bob 145, 147, 151, 233, 248, 252, 434
Sweeney, Warren 1171, 1180, 1191
Syms, Sylvia 82
"Syndicate Matter, The" 290-292, 1262, 1304

Tackna, Edith 217
"Takes a Crook Matter, The" 1163-1165, 1285, 1319
Tarplin, Maurice 190, 1091, 1092, 1116, 1119, 1121, 1133, 1167, 1173, 1184
Tatum, Jeanne 481, 544, 549, 586, 619, 624, 639, 694, 719, 740, 771, 775, 780, 793, 833, 840, 858, 864, 868, 880, 883, 905, 920, 963, 1003, 1010, 1031
"Tears of Night Matter, The" 576-581, 702, 1282, 1291, 1310
Tedrow, Irene 92, 472
"Tell-All Book Matter, The" 1302, 1321
"Telltale Tracks Matter, The" 876, 877-879, 1258, 1315, 1322

"Temperamental Tote Board Matter, The" 408-410, 1283, 1306
"Templeton Matter, The" 103, 708-710, 1270, 1288, 1313
"Terrible Torch Matter, The" 1155-1157, 1272, 1319
"Terrified Taun Matter, The" 384-386, 1283, 1305
Thatcher, Leora 1110, 1135, 1165
"Thelma Ibsen Matter, The" 269-271, 306, 465, 1262, 1288, 1304
Thomas, Hugh 96
Thomas, John 1061, 1137, 1138, 1163
Thompson, D. J. 73, 448, 472, 518, 619, 670, 773, 844, 883, 910
Thor, Larry 200, 217, 220, 221, 324, 468, 687, 1244
Thorson, Russell 472, 481, 509, 518, 535, 558, 600, 605, 624, 629, 644, 653, 687, 706, 717, 740, 759, 782, 798, 824, 831, 833, 847, 866, 877, 888, 915, 938, 958, 960, 982, 1000, 1003, 1017, 1019, 1028, 1029, 1033, 1036, 1038
"Three for One Matter, The" 1133-1135, 1269, 1319
"Three Sisters Matter, The" 775-777, 1279, 1314
Tice, Olin 190
"Time and Tide Matter, The" 805-807, 1282, 1314
"Tip-Off Matter, The" 907, 1231, 1232-1234, 1273, 1320
"Todd Matter, The" 8, 269, 304, 493-496, 1264, 1290, 1293, 1308
"Tolhurst Theft Matter, The" 231-233, 1279, 1303
"Tom Hickman Matter, The" 69, 153, 253, 1270, 1287, 1303, 1322
"Too Many Crooks Matter, The" 1119-1121, 1189, 1271, 1319
"Too Much Money Matter, The" 1021-1023, 1264, 1317
"Top Secret Matter, The" 5, 1167-1169, 1277, 1319

"Touch-Up Matter, The" 1069-1072, 1277, 1298, 1318
"Trans-Pacific Import Export Company, South China Branch" 142-144, 1259, 1302
"Trans-Pacific Matter – Part A, The" 1238-1239, 1259, 1290, 1304
"Trans-Pacific Matter – Part B, The" 1240-1241, 1259, 1290, 1304
"Trans-Pacific Matter Part 1, The" 1241-1242, 1259, 1290, 1306
"Trans-Pacific Matter Part 2, The" 1242-1244, 1259, 1290, 1306
Tremayne, Les 649, 687, 735, 764, 775, 840, 842, 917, 923
"True Love Matter, The" 1051-1053, 1055, 1262, 1296, 1318, 1323
Tully, Tom 271, 290, 292, 297, 336, 351, 365, 375, 412, 416
Turner, Fred 1227
Tuttle, Lurene 105, 147, 179, 576
"Twin Trouble Matter, The" 910-912, 1263, 1316
"Twins of Tahoe Matter, The" 1029-1031, 1269, 1317
"Twisted Twin Matter, The" 1015-1017, 1264, 1317
"Two Faced Matter, The" 851-853, 900, 1273, 1315
"Two Steps to Murder Matter, The" 1191-1193, 1284, 1320
"Two Tired Matter, The" 1067-1069, 1284, 1296, 1297, 1318, 1323
"Two's a Crowd Matter, The" 1078-1080, 1285, 1298, 1318

"Ugly Pattern Matter, The" 840-842, 1270, 1315
"Uncut Canary Matter, The" 378-380, 1261, 1305
"Underwood Matter, The" 282-284, 472, 1254, 1289, 1304
"Undried Fiddle Back Matter, The" 391-392, 1261, 1305, 1322
"Unholy Two Matter, The" 964-966, 1281, 1317

Unknown Cast 34, 36, 38, 40, 42, 44, 46, 48, 75, 85, 1048, 1051, 1053, 1063, 1069, 1200, 1202, 1235, 1236
Unknown Producer 1235, 1236
"Unworthy Kin Matter, The" 965, 1031-1033, 1278, 1317
"Upjohn Matter, The" 4, 264, 433-434, 522, 1258, 1292, 1306, 1322
"Urned Income Matter, The" 1002, 1044-1046, 1176, 1273, 1318

"Valentine Matter, The" 301, 452-456, 559, 1272, 1290, 1293, 130
Van Rooten, Luis 1072, 1116, 1165, 1167, 1178
Verdier, Bill 809
"Very Fishy Matter, The" 1055-1057, 1266, 1296, 1318
Victor, Paula 159
Vigran, Herb 24, 56, 500, 567, 576, 590, 704, 728, 747, 752, 793, 821, 842, 849, 853, 856, 869, 879, 888, 909, 918, 923, 929, 940, 945, 953, 967, 973, 977, 997, 1010, 1021, 1026, 1029
"Village of Virtue Matter, The" 824-826, 838, 1258, 1315
"Village Scene, The" 105-107, 1256, 1301
"Virginia Beach Matter, The" 79, 144-145, 1260, 1287, 1302
"Virginia Towne Matter, The" 89, 193-194, 1275, 1303
"Virtuous Mobster Matter, The" 8, 838-840, 1258, 1315
"Vivian Fair Matter, The" 175-176, 1275, 1302, 1321
"Vociferous Dolphin Matter, The" 10, 947, 1050, 1204-1206, 1279, 1320
Vola, Vicki 1155, 1204
"Voodoo Matter, The" 324-326, 1269, 1293, 1305

Wald, John 970, 971, 973, 975, 977, 978, 980, 981, 983, 985, 989, 991, 993, 995, 998, 1000, 1003, 1004, 1006, 1007, 1010, 1015, 1017, 1019, 1021, 1024, 1026, 1028, 1029, 1031, 1033, 1035, 1036, 1038, 1040, 1042
Walsh, George 1242, 1244
"Walter Patterson Matter, The" 265-267, 447, 1260, 1288, 1304
Walters, Joe 754
Warner, Gertrude 1074, 1089, 1090, 1128, 1137, 1138
Warnow, Mark 34, 36, 38, 40, 42, 44, 46
Waterman, Willard 64, 67, 73, 77, 86, 109, 125
"Wayward Clipper Matter, The" 1198-1200, 1284, 1296, 1320, 1323
"Wayward Diamonds Matter, The" 858-859, 1284, 1315
"Wayward Fireman Matter, The" 1065-1067, 1270, 1297, 1318
"Wayward Gun Matter, The" 1195-1197, 1254, 1320
"Wayward Heiress Matter, The" 4, 913, 915-917, 1048, 1232, 1272, 1316
"Wayward Killer Matter, The" 847-849, 1258, 1315
"Wayward Kilocycles Matter, The" 10, 947, 1048-1050, 1206, 1280, 1296, 1318
"Wayward Money Matter, The" 821-822, 1273, 1314
"Wayward Moth Matter, The" 811-812, 1141, 1280, 1314
"Wayward River Matter, The" 835-836, 1258, 1315
"Wayward Sculptor Matter, The" 917-918, 1282, 1316
"Wayward Trout Matter, The" 823-824, 1282, 1314
"Wayward Truck Matter, The" 7, 732-734, 1280, 1313
"Wayward Widow Matter, The" 752-754, 1274, 1314
"Weather or Not Matter, The" 1208-1210, 1280, 1320
Webb, Jane 127, 342, 373, 375
Webber, Peggy 96, 111, 140, 279, 310, 485, 713, 720, 728, 787, 893, 915
Weber, Karl 1178

"Weldon Bragg Matter, The" 171-172, 1263, 1302, 1321
"Well of Trouble Matter, The" 8, 1104-1106, 1277, 1318
Wentworth, Martha 54, 71, 115, 133, 189, 211, 280, 315, 331, 367
"What Goes Matter, The" 1033-1035, 1280, 1317
Whiting, Barbara 215
Whitney, Susan 586
"Who Took the Taxis for a Ride?" 49-51, 1273, 1300
"Who's Who Matter, The" 1063-1065, 1283, 1297, 1318
"Wholly Unexpected Matter, The" 1004-1006, 1282, 1317
"Will and a Way Matter, The" 925-926, 1266, 1316
"Willard South Matter, The" 189-190, 1265, 1302
"William Post Matter, The" 337-338, 1257, 1305
Willway, Lee 694, 895, 896
"Winnipesaukee Wonder Matter, The" 756-757, 1135, 1269, 1314, 1322
Winslowe, Paula 682, 685, 715, 775, 800, 844, 858, 859, 893, 983
"Winsome Widow Matter, The" 10, 905-907, 1234, 1266, 1316
Winters, Roland 609
Wipple, Barbara 1227
"Witness, Witness, Who's Got the Witness" 68-69, 153, 253, 1270, 1287, 1301
Wolcott, Florence 468
Wood, Jean 194
"Woodward Manila Matter, The" 161-163, 417-419, 1257, 1286, 1302, 1306
Wright, Ben 82, 117, 123, 130, 142, 151, 157, 165, 208, 235, 257, 326, 361, 386, 404, 485, 509, 649, 666, 677, 702, 724, 785, 800, 807, 858, 859, 931, 978, 987, 1012, 1042, 1242, 1244
Wright, Stewart 367, 370, 373, 375, 382, 644, 1048, 1051, 1053, 1063, 1069, 1234, 1237, 1244, 1250, 1286

Wright, Will 13, 24, 448, 456, 505, 522, 567, 581, 614, 658, 694, 702, 720, 737, 741, 745, 759, 769, 771, 773, 800, 802, 826, 835, 851, 853, 858, 868, 896, 909, 918, 922, 970, 980, 991, 998, 1242, 1244
"Wrong Doctor Matter, The" 4, 1117-1119, 1281, 1319
"Wrong Ending Matter, The" 916, 1046-1048, 1232, 1260, 1296, 1318, 1323
"Wrong Idea Matter, The" 1180-1182, 1262, 1319
"Wrong Man Matter, The" 955-956, 1263, 1316
"Wrong One Matter, The" 1140-1142, 1280, 1319
"Wrong Sign Matter, The" 1080-1082, 1278, 1298, 1299, 1318

"Yaak Mystery Matter, The" 1094-1096, 1264, 1318
Yafee, Ben 1206
"Yankee Pride Matter, The" 89, 149-151, 255-257, 1279, 1286, 1302, 1303, 1304, 1321, 1322
Yarborough, Barton 94, 175, 230
Young, Carleton 465, 468, 526, 535, 567, 708, 719
Young, Carleton G. 788, 819, 870, 896, 909, 918, 928, 967, 1042
Young, Dave 175, 311
"Youngstown Credit Group Matter, The" 239-241, 1257, 1303
"Yours Truly Matter, The" 748-749, 1282, 1314

Zerbe, Lawson 1059, 1065, 1072, 1077, 1078, 1082, 1087, 1110, 1116, 1119, 1126, 1143, 1144, 1146, 1152, 1153, 1173, 1180, 1182, 1191, 1193
"Zip Matter, The" 1193-1195, 1284, 1320
Zirato, Jr, Bruno 25, 1046, 1048, 1050, 1051, 1053, 1055, 1057, 1059, 1061, 1063, 1065, 1067, 1069, 1072, 1074, 1075, 1078, 1080, 1082, 1085, 1087, 1089,

1092, 1094, 1096, 1098, 1101, 1104, 1106, 1108, 1110, 1113, 1115, 1116, 1119, 1123, 1126, 1128, 1131, 1133, 1135, 1138, 1140, 1142, 1144, 1146, 1148, 1150, 1153, 1157, 1159, 1161, 1163, 1165, 1167, 1169, 1171, 1173, 1176, 1178, 1180, 1182, 1184, 1186, 1189, 1191, 1193, 1195, 1219, 1221

www.ingramcontent.com/pod-product-compliance
Lightning Source LLC
Chambersburg PA
CBHW061952300426
44117CB00010B/1304